The Beverage Testing Institute's
Buying Guide to
Wine

Introduction

This book would have been impossible to write 30 years ago. Even 20 years ago it would have been pretty thin. The intervening years, however, have seen exponential growth in the North American wine industry. This growth is not just limited to California. New regions are being developed, and states like Oregon and Washington are poised on the brink of stardom in their own right. What will the next ten years hold with New York, Virginia, and even parts of Canada continuing to develop apace? Of course, just as few could have foreseen today's market or the rise of these new appellations 30 years ago, will today's Texas or New Mexico become tomorrow's Washington? The dawn of the new century finds a newly awakened and powerful American wine industry, capable of making wines that compete with the finest in the world.

The statistics in this book are staggering—nearly 800 producers representing over 3,500 individual wines. There are over 900 Cabernets alone, and these are all very recent reviews, the figures haven't been padded by the inclusion of ten year-old Sauvignon Blancs. We review thousands of American wines each year, and were actually forced to trim current reviews for space considerations. For that reason, non-recommended wines are not included, and wines scoring 82 points or less are not printed with their tasting notes. This information can be found on our website, Tastings.com. The fact that there are just so many American wines out there these days says something about the vast array of choices available to the American wine consumer. This is where a book like this comes in handy. It is not only a great reference to almost every commercially significant wine produced in North America, but contains all sorts of handy information that allows you, the consumer, to make a more informed buying decision.

The first part of the book is arranged in chapters by state (or country in the case of Canada) and contains all wine reviews listed alphabetically by producer. This allows you to look up a specific producer or wine and to peruse reviews from New York State for instance. These sections also carry introductions that explain some of what is or has been going on in each of these areas. The second half of the book is arranged by grape varietal and wine style. Each of these chapters contains introductions to the wines in question, lists the top wines of that style reviewed in the first half of the book, and contains "Best Producer" lists. These lists are compiled with three quality tiers that tell you which wineries have a proven track record for producing the best wines of a given type. Best Producer lists are extremely useful, as it is sometimes difficult to find the exact wine you might be looking for. Should that be the case you can search for wines from a producer who is proven to be consistently excellent with the type of wine in question.

Finally, a number of the varietal sections contain information about what U.S. appellations (or regions where the grapes come from) are producing the best wines of a given grape—Chardonnay or Merlot for example. These "AVA" sections also tell you how wines produced in different regions may differ from each other. This means that instead of just letting me say which wine I like better, you can find an appellation that looks interesting, or makes wines to your taste, and start from there. This is a useful tool for the consumer to use in order to "whittle down the field." An in-depth explanation of the concept is to be found in Chapter Eight.

The various features allow you to approach what could otherwise be a fairly complex subject from a number of different simplifying angles. It has been designed with ease of use in mind, but also contains essential information that is easy to reference—all you wanted to know about U.S. Merlot in a snap, for instance. This, in combination with general information such as how to become a wine expert in ten easy steps (page 16), will have you off and running in no time. Never again should you be disappointed by an American wine purchase or intimidated by a restaurant wine list or a snooty sommelier.

About BTI

The Beverage Testing Institute (BTI) was founded in 1981, with a mission to create fair and reliable reviews. This led to the institute publishing a well-respected magazine, *International Wine Review*, from 1984 through 1990. Subsequently, the results of BTI tastings were featured first in *Wine & Spirits* magazine, and then in *Wine Enthusiast* magazine as an independently produced buying guide. Other publications, including the *Chicago Tribune* and the *Washington Post*, have showcased BTI reviews over the years.

In 1994, BTI began to review beer and spirits in addition to wine. Today, we are the largest full-time beverage review body in the world. In 1999 BTI will review more than 10,000 wines, beers, and spirits. We produce a bimonthly publication, *Tastings, the Journal*, which carries up-to-the-minute reviews and insight from the world of wine, beer, and spirits. *Tastings, the Journal* is supported by our website, Tastings.com, which contains hundreds of articles, links to all things gustatory, including thousands of winery and brewery listings, and a database of over 30,000 of our recent reviews, linked to retailers around the country so that you don't have to pull your hair out looking for that hard to find wine. Additionally, Tastings.com features the Insiders Club, a subscription service that alerts consumers to highly rated products from upcoming issues of the Journal. This puts you ahead of the crowd, before those products sell out. To subscribe, or to get more information about either *Tastings, the Journal* or the Insiders Club at Tastings.com, email us at journal@tastings.com; write to us at Beverage Testing Institute, 310 South Peoria Street, Suite 504A, Chicago, IL 60607; or phone us at 312-226-7857.

In addition to these endeavors, BTI produces a range of books. These include *Buying Guide to the Wines of North America, Buying Guide to Imported Wines, Buying Guide to Inexpensive Wines from Around the World, Buying Guide to Beer,* and *Buying Guide to Spirits.* They are all published by Sterling Publishers. Other publications that currently carry our reviews and musings include *Restaurant Hospitality* magazine, *All About Beer* magazine, Epicurious—the website of *Bon Appetit* and *Gourmet* magazines, AOL at keyword "Drinks," and Foofoo.com, to name a few.

BTI employs eight people on a full-time basis. BTI, in no particular order, is: Craig Goldwyn-web guy/guru, Jon Winsell-operations/man of databases, Richard Cooper-marketing/man of cigars, Charles Laverick-wine/outdoorsman, Marc Dornan-wine/beer/resident alien, Catherine Fallis-Journal/woman of words, Debra Bernstein-whip cracker/chef, Rochelle Calhoun-teamster/Latin dance instructor and Señor Alan Dikty-man of letters/spirits. As a group, we spend lots of time listening to Devo.

How BTI Reviews Are Created

My name is Charles Laverick. I am responsible for wine reviews at the Beverage Testing Institute, but I don't do it alone, and that is the difference between a BTI review and a review from a wine critic who is working alone. My colleague, Marc Dornan, sits in on nearly all reviewing sessions, as does an invited guest panelist chosen specifically for expertise in a given region. This panel of three convenes on a daily basis at 9:30 a.m. to conduct our wine reviews, and uses a proprietary methodology, which insures that BTI reviews are both consistent and meaningful.

The Quality Question

There are two widely used scales in the product-testing universe. These are the qualitative assessment scale and the consumer acceptance scale. While a consumer scale asks the taster whether or not they like a particular product and if so to what degree, a qualitative scale is focused on a given product's quality vis-à-vis its peers (i.e., Qualitative: "In the world of Cabernet is this a world class product?" Consumer: "Do you personally care for Cabernet or the flavors of this Cabernet in particular?").

Other critics don't fit neatly into either category, but tend to put a great deal of weight on their personal wine preferences, regardless of style. After some experimentation, we have come to the conclusion that a strict qualitative scale does the job better, as it more accurately reflects the consumer's understanding of the 100-point scale to which our reviews are ultimately translated. A 90 score signifies an excellent wine in the wider context of the wines of the world. Do consumers, or even professionals, like the flavors caused by malolactic fermentation in Chardonnay? Herbal Sauvignons? Oak-driven reds? We think these questions are best left to marketing professionals. Instead a BTI panelist will look at any style of wine as valid. We are not in an endless quest for thick wines with lots of oak or any other uniform wine style. We believe diversity should be celebrated and endeavor not to set out on any stylistic crusades or frame qualitative decisions along purely stylistic guidelines. A BTI panelist will set aside any personal prejudices about particular wine styles (oaked Chablis, modern Barolo, New Zealand Sauvignon, etc.) and judge wines solely on their own merits. Using this challenging set of criteria necessitates a small, well-trained cadre of tasting professionals.

Three's Company

While a consumer approach requires a broad base of panelists to get an accurate sample size, a qualitative approach requires a small number of professionals who specialize in whatever varietal or region is being addressed, and have demonstrated expertise as such. A BTI panel will most always contain exactly three panelists. Why three? Relying on a single taster carries with it a certain risk. After all everyone has a bad day. However, panels have their faults as well. Chief among them is the "law of averages." Two panelists give a product low marks while two give a product high marks—the net result? The data "averages" to describe a middle-of-the-road product, what none of the four originally thought. Borrowing an approach from the Australian show system (clever, those Antipodeans), we use a panel of three. This eliminates the inherent problem of averaging; helping to guarantee that what we print is what we meant to say. That's not to say that we won't on occasion have an extra individual in the room. Unlike some reviewers, we make a point of being transparent, welcome qualified visitors, and are happy to have them "audit" a session. Additionally, new panelists, or those without depth of experience in the category du jour will always "audit" the tasting (meaning their scores won't count) until such time as they are deemed ready. In order to achieve and maintain the desired level of consistency, the panel of three contains our two in-house tasting directors and one specifically invited expert for the "guest slot." This allows us to review very large categories with most panelists seeing the majority, if not all wines in that category. Finally, all panelists undergo a rigorous warm-up exercise that is not only educational, but allows each individual to determine whether or not they are "up to snuff" for the day's tasting. If there is the slightest doubt, that panelist is expected to disqualify himself before the tasting, and be replaced by one of the other trained in-house tasters whom we have on hand.

A Banded Approach

The scoring system that our panelists use is quite narrow, and hence our scoring tends to be highly repeatable. A score is given only after a thorough, objective assessment of a wine's qualities. We have devised a system based on the bands in the 100-point scale, which are widely recognized and roughly correspond to a five-star style system. These bands are:

96-100	Superlative
90-95	Exceptional
85-89	Highly Recommended
80-84	Recommended
<80	Not Recommended

After this thorough assessment of a wine's characteristics, a panelist is asked to place it in one of four quality bands in each of two rounds. All wines are initially tasted under "first round" parameters using a qualitative assessment that does not assess points for certain elements that are then added, but instead looks at overall quality. The first round scale is as such:

Round One

1 - A wine that one would not recommend in the wider context of today's global wine market (<80 points)

2 - A wine of sound commercial quality, though not overly exciting (80-84)

3 - A very good wine showing style and character, yet probably not of the highest merit (85-89)

4 - A wine that may be at the highest quality levels (potentially 90+)

Those wines that receive at least two scores of 4 are sent to the "merit round" whose scale is as follows:

Round Two

3 - A very good wine, yet upon comparison with examples of the highest quality, not of the highest merit (88-89 points)

4 - A truly excellent wine, of style and distinction (90-92)

5 - An outstanding wine, though not quite one of the world's finest (93-95)

6 - A world-class wine, providing one of the world's great wine experiences (96-100)

This banded approach allows our tasters to think in broad terms of general quality without getting mixed up in the minutiae of adding up points for "ageability," "color," or "aftertaste." We, just like the consumer, are addressing the wine in question only in its totality. Further, individual tasters do not have to concern themselves with what constitutes the differences between an 88 or an 86 or a 90 and a 91. Finally, one of the chief advantages of this system is the large percentage of wines tasted more than once. To witness, wines scoring over the critical 90 point barrier are without exception tasted twice, a virtual guarantee that a wine rated as such will be deserving of the accolades. Also, after the first round, all wines that show a wide disparity in scoring between panelists (controversial) are re-tasted at a later date under first round parameters, as are many low scoring wines.

A Novel Permutation

Final scores are reached using a novel mapping process that does not average the three scores but instead uses the mode, a statistic much closer to what the panelists, as a group, are really saying. If, for instance, a wine in the first round receives three scores of "3," it is placed in the upper center of the (85-89) band and given a final score of 88 points. Should the third score be a 4 or a 2, the wine in question would be given an 89 or an 86, respectively. The third score is used to move the final score up or down within the same band. Again, permutations that are controversial will be re-tasted. While the need to further narrow down scores within bands is a topic of some debate in the industry, we have taken the position that it is still in the consumer's interest to do so for the top four recommended bands: 80-84, 85-89, 90-95, and 96-100. Wines falling in the lowest band (<80) are simply noted as not recommended (NR) and no further breakdown is attempted. We realize that there are many conflicting views about the 100-point scale, but feel that we have devised the fairest system going for reaching individual points on that scale.

Description Is Key

In our continued attempt to lead the consumer "beyond the scores," we have been putting ever-greater emphasis on our descriptive evaluations. In order to continue this process, and also to insure thorough and consistent assessments, we use a comprehensive evaluation form in our tasting room. These forms translate directly to the final "tasting notes" that we try to print with every recommended wine (In instances where space doesn't permit this, all notes can be found on our website, www.tastings.com.) This form places an emphasis on objective structural information from color through intensity of finish. It covers several vital parameters and is amended with a final qualitative comment. This insures that all of our tasting notes are consistent in style, yet readable, while accurately conveying stylistic information to the consumer.

In order to make this descriptive information as consistent as possible (not to mention our qualitative assessments) we continue to rely heavily on our state-of-the-art tasting facility in Chicago. This room was specially designed to minimize external factors, and maximize our panelists concentration. Tasting at the same time of day, blind, under the same conditions, our panel continually works under ideal conditions. Hand in hand with our scorecard, we have specially designed tasting aids in order to standardize our tasting vocabularies. To this end we have even gone to the length of installing a state-of-the-art natural lighting system, paired with a standardized color palate for ever greater consistency. If all this sounds fanatical, it's because we are fanatical. Our institute is unique in the world of wine. We provide the world's only full-time professional reviewing service. This is not a contest, and couldn't be further from your typical "set 'em up and knock 'em down" wine fair. We take what we do seriously and train rigorously; both out of respect for producers and with an eye to providing the most trustworthy reviews a consumer can find.

Special Reports

Occasionally, we must travel to a wine region in order to cover it in a timely fashion. The best example would be Bordeaux, where we taste the new vintage from barrel on an annual basis, because the wine is sold in the futures market before it is bottled. These field tastings are referred to as "Special Reports," and an "SR" next to the tasting note designates reviews created in this fashion. This is to tell the reader that the review was not created under the ideal circumstances that we have established at our tasting lab in Chicago. Further, if the wine being reviewed was a barrel sample (a wine that has not finished aging or undergone the rigors of bottling), the score will be shown as a range—for instance 90-95. This is to make it clear to the reader that wines at this stage of evolution are tricky to evaluate, and that we are only aiming to put it into a general qualitative range based on its potential. Even when in the field, however, we strive to maintain as much of our methodology as possible, including a penchant for tasting blind. Lamentably, this is not always possible and that is why we do the vast majority of our tastings in Chicago where we can control all external factors.

Ten Things You Need to Know about Buying, Storing, and Serving Wine

1. Drink what you like.

Don't be intimidated. If you like a bit of sweetness to your wine, revel in it. If you just don't like red wine no matter what Morley Safer has to say, don't sweat it. Figure out what type of wine you like and get on with it. There are great examples of wine made in all styles. You pay for it and it should make you happy. If someone who presumes to know more than you do about wine gives you a hard time, get rid of them by referring to them as "cork dork" repeatedly or tell them that their Cabernet would be better on the rocks (see point ten).

2. Find a good retailer.

There are tons of wine shops around the country, both large and small, with people who are genuinely interested in wine waiting to answer your questions. If no one is willing to answer your questions, it is not a good wine shop. If they tell you what you should buy without asking you some fundamental questions—like what you like—it is not a good wine shop. In the end this person can steer you in the right direction and prevent the condition known as "overwhelming choice panic." Making a friend at a wine shop also may give you access to the allocated stuff that never hits the shelves. Your chances of getting a better wine for your money at a wine specialist (with assistance) as opposed to a grocery store (without assistance) are pretty good—plus you don't have to wait for an adult to come over and ring you up.

3. Pull from the bottom.

When in the wine shop, you will often notice that the wine is displayed vertically with a bottle on top and more of the same kind underneath it. Don't take the bottle on top; pull one from underneath. There are two reasons for this. One is that wine is sensitive to light, and fluorescent light in particular (hence the added protection of green or brown bottles). If your wine has been sitting there for a long time it may not be in quite the same condition as those that are a little more sheltered. Second, your new friend the retailer will have to come over and put one of the bottles from underneath in the display spot so that the next person knows what's there. This may endanger your chances of getting free samples and other handouts.

4. Beware the window and the vertical bottle.

Wine is not only sensitive to light; it is also sensitive to heat. If the wine shop in question is 90 degrees Fahrenheit in the summer or the wine is sitting on a shelf in front of a window, it is not a good wine shop. The heat will degrade the wine rather quickly, while constant temperature swings provided by exposure to sun, followed by cooler temperatures at night will accelerate the wine's demise at an alarming rate. Heat damaged wines can sometimes be spotted by the fact that the wine will have expanded and popped the cork up out of the bottle a half inch or so. In bad cases, there may even be a bit of "seepage." Finally, wines that don't have a high turnover rate should be stored horizontally, not upright. This is because when upright, the cork is no longer in contact with the wine. After some time the cork will dry out and contract, losing its seal. If the wine is then stored horizontally for a long period of time the wine may seep out the side. A sign of seepage (a sticky residue or stain) on the neck of the bottle under the capsule is not a good sign. If it is an old or rare wine, a cool, constant temperature over the years and horizontal storage should be prerequisites. If it seems like an unbelievable deal, there may be a reason. Show restraint.

5. Thou shalt not put wine near furnace.

When you bring wine home, don't forget everything you just learned. Wine does not like light, heat, temperature swings, or vibration. If you intend to keep it for a while don't put it next to the furnace. If it's a bottle for tonight, or next week, or next month, don't worry (real extremes excluded). If you intend to keep some wine around for a while though, find a decent spot for it. Storage doesn't have to be expensive. Put it on its side in a cool basement, or in a cooler part of the house that is usually dark, such as a closet. Though you may hear that ideal storage conditions are 55 degrees and about 70% humidity (to keep the cork moist and maintain the seal—very dry climates can dry a cork from the outside over a very extended period of time), the reality is that wine stored at a constant temperature of even 70 or 72 degrees Fahrenheit should be just fine. Remember that wild swings in temperature are worse. That being said, if you are a big shooter who invests lots of money, a cooling unit that also controls humidity is probably in order, especially if you are likely to have wine sitting around for a long time. It becomes a sickness, trust me. Plus, when you go to auction wine because you realize that your grandchildren will still be well provisioned with what you have left, the auction house will check "provenance." Has the wine been well stored over its lifetime? Poor cellar conditions will translate to lower bids. Seepage or popped corks probably mean rejection.

6. The myth of food pairing.

Cork dorks (see point one) like nothing better than to prattle on about food pairing. These inane people have given the average consumer the idea that they can't drink a particular wine without this or that type of food. Serving wine can lead to agitation and a condition known as corkophobia, whereby a wine's owner is afraid to pop the cork because they have been incapacitated by the thought of making a food pairing blunder. Here's the scoop. Drink what you like with food you like. While it is true that certain combinations may heighten the qualities of both food and wine, it is an impractical nightly ritual, and most wine is not meant to be a special occasion beverage. Rarely will a combination prove truly disastrous, and if you don't notice anyway does it really matter? One final inside secret. I am a wine critic. At home I drink red wine 95% of the time. I usually have wine with dinner. I do not have a breast of Muscovy duck sliced razor thin, dressed with a compote of rare Moroccan cherries and served on a melange of juvenile central Asian grains to go with a specific wine because it worked for someone else who is paid to come up with this drivel. Sometimes I have fish. Sometimes I have cheeseburgers. I then have a glass of red and never give it a second thought.

7. Get a grip on the glass.

Glassware has become a hot topic recently. There are companies that have designed specific glasses for every conceivable type of wine, from Napa Valley

Chardonnay to Chianti between two and three point five years of age grown on young vines and harvested on a Thursday under a waxing moon. Simple really, once the evil crystal cartels have their claws in you, you will have to buy a glass for every bottle you bring home. Where will you put them after a while? Also, with the profits they will be making from your initial purchases, they will design ever more perfect and riveting glasses, compelling you to buy them, always in search of glass-wine nirvana. The result of this spiraling descent into the fluffy cloud that is wine crystal? You will be penniless and on the street, with only a bottle, a paper bag, and your MD 20/20 super-sommelier 6450 glass to console you. To avoid this fate get yourself a set of simple glasses. Ideally, they should be tulip shaped and stemmed, with a slight taper inward toward the rim. This is so that when you give the wine a little swirl and put your nose to the top of the glass, the aromas will be right there for you. Don't fill the glass beyond a half to a third full for the simple reason that when you give it a little swirl you will spill it on yourself, or your date. If you like to drink your wine out of pewter tankards and it makes you happy, that's okay too, otherwise clear glass is a good idea, not these funny colored things that don't let you see the color of your wine. Since we actually evaluate wine for a living, we have researched glassware quite thoroughly. After lots of experimentation, we settled on the Riedel red wine glass from their "Overture" series. It works well for all types of wine, even Champagne, as the winemaker of Dom Perignon was amused to learn when visiting our office.

8. To decant or not to decant?

Rich red wines or ports that have been aged for five years or so—sometimes a little less, sometimes a lot more—can throw a sediment. This happens when some of the "stuffing" (technical term) falls out of solution as a dark-colored sandy-type substance, and settles on the bottom of the bottle. The problem is that when the bottle is shaken the wine turns cloudy and takes on a sort of gritty astringency when you drink it. The same effect can be had when the unshaken sediment from the bottom of the bottle is poured into your glass. How to solve this problem? Decanting. Get a carafe, or a decanter, or a water pitcher—anything that can hold the contents of the bottle. Light a candle or place the container over some other source of light. Take the bottle, which has been resting on its side or placed upright a couple of days before to allow "sedimental relocation" (hint), and open it while resisting the urge to shake it violently. Slowly pour from the bottle into the container with the neck of the bottle strategically positioned over the light source. It will look dark at first but don't panic. When about half the wine is poured out you will note the red color of the wine and be able to see clearly through to the light. Keep pouring, slowly tilting the bottle, and near the end you will notice a dark curl of sediment creeping up the bottle. Before it hits the neck, stop pouring. Congratulations, you have "decanted." Throw the little bit that's left out or cook with it. Decanting can also be done when drinking a youthful, full-bodied red that is muted and tannic. The interchange with oxygen helps to "open" the wine, simulating years of age in an hour or two. Be warned the cork dork who says that a wine bottle should be opened, then left on the table to "breathe." How much oxygen do you think 750 ml of wine gets from a dime-sized air space over an hour? Rather less than it will get from the act of pouring it into your glass I can assure you.

9. Don't serve it too cold.

Now that you are about to drink the wine that you have bought, stored, decanted, and generally fussed over—or not—do yourself a favor. Don't leave it on ice or in the arctic reaches of the refrigerator until it is so cold that you wouldn't want to put your tongue on the bottle. You are drinking a nice wine because good wine smells and tastes like something. If you don't like the taste of wine, however, over-chilling is a good tactic. It has the effect of dulling the wine's aromas and flavors. To chill, but not over-chill, an hour in the fridge is fine. In a restaurant, if the wine has been on ice for a while or a waiter brings you an arctic bottle and sets it back in the ice bucket, just pull it out and put it on the table. It will warm throughout the meal and open up in a few minutes time. While cold temperatures are something to watch with whites, Champagne is a bit of an exception. Champagne, due to its carbonation, has a tendency to be a bit rough at warmer temperatures, sort of like warm Coca-Cola. Bubbly needs a pretty good chill. If it is a really good Champagne (usually, but not always expensive is key here) don't over chill it for the same reasons as with whites, it will usually have a bit of age to it that has dulled the carbonation anyway. You paid the extra money because you think it tastes better than Cold Duck. Don't treat it like Cold Duck.

10. Or too hot.

You may have heard that red wines are best served at room temperature. This is true, but only partially. The adage meant European room temperature, and that usually referred to Britain. If you haven't been in a typical English home, take my word for it, it's chilly. There are Eskimos in Alaska who keep warmer igloos. The fact of the matter is a rich, high-alcohol (anything over 13%) red takes on a hot, rather aggressive profile where the alcohol dulls the aromas, at temperatures much above 70 or 72 degrees Fahrenheit. This is particularly true of the big, rich, ripe reds being produced in California, Australia, and other warm climate regions. When we taste reds at BTI, we serve them at about 67 or 68 degrees. When talking about something like Zinfandel, the difference is like night and day. At home I keep wines at cellar temperature, but if I have something that seems a bit warm, I'll throw the bottle in the fridge for ten minutes or so. Try heavy reds both ways, you'll be instantly converted. I even find that an ice cube can rescue a heavy red from being served too warm, particularly at a cocktail party or in the heat of summer. Many restaurants have the nasty habit of chilling the whites beyond recognition and then storing the reds somewhere above the grill, particularly in the United States. Even in France, however, they have not quite got the hang of it. At one particularly well-known French restaurant that shall remain nameless, I was subjected to a Cote-Rotie that had been stored near the restaurant's exquisite wood burning fire. The remedy, of course, was to ask for an ice bucket on which the decanter could rest for a few minutes and an ice cube for the wine in my glass. The inverse came later in the meal, with an old bottle of Sauternes that was being subjected to the polar treatment. The bottle was pulled and allowed to rest on the table. I gave no speeches and never treat such instances as a big deal, but that is how these wines show best. Even if it gave the sommelier something to snicker at for months on end, it made my dining companions and me happy. In the end, with wine, that's all that matters.

Part One:
Wines
of
North America

one

The Wines
of California

The Wines of California

California is on a roll. It seems as though people just can't get enough wine from the Golden State. The sunny, consistent, Mediterranean climate makes for big, ripe, fruity styles of wine with lots of alcohol and intensity. Producers are selling all they can make and planting vineyards on a grand scale to address the seemingly insatiable demand. Grape prices have never been higher for those who don't own their own vineyards, and land prices in glamour appellations such as the Napa Valley are at stratospheric levels. All of this adds up to one thing: It's a seller's market. California wine is getting more and more expensive at all levels. It is not unheard of for wines to double in price over two or three vintages. It has gone well beyond inflation in many instances and is getting into a "keeping up with the Joneses" situation. If a producer's neighbor raises prices, then why shouldn't he?

Cult Wine Mayhem

Industry insiders refer to an entire segment of new wineries and labels that seem to be popping up on a daily basis as "ego wineries," particularly in the more glamorous appellations where current land prices would never justify a land investment in pure business terms. These outfits are often started by someone who has made a fortune somewhere else. Fortunate, as the quickest way to make a small fortune in the wine business under the current terms is to start with a large one. Nonetheless, these enterprises are often started not to make money, but to create something. The goal is usually a "great" wine and everyone knows that great wine is expensive, right?

This leads us to the uniquely Californian phenomenon of wines with one or two vintages under the belt being sold for over $100 a bottle. A few people get together, make a bit of wine, it gets a favorable review, and before you can say "Screaming Eagle" someone is actually writing a check for something like $500, $600, do I hear $700 a bottle—sight unseen? What's a Ridge, or Stag's Leap, or Opus One to do? One can't blame these top shelf estates for taking modest 10% to 30% increases and gettin' while the gettins' good. At least they show breed and have a track record.

While this is the strangest wine market anyone has seen, there is one thing certain, it won't last. The Californians will find out what the Bordelaise have known for some time. Fine wine is a commodity and the market is cyclical. The next downturn in the stock market or the economy will bring with it a downturn in the super-premium wine market. These $50 and up wines are now just another commodity. They are not as much drunk as bought, sold, auctioned, and traded. When the party stops, the Opus Ones of the world will be fine, thank you very much. Their wines are great and they have built a loyal following over the last decade or three. As for some of the meteoric, flash-in-the-pan ego wineries? People will not be lining up to buy anymore, if that which they already bought is now worth a fraction of what they paid for it last year. Oh, by the way, how does it taste? These wines are more frequently admired than consumed. In the high-end California wine market today, as in the stock market, buyer beware, on the whole it is grossly overvalued.

Scale: Superlative (96-100), Exceptional (90-95), Highly Recommended (85-89), Recommended (80-84), Not Recommended (Under 80)

Stylistic Trends

There are also some worrying stylistic trends in California. Foremost among them is the retro-flashback to 1970s style, late harvest, high alcohol reds. I, and other people that actually drink wine in addition to just rating it, thought that these styles had been relegated to the back of the closet with pet rocks and platform heels. Come to think of it, platforms have come back haven't they? Perhaps Helen Turley owns a pair? Anyway, while the Californians spent much of the late '80s and early '90s admirably toiling away on concepts such as tannin management and soft extraction techniques that resulted in softer, better balanced, more accessible wines, the corresponding push for ever greater levels of ripeness, often in the name of "ripe tannins" and "flavor development" is now approaching the outer limits.

There are now a bevy of California reds over 15% alcohol, while 17% and up is not even uncommon anymore. Have you ever sat down to enjoy a bottle of red wine with a meal when that wine has 17% alcohol? How about a sweet, porty character due to the extreme ripeness? I will let these winemakers in on a secret. Only the British drink very high alcohol wines in warm climates—and they can't help it, they're British; they do it while wearing woolies and tweed. Yes, by the way, most of the country is warm much of the time. Even if we were in Alaska, however, overly alcoholic, porty reds are still too tough for most people to drink.

The insidious undercurrent here is that some would say these wines are made not to be drunk, but to be noticed—to reach out and grab the unsuspecting critic at a blind tasting—to jump out and say "Hey, look at me, I'm impressive." After all, critics spit, they don't actually try to drink a bottle or anything. No, that is up to the consumer who has just written a large check to acquire some of this massive, tannic, impenetrable elixir with the motor oil-like viscosity and the appropriately high rating. Once again, buyer beware, there is sometimes a difference between an impressive wine and a drinkable wine. Think about how you intend to use it before you buy it and when you read the tasting note, think about it again.

California at a Glance

Wines Reviewed:

2398

Producers/Brands Represented:

533

California Wine Is Good

Just so that no one gets the wrong impression so far, I would like to set the record straight. I like California wine. California wine is good. It is rich and flavorful and comes in a myriad of styles. The climate is forgiving and temperate and the wines are consistent. A number of producers are actually trying to hold the line on prices, and at the low end, say $8 or less per bottle, California still makes some of the world's best wine values. While the aforementioned wines that no one ever tastes grab the headlines, it is these more tangible California wines that bring a little sunshine to peoples' lives. California has the unique ability to make great wine at all levels, but sometimes gets caught up in its own sense of fashion. Perhaps that's the way it always is with California, just when you're ready to write it off as too crazy or far out, they seem to right the ship. For some reason, California always seems to make the most of its potential and make the rest of the world jealous in the process. For that reason, I think California wine will emerge better than ever in the next few years, but in the meantime, you will forgive me if I forego the expensive, but trendy motor oil, and keep buying from the vast majority of California producers who make delicious, balanced, reasonably priced wines.

Reviews

Acacia

1997 Chardonnay, Carneros $19.50.   **84**

Bright straw cast. Moderately full-bodied. Full acidity. Highly extracted. Minerals, citrus. Reined-in aromatically, with a lean and angular impression in the mouth. Firm and intense through the toasty finish.

1996 Chardonnay, Reserve, Carneros $30.   **82**

1995 Pinot Noir, Carneros $16.   **87**

Full cherry red. Medium-bodied. Moderately extracted. Moderately oaked. Mildly tannic. Rounded sweet and tart red fruit flavors have a vanilla oak edge that runs through the finish. Easygoing and straightforward.

1996 Pinot Noir, Reserve, Carneros $30.   **84**

Pale violet-ruby color. Medium-bodied. Moderately extracted. Mildly tannic. Red berries, minerals. Soft berry aromas lead a rounded mouthful of red berry flavors that concludes with some tannic grip. Acids are on the softer side, though this has some intensity and structure.

Acorn

1996 Dolcetto, Alegria Vineyards, Russian River Valley $18.   **87**

Bright purple. Medium-bodied. Full acidity. Highly extracted. Mildly oaked. Mildly tannic. Mint, dried herbs, black fruits. Pleasantly aromatic, with a full though lean palate feel. Finishes on an angular note.

Adastra

1996 Chardonnay, Carneros, Napa Valley $22.   **87**

Yellow-straw hue. Moderately full-bodied. Balanced acidity. Moderately extracted. Yellow apples, butter. Markedly buttery, toasty aromas. A full, rounded mouthfeel with juicy flavors that finish dryly. A generous, textured style.

Scale: Superlative (96-100), Exceptional (90-95), Highly Recommended (85-89), Recommended (80-84), Not Recommended (Under 80)

Adelaida

1996 Chardonnay, San Luis Obispo County $21.   86

Bright yellow-gold. Moderately full-bodied. Low acidity. Subtly extracted. Heavily oaked. Coconut, nuts. Generous flavors are dominated by sweet wood notes and a slight hint of maturity. Shows a broad low-acid mouthfeel and a lengthy oak-dominated finish.

1994 Cabernet Sauvignon, San Luis Obispo County $21.   86

Deep red-violet. Medium-bodied. Highly extracted. Moderately tannic. Black cherries, briar fruits, oak spice. Ripe, fleshy aromas show dark Cabernet fruit flavors complemented by chewy tannins. Not overly tough, but should soften with another year or two in the bottle.

1994 Calitage, San Luis Obispo County $27.   89

Bright ruby red. Medium-bodied. Moderately extracted. Moderately tannic. Red berries, vanilla. High-toned, fruity aromas follow through well on a particularly juicy palate, with elevated acids leaving the mouth refreshed. Tannins are supple and soft.

1995 Pinot Noir, HMR Vineyards, Paso Robles $24.   80

1995 Sangiovese, San Luis Obispo County $24.   90

Ruby purple. Medium-bodied. Balanced acidity. Highly extracted. Mildly oaked. Moderately tannic. Earth, red fruits. Dirty nose. Rustic, dry flavors finish with some grainy tannins. Very deep and concentrated, with great structure and plenty of new oak influence. Very ripe flavors.

1996 Zinfandel, San Luis Obispo County $19.   88

Bright cherry red. Medium-bodied. Balanced acidity. Moderately extracted. Moderately tannic. Pepper, red berries, minerals. Full, spicy, juicy fruit flavors have a big dash of pepper to complement them on the finish. Decent structure.

Adler Fels

1997 Chardonnay, Sonoma County $14.   82

1997 Chardonnay, Coleman Reserve, Sonoma County $16.   81

1997 Gewürztraminer, Sonoma County $11.   92

Deep yellow-gold. Penetrating, opulent lychee, spice, and melon aromas show great varietal intensity. A rich entry leads a full-bodied palate, with vibrant acidity and a glycerous texture. Extremely lengthy, flavorful finish. Drink now.

Aficionado Cellars

1996 Cabernet Sauvignon, Il Cuore, California $13.99.   83

Deep cherry red. Medium-bodied. Moderately extracted. Moderately oaked. Moderately tannic. Red fruits, cassis. Ripe berry fruit aromas lead solid, jammy flavors, with structure showing dry, fine-grained tannins that dry the mouth. A touch tough—better in a year or two.

Ahlgren

1996 Cabernet Franc, Bates Ranch, Santa Cruz Mountains $18.   89

Bright ruby purple. Medium-bodied. Balanced acidity. Moderately extracted. Mildly oaked. Mildly tannic. Red fruits, minerals, mint. Pleasantly aromatic, with a supple and generous quality to the palate. Smooth, harmonious, and well balanced, showing a sense of delicacy to the finish.

1993 Cabernet Sauvignon, Bates Ranch Reserve,
Santa Cruz Mountains $24.   80

Alban

1996 Grenache, Alban Estate Vineyard, Edna Valley $29.   92

Rich, opaque violet red to the rim. Powerful black fruit and vanilla aromas show a generous wood influence. A supple attack leads a moderately full-bodied palate, with velvety tannins. Lush, flavorful finish. Hedonistic and well balanced. Drink now.

1996 Reva Syrah, Edna Valley $23.   92

Deep purple, opaque to the rim. Intense blackberry, spicy oak, and olive flavors. Hefty wood tones. Firm entry. Full-bodied. Abundant grainy tannins. A rich, heavyweight style, with plenty of structuring tannin. Complex, intense varietal expression. Persistent rich finish. Drink within five years.

1996 Lorraine, Syrah, Edna Valley $29.   89

Deep purple, opaque, and luminous to the rim. Intense, fantastic oak, plum, blackberry, and coffee flavors. Hefty wood tones. Firm entry. Full-bodied. Plentiful grainy tannins. A heavyweight, with plenty of dry extract and spicy oak, and Rhone-like intensity. Lingering finish. Drink within five years.

Albertoni

1996 Barbera, California $13.99.   81
1996 Sangiovese, California $13.99.   86

Bright cherry red. Medium-bodied. Balanced acidity. Moderately extracted. Mildly tannic. Cherries, minerals, vanilla. Sweet berry aromas. Engaging and straightforward, with a soft, lingering finish.

Alderbrook

1997 Sauvignon Blanc, Dry Creek Valley $11.   84

Pale yellow-gold. Medium-bodied. Balanced acidity. Moderately extracted. Citrus, minerals. Yeasty, restrained aromas lead austere, tart citrus flavors with some mild dryness on the finish.

1997 Viognier, Russian River Valley $18.   81
1996 Cabernet Sauvignon, Sonoma County $16.   87

Deep purple. Moderately full-bodied. Balanced acidity. Highly extracted. Moderately oaked. Moderately tannic. Brown spices, game, earth. Forward and generous aromatics feature an unusual earthy touch. Quite firmly structured in the mouth, with hearty tannins that rear up on the finish.

1997 Pinot Noir, Russian River Valley $18.   81
1996 Zinfandel, OVOC, Sonoma County $16.   84

Deep blackish purple. Moderately full-bodied. Full acidity. Moderately extracted. Mildly oaked. Mildly tannic. Briar fruits, minerals, pickle barrel. Quite aromatic, with a fruit-centered palate feel. Crisp acidity lends a sense of vibrancy to the palate. Crisp through the finish.

Alexander Valley Vineyards

1997 Chardonnay, Wetzel Family Reserve, Alexander Valley $24.   83

Bright straw hue. Unusual blanched almond aromas seem to show a hint of oxidation. A rich entry leads a full-bodied palate with bright acidity and a mild sensation of sweetness. Brisk, vibrant finish. Drink now.

1996 Cabernet Franc, Wetzel Family Estate, Alexander Valley $20.   83

Bright ruby purple. Medium-bodied. Balanced acidity. Moderately extracted. Mildly tannic. Earth, minerals. Unusual aromatics lead a lighter-styled mouthfeel. Finishes on a lean, minerally note. Interesting, almost Old World in style.

1995 Cabernet Sauvignon, Alexander Valley $17.   85

Dark red. Medium-bodied. Moderately extracted. Mildly tannic. Blackberry, cassis, oak spice. Ripe black fruit aromas lead a plush, fruity palate, with some dry oak accents on the finish. Generously proportioned.

1996 Cabernet Sauvignon, Alexander Valley $17.50.   86

Bright ruby red with a slight fade. Medium-bodied. Balanced acidity. Moderately extracted. Moderately oaked. Mildly tannic. Earth, leather, black fruits. Distinctive, earthy aromatics lead a lean palate. Finishes with a slight note of bitterness.

1997 Syrah, Wetzel Family Estate, Alexander Valley $20.   81

Altamura

1995 Cabernet Sauvignon, Napa Valley $40.   91

Very deep purple-red hue. Intense, aromatic berry fruit and cordial aromas carry a slight oak influence. A lush entry leads to a moderately full-bodied palate with a stylish, lively mouthfeel, and velvety tannins. Supple and very lengthy flavorful finish. Exceptionally well balanced. Drink now or later.

1994 Sangiovese, Napa Valley $28.   90

Deep blackish ruby hue. Full-bodied. Balanced acidity. Highly extracted. Heavily oaked. Mildly tannic. Vanilla, black fruits. Quite aromatic and very modern in style, with a large-scaled, harmonious wave of dark fruit and toasty oak flavors. Rich and firmly structured, with exceptional length.

Amador Foothill Winery

1996 Fumé, Shenandoah Valley $8.   82

1996 Semillon, Shenandoah Valley $9.   86

Bright golden yellow. Medium-bodied. Full acidity. Moderately extracted. Kiwi, minerals, lemons. Clean tropical aromas follow through on a fresh, vibrant palate with a rounded mouthfeel. Well balanced.

1995 Sangiovese, Shenandoah Valley $12.   87

Deep ruby cast. Moderately full-bodied. Balanced acidity. Highly extracted. Mildly oaked. Moderately tannic. Overripe red fruits, herbs, wood. Shows a slightly Port-like quality and a touch of heat throughout. Rustic and full-framed, with tannins that bite down on the finish.

Anapamu

1996 Chardonnay, Central Coast $14.   90

Bright yellow-gold. Moderately full-bodied. Balanced acidity. Moderately extracted. Moderately oaked. Smoke, cream, tropical fruits. Aromatic and intense, with forward smoky flavors and a ripe creamy quality in the mouth. Shows fine balance through the lengthy finish.

1994 Cabernet Sauvignon, Monterey County $10.   83

Bright ruby red. Medium-bodied. Moderately extracted. Mildly tannic. Cherries, bell pepper, cedar. Rounded, plush, and soft, with a juicy character and very supple tannins that invite immediate drinking.

1996 Pinot Noir, Central Coast $14.   83

Pale cherry red. Moderately light-bodied. Subtly extracted. Mildly tannic. Red fruits, herbs, vanilla. Light, high-toned fruit aromas follow through on a lightly framed palate with subtle flavors that finish quickly.

S. Anderson

1997 Chardonnay, Carneros $22.   84

Bright pale gold. Generous aromas of honey and tropical fruits are rather unusual. A bright, fruity attack leads a moderately full-bodied palate with extravagant fruit intensity that follows through on the finish. A hedonistic, well-balanced style, though quite distinctive. Drink now.

1997 Chardonnay, Stags Leap District $22.   86

Pale yellow-straw hue. Aromatically restrained with an oaky note. A juicy attack is followed by a medium-bodied palate with moderate apple and pear flavors. The finish is clean, with good persistent acidity. Cleanly flavored and nicely textured.

1994 Cabernet Sauvignon, Richard Chambers Vineyard,
Stags Leap District $54.   95

Opaque ruby hue with purple highlights. Medium-bodied. Highly extracted. Moderately tannic. Red fruits, brown spice, cinnamon, chocolate. Bright, exotically spiced aromas. Elegant mouthfeel with concentrated red fruit flavors on entry that expand on the palate. The finish shows dry, textured tannins. This has cellaring structure.

1995 Cabernet Sauvignon, Richard Chambers Vineyard,
Stags Leap District $65.   94

Saturated blood-ruby red. Moderately full-bodied. Highly extracted. Moderately tannic. Spice, tobacco, black fruits. Dusty, exotic nose. Concentrated flavors show depth and a minerally edge persisting through a long finish that turns austere. Sublimely balanced and very approachable now.

1995 Merlot, Reserve, Stags Leap District $32.   89

Inky ruby color with purple highlights. Moderately full-bodied. Balanced acidity. Moderately extracted. Moderately oaked. Mildly tannic. Briar fruits, vanilla, minerals. Fruit centered with an aromatic and flavorful character. Light, bright, and well balanced on the palate. Some mildly astringent tannins pop up on the finish.

1996 Merlot, Reserve, Stags Leap District $40.   94

Bright purple-red, well saturated. Juicy, bright attack with plush, ripe flavors that are carried nicely by juicy acids. The tannins are particularly velvety and smooth on the finish. An elegant and concentrated style, which is drinking wonderfully. Drink now.

Anderson's Conn Valley Vineyards

1996 Chardonnay, Fournier Vineyard, Carneros $40.   86

Deep gold-straw color. Moderately full-bodied. Balanced acidity. Highly extracted. Moderately oaked. Butterscotch, pineapple. Thick, concentrated, and flavorful. This does veer toward the heavy buttery style, making for a rich finish.

1994 Cabernet Sauvignon, Estate Reserve, Napa Valley $40. 90

Very deep purple. Medium-bodied. Highly extracted. Mildly tannic. Vanilla, brown spice, plums. Sweet vanilla oak aromas. The tightly wound palate does not show much generosity in the middle at present. Fine-grained dry tannins dominate the finish.

1995 Cabernet Sauvignon, Estate Reserve, Napa Valley $48. 86

Bright ruby purple. Moderately full-bodied. Full acidity. Highly extracted. Mildly oaked. Moderately tannic. Vanilla, minerals, red fruits. Aromatically reserved, with a firm and linear mouthfeel. Firm tannins bite down on the finish. Needs time.

1993 Eloge, Napa Valley $60.   84

Deep ruby hue. Full-bodied. Full acidity. Highly extracted. Mildly oaked. Moderately tannic. Minerals, red fruits. Reserved and quite firm, with sturdy acidity and elevated tannins. Angular and quite lean through the finish. Needs time.

Angeline

1996 Zinfandel, Old Vine Cuvée, Mendocino County $11.   82

Antares

1996 Cabernet Sauvignon, California $30.   83

Bright purple red hue. Very ripe black fruit aromas with a note of anise. A firm entry leads to a moderately full-bodied palate with very flavorful black cherry and dry oak accents. Sturdy and well gripped through the finish.

1995 Merlot, California $24.99.   90

Deep ruby to the rim with brilliant clarity. Medium-bodied. Balanced acidity. Moderately extracted. Heavily oaked. Mildly tannic. Pencil shavings, plums, cedar. Pleasantly aromatic with a decided wood accent. In the mouth, this wine has the stuffing to balance out the oak, and all elements combine for an elegant, well-integrated finish.

Arciero

1995 Cabernet Franc, Paso Robles $10.50.   84

Pale ruby cast with a slight fade. Moderately light-bodied. Full acidity. Subtly extracted. Mildly oaked. Mildly tannic. Vanilla, citrus, red fruits. Lean and angular, with tart acidity through the finish. Flavors are wood driven and drying.

Scale: Superlative (96-100), Exceptional (90-95), Highly Recommended (85-89),
Recommended (80-84), Not Recommended (Under 80)

1995 Cabernet Sauvignon, Paso Robles $12.   82
1994 Nebbiolo, Paso Robles $9.95.   80
1995 Sangiovese, Paso Robles $14.99.   83
Bright ruby-garnet cast. Medium-bodied. Balanced acidity. Moderately extracted. Mildly oaked. Mildly tannic. Overripe red fruits, sweet herbs. Quite aromatic, with a slight Port-like note. Light and soft in the mouth, with some edgy acidity that props up the finish. Interesting.

Arrowood

1997 Chardonnay, Sonoma County $24.   82
1996 Chardonnay, Réserve Spéciale, Cuvée Michel Berthoud,
Sonoma County $38.   92
Bright straw hue. Elegant, yeasty, toasty aromas show a degree of complexity and a harmonious oak accent. A rich entry leads a moderately full-bodied palate with rounded acidity. The finish is creamy and persistent. A well-balanced and elegant style that is not overly weighty or flashy. Drink now.

1995 Cabernet Sauvignon, Sonoma County $35.   90
Bright ruby-purple hue. Generous red fruit and mineral aromas are concentrated and intense. A supple entry leads to a ripe, moderately full-bodied mouthfeel with velvety tannins. Forward, lengthy finish. Harmonious and elegant with exceptional balance and finesse. Drink now or later.

1994 Cabernet Sauvignon, Réserve Spéciale, Sonoma County $50.   92
Opaque ruby cast. Full-bodied. Balanced acidity. Moderately extracted. Mildly oaked. Mildly tannic. Minerals, chocolate, earth. Generous aromas are complex and forward. Full yet well structured in the mouth, with a supple, harmonious quality. Seamless through the lengthy finish.

Atlas Peak Vineyards

1997 Chardonnay, Atlas Peak, Napa Valley $16.   86
Bright pale yellow-gold. Moderate aromas of very subtle toasty oak and ripe citrus. A crisp entry leads a moderately full-bodied palate with ripe flavors and generous alcohol that combine with oak spice on the finish. Generous though well balanced by acids. Drink now.

1994 Cabernet Sauvignon, Atlas Peak, Napa Valley $18.   88
Deep ruby hue. Medium-bodied. Full acidity. Moderately extracted. Heavily oaked. Moderately tannic. Brown spices, cedar, red fruits. Exotic aromas feature a hefty wood accent. Firm and angular in the mouth, with a lean core of flavors. Crisp finish with some grip. Well balanced.

1995 Cabernet Sauvignon, Atlas Peak, Napa Valley $18.   80
1995 Cabernet Sauvignon, Consenso Vineyards, Atlas Peak,
Napa Valley $30.   83
Bright ruby with a slight fade. Forward, meaty, earthy, vanilla aromas show an oak accent and seem to be reductive. May blow off with aeration. A firm attack leads to a medium-bodied palate with grainy tannins. Subdued finish. Interesting, but could use a bit more grip through the finish. Drink now or later.

1995 Sangiovese, Reserve, Atlas Peak, Napa Valley $24.   86
Deep ruby red. Medium-bodied. Full acidity. Highly extracted. Moderately oaked. Moderately tannic. Bitter cherries, earth, minerals. Not very aromatic. Solid, flavorsome palate has bitter red fruit flavors and a large dose of spice in the finish. Quite an austere style.

Au Bon Climat

1997 Chardonnay, Santa Barbara County $18.   89
Medium yellow-straw hue. Smoky, yeasty aromas with ripe apple fruit. A fruity entry leads a moderately full-bodied palate with a glycerous, rich mouthfeel and juicy fruit acids persisting through the finish. Rather stylish. Drink now or later.

1996 Chardonnay, Le Bouge D'à Côte, Santa Barbara County $19.   89

Bright yellow-straw cast. Moderately full-bodied. Full acidity. Moderately extracted. Moderately oaked. Smoke, tart citrus. Striking smoky, yeasty aromas lead a tart citrus entry with a linear, bright follow-through showing bright acids and a youthful structure. Taut and young now.

1997 Chardonnay, Reserve Talley, Arroyo Grande Valley $25.   84

Bright yellow-straw hue. Restrained citrus, yeast, and mineral aromas. A crisp entry leads a moderately full-bodied palate with balanced acidity. Mildly buttery, stylish finish. Drink now.

1997 Chardonnay, Alban Vineyard, Edna Valley $35.   93

Deep straw hue. Exotic yeast, tropical fruit, and vanilla aromas show a harmonious oak influence. A zesty attack leads a moderately full-bodied palate with racy acidity. Intense, refreshing finish. Drink now or later.

95/96 Pinot Noir, Central Coast $19.   90

Pale garnet with a fading rim. Medium-bodied. Moderately extracted. Moderately oaked. Mildly tannic. Strong and exotic earthy, minerally nose. Plenty of herbal complexity, with crisp red fruit and a nice mouthfeel. Deceptively long finish with good varietal character. Drinking nicely now.

1996 Pinot Noir, La Bauge Au-Dessus, Santa Barbara County $25.   85

Pale ruby cast. Moderately full-bodied. Full acidity. Moderately extracted. Mildly oaked. Mildly tannic. Earth, minerals, dried herbs. Unusual earthy aromas lead a firm, intense mouthfeel that has spritzy acidity. Lean through the finish. Rather disjointed but perhaps just suffering from the pangs of youth.

1996 Pinot Noir, Sanford & Benedict Vineyard, Santa Ynez Valley $35.   90

Bright cherry-ruby cast. Moderately full-bodied. Full acidity. Moderately extracted. Mildly oaked. Mildly tannic. Minerals, spice. Quite aromatic, with complex minerally flavors throughout. Lean and zesty in the mouth, with a precise linear quality. Firm and intense through the lengthy finish.

1996 Pinot Noir, Piccho and Rincon, Arroyo Grande Valley $40.   92

Pale cinnamon-ruby cast. Moderately full-bodied. Full acidity. Highly extracted. Moderately oaked. Mildly tannic. Iron, minerals, spice. Intense, complex aromatics are a dead ringer for a first rate Vosne-Romanée. Firm and lean in the mouth, with an intensely minerally backbone. Finishes with fine grip and intensity. Should age well.

1996 Pinot Noir, Isabelle, California $50.   90

Violet red with a pale rim. Medium-bodied. Moderately extracted. Mildly oaked. Flowers, red berries, vanilla. Classically perfumed Pinot Noir aromas lead a mouthwatering, succulent palate with just a hint of dry astringency on the finish. Textbook.

Audubon

1996 Chardonnay, Sangiacomo Vineyards, Carneros, Sonoma $14.   81

1996 Merlot, Hopper Creek Vineyard, Napa Valley $20.   89

Deep ruby red with a fading rim. Earthy, herbal, spicy aromas have a woody character. Medium-bodied with a soft attack and developed, mature flavors. Moderately tannic with a powdery texture through the finish. This is near its optimum maturity. Drink now.

1997 Late Harvest Chardonnay, Trio C Vineyard, Napa Valley $12/375 ml. 84

Deep gold-straw hue. Forward honey and spice aromas. A sweet entry leads a medium-bodied palate. Soft, lush, and rounded. Drink now.

Babcock

1996 Pinot Noir, Santa Ynez Valley $30.   86

Full cherry red. Medium-bodied. Moderately extracted. Moderately oaked. Moderately tannic. Cherries, vanilla, minerals. Sweet, fleshy fruit aromas follow through on the palate. Has some grip on the finish, making for a solid style.

1997 Pinot Noir, Santa Barbara County $20.   89

Bright ruby hue with a violet rim. Medium-bodied. Moderately extracted. Cherries, minerals, vanilla. Sweet, ripe red fruit flavors are complemented by vanilla oak accents that linger through the finish. Stylish, though acids are a tad low, making for a soft, easy-drinking style.

1996 Sangiovese, Eleven Oaks, Santa Ynez Valley $18.   85

Deep blackish ruby cast. Moderately full-bodied. Balanced acidity. Moderately extracted. Moderately oaked. Mildly tannic. Leather, brown spices, earth. Quite aromatic, with a distinctive, gamey flavor profile. Rich, supple, and velvety in the mouth, with firm structure through the lengthy finish.

Baileyana

1997 Chardonnay, Edna Valley $17.   89

Bright gold-straw hue. Restrained butter and orange marmalade aromas. A crisp entry leads a moderately full-bodied palate with vibrant acidity. Lengthy, oak-kissed finish. Drink now or later.

Baily

1997 Montage, Temecula $11.   81
1997 Merlot, Temecula $15.95.   81

Bandiera

1997 Chardonnay, Coastal California $9.   83

Pale straw cast. Medium-bodied. Balanced acidity. Moderately extracted. Pears, melon. Features an agreeable fruit accent to the nose. Crisp and light in the mouth with a vibrant finish.

1997 Cabernet Sauvignon, Coastal, California $9.   83

Deep purple-red hue. Forward vanilla, black fruit, and mineral aromas belie a generous oak accent. A lush attack leads to a medium-bodied palate with velvety tannins and just enough acidity to lend a sense of buoyancy on the palate. Soft, flavorful finish. Drink now.

1995 Cabernet Sauvignon, Reserve 5, Napa Valley $14.   84

Saturated red-purple. Moderately full-bodied. Highly extracted. Moderately tannic. Spice, black fruits, licorice. Very ripe, generous aromas follow through on the palate, with a fruit-forward entry that concludes with a dry, short finish.

1996 Merlot, California $9.   81

Barefoot

1997 Chardonnay, Reserve, Sonoma County $9.99.   83

Bright yellow-straw hue. Unusual, subdued citrus and mineral aromas show a touch of heat. A lean entry leads a medium-bodied palate with rounded acidity. Quick buttery finish. Drink now.

NV White Zinfandel, California $3.99.   80

Bargetto

1997 Chardonnay, Regan Vineyards, Santa Cruz Mountains $18.   86

Pale straw hue. Subdued citrus and mineral aromas. A crisp entry, a medium-bodied palate, vibrant acidity. The finish is clean and racy. Drink now.

1997 Pinot Grigio, Central Coast $15.   87

Bright platinum cast. Moderately full-bodied. Balanced acidity. Moderately extracted. Smoke, citrus, minerals. Aromatic and flavorful, with a ripe melange of smoky flavors. Full in the mouth yet well balanced, with angular acidity. Shows fine grip and intensity on the finish.

1995 Cabernet Sauvignon, Santa Cruz Mountains $18.   88

Deep saturated ruby cast. Medium-bodied. Balanced acidity. Highly extracted. Mildly oaked. Moderately tannic. Spice, minerals. Pleasantly aromatic, with real complexity to the minerally flavors. Firm, lean, and angular through the precise finish.

1993 Cabernet Sauvignon, Bates Ranch, Santa Cruz Mountains $18.   86

Rich ruby red. Medium-bodied. Moderately extracted. Mildly tannic. Dill, brown spice, plums, earth. Outstanding spicy, earthy aromas reveal a supple, rounded palate with exotic brown spice notes through the finish. Attractive and juicy, but with a certain earthy note. Very approachable now.

1996 Merlot, California $18.   86

Deep ruby red to the rim with brilliant clarity. Moderately full-bodied. Balanced acidity. Highly extracted. Mildly oaked. Mildly tannic. Black fruits, sweet herbs, vanilla, earth. Though aromatically restrained, this wine is deeply flavored and lush on the palate. Well balanced and rich, with a pleasant herbal accent that adds complexity to the fruit flavors.

1996 Merlot, Santa Cruz Mountains $25.   86

Bright ruby red to the rim. Aggressive tea, herb, and mint aromas carry a slight oak accent. A soft attack is followed by a medium-bodied palate with juicy acidity and grainy tannins. Fades toward the finish. Unusual but interesting. Drink now.

1996 Merlot, Regan Vineyard, Santa Cruz Mountains $24.   84

Deep ruby hue with brilliant clarity. Medium-bodied. Full acidity. Moderately extracted. Moderately oaked. Moderately tannic. Red fruits, vanilla, minerals. Quite crisp, with buoy-ant acidity that turns sharp on a lighter-styled palate. Astringent tannins mark the finish.

1994 Pinot Noir, Santa Cruz Mountains $20.   88

Pale cherry red. Medium-bodied. Moderately extracted. Mildly tannic. Tart red berry and vanilla aromas show complexity. Crisp cherry flavors have a solid mineral note, with toasty oak spice on the finish.

Chaucers Mead, $9.   86

Deep yellow-straw cast. Moderately full-bodied. Low acidity. Moderately extracted. Honey, cream, vanilla. Fragrant and extremely pure in flavor, with a balanced, rounded mouthfeel. Finishes with fine length and mild sweetness.

Chaucers Raspberry Wine, $9/500 ml.   86

Deep ruby cast. Moderately full-bodied. Full acidity. Highly extracted. Raspberries, minerals. Pleasantly aromatic, with definitive red fruit overtones and a flavorful palate. Firm and concentrated, with vibrant acidity making for a tart finish. The sweetness provides a sense of roundness in the mouth. Lengthy and intense.

Barnett

1994 Cabernet Sauvignon, Spring Mountain District, Napa Valley $35.   87

Dark cherry red. Medium-bodied. Highly extracted. Quite tannic. Black cherries, currants, minerals, toasted oak. Solid and immensely dry through the finish, with mouthcoating tannins. Has some nice toasty qualities and black fruit flavors, though it needs time before it is approachable.

1995 Cabernet Sauvignon, Spring Mountain District, Napa Valley $35.   92

Deep ruby hue with a slight purple cast. Moderately full-bodied. Balanced acidity. Highly extracted. Moderately tannic. Anise, minerals, sweet herbs. Features an enticing and exotic high-toned array of flavors. Well structured and deep in the mouth, with firm tannins through the finish. Needs time.

Bartholomew Park

1996 Cabernet Sauvignon, Desnudos Vineyard, Sonoma Valley $35.   90

Deep purple-red hue. Intense plum, mineral, and herb aromas jump from the glass. A supple entry leads to a moderately full-bodied palate with excellent acidic grip and silky tannins. Lengthy, complex finish. Exquisitely balanced and harmonious. Drink now or later.

Scale: Superlative (96-100), Exceptional (90-95), Highly Recommended (85-89), Recommended (80-84), Not Recommended (Under 80)

34

1996 Merlot, Alta Vista Vineyards, Sonoma Valley $32.   94

Bright purple with a subtle fade. Intense red cherry and herb aromas. A supple attack leads a moderately full-bodied palate with velvety tannins and juicy acids. The lingering finish is flavorful and fruity. Drink now or later. Can improve with more age.

1995 Pinot Noir, Sonoma Valley $23.   82

Beaucanon

1997 Chardonnay, Reserve, Napa Valley $12.   89

Pale straw cast. Moderately full-bodied. Balanced acidity. Moderately extracted. Minerals, melon, citrus. Forward aromas feature a subtle spicy accent. Rich and fruity on entry, with a weighty midpalate. Finishes with lingering zesty acids.

1997 Chardonnay, Jacques de Coninck, Napa Valley $30.   87

Bright yellow-gold. Richly aromatic with full smoky, tropical accents. A lush entry leads a full-bodied palate with rich, rounded texture and generous alcohol. Finishes with a toasty oak accent and a note of warmth. Drink now.

1994 Cabernet Sauvignon, Napa Valley $14.   89

Medium cherry red. Medium-bodied. Moderately extracted. Moderately tannic. Red fruits, minerals, tea. Bright but rather lean, with a firm minerally backbone through to the finish. Solid, with well-extracted flavors and some firm tannins.

1995 Cabernet Sauvignon, Napa Valley $14.   86

Bright ruby violet. Medium-bodied. Highly extracted. Moderately tannic. Black fruits, brown spice. Lighter and crisp, showing a hint of very dry tannin on the finish. A fruit-centered, supple style that shows Cabernet flavors in a very balanced package. Suited to current drinking.

1996 Cabernet Sauvignon, Reserve, Napa Valley $14.   86

Bright crimson-red hue with a subtle fade to the rim. Muted aromas show oak spice and dark fruits. A crisp entry leads a medium-bodied palate with moderate cassis fruit flavors and a minerally, tannic grip through the finish. A lighter style with lively acids. Drink now.

1995 Merlot, Napa Valley $15.   81

1996 Merlot, Reserve, Napa Valley $15.   83

Full ruby-violet hue with a subtle fade. Crisp, fragrant aromas show red fruits and vanilla. Smooth on the attack, with a moderately full body and lush black cherry flavors. Finishes with fine-grained tannins and vanilla oak. Drink now or later. Can improve with more age.

Beaulieu

1997 Chardonnay, Coastal, California $9.99.   81

1997 Chardonnay, BV Carneros, Carneros $12.99.   83

Yellow-straw color. Medium-bodied. Balanced acidity. Moderately extracted. Moderately oaked. Lime zest, minerals. Straightforward citrus zest flavors with a minerally finish. An undemanding, easy-drinking style.

1996 Sauvignon Blanc, Napa Valley $10.95.   80

1996 Viognier, BV, Napa Valley $16.   84

Deep yellow-gold. Full-bodied. Low acidity. Moderately extracted. Mildly oaked. Toast, butter, oranges. Extremely full and ripe with a fat and unctuous palate feel. Has an oak accent with a buttery finish, making for an opulent style suited for near-term drinking.

1997 Pinot Noir Vin Gris, Signet Collection, Carneros $8.   84

Very pale russet hue. Generous strawberry and herb aromas. A lush entry leads a medium-bodied palate showing supple acidity. The finish is flavorful and stylish. Quite light, but showing interesting flavors. Drink now.

1994 Cabernet Sauvignon, Georges de Latour Private Reserve, Rutherford $50.   92

Dark cherry red. Medium-bodied. Highly extracted. Moderately tannic. Cassis, cherries, brown spice. Full toasty nose leads a dusty mouthful of concentrated, layered red fruit flavors, with generous oak spice notes lingering in the finish. Not fleshy, but still very generous and structured in its proportions. This should have good cellar potential.

1995 Cabernet Sauvignon, Georges de Latour Private Reserve, Rutherford $59.99.   92

Very deep, saturated ruby cast with a purple edge. Moderately full-bodied. Balanced acidity. Moderately extracted. Moderately oaked. Mildly tannic. Cassis, brown spices, minerals. Classic black currant aromas are intense and forward. Full, generous, and rich, with supple and abundant tannins lending a seamless quality through the finish. An elegant and refined wine.

1995 Grenache, Signet Collection, San Benito $8.   81

1994 Tapestry Reserve, Napa Valley $20.   90

Deep crimson red with purple highlights. Medium-bodied. Moderately extracted. Moderately tannic. Vanilla, toasted oak, black fruits. Harmonious, generous Cabernet fruit aromas. Solid midpalate with curranty fruit flavors and toasty notes throughout. Fine-grained, textured tannins through the finish.

1995 Tapestry Reserve, Napa Valley $24.99.   89

Saturated dark red. Moderately full-bodied. Highly extracted. Moderately tannic. Brown spice, black fruits, licorice. Spicy, dark fruit aromas have a dusty quality. Lush mouthfeel with cordial-like flavors up front, turning dry and spicy through the finish. Quite a classic structure.

1994 Merlot, Napa Valley $12.99.   85

Deep ruby red to the rim with brilliant highlights. Medium-bodied. Balanced acidity. Moderately extracted. Mildly tannic. Red fruits, dried herbs, minerals. Pleasant and well integrated, with firm structure and an angular presence on the palate. Finishes with dusty, drying tannins and lingering flavors.

1997 Pinot Noir, Carneros $16.   81

1995 Pinot Noir, Reserve, Carneros $29.95.   87

Full pinkish-tinged red. Medium-bodied. Moderately extracted. Heavily oaked. Mildly tannic. New oak dominates on the nose. Crisp blackberry and blueberry fruit flavors show through plenty of new oak on the palate. Some astringency on the finish. Quite high toned.

1996 Pinot Noir, Reserve, Carneros $30.   93

Deep violet red. Moderately full-bodied. Moderately extracted. Mildly tannic. Chocolate, vanilla, cherries. Perfumed, oak-accented aromas lead a full-flavored chocolatey mouthfeel, with a dusting of dry tannins through the finish. An elegant and flavorful style.

1996 Beauzeaux, Signet Collection, California $20.   87

Deep ruby red to the rim. Generous red fruit and mineral aromas. A supple attack leads a full-bodied palate showing dark fleshy fruits and chocolate flavors, with drying tannins. Clipped, deeply flavored finish. Well extracted and youthful, with a bit of an edge to the finish. Drink now or later. Can improve with more age.

1996 Ensemble, Signet Collection, California $25.   90

Deep ruby red to the rim. Generous red fruit and chocolate aromas. A supple attack leads a moderately full-bodied palate with silky tannins. Attractive, velvety finish. Quite stylish, and eminently drinkable. Drink within five years.

1995 Sangiovese, Signet Collection, Napa Valley $16.   83

Dark ruby red with a lightening rim. Medium-bodied. Balanced acidity. Moderately extracted. Moderately oaked. Moderately tannic. Earth, minerals. Austere aromas show some maturity. Uncompromisingly dry, assertive palate shows fine-grained tannins through the finish.

Scale: Superlative (96-100), Exceptional (90-95), Highly Recommended (85-89), Recommended (80-84), Not Recommended (Under 80)

36

1995 Syrah, Signet Collection, Dry Creek Valley $25.   92

Deep ruby red to the rim. Forward spice box, tobacco, and earth aromas show a hefty wood accent. A firm attack leads a moderately full-bodied palate with tannic grip and buoyant acidity. Lingering, flavorful, edgy finish. Quite stylish, with fine cool-climate varietal intensity. Drink now or later. Can improve with more age.

1996 Syrah, Signet Collection, North Coast $25.   87

Dark ruby red to the rim. Forward, overripe red fruit and mineral aromas show a judicious oak accent. A firm attack leads a medium-bodied palate that shows drying tannins. Angular, snappy finish. Compact and reserved. Drink now.

1996 Zinfandel, BV, Napa Valley $14.   84

Bright cherry red. Medium-bodied. Balanced acidity. Moderately extracted. Mildly oaked. Moderately tannic. Vanilla, black fruits. Ripe berry aromas lead a rounded palate with aggressive tannins drying the finish.

NV Muscat de Beaulieu, California $10.99/375 ml.   90

Deep tawny hue with orange highlights. Forward, spirity butterscotch and orange peel aromas. A rich entry leads a moderately full-bodied palate that has warm, spicy flavors. Liqueur-like. Showing fine intensity. Drink now.

Bel Arbor

1997 Chardonnay, California $5.99.   81
1997 White Zinfandel, California $5.99.   84

Very pale pink. Subdued citrus and berry aromas. A crisp entry leads a medium-bodied palate with a nice balance between sweetness and acidity. Shows decent intensity of flavor with a lengthy finish. Drink now.

1997 Merlot, California $6.99.   81

Bell

1994 Cabernet Sauvignon, Baritelle Vineyard, Rutherford $50.   86

Light, bright brick red. Moderately light-bodied. Moderately extracted. Mildly tannic. Bramble fruit, cherries, minerals. Rounded red fruit flavors, with a minerally, earthy, dry finish. Not fleshy, but it does show some structure and length in an austere manner.

1995 Cabernet Sauvignon, Baritelle Vineyard, Jackson Clone, Rutherford $50.   84

Bright brick red hue. Classic dusty, cedary aromas. A flavorful entry leads a medium-bodied palate with juicy mature fruit flavors and elegant cedary, dusty character. Evolved, softer tannins make this very attractive now. Drink now.

Bella Vigna

1997 Merlot, Twin Creeks Vineyard, Lodi $12.   86

Full ruby red with a subtle fade. Generously spicy aromas show a toasty oak accent with ripe fruity notes. A soft entry lead a medium-bodied palate with powdery, elegant tannins. Finishes with notably fine oak spice and fruit persistence. Very well balanced and varietally expressive. Drink now.

Belvedere

1997 Chardonnay, Sonoma County $10.   84

Bright straw hue. Muted citric aromas carry a very slight oak accent. A crisp entry is followed by a moderately full-bodied palate with creamy acidity. Rounded, buttery finish. Drink now.

1994 Cabernet Sauvignon, Dry Creek Valley $13.50.   89

Bright reddish purple. Medium-bodied. Highly extracted. Moderately tannic. Tobacco, plums, brown spice. Rich toasty aromas lead a ripe, rich mouthful of plummy fruits showing great texture and integration. Soft, rounded tannins linger through the finish.

1995 Cabernet Sauvignon, Dry Creek Valley $16.   89

Saturated blood red. Moderately full-bodied. Highly extracted. Moderately tannic. Currant, minerals. Jammy, ripe fruit aromas follow through on the palate. Chewy and rich, with a minerally note on the finish.

1996 Merlot, Dry Creek Valley $16.   88

Dark violet-red with a slight fade. Rich oaky aromas with black fruit accents. A lush attack leads a moderately full-bodied palate with fine-grained dry tannins and soft juicy acids. Short-term cellaring may help, but don't wait too long. Drink now or later.

1995 Merlot, Preferred Stock, Dry Creek Valley $24.   86

Very deep blackish ruby hue. Moderately full-bodied. Full acidity. Highly extracted. Heavily oaked. Moderately tannic. Vanilla, black fruits, menthol. Quite aromatic, with a big palate feel accented by mouthwatering acidity. Has a very deep core of fruit flavors but maintains a sense of lightness. Tannins grip down on the finish. It's a bit tough at present; mid-term (3-6 years) aging may make it more accessible.

1996 Pinot Noir, Anderson Valley $12.   88

Bright pale ruby cast. Medium-bodied. Full acidity. Moderately extracted. Mildly tannic. Iron, red fruits. Fragrant and intense, with an exotic minerally quality. Angular and zesty in the mouth, with bright flavors and a clean finish.

1995 Zinfandel, Dry Creek Valley $12.   84

Bright ruby purple to rim. Medium-bodied. Balanced acidity. Highly extracted. Moderately tannic. Briar fruits, chocolate, dried herbs. Fairly aromatic, with a firm and somewhat angular mouthfeel. Showing solid grip, but a little ungenerous.

Benziger

1996 Chardonnay, Carneros $13.   86

Bright yellow-gold. Medium-bodied. Balanced acidity. Moderately extracted. Moderately oaked. Coconut, yeast, apples. Sweet oak aromas follow through on a ripe, juicy palate, with a hint of dryness and spice on the finish.

1995 Tribute White, Sonoma Mountain $17.   91

Brilliant yellow-gold. Medium-bodied. Balanced acidity. Moderately extracted. Mildly oaked. Vanilla, citrus, butter. Toasty, zesty aromas. On the palate, a lovely overlay of vanilla with a hint of butter. Fine grip, concentration, and length, and drinking well now.

1996 Pinot Blanc, Imagery Series, Bien Nacido Vineyard, Santa Maria Valley $18.   81

1996 Fumé Blanc, Sonoma County $10.   90

Bright medium straw cast. Medium-bodied. Balanced acidity. Moderately extracted. Moderately oaked. Vanilla, smoke, citrus. Oak accents are pronounced on the nose. Spicy and oaky on the palate, with brisk citrus flavors elevated by racy acids.

**1996 Cabernet Franc, Imagery Series,
Rancho Salina & Blue Rock Vineyards, Sonoma County $22.**   89

Bright ruby purple. Medium-bodied. Balanced acidity. Moderately extracted. Moderately oaked. Mildly tannic. Vanilla, red fruits, minerals. Extremely aromatic, with an expensive oak overlay and a seamless core of red fruit flavors. Well balanced and harmonious, displaying a sense of delicacy. Refined and crisp through the lengthy, flavorful finish.

1995 Cabernet Sauvignon, Sonoma County $16.   90

Full dark red with bright highlights. Medium-bodied. Moderately extracted. Mildly tannic. Cassis, mint, black fruits, vanilla. Ripe, juicy berry aromas have sweet vanilla accents that are confirmed on the palate. Very rounded and open-knit in an accessible style. Plenty of sweet varietal Cabernet flavors.

1996 Cabernet Sauvignon, Sonoma County $17.   89

Dark ruby cast. Moderately full-bodied. Balanced acidity. Highly extracted. Moderately oaked. Mildly tannic. Black fruits, vanilla. Ripe and generous, with a fruit-forward personality and a lash of sweet vanilla oak. Generous on the palate, with mouthwatering acidity and angular tannins lending structure to the flavorful finish.

Scale: Superlative (96-100), Exceptional (90-95), Highly Recommended (85-89), Recommended (80-84), Not Recommended (Under 80)

1995 Cabernet Sauvignon, Ash Creek Vineyards Reserve, Alexander Valley $25.   86

Dark purple. Full-bodied. Balanced acidity. Highly extracted. Moderately oaked. Moderately tannic. Vanilla, black fruits. Generous aromas lead a dense and chunky palate feel. Ripe and flavorful throughout, with big tannins on the lengthy oak-tinged finish.

1995 Cabernet Sauvignon, Rancho Salina Vineyard, Sonoma Valley $28.   89

Bright red-purple. Moderately full-bodied. Moderately extracted. Moderately tannic. Black fruits, toasted oak. Bright berry aromas follow through on a vibrant palate that finishes with a toasty note and dry, fine-grained tannins. High-toned style.

1995 Cabernet Sauvignon, Reserve, Sonoma Mountain $35.   90

Saturated cherry red. Medium-bodied. Moderately extracted. Mildly tannic. Cassis, vanilla, spice. Rich, spicy, fleshy aromas lead a supple, textured palate with opulent fruit flavors and very supple tannins. Weighty and solid nonetheless.

1994 Tribute Red, Sonoma Mountain $25.   88

Deep reddish purple. Medium-bodied. Highly extracted. Moderately tannic. Cassis, vanilla, tobacco. Lots of chewy Cabernet fruit. Well-extracted dry tannins linger on the finish with sweet cedary notes. Very rounded and supple in the middle. Quite attractive now.

1995 Tribute Red, Sonoma Mountain $25.   91

Saturated dark ruby hue. Medium-bodied. Moderately extracted. Mildly tannic. Black fruits, coffee. Ripe, fleshy aromas follow through on an open-knit palate, with charred brown spice notes on the finish. Very supple.

1995 Merlot, Reserve, Sonoma County $32.   92

Deep blackish ruby hue. Moderately full-bodied. Balanced acidity. Highly extracted. Heavily oaked. Mildly tannic. Vanilla, black fruits, mint. Almost Australian in style, with a huge overlay of oak and a deep core of vibrant fruit flavors. Well integrated nonetheless, with solid grip and fine balance. Lingering flavorful finish.

1995 Pinot Noir, California $18.   88

Medium cherry red with purple highlights. Medium-bodied. Moderately extracted. Moderately oaked. Mildly tannic. Rounded, ripe berry flavors have a mild sweetness. A smooth, textured mouthfeel gives a polished feel. Plenty of sweet oak flavors make this very accessible.

Beringer

1997 Chardonnay, Founders' Estate, California $9.99.   82

1996 Chardonnay, Napa Valley $15.   86

Bright yellow-gold. Medium-bodied. Balanced acidity. Moderately extracted. Green apples, brown spice, vanilla. Typical aromas of oak spice and butter follow through with a textured, rounded palate feel, and a finish that shows spicy persistence.

1997 Chardonnay, Appellation Collection, Napa Valley $16.   83

Brilliant yellow-gold. Quite aromatic, showing browned butter and green apple aromas with a subtle oak accent. A crisp entry leads a medium-bodied palate with tart flavors and subtle oak spice. The finish is clean and quick. Rather lean. Drink now.

1996 Chardonnay, Private Reserve, Napa Valley $30.   90

Deep golden hue. Moderately full-bodied. Balanced acidity. Moderately extracted. Moderately oaked. Yeast, brown spices, bread dough. Ripe and opulent, with forward oak-accented aromatics and a big yeasty component. Weighty on the palate, yet balanced by appropriate acidity. Fine length and intensity on the finish.

1997 Chardonnay, Private Reserve, Napa Valley $36.   92

Brilliant golden yellow. Rich smoky, toasty oak aromas with yeast notes. A firm attack leads a moderately full-bodied palate with vibrant citrus flavors and lingering vanilla notes. Impressively concentrated. Drink now or later.

1996 Chardonnay, Sbragia-Limited Release, Napa Valley $35. 94

Bright yellow-gold. Moderately full-bodied. Full acidity. Moderately extracted. Moderately oaked. Yeast, yellow apples, brown spice. Rich butter and spice aromas follow through on the palate. Very spicy and direct, with a big up-front rush of flavors that taper through the finish. Extravagant yeasty qualities are a standout.

1996 Alluvium Blanc, Knights Valley $16. 82

1996 Sauvignon Blanc, Napa Valley $9. 90

Deep yellow-gold. Moderately full-bodied. Balanced acidity. Moderately extracted. Heavily oaked. Vanilla, brown spices, oranges. A hefty overlay of oak is supported by a core of ripe fruit flavors. Lush and rich in the mouth with a pleasant smoky finish.

1996 Viognier, Napa Valley $25. 87

Deep golden hue. Full-bodied. Balanced acidity. Moderately extracted. Moderately oaked. Toasted coconut, vanilla, tropical fruits. Wood accented, with a flavor profile dominated by oak. Attractive nonetheless, with a ripe palate feel that is rich yet well balanced by acidity through the finish. Made like a California Chardonnay.

1998 White Zinfandel, California $6. 81

1997 Rosé de Saignée, California $16. 89

Pale russet hue. Generous, rich bread dough and red fruit aromas. A soft entry leads a rich, moderately full-bodied palate that has great flavor intensity. Supple and stylish. Drink now.

1994 Cabernet Sauvignon, Knights Valley $20. 88

Bright crimson purple. Medium-bodied. Moderately extracted. Mildly tannic. Black cherries, vanilla. Bright dried fruit flavors on entry conclude with gentle tannins and vanilla sweetness, giving this a lighter note through the finish. Very attractive and well balanced. Drinking nicely now.

1995 Cabernet Sauvignon, Appellation Collection, Knights Valley $22. 86

Dark violet hue. Generous aromas of black cherry and vanilla. A fruity entry leads a medium-bodied palate with lush black fruits and soft tannins that fade quickly on the finish. Very user friendly. Drink now.

1993 Cabernet Sauvignon, Private Reserve, Napa Valley $65. 94

Opaque dark red-purple. Moderately full-bodied. Highly extracted. Quite tannic. Toasted oak, plums, cassis, pepper. Toasted oak and black fruit aromas. Tons of chewy black Cabernet fruit, with solid dry tannins through the finish. Assertive and structured, this should do well in the cellar.

1994 Cabernet Sauvignon, Private Reserve, Napa Valley $75. 97

Brilliant deep ruby red hue. Richly aromatic with generous vanilla oak accents and plush ripe cherry fruits. A silky entry leads a moderately full-bodied palate with plush, silky tannins and rich fruit flavors. Seamless and smooth through the finish. Drink now.

1996 Gamay Beaujolais, California $7. 81

1995 Alluvium Red, Knights Valley $30. 86

Saturated deep ruby-red hue. Generously aromatic with deeply fruited aromas of plums and dark fruits. Shows a toasty wood influence. A rich entry leads a moderately full-bodied palate with lush, supple fruit flavors and excellent mouthfeel. Tannins are fine grained and powdery. Harmonious, very approachable. Drink now or later.

1994 Merlot, Bancroft Ranch, Howell Mountain $45. 92

Deep blackish ruby hue. Full-bodied. Full acidity. Highly extracted. Heavily oaked. Quite tannic. Black fruits, cedar, earth. Extremely full and deep in style, with a hugely extracted core of complex flavors. Muscular throughout, though seemingly in balance, with very big, skillfully extracted tannins. Unapproachable now, this is a long-term (7–10 years) cellar candidate.

1995 Merlot, Bancroft Ranch, Howell Mountain $50. 90

Saturated dark purple-violet. Very woody aromas, with black cherry notes. A rich attack shows a marked oak influence, with fleshy fruit flavors in a tightly wound frame that concludes with a lingering dry oak finish. Drink within five years.

1996 Pinot Noir, Founders Estate, California $9.99.   **86**

Brilliant red-violet hue. Medium-bodied. Moderately extracted. Mildly tannic. Red fruits, vanilla. Generous and vibrant floral, fruity flavors explode on the palate and are supported by restrained, soft tannins. A fine, easy-drinking style.

1996 Pinot Noir, North Coast $16.   **89**

Pale ruby red with a subtly fading rim. Medium-bodied. Moderately extracted. Moderately oaked. Mildly tannic. Red fruits, vanilla, minerals. Bright, crisp aromas follow through on the palate with a sense of delicacy and fruit sweetness.

1995 Pinot Noir, Stanly Ranch, Los Carneros, Napa Valley $30.   **91**

Dark ruby cast. Medium-bodied. Highly extracted. Moderately tannic. Black fruit cordial, spice, tea. Rich, brooding aromas lead a solid, dry mouthful of flavors with fruit standing up to dry tannins and oak spice. Fine grip through the finish. This is showing solid, ageworthy structure.

1995 Zinfandel, Appellation Collection, North Coast $12.   **84**

Dark cherry red. Moderately light-bodied. Balanced acidity. Moderately extracted. Mildly oaked. Mildly tannic. Minerals, black fruits, pepper. A toasty nose with tarlike notes leads a lighter palate with black fruit focus, and a firm, minerally undernote that comes through on the finish.

1994 Port of Cabernet Sauvignon, Napa Valley $20.   **88**

Opaque blackish purple. Full-bodied. Balanced acidity. Highly extracted. Heavily oaked. Mildly tannic. Vanilla, cassis. Extraordinarily aromatic, with a melange of wood-accented black fruit flavors. Rich and deep in the mouth, with some drying wood tannins through the finish. Interesting.

1994 Botrytized Sauvignon Blanc-Semillon, Nightingale, Private Reserve, Napa Valley $22/375 ml.   **95**

Deep yellow-gold. Full-bodied. Balanced acidity. Moderately extracted. Heavily oaked. Toasted coconut, vanilla, tropical fruits. Outrageously toasty, with a hefty oak profile and a raft of botrytis-accented fruit flavors. Luxurious and complex in the mouth, with a supple, spicy finish. Hedonistic.

Bernardus

1996 Chardonnay, Monterey County $18.   **88**

Bright yellow-straw hue. Moderately full-bodied. Balanced acidity. Moderately extracted. Mildly oaked. Minerals, brown spices, citrus. Carries a judicious oak accent and a firm core of citric flavors. Vibrant and juicy, with oak spice lingering through the finish.

1994 Marinus, Carmel Valley $28.   **91**

Deep dark red. Medium-bodied. Moderately extracted. Moderately tannic. Cassis, tobacco, toasted oak. Elegantly structured, with fine integration of flavors that unfold on a solid palate. Some balanced tannins come through on the finish. Claret-like in character.

Bianchi

1996 Cabernet Sauvignon, Proprietor's Reserve, California $6.95.   **81**

Blackstone

1996 Merlot, California $10.   **85**

Dark ruby to the rim with brilliant clarity. Medium-bodied. Balanced acidity. Moderately extracted. Mildly tannic. Red fruits, vanilla. Straightforward and flavorful, with a well-integrated palate feel. Pleasantly structured through the finish.

1997 Merlot, California $10.   **84**

Pale ruby red with a bright cast. Sweet berry aromas follow through to a medium-bodied palate with sweet fruit and oak flavors. Acids are quite low and tannins are soft through the finish. An easy-drinking quaffer for near-term consumption.

1996 Merlot, Napa Valley $14.   82

Blossom Hill
1997 Chardonnay, California $4.99.   81
1996 Merlot, California $5.99.   80

Bogle
1997 Chardonnay, California $8.   81
1997 Sauvignon Blanc, California $7.   81
1997 Cabernet Sauvignon, California $10.   88
Saturated purple hue. Generous cassis and vanilla aromas with a judicious oak accent. A supple attack leads to a moderately full-bodied palate with lush tannins on the finish. Very fruit centered and well structured. Drink now or later.

1997 Merlot, California $9.   83
Brilliant violet with a bright cast. Aromas of cordials and vanilla oak. Medium-bodied, with clean black fruit flavors and sweet oak and juicy acids through the finish. Drink now.

1997 Petite Sirah, California $10.   92
Dark ruby purple. Moderately full-bodied. Highly extracted. Quite tannic. Plums, chocolate. Floral, bright fruity aromas follow through on the palate, with substantial tannins not turning too dry on the finish. This could use a few years, although is approachable now.

1995 Zinfandel, Old Vine Cuvée, California $11.   88
Bright blackish ruby hue. Moderately full-bodied. Full acidity. Moderately extracted. Mildly oaked. Mildly tannic. Vanilla, black fruits. Pleasant spicy oak nuances combine with a solid core of dark fruit flavors on the palate. Approachable, but showing solid concentration through the finish.

Bommarito
1997 Merlot, Napa Valley $12.   82

Bonny Doon
1996 Le Cigare Volant, California $22.   90
Bright, limpid purple-red to the rim. Powerful herb, red fruit, and vanilla aromas show a subtle wood accent. A soft attack leads a moderately full-bodied palate, with crisp acidity and mild tannic grip. The lingering finish is clean and flavorful. Bright, modern, and stylish. Drink now or later. Can improve with more age.

1997 Muscat Vin de Glacière, California $15/375 ml.   90
Pale yellow-copper hue. Forward, nutty apricot and tropical fruit aromas. A rich entry leads a moderately full-bodied palate featuring tons of sweetness. Flavorful and complex. Enticing in small measures. Drink now.

Bonterra
1997 Chardonnay, Mendocino County $12.   84
Bright yellow-straw hue. Subtle brown spice and citrus aromas carry a slight oak accent. A clean entry leads a medium-bodied palate that has decent acidity. Well balanced, flavorful finish. Drink now.

1995 Cabernet Sauvignon, North Coast $12.99.   87
Bright crimson red. Moderately light-bodied. Moderately extracted. Mildly tannic. Tart cassis, vanilla, cedar. Sweet fruit aromas. Crisp black fruit flavors keep the palate lively. Not particularly deep, though very accessible and good for early drinking.

1996 Cabernet Sauvignon, North Coast $13.   86
Saturated ruby blood-red hue. Lean, crisp aromas of tart black fruits and vanilla. A lean attack leads to a moderately full-bodied palate with vibrant acids and crisp, leaner fruit flavors. Finishes cleanly and quickly. A little ungenerous. Drink now or later.

Scale: Superlative (96-100), Exceptional (90-95), Highly Recommended (85-89), Recommended (80-84), Not Recommended (Under 80)

42

1996 Merlot, Mendocino County $17.   **86**

Bright ruby red. Unusual, high-toned anise, sweet herb, and mineral aromas. A crisp attack is followed by a lean, medium-bodied palate with juicy acidity and a bright, flavorful finish. A stylish lightweight. Drink now.

1996 Syrah, Mendocino County $25.   **91**

Deep, bright purple-red hue to the rim. Forward, perfumed, floral red fruit aromas. A supple attack leads a medium-bodied palate showing velvety tannins. Mouthwatering acidity lends a sense of buoyancy. Clean, flavorful finish. Stylish and elegant. Drink now.

Bonverre

1996 Chardonnay, California $8.   **81**

Bouchaine

1996 Chardonnay, Carneros $18.   **86**

Pale straw hue. Medium-bodied. Full acidity. Moderately extracted. Moderately oaked. Butter, minerals, lemon. Subtly smoky, buttery aromas lead a vibrant, crisp mouthful of tart fruit flavors that finish cleanly with minimal oak influence.

1995 Chardonnay, Estate Reserve, Carneros, Napa Valley $24.   **83**

Pale straw cast. Medium-bodied. Full acidity. Moderately extracted. Mildly oaked. Butter, vanilla, citrus. Stylishly textured, with a rounded, full mouthfeel and crisp acids lingering through the finish. Oak flavors are subtle.

1996 Cabernet Franc, Limited Release, Napa Valley $18.   **81**

1996 Pinot Noir, Carneros $19.   **84**

Pale violet hue. Medium-bodied. Moderately extracted. Mildly tannic. Vanilla, minerals, red fruits. Subtle fruity aromas lead a delicate, minerally palate that shows soft tannins and light berry fruit flavors.

1994 Pinot Noir, Reserve, Carneros $27.   **92**

Full cherry red. Medium-bodied. Moderately extracted. Moderately oaked. Moderately tannic. The rich, complex nose has a leathery accent. The gamey, supple, rounded palate is nicely textured. A long, complex finish has leather and earth notes with subtle oak spice. Drinking very well now.

1995 Pinot Noir, Reserve, Carneros $30.   **84**

Bright pale violet hue. Moderately light-bodied. Subtly extracted. Mildly tannic. Dried herbs, minerals, red fruits. Pronounced floral, dried herbal aromas lead a lightly framed palate with mild tannins and a quick finish.

Brophy Clark

1996 Pinot Noir, Arroyo Grande Valley $18.   **83**

Pale ruby cast. Medium-bodied. Balanced acidity. Moderately extracted. Mildly tannic. Minerals, dried herbs. Quite light in style with a decided herbal overtone. Lean and angular through the finish.

David Bruce

1997 Chardonnay, Santa Cruz Mountains $NA.   **85**

Bright yellow-straw hue. Pleasant earth and mineral aromas. A firm entry leads a medium-bodied palate, with crisp acids. Clipped finish. Drink now.

1994 Cabernet Sauvignon, Reserve, Santa Cruz Mountains $20.   **90**

Deep reddish purple. Medium-bodied. Highly extracted. Moderately tannic. Black fruits, dill, brown spice. Exotic pickled spice aromas. Rich, concentrated, and mouthfilling, with youthful vigor that does not mask its pure, ripe primary fruit flavors. Dry oak notes come through on the finish. Rather appealing now.

1996 La Rusticana d'Orsa, Santa Cruz Mountains $32.   **90**

Deep ruby purple to the rim. Generous spice, red fruit, and sweet herb aromas carry a hefty oak influence. A firm entry leads a moderately full-bodied palate, with robust tannins. Chewy, rich, and extracted, with a flavorful finish. Drink now or later.

1997 Petite Syrah, Central Coast $16. 88

Opaque purple. Moderately full-bodied. Highly extracted. Quite tannic. Black cherries, vanilla. Rich, peppery, explosively fruity aromas follow through to a thick, flavorsome palate with a textured mouthfeel and relatively supple finish, despite the impressive tannin levels.

1997 Petite Syrah, Ranchita Canyon, Paso Robles $18. 85

Very dark, opaque violet red. Brooding black fruit and mineral aromas show a generous oak influence. A hard entry leads a full-bodied palate that has big, robust tannins. An absolute monster; thick and rich with a tannic bite. Mid-term cellar candidate (3–6 years).

1996 Pinot Noir, Central Coast $16. 91

Deep cherry red. Medium-bodied. Moderately extracted. Mildly tannic. Black cherries, vanilla. Ripe black fruit aromas lead a smooth fruity palate. Bright primary flavors and soft tannins result in an opulent style. Supple and rounded, drinking well now.

1997 Pinot Noir, Central Coast $NA. 88

Rich ruby red with a slight fade. Generous red fruit, mineral, and dried herb aromas. A firm entry leads a moderately light-bodied palate that has drying tannins. Lingering, flavorful finish. Drink now.

1996 Pinot Noir, Sonoma County $NA. 89

Luminous, saturated ruby red. Fantastic flower and red fruit aromas carry a hefty oak accent. A firm entry leads a medium-bodied palate, with drying tannins. Structured, aromatic, and flavorful. Drink now or later.

1996 Pinot Noir, Russian River Valley $NA. 90

Bright, saturated ruby purple. Generous berry and mineral aromas show a big oak accent. A firm entry leads a moderately full-bodied palate, with crisp acids and drying tannins. A full, rich style. Drink now or later.

1995 Pinot Noir, Chalone $32. 94

Deep crimson purple. Medium-bodied. Highly extracted. Heavily oaked. Moderately tannic. Cocoa and berry aromas. Exotic, rich, deep black cherry and chocolate flavors expand on the palate and linger through a finish showing soft powdery tannins. A plush, ripe, rounded style that has the stuffing to keep and improve for a few years, though it is drinking nicely now.

1996 Pinot Noir, Chalone $32. 95

Dark cherry red. Moderately full-bodied. Highly extracted. Moderately tannic. Black cherries, anise, chocolate. Impressively rich, spicy aromas follow through on the palate, with solid tannins making for a structured style that will benefit from some cellar age. An intense and powerful style of New World Pinot.

1996 Pinot Noir, Santa Cruz Mountains $35. 86

Very dark ruby cast. Moderately full-bodied. Balanced acidity. Moderately extracted. Moderately oaked. Mildly tannic. Spice, minerals, black fruit. Forward aromas show depth and complexity. Ripe fruit flavors carry a spicy oak accent throughout. Firm and intense through the finish.

1995 Pinot Noir, Reserve, Russian River Valley $26. 92

Dark purple-red. Moderately full-bodied. Highly extracted. Moderately oaked. Moderately tannic. Sweet raspberry and vanilla aromas lead a juicy full palate, with chocolatey richness and a textured, generous mouthfeel. The finish is dominated by dry, fine-grained tannins. Excellent structure and weight.

1994 Pinot Noir, Estate Reserve, Santa Cruz Mountains $35. 91

Full ruby color. Medium-bodied. Highly extracted. Moderately oaked. Mildly tannic. Dark fruit aromas. Rich earthy, toasty character, with spicy black plum and cherry fruit flavors through a wonderful dry finish. Drinking nicely now.

1995 Zinfandel, Ranchita Canyon Vineyard, Paso Robles $15.   **91**
Deep blackish purple. Moderately full-bodied. Balanced acidity. Highly extracted.
Moderately oaked. Mildly tannic. Vanilla, black fruits, mint. Quite aromatic, with a very
full, focused palate feel. Firmly structured, intense, and lengthy, with a vibrant finish.
Great grip and depth.

1996 Zinfandel, Ranchita Canyon Vineyard, Paso Robles $15.   **88**
Deep blackish purple. Full-bodied. Balanced acidity. Highly extracted. Heavily oaked.
Mildly tannic. Brown spices, cedar, black fruits. Quite aromatic, with a hefty overlay of
wood spice and a deep core of fruit flavors. Full and rich on the palate, with enough
acidity to maintain a sense of balance.

Brutocao

1997 Chardonnay, Bliss Vineyard, Reserve, Mendocino $22.   **80**

1996 Sauvignon Blanc, Mendocino $10.50.   **82**

1995 Merlot, Hopland Ranch, Mendocino $18.   **85**
Deep blackish ruby hue. Moderately light-bodied. Balanced acidity. Moderately extracted.
Mildly oaked. Mildly tannic. Red fruits, mint, sweet herbs. Lighter in style, showing
straightforward crisp fruit flavors and a relatively firm structure. Oak becomes more
and more apparent on the finish.

1995 Zinfandel, Hopland Ranch, Mendocino $14.   **84**
Bright ruby-garnet cast. Moderately full-bodied. Balanced acidity. Moderately extracted.
Moderately oaked. Mildly tannic. Chocolate, minerals. Pleasantly aromatic, with a soft,
supple palate feel. Finishes on a generous note with velvety tannins and fine length.

Buehler

1995 Cabernet Sauvignon, Estate, Napa Valley $35.   **85**
Saturated deep ruby-brick red hue. Generously aromatic with an oak-spiced character
and ripe dark fruits. A firm attack leads a moderately full-bodied palate with generous
cassis flavors and solid gripping tannins. Impressively concentrated and ripe with a big
tannic kick through the finish. Soundly structured. Drink now or later.

Buena Vista

1996 Chardonnay, Carneros $14.   **84**
Pale straw hue. Medium-bodied. Full acidity. Moderately extracted. Crisp apples, tart
citrus. Clean and bright, with tart fruity flavors and vibrant acids playing out on the
finish. Very refreshing, with no oak flavors present.

1994 Cabernet Sauvignon, Carneros $16.   **85**
Deep reddish purple. Medium-bodied. Moderately extracted. Mildly tannic. Red berries,
vanilla. Full herbaceous berry-accented aromas follow through on the palate. Concentrated and focused, with a bright-fruit profile that extols its cool climate origins.

1995 Cabernet Sauvignon, Carneros $16.   **83**
Saturated dark red with purple highlights. Moderately full-bodied. Highly extracted.
Quite tannic. Cassis, minerals. Angular, with bright fruit flavors up front that give way
to brief, minerally tannins. Showing some tannic grip on the finish.

1993 Cabernet Sauvignon, Grand Reserve, Carneros $26.   **88**
Medium ruby red. Medium-bodied. Highly extracted. Moderately tannic. Red fruits,
vanilla, black tea. Concentrated on the entry with some rich fruity character. Solid
finish shows assertively dry tannins. Plenty of grip and authority through the finish.

1994 Cabernet Sauvignon, Grand Reserve, Carneros $28.95.   **86**
Saturated dark red. Moderately full-bodied. Highly extracted. Moderately tannic. Cassis,
vanilla, oak spice. Deep oak spice aromas follow through on the palate, with lush black
fruit flavors deferring to oak character. Tannins are ample and powdery, though not too
overbearing for current consumption.

1995 Merlot, Carneros $19.   86

Rich cherry red. Lean mineral aromas. A firm attack leads a medium-bodied palate with drying, angular tannins. Lean through the finish. This one walks on the tougher side of Merlot. Drink within 5 years.

1996 Pinot Noir, Sonoma Valley, Carneros $14.   80

1995 Pinot Noir, Grand Reserve, Carneros $26.   89

Cherry red with a pinkish hue. Medium-bodied. Moderately extracted. Mildly oaked. Moderately tannic. Perfumed vanilla oak aromas with fresh, crisp raspberry notes. Concentrated red fruit flavors on the palate, with some dry astringency through the finish. Has some cellaring structure.

1996 Zinfandel, The Celebration, Sonoma $19.50.   84

Bright ruby purple. Moderately full-bodied. Balanced acidity. Moderately extracted. Mildly tannic. Pepper, minerals, briar fruits. Somewhat reserved aromatically, with subtle peppery overtones. Ripe fruit flavors emerge on the compact palate. Finishes with some drying tannins.

Burgess

1994 Cabernet Sauvignon, Vintage Selection, Napa Valley $22.   87

Full crimson red with bright highlights. Medium-bodied. Moderately extracted. Mildly tannic. Vanilla, raspberries, red fruits. Attractive ripe berry aromas have vanilla oak accents. Fleshy forward flavors are rounded and accessible now. Hints of dry toasted character on the palate linger through the finish.

1995 Cabernet Sauvignon, Vintage Selection, Napa Valley $24.   86

Bright ruby purple. Moderately full-bodied. Balanced acidity. Moderately extracted. Heavily oaked. Moderately tannic. Vanilla, black fruits, earth. Pleasantly aromatic, with a hefty oak accent and a firm core of fruit flavors. Weighty and rich, with chunky tannins through the finish.

Buttonwood

1997 Sauvignon Blanc, Santa Ynez Valley $10.   84

Pale yellow-straw cast. Moderately light-bodied. Balanced acidity. Moderately extracted. White citrus, dried herbs. Very straightforward, showing simple citrus flavors in a very clean frame, leaving the palate refreshed.

1994 Cabernet Sauvignon, Santa Ynez Valley $16.   86

Dark garnet red. Medium-bodied. Highly extracted. Mildly tannic. Earthy, tobacco-scented aromas. Solid black Cabernet fruit on the palate gives way to a balanced dry finish showing cedary nuances. Quite dry overall, even slightly austere.

1995 Merlot, Santa Ynez Valley $18.   83

Very deep blackish ruby hue. Moderately full-bodied. Balanced acidity. Moderately extracted. Moderately oaked. Mildly tannic. Earth, cedar, black fruits. Profoundly earthy in style. Rich, well-structured mouthfeel. Some drying tannins on the flavorful finish.

Byington

1993 Cabernet Sauvignon, Bates Ranch, Santa Cruz Mountains $20.   89

Dark ruby red. Medium-bodied. Moderately extracted. Mildly tannic. Vanilla, red berries, anise, pepper. A somewhat toasty, spicy nose leads a bright red fruit entry that expands on the midpalate. Balanced astringency through the finish. Approachable now, with good acids keeping it lively.

1994 Cabernet Sauvignon, Smith Reichel Vineyard, Alexander Valley $18.   89

Dark brick red. Medium-bodied. Moderately extracted. Moderately tannic. Cooked fruit, brown spice, toasted oak. Jammy aromas lead a warm, generous palate, with dry assertive tannins through the finish. Angular and flavorsome.

Scale: Superlative (96-100), Exceptional (90-95), Highly Recommended (85-89), Recommended (80-84), Not Recommended (Under 80)

1994 Cabernet Sauvignon, Twin Mountains, Santa Cruz Mountains $14.50. 91
Full brick red. Medium-bodied. Highly extracted. Moderately tannic. Mint, brown spice, earth, red fruits. Exotic spicy, earthy aromas. A smooth but dry palate shows a seamless earthy quality through the finish. Seems to have mature flavors already, though it is still vigorous. Austere in a sophisticated manner.

1995 Merlot, Bradford Mountain, Sonoma County $20. 89
Very deep blackish ruby hue. Full-bodied. Full acidity. Highly extracted. Heavily oaked. Moderately tannic. Black fruits, lacquer. Quite aromatic, with a deep and brooding character. The dense core of flavor has a big overlay of oak notes. Still quite firm and tannic but well balanced. A candidate for mid-term (3–6 years) to long-term (7–10 years) aging.

1995 Pinot Noir, Central Coast $18. 86
Pale garnet red. Medium-bodied. Moderately extracted. Moderately oaked. Mildly tannic. Toasty, earthy nose with black cherry notes. Solid earthy backbone, with a minerally finish showing plenty of oak spice. A dry, assertive style that will show best with food.

1995 Pinot Noir, Willamette Valley $20. 89
Medium ruby red. Medium-bodied. Moderately extracted. Moderately oaked. Moderately tannic. Leather, earth, and black bramble fruit aromas are expressed well on the dry palate, with a lingering tobacco note on the finish. Quite austere.

Byron
1996 Pinot Blanc, Santa Maria Valley $16. 87
Bright golden hue. Moderately full-bodied. Full acidity. Moderately extracted. Mildly oaked. Toast, minerals, vanilla. Oak influences prevail on the nose and palate. In the mouth this wine is full though angular, with solid acidity.

1996 Pinot Gris, Santa Maria Valley $16. 84
Deep straw hue. Moderately full-bodied. Full acidity. Moderately extracted. Talc, oranges, lacquer. Marked aromas, with a distinctive high-toned note. Full on the palate, with racy acidity that balances out the finish.

1996 Pinot Noir, Santa Maria Valley $18. 93
Saturated dark ruby cast. Moderately full-bodied. Full acidity. Moderately extracted. Moderately oaked. Mildly tannic. Red fruits, dill pickle, wood. Generous aromas are in the classic Pinot range. Lush and supple on the palate, yet with a firm minerally backbone that lends a sense of balance.

1994 Pinot Noir, Reserve, Santa Barbara County $24. 86
Medium ruby red. Medium-bodied. Moderately extracted. Heavily oaked. Mildly tannic. Bright cherry fruit flavors up front, with plenty of toasted oak flavors coming through. Some warmth on the finish.

Cafaro
1995 Cabernet Sauvignon, Napa Valley $34. 89
Bright violet purple hue. Youthful crisp fruity aromas with a good overlay of new vanilla oak. A rich entry leads to a moderately full-bodied palate with crushed berry flavors and toasty new oak accents through the finish. Well stuffed and very youthful at present. Drink within 5 years.

1995 Merlot, Napa Valley $30. 88
Bright violet red. Sweet vanilla and red fruit aromas indicate generous oak accents. Moderately full-bodied with a bright attack, a midpalate with accents of crisp fruit, and velvety tannins through the finish. Drink now or later. Can improve with more age.

Cain

1996 Sauvignon Blanc, Musque, Ventana Vineyard, Monterey $16. 94

Bright yellow-gold. Medium-bodied. Balanced acidity. Moderately extracted. Earth, citrus, asparagus. Full citrus zest aromas follow through on a palate distinguished by its concentration, mouthfeel, and length. Very pure, cool climate Sauvignon Blanc flavors, with plenty of stuffing and earthy complexity.

1994 Cain Cuvée, Napa Valley $19. 85

Dark ruby purple. Medium-bodied. Moderately extracted. Mildly tannic. Tobacco, cassis. Varietally expressive aromas lead a straightforward palate with a certain lightness to the mouthfeel. Dry, fine-grained tannins on the finish.

1995 Cain Cuvée, Napa Valley $22. 86

Bright ruby cast. Moderately full-bodied. Balanced acidity. Moderately extracted. Mildly oaked. Mildly tannic. Chocolate, spice, minerals. Pleasantly aromatic, with a rich but firm palate feel. Turns lean and angular through the finish.

1994 Cain Five, Napa Valley $50. 91

Deep saturated ruby hue. Moderately full-bodied. Balanced acidity. Highly extracted. Mildly oaked. Moderately tannic. Minerals, cassis. Youthful and tightly wound with reined-in aromatics, but impressively structured. Shows breeding and elegance. Should gain complexity with mid- to long-term cellaring.

1995 Cain Five, Napa Valley $50. 87

Deep saturated ruby hue. Moderately full-bodied. Balanced acidity. Highly extracted. Mildly oaked. Moderately tannic. Minerals, brown spices, cassis. Aromas show oak spice and black fruits, with a firm, minerally backbone and a lean and taut structure. Built for the long haul.

Cakebread

1997 Chardonnay, Napa Valley $26. 84

Brilliant yellow-gold. Shows a very buttery nose. A tart attack leads a moderately full-bodied palate with strong butter and apple flavors that persist through the lengthy finish.

1996 Sauvignon Blanc, Napa Valley $14. 90

Bright straw cast. Moderately full-bodied. Full acidity. Moderately extracted. Mildly oaked. Brown spices, yeast, citrus. A hefty oak influence is backed up by a solid frame of fruit-derived flavors. Lush but well structured, with a zesty finish.

1994 Cabernet Sauvignon, Napa Valley $25. 88

Bright purple. Moderately light-bodied. Moderately extracted. Mildly tannic. Raspberries, cassis. Ripe raspberry and cassis aromas follow through on the juicy, open-knit palate. Very accessible, drink now.

1995 Cabernet Sauvignon, Napa Valley $30. 90

Bright ruby purple. Moderately full-bodied. Balanced acidity. Moderately extracted. Mildly oaked. Mildly tannic. Red fruits, minerals. Bright, fruit-centered aromatics are forward and generous. Supple and tasty in the mouth, with a gentle, velvety structure. Drinking very well.

1994 Cabernet Sauvignon, Reserve, Napa Valley $50. 91

Deep ruby purple. Moderately full-bodied. Balanced acidity. Moderately extracted. Moderately oaked. Mildly tannic. Black fruits, minerals, toast. Aromatic and generous, with a high-toned, fruit-centered quality. Supple and elegant in the mouth, with fine concentration and grip.

1995 Cabernet Sauvignon, Three Sisters, Napa Valley $75. 93

Deep ruby purple. Full-bodied. Balanced acidity. Highly extracted. Mildly oaked. Moderately tannic. Mint, red fruits, earth. Forward and distinctive aromatics lead a ripe and weighty mouthfeel. Concentrated and precise, with firm tannins. Fine length and intensity. Should develop beautifully.

Scale: Superlative (96-100), Exceptional (90-95), Highly Recommended (85-89), Recommended (80-84), Not Recommended (Under 80)

48

1995 Cabernet Sauvignon, Benchland Select, Napa Valley $75. **94**

Bright ruby purple. Moderately full-bodied. Balanced acidity. Moderately extracted.
Moderately oaked. Mildly tannic. Vanilla, minerals, red fruits. Bright and aromatic,
with a juicy, fruit-centered quality accented by judicious use of oak. Supple and flavorful
through the lengthy finish.

1995 Merlot, Napa Valley $28.50. **88**

Very deep ruby red to the rim with a purplish cast. Moderately full-bodied. Full
acidity. Highly extracted. Mildly tannic. Briar fruits, sweet herbs, minerals. Fruit driven,
with jammy, vibrant flavors. Brightly textured in the mouth with snappy acidity. Quite
accessible now, though it should gain complexity with mid-term (3–6 years) aging.

Calera

1997 Chardonnay, Central Coast $16. **89**

Deep straw cast. Moderately full-bodied. Balanced acidity. Moderately extracted. Bananas,
minerals. Aromatically reserved, with subtle malolactic flavors and a firm core of steely
acidity. Crisp through the finish.

1997 Viognier, Mount Harlan $30. **85**

Bright yellow-gold. Full-bodied. Balanced acidity. Moderately extracted. Tropical fruits,
butter, minerals. Rather reserved aromatically, but big, ripe, and flavorful on the palate,
with a rich buttery finish showing enough acidity to balance the weight.

1997 Pinot Noir, Central Coast $16. **86**

Very pale violet hue. Moderately light-bodied. Moderately extracted. Mildly tannic.
Dried herbs, red fruits, vanilla. Berry fruit and crisp herbal aromas follow through
on the palate. A light structure makes this very approachable now.

1994 Pinot Noir, Jensen, Mount Harlan $38. **86**

Medium cherry red. Medium-bodied. Moderately extracted. Moderately oaked.
Moderately tannic. Ripe raisiny, cherry aromas. Exotically scented with great persistence
throughout. Delicate yet full flavored. Dry tannins provide some grip on the finish, but
this is nice now.

1994 Pinot Noir, Mills, Mount Harlan $35. **86**

Bright cherry red. Medium-bodied. Moderately extracted. Moderately tannic. Red
berries, brown spice, minerals. Ripe, generous aromas lead a solidly flavorsome palate
with dry tannins giving a firm impression on the finish.

1995 Pinot Noir, Selleck, Twentieth Anniversary Vintage,
Mount Harlan $38. **91**

Cherry red with a violet rim. Medium-bodied. Moderately extracted. Moderately tannic.
Berry fruits, minerals, vanilla. Richly aromatic, with oak influences that come through
on the palate. Vibrant acids and good berry fruit flavors play on the finish. Shows some
dry tannins and will probably age well.

Callaway

1998 Chenin Blanc, California $7.50. **83**

Very pale straw cast. Pleasantly aromatic with white peach nuances. Juicy and flavorful
on the entry. Medium-bodied, with good flavor concentration following through to the
finish. Drink now.

1997 Pinot Gris, Temecula $12. **86**

Bright copper cast. Moderately full-bodied. Balanced acidity. Moderately extracted. Dried
herbs, minerals, gooseberries. Distinctively aromatic, with a big earthy, herbal streak. Full
and rich in the mouth with some racy acidity through the smoky finish.

1997 Sauvignon Blanc, Temecula $8. **84**

Pale platinum-straw hue. Medium-bodied. Balanced acidity. Moderately extracted.
Tropical fruits, dried herbs. Aromatic, with a juicy tropical character and an herbal
note that follows through on the finish.

1995 Cabernet Sauvignon, California $11.   **83**

Bright cherry red. Moderately light-bodied. Subtly extracted. Mildly tannic. Red fruits. Soft, candied aromas follow through, with candied fruit flavors and soft tannins on the finish.

1996 Dolcetto, Temecula $15.   **81**

1994 Nebbiolo, California $15.   **81**

Cambria

1996 Chardonnay, Reserve, Santa Maria Valley $36.   **88**

Bright yellow-straw cast. Moderately full-bodied. Balanced acidity. Moderately extracted. Moderately oaked. Yeast, cream, citrus. Ripe and impressive flavors show a complex yeasty note. Full and rounded in the mouth, with a distinct impression of fruit sweetness through the finish.

1995 Pinot Noir, Julia's Vineyard, Santa Maria Valley $27.   **89**

Dark red with a garnet rim. Moderately full-bodied. Highly extracted. Moderately oaked. Mildly tannic. Full-throttled spicy, mature aromas. Rich flavors of stewed cherries and berries with a distinctly earthy quality throughout. Tannins are grainy but not excessive for current drinking. Substantial style.

1996 Pinot Noir, Reserve, Santa Maria Valley $42.   **94**

Deep ruby cast. Moderately full-bodied. Balanced acidity. Moderately extracted. Moderately oaked. Mildly tannic. Vanilla, red fruits, minerals. Ripe and aromatic, with a core of lush fruit flavors and a hedonistic overlay of oak. Supple and generous through the finish. Exquisitely proportioned.

1996 Sangiovese, Tepusquet Vineyard, Santa Maria Valley $18.   **86**

Bright cherry red with a youthful rim. Medium-bodied. Balanced acidity. Moderately extracted. Moderately oaked. Mildly tannic. Raspberries, vanilla. Sweet, fleshy red fruit aromas follow through on the palate, with vanilla sweetness and juicy acids making this very approachable.

1996 Syrah, Tepusquet Vineyard, Santa Maria Valley $18.   **89**

Deep ruby purple, limpid and brilliant to the rim. Generous, sound vanilla and black fruit flavors. Firm entry. Moderately full-bodied. Moderate drying tannins. Bright, succulent fruit is not obscured by heavy oak. Lingering rich finish. Drinkable now, but can improve with more age.

Camelot

1997 Chardonnay, California $13.   **82**

Canyon Road

1997 Sauvignon Blanc, California $6.99.   **86**

Pale yellow-gold. Medium-bodied. Balanced acidity. Moderately extracted. Dried herbs, minerals, citrus. High-toned, zesty aromas. A dry citrusy attack, with some nice varietal character that lingers through the finish. This is very clean and racy with no distracting oak influences.

1995 Cabernet Sauvignon, Reserve, Sonoma County $18.   **88**

Dark saturated ruby to the rim. Moderately full-bodied. Full acidity. Moderately extracted. Mildly tannic. Black fruits, chocolate, minerals. Youthful and tightly wound, with a pleasant nose and deep, brooding flavors. Acidity lends structure through the angular finish.

Cardinale

1996 Royale, California $20.   **91**

Bright golden cast. Full-bodied. Balanced acidity. Moderately extracted. Heavily oaked. Smoke, yeast, cream. Quite heavily oaked, with a big smoky flavor profile. Luxuriant and rich, with yeasty complexity and enough acidity to maintain a sense of balance through the finish.

1995 Red Wine, California $70.   89

Saturated dark ruby hue. Moderately full-bodied. Moderately extracted. Moderately
oaked. Moderately tannic. Anise, brown spice, black fruits. Chocolatey aromas show
plummy, spicy accents that follow through on the palate. Finely wrought and flavorsome,
with a long, dry finish. This has plenty of ripe, developed Cabernet flavors.

Carmenet

1997 Chardonnay, Sangiacomo Vineyard, Carneros, Sonoma Valley $18.   83

Deep gold. Fat, oaky aromas. A rich, concentrated attack leads a moderately full-bodied
palate with solid flavors that seem closed in at present. Finishes tight and austere with
good acids and a touch of phenolic dryness. Drink now or later.

1997 Gewürztraminer, Sonoma Valley $14.   82

1996 Reserve White Meritage, Paragon Vineyard, Edna Valley $15.   86

Full golden yellow. Medium-bodied. Balanced acidity. Moderately extracted. Butter,
lemon, oak spice. Soft aromas with mild lemon cream notes. Good mouthfeel, and quite
flavorful, though lacking grip and intensity though the short finish.

1995 Cabernet Franc, Moon Mountain Vineyard, Sonoma Valley $25.   84

Deep, saturated ruby red hue. Subdued earth and red fruit aromas. A lush attack leads
to a moderately full-bodied palate with chunky tannins and decent acidic grip. Firm,
rich finish. Shows good weight and intensity but a little closed in at present. Drink now
or later.

1993 Moon Mountain Estate Reserve Meritage, Sonoma Valley $27.50.   91

Ruby color with a pale rim. Medium-bodied. Moderately extracted. Moderately tannic.
Dust, earth, red fruits. Dusty, earthy nose. Quite dry and austere, yet the tannins are
rounded. Not many primary fruit sensations here. Well integrated and smooth through
the finish. Exotic.

1995 Moon Mountain Estate Reserve Meritage, Sonoma Valley $40.   87

Bright ruby red. Medium-bodied. Moderately extracted. Moderately tannic. Black fruits,
spice. Bright, black berry fruit aromas follow through on a dry, oaky palate with a lean
finish. Tasty now, though it will be better in a year or so. Elegant.

1996 Merlot, Sangiacomo Vineyard, Carneros, Sonoma Valley $20.   89

Saturated, bright violet red. Generously aromatic with rich fruity aromas and toasted oak
accents. A lush entry leads a moderately full-bodied palate with smooth tannins and lush
fruity flavors. Very supple and lengthy, with plenty of toasty oak spice on the finish. Drink
now or later.

Carmody McKnight

1996 Cadenza, Paso Robles $22.50.   86

Saturated dark ruby hue. Ripe cordial-like aromas. A firm entry leads a moderately
full-bodied palate with a thick mouthfeel and generous dark fruit flavors. Finishes with
tough, gripping tannins. Solidly structured. Drink now or later.

Carneros Creek

1996 Pinot Noir, Fleur de Carneros, Carneros $12.   82

1997 Pinot Noir, Fleur de Carneros, Carneros $12.   82

1996 Pinot Noir, Carneros $18.   88

Bright cherry red. Medium-bodied. Moderately extracted. Heavily oaked. Moderately
tannic. A toasty, oak-accented nose leads bright raspberry and cherry fruit flavors. Rich
oak and rounded berry fruit flavors linger through a long toasty, smoky finish. Generous.

Maurice Carrie

1998 Johannisberg Riesling, California $7.95.   83

Bright pale straw cast. Ripe tropical fruit aromas have a zesty, minerally note. A lean
attack leads a medium-bodied palate showing sweet citrus flavors. Low in acid, with a
clipped finish. Drink now.

1996 Sauvignon Blanc, Temecula $7.95.   **84**

Bright pale straw hue. Medium-bodied. Balanced acidity. Moderately extracted. Lemon, yeast. Straightforward lemony aromas follow through on the palate with little complexity but reasonable acid balance and length.

Case

1994 Pinot Noir, Sleepy Hollow Vineyards, Monterey $26.   **89**

Medium garnet red. Medium-bodied. Moderately extracted. Mildly oaked. Mildly tannic. Rich, smoky red berry fruit aromas have a perfumed character. The elegant, focused palate has well-integrated flavors and a clean finish. Drinking nicely now.

Castle

1997 Chardonnay, Sonoma Valley $18.   **84**

Bright straw cast. Moderately full-bodied. Balanced acidity. Highly extracted. Yeast, citrus, nuts. Pleasantly aromatic, with a ripe and rounded mouthfeel. Finishes with an attractive nutty accent.

1997 Chardonnay, Los Carneros $22.   **81**

1997 Viognier, Ripken Vineyard, California $18.   **81**

1996 Cabernet Sauvignon, Nicolas Vineyard, Sonoma Valley $25.   **84**

Deep ruby red hue with a slight fade. Subdued and brooding mineral, earth, and red fruit aromas. A firm attack leads to a lean, medium-bodied mouthfeel with mildly astringent tannins. Firm, drying finish. Drink within five years.

1997 Cinsault, Dry Creek Valley $19.   **86**

Bright pale purple-red hue to the rim. Clean, forward berry and mineral aromas. A firm attack leads a medium-bodied palate, with drying tannins. Snappy, clean finish. A lighter style and tasty. Drink now.

1996 Merlot, Sonoma Valley $18.   **88**

Bright violet with a subtle fade. Crisp berry, herb, and vanilla aromas. A bright attack leads a medium-bodied palate with fine-grained tannins and juicy acids. Drink now.

1996 Merlot, Sangiacomo Vineyard, Carneros $25.   **89**

Deep, saturated purple-red. Generous mint and red fruit aromas carry a mild wood accent. A lush attack is followed by a medium-bodied, supple palate with crisp tannins and juicy acidity. The finish is lively and flavorful. Quite buoyant, with fine grip and intensity. Drink within 5 years.

1997 Pinot Noir, Los Carneros $22.   **84**

Bright violet red. Medium-bodied. Moderately extracted. Mildly tannic. Vanilla, red fruits. Toasty vanilla aromas lead a bright mouthful of tart red fruit flavors. A bite of dry tannins linger on the finish, giving this a note of astringency and solidity.

1997 Pinot Noir, Durell Vineyard, Los Carneros $30.   **87**

Brilliant violet cast. Medium-bodied. Moderately extracted. Moderately tannic. Berry fruits, minerals, oak spice. Intriguingly spiced and generous berry fruit aromas follow through on the palate in an expressive jammy manner, giving a sense of power and depth, with toasted spicy oak making a statement. Finishes with smooth, ripe tannins.

1997 Pinot Noir, Sangiacomo Vineyard, Los Carneros $30.   **89**

Bright violet hue. Medium-bodied. Moderately extracted. Mildly tannic. Vanilla, minerals, berry fruits. Toasted oak and berry fruit aromas follow through well on a lighter-framed palate, with bright, gripping acids making for a lively character. Acidity is marked and impressive.

1996 Syrah, Sonoma Valley $20.   **83**

Dark crimson color, limpid with a slight fade. Oak-influenced aromas. Generous, sound mineral, brown spice, and coffee flavors. Hefty wood tones. Firm entry. Moderately full-bodied. Moderate, drying tannins. Persistent finish. Rather distinctive and unusual. Drink now.

1996 Zinfandel, Sonoma County $16.   88

Bright blackish ruby cast. Medium-bodied. Full acidity. Moderately extracted. Mildly oaked. Mildly tannic. Briar fruits, wood. Pleasantly aromatic, with a fruit-accented palate feel. Lean and vibrant in the mouth, showing crisp acidity through the finish.

Castoro

1997 Chardonnay, Central Coast $12.   84

Bright yellow straw hue. Ripe green apple and butter aromas with vanilla. Ripe fruity on the entry, with a medium-bodied palate and nice notes of butter and oak matched by crisp acids. Well balanced and versatile. Drink now.

1995 Cabernet Sauvignon, Paso Robles $11.50.   85

Bright reddish purple. Medium-bodied. Moderately extracted. Mildly tannic. Red currant, dried herbs. Bright red fruit entry. A juicy palate has an herbal, toasty note through the finish. Quite straightforward, with some nice astringency running through it.

1996 Cabernet Sauvignon, Paso Robles $15.   86

Bright purple hue. Markedly ripe, jammy aromas. A fat entry leads a moderately full-bodied palate with a ripe core of fleshy fruit flavors and firm tannins clamping down on the medium-length finish. Rich and thick, though acids are rather soft. This should be better in a few years. Drink now or later.

1996 Zinfandel, Paso Robles $12.95.   86

Deep blackish purple cast. Moderately full-bodied. Full acidity. Moderately extracted. Moderately oaked. Mildly tannic. Black fruits, chocolate. Quite aromatic, with a full, flavorful palate feel. Lush and supple in the mouth, with vibrant acidity making for a bright finish. Big but well balanced.

1996 Zinfandel, Vineyard Tribute, Paso Robles $15.   81

Caymus

1994 Cabernet Sauvignon, Napa Valley $35.   92

Dark red-purple. Moderately full-bodied. Highly extracted. Moderately tannic. Cassis, plums, cedar. A bright, dense center of pure cassis fruit with good supporting tannins through the finish. Very well balanced. Has the structure to cellar, but it's approachable in youth.

1995 Cabernet Sauvignon, Napa Valley $65.   93

Deep blood red. Moderately full-bodied. Highly extracted. Moderately tannic. Lead pencil, cassis, minerals. Outstanding aromas are truly expressive. Rich tannins show exceptional balance with pure Cabernet fruit flavors that persist through a lengthy finish.

1994 Cabernet Sauvignon, Special Selection, Napa Valley $110.   95

Very deep ruby hue. Full-bodied. Balanced acidity. Highly extracted. Heavily oaked. Moderately tannic. Smoke, charred wood, black fruits. Quite aromatic, with a forward, smoky, toasted impression to the nose. Firm and full, though amazingly supple. Shows fine length and intensity. Approachable now, but far better to wait for further complexity to develop.

Cecchetti Sebastiani

1993 Cabernet Sauvignon, Napa Valley $30.   87

Dark crimson-ruby color. Medium-bodied. Moderately extracted. Moderately tannic. Plums, black fruits, black tea. Ripe black fruit aromas show a toasty note that is confirmed on the palate, with some dry, fine-grained tannins coming through on the finish. This has a meaty, savory quality.

Cedar Brook

1994 Cabernet Sauvignon, California $8.99.   84

Bright cherry red. Medium-bodied. Moderately extracted. Mildly tannic. Vanilla, red fruits. Sweet, forward aromas follow through on the open-knit palate and brief finish. Very simple and straightforward.

1996 Merlot, California $8.99.   83

Deep crimson-ruby color with brilliant highlights. Moderately light-bodied. Full acidity. Moderately extracted. Moderately oaked. Mildly tannic. Plums, black fruits, vanilla. Pleasantly aromatic and flavorful with a dark fruit accent. Juicy acidity lends a sense of vibrancy. Subtle oaky overtones come into play on the snappy finish.

1995 Zinfandel, California $8.99.   84

Bright blackish ruby color. Medium-bodied. Balanced acidity. Moderately extracted. Moderately oaked. Mildly tannic. Brown spices, coffee, black fruits. Oak nuances dominate the aromas and play out on the palate. Soft, supple, and velvety in the mouth, with a lingering finish.

Cedar Mountain

1997 Chardonnay, Blanches Vineyard, Livermore Valley $16.   89

Medium straw hue. Moderately full-bodied. Balanced acidity. Heavily oaked. Toasted coconut, brown spice, apples. Assertive yeasty, toasted oak aromas follow through on the palate, with complex yeast and wood accents dominating the finish. Stylish and flavorsome.

1994 Cabernet Sauvignon, Livermore Valley $20.   90

Dark red with purple highlights. Medium-bodied. Highly extracted. Mildly tannic. Black fruits, tobacco. Attractive ripe plum aromas. Concentrated black Cabernet fruit flavors expand on the palate, with dry but textured tannins keeping the finish firm.

1995 Cabernet Sauvignon, Blanches Vineyard, Livermore Valley $22.   88

Very deep blackish ruby hue. Opulent briar fruit and vanilla aromas show a decided wood accent. A lush entry leads to a thick, full-bodied palate with big velvety drying tannins. Ripe, flavorful finish. A big show style. Drink now or later.

1995 Duet, Livermore Valley $22.   88

Deep, saturated blackish ruby hue. Intense brown spice, black fruit, and licorice aromas show a generous oak accent. A rich entry leads to a thick full-bodied palate with robust velvety tannins. Features just enough acidity to maintain a sense of liveliness. Flavorful, persistent finish. A flashy showy style. Drink now or later.

1995 Merlot, Livermore Valley $21.50.   85

Very deep blackish purple hue. Medium-bodied. Full acidity. Highly extracted. Mildly tannic. Black cherries, cordial, sweet herbs, lacquer. Aromatic and fruit driven, with a dense core of very ripe fruit flavors. Vibrant acidity makes for a crisp, mildly astringent finish.

1996 Vintage Port, Amador County $19.50.   92

Opaque blackish ruby cast. Full-bodied. Balanced acidity. Highly extracted. Chocolate, black fruits, flowers. Shows amazing depth of concentration, with a fragrant and immensely flavorful palate feel. Rich and firmly structured, with just a hint of sweetness in the finish. A dead ringer for a high-end Portuguese wine. Intense and impressive.

Chalk Hill

1996 Chardonnay, Chalk Hill, Sonoma County $28.   86

Deep straw cast. Moderately full-bodied. Balanced acidity. Moderately extracted. Mildly oaked. Yeast, cream, smoke. Aromatic and full, with a ripe smoky quality throughout. Shows both complexity and richness, with a generous lengthy finish.

1996 Sauvignon Blanc, Chalk Hill, Sonoma County $19.   93

Deep green-gold. Moderately full-bodied. Balanced acidity. Moderately extracted. Moderately oaked. Vanilla, butter, oranges. Richly aromatic, with luxuriant oak accents. Full, round, and lush on the palate, with a velvety mouthfeel and a core of fruit flavor. Well balanced with fine length.

1994 Cabernet Sauvignon, Chalk Hill, Sonoma County $26.   88

Dark red. Medium-bodied. Moderately extracted. Moderately tannic. Tea, black fruits, brown spice. Sweet herbal notes on the nose lead a solidly flavored palate and a long dry finish showing lingering oak spice flavors. Some alcoholic warmth shows through.

Scale: Superlative (96-100), Exceptional (90-95), Highly Recommended (85-89),
Recommended (80-84), Not Recommended (Under 80)

1995 Cabernet Sauvignon, Chalk Hill, Sonoma County $32.   82

Chalone

1996 Chardonnay, Chalone $27.   88

Bright straw cast. Moderately full-bodied. Balanced acidity. Moderately extracted. Apples, pears, citrus. Ripe varietally pure Chardonnay aromas follow through on the palate. Full and rounded in the mouth, with a lush texture and well-defined, zesty finish.

1997 Chardonnay, The Pinnacles, Chalone $31.   88

Pale straw hue. Subdued mineral aromas. A lean entry leads an extracted, moderately full-bodied palate with steely flavors and very little oak influence. Shows clean varietal flavors and solid grip through the finish. May open with moderate age. Drink now or later.

1996 Chardonnay, Reserve, Chalone $45.   89

Deep straw cast. Moderately full-bodied. Balanced acidity. Highly extracted. Cream, citrus. Aromatically reserved, featuring a ripe and rounded mouthfeel. Broadly textured in the mouth, and full and rich through the finish.

1996 Chenin Blanc, Reserve, Chalone $20.   84

Medium gold hue. Mildly aromatic, with a hint of oak spice and key lime. A juicy entry leads a medium-bodied palate with a firm, structured character. Taut finish. Drink now or later.

1993 Pinot Noir, Reserve, Chalone $35.   88

Dark red with a subtle garnet cast. Medium-bodied. Moderately extracted. Moderately tannic. Black fruits, earth, spice. Rich, deep fruity aromas show an earthy note that follows through on the palate. Finishes with lingering astringency. A very sturdy style.

Chameleon

1996 Barbera, Amador County $14.   89

Bright pale ruby cast with a purple edge. Moderately light-bodied. Full acidity. Moderately extracted. Mildly oaked. Mildly tannic. Red fruits, minerals. Pleasantly aromatic and lighter in style, with a super-concentrated wave of briar fruit flavors. Vibrant acidity lends brightness throughout, and provides a clean, angular finish.

1996 Sangiovese, North Coast $16.   88

Cherry pink. Medium-bodied. Full acidity. Moderately extracted. Mildly tannic. Tart cherries, minerals. A lighter style with crisp, red fruit flavors and a solid, minerally underlay. Clean and fresh, with minimal new oak treatment. Uplifting acids give great grip.

Chappellet

1997 Chardonnay, Estate, Napa Valley $17.   88

Pale medium-straw hue. Ripe fruity aromas have a buttery, yeasty accent with obvious toasty oak notes. A smooth entry leads a moderately full-bodied palate with smooth texture and generous fruity flavors. Finishes with a note of yeasty complexity.

1997 Chardonnay, Signature Estate, Napa Valley $26.   91

Pale straw hue. Ripe apple and pear aromas. A lush entry leads a moderately full-bodied palate with a rounded mouthfeel and pure fruit flavors that linger through the finish. Particularly lengthy, with well-integrated toasty oak. Elegant.

1997 Dry Chenin Blanc, Napa Valley $11.   85

Pale straw hue. Subdued tropical fruit aromas. A rich entry leads a moderately full-bodied palate showing vibrant acidity. Full and intense in style. Drink now.

1997 Old Vine Cuvée, Special Select White Wine, Napa Valley $14.   88

Deep yellow-straw hue. Rich cream, pear, and spice aromas. A rich attack leads a concentrated, full-bodied palate, with firm acids and a drying finish. A powerful Chenin. Drink now or later.

1996 Cabernet Franc, Napa Valley $24.   86

Deep, saturated ruby red hue. Subdued red fruit and mineral aromas. A rich entry leads to a moderately full-bodied palate with robust tannins. Firm, flavorful finish. A big, ripe, extracted style. Drink now or later.

1995 Cabernet Sauvignon, Signature, Napa Valley $24.   89

Dark ruby hue. Moderately aromatic with distinct oak accent. A firm entry leads to a moderately full-bodied palate with a deep core of cassis. Finished with solid tannins and fine acidity. Well balanced and structured for further aging. Drink now or later.

1996 Merlot, Napa Valley $22.   89

Brilliant violet red. Generous black cherry aromas with vanilla accents. Bright, lush, and flavorsome on the entry, with a moderately full body and cedar and anise notes through the finish. Tannins are velvety and fine grained. Drink now or later. Can improve with more age.

1995 Sangiovese, Napa Valley $22.   89

Dark ruby red. Medium-bodied. Balanced acidity. Moderately extracted. Mildly oaked. Mildly tannic. Dried cherries, earth, licorice. Brooding, ripe aromas. Solid and mouthfilling, with excellent grip and length. Dry, austere finish.

Chateau Julien

1996 Chardonnay, Private Reserve "Sur Lie," Monterey County $15.   83

Pale straw cast. Medium-bodied. Full acidity. Moderately extracted. Vanilla, blanched almonds. Shows a hefty oak accent and a note of maturity. Lean and angular with a touch of dryness to the finish.

1995 Cabernet Sauvignon, Private Reserve, Monterey County $20.   86

Bright violet-red. Medium-bodied. Moderately extracted. Moderately tannic. Cherries, minerals, dried herbs. Crisp and lively bright red fruit flavors have an herbal note, with a bright, minerally finish showing some grip. Drinking well now.

1996 Cabernet Sauvignon, Private Reserve, Monterey County $25.   82

1996 Merlot, Grand Reserve, Monterey County $9.99.   86

Pale violet hue. Clean aromas of herbs, berry fruit, and vanilla. A soft entry leads a light-bodied palate with very gentle tannins. Easily quaffable. Drink now.

1996 Merlot, Private Reserve, Monterey County $20.   89

Bright violet red. Generous black cherry and vanilla aromas show a generous oak accent. A supple attack leads a medium-bodied palate with light, soft tannins and juicy acids. Drink now.

Chateau Montelena

1996 Chardonnay, Napa Valley $29.   86

Bright yellow-gold. Fresh aromas of ripe citrus with minimal oak influence. A crisp entry leads a medium-bodied palate with lemony flavors persisting through the finish. Well-balanced acidity. For youthful consumption.

1995 Cabernet Sauvignon, Calistoga Cuvée, Napa Valley $18.   87

Dark crimson appearance. Moderately full-bodied. Highly extracted. Moderately tannic. Black cherries, currants, oak spice. Decadent curranty, crushed black fruit flavors give this a strong fruity palate that is balanced by rounded soft tannins and spicy oak on the finish. Quite tight at present.

1996 Cabernet, Calistoga Cuvée, Napa Valley $25.   83

Bright violet red hue. Lighter, perfumed aromas do not show much weight. Rather simple and straightforward with a mildly reductive character.

1993 Cabernet Sauvignon, Montelena Estate, Napa Valley $40.   90

Saturated blood red. Moderately full-bodied. Highly extracted. Quite tannic. Currants, black cherries, black tea. Deep, ripe black fruit aromas follow through on the palate. Solid and dry through the finish. This will need some time to resolve the tannins.

Scale: Superlative (96-100), Exceptional (90-95), Highly Recommended (85-89), Recommended (80-84), Not Recommended (Under 80)

1994 Cabernet Sauvignon, Montelena Estate, Napa Valley $85.   92

Bright ruby-violet hue. Spicy oak accented aromas show fleshy dark fruit accents.
A firm entry leads a full-bodied palate with fleshy fruits and bright acids that give
this a well-gripped angular finish. Well structured, this will need a few more years.
Drink now or later.

Chateau Potelle

1995 Chardonnay, Central Coast $16.   84

Bright golden cast. Moderately full-bodied. Balanced acidity. Moderately extracted.
Minerals, vanilla. Subdued flavors play out on a soft and rounded palate. Features a
touch of viscosity tempered by acidity in the finish.

1996 Chardonnay, VGS, Mount Veeder, Napa Valley $38.   89

Bright gold. Rich buttery aromas with an oak accent. A smooth attack leads a
moderately full-bodied palate with a rounded mouthfeel and a soft finish. Fat
and generous with stylish touches. Drink now.

1996 Sauvignon Blanc, Napa Valley $11.   89

Very deep yellow-straw color. Moderately full-bodied. Full acidity. Moderately extracted.
Citrus, minerals, cream. Pleasantly aromatic, with a crisp fruit accent to the flavors that
follows through to a vibrant, snappy, intense finish.

1993 Cabernet Sauvignon, Mount Veeder, Napa Valley $29.   92

Deep ruby cast. Moderately full-bodied. Balanced acidity. Highly extracted. Moderately
tannic. Minerals, cassis. Tightly wound and firm, with reined-in flavors. Lean and angular
in the mouth, with a crisp yet weighty structure. Intense. Should open with time.

1994 Cabernet Sauvignon, VGS, Mount Veeder, Napa Valley $39.   89

Deep, saturated ruby red hue. Complex game, mineral, and red fruit aromas. A firm
attack leads to a moderately full-bodied palate with robust velvety tannins. Bursts with
flavor. Extremely lengthy concentrated finish. A well-balanced, graceful, and elegant
mountain wine. Drink now or later.

1995 Zinfandel, VGS, Mount Veeder, Napa Valley $35.   91

Solid red with purple highlights. Moderately full-bodied. Balanced acidity. Highly
extracted. Moderately oaked. Moderately tannic. Black fruits, chocolate, vanilla.
Rich, oak-forward aromas lead a thick mouthfeel of ripe briar fruits, with textured,
well-integrated tannins on the finish. Very stylish; expensive winemaking is evident.

Chateau Souverain

1997 Chardonnay, Sonoma County, Alexander Valley $13.   83

Pale straw cast. Medium-bodied. Balanced acidity. Moderately extracted. Minerals, cream.
Lean and crisp with a firm palate feel, finishing on an angular note.

1996 Chardonnay, Winemaker's Reserve, Russian River Valley $20.   87

Deep green-gold. Moderately full-bodied. Full acidity. Heavily oaked. Lemons, brown
spice. Youthful oak spice aromas lead a flavorsome, brashly oak-spiced mouthfeel of
generous fruit flavors with crisp acids. This should be better in a year or two.

1995 Cabernet Sauvignon, Alexander Valley $16.50.   89

Dark purple. Moderately full-bodied. Balanced acidity. Highly extracted. Mildly
oaked. Mildly tannic. Black fruits, chocolate. Tightly wound and dense, with restrained
aromatics. Silky mouthfeel. Lush, chewy tannins clamp down on the finish.

1994 Cabernet Sauvignon, Winemaker's Reserve, Alexander Valley $30.   90

Dark red with subtle purple highlights. Medium-bodied. Moderately extracted.
Mildly tannic. Earth, black fruits, oak. Rich oaky nose is confirmed on the palate.
Quite concentrated, with a viscous mouthfeel, though currently astringent through
the finish with dry oak character coming through.

1995 Cabernet Sauvignon, Winemaker's Reserve, Alexander Valley $35.   **86**

Deep, opaque purple red hue. Intense anise, vanilla, and mineral aromas show a forward oak accent. A supple attack leads to a moderately full-bodied palate with firm tannins and shy acidity. Closes up toward the finish. May open with some age. Drink now or later.

1996 Merlot, Alexander Valley $16.50.   **83**

Deep, dark ruby red. Subdued earth and black fruit aromas. A thick entry leads a full-bodied palate with chewy, velvety tannins and low levels of acidity. Big, fat, supple finish. Could use a bit more grip. Drink now.

Chateau St. Jean

1997 Chardonnay, Sonoma County $13. .   **84**

Bright green-straw cast. Medium-bodied. Balanced acidity. Moderately extracted. Minerals, cream, citrus. Aromatically reserved, with a rounded mouthfeel balanced by zesty acidity. A crisp, clean style.

1997 Chardonnay, Belle Terre Vineyard, Alexander Valley $24.   **84**

Bright straw hue. Subdued mineral and citrus aromas. A lush entry is followed by a medium-bodied palate with lean acidity. The finish is juicy and mouthwatering, though somewhat austere. Drink now or later.

1996 Chardonnay, Durell Vineyard, Carneros $24.   **88**

Deep yellow-gold. Moderately full-bodied. Balanced acidity. Highly extracted. Moderately oaked. Brown spice, citrus. A strong impression of oak and citrus on the nose follows through on the palate, with minerally leanness through the finish.

1996 Chardonnay, Robert Young Vineyard, Alexander Valley $24.   **92**

Bright straw hue. Forward, nutty, yeasty aromas show a degree of complexity. A ripe entry leads a moderately full-bodied palate with balanced acidity. The finish is lush, rounded and harmonious. Drink now.

1996 Fumé Blanc, Sonoma County $9.   **81**

1996 Fumé Blanc, La Petite Etoile Vineyard, Russian River Valley $13.   **88**

Bright pale straw cast. Medium-bodied. Balanced acidity. Moderately extracted. Moderately oaked. Brown spice, toasted oak, citrus zest. Generous toasty nose leads a bright spicy palate with toasted oak flavors to the fore. Has enough stuffing, grip, and citrus flavors to make for an assertive style that will stand up to richer foods.

1994 Cabernet Sauvignon, Cinq Cépages, Sonoma County $24.   **89**

Deep ruby cast. Moderately full-bodied. Balanced acidity. Moderately extracted. Mildly tannic. Chocolate, earth, cassis. Generous aromas have begun to reveal mature nuances. Supple yet firm in the mouth, with a velvety quality through the lengthy finish.

1995 Cabernet Sauvignon, Cinq Cépages, Sonoma County $24.   **89**

Deep saturated ruby red hue. Deep, brooding black fruit and chocolate aromas show a judicious oak accent. A supple entry leads to a moderately full-bodied palate with grippy tannins and marked acidity that enlivens the fruit flavors and helps to carry the wine's weightiness. Firm, stuffed finish. Drink now or later.

1992 Cabernet Sauvignon, Reserve, Sonoma County $45.   **94**

Deep ruby cast. Moderately full-bodied. Balanced acidity. Moderately extracted. Mildly oaked. Mildly tannic. Brown spices, red fruits, cedar. Generous aromas feature a well-integrated oak accent that merges with a firm core of fruit-centered flavors. Harmonious and supple, though well structured through the finish. Features fine grip and intensity.

1994 Cabernet Sauvignon, Reserve, Sonoma County $60.   **88**

Very deep ruby red hue. Intense black fruit and vanilla aromas show a hefty oak influence. A thick entry leads to a full-bodied palate with chewy grainy tannins. Rich, robust finish. A heavyweight, beginning to dry out. Drink within five years.

1996 Merlot, Sonoma County $18. 88

Saturated dark red. Oak-accented, generous berry fruit aromas. A flavorful attack leads a moderately full-bodied palate with persistent velvety tannins. Stylish and impressively concentrated. Drink now or later. Can improve with more age.

1994 Merlot, Reserve, Sonoma County $55. 97

Deep blood red. Richly aromatic with plummy, oaky aromas. A supple attack leads a moderately full-bodied palate with smooth tannins. The finish is most elegant. Already well developed and showing complexity, a rich, seamless wine with extraordinary finesse.

1995 Pinot Noir, Durell Vineyard, Carneros $30. 89

Full ruby red. Medium-bodied. Highly extracted. Moderately oaked. Mildly tannic. Earthy, crisp berry aromas lead a weighty palate that has a solid feel and plenty of tart red fruit flavors lingering through an assertive oaky finish.

1996 Pinot Noir, Durell Vineyard, Carneros $30. 81

1995 Johannisberg Riesling, Belle Terre Vineyards, Special Select Late Harvest, Alexander Valley $25/375 ml. 92

Deep copper hue. Exotic petrol and caramel aromas jump from the glass. A lean entry leads a complex, medium-bodied palate. Lots of sweetness balanced by firm acidity. Explodes with flavor. Intense and generous. Drink now.

Chateau Woltner

1996 Chardonnay, Howell Mountain, Napa Valley $13. 81

Chimére

1996 Pinot Blanc, Bien Nacido Vineyard, Santa Barbara County $13. 82

1996 Pinot Noir, Edna Valley $20. 84

Pale ruby-garnet cast. Medium-bodied. Full acidity. Moderately extracted. Heavily oaked. Mildly tannic. Brown spices, minerals. Quite fragrant, with a wood-dominated array of flavors. Rich though firm in the mouth, with an angular, earth-accented finish.

1996 Pinot Noir, Bien Nacido Vineyard-Mosby Vineyard, Santa Barbara County $23. 82

Chimney Rock

1997 Fumé Blanc, Napa Valley $13. 84

Pale straw cast. Medium-bodied. Full acidity. Highly extracted. Citrus, apples, minerals. Clean, racy, and austere in style, with precise and well-defined flavors through a vibrant, focused finish.

1994 Cabernet Sauvignon, Napa Valley $26. 88

Medium reddish purple. Medium-bodied. Moderately extracted. Mildly tannic. Violets, cassis, plums. Generous floral, ripe aromas lead an open-knit, juicy black fruit palate. Very supple, soft tannins on the finish.

1996 Cabernet Sauvignon, Napa Valley $30. 94

Deep violet-purple hue. Richly fruit forward aromas with sweet tobacco notes. A ripe entry leads to a lush fruity, moderately full-bodied palate with a light tannic structure and juicy acids. Very hedonistic. Drink now.

1994 Cabernet Sauvignon, Reserve, Stags Leap District $50. 90

Bright purple-red. Medium-bodied. Moderately extracted. Mildly tannic. Dried herbs, cassis, cedar, brown spice. Spicy black fruit aromas. Lively and vibrant on the palate, with full spicy oak flavors on the finish. Tannins are soft and rounded.

1995 Cabernet Sauvignon, Reserve, Stags Leap District $50. 94

Bright red with purple highlights. Moderately full-bodied. Highly extracted. Moderately tannic. Black cherries, cedar, vanilla. Scented, perfumed aromas lead a cordial-like array of fruit flavors that linger through the finish, with oak spice coming through. Supple and bright, yet with a pure, minerally intensity.

1994 Elevage, Stags Leap District $40.   **90**

Full reddish purple. Medium-bodied. Highly extracted. Moderately tannic. Cassis, toasted oak, brown spice. Full toasty aromas. Concentrated berry flavors, with generous oaky spice and a dry, fine-grained tannic finish. Showing some solid structure.

1995 Elevage, Stags Leap District $50.   **90**

Brilliant ruby red. Moderately full-bodied. Highly extracted. Moderately tannic. Mint, cassis, raspberries. Soft, supple, and harmonious, with an exotically bright and pure fruit center accented by leafy notes and oak spice. Tannins show great finesse, making for very attractive drinking now.

Christopher Creek

1996 Syrah, Russian River Valley $18.   **83**

Medium purple, brilliant with a slight fade. Generous tart berry fruit flavors. Subtle wood tones. An acidic entry leads a medium-bodied palate. Crisply acidic, lean, and dry, with some bright fruit underneath. Moderate, robust tannins and a finish that has grip. Drinkable now, but can improve with age.

Cilurzo

1996 Petite Sirah, Proprietor's Reserve, Temecula $14.95.   **80**

1997 Petite Sirah, Reserve, Temecula $19.95.   **84**

Opaque purple. Moderately full-bodied. Highly extracted. Moderately tannic. Big, generous core of blueberry flavors. Rather soft, low acids do not quite match the dry, powdery tannins.

Cinnabar

1997 Chardonnay, Santa Clara County-Santa Barbara County $16.50.   **88**

Deep green-straw cast. Moderately full-bodied. Full acidity. Highly extracted. Mildly oaked. Vanilla, minerals, citrus. Forward aromas carry a generous oak accent. Firm, rich, and ripe in the mouth, with a crisp, minerally backbone.

1996 Chardonnay, Santa Cruz Mountains $23.   **89**

Pale straw hue. Medium-bodied. Balanced acidity. Moderately extracted. Moderately tannic. Apples, spice. Ripe, spicy aromas lead a bright, fruity mouthful of apple flavors, with a supple, spicy finish that lingers.

1994 Cabernet Sauvignon, Saratoga Vineyard, Santa Cruz Mountains $25. **94**

Bright brick red. Medium-bodied. Moderately extracted. Mildly tannic. Minerals, red fruits, earth, brown spice. An attractive minerally, earthy nose leads a solid minerally palate with crisp fruity flavors and a lingering astringent finish. Fine, powdery tannins distinguish this wine. Austere in a sophisticated manner. Nice now, it should develop character with more age.

1995 Cabernet Sauvignon, Saratoga Vineyard, Santa Cruz Mountains $25. **87**

Deep ruby red with a slight fade. Medium-bodied. Balanced acidity. Moderately extracted. Moderately oaked. Mildly tannic. Brown spices, red fruits, minerals. Pleasantly aromatic, with a forward accent of spicy oak. Supple and velvety in the mouth, with fine length and smooth tannins.

1996 Xcellence, California $16.50.   **81**

1997 Merlot, Central Coast $18.   **87**

Medium, bright brick red. Sound ripe, evolved fruity aromas with plenty of oak spice accents. A mellow attack leads a medium-bodied palate with gentle tannins. A clean finish shows vanilla notes. Structured for near-term drinking.

Claudia Springs

1996 Pinot Noir, Anderson Valley $16.   **90**

Deep ruby-garnet hue. Moderately light-bodied. Balanced acidity. Moderately extracted. Mildly tannic. Dried herbs, minerals. Shows an herbal edge throughout. Quite light in style, yet broadens out somewhat on the finish. Stylish.

1996 Pinot Noir, Reserve, Anderson Valley $18.   91

Deep ruby purple. Medium-bodied. Full acidity. Moderately extracted. Mildly oaked. Mildly tannic. Minerals, berries, spice. High-toned aromas lead a lean and crisp palate. Bright fruit flavors linger through a complex spicy finish.

1996 Zinfandel, Vessar Vineyard, Redwood Valley $18.   89

Bright purple-red. Medium-bodied. Balanced acidity. Moderately extracted. Moderately oaked. Mildly tannic. Raspberries, vanilla. Very pure red berry aromas follow through on the palate, with some ripe tannins on the finish. Drinking very nicely now. Fruity and hedonistic.

Cline

1996 Marsanne, Los Carneros $20.   91

Bright golden cast. Full-bodied. Full acidity. Highly extracted. Mildly oaked. Tropical fruits, yeast, citrus. Exotically aromatic, with a huge range of complex flavors on the palate. Extremely full and rich in the mouth, yet there is quite racy acidity, and a zesty, spicy finish.

1996 Carignane, Ancient Vines, Contra Costa County $18.   91

Red-purple hue with slight fade. Moderately full-bodied. Highly extracted. Moderately tannic. Crisp cherries, coal tar, herbs. An impressive medicinal note on the nose, with faintly herbal and crisp fruit aromas that follow on the palate. Balanced dry tannins. Very complex.

1996 Mourvedre, Ancient Vines, Contra Costa County $18.   93

Blackish ruby hue. Medium-bodied. Highly extracted. Moderately tannic. Oak spice, mint, cherries. Fine eucalyptus aromas with a big blast of oak spice. Rich, fully extracted flavors and a generous mouthfeel are impressive. This will improve with a few years in the cellar.

1996 Mourvedre, Small Berry Vinyard, Contra Costa $28.   95

Bright ruby hue with a purple cast. Medium-bodied. Moderately extracted. Moderately tannic. Toasted oak spice, black fruits. Classy oak-accented aromas follow through on the palate, with solidly extracted flavors and firm tannins giving this a cellarworthy structure.

1996 Syrah, Caneros $18.   86

Rich purple, limpid and brilliant, with a slight fade. Generous, pleasant bramble fruit and vanilla flavors. Generous wood tones. Smooth entry. Moderately full-bodied with crisp acidity. Moderate silky tannins. Soft, supple extraction with plenty of balancing fruit acids. Subtle rich finish. Drink now.

1996 Zinfandel, Ancient Vines, Contra Costa County $18.   89

Deep blackish purple. Moderately full-bodied. Full acidity. Moderately extracted. Moderately oaked. Mildly tannic. Briar fruits, coffee, chocolate. Spicy oak notes emerge on the nose, and translate well to the fruit-centered palate. Vibrant acidity makes for a zesty, uplifting finish.

1996 Zinfandel, Big Break Vineyard, Contra Costa County $24.   97

Deep blackish purple. Full-bodied. Full acidity. Moderately extracted. Moderately oaked. Mildly tannic. Mint, black fruits, vanilla. Quite aromatic, with a full-throttled, flavorful character on the palate. Shows great richness and depth through the vibrant finish. Excellent grip and intensity.

1996 Zinfandel, Bridgehead Vineyard, Contra Costa County $24.   91

Deep blackish ruby hue. Full-bodied. Balanced acidity. Moderately extracted. Mildly oaked. Mildly tannic. Eucalyptus, chocolate, minerals. Extremely aromatic, with a rich, flavorful palate feel. Big but well balanced, with solid acidity making for a clean finish. Intense and lengthy.

1996 Zinfandel, Live Oak Vineyard, Contra Costa County $24.   95

Deep blackish purple. Full-bodied. Full acidity. Highly extracted. Moderately oaked. Mildly tannic. Vanilla, black fruits, minerals. Quite aromatic, with a flavorful, racy character on the palate. Deep and extracted, with vibrant acidity through the finish. Well balanced and intense.

1995 Muscat Canelli, Sonoma Valley $14/375 ml.   **88**

Deep yellow-straw hue. Generous caramel, orange, and spice aromas. A soft entry leads a moderately full-bodied palate showing lots of sweetness. Rich and rounded, with an attractive nutty complexity. Drink now.

Cloninger

1997 Chardonnay, Monterey $13.   **81**

1994 Cabernet Sauvignon, Monterey $13.   **87**

Saturated blackish red. Medium-bodied. Highly extracted. Mildly tannic. Dried herbs, blackberries. Full aromas have deep fruit accents with herbaceous notes. A solid and angular palate, with concentrated black fruit flavors showing a distinct herbal character through the finish

1996 Cabernet Sauvignon, Quinn Vineyard, Carmel Valley $14.   **89**

Opaque violet red. Moderately full-bodied. Moderately extracted. Moderately oaked. Mildly tannic. Dill, menthol, black fruits. Strong oak-accented aromas lead a crisp mouthful of tart fruit flavors, with spice emerging on the finish. Tannins are marginal.

Clos du Bois

1997 Chardonnay, Sonoma County $14.   **83**

Bright straw hue. Subdued mineral aromas carry a subtle tropical fruit accent. A lean entry leads a medium-bodied palate with angular acidity. Crisp finish. Well structured but not overly flavorful. Drink now.

1997 Chardonnay, Alexander Valley $15.   **83**

Pale straw hue. Medium-bodied. Full acidity. Moderately extracted. Citrus, minerals, vanilla. Tart and lean in flavors, though it has a sense of citric brightness and a clean finish that make for a very user-friendly style.

1997 Chardonnay, Calcaire Vineyard, Alexander Valley $18.   **86**

Bright yellow-gold. Moderately full-bodied. Balanced acidity. Moderately extracted. Mildly oaked. Vanilla, butter, green apples. A smooth mouthfeel with vanilla notes through the finish. Has a nice acidic cut that maintains a sense of balance.

1996 Chardonnay, Flintwood Vineyard, Dry Creek Valley $18.   **84**

Pale straw cast. Moderately full-bodied. Full acidity. Moderately extracted. Mildly oaked. Toasted oak, citrus. Pronounced smoky, buttery aromas lead an angular, citrus zest palate with a glycerous, full mouthfeel. Restrained, mildly smoky oak influences.

1995 Cabernet Sauvignon, Sonoma County $15.   **81**

1996 Cabernet Sauvignon, Sonoma County $15.   **83**

Deep cherry red with a slight fade. Generous spice and vanilla aromas show a hefty oak influence. A supple attack leads to a medium-bodied palate with ripe tannins. Soft, rounded finish. Pleasant, but lacks a bit for grip and intensity. Drink now.

1995 Cabernet Sauvignon, Alexander Valley Selection,
Alexander Valley $21.   **83**

Bright ruby cast. Medium-bodied. Balanced acidity. Moderately extracted. Mildly tannic. Dried herbs, red fruits, brown spices. Pleasantly aromatic, with a lively, lighter-styled mouthfeel. Juicy and angular through the finish.

1994 Cabernet Sauvignon, Briarcrest Vineyard, Alexander Valley $21.   **83**

Bright ruby red with a slight fade. Medium-bodied. Full acidity. Moderately extracted. Moderately tannic. Minerals, cassis. Lean, angular, and minerally, with a firm, linear quality. Picks up some mild astringency through the finish.

1995 Cabernet Sauvignon, Briarcrest Vineyard, Alexander Valley $30.   **83**

Deep garnet red hue. Subdued berry and mineral aromas. A soft entry leads to a moderately light-bodied palate with subtle tannins. Zesty acidity enlivens the palate. Clean, lean finish. Drink now.

Scale: Superlative (96-100), Exceptional (90-95), Highly Recommended (85-89), Recommended (80-84), Not Recommended (Under 80)

1995 Cabernet Sauvignon, Winemaker's Reserve, Alexander Valley $50.   **88**
Deep garnet hue. Pronounced minty aromas carry an herbal overtone. A lush entry leads
to a medium-bodied palate with lean tannins and zesty acidity. Flavorful, complex finish.
Lighter in style, but well balanced and harmonious. Drink now.

1994 Marlstone Vineyard, Alexander Valley $25.   **84**
Bright ruby red with a slight fade. Medium-bodied. Full acidity. Moderately extracted.
Mildly oaked. Mildly tannic. Brown spices, minerals. Aromatically reserved, with a lighter-
styled palate feel. Bright acids lend an angular, juicy quality. Pleasant, angular finish.

1996 Merlot, Sonoma County $17.   **84**
Pale ruby red with a subtle fade. Aromas of herbs and red fruits. A subtle entry leads a
light-bodied palate with gentle tannins and quick, clean finish. Drink now.

1995 Merlot, Selection, Alexander Valley $20.   **91**
Deep ruby hue to the rim with brilliant clarity. Medium-bodied. Full acidity. Moderately
extracted. Moderately oaked. Mildly tannic. Chocolate, black fruits, sweet herbs. Quite
rich in style, with a mouthfilling velvety palate feel. The tannins are very well integrated,
and the use of oak has been judicious. Lengthy chewy mouthfeel.

1996 Merlot, Alexander Valley $20.   **86**
Bright ruby red to the rim. Subdued herb and red fruit aromas. A soft entry is followed
by a moderately full-bodied, supple palate with low levels of acidity and chewy tannins.
Soft, fleshy finish.

1995 Zinfandel, Sonoma County $14.   **83**
Bright ruby-garnet cast. Medium-bodied. Balanced acidity. Subtly extracted. Mildly oaked.
Mildly tannic. Dried herbs, vanilla. Quite aromatic, with distinctive herbal overtones. Soft
and lush on the palate, with a supple finish.

Clos du Lac

1997 Zinfandel Blanc, Sierra Foothills $8.   **82**

1996 Cabernet Franc, Sierra Foothills- Amador County $15.   **83**
Bright ruby purple. Medium-bodied. Full acidity. Moderately extracted. Moderately
oaked. Moderately tannic. Minerals, cassis, chocolate. Generous aromas lead a ripe and
flavorful palate that shows complexity. Toughens a bit on the finish, where the tannins
rear up.

1997 Muscat Vin Doux Naturel, Sierra Foothills $12/375 ml.   **84**
Deep straw hue with a slight greenish cast. Moderately full-bodied. Full acidity. Highly
extracted. Flowers, sweet herbs, citrus. Quite forward in aromatics, with a touch of heat.
Full and round in the mouth, with a finish enlivened by buoyant acidity.

Clos du Val

1993 Cabernet Sauvignon, Napa Valley $24.   **87**
Dark ruby hue with purple highlights. Medium-bodied. Moderately extracted. Moderately
tannic. Black currants, black cherry. Dusty black fruit aromas. Rich black fruit flavors on
entry turn quite dry. Solid, dry, tealike, fine-grained tannins on the finish give this
authority and structure.

1995 Cabernet Sauvignon, Napa Valley $24.   **87**
Bright violet hue. A soft entry leads a medium-bodied palate with juicy acids and a lighter
fruit-centered palate. Finishes quickly and cleanly. Drink now.

1993 Cabernet Sauvignon, Reserve, Napa Valley $50.   **91**
Deep ruby hue with purple highlights. Medium-bodied. Highly extracted. Mildly
tannic. Chocolate, brown spice, black fruits. Rich black fruit aromas. Smooth, textured
mouthfeel shows great elegance. Clean lengthy finish shows persistent fruity nuances.
Fine balance, with complex flavors persisting.

1994 Cabernet Sauvignon, Reserve, Napa Valley $53.   92

Deep ruby hue with a slight purple cast. Moderately full-bodied. Full acidity. Highly extracted. Moderately oaked. Moderately tannic. Red fruits, vanilla, minerals. Generous aromas lead a firm and intense palate feel. Bright and juicy, with a sense of angularity. Focused and well balanced. Should age well.

1996 Merlot, Napa Valley $28.   84

Medium ruby red with a subtle fade. Pleasant herbal aromas. Moderately full-bodied with a supple attack and a rich texture giving way to firm tannins that grip the finish. Drink now or later. Can improve with more age.

1995 Pinot Noir, Carneros $20.   85

Cherry red with a pinkish tinge. Medium-bodied. Moderately extracted. Moderately oaked. Moderately tannic. Toasty, tart aromas lead tart red cherry flavors. Plenty of tart acids and astringent tannin through the finish. Quite tight and angular now, it should soften with a little time.

1995 Zinfandel, California $15.   85

Bright ruby-garnet cast. Medium-bodied. Balanced acidity. Moderately extracted. Mildly tannic. Tea, minerals. An interesting melange of earthy aromas plays out well on the palate, which is firm and well structured, in a rather reserved style. Fine grip and intensity; a Claret style.

Clos La Chance

1997 Chardonnay, Napa Valley $17.   91

Medium yellow-gold. Aromatically rich with buttery, smoky character and lots of ripe fruit. A rich entry leads a full-bodied palate with ripe fruit flavors and creamy texture. Lush through the finish.

1997 Chardonnay, Santa Cruz Mountains $19.   83

Bright straw hue. Unusual wool and earth aromas. A crisp entry leads a medium-bodied palate with vibrant acidity. Lean finish. Drink now.

1996 Chardonnay, Vintner's Reserve, Santa Cruz Mountains $27.   84

Brilliant yellow-straw hue. Intense buttery aromas. A rich entry leads a moderately full-bodied palate with creamy acidity. Generous lactic finish. Drink now.

1994 Cabernet Sauvignon, Santa Cruz Mountains $22.   90

Bright cherry red. Medium-bodied. Moderately extracted. Mildly tannic. Mint, toasted oak, cranberry. Pronounced minty, vanilla-kissed aromas. Lively red fruit flavors marry with assertive oak in a lightly framed palate showing clean astringency through the finish.

1995 Cabernet Sauvignon, Santa Cruz Mountains $21.   86

Bright ruby red with a slight fade. Medium-bodied. Balanced acidity. Moderately extracted. Moderately oaked. Mildly tannic. Spice, minerals, sweet herbs. Quite aromatic, showing a hefty oak accent. Light in the mouth, with a lean and angular finish.

1996 Cabernet Sauvignon, Santa Cruz Mountains $22.   86

Bright cherry garnet hue. Forward dried herb and brown spice aromas show a judicious oak accent. A lush entry leads to a moderately full-bodied palate with velvety tannins and a clean acidic cut. Ripe rounded finish.

1996 Merlot, Central Coast $18.   81

1996 Pinot Noir, Santa Cruz Mountains $24.   84

Bright ruby-garnet cast. Medium-bodied. Balanced acidity. Moderately extracted. Moderately oaked. Mildly tannic. Sandalwood, dill pickle. Generous aromas feature an exotic spicy quality. Lush and seamless in the mouth with a silky palate feel. The finish is lengthy and flavorful.

Scale: Superlative (96-100), Exceptional (90-95), Highly Recommended (85-89), Recommended (80-84), Not Recommended (Under 80)

Clos Pegase

1995 Cabernet Sauvignon, Napa Valley $22.99.   89

Deep ruby hue. Forward leather, berry, and mineral aromas. A lush entry leads to a moderately full-bodied palate with rich chewy tannins. Supple and persistent through the finish with classic dusty cherry flavors. Elegant but focused. Drink now or later.

1994 Cabernet Sauvignon, Hommage Reserve, Napa Valley $40.   93

Deep cherry red. Medium-bodied. Moderately extracted. Mildly tannic. Toasted oak, concentrated red berries. Elegant oaky aromas are well integrated, with some floral accents. Bright, plush fruit flavors show refinement and suppleness. Very attractive now, it is hard to see this tasting better with extended aging.

B.R. Cohn

1994 Cabernet Sauvignon, Olive Hill Vineyard, Sonoma Valley $32.   92

Deep reddish purple. Medium-bodied. Highly extracted. Moderately tannic. Cassis, vanilla, brown spice. Youthful, vibrant aromas that show vanilla and cassis notes. The solid, tightly wound palate has good depth of flavors and dense tannins that make this backward at present.

1995 Cabernet Sauvignon, Olive Hill Vineyard, Sonoma Valley $75.   94

Dark blood red. Moderately full-bodied. Highly extracted. Moderately tannic. Ripe black fruits. Rich cassis aromas follow through on a supple palate, with voluptuous flavors and impressive length. Very classic.

Concannon

1997 Chardonnay, Selected Vineyard, Central Coast $10.95.   86

Pale yellow-straw hue. Mildly aromatic with apricot character. A smooth attack leads a medium-light body with subtle oak flavors. Clean, rather short finish. Very user friendly.

1996 Chardonnay, Reserve, Livermore Valley $18.95.   83

Bright medium gold. Moderately aromatic with citrus and oak accents. A crisp entry leads a medium-bodied palate with straightforward citrus flavors. The persistent finish has full spicy oak notes. Drink now.

1997 Gewürztraminer, Limited Bottling, Arroyo Seco-Monterey $9.95.   83

Deep old-gold hue. Fat, overripe melon aromas show a slight herbal accent. A rich entry leads an oily, moderately full-bodied palate. Lean through the finish. Drink now.

1996 Marsanne, Santa Clara Valley $13.95.   84

Deep golden cast. Moderately full-bodied. Full acidity. Highly extracted. Oranges, blanched almonds, cream. Quite ripe aromatically. The entry is viscous, but it turns rather lean in the mouth with a sense of angularity and some mild bitterness to the finish.

1996 Assemblage White Reserve, Livermore Valley $12.95.   83

Bright straw cast. Moderately full-bodied. Balanced acidity. Moderately extracted. Citrus, toast, butter. Pleasantly aromatic, with a lush presence on the palate. Zesty acidity lends a counterpoint to the buttery finish.

1997 Orange Muscat, Limited Bottling, Yolo County $10.95.   84

Brilliant yellow-straw hue. Generous pear and ripe tropical fruit aromas jump from the glass. A lush entry leads a medium-bodied palate with moderate sweetness and zesty acidity. Rich, flavorful finish. Drink now.

1997 Johannisberg Riesling, Arroyo Seco-Monterey $9.95.   85

Bright yellow-gold. Distinctive minerally, mildly honeyed aromas seem to show a touch of botrytis. A heavy attack leads a moderately full-bodied palate with concentrated flavors and low acids. Mildly bitter notes through the finish. Interesting. Drink now.

1996 Sauvignon Blanc, Livermore Valley $7.95.   82

1996 Cabernet Sauvignon, Selected Vineyard, Central Coast $11.45.   82

1995 Cabernet Sauvignon, Reserve, Livermore Valley $19.95.   83

Bright cherry red with a garnet rim. Forward mineral, herb, and red fruit aromas. A lush entry leads to a medium-bodied palate with grippy tannins. Clipped, angular finish. Drink now.

1994 Assemblage Red Reserve, Central Coast $15.95.   86

Bright ruby red. Medium-bodied. Moderately extracted. Mildly tannic. Red berries, dried herbs, mild toasted oak. Ripe berry aromas have subtle toasty hints with herbaceous overtones. Open-knit, lively flavors make for an accessible style with a clean finish. Drink now.

1995 Assemblage Red Reserve, Livermore Valley $18.95.   81

1996 Mourvedre, Contra Costa County $16.95.   84

Ruby red, with a pale cast. Moderately extracted. Mildly tannic. Medium-bodied. Ripe fruits. Cooked, spicy, and jammy. Rather weak in acids, with dry, powdery tannins on the finish. The soft character suggests near-term drinking.

1996 Petite Sirah, Selected Vineyard, California $11.45.   83

Opaque purple-blue color. Full-bodied. Highly extracted. Quite tannic. Well-extracted flavors with dark, fleshy fruit character following through on the finish. Dry, thick tannins linger. Monolithic and intense.

1995 Petite Sirah, Reserve Vineyard, Central Coast $22.95.   84

Bright purple. Moderately full-bodied. Balanced acidity. Moderately extracted. Complex aromas show herbal, medicinal, briar fruit aromas. Lush, textured, and well proportioned, with tannins not drying the finish excessively.

1995 Zinfandel, Late Harvest, Limited Bottling, Livermore Valley $16.95.   86

Bright ruby cast. Medium-bodied. Full acidity. Moderately extracted. Mildly tannic. Dried herbs, red fruits. Fairly aromatic, with bright herbal overtones. Lean and crisp, with a hint of sweetness.

Conn Creek

1994 Cabernet Sauvignon, Limited Release, Napa Valley $22.   82

1994 Anthology, Napa Valley $44.   88

Deep red-violet. Moderately full-bodied. Highly extracted. Moderately tannic. Cassis, black fruits, brown spice. Fleshy, ripe fruit aromas follow through on a silky, textured, and rounded palate, with oak spice and velvety tannins defining the finish.

1995 Anthology, Napa Valley $44.   92

Deep ruby hue. Generous and exceptionally attractive vanilla and red fruit aromas carry a big sweet oak accent. A lush entrance leads to a moderately full-bodied palate that bursts with ripe fruit flavors. Rich velvety tannins and a juicy note of acidity provide support. Lengthy, attractive finish. Well balanced and eminently drinkable but structured to hold. Drink now or later.

Cook's

NV Spumante, American $4.29.   82

Cooper-Garrod

1996 Chardonnay, Santa Cruz Mountains $18.   80

1996 Cabernet Franc, Santa Cruz Mountains $18.   81

1994 Cabernet Sauvignon, Santa Cruz Mountains $25.   90

Bright crimson red with purple highlights. Medium-bodied. Moderately extracted. Mildly tannic. Plums, fresh herbs, earth. Exotic herbal-accented nose leads a fleshy, plummy palate with a very forward juicy character that makes this inviting to drink now.

Scale: Superlative (96-100), Exceptional (90-95), Highly Recommended (85-89), Recommended (80-84), Not Recommended (Under 80)

66

1995 Cabernet Sauvignon, Santa Cruz Mountains $28.   **93**

Deep ruby purple. Moderately full-bodied. Balanced acidity. Moderately extracted. Mildly tannic. Cassis, black fruits, minerals. Extraordinarily aromatic, showing a pure, fruit-centered flavor profile. Intense and lively, with fine length and grip. Harmony and elegance dominate.

1995 Cabernet Sauvignon, Proprietor's Reserve,
Santa Cruz Mountains $35.   **89**

Deep ruby purple. Moderately full-bodied. Balanced acidity. Moderately extracted. Mildly tannic. Red fruits, minerals. Intense and pure, with fruit-centered flavors and very little oak influence. Racy and lean, with fine intensity and grip.

Corbett Canyon

1997 Chardonnay, Reserve, Santa Barbara County $10.   **82**

1996 Sauvignon Blanc, Reserve, California $9.   **84**

Pale golden yellow. Medium-bodied. Balanced acidity. Moderately extracted. Mildly oaked. Lime, smoke, minerals. Aromatic buttery aromas. A brisk attack, with citrus flavors and a buttery malolactic note. Rather soft through the finish; it could use more grip and persistence.

1995 Cabernet Sauvignon, Reserve, Sonoma County $10.   **85**

Medium ruby-red hue. Moderately aromatic with dusty, soft cherry accents. A supple attack leads a medium-bodied palate with bright, soft fruity flavors showing development. Tannins are evolved and supple. Drink now.

Corison

1994 Cabernet Sauvignon, Napa Valley $35.   **89**

Bright reddish purple. Medium-bodied. Highly extracted. Moderately tannic. Cherries, eucalyptus, lead pencil. Full, complex aromas lead a crisp, astringent, full-flavored palate, with firm dry tannins on the finish. This has good focus and grip.

Cornerstone

1993 Cabernet Sauvignon, Beatty Ranch, Howell Mountain $32.   **91**

Deep blackish ruby color. Moderately full-bodied. Highly extracted. Moderately tannic. Cassis, plums, loam, toasted oak. A fine earthiness runs through the palate and is well supported by concentrated toasty black fruit flavors that persist through the finish. This has great length and balance. Good now, though cellaring can only help. Huge but elegant.

Cosentino

1997 Chardonnay, Napa Valley $18.   **87**

Bright straw cast. Moderately full-bodied. Full acidity. Highly extracted. River pebbles, tropical fruits, minerals. Focused aromatics have a pure fruit-driven quality throughout. Lean and intense through the zesty finish. Excellent grip and focus.

1997 Chardonnay, "The Sculptor" Reserve, Napa Valley $30.   **89**

Pale straw cast. Moderately full-bodied. Full acidity. Moderately extracted. Mildly oaked. Toast, minerals. Aromatically reserved, with an understated toasty accent. A generous mouthfeel reveals subtle flavors. Finishes with crisp, persistent fruit flavors.

1996 Cabernet Franc, Napa Valley $25.   **88**

Bright ruby cast. Medium-bodied. Balanced acidity. Moderately extracted. Heavily oaked. Mildly tannic. Spice, dill pickle, minerals. Oak-driven aromatics lead a lean and precise palate feel. Lengthy and flavorful through the finish. Weighty, yet well balanced.

1995 Cabernet Sauvignon, Napa Valley $18.   **85**

Bright ruby hue with subtle purple highlights. Medium-bodied. Moderately extracted. Moderately tannic. Cassis, cedar, tobacco. Soft black currant and cedar aromas follow through very nicely on the palate, with texture and a sense of elegance imparted by the velvety tannins. Delicious ripe varietal expression.

1996 Cabernet Sauvignon, Napa Valley $20.   84

Bright ruby red. Medium-bodied. Moderately extracted. Mildly tannic. Vanilla, red berries, minerals. A hint of herbal quality on the nose and palate. Lively and straightforward, for current drinking.

1994 Cabernet Sauvignon, Reserve, Napa Valley $40.   90

Bright cherry red. Medium-bodied. Moderately extracted. Moderately tannic. Toasted oak, vanilla, red berries. Rich, sweet oak-accented aromas follow through on the palate, with juicy berry flavors giving way to a firm spicy oak finish. Persistent toasty note.

1995 Cabernet Sauvignon, Reserve, Napa Valley $40.   88

Bright cherry red. Medium-bodied. Moderately extracted. Mildly tannic. Vanilla, cedar, red fruits. Oak-scented aromas lead a bright, juicy palate, with mildly chunky tannins playing on the finish. A firm, oaky style.

1994 The Poet Meritage, Napa Valley $30.   90

Dark ruby red. Medium-bodied. Highly extracted. Moderately tannic. Cassis, black fruits, subtle spice, eucalyptus. Fleshy, ripe aromas lead a smooth and textured palate that shows generous Cabernet fruit flavors and well-integrated soft tannins throughout. Plush, very harmonious, and forward drinking. Nice now.

1995 The Poet Meritage, Napa Valley $38.   89

Deep ruby hue with a pale rim. Moderately full-bodied. Highly extracted. Moderately tannic. Cedar, vanilla, cassis. Full oaky aromas lead a fleshy mouthful of ripe fruit flavors, with layers of silky tannins and oak spice through the finish. Very hedonistic and textured throughout.

1995 M. Coz Meritage, Napa Valley $75.   94

Dark violet red. Medium-bodied. Highly extracted. Moderately tannic. Toasted oak, brown spice, cassis. Scented, oak-driven aromas have complementary plush dark fruit flavors, with velvety tannins helping make this accessible. Has a fine mineral note through the finish. Very textured and stylish.

1996 Merlot, Reserve, Napa Valley $34.   92

Deep ruby-violet red with a subtle fade. Raspberry, herbal, and vanilla aromas. Moderately full-bodied. Lush and fruity on the attack, with a moderately full body, and bright acids lifting the lush tannins through the finish. Elegant and complex. Drink now.

1996 Merlot, Oakville, Napa Valley $60.   90

Bright cherry red. Very aromatic with outstandingly complex oaky accents and raspberry and violet scents. Moderately full-bodied with a big complement of exotic cherry flavors that conclude with a lingering, flavorful oak-accented finish. Drink now.

1996 Pinot Noir, Carneros $30.   86

Bright purple-tinged pale red. Medium-bodied. Moderately extracted. Heavily oaked. Mildly tannic. Plenty of cedar and vanilla aromas lead a palate of light, delicate red fruit flavors, with a nice mouthfeel. Vanilla oak flavors take over on the finish.

1996 Pinot Noir, Russian River Valley $50.   89

Bright cherry red with purple highlights. Medium-bodied. Moderately extracted. Moderately oaked. Mildly tannic. Floral, vanilla, and cedar aromas lead a bright, juicy palate, with concentrated raspberry and cherry flavors on the midpalate and plenty of vanilla oak dominating the finish. Somewhat youthful and angular.

1996 Zinfandel, The Zin, California $22.   81

Costa de Oro

1996 Chardonnay, Gold Coast Vineyards, Santa Maria Valley $18.   82

1997 Chardonnay, Gold Coast Vineyards, Santa Maria Valley $18.   81

Cottonwood Canyon

1994 Chardonnay, Santa Barbara County $24.   82

Scale: Superlative (96-100), Exceptional (90-95), Highly Recommended (85-89), Recommended (80-84), Not Recommended (Under 80)

68

1994 Chardonnay, Barrel Select, Santa Barbara County $29.   **86**

Bright yellow-gold. Moderately full-bodied. Balanced acidity. Moderately extracted. Heavily oaked. The color and aroma hint at maderization. Turns extremely woody on the palate, with a wave of sweet coconut flavors.

1994 Cabernet Sauvignon, Central Coast $24.50.   **90**

Pale ruby red. Moderately light-bodied. Moderately extracted. Mildly tannic. Red berries, chocolate, brown spice. High-toned oak-accented aromas show peppery notes. Elegant berry flavors on entry give way to a toasty, chocolatey finish. Well balanced and drinking well now. Subtlety and complexity evident.

1994 Synergy Classic, Central Coast $28.   **84**

Full garnet red. Medium-bodied. Moderately extracted. Mildly tannic. Brown spice, licorice. Mature, spicy aromas lead a ripe, soft palate with a mildly stewed-fruit flavor profile. Finishes with a minerally note. Not for further cellaring.

1995 Merlot, Central Coast $26.   **88**

Dark ruby with a garnet cast. Moderately light-bodied. Full acidity. Moderately extracted. Heavily oaked. Mildly tannic. Brown spices, cherries, minerals. Lighter in style and oak driven, this wine is both aromatic and flavorful. Relatively austere on the palate, with fine structural acidity and good length.

Coturri

1996 Zinfandel, Sonoma Mountain $21.   **84**

Deep blackish ruby color. Full-bodied. Balanced acidity. Moderately extracted. Mildly oaked. Mildly tannic. Chocolate, overripe fruits. Features a Port-like aromatic note, and carries the overripe theme through the palate. Thick and dense in the mouth, with an overtone of sweetness. Interesting, but not for everyone.

1996 Zinfandel, Freiberg Vineyards, Sonoma Valley $23.   **84**

Deep blackish purple. Full-bodied. Balanced acidity. Highly extracted. Moderately tannic. Dates, chocolate, earth. Deeply aromatic, with slight notes of overripeness and dark, brooding flavors. Thick and viscous in the mouth, showing an overtone of sweetness. Finishes with some chunky tannins.

1996 Zinfandel, P. Coturri Family Vineyards, Sonoma Valley $23.   **85**

Opaque blackish ruby hue. Moderately full-bodied. Balanced acidity. Highly extracted. Moderately tannic. Chocolate, black fruits. Aromatic, with deep, chocolatey flavors. Full, ripe, and thick, with chunky tannins through the finish. A mouthful.

Robert Craig

1994 Affinity, Napa Valley $33.   **90**

Saturated opaque reddish purple. Medium-bodied. Moderately extracted. Moderately tannic. Plums, black tea, licorice. Generous plummy aromas lead a full-flavored palate with weight and depth of flavors. Has a rounded mouthfeel, with some solidity to the tannins on the finish.

1995 Affinity, Napa Valley $35.   **89**

Saturated red-purple. Medium-bodied. Moderately extracted. Mildly tannic. Violets, chocolate, black fruits. Vibrant, fruity aromas lead a bright, juicy entry that gives way to slight tannins, with a mild, drying quality. A lighter-framed wine with firm structural elements that will allow it to age.

Creston

1995 Merlot, Paso Robles $16.   **82**

1995 Zinfandel, Paso Robles $13.   **83**

Bright ruby cast. Medium-bodied. Full acidity. Moderately extracted. Mildly tannic. Briar fruits. Quite aromatic, featuring a fruit-centered quality. Lighter in the mouth, with juicy acidity making for a vibrant finish.

Crichton Hall

1996 Chardonnay, Napa Valley $22. **88**

Bright yellow-gold. Medium-bodied. Balanced acidity. Moderately extracted. Mildly oaked. Ripe apples, citrus, butter. Rich, generous aromas of ripe fruits follow through on the palate, with a smooth, buttery texture and full and broad flavors. Well balanced and flavorful.

1996 Merlot, Napa Valley $26. **86**

Bright ruby red. Herbal, minerally aromas. Medium-bodied with a lean attack and crisp black fruit flavors that finish in a subtle manner. Drink now.

1995 Pinot Noir, Napa Valley $25. **87**

Pale pink-tinged red. Moderately light-bodied. Moderately extracted. Moderately oaked. Mildly tannic. Sweet, florally accented fruit aromas. Delicate strawberry and raspberry flavors unfold on the palate, with a dry oak-accented finish.

Cronin

1996 Chardonnay, Stuhlmuller Vineyard, Alexander Valley $18. **83**

Bright yellow-straw hue. Unusual blanched almond and mineral aromas. A lush entry is followed by a medium-bodied palate with lively bright acidity and a crisp, intense finish. Drink now.

Curtis

1997 Syrah Rosé, Santa Ynez Valley $8. **88**

Pale cherry red. Intense briar fruit and herb aromas jump from the glass. A fat entry leads a weighty, moderately full-bodied palate with rounded acidity. A full, rich, flavorful Rosé for the table. Drink now.

1997 Heritage, Old Vines Red, California $10. **85**

Bright purple-red hue to the rim. Generous red fruit, sweet herb, and mineral aromas. A crisp attack leads a medium-bodied palate that shows drying, astringent tannins. Clipped, snappy finish. Youthful and compact. Drink now or later. Can improve with more age.

1996 Syrah, Ambassador's Vineyard, Santa Ynez Valley $18. **87**

Medium cherry red, limpid, with a slight fade. Mild, sound herb, jammy black fruit, and olive flavors. Subtle wood tones. Soft entry. Medium-bodied. Soft, jammy fruit flavors dissipate quickly on a subtle, short finish. Delicate Rhone-like qualities. Drink now.

Cuvaison

1997 Chardonnay, Carneros $NA. **89**

Rich straw hue. Generous butter, citrus, and yeast aromas. A firm entry leads a moderately full-bodied palate. Features deep citrusy flavors with plenty of vanilla. Flashy, with a touch of phenolic dryness through the finish. Drink now.

1996 Chardonnay, Reserve, Napa Valley $NA. **92**

Bright yellow-gold. Generous leesy, ripe citrus, and roasted nut aromas. A soft entry leads a full-bodied palate, with balanced acidity. Nutty, ripe, and rich. A blowsy style, but well balanced. Drink now.

1994 Cabernet Sauvignon, Napa Valley $24.99. **93**

Dark reddish purple. Moderately full-bodied. Highly extracted. Moderately tannic. Cassis, currant, anise. Rich, concentrated black fruit flavors have supple integrated tannins giving this a rich center. Young and tight at present, though with plenty of attractive qualities.

1995 Cabernet Sauvignon, Napa Valley $NA. **88**

Dark, saturated ruby purple. Generous cassis and oak spice aromas. A firm entry leads a moderately full-bodied palate, with grainy tannins. Classic, varietal, and well gripped. Should age well. Mid-term cellar candidate (3–6 years).

Scale: Superlative (96-100), Exceptional (90-95), Highly Recommended (85-89), Recommended (80-84), Not Recommended (Under 80)

70

1996 Merlot, Carneros, Napa Valley $NA. **90**

Deep ruby red with a slight fade. Vanilla and ripe black fruit aromas show a pleasant wood accent. A firm entry leads a moderately full-bodied palate, with drying, well-gripped tannins. Good structure and fine, uplifting acidity. Well fruited and flavorful through the finish. Drink now or later.

1995 Pinot Noir, Eris, Carneros $18.99. **87**

Dark red. Medium-bodied. Moderately extracted. Moderately oaked. Mildly tannic. Toasted oak aromas with bramble fruit accents. On the palate, crisp black fruit flavors with a mineral edge and crisp acids. Spicy, toasty finish with some subtle gamey notes.

1996 Pinot Noir, Eris, Carneros $20. **82**

Dalla Valle

1993 Cabernet Sauvignon, Napa Valley $40. **90**

Saturated garnet-cherry red. Moderately full-bodied. Highly extracted. Moderately tannic. Plums, cassis, mineral. The solid, full-flavored palate has ripe black fruit flavors and generous minerally complexity that linger through the finish. This has the structure to cellar, though it is nice now.

Dark Star

1996 Cabernet Sauvignon, Paso Robles $19. **88**

Very deep saturated ruby cast. Full-bodied. Balanced acidity. Highly extracted. Moderately oaked. Moderately tannic. Black fruits, minerals, spice. Aromatically reserved, with a firm, concentrated, intense palate feel. Tannins clamp down on the finish.

1996 Ricordati, Paso Robles $20. **87**

Bright violet-red. Medium-bodied. Moderately extracted. Mildly tannic. Black fruits, mint, cedar. Mildly toasty, ripe, fleshy aromas follow through on the palate, with bright, spicy fruit flavors and soft tannins on the finish. A very accessible style.

Davis Bynum

1994 Cabernet Sauvignon, Hedin Vineyard, Russian River Valley $24. **87**

Bright ruby purple. Moderately full-bodied. Full acidity. Moderately extracted. Mildly tannic. Minerals, lead pencil, red fruits. Generous aromas are complex and unusual. Firm and angular in the mouth, with a bright, linear quality and vibrant acidity.

1994 Eclipse, Sonoma County $28. **87**

Bright ruby purple. Full-bodied. Full acidity. Highly extracted. Mildly tannic. Lead pencil, minerals, red fruits. Unusual aromas are complex and generous. Firm and angular in the mouth, with a clean, linear quality. Solid acidity says this is a good match for foods.

1995 Merlot, Laureles Estate Vineyard, Russian River Valley $24. **89**

Saturated dark violet red. Oaky, black raspberry, lead pencil aromas. A firm entry leads a full-bodied palate with plentiful chewy dry tannins and bright acidity marking the finish. Impressive and stylish with a hugely wrought, thickly textured mouthfeel, and a snappy, high-toned finish. Drink within 5 years.

1995 Pinot Noir, Limited Edition, Russian River Valley $28. **91**

Full, dark cherry red. Medium-bodied. Highly extracted. Moderately oaked. Mildly tannic. Dried herbs, leather, and black cherries on the nose lead a complex, flavorsome palate, with tobacco and cedar notes on the long finish. Dry, powdery tannins give some grip on the finish.

1996 Pinot Noir Limited Edition, Limited Edition,
Russian River Valley $28. **86**

Bright ruby cast. Moderately full-bodied. Full acidity. Highly extracted. Mildly oaked. Moderately tannic. Red fruits, minerals. Dark, minerally aromas lead a firm and extracted mouthfeel. Angular and intense through the finish.

De Loach

1993 Cabernet Sauvignon, OFS, Russian River Valley $25.   92

Bright, rich cherry red. Medium-bodied. Moderately extracted. Mildly tannic. Cassis, red fruits, dried herbs. Bright primary fruit aromas with subtle herbal notes. Harmonious and well integrated, with lots of bright red berry flavors expanding through the midpalate. Very attractive, giving lots of pleasure now.

1994 Cabernet Sauvignon, OFS, Russian River Valley $27.50.   90

Bright reddish purple. Medium-bodied. Highly extracted. Mildly tannic. Black tea, plums, brown spice. Generous spicy, curranty aromas lead rich, ripe flavors that expand on the silky palate and persist through a spicy finish. Very supple. Nice now, though a few years will only improve it.

1997 Pinot Noir, OFS, Russian River Valley $30.   81

1996 Zinfandel, Russian River Valley $18.   86

Deep blackish purple. Moderately full-bodied. Balanced acidity. Moderately extracted. Mildly oaked. Mildly tannic. Minerals, black fruits. Rather reserved aromatically, with a firm, taut, highly structured palate feel. Lean and angular through the finish. Could use a bit more time.

1996 Zinfandel, Barbieri Ranch, Russian River Valley $20.   94

Deep blackish purple. Moderately full-bodied. Balanced acidity. Moderately extracted. Moderately oaked. Mildly tannic. Black fruits, vanilla. Aromatic and flavorful, with a lush, velvety mouthfeel. Quite hedonistic, with velvety tannins through the finish.

1996 Zinfandel, Gambogi Ranch, Russian River Valley $20.   84

Bright blackish purple. Moderately full-bodied. Balanced acidity. Moderately extracted. Moderately oaked. Mildly tannic. Earth, briar fruits. Quite aromatic, with a distinctive earthy edge. Lush and velvety in the mouth, with a supple finish.

1996 Zinfandel, Papera Ranch, Russian River Valley $20.   89

Deep blackish purple. Moderately full-bodied. Balanced acidity. Moderately extracted. Moderately oaked. Mildly tannic. Black fruits, vanilla. Quite aromatic, with a fruit-centered palate that features harmonious oak overtones throughout. Lush, velvety, and supple, with a deep, intense finish.

1996 Zinfandel, Pelletti Ranch, Russian River Valley $20.   86

Bright blackish purple. Moderately full-bodied. Balanced acidity. Highly extracted. Mildly oaked. Moderately tannic. Minerals, black fruits. Rather reserved aromatically, with a firm, well-structured palate feel. Deeply flavored and intense, with tannins that bite down on the finish.

1996 Zinfandel, Saitone Ranch, Russian River Valley $20.   93

Deep blackish purple. Full-bodied. Full acidity. Highly extracted. Moderately oaked. Moderately tannic. Earth, chocolate, black fruits. Quite aromatic, with distinctive minerally overtones. Firm, deep, and focused, with an angular, juicy finish. Could use a bit more time to resolve itself.

1996 Zinfandel, OFS, Russian River Valley $27.50.   93

Deep blackish purple. Moderately full-bodied. Balanced acidity. Moderately extracted. Moderately oaked. Mildly tannic. Vanilla, black fruits. Quite aromatic, with a pleasant interplay between fruit and wood nuances. Lush and supple in the mouth, with an exceptionally lengthy finish.

de Lorimier

1996 Chardonnay, Alexander Valley $16.   86

Medium straw hue. Moderately full-bodied. Full acidity. Mildly oaked. Vanilla, green apples. Rich and zesty, with angular acids and broad flavors that give it a solid character. The finish is austere.

1996 Spectrum, Alexander Valley $14. **84**

Full golden hue. Medium-bodied. Low acidity. Moderately extracted. White peach, citrus. Floral aromas reveal a soft, rounded palate with much warmth on the finish. With a touch more acidity this would have perfect balance.

1994 Mosaic Meritage, Alexander Valley $20. **90**

Dark crimson red. Medium-bodied. Moderately extracted. Moderately tannic. Pepper, black fruits, plums, toasted oak. Rich plummy flavors unfold on the palate. The finish is bright and peppery. Fine acids give this a lively character and keep the finish fresh.

1995 Mosaic Meritage, Alexander Valley $24. **89**

Deep ruby purple. Full-bodied. Balanced acidity. Highly extracted. Mildly oaked. Moderately tannic. Minerals, black fruits. Aromatically reserved, with a firm and tightly wound palate feel. Aggressive tannins bite down on the finish.

1996 Merlot, Alexander Valley $18. **89**

Bright, opulent purple-red to the rim. Forward red fruit and vanilla aromas show a judicious oak accent. A generous, supple attack leads a moderately full-bodied palate with firm tannins. Flavorful and extremely lengthy through the finish. Well balanced and lush. Drink now.

De Rose

1997 Chardonnay, Cienega Valley $13.99. **81**

1996 Viognier, Cienega Valley $15/375 ml. **89**

Bright golden cast. Moderately full-bodied. Balanced acidity. Moderately extracted. Orange blossom, tropical fruits, yeast. Very aromatic, revealing tropical flavors along classic Viognier lines. Full and rich in the mouth, yet vibrant acidity gives fine balance through the finish.

1996 Cabernet Sauvignon, De Rose Family Vineyard, Dryfarmed Old Vines, Cienega Valley $17.95. **82**

1994 Zinfandel, Dry Farmed Old Vines, Cedolini Vineyards, Cienega Valley $19.95. **88**

Deep blackish ruby cast. Moderately full-bodied. Balanced acidity. Highly extracted. Heavily oaked. Moderately tannic. Red fruits, Bourbon. Quite aromatic, with a pervasive oak influence. Big and rich in the mouth, with a lengthy, drying finish.

1995 Zinfandel, Dry Farmed Old Vines, Cedolini Vineyards, Cienega Valley $19.95. **89**

Deep blackish ruby cast. Full-bodied. Low acidity. Highly extracted. Mildly oaked. Mildly tannic. Overripe black fruits. Fruit-centered aromatics carry a slight Port-like note through a thick, rich palate. Low acidity makes for a heavy finish.

1996 Zinfandel, Dry Farmed Old Vines, Cedolini Vineyards, Cienega Valley $19.95. **89**

Dark blackish purple. Full-bodied. Low acidity. Moderately extracted. Heavily oaked. Mildly tannic. Stewed fruits, chocolate, cedar. Extremely ripe, with a stewed note to the nose and a wave of toasty oak accents. The mouthfeel is thick and rich, with low acidity. Fat, generous, and flavorful through the finish.

Deaver

1997 Chardonnay, Sierra Foothills $11.99. **86**

Pale straw hue with a greenish tint. Mild aromas show a muted green apple note. A crisp entry leads a medium-bodied palate with bright acids and juicy apple flavors. Oak influence is very subtle. Drink now.

1996 Sangiovese, Amador County $16. **86**

Pale cherry red. Medium-bodied. Low acidity. Moderately extracted. Mildly tannic. Dried cherries. Oak-accented aromas follow through on the palate, with dried red fruit flavors lingering well through the finish.

1995 Zinfandel, Amador County $15.   86

Deep blackish ruby cast. Moderately full-bodied. Balanced acidity. Highly extracted. Mildly oaked. Mildly tannic. Black fruits, chocolate, minerals. Somewhat reserved aromatically, but rich, ripe, and concentrated on the palate. Full and intensely flavored, with a thick though well-balanced finish.

1994 Zinfandel, Old Vines, Amador County $12.99.   89

Deep blackish purple. Full-bodied. Balanced acidity. Highly extracted. Heavily oaked. Moderately tannic. Port, vanilla. Carries a slightly overripe note to the nose. Extremely full and rich on the palate, with a firm structure and hefty oak accents. The overall impression is of drinking a dry Port.

Deer Valley

1996 Sauvignon Blanc, Monterey County $3.99.   80

1995 Cabernet Sauvignon, California $5.99.   81

1996 Merlot, California $5.99.   80

Dehlinger

1997 Chardonnay, Russian River Valley $25.   83

Bright golden yellow. Restrained aromas show an oaky accent. Austere on the attack with a medium-bodied palate and subdued flavors. The finish seems tight and dry. Youthful, but has the stuffing to improve.

1995 Cabernet Sauvignon, Russian River Valley $28.   88

Deep ruby red hue with purple highlights. Bright briar fruit and mineral aromas. A soft attack leads to a medium-bodied palate with lean tannins and solid fruit ripeness. Clean through the finish with velvety fruit extract. Drink within five years.

1995 Syrah, Russian River Valley $35.   91

Dark purple, opaque, and brilliant to the rim. Intense, fantastic black cherry and blueberry flavors. Hefty wood tones. Smooth entry. Full-bodied. Plentiful drying tannins. Dense and richly extracted, with dry oak accents. Lingering rich finish. Intensely flavorful and hedonistic. Drink now or later. Can improve with more age.

1996 Syrah, Goldridge Vineyard, Russian River Valley $28.   91

Deep purple, opaque, and brilliant to the rim. Intense, fantastic ripe black cherry flavors. Generous wood tones. Supple entry. Moderately full-bodied. Moderate drying tannins. Fully extracted, deep, and rich through the lingering finish. Succulent, mildly overripe, and hedonistic. Drink now or later. Can improve with more age.

Delicato

1997 Cabernet Sauvignon, California $4.99.   84

Bright ruby-purple hue. A juicy attack leads to a medium-bodied palate with black cherry fruit flavors and mildly gripping tannins on the finish. Drink now.

1997 Merlot, California $4.99.   83

Bright violet hue. Herbal, berry fruit aromas have a vanilla accent. Medium-bodied, lush, and smooth through the finish with mild velvety tannins lingering. Straightforward and unchallenging. Drink now.

1997 Syrah, California $5.99.   81

Diamond Creek

1994 Cabernet Sauvignon, Red Rock Terrace, Napa Valley $50.   88

Bright, deep cherry red. Medium-bodied. Moderately extracted. Moderately tannic. Cassis, toasted oak, vanilla. Attractive toasty aromas lead a juicy, ripe Cabernet fruit palate, with some fine-grained tannins closing up the finish. Excellent acids and ripeness should allow this to develop in the cellar.

Scale: Superlative (96-100), Exceptional (90-95), Highly Recommended (85-89), Recommended (80-84), Not Recommended (Under 80)

74

1995 Cabernet Sauvignon, Red Rock Terrace, Napa Valley $75. **93**

Deep ruby purple. Moderately full-bodied. Balanced acidity. Moderately extracted. Mildly oaked. Mildly tannic. Red fruits, spice, minerals. Attractive aromas feature a ripe core of fruit flavors with a spicy oak accent. Firm and lean in the mouth, with a crisp but elegant structure. Finishes with some grainy tannins. Approachable, but worthy of cellaring.

1994 Cabernet Sauvignon, Volcanic Hill, Napa Valley $50. **90**

Deep opaque purple. Moderately full-bodied. Highly extracted. Moderately tannic. Minerals, flint, black fruits. Lean and steely, with an outstandingly long and dry palate showing firmness through the finish. Fine acids and tightly wound flavors indicate this will take some years to show its potential.

1995 Cabernet Sauvignon, Volcanic Hill, Napa Valley $75. **93**

Deep ruby purple. Moderately full-bodied. Balanced acidity. Moderately extracted. Mildly tannic. Minerals, cassis. Aromatic and elegant, with an emphasis on terroir, not winemaking. Lean and minerally, with exceptional balance and finesse. Fine grip and intensity.

Dolce

1995 Late Harvest Dessert Wine, Napa Valley $50/375 ml. **97**

Very deep yellow-gold. Moderately full-bodied. Balanced acidity. Moderately extracted. Moderately oaked. Vanilla, figs, apricots. Heavily botrytized, with a wave of toasty oak and ripe tropical flavors. Lush, rich, velvety mouthfeel and fine acids. Intense, it should develop with further age.

Domaine Carneros

1993 Brut, Carneros $19. **91**

Medium yellow-straw cast. Medium-bodied. Biscuit, ripe citrus, minerals. Fine toasty, biscuity aromas lead a richly flavored palate showing nutty development through the finish. Crisp, fine-beaded carbonation gives a vibrant mousse. Very stylish.

1992 Le Reve, Blanc de Blancs, Carneros $35. **93**

Bright green-straw cast. Moderately full-bodied. Full acidity. Biscuits, cream, toast. Classic biscuity aromas lead a refined and generous, though still quite youthful, mouthfeel. Shows fine balance and length, and a very satisfying degree of maturity now, though this has the vibrancy and weight to improve further with bottle age.

1995 Pinot Noir, Carneros $20. **86**

Bright magenta. Medium-bodied. Moderately extracted. Mildly tannic. Crisp, bright red berry fruit flavors are complemented by vanilla oak notes and a pleasing hint of astringency. Some weight is evident on the palate.

1996 Pinot Noir, Carneros $23.99. **83**

Pale ruby red. Medium-bodied. Moderately extracted. Mildly tannic. Strawberries, vanilla. Soft berry fruit aromas follow through on the palate, with vanilla oak accents lingering on the finish. Soft acids make for an easy-drinking style. This is not structured for aging.

Domaine Chandon

NV Blanc de Noirs, Carneros $18. **86**

Pale copper cast. Moderately full-bodied. Full acidity. Highly extracted. Minerals, toast, red fruits. Subtle aromas lead a big, forceful, well-balanced mouthfeel. Vibrant, crisp, and weighty through the substantial finish.

NV Brut Cuvée, Napa County $18. **88**

Pale straw hue with a brilliant cast. Medium-bodied. Yeast, bread, citrus. A creamy mouthfeel shows vibrant, fine-beaded carbonation. The flavors have a clean citrusy streak through the finish, though there are hints of smoky yeast complexity.

1998 25th Anniversary Reserve Cuvée, Napa County $24. **89**

Medium green-straw color. Medium-bodied. Burnt coffee, mocha, citrus. Smoky aromas. Generously proportioned and structured, showing a creamy mouthfeel and fine concentration of flavors. Nice now, though this should be smokier in a year or two.

1996 Pinot Noir, Carneros $28.95.   87

Dark ruby cast. Medium-bodied. Moderately extracted. Moderately tannic. Leather, earth, black fruits. Some classic aromas and flavors are present, though this is generously proportioned and weighty. Complex and stylish.

Domaine de la Terre Rouge

1994 Noir, Grande Année, Sierra Foothills $20.   83

Deep brick red with a fading rim. Lean aromas of herbs, minerals, and earth. A supple attack leads a medium-bodied palate, with drying tannins. Clipped, linear finish. Drink now.

1997 Tête-à-Tête, Sierra Foothills $12.   81

1996 Syrah, Sentinel Oak Vineyard, Pyramid Block,
Shenandoah Valley $25.   86

Deep, opaque ruby color, with a slight fade. Chocolate and black fruit flavors. Medium-bodied. Well extracted, with dry, grainy tannins. Tough and structured but impressively flavorsome. Drink within five years.

Domaine Napa

1996 Chardonnay, Sonoma County $13.99.   81

1996 Chardonnay, Napa Valley $15.99.   84

Burnished gold hue. Delicate floral nose. Medium-bodied lemon-dominated palate with weight and richness of mouthfeel yet showing an acid spike through the finish. Rather a strange style.

1996 Fumé Blanc, Napa Valley $9.99.   87

Very deep straw hue. Moderately full-bodied. Balanced acidity. Moderately extracted. Minerals, citrus. Aromatically reserved, with a full but soft mouthfeel. Picks up some nice grip through the finish.

Domaine Saint George

1997 Chardonnay, Select Reserve, California $5.99.   83

Pale straw cast. Medium-bodied. Balanced acidity. Moderately extracted. Minerals, citrus, pears. Aromatically reserved, with a crisp yet rounded structure. Shows a lingering citric finish.

1996 Fumé Blanc, Select Reserve, California $7.   83

Bright golden yellow. Medium-bodied. Balanced acidity. Moderately extracted. Moderately oaked. Vanilla, toasted oak, ripe citrus. Full toasty oak aromas lead a buttery, ripe citrus palate with smoky oak overtones through the finish. A softer, appealing style.

1997 Cabernet Sauvignon, Select Reserve, California $10.   83

Bright cherry purple hue. Decidedly berry-like, vanilla aromas. A crisp attack leads to a medium-bodied palate with a fruity center and mild tannins. Finishes in a lean, brief manner. Drink now.

1995 Cabernet Sauvignon, STG, Russian River Valley $15.   81

Dominus

1992 Napanook Vineyard, Napa Valley $50.   88

Deep ruby to the rim. Moderately full-bodied. Balanced acidity. Highly extracted. Moderately oaked. Quite tannic. Dry. Reminiscent of tea, herbs, cassis. Distinctive herbal aromatics are overshadowed by a wave of tannins on the palate of this Bordelaise-styled wine. Focused in structure, this is relatively inaccessible. Seems rather heavy on the tannins without requisite stuffing to balance, but this may be resolved with cellaring.

Scale: Superlative (96-100), Exceptional (90-95), Highly Recommended (85-89), Recommended (80-84), Not Recommended (Under 80)

76

1994 Napanook Vineyard, Napa Valley $75.   95

Opaque blood red. Moderately full-bodied. Highly extracted. Quite tannic. Bitter chocolate, black fruits, earth. An exotic, powerfully earthy nose reveals a big dry mouth-ful of concentrated mineral and earth, with tightly wound fruit flavors showing through. This has impressive structure, with firm dry tannins and an austere feel throughout.

1995 Cabernet Sauvignon, Napanook Vineyard, Napa Valley $95.   95

Deep ruby red with a slight fade. Moderately full-bodied. Balanced acidity. Moderately extracted. Mildly oaked. Moderately tannic. Minerals, pencil shavings, earth. A Francophilic style, with restrained and complex mineral and earth-accented flavors. Supple on entry, with a lush quality up front and firm tannins on the finish. Needs time.

Douglass Hill

1997 Chardonnay, Napa Valley $15.99.   81

1995 Cabernet Franc, Napa Valley $16.   84

Bright garnet hue. Unusual mint and vanilla aromas show a big oak accent. A crisp attack leads to a medium-bodied palate with drying tannins and zesty acidity. Features a cedary, mature quality to the finish. Lighter styled but interesting. Drink now.

1995 Cabernet Sauvignon, Napa Valley $16.   81

Dover Canyon

1997 Chardonnay, Cougar Ridge Vineyard, Central Coast $16.   84

Pale golden cast. Moderately full-bodied. Full acidity. Moderately extracted. Mildly oaked. Toast, cream, citrus. Generous aromas show a pleasant leesy note that adds a measure of complexity to a firm core of wood-accented fruit flavors. Zesty and stylish, with good grip to the finish.

1996 Cabernet Sauvignon, Paso Robles $18.   86

Deep, saturated ruby purple. Moderately full-bodied. Balanced acidity. Highly extracted. Mildly oaked. Moderately tannic. Licorice, wood, minerals. Unusual aromatics lead a firm and flavorful palate. Firm tannins bite down on the finish.

1995 Ménage, Paso Robles $22.   88

Bright violet-red. Medium-bodied. Moderately extracted. Mildly tannic. Cassis, leaves, vanilla. Leafy, ripe aromas lead a soft, lush palate of berry flavors, with silky tannins giving a forward, accessible structure. Drinking very well now.

1996 Ménage, Paso Robles $28.   88

Bright violet-ruby hue. Generously aromatic with a ripe nose of cassis aromas. A firm entry leads a moderately full-bodied palate with a ripe core of black currant flavors and solid, gripping tannins that clamp down on the finish. A solidly structured wine with plenty of youthful character. Drink now or later.

1996 Merlot, Reserve, Central Coast $24.   89

Saturated crimson red. Distinctive aromas of blackberries and spice. A firm attack leads a moderately full-bodied palate with tough, chunky tannins and crisp acids. Finishes with flavors and grip. Well structured and solid, best to give it a year or two. Drink now or later. Can improve with more age.

Dry Creek Vineyard

1997 Chardonnay, Sonoma County $16.   87

Deep yellow-straw hue. Generous tropical fruit and citrus aromas show a judicious oak accent. A lush entry leads a full-bodied palate with rounded acidity. Weighty, rich finish. Drink now.

1997 Chardonnay, Reserve, Sonoma County $20.   90

Deep yellow-straw hue. Forward brown spice and citrus aromas show a hefty oak accent. A lush attack leads a full-bodied palate with rounded, creamy acidity and generous yeasty flavors. Ripe, lengthy finish. Rich but well balanced. Drink now.

1996 Fumé Blanc, Reserve, Dry Creek Valley $15.75.   87

Medium yellow-straw hue. Medium-bodied. Balanced acidity. Moderately extracted. Mildly oaked. Dried herbs. Smoky, citrusy aromas follow through well on the palate. Ripe, smoothly textured mouthfeel. Finishes with lingering smoke and oak spice notes.

1995 Cabernet Franc, Vintner's Selection, Dry Creek Valley $25.   83

Bright ruby purple. Medium-bodied. Balanced acidity. Moderately extracted. Mildly tannic. Green herbs, minerals, earth. Carries a green streak through to the lighter-styled palate. Lacks somewhat for grip or intensity. Overcropped and vapid.

1996 Cabernet Sauvignon, Dry Creek Valley $18.75.   93

Bright red-purple. Medium-bodied. Highly extracted. Mildly tannic. Black cherries, anise, dried herbs. A very ripe, plummy nose follows through on the palate, with dry, powdery tannins clamping down on the finish.

1995 Cabernet Sauvignon, Reserve, Dry Creek Valley $27.   94

Saturated red-purple. Moderately full-bodied. Highly extracted. Moderately tannic. Black cherries, licorice. Fleshy, ripe aromas lead an intense mouthful of dark fruit flavors, with firm tannins giving a dry, angular finish at present.

1995 Meritage, Dry Creek Valley $25.   88

Bright red-purple. Moderately full-bodied. Highly extracted. Moderately tannic. Black cherries, brown spice, anise. A dusty nose leads an intense burst of ripe black fruits, with powdery tannins drying the finish. Impressive, but needs time.

1996 Meritage, Sonoma County $25.   84

Bright violet-purple hue. Perfumed aromas of cedar, vanilla and berry fruits. A fruity attack leads a medium-bodied palate with silky tannins and juicy red cherry flavors. Very attractive and fruit forward. Drink now.

1996 Merlot, Sonoma County $18.75.   81

1995 Merlot, Reserve, Dry Creek Valley $30.   81

1995 Zinfandel, Old Vines, Sonoma County $16.   86

Deep blackish ruby hue. Moderately full-bodied. Balanced acidity. Moderately extracted. Mildly oaked. Mildly tannic. Mint, dried herbs, red fruits. Quite aromatic, with distinctive herbal overtones. A lush but well-structured palate feel, with solid grip through the finish.

1995 Zinfandel, Reserve, Sonoma County $25.   89

Bright ruby-garnet hue. Moderately full-bodied. Balanced acidity. Moderately extracted. Heavily oaked. Mildly tannic. Vanilla, black fruits. Spicy oak notes emerge on the nose and dominate the palate. Lush and velvety in the mouth, with a supple quality. Picks up some very mild tannins on the finish.

Duckhorn

1997 Sauvignon Blanc, Napa Valley $14.   83

Bright yellow-gold. Medium-bodied. Full acidity. Moderately extracted. Tart tropical fruits, lemons. Quite ripe, with a full complement of flavors. Angular acidity follows through on the short finish.

1994 Cabernet Sauvignon, Napa Valley $35.   88

Solid blackish red. Medium-bodied. Highly extracted. Moderately tannic. Plums, earth, black tea. Rich spicy, plummy nose leads an assertive entry, with impressive austere, dry tannins on the finish. Angular and structured, this will be better in a few years.

1995 Cabernet Sauvignon, Napa Valley $32.   82

1995 Paraduxx, Napa Valley $20.   93

Deep blackish purple. Full-bodied. Balanced acidity. Highly extracted. Heavily oaked. Mildly tannic. Vanilla, black fruits. Pleasantly aromatic, with a bright, fruit-centered overtone and generous oak seasoning. Full, but well structured on the palate, with a lean finish.

Scale: Superlative (96-100), Exceptional (90-95), Highly Recommended (85-89), Recommended (80-84), Not Recommended (Under 80)

78

1996 Decoy Migration, Napa Valley $15.   81

1993 Merlot, Howell Mountain, Napa Valley $30.   90

Very deep blackish ruby hue to the rim. Moderately full-bodied. Balanced acidity. Highly extracted. Mildly oaked. Moderately tannic. Chocolate, black fruits, minerals. Deep and well extracted, this is a very dense wine. A rich core of flavor is ensconced in a notably firm structure, with a wave of velvety tannins at the finish. Solid balance bodes well for mid-term (3–6 years) to long-term (7–10 years) aging.

1995 Merlot, Napa Valley $28.   90

Deep ruby to the rim with a slight purplish cast. Moderately full-bodied. Balanced acidity. Highly extracted. Moderately oaked. Mildly tannic. Brown spices, dusty cherries, minerals. Quite aromatic, with a firm and concentrated character on the palate. Flavorful throughout, with dusty tannins and a lingering finish.

1996 Merlot, Napa Valley $32.   88

Saturated violet hue. Aromas show a youthful, oaky character with dark fleshy fruit accents. A crisp entry leads a moderately full-bodied palate with ample fine-grained tannins and an impressive concentration of fruit flavors. Dense and well structured. Drink now or later.

Dunn

1993 Cabernet Sauvignon, Napa Valley $35.   92

Opaque dark purple. Moderately full-bodied. Highly extracted. Quite tannic. Cassis, blackberries, earth, black tea. Very impressive tightly wound flavors have all the classic hallmarks of the variety. Tight midpalate and great supporting tannins through the finish suggest the possibility of a long cellar life.

Dunnewood

1996 Sauvignon Blanc, Coastal Series, Vintner's Select, Mendocino $5.99.   86

Pale green-gold. Medium-bodied. Balanced acidity. Moderately extracted. Lemon, mineral. A clean herbaceous, mildly buttery nose delivers faithfully on the palate. A little light in flavors but the mouthfeel is a plus point.

1997 White Zinfandel, California $5.99.   80

1996 Cabernet Sauvignon, Coastal Series, North Coast $7.99.   80

1994 Cabernet Sauvignon, Dry Silk, Napa Valley $9.99.   87

Brilliant violet-red hue. Generously aromatic with a spicy, pickle note and well-defined crisp fruits. A bright entry leads to a medium-bodied palate with sensational bright acids and deep black cherry flavors that finish cleanly with a lingering note of oak subtlety. Solid, in a more reserved, classical style. Drink now or later.

1996 Merlot, North Coast $8.99.   81

1996 Pinot Noir, North Coast $7.99.   83

Medium dark ruby hue. Medium-bodied. Moderately extracted. Moderately tannic. Minerals, earth. Austere earthy aromas lead a tight, somewhat lean mouthful of flavors with a touch of fruit generosity.

Durney

1993 Cabernet Sauvignon, Carmel Valley $20.   85

Deep ruby red. Medium-bodied. Moderately extracted. Moderately tannic. Earth, brown spice, tomato. Rustic aromas of leather and earth follow through on the palate. The flavors manage to be both ripe and austere. Not for keeping.

Eberle

1997 Chardonnay, Paso Robles $15.   84
Bright yellow-straw hue. Generous spice and tropical fruit aromas carry a slightly unusual honeyed quality. A crisp entry leads a medium-bodied palate with zesty acidity. Ripe, intense finish. Drink now.

1997 Counoise Rose, Lauridsen Vineyard, Paso Robles $11.   84
Pale cherry-garnet hue. Forward spice and berry aromas. A rich entry leads a moderately full-bodied palate, with a wave of exotic, smoky fruit flavors. Acidity is on the low side, making for a big, heavy Rosé. Drink now.

1996 Cabernet Sauvignon, Paso Robles $20.   86
Pale ruby-red hue with a fading rim. Very aromatic with a spice box quality and a suggestion of ripe berry fruits. A ripe, juicy entry leads a medium-bodied palate with attractive sweet cherry and toasty oak flavors. Finishes with very gentle tannins. Very supple and forward, this is drinking well now. Drink now.

1996 Côtes-du-Rôbles, Paso Robles $13.   83
Pale orange-red hue. Subdued herb and mineral aromas. Moderately light-bodied. A crisp attack leads a light-bodied palate with drying tannins. The finish is clipped and clean. A lightweight with grip. Drink now.

1996 Zinfandel, Sauret Vineyard, Paso Robles $18.   82

1998 Muscat Canelli, Paso Robles $11.   83
Bright yellow-straw hue. Attractive orange blossom and honeyed citrus aromas. A rich entry leads a medium-bodied palate showing mild sweetness. Soft and lush. Drink now.

Echelon

1997 Chardonnay, Central Coast $12.50.   81

Edgewood

1997 Chardonnay, Napa Valley $18.   88
Bright yellow-gold. A rich smoky, leesy nose shows toasty oak influences. A spicy attack leads a moderately full-bodied palate with glycerous smoothness and a lingering yeasty finish. Very elegant and rich. Drink now.

1995 Cabernet Sauvignon, Napa Valley $20.   86
Saturated red-purple. Moderately full-bodied. Highly extracted. Moderately tannic. Back fruits, licorice. Solid, tightly wound, concentrated fruit flavors and impressive structural tannins that give a firm, reserved note to the finish.

1996 Cabernet Sauvignon, Napa Valley $20.   83
Deep purple red hue. Lean, brooding mineral and black fruit aromas carry an earthy edge. A firm attack leads to a medium-bodied palate with big, astringent tannins. Clipped finish. On the tough side.

1996 Malbec, Napa Valley $18.   83
Rich ruby purple hue. Generous vanilla and briar fruit aromas show a judicious oak accent. A lush attack leads to a moderately full-bodied palate with big supple tannins. Rich, intense finish. Drink now.

1993 Cellarette Cuvée, Napa Valley $22.50.   87
Full red-purple. Medium-bodied. Moderately extracted. Moderately tannic. Cassis, black fruits, brown spice. Soundly structured, with attractive toasty oak notes lingering through the finish. Tart and juicy, with vanilla oak notes throughout.

1994 Merlot, Napa Valley $19.99.   82

1995 Petite Sirah, Napa Valley $14.   81

1995 Zinfandel, Napa Valley $14.   86
Opaque dark red. Medium-bodied. Balanced acidity. Highly extracted. Moderately oaked. Ripe black fruits, vanilla. Ripe nose reminiscent of Port. Solid and compact palate, with dry, dusty tannins on the finish. Rather structured, and lacking midpalate stuffing.

Scale: Superlative (96-100), Exceptional (90-95), Highly Recommended (85-89), Recommended (80-84), Not Recommended (Under 80)

80

Edmeades

1996 Chardonnay, Anderson Valley $18. 89

Rich gold. Very ripe tropical aromas have a citrus zest quality and spicy oak influence. A rich attack leads a full-bodied palate with concentrated ripe fruit flavors, bright acids, and well-balanced oak flavors. Quite a powerful style, yet well structured. Drink now or later.

1996 Petite Sirah, Eagle Point Vineyard, Mendocino $20. 87

Opaque blackish red. Full-bodied. Highly extracted. Quite tannic. An extremely chewy texture shows the massive extract of this wine. Monolithic and tough, with a mild, cooked-fruit character.

1995 Pinot Noir, Anderson Valley $20. 86

Bright cherry red. Medium-bodied. Moderately extracted. Moderately oaked. Moderately tannic. Brown spice nuances on the nose. Crisp, focused cherry and berry flavors have plenty of firm oak in support, with dry tannins coming through on the finish.

1996 Pinot Noir, Anderson Valley $20. 93

Deep ruby cast. Moderately full-bodied. Balanced acidity. Moderately extracted. Mildly oaked. Mildly tannic. Spice, minerals, tomato vine. Quite aromatic, with real complexity. Generous yet firm in the mouth, with an angular, spicy finish. Shows fine persistence and intensity.

Edmunds St. John

1996 Syrah, California $18. 93

Rich, hazy garnet red with a slight fade. Intense, powerful medicinal, old-vine, spice cabinet, and game aromas. A supple attack leads a moderately full-bodied palate that has tannic grip. Lengthy, flavorful finish. Individualistic, but not everyone's cup of tea. Drink now or later. Can improve with more age.

Edna Valley Vineyard

1997 Chardonnay, Paragon Vineyard, Edna Valley $18. 83

Deep yellow-straw hue. Restrained mineral aromas show a slightly earthy edge. A rich entry leads a full-bodied palate with angular acidity. Well structured but not overly flavorful. Drink now.

Ehlers Grove

1997 Chardonnay, Winery Reserve, Carneros, Napa Valley $30. 86

Bright golden yellow. Ripe subtly honeyed aromas. A crisp attack leads a moderately full-bodied palate with bright acids and deep flavors. Well balanced and structured. Drink now or later.

El Molino

1995 Pinot Noir, Napa Valley $41.95. 90

Full ruby hue with a lightening rim. Medium-bodied. Moderately extracted. Moderately tannic. Minerals, black fruits, leather. A distinctively minerally, oak-spiced nose leads a solid, well-gripped palate, with structuring tannins showing well through the finish. Elegant yet firm.

Elkhorn Peak

1997 Chardonnay, Fagan Creek Vineyard, Napa Valley $18. 89

Medium straw hue. Generously aromatic with pure ripe fruit and smoky oak aromas. A juicy attack leads a moderately full-bodied palate with a succulent fruity character and judicious oak accents. A big, ripe, lush style.

1995 Pinot Noir, Fagan Creek Vineyard, Napa Valley $26. 89

Pale cherry red. Medium-bodied. Moderately extracted. Moderately oaked. Mildly tannic. Perfumed new oak aromas have a dill accent, leading a rounded palate with good weight. Full cherry fruit flavors are complemented by toasty notes through the finish.

1996 Pinot Noir, Fagan Creek Vineyard, Napa Valley $26.   **86**

Pale ruby red. Medium-bodied. Moderately extracted. Mildly oaked. Mildly tannic. Red berries, dried herbs, vanilla. Soft red fruit aromas follow through well on a generous palate, with light, gripping tannins and relatively soft acids making for an accessible style.

Eos

1996 Zinfandel, Paso Robles $15.99.   **82**

Equinox

NV Harmony Cuvée Brut, Santa Cruz Mountains $27.   **90**

Bright yellow-gold. Medium-bodied. Full acidity. Charred yeast, roasted coffee. Complex smoky, yeasty aromas lead a taut, concentrated palate, with bright acids and fine toasty yeast notes. The lengthy dry finish has an assertive character. Shows soft carbonation, with a fine bead.

1992 Cuvée de Chardonnay, Blanc de Blanc, Santa Cruz Mountains $33.   **92**

Bright yellow-straw cast. Moderately full-bodied. Full acidity. Smoke, toast, blanched almonds. Outstandingly complex, highly smoky yeast aromas. Forceful and intense palate, with vibrant carbonation and intense Chardonnay character that makes for a very bright and flavorful mouthful.

Estancia

1997 Chardonnay, Pinnacles, Monterey County $11.   **83**

Deep golden yellow. Aromas show a marked oak accent. A rich entry leads a full-bodied palate that does not show matching fruit generosity on the midpalate. Alcohol, wood, and glycerine are the key elements.

1997 Chardonnay, Reserve, Monterey $19.   **83**

Bright golden yellow. Moderately aromatic with toasted oak character making an impression. An angular entry leads a moderately full-bodied palate with glycerine and alcohol outdoing fruit flavors. Finishes with a lean note.

1996 Fumé Blanc, Pinnacles, Monterey County $10.   **94**

Deep golden luster. Moderately full-bodied. Balanced acidity. Highly extracted. Moderately oaked. Dried herbs, toasted oak, citrus. Assertive oak aromas with a strong dried herbal accent. Rich, mouthfilling herbal flavors with a fine smoky oak note through the finish. Very hedonistic, though this is not for the cellar—drink it now.

1995 Cabernet Sauvignon, California $12.   **86**

Full ruby red. Medium-bodied. Balanced acidity. Moderately extracted. Moderately tannic. Lead pencil, cassis, minerals. Bright, varietally correct aromas show an oak spice note that follows through on the palate. Firm yet generous, this is drinking nicely now.

1996 Cabernet Sauvignon, California $12.   **80**

1996 Duo, Alexander Valley $18.   **83**

Bright blackish ruby cast. Moderately full-bodied. Full acidity. Highly extracted. Mildly tannic. Black fruits, minerals. Rather reserved aromatically, but the deep fruit flavors are highlighted by racy acidity. Finishes with a mildly bitter note.

1994 Red Meritage, Alexander Valley $18.   **91**

Bright cherry red. Medium-bodied. Highly extracted. Mildly tannic. Chocolate, toasted oak, cinnamon. A gorgeously rich and generous nose leads a full-flavored toasty palate, with an outstanding lingering chocolatey finish. Very harmonious and balanced.

1995 Red Meritage, Alexander Valley $22.   **86**

Bright ruby with a slight fade. Medium-bodied. Balanced acidity. Moderately extracted. Moderately oaked. Mildly tannic. Brown spices, cedar. Quite aromatic, with a definite oak accent. Lighter-styled but lush through the wood-driven finish.

Scale: Superlative (96-100), Exceptional (90-95), Highly Recommended (85-89), Recommended (80-84), Not Recommended (Under 80)

1996 Merlot, Sonoma County $14.   88
Bright violet-ruby hue. Black fruit and herb aromas. A supple attack leads a moderately full-bodied palate with firm, dry tannins. Finishes with an angular tannic grip. Drink now or later. Can improve with more age.

1997 Pinot Noir, Monterey $12.   84
Pale cherry red. Medium-bodied. Moderately extracted. Mildly tannic. Fruit cordial, vanilla. Ripe, cordial-like aromas follow through on the palate with a range of jammy flavors. Finishes with soft tannins.

1996 Pinot Noir, Pinnacles, Monterey $12.   80
1996 Pinot Noir, Reserve, Monterey $18.   87
Deep cherry red. Medium-bodied. Moderately extracted. Cherries, dried herbs, vanilla. Ripe red fruit aromas lead a generous palate, with crisp fruity flavors that show a marked oak impression through the finish. Opulently fruity, with fine length.

Estate Cellars
NV Cabernet Sauvignon, California $7.99.   80

Estrella
1997 Chardonnay, California $5.99.   81
1995 Sauvignon Blanc, Proprietor's Reserve, California $9.99/1.5 L. 83
Pale straw. Medium-bodied. Balanced acidity. Moderately extracted. Mildly oaked. Dried herbs, citrus. Nice herbal suggestion on the nose follows through on a rounded, crisp palate with a lively acid balance.

1998 White Zinfandel, California $4.99.   80
1996 Cabernet Sauvignon, Proprietor's Reserve, California $5.99.   81
1996 Pinot Noir, Proprietor's Reserve, California $9.99/1.5 L.   81
1996 Zinfandel, Proprietor's Reserve, California $9.99/1.5 L.   82

Etude
1995 Pinot Noir, Carneros $33.50.   89
Bright cherry red. Medium-bodied. Highly extracted. Moderately oaked. Mildly tannic. Full red fruit and vanilla aromas. Concentrated flavors, with a fine, weighty palate that is not hugely fruity. Fine-grained tannins on the dry finish. This has some structure for cellaring.

1996 Pinot Noir, Carneros $30.   83
Dark violet hue. Medium-bodied. Moderately extracted. Mildly tannic. Blackberries, minerals. Crisp, tart black fruit flavors. The rather ripe black fruit flavors are backed up with oak spice and very mild tannins.

Falconer
1983 Blanc de Blancs RD, San Luis Obispo County $19.95.   90
Deep gold. Moderately full-bodied. Full acidity. Highly extracted. Bread dough, almonds, caramel. Forward, toasty aromas indicate an attractive level of maturity. Surprisingly youthful in the mouth, with sturdy acidity and aggressive, refreshing carbonation. Balanced and flavorful, in a rustic style.

Fanucchi
1996 Zinfandel, Fanucchi Wood Road Vineyard, Old Vine,
Russian River Valley $33.75.   84
Opaque blackish purple. Full-bodied. Balanced acidity. Highly extracted. Mildly oaked. Moderately tannic. Lacquer, black fruits. Reserved aromatically, with a hugely extracted, dense mouthfeel. Brooding flavors are tightly wrapped in the highly structured palate. Finishes with a lash of tannin. Impressive, but perhaps a bit too tough.

Far Niente

1997 Chardonnay, Napa Valley $40.   86

Pale yellow-straw hue. Oaky, blanched almond aromas. A tart entry leads a medium-bodied palate with spiky acidity and phenolic dryness through the finish.

1994 Cabernet Sauvignon, Napa Valley $55.   90

Full dark red. Medium-bodied. Highly extracted. Moderately tannic. Plums, dried herbs, minerals. Bright black fruit flavors on entry. Good viscous mouthfeel with some earthy qualities and solid dry tannins on the finish. Herbal notes add complexity.

1995 Cabernet Sauvignon, Napa Valley $70.   91

Very deep ruby hue. Generous brown spice and red fruit aromas show a refined oak accent and a complex gamey edge. A lush attack leads to a moderately full-bodied palate with ripe velvety tannins. Rich, flavorful finish. A big but well-balanced style. Drink now or later.

Farella-Park

1994 Cabernet Sauvignon, Napa Valley $28.   87

Deep dark red with purple highlights. Medium-bodied. Moderately extracted. Moderately tannic. Black fruits, black tea, brown spice. Solid dark fruit flavors are matched by some tough tannins that make for an assertive finish. This should be better in a few years.

1995 Cabernet Sauvignon, Napa Valley $32.   85

Saturated, opaque red-purple. Moderately full-bodied. Highly extracted. Quite tannic. Cassis, minerals, oak spice. Very pure, cordial-like fruit aromas lead a concentrated mouthfeel, with dense, fine-grained tannins drying the finish. Heavily extracted and firm, this will need years of cellaring.

1995 Merlot, Napa Valley $24.   88

Deep ruby hue to the rim. Moderately full-bodied. Balanced acidity. Highly extracted. Mildly oaked. Mildly tannic. Black fruits, earth, minerals. Quite firm in style, with a dense and highly extracted mouthfeel. Robust tannins clamp down on the palate, but its balance is such that it should mellow nicely with mid-term (3–6 years) aging.

Gary Farrell

1996 Chardonnay, Allen Vineyard, Russian River Valley $28.   94

Brilliant yellow-gold. Moderately full-bodied. Balanced acidity. Peach, apples, yeast, vanilla. Fruit-laden aromas are a standout. Generously textured, with full juicy flavors showing impressive persistence through the finish. Some oaky character remains as a well-integrated background component, adding to the complexity.

1995 Cabernet Sauvignon, Hillside Selection, Sonoma County $24.   86

Saturated bright purple. Medium-bodied. Full acidity. Moderately extracted. Mildly tannic. Minerals, black fruits. Aromatically reserved, with a core of primary fruit on the palate. Bright and zesty, with acidity to the fore and an angular, crisp finish.

1996 Merlot, Russian River Valley $22.   91

Saturated bright purple. Crisp berry fruit and vanilla aromas. A vibrant attack leads a medium-bodied palate with velvety, supple tannins. Finishes with a lingering fruit persistence. Drink now.

1995 Merlot, Ladi's Vineyard, Sonoma County $22.   86

Very deep blackish ruby hue with a slight purplish cast. Medium-bodied. Full acidity. Highly extracted. Mildly oaked. Moderately tannic. Black fruits, black pepper, menthol. Quite youthful and a bit closed. Features a tightly wound core of dark flavors and juicy acidity. Tannins close in on the finish.

1995 Pinot Noir, Anderson Valley $30.   90

Dark ruby red. Medium-bodied. Highly extracted. Quite tannic. Nice leathery, meaty aromas. Dry dark fruit flavors have a tar and licorice note, with tealike tannins on the finish. Rather tough now. Austere style.

Scale: Superlative (96-100), Exceptional (90-95), Highly Recommended (85-89), Recommended (80-84), Not Recommended (Under 80)

1996 Pinot Noir, Russian River Valley $22.50.　　　　**88**

Bright pale ruby cast. Moderately light-bodied. Full acidity. Moderately extracted. Mildly oaked. Mildly tannic. Cherries, raspberries, vanilla. Fruit centered and delicate, with a flavorful, zesty quality and a light frame. Crisp and racy finish.

1995 Pinot Noir, Allen Vineyard, Russian River Valley $40.　　　　**90**

Bright purple-red. Medium-bodied. Highly extracted. Moderately oaked. Moderately tannic. Bright raspberry fruit aromas with vanilla accents follow through on the palate, with up-front juicy acids highlighting dry, tealike tannins on the finish. Sound structure.

1996 Pinot Noir, Bien Nacido Vineyard, Santa Barbara County $28.　　　　**87**

Pale ruby purple. Medium-bodied. Full acidity. Moderately extracted. Mildly oaked. Moderately tannic. Raspberries, minerals. Restrained berryish aromas lead a firm and intense mouthfeel with excellent fruit persistence. Vibrant and zesty finish. Lighter in style but packed with flavor.

1995 Pinot Noir, Rochioli Vineyard, Russian River Valley $50.　　　　**89**

Deep ruby cast. Medium-bodied. Full acidity. Moderately extracted. Mildly oaked. Mildly tannic. Iron, earth, berries. Generous aromatics show a degree of minerally complexity. Fine depth of flavor in the mouth, with a lingering and intense finish.

1996 Zinfandel, Old Vine Selection, Sonoma County $22.50.　　　　**91**

Bright purple. Moderately full-bodied. Full acidity. Moderately extracted. Mildly oaked. Mildly tannic. Briar fruits, vanilla. Quite aromatic, with a vibrant, fruit-centered mouthfeel. Lush and generous, with a lengthy finish.

Fenestra

1996 Semillon, Livermore Valley $9.50.　　　　**89**

Bright full-gold hue. Moderately full-bodied. Balanced acidity. Moderately extracted. Moderately oaked. Vanilla, oak spice, tropical fruits. Rich, toasty aromas lead a rounded, glycerous mouthfeel with juicy tropical flavors. Acids give this fine structure and it should improve with further age.

1995 Cabernet Franc, Santa Lucia Highlands $12.50.　　　　**81**

1994 Cabernet Sauvignon, Livermore Valley $13.50.　　　　**83**

Bright ruby hue with a slight garnet cast. Moderately full-bodied. Balanced acidity. Highly extracted. Heavily oaked. Moderately tannic. Brown spices, minerals. Quite aromatic, with a hefty oak accent. Thick and rich in the mouth. Tannins bite down on the finish.

1992 Cabernet Sauvignon, Smith & Hook Vineyard,
Santa Lucia Highlands $14.　　　　**84**

Bright brick red. Medium-bodied. Moderately extracted. Mildly tannic. Loam, minerals, spice. Mature aromas are showing through. A refined palate of minerals and faded fruit flavors conveys a sense of elegance and maturity.

Ferrari-Carano

1996 Chardonnay, Alexander Valley $21.　　　　**93**

Yellow-gold. Moderately full-bodied. Balanced acidity. Moderately extracted. Vanilla, smoke, lemon, quince. Rich smoky aromas. Sweetly fruity and generous, with a supple, creamy mouthfeel. Shows a persistent, fine, juicy, flavorful finish.

1995 Chardonnay, Reserve, 87%Napa County, 13%Sonoma County $34.　　　　**94**

Bright yellow-gold. Moderately full-bodied. Balanced acidity. Moderately extracted. Moderately oaked. Smoke, yeast, crisp apples. Outstanding bright acids perfectly frame this intensely fruity style that shows extravagant texture and well-balanced oak spice. Outstanding Champagne-like smoky yeast complexity.

1993 Cabernet Sauvignon, Sonoma County $22.50.　　　　**90**

Dark red with purple highlights. Medium-bodied. Highly extracted. Moderately tannic. Olive, vanilla, cedar, cassis. Generous aromas reveal ripe, fleshy Cabernet fruit on the palate, with balanced powdery tannins through the finish. Solidly structured with plenty of stuffing.

1994 Cabernet Sauvignon, Sonoma County $28.　　　　　91

Dark ruby cast. Moderately full-bodied. Balanced acidity. Moderately extracted. Moderately oaked. Mildly tannic. Chocolate, earth, black fruits. Pleasantly aromatic, with a full, rich mouthfeel. Supple, lush, and velvety, showing a firm structure through the finish. Well balanced.

1995 Siena, Sonoma County $28.　　　　　86

Deep blackish ruby hue. Moderately full-bodied. Balanced acidity. Moderately extracted. Mildly oaked. Mildly tannic. Red fruits, minerals, spice. Pleasantly aromatic, with a lush, though well-structured palate feel. Picks up a pleasant angular note on the finish.

1992 Reserve Red, Sonoma County $47.　　　　　91

Bright reddish purple. Medium-bodied. Highly extracted. Moderately tannic. Black cherry, mint, cassis. Elegant perfumed nose of mint and cassis leads a concentrated palate of black cherry fruits with ample supple tannins showing great integration. Soundly structured, this should be worth holding on to.

1993 Tresor Reserve, Sonoma County $55.　　　　　94

Deep blackish ruby cast. Moderately full-bodied. Balanced acidity. Moderately extracted. Mildly tannic. Earth, black fruits, mushrooms. Generous aromas have an exotic and complex quality beginning to hint at maturity. Large scaled and firm in the mouth, with a lengthy finish. Shows fine grip and intensity.

1995 Merlot, Sonoma County $25.　　　　　83

Saturated dark red. Deeply woody, oak spice aromas. A firm attack leads a moderately full-bodied palate with firm fine-grained tannins. Drink now.

1995 Zinfandel, Sonoma County $18.　　　　　86

Dark blackish ruby hue with a purple edge. Moderately full-bodied. Balanced acidity. Moderately extracted. Mildly oaked. Mildly tannic. Chocolate, black fruits, vanilla. Pleasantly aromatic, with deep fruit flavors throughout. Full and lush on the palate, but well structured, with chunky tannins through the finish.

Gloria Ferrer

NV Blanc de Noirs, Carneros $15.　　　　　86

Pale copper hue with a subtle pinkish overtone. Full-bodied. Full acidity. Highly extracted. Minerals, red fruits. Aromatically reserved, with a forceful and austere mouthfeel featuring vibrant carbonation. Intense and racy through the finish.

NV Brut, Sonoma County $15.　　　　　83

Bright pale gold hue. Medium-bodied. Full acidity. Grapefruit, yeast. Steely, bright citrus aromas have a fresh yeasty note that follows through on the flavor-packed palate and persistent finish. Shows lively medium-beaded carbonation.

1989 Carneros Cuvée Brut, Carneros $28.　　　　　92

Brilliant yellow-gold. Moderately full-bodied. Full acidity. Nuts, spice, baked fruit. Rich, complex aromas show a toasty, nutty character, indicating maturity that is confirmed on the palate. Concentrated, fine-beaded carbonation supplies a tight mousse. This shows persistence of flavors.

1990 Royal Cuvée Brut, Vintage Reserve, Carneros $20.　　　　　88

Medium straw cast. Medium-bodied. Full acidity. Spice, toast, citrus zest. Generous bready aromas. Full carbonation with a frothy mouthfeel. Very lively and concentrated, with a long, zesty finish.

1996 Pinot Noir, Carneros $19.　　　　　83

Pale ruby-violet hue. Medium-bodied. Low acidity. Subtly extracted. Red fruits, vanilla. Soft, perfumed aromas lead a rounded, fat, pleasant mouthful of flavors. This lacks structure to develop further in the bottle.

Fetzer

1997 Chardonnay, Sundial, California $7.99.　　　　　81

Scale: Superlative (96-100), Exceptional (90-95), Highly Recommended (85-89), Recommended (80-84), Not Recommended (Under 80)

1997 Chardonnay, Barrel Select, Mendocino County $11.99. 81
1996 Chardonnay, Reserve, Mendocino County $20. 88

Rich yellow-straw hue. Generous brown spice and pear aromas show a judicious oak accent. A fat entry leads a moderately full-bodied palate with shy acidity. Rounded, buttery finish. Hedonistically attractive but will not keep. Drink now.

1997 Gewürztraminer, California $5.99. 82
1997 Johannisberg Riesling, California $6.99. 88

Medium yellow-straw color. Rich aromas of ripe stone fruits and petrol are classic, pure Riesling. A rich attack follows through well on the medium-bodied palate, with oily flavors through the finish. Drink now.

1997 White Zinfandel, California $5.99. 80
1996 Cabernet Sauvignon, Valley Oaks, California $8.99. 81
1995 Cabernet Sauvignon, Barrel Select, North Coast $14.99. 87

Saturated dark ruby hue. Elegant aromas of lavish oak and rich cassis and plum. A lush entry leads to a moderately full-bodied palate with velvety, abundant tannins and sweet cedary oak flavors that persist through the finish. Very supple and mouthfilling. Drink now.

1994 Cabernet Sauvignon, Reserve, Napa Valley $28. 93

Dark ruby hue. Markedly ripe, oak-accented aromas have a sweet vanilla note. A soft entry leads a moderately full-bodied mouthfeel with clean acidity and ripe black fruit flavors that give way to a dark chocolate note on the finish. A thicker, rich style. Drink now or later.

1997 Merlot, Eagle Peak, California $8.99. 83

Bright violet-ruby hue. Moderately aromatic with weedy and oak accents and plummy fruit. A supple entry leads a medium-bodied palate with berry fruit flavors matched by supple tannins and lingering oak flavors. Well balanced with fine acidity and good grip on the finish. Drink now.

1995 Merlot, Barrel Select, Sonoma County $13.99. 85

Deep blackish ruby hue with brilliant clarity. Moderately light-bodied. Balanced acidity. Moderately extracted. Mildly oaked. Mildly tannic. Red fruits, vanilla. Lighter in style, with a soft mouthfeel. Straightforward fruit flavors are accented by a kiss of oak.

1996 Merlot, North Coast $14.99. 85

Bright ruby red to the rim. Clean cherry and mineral aromas. A lean attack leads a medium-bodied palate with firm tannins and juicy acidity, and a crisp, clipped finish. Racy and refreshing. Drink now.

1995 Merlot, Reserve, North Coast $22. 88

Bright ruby red to the rim. Attractive red fruit and vanilla aromas show an attractive wood accent. A crisp attack leads a medium-bodied palate with vibrant acidity and subdued tannins. Flavorful, ripe, wood-accented finish. Lighter in style but well balanced and tasty. Drink now.

1996 Pinot Noir, California $12.99. 84

Bright ruby cast. Medium-bodied. Balanced acidity. Moderately extracted. Mildly tannic. Minerals, red fruits. Lean aromas lead a firm and grippy mouthfeel. Full yet lean through the finish.

1995 Pinot Noir, Bien Nacido Vineyard Reserve,
Santa Barbara County $24. 88

Bright cherry red. Medium-bodied. Moderately extracted. Moderately oaked. Mildly tannic. Full, generous, rounded cherry and raspberry fruit flavors fill the palate. Nice bright acids with a hint of herbal character on the finish.

1993 Port, Mendocino County $18.99. 82

Ficklin

Tinta Port, California $12.   86

Deep ruby-garnet cast. Medium-bodied. Balanced acidity. Moderately extracted. Brown spices, toast. Pleasantly aromatic, with a gentle woody note and a touch of heat. Ripe and full in the mouth, with a lingering, flavorful finish.

1988 Vintage Port, California $25.   91

Deep ruby-garnet cast. Moderately full-bodied. Balanced acidity. Moderately extracted. Overripe red fruits, tea, minerals. Quite aromatic and complex, with a mature, flavorful palate feel. Full but well structured, with a sense of leanness through the finish, provided by buoyant acidity.

10 Year Old Tawny Port, California $22.   92

Opaque mahogany cast with a greenish fade to the rim. Full-bodied. Full acidity. Highly extracted. Salted pecans, rancio, treacle. Extraordinarily flavorful, with a well-aged, Oloroso Sherry edge to the complex flavors. Thick, rich, and concentrated on the palate, with great intensity and style.

Fife

1995 Merlot, Napa Valley $20.   80
1996 L'Attitude 39, Mendocino $18.   84

Deep ruby red to the rim. Generous earth, herb, and spice aromas show a moderate wood accent. A soft attack leads a medium-bodied palate that has tannic grip. The finish is supple and flavorful. Well balanced. Drink now.

1996 Max Cuvée, Napa Valley $30.   88

Very dark, opaque violet red to the rim. Brooding, intense black fruit, vanilla, and mineral aromas show a generous wood accent. A firm attack leads a full-bodied palate, with abundant robust, chunky tannins. The finish is flavorful and tannic. A monster show style, displaying extract, color, and tannin galore, it is not for the faint of heart. Good for long-term (7–10 years) cellaring.

1995 Zinfandel, Redhead Vineyard, Redwood Valley $18.50.   84

Bright blackish ruby cast. Moderately full-bodied. Balanced acidity. Highly extracted. Mildly oaked. Moderately tannic. Minerals, red fruits, black pepper. Somewhat reserved aromatically, with a firm, compact palate feel. Lean and austere through the concentrated finish.

J. Filippi

Fondante Ciello, Chocolate Port, California $18/500 ml.   80

Firestone

1997 Chardonnay, Santa Ynez Valley $13.   83

Bright straw hue. Forward mineral and spice aromas show a restrained oak accent. A crisp entry leads a medium-bodied palate with racy acidity. Sharp, cleansing finish. Drink now.

1997 Gewürztraminer, Carranza Mesa Vineyard, Santa Ynez Valley $9.   82
1997 Riesling, Santa Barbara County $7.   89

Medium green-gold hue. Exotic aromas of petrol and minerals. A rich entry leads a medium-bodied palate with a glycerous mouthfeel, peach flavors, and an oily texture that sets this apart. Lingering, rich finish. An excellent match with pork or other white meats. Drink now or later.

1993 Reserve Red, Santa Ynez Valley $30.   89

Dark red. Moderately full-bodied. Moderately extracted. Mildly tannic. Plums, toasted oak, chocolate. Attractive rich black fruit aromas have tobacco accents. The rounded mouthfeel has generous ripe flavors and sweet, spicy, chocolatey notes on the finish. Drinking nicely now.

Scale: Superlative (96-100), Exceptional (90-95), Highly Recommended (85-89), Recommended (80-84), Not Recommended (Under 80)

1995 Merlot, Santa Ynez Valley $14.   83

Deep blackish ruby hue. Medium-bodied. Balanced acidity. Moderately extracted. Mildly tannic. Earth, black fruits. Aromatics are quite earthy. Compact palate feel. Features some mild astringency and an herbal note to the finish.

1995 Port, Santa Ynez Valley $20.   82

Fisher

1997 Chardonnay, Coach Insignia, Sonoma County $25.   82

1997 Chardonnay, Whitney's Vineyard, Sonoma County $40.   89

Bright straw hue. Restrained, youthful yeasty aromas. A lush entry leads a full-bodied palate with rounded yet vibrant acidity. Features a substantial, harmonious mouthfeel and a crisp finish. Should open with age. Midterm cellar candidate.

1995 Cabernet Sauvignon, Coach Insignia, Napa Valley $25.   91

Bright ruby purple. Moderately full-bodied. Balanced acidity. Highly extracted. Moderately tannic. Minerals, cassis, earth. Pleasantly aromatic, with a firm and intense palate feel. Crisp, lean, and angular through the finish.

1996 Coach Insignia Red, Napa County $30.   84

Deep ruby-violet hue. Rich, ripe aromas show a deeply fruited character, somewhat reserved. A lush entry leads a moderately full-bodied palate with dense dark fruit flavors and finely wrought grainy tannins. Stuffed, well-gripped, and flavorful. This has cellarable structure. Drink now or later.

1994 Cabernet Sauvignon, Lamb Vineyard, Napa Valley $50.   95

Opaque red with bright purple highlights. Full-bodied. Highly extracted. Moderately tannic. Currants, black fruit, tea. Weighty and massively full on the palate. Dense and chewy, with assertive dry tannins making it backward at present. Excellent structure for long-term (7–10 years) cellaring.

1995 Cabernet Sauvignon, Lamb Vineyard, Napa Valley $50.   92

Deep, saturated ruby hue. Moderately full-bodied. Balanced acidity. Highly extracted. Moderately tannic. Black fruits, minerals. Features a youthful, minerally array of flavors. Tight and firm, but showing great depth and intensity. Firm tannins rise on the finish. A long-term (7–10 years) cellar candidate.

1994 Cabernet Sauvignon, Wedding Vineyard, Sonoma County $50. 92

Very deep ruby hue with a slight purple cast. Full-bodied. Balanced acidity. Highly extracted. Moderately tannic. Currants, black fruit, tea. Aromatically reserved, with a powerful, tightly wound palate feel. Dense and brooding, though not thick or heavy, with excellent structure. Tannins clamp down on the finish, though this should open with long-term (7–10 years) aging.

1996 Merlot, RCF Vineyard, Napa Valley $30.   89

Bright violet red. Generous cherry fruit aromas are appealing, with a minerally note. Lush on the attack, with a moderately full-bodied palate that shows concentrated black cherry flavors lifted by juicy acids. Fine-grained tannins supply some grip on the minerally finish. Drink now or later. Can improve with more age.

Flora Springs

1997 Chardonnay, Reserve, Napa Valley $24.   88

Full golden yellow. Very aromatic with rich, ripe smoky aromas. A lush entry is followed by a full-bodied palate with tropical ripeness and oaky accents that linger on the finish. A big, bold style.

1995 Cabernet Sauvignon, Cypress Ranch, Napa Valley $40.   90

Opaque purple. Full-bodied. Highly extracted. Quite tannic. Pepper, licorice, black fruit. Heavyweight, dry, and big-shouldered, with drying, earthy tannins clamping down on the finish. This will need rare meaty fare for near-term consumption.

1994 Trilogy, Napa Valley $30.   90

Dark cherry red. Medium-bodied. Highly extracted. Moderately tannic. Earth, black fruits, brown spice. Rich earthy, minty nose with toasty accents leads a solid, mouthfilling palate, with some assertive structure giving authority and grip through the finish.

1995 Trilogy, Napa Valley $40.   93

Deep ruby cast. Moderately full-bodied. Balanced acidity. Moderately extracted. Moderately oaked. Mildly tannic. Mint, red fruits, vanilla. Aromatic and harmonious, with a lush, supple entry. Exquisitely made, with gentle extraction making for a velvety mouthfeel. Flavorful and generous through the lengthy finish.

1996 Trilogy, Napa Valley $45.   90

Saturated dark violet red hue. Intensely aromatic with bright cassis and tobacco notes. A rich entry leads a full-bodied palate with a deep core of lushly extracted fruit flavors with waves of spice and licorice through the lengthy finish.

1995 Merlot, Napa Valley $16.   87

Very deep ruby hue to the rim. Medium-bodied. Balanced acidity. Highly extracted. Mildly oaked. Mildly tannic. Black fruits, chocolate, minerals. Somewhat perfumed in character, with a dense mouthfeel. Chewy tannins come out on the lingering finish.

1995 Merlot, Windfall Vineyard, Napa Valley $32.   93

Deep, opaque blackish ruby hue. Moderately full-bodied. Balanced acidity. Highly extracted. Moderately oaked. Mildly tannic. Black fruits, brown spices, mint. Quite aromatic, with a big, rich mouthfilling character. Features a chewy texture with velvety tannins, and a lengthy flavorful finish.

1996 Merlot, Windfall Vineyard, Napa Valley $40.   92

Saturated dark ruby hue. Dense aromas of oak, dark fruits, and earth. A firm entry leads a full-bodied palate with very dense flavors showing great depth of fruit and a heavy oak accent that lingers on the finish. Tannins are dry and dusty. A big, dense wine with a thick mouthfeel. Drink now or later.

1996 Pinot Noir, Lavender Hill Vineyard, Carneros $20.   82

Thomas Fogarty

1997 Chardonnay, Monterey $17.50.   80
1997 Chardonnay, Santa Cruz Mountains $19.   80
1996 Chardonnay, Estate Reserve, Santa Cruz Mountains $28.   84

Bright yellow-gold. Moderately full-bodied. Full acidity. Highly extracted. Moderately oaked. Nuts, spice, citrus. Reserved nutty aromas lead a weighty, solid mouthful of broad flavors held together by firm acids that stretch out through the finish.

1997 Gewürztraminer, Monterey $12.50.   89

Deep yellow-straw hue. Bold, generous flower and spice aromas. A lush entry leads a moderately full-bodied palate, with mild sweetness offset by vibrant acidity. Ripe, flavorful finish. Drink now.

1996 Cabernet Sauvignon, Napa Valley $25.   89

Saturated deep violet hue. Aromatically reserved with cherry fruit and vanilla. A crisp entry leads a medium-bodied palate with bright cherry fruit flavors and mild but dry fine-grained tannins. Youthful and angular with fine varietal flavors. Drink now or later.

1996 Cabernet Sauvignon, Santa Cruz Mountains $25.   90

Deep ruby hue. High-toned anise, vanilla, and brown spice aromas carry a big oak accent. A lush attack leads to a moderately full-bodied palate with velvety tannins and bright acidity. Supple, harmonious, wood-accented finish. A very stylish wine, drinking beautifully now. Drink now.

1996 Merlot, Santa Cruz Mountains $23.   85

Bright, saturated ruby red. High-toned red fruit and mineral aromas. A crisp attack, and a moderately light-bodied palate with zesty acidity and subtle tannins. Bright, fruit-forward finish. Drink now.

Scale: Superlative (96-100), Exceptional (90-95), Highly Recommended (85-89), Recommended (80-84), Not Recommended (Under 80)

1996 Pinot Noir, Santa Cruz Mountains $27.   86

Deep ruby cast. Moderately full-bodied. Low acidity. Moderately extracted. Mildly tannic.
Anise, black fruits. Forward aromas carry an unusual high-toned quality. Broad in the
mouth, with low acidity levels fleshing out the finish.

1995 Pinot Noir, Estate Reserve, Santa Cruz Mountains $30.   89

Full cherry red. Medium-bodied. Highly extracted. Moderately oaked. Moderately tannic.
Full oak and red fruit aromas. Concentrated raspberry and cherry flavors have plenty of
dry oak accents in support. Youthful and tight at present.

1996 Sangiovese, Estate Reserve, Santa Cruz Mountains $27.50.   91

Saturated ruby purple. Medium-bodied. Balanced acidity. Highly extracted. Moderately
oaked. Moderately tannic. Vanilla, red fruits. Solid, tight palate of red fruits, with a heavy
influence of new oak barrels that give it a strong vanilla note and a dry finish. Quite silky
and stylish.

Foley

1996 Chardonnay, Barrel Select, Santa Barbara County $25.   94

Deep straw cast. Moderately full-bodied. Full acidity. Moderately extracted. Moderately
oaked. Citrus, vanilla, brown spices. Generous aromas feature a big oak component and
join a core of zesty citrus flavors in the mouth. Sumptuous and flavorful, with a fine acid
backbone that make for a firm and lengthy finish.

1997 Chardonnay, Barrel Select, Santa Barbara County $28.   98

Deep gold. Nutty, generously oaky aromas are very Burgundian. Very fruity on the attack,
leading a moderately full-bodied palate with vibrant acids to match the rich fruity center.
Persistent fruit character through the finish. Very impressively concentrated, with lavish
winemaking. Drink now or later.

1997 Chardonnay, Bien Nacido Vineyard, Santa Maria Valley $24.   95

Deep yellow-straw hue. Opulent tropical fruit and toasted coconut aromas indicate a
sweet wood influence. A crisp entry leads a moderately full-bodied palate with racy
acidity. Shows great intensity of flavor and excellent grip, and a complex, stylish finish.
Drink now.

1996 Sauvignon Blanc, Santa Barbara County $14.   93

Yellow-straw hue. Medium-bodied. Balanced acidity. Highly extracted. Lemon, limes,
minerals. Forceful and intense on the palate. This has a smoky theme through the finish.
Showing no shortage of character, this is an exuberant California interpretation of the
Pessac style.

1995 Cabernet Sauvignon, La Cuesta Vineyard, Santa Ynez Valley $27.   88

Full cherry red with subtle purple highlights. Medium-bodied. Moderately extracted.
Mildly tannic. Plums, cassis, licorice, earth. Bright black fruit flavors reveal smoky
Cabernet fruit character. The lingering finish has plenty of complexity. Well balanced
and full of character.

1996 Pinot Noir, Santa Maria Hills Vineyard, Santa Maria Valley $25.   87

Dark ruby purple. Full-bodied. Full acidity. Highly extracted. Moderately tannic. Anise,
chocolate, tea. Aromatic and complex, with an unusual array of flavors. Full, firm, and
zesty in the mouth, showing great intensity. Finishes with a hint of bitterness.

1997 Pinot Noir, Santa Maria Hills Vineyard, Santa Maria Valley $32.   89

Bright saturated ruby purple. Moderately full-bodied. Full acidity. Highly extracted.
Moderately tannic. Dried herbs, tea, iron. Forward aromas are complex and distinctive.
Full throttled in the mouth, with real intensity and depth of flavor. Lengthy and
persistent.

Folie à Deux

1993 Fantaisie Brut, Napa Valley $18.   85

Bright yellow-straw hue. Medium-bodied. Full acidity. Yeast, minerals, citrus. Developed,
yeasty aromas are distinctive. Crisp and bright on the palate, with an angular, drying
finish that could use another year to resolve.

1995 Cabernet Sauvignon, Napa Valley $18.   **87**

Medium ruby red. Medium-bodied. Moderately extracted. Mildly tannic. Red berries, brown spice. Vanilla and spice nose shows berry fruit accents that are confirmed on the palate. God oak spice flavors through the finish. Balanced and appealingly straightforward.

1995 Cabernet Sauvignon, Reserve, Napa Valley $22.   **88**

Dark ruby center with purple highlights. Medium-bodied. Moderately extracted. Mildly tannic. Plums, pepper, brown spice. An assertively spicy, peppery nose is confirmed on the palate, with full black fruit flavors giving a sense of depth.

1996 Sangiovese, Amador County $16.   **85**

Bright blackish garnet cast. Moderately full-bodied. Low acidity. Moderately extracted. Mildly tannic. Overripe red fruits, dried herbs. Extremely ripe, with a hint of Port. Soft and flabby in the mouth, this could use a bit more grip.

1996 Zinfandel, Old Vine, Amador County $18.   **86**

Deep blackish ruby cast. Medium-bodied. Balanced acidity. Moderately extracted. Mildly oaked. Mildly tannic. Chocolate, minerals. Reserved aromatically, with a lighter-styled though flavorful mouthfeel. Soft and velvety through the finish.

1996 Zinfandel, Eschen Vineyard Old Vine, Fiddletown $22.   **87**

Bright blackish ruby hue. Moderately full-bodied. Balanced acidity. Highly extracted. Mildly oaked. Mildly tannic. Black fruits, minerals. Somewhat reserved aromatically, with a full, ripe mouthfeel. Highly structured, with lean tannins and a lengthy finish.

Foppiano

1996 Petite Sirah, Russian River Valley $16.   **83**

Opaque, saturated purple-red hue. Restrained spicy wood and black fruit aromas. A lush attack leads a very full-bodied palate, with robust astringent tannins. The finish is thick, with grip. Lots of stuffing but rather shy of flavor. Drink now or later. Can improve with more age.

Forest Glen

1997 Chardonnay, California $9.99.   **90**

Rich golden yellow. Powerful toasted wood, citrus, and cream aromas show a hefty oak accent. A ripe attack leads a moderately full-bodied palate with juicy acidity. Flavorful, lengthy finish. Shows a lot of style. Drink now or later.

1996 Cabernet Sauvignon, California $9.99.   **84**

Bright crimson-purple hue. Markedly toasty oak-accented aromas with ripe cassis notes. A firm entry leads to a medium-bodied wine with plenty of dry oaky flavors and a bright fruity backdrop with grainy tannins. Drink now.

1997 Merlot, California $9.99.   **83**

Full violet ruby hue. Oak-accented aromas follow through on the medium-bodied palate with up-front brambly fruit flavors and an earthy dry note coming through on the finish.

1996 Sangiovese, California $9.99.   **87**

Bright cherry red. Moderately light-bodied. Balanced acidity. Moderately extracted. Moderately oaked. Mildly tannic. Red berries, vanilla. Soft, rounded, and supple. Finishes with velvety tannins and vanilla flavors.

1996 Shiraz, California $9.99.   **84**

Medium red-purple. Red currants, vanilla, and mineral flavors. Hint of wood tones. A firm entry leads a medium-bodied palate. Moderate, drying tannins. Fruit flavors are rather muted. Subtle, short finish. Dry and lean, this will work best with food. Drink now.

Forest Hill

1995 Chardonnay, Private Reserve, Napa Valley $60.   **81**

Scale: Superlative (96-100), Exceptional (90-95), Highly Recommended (85-89), Recommended (80-84), Not Recommended (Under 80)

Forest Ville

1997 Chardonnay, California $5.99.   83

Bright yellow-straw hue. Subtle mineral and citrus aromas. A creamy entry leads a medium-bodied palate with rounded acidity. The finish is clean and weighty. Drink now.

1997 Gewürztraminer, California $5.99.   86

Deep yellow-straw hue. Generous spice, citrus, and orange rind aromas. A lush entry leads a moderately full-bodied palate, with marked sweetness offset by solid acidity. Flavorful and intense. Drink now.

1996 Johannisberg Riesling, California $5.99.   81

1995 Sauvignon Blanc, California $5.99.   83

Bright pale yellow. Medium-bodied. Balanced acidity. Moderately extracted. Mildly oaked. Vanilla, citrus. Faintly smoky aromas lead a simple palate, with faint varietal flavors and a hint of oak influence on the finish.

1997 White Zinfandel, California $4.99.   81

1998 White Merlot, California $5.99.   82

1996 Cabernet Sauvignon, California $5.99.   81

1997 Merlot, California $5.99.   86

Bright violet red. Attractive vanilla and cherry fruit aromas. Medium-bodied, open-knit style with generous red fruit and oak accents through the clean finish. Very user friendly and supple.

1997 Shiraz, California $5.99.   84

Pale cherry-purple color, limpid and brilliant, with a slight fade. Subtle, pleasant herb, black fruit, and vanilla flavors. Hint of wood tones. A soft entry and a medium-bodied palate. Light, drying tannins. Subtle, short finish. This is a jammy, lighter style to drink now.

Forman

1996 Chardonnay, Napa Valley $28.   81

1994 Cabernet Sauvignon, Napa Valley $38.   88

Bright crimson red. Medium-bodied. Moderately extracted. Moderately tannic. Cherries, berries, vanilla. Bright aromas lead tightly wound cherry fruit flavors. Solid, though not a heavyweight in style. Oak flavors are in fine balance. Has a youthful character.

1995 Cabernet Sauvignon, Napa Valley $40.   91

Deep violet purple. Medium-bodied. Highly extracted. Moderately tannic. Cassis, spice. Bright through the finish, which has some grip and a dusting of fine-grained tannins. The mouthfeel is rich and deep.

Fox Hollow

1997 Chardonnay, California $8.99.   83

Deep yellow-straw hue. Subdued citrus and spice aromas. A full entry is followed by a moderately full-bodied palate with edgy acidity and a subtle finish. Drink now.

1995 Cabernet Sauvignon, California $8.99.   86

Bright cherry red with subtle purple cast. Ripe fruit-centered aromas show cassis and subtle oak influence. A lush entry leads to a medium-bodied palate with lush, supple tannins and generous, ripe fruit flavors that linger on the finish. Drink now.

1997 Merlot, California $8.99.   86

Bright violet red. Faintly fleshy aromas lead a soft attack with vanilla oak and black fruit flavors on a medium-bodied palate. Finishes with mild, grainy tannins. A soft, lush easy-drinking style. Drink now.

1997 Pinot Noir, Monterey County $8.99.   83

Bright violet red. Cherries, vanilla. Crisp, vibrant, fruity aromas follow through on a supple palate with precise black cherry flavors.

1996 Shiraz, California $8.99.   86

Pale purple, limpid, and brilliant, with a slight fade. Subtle, pleasant cherry and vanilla flavors. Hint of wood tones. Smooth entry. Moderately light-bodied. Very mild, silky tannins. Structurally light, with up-front bright fruit flavors carried by fruit acidity. Subtle, short finish. Straightforward and quaffable. Drink now.

Foxen

1995 Pinot Noir, Sanford & Benedict Vineyard, Santa Ynez Valley $28.   89

Bright ruby red. Medium-bodied. Moderately extracted. Moderately oaked. Mildly tannic. Elegant, complex aromas. Rich black and red berry fruit flavors, with lingering sweet tobacco and vanilla notes.

Foxridge

1997 Chardonnay, Carneros $9.99.   86

Pale straw hue. Medium-bodied. Balanced acidity. Moderately extracted. Citrus, apples. Clean, fruity aromas. Bright, lively, and juicy, with a crisp finish that does not show much oak influence.

Franciscan

1995 Chardonnay, Oakville Estate, Cuvée Sauvage, Napa Valley $30.   91

Deep yellow-gold. Full-bodied. Balanced acidity. Highly extracted. Moderately oaked. Lanolin, minerals, spices. Forward and aromatic, with complex and enticing flavors. Rich, lush, and opulent in the mouth. Acidity provides a backbone, though this is rich through the finish.

1996 Chardonnay, Oakville Estate, Cuvée Sauvage, Napa Valley $30.   94

Full gold. Generous aromas of toasted oak, yeast, ripe fruits, and butter. An opulent attack leads a moderately full body with rich flavors that taper to an oaky, leesy finish. Very stylish and decadent. Some bottle age should help this settle down. Drink now or later.

1997 Chardonnay, Oakville Estate, Napa Valley $15.   86

Bright gold. Moderate aromas of browned butter and tropical fruits. A rich entry leads a full-bodied palate with opulent texture, though the fruit flavors are somewhat restrained. The finish is clean. Drink now.

1994 Cabernet Sauvignon, Oakville Estate, Napa Valley $17.   90

Deep red. Moderately full-bodied. Highly extracted. Mildly tannic. Plums, cassis, toasted oak. Ripe, faintly Port-like nose. Rich, supple black fruit flavors unfold on the palate and linger through the toasty finish. Very plush and generously fruity style.

1995 Cabernet Sauvignon, Oakville Estate, Napa Valley $17.   86

Deep ruby red with a slight fade. Moderately full-bodied. Balanced acidity. Moderately extracted. Mildly oaked. Mildly tannic. Cassis, minerals, spice. Pleasantly aromatic, with a firm palate feel. Focused and angular through the finish, with a big, chunky character.

1994 Oakville Estate, Magnificat Meritage, Napa Valley $25.   91

Dark blood red. Medium-bodied. Moderately extracted. Moderately tannic. Toasted oak, black currants, plums. Full berry fruit aromas have a toasty accent. Ripe, bright black fruit flavors fill the palate and linger through the finish. Delicious, with lots of primary fruit flavors making it irresistible.

1995 Oakville Estate, Magnificat Meritage, Napa Valley $30.   89

Deep ruby hue with a slight fade to the rim. Moderately full-bodied. Balanced acidity. Moderately extracted. Heavily oaked. Mildly tannic. Brown spices, leather, red fruits. Generous aromas are largely oak driven, with a big spicy overlay of flavor throughout. Soft and supple in the mouth, with a well-structured, somewhat angular finish.

1996 Merlot, Napa Valley $17.   84

Dark ruby hue with a slight fade. Generous fruit and vanilla aromas. Medium-bodied, with a lush, ripe attack that follows through on the midpalate with fine-grained tannins and vanilla oak. Drink now or later. Can improve with more age.

Franus

1994 Cabernet Sauvignon, Napa Valley $25.   86

Solid, opaque blackish red. Moderately full-bodied. Highly extracted. Moderately tannic. Earth, plums, black fruits. Full meaty aromas lead a deeply textured palate, with lots of integrated dry, fine-grained tannins providing excellent grip. Plenty of fleshy fruit flavors here. Medium-term cellaring.

Freemark Abbey

1996 Chardonnay, Napa Valley $20.   81

1996 Chardonnay, Carpy Ranch Vineyard, Napa Valley $26.   84

Deep straw cast. Moderately full-bodied. Balanced acidity. Moderately extracted. Minerals, citrus, butter. Aromatically reserved, with a lean and zesty presence on the palate. Crisp and angular through the finish.

1994 Cabernet Sauvignon, Napa Valley $19.99.   88

Bright reddish purple. Medium-bodied. Moderately extracted. Moderately tannic. Plums, cassis, cedar. Generous, rounded, plush, bright Cabernet fruit flavors unfold on the silky palate. The tannins are still quite dry and youthful through the finish.

1995 Cabernet Sauvignon, Napa Valley $24.   87

Bright ruby hue. Interesting mint, earth, and mineral aromas. A lean attack leads to a medium-bodied palate with earthy flavors and supple tannins. A ripe, fruity quality emerges on the finish. Stylish and flavorful. Drink now.

1992 Cabernet Sauvignon, Bosché Estate, Napa Valley $27.99.   92

Deep ruby red. Medium-bodied. Moderately extracted. Moderately tannic. Black cherries, toasted oak. Expressive, integrated aromas have a toasty accent. Rich but supple entry shows a velvety character, with plenty of vigorous tannins coming through on the finish. Nice now, but this will soldier on in the cellar.

1994 Cabernet Sauvignon, Bosché Estate, Napa Valley $44.   92

Bright ruby hue to the rim. Opulent red fruit and mineral aromas carry a subtle oak accent. A crisp entry leads to a moderately full-bodied palate with lush, chewy tannins. Zesty acidity lends buoyancy to the flavors. Ripe, racy finish. Approachable and well balanced with the structure to age beautifully. Drink now or later.

1992 Cabernet Sauvignon, Sycamore Vineyard, Napa Valley $26.49.   90

Full ruby red. Medium-bodied. Moderately extracted. Mildly tannic. Black bramble fruits, lead pencil, chalk. Lead pencil aromas lead a velvety palate, with fine chalky tannins coming through on the finish. Balanced and very well integrated. Drinking nicely now.

1993 Cabernet Sauvignon, Sycamore Vineyard, Napa Valley $28.99.   89

Deep ruby cast. Moderately full-bodied. Balanced acidity. Moderately extracted. Moderately oaked. Mildly tannic. Vanilla, red fruits, minerals. Generous aromas lead a supple and harmonious palate feel. Gentle and velvety, though quite flavorful, with fine length.

Freestone

1994 Cabernet Sauvignon, Napa Valley $15.   89

Ruby-red center with a pale rim. Medium-bodied. Moderately extracted. Mildly tannic. Vanilla, black cherries, brown spice. Straightforward red and black fruit flavors with a rounded mouthfeel and a tart spicy edge running through the finish. Very accessible and drinking well now.

Frey

1997 Cabernet Sauvignon, Butow Vineyards, Redwood Valley $10.50.   **89**

Bright purple-red hue. Intense black fruit and vanilla aromas show a sweet oak accent. A ripe attack leads to a moderately full-bodied palate with juicy acidity and lush tannins. Flavorful, lengthy finish. Shows excellent cut and integration. Well balanced and stylish. Drink now or later.

Frick

1994 Zinfandel, Dry Creek Valley $15.   **84**

Bright blackish purple. Medium-bodied. Full acidity. Highly extracted. Mildly tannic. Briar fruits, minerals. Quite aromatic, with a high-toned quality. Light, juicy, and angular in the mouth. Finishes on a tart note.

Gabrielli

1995 Pinot Noir, Floodgate Vineyard, Anderson Valley $17.   **88**

Full cherry red. Medium-bodied. Moderately extracted. Moderately oaked. Moderately tannic. Ripe berry and vanilla aromas lead a sweet berry fruit entry that turns quite dry and assertive through the finish. Plenty of depth of flavor and a solid structure, with well-balanced oakiness.

Gainey

1996 Chardonnay, Limited Selection, Santa Barbara County $28.   **87**

Bright straw cast. Medium-bodied. Full acidity. Moderately extracted. Toast, yeast, citrus. Fine toasty aromas. Light on the palate, with delicate yet complex flavors. Crisp and stylish through the zesty finish.

1998 Riesling, Central Coast $10.   **83**

Pale straw hue. Tart citrus aromas with a floral note. Crisp on entry, leading a medium-bodied palate with leaner citrus flavors lingering on the finish. Drink now.

1996 Cabernet Franc, Limited Selection, Santa Ynez Valley $20.   **86**

Rich ruby hue with a slight fade. Generous wood and black fruit aromas. A lush entry leads to a moderately full-bodied palate with firm tannins. Rich, tannic finish. Big, but rather tough at present. Drink now or later.

1996 Merlot, Santa Ynez Valley $16.   **87**

Deep, saturated ruby red. Forward cedar, black fruit, and vanilla aromas show a big oak accent. A soft attack leads a full-bodied, lush mouthfeel with robust powdery tannins. The finish is rich and flavorful. Shows depth and intensity on a generous frame. Drink now or later. Can improve with more age.

1996 Pinot Noir, Limited Selection, Santa Maria Valley $28.   **89**

Deep ruby-garnet cast. Moderately full-bodied. Full acidity. Moderately extracted. Moderately oaked. Mildly tannic. Spice, red fruits, sweet wood. Generous aromas feature ripe fruit and sweet oak overtones. Lush and flavorful in the mouth, yet underpinned by a firm, minerally backbone and zesty acidity. Finishes with fine length and intensity.

Gallo Sonoma

1997 Chardonnay, Russian River Valley $14.   **88**

Bright yellow-gold. Generous ripe citrus aromas with judicious oak and yeast accents. A generous, lush attack leads a moderately full-bodied palate with broad, full fruit flavors that persist through the finish. Hedonistic. Drink now.

1996 Chardonnay, Estate, Northern Sonoma $38.   **94**

Deep yellow-straw hue. Forward, flashy aromas show a buttery, yeasty opulence and a big oak accent. A rich entry leads a full-bodied palate with racy acidity lending balance. Big and intensely flavored with fine grip and a lengthy, persistent finish. A great show style. Drink now or later.

1996 Chardonnay, Laguna Ranch Vineyard, Russian River Valley $20.   **87**
Bright yellow-gold. Moderately full-bodied. Balanced acidity. Highly extracted. Moderately oaked. Smoke, toast, citrus. Aromatically complex, with a pleasant toasty accent and a core of citric flavors. Rich and ripe through the finish.

1996 Chardonnay, Stefani Vineyard, Dry Creek Valley $18.   **86**
Bright straw cast. Moderately full-bodied. Balanced acidity. Moderately extracted. Mildly oaked. Cream, brown spices, citrus. Ripe and opulent, with a lush, rounded texture offset by zesty acidity. Rich and lengthy through the finish.

1994 Cabernet Sauvignon, Sonoma County $12.   **87**
Deep garnet hue. Generous cedar and brown spice aromas show a mellow oak accent. A rich entry leads to a full-bodied palate with silky tannins and excellent acidic structure. Firm, flavorful finish. A harmonious and very elegant wine. Drink now or later.

1994 Cabernet Sauvignon, Barrelli Creek Vineyard, Alexander Valley $20.   **90**
Deep ruby hue. Moderately full-bodied. Balanced acidity. Moderately extracted. Heavily oaked. Mildly tannic. Toasted coconut, plums. Quite fragrant, with a hefty oak overlay and a dense, chewy palate feel. Lush and supple through the lengthy finish.

1993 Cabernet Sauvignon, Frei Ranch Vineyard, Dry Creek Valley $18.   **91**
Blackish red. Moderately full-bodied. Highly extracted. Moderately tannic. Brown spice, black fruits, earth. Exotic, spicy nose shows dark fruit flavors. The concentrated, assertively full-flavored palate has rich earthy qualities, with exotic spices lingering on the dry finish. Tannins are quite dry and authoritative.

1994 Cabernet Sauvignon, Frei Ranch Vineyard, Dry Creek Valley $18.   **93**
Saturated dark red. Moderately full-bodied. Highly extracted. Moderately tannic. Briar fruits, anise, toasted coconut. Powerful spicy aromas lead expressive black fruit flavors, with ripe tannins that conclude with a touch of dryness. Very flavorsome and drinking well now.

1993 Cabernet Sauvignon, Stefani Vineyard, Dry Creek Valley $18.   **88**
Opaque black cherry hue. Moderately full-bodied. Highly extracted. Quite tannic. Black fruits, black tea, earth, brown spice. Ripe plummy flavors on entry expand on the midpalate giving a fleshy quality. Assertively dry, with strapping tannins through the finish.

1994 Cabernet Sauvignon, Stefani Vineyard, Dry Creek Valley $18.   **86**
Very deep ruby red hue. Intensely fragrant brown spice and licorice aromas show a dominant wood influence. A lush attack leads to a full-bodied palate with big grainy tannins. Firm, flavorful finish. A big showy style, drinking well now, but lacking long term acidity. Drink within five years.

1993 Cabernet Sauvignon, Estate, Northern Sonoma $45.   **90**
Dark blackish red. Moderately full-bodied. Highly extracted. Quite tannic. Black tea, black fruits, cinnamon, brown spice, plums. Enticing spicy nose. Vigorous and youthful, with ripe extracted flavors on entry turning dry and assertive through the finish.

1994 Cabernet Sauvignon, Estate, Northern Sonoma $54.99.   **93**
Deep ruby hue. Subdued mineral and earth aromas show a slight oak influence. A firm attack leads to a medium-bodied palate with strong tannins and shy acidity. Firm, intense finish. Drink within five years.

1994 Valdigue, Barrelli Creek Vineyard, Alexander Valley $13.   **89**
Deep cherry red. Medium-bodied. Moderately extracted. Mildly tannic. Briar fruit, chocolate. Mature, earthy aromas lead a deeply flavored, fleshy mouthful of mature-tasting fruit with dark chocolatey notes through the finish.

1996 Merlot, Sonoma County $11.   **87**
Deep, saturated purple-red. Subdued overripe red fruit aromas. A firm attack followed by a medium-bodied palate with robust tannins. The finish is lean and flavorful. Overall, on the firm side. Drink now.

1996 Pinot Noir, Russian River Valley $11.99.   **84**

Light ruby red with a slight fade. Moderately full-bodied. Balanced acidity. Moderately extracted. Mildly tannic. Minerals, chocolate. Aromatically reserved, with a weighty impression on the palate. Tasty, but somewhat lacking in finesse.

1995 Zinfandel, Barrelli Creek Vineyard, Alexander Valley $14.   **87**

Opaque blackish cast. Full-bodied. Balanced acidity. Moderately extracted. Moderately oaked. Mildly tannic. Chocolate, black fruits. Quite aromatic, deep, and brooding. Lush, rich, and flavorful on the palate, with a thick, velvety quality. Supple and well balanced through the finish.

1995 Zinfandel, Frei Ranch Vineyard, Dry Creek Valley $14.   **84**

Deep blackish purple. Medium-bodied. Balanced acidity. Moderately extracted. Mildly oaked. Mildly tannic. Black fruits, minerals. Somewhat reserved aromatically, with a lighter-styled, minerally palate feel. Firm and compact through the finish, with solid grip. A lean and elegant style.

Gan Eden

1997 Black Muscat, San Joaquin County $14.   **85**

Pale cherry red. Exotic rose and black cherry aromas spring from the glass. A crisp entry leads a moderately light-bodied palate that has mild sweetness. Snappy and flavorful. Drink now.

1997 Gewürztraminer, Late Harvest, Monterey County $14.   **80**

Geyser Peak

1994 Shiraz-Cabernet, Sparkling, Alexander Valley $19.99.   **84**

Full cherry red. Medium-bodied. Vanilla, plums. Red wine aromas have an oak-aged Shiraz impression that follows through in a lighthearted manner on the palate. For those who like their red wine with bubbles; or possibly the ideal barbecue wine.

1997 Chardonnay, Sonoma County $14.   **82**

1996 Chardonnay, Reserve, Alexander Valley $23.   **90**

Bright yellow-straw hue. Opulent brown spice and tropical fruit aromas show a sweet oak influence. A rich attack leads a full-bodied palate with vibrant acidity. Juicy, intense finish. Drink now.

1997 Sauvignon Blanc, Sonoma County $8.50.   **82**

1996 Cabernet Franc, Winemaker's Selection, Alexander Valley $20.   **83**

Bright ruby purple hue. Subdued mineral and anise aromas. An angular entry leads to a medium-bodied palate with austere, mildly astringent tannins. Firm, flavorful finish. On the tough side. Drink within 5 years.

1994 Cabernet Sauvignon, Reserve, Alexander Valley $28.   **88**

Saturated, deep crimson red. Medium-bodied. Highly extracted. Moderately tannic. Cassis, black fruits, brown spice, tea. Toasty aromas have black fruit accents. Compact on the midpalate, with some angular tannins on the finish. A solid wine with good structure.

1995 Cabernet Sauvignon, Reserve, Alexander Valley $24.99.   **89**

Dark purple. Full-bodied. Balanced acidity. Highly extracted. Heavily oaked. Moderately tannic. Oriental spices, lacquer, minerals. Outrageously aromatic, with a huge oak accent. Firm, concentrated, and tightly wound in the mouth, with a wallop of tannins through the finish. Needs time.

1996 Malbec, Winemaker's Selection, Alexander Valley $20.   **85**

Deep, brilliant purple red hue. Unusual, high-toned anise and mineral aromas. A crisp attack leads to a rich, moderately full-bodied mouthfeel, with zesty acidity. Vibrant, flavorful finish. Well balanced and carries its weight well. Drink within five years.

Scale: Superlative (96-100), Exceptional (90-95), Highly Recommended (85-89), Recommended (80-84), Not Recommended (Under 80)

1994 Reserve Alexandre Meritage, Alexander Valley $28.   88

Full cherry red with a bright cast. Medium-bodied. Moderately extracted. Mildly tannic.
Red berries, cassis, dried herbs, toasted oak. Rounded, soft, and supple on entry, with
bright fruity flavors lingering on the finish. Excellent balance and an appealing juicy
character make for pleasurable early drinking.

1995 Reserve Alexandre Meritage, Alexander Valley $24.99.   88

Deep ruby purple. Moderately full-bodied. Balanced acidity. Highly extracted. Moderately
oaked. Mildly tannic. Vanilla, cassis, licorice. Pleasantly aromatic, with intertwined wood
and fruit flavors. Well balanced and lean through the finish, with crisp acidity.

1996 Reserve Alexandre Meritage, Alexander Valley $32.   84

Bright purple red hue. Forward berry and mineral aromas carry a slight oak accent.
A lighter entry leads to a moderately light-bodied palate with subtle tannins. Shows some
grip to the finish. Almost a quaffer. Lacks intensity or depth. Drink now.

1996 Merlot, Reserve, Alexander Valley $32.   88

Deep, saturated purple-red. Intense anise and vanilla aromas show a dominant oak
accent. A rich entry leads a moderately full-bodied, chunky palate with big drying
tannins. Firm, structured finish. Could use a bit more time to resolve its structure.
Good for long-term cellaring.

1996 Petite Sirah, Winemaker's Selection, Alexander Valley $20.   88

Saturated purple. Moderately full-bodied. Highly extracted. Quite tannic. Significantly
oaky aromas follow through on the palate, with black cherry flavors. Dry, astringent
tannins have a chalky character on the finish.

1996 Petite Verdot, Winemaker's Selection, Alexander Valley $20.   86

Opaque, saturated purple red hue. Subdued anise and mineral aromas carry a big oak
accent. A thick entry leads to a full-bodied palate with big firm tannins. Shows breadth of
flavor before the tannins bite into the finish. Impressively extracted. Drink now or later.

1996 Shiraz, Sonoma County $16.   86

Medium purple color, limpid and brilliant, with a slight fade. Generous, pleasant
aromas of vanilla, black fruits, flowers. Generous wood tones. A firm entry leads a
medium-bodied palate, with crisp acidity. Moderate, drying tannins. Crisp and lean
on the midpalate, with bright fruit. Lingering finish. Drink now.

1996 Shiraz, Reserve, Sonoma County $32.   87

Deep purple, opaque, and brilliant. Generous, pleasant blackberry and mineral flavors.
Generous wood tones. Firm entry. Moderately full-bodied, with crisp acidity and plentiful
grainy tannins. Dry, lean, and angular, though well extracted. Lingering finish. Fine
American oak accents.

1995 Zinfandel, Sonoma County $15.   83

Bright blackish purple. Moderately full-bodied. Full acidity. Moderately extracted.
Mildly oaked. Mildly tannic. Red fruits, minerals. Fruit-centered and relatively high-toned
aromas. Full, but quite lively on the palate, with well-balanced acidity.

1995 Henry's Reserve Shiraz Port, Alexander Valley $15/375 ml.   87

Opaque dark cherry red. Medium-bodied. Moderately extracted. Reminiscent of
blackberries, plums, black tea. Rich, plummy black fruit aromas open up on the
midpalate. Finishes with a dry, solid layer of tannins that suggest this will soften with
some age. Good balance.

Girard

1994 Cabernet Sauvignon, Napa Valley $25.   90

Dark crimson center with purple highlights. Moderately full-bodied. Moderately
extracted. Moderately tannic. Cassis, cedar. Toasty oak nose shows black fruit accents.
Pure, focused black Cabernet fruit is supple and generous, with textured, rounded
tannins on a very persistent fruity finish.

1995 Cabernet Sauvignon, Napa Valley $28. **92**

Bright ruby purple. Moderately full-bodied. Balanced acidity. Moderately extracted. Moderately oaked. Mildly tannic. Licorice, mint. Unusual, high-toned aromatics are stylish and complex. Lean and angular in the mouth, with a focused and well-defined personality. Crisp, lengthy finish.

1994 Cabernet Sauvignon, Reserve, Napa Valley $40. **91**

Full purple-red. Medium-bodied. Highly extracted. Moderately tannic. Cassis, toasted oak. The tight, focused fruity nose shows generous oaky accents. Great concentration and fine-toasted character, with good tannic grip through the finish. Youthful and vigorous, this will need time to show its best.

Glen Ellen

1995 Viognier, Expressions, San Benito County $11/375 ml. **87**

Bright golden cast. Full-bodied. Balanced acidity. Moderately extracted. Mildly oaked. Cinnamon, orange peel, pine. Outrageously aromatic, with a huge and complex bouquet. The exotic flavors are well translated onto a rich and supple palate. Good grip and fine length.

1996 Cabernet Sauvignon, Proprietor's Reserve, California $6. **81**

1997 Gamay Beaujolais, Proprietor's Reserve, California $5. **81**

Grand Cru

1996 Gewürztraminer, California $7.99. **80**

1996 Johannisberg Riesling, California $7.99. **83**

Gold-straw hue. Aromatically intense, with petrol and mineral accents. Concentrated flavors on the attack, leading a moderately full-bodied palate, with sweetness up front giving way to leaner, dryer flavors on the finish. Rather unusual. Drink now.

1995 Sauvignon Blanc, California $7.99. **83**

Brilliant pale yellow-gold. Medium-bodied. Balanced acidity. Moderately extracted. Heavily oaked. Vanilla, smoke, ripe citrus. Assertive French oak aromas. A heavy smoky note pervades the palate and lingers through the finish. Solid weight and mouthfeel. Some will like the oak dominance and others will hate it.

1996 Cabernet Sauvignon, Premium Selection, California $7.99. **83**

Bright cherry red hue. Aromas show toasted oak, vanilla, and black fruits. A light, fruity attack leads to a medium-bodied palate with smooth tannins and a lively finish. Drink now.

1997 Merlot, California $7.99. **86**

Violet purple with a bright cast. Bright fruity aromas have cherry and vanilla accents. Medium-bodied, flavorful, and fruity on the attack, showing fine grip and grainy tannins through the finish. Drink now or later. Can improve with more age.

1995 Pinot Noir, Premium Selection, California $7.99. **80**

1997 Syrah, California $7.99. **83**

Medium crimson purple, limpid and brilliant, with a slight fade. Subtle, sound cherry, berry fruit, and vanilla flavors. Subtle wood tones. Smooth entry. Medium-bodied. Moderate, velvety tannins. Lingering rich finish. Peppery, jammy, youthful, and supple. Drink now.

1996 Zinfandel, Premium Selection, California $7.99. **84**

Deep blackish purple. Medium-bodied. Balanced acidity. Moderately extracted. Heavily oaked. Moderately tannic. Vanilla, black fruits. Hefty oak notes dominate the nose and join ripe berry flavors on the palate. Lighter in style and relatively soft, with a pleasant, lingering finish.

Scale: Superlative (96-100), Exceptional (90-95), Highly Recommended (85-89), Recommended (80-84), Not Recommended (Under 80)

100

Granite Springs

1995 Zinfandel, El Dorado $11.50.   86

Bright blackish ruby cast. Moderately full-bodied. Balanced acidity. Moderately extracted. Moderately oaked. Mildly tannic. Chocolate, black fruits. Quite aromatic, with a firm and flavorful mouthfeel. Well balanced and deep through the finish.

Green & Red

1996 Zinfandel, Chiles Valley Vineyards, Napa Valley $18.   84

Bright blackish ruby cast. Medium-bodied. Balanced acidity. Subtly extracted. Mildly tannic. Red fruits, minerals. Rather reserved aromatically, with a lighter-styled, lean palate feel. Focused and angular through the finish.

Grey Wolf

1995 Cabernet Sauvignon, Paso Robles $20.   83

Deep ruby cast. Moderately full-bodied. Balanced acidity. Moderately extracted. Moderately oaked. Mildly tannic. Brown spices, red fruits, minerals. Shows a spicy oak accent throughout. Lean and firm in the mouth. Acidity makes for a bright, juicy finish.

1994 Barton Family Reserve Meritage, Paso Robles $19.   87

Deep crimson red. Moderately full-bodied. Highly extracted. Moderately tannic. Cassis, licorice, mint. Solid, structured style. Features a full-flavored, viscous mouthful of dark fruit flavors that linger through the finish. Impressively proportioned wine in a classic style. A heavyweight.

1995 Barton Family Reserve Meritage, Paso Robles $22.   89

Dark violet red with a subtle fade. Medium-bodied. Moderately extracted. Moderately tannic. Tobacco, earth, black fruits. Ripe dark fruit aromas with earthy overtones. Weighty and flavorsome, though open-knit in structure. Earthy tannins on the finish ride lightly on the palate. Best consumed when still relatively young.

1995 Merlot, Reserve, Paso Robles $17.   83

Deep ruby purple. Medium-bodied. Balanced acidity. Moderately extracted. Mildly oaked. Mildly tannic. Earth, licorice, black pepper. Slightly funky aromatics, with a lighter-styled, crisp palate. Finishes with some wood notes and mild astringency.

Grgich Hills

1997 Chardonnay, Napa Valley $30.   88

Bright golden yellow. Moderately aromatic with subtle butter, vanilla, and ripe fruits. A juicy entry leads a moderately full-bodied palate with ripe, generous citrus flavors and a subtle oak impression on the finish. Drink now.

1996 Fumé Blanc, Napa Valley $18.   87

Deep straw cast. Moderately full-bodied. Full acidity. Highly extracted. Citrus, minerals. Aromatic, with a firm and angular though flavorful mouthfeel. Crisp through the finish with a hint of bitterness.

1994 Cabernet Sauvignon, Napa Valley $30.   91

Saturated, deep reddish purple. Medium-bodied. Highly extracted. Moderately tannic. Cassis, black fruits, minerals. Very aromatic nose. The compact palate has a crisp edge. Solid dry tannins are accentuated by fine acids. Very well structured and lively, though not yet showing its best.

1995 Cabernet Sauvignon, Napa Valley $45.   93

Bright ruby red hue. Generous red fruit and vanilla aromas carry a sweet oak accent. A crisp entry leads to a medium-bodied palate buoyed by juicy acidity. Flavorful, vibrant finish. Stylish and well balanced with particularly admirable acidity. Drink now or later.

1994 Cabernet Sauvignon, Yountville Selection, Napa Valley $85.   **93**

Bright purple-red hue. Intense and exotic spice, floral, and anise aromas. A lean entry leads to a medium-bodied palate with grippy tannins. Shows admirable restraint and finesse in these days of high alcohol show monsters. Lively, buoyant finish. Well balanced and showing excellent grip and intensity through the finish. Drink now or later.

1995 Zinfandel, Sonoma County $18.   **88**

Dark ruby purple. Moderately full-bodied. Balanced acidity. Moderately extracted. Mildly oaked. Mildly tannic. Chocolate, black fruits. Reserved in style, with a firm, focused mouthfeel. Rich nonetheless, with deep fruit and mineral flavors. More of a Claret style.

1995 Violetta, Late Harvest, Napa Valley $40/375 ml.   **90**

Deep tawny amber hue. Exotic toffee and caramel aromas show a touch of rancio. A lush entry leads a medium-bodied palate with lean acids and mild sweetness. Well balanced, with complex, Sherried flavors. Drink now.

Groth

1995 Cabernet Sauvignon, Napa Valley $30.   **89**

Deep ruby cast. Medium-bodied. Balanced acidity. Moderately extracted. Mildly oaked. Mildly tannic. Minerals, red fruits. Elegant and reserved, with firm and focused flavors. Crisp and lean through the angular finish.

Guenoc

1997 Chardonnay, North Coast $15.50.   **84**

Pale straw cast. Medium-bodied. Full acidity. Moderately extracted. Minerals, citrus zest, dried herbs. Lean and angular, with an herbal cast. Firm and zesty through the finish.

1996 Chardonnay, Reserve, Genevive Magoon Vineyard, Guenoc Valley $25.   **90**

Full yellow-straw hue. Moderately full-bodied. Balanced acidity. Highly extracted. Moderately oaked. Yeast, smoke, ripe citrus. Smoky aromas follow though on a structured, firm palate, with nutty depth and a spicy finish. Still youthful and tight, this should improve.

1997 Chardonnay, Reserve, Genevive Magoon Vineyard, Guenoc Valley $25.   **89**

Pale yellow-straw color. Moderately full-bodied. Balanced acidity. Highly extracted. Vanilla, smoke, green apples. A tart and vibrant core of crisp fruit and a good dollop of oak spice through the finish give this a lingering complexity.

1996 Chardonnay, "Unfiltered" Reserve, Genevive Magoon Vineyard, Guenoc Valley $30.   **91**

Yellow-straw hue. Moderately full-bodied. Full acidity. Moderately extracted. Mildly oaked. Citrus, vanilla, spice. Perfumed vanilla and spice aromas. Vibrant and angular on the palate, with racy citric acids and oak spice vying for attention through the finish.

1997 Chardonnay, "Unfiltered" Reserve, Genevive Magoon Vineyard, Guenoc Valley $30.   **92**

Bright yellow-straw color. Medium-bodied. Full acidity. Moderately extracted. Moderately oaked. Vanilla, yeast, apples. Attractive yeasty aromas. Vibrant and racy, with crisp flavors complemented by smoke and vanilla notes that emerge on the finish along with notable yeast complexity.

1996 Sauvignon Blanc, North Coast $13.50.   **84**

Pale straw cast. Medium-bodied. Balanced acidity. Moderately extracted. Mildly oaked. Smoke, citrus zest. Smoky tropical aromas lead a rounded fruit-centered palate. Not weighty, but delightful in flavor intensity and purity.

1996 Cabernet Sauvignon, California $12.   **84**

Bright cherry red. Medium-bodied. Moderately extracted. Mildly tannic. Red fruits, vanilla, minerals. Plush fruit-centered aromas follow through on the palate, with a brief, dry finish.

Scale: Superlative (96-100), Exceptional (90-95), Highly Recommended (85-89), Recommended (80-84), Not Recommended (Under 80)

102

1995 Cabernet Sauvignon, North Coast $15.50. **84**

Dark, saturated ruby hue. Medium-bodied. Full acidity. Moderately extracted. Mildly tannic. Minerals, red fruits. Firm and minerally, with a zesty palate feel. Vibrant, mouthwatering acidity makes for a bright if slightly austere finish.

1994 Cabernet Sauvignon, Beckstoffer IV Reserve, Napa Valley $40.50. **88**

Bright purple. Moderately full-bodied. Full acidity. Moderately extracted. Moderately oaked. Mildly tannic. Vanilla, black fruits, minerals. Aromatic and intense, with a bright, fruit-centered quality. Crisp and lean through the juicy finish.

1995 Cabernet Sauvignon, Beckstoffer IV Reserve, Napa Valley $40.50. **86**

Bright purple. Moderately full-bodied. Full acidity. Moderately extracted. Mildly oaked. Mildly tannic. Licorice, red fruits, minerals. Bright, zesty, angular, and crisp, in a high-toned, fruit-accented style. The finish is lean and flavorful.

1994 Cabernet Sauvignon, Bella Vista Reserve, Napa Valley $30.50. **85**

Deep ruby purple. Moderately full-bodied. Highly extracted. Moderately tannic. Beets, minerals. Earthy, austere aromas. Fleshy dark fruit flavors are overtaken by lean, slightly bitter notes on the finish.

1995 Cabernet Sauvignon, Bella Vista Reserve, Napa Valley $30.50. **89**

Dark ruby-brick red. Medium-bodied. Highly extracted. Heavily oaked. Moderately tannic. Vanilla, chocolate, berry fruits. Strong oak accents on the nose. Deep and voluptuous dark fruit flavors, with a full complement of earthy, chocolatey notes persisting through the finish. Very supple up front, though oak tannins dry the finish.

1995 Meritage, California $18.50. **86**

Bright violet-red. Medium-bodied. Moderately extracted. Moderately tannic. Brown spice, red cherries, minerals. Dusty, oak-spiced aromas follow through on a crisp, minerally palate, with dry, minerally tannins highlighted by the vibrant acids. Firm and dry.

1995 Petite Sirah, California $15.50. **84**

Dark purple. Moderately full-bodied. Highly extracted. Moderately tannic. Succulent dark cherry fruit aromas. Well gripped and solidly extracted, with dry tannins on the finish.

1996 Zinfandel, California $11. **86**

Deep blackish purple. Medium-bodied. Full acidity. Highly extracted. Moderately tannic. Black fruits, minerals. Rather unyielding aromatically, with a firm, highly structured, intense palate feel. Features a core of brooding black fruit flavors, and finishes with solid tannins.

1994 Vintage Port, California $25. **87**

Dark cherry red with a ruby cast. Medium-bodied. Balanced acidity. Moderately extracted. Moderately oaked. Moderately tannic. Reminiscent of tobacco, lacquer, brown spice, baked raspberry tart. Compact texture. A brawny style, with youthful tannins up front. Sweet berry notes are nicely accented by soft, plush earthy components. A polished style, if a bit coarse at the present. Should cellar well.

Guglielmo

1997 Chardonnay, Vineyard Selection Series, Monterey County $9.95. **81**

1997 Chardonnay, Private Reserve, Monterey County $14. **86**

Emphatic deep gold. Butter and oak-spiced aromas show a subdued fruity character. A lean entry leads a moderately full-bodied palate with lush buttery qualities. Fruit flavors are faint through the finish. Drink now.

Gundlach Bundschu

1997 Chardonnay, Rhinefarm Vineyards, Sonoma Valley $16. **83**

Bright straw hue. Lean minerally aromas. A crisp entry leads a moderately light-bodied palate with racy acidity. Shows little if any oak influence. Clean, tart finish. Drink now.

1997 Chardonnay, Sangiacomo Ranch, Sonoma Valley $18. **80**

1997 Gewürztraminer, Rhinefarm Vineyards, Sonoma Valley $12. **81**
1996 Cabernet Sauvignon, Rhinefarm Vineyards, Sonoma Valley $24. **87**

Deep purple red hue. Intense and unusual floral, anise, and mineral aromas. A supple entry leads to a ripe and rounded moderately full-bodied palate. Rich, herb-tinged finish shows complexity. A well-balanced, well-structured style. Drink now or later.

1996 Merlot, Rhinefarm Vineyards, Sonoma Valley $21. **89**

Deep ruby-violet red. Generous, spicy oak-accented aromas show dill and cedar notes. A rich attack is followed by a moderately full-bodied palate with chewy tannins and softer acids. Drink now or later. Can improve with more age.

Hacienda

1997 Chardonnay, Clair de Lune, California $6.99. **82**
1996 Cabernet Sauvignon, Clair de Lune, California $6.99. **86**

Bright cherry red hue. Attractive cedar, vanilla, and cassis aromas. A rich entry leads to a moderately full-bodied palate with lush, velvety tannins and generous cassis fruit flavors. Drink now.

1997 Merlot, Clair de Lune, California $6.99. **84**

Deep, dark violet hue. Brambly, ripe fleshy aromas. Medium-bodied, with bright blackberry and cherry flavors up front, and subtle velvety tannins and obvious vanilla oak flavors lingering on the finish. Drink now.

1996 Pinot Noir, Clair de Lune, California $6.99. **86**

Pale violet red. Moderately light-bodied. Moderately extracted. Mildly tannic. Vanilla, red berries. Perfumed, sweetish aromas lead a bright and fruity palate with lively acids providing solid grip.

1996 Shiraz, Clair de Lune, California $6.99. **84**

Medium cherry red, limpid and brilliant to the rim. Generous, sound cedar and cherry flavors. Generous wood tones. Smooth entry. Medium-bodied. Moderate velvety tannins. Oak dominated, with brown spice notes. Subtle finish. Drink now.

Hagafen

1997 Chardonnay, Napa Valley $13.50. **83**

Pale straw cast. Moderately full-bodied. Full acidity. Moderately extracted. Citrus, minerals. Aromatically reserved, with lean, crisp, focused flavors. Ripe and zesty through the finish.

1997 Chardonnay, Reserve, Napa Valley $18. **87**

Bright straw cast. Moderately full-bodied. Balanced acidity. Moderately extracted. Mildly oaked. Spice, melon, minerals. Forward aromas carry a spicy oak overlay. Bright and crisp in the mouth, with an angular, zesty finish.

1998 Johannisberg Riesling, Napa Valley $12. **86**

Pale straw hue. A lean attack leads a medium-bodied palate with stone fruit flavors and subtle herbal notes through the finish. Mildly off-dry style. Drink now.

1996 Cabernet Franc, Napa Valley $18. **87**

Bright ruby cast. Medium-bodied. Balanced acidity. Moderately extracted. Moderately oaked. Moderately tannic. Red fruits, vanilla. Aromatic and deeply flavored, with a core of ripe fruit flavors and a generous oak accent. Firm and intense in the mouth, with a lengthy finish. Approachable, but should continue to improve.

1995 Cabernet Sauvignon, Napa Valley $20. **85**

Opaque, deep purple-red. Medium-bodied. Highly extracted. Moderately tannic. Black fruit, plums, brown spice. Violets and spice in the nose follow through on the palate. Concentrated flavors, with a tart edge and plenty of soft tannins that give texture. A bit young and aggressive.

1996 Cabernet Sauvignon, Napa Valley $24.   80
1996 Pinot Noir, Napa Valley $13.   86
Strawberry red. Moderately light-bodied. Moderately extracted. Moderately oaked.
Mildly tannic. Vanilla and strawberry aromas are well conveyed on the palate. Crisp
and juicy through the finish. Well balanced, very drinkable.

Hahn Estates
1997 Chardonnay, Monterey $11.   83
Deep straw cast. Moderately full-bodied. Balanced acidity. Moderately extracted. Mildly
oaked. Lychee, spice, butter. Generous flavors carry an aromatic varietal overtone. Ripe
and rounded, with a buttery note to the finish.
1996 Cabernet Franc, Santa Lucia Highlands $10.   83
Bright ruby cast. Moderately light-bodied. Balanced acidity. Subtly extracted. Mildly
tannic. Vegetables, minerals. Shows a green streak throughout. Light though firmly
structured in the mouth, with a lean finish.
1996 Red Meritage, Santa Lucia Highlands $15.   87
Saturated dark ruby red hue. Very ripe fruit with an herbal streak. A tart entry leads a
moderately full-bodied palate with bright fruit flavors and racy tart acids that give this
great cut through the finish. Finishes very cleanly. Drink now.

Hallcrest
1991 Cabernet Sauvignon, Covington Vineyards,
El Dorado County $22.50.   85
Dark blackish red. Medium-bodied. Moderately extracted. Moderately tannic. Plums,
black tea, earth. Leafy, earthy aromas are confirmed on the palate. Bright acids keep
this lively and accentuate the tough tannins that make for an assertive finish.

Handley
1993 Brut, Anderson Valley $22.   84
Bright yellow-gold. Medium-bodied. Full acidity. Baked bread, ripe citrus. Bright, lively,
and clean, with a high-toned, fruity accent. Flavors show impressive concentration
through the finish.
1997 Chardonnay, Anderson Valley $18.   81
1997 Chardonnay, Dry Creek Valley $18.   83
Medium gold. Moderate aromas show alcohol. A bright, tart entry is followed by a
medium-bodied palate that has straightforward tart fruit flavors that finish quickly, with
mild oak influences. Drink now.
1997 Pinot Gris, Anderson Valley $18.   83
Bright platinum cast. Medium-bodied. Full acidity. Moderately extracted. Smoke,
minerals. Reserved aromatically, with a lean, racy, vibrant palate feel. Finishes with
a telltale smoky richness.

Hanna
1996 Chardonnay, Russian River Valley $16.   83
Brilliant yellow-gold. Moderately full-bodied. Balanced acidity. Moderately extracted.
Mildly oaked. Honey, apples, spice. Curiously honeyed, rich aromas lead a juicy, fruity
mouthful of flavors with a clean, mouthwatering finish. Rather distinctive.
1995 Cabernet Sauvignon, Alexander Valley $20.   90
Bright ruby purple. Medium-bodied. Balanced acidity. Moderately extracted. Moderately
oaked. Mildly tannic. Black fruits, brown spices, minerals. Generous aromatics lead a
lean and pure mouthfeel, with precise fruit flavors. Crisp and angular, with excellent
definition to the lengthy finish.

1995 Merlot, Alexander Valley $21.   89

Deep ruby with a slight purplish cast. Medium-bodied. Balanced acidity. Moderately extracted. Mildly oaked. Mildly tannic. Plums, minerals, sweet herbs. Still a little reined in aromatically, with a youthful, compact palate. Fruit driven and very dense in flavor through the finish. Has some chunky tannins that should be mitigated with mid-term (3–6 years) cellaring.

Harmony

1997 Chardonnay, San Luis Obispo County $14.50.   85

Deep yellow-straw hue. Opulent vanilla, citrus, and cream aromas show a hefty oak accent. A firm entry leads a moderately full-bodied palate with rounded acidity. Extremely lengthy buttery finish. Rather wood dominated, but hedonistically interesting.

1997 Johannisberg Riesling, Paso Robles $9.   84

Medium gold hue. Classical aromas of petrol and green apples. A bright attack leads a medium-bodied palate, with rich flavors and an oily note through the finish. Fine, pure Riesling character. Drink now.

Harrison

1994 Cabernet Sauvignon, Napa Valley $33.   89

Dark crimson with subtle purple highlights. Medium-bodied. Moderately extracted. Mildly tannic. Cassis, plums, cedar. Rich, ripe Cabernet aromas. Smooth and velvety, with textured black fruit flavors and supple tannins on the finish. Quite a polished style that is very accessible for current drinking.

Hartford Court

1996 Chardonnay, Seascape Vineyard, Sonoma Coast $35.   89

Deep golden cast. Full-bodied. Balanced acidity. Highly extracted. Moderately oaked. Brown spices, tropical fruits, yeast. Generous aromatics lead a rich mouthfeel buttressed by firm acidity. Ripe and intense yet well balanced, with complex flavors.

1995 Pinot Noir, Dutton Ranch-Sanchietti Vineyard, Russian River Valley $29.   84

Medium reddish purple. Medium-bodied. Moderately extracted. Moderately oaked. Moderately tannic. An oak-dominated nose leads a mild black cherry and pepper palate, with bitter notes on the finish.

1995 Pinot Noir, Arrendell Vineyard, Russian River Valley $34.   87

Dark reddish purple. Medium-bodied. Highly extracted. Moderately oaked. Moderately tannic. Generous black cherry and raspberry aromas have a chocolate richness through the finish. Plenty of stuffing, but also lots of toasted oak through the finish.

1996 Pinot Noir, Arrendell Vineyard, Russian River Valley $42.   88

Bright saturated ruby purple. Moderately full-bodied. Balanced acidity. Highly extracted. Mildly oaked. Moderately tannic. Minerals, chocolate, black fruits. Bright aromas lead a weighty and intense mouthfeel. Competent, but seems to lack that extra dimension and ends up seeming a tad hollow.

Hartwell

1997 Chardonnay, Stags Leap District, Napa Valley $39.99.   84

Bright yellow-gold. Moderate aromas of citrus zest and oak spice. A crisp entry leads a medium-bodied palate with bright citrus flavors. Finishes with a note of dryness and oak spice. Well balanced, with bright acids. Drink now.

1994 Cabernet Sauvignon, Sunshine Vineyard, Stags Leap District $45. 85

Garnet-brick red. Medium-bodied. Moderately extracted. Mildly tannic. Earth, black fruit, currant. Minty accents on the nose. An austere, earthy palate has toasty, spicy flavors lingering on the finish. Nice now, this does not need further cellaring.

1995 Cabernet Sauvignon, Sunshine Vineyard, Stags Leap District $80.   **94**

Opaque blood red. Moderately full-bodied. Highly extracted. Quite tannic. Cassis, licorice, earth. Deep, fleshy aromas have an earthy accent that follows on a rich, spicy mouthful of flavors, concluding firmly with assertive tannins.

Havens

1994 Bourriquot, Napa Valley $28.   **88**

Deep reddish purple. Medium-bodied. Highly extracted. Moderately tannic. Plums, black fruits, bitter chocolate, brown spice. Full, assertive, and rich, with deep savory flavors that linger through a chalky, bitter-chocolate finish. Approachable now, though this should be better in a few years.

1996 Merlot, Napa Valley $20.   **84**

Bright ruby hue with a subtle fade. Clean cherry fruit and vanilla aromas. Soft on the attack, with a medium-bodied palate and ripe berry flavors that finish with soft tannins. Drink now.

Hawk Crest

1997 Chardonnay, California $10.   **81**
1996 Sauvignon Blanc, Stag's Leap Wine Cellars, California $8.   **82**
1996 Cabernet Sauvignon, California $12.   **81**

Haywood

1997 Chardonnay, Vintner's Select, California $7.99.   **81**
1996 Cabernet Sauvignon, California $8.50.   **81**
1997 Merlot, California $7.99.   **86**

Bright violet-ruby red. Perfumed, fruity aromas have a berry fruit quality. Medium-bodied, lush on the attack with velvety tannins and juicy berry fruit flavors. Finishes with soft, lush tannins. Well stuffed and flavorsome. Drink now.

1995 Zinfandel, Los Chamizal Vineyard, Sonoma Valley $18.   **84**

Dark ruby purple. Moderately full-bodied. Balanced acidity. Moderately extracted. Mildly tannic. Black fruits. Pleasantly aromatic, with a ripe, luxuriant array of fruit-centered flavors on the palate. Lush in texture and well balanced, with a focused finish.

1995 Zinfandel, Rocky Terrace, Los Chamizal Vineyard, Sonoma Valley $25.   **87**

Dark ruby purple to the rim. Moderately full-bodied. Balanced acidity. Moderately extracted. Moderately oaked. Mildly tannic. Brown spices, black fruits, chocolate. Quite aromatic, with a hefty oak accent and a flavorful palate feel. Lush and deep in the mouth, with a velvety quality. Finishes with some mild, dusty tannins.

Heartswood

1995 Chardonnay, Private Reserve, Monterey $9.99.   **86**

Deep yellow-straw cast. Moderately full-bodied. Balanced acidity. Moderately extracted. Flowers, spice. Forward, generous aromas show an opulent spicy accent. Lush, generous, and rounded in the mouth, with a note of viscosity.

Heiss

1997 Chardonnay, Santa Clara Valley $25.   **88**

Pale yellow-green. Medium-bodied. Full acidity. Moderately extracted. Moderately oaked. Lemon, minerals. Clean, bright primary fruit flavors with a considerable overlay of spicy, nutty oak accents that make for a complex finish.

Heitz

1997 Chardonnay, Cellar Selection, Napa Valley $18. 84
Medium yellow-gold. Melon and pear aromas have a buttery accent. A thick entry leads a full-bodied palate with a heavy malolactic character. Finishes in a thick alcoholic manner. Very generous.

1992 Cabernet Sauvignon, Napa Valley $20. 89
Bright brick red. Medium-bodied. Moderately extracted. Mildly tannic. Cassis, mineral, mint, dried herbs. Subtle herbal, minty aromas lead a solid, full-flavored palate, with a firm minerally backbone and a hint of firm tannins on the finish. Plenty of character.

1993 Cabernet Sauvignon, Napa Valley $21. 86
Deep ruby-garnet cast. Moderately full-bodied. Balanced acidity. Moderately extracted. Mildly oaked. Moderately tannic. Mint, earth, chocolate. Forward aromas have a high-toned accent and a deep, earthy quality. Rich in the mouth, with an angular, structured finish.

1994 Cabernet Sauvignon, Napa Valley $25. 86
Dark ruby hue. Plummy, very ripe aromas. A heavy entry leads a full-bodied palate with a thick mouthfeel and low acidity. Big shouldered and chocolatey with very tough tannins that dry the finish. This will need much more time. Drink now or later.

1993 Cabernet Sauvignon, Bella Oaks Vineyard, Napa Valley $28. 86
Deep ruby cast. Moderately full-bodied. Balanced acidity. Moderately extracted. Mildly tannic. Red fruits, mint, minerals. Light in style, with a pure, focused palate feel. Crisp and intense through the flavorful finish.

1994 Cabernet Sauvignon, Bella Oaks Vineyard, Napa Valley $35. 83
Fading ruby with a garnet rim. Weak, mildly herbal aromas seem rather tired. A weak entry leads a medium-bodied palate with dilute flavors and a dull woody finish. Not showing much concentration or the ability to age any further. Drink now.

1992 Cabernet Sauvignon, Martha's Vineyard, Napa Valley $68. 93
Dark blood red. Medium-bodied. Moderately extracted. Moderately tannic. Cassis, plums, mint, minerals, tea. A ripe, somewhat earthy nose shows minty accents. Very attractive bright black fruit flavors have a solid underlying minerally base, with astringent tannins keeping the finish dry. Very impressive now, though this can only improve.

1992 Cabernet Sauvignon, Trailside Vineyard, Napa Valley $48. 87
Bright blood red. Medium-bodied. Highly extracted. Moderately tannic. Cassis, mint, minerals. A very particularly eucalyptus nose. Rich, supple Cabernet fruit flavors unfold on the palate, with dusty tannins lingering on the minty finish.

1993 Cabernet Sauvignon, Trailside Vineyard, Napa Valley $48. 91
Deep ruby hue with a slight purple edge. Moderately full-bodied. Balanced acidity. Moderately extracted. Mildly oaked. Mildly tannic. Licorice, mint, minerals. Aromatic and complex, with an emphasis on pure fruit flavors showing terroir, not winemaking. Supple and gentle in the mouth, with fine intensity through the finish.

1996 Grignlino Port, Napa Valley $18. 83
Deep blackish purple. Medium-bodied. Low acidity. Moderately extracted. Black fruits, licorice. Pleasantly aromatic and solidly fruit centered, with a touch of heat. Ripe, flavorful, and straightforward on the palate, with a decidedly sweet finish.

Helena View

1995 Cabernet Franc, Johnston Vineyards, Napa Valley $30. 84
Bright ruby-garnet cast. Medium-bodied. Balanced acidity. Moderately extracted. Heavily oaked. Mildly tannic. Spice, cherries. Quite aromatic, with oak-driven flavors throughout. Light in the mouth, with a lean, angular finish.

1992 Cabernet Sauvignon, Napa Valley $20.   90
Full brick red. Medium-bodied. Moderately extracted. Mildly tannic. Vanilla, toasted oak. Minty, mature nose is well expressed on the palate. Very toasty through the finish. Oaky style with astringency running through the finish. Drinking very well now.

1994 Cabernet Sauvignon, Napa Valley $32.50.   86
Pale cherry red. Medium-bodied. Moderately extracted. Mildly tannic. Oak spice, red fruits. Supple and juicy, in a very straightforward, early-drinking manner. Harmonious, if lighter in style.

1995 Cabernet Sauvignon, Napa Valley $32.50.   84
Pale cherry red. Medium-bodied. Moderately extracted. Mildly tannic. Dill, red fruits. An aromatic, oaky nose follows through on a lightweight palate with straightforward berry flavors. Nicely balanced, drinking well now.

1995 Cabernet Sauvignon, Tradition, Napa Valley $38.   85
Mature pale garnet red. Medium-bodied. Moderately extracted. Mildly tannic. Leather, spice, black fruits. Showing perfumed, mature character on the palate, with light, leathery flavors and a touch of tannic bite. Not for further keeping.

Hendry

1993 Cabernet Sauvignon, Block 8, Napa Valley $22.   93
Opaque blackish red. Medium-bodied. Highly extracted. Moderately tannic. Sweet herbs, black cherries, mint, brown spice. Exotic, fresh herbal aromas. Rich and concentrated black fruit flavors on the palate have a minty accent that lingers through a solid finish. Very attractive now, though it has sound structure for cellaring.

1995 Cabernet Sauvignon, Block 8, Napa Valley $24.   90
Bright ruby cast. Medium-bodied. Balanced acidity. Moderately extracted. Mildly oaked. Mildly tannic. Mint, red fruits. Forward, distinctive aromatics feature a decidedly minty accent. Lighter in style, with a supple quality and a juicy, flavorful finish.

1995 Zinfandel, Block 7, Napa Valley $18.   89
Deep ruby cast. Medium-bodied. Balanced acidity. Moderately extracted. Moderately oaked. Mildly tannic. Brown spices, mint, red fruits. Shows a flashy, spicy oak accent to the nose, with a core of bright fruit flavors in the mouth. Well balanced and lively, with an uplifting, lengthy finish.

Herzog

1997 Chardonnay, Baron Herzog, California $12.95.   88
Brilliant yellow-straw hue. Generous brown spice and pear aromas show a hefty oak accent. A rich entry leads a moderately full-bodied palate with rounded acidity. The finish is ripe and stylish. Drink now.

1996 Chardonnay, Special Reserve, Russian River Valley $19.99. 86
Bright pale gold. Medium-bodied. Balanced acidity. Moderately extracted. Brown spice, citrus, butter. Smoky, zesty aromas lead a smooth, spicy mouthful of flavors with a rounded texture through the finish.

1998 White Zinfandel, Baron Herzog, California $6.95.   80

1995 Cabernet Sauvignon, Baron Herzog, California $13.99.   86
Bright crimson red with a purple rim. Medium-bodied. Moderately extracted. Mildly tannic. Cassis, black fruits, currant, oak spice. Soft, rounded berry fruit flavors unfold on the palate. A ripe, fruity style with nice oak spice on the finish.

1996 Cabernet Sauvignon, Baron Herzog, California $13.99.   86
Bright cherry red. Medium-bodied. Moderately extracted. Mildly tannic. Vanilla, cassis. Clean, fruity accents follow through on the palate, with a supple character and a mild note of minerally astringency through the finish.

1994 Cabernet Sauvignon, Special Reserve, Alexander Valley $26.69. 91
Dark crimson with subtle purple highlights. Medium-bodied. Highly extracted. Mildly tannic. Vanilla, tobacco, black fruits. Sweet, ripe fruity aromas. Rich, flavor-packed palate has ripe chocolatey accents and a lingering toasty finish. Very attractive and forward.

1995 Cabernet Sauvignon, Special Reserve, Alexander Valley $25.99.　　　91
Very deep ruby hue. Moderately full-bodied. Balanced acidity. Moderately extracted. Moderately oaked. Mildly tannic. Vanilla, spice, black fruits. A toasty nose melds seamlessly with a firm core of fruit flavors on the palate. Balance and elegance are key, with a focused and well-structured though supple finish. Fine length and intensity.

1997 Gamay, Baron Herzog, Paso Robles $7.95.　　　83
Pinkish red. Moderately light-bodied. Subtly extracted. Mildly tannic. Herbs, flowers, citrus. Crisp herbaceous aromas lead a taut, vibrant palate with a cleansing finish.

1996 Zinfandel, Baron Herzog, California $12.99.　　　86
Bright ruby purple. Medium-bodied. Full acidity. Moderately extracted. Moderately oaked. Mildly tannic. Vanilla, briar fruits. Toasty oak nuances emerge on the nose and join a wave of bright, fruit-centered flavors in the mouth. Lighter in style, with a sense of liveliness brought forth by buoyant acidity.

Hess Collection
1996 Chardonnay, Napa Valley $15.　　　89
Bright yellow-gold. Medium-bodied. Balanced acidity. Moderately extracted. Mildly oaked. Yeast, citrus. Smooth, rounded mouthfeel has a ripe core of fruit flavors with restrained oak spice not overwhelming the ensemble. Very appealing and direct, with a nice mouthfeel.

1993 Cabernet Sauvignon, Mount Veeder, Napa Valley $20.　　　94
Bright dark red. Medium-bodied. Highly extracted. Moderately tannic. Vanilla, toasted oak, cassis, plums. Delicious toasty oak aromas lead an elegantly fruity palate, with juicy ripe accents and firm oak spice flavors on the finish. A little too vigorous now, it should settle with a few years aging.

1994 Cabernet Sauvignon, Mount Veeder, Napa Valley $19.75.　　　91
Deep ruby purple. Moderately full-bodied. Balanced acidity. Moderately extracted. Moderately oaked. Moderately tannic. Vanilla, red fruits, minerals. Forward, fruit-centered flavors feature a spicy oak accent. Rich and firm in the mouth, with abundant ripe tannins. Lengthy finish.

1995 Cabernet Sauvignon, Mount Veeder, Napa Valley $24.75.　　　92
Deep, saturated ruby red hue. Powerful briar, brown spice, and mineral aromas. A lush entry leads to a moderately full-bodied palate with complex gamey flavors and velvety tannins. Generous and supple finish with fine length. Approachable, but has the extract to age. Drink now or later.

1995 Merlot, Mount Veeder, Napa Valley $22.50.　　　84
Bright ruby red. Generous mocha and plum aromas have an oaky accent. Full-bodied, with a firm attack and solidly structured palate firmly gripped by tannins and showing complex, evolved flavors. Judiciously oaked. Drink now or later. Can improve with more age.

Hidden Cellars
1996 Chauche Gris, Mendocino $11.　　　84
Bright golden hue. Full-bodied. Balanced acidity. Moderately extracted. Cream, oranges. Rather reserved aromatically, but quite full and rich on the palate, with a mouthfilling character. Snappy acidity lends a sense of balance to the finish. A big wine for rich food, and consumption over the near term.

1996 Sauvignon Blanc, Mendocino $13.　　　84
Bright golden yellow. Medium-bodied. Balanced acidity. Moderately extracted. Mildly oaked. Butter, yeast, brown spice. Soft, vanilla-accented aromas lead a textured mouthfeel, with buttery character balanced by zesty acids on the mildly oak-spiced finish.

Scale: Superlative (96-100), Exceptional (90-95), Highly Recommended (85-89), Recommended (80-84), Not Recommended (Under 80)

1996 Sorcery Red, Mendocino $28. 86

Bright blackish ruby cast. Medium-bodied. Balanced acidity. Highly extracted. Moderately oaked. Quite tannic. Vanilla, briar fruits. Very aromatic, with a lighter-styled mouthfeel. Finishes with impressively firm tannins. Rather tough at present.

1995 Zinfandel, Mendocino Heritage, Hildreth Ranch, Mendocino $25. 86

Deep blackish ruby cast. Moderately full-bodied. Balanced acidity. Moderately extracted. Mildly oaked. Mildly tannic. Chocolate, black fruits, forest floor. Quite aromatic, with a soft, supple, flavorful palate feel. Crisp and focused through the finish.

1996 Zinfandel, Mendocino Heritage, Ford-Hitzman Vineyards, Mendocino $32. 89

Deep blackish ruby cast. Moderately full-bodied. Balanced acidity. Moderately extracted. Moderately oaked. Mildly tannic. Brown spices, chocolate, black fruits. Quite aromatic, with a hefty wood accent to the core of bright fruit flavors. Supple and rich in the mouth, with velvety tannins through the finish.

1996 Zinfandel, Old Vines, Mendocino $18. 85

Bright blackish ruby cast. Moderately full-bodied. Balanced acidity. Highly extracted. Moderately oaked. Quite tannic. Stewed red fruits, wood. Intensely aromatic, with a hint of overripeness and a touch of heat. Firm and compact in the mouth, with a tannic finish.

William Hill

1997 Chardonnay, Napa Valley $14.50. 86

Bright yellow-gold. Restrained yeasty and buttery aromas. A rich entry leads a moderately full-bodied palate with ripe, full fruit flavors and judicious oak. Generous alcohol gives this a degree of warmth on the finish.

1997 Chardonnay, Reserve, Napa Valley $20. 86

Medium straw cast. Moderately full-bodied. Balanced acidity. Moderately extracted. Mildly oaked. Apples, melon, butter. Floral, fruity aromas. Weighty, buttery smooth, and very conventional, with reserved fruit expression and glycerous texture.

1995 Cabernet Sauvignon, Napa Valley $16. 82

1996 Cabernet Sauvignon, Napa Valley $18. 86

Deep violet-red hue. Very ripe fleshy fruit aromas. A lush attack leads a moderately full-bodied palate with a rich center of cassis fruits and softer acids. Finishes with textured, supple tannins. A hedonistic style. Drink now.

1994 Cabernet Sauvignon, Reserve, Napa Valley $27. 90

Deep red-purple with a lightening rim. Medium-bodied. Moderately extracted. Moderately tannic. Vanilla, violets. Floral aromas. Tight and angular, with grainy, aggressive tannins drying the finish. This has all the attributes of a very youthful wine that will need time.

1995 Cabernet Sauvignon, Reserve, Napa Valley $27. 88

Saturated dark violet hue. Generously aromatic black cherry and vanilla aromas. A fruity attack leads a moderately full-bodied palate with bright fruit forward flavors and judicious, supple tannins. Very generous and fruity. Drink now.

1996 Merlot, Napa Valley $19. 84

Bright violet purple. Generous raspberry aromas. Medium-bodied, with a supple attack and a rounded, ripe mouthful of red fruit flavors with soft acids and mild tannins. Drink now.

HMR Winery

1997 Muscat Canelli, Paso Robles $11. 80

Hop Kiln

1996 Zinfandel, Sonoma County $16.   90

Dark ruby purple. Moderately full-bodied. Balanced acidity. Moderately extracted. Mildly tannic. Briar fruits, chocolate. Quite aromatic, with a deep, fruit-centered character. Lush, but well structured on the palate. Shows good grip and intensity through the finish.

1996 Primitivo Zinfandel, Sonoma County $22.   90

Deep blackish purple. Moderately full-bodied. Full acidity. Highly extracted. Mildly tannic. Red fruits, chocolate, black pepper. Quite aromatic, with a deep, fruit-centered character. Firmly structured and tight on the palate, with excellent grip through the finish. Should evolve nicely.

Robert Hunter

1992 Brut de Noirs, Sonoma Valley $25.   85

Deep straw cast. Full-bodied. Full acidity. Highly extracted. Yeast, toast, minerals. Forward aromas feature an intense, mature, yeasty quality. Full-throttled and rich in the mouth, with vibrant carbonation and a generous, lengthy finish.

Huntington

1997 Chardonnay, Sonoma County $9.99.   84

Deep straw cast. Medium-bodied. Full acidity. Moderately extracted. Minerals, citrus. Aromatically reserved, with a ripe and rounded mouthfeel. Shows some zesty acidity and a touch of spice through the finish.

1997 Chardonnay, Cairns Cuvée, Alexander Valley $16.   89

Bright straw hue. Attractive pear and apple aromas show varietal intensity and subdued oak influence. A brisk entry leads a full-bodied palate with racy, vibrant acidity. Shows grip and intensity through the juicy finish. Structured to improve with moderate age. Midterm cellar candidate (3–6 years).

1996 Cabernet Sauvignon, California $10.   81

1996 Merlot, California $10.   84

Bright ruby red. Attractive red fruit aromas. A crisp attack is followed by a moderately light-bodied palate with juicy acidity and modest tannins. Lean finish. A bright quaffer to be consumed in the near term.

Husch

1997 Chardonnay, Mendocino $12.50.   84

Pale yellow-straw hue. Pleasant citrus and toast aromas carry a slight oak accent. A firm entry leads a medium-bodied palate with racy acidity. Crisp, flavorful finish. Relatively light in style and well structured. Drink now or later.

1997 Chardonnay, La Ribera Vineyards, Mendocino $16.   83

Pale straw hue. Restrained biscuit and toast aromas. A crisp entry leads a ripe, medium-bodied palate that shows zesty acidity. Subtle, well-structured finish. A clean, racy style. Drink now.

1996 Chardonnay, Special Reserve, Anderson Valley $22.   87

Full golden yellow. Heavy buttery, ripe aromas show a pear and yeast character. A rich attack leads a moderately full-bodied palate with oak spice and butter flavors. The fruit flavors are muted. Rather thick, though the acids show through.

1998 Chenin Blanc, Mendocino $8.50.   84

Pale straw hue. Moderately aromatic, showing sweet apple and peach nuances. A juicy entry leads a medium-bodied palate, with clean, fruity flavors that linger on the finish. Drink now.

1998 Gewürztraminer, Anderson Valley $11.   86

Pale straw hue. Lean aromas are youthful and undeveloped, with a sulfurous note that should diminish with further bottle age. A crisp entry leads a medium-bodied palate that has a touch of sweetness and vibrant acidity. The finish is clean and crisp. Could use a few more months to come together. Drink now or later.

1996 Sauvignon Blanc, La Ribera Vineyard, Mendocino $10.50.   88

Deep straw cast. Moderately full-bodied. Full acidity. Moderately extracted. Mildly oaked. Yeast, oranges, spice. Very aromatic, with a full range of flavors and a toasty oak influence. Crisp and vibrant finish. Smoky aromas lead a bright, citrus-centered palate with smoky overtones. Finishes assertively with snappy acidity.

1995 Cabernet Sauvignon, Mendocino $16.50.   84

Violet-ruby hue with a fading rim. Medium-bodied. Moderately extracted. Mildly tannic. Red fruits, minerals. Crisp, minerally aromas, with bright red fruit flavors that fade quickly. A straightforward, snappy style with a leaner character that invites current drinking.

1996 Cabernet Sauvignon, Mendocino $16.50.   86

Bright saturated ruby hue. Generous briar fruit, sour cherry, and vanilla aromas show a pleasant wood accent. A crisp attack leads to a medium-bodied palate with lean grippy tannins and zesty acidity. Racy finish. Lighter in style, but flavorful and intense. Drink now.

1994 Cabernet Sauvignon, La Ribera Vineyard, Mendocino $15.   88

Bright crimson red. Medium-bodied. Moderately extracted. Mildly tannic. Black cherries, dried herbs. Lively black fruit aromas are confirmed on the palate and accentuated by bright acids that give this a lean feel through the finish. Quite lengthy. Very attractive for early drinking.

1995 Pinot Noir, Anderson Valley $16.   88

Pale cherry red. Medium-bodied. Moderately extracted. Mildly oaked. Mildly tannic. Supple, rounded red cherry flavors have good weight and depth. Lingering astringency reveals some dry tannins. Nice now, with the appropriate food.

1995 Pinot Noir, Reserve, Anderson Valley $29.   81

1998 Muscat Canelli, Mendocino $14.   83

Bright straw hue with a slight spritz. Subdued mineral and talc aromas. A zesty entry leads a moderately light-bodied palate, with mild sweetness offset by racy acidity. Rather light in style, but clean and refreshing. Drink now.

1998 Gewürztraminer, Late Harvest, Anderson Valley $14/375 ml.   85

Deep straw hue. Subdued spicy aromas show a varietal Gewürztraminer accent. A lean entry leads a medium-bodied palate that shows sharp acidity and moderate sweetness. Very clean, with a well-cut finish. Drink now.

Indigo Hills

1997 Chardonnay, Mendocino County $11.   88

Bright straw cast. Medium-bodied. Full acidity. Moderately extracted. Minerals, apples, citrus. Crisp, zesty aromas lead a firm mouthful of bright flavors that remain pure, vibrant, and crisp through the finish, with a subtle toasty accent lingering.

1995 Cabernet Sauvignon, Paso Robles $9.   83

Deep ruby-purple hue. Dark berry fruit and herbal notes on the nose. Shows a marked oak accent. A rich attack leads a moderately full-bodied palate with ripe berry flavors up front and lingering supple tannins on the finish. Not structured for cellaring, this is nice now.

1996 Pinot Noir, Mendocino County $12.   84

Full cherry red. Medium-bodied. Moderately extracted. Mildly tannic. Red fruits, minerals, brown spices. Jammy fruit aromas lead a fleshy, rounded palate with soft tannins lingering on the finish.

Iron Horse

1993 Brut, Sonoma County $23.50. 90
Brilliant pale gold hue. Moderately full-bodied. Full acidity. Minerals, yeast, citrus. Firm, yeasty aromas. Bright and lively, with full acids highlighting the clean citrus and mineral flavors. Youthful at present, this has the structure to benefit from further cellaring.

1993 Russian Cuvée, Sonoma County $23.50. 89
Brilliant pale gold hue. Medium-bodied. Full acidity. Bread, citrus, tart tropical fruits. Soft, leesy aromas lead a concentrated, juicy, bright mouthful of flavors that persist well through the finish. Soundly structured, this will benefit from extra bottle age.

1993 Vrais Amis, Sonoma County $28. 89
Bright yellow-gold. Medium-bodied. Full acidity. Bread, ripe citrus. Vibrant, lively carbonation. Well-defined, bright, fruity flavors are lifted by lively acids. A fine aperitif style, though quite tight at present; another year or two of cellaring will be rewarded.

1993 Brut Rose, Sonoma County $28. 90
Deep pinkish salmon cast. Full-bodied. Full acidity. Highly extracted. Red fruits, minerals, toast. Ripe, toasty aromas lead a forceful and intense palate. Tightly wound and firm, though bursting with flavor. Probably best with food now, though this has the stuffing to cellar well.

1991 Blanc de Blancs, Sonoma County $30. 91
Bright pale golden cast. Full-bodied. Full acidity. Highly extracted. Bread dough, cream, toast. Tight and youthful, with a forceful and powerful structure. Firm and intense in the mouth, with classic but reserved flavors. Impressive now, though this will blossom with mid-term (3–6 years) cellaring.

1989 Brut LD, Sonoma County Green Valley $45. 92
Straw color. Medium-bodied. Full acidity. Reminiscent of biscuit, minerals, stone fruits. Rich aromas lead a tightly wrought, complex, flavorsome palate with a strong impression of yeast on the midpalate through the finish. Should cellar well.

1990 Blanc de Blancs LD, Sonoma County, Green Valley $45. 92
Bright pale yellow-gold. Medium-bodied. Full acidity. Moderately extracted. Lemons, roasted coffee, minerals. Pronounced smoky, roasted coffee aromas lead a tight, concentrated palate and a lingering finish. Very focused citrus flavors. This is probably a few years away from optimum maturity, although it is drinkable now.

1997 Chardonnay, Sonoma County, Green Valley $22. 83
Pale straw cast. Medium-bodied. Balanced acidity. Moderately extracted. Dried herbs, minerals. Lean and crisp, with brisk acidity lending a sense of balance. Nicely textured and well balanced, if light on flavors.

1997 Sauvignon Blanc, Cuvée Joy, Alexander Valley $18. 84
Pale golden yellow. Medium-bodied. Balanced acidity. Moderately extracted. Citrus zest, minerals. Bright citrus aromas are followed by straightforward citrus flavors that could use more clarifying acidity on the warm finish.

1997 Fumé Blanc, Alexander Valley $18. 83
Pale yellow-straw hue. Medium-bodied. Low acidity. Moderately extracted. White citrus, dried herbs. Acids are quite soft; this has a very rounded, almost glycerous mouthfeel, though the flavors are straightforward.

1997 Viognier, Alexander Valley $18. 86
Bright yellow-gold. Full-bodied. Balanced acidity. Highly extracted. Mildly oaked. Melon, tropical fruits, talc. Quite aromatic, with a ripe and complex array of flavors. Full and rich on the palate, but balanced by a zesty note of acidity. Finishes with a slight wood accent.

1994 Cabernet Sauvignon, Alexander Valley $20. 86
Saturated, deep reddish purple. Medium-bodied. Moderately extracted. Mildly tannic. Black fruits, cassis, brown spice, chocolate. Ripe spicy aromas lead a velvety palate and a powdery tannic finish. Some firm astringency runs through this.

Scale: Superlative (96-100), Exceptional (90-95), Highly Recommended (85-89), Recommended (80-84), Not Recommended (Under 80)

1995 Cabernet Sauvignon, Alexander Valley $22. **82**

1996 Pinot Noir, Green Valley, Sonoma County $23. **89**

Bright cherry red with pink highlights. Medium-bodied. Moderately extracted. Moderately oaked. Mildly tannic. Floral, candied cherry aromas. Very full, with a juicy mouthfeel and a nice glycerous touch through the finish. Fine concentration of smooth cherry flavors with plenty of vanilla oak notes in support.

1997 Pinot Noir, Green Valley, Sonoma County $24. **84**

Pale ruby-garnet cast. Moderately light-bodied. Full acidity. Subtly extracted. Mildly oaked. Mildly tannic. Red fruits, minerals. Features a grapey, primary fruit quality to the nose. Light and zesty in the mouth with a hint of wood spice. Drying fruity finish.

1995 Sangiovese, Alexander Valley $16. **86**

Bright cherry red. Moderately light-bodied. Balanced acidity. Moderately extracted. Mildly tannic. Cherries, earth, oak. Hints of floral, high-toned fruits. Lively dried fruit flavors are well focused, with a minerally, lean backbone through the finish.

J Wine Co.

1994 J Brut, Sonoma County $28. **90**

Pale yellow-straw hue. Medium-bodied. Full acidity. Tart apples, citrus, yeast. Bright, fruity, doughy aromas. Clean, crisp flavors with fine-beaded carbonation and subtle yeast complexity. This is a not a heavyweight style, but is characterized by finesse and poise.

Marcus James

NV White Zinfandel, Special Reserve, $6.99. **80**

Jarvis

1996 Chardonnay, Napa Valley $38. **90**

Bright straw cast. Moderately full-bodied. Balanced acidity. Moderately extracted. Minerals, green apples, butter. Aromatically reserved, yet with a focused and precise set of flavors on the palate. Rich but well structured, with a lengthy spicy finish.

1996 Chardonnay, Reserve, Napa Valley $48. **90**

Bright gold. Aromatically generous with a fine smoky, toasted-oak note and buttery richness. A smooth entry leads a moderately full-bodied palate with a rich, rounded mouthfeel showing some intensity. Very stylish.

1996 Cabernet Franc, Napa Valley $44. **93**

Deep ruby purple. Moderately full-bodied. Balanced acidity. Highly extracted. Moderately oaked. Mildly tannic. Black fruits, minerals, spice. Aromatic and rich, with a weighty core of ripe fruit flavors and a judicious oak accent. Supple and harmonious in the mouth, with a very lengthy, exotically flavored finish.

1993 Cabernet Sauvignon, Napa Valley $55. **93**

Deep red. Medium-bodied. Highly extracted. Mildly tannic. Red fruits, cassis, toasty oak spice. Very attractive spicy aromas. Distinguished by a silky mouthfeel with concentrated plush flavors that linger through the finish. Beautifully integrated flavors leave a luxurious impression.

1994 Cabernet Sauvignon, Napa Valley $58. **98**

Opaque red with a brick rim. Moderately full-bodied. Highly extracted. Moderately tannic. Mineral, chocolate, black fruits. Dusty, spicy aromas lead a solid, mineral-packed mouthful of flavors through a long, drying finish. Has a pleasing note of austerity that makes for a classic, highly sophisticated character. Drinking very well now.

1993 Cabernet Sauvignon, Reserve, Napa Valley $75. **97**

Saturated dark red. Moderately full-bodied. Highly extracted. Moderately tannic. Cassis, oak spice, lead pencil. Fleshy, minerally aromas follow through on the palate with a sense of concentration and austerity through the finish. Very classy and reserved, in a Claret-like manner.

1993 Lake William, Napa Valley $45.   **92**

Deep ruby hue with a pale purple-tinged rim. Medium-bodied. Moderately extracted.
Mildly tannic. Pepper, spice, black bramble fruits. High-toned aromas show complexity.
Spicy, almost pickled red berry fruit flavors through the finish are highlighted by bright
acids. Very nice now, and full of exotic spicy flavors.

1996 Lake William, Napa Valley $48.   **94**

Saturated red-purple. Moderately full-bodied. Highly extracted. Moderately tannic.
Vanilla, smoke, red fruits. Rich, smoky aromas have high-toned fruity accents that follow
through on the palate, showing concentration and vibrancy through a spicy finish.

1996 Merlot, Napa Valley $46.   **86**

Deep violet-ruby hue. Generously aromatic with chocolate and ripe black cherry aromas.
Medium-bodied, with a lively attack that develops into bright fleshy fruit flavors that
linger through the supple finish. Drink now.

Jekel

1997 Chardonnay, FOS Reserve, Monterey $22.   **85**

Medium golden yellow. Richly aromatic with a heavy dose of oak spice and yeasty
character. A fat entry leads a full-bodied palate with glycerine and alcohol to the fore.
Tart apples, butter, and spice flavors. Moderately short finish. Drink now.

1998 Johannisberg Riesling, Monterey $10.   **84**

Bright pale gold hue. Generous apple and tropical fruit aromas. A juicy, moderately
sweet attack leads a medium-bodied palate, with clean, straightforward flavors through
the finish. Drink now.

1996 Cabernet Franc, Sanctuary Estate Reserve, Monterey $18.   **84**

Bright ruby red hue. Forward mineral and red fruit aromas. A crisp attack leads to a
medium-bodied palate with lean tannins. Firm, angular finish. Rather austere but well
structured. Drink within 5 years.

1996 Malbec, Sanctuary Estate Reserve, Monterey $18.   **82**

1994 Sanctuary Estate Meritage, Monterey $16.   **80**

1995 Sanctuary Estate Meritage, Monterey $25.   **87**

Saturated dark ruby-red hue. Aromatically reserved. A firm entry leads a medium-bodied
palate with fine-grained tannins and racy, bright fruit flavors. Medium-length finish shows
a minerally quality. Wood flavors are well integrated. Drink now or later.

1996 Merlot, California $12.   **84**

Brickish ruby hue with a subtle fade. Spicy, woody aromas. A crisp attack followed by
mildly astringent tannins on the medium-bodied palate. Well gripped by tannins and
acids on the finish. Drink now.

1996 Merlot, Sanctuary Estate Reserve, Monterey $18.   **88**

Bright violet-crimson hue. Generous rich aromas of black fruits and brown spice.
A supple, smooth attack leads a moderately full-bodied palate with velvety, drying
tannins. Generously fruity and deep, with a persistent finish. Drink now or later. Can
improve with more age.

1996 Petit Verdot, Sanctuary Estate Reserve, Monterey $18.   **84**

Deep ruby red hue. Forward herb and cola aromas. A lean attack leads to a moderately
light-bodied palate with grippy tannins. Crisp, zesty finish. An interesting but very light
interpretation of Petite Verdot. Drink now.

1996 Pinot Noir, Gravelstone, Monterey $13.   **83**

Pale cherry red. Medium-bodied. Moderately extracted. Mildly tannic. Red berry fruits,
minerals. Perfumed aromas follow through on the palate, with lean flavors showing a
minerally edge on the finish.

Scale: Superlative (96-100), Exceptional (90-95), Highly Recommended (85-89),
Recommended (80-84), Not Recommended (Under 80)

1997 Late Harvest Johannisberg Riesling, Monterey $25/375 ml.　83
Deep bronze hue. Lean brown spice and lacquer aromas show a nutty, buttery note.
A lush entry leads a medium-bodied palate that has marked sweetness. Straightforward,
nutty, toffee-flavored finish. Drink now.

Jepson
1994 Blanc de Blanc, Burnee Hill Vineyard, Mendocino County $19.　80
1996 Chardonnay, Mendocino County $15.　89
Bright yellow-gold. Medium-bodied. Full acidity. Moderately extracted. Citrus, lemons,
vanilla. Crisp and lively on the palate, with a lemony firmness running through the finish
that stands up to the buttery, oaky character. A flavorful and firm style.
1997 Sauvignon Blanc, Mendocino County $10.　81
1997 Viognier, Mendocino County $15.　81
1995 Pinot Noir, Sonoma County $15.　80

Jessandra Vittoria
1995 Cabernet Sauvignon, Sonoma Valley $30.　88
Opaque blackish red. Medium-bodied. Highly extracted. Moderately tannic. Black fruits,
allspice. Full aromas of dust and spice are rather distinctive. A full, concentrated palate
follows the aromas with a marked spicy, tangy, tart note on the finish. Not to everyone's
liking, perhaps, but bursting with character.

Jordan
1994 Cabernet Sauvignon, Alexander Valley $34.　88
Bright ruby purple. Medium-bodied. Full acidity. Moderately extracted. Mildly oaked.
Mildly tannic. Red fruits, minerals, brown spices. Pleasantly aromatic, with a core of ripe
fruit flavors. A lighter style, with a sense of crispness through the finish. Well balanced.

Jory
1997 Chardonnay, El Nino, Central Coast $15.　81
1997 Chardonnay, Lion Oaks Ranch, Selected Clone,
Santa Clara Valley $30.　84
Bright yellow-straw hue. Medium-bodied. Full acidity. Moderately extracted. Mildly oaked.
Minerals, grape skins. Muted aromas lead a clean, bright, angular palate with dry notes
lingering on the finish.
1996 Black Hand, Mano Nera Red, California $13.　83
Deep ruby purple. Moderately full-bodied. Balanced acidity. Highly extracted. Mildly
oaked. Mildly tannic. Briar fruits, vanilla. Lighter in style, with vibrant fruit flavors. Juicy,
with a clean edge of acidity to the finish.

Joullian
1996 Chardonnay, Monterey $15.50.　88
Pale straw cast. Medium-bodied. Full acidity. Moderately extracted. Minerals, citrus, toast.
Toasty, zesty aromas precede generous yet precise flavors highlighted by crisp and zesty
acids that persist through the finish.
1996 Sauvignon Blanc, Family Reserve, Carmel Valley $16.50.　83
Pale straw. Medium-bodied. Balanced acidity. Moderately extracted. Apples, lemons.
Very straightforward, bright, clean fruity flavors give way to a warm alcohol finish
showing a touch of oak spice.
1996 Zinfandel, Sias Cuvée, Carmel Valley $16.　80

Judd's Hill

1995 Cabernet Sauvignon, Napa Valley $28.   89

Saturated violet red. Moderately full-bodied. Highly extracted. Moderately tannic. Violets, cassis, vanilla. Solid, gripping tannins with highlighted fruit flavors showing great intensity. Rich and well structured, this will be better in a few years.

Justin

1997 Chardonnay, Native Yeast, Paso Robles $18.50.   82
1997 Chardonnay, Reserve, Paso Robles $18.   86

Bright straw hue. Subdued mineral and coconut aromas show a slight wood accent. A lush entry is followed by a medium-bodied palate with rounded acidity, and a crisp, buttery finish. Drink now.

1995 Cabernet Sauvignon, Paso Robles $20.   84

Deep ruby cast. Moderately full-bodied. Balanced acidity. Moderately extracted. Mildly tannic. Minerals, black fruits. Aromatically reserved, but full and flavorful in the mouth. Angular through the finish.

1996 Cabernet Sauvignon, Paso Robles $20.   84

Full ruby red hue. Aromas are jammy and herbal. A crisp entry leads a medium-bodied palate with chewy cassis fruit flavors and moderate tannins that take a greenish turn through the finish. Rather angular. Drink now.

1995 Justification, Paso Robles $22.50.   81
1994 Isosceles, Paso Robles $32.50.   88

Saturated dark blackish red with purple highlights. Moderately full-bodied. Highly extracted. Quite tannic. Toasted oak, cassis, blackberries, brown spice. Ripe, brooding nose. Dense, mouthfilling Cabernet fruit flavors. The textured mouthfeel shows richness and a chewy character through the richly tannic finish. Solidly structured and backward, it needs three to four years to show at its best.

1995 Isosceles, Paso Robles $36.50.   84

Medium ruby-red hue with a subtle fade. Subtle aromas have a lean character, showing red fruits and herbs. A bright entry leads a medium-bodied palate with racy acids and tart red fruit flavors. Finishes with a note of green tannins. Drink now.

1996 Merlot, Reserve, Paso Robles $25.   86

Bright, deep purple-red. Intense mint, plum, and overripe black fruit aromas. A crisp attack leads a medium-bodied palate with vibrant acidity and firm tannins. The finish is on the light side, but juicy and flavorful. A racy, cheerful style. Drink now.

1995 Nebbiolo, San Luis Obispo County $22.50.   84

Bright blackish ruby cast. Moderately full-bodied. Low acidity. Moderately extracted. Mildly tannic. Red fruits, minerals. Rather reserved aromatically, with austere minerally flavors on the palate. Low acidity levels make for a lush entry. Could use a bit more grip.

1995 Sangiovese, San Luis Obispo County $22.50.   83

Cherry red with a subtle fade. Medium-bodied. Balanced acidity. Moderately extracted. Mildly tannic. Red berries. Soft red berry flavors, with mild oak/spice notes on the finish. A rounded, easy-drinking style.

1996 Obtuse, Paso Robles $22.50.   86

Opaque blackish purple. Full-bodied. Balanced acidity. Highly extracted. Mildly tannic. Black fruits, minerals. Quite aromatic, with a full and flavorful palate feel. Round and rich, though well structured through the finish.

Kautz Ironstone

1997 Chardonnay, Kautz, Library Collection, California $14.99.   81

Scale: Superlative (96-100), Exceptional (90-95), Highly Recommended (85-89), Recommended (80-84), Not Recommended (Under 80)

Robert Keenan

1997 Chardonnay, Napa Valley $18.　　　　　　　　　　　　84

Bright straw cast. Moderately full-bodied. Full acidity. Moderately extracted. Minerals, green apples. Aromatically reserved, with precise and focused flavors. Firm and quite lean, with mouthwatering acidity making for a clean, refreshing finish.

1993 Cabernet Sauvignon, Hillside Estate, Spring Mountain District, Napa Valley $23.　　　　　　　　　　89

Saturated, opaque dark purple. Moderately full-bodied. Highly extracted. Quite tannic. Black fruits, black tea, tobacco, earth. Inky, solid palate has tightly wound flavors with firm, dry tealike tannins making it a little mean at present. A structural monster.

1994 Cabernet Sauvignon, Hillside Estate, Spring Mountain District, Napa Valley $24.　　　　　　　　　　92

Deep saturated ruby purple. Full-bodied. Balanced acidity. Highly extracted. Heavily oaked. Quite tannic. Vanilla, black fruits, minerals. All systems go, in a full-throttled, hearty, chunky wine with very modern, fruit-centered, wood-accented flavors. Finishes with a wallop of tannin. A show style that needs a lengthy tour of duty in the cellar.

1996 Merlot, Napa Valley $30.　　　　　　　　　　　　89

Dark violet red. Ripe fruit aromas. A soft, fruity attack leads a generously fruity midpalate with mild powdery tannins on the finish. Drink now.

Kendall-Jackson

1996 Chardonnay, Camelot Vineyard, Santa Maria Valley $19.　　　　85

Bright yellow-straw cast. Moderately full-bodied. Low acidity. Moderately extracted. Heavily oaked. Brown spices. A big, oaky style with forward oaky aromas and substantial texture on the palate, though it lacks grip on the finish.

1996 Chardonnay, Paradise Vineyard, Arroyo Seco $18.　　　　　85

Deep yellow-straw cast. Moderately full-bodied. Full acidity. Highly extracted. Minerals, citrus. Crisp, lean, and intense, with a subtle yeasty overtone. The finish is vibrant.

1997 Chardonnay, Vintner's Reserve, California $16.　　　　　83

Bright yellow-gold. Medium-bodied. Balanced acidity. Moderately extracted. Spicy, yeasty aromas show an oak influence that comes through on the palate. Bright sweet lemon flavors provide a lively note.

1996 Chardonnay, Grand Reserve, California $26.　　　　　　80

1997 Chardonnay, Grand Reserve, California $26.　　　　　　90

Brilliant golden yellow. Generous toast, yeast, and cream flavors show a judicious oak accent. A smooth attack is followed by a moderately full-bodied palate with balanced acidity. The finish is persistent and flavorful. Overall, a rich and intense wine. Drink now or later.

1997 Chenin Blanc, Vintner's Reserve, California $11.　　　　　83

Medium yellow-gold. Moderately aromatic, with a sweet citrus note. A juicy entry leads a medium-bodied palate, with fine concentration and some glycerous richness. Finishes with a note of citrus zest. Drink now.

1997 Johannisberg Riesling, Vintner's Reserve, California $11.　　　86

Deep yellow-gold. Aromatically generous, with big ripe fruit character. A rich, moderately sweet entry leads a medium-bodied palate. Pure green apple flavors linger through the finish. A soft, juicy style. Drink now.

1995 Cabernet Franc, Buckeye Vineyard, Alexander Valley $20.　　　86

Very deep ruby hue. Medium-bodied. Balanced acidity. Moderately extracted. Mildly tannic. Licorice, minerals. High-toned aromas lead a weighty but firm and angular mouthfeel that fades toward the finish.

1995 Cabernet Franc, Grand Reserve, California $18.　　　　　83

Deep, saturated ruby garnet hue. Subdued mineral and black fruit aromas. A rich attack leads to a moderately full-bodied palate with robust chunky tannins. Big, firm finish. Full throttle but rather monolithic. Drink now or later.

1994 Cabernet Sauvignon, Buckeye Vineyard, Alexander Valley $24.   **89**

Deep crimson red with purple highlights. Moderately full-bodied. Moderately extracted. Moderately tannic. Toasted oak, black currants, brown spice. Generous oak-accented, rich black fruit aromas are confirmed on the palate. Well-balanced tannins are plush and rounded on the palate with good texture through the finish. Quite structured.

1995 Cabernet Sauvignon, Buckeye Vineyard, Alexander Valley $27.   **88**

Deep ruby purple. Moderately full-bodied. Balanced acidity. Moderately extracted. Mildly oaked. Moderately tannic. Minerals, black fruits, vanilla. Aromatically reserved, but flavorful and rich on the palate. Firm structure throughout, with tannins clamping down on the finish.

1994 Cabernet Sauvignon, Vintner's Reserve, California $18.   **88**

Full brick red. Medium-bodied. Moderately extracted. Mildly tannic. Black fruits, earth, brown spice. Dusty black fruit aromas reveal a well-balanced palate with generous ripe flavors and a spicy accent through the finish.

1995 Cabernet Sauvignon, Vintner's Reserve, California $18.   **83**

Bright cherry red. Medium-bodied. Moderately extracted. Moderately tannic. Cassis, tea. Jammy, black fruit aromas lead ripe, fruity flavors with a streak of powdery, dry tannins on the finish. Backward now.

1994 Cabernet Sauvignon, Grand Reserve, California $41.   **89**

Deep reddish purple. Medium-bodied. Highly extracted. Mildly tannic. Mint, vanilla, black fruits. Attractive mint-nuanced aromas. Solid, chewy Cabernet fruit on the palate gives way to dry, powdery tannins through the finish. Good acids give this a tart edge.

1995 Cabernet Sauvignon, Grand Reserve, California $42.   **87**

Saturated dark red-purple hue. Brooding black fruit, toasted oak aromas. A tough entry leads to a full-bodied palate with well-extracted fruit flavors and whopping, chewy, drying tannins that grip the finish. Very dry and tough at present. Drink within five years.

1995 Merlot, Buckeye Vineyard, Alexander Valley $29.   **84**

Deep, saturated ruby hue. Interesting, high-toned anise, chocolate and red fruit aromas show a hearty oak accent. A lush entry leads a rounded, medium-bodied palate with drying tannins and low levels of acidity. The finish is fat and rich. Eminently drinkable. Drink now.

1996 Merlot, Vintner's Reserve, California $19.   **83**

Full ruby red. Oak-dominated aromas with brambly accents. Medium-bodied, with a lush entry and an oaky palate showing dry, powdery tannins on the finish. Relatively low acids make for a softer, rounded style.

1995 Merlot, Grand Reserve, California $42.   **86**

Full ruby red. Distinctly oak-accented aromas. Dry and well gripped on the medium-bodied palate with oak dominating the ripe, plummy black fruit flavors. Finishes in a dry cedary manner.

1997 Pinot Noir, Vintner's Reserve, California $30.   **82**

1996 Pinot Noir, Grand Reserve, California $30.   **88**

Pale violet red. Moderately light-bodied. Moderately extracted. Mildly tannic. Vanilla, berry fruits, cherry. Bright berry and vanilla aromas lead a supple, brightly fruity palate with a clean, crisp finish.

1996 Syrah, Vintner's Reserve, California $16.   **86**

Dark purple, limpid, and brilliant to the rim. Sound black cherry and bitter chocolate flavors. Mild wood tones. A firm entry leads a medium-bodied palate with balanced acidity. Moderate, drying tannins. Sweet fruit, chocolate, and wood notes work well through the subtle bitter finish. Drink now or later. Can improve with more age.

1995 Syrah, Grand Reserve, California $20.   **86**

Medium cherry red, limpid with a slight fade. Subtle, pleasant berry fruit and cedar flavors. Hint of wood tones. A smooth entry and a medium-bodied palate. Moderate drying tannins on a subtle finish. Fleshy black fruit flavors make this attractive. Spicy, oak-accented style. Drink now.

Scale: Superlative (96-100), Exceptional (90-95), Highly Recommended (85-89),
Recommended (80-84), Not Recommended (Under 80)

1996 Zinfandel, Vintner's Reserve, California $16.   **84**

Bright blackish purple. Moderately full-bodied. Balanced acidity. Moderately extracted. Mildly oaked. Moderately tannic. Black fruits, vanilla. Carries an oaky nuance on the nose, and merges with a nice fruit-centered core of flavors. Lighter in style, with some hefty tannins toward the finish.

1997 Chardonnay, Select Late Harvest, California $40/375 ml.   **89**

Brilliant deep gold. Rich apricot and honey aromas. A lush attack leads a medium-bodied palate with attractive, intensely juicy tropical flavors. Acids and sugars strike a fine balance. Subtly botrytized.

Kathryn Kennedy

1994 Cabernet Sauvignon, Santa Cruz Mountains $75.   **95**

Opaque reddish purple. Moderately full-bodied. Highly extracted. Moderately tannic. Black cherries, brown spice, anise. A spicy pickled nose leads a pure, concentrated palate with very focused primary fruit flavors on entry that dominate the midpalate. Acid levels are impressively high. Still a little tight.

1995 Cabernet Sauvignon, Santa Cruz Mountains $110.   **94**

Saturated ruby purple. Moderately full-bodied. Full acidity. Highly extracted. Moderately tannic. Cherry cordial, minerals. Pure fruit aromas are defined with great intensity and focus. Terroir is magnified in the form of a ripe, minerally character, with little if any wood influence. Admirably restrained. Approachable, but should become more complex with age.

1996 Lateral, California $35.   **83**

Bright ruby with a pale rim. Moderately light-bodied. Moderately extracted. Mildly tannic. Dried herbs, raspberry, red berries. Perfumed, fruity, and lighter in style, with bright red berry flavors and a dusting of mineral through the finish.

1996 Syrah, Maridon Vineyard, Santa Cruz Mountains $38.   **93**

Very dark purple, opaque and brilliant to the rim. Generous, fantastic plum and vanilla flavors. Generous wood tones. Supple entry. Full-bodied, with plentiful velvety tannins. Lingering rich finish. A lush, supple, well-extracted style showing great varietal character. Drink now or later. Can improve with age.

Kenwood

1997 Chardonnay, Sonoma County $15.   **81**

1997 Chardonnay, Reserve, Sonoma Valley $22.   **83**

Pale straw hue. Medium-bodied. Balanced acidity. Moderately extracted. Mildly oaked. Vanilla, apples, minerals. An oak-spiced nose leads a crisp appley palate of flavors with a light, clean finish. Very quaffable.

1996 Sauvignon Blanc, Sonoma County $10.   **84**

Deep green-straw cast. Moderately full-bodied. Full acidity. Moderately extracted. Dried herbs, minerals. Quite aromatic, with a distinctive herbal Sauvignon Blanc personality. Full but zesty in the mouth, with vibrant acidity through the finish.

1996 Sauvignon Blanc, Reserve, Sonoma Valley $15.   **86**

Medium yellow-straw hue. Medium-bodied. Balanced acidity. Moderately extracted. Mildly oaked. Vanilla, citrus zest, oak spice. Pleasant smoky nose. Rounded, somewhat soft mouthfeel, with a faintly oak-spiced finish. Easy going, open-knit style.

1994 Cabernet Sauvignon, Sonoma Valley $18.   **87**

Full reddish purple. Medium-bodied. Moderately extracted. Mildly tannic. Blackberry, cassis, cedar. Vanilla-scented nose leads a chewy mouthful of black Cabernet fruit, with finely balanced powdery tannins on the finish. Attractive now.

1995 Cabernet Sauvignon, Sonoma Valley $18.   **88**

Bright red with a pale ruby rim. Medium-bodied. Moderately extracted. Moderately tannic. Mineral, red fruits. Earthy, ferric nose seems odd. Brisk berry flavors pass quickly, leaving a minerally, dry finish.

1994 Cabernet Sauvignon, Jack London Vineyard, Sonoma Valley $25.   **91**

Dark garnet red. Medium-bodied. Moderately extracted. Mildly tannic. Earth, licorice, black fruits, brown spice. Deep, rich earthy nose leads a supple palate with black fruit and licorice flavors. Austere yet soft on the finish. Very approachable now, probably not for long-term (7–10 years) cellaring.

1995 Cabernet Sauvignon, Jack London Vineyard, Sonoma County $25.   **90**

Dark ruby red. Medium-bodied. Moderately extracted. Moderately tannic. Cassis, mineral, brown spice. Dark, fleshy aromas lead a tight, minerally palate showing good grip, with generous Cabernet fruit flavors showing through. A lighter style whose tannins are in fine balance.

1995 Cabernet Sauvignon, Yulupa, Sonoma County $25.   **83**

Bright ruby hue. Medium-bodied. Balanced acidity. Moderately extracted. Mildly tannic. Minerals, red fruits. Subtle aromas point to a more reserved style, with a lighter-styled palate feel and crisp flavors that follow through on the finish. Drinking well now.

1995 Merlot, Sonoma County $20.   **89**

Deep blackish ruby color with brilliant clarity. Medium-bodied. Balanced acidity. Highly extracted. Mildly oaked. Mildly tannic. Black fruits, vanilla. Bright and forceful, with a juicy quality to the dark fruit flavors. Well integrated and nicely balanced. There is a kiss of oak on the finish.

1995 Merlot, Jack London Vineyard, Sonoma Valley $25.   **89**

Deep ruby with a purplish cast. Moderately full-bodied. Full acidity. Moderately extracted. Mildly tannic. Black fruits, earth, black olives. A little reserved aromatically and somewhat tight on the palate. Still, it features a very deep core of dark flavors and a veil of velvety tannins. Well balanced. Should open with mid-term (3–6 years) cellaring.

1995 Merlot, Massara, Sonoma Valley $25.   **89**

Very deep blackish ruby hue with a purple cast. Moderately full-bodied. Full acidity. Highly extracted. Mildly tannic. Black fruits, earth, dried herbs. Still quite closed, though very deep and extracted. Features a vibrant note of acidity and rich tannins through the finish. Will need time to open up more fully.

1995 Pinot Noir, Russian River Valley $17.   **84**

Pale garnet red. Moderately light-bodied. Subtly extracted. Mildly oaked. Mildly tannic. A pleasant mouthful of dried red fruits and minerals with a touch of tobacco through the finish. Has nice varietal character, though it is quite light.

1995 Pinot Noir, Olivet Lane, Russian River Valley $22.   **88**

Pale garnet red. Moderately light-bodied. Moderately extracted. Mildly oaked. Mildly tannic. Strawberry aromas lead a well-balanced palate with crisp cherry flavors, and fine powdered tannins and minerals through the finish.

1995 Zinfandel, Sonoma Valley $15.   **86**

Bright blackish ruby cast. Medium-bodied. Balanced acidity. Moderately extracted. Mildly tannic. Black fruits, minerals. Reserved aromatically, with a firm, well-structured palate feel. Though tightly wound, a core of dark fruit flavors emerges here and there. Shows fine grip on the finish. Well balanced; should open in the near term.

1995 Zinfandel, Jack London Vineyard, Sonoma Valley $20.   **82**

1995 Zinfandel, Upper Weise Ranch, Sonoma Valley $20.   **86**

Bright blackish ruby cast. Moderately full-bodied. Balanced acidity. Moderately extracted. Mildly oaked. Mildly tannic. Black fruits, spice. Lighter in style, with a high-toned, lively presence on the palate. Flavorful throughout, however, with a crisp, balanced finish.

Kistler

1993 Cabernet Sauvignon, Kistler Vineyard, Sonoma Valley $30.   **85**

Deep dark ruby red. Moderately full-bodied. Highly extracted. Moderately tannic. Earth, blackberry, black tea, black fruits. Exotically earthy nose with herbal accents. The deeply layered palate shows an austere character, with plenty of tealike notes through the finish. Rich and savory.

Scale: Superlative (96-100), Exceptional (90-95), Highly Recommended (85-89), Recommended (80-84), Not Recommended (Under 80)

Korbel

NV Chardonnay Brut, California $12.99.   83

Medium yellow-straw cast. Medium-bodied. Spice, tropical fruits. Yeasty, spicy aromas lead a generously flavored palate showing weight and some citrus length. The flavors are very attractive, though the bubbles are rather large.

NV Natural Sparkling Wine, California $12.99.   83

Pale yellow-gold. Medium-bodied. Citrus zest, canned pears. Powdery, zesty aromas follow through on the palate, with a dry finish that has an authoritative grip. Full, crisp carbonation.

NV Rouge Sparkling Wine, California $12.99.   84

Pale cherry red. Medium-bodied. Rose petals, cherries. A floral, dark fruit impression is conveyed on the nose and palate, with the very slightest suggestion of dry tannin on the finish. Novel, but undeniably appealing.

1994 Cabernet Sauvignon, Alexander Valley $18.99.   90

Medium cherry red. Medium-bodied. Moderately extracted. Mildly tannic. Black pepper, brown spice, bright black fruits. Wonderfully spiced aromatics lead a well-balanced palate with supple character and generous flavors. Very bright, with good acids lingering through the finish.

Charles Krug

1996 CK Mondavi Zinfandel, California $7.   81

1995 Cabernet Sauvignon, Napa Valley $16.   84

Bright brick red. Medium-bodied. Moderately extracted. Mildly tannic. Mint, berries. Bright oak and berry aromas lead a succulent and juicy mouthful of flavors, with oak playing a prominent role. Drink now.

1994 Peter Mondavi Family, Generations, Napa Valley $30.   85

Bright ruby red with a distinct fade on the rim. Medium-bodied. Highly extracted. Moderately tannic. Allspice, vanilla, red fruits. Dusty, spicy aromas lead a similar flavor profile, with dusty tannins lingering on the finish. The finish falls off quickly.

1994 Cabernet Sauvignon, Vintage Selection, Napa Valley $47.   88

Deep ruby hue with a fading rim. Medium-bodied. Moderately extracted. Moderately tannic. Brown spice, black fruits, caramel. Very ripe black fruit aromas are complemented by a toasted oak note that comes through on the finish. Ripe and full, this is drinking well now.

1994 Merlot, Reserve, Napa Valley $21.50.   89

Deep crimson red with a slight fade to the rim. Medium-bodied. Balanced acidity. Moderately extracted. Heavily oaked. Mildly tannic. Red fruits, dill pickle, brown spices. Quite aromatic, with well-extracted fruit flavors mingling with complex oak accents. Nicely integrated, with some dusty tannins and a lingering drying finish.

1996 Pinot Noir, Carneros $16.   81

1995 Sangiovese, Reserve, Napa Valley $16.   83

Browning garnet hue. Medium-bodied. Moderately extracted. Moderately oaked. Mildly tannic. Earth, brown spice. Mature spicy aromas. Rather rustic and dry, with little primary fruit character showing.

1995 Zinfandel, Napa Valley $11.   81

Kunde

1996 Chardonnay, Kinneybrook Vineyard, Sonoma Valley $20.   86

Medium yellow-gold. Moderately full-bodied. Balanced acidity. Moderately extracted. Mildly oaked. Yeast, vanilla, apples. Rich yeasty aromas follow through on a generous mouthfeel, with a pleasant doughy quality throughout that should develop further with a few months of cellaring.

1996 Chardonnay, Wildwood Vineyard, Sonoma Valley $20.   87

Bright pale straw color. Medium-bodied. Balanced acidity. Moderately extracted. Mildly oaked. Vanilla, apple. Shows a light touch of oak on the nose, with clean appley flavors on a brief finish. Balanced and flavorful, with a supple texture that stands out.

1996 Chardonnay, Reserve, Sonoma Valley $22.   84

Bright yellow-gold. Moderately full-bodied. Balanced acidity. Moderately extracted.
Moderately oaked. Vanilla, apples, yeast. Doughy aromas seem reserved now. A weighty,
generous mouthfeel has a spicy persistence, with acids rearing up on the finish.

1997 Viognier, Sonoma Valley $18.   83

Bright yellow-gold. Moderately full-bodied. Balanced acidity. Moderately extracted.
Citrus, minerals. Citrus zest aromas lead a full, ripe palate that is well balanced by
structural acidity. Could use a little more intensity of flavor.

1994 Cabernet Sauvignon, Sonoma Valley $17.   90

Dark red with subtle purple highlights. Medium-bodied. Highly extracted. Moderately
tannic. Loam, cinnamon, vanilla, dark fruits. Toasty nose shows a singular earthy note
that follows through on the assertively flavored palate. Good acids give this a lively feel
through the finish. Well balanced and harmonious.

1995 Cabernet Sauvignon, Sonoma Valley $20.   93

Saturated dark red. Medium-bodied. Moderately extracted. Moderately tannic. Black
fruits, minerals, vanilla. Reserved, fleshy aromas lead a chunky yet bright mouthful of
flavors, with dry, powdery tannins through the finish. Well balanced and noble, with
poise and elegance.

1997 Merlot, Sonoma Valley $17.   86

Bright violet purple. Warm, very ripe berry fruit aromas. A juicy attack leads a moderately
full-bodied palate with powdery tannins and some alcohol warmth. Firm dry tannins on
the finish. Drink within five years.

La Crema

1997 Chardonnay, Cold Coast Vineyards, Sonoma Coast $19.   91

Bright yellow-straw hue. Generous yeast and vanilla aromas carry a hefty oak accent.
A lush entry leads a moderately full-bodied palate buoyed by crisp acidity. The finish is
intense and flavorful. Drink now or later.

1996 Chardonnay, Reserve, Sonoma Coast $27.   82
1995 Pinot Noir, Sonoma Coast $21.   86

Medium cherry red. Moderately light-bodied. Moderately extracted. Moderately
oaked. Mildly tannic. Red berry fruit aromas. Cranberry and strawberry flavors have
an astringent backbone, with sweet tobacco notes lingering on the finish.

1996 Pinot Noir, Sonoma Coast $20.   83

Pale ruby cast. Moderately light-bodied. Full acidity. Subtly extracted. Mildly tannic.
Sweet herbs, minerals, red fruits. Lean and stylish, with varietal Pinot aromas and a clean,
angular finish. Crisp and tasty.

1995 Pinot Noir, Reserve, Sonoma Coast $26.   87

Bright pale cherry red with purple highlights. Medium-bodied. Moderately extracted.
Moderately oaked. Mildly tannic. Bright, tart cherry flavors have tobacco and spice
accents. Lengthy astringent finish. Dry and somewhat austere. Some complex chocolate
notes.

1996 Pinot Noir, Reserve, Sonoma Coast $27.   86

Bright saturated ruby cast. Medium-bodied. Full acidity. Moderately extracted. Mildly
tannic. Minerals, black fruits. A racy, fruit-driven nose leads a firm and intense palate feel.
Crisp, lean, and vibrant through the finish.

1996 Zinfandel, Reserve, Sonoma County $22.   86

Bright purple. Moderately full-bodied. Full acidity. Moderately extracted. Mildly oaked.
Mildly tannic. Briar fruits, vanilla. Aromatic, with a pleasant interplay between fruit and
oak nuances. Well balanced and lively, with subtle tannins through the finish.

Scale: Superlative (96-100), Exceptional (90-95), Highly Recommended (85-89),
Recommended (80-84), Not Recommended (Under 80)

La Jota

1995 Cabernet Sauvignon, Howell Mountain Selection, Howell Mountain, Napa Valley $30.   93

Saturated ruby cast. Moderately full-bodied. Balanced acidity. Highly extracted. Moderately oaked. Moderately tannic. Mint, plums, cedar. Pleasantly aromatic, with a deep black fruit core accented by spicy oak nuances. Deep and full in the mouth, with robust yet velvety tannins. Exceptional balance and depth. Should be more approachable in five to ten years.

1996 Cabernet Sauvignon, Howell Mountain Selection, Howell Mountain, Napa Valley $34.   87

Deep ruby hue. Generous vanilla and mineral aromas show a decided oak accent. A rich entry leads to a moderately full-bodied palate with grippy tannins. Firm, authoritative finish. Quite rich and stylish, but could use a bit more acidity toward the finish. Drinking well now. Drink now or later.

1996 Cabernet Sauvignon, 15th Anniversary, Howell Mountain, Napa Valley $58.   96

Deep, opaque purple-red hue. Intense and attractive vanilla, black fruit, and mineral aromas. A lush attack leads to a full-bodied, mouthfilling palate with velvety, chewy tannins. Outstanding, lengthy finish. Big and rich, but carries its weight seamlessly. Approachable now but exquisitely balanced and quite age worthy.

Laetitia

1993 Elegance Brut Rose, San Luis Obispo County $23.   87

Pale salmon cast. Full-bodied. Full acidity. Highly extracted. Charred yeast, minerals. Forward, charred-yeast nuances feature prominently in the flavor profile. Full-throttled and firm in the mouth, with aggressive carbonation and a rich, zesty finish. This will show best with food.

1993 Elegance Brut, California $23.   88

Deep yellow-gold. Moderately full-bodied. Full acidity. Mature, faintly maderized aromas. Broad flavors show plenty of black grape character, with a mouthfilling presence and lengthy finish. A forceful, big-shouldered style that will match with food.

1996 Chardonnay, Reserve, San Luis Obispo County $18.   86

Deep yellow-straw hue. Intense vanilla, citrus, and mineral aromas show judicious oak influences and a slightly earthy overtone. A firm entry leads a moderately full-bodied palate with crisp acidity. Subtle nutty finish. Drink now.

1996 Pinot Blanc, Reserve, San Luis Obispo County $17.   88

Deep golden cast. Moderately full-bodied. Full acidity. Moderately extracted. Heavily oaked. Smoke, tropical fruits, butter. Quite aromatic, with heavily toasted oak and ripe fruit flavors. This is a full-throttled style with a flavorful palate and vibrant acidity making for a brisk finish.

1996 Pinot Blanc, La Colline Vineyard Designated Reserve, $25.   88

Bright golden hue. Moderately full-bodied. Full acidity. Moderately extracted. Moderately oaked. Toasted coconut, butter, tropical fruits. Oak influence is readily apparent on the nose and plays out on the palate with a bevy of ripe tropical flavors. Quite full and weighty, with vibrant acidity through the finish.

1996 Pinot Noir, San Luis Obispo County $29.   82

1996 Pinot Noir, Laetitia Vineyard, San Luis Obispo County $29.   93

Deep ruby purple. Full-bodied. Balanced acidity. Highly extracted. Moderately oaked. Mildly tannic. Vanilla, red fruits, sweet herbs. Lavish oak accents are prominently featured, with a lush core of berry flavors lending balance in the mouth. Big and supple, with fine weight and intensity through the finish.

1996 Pinot Noir, Les Galets Vineyard, San Luis Obispo County $29.   91

Dark blackish ruby cast. Moderately full-bodied. Balanced acidity. Highly extracted. Moderately oaked. Moderately tannic. Vanilla, black fruits, minerals. Fragrant and intense, with a linear minerally quality featuring fruit and sweet wood accents. Extracted and intense, showing a very firm structure, yet it seems to have the requisite stuffing to balance everything out in the end.

1996 Pinot Noir, Reserve, San Luis Obispo County $18.   86

Deep ruby cast. Moderately full-bodied. Full acidity. Highly extracted. Moderately tannic. Earthy, herbal aromas lead a deep and extracted palate with a firm minerally core. Angular through the finish with a hint of bitterness.

Lake Sonoma

1995 Zinfandel, Heck Cellar Selection, Dry Creek Valley $17.   84

Deep ruby hue with a slight fade. Moderately full-bodied. Balanced acidity. Highly extracted. Mildly oaked. Moderately tannic. Cedar, earth, red fruits. Aromatically reserved, with a touch of heat. Firm and flavorful on the palate, with chunky tannins through the finish.

Lakespring

1996 Chardonnay, California $11.99.   83

Deep straw hue. Forward tropical fruit and melon aromas. A vibrant entry is followed by a full-bodied mouthfeel with crisp acidity and a clean finish. Drink now.

Lambert Bridge

1997 Chardonnay, Sonoma County $18.   88

Pale straw hue. Generous yeast and toast aromas. A lush entry leads a moderately full-bodied palate with crisp acidity. Elegant, flavorful, and well-structured finish. Drink now.

1997 Chardonnay, Abbe Vineyard, Dry Creek Valley $24.   84

Intense deep gold. Impressive aromas of toasted oak, yeast, and lush fruit. Forceful on the attack with a moderately full body and a big oaky influence on the palate. Bright acids give good structure. Finishes with an assertive oaky note. Bottle age should help. Drink now or later.

1994 Crane Creek Cuvée, Dry Creek Valley $28.   92

Dark blackish red with purple highlights. Moderately full-bodied. Highly extracted. Moderately tannic. Plums, anise, brown spice. Rich, well-extracted flavors show plenty of chewy Cabernet fruit character, with fine-textured tannins on the finish. Well balanced and solidly structured.

1995 Crane Creek Cuvée, Dry Creek Valley $32.   85

Very deep, saturated purple-red hue. Deep, brooding anise and mineral aromas. A firm entry leads to a ripe and intense mouthfeel with big chewy tannins. Firm, concentrated finish. Somewhat reserved at present but strikes an admirable balance between structure and extract. Good for long-term cellaring.

1996 Merlot, Sonoma County $20.   88

Bright violet red. Generous berry and earth aromas. A rich attack leads a moderately full-bodied palate with balanced velvety tannins. Drink now.

1996 Zinfandel, Dry Creek Valley $20.   91

Deep ruby purple. Moderately full-bodied. Full acidity. Moderately extracted. Mildly oaked. Mildly tannic. Vanilla, briar fruits. Quite aromatic, with a lush, concentrated, fruit-centered palate feel. Lengthy and vibrant through the finish, with dusty tannins.

Scale: Superlative (96-100), Exceptional (90-95), Highly Recommended (85-89), Recommended (80-84), Not Recommended (Under 80)

Lamborn Family

1995 Zinfandel, The French Connection, Unfiltered, Howell Mountain, Napa Valley $22.50.   **93**

Full dark cherry cast. Moderately full-bodied. Highly extracted. Moderately tannic. Pepper, black fruits, red fruits. Good glycerous mouthful. Concentrated and intense, with great acid balance and finesse. Very structured, with ripe tannins giving an astringent finish. Quite classy.

Landmark

1997 Chardonnay, Overlook, Sonoma County/Santa Barbara County/Monterey County $22.   **89**

Yellow-gold. Medium-bodied. Balanced acidity. Moderately extracted. Sweet citrus fruits, oak spice, yeast. Sweetly aromatic, with subtle smoky accents and a bright, zesty core of flavors. Very supple and silky texture makes for a refined style.

1996 Chardonnay, Damaris Reserve, Sonoma County $32.   **88**

Deep yellow-gold. Moderately full-bodied. Balanced acidity. Moderately extracted. Cream, citrus, toast. Ripe and full yet tightly wound, with a big, weighty mouthfeel that shows a creamy, well-toasted character that remains rich through the finish.

1995 Pinot Noir, Grand Detour, Sonoma County $30.   **82**

Lang

1995 Zinfandel, Twin Rivers Vineyards, El Dorado $14.   **80**

Langtry

1996 White Meritage, Guenoc Valley $21.   **87**

Deep straw cast. Moderately full-bodied. Balanced acidity. Moderately extracted. Moderately oaked. Toasted coconut, cream. Luxuriant oaky notes are readily apparent on the nose and translate well to the palate. Rich and lush in style with solid acidity through the finish.

1994 Red Meritage, Napa Valley $41.   **87**

Bright reddish purple. Medium-bodied. Moderately extracted. Moderately tannic. Cassis, black tea, tobacco. Rich, pure cassis fruit aromas lead a tight mouthful of dark fruit flavors that linger through a fine-grained tannic finish. This has some solidity and structure. Very classic style.

1995 Red Meritage, North Coast $41.   **87**

Bright red-purple. Medium-bodied. Moderately extracted. Moderately tannic. Black fruits, minerals, brown spice. Youthful aromas. Angular and tough, with alcohol showing on the finish. Hard to appreciate at present.

Latcham Vineyards

1995 Zinfandel, El Dorado $10.   **83**

Deep blackish ruby cast. Moderately full-bodied. Balanced acidity. Moderately extracted. Mildly oaked. Mildly tannic. Minerals, black fruits. Rather reserved aromatically, with a firm, structured palate feel. Compact and flavorful, with a bit of tannic bite to the finish.

1995 Zinfandel, Special Reserve, El Dorado $14.   **84**

Deep blackish purple. Moderately full-bodied. Balanced acidity. Highly extracted. Mildly oaked. Moderately tannic. Plums, minerals. Quite aromatic, with a decidedly minerally note. Firm and dense on the palate, though well structured, with a precise and focused finish.

Laurel Glen

1994 Cabernet Sauvignon, Sonoma Mountain $38. **90**

Opaque reddish purple. Moderately full-bodied. Highly extracted. Quite tannic.
Green olive, eucalyptus, earth, bright fruits. Bright fruity flavors on entry are quickly
overwhelmed by huge dry, firm tannins through the finish. This is a densely structured
wine that will need years to resolve its tannins. Impressive but not showing its paces yet.

1995 Cabernet Sauvignon, Sonoma Mountain $38. **90**

Opaque, saturated purple. Full-bodied. Highly extracted. Quite tannic. Black fruits, tea.
Inky, deep, and impenetrable at present. Plenty of dark fruit flavors and big tannins. Not
a pleasure to drink now; needs years in the cellar.

Domaine Laurier

1996 Chardonnay, Reserve, Sonoma County $16. **91**

Deep yellow-straw hue. Pungent lemon and vanilla aromas show a powerful oak
influence. A crisp entry leads a moderately full-bodied palate balanced by vibrant
acidity. Persistent, intense finish. Perhaps a tad manipulated, but impressive. Drink now.

Laurier

1996 Chardonnay, Sonoma County $15. **88**

Bright yellow-gold. Generous citrus and vanilla aromas show an integrated wood accent.
A lush entry is followed by a moderately full-bodied palate with creamy acidity and a soft,
gentle finish. Stylish. Drink now.

1996 Pinot Noir, Sonoma County $16.99. **84**

Deep saturated ruby cast. Medium-bodied. Balanced acidity. Moderately extracted.
Moderately oaked. Mildly tannic. Vanilla, minerals, red fruits. Fragrant and intense,
though rather light in frame. Finishes on an intense, angular note. Shows fine grip.

Daniel Lawrence

1997 Chardonnay, Ricci Vineyard, Carneros $12. **81**

1996 Chardonnay, Vineyard Reserve, Santa Cruz Mountains $15. **89**

Bright golden yellow. Moderately full-bodied. Balanced acidity. Highly extracted.
Moderately oaked. Green apples, vanilla, butter. Generously aromatic, with a leesy,
ripe character coming through on a deeply flavored palate that shows opulent fruity
flavors, texture, and length. Very stylish.

1997 Chardonnay, Reserve, Santa Cruz Mountains $15. **84**

Pale yellow-gold. Medium-bodied. Balanced acidity. Moderately extracted. Moderately
oaked. Apples, white peach, vanilla. Fragrant, almost floral aromas lead a juicy, crisp
palate with judicious oak accents on the finish. Very bright and fresh.

1997 Merlot, Kathleen's Cuvée, Alexander Valley $11.99. **83**

Bright purple-red. Lean mineral and red fruit aromas. A crisp attack leads a light-bodied
palate with gentle tannins. The finish is light and fruity. A quaffer. Drink now.

Lazy Creek

1995 Pinot Noir, Anderson Valley $16. **86**

Pale ruby red. Medium-bodied. Moderately extracted. Mildly oaked. Mildly tannic.
Slightly warm aromas have mild vanilla and cherry notes. Crisp, simple cherry-berry
flavors linger through a mildly astringent finish. Shows some good varietal character.

Le Ducq

1994 Cabernet Sauvignon, Sylviane, Napa Valley $30. **89**

Deep reddish purple. Medium-bodied. Moderately extracted. Moderately tannic. Cassis,
bramble fruits, toasted oak, brown spice. Good toasty nose with suggestive dark fruit
notes. Solid, textured mouthfeel, with tight black Cabernet fruit flavors and good dry
tannins through the finish. Time will improve this.

1995 Cabernet Sauvignon, Sylviane, Napa Valley $30.   **88**

Deep ruby purple. Moderately full-bodied. Balanced acidity. Highly extracted. Mildly oaked. Moderately tannic. Black fruits, minerals. Rather reserved in style, but showing a ripe, fruit-centered quality. Firm, chunky tannins bite into the finish.

1993 Meritage, Napa Valley $91.   **92**

Deep ruby cast. Full-bodied. Balanced acidity. Moderately extracted. Mildly oaked. Mildly tannic. Earth, red fruits, minerals. Aromatically subdued, but rich and flavorful in the mouth. Ripe and seductive, with a velvety quality through the finish.

1994 Meritage, Napa Valley $99.   **93**

Saturated ruby cast. Moderately full-bodied. Balanced acidity. Moderately extracted. Moderately oaked. Mildly tannic. Brown spices, red fruits, minerals. Forward, generous aromas lead a rich and supple palate, buttressed by ripe tannins. Well balanced and built for aging, though this can be enjoyed now.

1995 Meritage, Napa Valley $65.   **89**

Deep ruby cast. Moderately full-bodied. Balanced acidity. Highly extracted. Moderately oaked. Mildly tannic. Chocolate, red fruits, minerals. Aromatically reserved, with a weighty, chunky quality. Big tannins bite down on the finish.

1994 Merlot, Sylviane, Napa Valley $30.   **90**

Very deep blackish ruby hue. Moderately full-bodied. Balanced acidity. Mildly oaked. Moderately tannic. Black fruits, chocolate, minerals. Beautifully textured, with a rich, lush mouthfeel and dense, dark flavors. Well balanced, with a cascade of velvety tannins at the finish. Approachable now, it should mellow nicely with near-term to mid-term (3–6 years) aging.

1995 Merlot, Sylviane, Napa Valley $30.   **86**

Deep blackish ruby hue. Moderately full-bodied. Balanced acidity. Highly extracted. Mildly oaked. Quite tannic. Black fruits, vanilla, lacquer. Assertive dark flavors are plentiful on a very firmly structured palate. Tannins really rear up on the finish, making this wine a bit tough and compact.

Lewis Cellars

1997 Chardonnay, Reserve, Napa Valley $34.99.   **90**

Bright pale gold. Reserved, tight aromas have a subtle yeasty accent. A bright entry leads a medium-bodied, flavor-packed palate, with subtle oaky notes and intense citrus zest character. An opulently textured style. Drink now or later.

Limerick Lane

1996 Zinfandel, Collins Vineyard, Russian River Valley $24.   **88**

Bright blackish purple. Moderately full-bodied. Low acidity. Moderately extracted. Moderately oaked. Mildly tannic. Vanilla, overripe red fruits, roasted nuts. Quite aromatic, with a lighter-styled and vibrant mouthfeel. Flavorful and lean through the zesty finish.

LinCourt

1997 Chardonnay, Santa Barbara County $14.   **89**

Deep gold. Rather developed oak spice aromas. Possibly a touch maderized. A rich entry leads a full-bodied palate with mature flavors and a thick alcoholic mouthfeel. Interesting now, but maybe not for cellaring.

1996 Syrah, Santa Barbara County $14.   **90**

Opaque, brilliant dark crimson hue to the rim. Intense black fruit cordial, briar, oak spice, and pickle flavor elements. Hefty wood tones. Supple entry. Full-bodied with plentiful velvety tannins. Lots of everything here in a supple, well-extracted style. Lingering, rich finish. Intense, concentrated, and stuffed. Drinkable now, but can improve with age.

Liparita
1997 Chardonnay, Carneros $24.   **85**

Full gold. Aromatically restrained with oaky notes. A soft entry leads a full-bodied palate with a generous texture and restrained acids, but dulled flavors. Finishes quickly. Drink now.

Livingston
1995 Cabernet Sauvignon, Stanley's Selection, Napa Valley $24.   **89**

Dark ruby cast. Moderately full-bodied. Balanced acidity. Highly extracted. Moderately oaked. Mildly tannic. Cassis, licorice, minerals. Aromatic and complex, with an emphasis on terroir, not winemaking. Firm though supple in the mouth, with a sense of brightness to the lengthy finish. Seamless.

Lockwood
1997 Chardonnay, Monterey $14.99.   **86**

Medium-full yellow-gold. Generous aromas of sweet wood and tart fruits. A bright entry leads a moderately full-bodied palate with angular acids. Fruit flavors are generous and ripe with judicious oak accents through the finish.

1996 Chardonnay, Partners' Reserve, Monterey $19.99.   **80**

1994 Cabernet Sauvignon, Partners' Reserve, Monterey $21.   **87**

Deep purple-tinged red. Medium-bodied. Highly extracted. Mildly tannic. Red berries, spice, vanilla. Spicy aromas lead a somewhat lean though reasonably concentrated mouthful of red berry fruit flavors through a long minerally finish. Well balanced and harmonious.

1996 Cabernet Sauvignon, Partners' Reserve, Monterey $19.99.   **83**

Full dark ruby-purple hue. Toasty black cherry and toasted oak aromas. A rich entry leads a moderately full-bodied palate with a rich center of dark fruits and chewy dry tannins that grip the finish. Solidly structured, ripe style. Drink now or later.

1995 Merlot, Monterey County $18.   **90**

Deep blackish ruby hue with purple highlights. Moderately full-bodied. Balanced acidity. Moderately extracted. Moderately oaked. Mildly tannic. Plums, vanilla, green herbs. Aromatic and quite flavorful, with real complexity. Quite snappy on the palate, with good grip and a lengthy oak-accented finish.

1996 Merlot, Monterey County $17.99.   **86**

Bright crimson-ruby hue. Good aromas of herbs with minerally edges. A crisp attack leads a medium-bodied palate with lean, dry tannins and lively acids. Drink now.

1995 Merlot, Partners' Reserve, Monterey County $24.   **92**

Very deep, opaque blackish ruby hue with purple highlights. Moderately full-bodied. Balanced acidity. Highly extracted. Heavily oaked. Mildly tannic. Black fruits, vanilla, minerals. Quite deeply flavored, with a pure expression of dark fruit flavors intertwined with wood and mineral notes. Well structured on the palate, with a hint of austerity and a lengthy finish.

1996 Merlot, Partners' Reserve, Monterey $24.99.   **91**

Bright purple-red. Attractive toasty vanilla and berry aromas. A supple attack leads a moderately full-bodied palate with generous ripe tannins and juicy acids. Finishes with lingering toasty notes and bright fruits. Drink now or later. Can improve with more age.

1996 Syrah, Monterey $16.   **83**

Dark ruby color, limpid with a slight fade. Coal tar, herbs, black fruits. Medium-bodied. Pruney, ripe, and soft, with a flabby finish. Drink now or later. Can improve with age.

Scale: Superlative (96-100), Exceptional (90-95), Highly Recommended (85-89), Recommended (80-84), Not Recommended (Under 80)

J. Lohr

1997 Chardonnay, Cypress, California $10.   84

Bright yellow-straw hue. Powerful banana and vanilla aromas show a big sweet oak accent.
A rich entry leads a full-bodied palate that has creamy acidity. Rounded, opulent finish.
Drink now.

1997 Chardonnay, Riverstone, Monterey $14.   91

Medium golden yellow. Quite aromatic with butter and apple aromas marked by vanilla
oak influence. A rich entry leads a moderately full-bodied palate with nutty oak flavors
coming through on the persistent finish. Excellent match with lobster, crab, or any rich
white fish. Drink now or later.

1996 Merlot, Cypress, California $10.50.   87

Deep ruby purple with brilliant highlights. Moderately full-bodied. Balanced acidity.
Highly extracted. Mildly oaked. Moderately tannic. Cherry cordial, licorice, bacon.
Aromatic and deeply flavored, with a sturdy, well-structured palate feel. Velvety tannins
bite into the finish, but the stuffing indicates that near-term cellaring should help open
up this wine.

1996 Syrah, South Ridge, Paso Robles $14.   88

Dark black cherry color, limpid and brilliant. Generous, sound bramble fruit and
vanilla flavors. Subtle wood tones. Smooth entry. Moderately full-bodied with crisp acidity.
Moderate drying tannins. Chunky, rich, and fruity. Lengthy finish. Drinkable now, but
can improve with age.

Lokoya

1995 Chardonnay, Wild Yeast, Napa Valley $30.   80

1995 Cabernet Sauvignon, Diamond Mountain, Napa Valley $100.   89

Deep, saturated blackish ruby hue. Intense chocolate, herb, and mineral aromas show
judicious oak usage. A lush entry leads to a thick, full-bodied mouthfeel with big velvety
tannins. Firm, grippy finish. A real heavyweight in every respect. A very ripe style that is
rather fatiguing at present. Good for long-term cellaring.

1995 Cabernet Sauvignon, Mount Veeder, Napa Valley $100.   87

Deep, saturated purple-red hue. Brooding, intense red fruit and mineral aromas show
a firm oak accent. A structured entry leads to a full-bodied palate with a big tannic
wallop. Clipped, tannic finish. Quite tough at present. May come around with years
of cellaring. Seems to have the fruit to hold out but rather shy of acidity. Good for
long-term cellaring.

1995 Cabernet Sauvignon, Rutherford, Napa Valley $100.   95

Very deep, intense ruby hue. Powerful brown spice, cedar, and berry aromas carry a
hefty wood accent. A lush entry leads to an extraordinarily flavorful palate with cordial-
like intensity. Chewy tannins are buttressed by sturdy acidity. Intense flavorful finish. Lots
of wood to be sure, but has the fruit extract to carry the day. Drink now or later.

Lolonis

1996 Chardonnay, Private Reserve, Redwood Valley, Mendocino $25.   88

Bright green-gold. Medium-bodied. Full acidity. Moderately extracted. Mildly oaked.
Vanilla, white peach. Warm, smoky aromas lead a silky, rounded palate featuring sweet
citrus flavors. Broad texture makes for a substantial style.

1996 Cabernet Sauvignon, Redwood Valley $17.   81

1994 Cabernet Sauvignon, Private Reserve, Mendocino County $25.   89

Deep, saturated ruby-red hue. Perfumed brown spice and black fruit aromas carry a
pronounced wood accent. A lush attack leads to a moderately full-bodied palate with
integrated tannins. Harmonious and well balanced with the structure to contain the
ripeness. Flavorful, grippy finish. Developing beautifully. Drink now or later.

1996 Merlot, Private Reserve, Redwood Valley $25.   84

Bright purple-red. Generous overripe berry fruit and chocolatey aromas. A lush entry leads a thick, full-bodied palate with comparatively low acidity levels and chunky tannins. Big, rich finish. This is a heavier style in need of food. Drink now.

1995 Zinfandel, Redwood Valley $17.   89

Deep blackish purple. Moderately full-bodied. Balanced acidity. Moderately extracted. Moderately oaked. Mildly tannic. Chocolate, black fruits. Quite aromatic, with a rich, supple mouthfeel. Ripe and velvety through the long, flavorful finish.

1995 Zinfandel, Private Reserve, Redwood Valley $25.   86

Deep blackish purple. Moderately full-bodied. Balanced acidity. Moderately extracted. Moderately oaked. Mildly tannic. Chocolate, black fruits. Pleasantly aromatic, with well-integrated oak and fruit flavors. Rich and supple in the mouth, with chunky tannins through the finish.

Longoria

1995 Cabernet Franc, Blues Cuvée, Santa Ynez Valley $21.   81

1997 Pinot Noir, Bien Nacido Vineyard, Santa Maria Valley $32.   82

Lyeth

1995 Meritage, North Coast $9.   81

MacRostie

1997 Chardonnay, Carneros $17.99.   84

Medium-bright gold. Mild aromas of butter with heavy oak accents. A dull entry leads a moderately full-bodied palate with dry flavors that come through on the finish. Not very generous. Drink now.

1996 Merlot, Carneros $26.   86

Saturated ruby red. Muted, minerally, floral aromas. A stern attack leads a moderately full-bodied palate with drying tannins. The finish is tannic, though flavorful. Well structured, and rather tight at present. Drink now or later. Can improve with more age.

1995 Pinot Noir, Carneros $17.75.   88

Pale bright cherry red. Medium-bodied. Moderately extracted. Mildly oaked. Mildly tannic. Rich perfumed red fruit aromas show nice varietal character. Crisp and fruity on the palate, with supple berry flavors. A hint of tannin and toasted oak on the finish.

1995 Pinot Noir, Reserve, Carneros $25.   91

Bright translucent blood red. Medium-bodied. Moderately extracted. Moderately oaked. Mildly tannic. Excellent rich Pinot Noir fruit aromas show great varietal character, with eucalyptus notes. Supple, rounded, and delicate through the lingering finish. A toasty chocolate note adds appeal. Drinking nicely now.

Maddalena

1996 Cabernet Sauvignon, Central Coast $9.95.   81

1996 Merlot, San Simeon Reserve, Central Coast $14.95.   82

Madroña

1993 Quintet, El Dorado $15.   86

Deep ruby-violet hue Moderately full-bodied. Highly extracted. Quite tannic. Leather, earth, minerals. Austere dark fruit aromas lead a dry, minerally mouthful of flavors, with an earthy finish. Tannins are quite demanding and tough at present.

1996 Zinfandel, Reserve, El Dorado $16.   86

Deep blackish purple. Full-bodied. Balanced acidity. Moderately extracted. Moderately oaked. Moderately tannic. Black fruits, chocolate. Rather reserved aromatically, but supple and rich, with a chunky, generous mouthfeel. Deeply flavored through the finish.

Scale: Superlative (96-100), Exceptional (90-95), Highly Recommended (85-89), Recommended (80-84), Not Recommended (Under 80)

132

Marcelina

1996 Chardonnay, Napa Valley $20. — 83

Bright yellow-straw cast. Moderately full-bodied. Balanced acidity. Highly extracted. Minerals, citrus peel. Bright and aromatic, with a full impression in the mouth and a firm, pithy finish. Solid and flavorful.

1993 Cabernet Sauvignon, Napa County $20. — 85

Medium ruby red with ripe aromas. A thick entry leads a moderately full-bodied palate with ripe, mature fruit flavors and tough chewy tannins. Seems rather old fashioned. Drink now.

Marietta

1996 Cabernet Sauvignon, Sonoma County $17. — 89

Saturated dark ruby hue. Ultra ripe primary fruit-forward aromas. A juicy entry leads a moderately full-bodied palate of jammy ripe fruit flavors with supple, silky tannins lingering on the finish. Low acids give a thickish mouthfeel. Drink now.

1996 Syrah, California $16. — 89

Deep dark red, limpid, and brilliant to the rim. Generous, appealing blackberry, bramble fruit, and cinnamon flavors. Generous wood tones. Smooth entry. Moderately full-bodied. Plentiful velvety tannins. Very bright flavors. Lingering rich finish. Fruit forward, fleshy, and hedonistic. Drink now or later. Can improve with more age.

Markham

1994 Cabernet Sauvignon, Napa Valley $15.49. — 89

Deep reddish purple. Medium-bodied. Highly extracted. Mildly tannic. Black cherries, chocolate, brown spice. Rich, mouthfilling, and textured, with full, rounded flavors and ample soft tannins through the finish. Very polished and plush. Attractive for current drinking.

1995 Cabernet Sauvignon, Napa Valley $19. — 88

Bright violet-red. Medium-bodied. Moderately extracted. Moderately tannic. Black fruits, minerals. Juicy, supple, and well balanced. This is well suited for current drinking, with a fine finish of powdery tannins giving grip.

1995 Merlot, Napa Valley $18. — 88

Very deep ruby to the rim with brilliant clarity. Moderately full-bodied. Balanced acidity. Subtly extracted. Moderately tannic. Licorice, plums, earth. Still reined in aromatically, this youthful wine opens up on the palate with fruit-driven flavors. Chewy tannins bite into the finish.

1996 Merlot, Napa Valley $19. — 86

Deep, saturated ruby red. Bright candied red fruit aromas show a subtle oak accent. A crisp attack leads a medium-bodied palate with vibrant acidity and mild tannins. The finish is generous, soft, and flavorful. An effusively clean and fruity effort. Drink now.

1995 Merlot, Reserve, Napa Valley $38. — 89

Deep, saturated ruby red. Generous red fruit and vanilla aromas show a modest oak accent. A lush attack leads a medium-bodied palate with drying, woody tannins. The finish is supple and rounded. A mellow style, but well balanced and structured. Drink now.

1995 Zinfandel, Napa $16. — 92

Blood red with a subtle purple note. Medium-bodied. Balanced acidity. Moderately extracted. Moderately oaked. Mildly tannic. Black fruits, bittersweet chocolate. Rich, ripe fruit flavors reveal some depth and persistence on the palate, with a good dose of vanilla oak seasoning. Pleasantly chewy, with great balance.

Martin Brothers (Renamed Martin & Weyrich, Spring 1999)

1995 Cabernet Sauvignon, Etrusco, Paso Robles $18. 89

Medium ruby red. Medium-bodied. Moderately extracted. Mildly tannic. Red berry fruits, chocolate, minerals. Developed aromas show an earthy generosity that is confirmed on the palate, with brisk acids and ripe fruit flavors. Seasoned with a dose of oak spice that emerges on the finish.

NV Insieme Red, Central Coast $10. 81

1996 Nebbiolo, Central Coast $11. 81

1995 Nebbiolo, Vecchio, Central Coast $20. 84

Bright blackish ruby cast. Moderately full-bodied. Full acidity. Highly extracted. Mildly oaked. Mildly tannic. Red fruits, flowers, earth. Quite aromatic, with a distinctive earthy, herbal edge. Finishes on a lean note, with angular acidity.

1996 Sangiovese, Il Palio, Central Coast $12. 80

1998 Moscato Allegro, California $10. 86

Bright golden hue with a slight spritz. Forward melon and pear aromas. A vibrant entry leads a flavorful palate displaying juicy acidity and mild sweetness. Lively and refreshing. Drink now.

Martinelli

1996 Chardonnay, Gold Ridge, Russian River Valley $20. 95

Deep, saturated yellow-straw hue. Powerful yeast, cream, and spice aromas show a hefty oak accent. A rich entry leads a full-bodied but balanced palate. Extremely flavorful and big; this is a showy, opulent style. Drink now.

1996 Chardonnay, Charles Ranch, Sonoma Coast $30. 86

Deep, saturated yellow-straw hue. Generous cream and hazelnut aromas carry a toasty oak influence. A supple entry leads a moderately full-bodied palate. A big, rich style with shy acidity. On the fat side, but flavorful and opulent, with a touch of wood. Drink now.

1997 Gewürztraminer, Russian River Valley $12. 93

Deep, saturated green-gold hue. Powerful, varietally intense lychee, spice, and sweet citrus aromas. A rich entry leads a full-bodied palate, with crisp acidity and a hint of sweetness. Big, intense, and rich, with great power. Drink now.

1996 Pinot Noir, Martinelli Vineyard, Russian River Valley $25. 88

Pale ruby-garnet cast. Moderately full-bodied. Balanced acidity. Moderately extracted. Moderately oaked. Mildly tannic. Green herbs, spice, minerals. Unusual aromatics lead a full and flavorful impression in the mouth. Ripe and zesty through the warming finish.

1997 Zinfandel, Louisa & Giuseppe, Russian River Valley $18. 91

Opaque, saturated violet red. Powerful, brooding black fruit, anise, and spice aromas. A jammy entry leads a full-bodied palate, with shy acidity and velvety tannins. Hedonistic and rich, with hefty ripeness, but there is a dry, savory edge to the finish. Drink now.

1996 Zinfandel, Jackass Vineyard, Russian River Valley $25. 96

Deep blackish ruby hue with a slight haze. Full-bodied. Balanced acidity. Highly extracted. Heavily oaked. Mildly tannic. Pickle barrel, black fruits, pomegranate, spice cabinet. Redolent of wood seasoning, with a distinctive pickled note often associated with American oak. Full and rich on the palate, with a thick, velvety texture. Lengthy and supple through the finish. Exotic and intense.

1997 Muscat Alexandria, Jackass Hill, Russian River Valley $18/375 ml. 90

Bright straw hue. Perfumed flower, peach blossom, and Muscat aromas. A rich entry leads a moderately sweet, full-bodied palate. Extremely flavorful, with an unctuous, viscous texture. Drink now.

Scale: Superlative (96-100), Exceptional (90-95), Highly Recommended (85-89), Recommended (80-84), Not Recommended (Under 80)

Louis Martini

1997 Chardonnay, North Coast $10.   83
Pale straw cast. Medium-bodied. Full acidity. Moderately extracted. Flowers, citrus.
Vibrant aromas have an unusual overtone. Lean, crisp, and zesty through the finish.

1996 Chardonnay, Reserve, Russian River Valley $18.   82

1996 Sauvignon Blanc, Napa Valley $9.   80

1994 Barbera, Heritage Collection, Lake County $12.   87
Bright blackish ruby cast. Medium-bodied. Full acidity. Moderately extracted. Mildly
tannic. Red fruits, minerals. Rather reserved aromatically, but flavorful and very well
structured on the palate. Finishes on an austere, minerally note, and shows admirable
restraint. Will be excellent at the table.

1994 Cabernet Sauvignon, Reserve, Napa Valley $18.   91
Bright red-purple. Moderately full-bodied. Highly extracted. Moderately tannic. Cassis,
minerals, vanilla. Rich, spiced black fruit aromas follow through on the palate, with fine
grip and balance making for an approachable style that will age well.

**1994 Cabernet Sauvignon, Monte Rosso Vineyard Selection,
Sonoma Mountain $30.**   92
Dark blackish red with purple highlights. Medium-bodied. Moderately extracted. Mildly
tannic. Vanilla, black fruits, brown spice, earth. Oak-accented aromas lead an earthy but
rounded palate with assertive and complex flavors and soft tannins through the finish.
Harmonious and very forward.

**1995 Cabernet Sauvignon, Monte Rosso Vineyard Selection,
Sonoma Valley $35.**   87
Saturated blood red. Moderately full-bodied. Highly extracted. Moderately tannic.
Jammy black fruits, brown spice. Dusty, ripe aromas lead a firm palate, with gripping
tannins and fine persistence through the finish. Tannins have a dry, powdery quality.
A more old-fashioned style.

1995 Merlot, Reserve, Russian River Valley $18.   88
Blood red with a brick-red rim. Leathery, extravagantly spiced black fruit aromas show
a distinct oak influence. A bright entry leads a medium-bodied palate with slight but
powdery dry tannins. The lingering, spicy finish shows complex flavors. Very evolved
and mature tasting. Drink now.

1993 Zinfandel, Heritage Collection, Sonoma Valley $12.   86
Bright ruby cast. Moderately full-bodied. Balanced acidity. Moderately extracted. Mildly
tannic. Minerals, red fruits. Reserved aromatically, with distinctive minerally nuances.
Features an elegant, balanced character with a firm, focused finish. Artfully crafted for
those who tire of "Zin monsters."

Martini & Prati

1996 Pinot Bianco, Monterey $10.   84
Deep golden cast. Moderately full-bodied. Balanced acidity. Moderately extracted.
Flowers, citrus, tropical fruits. Quite aromatic, with some complexity to the flavors.
Full though angular on the palate, with steely acidity through the finish.

1996 Vino Grigio, California $12.50.   88
Bright golden cast. Moderately full-bodied. Full acidity. Moderately extracted. Tropical
fruits, spice, cream. Ripe aromas follow through on the palate, with a sense of richness
to the fruit-accented flavors. Full and lush, with zesty acidity providing good grip.

1993 Fuoco di Sant Elmo, California $20.   82

1995 Zinfandel, California $15.   82

1996 Zinfandel, Reserve, Russian River Valley $18.   90
Deep blackish purple. Full-bodied. Balanced acidity. Moderately extracted. Heavily oaked.
Mildly tannic. Vanilla, black fruits. Extremely aromatic, with real intensity to the dark
fruit flavors and a hedonistic wave of toasty oak accents. Lush and exotic on the palate,

with velvety tannins. Intense and charming, not unlike a top Aussie Shiraz.

Paul Masson
Rich Ruby Port, California $5.99.   82

Matanzas Creek
1996 Chardonnay, Sonoma Valley $30.   88
Brilliant yellow-straw hue. Subdued mineral and citrus aromas. A crisp entry leads a moderately full-bodied palate with firm acidity and fine intensity. The finish is creamy and generous. A well-structured wine that should open with some aging. Midterm cellar candidate (3–6 years).

1995 Chardonnay, Journey, Sonoma Valley $95.   94
Deep straw hue. Opulent vanilla, yeast, and orange aromas show an attractive leesy quality and generous oak influence. A firm entry leads a full-bodied palate that has lean, intense acidity. Flavorful and complex through the racy finish. Drink now.

1996 Sauvignon Blanc, Sonoma County $18.   91
Bright golden yellow. Medium-bodied. Balanced acidity. Moderately extracted. Moderately oaked. Lime zest, brown spice, minerals. Toasty tart citrus aromas lead a solid palate, with a minerally backbone and toasty oak spices on the finish. Well structured, with a good mouthfeel. This would be a good food partner.

1996 Merlot, Sonoma Valley $47.   88
Dark ruby red. Muted aromas show a mild oaky character. A soft entry leads a moderately full-bodied palate with plenty of fine-grained tannins and dark fruit flavors. Rather heavily extracted flavors make for a leaner style with a drying finish.

1994 Merlot, Journey, Sonoma Valley $155.   94
Saturated dark violet-ruby hue. Impressively powerful, dense oak-accented black fruit and olive aromas show great complexity. A firm attack leads a full-bodied palate with fine-grained gripping tannins and powerful, concentrated flavors. Rather a dry finish with spice and minerals lingering. Good for long-term cellaring.

Maxus
1991 Midnight Cuvée, California $19.99.   90
Deep salmon cast. Full-bodied. Red fruits, toast. Generous aromas show a complex character with oak nuances. Rich, ripe, and rounded in the mouth, with fine weight and intensity. Subtle red fruit flavors linger on the finish.

1991 Brut, California $19.99.   90
Full yellow-gold. Moderately full-bodied. Nuts, apples. Developed nutty, bready aromas follow through on a soft yet generous palate showing good maturity and length. Plush, rich, and full-flavored. For those who like mature styles.

1991 English Cuvée, California $29.99.   91
Full golden yellow. Moderately full-bodied. Bread, nuts, baked apples. Profoundly rich, developed aromas show a powerful yeast accent that comes through on the palate, with rich flavors and soft acids. A very hedonistic and voluptuous style.

Mayacamas
1992 Cabernet Sauvignon, Napa Valley $30.   89
Deep ruby red with a slight fade. Medium-bodied. Balanced acidity. Moderately extracted. Mildly tannic. Mushroom, minerals, licorice. Aromatic and intense, with a high-toned, earthy quality throughout. Lean and angular on the palate, with a crisp finish.

1993 Cabernet Sauvignon, Napa Valley $38.   86
Deep cherry red with a garnet rim. Interesting and mature forest, earth, and herb aromas. A lush entry leads to a medium-bodied palate with grippy tannins and a well-balanced structure. Angular, flavorful finish. Showing some mature complexities and

drinking well now. Drink within five years.

1993 Sauvignon Blanc, Late Harvest, Napa Valley $16/375 ml.   **86**

Deep bronzed golden hue. Moderately full-bodied. Balanced acidity. Moderately extracted. Mildly oaked. Petrol, rancio, tropical fruits. Quite complex aromas, with a rich, lush, viscous palate feel. Carries an almost Alsatian tone of exoticism. A touch of acidity keeps the finish lively. Individualistic style.

Peter McCoy

1996 Chardonnay, Clos de Pierres, Knights Valley $39.   **90**

Yellow-straw hue with a slight haze. Moderately full-bodied. Balanced acidity. Highly extracted. Mildly oaked. Yeast, cream, citrus. Forward aromas are quite complex, showing a big yeasty, creamy accent. Full and rich in the mouth with an opulent and rounded character. Flavorful through the finish.

McDowell

1996 Viognier, Mendocino $15.   **84**

Deep straw cast. Full-bodied. Full acidity. Moderately extracted. Minerals. Rather reserved aromatically, with a generous mouthfeel buttressed by vibrant and racy acidity. Well structured, but neutral in the flavor department.

1997 Grenache Rosé, Mendocino $9.   **83**

Very pale pinkish salmon hue. Subdued berry and citrus aromas. A crisp entry leads a taut, moderately light-bodied palate that has vibrant acidity. The finish is clean and flavorful. Drink now.

1997 Syrah, Mendocino $12.   **85**

Bright purple-red hue to the rim. Subdued earth, herb, and red fruit aromas. A firm attack leads a moderately full-bodied palate, with aggressive astringent tannins. Lacks somewhat for acidic grip. Tannic, earthy finish. Rather tough at present, with a funky edge that should blow off. Drink within five years.

McIlroy

1996 Zinfandel, Porter-Bass Vineyard, Russian River Valley $18.   **86**

Bright blackish ruby cast. Moderately full-bodied. Balanced acidity. Moderately extracted. Mildly oaked. Mildly tannic. Black fruits, minerals. Pleasantly aromatic, with a deep fruit core. Lush but firm in the mouth, with chunky tannins through the finish.

McKeon-Phillips

1996 Chardonnay, Reserve, Santa Barbara County $21.33.   **88**

Deep yellow-straw cast. Moderately full-bodied. Balanced acidity. Moderately extracted. Moderately oaked. Vanilla, spice, citrus. Generous aromas feature a hefty wood accent that follows through on a ripe, rounded mouthfeel. The finish is crisp and flavorful.

Mer et Soleil

1993 Chardonnay, Central Coast $30.   **94**

Moderately full-bodied. Lots of acid. Lots of fruit. Lots of oak. Dry. Reminiscent of baking bread, citrus, pears, butterscotch. Rich, piquant fruit is swamped by layers of aromatic oak. Rounded in the mouth, immensely proportioned, and chock full of succulent, stunningly complex flavors. This is a big-boned Chardonnay, kept in balance by its fabulous lingering acidity.

1994 Chardonnay, Central Coast $31.99.   **93**

Very deep gold. Medium-bodied. Balanced acidity. Moderately extracted. Heavily oaked. Dry. Reminiscent of citrus, brown spice. Big flavors reveal a strongly oak-influenced palate with some bright citrus fruit underneath. Generous, slightly oily texture is kept lively by some good acidity.

1995 Chardonnay, Central Coast $35.   **93**

Bright yellow-gold. Medium-bodied. Highly extracted. Heavily oaked. Full vanilla oak aromas lead an oak-accented palate with plenty of tropical nuances, and spice and smoke on the finish. The acid balance is zippy, making this a powerful yet polished style.   137

1996 Chardonnay, Central Coast $34.99. 92

Bright yellow-straw hue. Forcefully aromatic with oaky, nutty accents. A flavorful attack leads a moderately full-bodied palate with complex flavors of yeast, toasted oak, and tart apples. Well structured and assertive through the finish. This would be an excellent match with lobster, crab, or any rich white fish. Drink now.

Meridian

1997 Chardonnay, Santa Barbara County $11. 84

Bright green-straw hue. Medium-bodied. Balanced acidity. Vanilla, sweet citrus. Appealing vanilla and sweet fruit aromas lead a direct, juicy mouthful of fruit flavors that linger through the finish.

1996 Chardonnay, Coastal Reserve, Edna Valley $15. 89

Bright yellow-gold. Moderately full-bodied. Balanced acidity. Moderately extracted. Mildly oaked. Cream, minerals, citrus. Forward aromas feature a complex yeasty note. Big and ripe in the mouth, with an opulent, creamy texture. Lengthy flavorful finish.

1997 Sauvignon Blanc, California $8.50. 83

Bright yellow-gold. Medium-bodied. Balanced acidity. Moderately extracted. Mildly oaked. Butter, vanilla, citrus. Rich buttery aromas with a smoky note. Rounded, mouthfilling flavors with plenty of glycerin and alcohol. Well proportioned, showing Chardonnay structure and character.

1995 Cabernet Sauvignon, California $12. 86

Bright ruby hue to the rim. Moderately full-bodied. Balanced acidity. Moderately extracted. Moderately oaked. Mildly tannic. Cedar, red fruits. Pleasantly aromatic, with a well-integrated oak accent and a core of ripe fruit flavors. Understated, elegant, and well balanced.

1994 Cabernet Sauvignon, Coastal Reserve, California $20. 86

Deep ruby red to the rim. Moderately full-bodied. Balanced acidity. Moderately extracted. Moderately oaked. Mildly tannic. Cherry cordial, vanilla. Generous aromas feature a hefty oak accent. Firm and flavorful in the mouth, with angular tannins through the finish.

1995 Merlot, California $13. 83

Very deep red with brilliant highlights. Medium-bodied. Balanced acidity. Subtly extracted. Mildly tannic. Red fruits, vanilla, black tea. Lighter in style, with straightforward fruit-driven flavors and an accent on acidity at the finish.

1997 Pinot Noir, Santa Barbara $14. 85

Bright pale ruby cast. Moderately light-bodied. Full acidity. Moderately extracted. Moderately tannic. Minerals, red fruits. Lean, minerally aromas lead a firm and tightly wound palate feel. Angular through the finish, with a hint of bitterness.

1996 Pinot Noir, Coastal Reserve, Santa Barbara County $20. 88

Deep ruby cast. Moderately full-bodied. Balanced acidity. Moderately extracted. Moderately oaked. Mildly tannic. Spice, minerals, red fruits. Forward aromatics carry a prominent oak accent. Ripe and full in the mouth, with a sense of richness. Finishes with grainy tannins.

1996 Syrah, Paso Robles $14. 88

Deep purple-red, limpid, and brilliant to the rim. Generous, fantastic cedar and red currant flavors. Firm entry. Medium-bodied with crisp acidity. Moderate, grainy tannins. Well gripped through the finish, with fine structuring acids. Lingering finish. Bright and lively, with a nice oak overlay. Drink now.

1996 Zinfandel, Paso Robles $12. 86

Deep blackish ruby cast. Medium-bodied. Balanced acidity. Moderately extracted. Heavily oaked. Mildly tannic. Vanilla, black fruits. A fragrant oak influence is readily apparent on the nose, and joins a restrained core of fruit flavors in the mouth. Well balanced and elegant, in a sturdy Claret style.

Merryvale

1997 Chardonnay, Starmont, Napa Valley $20. 83

Deep straw cast. Moderately full-bodied. Full acidity. Moderately extracted. Minerals, flint, butter. Unusual high-toned aromas are focused and precise. Turns full and rich in the mouth, with a tapering finish.

1996 Chardonnay, Reserve, Napa Valley $30. 85

Bright yellow-straw cast. Medium-bodied. Full acidity. Moderately extracted. Mildly oaked. Smoke, toast, citrus. Shows a forward toasty oak accent throughout. Light in the mouth, with a bright, zesty texture. Crisp and vibrant finish.

1996 Vignette, Napa Valley $22. 93

Deep green-gold. Moderately full-bodied. Balanced acidity. Moderately extracted. Mildly oaked. Figs, lanolin, toast. Features classic nutty Semillon aromas with a judicious overlay of oak. Rich and flavorful in the mouth, and well balanced through a very lengthy finish. A decidedly harmonious style.

1996 Sauvignon Blanc, Napa Valley $17. 89

Deep yellow-gold. Full-bodied. Full acidity. Highly extracted. Mildly oaked. Butter, vanilla, citrus. Full and toasty on the nose with very ripe overtones. Mouthfilling and vibrant through the lengthy finish. A well-structured, assertive Fumé style.

1996 Cabernet Sauvignon, Hillside, Napa Valley $18. 86

Saturated violet red. Medium-bodied. Highly extracted. Moderately tannic. Red berries, minerals. Bright, juicy, and somewhat cordial-like flavors, with a mild note of green tannins on the finish. Acids remain quite lively, accentuating a dry, tannic finish.

1994 Cabernet Sauvignon, Napa Valley $27. 87

Dark saturated ruby appearance. Medium-bodied. Highly extracted. Moderately tannic. Cassis, plums, licorice, chocolate, black tea. Generous black fruit aromas lead a solid palate with deep flavors. Solid tannins on the finish. Well structured, this should improve with some maturity.

1995 Cabernet Sauvignon, Reserve, Napa Valley $30. 91

Dark blood-violet red. Moderately full-bodied. Highly extracted. Quite tannic. Cassis, cedar, mineral. A concentrated, fruit-packed palate with toasty overtones. Firm-edged tannins show on the finish. This will need some time to resolve its firm structure.

1993 Profile, Napa Valley $48. 88

Opaque garnet red. Moderately full-bodied. Highly extracted. Quite tannic. Licorice, brown spice, black fruits. A brooding nose leads a full-flavored palate that is tightly wound. Firm dry finish. This needs cellaring to show its potential.

1994 Profile, Napa Valley $55. 96

Saturated, opaque blood red. Moderately full-bodied. Highly extracted. Quite tannic. Nutmeg, oriental spice, cassis. Exotic, oriental-spiced aromas are intriguing. Solidly extracted, with very tight, grainy tannins. This is a wine for long-term (7–10 years) cellaring; needs more bottle age to show its best.

1995 Profile, Napa Valley $66. 91

Bright ruby-violet hue. Ripe plummy aromas with a dusty, spiced accent. A firm entry leads a medium-bodied palate with very tight tannins and good fruit concentration. Well gripped and dry through the finish. Drink now or later.

1995 Merlot, Reserve, Napa Valley $32. 90

Very deep blackish ruby hue to the rim. Moderately full-bodied. Balanced acidity. Highly extracted. Moderately oaked. Moderately tannic. Chocolate, black fruits, licorice. Deep and flavorful with a dense core of extract. Though firmly structured, this wine is well balanced, with a lingering finish. Approachable now but will improve with mid-term (3–6 years) aging.

1996 Merlot, Reserve, Napa Valley $32. 86

Saturated dark ruby hue. Restrained aromas show a woody character with muted fruit. A lean entry leads a full-bodied palate with tough, drying tannins masking fruit flavors. Finishes in a rustic, dry manner. This seems to be drying out.

Peter Michael

1996 Chardonnay, "Clos du Ciel," Napa County $38.   90

Bright yellow-gold. Moderately full-bodied. Full acidity. Moderately extracted. Lime, lemon zest, spice. Bright, zesty fruit flavors have a piercing purity that is not dulled by considerable oak spice and yeasty notes. This is bright and youthful at present, with a very distinctive character.

1996 Chardonnay, "Belle Côte," Knights Valley $42.   89

Bright yellow-straw cast. Moderately full-bodied. Full acidity. Mildly oaked. Cream, citrus, yeast. Forward aromatics carry a complex yeasty quality throughout. Bright and firm in the mouth with zesty acidity through the finish.

1996 Sauvignon Blanc, L'Apres-Midi, Napa County $20.   91

Full bright yellow-gold. Moderately full-bodied. Full acidity. Highly extracted. Moderately oaked. Toasted oak, ripe citrus. Very aromatic, with distinct oak and smoky yeast influences. Rich, heavily toasted flavors with fine concentration and grip through the finish. Nice now, though this should develop further with short-term (1–2 years) cellaring.

1994 Les Pavots Red, Knights Valley $35.   90

Saturated red. Medium-bodied. Highly extracted. Moderately tannic. Black cherries, plums, vanilla, tobacco. Chewy Cabernet fruit flavors lead cigar box notes on the finish, which is quite dry from the assertive tannins. Shows some good structure; quite a heavyweight.

Michel-Schlumberger

1993 Cabernet Sauvignon, Dry Creek Valley $19.50.   86

Deep purple-red. Medium-bodied. Moderately extracted. Mildly tannic. Tart red fruits, minerals. Rather crisp and tart, with focused cherry fruit flavors up front that give way to lemony acids and minerally notes on the finish.

1994 Cabernet Sauvignon, Dry Creek Valley $20.   90

Saturated red-purple. Moderately full-bodied. Highly extracted. Quite tannic. Red fruits, minerals. Youthful and tannic, showing a floral nose and deep palate with firm tannins and vibrant berry fruit flavors. This needs time.

1995 Cabernet Sauvignon, Dry Creek Valley $22.   81

1993 Cabernet Sauvignon, Schlumberger Reserve, Dry Creek Valley $35.   86

Black cherry red. Medium-bodied. Moderately extracted. Moderately tannic. Black cherries, mineral, spice. Aromas of mineral and black fruits follow on the palate. The finish turns dry, with a mildly bitter note. A lean, taut style.

1996 Merlot, Sonoma County $21.   83

Bright ruby-violet red. Lean herbal and red fruit aromas. A mild attack leads a medium-bodied palate with slight drying tannins and low acids. Drink now.

1996 Syrah, Coastal California $20.   86

Deep ruby red, opaque and brilliant, with a slight fade. Medium-bodied. Tart berry, raspberry, and mineral flavors. Lively acids make for an aggressive, puckering mouthful. Flavorsome and youthful. Drinkable now, but can improve with more age.

Midnight Cellars

1996 Chardonnay, Central Coast $19.   84

Deep straw cast. Medium-bodied. Full acidity. Highly extracted. Mildly oaked. Brown spices, minerals. Subdued aromas carry a pleasant oak accent. Crisp, lean, and very zesty through the finish.

1995 Cabernet Franc, Crescent, Paso Robles $15.   87

Bright ruby purple. Medium-bodied. Balanced acidity. Moderately extracted. Mildly oaked. Mildly tannic. Red fruits, brown spices, minerals. Aromatic, with a flavorful palate. Lean and angular through the finish, showing a firm structure on a lighter frame.

Scale: Superlative (96-100), Exceptional (90-95), Highly Recommended (85-89), Recommended (80-84), Not Recommended (Under 80)

140

1995 Cabernet Sauvignon, Nocturne, Paso Robles $15. 84

Bright ruby purple. Moderately full-bodied. Balanced acidity. Highly extracted. Heavily oaked. Moderately tannic. Black cherries, vanilla. Quite aromatic, with a hefty oak overlay and an intense, cordial-like fruit accent. Ripe and flavorful, with decent acidity and firm tannins on the finish.

1995 Merlot, Eclipse, Paso Robles $19. 89

Deep ruby red with a blackish hue. Moderately full-bodied. Balanced acidity. Highly extracted. Heavily oaked. Mildly tannic. Plums, vanilla, cordial. Fruit driven and quite aromatic, with a sense of sweetness to the flavors. Velvety, lush, and quite supple in the mouth, with a lengthy oak-tinged finish.

Mietz

1995 Merlot, Sonoma County $21. 89

Deep blackish ruby with a slight purplish cast. Moderately full-bodied. Balanced acidity. Highly extracted. Mildly oaked. Mildly tannic. Black fruits, vanilla, sweet herbs. Aromatic and flavorful with a sense of richness to the palate. Vibrant acidity lends some buoyancy to the dark fruit flavors. Tannins are still a bit chunky in the finish. Should integrate nicely in the near term.

Milano

1995 Zinfandel, Sanel Valley Vineyard, Mendocino County $12. 82

Mill Creek

1996 Merlot, Dry Creek Valley $17.50. 84

Bright violet hue with a slight fade. Anise and black plum aromas. A smooth attack leads a medium-bodied palate with soft tannins and juicy acids. Drink now.

Mirassou

1997 Chardonnay, Family Selection, Monterey County $11.95. 83

Pale straw cast. Medium-bodied. Full acidity. Moderately extracted. Minerals, bread dough. Firm, lean, and crisp, with a measure of austerity throughout. Angular, brisk finish.

1996 Pinot Blanc, Harvest Reserve, Monterey County $15.95. 81

1998 Riesling, Family Selection, Monterey County $7.50. 84

Pale straw hue. Aromas of butter, flowers, and tart apple, with an herbal twist. A soft entry leads a medium-bodied palate, with juicy fruit flavors lingering on the finish. Drink now.

1998 White Zinfandel, Family Selection, California $6.95. 80

1993 Cabernet Sauvignon, Monterey County $11.95. 85

Bright cherry red. Moderately light-bodied. Moderately extracted. Mildly tannic. Mint, cranberry, minerals. Attractive minty nose leads a crisp, clean palate, with bright red fruit flavors and a mildly astringent finish. Quite light in style but well balanced.

1994 Cabernet Sauvignon, Harvest Reserve, Napa Valley $17.95. 86

Bright purple-red. Moderately light-bodied. Moderately extracted. Mildly tannic. Tart cherries, raspberries. High-toned red fruit flavors give this wine a bright feel through the finish. Though the flavors are not especially deep, there is an appealingly accessible balance with plenty of bright fruity character.

1995 Cabernet Sauvignon, Harvest Reserve, Napa Valley $17.95. 87

Bright violet-red with a weak rim. Medium-bodied. Moderately extracted. Mildly tannic. Red fruits, vanilla. Bright berry fruit aromas follow through on a juicy, bright palate, with clean flavors and lively acids making for an easy-drinking style. Best drunk in its youth.

1990 Petite Sirah, Monterey County $35. 84

Full brick red with a subtly fading rim. Moderately full-bodied. Moderately extracted. Moderately tannic. Tobacco and currant aromas follow through on the palate, with a heavy spice and coffee character coming through on the finish. Very interesting and complex, showing marked maturity.

1996 Petite Sirah, Monterey County $11.95.   83

Opaque purple. Moderately full-bodied. Highly extracted. Quite tannic. Herbal and
blueberry aromas follow through on a palate that shows a thick, textured mouthfeel.
Impressive grainy tannins on the finish.

1995 Pinot Noir, Family Selection, Central Coast $10.95.   89

Pale ruby hue. Moderately light-bodied. Moderately extracted. Mildly oaked. Mildly
tannic. Crisp red berry fruit aromas have gamey notes. Lean and crisp, with subtle
astringency through the finish. Nice oak spice notes linger. Well balanced and drinking
well now.

1996 Pinot Noir, Family Selection, Monterey County $10.95.   83

Very pale red. Moderately light-bodied. Subtly extracted. Red fruits, dried herbs,
minerals. Crisp fruity aromas lead a lightly framed palate with lean, bright flavors
and a clean finish.

1995 Pinot Noir, Harvest Reserve, Monterey County $15.95.   85

Bright cherry red. Medium-bodied. Moderately extracted. Mildly oaked. Mildly tannic.
Smooth spicy cherry and berry flavors linger through the finish, with pleasing hints of
tannin and vanilla oak.

1996 Pinot Noir, Harvest Reserve, Monterey County $15.95.   86

Bright violet purple. Medium-bodied. Moderately extracted. Vanilla, cherries.
Sweet oak-driven aromas follow through well on the palate with supple fruity flavors.
Clean finish.

1988 Zinfandel, Harvest Reserve, Santa Clara Valley $32.50.   86

Fading garnet with browning pale rim. Moderately light-bodied. Low acidity. Subtly
extracted. Mildly tannic. Spice, stewed fruits. Very mature aromas have a stewed character
that is either interesting or off-putting, depending on your tastes. The flavors follow the
aromas, with dusty spice and stewed flavors. Graceful and mellow, with a soft mouthfeel.
Unrecognizable as Zinfandel.

1995 Zinfandel, Harvest Reserve, Santa Clara Valley $15.95.   80

1997 Johannisberg Riesling, Late Harvest, San Vicente Ranch,
Monterey County $15.95.   89

Deep straw hue. Attractive honeyed pineapple and tropical fruit aromas. A rich entry
leads a moderately full-bodied palate that has an oily texture and complex petrol
overtones. Sweet, but well balanced and extremely flavorful. Drink now.

Mission View

1995 Cabernet Franc, Paso Robles $13.50.   85

Bright ruby purple. Medium-bodied. Balanced acidity. Highly extracted. Moderately
oaked. Mildly tannic. Bacon fat, vanilla, minerals. Oak-driven flavors play out on a
lighter-styled palate. Lean and drying through the finish.

1996 Cabernet Sauvignon, Paso Robles $12.75.   84

Pale crimson with a purple fading rim. Sweet vanilla aromas with a note of cherry fruits.
A bright entry leads a medium-bodied palate with sweet fruit flavors and rather slight
tannins. Finishes with a note of warmth. Drink now.

1995 Merlot, Limited Release, Paso Robles $14.50.   81

1996 Merlot, Midnight Mischievous, Paso Robles $15.   81

1996 Zinfandel, Eastside Ecstasy, Paso Robles $13.50.   86

Bright ruby cast. Moderately full-bodied. Balanced acidity. Highly extracted. Moderately
tannic. Briar fruits. The generous fruit flavors carry a slight sense of overripeness. Firm
and compact on the palate, with an overtone of sweetness, and hefty tannins through
the finish.

Scale: Superlative (96-100), Exceptional (90-95), Highly Recommended (85-89),
Recommended (80-84), Not Recommended (Under 80)

Robert Mondavi

1996 Chardonnay, Napa Valley $19.   **87**

Bright yellow-gold. Medium-bodied. Balanced acidity. Moderately extracted. Vanilla, tart apple, spice. Crisp and bright, with citrus flavors and mild buttery texture; an elegant style. Shows good grip through the finish.

1996 Chardonnay, Carneros $25.   **81**

1996 Chardonnay, Reserve, Napa Valley $30.   **92**

Bright golden yellow. Moderately full-bodied. Balanced acidity. Moderately extracted. Moderately oaked. Ripe apples, vanilla, brown spice. Ripe toasty, spicy aromas. Broad and textured, with generous apple flavors and toasted oak accents throughout, and a flavorful finish.

1996 Sauvignon Blanc, Coastal, North Coast $8.   **81**

1996 Fumé Blanc, Napa Valley $12.   **83**

Deep yellow-straw hue. Moderately full-bodied. Full acidity. Moderately extracted. Mildly oaked. Vanilla, citrus, yeast. Oak influence is readily apparent on the nose and combines with a pleasant yeasty note to add a measure of complexity to the palate. Well balanced, with good intensity.

1994 Fumé Blanc, To-Kalon Vineyard Reserve, Napa Valley $20.   **89**

Deep yellow-gold. Moderately full-bodied. Full acidity. Moderately extracted. Moderately oaked. Brown spices, citrus, minerals. Quite aromatic, with a hefty note of barrel influence balanced by crisp fruit flavors. Full though vibrant on the palate, with a snappy finish.

1995 Fumé Blanc, To-Kalon Vineyard Reserve, Napa Valley $22.   **87**

Bright yellow-gold. Moderately full-bodied. Full acidity. Moderately extracted. Citrus, minerals. Youthful, with reserved aromatics and a tightly wound palate feel. Good intensity, with a firm structure through the finish. Should develop further with near-term cellaring.

1995 Cabernet Sauvignon, Coastal, North Coast $10.95.   **84**

Deep ruby hue to the rim. Medium-bodied. Balanced acidity. Moderately extracted. Mildly tannic. Dried herbs, earth, red fruits. Somewhat light in style, with an earthy quality throughout. Lean and angular through the finish.

1994 Cabernet Sauvignon, Napa Valley $22.   **87**

Dark reddish purple. Medium-bodied. Highly extracted. Moderately tannic. Cassis, plums, brown spice. Rather dry and austere at present, with some lean fruit flavors on the midpalate and solid tannins through the finish. Decently structured, this could happily take more cellar time.

1995 Cabernet Sauvignon, Napa Valley $21.   **91**

Saturated red with violet highlights. Medium-bodied. Highly extracted. Moderately tannic. Cassis, earth, brown spice. Rich black fruit aromas follow through on the palate, with earthy tannins giving grip. Solid and flavor-packed; nice both now and a few years hence.

1994 Cabernet Sauvignon, Oakville, Napa Valley $28.   **87**

Dark red. Medium-bodied. Moderately extracted. Moderately tannic. Black fruits, plums, cedar. Robustly flavorful, with chewy black fruit flavors and rich tannins on the finish. This is approachable and enjoyable now, but will benefit from one to two more years in bottle.

1995 Cabernet Sauvignon, Oakville, Napa Valley $27.   **87**

Deep ruby cast. Moderately full-bodied. Balanced acidity. Moderately extracted. Moderately oaked. Mildly tannic. Brown spices, cassis, minerals. Pleasantly aromatic, with a lush and supple mouthfeel that is buttressed by a firm, minerally backbone. Showing complexity and a sense of terroir. Well balanced and lengthy.

1995 Cabernet Sauvignon, SLD, Napa Valley $27.   88
Saturated red-purple. Moderately full-bodied. Highly extracted. Moderately tannic. Cassis, mint, cedar. Crisp yet full fruit-laden aromas follow through on the palate, with plenty of mineral stuffing and some hard-edged tannins that will need a few years to resolve.

1994 Cabernet Sauvignon, Reserve, Napa Valley $75.   89
Dark reddish purple. Moderately full-bodied. Highly extracted. Quite tannic. Cassis, black fruits, minerals. Somewhat meaty aromas. Well structured and proportioned, with impressive tannins drying out the finish. Solidly extracted flavors make for an assertive style that would benefit from some extra fleshiness on the midpalate.

1995 Cabernet Sauvignon, Reserve, Napa Valley $75.   93
Saturated dark red. Moderately full-bodied. Highly extracted. Quite tannic. Earth, mineral. Rich aromas, hinting of dark fruits and earth. Dense, gripping palate of fleshy dark fruits and granular tannins. Big-shouldered and rather young at present, though drinkable.

1997 Merlot, Coastal, Central Coast $14.   84
Bright crimson red. Clean aromas of minerals and herbs. A crisp attack leads a medium-bodied palate with light drying tannins and lively acids that provide some grip. There are nice fruit accents throughout. The finish is clean and quick. Drink now.

1995 Merlot, Napa Valley $26.   87
Deep blackish ruby hue. Medium-bodied. Balanced acidity. Moderately extracted. Moderately oaked. Mildly tannic. Dried herbs, black fruits, leather. Pleasantly aromatic with a hefty oak accent. The core of fruit flavors gains complexity from an herbal streak. Relatively supple in structure, with some dusty tannins on the finish.

1996 Merlot, Napa Valley $26.   86
Deep ruby red. Pleasant aromas show an oaky quality. Medium-bodied, with a ripe, lush entry and plummy flavors that conclude with a dry cedary note. Drink now or later. Can improve with more age.

1996 Pinot Noir, Coastal, Central Coast $10.95.   80
1995 Pinot Noir, Napa Valley $18.   88
Medium cherry red. Medium-bodied. Moderately extracted. Moderately oaked. Moderately tannic. Rich cherry pie aromas with vanilla accents lead a rounded palate with some depth of fruit flavors. A hint of astringent tannins gives some authority to the finish.

1996 Pinot Noir, Napa Valley $19.   84
Pale violet red. Medium-bodied. Moderately extracted. Mildly oaked. Mildly tannic. Red fruits, minerals. A note of herbal greenness shows on the nose and follows through on the palate, with tart berry flavors and a dry, astringent finish. Good grip, though not great depth.

1995 Pinot Noir, Carneros $26.   88
Medium cherry red with a pale rim. Medium-bodied. Moderately extracted. Moderately oaked. Mildly tannic. Perfumed vanilla and red fruit aromas. Crisp, juicy raspberry and strawberry flavors with just a hint of tannin on the finish. Nice now, this has some weight and structure.

1996 Pinot Noir, Carneros $26.   84
Full ruby red with a lightening rim. Medium-bodied. Moderately extracted. Mildly tannic. Minerals, vanilla. Rustic aromas with a red fruit accent lead a lean, minerally palate with some grip on the finish. Probably best over the near term.

1995 Pinot Noir, Reserve, Napa Valley $31.   89
Cherry red with subtle purple highlights. Medium-bodied. Moderately extracted. Moderately oaked. Moderately tannic. Complex, rich, rounded aromas of toast and ripe cherry fruit. The solid palate has tightly wound flavors, with a veneer of dry tannin throughout.

1996 Pinot Noir, Reserve, Napa Valley $36.   90

Pale violet red. Medium-bodied. Moderately extracted. Mildly tannic. Red berry fruits, vanilla. Subtly perfumed, fruity aromas lead a linear and precise palate with red fruit flavors and oak spice. Finishes with fine minerally persistence.

1995 Zinfandel, Coastal, North Coast $10.   81

1996 Zinfandel, Napa Valley $18.   87

Deep blackish ruby cast. Moderately full-bodied. Balanced acidity. Moderately extracted. Mildly oaked. Mildly tannic. Red fruits, brown spices. Somewhat reserved aromatically, with a flavorful, rich palate feel. Made in a Claret style with a well-integrated oak nuance woven throughout. Firm and well structured through the finish.

La Famiglia di Robert Mondavi

1996 Tocai Friulano, California $18.   89

Deep golden cast. Moderately full-bodied. Full acidity. Moderately extracted. Petrol, minerals, lime peel. Almost Riesling-like aromatically, with a full and rich palate feel. Angular acidity makes for a very lean and focused finish. An unusual though extremely interesting wine.

1996 Pinot Grigio, California $16.   86

Bright golden hue. Moderately full-bodied. Balanced acidity. Moderately extracted. Smoke, citrus, cream. Pleasantly aromatic, with a full, rich mouthfeel. Buoyant acidity enlivens the palate and makes for a zesty finish.

1995 Barbera, California $18.   83

Bright ruby purple. Moderately full-bodied. Full acidity. Moderately extracted. Mildly tannic. Black pepper, dried herbs, overripe black fruits. Unusual aromatics, with a slight Port-like note. Full but lean on the palate, with a concentrated finish.

1995 Sangiovese, California $22.   82

Monterey Peninsula Winery

1996 Pinot Noir, Sleepy Hollow Vineyard, Monterey County $16.99.   81

1995 Zinfandel, Naraghi Vineyard, Monterey County $14.99.   85

Bright ruby-garnet cast. Medium-bodied. Low acidity. Moderately extracted. Mildly tannic. Cherry tomatoes, stewed fruits. Engaging, mildly overripe notes in the nose. Light on the palate, with low acidity through the finish. A distinctive style, though very quaffable.

Monterey Vineyard

1996 Sauvignon Blanc, Monterey County $5.50.   82

Monterra

1997 Chardonnay, San Bernabé Ranch, Monterey County $8.99.   86

Pale straw hue. Yeasty, yellow apple aromas. A juicy entry leads a medium-bodied palate with judicious oak flavors and subtle yeasty notes. The subtle, lingering finish shows some juicy acidity. Drink now.

1995 Cabernet Sauvignon, Monterey County $9.99.   84

Bright violet-purple. Medium-bodied. Moderately extracted. Mildly tannic. Black fruits, flowers. Floral aromas lead a simple array of berry fruit flavors that finish with soft tannins. Quaffing style.

1996 Cabernet Sauvignon, Promise, Monterey County $9.99.   87

Deep purple red hue. Generous black fruit and vanilla aromas show a judicious oak component. A lush attack leads to a medium-bodied palate with soft, velvety tannins. Supple, harmonious finish. Rather shy of acidity, but very tasty in the near term. Drink now.

1995 Merlot, Monterey County $9.99. 85

Deep blackish ruby hue to the rim. Medium-bodied. Balanced acidity. Moderately extracted. Mildly tannic. Currants, minerals, black fruits. Clean and forceful, with a lighter-styled palate and solid structure. Features a hint of astringency on the snappy finish.

1996 Merlot, Promise, Monterey $9.99. 84

Bright crimson-violet hue, well saturated. Ripe, jammy black fruit aromas. The medium-bodied palate shows low acidity, and thick tannins come forward on an earthy finish. Drink now.

1996 Syrah, Monterey County $9.99. 86

Rich purple, limpid and brilliant, with a slight fade. Medium-bodied. Blueberry and vanilla flavors. A soft, round fruit-forward style with fine persistence of fruit flavors. Supple and easy drinking. Drink now.

Montevina

1997 Nebbiolo, Rosato, Amador County $7.50. 86

Bright pink. Medium-bodied. Full acidity. Moderately extracted. Minerals, citrus, red fruits. Pleasantly aromatic, with a clean, green edge. Ripe and full in the mouth, with an uplifting finish and a hint of sweetness.

Monthaven

1996 Chardonnay, Monterey $10. 84

Bright yellow-straw cast. Moderately full-bodied. Full acidity. Highly extracted. Moderately oaked. Yeast, brown spices, minerals. Shows a big oak accent to the firm backbone of minerally flavors. Aggressive in the mouth, with a forceful angular quality and a dry note on the finish.

1997 Chardonnay, Napa Valley $9.99. 87

Bright green-gold. Extravagant toasted coconut, smoke, and ripe fruit aromas. A sumptuous attack leads a full-bodied palate with impressive buttery richness and glycerous smoothness. Impressive depth of fruit flavors. Finishes with leesy complexity.

1995 Cabernet Sauvignon, Napa Valley $9.99. 86

Blood red. Medium-bodied. Moderately extracted. Moderately tannic. Black fruits, earth. Reserved aromas lead a chunky, broad palate of flavors, with powdery tannins. Pleasantly rustic, with a spicy finish.

1995 Carignane, California $14. 83

Brick red with a slight fade. Medium-bodied. Moderately extracted. Mildly tannic. Anise, black fruits. Lean and firmly structured, with dusty tannins and black fruit flavors lingering through the finish. A flavorful, rustic style.

1996 Syrah, California $9.99. 81

1995 Zinfandel, Napa Valley $9.99. 87

Full dark cherry red. Medium-bodied. Balanced acidity. Moderately extracted. Mildly oaked. Mildly tannic. Black fruits. Very straightforward; a burst of solid black fruit flavors tapers off with indecent haste. Quite generous.

1996 Zinfandel, California $9.99. 80

Monticello

1996 Chardonnay, Wild Yeast Corley Reserve, Napa Valley $32.50. 88

Deep yellow-straw cast. Moderately full-bodied. Full acidity. Moderately extracted. Mildly oaked. Bread dough, vanilla, citrus. Spicy aromas feature a distinctive doughy note. Rich but angular in the mouth, and lean through the finish.

1995 Cabernet Sauvignon, Jefferson Cuvée, Napa Valley $22.   84

Medium ruby red. Medium-bodied. Moderately extracted. Mildly tannic. Lead pencil, black fruits. Restrained, elegant, oak-spiced aromas lead a harmonious, supple mouthful of attractive Cabernet fruit flavors, with drying tannins on the finish. Nice now.

1994 Cabernet Sauvignon, Corley Reserve, Napa Valley $35.   88

Deep violet-red color. Medium-bodied. Moderately extracted. Mildly tannic. Oak spice, black fruits. Bright, oaky aromas lead crisp berry fruit flavors with a vanilla and spice theme through the finish.

1994 Merlot, Corley Reserve, Napa Valley $28.   90

Deep ruby red to the rim with brilliant highlights. Moderately full-bodied. Balanced acidity. Highly extracted. Moderately oaked. Moderately tannic. Red fruits, minerals, vanilla. Quite aromatic, with a firmly structured mouthfeel and a deep core of flavor. Well-integrated oak accents add complexity to the minerally fruit notes. Solid acidity rounds out the package.

1996 Pinot Noir, Napa Valley $22.   84

Pale ruby cast. Medium-bodied. Moderately extracted. Mildly tannic. Oak spice, berry fruits. Spicy, fruity aromas lead a soft, fruit-forward palate, with a generous amount of oak spice lingering on the finish.

Montpellier

1997 Chardonnay, California $6.99.   81

1997 White Zinfandel, California $5.99.   80

1996 Cabernet Sauvignon, California $6.99.   84

Bright ruby red with a slight fade. Unusual aromas of tart berries and dust. A crisp entry leads a moderately full-bodied palate with hollow fruit flavors and firm, drying tannins. Drink now.

1997 Merlot, California $6.99.   84

Bright violet hue with a fading rim. Floral, vanilla oak aromas. Jammy flavors on the attack with a soft, fruity character through the finish. A lighter-bodied wine with easy drinkability.

1997 Syrah, California $6.99.   84

Medium purple, limpid and brilliant, with a slight fade. Mild, pleasant black cherry and vanilla flavors. Mild wood tones. Smooth entry, moderately light-bodied with balanced acidity. Mild, silky tannins. Bright fruity accents throughout. Structurally light. Subtle, short finish. Appealingly straightforward, with a soft, fruity character. Drink now.

1996 Zinfandel, California $6.99.   80

Morgan

1997 Chardonnay, Monterey $20.   84

Rich gold. Aromas show a degree of smoky development/maderization. A viscous entry leads a full-bodied palate with warming alcohol coming through. Drink now.

1996 Chardonnay, Reserve, Monterey $25.   91

Medium yellow-gold. Smoky, vanilla-scented aromas with yeasty accents. A bright entry leads a medium-bodied palate with a taut structure and fine depth of fruit and oak flavors. Finishes with lingering smoky complexity. Drink now or later.

1997 Sauvignon Blanc, Sonoma-Monterey $13.   85

Full golden yellow. Medium-bodied. Full acidity. Moderately extracted. Lime, lemon zest, minerals. High-toned, zesty aromas lead a full, rounded mouthfeel with good citrus flavors and a minerally finish. Fresh and lively style.

1996 Pinot Noir, Monterey $20.   83

Pale cherry red. Moderately light-bodied. Moderately extracted. Mildly tannic. Vanilla, berries. Floral, oaky aromas follow through on the palate, with soft tannins through the finish.

1995 Pinot Noir, Reserve, Monterey $28.   87

Medium cherry-garnet hue. Medium-bodied. Moderately extracted. Moderately oaked. Mildly tannic. Tomato vine, brown spice, and sour cherry flavors abound, with bright acids through the finish. Quite complex and flavorsome. This has a minerally feel throughout. Well balanced and nice to drink now.

1996 Pinot Noir, Reserve, Monterey $32.   88

Bright violet red. Medium-bodied. Moderately extracted. Mildly tannic. Red berries, flowers, vanilla. Bright perfumed aromas lead juicy, vibrant fruit flavors, with a generous vanilla oak influence coming through on the finish.

1996 Syrah, Monterey $20.   84

Rich, limpid, brilliant ruby purple with a slight fade. Medium- to light-bodied. Bramble fruit and vanilla aromas. Juicy and immediate, and lifted by good fruit acids. Drink now.

Moshin

1995 Pinot Noir, Russian River Valley $16.   86

Medium cherry red. Moderately light-bodied. Moderately extracted. Mildly tannic. Leathery, raspberry-accented aromas. Well-concentrated, focused raspberry flavors on the palate with an oaky backnote. Dry, powdery tannins give a dry finish.

Mount Eden

1997 Chardonnay, MacGregor Vineyard, Edna Valley $17.99.   84

Deep golden yellow. Forward smoke, yeast, and charred oak aromas carry a big wood accent. A lean entry leads a moderately full-bodied palate with rounded acidity. Lean, buttery finish. Drink now.

1995 Cabernet Sauvignon, Santa Cruz Mountains $20.   88

Deep ruby purple. Medium-bodied. Balanced acidity. Moderately extracted. Mildly tannic. Licorice, minerals, flowers. High-toned aromatics are forward and intense. Somewhat light in the mouth, with a lean and angular impression. Crisp and bright through the finish.

1993 Cabernet Sauvignon, Old Vine Reserve, Santa Cruz Mountains $35.   94

Deep blackish red with purple highlights. Moderately full-bodied. Highly extracted. Moderately tannic. Brown spice, toasted oak, licorice, black fruits. Brooding dark fruit aromas. Thick, chewy black Cabernet fruit dominates the palate. An assertively dry finish shows fine-grained tannins and rich oak spice flavors. A big-shouldered wine in need of cellaring.

1995 Cabernet Sauvignon, Old Vine Reserve, Santa Cruz Mountains $39.99.88

Very deep blackish ruby hue. Intense chocolate and anise aromas show a pronounced oak influence. A firm entry leads to a full-bodied palate with lush thick tannins and a marked note of acidity that enlivens the flavors. Firm, intense finish. A big brooding style, rather awkward at present, but with the stuffing to blossom with age. Good for long-term cellaring.

Mount Palomar

1996 Cortese, Castelletto, Temecula $16.   93

Bright golden cast. Moderately full-bodied. Balanced acidity. Moderately extracted. Blanched almonds, cream, oranges. Attention-grabbing aromas, with lush and exotic flavors. Rich and rounded in the mouth with buoyant acidity that enlivens a flavorful finish.

1997 Rey Sol Le Mediterrane Blanc, Temecula $16.   87

Deep golden cast. Full-bodied. Balanced acidity. Moderately extracted. Honey, yeast, tropical fruits, butter. Aromatic, with big, ripe, honeyed flavors. Full and rich in the mouth, though well balanced with juicy acidity.

1997 Roussane, Rey Sol, Temecula $18.   86

Deep golden cast. Full-bodied. Low acidity. Moderately extracted. Bananas, cream. Extremely fat and ripe, with a buttery accent. Full and tropical in flavor with a weightiness that is accentuated by low levels of acidity.

1997 Viognier, Rey Sol, Temecula $18.   84

Very deep golden hue. Full-bodied. Low acidity. Moderately extracted. Mildly oaked. Oranges, vanilla. Aromatic, with extremely ripe fruit notes offset by subtle oak accents. Full and rich in the mouth with low levels of acidity.

1996 Rey Sol Le Mediterrane Old Vines Selection Red, South Coast $10.   85

Bright garnet red with a slight fade. Forward earth and leather aromas. A soft attack leads a medium-bodied palate that lacks tannic grip. The finish is flat and earthy. This wine is in search of a bit more structure. Drink now.

1994 Sangiovese, Castelletto, Temecula $18.   84

Dark ruby red with a subtle fade. Medium-bodied. Balanced acidity. Moderately extracted. Moderately oaked. Mildly tannic. Red fruits, oak spice. Powerfully aromatic, spicy aromas. Good weight and roundness to the mouthfeel, with crisp red fruit flavors that turn dry and spicy through the finish.

Mount Veeder Winery

1995 Cabernet Sauvignon, Napa Valley $30.   91

Deep ruby hue. Moderately full-bodied. Balanced acidity. Moderately extracted. Mildly oaked. Mildly tannic. Red fruits, brown spices, minerals. Forward aromas reveal well-integrated fruit and wood flavors. Soft and supple, with generosity and elegance. Well balanced and lengthy.

1993 Reserve, Napa Valley $40.   95

Dark blood red. Medium-bodied. Highly extracted. Moderately tannic. Red currants, cassis, cedar. Ripe berry aromas reveal bright, high-toned fruit flavors that show a ripe juicy character up front. Firm tannins clamp down on the finish, though this is quite approachable now with rich food.

1995 Reserve, Napa Valley $50.   92

Deep, saturated ruby purple hue. Brooding brown spice, mineral, and leather aromas. A firm attack leads to a moderately full-bodied palate with grippy tannins and solid acidity for balance. Lengthy, flavorful finish. Approachable now but well balanced and built for age. Carries its weight admirably. Drink now or later.

Mumm Cuvée Napa

NV Blanc de Noir, Napa Valley $15.95.   88

Bright pale pink cast. Moderately full-bodied. Full acidity. Red fruits, minerals, citrus. Forward, attractive aromas carry a pleasant fruity overtone. Soft and generous in the mouth, with crisp acidity and fine balance.

NV Brut Prestige, Napa Valley $15.95.   87

Bright pale gold hue. Medium-bodied. Citrus, minerals. Juicy, bright, clean, fruity aromas follow through well on the palate, with crisp carbonation and moderate bead size.

Murphy-Goode

1997 Chardonnay, Sonoma County $15.   84

Bright straw hue. Subdued aromas carry a crisp appley note. A lean entry leads a moderately light-bodied palate with crisp acidity. Crisp, clipped finish. Drink now.

1996 Chardonnay, Island Block Reserve, Alexander Valley $24.   89

Deep yellow-straw hue. Generous pear and tropical fruit aromas. A crisp entry leads a medium-bodied palate that shows zesty acidity. The finish is clean and snappy. Drink now.

**1996 Chardonnay, J&K Murphy Vineyard Reserve,
Russian River Valley $24.**   89

Full yellow-gold. Spicy, yellow apple aromas. A fresh entry leads a medium-bodied palate with crisp fruity flavors that persist through the finish. Shows good varietal flavors. Drink now.

1996 Pinot Blanc, Sonoma County $13.50.   85

Bright golden cast. Medium-bodied. Full acidity. Moderately extracted. Moderately oaked. Toasted coconut, minerals. Marked oak spice on the nose also dominates the flavors on the palate. Clean and brisk in structure, with vibrant acidity making for a snappy finish.

1997 Fumé Blanc, Sonoma County $11.50.   86

Bright yellow-gold. Medium-bodied. Full acidity. Moderately extracted. Citrus zest, minerals. Bright, zesty aromas follow through on the palate with lively acids playing through the finish. Shows some clean varietal character in the herbal notes.

1996 Fumé, Reserve, Alexander Valley $16.50.   92

Full yellow-gold. Moderately full-bodied. Balanced acidity. Moderately extracted. Moderately oaked. Brown spice, ripe citrus fruits. Nice toasty oak accents on the nose lead a spicy, flavorsome palate, showing a structured character and some dryness on the finish. Nice now, this should be better in a year or two.

1996 Fumé II, The Deuce, Alexander Valley $24.   93

Bright yellow-straw color. Medium-bodied. Balanced acidity. Moderately extracted. Mildly oaked. Toasted oak, butter, peach. Smoky, vanilla aromas lead a rounded mouthfeel with buttery character and a pronounced spicy finish. An extravagant texture with exotic smoky flavors are the keynotes of this hedonistic wine. Sublimely balanced.

1995 Cabernet Sauvignon, Alexander Valley $20.   89

Medium cherry red. Medium-bodied. Moderately extracted. Mildly tannic. Dried herbs, red fruits, chocolate. Crisp herbal aromas show an oak influence. Crisp fruity flavors give way to dry oaky and herbal notes through the finish. A subtle, elegant style.

1996 Cabernet Sauvignon, Alexander Valley $19.   81

1994 Cabernet Sauvignon, Murphy Ranch, Alexander Valley $25.   88

Medium-dark cherry red. Medium-bodied. Moderately extracted. Mildly tannic. Brown spice, red fruits. An elegant spicy nose leads a supple palate, with nice crisp fruity flavors that finish cleanly. Distinguished by some subtlety of flavors, a good mouthfeel, and bright acids.

1994 Cabernet Sauvignon, Brenda Block, Alexander Valley $30.   91

Full dark cherry red. Medium-bodied. Highly extracted. Moderately tannic. Brown spice, chocolate, berry fruits. The smooth, velvety mouthfeel has generous and rich flavors through the finish. Quite concentrated. Elegant and structured, with ample soft tannins. Nice now but can cellar.

1996 Zinfandel, Sonoma County $16.   87

Bright ruby cast. Moderately full-bodied. Balanced acidity. Moderately extracted. Mildly oaked. Mildly tannic. Black fruits. Aromatic, with a lovely interplay between fruit and oak notes. Soft and lush through the finish.

Mystic Cliffs

1997 Chardonnay, California $8.   81

1995 Cabernet Sauvignon, California $6.99.   88

Bright cherry red. Medium-bodied. Moderately extracted. Mildly tannic. Toasted oak, vanilla, red fruits. A bright, fruity nose leads a juicy, open-knit palate with a hint of oak spice and astringency on the finish.

Nalle

1996 Zinfandel, Dry Creek Valley $20.   86

Bright blackish purple. Moderately full-bodied. Balanced acidity. Highly extracted.
Mildly oaked. Moderately tannic. Black fruits, minerals. Quite aromatic, with a pure,
fruit-centered flavor profile. Lean and well structured through the finish. Rather
tough at present.

Napa Creek

1997 Chardonnay, Lodi $8.99.   81
1996 Cabernet Sauvignon, Lodi $8.99.   81
1996 Merlot, Lodi $8.99.   80

Napa Ridge

1997 Chardonnay, Coastal Vines, North Coast $9.   81
1995 Chardonnay, Reserve, Napa Valley $15.   81
1996 Cabernet Sauvignon, Central Coast $10.   89

Bright crimson red hue. Generous aromas show black cherry fruit and sweet oak accents.
A flavorful, fruity entry leads a medium-bodied palate with fleshy, ripe fruit flavors and
rounded tannins. Finishes with lingering fruit persistence and well-integrated oak flavors.
Drink now or later.

1995 Cabernet Sauvignon, Coastal Reserve, Napa Valley $15.   84

Bright violet-purple hue. Fruit-forward, ripe aromas have a nice vanilla oak accent.
A firm entry leads a medium-bodied palate with cherry fruit flavors and dry tannins.
Flavors dissipate quickly. Drink now.

1996 Pinot Noir, Coastal, North Coast $19.   85

Pale cherry red with a pink tinge. Moderately light-bodied. Moderately extracted.
Moderately oaked. Mildly tannic. Mildly jammy, vanilla-accented aromas lead a bright
sweet fruit mouthful, with a lingering fruity, vanilla oak finish. Very pleasant and
straightforward.

Newlan

1997 Chardonnay, Napa Valley $16.   83

Bright yellow-gold. Subtle oak aromas with ripe buttery accents. A soft entry leads a
moderately full-bodied palate with generous texture and mouthfeel, though fruit flavors
are restrained. Finishes with a note of oak and alcohol. Drink now.

1995 Cabernet Sauvignon, Napa Valley $20.   88

Saturated ruby-violet hue. Moderately full-bodied. Highly extracted. Moderately tannic.
Vanilla, spice, black fruits. Lively, high-toned fruit flavors, bright and well gripped by
tannins through the finish.

1995 Pinot Noir, Napa Valley $19.   90

Bright red with purple hints. Medium-bodied. Moderately extracted. Moderately oaked.
Mildly tannic. Floral, aromatic fruity nose has violet accents. Bright and fruity, with a
mineral accent. Crisp acids keep the palate fresh. Tannins on the finish are slight.

1995 Pinot Noir, Reserve, Napa Valley $28.   88

Pale garnet red. Medium-bodied. Moderately extracted. Mildly oaked. Mildly tannic.
Baked cherries with a spicy accent make for complex aromas. Full flavored on the palate,
with good weight. Very spicy oak finish. A dry style.

1996 Zinfandel, Napa Valley $18.   83

Deep blackish purple. Moderately full-bodied. Full acidity. Moderately extracted. Mildly
oaked. Moderately tannic. Briar fruits, earth. Quite aromatic, showing distinct earthy
overtones. Full and rich in the mouth, with elevated acidity making for a crisp finish.

Newton

1997 Chardonnay, Napa County $25.   94

Bright yellow-gold. Moderately full-bodied. Balanced acidity. Highly extracted. Vanilla, toasted oak, ripe citrus. Aromatically complex, with assertive yeasty accents. A rich, creamy mouthful shows plush texture with balanced oak spice, vanilla, and ripe fruit components. The finish is very lush and generous.

1995 Cabernet Sauvignon, Napa Valley $36.99.   89

Deep purple red hue. Brooding mineral and berry cordial aromas. A firm entry leads to a full-bodied palate with robust grippy tannins and a real structural edge. Firm, angular finish. Has all the components to age beautifully, and needs it. Good for long-term cellaring.

1996 Merlot, Napa Valley $32.   87

Saturated dark ruby hue. Moderately full-bodied with concentrated black cherry flavors and a lush, tannic structure that grips the finish. Drink now or later. Can improve with more age.

Neyers

1997 Chardonnay, Carneros $27.99.   85

Dark gold. Very ripe aromas have a tropical note. A lush entry is followed by a full-bodied palate with rounded texture and concentrated flavors that linger on the finish. This is a rich, leesy style with impressive weight. Drink now or later.

1995 Cabernet Sauvignon, Napa Valley $40.   89

Deep red-violet. Moderately full-bodied. Moderately extracted. Moderately tannic. Brown spice, black fruits, licorice. Oak spice shows strongly on the nose, with a restrained, dry palate finishing quickly. Quite an austere style.

1996 Merlot, Napa Valley $28.   91

Pale ruby hue with a fading rim. Intriguing earthy, oak-accented aromas. Medium-bodied with a crisp attack and understated, complex flavors on the midpalate. The tannins are subtle and evolved. The finish lingers, with complex, mature flavors. Drink now.

Nichols

1997 Chardonnay, Edna Ranch Vineyard, Edna Valley $32.   86

Bright straw cast. Moderately full-bodied. Low acidity. Moderately extracted. Mildly oaked. Earth, vanilla, butter. Generous aromas carry a slightly unusual quality. Ripe and full in the mouth with a fat texture. Balanced by a hint of acidity in the finish.

1996 Chardonnay, Paragon Vineyard, Edna Valley $32.   87

Bright yellow-straw cast. Moderately full-bodied. Balanced acidity. Moderately extracted. Mildly oaked. Yeast, toast, citrus. Forward aromas carry a complex yeasty accent. Vibrant and crisp in the mouth, with zesty citric flavors through a snappy finish.

1996 Pinot Noir, Cottonwood Canyon Vineyard, Santa Barbara County $33.   90

Very pale ruby red. Moderately light-bodied. Moderately extracted. Mildly oaked. Mildly tannic. Lean, herbal, meaty aromas. A smooth, glycerous mouthfeel, with some bitter cherry flavors through the minerally finish. Quite sophisticated and seamless. More flavorful and intense than it first seems.

1996 Pinot Noir, Pisoni Vineyard, Monterey County $42.   91

Very deep black cherry color. Medium-bodied. Highly extracted. Moderately oaked. Moderately tannic. Rich dark fruit aromas have cedar and tobacco notes. Rich, concentrated fruit flavors linger through a long, complex finish with nice toasty character. Drinking well now, though it could be cellared.

Scale: Superlative (96-100), Exceptional (90-95), Highly Recommended (85-89), Recommended (80-84), Not Recommended (Under 80)

1996 Pinot Noir, Reserve, Central Coast $45.   **90**

Full cherry red with slight purple highlights. Medium-bodied. Moderately extracted. Moderately oaked. Mildly tannic. Hints of tar, black fruit, and tobacco. Complex, ripe aromas. Smooth, elegant texture, with ripe plum flavors through a complex, lengthy finish. Nice now, this should improve with one to two years of cellaring.

1996 Zinfandel, Cienega Valley Vineyards, Central Coast $24.   **80**

Niebaum-Coppola

1997 Chardonnay, Napa Valley $20.   **88**

Bright green-straw cast. Medium-bodied. Balanced acidity. Moderately extracted. Mildly oaked. Ripe lemons, apples. Very sweet, juicy fruit flavors are clean and direct, with a subtle vanilla oak influence that lingers through the finish.

1996 Cabernet Franc, Napa Valley $20.   **90**

Bright ruby purple. Moderately full-bodied. Balanced acidity. Moderately extracted. Moderately oaked. Mildly tannic. Licorice, black fruits, coffee. Showing some aromatic complexity, with well-integrated fruit and wood flavors. Firm and well balanced, with deep flavors and acidity making for a buoyant finish. Stylish.

1997 Cabernet Sauvignon, Francis Coppola Diamond Series Black Label Claret, North Coast $17.   **80**

1992 Rubicon, Rutherford, Napa Valley $45.   **91**

Nearly opaque dark blood red. Medium-bodied. Highly extracted. Moderately tannic. Plums, cassis, black tea, chocolate. A plummy nose leads a dense, tight palate with concentrated, tightly wound flavors that linger through the finish. Still quite closed, this should cellar well.

1994 Rubicon, Rutherford, Napa Valley $65.   **92**

Deep ruby purple. Moderately full-bodied. Balanced acidity. Moderately extracted. Moderately oaked. Mildly tannic. Black fruits, chocolate, brown spices. Enticingly aromatic, with a large-framed though supple mouthfeel. Shows great intensity of flavor, with fine depth. Exceptional length, with acidity lending balance to the finish. Approachable, but structured for long-term (7–10 years) aging.

1995 Rubicon, Rutherford, Napa Valley $65.   **93**

Saturated dark ruby hue. Exotically spicy aromas show dark fruits and rich oak spice. A rich entry leads to a moderately full-bodied palate with a fleshy core of cordial-like fruit and well-integrated lush oak spice that comes through strongly on the finish. Hedonistic and drinking well now. Drink now.

1995 Merlot, Francis Coppola Family Wines, Napa Valley $32.   **92**

Very deep ruby to the rim with a purplish cast. Medium-bodied. Balanced acidity. Moderately extracted. Mildly oaked. Mildly tannic. Licorice, black fruits, sweet herbs. Flavorful and extremely well integrated, with a real sense of depth to the palate. Solid acidity enlivens the lengthy finish.

1996 Merlot, Napa Valley $32.   **89**

Saturated violet purple. Generously aromatic with an oaky character. Full-bodied, with a lush, velvety mouthfeel, broad fleshy cherry fruit flavors, and plenty of vanilla oak accents through the finish. Drink now or later. Can improve with more age.

1996 Zinfandel, Edizione Pennino, Napa Valley $26.   **88**

Dark cherry red. Medium-bodied. Balanced acidity. Moderately extracted. Moderately tannic. Tobacco, plums. Forward, attractive aromas lead a seductive, richly wrought palate, with ample tannins providing structure and grip on the finish.

Norman

1995 Cabernet Sauvignon, Paso Robles $17.　　　　　　　　　81

1996 No Nonsense Red, Claret, Paso Robles $15.　　　　　　82

1995 Pinot Noir, William Cain Vineyard, Paso Robles $18.　　87

Cherry red with a garnet rim. Medium-bodied. Moderately extracted. Moderately oaked. Mildly tannic. Fragrant brown spice aromas have a cinnamon accent. Nice soft Pinot fruit flavors on entry have plenty of plum, chocolate, and toast flavors through the finish. Drinking nicely now, with just a hint of dry tannins.

Oakville Ranch

1996 Chardonnay, ORV, Oakville $32.　　　　　　　　　　85

Bright straw cast. Medium-bodied. Balanced acidity. Moderately extracted. Minerals, butter. Aromatically subdued, with subtle flavors. Ripe and lush in the mouth with a textured quality. Buttery through the finish.

1996 Chardonnay, Vista Vineyard, California $26.　　　　　84

Bright straw cast. Moderately full-bodied. Balanced acidity. Moderately extracted. Green apples, melon, cream. Ripe and forward, with fruit-centered flavors and an opulent texture. Shows generosity through the well-balanced buttery finish.

1994 Cabernet Sauvignon, Napa Valley $30.　　　　　　　87

Dark blackish purple. Moderately full-bodied. Highly extracted. Moderately tannic. Cassis, plums, black tea. Pure cassis aromas lead a fleshy, bright palate, with chewy fruit flavors and ample soft tannins through the finish. Attractive now, but this will be better with some age.

1995 Cabernet Sauvignon, Napa Valley $35.　　　　　　　89

Very deep ruby purple. Moderately full-bodied. Balanced acidity. Highly extracted. Mildly oaked. Quite tannic. Minerals, cassis. Aromatically reserved, with a tightly wound, dense mouthfeel. Aggressive tannins merge with a firm, minerally backbone to suggest long-term (7–10 years) cellaring.

1994 Robert's Blend, Napa Valley $45.　　　　　　　　　91

Opaque blackish purple. Medium-bodied. Highly extracted. Moderately tannic. Cassis, black fruits, tobacco. Ripe cassis aromas with cedary notes are fully expressed on the palate. Bright Cabernet fruit flavors linger through a tobacco-accented finish. Very plush and generous style.

1995 Robert's Blend, Napa Valley $45.　　　　　　　　　89

Saturated ruby purple. Moderately full-bodied. Balanced acidity. Highly extracted. Moderately oaked. Moderately tannic. Vanilla, minerals, briar fruits. Pleasantly aromatic, with a firm and intense mouthfeel. Firm tannins bite down on the finish. Needs time.

1995 Merlot, Napa Valley $35.　　　　　　　　　　　　90

Saturated dark violet red with purple highlights. Rich, brooding aromas have a lush dark-fruit character with oaky accents. Rich and lush on entry with fantastic grip and fine-grained tannins. Mouthfilling fruity flavors with excellent structure. Good for long-term cellaring.

1996 Zinfandel, Napa Valley $20.　　　　　　　　　　　82

Obester

1996 Sauvignon Blanc, Mendocino $9.95.　　　　　　　　84

Medium straw hue. Moderately light-bodied. Balanced acidity. Moderately extracted. Dried herbs, vanilla, citrus. Bright zesty aromas have a subtle smoky accent. Crisp and flavorful on the palate, this finishes cleanly with an acid snap and a hint of dryness.

1995 Sangiovese, 20th Anniversary, Mendocino County $13.95.　　87

Bright ruby hue with a pink rim. Medium-bodied. Full acidity. Moderately extracted. Moderately oaked. Mildly tannic. Red fruits, bitter cherries, vanilla. High-toned fruity aromas lead a brisk, minerally palate with dry oak notes on the finish. Lively style.

Scale: Superlative (96-100), Exceptional (90-95), Highly Recommended (85-89), Recommended (80-84), Not Recommended (Under 80)

154

Ojai

1996 Chardonnay, Talley Vineyard, Arroyo Grande Valley $24.   83

Bright straw cast. Medium-bodied. Full acidity. Moderately extracted. Minerals, citrus. Aromatically reserved, with a crisp and angular presence in the mouth. Acidity turns tart on the finish.

Opus One

1992 Oakville, Napa Valley Red $65.   97

Moderately full-bodied. Medium acid. Lots of fruit. Medium oak. Lots of tannin. Dry. Reminiscent of earth, cassis, black fruits, cherry tobacco. Displays stunning depth and breadth of flavor. Dark, luscious black fruit is surprisingly approachable, but fine acidity and a firm lattice of tannins insure long-term aging potential. Deep, elegantly structured, and very complex.

1993 Oakville, Napa Valley Red $85.   96

Deep ruby to the rim with purplish highlights. Moderately full-bodied. Balanced acidity. Highly extracted. Highly oaked. Moderately tannic. Dry. Reminiscent of vanilla, black cherries, leather. Attractive aromatic qualities play out on a solidly crafted and balanced framework. Quite deep with impressive length, it is slightly more closed than recent vintages but should cellar beautifully.

1994 Oakville, Napa Valley Red $90.   94

Opaque dark red. Medium-bodied. Highly extracted. Quite tannic. Cassis, black cherries, mint, black tea. Rich plummy aromas lead a focused, tight palate, with concentrated black Cabernet fruit flavors and stern tannins on the finish. Solidly structured, this wine needs cellaring to reveal its potential.

1995 Oakville, Napa Valley Red $100.   99

Deep ruby cast. Moderately full-bodied. Balanced acidity. Moderately extracted. Heavily oaked. Moderately tannic. Leather, earth, black fruits. Aromatic and concentrated, with complexity to the flavors throughout. Lush, supple, and harmonious, showing velvety tannins and a lengthy finish. Almost approachable, but best in a few years.

Orfila

1997 Chardonnay, Ambassador's Reserve, San Diego & San Luis Obispo Counties $14.98.   81

1995 Merlot, Coastal, California $16.   86

Deep ruby red with a slight fade to the rim. Medium-bodied. Full acidity. Moderately extracted. Heavily oaked. Mildly tannic. Dusty cherries, toasted coconut, vanilla. A heavy wood accent with a drying palate feel. Nonetheless, it features a core of dusty fruit flavors that support the oak and lead to an angular, well-defined finish. A little bit like a Rioja in style. Attractive and interesting.

1995 Merlot, Ambassador's Reserve, San Diego County $25.   82

1996 Merlot, Ambassador's Reserve, San Diego County $25.   84

Medium ruby hue with a slight fade. Berry fruit and generous oak accents on the nose. A supple entry leads a medium-bodied palate with soft jammy fruit flavors and pleasant oak spice through the rounded finish. Drink now.

Tawny Port, California $14.98/500 ml.   83

Deep orange-copper cast with a definite haze. Medium-bodied. Balanced acidity. Moderately extracted. Caramel, toffee. Pleasantly aromatic, with a gentle woody tone throughout. Light and straightforward on the palate. Finishes with a touch of heat.

The Organic Wine Works

1997 Merlot, California $16.   80

Page Mill

1997 Chardonnay, Bien Nacido Vineyard, Santa Maria Valley $18.   81

1997 Chardonnay, Garbett Vineyard, Matadero Valley,
Santa Clara County $20. 86

Bright yellow-straw color. Moderately full-bodied. Balanced acidity. Highly extracted.
Moderately oaked. Smoke, butter, lemons. Forceful burnt butter aromas lead a firm,
tart mouthful of flavors with mineral and oak spice character gripping the finish.

1997 Sauvignon Blanc, French Camp Vineyard, San Luis Obispo $11. 85

Medium yellow-straw color. Medium-bodied. Balanced acidity. Moderately extracted.
Grapefruit, smoke. Ripe, smoky, citrusy aromas follow through well on a textured palate,
with a smooth and flavorful finish.

1993 Cabernet Sauvignon, Napa Valley $20. 82

1995 Macaire, Napa Valley $32. 89

Bright ruby cast. Moderately full-bodied. Balanced acidity. Moderately extracted.
Moderately oaked. Mildly tannic. Minerals, red fruits, dried herbs. Pleasantly aromatic,
with real complexity to the range of flavors. Soft and supple in the mouth, with a leafy
quality that is very Merlot-like. Well balanced.

1996 Pinot Noir, Bien Nacido Vineyard, Santa Maria Valley $20. 81

Pahlmeyer

1995 Red, Napa Valley $60. 94

Deep ruby cast. Moderately full-bodied. Balanced acidity. Highly extracted. Moderately
oaked. Moderately tannic. Cedar, black fruits, earth. Forward aromas show breeding and
complexity. Firm and deep in the mouth, with fine concentration and length. Balanced
for long-term (7–10 years) aging.

Paradise Ridge

1995 Blanc de Blanc, Private Reserve, Sonoma County $19. 81

1997 Chardonnay, Nagasawa Vineyard, Sonoma County $15.95. 84

Bright yellow-straw hue. Unusual, high-toned blanched almond and mineral aromas.
A lean entry leads a medium-bodied palate with firm extraction and angular acidity.
Finishes with a phenolic, mildly astringent quality. Drink now.

1997 Chardonnay, Barrel Select, Nagasawa Vineyard,
Sonoma County $17.95. 89

Bright straw hue. Generous vanilla and spice aromas show an integrated oak accent.
A firm entry is followed by a moderately full-bodied palate with lush acidity and a
rounded, ripe finish. Well balanced. Drink now.

1996 Cabernet Sauvignon, North Coast $18.95. 83

Pale ruby-purple hue. Cedar, vanilla aromas. A bright entry leads to medium-bodied
palate with vibrant red fruit flavors and light but dry gripping tannins. Drink now.

Paraiso Springs

1997 Chardonnay, Santa Lucia Highlands $16. 89

Pale yellow-straw hue. Moderate vanilla, smoke, and clean apple aromas. A fruity entry
leads a medium-bodied palate with a ripe fruity center and judicious oak accents.
Drink now.

1997 Gewürztraminer, Santa Lucia Highlands $9. 87

Bright straw hue. Clean, intense mineral and honeyed tropical fruit aromas. A lean
entry leads a medium-bodied palate that has an assertive acidic edge. Firm through the
dry finish. Taut and stylish. Drink now.

1997 Riesling, Santa Lucia Highlands $9. 90

Bright yellow-gold. Intense varietally pure aromas of petrol, minerals, and peach.
A flavorful attack leads a medium-bodied palate, with mild sweetness and good acid
balance through the finish. Quite stylish. Drink now.

Scale: Superlative (96-100), Exceptional (90-95), Highly Recommended (85-89),
Recommended (80-84), Not Recommended (Under 80)

1995 Pinot Noir, Santa Lucia Highlands $18.   86

Dark garnet red. Medium-bodied. Moderately extracted. Moderately tannic. Faintly
stewed red fruit aromas have an earthy accent. Interesting cherry and tomato flavors
linger through an herbal finish. Plenty of character, though maybe not everyone's
preference.

1996 Pinot Noir, Santa Lucia Highlands $22.50.   89

Pale red with a subtle garnet rim. Medium-bodied. Moderately extracted. Mildly tannic.
Game, red berries. Elegant perfumed aromas follow through well on the palate, with
sweet fruit flavors and subtle tannins. Gamey flavors linger on the finish.

1996 Syrah, Santa Lucia Highlands $22.50.   86

Dark purple, limpid and brilliant to the rim. Plentiful drying tannins. Medium-bodied.
Juicy, fleshy fruit flavors with a supple finish. A touch of game and berries in a soft
structure make for attractive early drinking.

Parducci

1996 Chardonnay, Carneros Bighorn Ranch, Reserve, Napa Valley $20.   86

Pale straw hue. Medium-bodied. Balanced acidity. Moderately extracted. Moderately
oaked. Butterscotch, blanched almonds. Heavy buttery aromas follow through on the
palate, which shows an oaky accent. Citrusy flavors stay in the background.

1995 Cabernet Sauvignon, Mendocino $10.   86

Bright reddish purple. Medium-bodied. Moderately extracted. Mildly tannic. Black
berry fruits, vanilla. Ripe, deep fruit flavors have a juicy feel on the palate, with a clean
lingering finish showing very soft tannins. Lots of primary fruit flavors make this very
accessible and forward.

1996 Cabernet Sauvignon, Vineyard Select, North Coast $10.   86

Bright purple-red hue. Attractive toasted oak and cassis aromas. A smooth entry leads
to a moderately full-bodied palate with lively, bright fruit flavors and very fine grippy
tannins on the finish. Well balanced and flavorsome. Drink now or later.

1997 Merlot, California $10.   81

1997 Syrah, Mendocino $10.   83

Bright ruby red to the rim. Generous herb, red fruit, and vanilla aromas show a subtle
wood accent. A soft attack leads a medium-bodied palate, with supple tannins. The
angular finish has some grip. A lighter-styled quaffer. Drink now.

Fess Parker

1997 Chardonnay, Santa Barbara County $16.   87

Bright green-gold. Smoky, yeasty aromas show subtle, well-integrated oak. A fruity entry
leads a moderately full-bodied palate with a lush center of ripe Chardonnay fruit and
complex leesy notes persisting through the finish.

1997 Chardonnay, American Tradition Reserve,
Santa Barbara County $22.   88

Rich gold-straw hue. Intense yeast, mineral, and vanilla aromas show a harmonious oak
accent. A lush entry leads a full-bodied palate with angular acidity and complex, intense
flavors. Powerful, assertive finish. Drink now.

1997 Chardonnay, American Tradition Reserve, Marcella's Vineyards,
Santa Barbara County $24.   89

Deep golden yellow. Intense tropical fruit, cream, and yeast aromas show judicious
wood influence. A ripe entry is followed by a full-bodied palate with balanced acidity
and a rich, flavorful finish. A big, weighty, intense style. Drink now.

1996 Viognier, Santa Barbara County $22.   91

Bright golden hue. Moderately full-bodied. Balanced acidity. Moderately extracted.
Flowers, citrus, minerals. Perfumed aromas, with a complex array of flavors. Well
structured and zesty on the palate, with vibrant acidity that does not mask the ripeness.
Has the hallmarks of classic Viognier.

1996 Pinot Noir, Santa Barbara County $18.   85

Pale ruby-garnet cast. Medium-bodied. Balanced acidity. Moderately extracted. Mildly
oaked. Mildly tannic. Minerals, dried herbs. Aromatically reserved, with a lean and
angular palate feel. Finishes with some mild bitterness.

1995 Pinot Noir, American Tradition Reserve, Santa Barbara County $28.   90

Dark red. Medium-bodied. Highly extracted. Moderately oaked. Mildly tannic. Earthy
black fruit aromas. Licorice, earth, and black cherries come through on the palate.
Long finish. Plenty of character here.

1996 Pinot Noir, American Tradition Reserve, Santa Barbara County $26.   86

Pale ruby-garnet cast. Moderately full-bodied. Full acidity. Moderately extracted. Heavily
oaked. Moderately tannic. Sweet wood, red fruits, minerals. Aromatic and distinctive,
though largely wood driven in flavor. Lean and angular in the mouth, with a lengthy
spicy finish.

1996 Syrah, Santa Barbara County $18.   88

Deep, dark red, limpid to the rim. Hefty wood tones. Firm entry. Moderately full-bodied.
Moderate, grainy tannins. Chewy and flavorsome, with muted, unusual black fruit, spice,
and earth flavors. Lingering rich finish. Well structured, concentrated, and youthful.
Drink now.

*1996 Syrah, American Tradition Reserve, Rodney's Vineyard, Santa Barbara
County $30.*   89

Dark brick red, limpid and dull to the rim. Hefty wood tones. Firm entry. Full-bodied.
Plentiful, drying tannins. Shows a developed, woody character with rather muted,
unusual brown spice, fruit, and earth flavors. Short finish. Drink now.

Patz & Hall

1997 Chardonnay, Napa Valley $30.   91

Brilliant pale yellow-gold. Stylish yeasty, smoky aromas. A smoky entry leads a medium-
bodied palate with great focus of flavors. The acid balance is notably good. Finishes with
a crisp, toasty note. Drink now or later.

1997 Chardonnay, Carr Vineyard, Mount Veeder $42.   89

Full gold. Rich buttery aromas. A lush attack leads a full-bodied palate with a rounded,
generous mouthfeel. Acids come through on the finish. A weighty, fat style although
the acids are in balance. Drink now.

1997 Chardonnay, Hyde Vineyard, Carneros $36.   92

Bright yellow-gold. Buttery, smoky aromas. A rich attack leads a moderately full-bodied
palate with tart acids. Rich, opulent style with classy notes of oak and lees balanced by
good acidity through the finish. Drink now.

1996 Pinot Noir, Russian River Valley $30.   86

Pale ruby-garnet cast. Medium-bodied. Balanced acidity. Moderately extracted. Mildly
tannic. Dried herbs, minerals. Aromatically reserved, with a lean, minerally quality
throughout. Lingering dusty finish.

Peachy Canyon

1995 Zinfandel, Dusi Ranch, Paso Robles $22.   81

Robert Pecota

1998 Dry Chenin Blanc, Monterey County $11.   84

Pale straw hue. Sweet pineapple and mineral aromas. A juicy entry leads a medium-bodied palate, with good tropical fruit flavor concentration and a zesty finish. Very pleasant.

1997 Sauvignon Blanc, California $11.   83

Pale platinum-gold. Medium-bodied. Balanced acidity. Moderately extracted. Citrus,
minerals. Restrained smoky aromas. Straightforward flavors are carried by lively acids
through a reasonably clean finish. Lacks only some flavor intensity on the midpalate.

1995 Cabernet Sauvignon, Kara's Vineyard, Napa Valley $25.   83

Bright red-purple. Moderately full-bodied. Moderately extracted. Moderately tannic. Black fruits, minerals. Pickled and bright on the palate, with crisp acids and powdery tannins that dry the finish.

1996 Cabernet Sauvignon, Kara's Vineyard, Napa Valley $29.   84

Bright violet-red hue. Youthful primary fruit aromas show a cherry fruit and vanilla. A bright, fruity entry leads a moderately full-bodied palate with dry, grainy tannins that grip the finish. Youthful. Well structured. Drink now or later.

1995 Merlot, Steven Andre Vineyard, Napa Valley $25.   87

Very deep ruby red with a purplish cast. Moderately full-bodied. Full acidity. Moderately extracted. Mildly tannic. Red fruits, minerals. Lighter in style, with acidity to the fore on the bright palate. Quite minerally throughout, with a crisp, angular finish.

1996 Merlot, Steven Andre Vineyard, Napa Valley $29.   86

Bright purple-red to the rim. Generous berry and mineral aromas show a spicy oak accent. A firm attack leads a lean, medium-bodied palate with tannic grip. The finish is tart and angular. Surprisingly light in style, but structured and snappy, clean and precise. Drink now or later. Can improve with more age.

1998 Muscat Canelli, Moscato d'Andrea, Napa Valley $11/375 ml.   86

Bright yellow-straw hue. Generous nutty pear and honey aromas. A lush entry leads a medium-bodied palate showing mild sweetness offset by lean acids. Lighter in style, but well flavored. Drink now.

Pedroncelli

1997 Chardonnay, F. Johnson Vineyard, Dry Creek Valley $13.   88

Medium yellow-gold. Mild aromas of yellow apples and heavily charred oak. Crisp on the attack with a moderately full body and tart fruit flavors standing up to the alcohol. Rather angular through the finish. Drink now.

1998 Zinfandel Rosé, Vintage Selection, Sonoma County $8.   92

Very deep raspberry pink. Intense, grapey, red fruit aromas. A firm entry leads a medium-bodied palate that has tons of flavor and great acidity. A powerful, stylish Rosé. Drink now.

1995 Cabernet Sauvignon, Morris Fay Vineyard, Alexander Valley $13.   86

Bright ruby cast. Medium-bodied. Balanced acidity. Moderately extracted. Mildly tannic. Minerals, dried herbs. Lighter in style, with a slightly herbal character. Lean flavors linger through the finish.

1995 Cabernet Sauvignon, Three Vineyards, Dry Creek Valley $12.50.   88

Deep cherry red. Medium-bodied. Highly extracted. Moderately tannic. Earth, black fruits, tobacco. Brooding, earthy nose with smoky notes leads a rich, chewy, impressively proportioned palate. Textured tannins linger on the finish.

1996 Cabernet Sauvignon, Three Vineyards, Dry Creek Valley $12.   88

Bright red-purple. Medium-bodied. Highly extracted. Moderately tannic. Red fruits, mineral. Mineral and red fruit aromas lead a dry palate, with fine-grained tannins showing on the finish. A youthful, vibrant style.

1996 Pinot Noir, F. Johnson Vineyard, Dry Creek Valley $13.   83

Pale ruby cast. Moderately light-bodied. Full acidity. Subtly extracted. Mildly tannic. Sweet herbs, minerals, meat. Unusual aromas lead a very light palate. Crisp through the finish.

1995 Pinot Noir, Single Vineyard Selection, Dry Creek Valley $13.   84

Very pale ruby hue with a light rim. Moderately light-bodied. Moderately extracted. Mildly oaked. Mildly tannic. Strawberry and vanilla-scented aromas lead a light, somewhat delicate palate with a minerally finish. Well balanced and very drinkable, with plenty of varietal character.

1996 Zinfandel, Mother Clone, Special Vineyard Selection, Dry Creek Valley $12.   **90**

Deep blackish ruby color with a brilliant cast. Moderately full-bodied. Low acidity. Moderately extracted. Mildly oaked. Mildly tannic. Briar fruits, minerals, chocolate. Quite aromatic, with a flavorful palate feel. Soft and generous in the mouth, with low acidity. Finishes with mild astringency.

1996 Zinfandel, Pedroni-Bushnell Vineyard, Single Vineyard Selection, Dry Creek Valley $13.   **86**

Deep blackish ruby hue with a purple edge. Moderately full-bodied. Balanced acidity. Moderately extracted. Mildly tannic. Black fruits, earth, chocolate. Aromatic and quite deeply flavored, with brooding, dark fruit notes. Surprisingly soft and supple on entry, with some mild astringency through the finish.

Peirano

1997 Cabernet Sauvignon, Lodi $8.99.   **83**

Bright ruby hue. Subdued mineral and anise aromas. A crisp attack leads to a medium-bodied palate with crisp acidity and grippy tannins. Fades toward the finish. Drink now.

1997 Merlot, Six Clones, Lodi $9.99.   **81**

Peju Province

1997 Chardonnay, Napa Valley $18.   **92**

Bright yellow-gold. Medium-bodied. Balanced acidity. Moderately extracted. Moderately oaked. Coconut, green apples, oak spice. Very appealing toasted oak aromas show a bright citrus accent that comes through on the palate. Outstanding lingering smoky finish.

1997 Chardonnay, HB Vineyard, Napa Valley $26.   **88**

Bright yellow-straw hue. Moderately full-bodied. Balanced acidity. Moderately extracted. Mildly oaked. Butter, spice, yellow apples. Complex yeasty aromas have a forceful character. Generously fruity, textured, and supple, this strikes all the right notes and finishes cleanly.

1997 Provence-A California Table Wine, California $16.50.   **86**

Brilliant, saturated pale purple. Lean herb and cherry aromas. A zesty entry leads a medium-bodied palate with vibrant acidity. Deep fruit flavors roll through the finish. Powerful, but a tad austere. Should open with a few more months of aging. Drink now or later.

1995 Cabernet Franc, Napa Valley $25.   **84**

Bright ruby hue with a garnet rim. Forward vanilla and spice aromas show a dominant oak influence. A lush entry leads to a medium-bodied palate with velvety tannins and a core of chocolatey flavors. Rich, generous, flavorful finish. Lower acidity levels make for a lush attractive wine, but not a keeper. Drink now.

1995 Cabernet Sauvignon, Napa Valley $28.   **93**

Bright saturated ruby cast. Moderately full-bodied. Balanced acidity. Moderately extracted. Heavily oaked. Mildly tannic. Briar fruits, coconut, vanilla. Outrageously aromatic, with a forward and intense flavor profile. Shows great definition despite a supple, open-knit structure. Velvety and stylish.

1994 Cabernet Sauvignon, H.B. Vineyard, Napa Valley $55.   **94**

Opaque dark crimson appearance. Moderately full-bodied. Highly extracted. Moderately tannic. Sweet herbs, black currant, brown spice, chocolate. Exotic spicy nose has sweet herbal overtones. A concentrated center of generous black juicy fruits is kept in check by firm dry tannins. Very structured and powerful.

1995 Cabernet Sauvignon, Estate Bottled, Napa Valley $55.   95

Deep ruby purple. Moderately full-bodied. Balanced acidity. Moderately extracted. Moderately oaked. Mildly tannic. Oriental spices, cassis, ginger. Exotically aromatic, with complexity throughout. Supple and generous in the mouth. Carries its weight effortlessly, with great refinement and style.

1995 Merlot, Napa Valley $35.   90

Bright cherry red, well saturated. Generous ripe aromas have a toasty oak accent. Moderately full-bodied with a firm attack and concentrated black fruit flavors that are well matched by ripe, chewy dry tannins that clamp down on the finish. Drink now or later. Can improve with more age.

1997 Chardonnay, Late Harvest, Napa Valley $35/375 ml.   80

Robert Pepi

1997 Malvasia Bianca, Central Coast $14.   88

Deep yellow-straw hue. Enticing flower and herb aromas are perfumed and exotic. A rich entry leads a moderately full-bodied palate showing crisp, juicy acidity. Drying finish. A real flavor bomb with a lean structure; an antidote for Chardonnay. Drink now.

1996 Barbera, Sonoma County $19.   84

Deep blackish purple. Medium-bodied. Full acidity. Moderately extracted. Mildly oaked. Mildly tannic. Earth, dried herbs, black fruits. Forward, interesting aromatics lead a lush palate feel buoyed by crisp acidity. Lean, focused finish.

1995 Sangiovese, Colline di Sassi, Napa Valley $25.   84

Dark ruby hue. Medium-bodied. Balanced acidity. Highly extracted. Moderately oaked. Mildly tannic. Earth, black fruits, brown spice. Spicy, earthy aromas lead a solid mouthful of earthy black fruits that turns dry on the finish. Rather ripe and chewy.

Pepperwood Grove

1997 Cabernet Sauvignon, California $7.   83

Pale cherry-red hue. Vanilla and red cherry aromas show a marked sweet oak influence. A soft attack leads to a medium-bodied palate with a juicy cherry fruit flavors and mild velvety tannins. Drink now.

1997 Merlot, California $7.   81

1997 Pinot Noir, California $6.99.   83

Very pale violet hue. Moderately light-bodied. Subtly extracted. Mildly tannic. Cherries, vanilla. Vibrant, sweet, fruity aromas follow through on the palate, with a crisp finish that makes for a fresh style.

1996 Zinfandel, California $6.99.   81

Perry Creek

1997 Chardonnay, El Dorado $12.   84

Pale straw hue. Clean aromas of mild apple fruit with very subtle oak. A clean attack leads a medium-bodied palate with bright fruit flavors that have refreshing varietal character. Acids are crisp through the finish. Drink now.

1996 Cabernet Sauvignon, El Dorado $12.50.   83

Deep garnet hue. Generous spice and mineral aromas. A lush entry leads to a moderately full-bodied palate with mildly astringent tannins. Ripe, rounded finish. Decent, but lacking grip and intensity. Drink now.

1996 Merlot, El Dorado $12.   81

1996 Sangiovese, El Dorado $15.   81

1996 Zinfandel, Zin Man, Sierra Foothills $12.   81

Pesenti

1995 Cabernet Sauvignon, Paso Robles $20.   **80**

1996 Cabernet Sauvignon, Paso Robles $15.   **86**

Deep ruby-purple hue. Moderate aromas show a sweet oak accent and ripe berry fruits. A fruity entry leads a medium-bodied palate with broad cherry fruit flavors and soft tannins lingering on the finish. Generously fruity with some underlying structure. Drink now.

1995 Zinfandel, Paso Robles $16.   **84**

Deep blackish ruby cast. Moderately full-bodied. Full acidity. Moderately extracted. Mildly oaked. Moderately tannic. Minerals, stewed fruits, wood. Quite aromatic, with a full but lean palate feel. Elevated acidity makes for an angular, juicy finish.

1996 Zinfandel, Paso Robles $16.   **84**

Deep blackish purple. Moderately full-bodied. Balanced acidity. Moderately extracted. Moderately oaked. Mildly tannic. Black fruits, brown spices. Pleasantly aromatic, with a solid interplay between fruit and wood nuances. Soft and supple on the palate, and well structured through the finish.

1997 Zinfandel Port, Second Estate Reserve, Paso Robles $20/500 ml.   **84**

Opaque blackish purple. Full-bodied. Full acidity. Highly extracted. Moderately tannic. Briar fruits, minerals. Extremely aromatic and wholly fruit-centered, with a ripe, jammy quality throughout. Full-throttled and intense, this wine is really showing its youth. Not for the faint of heart.

Peterson

1996 Cabernet Sauvignon, Bradford Mountain Vineyard,
Dry Creek Valley $25.   **88**

Very deep, saturated purple red hue. Intense vanilla and red fruit aromas show a big oak accent. A supple attack leads to a medium-bodied palate with ripe, supple tannins. Rich, rounded finish. A ripe and generous style. Drink within five years.

1996 Merlot, Dry Creek Valley $22.50.   **87**

Bright, saturated purple-red. Subdued mineral, chocolate, and red fruit aromas. A lean entry leads a medium-bodied palate with mildly astringent tannins and a firm, clipped finish. Rather austere but shows depth. Drink now.

1995 Zinfandel, Dry Creek Valley $14.   **84**

Deep blackish ruby cast. Moderately full-bodied. Balanced acidity. Highly extracted. Moderately oaked. Moderately tannic. Spice, chocolate, dried herbs. Somewhat reined in aromatically, with a firm, austere palate feel. Rather lean through the finish.

Pezzi King

1997 Chardonnay, Sonoma County $21.   **91**

Bright straw hue. Forward citrus and vanilla aromas show a pleasant oak accent. A crisp entry leads a moderately full-bodied palate with rounded acidity. Vibrant, persistent finish. Rich, but well balanced. Drink now.

1995 Cabernet Sauvignon, Dry Creek Valley $25.   **89**

Saturated cherry red. Moderately full-bodied. Highly extracted. Moderately tannic. Black cherries, minerals, brown spice. Deep, concentrated flavors are tightly wound, with fine-grained tannins clamping down on the finish. This will be better in a year or two.

1996 Cabernet Sauvignon, Dry Creek Valley $26.   **84**

Bright ruby red hue to the rim. Generous red fruit and vanilla aromas show a judicious oak accent. A soft entry leads to a medium-bodied palate with velvety tannins. Fruit-centered, ripe finish. Supple and eminently drinkable. Drink now.

Scale: Superlative (96-100), Exceptional (90-95), Highly Recommended (85-89),
Recommended (80-84), Not Recommended (Under 80)

Joseph Phelps

1996 Chardonnay, Los Carneros $22.   84

Bright pale straw cast. Medium-bodied. Full acidity. Moderately extracted. Moderately oaked. Menthol, vanilla, minerals. Assertively oaky aromas lead a lean palate, with vanilla flavors lingering through the finish. The creamy texture is a plus.

1996 Chardonnay, Ovation, Napa Valley $40.   89

Bright straw cast. Moderately full-bodied. Balanced acidity. Moderately extracted. Mildly oaked. Tropical fruits, minerals, yeast. Ripe and opulent, with complex if understated flavors. A weighty mouthfeel is balanced by zesty acidity. Lean through the finish.

1996 Viognier, Vin du Mistral, Napa Valley $28.   90

Deep straw cast. Full-bodied. Balanced acidity. Moderately extracted. Apples, minerals, flowers. Quite aromatic, with a complex array of flavors. Full and rich on the palate, showing a buttery character that is well balanced by acidity.

1994 Cabernet Sauvignon, Napa Valley $24.   90

Opaque dark purple-red. Medium-bodied. Highly extracted. Moderately tannic. Vanilla, brown spice, plums. Rich, spicy ripe fruit aromas lead a solid-textured palate with a powdery mouthfeel and impressive ripe flavors. Well integrated and quite plush. Lively high-toned fruity character.

1995 Cabernet Sauvignon, Napa Valley $27.   90

Deep ruby cast. Moderately full-bodied. Balanced acidity. Moderately extracted. Moderately oaked. Moderately tannic. Licorice, black fruits, earth. Big and weighty in style, with a rich and lush mouthfeel. Chunky tannins rear up on the finish.

1996 Cabernet Sauvignon, Napa Valley $30.   91

Saturated ruby-violet hue. Generously aromatic with big plummy fruit aromas and toasty vanilla notes. A rich attack leads a full-bodied palate with a thick, chewy mouthfeel and lush ripe cherry fruit flavors complimented by generous, supple tannins. A big, chewy wine that has the structure to age further. Drink now or later.

1994 Cabernet Sauvignon, Backus Vineyard, Napa Valley $70.   92

Opaque dark red-purple. Moderately full-bodied. Highly extracted. Moderately tannic. Cassis, plums, black tea. Ripe, brooding fleshy fruit aromas lead a thick, concentrated palate. Tight tannins envelope the finish. Needs some years to resolve the tannins. Structurally impressive.

1995 Cabernet Sauvignon, Backus Vineyard, Napa Valley $70.   93

Saturated ruby purple. Full-bodied. Balanced acidity. Highly extracted. Moderately oaked. Moderately tannic. Black fruits, minerals, mint. Aromatically reserved, with a dense and youthful palate feel. Tightly wound and stuffed with flavor. Shows excellent grip and intensity through the finish. Needs time to show its best.

1994 Insignia, Napa Valley $70.   93

Solidly opaque dark purple. Moderately full-bodied. Highly extracted. Moderately tannic. Violets, cassis, tobacco, cedar. Violet-edged dark berry fruit aromas. A solid, layered palate has fruity depth and richness, with a long, flavorful finish showing ample soft tannins. Still youthful, though very accessible now.

1995 Insignia, Napa Valley $75.   92

Dark ruby purple. Full-bodied. Balanced acidity. Highly extracted. Heavily oaked. Moderately tannic. Cocoa, earth, black fruits. Powerfully aromatic, displaying great depth and intensity. Complex throughout, with a weighty, extracted quality buttressed by firm tannins. A long-term (7–10 years) cellar candidate.

1995 Merlot, Napa Valley $26.   90

Deep blackish ruby hue with a slight purple cast. Moderately full-bodied. Balanced acidity. Moderately extracted. Moderately oaked. Mildly tannic. Black fruits, chocolate, minerals. Aromatic and complex, with a range of dense flavors and a judicious oak accent. Lush and chewy in the mouth with a firm structure. Velvety tannins rise on the finish.

1996 Merlot, Napa Valley $30.   89

Saturated dark ruby-violet hue. Rich, generous aromas show a chocolatey, toasty oak accent with dark fruits. A rich entry leads a full-bodied palate with deep fruit flavors and lush, textured tannins through the finish. Impressively dense, with chocolatey and plum flavors. Drink now or later.

1996 Le Mistral, California $25.   92

Deep purple-red hue to the rim. Forward perfumed red fruit, earth, and vanilla aromas with a mild wood accent. A smooth attack leads a full-bodied palate with abundant velvety tannins. Persistent, flavorful finish. Rich, elegant, and wonderfully made with the latest in soft extraction techniques. Drink now or later. Can improve with more age.

Philippe-Lorraine

1995 Cabernet Sauvignon, Napa Valley $17.50.   80
1996 Cabernet Sauvignon, Napa Valley $18.50.   92

Bright ruby with a slight garnet cast. Intense kirsch, vanilla, and cordial-like aromas show a big wood accent. A lush attack leads to a medium-bodied palate with ripe tannins. Exceptionally flavorful and attractive, fruit-centered finish. Unusual but hedonistic. Drink within five years.

1996 Merlot, Napa Valley $21.   91

Dark ruby-violet hue. Well-developed oaky, earthy, black fruit aromas. Firm on the attack with lushly extracted flavors and dry tannins through the finish. Quite complex and evolved, though it could use some cellar time and would improve with more age. Drink now or later.

R.H. Phillips

1997 Chardonnay, Barrel Cuvée, Dunnigan Hills $8.   80
1997 Sauvignon Blanc, Night Harvest, Dunnigan Hills $7.   81
1996 Syrah, EXP, Dunnigan Hills $12.   86

Dark ruby color, limpid with a slight fade. Medium-bodied. Cooked fruit flavors. Crisp, fruity, and well supported by grainy tannins and bright acids. Fruit-centered and relatively firmly structured. Drink now.

Pietra Santa

1996 Sangiovese, San Benito County $20.   82

Pine Ridge

1997 Chardonnay, Knollside Cuvée, Napa Valley $17.50.   86

Pale green-straw hue. Moderately full-bodied. Balanced acidity. Moderately extracted. Moderately oaked. Apples, butter, minerals. Soft vanilla and butter aromas follow through on the palate, with a lush mouthfeel and sweet, bright apple flavors that linger on the finish.

1997 Chardonnay, Dijon Clones, Napa Valley, Carneros $24.   84

Greenish gold. Medium-bodied. Full acidity. Moderately extracted. Lime, lemon. Bright citrus zest aromas. Crisp and tart, with a firm citrus edge that turns dry on the finish.

1994 Cabernet Sauvignon, Howell Mountain, Napa Valley $35.   91

Opaque blackish red. Moderately full-bodied. Highly extracted. Quite tannic. Earth, minerals, black fruits, black tea. Austere, closed-up nose. The tightly wound palate is not showing much generosity, though concentrated black fruit flavors are evident and hugely impressive. Tough through the finish. Needs long-term cellaring.

1995 Cabernet Sauvignon, Howell Mountain, Napa Valley $37.50.   94

Dark ruby purple. Full-bodied. Balanced acidity. Highly extracted. Moderately oaked. Quite tannic. Chocolate, licorice, brown spices. Exotic aromas show breeding and complexity. Deep and profound in the mouth, with a wave of brooding flavors. Firm tannins clamp down on the rich finish. Needs time.

Scale: Superlative (96-100), Exceptional (90-95), Highly Recommended (85-89), Recommended (80-84), Not Recommended (Under 80)

164

1996 Cabernet Sauvignon, Howell Mountain, Napa Valley $40. 97

Deep, opaque purple-red hue. Forward, intense vanilla and cordial-like blackberry aromas. A lush concentrated entry leads to a full-bodied supple palate feel with robust velvety tannins. Flavorful, stylish finish. Concentrated and impressive, yet very well balanced. Drink now or later.

1994 Cabernet Sauvignon, Stags Leap District, Napa Valley $35. 86

Full raspberry red. Medium-bodied. Moderately extracted. Mildly tannic. Raspberries, cassis, anise. Crisp, high-toned aromas. Bright, juicy raspberry and black fruit flavors expand vibrantly on the palate, with soft tannins through the finish and attractive minerally accents. Nice now.

1995 Cabernet Sauvignon, Stags Leap District, Napa Valley $37.50. 93

Saturated violet red. Moderately full-bodied. Highly extracted. Moderately oaked. Moderately tannic. Licorice, black fruits, earth. Toasty, dark fruit aromas follow through on the palate, with a vibrant, fruity center and dry, earthy notes through the lean finish. Impressively structured, though this is giving pleasure now.

1996 Cabernet Sauvignon, Stags Leap District, Napa Valley $40. 95

Brilliant ruby hue. A rich entry leads a moderately full-bodied palate with forcefully intense dark fruit flavors and voluptuous supple tannins that linger through the finish. Very hedonistic and persistent. Drink now or later.

1995 Cabernet Sauvignon, Rutherford, Napa Valley $24. 90

Deep ruby hue with a slight purple cast. Moderately full-bodied. Balanced acidity. Moderately extracted. Mildly oaked. Mildly tannic. Cassis, vanilla. Pleasantly aromatic, with a soft, supple, and harmonious palate feel. Gentle and well balanced, and quite flavorful through the finish.

1996 Cabernet Sauvignon, Rutherford, Napa Valley $25. 90

Medium ruby-violet hue. Attractively aromatic with deep cordial-like aromas. A richly fruity entry leads a moderately full-bodied palate with fantastic fruit intensity with cordial-like flavors that persist through a long finish. Drink now or later.

1994 Andrus Reserve, Napa Valley $85. 94

Dark reddish purple. Moderately full-bodied. Highly extracted. Moderately tannic. Black fruits, loam, minerals. Austere minerally nose leads a concentrated minerally palate with austere black fruit flavors that show amazing persistence on the finish. This wine impresses with its weight and persistence.

1995 Andrus Reserve, Napa Valley $85. 91

Deep ruby purple. Moderately full-bodied. Balanced acidity. Moderately extracted. Moderately oaked. Mildly tannic. Licorice, minerals, cassis. High-toned aromas lead a precise and well-defined palate feel. Crisp and intense through the angular finish. Shows fine grip and very judicious use of wood.

1996 Merlot, Crimson Creek, Napa Valley $25. 89

Bright violet-ruby hue. Lean, restrained aromas have a minerally, black fruit quality Moderately full-bodied, with a firm attack, minerally backbone, and some tough tannins. Rather angular through the finish, but well structured. Drink now or later. Can improve with more age.

1996 Merlot, Carneros $35. 94

Semi-saturated dark ruby hue. Generous dark chocolate and plum aromas. A rich attack leads a moderately full-bodied palate with chunky, soft tannins and a deeply flavorful finish. Drink now or later. Can improve with more age.

1993 Black Diamond Port, Napa Valley $16/375 ml. 80

Piper Sonoma

NV Brut, Sonoma $14. 87

Bright straw cast. Medium-bodied. Full acidity. Toast, citrus peel. Forward aromas feature a subtle yeast accent. Crisp, bright, and austere through the finish, yet showing fine biscuity nuances.

NV Blanc de Noir, Sonoma $15.   **90**

Deep straw cast. Moderately full-bodied. Yeast, toast, bread dough. Forward, mature aromatics are complex and yeasty. Smooth and supple in the mouth, with a silky texture. This seems very generous and developed, with signs of extended bottle age.

Plam

1994 Cabernet Sauvignon, Vintner's Reserve, Napa Valley $30.   **90**

Dark garnet-red center. Medium-bodied. Highly extracted. Moderately tannic. Cassis, earth, chocolate, brown spice. Deep spicy aromas suggest concentrated black fruit flavors that are confirmed on the palate. The solid, chewy mouthfeel concludes with an assertive finish.

1995 Cabernet Sauvignon, Vintner's Reserve, Napa Valley $30.   **94**

Saturated, opaque purple. Full-bodied. Highly extracted. Quite tannic. Spice, cassis, chocolate. Rich, deep, fruity aromas show a heavy oak spice accent. Weighty, heavily wrought texture and flavors convey power and structure. This needs time.

1995 Merlot, Vintner's Reserve, Napa Valley $25.   **93**

Deep blackish ruby color. Moderately full-bodied. Balanced acidity. Highly extracted. Heavily oaked. Mildly tannic. Cedar, cherry cordial, brown spices. Supple on the entry and extremely aromatic and flavorful on the palate, with some dusty tannins. Very lengthy finish. Quite solid and well balanced.

Prager Winery & Port Works

1993 Petite Sirah, Royal Escort LBV Port, Napa Valley $38.50.   **88**

Deep blackish ruby cast. Moderately full-bodied. Full acidity. Highly extracted. Mildly tannic. Brown spices, black fruits, chocolate. Oaky aromas, with spicy flavors throughout. Full though drying on the palate, with a deep core of dark fruit flavors. Finishes with a touch of heat.

Noble Companion 10 Year Old Tawny Port, Napa Valley $45.   **89**

Deep mahogany cast. Moderately full-bodied. Full acidity. Highly extracted. Mildly tannic. Salted nuts, treacle, brown spices. Carries a fiery impression on the nose. Full throttled and flavorful on the palate, with some Sherry-like complexities. The lengthy finish is a touch hot.

Pride Mountain

1996 Cabernet Franc, Sonoma County $25.   **89**

Deep ruby purple. Moderately full-bodied. Balanced acidity. Highly extracted. Moderately oaked. Moderately tannic. Vanilla, black fruits. Aromatic and modern, with a forward, fruit-and-wood flavor profile. Full and round in the mouth, with a drying, flavorful finish. Well balanced.

1996 Cabernet Sauvignon, Napa Valley $29.99.   **98**

Saturated black-ruby hue. Chocolate and anise aromas are quite distinctive. A rich entry leads to a full-bodied palate showing enormous density of flavors and a rich, rounded mouthfeel that finishes with toasty oak accents. A voluptuous style that is very approachable now. Drink now or later.

Quady

Batch 88 Starboard, California $11.50.   **89**

Deep ruby-garnet cast. Full-bodied. Balanced acidity. Highly extracted. Chocolate, tea, black fruits. Aromatic and quite complex, with a wide range of flavors throughout. Lush, rounded, and well balanced on the palate, with a lengthy finish.

1993 LBV Port, Amador County $12.   **91**

Deep blackish garnet cast. Moderately full-bodied. Balanced acidity. Highly extracted. Chocolate, brown spices, black fruits. Carries a generous wood accent throughout, with a deeply flavored, supple palate feel. Shows fine grip and intensity, with excellent length.

Scale: Superlative (96-100), Exceptional (90-95), Highly Recommended (85-89), Recommended (80-84), Not Recommended (Under 80)

166

1989 Frank's Vineyard Vintage Starboard, California $19.   90

Deep ruby cast with a brick rim. Moderately full-bodied. Balanced acidity. Moderately extracted. Mild sweetness. Reminiscent of black fruits, earth, dried apricots. Rich earthy aromas introduce this full-flavored Port with a firm, woody character. The sweetness is subsumed by well-balanced acidity and wood influences. Finishes with complex, Sherry-like tones.

1990 Frank's Vineyard Vintage Starboard, California $19.   89

Black-ruby hue with brickish rim. Moderately full-bodied. Balanced acidity. Highly extracted. Medium sweetness. Reminiscent of black fruits, vanilla, butterscotch. Rich and ripe tasting, and very nicely textured, with grainy tannins lingering in a long, flavorful finish. Evolving nicely and destined for further improvement.

1990 Vintage Starboard, Amador County $21.50.   93

Opaque blackish garnet cast. Moderately full-bodied. Balanced acidity. Moderately extracted. Minerals, black fruits, olives. Quite aromatic, with pleasant mature nuances throughout. Rich, supple, and velvety in the mouth, with a very lengthy finish. Classic and stylish.

1997 Black Muscat, Elysium, California $12.   86

Saturated pale cherry-garnet hue. Generous herb and red fruit aromas carry a spiritish accent. A lush entry leads a full-bodied palate that has lots of sweetness and lean acidity. Perfumed through the finish. Full throttled. Drink now.

1997 Orange Muscat, Essensia, California $12.   86

Deep copper hue. Exotic, spiritish orange peel and mineral aromas. A lush entry leads a moderately full-bodied, sweet palate with a pithy finish. This vintage of Essensia is moving toward the rustic side, with an herbal overtone. Drink now.

Quail Ridge

1996 Sauvignon Blanc, Reserve, Rutherford River Ranch, Napa Valley $14.99.   82

1994 Cabernet Sauvignon, Napa Valley $14.99.   85

Pale purplish red. Moderately light-bodied. Moderately extracted. Moderately tannic. Crisp berries, minerals. Quite lean in style, with some juicy flavors up front, and astringency running through the palate to give a somewhat compact finish.

1995 Cabernet Sauvignon, Napa Valley $15.99.   86

Pale, bright cherry red with purple highlights. Moderately light-bodied. Moderately extracted. Mildly tannic. Raspberries, cherries, cedar. Crisp fruity aromas follow through on an open-knit palate with accessible flavors. Nice now, but not for the long haul.

1996 Cabernet Sauvignon, Napa Valley $22.   84

Medium violet-purple hue. Restrained sweet herbal aromas. A light entry leads to a lighter-bodied palate with subtle flavors and a minerally grip through the finish. Rather restrained in style. Drink now.

1993 Cabernet Sauvignon, Volker Eisele Vineyard Reserve, Napa Valley $39.99.   92

Full cherry red with a subtle brick cast. Medium-bodied. Moderately extracted. Moderately tannic. Violets, black currants, spice. Hugely perfumed with enticing violet hints. An elegant and delicate palate shows well-integrated, noble, fine-grained tannins and great persistence of flavors through the finish. Attractive now, though more age will probably improve it.

1995 Cabernet Sauvignon, Volker Eisele Vineyard Reserve, Napa Valley $40.   88

Medium ruby hue. Leaner, reserved aromas show a minerally overtone. A firm entry leads to a medium-bodied palate with firm flavors and a tannic structure and acidity that makes for a well-gripped finish. Fruit flavors are tightly focused, bright, and cherry-like. Drink now or later.

1995 Merlot, California $19.99. 82

Quatro
1997 Chardonnay, Sonoma County $9.99. 81
1996 Merlot, Sonoma County $12. 89
Brilliant violet red. Generous cherry fruit and vanilla aromas. A vibrant attack leads a medium-bodied palate with balanced fine-grained tannins. Finishes with juicy, fruity persistence. This is a concentrated, stylish wine to be consumed now or later. Can improve with more age.

Quinta da Sonora
1996 Vinho Tinto, Sierra Foothills $18. 87
Deep blackish purple. Moderately full-bodied. Balanced acidity. Highly extracted. Mildly oaked. Mildly tannic. Blueberries, minerals, vanilla. Exotically aromatic, with a lush, flavorful mouthfeel. Full and lean through the finish. Intense and well balanced.

Quintessa
1995 Red, Rutherford $75. 90
Bright ruby-garnet hue. Mature coffee and oak spice aromas show a developed, tertiary character. A firm entry leads to a moderately full-bodied palate with rounded fruit flavors and plenty of spicy oak notes through the finish. Elegant, and drinking very nicely now.

Qupé
1997 Chardonnay, Bien Nacido Vineyard, Santa Barbara County $18. 93
Pale straw hue. Mildly aromatic with apple character. A crisp entry leads a medium-bodied palate with zesty citrus flavors and no oak influences. The finish is clean. This would be an excellent match with sole or delicate fish.
1996 Chardonnay, Bien Nacido Reserve, Santa Barbara County $25. 90
Medium yellow-gold. Generous aromas of toasty oak and ripe fruit. A juicy entry leads a moderately full-bodied palate with bright acids to match the full citrus fruits. Alcohol seems a bit on the high side. Finishes with judicious oak spice flavors. Drink now or later.
1996 Los Olivos Red Cuvée, Ibarra, Young, and Stolpman Vineyards, Santa Barbara County $18. 90
Bright purple-red to the rim. Forward black fruit, earth, and spice aromas show a subtle wood influence. A soft attack leads a medium-bodied palate showing velvety tannins. Supple, lengthy, flavorful finish. Harmonious and complete. Drink now.
1997 Syrah, Central Coast $13.50. 84
Pale purple, limpid, with a fading rim. Subtle, clean flower and crisp berry flavors. Firm entry. Moderately light-bodied with crisp acidity. Has a relatively light frame. The finish is clipped and short. Drink now.
1996 Syrah, Bien Nacido Reserve, Santa Barbara County $25. 89
Dark ruby purple, limpid and brilliant, with a slight fade. Generous, sound black fruit, cherry, and vanilla flavors. Generous wood tones. Smooth entry. Moderately full-bodied. Moderate thick tannins. Lingering finish. Thick, chewy, and fruity. Drink now.
1996 Syrah, Bien Nacido Hillside Estate, Santa Barbara County $35. 92
Dark crimson purple, limpid and brilliant to the rim. Generous, ripe, juicy berry fruit and jammy black fruit flavors. Soft entry. Moderately full-bodied. Moderate drying tannins. Rather weak on the finish. Drink now.

Ramey
1996 Chardonnay, Hyde Vineyard, Carneros, Napa Valley $45. 91
Bright gold. Smoky, buttery aromas with obvious oak influence. A bright attack leads a moderately full-bodied palate with impressive flavor concentration. Finishes with persistent flavors and lingering oak spice. Drink now or later.

Ramspeck

1995 Cabernet Sauvignon, Napa Valley $18.   85

Blackish red. Medium-bodied. Highly extracted. Moderately tannic. Earth, pencil lead, brown spice, black fruits. Quite an austere style, with a solid minerally presence on the midpalate. Good grip through the finish, with a firm chalky feel. Time will probably help this one.

Rancho Sisquoc

1994 Cabernet Sauvignon, Santa Maria Valley $18.   88

Bright purple-crimson color. Medium-bodied. Highly extracted. Moderately tannic. Cigar box, black cherries. Cedar and tobacco in the nose. Concentrated black cherry flavors on entry linger through a well-balanced finish showing fine soft tannins that provide a supple character.

1996 Cabernet Sauvignon, Santa Maria Valley $20.   90

Deep ruby-red hue. Generous aromas show chocolate and dark fruit accents. A rich entry leads a full-bodied palate with fully extracted flavors and plenty of spicy oak flavors that linger through a persistent finish. Very well balanced with plenty of structure and flavor concentration to allow this to improve.

1995 Merlot, Santa Maria Valley $18.   89

Deep blackish ruby color. Medium-bodied. Balanced acidity. Moderately extracted. Moderately oaked. Mildly tannic. Red fruits, minerals, vanilla. Aromatic and focused, with concentrated red fruit flavors. Firmly structured, with cleansing acidity in the lengthy oak-tinged finish. Well balanced.

1996 Merlot, Santa Maria Valley $20.   86

Deep, saturated purple-red. Unusual, high-toned earth and mineral aromas show a reductive note, but seem to blow off with aeration. A lean entry leads a medium-bodied palate with racy acidity and tannic grip. The finish is crisp and linear. Well structured. Drink now or later. Can improve with more age.

Kent Rasmussen

1996 Petite Sirah, Ramsay, Napa Valley $20.   84

Bright purple. Moderately full-bodied. Highly extracted. Floral, bright black fruit aromas. Tannins are very dry and fine grained, making this rather tough at present.

1995 Pinot Noir, Carneros $26.   81

1996 Pinot Noir, Carneros $27.   80

1996 Syrah, Ramsay Reserve, Napa Valley $20.   89

Deep purple, opaque, and brilliant, with a slight fade. Generous, pleasant briary bramble fruit and oak spice flavors. Hefty wood tones. Firm entry. Moderately full-bodied. Angular, with plentiful hard-edged tannins through the clipped bitter finish. Good structure, though tough now. Drink within five years.

Ravenswood

1994 Rancho Salina Vineyards Red, Sonoma Valley $30.   89

Dark ruby color. Medium-bodied. Moderately extracted. Moderately tannic. Earth, brown spice, black fruits. Exotic dark fruit and spice aromas lead a solid, full-flavored palate, with well-balanced dry tannins on the finish. Quite complex though harmonious in its flavors.

1995 Rancho Vineyards Red, Sonoma Mountain $30.   91

Blood red with a subtle garnet cast. Medium-bodied. Moderately extracted. Moderately tannic. Earth, brown spice, black fruits. Dusty, spicy aromas follow through on the palate, with ripe black fruit flavors and a bite to the dry tannins.

1995 Pickberry Vineyards Red, Sonoma Mountain $35.   90

Bright blood red. Moderately full-bodied. Highly extracted. Moderately tannic. Bramble fruits, cedar, sage. Smoky, ripe aromas lead a fleshy entry, with fine-grained, angular tannins drying the finish. A well-balanced, generous style that will need a few more years.

1996 Zinfandel, Sonoma County $15.25.   88

Deep blackish ruby hue. Medium-bodied. Full acidity. Moderately extracted. Mildly oaked. Mildly tannic. Black fruits, minerals. Quite aromatic, with a high-toned, fruit-centered palate feel. Crisp, vibrant, and tasty in a lighter style, with a lengthy finish.

1996 Zinfandel, Dickerson Vineyard, Napa Valley $24.   91

Bright blackish ruby cast. Moderately full-bodied. Balanced acidity. Highly extracted. Moderately oaked. Mildly tannic. Black fruits, minerals, vanilla. Quite aromatic, with a firm, angular palate feel. Shows fine depth and length, with a taut finish. Intense and "well gripped."

1996 Zinfandel, Monte Rosso, Sonoma Valley $24.   95

Deep blackish ruby hue. Full-bodied. Full acidity. Highly extracted. Moderately oaked. Moderately tannic. Minerals, black fruits. Pleasantly aromatic, with a concentrated, angular palate feel that shows great depth. Firmly structured and intense, with a lengthy finish.

1996 Zinfandel, Old Hill Vineyard, Sonoma Valley $26.   91

Bright blackish ruby cast. Moderately full-bodied. Balanced acidity. Moderately extracted. Mildly oaked. Mildly tannic. Red fruits, black pepper, licorice. Quite aromatic, with a velvety, lush palate feel. Deeply flavored and very well balanced, with lean tannins through the finish.

1996 Zinfandel, Wood Road Belloni, Russian River Valley $24.   94

Bright blackish purple. Full-bodied. Balanced acidity. Highly extracted. Moderately oaked. Moderately tannic. Chocolate, sweet herbs, black fruits. Quite aromatic, with great complexity to the range of flavors. Deep and intense, with a lush, velvety texture. Firm through the finish.

Martin Ray

1996 Chardonnay, Mariage, California $20.   86

Bright yellow-gold. Medium-bodied. Balanced acidity. Moderately extracted. Toasted oak, citrus, brown spice. Nutty, yeasty aromas lead a rich, rounded mouthfeel, with lush citrus fruit flavors and spicy oak on the finish. A generous style.

1997 Chardonnay, Marriage, California $20.   88

Bright straw hue. Generous brown spice aromas carry an intense oak accent. A firm attack leads a rounded, moderately full-bodied mouthfeel with creamy acidity. Generous, flavorful finish. Drink now.

1995 Cabernet Sauvignon, Santa Cruz Mountains $25.   89

Deep saturated ruby cast. Moderately full-bodied. Balanced acidity. Highly extracted. Heavily oaked. Moderately tannic. Dill pickle, spice, minerals. Quite aromatic, with a flavor profile dominated by American oak. Ripe and full in the mouth, with grainy tannins through a drying finish.

1994 Cabernet Sauvignon, Saratoga Cuvée, California $35.50.   89

Deep red. Medium-bodied. Highly extracted. Moderately tannic. Black fruits, earth, minerals. An earthy, assertive nose leads a rather young and tight palate, with plenty of firm spicy oak flavors on the finish. Quite austere, and with sound structure and some depth, this will be best with richer foods.

1995 Cabernet Sauvignon, Saratoga Cuvée, California $25.   89

Saturated blood red. Medium-bodied. Moderately extracted. Heavily oaked. Moderately tannic. Black fruits, brown spice. Dense black fruit aromas follow through on the palate, with plentiful soft tannins. The balanced finish shows some firmness, yet this is drinking well now. Very oak-influenced style.

1995 Cabernet Sauvignon, Diamond Mountain, Napa Valley $45.   93

Deep ruby cast. Moderately full-bodied. Balanced acidity. Highly extracted. Moderately oaked. Moderately tannic. Brown spices, minerals, pencil shavings. Quite aromatic, with a big toasty oak accent. Firm, lean, and tightly wound in the mouth, with very robust tannins. Needs time.

Scale: Superlative (96-100), Exceptional (90-95), Highly Recommended (85-89), Recommended (80-84), Not Recommended (Under 80)

170

1995 Pinot Noir, California $36.   90

Full cherry-garnet red with a light rim. Medium-bodied. Moderately extracted. Moderately oaked. Mildly tannic. Vanilla and cherry aromas. Full berry flavors are defined by crisp acids that give this a lively and generous palate presence with impressive concentration of flavors. Vanilla notes linger on the finish.

1996 Pinot Noir, California $19.   86

Bright ruby cast. Medium-bodied. Balanced acidity. Moderately extracted. Moderately oaked. Mildly tannic. Brown spices, minerals, red fruits. Bright aromas carry a ripe berry quality. Oak spice makes for a drying quality through the finish.

Raymond

1997 Chardonnay, Amberhill, California $10.   83

Deep yellow-straw hue. Generous spice, mineral, and vegetable aromas. A rich attack leads a ripe, moderately full-bodied palate with rounded acidity. The finish is rich and flavorful. Drink now.

1997 Chardonnay, Monterey $13.   86

Bright yellow-gold. Ripe buttery aromas. A vibrant entry leads a moderately full-bodied palate with a bright, lush, citrus center and full alcohol to match the acids. Finishes with lingering fruit acids. Very flavorful.

1997 Chardonnay, Reserve, Napa Valley $15.   83

Dark yellow-straw hue. Toast, green apple, and yeast aromas. A juicy entry leads a moderately full-bodied palate with a juicy, fruity center and a lingering oak spice finish. Drink now.

1996 Chardonnay, Generations, Napa Valley $27.   88

Full yellow-straw hue. Rich smoky aromas with a toasty oak accent. A rich attack leads a moderately full-bodied palate with a rounded mouthfeel and alcohol heat showing on the finish. Drink now.

1996 Sauvignon Blanc, Valley Reserve, Napa Valley $11.   86

Deep yellow-gold. Moderately full-bodied. Full acidity. Highly extracted. Mildly oaked. Yeast, minerals, citrus. Quite aromatic, with complex flavors and a distinctive yeasty note. Crisp and vibrant through the snappy finish.

1996 Cabernet Sauvignon, Amberhill, California $10.   81

1995 Cabernet Sauvignon, Napa Valley $15.   84

Violet-red with a lightening rim. Medium-bodied. Moderately extracted. Mildly tannic. Brown spice, black fruits. Spicy oak aromas lead soft black fruit flavors. Supple, with generous alcohol showing on the finish. For current drinking.

1994 Cabernet Sauvignon, Reserve, Napa Valley $20.   86

Bright reddish purple. Medium-bodied. Moderately extracted. Mildly tannic. Cassis, plums, tobacco. Rather full, ripe aromas show fleshy cassis-like notes. Supple, rounded, and attractive, with soft tannins on the finish and tobacco notes. Drink now.

1995 Cabernet Sauvignon, Reserve, Napa Valley $20.   86

Bright violet-purple with a lightening rim. Moderately full-bodied. Moderately extracted. Moderately tannic. Blueberries, spice. Ripe and smooth, with fine-textured tannins in a supple, friendly style that has enough juicy acidity to provide focus.

1996 Cabernet Sauvignon, Reserve, Napa Valley $23.   87

Bright ruby hue. Subdued mineral and berry aromas. A crisp attack leads to a medium-bodied palate with acidic vibrancy and grippy tannins. Clean, stylish finish. Straightforward and attractive. Drink now.

1994 Cabernet Sauvignon, Generations, Napa Valley $35.   88

Deep reddish purple. Medium-bodied. Highly extracted. Mildly tannic. Toasted oak, vanilla, cassis. Rich toasted oak aromas. Elegant, smooth, and supple, with fine concentration and full toasty oak components that linger through the finish. Nice now.

1995 Cabernet Sauvignon, Generations, Napa Valley $50.   **90**

Deep purple-red hue. Vibrant berry and oak aromas show a typical Australian show wine accent. A lean entry leads to a moderately full-bodied palate with vibrant acidity and gripping tannins. Firm, vibrant, flavorful finish. Quite modern, with direct flavors, but a well-crafted and tasty style. Drink now or later.

Reliz Canyon

1997 Chardonnay, Arroyo Seco $14.   **83**

Pale straw cast. Medium-bodied. Full acidity. Moderately extracted. Minerals, citrus peel. Lean and quite austere, with a pithy, citric quality. Firm and intense through the finish.

1996 Merlot, Monterey $13.95.   **86**

Violet red. Lean aromas of minerals, red fruits, and herbs. A bright attack, a medium-bodied palate, vibrant acids and light, gripping tannins. Drink now.

Renaissance

1995 Chardonnay, Reserve, North Yuba $19.99.   **89**

Bright gold-straw hue. Medium-bodied. Full acidity. Moderately extracted. Mildly oaked. White citrus, vanilla. Clean citrusy aromas lead a bright, lively mouthful of flavors that turn firm and minerally through the finish, with subtle oak spice emerging. A crisp and lean style.

1998 Riesling, Demi-Sec, North Yuba $11.99.   **81**

1997 Sauvignon Blanc, North Yuba $10.   **87**

Bright yellow-gold. Medium-bodied. Balanced acidity. Moderately extracted. Minerals, dried herbs, citrus fruits. Wet wool aromas similar to Loire Sauvignon Blanc. A bright citrus streak through the palate gives this a vivacious character.

1996 Sauvignon Blanc, Barrel Select, North Yuba $12.   **84**

Bright yellow-gold. Medium-bodied. Low acidity. Moderately extracted. Mildly oaked. Butter, citrus. Rich buttery aromas are followed by similar flavors on the palate. A hint of smoky oak comes through on the finish.

1995 Cabernet Sauvignon, North Yuba $13.99.   **82**

1994 Cabernet Sauvignon, Reserve, North Yuba $19.99.   **86**

Deep ruby red to the rim. Moderately full-bodied. Balanced acidity. Highly extracted. Moderately tannic. Earth, chocolate, minerals. Carries an earthy accent throughout. Full, but firmly structured, with firm tannins through the finish.

1995 Sauvignon Blanc, Late Harvest, North Yuba $19.99.   **84**

Deep yellow-gold. Medium-bodied. Full acidity. Moderately extracted. Mildly oaked. Yeast, toast, vanilla. Heavily toasted in the nose, with a distinctive yeasty character. Thick and sweet yet extremely vibrant acidity gives a mouthwatering finish.

Renwood

1996 Viognier, Amador County $21.95.   **82**

1996 Barbera, Amador County $18.95.   **81**

1994 Vintage Port, Shenandoah Valley $21.95/500 ml.   **84**

Deep blackish garnet cast. Moderately full-bodied. Balanced acidity. Moderately extracted. Minerals, earth, black fruits. Fragrant and flavorful, with a deep and brooding array of flavors. Well balanced, with measured sweetness to the finish.

1996 Zinfandel, Amador Ice, Amador County $9.95/375 ml.   **81**

Richardson

1995 Cabernet Sauvignon, Horne Vineyard, Sonoma Valley $18.   **89**

Opaque dark red with bright purple accents. Moderately full-bodied. Highly extracted. Moderately tannic. Mint, vanilla, and red and black fruits. Very aromatic cedary, minty nose shows oak accents. Big minty mouthful, with a solid structured feel through a balanced but astringent finish.

1996 Cabernet Sauvignon, Horne Vineyard, Sonoma Valley $22.　　　94

Saturated red-purple. Moderately full-bodied. Moderately extracted. Moderately oaked. Moderately tannic. Bright black fruits, mint, minerals. Abundant fruit-forward aromas jump out of the glass. Bright and vibrant, with a chewy, textured character and supple tannins that are nice now.

1994 Synergy, Sonoma Valley $17.　　　85

Medium cherry red. Medium-bodied. Moderately extracted. Mildly tannic. Tea, red fruits, vanilla. Simple berry and vanilla aromas. Straightforward, with crisp fruity flavors on a simple palate. Does not show extravagant weight or concentration, though the balance is good.

1996 Synergy, Sonoma Valley $20.　　　92

Bright red-purple. Moderately full-bodied. Moderately extracted. Moderately oaked. Mildly tannic. Red fruits, vanilla. Fleshy red fruit aromas. Velvety fruit-centered flavors have a supple, polished character with great persistence through the finish.

1996 Pinot Noir, Sangiacomo Vineyard, Carneros $19.　　　89

Bright cherry red with a pinkish tinge. Medium-bodied. Moderately extracted. Mildly tannic. Bright perfumed, fruity aromas have dill note. Racy, well-defined fruit flavors on the palate show a crisp vanilla accent through the finish. Very fruity and lively.

1997 Syrah, Sonoma Valley $22.50.　　　86

Rich purple, limpid, and brilliant to the rim. Subtle, sound leather, spice, and black fruit flavors. Generous wood tones. Firm entry. Moderately full-bodied. Plentiful drying tannins. Dry and lean, with some leathery overtones. Clipped finish. Nice briar and minty notes, though a little dirty. Flavorsome. Drink now.

Ridge

1997 Chardonnay, California $NA.　　　91

Deep, saturated yellow-straw hue. Generous citrus, cream, and spice aromas. A supple entry leads a moderately full-bodied but well-balanced palate. Rounded and rich, with great persistence. Drink now.

1996 Chardonnay, Santa Cruz Mountains $25.　　　92

Bright golden luster. Moderately full-bodied. Full acidity. Highly extracted. Honeysuckle, peaches, apples. Rich honeyed aromas lead a bright, vibrantly fruity mouthful with a degree of generosity that follows through the engagingly honeysuckle-like finish.

1997 Coast Ridge Red, California $NA.　　　86

Brilliant, saturated ruby purple. Generous red fruit, mineral, and flower aromas. A crisp entry leads a medium-bodied palate, with drying tannins. Bright fruity finish. Drink now.

1995 Cabernet Sauvignon, Santa Cruz Mountains $22.　　　93

Opaque reddish purple. Moderately full-bodied. Highly extracted. Quite tannic. Black plums, toasted oak, black tea. The nose is muted but suggestively rich, with toasty accents. Extraordinarily thick and viscous mouthfeel. Whopping tannins on the finish make this tough at present. Fruit flavors are immensely concentrated and bright. This wine needs cellaring.

1993 Cabernet Sauvignon, Monte Bello, Santa Cruz Mountains $55.　　　96

Opaque blackish red. Moderately full-bodied. Highly extracted. Moderately tannic. Toasted oak, ripe plums, minerals, allspice. Toasty, dill-accented nose with suggestive dark fruit notes. Rich, dense, concentrated, and chewy. Hugely proportioned, with great depth of flavors. Tannins are rather dry and constraining on the finish at present. Densely structured.

1994 Cabernet Sauvignon, Monte Bello, Santa Cruz Mountains $65.　　　95

Deep, saturated ruby purple. Moderately full-bodied. Balanced acidity. Moderately extracted. Mildly oaked. Moderately tannic. Cassis, minerals, toast. Very aromatic, with a firm, minerally backbone to the fruit-forward flavors. Oak seems to play a minor supporting role. Elegant and exceptionally well balanced, with a crisp finish. Not a show wine, but a style that blossoms with age.

1995 Cabernet Sauvignon, Monte Bello, Santa Cruz Mountains $70.   92

Deep, saturated ruby purple. Full-bodied. Full acidity. Highly extracted. Moderately oaked. Moderately tannic. Vanilla, black fruits, minerals, flowers. Extremely aromatic, with a ripe core of intense fruit flavors bolstered by judicious use of oak. Deep, impressive, and intense, with a firm but velvety palate feel. Very approachable, but cellaring will undoubtedly bring out a great measure of complexity.

1995 Merlot, Santa Cruz Mountains $40.   90

Very deep blackish ruby hue with a slight purple cast. Moderately full-bodied. Full acidity. Moderately extracted. Mildly oaked. Moderately tannic. Red fruits, dried herbs, minerals. Still a bit reserved aromatically, this youthful wine fills out on the palate. Flavors are complex, with a hefty mineral accent. Full acidity and a firm structure are in balance with the level of extract. Will need some aging to fully reveal itself. Elegant.

1996 Merlot, Monte Bello Ridge, Santa Cruz Mountains $40.   93

Saturated purple-red. Deep, profound black fruit and vanilla aromas show a judicious oak accent. A firm attack leads a moderately full-bodied palate with firm tannins and juicy acidity, followed by a crisp finish. The wine literally bursts with flavor. Drink now or later. Can improve with more age.

1997 Mataro, Bridgehead, Contra Costa County $NA.   88

Bright, saturated ruby purple. Generous red fruit, earth, and mineral aromas. A firm entry leads a medium-bodied palate, with velvety tannins. Quite stylish. Drink now.

1996 Petite Sirah, York Creek, Spring Mountain, Napa Valley $NA.   90

Deep, saturated ruby purple. Generous black fruit and wood aromas show a hefty oak influence. A firm entry leads a full-bodied palate, with robust tannins. Aromatic and stuffed, with a big tannic finish. Needs time. Mid-term cellar candidate (3–6 years).

1996 Zinfandel, Dusi Ranch, Paso Robles $25.   95

Deep blackish ruby cast. Moderately full-bodied. Balanced acidity. Moderately extracted. Mildly oaked. Mildly tannic. Chocolate, black fruits. Somewhat reserved aromatically, but rich and flavorful on the palate. Amazingly lush, with a supple, velvety texture. Quite well balanced; should gain in complexity with age.

1997 Zinfandel, Late Picked, Paso Robles $NA.   89

Dark, saturated violet-red. Fantastic black fruit and chocolate aromas carry distinctive floral overtones. A firm entry leads a moderately full-bodied palate with velvety tannins. Big and rich with a sweetish edge, but balanced by solid acidity. Drink now.

1995 Zinfandel, Geyserville, Sonoma County $22.   92

Deep blackish ruby cast. Moderately full-bodied. Balanced acidity. Moderately extracted. Heavily oaked. Mildly tannic. Brown spices, sandalwood, black fruits. Quite aromatic, with a hefty overlay of spicy wood notes, and a firm core of ripe fruit flavors. Lush and generous through the lengthy finish.

1996 Zinfandel, Lytton Springs, Dry Creek Valley $25.   92

Deep blackish purple. Moderately full-bodied. Balanced acidity. Highly extracted. Moderately tannic. Black fruits, chocolate, pepper. Rather reserved aromatically, with a firm, focused palate feel. Elegant in the mouth, showing a seamless texture and a lean finish. Should reward mid-term (3–6 years) aging.

1995 Zinfandel, Pagani Ranch, Late Picked 100 Year Old Vines, Sonoma Valley $22.   91

Deep blackish purple. Full-bodied. Balanced acidity. Moderately extracted. Mildly oaked. Mildly tannic. Black pepper, briar fruits, licorice. Quite aromatic, with a rich, opulent texture. Extremely ripe and lush, with a weighty, flavorful mouthfeel. Carries a hint of Port throughout. Finishes with some mild astringency.

1996 Zinfandel, Sonoma Station, Sonoma County $18.   88

Bright blackish purple. Medium-bodied. Balanced acidity. Moderately extracted. Mildly oaked. Mildly tannic. Briar fruits, vanilla. Quite aromatic, with a lighter-styled, fruit-centered palate feel. Nicely textured, featuring solid grip through the lengthy, flavorful finish.

1997 Zinfandel, Sonoma Station, Sonoma County $NA.   **89**

Brilliant, saturated purple. Forward briar fruit and mineral aromas. A crisp entry leads a medium-bodied palate, with marked acidity and grainy tannins. Lots of fruit, with a great acidic cut. Drink now.

1995 Zinfandel, York Creek, Spring Mountain $22.   **88**

Bright blackish ruby hue. Moderately full-bodied. Balanced acidity. Highly extracted. Mildly oaked. Moderately tannic. Minerals, chocolate. Made in a reserved Claret style. Taut and firm in structure, with a minerally backbone. Finishes with mild astringency.

River Run

1996 Carignane, Wirz Vineyard, Cienega Valley $15.   **86**

Crimson hue with a pale, fading rim. Medium-bodied. Moderately extracted. Mildly tannic. Raspberry notes. Generous berry fruit aromas show a ripe, jammy character. Well gripped and lively on the palate with a fruit center. Supple tannins on the finish.

1997 Malbec, Mannstand Vineyard, Santa Clara County $18.   **82**

1996 Merlot, California $15.   **87**

Very deep purplish ruby hue. Moderately full-bodied. Full acidity. Highly extracted. Mildly oaked. Mildly tannic. Black fruits, plums, vanilla. Deep and brooding, with a rich, chewy texture. Attractive fruit flavors are highlighted by vibrant acidity. Clean through the finish, with velvety tannins.

Rochioli

1995 Chardonnay, Estate, Russian River Valley $25.   **93**

Medium straw hue. Clean citrus, mineral, and hazelnut aromas. A firm entry leads a medium-bodied palate showing crisp acids. A vibrant style with some grip and leesy complexity. Quite flavorful, with great balance. Opulent yet restrained. Meursault-like. Drink now or later.

1997 Sauvignon Blanc, Russian River Valley $16.   **86**

Pale straw cast. Medium-bodied. Balanced acidity. Moderately extracted. Apple, gooseberry. High-toned aromas. A hint of sweetness with high-toned tropical fruit flavors on the palate. Clean, simple, and juicy, showing some intriguing varietal character.

1995 Pinot Noir, Russian River Valley $34.99.   **89**

Medium red-purple. Medium-bodied. Moderately extracted. Moderately oaked. Mildly tannic. Floral and vanilla aromas. Bright vanilla-edged raspberry and cherry fruit flavors. Light, fine-grained tannins on the finish. Still a little tight.

1996 Pinot Noir, Russian River Valley $35.   **86**

Pale ruby cast. Medium-bodied. Full acidity. Moderately extracted. Mildly tannic. Minerals, red fruits, vanilla. Unusual aromas lead a brisk and angular palate feel. Lean but flavorful through the finish.

1997 Pinot Noir, Sonoma Valley $25.   **90**

Pale cherry red with a slight fade. Interesting dusty cherry and herb aromas carry a mild oak accent. A supple entry leads a medium-bodied palate, with velvety tannins. Well balanced and elegant, with crisp Pinot flavors. Light but elegant. Drink now.

Rocking Horse

1994 Cabernet Sauvignon, Garvey Family Vineyard, Rutherford $25.   **88**

Dark reddish purple. Medium-bodied. Moderately extracted. Moderately tannic. Black cherry, cassis, black tea, brown spice. Solid, chewy black Cabernet fruit flavors turn dry, with fine-grained tannins dominating the finish. Soundly structured.

1996 Zinfandel, Lamborn Vineyard, Howell Mountain $18.   **94**

Bright cherry red. Medium-bodied. Balanced acidity. Moderately extracted. Moderately tannic. Cherries, minerals, vanilla. Intense, pure, black cherry aromas follow through on the palate, with elegant, concentrated flavors. Tightly wound yet still very stylish. Cellar.

Roederer Estate

NV Brut, Anderson Valley $17. 89

Pale yellow-straw hue. Medium-bodied. Full acidity. Smoke, citrus, minerals. Aromas are smoky, yet they have a piercing citrus note. The aromas follow through on the palate, with concentrated flavors and bright acids. Fine-beaded, pinpoint bubbles are a standout. Sound structure and persistence indicate that this could gain more complexity in a year or two.

NV Brut Rose, Anderson Valley $21. 92

Pale copper hue with a pinkish overtone. Moderately full-bodied. Minerals, citrus, red fruits. Reserved and elegant, with classic flavors. Well-balanced carbonation adds a refreshing note and elegant mousse to the silky mouthfeel. Very stylish and refreshing, and drinking well now.

1992 L'Ermitage, Anderson Valley $35. 93

Brilliant yellow-gold. Medium-bodied. Full acidity. Smoke, ripe citrus. Profoundly complex, smoky aromas. Rich, round, and flavorsome, with fine-beaded bubbles and complex yeasty accents that persist through the finish. Very elegant and classic, showing the refinement of tête de cuvée Champagne.

Rombauer

1997 Chardonnay, Carneros $25.75. 87

Brilliant yellow-gold. Moderately full-bodied. Balanced acidity. Highly extracted. Moderately oaked. Vanilla, smoke, tropical fruit. Plenty of sweet tropical fruit and toasty oak flavors compete for attention right through the lengthy finish. Shows a concentrated character.

Rosenblum

1997 Chardonnay, Edna Valley $23. 86

Bright yellow-straw cast. Moderately full-bodied. Full acidity. Moderately extracted. Earth, citrus. Shows a slightly unusual earthy note on the nose. Crisp and linear in the mouth. Finishes with a vibrant wood-accented note.

1996 Semillon-Chardonnay, Livermore Valley $11. 86

Bright yellow-gold. Moderately light-bodied. Full acidity. Moderately extracted. Figs, dried herbs, lemons, minerals. Bright and vibrant, with a nice figgy twist through a racy and flavorsome finish.

1997 Viognier, Santa Barbara County $15. 91

Bright straw cast. Moderately full-bodied. Full acidity. Moderately extracted. Tropical fruits, oranges, flowers. Quite aromatic, with an extremely ripe and complex fruit-centered flavor profile. Vibrant acidity balances the weightiness of the wine through a fine and intense finish.

1995 Cabernet Sauvignon, Hendry Vineyard, Reserve, Napa Valley $40. 87

Deep blood-brick red. Moderately full-bodied. Highly extracted. Moderately oaked. Mildly tannic. Eucalyptus, black fruits, brown spice. Rich, minty aromas, with an earthy backnote that follows through on the palate. Lengthy, powdery tannins, yet a very flavorful finish.

1995 Holbrook Mitchell Trio, Napa Valley $35. 89

Bright violet-red. Medium-bodied. Moderately extracted. Mildly tannic. Licorice, minerals, cassis. Earthy notes on the nose come through on the palate, with good minerally grip, fine acids, and bright black fruit flavors.

1996 Holbrook Mitchell Trio, Napa Valley $35. 87

Bright red-purple. Medium-bodied. Moderately extracted. Moderately oaked. Mildly tannic. Cassis, licorice, oak spice. Warm, spicy aromas lead a bright, lively palate, with great balance evident. Oak accents play a substantial role.

1995 Merlot, Lone Oak Vineyard, Russian River Valley $20.   **90**

Blackish ruby hue. Medium-bodied. Full acidity. Highly extracted. Moderately oaked. Mildly tannic. Vanilla, black fruits, mint. Quite racy in style, with vibrant acidity that makes the fruit flavors seem juicy. Features a well-integrated oak overlay and a clean, snappy finish with some mild astringency. Fine length.

1997 Mourvedre, Chateau La Paws, Côte du Bone, Contra Costa County $9.50.   **86**

Pale ruby red with a slight fade. Medium-bodied. Moderately extracted. Mildly tannic. Raspberry, cola, vanilla. Soft, berryish, and fruit centered, with a supple lingering finish. Very high drinkability factor.

NV Zinfandel, Vintners Cuvée XVI, California $9.50.   **85**

Deep ruby purple. Moderately full-bodied. Balanced acidity. Moderately extracted. Mildly tannic. Red berries, minerals. Bright, fruit-centered aromatics lead a lighter-styled, lively palate feel. Precocious and tasty, with good grip to the finish. Well balanced.

1996 Zinfandel, Contra Costa County $15.   **82**

1996 Zinfandel, Annette's Reserve, Rhodes Vineyard, Redwood Valley $20. **95**

Deep reddish purple. Medium-bodied. Highly extracted. Moderately oaked. Mildly tannic. Coffee, chocolate, raspberries. Exotically ripe, expressive aromas follow through well on the explosively fruity palate. A fine dusting of tannins gives this some needed grip through the finish. Exciting.

1996 Zinfandel, Ballentine Vineyard, Napa Valley $19.   **83**

Bright cherry purple. Medium-bodied. Balanced acidity. Moderately extracted. Mildly oaked. Mildly tannic. Briar fruits, vanilla. Juicy, supple sweet fruit flavors. This is a softer style with low acids.

1996 Zinfandel, Continente Vineyard, Old Old Vine, Contra Costa County $20.   **86**

Deep blackish ruby cast. Full-bodied. Balanced acidity. Moderately extracted. Moderately oaked. Mildly tannic. Black fruits, brown spices, chocolate. Quite aromatic, with a spicy oak overlay and a lush palate feel featuring solid fruit concentration. Rich and ripe through the finish.

1996 Zinfandel, Harris Kratka Vineyard, Alexander Valley $22.   **91**

Deep blackish ruby cast. Full-bodied. Balanced acidity. Moderately extracted. Heavily oaked. Mildly tannic. Chocolate, black fruits. Quite aromatic, with a big, lush, chocolatey character in the mouth. Smooth and supple, with a thick, velvety texture. Intense and enticing.

1996 Zinfandel, Reserve, Hendry Vineyard, Napa Valley $22.   **88**

Bright cherry red. Medium-bodied. Balanced acidity. Moderately extracted. Mildly oaked. Mildly tannic. Plums, berry fruits, chocolate. The smooth, rich, textured mouthfeel shows plenty of hedonistic fruit flavors and vanilla oak nuances.

1996 Zinfandel, Richard Sauret Vineyard, Paso Robles $17.   **90**

Bright blackish purple. Moderately full-bodied. Balanced acidity. Moderately extracted. Mildly oaked. Mildly tannic. Chocolate, black fruits. Intensely aromatic, with a supple and deeply flavored mouthfeel. Well balanced and seductive through the finish.

1996 Zinfandel, Rockpile Vineyard, Dry Creek Valley $22.   **91**

Dark ruby purple to the rim. Moderately full-bodied. Full acidity. Moderately extracted. Mildly oaked. Mildly tannic. Briar fruits, vanilla. Quite aromatic, with a solid interplay between oak and fruit flavors. Lush and rich in the mouth, with buoyant acidity that keeps everything lively through the finish. Well balanced and intense.

1996 Zinfandel, Samsel Vineyard, Maggie's Reserve, Sonoma Valley $28.   **95**

Bright ruby purple. Moderately full-bodied. Full acidity. Moderately extracted. Mildly oaked. Mildly tannic. Briar fruits. Quite aromatic, with a big, fruit-centered flavor profile. Lush and rich in the mouth, yet with the requisite acidity to keep things lively. Quite pure, finishing with excellent grip.

1996 Zinfandel, White Cottage Vineyard, Howell Mountain $21.   95
Dark cherry red. Medium-bodied. Balanced acidity. Moderately extracted. Moderately tannic. Plums, black fruits. A deep, fleshy, fruit-centered style with an underlying concentration of flavors backed by some fine tannins. Very ripe, almost soft, this is currently drinking well. May not have the stuffing to cellar extensively. Hedonistic.

1994 Zinfandel, Late Harvest, Sonoma County $15/375 ml.   89
Opaque blackish ruby hue. Moderately full-bodied. Balanced acidity. Moderately extracted. Mildly oaked. Mildly tannic. Chocolate, black fruits. Quite aromatic, with a fruit-centered, Portlike mouthfeel. Rich and dense through the finish. Quite flavorful; made for chocolate.

1994 Port, California $10/375 ml.   82

1991 Late Harvest Sauvignon Blanc, Concento d'Oro,
Napa Valley $15/375 ml.   81

Stephen Ross
1997 Chardonnay, Edna Ranch, Edna Valley $18.50.   88
Deep straw hue. Reserved mineral, wool, and citrus aromas. A lean entry leads a medium-bodied palate with angular acidity. Firm, phenolic finish. Drink now.

1997 Chardonnay, Bien Nacido Vineyard, Santa Maria Valley $20.   90
Bright yellow-straw hue. Restrained and stylish yeast, toast, and mineral aromas. A firm entry is followed by a medium-bodied palate with crisp acidity and a ripe, persistent finish. Exceptionally well balanced. Drink now.

1996 Pinot Noir, La Colline Vineyard, Arroyo Grande Valley $20.   86
Pale cherry red with subtle purple highlights. Medium-bodied. Moderately extracted. Moderately oaked. Mildly tannic. Crisp and well-defined red cherry and berry flavors have an herbal, minerally theme through the finish. Very bright.

1996 Pinot Noir, Edna Ranch, Edna Valley $22.   86
Reddish purple with a bright rim. Medium-bodied. Moderately extracted. Moderately tannic. Crisp candied cherry flavors up front turn very dry and minerally through the finish. Tight, fine-grained tannins make this tough at present, though the structure is impressive.

1996 Pinot Noir, Bien Nacido Vineyard, Santa Maria Valley $24.   87
Bright purple. Medium-bodied. Moderately extracted. Moderately oaked. Mildly tannic. Clean, smooth, and juicy, with sweet cherry flavors through the finish highlighted by herbal notes and mild citrus acidity. Tannins are very soft, with subtle oak accents.

Round Hill
1997 Chardonnay, California $8.   84
Pale green-gold. Medium-bodied. Full acidity. Moderately extracted. Tart citrus, flowers. Tart yet floral aromas lead a vibrant, angular palate with straightforward flavors that finish quickly.

1995 Cabernet Sauvignon, California $9.   80
1992 Cabernet Sauvignon, 20th Anniversary Release, Napa Valley $24.   84
Deep ruby-violet hue. Medium-bodied. Moderately extracted. Moderately tannic. Minerals, anise, earth. Lean, dry aromas lead a tough, dry mouthful of flavors, with green tannins making for a dry finish.

1996 Merlot, California $8.   81

J. Runquist
1995 Zinfandel, Z, Massoni Ranch, Amador County $18.   81

Rust Ridge

1995 Cabernet Sauvignon, Napa Valley $24.　　　　　　　**89**

Deep brick red. Medium-bodied. Moderately extracted. Moderately tannic. Licorice, black fruits, cherries. Ripe, earthy, developed aromas indicate a harmony that follows through on the palate. Broad, softer flavors come together well. Finishes with good grip. Excellent for current drinking.

1996 Zinfandel, Napa Valley $18.　　　　　　　**86**

Bright cherry red. Medium-bodied. Balanced acidity. Moderately extracted. Moderately oaked. Mildly tannic. Vanilla, cherries, raspberries. Attractive vanilla and berry aromas follow through on a balanced palate, showing stylish winemaking. Very drinkable, succulent, and lush.

Rutherford Grove

1995 Merlot, Napa Valley $9.99.　　　　　　　**80**

Rutherford Hill

1995 Merlot, Reserve, Napa Valley $40.　　　　　　　**90**

Deep opaque ruby to the rim with a slight purplish cast. Moderately full-bodied. Balanced acidity. Highly extracted. Heavily oaked. Moderately tannic. Brown spices, mint, red fruits. Oak-driven aromatics lead a well-integrated, finely wrought mouthfeel with a deep core of fruit flavors. Well balanced and nicely crafted, with chewy tannins and a lengthy finish buoyed by juicy acidity.

1996 Merlot, Reserve, Napa Valley $44.　　　　　　　**94**

Saturated bright ruby red with violet highlights. Fabulously fruity aromas. Full-bodied and rich on the attack with lush fruit flavors and velvety tannins that are well integrated and carry through the lengthy finish. A rich and hedonistic style. Drink now or later. Can improve with more age.

1995 Sangiovese, 21st Anniversary, Napa Valley $30.　　　　　　　**91**

Ruby red. Medium-bodied. Full acidity. Moderately extracted. Moderately oaked. Mildly tannic. Mint, vanilla, tart cherries. Bright and lively, with juicy acids and bright flavors underscored by minerally austerity and dried red fruit flavors. Very tasty.

Rutherford Ranch

1997 Chardonnay, Napa Valley $10.　　　　　　　**81**

1993 Cabernet Sauvignon, Napa Valley $12.　　　　　　　**89**

Medium brick-cherry color. Medium-bodied. Moderately extracted. Mildly tannic. Red fruits, toasted oak, minerals. Subtle toasty nose. Juicy red fruit flavors on the palate linger on the finish. Good balance for early drinking, but not for extended keeping.

1995 Cabernet Sauvignon, Napa Valley $12.　　　　　　　**80**

1995 Merlot, Napa Valley $13.　　　　　　　**80**

Rutherford Vintners

1997 Chardonnay, Stanislaus County $8.99.　　　　　　　**85**

Pale straw hue. Faint melony aromas. A clean entry leads a medium-bodied palate with peach and apple flavors that linger on the medium-length finish. No oak influence. Drink now.

1995 Fumé Blanc, Barrel Select, North Coast $8.99.　　　　　　　**86**

Very deep golden hue. Moderately full-bodied. Full acidity. Moderately extracted. Mildly oaked. Brown spice, menthol, lime, lemons. Minty aromas and toasty oak spice make a strong impression, with a bright center of zesty fruit flavors filling the palate. Well structured, with good grip.

1997 White Zinfandel, Lodi $5.99.　　　　　　　**84**

Saturated raspberry pink. Generous talc and berry aromas. A lush entry leads a medium-bodied palate that has good flavor intensity. Decent acid-sugar balance through the finish. Drink now.

1996 Cabernet Sauvignon, Lodi $8.99.   **84**

Ruby hue with a pale violet rim. Moderately light-bodied. Moderately extracted. Mildly tannic. Black fruits, flowers. Aromas of dark Cabernet fruit with floral accents. Juicy, straightforward, and light in style.

1997 Merlot, Stanislaus County $8.99.   **84**

Light violet hue. Light fruit-scented, floral aromas are quite fragrant. A juicy attack reveals a lighter-bodied palate with crisp acidity and a clean finish. Drink now.

1997 Shiraz, Stanislaus County $8.99.   **83**

Dark ruby color, with a fading rim. Cherry and vanilla flavors. Medium-bodied. Tart aromas lead crisp fruit flavors through a drying finish. Drink now.

1996 Zinfandel, Lodi $8.99.   **84**

Bright red-purple. Medium-bodied. Balanced acidity. Moderately extracted. Mildly tannic. Red berries. Superripe, fleshy berry aromas follow through on the palate. Generous and round, with soft tannins. Easy drinking.

Rutz

1996 Chardonnay, Russian River Valley $20.   **81**

1996 Chardonnay, Dutton Ranch, Russian River Valley $30.   **85**

Bright yellow-gold. Moderately full-bodied. Full acidity. Apples, vanilla, spice. Vibrant and intense, this has a tight core of bright Chardonnay flavors and a weighty mouthfeel that features oak spice on the finish. It should be better in a year.

1996 Pinot Noir, Sleepy Hollow Vineyard, Monterey $30.   **81**

Saddleback

1997 Pinot Blanc, Napa Valley $13.50.   **86**

Deep straw cast. Medium-bodied. Full acidity. Highly extracted. Mildly oaked. Butter, minerals, tropical fruits. Quite buttery aromas and flavors, with a lean and angular palate feel that still conveys a sense of ripeness. Good lengthy finish.

1996 Cabernet Sauvignon, Napa Valley $32.   **87**

Saturated dark ruby hue. Dark fruit aromas with earth and anise. A flavorful entry leads a medium to moderately full-bodied palate with rich black cherry and wood flavors. Tannins are well balanced and moderately supple through the finish. Drink now.

Saintsbury

1996 Chardonnay, Reserve, Carneros $28.   **84**

Brilliant yellow-gold. Moderately full-bodied. Balanced acidity. Moderately extracted. Moderately oaked. Smoke, green apples. The toasty, smoky nose shows a crisp fruity accent that comes through on the palate with a decidedly crisp mouthfeel.

1995 Pinot Noir, Reserve, Carneros $28.   **91**

Dark cherry red. Medium-bodied. Highly extracted. Moderately oaked. Moderately tannic. Black cherry and bramble fruit aromas lead a mouthful of dark fruit flavors, with an earthy licorice note through the finish. Plenty of flavors and structure here.

1996 Pinot Noir, Reserve, Carneros $34.   **86**

Dark violet red with a lightening rim. Medium-bodied. Moderately extracted. Moderately oaked. Moderately tannic. Raspberries, oak spice, minerals. Perfumed sweet aromas show an oaky note. Full-flavored and fruity on the palate, with a firm, lingering spicy finish. Flavorful and varietally faithful.

Salmon Creek

1996 Chardonnay, Los Carneros, Sonoma County $16.   **86**

Bright yellow-gold. Generous aromas of oak and crisp citrus fruits. A bright attack leads a moderately full-bodied palate with zesty flavors and oak spice. Finishes with a note of dryness. Drink now.

Scale: Superlative (96-100), Exceptional (90-95), Highly Recommended (85-89), Recommended (80-84), Not Recommended (Under 80)

180

San Saba

1997 Chardonnay, Monterey $20. 93

Dark golden cast. Moderately full-bodied. Balanced acidity. Highly extracted. Moderately oaked. Butterscotch, vanilla, ripe citrus. Features a rich, viscous, buttery texture and a strong sensation of yeast and vanilla oak flavors. Decadent, though a softer style.

1994 Cabernet Sauvignon, Monterey $17. 85

Deep garnet red. Medium-bodied. Moderately extracted. Mildly tannic. Bell pepper, stems, red berries. Very distinctively herbal nose leads a soft, rounded mouthfeel with berry flavors that give way to an herbal finish.

1995 Merlot, Monterey $20. 81

Sanford

1997 Chardonnay, Santa Barbara County $18. 85

Pale straw hue. Muted aromas. Rather heavy on the medium-bodied palate with soft acids accentuating the warm finish.

1995 Pinot Noir, Santa Barbara County $20. 90

Rich ruby red. Medium-bodied. Moderately extracted. Moderately oaked. Mildly tannic. Meaty, leathery, dusty cherry aromas lead a smooth, rounded palate. Shows a delightful balance and full Pinot Noir fruit character. Lovely finish with lingering cinnamon notes.

Santa Barbara Winery

1996 Chardonnay, Reserve, Santa Ynez Valley $24. 90

Bright yellow-straw cast. Moderately full-bodied. Balanced acidity. Moderately extracted. Tropical fruits, cream, citrus. Generous aromas feature a rich fruity quality. Opulent and textured in the mouth, with a lengthy, complex finish. Generous and elegant.

Santa Rita Creek

1995 Pinot Noir, Paso Robles $14.50. 85

Pale cherry red with a purple cast. Moderately light-bodied. Moderately extracted. Moderately oaked. Mildly tannic. Crisp, faintly candied cherry flavors lead a very balanced palate, with bright cherry and berry flavors and plenty of vanilla oak through the cleanly astringent finish.

Santino

1997 Harvest White Zinfandel, Shenandoah Valley $4.95. 81

1996 Satyricon, California $11.95. 84

Bright garnet red with a slight fade. Attractive, generous leather, herb, and mineral aromas. A supple attack leads a medium-bodied palate, with drying, mildly astringent tannins. The finish is lean and angular. Rather edgy. Drink now.

1995 Zinfandel, California $10. 84

Deep blackish ruby hue. Full-bodied. Full acidity. Highly extracted. Mildly oaked. Mildly tannic. Brown spices, chocolate. Oak overtones are readily apparent on the nose, and play out on the palate. Thick and chunky, with a drying, dusty finish. A tad rustic.

1996 Muscato del Diavolo, Amador County $9.95/500 ml. 80

V. Sattui

1997 Chardonnay, Napa Valley $16.75. 83

Pale green-straw hue. Subdued yeasty aromas. Clean on the attack, leading a moderately full-bodied palate with a glycerous mouthfeel and short flavors. Drink now.

1997 Chardonnay, Carsi Vineyard, Napa Valley $18. 86

Green-gold. Rich tropical aromas with a toasted coconut note. The attack is rich, leading a full-bodied palate and a glycerous mouthfeel. Flavors of juicy apples and smoky oak persist through the finish. Very elegant and refined.

1997 Chardonnay, Carsi Vineyard, Old Vine, Napa Valley $19.75. 83

Full yellow-gold. Ripe aromas of melon, apple, and smoky yeast with obvious wood influence. A rich attack leads a rather thick, full-bodied palate with a glycerous mouthfeel and tropical generosity through the finish. Drink now.

1998 Gewürztraminer, Sonoma County $11.25. 83

Bright straw hue. Intense spice and banana aromas jump from the glass. A racy entry leads a medium-bodied palate, with mild sweetness offset by crisp acidity. Refreshing finish. A quaffer. Drink now.

1998 Dry Johannisberg Riesling, Napa Valley $11.25. 86

Medium golden hue. Very classic aromas of petrol with herbal, minerally nuances. A soft entry leads a medium-bodied palate, with a rounded mouthfeel and impressive, deep petrol flavors. A streak of acid comes through on the finish. Very stylish. Drink now or later.

1998 Off-Dry Johannisberg Riesling, Napa Valley $11.25. 83

Medium gold hue. Very aromatic with a whiff of petrol and some tropical character. A sweet, tropical attack leads a medium-bodied palate, with glycerous richness and off-dry sweetness through the finish. Drink now.

1996 Sauvignon Blanc, Suzanne's Vineyard, Napa Valley $11.25. 82

1997 White Zinfandel, California $7.75. 82

1997 Gamay Rouge, California $13.75. 80

1995 Cabernet Sauvignon, Napa Valley $17.50. 83

Saturated ruby purple. Moderately full-bodied. Highly extracted. Quite tannic. Earth, anise. Lean, tough aromas. Tough and heavily wrought tannins give this a formidable structure that is hard to penetrate.

1994 Cabernet Sauvignon, Morisoli Vineyard, Napa Valley $25. 86

Opaque dark purple. Medium-bodied. Highly extracted. Mildly tannic. Black plums, brown spice, minerals. Crisp, juicy black fruit flavors seem tight and high toned. Some dry tannins and vigorous acids are restraining this at present.

1995 Cabernet Sauvignon, Morisoli Vineyard, Napa Valley $25. 89

Bright ruby purple. Moderately full-bodied. Balanced acidity. Highly extracted. Mildly oaked. Quite tannic. Minerals, black fruits. Aromatically reserved, with a dense and brooding palate feel. Firm, chunky tannins make for a tough and unyielding impression in the mouth. Perhaps it will open after some cellar time.

1994 Cabernet Sauvignon, Preston Vineyard, Napa Valley $30. 85

Deep purple. Medium-bodied. Highly extracted. Moderately tannic. Blackberries, plums, brown spice, minerals. Bright, compact red fruit flavors are kept in check by aggressive acids and dry tannins. This is not showing at its best right now, but seems to have all the structural elements to develop with cellaring.

1995 Cabernet Sauvignon, Preston Vineyard, Napa Valley $27. 89

Brilliant violet hue. Moderately full-bodied. Balanced acidity. Highly extracted. Mildly oaked. Moderately tannic. Briar fruits, vanilla, minerals. Reined-in aromatics lead a firm and intense palate feel. Fruit centered, with a very sturdy structure. Needs time.

1994 Cabernet Sauvignon, Rosenbrand Family Reserve, Napa Valley $60. 91

Brilliant violet cast. Full-bodied. Balanced acidity. Highly extracted. Mildly oaked. Moderately tannic. Flowers, minerals, spice. Intense and unusual aromatics lend a sense of complexity throughout. Generous and supple on the entry, with firm tannins rearing up on the finish. Needs time to mellow; all the components of a long-term (7–10 years) cellar candidate are present.

1994 Cabernet Sauvignon, Suzanne's Vineyard, Napa Valley $20. 85

Dark purple. Medium-bodied. Highly extracted. Moderately tannic. Cherries, cassis, minerals, toasted oak. Vibrant toasty aromas show strong oak accents that are confirmed on the bright, juicy, fruity palate. Young and lively, with fine acids and a minerally edge.

1995 Cabernet Sauvignon, Suzanne's Vineyard, Napa Valley $22.50.   **88**

Saturated dark red-purple. Moderately full-bodied. Highly extracted. Quite tannic. Earth, spice, black fruits. Dense and dry, with chunky tannins drying the finish. A powerful style that will need time to resolve its tannins.

1995 Zinfandel, Howell Mountain, Napa Valley $18.   **89**

Opaque center with purple highlights. Medium-bodied. Balanced acidity. Highly extracted. Moderately oaked. Quite tannic. Toasted coconut, black fruits, minerals. An attractive toasty nose leads a solid, tight, minerally palate showing dry, fine-grained tannins. Solidly structured.

1995 Zinfandel, Suzanne's Vineyard, Napa Valley $16.75.   **86**

Blood red. Medium-bodied. Balanced acidity. Moderately extracted. Moderately oaked. Moderately tannic. Red fruits, chocolate, brown spice. Rich and fleshy, with an expansive midpalate and some angular tannins.

1997 Muscat, California $12.   **85**

Brilliant yellow-straw hue. Reserved orange blossom and lacquer aromas. A vibrant entry leads a medium-bodied palate that has crisp acids and moderate sweetness. The finish is clean, flavorful, and refreshing. Drink now.

Saucelito Canyon

1996 Zinfandel, Arroyo Grande Valley $19.   **86**

Opaque red-purple. Moderately full-bodied. Balanced acidity. Highly extracted. Moderately oaked. Moderately tannic. Red fruits. Intensely fleshy red berry aromas. Solid, rather tight palate has plenty of stuffing and a glycerous mouthfeel. Finish has a mildly bitter note.

Savannah-Chanel

1997 Chardonnay, Santa Cruz Mountains $20.   **86**

Bright yellow-straw hue. Moderately full-bodied. Balanced acidity. Highly extracted. Apples, smoke, spice. Markedly floral, oak-spiced aromas follow through on the deeply flavored palate. Finishes with a lingering sense of tartness and spice.

1996 Cabernet Franc, Santa Cruz Mountains $26.   **83**

Bright ruby cast. Medium-bodied. Balanced acidity. Moderately extracted. Mildly oaked. Mildly tannic. Spice, minerals, red fruits. A spicy oak nuance in the nose leads a lighter-styled, angular palate feel. Taut and flavorful through the finish.

1995 Cabernet Franc, Library Selection, Santa Cruz Mountains $35.   **80**

Schramsberg

1994 Blanc de Blancs, Napa Valley $26.   **92**

Bright straw cast. Full-bodied. Full acidity. Minerals, citrus zest. Bright citrus zest and doughy aromas. Firm, concentrated, and lively on the palate. This wine shows a degree of intensity through the finish that bodes well for its cellar life.

1992 Blanc de Noirs, Napa Valley $27.   **91**

Bright pale gold. Full-bodied. Butter, yeast, toast. Developed, toasty, rich aromas lead a rich and ripe mouthfeel. Shows excellent weight and concentration, with fine length and intensity. Complex and attractive now, with a fine, frothy mousse.

1992 J.Schram, Napa Valley $65.   **91**

Full yellow-straw hue. Moderately full-bodied. Smoke, roasted coffee, tropical fruit. Rich, rounded, and leesy, with evident smoky maturity. Very generous and textured, and drinking very well now. This shows outstanding yeast complexity and a finely beaded mousse.

Schuetz Oles

1996 Zinfandel, Napa Valley $12.   84

Deep blackish ruby cast. Moderately full-bodied. Balanced acidity. Highly extracted.
Moderately oaked. Moderately tannic. Tea, brown spices, minerals. Complex aromatics,
with a firm, austere palate feel. Astringent tannins clamp down on the finish, but the
flavor keeps going. Needs a bit of time.

1996 Zinfandel, Korte Ranch, Napa Valley $18.   88

Deep blackish ruby hue. Moderately full-bodied. Full acidity. Moderately extracted.
Mildly oaked. Mildly tannic. Briar fruits, spice. Pleasantly aromatic, with a firm, flavorful,
well-structured palate feel. Angular and clean through the finish.

Schug

1997 Chardonnay, Carneros $18.   86

Pale yellow-straw color. Moderately full-bodied. Balanced acidity. Moderately extracted.
Melon, apple. Clean, ripe Chardonnay aromas lead a mouthful of juicy flavors, with a
very light touch of oak. Clean and crisp.

1996 Chardonnay, Heritage Reserve, Carneros $25.   86

Yellow-straw hue. Medium-bodied. Balanced acidity. Moderately extracted. Moderately
oaked. Brown spice, ripe apples, smoke. Decidedly yeasty, smoky aromas strike a pungent
note. Flavorful and rounded on the palate, with a brown spice note on the finish.

1995 Cabernet Sauvignon, North Coast $18.   81
1996 Cabernet Sauvignon, North Coast $18.   82
1995 Cabernet Sauvignon, Heritage Reserve, Sonoma Valley $40.   89

Bright red with a lightening purple rim. Moderately full-bodied. Highly extracted.
Heavily oaked. Moderately tannic. Dill, spice, black fruits. Powerful oak spice aromas
dominate, showing through on the palate along with crisp cassis fruit flavors.

1996 Merlot, North Coast $18.   83

Bright ruby red to the rim. Lean mineral and red fruit aromas. A crisp entry leads to
a medium-bodied palate with tannic grip, followed by an angular finish. Tasty, but it
lacks a little stuffing. Drink now.

1996 Merlot, Heritage Reserve, Carneros $30.   84

Bright ruby red with a subtle fade. Vibrant red berry and herb aromas carry a marked
cedary oak accent. A lively attack leads a moderately full-bodied palate with firm tannins.
The finish is clean and lightly tannic. Drink now.

1996 Pinot Noir, Carneros $18.   82
1995 Pinot Noir, Heritage Reserve, Carneros $30.   89

Medium cherry red with a pale rim. Medium-bodied. Moderately extracted. Moderately
oaked. Mildly tannic. Cherry fruit aromas with spicy accents. Assertive and crisp, with
bright acids and well-defined fruit flavors. Amazingly persistent on the finish, with
concentrated red fruit flavors lingering.

Sea Ridge Coastal

1997 Chardonnay, California $9.99.   84

Deep yellow-straw hue. Big brown spice and mineral aromas. A full attack leads a
moderately full-bodied palate with rounded acidity. Generous, flavorful finish. Drink now.

1995 Cabernet Sauvignon, California $10.   86

Saturated purple-red hue. Vibrant fruity, cassis aromas with judicious vanilla oak notes.
A crisp entry leads to a moderately full-bodied palate with bright fruit-centered character
and grainy, gripping tannins. Well structured and varietally expressive.

1996 Pinot Noir, California $10.   81

Scale: Superlative (96-100), Exceptional (90-95), Highly Recommended (85-89),
Recommended (80-84), Not Recommended (Under 80)

1996 Shiraz, California $10. **84**

Pale red, transparent, with a fading rim. Mild, soundly baked red fruit, vanilla, and cherry flavors. Hint of wood tones. Soft entry. Moderately light-bodied. A lighter style, very quaffable. Drink now.

1996 Zinfandel, California $10. **81**

Seavey

1993 Cabernet Sauvignon, Napa Valley $28. **90**

Dark crimson-ruby appearance. Medium-bodied. Highly extracted. Moderately tannic. Cooked black fruits, meat, allspice. Full, rich fruity aromas have a savory, meaty accent. Ripe black fruit flavors unfold on the palate, with some dry dusty tannins on the finish.

Seghesio

1996 Zinfandel, Sonoma County $11. **84**

Deep blackish purple. Moderately full-bodied. Low acidity. Highly extracted. Mildly oaked. Moderately tannic. Minerals, black fruits, pepper. Rather reserved aromatically, with a lean, firm palate feel. Deeply flavored, with a minerally, austere finish.

Sequoia Grove

1997 Chardonnay, Carneros, Napa Valley $16.99. **81**

1995 Cabernet Sauvignon, Napa Valley $22.99. **86**

Bright ruby with a slight fade. Generous, high-toned anise, mineral, and red fruit aromas. A crisp entry leads to a supple, medium-bodied palate with grippy tannins and zesty acidity. Vibrant finish. Somewhat lighter in style, but well balanced. Drink now.

1995 Cabernet Sauvignon, Reserve, Napa Valley $35. **89**

Deep ruby purple. Moderately full-bodied. Balanced acidity. Moderately extracted. Moderately oaked. Moderately tannic. Brown spices, red fruits. Pleasantly aromatic, with a supple entry quickly backed up by firm tannins. The flavorful finish has grip. Approachable, but needs time.

Sequoia Ridge

1996 Chardonnay, California $8.99. **83**

Yellow-straw hue. Medium-bodied. Balanced acidity. Moderately extracted. Vanilla, yeast, sweet lemon. Floral aromas lead a juicy, soft mouthful of flavors, with nice persistence of sweet lemon flavors.

Seven Peaks

1997 Chardonnay, Reserve, Edna Valley $16. **90**

Brilliant yellow-straw hue. Zesty vanilla, mineral, and citrus aromas. A lean entry is followed by a medium-bodied palate with angular acidity. The finish is creamy and complex. Drink now.

1996 Cabernet Sauvignon, Central Coast $11. **88**

Saturated violet-purple hue. Very rich aromas show a ripe cassis and toasted oak accent. A rich entry leads a full-bodied palate with fleshy flavors with significant new oak character. Very youthful and structured, with dry gripping tannins clamping on the finish. Drink now or later.

1996 Shiraz, Paso Robles $16. **86**

Dark ruby color, limpid to the rim. Generous, pleasant tart black fruit, plum, and vanilla flavors. Subtle wood tones. Firm entry. Moderately full-bodied with crisp acidity. Plentiful drying tannins. Solid, angular, and fruity. Lingering dry finish. Drinkable now, but can improve with age.

Shafer

1996 Chardonnay, Red Shoulder Ranch, Carneros, Napa Valley $30.   **93**

Yellow-straw color. Moderately full-bodied. Full acidity. Moderately extracted. Lime, citrus, oak spice. Vibrant, lively, and structured, with impressive concentration and a lingering persistence of citric acids. This should develop more complexity with further bottle age.

1997 Chardonnay, Red Shoulder Ranch, Carneros, Napa Valley $35.   **94**

Brilliant yellow-straw color. Richly aromatic with butter, yeast, and green apple. A rich entry leads a moderately full-bodied palate with a generous oak accent and rich finish showing leesy complexity. The mouthfeel is particularly fine. Drink now or later.

1994 Cabernet Sauvignon, Stags Leap District, Napa Valley $28.   **90**

Opaque bright reddish purple. Medium-bodied. Highly extracted. Moderately tannic. Crisp berries, minerals, brown spice. Assertive, bright fruity aromas. Concentrated and tightly wound flavors on the palate show fruity depth. Plenty of high-toned Cabernet fruit flavors here that will soften with some time in bottle.

1995 Cabernet Sauvignon, Stags Leap District, Napa Valley $30.   **93**

Saturated dark red with violet highlights. Moderately full-bodied. Highly extracted. Moderately tannic. Tobacco, cedar, cassis. Rich, smooth, and supple, with textured, layered tannins and a fruity middle. Elegant, yet weighty.

1996 Cabernet Sauvignon, Stags Leap District, Napa Valley $35.   **89**

Bright violet-purple hue. Ripe cherry aromas with subtle charred accents. A soft entry leads to a moderately full-bodied palate with rich cherry fruit flavors and plush tannins that could use a touch more acidity to keep them in check. Drink now or later.

1993 Cabernet Sauvignon, Hillside Select, Stags Leap District, Napa Valley $60.   **93**

Deep opaque purple. Medium-bodied. Highly extracted. Moderately tannic. Red cherries, cocoa, cedar. Angular and minerally, with some solid tannins contrasting with the crisp red fruit flavors. Shows some structure and depth. This will resolve itself more harmoniously with time.

1994 Cabernet Sauvignon, Hillside Select, Stags Leap District, Napa Valley $85.   **95**

Saturated dark violet-red. Moderately full-bodied. Highly extracted. Moderately oaked. Moderately tannic. Tobacco, black cherries, minerals. Fantastically rich aromas lead a seamlessly smooth mouthful that remains structured yet harmonious through a long, cedary finish. Exotic and very drinkable now, yet will be better in a few years.

1995 Firebreak, Napa Valley $27.   **87**

Deep blackish ruby cast. Moderately full-bodied. Balanced acidity. Moderately extracted. Moderately oaked. Mildly tannic. Black fruits, minerals, spice. Pleasantly aromatic, with a gentle oak overlay and a core of dark fruit flavors. Full and firm on the palate, with an angular quality and lush tannins. Modern in style and well crafted.

1995 Merlot, Napa Valley $28.   **89**

Very deep ruby hue with a slight purplish cast. Medium-bodied. Balanced acidity. Moderately extracted. Moderately oaked. Mildly tannic. Black fruits, cedar, earth. Pleasantly aromatic, with a lighter-styled palate feel that is very well balanced. Quite vibrant through the bright, flavorful finish.

1996 Merlot, Napa Valley $32.   **89**

Well-saturated violet hue. Ripe plum, earth, and tobacco aromas. Moderately full-bodied with a rich, lush attack and velvety, abundant tannins through the finish. Drink now.

Shale Ridge

1997 Chardonnay, Monterey $9.99.   **86**

Pale yellow-straw hue. Apple and pear aromas show no wood influence. A soft entry leads a medium-bodied palate with juicy fruit flavors that linger briefly through the finish. Very easy drinking and versatile. Drink now.

Scale: Superlative (96-100), Exceptional (90-95), Highly Recommended (85-89), Recommended (80-84), Not Recommended (Under 80)

186

1997 Cabernet Sauvignon, Monterey County $9.99. 83

Saturated ruby-purple hue. Aromatically reserved with ripe, jammy notes. A firm entry leads a moderately full-bodied palate with tough, firm tannins that coat the mouth. Rather jammy and structured. Drink now or later.

1997 Merlot, Monterey $9.99. 83

Violet-ruby hue with a subtle fade. Unusual aromas of herbs and black fruits. A supple attack, with a moderately full-bodied palate that remains supple despite the chewy tannins. Drink now.

Charles Shaw

1997 Chardonnay, California $8.99. 85

Old gold hue. Muted mineral and spice aromas. A lean entry is followed by a medium-bodied palate with angular acidity, and a clean finish. Not overly flavorful, but well structured. Drink now.

1996 Cabernet Sauvignon, California $8.99. 86

Bright crimson hue. Herbs and black fruit aromas with mild oak accents. A crisp attack leads to a medium-bodied palate with fine grained grippy tannins through the finish. Drink now.

1997 Merlot, California $8.99. 88

Full violet red. Cherry fruit aromas lead a bright, crisp, moderately light-bodied palate with powdery tannins dominating the finish. Good structure and grip, with generous fruit flavors.

1996 Pinot Noir, California $8.99. 84

Cherry red with violet highlights. Medium-bodied. Moderately extracted. Mildly tannic. Red fruits, vanilla. Berryish, oak-accented aromas follow through on the palate, with tart fruit flavors and mild astringency lingering on the finish.

1996 Shiraz, California $8.99. 83

Medium crimson red, limpid, with a slight fade. Subtle, pleasant cherry, vanilla, and mineral flavors. Hint of wood tones. Soft entry, moderately light-bodied. Mild drying tannins. Subtle, short finish. Jammy and mildly oak spiced. A lighter style. Drink now.

Shenandoah Vineyards

1996 Cabernet Sauvignon, Amador County $11.95. 86

Deep ruby-red hue to the rim. Generous brown spice, licorice, and black fruit aromas show a hefty oak accent. A firm entry leads to a moderately full-bodied mouthfeel with big grippy tannins and shy acidity. Big, tannic finish. A flashy style, but without the acidity to age well for the long term. Drink within five years.

1996 Sangiovese, Amador County $12. 81

1996 Zinfandel, Special Reserve, Amador County $9. 84

Deep blackish ruby cast. Moderately full-bodied. Balanced acidity. Moderately extracted. Mildly oaked. Mildly tannic. Chocolate, black fruits. Pleasantly aromatic, with a core of deep fruit flavors and toasty oak overtones. Thick and rich in the mouth, with a generous, chunky finish.

1996 Zinfandel, Vintners Selection, Shenandoah Valley $15. 86

Bright blackish ruby cast. Moderately full-bodied. Balanced acidity. Highly extracted. Heavily oaked. Moderately tannic. Vanilla, red fruits. Quite aromatic, with a hefty wood component and a sturdy core of red fruit flavors. Firm and well structured on the palate, with a lengthy, flavorful, tannic finish.

Siduri

1997 Pinot Noir, Van Der Kamp Vineyards, Old Vines, Sonoma Mountain $40. 81

Sierra Vista

1994 Cabernet Sauvignon, Five Star Reserve, El Dorado $24. **90**

Saturated blackish red with purple highlights. Moderately full-bodied. Highly extracted. Moderately tannic. Chocolate, toasted oak, black fruits. Big toasty oak nose reveals a concentrated dry palate with fine fruity flavors that are subordinated to an expressively toasty finish. Quite full throttled.

1997 Syrah, Herbert Vineyard, El Dorado $18. **83**

Deep purple, opaque to the rim. Cooked fruits, berries, mocha flavors. Medium-bodied. Thick and heavy, with ripe, well-extracted flavors not quite matched by the acids. A touch blowsy and ponderous. Drink now.

1996 Syrah, Red Rock Ridge, El Dorado $18. **83**

Rich ruby purple, limpid with a slight fade. Medium-bodied. Ripe berry fruit and chocolate flavors. Fleshy, very ripe, and textured through the finish. Jammy and a touch flabby. Drink now.

1996 Zinfandel, Herbert Vineyard, El Dorado $15. **86**

Deep blackish purple. Moderately full-bodied. Balanced acidity. Moderately extracted. Mildly oaked. Moderately tannic. Brown spices, briar fruits. Aromatic and fruit-centered, with a big, flavorful palate feel. A little rugged through the finish.

1996 Zinfandel, Reeves Vineyard, El Dorado $15. **93**

Deep blackish purple. Moderately full-bodied. Balanced acidity. Moderately extracted. Moderately oaked. Mildly tannic. Black fruits, vanilla. Quite aromatic, with a generous, vanilla-accented core of fruit flavors. Rich and full, though extremely well balanced. It carries its weight effortlessly through the lengthy finish.

Signorello

1997 Chardonnay, Napa Valley $30. **89**

Bright full gold. Aromas show a strong yeasty accent with a heavy oak influence. A flavorful entry leads a moderately full-bodied palate with spicy oak and ripe fruit flavors that finish with alcohol warmth.

1996 Chardonnay, Founder's Reserve, Napa Valley $45. **90**

Deep golden cast. Full-bodied. Balanced acidity. Highly extracted. Moderately oaked. Butter, brown spices, yeast. Ripe and opulent, displaying forward aromatics. Full and rich, with a textured, weighty mouthfeel and vibrant acidity lending balance through the finish.

1996 Chardonnay, Hope's Cuvée, Napa Valley $60. **90**

Bright yellow-straw cast. Moderately full-bodied. Balanced acidity. Moderately extracted. Mildly oaked. Yeast, brown spices. Shows a big, forward toasted yeast note throughout. Ripe and rich in the mouth with a zesty, vibrant finish. Generous and complex.

1997 Chardonnay, Hope's Cuvée, Napa Valley $60. **93**

Bright yellow-gold. Smoky, notably yeasty aromas. An oaky attack leads a moderately full-bodied palate with concentrated ripe fruit flavors and spicy complexity through the finish. The extravagant mouthfeel points to serious pedigree. Has the structure to improve over time. Drink now or later.

1996 Semillon, Napa Valley $20. **87**

Dark golden hue. Moderately full-bodied. Balanced acidity. Highly extracted. Mildly oaked. Vanilla, brown spice, tart tropical fruits. Resinous oak aromas lead a big, full, rich, rounded, glycerous palate. A very ripe, full-blown style, with a warm spicy finish.

1995 Cabernet Franc, Napa Valley $35. **90**

Deep ruby cast. Medium-bodied. Balanced acidity. Moderately extracted. Moderately oaked. Mildly tannic. Spice, minerals, cassis. Perfumed and stylish, with a firm, minerally backbone and a lush, velvety overlay. Supple yet well balanced, with a crisp, flavorful finish.

Scale: Superlative (96-100), Exceptional (90-95), Highly Recommended (85-89), Recommended (80-84), Not Recommended (Under 80)

1994 Cabernet Sauvignon, Napa Valley $30.   90

Dark blood red with subtle purple highlights. Moderately full-bodied. Highly extracted. Moderately tannic. Toasted oak, cassis, plums, brown spice. Rich oaky nose suggests ripe black fruits that are confirmed on the palate. The chewy, ripe palate is full and rounded, with plenty of toasted character on the dry finish.

1995 Cabernet Sauvignon, Napa Valley $30.   92

Saturated dark ruby red. Moderately full-bodied. Highly extracted. Moderately tannic. Toasted oak, brown spice, black fruits. Brooding aromas show oak spice and dark fruits. Rich, finely wrought mineral and earth flavors are well matched with dark fruits. Although drinkable now, this will be better with a few miles in the cellar.

1996 Cabernet Sauvignon, Napa Valley $35.   91

Rich ruby hue with a subtly fading rim. Generously oak spiced aromas. A rich entry leads a moderately full-bodied palate with juicy, bright plummy fruit and generous chocolatey flavors and leathery tannins through the finish. Drinking very well now. Drink now.

1994 Cabernet Sauvignon, Founder's Reserve, Napa Valley $55.   93

Dark crimson red. Moderately full-bodied. Highly extracted. Black pepper, plums, cassis, toasted oak. Rich black fruit in the nose, with toasty overtones. Concentrated curranty flavors are very accessible now. The persistent fruity finish has balanced tannins and toasty oak flavors.

1995 Cabernet Sauvignon, Founder's Reserve, Napa Valley $55.   93

Saturated violet red. Moderately full-bodied. Highly extracted. Moderately tannic. Berry fruits, vanilla, minerals. Youthful, vibrant, concentrated aromas lead a high-toned, bright mouthful of mineral and fruit flavors, with oak spice playing on the finish. Sprightly and young, yet very harmonious.

1996 Cabernet Sauvignon, Founder's Reserve, Napa Valley $75.   92

Bright ruby hue with a subtly fading rim. Generous developed aromas a show marked oak accent. A plush entry leads a moderately full-bodied palate with rich black fruit flavors and grainy tannins that linger on the finish. Has a well-integrated, oaky character and is very approachable now. Drink now or later.

1996 Petite Sirah, 110 Year Old Vines, Napa Valley $25.   88

Opaque dark purple. Full-bodied. Highly extracted. Quite tannic. Fleshy, chunky, and rich, with generous plum and blackberry fruit flavors. Significantly oaky. Tannins do not dominate. A blockbuster to cellar for a few years.

1995 Pinot Noir, Las Amigas Vineyard, Carneros $48.   92

Nearly opaque dark red. Moderately full-bodied. Highly extracted. Moderately tannic. Earthy black fruit aromas lead a fully extracted palate with licorice and black bramble fruit flavors. Solid fine-grained tannins come through on the dry finish, where some mild bitterness and nutmeg notes pop up.

1996 Pinot Noir, Las Amigas Vineyard, Carneros $45.   91

Dark ruby-violet hue. Medium-bodied. Moderately extracted. Moderately tannic. Black fruits, oak spice, minerals. Solid, well-proportioned character, with firm tannins and a core of black fruit flavors. This is approachable now but will be better with age.

1995 Pinot Noir, Martinelli Vineyard, Russian River Valley $48.   88

Very dark reddish purple. Moderately full-bodied. Highly extracted. Moderately oaked. Moderately tannic. Leathery, earthy aromas are very pronounced and complex. Black cherry and licorice flavors on the palate. Very backward and difficult now, this is one for the cellar.

1996 Pinot Noir, Martinelli Vineyard, Russian River Valley $45.   89

Deep ruby red with a slight fade. Moderately full-bodied. Balanced acidity. Highly extracted. Moderately oaked. Mildly tannic. Spice, chocolate, pickle barrel. The deep, complex aromas are pleasantly perfumed. Firm and weighty in the mouth, with an intense, darkly flavored finish.

1996 Syrah, Napa Valley $30.   **93**

Deep ruby red, limpid with a slight fade. Intense toasted oak spice, red fruit, and olive flavors. Hefty wood tones. A firm entry leads a moderately full-bodied palate. Moderate, drying tannins. Well developed and oaky. Lingering finish. Drink now.

1994 Zinfandel, Napa Valley $25.   **88**

Full cherry red. Medium-bodied. Moderately extracted. Moderately oaked. Moderately tannic. Black raspberries, vanilla, pepper. Extroverted, vanilla-scented berry aromas lead a bright, fruity palate; tannins are approachable now, giving the finish some dry authority.

1995 Zinfandel, Napa Valley $25.   **87**

Deep blackish ruby cast. Full-bodied. Full acidity. Moderately extracted. Moderately oaked. Mildly tannic. Vanilla, dried herbs, black fruits. Quite aromatic, with a firm, flavorful palate feel. Deep and intense through the lengthy finish.

1996 Zinfandel, Russian River Valley $25.   **89**

Deep blackish ruby cast. Moderately full-bodied. Balanced acidity. Moderately extracted. Moderately oaked. Mildly tannic. Pepper, black fruits, minerals. Rather reserved aromatically, with a firm, highly structured palate feel. Elegant and well balanced, in more of a Claret style.

Silver Oak

1993 Cabernet Sauvignon, Alexander Valley $38.   **92**

Dark blackish red. Medium-bodied. Highly extracted. Moderately tannic. Toasted oak, licorice, black fruits, brown spice. Exotically rich toasty aromas lead a deep, flavorful, well-extracted palate, with a long toasty finish that has lingering fruit flavors.

1994 Cabernet Sauvignon, Alexander Valley $45.   **91**

Deep ruby hue. Medium-bodied. Balanced acidity. Moderately extracted. Moderately oaked. Mildly tannic. Vanilla, red fruits. Pleasantly aromatic, with a somewhat light palate feel. Toasty oak plays a part throughout, with crisp acidity. Elegant and well balanced. Drinking well.

1993 Cabernet Sauvignon, Napa Valley $50.   **90**

Full brick red. Medium-bodied. Moderately extracted. Moderately tannic. Black cherries, cedar, cinnamon. Generous oak-spiced aromas show some mature accents. Rounded and extravagantly spicy, though not a heavyweight style. This is very approachable now and is not in need of extensive cellaring.

1994 Cabernet Sauvignon, Napa Valley $65.   **90**

Dark ruby hue. Rich, very aromatic spicy oak aromas with fleshy dark fruits. A rich entry leads a supple, moderately full-bodied palate with dark black cherry fruits and elegant powdery tannins that linger. Very well balanced and showing very distinctive flavors of American oak. Drink now or later.

Silver Ridge

1997 Chardonnay, California $9.99.   **88**

Brilliant yellow-straw hue. Generous vanilla and cream aromas carry an attractive oak accent. A rounded entry leads a medium-bodied palate with balanced acidity. Lengthy, flavorful finish. Drink now.

1995 Cabernet Sauvignon, California $9.99.   **81**

1997 Merlot, California $9.99.   **81**

1996 Pinot Noir, California $9.99.   **84**

Pale violet hue. Moderately light-bodied. Subtly extracted. Mildly tannic. Red fruits, vanilla. Smooth yet crisp, with berry fruit flavors and balanced oak notes through the finish. Easy drinking.

1996 Syrah, California $9.99.   **82**

Scale: Superlative (96-100), Exceptional (90-95), Highly Recommended (85-89),
Recommended (80-84), Not Recommended (Under 80)

190

Silverado

1994 Cabernet Sauvignon, Napa Valley $22.50.　　　　　91

Full reddish purple. Medium-bodied. Moderately extracted. Moderately tannic. Mint, cherries, black fruits. High-toned spicy oak nose has minty notes. The full-flavored palate has a firm overlay of attractive oak flavors that linger through the finish. Nice now, though this will probably come together with a few years of aging.

1995 Cabernet Sauvignon, Napa Valley $25.　　　　　88

Saturated deep red-purple. Moderately full-bodied. Highly extracted. Moderately tannic. Mineral, spice, black fruits. Oak-centered aromas lead a crisp black fruit palate, with noble, fine-grained tannins supplying a firm, structured finish.

1994 Cabernet Sauvignon, Limited Reserve, Napa Valley $50.　　　　　93

Opaque appearance with bright purple highlights. Moderately full-bodied. Highly extracted. Moderately tannic. Violets, cherries, cedar, tobacco. Vivacious berry fruit aromas follow through on the palate. Rounded, viscous mouthfeel shows great depth and persistence. Quite supple now, though this could profitably use cellar time.

1995 Merlot, Napa Valley $22.50.　　　　　94

Very deep ruby hue to the rim. Medium-bodied. Balanced acidity. Moderately extracted. Moderately oaked. Mildly tannic. Mint, red fruits, chocolate. Big, rich, and fruit driven in style, with pleasant mint and barrel accents that add complexity. Well balanced and extremely lush on the palate, with fine length.

Silverado Hill

1995 Cabernet Sauvignon, Napa Valley $13.　　　　　80

Simi

1996 Chardonnay, Sonoma County $17.　　　　　86

Pale straw cast. Medium-bodied. Full acidity. Moderately extracted. Green apples, minerals. Crisp and clean, with precisely defined flavors and a linear structure. Firm acidity makes for a zesty finish.

1996 Chardonnay, Carneros $21.　　　　　84

Deep yellow-straw color. Moderately full-bodied. Balanced acidity. Moderately extracted. Butterscotch, apple. Thick, generous, and flavorful, with a subtle note of vanilla oak. Shows a creamy mouthfeel with yeasty overtones that emerge on the finish.

1995 Chardonnay, Reserve, Sonoma County $29.　　　　　88

Bright yellow-gold. Forward aromas show a subtle oak accent and a citric core. The moderately full-bodied palate has flavors of brown spices, citrus and cream, with mild oak notes and assertive acidity. Full yet angular in the mouth with a crisp spicy finish.

1995 Sendal, Sonoma County $20.　　　　　85

Deep golden cast. Moderately full-bodied. Balanced acidity. Moderately extracted. Figs, citrus, nuts. Quite aromatic, with a richly luxuriant flavor profile. Solid acidity makes for a racy and buoyant finish.

1996 Sauvignon Blanc, Sonoma County $14.　　　　　84

Medium straw hue. Medium-bodied. Balanced acidity. Moderately extracted. White peach, apples. Reserved, perfumed aromas reveal orchard fruit flavors up front, with some alcohol warmth and dryness on the finish.

1994 Cabernet Sauvignon, Alexander Valley $19.　　　　　89

Bright reddish purple. Medium-bodied. Moderately extracted. Mildly tannic. Black cherries, plums. Attractive fruity, ripe berry-accented nose leads a smooth, lush palate and with a simple finish. A very fruit-forward style that is drinking well now.

1995 Cabernet Sauvignon, Alexander Valley $22.　　　　　87

Bright ruby hue. Moderately full-bodied. Balanced acidity. Moderately extracted. Mildly tannic. Black fruits, minerals. Generous aromas feature a decided fruit accent. Rich and stylish in the mouth, with velvety tannins lending structure. Well balanced and lengthy.

1994 Cabernet Sauvignon, Reserve, Sonoma County $46.　　　91

Deep ruby purple. Moderately full-bodied. Balanced acidity. Moderately extracted. Mildly oaked. Mildly tannic. Minerals, black fruits, brown spices. Pleasantly aromatic, with a soft and supple palate feel. Rich and velvety in the mouth, with a seamless quality through the lengthy finish.

1996 Shiraz, Sonoma County $18.50.　　　84

Medium purple, limpid and brilliant, with a slight fade. Mild, sound flower, cherry, vanilla, and cedar flavors. Subtle wood tones. Supple entry. Medium-bodied with crisp acidity. Moderately short finish. A light, easy-drinking style with a delicate finish. Drink now.

Smith & Hook

1996 Viognier, Arroyo Seco $18.　　　87

Deep golden cast. Full-bodied. Low acidity. Highly extracted. Oranges, cream, talc. Very aromatic, with unusual though complex flavors. Extremely full in the mouth with relatively low acidity. Finishes with an angular, assertive note.

1994 Cabernet Sauvignon, Santa Lucia Highlands $18.　　　87

Black cherry red. Medium-bodied. Moderately extracted. Mildly tannic. Dill, black fruits, minerals. Mildly toasty nose and a lean, crisp palate with fine acids give this wine presence on the palate. Rather similar to though lighter than its pricier stablemate.

1995 Cabernet Sauvignon, Santa Lucia Highlands $18.　　　89

Bright brick red. Medium-bodied. Moderately extracted. Mildly tannic. Spice, minerals, red fruits. Dusty, spicy, almost meaty aromas lead an elegant mouthful of leaner flavors, with bright acids and mild tannins providing some grip and lending a food-friendly balance. This is an Old World style.

1996 Cabernet Sauvignon, Santa Lucia Highlands $18.　　　82

1994 Cabernet Sauvignon, Masterpiece Edition,
Santa Lucia Highlands $35.　　　90

Dark black cherry color. Medium-bodied. Highly extracted. Mildly tannic. Dill, black fruits, minerals. Toasty, oak-accented nose leads a deep, fruity palate with full flavors and complex oaky accents through the finish. Shows great balance and harmony. Dry tannins on the lengthy finish.

1995 Cabernet Sauvignon, Masterpiece Edition,
Santa Lucia Highlands $40.　　　86

Brick red with garnet highlights. Medium-bodied. Moderately extracted. Mildly tannic. Minerals, earth, brown spice. Mature, oriental spice aromas lead a lighter-styled, fading palate, with subtlety the key word. This has bright acids and a sense of refinement, though not for keeping. Not for those seeking extravagantly fruity Cabernet styles, this is more of an Old World style.

1995 Merlot, Santa Lucia Highlands $19.95.　　　87

Deep ruby with a blackish cast. Medium-bodied. Full acidity. Moderately extracted. Moderately oaked. Mildly tannic. Cedar, black fruits, minerals, green herbs. Oak figures prominently in the aromatics. Crisp and angular in the mouth, with complex flavors and an herbal tinge to the clean, snappy finish.

1996 Merlot, Santa Lucia Highlands $19.　　　81

Sobon

1997 Roussanne, Shenandoah Valley $15.　　　82

1997 Rhone Rose, Shenandoah Valley $9.　　　88

Brilliant pale cherry hue. Forward red fruit and mineral aromas have a lean citric edge. A firm entry leads a moderately full-bodied palate showing vibrant acidity. Flavorful, intense, and refreshing. Drink now.

Scale: Superlative (96-100), Exceptional (90-95), Highly Recommended (85-89), Recommended (80-84), Not Recommended (Under 80)

1996 Syrah, Shenandoah Valley, California $15.   **84**

Medium ruby color, limpid, with a slight fade. Medium-bodied. Herbal and berry flavors. Light, bright fruity flavors with mild drying tannins. A touch herbal, but juicy and balanced. Drink now.

1996 Zinfandel, Cougar Hill, Shenandoah Valley $15.   **84**

Bright ruby-garnet cast. Medium-bodied. Balanced acidity. Moderately extracted. Mildly oaked. Mildly tannic. Black fruits, minerals, vanilla. Reserved aromatically, with gentle, spicy oak overtones. Lush and generous through the finish. Well balanced.

1996 Zinfandel, Lubenko Vineyard, Fiddletown $15.   **84**

Bright blackish ruby cast. Moderately full-bodied. Full acidity. Moderately extracted. Mildly oaked. Mildly tannic. Briar fruits, minerals. Quite aromatic, with a full though angular palate feel. Vibrant acidity provides a juicy finish.

1996 Zinfandel, Rocky Top, Shenandoah Valley $15.   **80**

Sonoma Creek

1997 Cabernet Sauvignon, Sonoma County $11.95.   **84**

Bright ruby red with a slight purple cast. Medium-bodied. Balanced acidity. Moderately extracted. Moderately oaked. Mildly tannic. Bramble fruits, vanilla. Pleasantly aromatic, with a crisp, generous, fruit-centered personality. Clean and angular through the flavorful finish. A cheerful quaffing style.

1995 Cabernet Sauvignon, Reserve, Sonoma Valley $17.95.   **92**

Saturated cherry red. Moderately full-bodied. Moderately extracted. Mildly tannic. Black cherries, vanilla. Sweet black fruit aromas follow through on a soft, fleshy palate with soft, rounded tannins through the finish. Very hedonistic.

1995 Cabernet Sauvignon, Rancho Salina Vineyard, Sonoma Valley $28.95. **91**

Saturated ruby purple. Moderately full-bodied. Highly extracted. Moderately tannic. Black cherries, cedar. Rich, luxuriously decadent aromas lead a vibrant palate of fleshy black fruits with complex cedar nuances. Drinking very well now.

1995 Cabernet Sauvignon, Van der Kamp Vineyard, Sonoma Mountain $28.95.   **89**

Saturated red-purple. Moderately full-bodied. Highly extracted. Moderately tannic. Vanilla, cassis. Spicy oak and jammy red fruit aromas follow through on a rounded, fleshy palate, with a good degree of berry intensity.

1995 Meritage, Sonoma Valley $17.95.   **89**

Saturated cherry red. Moderately full-bodied. Moderately extracted. Mildly tannic. Black berry fruits, dried herbs. Brash berry fruit flavors leap from the glass. Shows a soft herbal tinge and a good acid cut throughout. Ripe, ample tannins give this cellaring structure, though it is drinkable now.

Sonoma-Cutrer

1997 Chardonnay, Russian River Ranches, Russian River Valley $16.99.   **81**

1996 Chardonnay, The Cutrer, Sonoma County $27.99.   **91**

Brilliant straw hue. Reserved steely aromas show a slight wood accent. A brisk entry leads a full-bodied palate with flinty, minerally flavors and sharp acidity. Rich, intense finish. Shows fine cut, and has a Chablis-like edge. Drink now or later.

1996 Chardonnay, Les Pierres, Sonoma County $29.99.   **92**

Bright straw hue. Subdued mineral and citrus aromas show a subtle leesy quality and mild oak influences. The entry is crisp, followed by a full-bodied palate with brisk acidity. Authoritative, if somewhat austere finish. This needs time to develop and is a midterm cellar candidate.

Sonoma-Loeb

1997 Chardonnay, Sonoma County $20.   83

Bright yellow-straw cast. Medium-bodied. Balanced acidity. Moderately extracted.
Minerals, citrus. Aromatically reserved, with a ripe and rounded mouthfeel. Shows
a gentle fade to the finish.

1997 Chardonnay, Private Reserve, Sonoma County $30.   84

Deep straw cast. Moderately full-bodied. Balanced acidity. Moderately extracted.
Mildly oaked. Minerals, cream, spice. Ripe and rounded, with a soft, creamy texture
and subdued flavors. Rich and generous through the finish.

Sonora Winery & Port Works

1996 Zinfandel, Old Vine, Story Vineyard, Amador County $18.   84

Deep blackish ruby cast. Moderately full-bodied. Low acidity. Moderately extracted.
Mildly oaked. Mildly tannic. Brown spices, stewed black fruits. Quite aromatic, with a
big, full-throttled, flavorful palate feel. Somewhat lacking in acidity. Chunky tannins
dominate the finish. Not for the faint of heart.

1996 Zinfandel, Old Vine, TC Vineyard, Amador County $18.   81

1992 Vintage Port, Sierra Foothills $15.99/500 ml.   80

1994 Vintage Port, Sierra Foothills $16/500 ml.   86

Opaque blackish purple. Moderately full-bodied. Low acidity. Highly extracted. Mildly
tannic. Minerals, black fruits. Rather reserved aromatically, but opens up on the palate,
displaying a lush, rounded mouthfeel. Deep, brooding, and intense, with marked
sweetness to the finish. Could use a few more years of age.

Soquel

1994 Cabernet Sauvignon, Santa Cruz Mountains $22.   85

Solid blood red. Medium-bodied. Highly extracted. Moderately tannic. Brown spice,
dust, chocolate. Dry, dusty nose has full brown spice accents. The palate is powdery,
with well-integrated tannins and a chocolatey note through the finish. Fruit flavors are
a little austere.

1994 Cabernet Sauvignon, Partner's Reserve, Santa Cruz Mountains $40.   91

Deep garnet red. Moderately full-bodied. Highly extracted. Moderately tannic. Dill, sage,
black plums, anise, earth. An exotically spiced, herbal nose leads a thick, concentrated
palate with a chewy mouthfeel and a lengthy finish showing impressive noble tannins.
A complex blockbuster.

1995 Cabernet Sauvignon, Partner's Reserve, Santa Cruz Mountains $40.   91

Saturated, opaque red-purple. Moderately full-bodied. Highly extracted. Quite tannic.
Cedar, vanilla, cassis. Dense, sweet-edged aromas lead an inky, dry palate that has
ample fine-grained tannins, but also a sense of generosity showing through. Impossibly
young now.

Sparrow Lane

1996 Zinfandel, Reserve, Beatty Ranch, Howell Mountain $25.   90

Opaque dark red with purple highlights. Moderately full-bodied. Balanced acidity.
Highly extracted. Moderately oaked. Moderately tannic. Black fruits. Impressively rich
fruit-centered aromas lead a glycerous mouthful of dark fruit flavors, with oak accents
coming though. A rather big-shouldered style that is drinkable now.

Spottswoode

1996 Sauvignon Blanc, Napa Valley $18.   89

Bright metallic emerald color. Medium-bodied. Balanced acidity. Moderately extracted.
Reminiscent of ripe lemons, pineapple. Clean fruity aromas with some buttery notes.
Silky mouthfeel with a hint of zest on the finish. Very refined and elegant.

Scale: Superlative (96-100), Exceptional (90-95), Highly Recommended (85-89),
Recommended (80-84), Not Recommended (Under 80)

1992 Cabernet Sauvignon, Napa Valley $39. **92**

Medium-bodied. Medium acid. Medium fruit. Lots of oak. Medium tannin. Dry. Reminiscent of leather, cassis, vanilla, nutmeg. Dense and well integrated, with a firm backbone. Wood tones dominate delicately balanced fruit. 94% Cabernet Sauvignon accented with 6% Cabernet Franc.

1993 Cabernet Sauvignon, Napa Valley $42. **94**

Deep ruby to the rim with a subtle purplish cast. Moderately full-bodied. Balanced acidity. Highly extracted. Moderately oaked. Moderately tannic. Dry. Reminiscent of vanilla, cassis, black cherries. Extremely deep and rich in flavor, this wine has an excellent level of extraction while maintaining a sense of balance and lushness. Soft tannins come through in the finish and give a sense of depth and richness. Though accessible now, it should be even better in five years. A classic California Cabernet.

1994 Cabernet Sauvignon, Napa Valley $45. **93**

Full bright crimson appearance. Medium-bodied. Moderately extracted. Mildly tannic. Red berries, cassis, brown spice. Full berry fruit aromas. Bright, juicy primary fruit flavors expand on the palate. Fine concentration and focus, with a lingering spicy oak finish. Drinking well now.

1995 Cabernet Sauvignon, Napa Valley $55. **92**

Deep ruby purple. Moderately full-bodied. Balanced acidity. Highly extracted. Moderately oaked. Moderately tannic. Vanilla, red fruits, minerals. Quite fragrant, in a modern style, with a stylish interplay between fruit and wood. Shows fine depth, focus, and structure in the mouth, with a lengthy finish. Should develop beautifully.

Spring Mountain Vineyard

1993 Miravalle-Alba-Chevalier Red, Napa Valley $28. **93**

Dark black cherry color. Medium-bodied. Moderately extracted. Moderately tannic. Earth, minerals, cassis. Toasty, dusty aromas lead a rich chewy palate with great depth of flavors revealing layers of earthy complexity. The tannins are firm and dry, but do not dominate totally. Structured for keeping.

1994 Miravalle-Alba-Chevalier Red, Napa Valley $28.99. **83**

Saturated dark ruby hue. Moderately full-bodied. Highly extracted. Quite tannic. Black fruits, dark chocolate, brown spice. Rich, spicy aromas follow through well on the palate, with spicy berry notes playing out through the finish. The tannins are chunky, though not out of balance.

St. Amant

1995 Vintage Port, Amador County $28. **85**

Saturated blackish red. Medium-bodied. Highly extracted. Moderately tannic. Reminiscent of blueberry, chocolate, raspberries. Complex, exotic plummy nose. Deeply extracted and flavorsome, though somewhat compact on the palate at present, with dry tannins on the finish. Needs some time.

St. Clement

1997 Chardonnay, Abbots Vineyard, Carneros, Napa Valley $20. **89**

Rich yellow-gold. Ripe aromas of butter and toasted oak. A spicy attack leads a moderately full-bodied palate with rich, lush texture and yeasty notes. This is a big, alcoholic style that maintains reasonable acid balance and shows stylish touches. Drink now.

1997 Sauvignon Blanc, Napa Valley $13. **84**

Deep straw cast. Moderately full-bodied. Balanced acidity. Moderately extracted. Minerals, citrus. Seemingly quite youthful, this wine is rather reserved aromatically, with a lush entry on the palate, becoming tighter and more angular through the finish.

1994 Cabernet Sauvignon, Napa Valley $25. 90

Full dark red with bright purple highlights. Medium-bodied. Moderately extracted. Mildly tannic. Black fruits, oak spice. Concentrated midpalate, with solid black fruit flavors, and a hint of imposing tannin on a good, long toasty finish. Solid structure, classic style.

1995 Cabernet Sauvignon, Napa Valley $26. 87

Dark ruby-violet hue. Medium-bodied. Highly extracted. Moderately tannic. Cassis, vanilla. Succulent and luxurious, with finely polished tannins and harmoniously ripe flavors. Bursting with textbook Cabernet flavors, in a lighter style.

1994 Cabernet Sauvignon, Howell Mountain, Napa Valley $45. 92

Opaque bright purple. Moderately full-bodied. Highly extracted. Moderately tannic. Crisp cassis, black fruits, chalk. Ripe, high-toned fruity aromas lead a bright fruity entry that expands on the midpalate, with surprisingly accessible tannins coming through on the finish. Youthful and vigorous still.

1995 Cabernet Sauvignon, Howell Mountain, Napa Valley $45. 93

Saturated dark ruby purple. Moderately full-bodied. Balanced acidity. Moderately extracted. Mildly oaked. Mildly tannic. Licorice, minerals, chocolate. Exotic, high-toned aromas lead a supple, smooth palate feel. Concentrated yet elegant, with very fancy extraction resulting in abundant silky tannins. Approachable but ageworthy.

1995 Oroppas, Napa Valley $35. 90

Dark ruby with bright purple highlights. Medium-bodied. Moderately extracted. Mildly tannic. Licorice, cassis, plums, pepper. Generous, ripe black fruit aromas reveal a supple and rounded mouthfeel. The finish is long, with lingering black fruit flavors. A ripe, expressive style.

1996 Oroppas, Napa Valley $35. 94

Bright red-purple. Moderately full-bodied. Highly extracted. Moderately tannic. Cassis, black fruits, vanilla. Very lush, fruit-forward aromas follow through on the palate, with a rounded texture and a silky mouthfeel through the finish. Very hedonistic and supple.

1994 Merlot, Napa Valley $24. 87

Deep ruby red to the rim with brilliant highlights. Medium-bodied. Balanced acidity. Moderately extracted. Mildly oaked. Mildly tannic. Red fruits, chocolate, anise. Still youthful, with a tightly wound dense core of flavor. Rich and thick, but well balanced, with a lingering finish. Should develop some complexity with aging.

1995 Merlot, Napa Valley $24. 84

Deep ruby to the rim with brilliant highlights. Medium-bodied. Balanced acidity. Moderately extracted. Mildly oaked. Mildly tannic. Red fruits, anise, minerals. Lighter in style, with bright flavors. A well-balanced and lingering finish.

1996 Merlot, Napa Valley $24. 83

Well-saturated bright violet hue. Black cherry and herb aromas. Medium-bodied, with a flavorful attack and crisp, generous fleshy fruit flavors that are well balanced by moderate tannic astringency through the finish. Drink now.

1995 Merlot, Columbia Valley $22. 90

Deep blackish ruby hue with brilliant clarity. Medium-bodied. Balanced acidity. Moderately extracted. Moderately oaked. Mildly tannic. Chocolate, minerals, red fruits. Supple and velvety in the mouth, with well-integrated, complex flavors. Quite balanced, this should cellar nicely.

St. Francis

1997 Chardonnay, Sonoma County $12.99. 84

Bright straw hue. Subdued mineral and earth aromas carry a slight oak accent. A lush entry is followed by a medium-bodied palate with rounded acidity and a clean, gentle finish. Drink now.

1997 Chardonnay, Reserve, Sonoma County $22.99.   91

Deep yellow-straw color. Opulent toasted-coconut aromas show a dominant
oak accent. A crisp entry leads a full-bodied palate with vibrant acidity. Complex,
leesy flavors with a slightly buttery quality through the finish. Showy. Drink now.

1995 Cabernet Sauvignon, Sonoma County $10.99.   87

Full dark cherry red. Medium-bodied. Moderately extracted. Mildly tannic. Plums, cassis,
tobacco. Full-flavored, fleshy dark fruit flavors are forward and attractive, giving an
impression of fatness on the midpalate. Soft, supple tannins on the finish. Nice now.

1996 Cabernet Sauvignon, Sonoma County $13.99.   84

Bright cherry garnet hue. Subdued mineral, earth, and berry aromas. A soft attack leads
to a medium-bodied palate with firm and drying tannins. Lean finish. On the tough side.
Drink within five years.

1994 Cabernet Sauvignon, Reserve, Sonoma Valley $30.   96

Opaque blackish red. Moderately full-bodied. Highly extracted. Quite tannic. Black fruits,
licorice, earth, brown spice. Dark, brooding aromas. The solid, tightly wound palate has
an extravagantly concentrated and ripe mouthfeel. Big fine-grained tannins come
through on the long finish. Great structure should allow this to cellar for a decade.

1995 Cabernet Sauvignon, Reserve, Sonoma Valley $33.99.   91

Opaque, saturated blackish ruby hue. Flashy toasted coconut and chocolate aromas show
a huge American oak influence. A thick and supple entry leads to a full-bodied palate
with waves of flavor and robust velvety tannins. Very fancy extraction indeed. Soft, very
flavorful finish. Without the acidity to be a long-term ager but carries its weight well.
A showy hedonistic style. Drink within five years.

1995 Merlot, Sonoma County $18.   89

Deep blackish ruby hue. Moderately full-bodied. Balanced acidity. Highly extracted.
Moderately oaked. Moderately tannic. Earth, black fruits, incense. Somewhat unusual
aromatics, with a slight funky quality. Rich and chewy in the mouth with a thick character
and chunky tannins. Lingering perfumed finish. Perhaps it's in a bit of an awkward stage
aromatically; give it benefit of the doubt.

1996 Merlot, Sonoma County $23.99.   92

Blood red with a garnet cast and a slight fade. Well-developed aromas show leathery,
spicy, oaky accents. A crisp attack leads a medium-bodied palate with developed earthy
tannins. Finishes with spicy complexity.

1994 Merlot, Reserve, Sonoma Valley $29.   93

Very deep blackish ruby hue. Moderately full-bodied. Balanced acidity. Highly extracted.
Heavily oaked. Mildly tannic. Brown spices, black fruits, sweet herbs. Deeply aromatic
with a big overlay of sweet oak. In the mouth, there is great density of fruit and a chunky
texture. Well integrated and well balanced, with velvety tannins.

1995 Merlot, Reserve, Sonoma Valley $33.99.   93

Deep brick red. Chocolate and brown spice aromas. A supple attack leads a moderately
full-bodied palate with evolved tannins and soft acids, and a solid grip. Complex flavors
of minerals and spice linger on the earthy finish. Drink now.

1996 Zinfandel, Old Vines, Sonoma County $20.   94

Deep blackish ruby hue. Moderately full-bodied. Balanced acidity. Highly extracted.
Moderately oaked. Mildly tannic. Brown spices, black fruits. Toasty oak nuances on the
nose merge with a wave of dark fruit flavors in the mouth. Lush, deep, and rich, with a
velvety, supple finish. Fine length and intensity.

1996 Zinfandel, Pagani Vineyard Reserve, Sonoma Valley $28.   95

Saturated, deep blackish ruby hue. Full-bodied. Balanced acidity. Highly extracted.
Moderately oaked. Mildly tannic. Vanilla, black fruits, tar. An opaque color belies this
wine's depth and structure, with brooding aromas and a wave of dark flavors on the
palate. Rich and forceful, though very well integrated. The toasted coconut nuances
of American oak are unmistakable; the combination is reminiscent of a top-flight
Aussie Shiraz.

St. Supéry

1996 Chardonnay, Dollarhide Ranch, Napa Valley $12.50. 86

Bright straw cast. Moderately full-bodied. Full acidity. Moderately extracted. Citrus, melon, minerals. Quite aromatic, with bright fruit flavors to the fore. Zesty and intense in the mouth, with a clean, snappy finish.

1996 Meritage, Napa Valley $20. 82

1997 Sauvignon Blanc, Dollarhide Ranch, Napa Valley $9.90. 91

Very deep straw hue. Moderately full-bodied. Full acidity. Highly extracted. Dried herbs, citrus, cream. Ripe and flavorful with marked complexity. Rich and full in the mouth, with a supple texture and a lengthy, herb-tinged finish.

1994 Cabernet Sauvignon, Napa Valley $15.75. 90

Deep cherry red. Medium-bodied. Moderately extracted. Mildly tannic. Currants, cassis, licorice. Rich, ripe berry aromas lead a supple, rounded, ripe palate with some pleasing spice notes and hints of firm tannin on the finish. Very attractive now.

1995 Cabernet Sauvignon, Dollarhide Ranches, Rutherford $16.50. 80

1994 Red Meritage, Napa Valley $40. 89

Bright violet red. Medium-bodied. Moderately extracted. Heavily oaked. Moderately tannic. Vanilla, red fruits. Crisp vanilla, oak-accented aromas lead a lively palate dominated by an oak astringency that grips the midpalate and finish.

1995 Red Meritage, Napa Valley $40. 88

Medium brick red hue. Moderately aromatic with a full oak-spiced nose showing ripe, mature fruits. A firm attack leads a medium-bodied palate with softer acids and lighter tannins. Oak spice flavors come to the fore and linger on the finish. Supple, balanced, and harmonious. Drink now.

1995 Merlot, Dollarhide Ranches, Napa Valley $16.50. 83

Deep ruby red to the rim, with brilliant clarity. Medium-bodied. Balanced acidity. Moderately extracted. Moderately tannic. Dried herbs, earth, red fruits. Veers to the herbal end of the spectrum, with a lighter-styled palate. Tannins clamp down on the lush mouthfeel.

1996 Merlot, Dollarhide Ranches, Napa Valley $16.50. 81

Stag's Leap Wine Cellars

1997 Chardonnay, Napa Valley $26. 84

Bright yellow-gold. Aromatically restrained with subtle oak and yeast notes. A spicy attack leads a moderately full-bodied palate with tart acids and a note of alcohol warmth. Rich, textured mouthfeel.

1996 Chardonnay, Beckstoffer Ranch, Napa Valley $30. 87

Bright straw cast. Medium-bodied. Full acidity. Moderately extracted. Mildly oaked. Minerals, coconut, citrus. Aromatic and forward, showing a definite sweet oak component. Crisp and zesty, with a refreshing vibrant note to the lengthy finish.

1996 Chardonnay, Reserve, Napa Valley $37. 90

Bright straw cast. Moderately full-bodied. Balanced acidity. Moderately extracted. Mildly oaked. Green apples, melon, brown spices. Aromatic and flavorful, with a crisp, focused, and well-defined presence on the palate. Elegant and stylish, with a balanced, lengthy finish.

1995 Cabernet Sauvignon, Napa Valley $26. 89

Dark blood-ruby hue. Medium-bodied. Highly extracted. Moderately tannic. Minerals, cassis, oak spice. Lean, taut, and reserved, with fine structure. This shows plenty of pedigree, though it is not a powerful style. Drinking well now, though it has the structure to age gracefully.

Scale: Superlative (96-100), Exceptional (90-95), Highly Recommended (85-89), Recommended (80-84), Not Recommended (Under 80)

1994 Cabernet Sauvignon, Fay, Napa Valley $50.   94

Dark ruby red. Medium-bodied. Moderately extracted. Moderately tannic. Plums, cassis, cherries, earth. A big, rich mouthful of black fruit and earth, with black fruit flavors and fine-grained tannins on the finish. This is drinking very well now.

1995 Cabernet Sauvignon, Fay, Napa Valley $70.   94

Saturated blood red. Moderately full-bodied. Moderately extracted. Moderately tannic. Toasted oak, cassis, mineral. Charred aromas have a fleshy accent that follows through on the palate. Rich, juicy middle, and layers of ripe tannins that linger through the finish. Has a great mineral accent throughout.

1994 Cabernet Sauvignon, SLV, Napa Valley $50.   93

Dark ruby red. Medium-bodied. Moderately extracted. Moderately tannic. Plums, earth, brown spice. Intriguingly earthy spiced aromas. The deeply flavored palate has an earthy richness and smoothness through to its spicy conclusion. Very ripe and supple, and drinking well now.

1995 Cabernet Sauvignon, SLV, Napa Valley $70.   94

Saturated blood red. Moderately full-bodied. Highly extracted. Moderately tannic. Mineral, fleshy berries, brown spice. Mineral-rich aromas have plenty of cassis backing. Concentrated flavors show intensity and harmony, with a noble, earthy finish that turns powdery and dry. This is very elegant now, yet will cellar well.

1994 Cabernet Sauvignon, Cask 23, Napa Valley $100.   96

Deep ruby hue with purple highlights. Medium-bodied. Highly extracted. Moderately tannic. Plums, black fruits, brown spice. Elegant toasty nose. Deep, chewy black fruit flavors fill the palate, with earthy richness coming through on the long dry finish. Shows some structure, but is very approachable. Exhibits a seemingly strong "gout de terroir."

1995 Cask 23, Napa Valley $120.   97

Saturated blood-ruby red. Moderately full-bodied. Highly extracted. Quite tannic. Cassis, oak spice, licorice. Brown spice and expressive Cabernet fruit aromas open up on the palate. Forceful, abrupt dry tannins give a firm finish through which generous fruit is still very marked.

1994 Merlot, Napa Valley $26.   88

Very deep ruby red with brilliant highlights. Medium-bodied. Balanced acidity. Moderately extracted. Mildly oaked. Mildly tannic. Currant, minerals, vanilla. Restrained and elegant in style, with a balanced mouthfeel. Complex flavors are buttressed by steely acidity and some tannic grip on the finish. Should open beautifully with mid-term (3–6 years) cellaring. Has more than a little Bordeaux in its overall style.

Staglin

1994 Cabernet Sauvignon, Rutherford, Napa Valley $37.   88

Deep cherry red. Medium-bodied. Highly extracted. Quite tannic. Cherries, cassis, chalk. Dusty, spicy nose leads a full mouthful of cherry-accented Cabernet fruit flavors, with firm powdery tannins coming through on the finish.

1995 Cabernet Sauvignon, Rutherford, Napa Valley $42.50.   92

Bright ruby purple. Moderately full-bodied. Balanced acidity. Moderately extracted. Moderately oaked. Mildly tannic. Cassis, vanilla. Quite aromatic, with a pure and expressive fruit-centered quality accented by judicious use of oak. Focused and flavorful, displaying fine length and intensity.

1996 Sangiovese, Stagliano, Rutherford, Napa Valley $35.   90

Bright reddish purple. Medium-bodied. Balanced acidity. Moderately extracted. Mildly tannic. Raspberries, cherries, chocolate. High-toned red fruit aromas follow through on a clean, lively palate. Quite bright, with great balance.

Stags' Leap Winery

1997 Chardonnay, Napa Valley $21.   86

Pale yellow-straw hue. Aromatically subdued with mild green apple and vanilla accents. A clean attack leads a medium-bodied palate with brief fruit flavors and a quick oaky finish. Drink now.

1995 Cabernet Sauvignon, Napa Valley $30.   86

Dark violet-red hue. Dusty, minerally aromas are elegant. A firm entry leads a moderately full-bodied palate with firmer, leaner flavors having a sense of depth and a fine, spicy note. Classically structured and nice now. Drink now or later.

1995 Merlot, Napa Valley $28.   87

Very deep ruby hue to the rim. Moderately full-bodied. Balanced acidity. Highly extracted. Moderately oaked. Mildly tannic. Cassis, dried herbs, brown spices. Quite aromatic, with a complex and flavorful palate to match. Well structured, with drying, dusty tannins through the finish. Fine length.

1996 Merlot, Napa Valley $28.   84

Bright violet hue with a lightening rim. Relatively light floral aromas. Moderately light-bodied with a juicy attack and weaker flavors on the midpalate. Finishes with very subtle tannins and a buttery note. Drink now.

1995 Petite Sirah, Napa Valley $22.   90

Dark crimson purple. Medium-bodied. Moderately extracted. Quite tannic. Solid, well gripped, and dry through the finish. Rich blackberry, mint, and anise flavors show through, giving this a sense of proportion and balance.

Steele

1997 Chardonnay, Steele Cuvée, California $18.   84

Pale green-gold. Medium-bodied. Balanced acidity. Moderately extracted. Mildly oaked. Melon, peach, vanilla. Juicy, ripe tropical flavors linger through the finish. Shows a judicious touch of oak seasoning. An easy-drinking style.

1996 Chardonnay, Bien Nacido Vineyard, Santa Barbara County $26.   91

Bright golden cast. Moderately full-bodied. Balanced acidity. Moderately extracted. Mildly oaked. Yeast, cream, vanilla. Shows a marked leesy accent to the generous aromas. Ripe, rounded, and very flavorful in the mouth, with enough acidity to retain a sense of balance through the finish. Stylish.

1996 Chardonnay, Du Pratt Vineyard, Mendocino County $26.   86

Bright yellow-gold. Medium-bodied. Balanced acidity. Mildly oaked. Green apples, vanilla. Distinctive yeasty aromas with spicy, toasty accents follow through on the palate, with tart fruit flavors and a dry finish.

1996 Chardonnay, Durell Vineyard, Carneros $26.   91

Brilliant golden luster. Medium-bodied. Balanced acidity. Moderately extracted. Smoky oak, tropical fruits. Smoky tropical aromas follow through on a supple, silky palate with marked depth of flavors and a lingering finish showcasing smoky flavors. Very stylish.

1996 Chardonnay, Goodchild Vineyard, Santa Barbara County $26.   84

Bright yellow-gold. Moderately full-bodied. Full acidity. Moderately extracted. Minerals, lanolin. Aromatically reserved, with a lean and racy quality. Angular and austere through the finish.

1996 Chardonnay, Lolonis Vineyard, Mendocino County $28.   84

Bright yellow-straw hue. Moderately full-bodied. Balanced acidity. Moderately extracted. Moderately oaked. Vanilla, pears, apples. Warm, spicy aromas follow through on the palate, with a hot finish showing oak spice and mild drying flavors.

1996 Chardonnay, Parmlee-Hill Vineyard, Sonoma Valley $26.   88

Deep golden yellow. Moderately full-bodied. Balanced acidity. Highly extracted. Moderately oaked. Apples, butter. Big and rounded, with a very buttery texture and flavor. Plush and generous in the mouth, showing a leesy richness. A softer style with low acids.

1996 Chardonnay, Sangiacomo Vineyard, Carneros $24.   84

Bright yellow-gold. Medium-bodied. Balanced acidity. Moderately extracted. Moderately oaked. Vanilla, peach, apple. Firmly structured, with oak spice and smoky accents that emerge in the finish, yet this has a core of ripe Chardonnay flavors that fill the midpalate.

Scale: Superlative (96-100), Exceptional (90-95), Highly Recommended (85-89), Recommended (80-84), Not Recommended (Under 80)

200

1994 Cabernet Sauvignon, Anderson Valley $28.   89

Saturated reddish purple. Medium-bodied. Highly extracted. Moderately tannic. Plums, black fruits, black tea. Ripe, generous fruity nose has vanilla notes. The solid, compact palate has fine depth of flavors and good acids to balance. Not very forthcoming at present, with firm tannins on the finish. One to two years cellaring?

1995 Pinot Noir, Anderson Valley $23.   90

Full ruby red. Medium-bodied. Moderately extracted. Heavily oaked. Moderately tannic. Rich new oak aromas with ripe berry accents. A solid, flavorsome palate, with plenty of tannic grip and bright fruit flavors. The finish is dry and oaky.

1995 Pinot Noir, Bien Nacido Vineyard, Santa Barbara County $34.   91

Dark reddish purple. Medium-bodied. Highly extracted. Moderately oaked. Moderately tannic. Tarry nose. Toasty, juicy black cherry aromas lead a full, rich mouthful of dark fruits. The toasty finish lingers impressively with black cherry flavors. Nice now, better in a year or two.

1996 Zinfandel, Catfish Vineyard, Clear Lake $18.   95

Deep blackish purple. Moderately full-bodied. Balanced acidity. Moderately extracted. Moderately oaked. Mildly tannic. Vanilla, black fruits. Quite aromatic, with an excellent interplay between fruit and spicy wood notes. Lush though well balanced in the mouth. Intense and lengthy.

1996 Zinfandel, Du Pratt Vineyard, Mendocino $20.   93

Opaque blackish purple. Moderately full-bodied. Full acidity. Moderately extracted. Moderately oaked. Mildly tannic. Blueberries, chocolate. Outrageously aromatic, with a melange of oak-tinged flavors that explode on the palate. Rich, supple, and velvety, with bright acidity making for a lively finish. Excellent grip and intensity.

1996 Zinfandel, Pacini Vineyard, Mendocino $16.   92

Deep blackish ruby cast. Moderately full-bodied. Balanced acidity. Highly extracted. Heavily oaked. Mildly tannic. Vanilla, black cherries. Quite aromatic, with large amounts of attractive oak nuances accenting a rich core of chocolatey fruit. Supple, deep, and rich, with a lengthy finish.

Robert Stemmler

1995 Pinot Noir, Sonoma County $26.   87

Pale cherry red with a pinkish hue. Moderately light-bodied. Moderately extracted. Moderately oaked. Mildly tannic. Crisp and angular, with lean flavors of tart red fruits and a minerally, astringent finish. Earthy, with mild leathery notes.

Sterling

1997 Chardonnay, Napa Valley $15.   88

Bright straw cast. Moderately full-bodied. Balanced acidity. Moderately extracted. Mildly tannic. Citrus, butter, minerals. Creamy citrus aromas lead a smooth-textured mouthful of butter and lemon flavors with fine persistence. Oak character is quite reserved and well integrated.

1996 Sauvignon Blanc, North Coast $10.   84

Pale straw hue. Medium-bodied. Balanced acidity. Moderately extracted. White citrus, dried herbs. Aromatically reserved. Clean and unoaked, with an appropriate herbal note that intensifies on the finish.

1995 Merlot, Napa Valley $14.   86

Very deep ruby hue to the rim. Medium-bodied. Balanced acidity. Moderately extracted. Mildly oaked. Mildly tannic. Red fruits, vanilla, minerals. Straightforward and well crafted, with pleasant fruit flavors and oak accents. Nicely structured, though quite drinkable.

Stevenot

1996 Zinfandel, Sierra Foothills $12.   81

Stone Creek

1997 Chardonnay, California $6.89.   82

1995 Cabernet Sauvignon, California $6.89.   89

Bright cherry red. Medium-bodied. Subtly extracted. Mildly tannic. Berry fruits, vanilla. Jammy, ripe aromas lead soft fruity flavors, with a very ripe accent and quick finish. An open-knit style, this is soft and easy drinking, and will be best in its youth.

1996 Cabernet Sauvignon, Special Selection, California $6.89.   83

Pale bright ruby red hue. Muted minerals and red berry aromas. A crisp attack leads to a medium-bodied palate with fine grained tannins and crisp berry fruit flavors. Drink now.

1996 Cabernet Sauvignon, Chairman's Reserve, North Coast $15.50.   83

Bright ruby-crimson red hue. Markedly ripe fruit cordial-like aromas with vanilla accents. A light entry leads to a medium-bodied palate with weak fruit flavors that finish quickly, showing very slight tannins. Drink now.

1996 Pinot Noir, Sonoma County $13.50.   83

Pale pinkish red. Moderately light-bodied. Moderately extracted. Mildly tannic. Floral, candied red fruit aromas. Simple sweet fruit flavors, with a clean, mildly juicy palate through to a quick finish. Highly quaffable.

Stonegate

1996 Sauvignon Blanc, Napa Valley $9.50.   88

Bright yellow-gold. Moderately full-bodied. Full acidity. Highly extracted. Heavily oaked. Brown spices, oranges. Very aromatic with a toasty oak overlay. Extremely vibrant acidity produces a bracing finish. A clean and focused style.

1995 Cabernet Sauvignon, Napa Valley $18.   86

Bright violet-red. Medium-bodied. Highly extracted. Moderately tannic. Black berry fruits, licorice. Fruit-centered, bright, and fleshy, with chunky tannins that are not so dry as to prevent pleasure. A solid, fruity style.

1996 Sauvignon Blanc, Late Harvest, Napa Valley $15/375 ml.   84

Very deep bronzed golden hue. Full-bodied. Balanced acidity. Moderately extracted. Toasted coconut, figs, smoke. Quite aromatic, with a big oak overlay and a core of figgy Semillon flavors. Lush and viscous in the mouth, but has enough acidity to avoid a cloying finish.

Stonehedge

1997 Chardonnay, California $10.   83

Deep straw cast. Moderately full-bodied. Balanced acidity. Moderately extracted. Butter, cream. Aromatically reserved, with a ripe buttery quality in the mouth. A touch of acidity lends some balance to the rich finish.

1996 Sauvignon Blanc, California $10.   81

1995 Cabernet Sauvignon, Napa Valley $12.99.   85

Bright cherry red. Medium-bodied. Moderately extracted. Moderately tannic. Minerals, black fruits. A straightforward, angular, mineral-dominant style with a dry finish, though it has enough flesh to carry the tougher structural elements. Subtle oak influence.

1994 Malbec, Napa Valley $12.99.   83

Deep purple with a lightening rim. Moderately light-bodied. Moderately extracted. Moderately tannic. Vanilla, flowers, red fruit. Solid black fruit aromas follow through on the palate, with licorice-like notes through the finish. Tannins are ripe and chewy, though this tends toward the bland.

1995 Zinfandel, Napa Valley $14.99.   87

Opaque dark red. Medium-bodied. Balanced acidity. Highly extracted. Mildly oaked. Moderately tannic. Blackberries. Quite tough and solid, with heavily wrought flavors and no sign of a fruity center. The tannins are rather dry and fine grained.

Scale: Superlative (96-100), Exceptional (90-95), Highly Recommended (85-89), Recommended (80-84), Not Recommended (Under 80)

202

Stonestreet

1996 Chardonnay, Sonoma County $24.　　　　81

1997 Gewürztraminer, Anderson Valley $16.　　　　88

Deep yellow-straw hue. Intense spice and lychee aromas jump from the glass. A rich entry leads a full-bodied, oily palate. Fat and weighty, with a rounded, flavorful finish. Drink now.

1994 Cabernet Sauvignon, Alexander Valley $35.　　　　90

Opaque deep reddish purple. Medium-bodied. Highly extracted. Mildly tannic. Plums, tobacco, vanilla. Oak-accented aromas show full fruity notes. Rounded, full plummy flavors expand on the palate, with ample soft tannins on the finish. Lovely texture. Approachable now.

1995 Cabernet Sauvignon, Alexander Valley $37.　　　　88

Deep ruby hue. Moderately full-bodied. Balanced acidity. Highly extracted. Mildly oaked. Moderately tannic. Black fruits, minerals, chocolate. Firm and concentrated, with a lush but tightly wound palate feel. Tannins rear up on the finish.

1994 Legacy, Alexander Valley $50.　　　　91

Bright reddish purple. Medium-bodied. Highly extracted. Moderately tannic. Tobacco, vanilla, cedar, black fruits. Plush, elegant aromas are strikingly attractive, leading a rounded, velvety palate, with textured tannins and a lingering cedary finish. A charmer, drinking nicely now.

1995 Legacy, Alexander Valley $65.　　　　91

Dark ruby cast. Full-bodied. Balanced acidity. Highly extracted. Heavily oaked. Moderately tannic. Spice, black fruits. Generous aromas lead a lush, velvety mouthfeel with a very firm structure. Tightly wound through the finish. Tannins clamp down hard. Needs time.

1995 Merlot, Alexander Valley $37.　　　　82

1995 Pinot Noir, Russian River Valley $30.　　　　90

Full ruby red. Medium-bodied. Moderately extracted. Moderately oaked. Moderately tannic. Rich tobacco and vanilla aromas lead a seductively rounded palate, with well-framed cherry fruit flavors and textured soft tannins showing great integration. Very polished style.

1996 Pinot Noir, Russian River Valley $33.　　　　83

Bright ruby-garnet cast. Moderately full-bodied. Balanced acidity. Moderately extracted. Heavily oaked. Mildly tannic. Sandalwood, spice, minerals. Quite aromatic, with a hefty oak overlay. Shows quite a bit of weight in the mouth, but lacks a bit for grip.

Storrs

1997 Chardonnay, Ben Lomond Mountain, Santa Cruz Mountains $24.　　　　93

Bright yellow-gold. Moderately full-bodied. Balanced acidity. Highly extracted. Moderately oaked. Smoke, butter, green apples. Exotically rich, generous aromas have a yeasty, spicy character that comes through on an impressively deep and persistent palate with an opulent set of flavors.

1995 Pinot Noir, Sunnyknoll Ranch, Santa Cruz Mountains $20.　　　　86

Bright red. Medium-bodied. Balanced acidity. Moderately extracted. Moderately oaked. Mildly tannic. Rich and toasty. French oak aromas have a vanilla theme with bright red fruit accents. Lively berry fruit flavors show sweetness on the entry, then become drier and more oaky through the finish. Drinking well now.

Storybook Mountain

1995 Zinfandel, Eastern Exposures, Napa Valley $19.50.　　　　90

Bright reddish purple. Medium-bodied. Balanced acidity. Highly extracted. Quite tannic. Black fruits, tea. This is a thick, extracted monster of a wine, with heavy, dry tannins. Rather tight and not much fruit in the middle yet. Not approachable now, but it has the structure to age well.

1996 Zinfandel, Mayacamas Range, Napa Valley $18.50.   84

Bright blackish purple. Medium-bodied. Balanced acidity. Moderately extracted. Mildly oaked. Mildly tannic. Pepper, briar fruits, vanilla. Quite aromatic, with a firm, minerally palate feel. Lighter in style, but well structured, with an angular finish.

Stratford

1996 Chardonnay, California $12.   84

Bright yellow-straw hue. Medium-bodied. Balanced acidity. Moderately extracted. Moderately oaked. Vanilla, menthol, lime. High-toned aromas have a marked menthol note. Crisp, bright citrus flavors with a fine complement of oak spice through the finish.

Rodney Strong

1997 Chardonnay, Chalk Hill, Sonoma County $16.   84

Bright yellow-green. Moderately full-bodied. Balanced acidity. Moderately extracted. Mildly oaked. Green apples, vanilla. Bright green apple aromas follow through well on a bright, clean, persistently flavorsome palate.

1996 Chardonnay, Chalk Hill Vineyard Reserve, Northern Sonoma $24.   87

Yellow-straw hue. Medium-bodied. Balanced acidity. Moderately extracted. Mildly oaked. Butter, vanilla, apples. Aromatically reserved, this shows a rounded texture and good weight, with elegant toasty flavors and a soft frame.

1997 Sauvignon Blanc, Charlotte's Home, Northern Sonoma $10.   82

1995 Cabernet Sauvignon, Sonoma County $13.   86

Bright ruby cast. Medium-bodied. Balanced acidity. Moderately extracted. Moderately oaked. Mildly tannic. Minerals, brown spices. Pleasantly aromatic, with a spicy oak overlay and a core of red fruit flavors on the palate. Lush and well integrated, with a lengthy finish.

1996 Cabernet Sauvignon, Sonoma County $14.   84

Medium ruby-violet hue. Smoky, cedary aromas. A supple entry leads a medium-bodied palate with cassis and black cherry fruit flavors. Tannins are supple and smooth through the finish.

1993 Cabernet Sauvignon, Alexander's Crown Vineyard,
Northern Sonoma $22.   88

Bright brick red. Medium-bodied. Moderately extracted. Moderately tannic. Minerals, red fruits, brown spice. Brisk and lively, with a firm, minerally backbone and bright fruit acids through the finish. Quite high toned and elegant.

1995 Cabernet Sauvignon, Alexander's Crown Vineyard,
Northern Sonoma $24.   86

Bright ruby cast. Moderately full-bodied. Balanced acidity. Moderately extracted. Mildly tannic. Minerals, black fruits. Aromatically reserved, with a firm, minerally personality. Well structured and lean through the finish.

1993 Cabernet Sauvignon, Reserve, Northern Sonoma $30.   89

Full cherry red. Medium-bodied. Moderately extracted. Moderately tannic. Red berries, tea, minerals. Red berry and tea aromas lead a harmonious and balanced palate, with some firm powdery tannins on the finish. Quite lean, with an austere but focused character.

1994 Cabernet Sauvignon, Reserve, Northern Sonoma $35.   89

Dark ruby hue. Moderately full-bodied. Balanced acidity. Moderately extracted. Moderately oaked. Mildly tannic. Brown spices, black fruits, minerals. Generous aromas feature a pleasant interplay between fruit and wood notes. Harmonious, supple, and velvety in the mouth, with a flavorful, well-structured finish.

1996 Merlot, Sonoma County $16.   88

Medium ruby hue with a slight fade. Perfumed oaky aromas. A supple attack, a medium-bodied palate and light drying tannins on the finish. Drink now or later. Can improve with more age.

Scale: Superlative (96-100), Exceptional (90-95), Highly Recommended (85-89), Recommended (80-84), Not Recommended (Under 80)

1996 Pinot Noir, Russian River Valley $17.   **84**
Pale ruby-garnet cast. Medium-bodied. Balanced acidity. Subtly extracted. Moderately oaked. Mildly tannic. Spice, licorice. Quite aromatic, with a spicy wood note and an unusual high-toned quality. Full in the mouth, yet lacking somewhat for grip. Unusual.

1995 Zinfandel, Old Vines, Northern Sonoma $16.   **82**

Summerfield
1997 Chardonnay, Vintner's Reserve, California $7.99.   **82**

Summers
1997 Chardonnay, Napa Valley $30.   **80**

Sunstone
1997 Chardonnay, Santa Barbara County $20.   **84**
Bright yellow-gold. Medium-bodied. Balanced acidity. Moderately extracted. Mildly oaked. Apples, spice, butter. Buttery, spicy aromas follow through on a silky smooth palate with a subtle fruity expression and a textural richness through the finish.

1996 Cabernet Sauvignon, Santa Barbara County $20.   **81**

1997 Syrah, Reserve, Santa Barbara County $28.   **83**
Dark crimson, limpid, with a slight fade. Ripe earth, black fruit, and tomato flavors. Generous wood tones. Firm entry. Moderately full-bodied. Plentiful drying tannins. Solidly structured. Lingering rich finish. A strange earthy accent mutes the fruit character. Drink now.

Joseph Swan
1997 Chardonnay, Estate Vineyard, Russian River Valley $22.50.   **89**
Deep, saturated yellow-straw hue. Generous vanilla, brown spice, and citrus aromas show a hefty oak influence. A firm entry leads a moderately full-bodied palate, with crisp acids. A rich, rounded, flavorful style with solid acidity. Drink now or later.

1996 Mourvedre, Russian River Valley $15.   **82**

1997 Pinot Noir, Lone Redwood Ranch, Russian River Valley $10.   **80**

1997 Pinot Noir, Saralee's Vineyard, Russian River Valley $16.   **81**

1996 Pinot Noir, Estate, Russian River Valley $30.   **83**
Bright ruby purple with a slight fade. Briar fruit, spice, and red fruit aromas. A firm entry leads a medium-bodied palate with crisp, drying tannins. A strangely flavored Pinot, but it shows some jammy richness and decent grip toward the finish. Drink now.

Swanson
1998 Sangiovese, Rosato, Napa Valley $14.   **87**
Deep cherry red. Attractive toasty aromas show a subtle oak accent. A lush entry leads a moderately full-bodied palate, with crisp acids and ripe fruit flavors. Angular, edgy finish. Drink now.

1994 Cabernet Sauvignon, Napa Valley $24.   **86**
Dark cherry red. Medium-bodied. Moderately extracted. Mildly tannic. Plums, tobacco. Plummy aromas with tobacco accents follow through on the palate. Soft and almost jammy, with bright acids and soft tannins throughout.

1995 Alexis, Napa Valley $40.   **87**
Saturated violet-ruby hue. Medium-bodied. Moderately extracted. Moderately tannic. Vanilla, brown spice, black currants. Attractive toasty aromas follow through, with spicy, supple flavors showing a fine fruit center, and a silky finish. Nice now.

1995 Merlot, Napa Valley $24.   **91**
Deep ruby red to the rim. Moderately full-bodied. Balanced acidity. Highly extracted. Moderately oaked. Mildly tannic. Mint, brown spices, red fruits. Aromatic and flavorful, with real complexity. In the mouth this wine is chewy and lush, showing solid balance and a firm structure. Velvety tannins rise up in the lengthy finish.

1996 Syrah, $40.   88

Dark red-purple color, limpid, with a slight fade. Generous, sound notes of spicy red berries and currants. Firm entry, moderately full-bodied. Plentiful drying tannins. Well extracted, structured. Lingering rich finish. Well wrought and solidly extracted. Drink within five years.

Sylvester

1995 Cabernet Sauvignon, Kiara Reserve, Paso Robles $13.50.   83

Pale ruby cast. Medium-bodied. Moderately extracted. Moderately oaked. Mildly tannic. Red fruits, vanilla. Pleasantly aromatic, with well-integrated fruit and wood flavors. Firm and angular through the finish.

Tablas Creek

1996 Tablas Hills Cuvée Rouge, Paso Robles $19.99.   88

Bright ruby red to the rim. Generous red fruit, herb, and vanilla aromas show an attractive wood accent. A firm attack leads a medium-bodied palate that has tannic grip. The finish is angular and flavorful. Shows fine grip and intensity. Drink within five years.

Taft Street

1996 Sauvignon Blanc, Russian River Valley $9.   81

Talbott

1996 Chardonnay, Cuvée Cynthia, Monterey $45.   91

Deep straw cast. Medium-bodied. Full acidity. Moderately extracted. Mildly oaked. Yeast, toast, minerals. Outrageously aromatic, with a distinctive yeasty complexity. Surprisingly light in the mouth, showing a sense of delicacy and elegance through the lengthy finish.

1995 Chardonnay, Diamond T Estate, Monterey $45.   90

Deep straw cast. Moderately full-bodied. Full acidity. Highly extracted. Mildly oaked. Toasted coconut, minerals, citrus zest. Aromatic and generous, with a range of complex yeasty flavors. Zesty, vibrant, and extremely intense in the mouth, with excellent acidity through the lengthy finish.

Talley

1996 Chardonnay, Arroyo Grande Valley $20.   81
1997 Chardonnay, Arroyo Grande Valley $22.   87

Medium gold. Generous tropical aromas. A lush attack leads a moderately full-bodied palate with muted fruit flavors and a notably alcoholic mouthfeel. Quite a generous style. Drink now.

Iván Tamás

1997 Chardonnay, Central Coast $8.95.   83

Pale yellow-straw hue. Clean fruity aromas of apples lead a medium-bodied palate with no oak influence obvious. Acids are juicy and fruit flavors are clean through the finish. Drink now.

1996 Chardonnay, Reserve, Central Coast $15.   84

Medium yellow-gold. Straightforward aromas of apples and citrus with subtle oak accents. A crisp entry leads a moderately full-bodied palate with angular acids and a sensation of alcohol on the finish. Drink now.

1994 Cabernet Sauvignon, Reserve, Livermore Valley $15.   81

Scale: Superlative (96-100), Exceptional (90-95), Highly Recommended (85-89), Recommended (80-84), Not Recommended (Under 80)

Temecula Crest

1997 Sauvignon Blanc, Temecula $9.95.   85

Pale straw hue. Medium-bodied. Full acidity. Moderately extracted. Tart apples, leaves, grapefruit. High-toned grapefruit aromas lead simple tart apple flavors with a minerally backbone. Zesty, clean character.

1996 Nebbiolo, Temecula $18.   83

Bright ruby-garnet cast. Medium-bodied. Full acidity. Highly extracted. Mildly tannic. Minerals, earth. Somewhat reserved in flavor, but structurally quite interesting, with a lean, mildly astringent note. Would make a decent table wine.

Terra d'Oro

1995 Barbera, Montevina, Amador County $18.   87

Deep blackish ruby cast. Moderately full-bodied. Balanced acidity. Highly extracted. Moderately oaked. Mildly tannic. Vanilla, black fruits, minerals. Extremely aromatic, with a hefty oak overlay and a sturdy core of dark fruit flavors. Rich, though quite firm through the finish. Well balanced, with fine intensity.

1995 Sangiovese, Montevina, Amador County $16.   87

Full ruby red. Medium-bodied. Balanced acidity. Moderately extracted. Moderately oaked. Vanilla, red fruits, earth. Softer juicy red fruit flavors defer to dry, dusty tannins. Acids seem a tad low to allow this to age; drink it soon.

1995 Zinfandel, Montevina, Amador County $16.   82

The Terraces

1994 Cabernet Sauvignon, Napa Valley $49.99.   94

Bright ruby cast. Moderately full-bodied. Balanced acidity. Moderately extracted. Heavily oaked. Mildly tannic. Vanilla, red fruits, brown spices. Extremely aromatic, with a generous oak accent to a bright core of precisely defined red fruit flavors. Stylish, well integrated, and well balanced, with real distinction. Shows fine grip to the intense finish. Though tasty now, it will be better with further cellaring.

Tessera

1996 Chardonnay, California $10.   81

Testarossa

1997 Chardonnay, Santa Maria Valley $26.   85

Bright yellow-straw cast. Moderately full-bodied. Balanced acidity. Moderately extracted. Mildly oaked. Brown spices, citrus. Generous aromas show a spicy accent. Ripe and rounded in the mouth, with a crisp, snappy finish.

1996 Chardonnay, Chalone Appellation, Monterey County $29.   87

Pale straw cast. Medium-bodied. Full acidity. Moderately extracted. Mildly oaked. Vanilla, citrus, minerals. Light in the mouth though quite flavorful, with an oak-accented, yeasty array of flavors. Bright and zesty through the finish.

1996 Chardonnay, Bien Nacido Vineyard, Santa Maria Valley $29.   83

Bright yellow-straw cast. Moderately full-bodied. Balanced acidity. Moderately extracted. Minerals, tropical fruits. Aromatically reserved, and marked by a ripe and rounded texture. Crisp through the finish, with a hint of wood spice lingering.

Thackrey

NV Pleiades VII Old Vines Red, California $28.   86

Bright garnet red with a slight fade. Generous medicinal and red fruit aromas. A soft attack leads a medium-bodied palate showing silky tannins. Lengthy, supple finish. Old-vine complexity of flavor is married to easy drinkability. Drink now.

1993 Syrah, Orion, Old Vines Rossi Vineyard, St. Helena, Napa Valley $30. 95

Opaque purplish black. Full-bodied. Full acidity. Lots of fruit. Moderately oaked. Quite tannic. Dry. Reminiscent of vanilla, black fruits, minerals, passion flowers. This vintage's structure is stunning. Hugely extracted, superripe black fruit is supported by a frame of rugged, lasting tannins. Beautifully integrated acidity results in a lively showstopper, explosive with flavor and exquisitely balanced.

1994 Syrah, Orion, Old Vines Rossi Vineyard, St. Helena, Napa Valley $30. 94

Blackish ruby purple. Full-bodied. Balanced acidity. Highly extracted. Quite tannic. Dry. Reminiscent of rosemary, eucalyptus, marionberry, lavender, sandalwood. Jammy, rich texture. A potpourri of exotic fragrances beautifully enhanced by succulent, lip-smacking black fruits. Quite tannic at present, this is now in a preview stage of greatness.

1995 Syrah, Orion, Old Vines Rossi Vineyard, St. Helena, Napa Valley $45. 97

Deep, impenetrable blackish purple. Full-bodied. Balanced acidity. Highly extracted. Quite tannic. Eucalyptus, sweet herbs, black fruits, tar. Inimitable in style, with a signature complex nose that has a medicinal, classic Syrah character. Extremely concentrated with great depth and a lash of tannin. Approachable now only by virtue of its outstanding balance. A show wine, not an everyday drink.

1996 Syrah, Orion, Old Vines Rossi Vineyard, St. Helena, Napa Valley $60. 95

Very dark purple, opaque and brilliant to the rim. Powerful, fantastic coal tar, black fruit, and oak spice flavors. Hefty wood tones. Smooth entry. Full-bodied. Abundant grainy tannins. Monster extraction with lots of everything in a structured frame. Persistent rich finish. Good for long-term (7–10 years) cellaring.

Thornton

1990 Brut Reserve, California $25. 84

Bright yellow-gold. Moderately full-bodied. Baked fruit, spice. Mature, faintly bready aromas lead a rich, moderately alcoholic mouthfeel, with baked fruit flavors predominating.

1998 Grenache Rosé, Collins Ranch, Cucamonga Valley $7.99. 90

Saturated, deep raspberry pink hue. Attractive, forward red fruit and licorice aromas. A rich entry leads a moderately full-bodied palate showing rounded acidity. Generous and quite flavorful. Drink now.

1996 Cabernet-Merlot, South Coast, South Coast $17. 86

Ruby-garnet hue with a fading rim. Medium-bodied. Moderately extracted. Moderately tannic. Leather, spice. Mature, developed aromas lead a dry palate showing leathery tannins and a silky mouthfeel. Flavors take a meaty character. Not for those seeking a fruit-centered style.

1995 Zinfandel, Old Vine, South Coast $18. 82

Titus

1994 Cabernet Sauvignon, Napa Valley $22. 90

Saturated dark crimson color. Medium-bodied. Highly extracted. Moderately tannic. Plums, black fruits, brown spice, chocolate. Rich, ripe fruit aromas lead a palate showing solid black Cabernet fruit flavors that are complemented by balanced powdery tannins on the finish.

1996 Zinfandel, Napa Valley $17. 84

Bright reddish purple. Medium-bodied. Balanced acidity. Moderately extracted. Mildly oaked. Moderately tannic. Red fruits. Rather brash, with bright red fruits and solid tannins giving an angular structure.

Topolos

1996 Alicante Bouschet, Old Vines, Sonoma County $18.   86

Dark, opaque purple red to the rim. Generous, unusual prune, black fruit, and sandalwood aromas suggest mild wood treatment. A firm attack leads a full-bodied palate that shows marked acidity and drying tannins. Persistent, flavorful, tannic finish. Drink now.

1996 Zinfandel, Bella Lisa, Russian River Valley $16.   84

Bright blackish ruby cast. Medium-bodied. Balanced acidity. Moderately extracted. Mildly oaked. Mildly tannic. Stewed fruits, brown spices. Carries a slightly overripe note through a lighter-styled palate feel. Lean through the finish. Lacks intensity.

1995 Zinfandel, Piner Heights, Russian River Valley $16.50.   86

Bright blackish ruby cast. Medium-bodied. Balanced acidity. Moderately extracted. Moderately oaked. Mildly tannic. Brown spices, black fruits, sweet herbs. Quite aromatic, with a wave of complex, slightly pruney flavors. Full and ripe on the palate, with some chunky tannins in the finish.

1996 Zinfandel, Rossi Ranch, Sonoma Valley $24.75.   84

Deep blackish ruby cast. Full-bodied. Balanced acidity. Highly extracted. Mildly oaked. Moderately tannic. Stewed fruits, minerals. Slightly overripe, with a full, flavorful mouthfeel. Carries a strange salty note through the palate. Unusual.

Marimar Torres

1996 Chardonnay, Don Miguel Vineyard, Sonoma County,
Green Valley $25.   81

1995 Pinot Noir, Don Miguel Vineyard, Sonoma County, Green Valley $25. 86

Bright saturated ruby cast. Medium-bodied. Full acidity. Moderately extracted. Mildly oaked. Mildly tannic. Minerals, red fruits. Generous aromas feature a racy fruit-centered note that plays out on the palate. Vibrant and clean in the mouth, with grip and intensity through the finish.

Trefethen

1994 Cabernet Sauvignon, Napa Valley $24.   86

Opaque bright purple. Medium-bodied. Highly extracted. Mildly tannic. Flowers, red fruits, minerals. High-toned floral and raspberry aromas. Very bright acids. Concentrated red fruit flavors have great clarity, with a clean minerally finish.

1995 Cabernet Sauvignon, Napa Valley $24.   84

Bright violet-red. Medium-bodied. Highly extracted. Moderately tannic. Black cherries, mineral. Lighter styled and juicy, with bright cherry flavors and a supple finish. Drinking well now.

Trentadue

1995 Carignane, Sonoma County $12.   87

Dark crimson. Moderately full-bodied. Moderately extracted. Mildly tannic. Plummy, black cherry flavors follow through with a generous palate feel and mouthcoating tannins. Drinking well now, though it will develop in the future. Very modern and well-extracted.

1994 Merlot, Alexander Valley $18.   85

Deep ruby with a slight garnet fade and brilliant clarity. Medium-bodied. Full acidity. Moderately extracted. Mildly tannic. Dusty cherries, sweet herbs, mint. Lighter in style, with bright and lively flavors and vibrant acidity on the palate. Some dusty tannins at the finish.

1995 Petite Sirah, Sonoma County $16.   83

Dark saturated ruby red. Highly extracted. Medium-bodied. Moderately tannic. Minty, black fruit aromas follow through. Lush fruit flavors with moderate tannins give this a very forward fruit-centered character that invites current drinking.

1995 Sangiovese, Alexander Valley $18.   **89**

Dark ruby color. Medium-bodied. Balanced acidity. Moderately extracted. Moderately oaked. Mildly tannic. Eucalyptus, tart cherries, minerals. Very aromatic. The bright, vibrant palate has tight, minerally focus with high-toned fruit flavors.

1994 Merlot Port, Alexander Valley $20.   **84**

Bright cherry red. Medium-bodied. Balanced acidity. Moderately extracted. Mildly oaked. Mildly tannic. Reminiscent of plums, mint, mocha. Soft, moderately lush texture. A bright plummy nose leads a racy palate with high-toned fruity flavors, delicate brown spice, and some gentle tannins in the finish.

1994 Petite Sirah Port, Alexander Valley $20.   **88**

Opaque reddish purple. Moderately full-bodied. Highly extracted. Reminiscent of cherry, apple, black fruits. Sweet plummy entry expands on the midpalate, with the finish showing tannic grip and spicy notes. A bit unapproachable now, but should soften up beautifully with time.

Tria

1995 Labyrinth Red, California $18.   **86**

Deep ruby hue with a garnet edge. Generous vanilla and red fruit aromas. A lush entry leads to a medium-bodied palate with lean tannins and zesty acidity. Ripe, well-cut finish. Showing some intensity. Drink now.

1996 Pinot Noir, Monterey $20.   **85**

Bright ruby red. Medium-bodied. Moderately extracted. Moderately oaked. Mildly tannic. Leather, black fruits. Spicy, perfumed aromas lead a mouthful of dark fruit flavors, with oak spice rearing up on the finish. Flavorful.

1996 Zinfandel, Dry Creek Valley $18.   **89**

Deep blackish purple. Full-bodied. Balanced acidity. Highly extracted. Mildly oaked. Moderately tannic. Minerals, chocolate. Quite firm and flavorful, with a highly structured palate feel. Rich and intense, with chunky tannins through the finish.

Tribaut

NV Blanc de Blancs Brut, California $9.   **86**

Deep golden cast. Medium-bodied. Full acidity. Subtly extracted. Butter, minerals. Rather overtly mature, with big toasty aromas that follow through on the palate. Shows buttery richness, though not a lengthy finish. Although the maturity is exaggerated, this has attractive character.

NV Blanc de Noirs Brut, California $9.   **80**

M. Trinchero

1996 Chardonnay, Founder's Estate, Napa Valley $25.   **83**

Pale straw hue. Very distinctive aromas show assertive toasted oak and smoky yeast. A woody attack leads a moderately full-bodied, brightly acidic palate dominated by oak-accented flavors.

1995 Cabernet Sauvignon, Founder's Estate, Napa Valley $30.   **84**

Dark violet-red. Medium-bodied. Moderately extracted. Moderately tannic. Earth, licorice, black fruits. Dry and compact, with alcohol supplying a rounded mouthfeel. The finish is rather short and powdery.

1996 Cabernet Sauvignon, Founder's Estate, California $30.   **88**

Intense, saturated neon purple hue. Very aromatic with violet and anise aromas. A firm attack leads to a full-bodied palate with dense, dry tannins drying the palate. Quite tough and unyielding now, but the acids are excellent. Drink within five years.

Scale: Superlative (96-100), Exceptional (90-95), Highly Recommended (85-89), Recommended (80-84), Not Recommended (Under 80)

Truchard

1996 Chardonnay, Carneros, Napa Valley $24.   91

Pale green-gold. Moderately full-bodied. Full acidity. Moderately extracted. Moderately oaked. Vanilla, spice, lemons. Very aromatic, with plush fruity, smoky aromas following through on the palate. Shows a supple and silky mouthfeel, with a lingering finish.

1995 Cabernet Sauvignon, Carneros, Napa Valley $24.   88

Saturated dark ruby red. Moderately full-bodied. Moderately extracted. Moderately tannic. Spice, crisp berries, cherry tomato. Lively, engaging aromas. Berrylike flavors burst on the palate with balanced, powdery tannins giving some authority on the finish. Very nice now.

1994 Cabernet Sauvignon, Reserve, Carneros, Napa Valley $32.   90

Full ruby hue with violet highlights. Medium-bodied. Moderately extracted. Mildly tannic. Cassis, cedar. Soft, silky, and supple, this has a refined balance with succulent Cabernet fruit flavors. Soft tannins caress the finish, which shows fine persistence. Drinking very nicely now.

1996 Pinot Noir, Carneros, Napa Valley $25.   83

Pale violet-ruby hue. Medium-bodied. Subtly extracted. Mildly tannic. Red fruits, strawberries, vanilla. Perfumed fruity aromas lead a supple, smooth, silky mouthful of flavors with attractive vanilla accents throughout. A delicate style.

1996 Zinfandel, Carneros, Napa Valley $18.   90

Deep blackish ruby cast. Medium-bodied. Full acidity. Moderately extracted. Moderately oaked. Mildly tannic. Mint, brown spices, red fruits. Quite aromatic, with a lively, high-toned array of flavors on the palate. Supple and well balanced, with a lengthy finish. Eminently drinkable.

Tulocay

1997 Chardonnay, Napa Valley $16.   84

Medium yellow-straw color. Aromas show a marked yeasty note that verges on cheesy. Assertively smoky on the attack, with a full body and deep woody flavors, though it is rather short on fruit. Finishes quickly.

1994 Cabernet Sauvignon, Cliff Vineyard, Napa Valley $22.   87

Deep, dark brick red. Moderately full-bodied. Highly extracted. Moderately tannic. Mineral, earth, black plums. The firm, hard-edged palate has deep black fruit flavors up front, with a strong minerally underlay. A little tough now but not impenetrable. Time should resolve this.

1996 Cabernet Sauvignon, Cliff Vineyard, Napa Valley $21.   89

Saturated blackish-ruby hue. Restrained aromas show anise and black fruits. A firm entry leads a moderately full-bodied palate with deeply extracted flavors that finish dryly with a lingering woody note. Rather tough at present. Drink now or later.

1996 Pinot Noir, Haynes Vineyard, Napa Valley $18.   84

Pale ruby red. Moderately light-bodied. Subtly extracted. Mildly tannic. Minerals, oak spice, berry fruits. Lean, high-toned aromas lead a brisk, tart fruit palate with fine grip and a minerally finish. Nice now, it does not have the stuffing for long aging.

Turley

1996 Zinfandel, Old Vines, California $30.   92

Deep blackish ruby hue. Full-bodied. Balanced acidity. Highly extracted. Heavily oaked. Mildly tannic. Black fruits, vanilla. Quite aromatic, with a big, ripe, fruit-centered palate feel. Firm and rich, with a deep, lengthy finish. Weighty but well balanced.

1995 Zinfandel, Moore "Earthquake" Vineyard, Napa Valley $35.   86

Deep ruby-garnet hue with a slight haze. Moderately full-bodied. Low acidity. Moderately extracted. Mildly tannic. Overripe red fruits, brown spices. Quite aromatic, with a full, ripe, rich palate feel. Almost viscous, with a distinct impression of sweetness. Made in a late-harvest style, it features a Port-like note throughout. Soft and luxuriant through the finish, with good length. Surprisingly open-knit, given its weight.

1996 Zinfandel, Hayne Vineyard, Napa Valley $35.   95

Deep blackish ruby cast with a slight haze. Full-bodied. Low acidity. Highly extracted. Moderately oaked. Mildly tannic. Black fruits, earth, chocolate. Rather reserved aromatically, with a deep, brooding quality throughout. Dark, firm, and extracted, with a ripe, chocolatey quality. Big and weighty but well balanced, with a highly structured, lengthy finish.

Turnbull

1994 Cabernet Sauvignon, Napa Valley $22.   88

Dark garnet-ruby color. Medium-bodied. Highly extracted. Moderately tannic. Plums, ground spice, earth. Deep fleshy aromas with full spicy accents lead a rounded, juicy entry that turns rather earthy and authoritatively dry on the finish.

1995 Cabernet Sauvignon, Napa Valley $20.   88

Deep saturated ruby hue. Moderately full-bodied. Balanced acidity. Moderately extracted. Moderately oaked. Mildly tannic. Red fruits, vanilla. Generous aromas reveal a full and well-balanced palate. Firm and angular through the lengthy, flavorful finish.

Turning Leaf

1995 Chardonnay, Reserve, Sonoma County $10.   84

Bright yellow-straw cast. Moderately full-bodied. Balanced acidity. Highly extracted. Mildly oaked. Citrus, cream, brown spices. Forward aromas carry an enticing spicy accent and a full mouthfeel but also hint at a degree of maturity. The finish is lean and angular.

1994 Cabernet Sauvignon, Reserve, Sonoma County $10.   81

1995 Merlot, Sonoma County $10.   80

1996 Merlot, Winemaker's Choice Reserve, Sonoma County $12.   81

1995 Pinot Noir, Reserve, Sonoma County $10.99.   85

Pale pinkish cherry red. Moderately light-bodied. Moderately extracted. Mildly tannic. Vanilla and raspberry aromas. Simple crisp red fruit palate with dry fine-grained tannins on the finish.

1996 Pinot Noir, Winemaker's Choice Reserve, California $12.   82

Twin Hills

1993 Cabernet Sauvignon, Paso Robles $15.   83

Deep blackish ruby cast. Moderately full-bodied. Full acidity. Moderately extracted. Mildly oaked. Moderately tannic. Sandalwood, minerals, black fruits. Reined-in, wood-accented aromatics lead a firm and angular palate feel. Crisp through the finish.

1994 Zinfandel, Paso Robles $15.   80

Zinfandel Port, Lot XCII, Paso Robles $25.   89

Deep garnet cast. Moderately full-bodied. Full acidity. Highly extracted. Roasted salted nuts, rancio, treacle. Extraordinarily aromatic, with an notable Sherry-like quality to the complex flavors. Rich and intense, with a roasted accent and an angular finish provided by juicy acidity.

M.G. Vallejo

1997 Chardonnay, California $6.99.   81

1997 White Zinfandel, California $6.   82

1996 Pinot Noir, California $6.99.   82

Valley of the Moon

1995 Zinfandel, Sonoma Valley $25.   90

Bright blackish ruby cast. Moderately full-bodied. Full acidity. Moderately extracted. Mildly tannic. Black fruits, earth. Pleasantly aromatic, with deep, brooding flavors. Rich on the palate, with a finish enlivened by buoyant acidity. Zesty.

Scale: Superlative (96-100), Exceptional (90-95), Highly Recommended (85-89),
Recommended (80-84), Not Recommended (Under 80)

Van Asperen

1997 Chardonnay, Napa Valley $12.   81

1994 Cabernet Sauvignon, Napa Valley $15.   84

Bright violet red. Medium-bodied. Moderately extracted. Moderately tannic. Cassis, minerals, vanilla. Bright, crisp aromas follow through on a lively palate with minerally backbone. A leaner style.

1995 Cabernet Sauvignon, Napa Valley $18.   84

Bright cherry red hue. Subdued, lean mineral and earth aromas. A lean entry leads to a moderately light-bodied palate with candied flavors, bright acidity, and grippy tannins. Snappy, flavorful finish. A straightforward but tasty style. Drink now.

1994 Cabernet Sauvignon, Signature Reserve, Napa Valley $28.   86

Bright purple red hue. Pronounced vanilla, mineral, and herb aromas show a judicious oak accent. A lean entry leads to a medium-bodied palate with crisp tannins and vibrant acidity. Generous, flavorful finish. Well balanced. Drink within five years.

1996 Merlot, Napa Valley $15.   83

Bright violet hue with a pale cast. Mildly floral aromas. Medium-bodied, with a soft attack and rounded, lighter flavors and a clean finish. Drink now.

1995 Zinfandel, Napa Valley $10.   82

Van Roekel

1996 Viognier, Temecula $10.95.   82

1997 Rosé of Syrah, Temecula $9.95.   80

1996 Zinfandel, Temecula $13.95.   80

1994 Sweet Salud, Temecula $15.95.   83

Deep golden cast. Medium-bodied. Full acidity. Moderately extracted. Tropical fruits, honey, dried herbs. Aromatic, with a full though angular palate feel. Acidity is extremely vibrant through the finish.

Venezia

1996 Chardonnay, Big River Ranch, Alexander Valley $19.99.   86

Bright yellow-straw cast. Moderately full-bodied. Full acidity. Heavily oaked. Yeast, oak spice, ripe citrus. Complex, toasty aromatics lead a brightly acidic yet full-flavored and weighty palate featuring spicy oak and citrus acids through the finish.

1997 Chardonnay, Regusci Vineyards, Napa Valley $20.   89

Brilliant yellow-gold. Ripe, generous aromas of butter, smoke, and tropical fruits. A rich, fruity entry leads a full-bodied palate with a juicy center and plenty of yeasty, oaky accents emerging on the finish. Drink now.

1995 Cabernet Sauvignon, Meola Vineyards, Alexander Valley $20.   87

Deep crimson red. Medium-bodied. Moderately extracted. Moderately tannic. Toasted oak, vanilla, black fruits. High-toned floral aromas show oaky accents that are confirmed on the palate. Tending toward austere, with tightly wound black fruit flavors and plenty of dry oaky character through the finish.

1996 Cabernet Sauvignon, Meola Vineyards, Alexander Valley $19.99.   88

Very deep ruby purple. Moderately full-bodied. Balanced acidity. Moderately extracted. Moderately oaked. Mildly tannic. Vanilla, cassis, minerals. Generous aromas feature a toasty oak accent. Acidity lends a sense of brightness to the core of fruit flavors. Firm, lengthy finish.

1996 Sangiovese, Alegria Vineyards, Russian River Valley $19.99.   85

Bright purple red. Medium-bodied. Balanced acidity. Moderately extracted. Moderately tannic. Vanilla, black fruits, minerals. A dry, assertive character is imparted by oak influences, with high-toned dried red fruit flavors coming through.

1996 Sangiovese, Nuovo Mondo, North Coast $19.99.   **84**

Bright reddish purple. Moderately light-bodied. Balanced acidity. Moderately extracted. Mildly tannic. Red fruits, vanilla. Rather soft on the finish. Rounded cherry flavors finish quickly.

1996 Sangiovese, Van Noy Vineyards, Russian River Valley $19.99.   **84**

Bright cherry purple. Medium-bodied. Balanced acidity. Moderately extracted. Moderately oaked. Moderately tannic. Red fruits, vanilla. Youthful, high-toned fruity "aromas. Crisp, red fruit flavors elevate a dry oak background that follows through on the finish.

Venge

1996 Sangiovese, Penny Lane Vineyard, Oakville, Napa Valley $20.   **86**

Dark ruby. Medium-bodied. Balanced acidity. Moderately extracted. Mildly oaked. Mildly tannic. Black fruits, earth. Very soft and fleshy, with dark, berry-accented flavors. Velvety tannins. Lush and textured.

Via Firenze

1995 Dolcetto, Napa Valley $14.99.   **84**

Bright ruby cast. Medium-bodied. Full acidity. Moderately extracted. Mildly tannic. Red fruits, minerals. Somewhat reserved aromatically, but turns quite flavorful on the palate. Lean, concentrated, and focused, with a firm, angular finish. Intense and well balanced.

1996 Sangiovese, Tuscan Collection, Mendocino $17.99.   **81**

Viader

1993 Red, Napa Valley $30.   **89**

Full crimson red. Medium-bodied. Moderately extracted. Moderately tannic. Ripe berries, currants, anise. Full, ripe fruity aromas follow through well on the palate, with plush tannins highlighting the finish. Drinking nicely now.

Vigil

1996 A. Nice, Chardonnay, California $12.   **84**

Deep straw cast. Medium-bodied. Full acidity. Moderately extracted. Dried herbs, minerals, butter. Forward high-toned aromas lead a ripe mouthfeel with a textured buttery quality. Crisp acidity makes for a refreshing finish.

1997 Cabernet Franc, Solari Vineyard, Napa Valley $25.   **84**

Deep, saturated purple-red hue. Opulent, unusual ginger and black fruit aromas carry a big oak accent. A lush entry leads to a moderately full-bodied palate with supple velvety tannins. Rich, chocolatey finish. Rather unusual flavors, but not unattractive. Drink now or later.

1995 Valiente Claret, Napa Valley $20.   **86**

Bright reddish purple. Medium-bodied. Moderately extracted. Mildly tannic. Red fruits, minerals, chocolate. Quite light on the midpalate, though the flavors have a juicy quality. Chocolatey flavors and a minerally backbone come through on the finish.

1996 Valiente Claret, Napa Valley $22.   **86**

Bright ruby purple. Medium-bodied. Full acidity. Highly extracted. Moderately oaked. Moderately tannic. Menthol, red fruits, vanilla. Forward aromas carry an overtly minty quality. Racy and lean in the mouth all the way through the flavorful finish, with a firm structure.

1996 Zinfandel, Tres Condados, California $12.99.   **84**

Bright blackish purple. Moderately full-bodied. Balanced acidity. Moderately extracted. Mildly tannic. Black fruits, minerals. Reserved aromatically, but features a solid core of brooding, dark fruit flavors. Well structured and firm, with good grip to the finish.

Villa Mt. Eden

1997 Chardonnay, California $10. 88

Bright yellow-gold. Ripe smoky, browned butter aromas. A rich, flavorful entry leads a moderately full-bodied palate with impressively concentrated fruit flavors, juicy acids, and well-integrated oak character. Persistent fruity finish. Drink now or later.

1997 Chardonnay, Grand Reserve, Bien Nacido Vineyard,
Santa Maria Valley $18. 88

Bright yellow-gold. Ripe fruity aromas show yeast, butter, and well-integrated oak. A smooth entry leads a medium-bodied palate with good fruit emphasis and a generous mouthfeel. Finishes with a lingering yeasty note. Stylish. Drink now or later.

1996 Chardonnay, Signature Series, Bien Nacido Vineyard,
Santa Maria Valley $30. 93

Deep gold. Powerfully aromatic with very ripe fruits, and rich leesy and oaky accents. A sumptuous attack leads a full-bodied palate with a smooth, textured mouthfeel. Flavors are quite concentrated with deep fruity character. Finishes with leesy complexity. Drink now or later.

1995 Cabernet Sauvignon, California $11. 82

1995 Cabernet Sauvignon, Grand Reserve, Napa Valley $20. 89

Deep brick-violet hue. Ripe fleshy aromas with a woody accent. A smooth attack leads a moderately full-bodied palate with a thickish mouthfeel and softer acidity, allied to supple but richly textured tannins. Generous, rich style. Very approachable now. Drink now.

1994 Cabernet Sauvignon, Signature Series, Mendocino $50. 90

Blackish red with purple highlights. Medium-bodied. Highly extracted. Moderately tannic. Plums, black fruits, black tea, brown spice. Oaky aromas have fleshy accents that are confirmed on the palate. Impressively rich and deep, with well-extracted flavors through a dry oaky finish. Short- to medium-term cellaring should round this out.

1995 Cabernet Sauvignon, Signature Series, Mendocino $45. 90

Saturated dark red with purple highlights. Moderately full-bodied. Highly extracted. Heavily oaked. Moderately tannic. Vanilla, oak spice, black fruits. Dense oak-dominated aromas follow through on the palate. Deep, rich, and chocolatey, though under the thumb of its oak at present. This should be better in a year or two.

1996 Zinfandel, California $12. 84

Bright blackish ruby hue. Moderately full-bodied. Balanced acidity. Highly extracted. Moderately oaked. Moderately tannic. Brown spices, black fruits. Pleasantly aromatic, with a flavorful palate feel. Firm and well structured, with dusty tannins through the finish. Nicely balanced and lengthy.

1996 Zinfandel, Grand Reserve, Monte Rosso Vineyard,
Sonoma Valley $20. 84

Deep blackish ruby cast. Full-bodied. Full acidity. Highly extracted. Moderately tannic. Black fruits, pepper. Reserved aromatically but full-throttled on the palate, with prickly acidity and a thick texture. Carries a slightly overripe undercurrent, with a suggestion of sweetness.

Volker Eisele

1995 Cabernet Sauvignon, Napa Valley $30. 85

Deep ruby cast. Full-bodied. Balanced acidity. Highly extracted. Mildly oaked. Moderately tannic. Earth, spice, dried herbs. Pleasantly aromatic, showing a firm and chunky palate feel. Rich and weighty, with a wave of tannins that bite into the finish. Needs time.

1996 Cabernet Sauvignon, Napa Valley $30. 85

Bright violet-red hue. Aromatically reserved with an herbal note to the nose. A firm entry leads a medium-bodied palate with very tough, youthful tannins gripping the finish. Rather youthful and angular. Drink now or later.

Von Strasser

1994 Cabernet Sauvignon, Diamond Mountain, Napa Valley $32.   90

Saturated purple-red. Moderately full-bodied. Highly extracted. Moderately tannic. Red fruits, crisp blackberries, minerals. Bright, high-toned fruit aromas lead a lively, concentrated palate, with minerally austerity coming through on the finish. Promising structure bodes well for keeping.

1995 Cabernet Sauvignon, Diamond Mountain, Napa Valley $36.   87

Dark, saturated ruby purple. Full-bodied. Balanced acidity. Highly extracted. Moderately oaked. Quite tannic. Vanilla, minerals, black fruits. Shows a toasty oak accent on the nose, but closes down completely in the mouth, with a wave of astringent tannins. Rather severe, this will need extended cellaring.

Voss

1997 Sauvignon Blanc, Napa Valley $12.50.   95

Deep straw cast. Moderately full-bodied. Full acidity. Highly extracted. Dried herbs, pineapple, gooseberries. Markedly pungent, with forceful New Zealand-style herbal flavors. Crisp and extremely vibrant, with a juicy mouthfeel and a lengthy, flavorful finish. Very stylish.

1995 Merlot, Napa Valley $20.   89

Deep ruby red to the rim. Medium-bodied. Balanced acidity. Moderately extracted. Mildly oaked. Moderately tannic. Black fruits, earth, minerals. Compact in style, with a youthful core of flavors wrapped in a shroud of velvety tannins. Well balanced, it should mellow with age.

1996 Merlot, Napa Valley $18.   84

Bright, pale ruby red. Generous red fruit, vanilla, and herb aromas show an attractive wood accent. A crisp attack is followed by a moderately light-bodied palate with a vibrant, fruity finish. Eminently drinkable and tasty. Drink now.

1995 Shiraz, Napa Valley $16.   88

Deep, opaque purple-red hue. Generous sweet wood, vanilla, and berry aromas show a dominant oak accent. A rich, lush attack leads a full-bodied palate, with abundant velvety tannins. Big, chunky finish. Drink within five years.

1996 Botrytis Sauvignon Blanc, Napa Valley $18.50/375 ml.   89

Very deep bronzed golden hue. Full-bodied. Full acidity. Moderately extracted. Apricots, honey, vanilla. Heavily botrytized, with a complex wave of flavors on the palate. Though quite viscous, this wine features excellent acidic grip through the finish. An intense style.

Weinstock

1996 Chardonnay, California $10.99.   83

Yellow-straw color. Medium-bodied. Balanced acidity. Moderately extracted. Mildly oaked. Vanilla, spice, apples. Light oak spice aromas lead a bright, straightforward mouthful of flavors with buttery texture and enough acid to keep the finish fresh.

1997 Contour, Clarksburg $8.95.   82

1998 Contour, Clarksburg $8.95.   86

Very pale straw cast. Quite aromatic, with a big floral, fruity character. A lush entry leads a medium-bodied palate, with sweet tropical flavors carrying through to the finish. Drink now.

1997 Sauvignon Blanc, California $8.99.   81

1998 White Zinfandel, California $6.95.   84

Pale pink. Subdued berry and mineral aromas. A crisp entry leads a medium-bodied palate with sharp fruit acidity balanced by mild sweetness. Very clean and refreshing. Vibrant. Drink now.

Scale: Superlative (96-100), Exceptional (90-95), Highly Recommended (85-89), Recommended (80-84), Not Recommended (Under 80)

1997 Gamay, Paso Robles $7.49.　　　　　　　　　　　　　　84

Bright neon violet hue. Medium-bodied. Moderately extracted. Mildly tannic. Black fruits. Grapey and fresh on the nose and through the palate, with clean lightly astringent notes on the finish. Very tasty and balanced.

NV Pinot Noir, Reserve, American $7.99.　　　　　　　　　80

Wellington

1994 Cabernet Sauvignon, Mohrhardt Ridge Vineyard,
Sonoma County $15.　　　　　　　　　　　　　　　　87

Opaque blackish red-purple. Moderately full-bodied. Highly extracted. Moderately tannic. Plums, cassis, earth, brown spice. Heavyweight black fruit flavors are complemented by a voluptuous mouthfeel, with fine, supple tannins that show a hint of firmness on the finish. Attractive now.

1995 Merlot, Sonoma Valley $16.　　　　　　　　　　　89

Deep ruby hue with a purplish cast. Moderately full-bodied. Balanced acidity. Highly extracted. Moderately oaked. Moderately tannic. Red fruits, licorice, vanilla. Aromatic and quite rich in style with a chewy palate feel. Tannins have some grip in the mouth, but the finish is still relatively lengthy. Tasty but serious.

Wente

NV Brut Reserve, Arroyo Seco $14.　　　　　　　　　　81
1997 Chardonnay, Central Coast $11.　　　　　　　　　83

Pale yellow-straw hue. Generous ripe aromas have a buttery accent. A rich attack leads a moderately full-bodied palate with tropical flavors and judicious oak. The acidity is well balanced and fresh. The finish is persistent, with a touch of oak spice.

1996 Chardonnay, Riva Ranch Reserve, Arroyo Seco, Monterey $16.　　86

Pale straw cast. Moderately full-bodied. Full acidity. Moderately extracted. Mildly oaked. Minerals, spice, cream. Generous spicy aromas lead a ripe and creamy mouthfeel. Lushly textured through the zesty finish.

1996 Cabernet Sauvignon, Livermore Valley $11.　　　　80
1994 Cabernet Sauvignon, Charles Wetmore Reserve, Livermore Valley$22.　89

Pale cherry red. Moderately light-bodied. Moderately extracted. Mildly tannic. Red berries, brown spice, minerals. Smooth and juicy mouthfeel, with a soft finish showing lingering brown spice notes. Nicely balanced and very approachable now. A lighter style but well balanced, with a generous character.

1995 Cabernet Sauvignon, Charles Wetmore Reserve,
Livermore Valley $24.　　　　　　　　　　　　　　81
1996 Merlot, Crane Ridge Reserve, Livermore Valley $16.　　84

Deep, saturated ruby red. Generous dusty cherry and mineral aromas. A soft attack leads a medium-bodied palate, with tannic grip and a structured, flavorful finish. Well balanced and intense. Drink now or later. Can improve with more age.

Mark West

1996 Chardonnay, Russian River Valley $15.　　　　　89

Bright yellow-gold. Moderately full-bodied. Full acidity. Moderately extracted. Moderately oaked. Lemons, spice. Bright, zesty aromas show a touch of spice. A crisp, lively mouthful of vibrant flavors grips the palate through the finish.

Whitcraft

1996 Pinot Noir, Bien Nacido Vineyard, Santa Maria Valley $34.99.　　88

Dark red with purple highlights. Medium-bodied. Highly extracted. Heavily oaked. Moderately tannic. Brooding, earthy aromas have a ferric note. Fruity black cherry richness up front gives way to a solid, lingering earthy finish that is not too dry. Well structured, and quite distinctive.

Whitehall Lane

1997 Chardonnay, Napa Valley $16. 84

Brilliant yellow-gold. Smooth smoky aromas. A spicy entry leads a moderately full-bodied palate with alcohol warmth showing through the tart acids. Drink now.

1996 Cabernet Sauvignon, Napa Valley $22. 88

Dark red-violet. Medium-bodied. Highly extracted. Moderately tannic. Ripe berries, vanilla. Very ripe, fruit-laden aromas show rich oak accents that follow through on a rich, softer-styled palate. The finish has ample velvety tannins. Drinking well now.

1994 Cabernet Sauvignon, Morisoli Vineyard Reserve, Napa Valley $36. 92

Opaque, dark ruby purple. Medium-bodied. Highly extracted. Moderately tannic. Cassis, black fruits, tobacco. Impressively generous and concentrated black Cabernet fruit flavors are complemented by lovely sweet tobacco and cedar notes through the finish. Mouthfeel is textured and plush.

1995 Cabernet Sauvignon, Morisoli Vineyard Reserve, Napa Valley $40. 90

Deep ruby purple. Moderately full-bodied. Balanced acidity. Moderately extracted. Heavily oaked. Mildly tannic. Black fruits, vanilla, spice. Quite aromatic, displaying a hefty oak overlay and a dense core of pure black fruit flavors. Concentrated and harmonious, with an overtone of sweetness to the wood flavors through the finish.

1995 Merlot, Napa Valley $20. 88

Deep blackish ruby hue. Balanced acidity. Highly extracted. Moderately oaked. Quite tannic. Chocolate, black fruits, minerals. Deeply flavored though still very tightly wound. Big, aggressive tannins rear up on the finish, but the level of extract should outlast them. Mid-term to long-term (7–10 years) cellaring will help it open up.

1996 Merlot, Napa Valley $22. 88

Semi-saturated brick-red hue. Generously aromatic with toasty vanilla accents on the nose. A lush, supple attack shows generous cherry fruit flavors. Quite oaky on the palate, with softer tannins through the finish. Drink now.

1995 Merlot, Leonardini Vineyard Reserve, Napa Valley $36. 93

Inky ruby hue with a purple cast. Full-bodied. Balanced acidity. Highly extracted. Heavily oaked. Quite tannic. Toasted coconut, black fruits, minerals. Quite attractive aromatically with a big oak overlay. A dense and focused core of fruit presents itself on the rich and velvety palate. Finishes with a wave of thick tannins. Sturdy but well balanced. Mid-term to long-term (7–10 years) cellaring recommended.

1996 Merlot, Leonardini Vineyard Reserve, Napa Valley $40. 92

Well-saturated bright violet red. Ripe fruit-laden aromas with a marked oaky accent. A soft, fruity attack is followed by rounded fruity flavors that fill the midpalate. Finishes with very supple, softer tannins. Drink now.

Wild Horse

1996 Cabernet Sauvignon, Paso Robles $16. 81

1997 Valdigue, Paso Robles $13. 83

Full purple-red. Medium-bodied. Moderately extracted. Mildly tannic. Jammy red fruits, candied berries. Jammy, ripe aromas lead a mildly overripe mouthful of flavors with very soft tannins on the finish.

1995 Grenache, Cienega Valley $13. 84

Pale garnet red with a slight fade. Generous overripe red fruit and mineral aromas. A firm attack leads a moderately light-bodied palate, with mildly astringent tannins. Lean, angular finish. Solid grip but lacks generosity. Drink now.

1995 Merlot, Central Coast $18. 85

Deep blackish ruby hue with brilliant clarity. Medium-bodied. Full acidity. Moderately extracted. Mildly tannic. Black fruits, minerals. Straightforward and well structured, with crisp acidity. Clean, angular finish.

Scale: Superlative (96-100), Exceptional (90-95), Highly Recommended (85-89), Recommended (80-84), Not Recommended (Under 80)

1996 Merlot, Central Coast $16.   **84**

Bright brick red. Lean aromas of minerals and spice. A crisp attack leads a medium-bodied palate with light, grainy tannins. The finish is crisp, with tart fruit flavors persisting nicely. Drink now.

1995 Merlot, Paso Robles $18.   **85**

Deep ruby red with brilliant clarity. Medium-bodied. Balanced acidity. Moderately extracted. Mildly tannic. Black fruits, sweet herbs. Quite focused and very fruit driven. Clean and crisp on the palate, with noticeable acidity and a tart cranberry-accented finish.

1995 Merlot, Unbridled, Paso Robles $28.   **88**

Very deep blackish ruby hue. Moderately full-bodied. Balanced acidity. Moderately extracted. Heavily oaked. Mildly tannic. Leather, black fruits, minerals. Leathery, gamey oak influences mingle with a core of deep fruit flavors. A tad austere on the palate, with a structured, focused mouthfeel. Clean and racy finish.

1996 Mourvedre, James Berry Vineyard, Paso Robles $16.   **86**

Ruby red. Medium-bodied. Moderately extracted. Moderately tannic. Black cherry. Firm and well extracted, with dark fruit flavors giving way to a lengthy finish showing a degree of tannic toughness.

1997 Pinot Noir, Central Coast $19.   **84**

Bright violet red. Medium-bodied. Moderately extracted. Mildly tannic. Flowers, berry fruits, vanilla. Light floral aromas lead a brisk palate, with berry fruit flavors, crisp acids, and subtle vanilla oak notes lingering. Shows a bitter note on the finish.

1996 Syrah, Central Coast $16.   **80**

1996 Syrah, James Berry Vineyard, Paso Robles $18.   **86**

Deep ruby purple, limpid, and brilliant to the rim. Mild, sound herb, mineral, and berry fruit flavors. Subtle wood tones. Firm entry. Moderately full-bodied with crisp acidity. Plentiful grainy tannins. Bright, crisp, and well gripped. Clipped finish. Rather tightly wound, with some tart herbal flavors.

Wildhurst

1996 Sauvignon Blanc, Clear Lake $9.   **81**

1996 Merlot, Clear Lake $14.   **86**

Deep ruby to the rim with brilliant clarity. Medium-bodied. Balanced acidity. Moderately extracted. Mildly tannic. Black fruits, sweet herbs, minerals. Lighter in style, with an angular presence on the palate. The flavors push through some dusty tannins. Pleasant.

1996 Zinfandel, Clear Lake $13.50.   **86**

Bright blackish ruby cast. Moderately full-bodied. Balanced acidity. Moderately extracted. Mildly oaked. Mildly tannic. Black fruits. Fruit-centered and aromatic, with a rich, ripe, lush palate feel. Quite flavorful, with solid length and velvety tannins. Oak nuances come through in the finish.

Windsor

1996 Blanc de Noir, Sonoma County $14.   **82**

1997 Chardonnay, California $10.50.   **81**

1996 Chardonnay, Barrel Fermented, Private Reserve, Russian River Valley $15.   **86**

Bright green-gold. Moderately full-bodied. Full acidity. Moderately extracted. Moderately oaked. Vanilla, spice, lemon zest. Bright lemony aromas show a spicy note that comes through well on the palate with bright citrus-accented flavors.

1997 Chardonnay, Barrel Fermented, Private Reserve, Russian River Valley $16.   **84**

Yellow-gold. Dull nutty aromas show an oak accent. A simple attack leads a medium-bodied palate with subdued apple flavors. Not very clean. Drink now.

1997 Chardonnay, Murphy Ranch, Private Reserve, Alexander Valley $14. **84**

Bright straw hue. Unusual nutty, tropical aromas. A lean entry leads a medium-bodied palate with crisp acidity. The finish is lean and vibrant, with very little oak influence. Well structured. Drink now.

1996 Chardonnay, Preston Ranch, Private Reserve,
Russian River Valley $14. **86**

Bright yellow-gold. Moderately full-bodied. Full acidity. Moderately oaked. Apples, vanilla, yeast. Smoky, yeasty aromas lead a rounded mouthfeel showing silky character and bright Chardonnay fruit flavors.

1997 Chardonnay, Preston Ranch, Private Reserve,
Russian River Valley $15. **82**

1996 Chardonnay, Shelton Signature Series, Russian River Valley $16. **83**

Deep green-gold. Moderately full-bodied. Full acidity. Moderately extracted. Nutmeg, lemon zest. Forcefully spicy aromas lead a deeply flavored though not hugely fruity palate, with heavy oak accents showing.

1997 Chardonnay, Shelton Signature Series, Russian River Valley $17. **81**

1996 Chardonnay, Private Reserve Estate, Russian River Valley $20. **85**

Deep gold-straw hue. Moderately full-bodied. Balanced acidity. Heavily oaked. Brown spice, vanilla, citrus. Rich, broad aromas accented with oak spice lead a nutty, full-flavored palate that has a rich, smooth texture.

1997 Chardonnay, Private Reserve Estate, Russian River Valley $21. **83**

Deep golden yellow. Oak, butter, and apple aromas. A rounded attack leads a moderately full-bodied palate with generous alcohol providing good mouthfeel. The flavors remain clean throughout. Drink now.

1998 Muscat Canelli, Late Harvest, Murphy Ranch,
Alexander Valley $13.50. **85**

Brilliant yellow. Enticing tropical fruit, citrus, and spice aromas. A lush entry leads a rounded, medium-bodied palate showing marked sweetness. Spritzy acidity enlivens the spicy finish. Drink now.

1997 Fumé Blanc, North Coast $9.50. **82**

1997 Fumé Blanc, Private Reserve, Middle Ridge Vineyard,
Mendocino County $11. **82**

1997 Semillon, Private Reserve, North Coast $14. **84**

Bright green-gold. Medium-bodied. Balanced acidity. Moderately extracted. Figs, nuts, kiwi fruit. Striking varietal aromas follow through on a lighter palate with good concentration of flavors and juicy acids. Stylish.

1998 Rosé du Soleil, California $12. **81**

1994 Cabernet Sauvignon, Private Reserve, Alexander Valley $20. **89**

Bright dark ruby hue. Moderately full-bodied. Balanced acidity. Moderately extracted. Moderately oaked. Mildly tannic. Cassis, brown spices. Pleasantly aromatic, showing toasty oak nuances. Firm and lean on the palate, with excellent grip. Angular, juicy finish. Well balanced.

1995 Cabernet Sauvignon, Private Reserve, Alexander Valley $21. **82**

1994 Cabernet Sauvignon, Private Reserve, Mendocino County $22. **86**

Dark red with crimson highlights. Medium-bodied. Moderately extracted. Moderately tannic. Crisp berry fruits, minerals. High-toned berry fruit aromas lead a bright and crisp palate, with solid astringency running through the finish.

1994 Cabernet Sauvignon, Private Reserve, Dry Creek Valley $22. **90**

Bright ruby hue. Medium-bodied. Moderately extracted. Mildly tannic. Crisp black cherries, brown spice. Bright fruity aromas lead an understated palate, with crisp juicy fruit flavors expanding on the midpalate, and a solid, astringent finish highlighted by fine acids.

Scale: Superlative (96-100), Exceptional (90-95), Highly Recommended (85-89), Recommended (80-84), Not Recommended (Under 80)

220

1994 Cabernet Sauvignon, River West Vineyard, Russian River Valley $18. 85
Bright ruby red with a slight fade. Medium-bodied. Balanced acidity. Moderately extracted. Mildly tannic. Minerals, dried leaves, herbs. Pleasantly aromatic, with a wave of early-maturing flavors. Crisp and lean in the mouth, with an angular finish.

1995 Cabernet Sauvignon, River West Vineyard, Russian River Valley $18. 82

1994 Cabernet Sauvignon, Shelton Signature Series, Sonoma County $21. 88
Bright ruby cast. Medium-bodied. Balanced acidity. Moderately extracted. Mildly oaked. Mildly tannic. Minerals, red fruits, vanilla. Pleasantly aromatic, with a firm, fruit-centered palate and a generous oak overlay. Lean and angular through the flavorful finish.

1995 Cabernet Sauvignon, Shelton Signature Series, Sonoma County $22. 89
Deep ruby hue. Reserved, unusual anise and berry aromas. A lean entry leads to a medium-bodied palate with supple tannins and bright acidity. Crisp, spicy finish. Drink now.

1996 Carignane, Mendocino County $10. 89
Dark crimson hue with a purple tinge. Moderately full-bodied. Highly extracted. Mildly tannic. Raspberries, cherries. Smooth and fleshy, with a fruit-centered character. Supple tannins on the finish. Very approachable, though chewy tannins come through on the finish.

1993 Private Reserve Meritage, Sonoma County $22. 86
Full cherry red. Medium-bodied. Highly extracted. Moderately tannic. Bitter chocolate, red berries, minerals. A smoky nose leads crisp red fruit flavors showing great elegance through a lingering dry finish. A harmonious integration of flavors distinguishes this wine.

1995 Private Reserve Meritage, Sonoma County $20. 88
Bright ruby cast. Medium-bodied. Balanced acidity. Moderately extracted. Mildly oaked. Mildly tannic. Minerals, red fruits, brown spices. Aromatically generous and quite flavorful on the palate. Crisp acidity makes for a lively, buoyant quality through the finish.

1995 Merlot, Private Reserve, Sonoma County $18. 86
Deep ruby red to the rim. Medium-bodied. Balanced acidity. Moderately extracted. Mildly oaked. Mildly tannic. Black fruits, minerals, vanilla. Straightforward in character with ripe fruit flavors. Minerally accents lend complexity. Soft and fleshy in the mouth, with some velvety tannins on the finish.

1995 Merlot, Shelton Signature Series, Sonoma County $23.50. 90
Deep blackish ruby hue with brilliant clarity. Moderately full-bodied. Balanced acidity. Highly extracted. Moderately oaked. Moderately tannic. Black fruits, vanilla, mint. Deeply flavored and very New World in style, with a big oak overlay and a sense of sweetness to the ripe fruit flavors. Rich though well balanced, with some chewy tannins and a lengthy finish.

1996 Merlot, Shelton Signature Series, Sonoma County $24.50. 88
Bright violet hue. Aromas of cherry fruits and vanilla. A firm attack is followed by a medium-bodied palate with dry tannins that provide grip. Drink now.

1996 Petite Sirah, North Coast $12. 86
Bright red-purple. Moderately full-bodied. Highly extracted. Moderately tannic. Oak spice, red fruits. Heavily oak-accented aromas have a bright fruit underlay that follows through on the palate. Well balanced, and drinking well now.

1995 Pinot Noir, Private Reserve, North Coast $13. 84
Pale cherry red. Moderately light-bodied. Moderately extracted. Moderately oaked. Mildly tannic. Quite straightforward, with bright cherry fruit accents and a short vanilla-kissed finish.

1995 Pinot Noir, Shelton Signature Series, California $16. 88
Pale cherry red with pinkish highlights. Medium-bodied. Moderately extracted. Moderately oaked. Moderately tannic. Nice vanilla and dried herbal nuances on the nose. Bright, crisp raspberry and cherry flavors fill the palate, with some toasty oak notes lingering through the finish. Quite elegant.

1996 Pinot Noir, Shelton Signature Series, Russian River Valley $16. **80**

1997 Syrah, Private Reserve, Sonoma County $15. **81**

1996 Zinfandel, Sonoma County $9.75. **84**

Bright ruby hue. Medium-bodied. Balanced acidity. Subtly extracted. Mildly oaked. Mildly tannic. Black fruits, spice. Fairly aromatic, with a lighter-styled palate feel. Crisp and flavorful through the finish. Good grip.

1996 Zinfandel, Private Reserve, Mendocino County $13.50. **81**

1996 Zinfandel, Old Vines Private Reserve, Russian River Valley $13.50. **84**

Bright ruby with a slight garnet cast. Medium-bodied. Balanced acidity. Subtly extracted. Mildly oaked. Mildly tannic. Stewed fruits, vanilla. Carries a slightly overripe note in the aromatics and through the palate. Lighter in style, with a soft character. Tasty, but lacks intensity.

1996 Zinfandel, Shelton Signature Series, Alexander Valley $14.50. **86**

Bright blackish ruby cast. Medium-bodied. Balanced acidity. Moderately extracted. Mildly oaked. Mildly tannic. Black fruits, brown spices, minerals. Somewhat reserved in style, with a firm, balanced mouthfeel. Made in more of a Claret style, with elegant interplay between fruit and oak nuances. Shows solid grip through the finish.

Rare Port, California $13. **85**

Deep blackish garnet cast. Moderately full-bodied. Balanced acidity. Moderately extracted. Brown spices, raisins. Made in more of a tawny style, with an obvious wood accent to the flavors. Ripe, thick, and lush. Well-balanced finish with a touch of heat.

1997 Sauvignon Blanc, Murphy Ranch Special Select Late Harvest Private Reserve, Alexander Valley $25. **87**

Bright yellow-gold. Moderately full-bodied. Full acidity. Moderately extracted. Stone fruits, pears. Very aromatic, with pure and expressive fruit flavors. Thick and viscous in the mouth with solid acidity that helps moderate a very sweet finish.

Windwalker

1996 Barbera, Cooper Vineyard, Amador County $12.50. **84**

Bright ruby cast. Medium-bodied. Balanced acidity. Moderately extracted. Mildly oaked. Mildly tannic. Vanilla, red fruits. Rather reserved aromatically, with a flavorful, rounded palate feel. Finishes on a lean note.

1996 Merlot, El Dorado $11.25. **81**

Woodbridge

1996 Chardonnay, Twin Oaks, California $10. **81**

1997 Merlot, California $10. **81**

Woodside

1994 Brut, Santa Cruz Mountains $22. **82**

1993 Cabernet Sauvignon, Santa Cruz Mountains $25. **90**

Bright raspberry red. Medium-bodied. Highly extracted. Mildly tannic. Raspberries, cherries, dried herbs, sweet tobacco. Concentrated crisp red fruit flavors up front expand on the midpalate, with noble fine-grained tannins coating the mouth on the finish. Balanced and approachable now, but it will be better in a few years.

York Mountain Winery

1994 Pinot Noir, William Cain Vineyard, San Luis Obispo County $14. **87**

Pale ruby red. Medium-bodied. Moderately extracted. Mildly oaked. Mildly tannic. Perfumed aromas of jasmine. Mellow, well-integrated flavors of floral red fruits and dry minerals through the finish. Has enough grip for richer foods. Stylish and well balanced.

Scale: Superlative (96-100), Exceptional (90-95), Highly Recommended (85-89), Recommended (80-84), Not Recommended (Under 80)

1996 Zinfandel, San Luis Obispo County $14.   82

Yorkville

1996 Eleanor of Aquitaine, Randle Hill Vineyard, Mendocino $16.   86

Very deep straw cast. Full-bodied. Balanced acidity. Moderately extracted. Moderately oaked. Yeast, toast, citrus, sweet herbs. Aromatic and complex, with a generous yeasty flavor profile. Lush and rich in the mouth, with fine length and intensity.

1997 Semillon, Randle Hill Vineyard, Mendocino $12.   82

1996 Cabernet Franc, Rennie Vineyard, Mendocino County $14.   86

Bright ruby purple. Moderately light-bodied. Full acidity. Subtly extracted. Moderately oaked. Mildly tannic. Cherries, vanilla. Tart and crisp, with bright vanilla-accented fruit flavors. Lean and zesty through the brisk finish.

1995 Richard the Lion-Heart, Mendocino County $20.   88

Saturated bright violet-ruby hue. Medium-bodied. Moderately extracted. Mildly tannic. Minerals, red fruits. Perfumed berry fruit aromas. Linear, angular palate shows a crisp flavor profile, with very spiky, tart acids highlighting the brisk fruit flavors and dusty tannins.

Zabaco

1996 Chardonnay, Russian River Valley $14.   92

Rich gold. Aromatically lush with buttery, leesy, and oaky character showing. A lush attack leads a full-bodied palate with hedonistic texture and concentrated flavors. Finishes with an authoritative oaky accent.

1994 Zinfandel, Sonoma County $9.   85

Deep blackish ruby cast. Moderately full-bodied. Balanced acidity. Moderately extracted. Mildly oaked. Mildly tannic. Black fruits, wood. Pleasantly aromatic, with a distinct woody note throughout. Firm, lean, and angular through the finish. Features some drying wood tannins.

Zaca Mesa

1996 Roussanne, Zaca Vineyards, Santa Barbara County $16.50.   86

Very deep golden cast. Full-bodied. Low acidity. Highly extracted. Mildly oaked. Yeast, toast, minerals. Spicy yeast notes dominate the nose. Quite full on the palate with a rather heavy quality, and a hint of a wood accent on the finish.

1996 Z Cuvée Red, Santa Barbara County $16.50.   84

Cherry red with a slight fade. Generous earth and mineral aromas. A firm attack leads a medium-bodied palate, with drying tannins. Compact, flavorful finish. Shows fine grip and intensity. Drink now.

1996 Syrah, Zaca Vineyards, Santa Barbara County $20.   88

Deep purple, limpid and luminous to the rim. Generous high-toned, crisp, jammy fruit flavors. Subtle wood tones. Firm entry. Moderately full-bodied with crisp acidity. Moderate grainy tannins. Dry and rather lean on the palate. Subtle finish. Concentrated, well extracted, and rather youthful. Drink now or later. Can improve with more age.

Joseph Zakon

1998 Sweet White Muscat, Muscatini, California $8.50.   82

1998 Sweet Red Muscat, Muscatini, California $8.50.   80

Zayante

1995 Zinfandel, Santa Cruz Mountains $14.   87

Deep blackish ruby color. Full-bodied. Full acidity. Highly extracted. Mildly oaked. Quite tannic. Cigars. A pungent, tobacco-tinged nose leads a full-throttled, tannic, acidic mouthfeel. Tough, bracing finish.

ZD

1997 Chardonnay, California $26.   88

Deep straw cast. Moderately full-bodied. Balanced acidity. Moderately extracted. Mildly oaked. Yeast, toast, minerals. Forward aromas carry a distinctive yeasty nuance. Rich in the mouth, yet well balanced by zesty acidity that gives it a solid structure.

1995 Chardonnay, Library Select, California $34.   86

Deep golden hue. Full-bodied. Balanced acidity. Moderately extracted. Moderately oaked. Honey, nuts, cream. Ripe and rich, with generous, exotic aromas and a pronounced yeasty quality. Full and weighty in the mouth, with a lengthy, flavorful finish. Showing some maturity.

1994 Cabernet Sauvignon, Napa Valley $30.   87

Dark, solid red-purple. Moderately full-bodied. Highly extracted. Quite tannic. Earth, black tea, plums. Earthy, austere nose. The palate is solid and well extracted, with strong fine-grained tannins through the finish. Not showing much generosity now, this is a bit of a dormant monster. Needs time.

1996 Cabernet Sauvignon, Napa Valley $38.   84

Saturated dark ruby hue. Generously aromatic with a rich oak accent. A firm entry leads a solid, full-bodied palate with bright acids and firm powdery tannins. Rich and solidly structured, this should improve with age. Drink now.

1993 Cabernet Sauvignon, Reserve, Napa Valley $45.   90

Opaque brickish ruby color. Moderately full-bodied. Highly extracted. Quite tannic. Earth, black tea, mineral, plums. Dark, brooding aromas. The weighty palate show serious extracted flavors and an earthy dry character. Needs plenty of time to soften its components.

1995 Pinot Noir, Carneros $24.   90

Pale ruby-cherry red. Medium-bodied. Moderately extracted. Moderately oaked. Mildly tannic. Perfumed aromas of vanilla and red berry fruits. Silky smooth, with flavors of coffee, licorice, and black fruits. The textured mouthfeel reveals soft tannins and tobacco and spice flavors on the finish.

two

The Wines
of Washington

An Introduction: The Wines of Washington

In a remarkably brief period of time, Washington State has established itself as one of the nation's premier viticultural regions. Boutique wines such as Leonetti, Andrew Will, and Quilceda Creek have enjoyed remarkable success, and are often under severe allocation. While such specialty wines are indeed worth seeking out, there are also some great Washington wines that enjoy wide distribution and consistent supply, while being sold at attractive price points.

Chateau Ste. Michelle, Hogue, and the Columbia Winery broke new ground in Washington in the '70s and early '80s, paving the way for national consumer acceptance of Washington State wines, and the proliferation of boutique wineries in the last decade. Their success was built largely on their ability to produce excellent wines at very attractive prices. While they all still have wide ranging portfolios with many wines still at attractive price points they have also refined and expanded their production at the top end. Vineyard-designated bottlings from Ste. Michelle and Columbia in particular figure among the finest produced in the state, and often the country, vintage after vintage. Furthermore, with their solid distribution networks, these limited-production wines are available both far and wide.

Chateau Ste. Michelle

Largest and probably best known of the trio is Chateau Ste. Michelle, or more accurately, the wine group known as Stimson Lane. Though tracing its roots back to just after Prohibition, Ste. Michelle came into its own in the early '70s and spun off another winery, Columbia Crest, in the early '80s. Both wineries are owned by parent company, Stimson Lane. Since its inception, Columbia Crest has actually outstripped Chateau Ste. Michelle's own production, becoming the largest winery in the Northwest. While Columbia Crest has focused on moderately priced wines, Ste. Michelle has been largely free to pursue a range of premium wines. This has led to the acquisition of some of the state's best vineyard land and the rapid development of a wide range of vineyard-designated wines. In true Ste. Michelle style, success has been swift and spectacular. Wines from Canoe Ridge, Cold Creek, and Horse Heaven Hills have proven exceptional so far, while new bottlings, such as the recent Chateau Reserve line, are being released every year. This has given Stimson Lane, from Columbia Crest through the specialty wines of Ste. Michelle, one of the widest ranging and highest quality portfolios of wine in the nation.

Columbia Winery

Known as Associated Vintners until 1984, Columbia is Washington's oldest continuously operating premium grape winery, dating to 1962. A psychology professor at the University of Washington and a number of his colleagues, whose subsequent research provided much of the impetus for Washington's grape planting boom, founded it. In 1979 David Lake, a Master of Wine, arrived to take on the winemaking duties, and he has been on board ever since. Lake's wines tend to be quite refined in style, and though long lived, recent vintages have been getting more and more accessible in youth. Of particular note are bottlings from the Red Willow Vineyard, one of the state's finest. This property, owned by respected Washington grower Mike Sauer, has been contracted to Columbia for

Scale: Superlative (96-100), Exceptional (90-95), Highly Recommended (85-89), Recommended (80-84), Not Recommended (Under 80)

several years, and provides a number of limited production wines, including what was the state's first commercial Syrah. Further developments should be interesting as this vineyard now contains recent experimental plantings of such exotic varieties as Sangiovese, Nebbiolo, and even Tempranillo.

Hogue Cellars

In 1949 the Hogue family started a farm in the heart of Washington's Yakima Valley. Hops, asparagus, potatoes, and a number of other crops formed the backbone of the family's production until the late '70s when the patriarch's son, Mike Hogue, decided to plant grapes and make wine. A fortuitous decision, as those early wines, produced in a small concrete shed on the property, won quick acclaim. This began what has been a truly meteoric rise, as Hogue is now among the state's largest wineries. In the late '80s their Riesling gained a national following while Chardonnay and Merlot have followed in the '90s. The year 1989 saw the building of a new winery. For the Hogue family, however, this rapid expansion has not greatly changed their refreshing sense of perspective on what for them is just a special part of the family business. Mike Hogue explains, "We've always had a lot of pride in what we produce, but as soon as the crop was brought in and sold, our identity was lost. With wine it's different. It's our wine, with our pride in it, and the family's name on the label." Something, no doubt, many a consumer understands all to well.

Walla Walla and the Canoe Ridge

While Washington's large wineries have made a splendid reputation for producing high quality wines at reasonable prices, the process has come full circle and paved the way for consumer acceptance of the boutique wineries that have sprung up in the last decade. Much attention in particular should be paid to the exciting wines coming from the Walla Walla Valley and Canoe Ridge. This is true not only of the widely successful Merlot but also of Cabernet and Chardonnay along with some interesting varietals such as Syrah and Semillon.

Washington at a Glance

Wines Reviewed:

319

Producers/Brands Represented:

51

The AVA system in Washington is still underdeveloped, with a huge swath of land entitled to use the Columbia Valley appellation. More recently, however, a continuing recognition of the diversity of the state's wines has led to the creation and pursuit of more precise appellations. The Walla Walla Valley, recently recognized as an official appellation, is one such area.

Long home to a famous onion-producing industry (Walla Walla Sweets), the Walla Walla Valley is in the extreme southeastern portion of the state, and spills over the border into northeastern Oregon. This quirk of political map drawing makes Walla Walla one of the very few cross-state appellations in the country. Lying in the rain shadow of the towering Cascades to the west, the area, like all of eastern Washington, is semi-arid. Agriculture is made possible through the use of irrigation. For most this means precisely controlled drip irrigation that puts the water where it is needed, when it is needed, and in the quantities required. Of the potential vineyard acreage in Walla Walla, only a tiny percentage has been planted thus far, making the area's potential for growth quite exciting. The only limiting factor will be ever-growing demands on the Columbia River and its tributaries for water rights.

Leonetti Cellar, founded in 1977, was Walla Walla's first winery, and foreshadowed the development of the area as a boutique wine haven. Walla Walla wines tend to be lush and endearing with a heavy reliance on oak seasoning. The Merlots of Leonetti, Waterbrook, L'Ecole No. 41, Patrick M. Paul, and the like are highly coveted and eminently accessible. As for Chardonnay, many of the wines swing for the fences, but can always rely on the telltale acidity that Washington wines usually possess for balance. It must be noted that similarities among the area's wines have much to do with winemaking practices, as many of these wineries' bottlings utilize grapes grown outside the Walla Walla Valley. As opposed to offering proof of Walla Walla's supremacy for grape growing, the region's wines actually show how a close-knit winemaking community has helped with the exchange of ideas and allowed the enological equivalent of an artistic colony to develop.

Unlike Walla Walla, the wines of a new micro-appellation (as yet unofficial), Canoe Ridge, owe their startling quality to the region itself, in addition to the skill of the winemakers. Lying well to the west of Walla Walla on the banks of the Columbia River, Canoe Ridge is a 1,000 foot hill rising from the river and looking out over the barren scrub land on the Oregon side. Named by Lewis and Clark on a 19th century expedition through the area, the hill resembles an overturned canoe. It is jointly owned, in its entirety, by Chateau Ste. Michelle and the Canoe Ridge Winery, a member of the prestigious Chalone family of wineries. Planted only in the late '80s, it would be an understatement to say that the initial releases have shown promise. They are already some of the best Merlots in the state and the country, while the Chardonnays have proven exceptional as well. Somewhat more restrained than many Walla Walla wines, Canoe Ridge wines show attractive fruit, while being relatively elegant and restrained. As an added bonus the wines are blessedly devoid of harsh tannins.

With Washington wines on the whole that's much of the idea. Often referred to as one-third California and two-thirds Bordeaux, the region's wines offer the ripe and forward qualities of fine New World wines with the crispness and drinkable structure of the Old. Never overpowering or alcoholic, Washington wines are best defined in one word: balance.

Reviews

Apex

1997 Chardonnay, Columbia Valley $17.99.   90

Yellow-straw hue. Spicy oak-accented aromas. A buttery entry leads a moderately full-bodied palate with ripe, fruity flavors. Finishes with a hint of dryness and plenty of spicy oak. This is a well-balanced wine, with fine acids. Drink now or later.

1997 Dry Gewürztraminer, Barrel Fermented, Columbia Valley $13.   80

1994 Cabernet Sauvignon, Columbia Valley $35.   90

Saturated brick red. Moderately full-bodied. Highly extracted. Moderately tannic. Cassis, oak spice, earth. Chocolatey dark fruit aromas lead a tight, packed palate showing rich, dry tannins and earthy intensity. Well structured, this could improve with further age.

1995 Cabernet Sauvignon, Columbia Valley $35.   89

Saturated violet-purple hue. Aromas show a pure cassis fruit expression with marked oak influence. A flavorful, fruity entry leads to a moderately full-bodied palate with supple cabernet tannins gripping the finish. Fruit flavors persist well through the finish. Drink now or later.

1994 Merlot, Columbia Valley $28.99.   92

Dark cherry red. Moderately full-bodied. Highly extracted. Moderately oaked. Moderately tannic. Reminiscent of cedar, tobacco, plums. Rich plummy nose leads a fleshy, rounded palate with hugely attractive spice and tobacco notes through the lengthy finish.

1995 Merlot, Columbia Valley $40.   92

Deep blackish ruby hue to the rim with brilliant highlights. Medium-bodied. Balanced acidity. Highly extracted. Moderately oaked. Mildly tannic. Red fruits, oriental spice, minerals. Quite aromatic, with an extremely complex array of flavors on the palate. Well integrated, finely wrought, and elegant in style, with solid balance and a pleasant, harmonious finish.

1996 Merlot, Columbia Valley $35.   87

Rich ruby red with a slight fade. Powerful cedar and spice aromas show a dominant wood accent. A rich, rounded attack leads a moderately full-bodied palate with chewy, velvety tannins. The finish is supple and flavorful. A generous and mellow wine. Drink within five years.

1995 Pinot Noir, Willamette Valley $20.   89

Bright reddish purple. Medium-bodied. Moderately extracted. Mildly tannic. Reminiscent of strawberries, raspberries. Crisp and clean, with bright fruit. Flavors are subtle with a nice but mildly astringent finish. Eminently quaffable.

1996 Pinot Noir, Willamette Valley $20.   80

1996 Pinot Noir, Washington $20.   84

Bright ruby cast. Medium-bodied. Balanced acidity. Moderately extracted. Mildly oaked. Moderately tannic. Dried herbs, chocolate, earth. Aggressive herbal aromas lead a lush mouthfeel of some substance. Fine-grained tannins on the finish.

1997 Gewürztraminer, Ice Wine, Columbia Valley $35/375 ml.   92

Deep yellow-straw hue. Intense, pure tropical fruit and toasted coconut aromas. A rich entry leads a sweet, medium-bodied palate balanced by a firm edge of acidity. Shows great length and intensity through the finish. Drink now.

Arbor Crest

1996 Sauvignon Blanc, Washington $7.25.   86

Pale straw hue. Medium-bodied. Balanced acidity. Moderately extracted. White peach, apples. Ripe fruity aromas with a slight tropical edge. Juicy and clean on the palate with decent mouthfeel and no use of oak evident.

1995 Cabernet Sauvignon, Cameo Reserve, Washington $13.   **87**

Blood red with violet highlights. Moderately full-bodied. Highly extracted. Moderately tannic. Dried herbs, red fruits. Subtle, mildly herbal aromas lead a gently fruity palate. A lean style with mild tannins showing on the finish.

Badger Mountain

1995 Merlot, Columbia Valley $14.   **81**

Barnard Griffin

1997 Chardonnay, Washington $12.95.   **88**

Bright golden hue. Moderately full-bodied. Full acidity. Moderately extracted. Moderately oaked. Brown spices, butter, citrus. Generous aromas carry a judicious oak accent. Crisp and zesty, with a vibrant core of minerally, fruity flavors that remain refreshing through the finish.

1996 Chardonnay, Reserve, Columbia Valley $17.95.   **86**

Deep yellow-straw cast. Moderately full-bodied. Full acidity. Moderately extracted. Mildly oaked. Brown spices, butter, minerals. Forward aromas carry a subtle oak accent to a core of firm citric flavors. Crisp and lean through the finish.

1995 Cabernet Sauvignon, Washington $16.95.   **87**

Bright cherry red. Medium-bodied. Moderately extracted. Mildly tannic. Black cherries, minerals. Bright, juicy aromas follow through on a velvety palate with elegant tannins. Supremely drinkable.

1996 Cabernet Sauvignon, Columbia Valley $16.95.   **91**

Saturated bright violet-purple hue. Youthful aromas show primary character of black fruits and oak spice. Bright lively attack leads to a medium-bodied palate with focused cassis fruit flavors and grainy, gripping tannins. A very youthful, somewhat tough wine. Drink now or later.

1995 Merlot, Washington $16.95.   **87**

Very deep ruby hue to the rim. Medium-bodied. Balanced acidity. Moderately extracted. Mildly oaked. Mildly tannic. Red fruits, minerals, pencil shavings. Well balanced, with complex yet integrated flavors, though a tad austere in the mouth. Lengthy finish. A very solid food wine.

1997 Merlot, Columbia Valley $16.95.   **84**

Brilliant purple-red to the rim. Perfumed berry and mineral aromas. A crisp attack leads a moderately light-bodied palate with firm tannins. Bright, flavorful, zesty finish. A well-balanced, tasty, lighter-styled wine. Drink within five years.

1997 Merlot, Ciel du Cheval Vineyard, Columbia Valley $39.   **89**

Bright purple-red to the rim. Attractive floral, spice, and red fruit aromas show a moderate oak accent. A crisp attack leads a medium-bodied palate with lean tannins. The finish is ripe and flavorful. Almost delicate in style, but well balanced and full of flavor. Drink now or later. Can improve with more age.

1994 Merlot, Reserve, Columbia Valley $24.   **92**

Deep reddish purple. Medium-bodied. Highly extracted. Moderately oaked. Mildly tannic. Reminiscent of raspberries, toasted oak, brown spices. Very distinctive nose of ripe fruits. Nice toasty notes accent the fruity palate, with an elegant finish.

1995 Merlot, Reserve, Columbia Valley $26.95.   **90**

Very deep blackish ruby color. Medium-bodied. Balanced acidity. Moderately extracted. Moderately oaked. Mildly tannic. Bacon, brown spices, red fruits. Quite aromatic, with a concentrated wave of flavors on the palate. Well-balanced and elegant mouthfeel, with fine length and some dusty tannins on the finish.

Bookwalter

1997 Chardonnay, Columbia Valley $8.   86

Bright straw cast. Medium-bodied. Full acidity. Moderately extracted. Minerals, citrus. Clean and focused, with pure fruit flavors. Zesty, angular, and refreshing through the finish.

1997 Chardonnay, Vintner's Select, Washington $18.   88

Pale straw hue. Ripe apple, smoky aromas. A smooth attack leads a moderately full-bodied palate with a weighty mouthfeel and toasted oak flavors that persist through the finish. Texturally impressive, with a marked oak accent. Drink now.

1998 Chenin Blanc, Washington $6.   81

1998 Johannisberg Riesling, Washington $6.   81

NV Red, Washington $10.   83

Full brick red with a garnet cast. Medium-bodied. Moderately extracted. Moderately tannic. Dried herbs, earth. Herbal, mature aromas follow through on the palate, with dusty, dry tannins making for a lean finish.

1996 Cabernet Sauvignon, Vintner's Select, Washington $39.   84

Deep ruby red hue. Generous spice, mineral, and red fruit aromas. A firm attack leads to a moderately full-bodied palate with robust grippy tannins. Angular, austere finish. Well flavored, but rough. Drink within five years.

1995 Merlot, Washington $15.   80

W.B. Bridgman

1997 Chardonnay, Columbia Valley $10.99.   86

Yellow-straw hue. Aromas of yellow apples and butter. A soft entry leads a moderately full-bodied palate with fruit-centered flavors and soft acids that make for a quick finish. The mouthfeel shows a full buttery quality. Drink now.

1994 Cabernet Sauvignon, Columbia Valley $15.   88

Full cherry red. Medium-bodied. Moderately extracted. Moderately tannic. Juicy red fruits, vanilla, toasted oak. Nice spice and vanilla nose. Crisp and juicy, with a firm, astringent finish. The dry and austere style may not be to everyone's taste, but it is sure to match well with richer foods.

1995 Cabernet Sauvignon, Columbia Valley $13.99.   87

Deep red-violet. Medium-bodied. Highly extracted. Moderately tannic. Mineral, oak spice. Austere aromas show oak spice accents. Dry, lean flavors have some Cabernet fruit character, with minerals defining the finish.

1996 Cabernet Sauvignon, Columbia Valley $14.   86

Brick red with a fading rim. Aromatically reserved with tertiary, mature character. A lean entry leads a moderately full-bodied palate with muted fruit flavors and tart acidity. Drink now.

1994 Merlot, Columbia Valley $14.99.   83

Cherry red. Moderately full-bodied. Moderately extracted. Moderately oaked. Reminiscent of cedar, herbs, black cherry. Crisp herbal-accented nose leads a firm, slightly austere palate with an imposing finish. Fairly assertive.

1995 Merlot, Columbia Valley $14.99.   85

Very dark ruby hue to the rim. Medium-bodied. Balanced acidity. Moderately extracted. Mildly oaked. Mildly tannic. Minerals, red fruits. Still a bit unyielding aromatically, with a youthful character. Well balanced, though somewhat austere on the palate, this wine should work quite well with food.

1996 Merlot, Washington $16.   82

1997 Syrah, Columbia Valley $18.   88

Bright purple-red to the rim. Subdued red fruit and mineral aromas show a mild wood accent. A crisp attack leads a medium-bodied palate, with tannic grip and bright acidity, and a snappy, flavorful finish. Clean and stylish, with cool climate varietal intensity. Drink now.

Canoe Ridge Vineyard

1997 Chardonnay, Columbia Valley $14.   88
Brilliant yellow-gold. Ripe but very subtle oaky aromas. A creamy attack leads a medium-bodied palate that has a lush, textured mouthfeel. Finishes with good fruit persistence. Drink now.

1995 Cabernet Sauvignon, Columbia Valley $22.   90
Dark ruby red with a subtle fade to the rim. Dark fruited aromas with anise notes and a perception of oak. A firm entry leads to a full-bodied palate with firm tannins gripping the finish. Quite structured and gripping on the finish. Drink now or later.

1994 Merlot, Columbia Valley $18.   90
Deep cherry red with a light garnet cast. Moderately full-bodied. Moderately extracted. Moderately tannic. Reminiscent of red fruits, brown spice, dried herbs. Austere nose. Lively ripe fruit on entry with supple tannins through the finish give this a rounded character. Fashioned in a balanced, subtle mold.

1995 Merlot, Columbia Valley $18.   89
Very deep blackish ruby hue to the rim. Moderately full-bodied. Balanced acidity. Highly extracted. Mildly oaked. Mildly tannic. Chocolate, minerals, red fruits. Still a bit closed, with a youthful core of dense, chewy flavors. Pleasantly textured and a bit thick, but well balanced. Should mellow and open with mid-term (3–6 years) aging.

1996 Merlot, Columbia Valley $19.   88
Rich garnet red. Muted spice and mineral aromas show a modest wood accent. A lush attack leads a moderately full-bodied palate with drying, astringent tannins. The finish has plenty of flavor, though it is slightly tough. Drink within five years.

Cascade Ridge

1997 Chardonnay, Columbia Valley $15.   82
1996 Cabernet Sauvignon, Columbia Valley $19.99.   80
1995 Merlot, Columbia Valley $19.99.   80

Caterina

1997 Chardonnay, Columbia Valley $15.   86
Pale yellow-gold. Ripe aromas of butter and yellow apples, showing judicious oak influences. A rich attack leads a moderately full-bodied palate with a glycerous, smooth mouthfeel and juicy apple flavors through the clean finish. Drink now.

1997 Sauvignon Blanc, Columbia Valley $11.   81
1995 Cabernet Sauvignon, Columbia Valley $19.   87
Full blackish red with purple highlights. Medium-bodied. Moderately extracted. Mildly tannic. Tart cherry, currant, minerals. A bright fruity impression on entry is carried by good acids, but the main impression is of minerally concentration and fine austerity through a long finish. Drinking well now.

1995 Cabernet Sauvignon, Wahluke Slope Vineyard Reserve, Columbia Valley $32.   88
Dark ruby hue with purple highlights. Medium-bodied. Moderately extracted. Moderately tannic. Lemons, red fruits, tobacco. Bright acids give this an assertive palate with crisp, full fruity flavors. Fine concentration and persistence through the finish. Shows a fine earthy "gout de terroir" throughout.

1994 Merlot, Columbia Valley $16.   89
Dark red appearance. Medium-bodied. Highly extracted. Moderately tannic. Reminiscent of black tea, plums, minerals. Dark fruity aromas with some dry accents. A well-structured palate with concentrated flavors and fine astringent tannins through the finish.

1995 Merlot, Columbia Valley $18.   80

Scale: Superlative (96-100), Exceptional (90-95), Highly Recommended (85-89), Recommended (80-84), Not Recommended (Under 80)

1996 Merlot, Columbia Valley $18.   88

Bright garnet red. Generous spice and red fruit aromas belie a forward wood accent.
A crisp attack is followed by a medium-bodied, substantive palate with firm tannins and
a flavorful, lingering finish. Rather light in style, but it has some grip and is quite tasty.
Drink within five years.

Chateau Ste. Michelle

1996 Chardonnay, Columbia Valley $14.   86

Bright yellow-straw cast. Moderately full-bodied. Balanced acidity. Moderately extracted.
Mildly oaked. Minerals, citrus, cream. Aromatically reserved, with a generous rounded
texture. The finish is crisp.

1996 Chardonnay, Canoe Ridge Estate Vineyard, Columbia Valley $28.   88

Bright yellow-straw cast. Moderately full-bodied. Full acidity. Moderately extracted.
Minerals, yeast, toast. Aromatically reserved, showing lean, minerally flavors in the
mouth. Texturally interesting, with a sense of lushness and a zesty, angular finish.

1996 Chardonnay, Cold Creek Vineyard, Columbia Valley $26.   90

Bright yellow-straw cast. Moderately full-bodied. Balanced acidity. Moderately extracted.
Mildly oaked. Brown spices, minerals, citrus. Generous aromatics feature a hint of oak.
Firm and flavorful in the mouth, with a core of steely fruit flavors that persist through
a lengthy, vibrant finish.

1996 Chardonnay, Indian Wells Vineyard, Columbia Valley $26.   92

Bright yellow-gold. Moderately full-bodied. Full acidity. Moderately extracted. Mildly
oaked. Minerals, brown spices. Aromatically reserved, with a firm and concentrated
palate feel. Opens up toward the finish, with a hint of oak. Should develop further with
some short-term (1–2 years) to mid-term (3–6 years) cellaring.

1996 Chardonnay, Reserve, Columbia Valley $31.   89

Bright straw cast. Medium-bodied. Full acidity. Moderately extracted. Minerals, citrus zest.
Clean, crisp, and angular, with a sense of reserved richness. Firm and weighty through
the steely, angular finish.

1996 Sauvignon Blanc, Barrel Fermented, Columbia Valley $10.   83

Bright pale straw hue. Medium-bodied. Balanced acidity. Moderately extracted. Mildly
oaked. Peach, sweet herbs. Sweet herbal and ripe citrus aromas. Fruity and forward, with
very subtle toasty oak notes that stay in the background.

1996 Sauvignon Blanc, Horse Haven Vineyard, Columbia Valley $15.   84

Pale straw cast. Medium-bodied. Balanced acidity. Moderately extracted. Lime, dried
herbs, minerals. Subtle herbal aromas with high-toned citrus notes. Bright and lively on
the palate, with a clean finish.

1994 Cabernet Sauvignon, Columbia Valley $16.   85

Deep garnet red. Medium-bodied. Moderately extracted. Quite tannic. Plums, currants,
minerals, brown spice. Rich, ripe black fruit aromas are confirmed on the palate. Some
tough angular tannins come through on the finish, giving an assertive character. Best
with rich foods.

1995 Cabernet Sauvignon, Columbia Valley $16.   90

Dark purple-red. Medium-bodied. Moderately extracted. Moderately tannic. Cassis, oak
spice. Generous aromas. Textured and rich, with polished flavors and powdery tannins.
Shows textbook Cabernet character.

1996 Cabernet Sauvignon, Columbia Valley $16.   90

Dark ruby hue with a violet cast. Muted aromas show an anise and dark chocolate note.
A firm entry leads a moderately full-bodied palate with inky, austere flavors. Nice finish.
Should age well.

1995 Cabernet Sauvignon, Cold Creek Vineyard, Columbia Valley $27.   95

Bright violet-red with a subtle fade to the rim. Medium-bodied. Moderately extracted.
Moderately tannic. Cassis, mineral, oak spice. Bright Cabernet fruit aromas show through
on the nose and follow up on the palate, with supple tannins on the finish, and fine,
minerally intensity throughout. Nice now, though this will age further.

1995 Cabernet Sauvignon, Horse Heaven Vineyard, Columbia Valley $27.   **94**

Bright purple-red. Moderately full-bodied. Highly extracted. Moderately tannic. Vanilla, ripe black cherries. Perfumed, oak-accented nose. Fleshy primary fruit flavors up front give way to silky tannins that progress through a dry finish. Intense and generous.

1994 Ethos Red, Columbia Valley $31.   **90**

Saturated cherry red with purple highlights. Medium-bodied. Highly extracted. Moderately tannic. Vanilla, ripe cherries, cassis, chocolate. Ripe chocolatey aromas lead a concentrated palate, with full, ripe flavors and fine-grained tannins on the finish. Impressively structured.

1994 Artist Series Red Meritage, Columbia Valley $50.   **91**

Dark crimson red with subtle purple highlights. Moderately full-bodied. Highly extracted. Moderately tannic. Toasted oak, brown spice, cassis, black fruits. A restrained toasty nose hints at richness that comes through on the palate. Fine-textured mouthfeel. Rich layered tannins taper through the finish. Big in all departments, with great structure.

1995 Artist Series Red Meritage, Columbia Valley $50.   **94**

Deep violet red. Moderately full-bodied. Moderately extracted. Moderately tannic. Cassis, mineral, oak spice. Supremely elegant aromas reveal a sumptuously textured, intense palate with a degree of persistence and length on the finish that shows its class. Very nice now, though this has all the elements to age further.

1994 Merlot, Columbia Valley $17.   **87**

Deep cherry red. Moderately full-bodied. Highly extracted. Quite tannic. Reminiscent of black fruits, tea. A solid mouthful with rich fruit accents under a layer of imposing tannins. Quite tough at present but structurally sound. This should age well.

1996 Merlot, Columbia Valley $18.   **88**

Bright, saturated ruby red. Subdued red fruit aromas. A lush attack leads a medium-bodied palate with lean tannins. The finish is flavorful and clean. A tasty effort in a lighter style, showing a bit of an edge to its tannins. Drink now.

1995 Merlot, Canoe Ridge Estate Vineyard, Columbia Valley $31.   **90**

Deep blackish ruby hue with brilliant clarity. Medium-bodied. Balanced acidity. Moderately extracted. Moderately oaked. Moderately tannic. Black fruits, vanilla, licorice. Pleasantly aromatic, with a lighter-styled palate and firm structure. Well balanced and finely wrought, though still a bit tight, with a lengthy finish nonetheless. Near-term cellaring might be helpful in resolving some scrappy tannins.

1994 Merlot, Cold Creek Vineyard, Columbia Valley $28.   **92**

Intense dark red with purple highlights. Full-bodied. Highly extracted. Heavily oaked. Moderately tannic. Reminiscent of cedar, pine, black fruits, tea. Deep, dark fruit and oak accents in the nose. Solid, dense palate with fruity depth and a firm but lengthy finish. Highly structured, though a bit tight for current enjoyment.

1995 Merlot, Horse Heaven Vineyard, Columbia Valley $31.   **88**

Very deep ruby red with a slight purplish cast. Medium-bodied. Balanced acidity. Moderately extracted. Mildly oaked. Mildly tannic. Minerals, red fruits, sweet herbs. Still a bit closed, with a touch of austerity on the palate. Elegant and well balanced, this is a solid table wine.

1994 Merlot, Indian Wells Vineyard, Columbia Valley $30.   **90**

Deep crimson color. Moderately full-bodied. Highly extracted. Moderately oaked. Moderately tannic. Reminiscent of black fruits, tea, chocolate. Silky entry with deep fruity flavors gives way to textured tannins through a lengthy, firm toasty finish. Elegant and generously proportioned, with enough structure to cellar well.

1995 Merlot, Indian Wells Vineyard, Columbia Valley $31.   **85**

Very deep blackish ruby hue. Medium-bodied. Balanced acidity. Highly extracted. Mildly oaked. Quite tannic. Minerals, red fruits. Quite closed and compact, with an angular feeling to the lighter-styled palate. Finishes with a wave of astringent tannins.

Scale: Superlative (96-100), Exceptional (90-95), Highly Recommended (85-89), Recommended (80-84), Not Recommended (Under 80)

234

1994 Merlot, Chateau Reserve, Columbia Valley $40.　　　　**96**

Very deep reddish purple. Full-bodied. Highly extracted. Moderately oaked. Quite tannic. Reminiscent of black fruits, licorice, tea, brown spice. Rich, brooding dark fruit nose. Solid, generously textured mouthfeel with great depth and full layered tannins through the finish. Substantial and structured. Though drinking nicely now, this could be cellared.

1995 Merlot, Chateau Reserve, Columbia Valley $42.　　　　**92**

Very deep ruby hue with brilliant clarity. Moderately full-bodied. Balanced acidity. Moderately extracted. Moderately oaked. Mildly tannic. Vanilla, red fruits, minerals. Still a bit reined-in aromatically, this youthful wine is lighter in style on the palate. Chalky tannins intrude on the palate, but the flavors expand through the finish. Mid-term cellaring should round it out and provide more complexity, though it is tasty now.

1995 Syrah, Reserve, Columbia Valley $28.　　　　**85**

Bright purple-red to the rim. Subdued earth and black fruit aromas show a subtle wood accent. A soft attack leads a moderately full-bodied palate showing velvety tannins. Lush, earthy finish. Interesting, but somewhat lacking in acidic grip. Drink now.

1995 Semillon, Late Harvest, Reserve, Columbia Valley $20.　　　　**87**

Deep bronzed golden hue. Full-bodied. Balanced acidity. Moderately extracted. Moderately oaked. Tropical fruits, pears, honey. Oak aromas, with a rich and viscous core of buttressing tropical fruit flavors. Luxuriant and velvety with a hint of acidity that keeps the sweetness in balance.

Chinook
1993 Merlot, Yakima Valley $21.50.　　　　**84**

Deep cherry red. Medium-bodied. Moderately extracted. Mildly tannic. Reminiscent of raspberries, dried herbs. Huge herb- and berry-scented nose. Ripe, fleshy fruit accent on the palate lingers through a soft finish. Very attractive now.

Claar
1997 Chardonnay, Columbia Valley $10.99.　　　　**87**

Brilliant yellow-gold. Heavy buttery aromas. A rich attack leads a full-bodied palate with broad, ripe apple flavors and full buttery qualities. This is a big, flavorful style with good acid balance. Very structured and tight, maybe further age will enhance it. Drink now or later.

1997 Dry Riesling, Columbia Valley $5.99.　　　　**81**

1997 White Riesling, Columbia Valley $5.99.　　　　**83**

Pale straw hue. Clean aromas of citrus zest and minerals. An off-dry entry leads a medium-bodied palate, with juicy acids and a quick finish. Drink now.

1997 Riesling, Botrytisized Ice Wine, Columbia Valley $29.99/375 ml.　　　　**90**

Brilliant pale amber hue. Forward spice and pear aromas. A rich entry leads a viscous, moderately full-bodied palate. Quite sweet, with rounded acidity. Polished and supple. Drink now.

Columbia Crest
1997 Chardonnay, Columbia Valley $9.　　　　**86**

Medium pale straw hue. Moderate aromas of butter, citrus, and oak spice. A crisp entry leads a medium-bodied palate with tangy fruit and brown spice flavors that linger on the finish. Nice texture and mouthfeel. Drink now.

1997 Chardonnay, Estate Series, Columbia Valley $14.　　　　**88**

Full yellow-gold. Aromatically complex with butterscotch and vanilla character. A smoky entry leads a moderately full-bodied palate with assertive smoke and toasty oak flavors that are well integrated with fruity, buttery character. Acids are balanced through the oak-spiced finish. Very stylish, layered, and complex.

1996 Chardonnay, Reserve, Columbia Valley $18.   88

Bright yellow-straw cast. Moderately full-bodied. Balanced acidity. Moderately extracted.
Minerals, citrus. Crisp, subtly oaky aromas, and a ripe, generous mouthfeel. Shows lean
flavors, with a hint of wood to the finish.

1996 Semillon-Chardonnay, Columbia Valley $8.   83

Pale straw hue. Moderately light-bodied. Balanced acidity. Moderately extracted. Citrus
zest, minerals. Faint lemon zest aromas follow through on a light, crisp palate without a
lot of fruit flavors.

1996 Sauvignon Blanc, Estate Series, Columbia Valley $9.   86

Pale yellow-gold. Medium-bodied. Balanced acidity. Moderately extracted. Mildly oaked.
Smoke, butter, citrus. Soft and juicy, with a layer of mildly smoky oak flavors. Rounded,
textured mouthfeel and lengthy finish.

1995 Cabernet Sauvignon, Columbia Valley $11.   83

Full ruby red. Medium-bodied. Moderately extracted. Moderately tannic. Cordial,
minerals, oak spice. Ripe, jammy aromas follow through on the palate, with some
firmness and spice on the finish.

1994 Cabernet Sauvignon, Estate Series, Columbia Valley $17.   89

Deep blood red. Medium-bodied. Moderately extracted. Mildly tannic. Brown spice,
black fruits, minerals. Fleshy, ripe black fruit aromas follow through well on the palate.
A lush entry turns dry, with minerally grip on the finish. Drinking very well now.

1995 Cabernet Sauvignon, Estate Series, Columbia Valley $21.   88

Deep brick red hue with a subtle browning rim. Ripe aromas show developed
character. A rich entry leads a full-bodied palate with chewy black fruits and a dry
anise-like finish with lingering chocolatey notes. Quite mature at present, though
this can develop further. Drink now or later.

1994 Reserve Red, Columbia Valley $20.   89

Dark blood red with a garnet cast. Medium-bodied. Highly extracted. Quite tannic.
Earth, brown spice, black tea, black fruits. Rich toasted oak nose. Concentrated spicy
black fruit flavors, with rustic tannins on the finish. A little tough now; hopefully time
will help.

1995 Reserve Red, Columbia Valley $22.   89

Saturated dark ruby red hue. Ripe, somewhat nutty, oak-influenced aromas. A firm attack
leads a moderately full-bodied palate with dry tannins and focused fruit flavors finishing
with a complex oak-spiced note. Drink now or later.

1996 Merlot, Columbia Valley $16.   89

Bright, deep ruby red to the rim. Generous vanilla and red fruit aromas show a forward
oak accent. A lush attack leads a moderately full-bodied mouthfeel with firm tannins and
a rounded, flavorful finish. Forward and quite drinkable. Drink now.

1994 Merlot, Estate Series, Columbia Valley $19.   88

Very deep ruby red to the rim with brilliant clarity. Moderately full-bodied. Balanced
acidity. Highly extracted. Moderately oaked. Moderately tannic. Red fruits, brown
spices. Fruit and wood nuances have intertwined to form a harmonious whole. Quite
firmly structured, with a lash of tannin at the finish. Should mellow with mid-term
(3–6 years) aging.

1995 Merlot, Estate Series, Columbia Valley $22.   90

Rich ruby red with a slight fade. Powerful spice, red fruit, and mineral aromas carry
a prominent oak accent. A rich attack leads a supple, moderately full-bodied palate
displaying velvety tannins. The finish is lengthy and flavorful. Generous and well
rounded, with a nice balance between oak and fruit flavors. Drink within five years.

1996 Syrah, Reserve, Columbia Valley $22.   90

Bright, deep ruby red to the rim. Perfumed red fruit and vanilla aromas carry a generous
oak accent. A soft attack leads a medium-bodied palate, with silky tannins and buoyant
acidity. The finish is persistent and flavorful. Very modern in style, with a hedonistic and
eminently drinkable personality. Drink now.

Columbia Winery

1996 Chardonnay, Otis Vineyard, Yakima Valley $19.　　　　　**91**

Bright yellow-straw cast. Moderately full-bodied. Full acidity. Moderately extracted. Moderately oaked. Brown spices, citrus, minerals. Aromatically complex, with a range of fruit, yeast, and wood influences. All are carried on a lean and vibrant frame that provides a refreshing and well-balanced finish.

1996 Chardonnay, Wyckoff Vineyard, Yakima Valley $19.　　　　　**90**

Bright yellow-gold. Moderately full-bodied. Full acidity. Moderately extracted. Mildly oaked. Vanilla, citrus, minerals. Aromatically generous, with a firm core of citric flavors accented by judicious use of oak. Zesty and intense with a lengthy finish.

1998 Gewürztraminer, Yakima Valley $6.　　　　　**86**

Bright straw hue. Generous spice and honeyed melon aromas. A rich entry leads a medium-bodied palate showing marked sweetness offset by crisp acidity. Clean, well-balanced finish. Drink now.

1996 Pinot Gris, Yakima Valley $10.99.　　　　　**85**

Bright golden cast. Medium-bodied. Full acidity. Highly extracted. Minerals, grapefruit zest. Rather unyielding in aromatics, with a clean, racy, mildly bitter palate feel. A buttery note emerges in the finish.

1995 Semillon, Columbia Valley $9.　　　　　**82**

1996 Semillon, Reserve Sur Lie, Columbia Valley $10.99.　　　　　**80**

1995 Cabernet Franc, Red Willow Vineyard, David Lake Signature Series, Yakima Valley $20.99.　　　　　**86**

Bright ruby cast. Moderately full-bodied. Full acidity. Moderately extracted. Mildly oaked. Moderately tannic. Earth, minerals. Lean and reserved, with a firm, minerally character. Quite linear through the vibrant finish. A solid table wine.

1996 Cabernet Franc, Red Willow Vineyard, avid Lake Signature Series, Yakima Valley $19.　　　　　**86**

Bright ruby hue. Attractive candied cherry and spice aromas. A firm attack leads a medium-bodied palate that shows lean, gripping tannins. The finish is firm and angular. Tightly wound and focused, with a crisp, sturdy structure. Drink now or later. Can improve with more age.

1994 Cabernet Sauvignon, Otis Vineyard, David Lake Signature Series, Yakima Valley $23.　　　　　**93**

Saturated blood red. Moderately full-bodied. Highly extracted. Moderately tannic. Cassis, mineral, spice. Intense and rich, with supple tannins and extraordinary purity of flavors that persist for a mile on the finish.

1995 Cabernet Sauvignon, Otis Vineyard, David Lake Signature Series, Yakima Valley $24.　　　　　**83**

Pale ruby-red hue. Oak accents are very pronounced on the nose. A vibrant entry leads a medium-bodied palate with oak astringency dominating the flavors. Finishes with a note of bitterness. Drink now.

1994 Cabernet Sauvignon, Red Willow Vineyard, David Lake Signature Series, Yakima Valley $23.　　　　　**91**

Deep cherry red with a bright rim. Medium-bodied. Highly extracted. Moderately tannic. Red berries, pomegranate. Exotic primary fruit aromas follow through on the palate, showing intensity that is matched by ultra-fine, dry tannins. Very silky.

1995 Cabernet Sauvignon, Red Willow Vineyard, David Lake Signature Series, Yakima Valley $29.　　　　　**89**

Saturated violet hue. Anise and earth aromas show little fruit generosity. A firm entry leads a moderately full-bodied palate, with dry, powdery tannins through the finish. This seems rather tough at present, but will soften nicely.

1994 Cabernet Sauvignon, Sagemoor Vineyard, David Lake Signature Series, Columbia Valley $23.   88

Deep ruby red. Moderately full-bodied. Highly extracted. Moderately tannic. Cordial, black fruits, spice. Very ripe dark fruit aromas have a jammy note that follows through with very generous flavors and fine persistence. Tannins show a powdery quality.

1995 Cabernet Sauvignon, Reserve, Yakima Valley $15.   88

Deep ruby-violet hue with a subtle fade. Richly fruited aromas show classic cassis notes with generous oak accents. A rich entry leads a full-bodied palate with chewy fruit flavors and chunky, rich tannins. This is a very big wine with plenty of stuffing through a long flavorful finish. Drink within five years.

1994 Merlot, Columbia Valley $14.   88

Deep cherry color. Moderately full-bodied. Highly extracted. Moderately oaked. Moderately tannic. Reminiscent of black fruits, chocolate, tea. Rich berry-accented nose. Chewy, thick mouthfeel with a complex fleshy character on the palate, and some austere tealike tannins through the finish.

1994 Merlot, Red Willow Vineyard, David Lake Signature Series, Yakima Valley $23.   90

Bright reddish purple. Medium-bodied. Moderately extracted. Moderately oaked. Moderately tannic. Reminiscent of red fruits, minerals, toasted oak. Vibrant entry gives way to minerally undertones through the firm toasty finish. An elegant, structured style that should cellar well.

1995 Merlot, Red Willow Vineyard, David Lake Signature Series, Columbia Valley $23.   90

Deep blackish ruby hue. Medium-bodied. Full acidity. Moderately extracted. Mildly oaked. Mildly tannic. Red fruits, vanilla, minerals. Lighter in style and very well balanced. The core of flavor has a measure of complexity and a judicious oak accent. Well integrated, with a firm, angular finish. A solid table wine.

1996 Milestone Merlot, Red Willow Vineyard, David Lake Signature Series, Yakima Valley $24.   86

Bright ruby red with a slight fade. Attractive, high-toned wood, anise, and red fruit aromas show a judicious oak accent. A crisp attack leads a medium-bodied palate with firm tannins. Angular, flavorful finish. Relatively light in style, but tasty and well structured. Drink within five years.

1995 Pinot Noir, Washington $11.99.   81

1997 Pinot Noir, Washington $12.   81

1996 Syrah, Red Willow Vineyard, Yakima Valley $29.   87

Bright saturated ruby red to the rim. Clean mineral and red fruit aromas carry a very subtle oak accent. A firm attack leads a medium-bodied palate, with tannic grip. A snappy, compact finish. Quite modern in style and somewhat closed at present, but the balance bodes well for mid-term (3–6 years) aging. Drink now or later. Can improve with more age.

1998 Riesling, Cellarmaster's Reserve, Columbia Valley $7.   84

Pale straw hue. Modest appley aromas. A sweet, juicy entry leads a medium-bodied palate, with ripe, tangy flavors through the finish. Drink now.

Covey Run

1997 Chardonnay, Washington $9.   83

Pale gold. Zesty citrus aromas. A fruity, tart entry leads a moderately full-bodied palate with a rounded mouthfeel and concentrated, pure Chardonnay flavors lifted by good acids through the finish. Oak is subtle. Impressive flavors and structure. Drink now or later.

1996 Chardonnay, Reserve, Yakima Valley $13.   84

Full yellow-gold. Moderate aromas show a spicy oak accent. A crisp attack leads a medium-bodied palate with tart apple flavors that linger on the nutty finish. Drink now.

1996 Chardonnay, Celilo Vineyard, Washington $25. **86**

Bright straw cast. Moderately full-bodied. Full acidity. Moderately extracted. Mildly oaked. Minerals, citrus, toast. Rather reserved in style, though well structured, with a weighty palate balanced by a crisp and zesty structure.

1998 Gewürztraminer, Washington $6. **82**

1997 Gewürztraminer, Celilo Vineyard, Washington $12. **85**

Bright straw hue. Lean, minerally aromas show an edge of residual sulfur that should disappear with a bit more bottle age. A lush entry leads a medium-bodied palate that has a slight hint of sweetness offset by bright acidity. The finish is spicy and flavorful. A clean wine. Drink now.

1996 Fumé Blanc, Columbia Valley $8. **86**

Medium straw cast. Medium-bodied. Balanced acidity. Moderately extracted. Dried herbs, citrus, minerals. Crisp herbal aromas have a wet wool note. Good grip and intensity on the palate, with a fine lengthy finish.

1995 Cabernet Sauvignon, Columbia Valley $12.99. **85**

Deep ruby red. Moderately full-bodied. Moderately tannic. Herbs, cordial. Cooked, herbal aromas lead a thick, solid mouthful of dry flavors, with precocious tannins coming through on the finish.

1996 Cabernet Sauvignon, Columbia Valley $12.99. **86**

Bright ruby-violet hue. Generously aromatic with a heavy oak accent and vibrant Cabernet fruits. A bright entry leads a moderately full-bodied palate with notes of bitterness and astringency lingering on the finish.

1996 Cabernet Sauvignon, Reserve, Columbia Valley $24. **86**

Saturated dark ruby hue. Rich chocolatey aromas have a dark fruity accent. A plush entry leads to a moderately full-bodied palate with rich chocolatey character that lingers though the long finish. Very oak accented, but this has flesh beneath.

1994 Cabernet Sauvignon, Whiskey Canyon Vineyard,
Yakima Valley $28. **88**

Saturated red-garnet hue. Moderately full-bodied. Highly extracted. Moderately tannic. Black fruits, minerals. Mature aromas lead a weighty, dry palate, with grainy tannins lingering through the finish. This is showing mature flavors, but there is still plenty of life here.

1995 Malbec, Buoy Vineyard, Yakima Valley $16. **80**

1996 Cabernet-Merlot, Washington $10. **84**

Bright red-violet. Moderately light-bodied. Moderately extracted. Mildly tannic. Ripe berry fruits, vanilla. Bright berry fruit aromas lead a simple, crisp mouthful of similar flavors, with a hint of tannic bite for balance.

1995 Merlot, Columbia Valley $12.99. **83**

Deep ruby hue with brilliant clarity. Medium-bodied. Full acidity. Moderately extracted. Mildly oaked. Mildly tannic. Chocolate, minerals, red fruits. A light style with some complexity to its range of flavors. Quite crisp on the palate and a bit tart through the finish.

1994 Merlot, Reserve, Yakima Valley $23. **88**

Deep cherry red. Moderately full-bodied. Highly extracted. Reminiscent of black fruits, brown spice, minerals. Brooding dark fruit nose. Rich, ripe, and dense, with a chewy mouthfeel and ample supple tannins through the lengthy finish. Well structured, this should develop character with further age.

1995 Merlot, Reserve, Yakima Valley $23. **85**

Deep ruby red to the rim. Medium-bodied. Balanced acidity. Highly extracted. Mildly oaked. Moderately tannic. Red fruits, sweet herbs, vanilla. Aromatic and fairly complex, with a bit of an earthy, herbal streak. The palate is still tightly wound and compact, and chunky tannins rear up in the finish.

DeLille

1994 D2, Yakima Valley $22. 92

Full purple-tinged cherry red. Medium-bodied. Highly extracted. Mildly tannic.
Cassis, bramble fruits, red fruits. Inviting toasty aromas lead a focused palate with
good concentration of flavors and a lingering toasty finish. Superbly balanced, with
noble fine-grained tannins defining the finish.

1996 D2, Yakima Valley $24. 86

Bright violet-red hue. Aromatically restrained with clean, faintly herbal character.
A crisp entry leads to a medium-bodied palate with lighter berry fruit flavors and slight,
smoother tannins. Drink now.

1994 Chaleur Estate, Yakima Valley $32. 96

Dark black cherry with purple highlights. Moderately full-bodied. Highly extracted.
Quite tannic. Bittersweet chocolate, chalk, black cherries. Wonderfully deep black cherry
fruit flavors on the midpalate. Very impressive chalky, powdery tannins on the finish.
Very structured, this needs plenty of time. Youthful and vigorous.

1995 Chaleur Estate, Yakima Valley $34. 94

Deep red-violet. Moderately full-bodied. Highly extracted. Moderately tannic. Black fruits,
oak spice. Silky, ultrafine tannins leave a dry impression. Finely wrought and impressively
concentrated. This will be even better with some further cellar age.

1996 Chaleur Estate, Yakima Valley $38. 96

Semi-saturated dark ruby hue. Fleshy intensely fruity aromas have a chocolatey note. A
firm attack leads a moderately full-bodied palate with rich cassis and anise and chocolate
flavors. Tannins are well balanced, providing good grip on the finish. Drink now or later.

Dunham

1995 Cabernet Sauvignon, Columbia Valley $28. 93

Dark brick red. Moderately full-bodied. Highly extracted. Moderately tannic. Spice, black
fruits. Exotically spicy aromas show an oaky accent. Very full flavored and complex on the
palate, with notable intensity and depth. Long, long spicy finish.

E.B. Foote

1997 Chardonnay, Columbia Valley $12. 83

Pale yellow-gold. Tart apple aromas. A bright entry is followed by a medium-bodied
palate with crisp flavors that finish cleanly. Refreshing. Drink now.

1995 Cabernet Sauvignon, Columbia Valley $15. 87

Brick-ruby red. Medium-bodied. Moderately extracted. Moderately tannic. Black pepper,
dried herbs, black fruits. Jammy, herbal aromas lead a thick mouthfeel, with mineral and
herb flavors persisting.

1994 Cabernet Sauvignon, Cellar Reserve, Columbia Valley $32. 88

Opaque blood red. Moderately full-bodied. Highly extracted. Moderately tannic.
Chocolate, red fruits, earth. Very ripe to slightly overripe aromas lead a soft, viscous,
yet earthy palate with a deep black fruit character showing through. Low acid makes
for a very velvety mouthfeel, though the flavors finish dryly.

1996 Cabernet-Merlot, Columbia Valley $15. 82

1994 Merlot, Columbia Valley $12. 82

1995 Merlot, Columbia Valley $15. 84

Deep blackish ruby hue. Moderately light-bodied. Full acidity. Moderately extracted.
Mildly tannic. Chocolate malt, lacquer, plums. Extremely aromatic, with a very chocolatey
character and a mild oxidized note. Notably ripe fruit flavors come through on a lush
and velvety mouthfeel. Lengthy finish. Unusual but tasty.

Scale: Superlative (96-100), Exceptional (90-95), Highly Recommended (85-89),
Recommended (80-84), Not Recommended (Under 80)

Glen Fiona

1997 Syrah, Walla Walla Valley $35.   91

Opaque, saturated violet red. Intense sweet fruit and vanilla aromas, with a generous wood accent and a touch of heat. A lush attack leads a full-bodied palate showing grainy tannins. Rich, ripe finish. A thick, stuffed blockbuster style. Drink now or later. Can improve with more age.

Gordon Brothers

1997 Chardonnay, Columbia Valley $15.49.   81

1996 Cabernet Sauvignon, Columbia Valley $15.49.   88

Deep brick red. Medium-bodied. Moderately extracted. Moderately tannic. Mineral, black fruits, vanilla. Supple, well-rounded wine with juicy Cabernet fruit flavors and mineral notes on the finish. Very Claret-like.

1994 Tradition, Columbia Valley $19.99.   88

Deep ruby red. Medium-bodied. Moderately extracted. Mildly tannic. Red berry fruits, plums. Meaty, fleshy aromas are very inviting. A rounded, sumptuous palate shows soft, integrated tannins that linger through the finish. This reflects a high proportion of Merlot.

1994 Merlot, Columbia Valley $16.99.   87

Deep ruby with a slight garnet fade at the rim. Moderately full-bodied. Full acidity. Moderately extracted. Mildly oaked. Mildly tannic. Brown spices, red fruits. Pleasantly aromatic, with a nicely balanced, well-integrated palate feel. Solid though unobtrusive structure, and a dusty, mildly tannic finish.

Hedges

1997 Fumé Chardonnay, Columbia Valley $8.   84

Bright pale golden hue. Medium-bodied. Full acidity. Moderately extracted. Grassy lemon zest nose. Juicy flavors with a hint of sour apple dryness on the finish.

1997 Cabernet-Merlot, Washington $10.   81

1994 Red Mountain Reserve, Columbia Valley $30.   91

Opaque blackish red with purple highlights. Medium-bodied. Highly extracted. Moderately tannic. Black cherries, black tea. Concentrated black cherry flavors have a dry feel through the astringent finish. Impressive and structured, with solid tannins making it a little backward at present.

1995 Red Mountain Reserve, Columbia Valley $30.   89

Deep, opaque violet-red hue. Brooding chocolate, black fruit, and mineral aromas. A lush entry leads to a full-bodied palate with firm tannins. Rich, structured finish. Rather tough at present, but has the extract to outlast the tannins. Good for long-term cellaring.

1995 Three Vineyards, Columbia Valley $20.   90

Saturated, opaque red-purple. Moderately full-bodied. Highly extracted. Quite tannic. Black fruits, earth, minerals. Taut, angular, and tough to appreciate now. This has the structure and depth to cellar well.

Hogue

1997 Chardonnay, Columbia Valley $13.95.   86

Brilliant green-gold. Very pure fruit-centered aromas of green apples. A smooth entry leads a moderately full-bodied palate with pure Chardonnay flavors and very restrained vanilla oak notes. Acids are markedly crisp through the finish. Well structured. Drink now or later.

1997 Chardonnay, Barrel Select, Columbia Valley $8.95.   84

Brilliant yellow-gold. Ripe yellow apple and toasty oak aromas. A smooth entry leads a moderately full-bodied palate with creamy texture and lingering fruit and oak spice notes on the finish. Drink now or later.

1997 Chardonnay, Genesis, Sunnyside Vineyard, Yakima Valley $19.99.   89

Bright yellow-gold. Stylish aromas of wax and spice. A smooth entry leads a moderately full-bodied palate with lush, ripe flavors and well-integrated toasty nuances that persist through the finish. Well balanced, elegant, and refined.

1996 Semillon-Chardonnay, Columbia Valley $8.   86

Full golden straw hue. Medium-bodied. Balanced acidity. Moderately extracted. Nuts, figs, melon. Nutty aromas lead a surprisingly fresh-tasting palate, with an oily, glycerous mouthfeel and generous tropical flavors. Very concentrated.

1997 Fumé Blanc, Columbia Valley $8.   84

Pale platinum cast. Medium-bodied. Full acidity. Moderately extracted. Tart honeydew, citrus. High-toned fruity aromas lead a crisp palate that leaves the mouth refreshed. Not intensely flavorful but showing attractive aromatic character.

1996 Semillon, Columbia Valley $8.   86

Yellow-straw cast. Medium-bodied. Full acidity. Highly extracted. Tart kiwi, lemons, minerals. High-toned citrus aromas lead a bright, minerally palate. This straightforward style finishes cleanly with lingering juicy acids.

1994 Cabernet Franc, Genesis, Columbia Valley $15.   85

Bright ruby hue with a fade to the rim. Moderately full-bodied. Full acidity. Highly extracted. Moderately tannic. Minerals, red fruits. Lean and austere in style, with a firm structure. Finishes on a vibrant, earthy note.

1995 Cabernet Sauvignon, Columbia Valley $14.95.   83

Dark ruby with a fading rim. Muted aromas show a pickled herbal note. Shows a considerable American oak influence. A light entry leads to a medium-bodied palate with mild fruit sensations and some light bitterness through the finish. Drink now.

1994 Cabernet Sauvignon, Barrel Select, Columbia Valley $14.   87

Deep blood red. Medium-bodied. Moderately extracted. Mildly tannic. Black fruits, minerals, smoke. Crisp plummy flavors have a smoky accent, with clean herbal notes coming through on the finish. Drink now.

1995 Cabernet Sauvignon, Genesis, Champoux Vineyard, Columbia Valley $22.99.   92

Saturated violet-purple hue. Intensely rich dark fruit aromas with toasted oak accents. A firm entry leads to a full-bodied palate with deep, fleshy fruit flavors and rich tannins that coat the mouth. This needs much more time to resolve its youthful exuberance. Drink within five years.

1995 Cabernet Sauvignon, Reserve, Columbia Valley $30.   86

Bright violet-red hue. Crisp cassis and vanilla aromas show generous oak influence. A crisp entry leads to a moderately full-bodied palate with lively acids and balanced dry tannins. Showing a classic Cabernet structure. Drink now or later.

1997 Cabernet-Merlot, Columbia Valley $8.95.   80

1994 Merlot, Columbia Valley $15.   86

Ruby with a violet cast. Medium-bodied. Moderately extracted. Moderately oaked. Reminiscent of green tea, cigar box, minerals. Straightforward berry flavors up front, with solid tannins showing some green notes through the finish.

1996 Merlot, Barrel Select, Columbia Valley $14.95.   84

Bright, pale ruby red. Generous red fruit, mineral, and vanilla aromas show a slight oak accent. A ripe attack leads a medium-bodied palate with lean tannins and a lush, flavorful finish. Eminently drinkable, with ripe flavors and a clean, precise structure. Drink within five years.

1994 Merlot, Genesis, Columbia Valley $23.   87

Very deep ruby red with a slight garnet cast. Moderately full-bodied. Balanced acidity. Highly extracted. Mildly oaked. Moderately tannic. Black fruits, sandalwood, licorice. Still reined-in aromatically, this youthful wine is tightly wound and dense on the palate. Deeply flavored and well balanced, with some unresolved tannins at the finish. Needs some mid-term (3–6 years) aging to round itself out.

1996 Syrah, Genesis, Columbia Valley $15.   86

Bright saturated ruby red to the rim. Generous red fruit and spice aromas with a prominent oak accent. A firm attack leads a medium-bodied palate showing astringent tannins. Intense, flavorful finish. A firm, lean, and compact style. Drink now or later. Can improve with more age.

Hoodsport

1997 Merlot, Yakima Valley $14.99.   81

Hyatt

1994 Cabernet Sauvignon, Reserve, Yakima Valley $32.   87

Garnet-cherry red. Medium-bodied. Moderately extracted. Moderately tannic. Herbs, oak spice, red fruits. Lean, herbal-accented nose leads a concentrated palate, with tight red fruit flavors and edgy tannins showing some authority on the finish. This should show best with richer foods.

1995 Cabernet Sauvignon, Reserve, Yakima Valley $32.   88

Deep reddish purple. Medium-bodied. Highly extracted. Mildly tannic. Cassis, red berries, minerals. A tight, high-toned nose reveals an angular, compact palate showing youthful vibrancy. Some dry minerally undertones, with astringent tannins. Needs time for optimum pleasure.

1994 Merlot, Yakima Valley $14.99.   88

Ruby red. Medium-bodied. Moderately extracted. Moderately oaked. Reminiscent of black fruits, tea, minerals. Brooding dark fruit in the nose. A lean fruity style with some austerity on the palate and reasonably firm tannins through the finish. Solid.

1994 Merlot, Reserve, Yakima Valley $29.99.   90

Ruby red. Moderately full-bodied. Moderately extracted. Heavily oaked. Moderately tannic. Reminiscent of tea, dried herbs, black fruits. Brooding oak-accented aromas. A solid, mouthfilling style with tightly wound flavors on the midpalate and a lengthy austere finish.

Kestrel

1996 Chardonnay, Columbia Valley $22.   93

Bright yellow-gold. Outstanding aromas of butterscotch and ripe fruits. A toasty attack leads a full-bodied palate with a lush texture and ripe fruit flavors. Exotic brown spice comes through on the finish. Very stylish. Drink now or later.

1995 Cabernet Sauvignon, Columbia Valley $22.   94

Bright violet-purple hue. Aromas show complex oak influence with crisp black fruits. A lively entrance leads to a moderately full-bodied palate with dry tannins covering the fruit expression now. Time should help this, though this is highly structured and very marked by complex oak spice. Drink now or later.

1996 Merlot, Columbia Valley $28.   84

Medium-dark ruby hue. Restrained very woody aromas. A firm entry leads a medium-bodied palate with dull fruit flavors and a dry astringent finish. Rather lean, this does not have the stuffing to improve. Drink now.

Kiona

1997 Chardonnay, Washington $11.   83

Dark straw cast. Moderately full-bodied. Balanced acidity. Moderately extracted. Minerals, flint, butter. Shows a big minerally quality throughout. Ripe and rounded in the mouth with a buttery texture moderated by crisp acids.

1997 Chardonnay, Reserve, Columbia Valley $19. **82**

1996 Cabernet Sauvignon, Washington $14.99. **86**

Bright purple-red. Medium-bodied. Moderately extracted. Moderately tannic. Sweet plums, black cherries, tobacco. Youthful appearance and aromas. Sweet, supple fruit flavors with good texture and mouthfeel. Dry, fine-grained tannins distinguish the finish.

1997 Cabernet Sauvignon, Washington $17.99. **87**

Saturated ruby hue. Ripe fruity aromas with a touch of vanilla oak. A soft entry leads to a medium-bodied palate with concentrated, fruit-forward character that fills the mouth. Finishes with soft, supple tannins. Drink now.

1995 Cabernet Sauvignon, Reserve, Yakima Valley $29.99. **92**

Saturated blood red. Moderately full-bodied. Highly extracted. Moderately oaked. Moderately tannic. Brown spice, sandalwood, licorice, earth. Rich, spicy aromas lead a concentrated, broad palate of spice flavors with sweet black fruit notes showing through a long finish. Very stylish, drinking well now.

1997 Cabernet-Merlot, Columbia Valley $9.99. **83**

Bright violet-red. Moderately light-bodied. Moderately extracted. Mildly tannic. Flowers, dried herbs. Engaging floral aromas lead a light-framed palate with bright floral flavors. Finishes with a hint of dry tannins.

1995 Merlot, Columbia Valley $18. **83**

Deep ruby color. Medium-bodied. Highly extracted. Moderately tannic. Reminiscent of ripe berries, brown spice, licorice. Fleshy berry aromas. Rich, expansive fruity palate with a mouthfilling character and some fine tannins on the lengthy finish. Would cellar well, although approachable now.

1996 Merlot, Washington $19.99. **82**

L'Ecole No. 41

1997 Chardonnay, Washington $19.50. **87**

Bright pale golden cast. Moderately full-bodied. Full acidity. Moderately extracted. Mildly oaked. Minerals, brown spices, butter. Generous aromas feature a judicious oak accent. Ripe and lush in the mouth, with zesty acidity providing balance to the finish.

1996 Semillon, Washington $13.50. **87**

Deep yellow-gold. Moderately full-bodied. Full acidity. Highly extracted. Figs, lemons, minerals, brown spice. An impressive array of spicy aromas leads an expansive palate held together by bright acids. Firm and concentrated, with a generous mouthfeel and understated oak accents.

1994 Cabernet Sauvignon, Columbia Valley $24. **90**

Dark blood red with subtle purple highlights. Medium-bodied. Highly extracted. Mildly tannic. Dill, tobacco, currants, black fruits. A very pronounced oak-accented nose follows through on the palate, with chewy, curranty black fruits on the midpalate. Full and long toasty finish. Very attractive.

1995 Cabernet Sauvignon, Columbia Valley $25. **94**

Saturated brick red. Moderately full-bodied. Highly extracted. Moderately oaked. Moderately tannic. Dill, coconut, black fruits. Extravagant spice aromas follow through on a densely flavored palate that has a surprisingly supple character, inviting current drinking.

1996 Cabernet Sauvignon, Columbia Valley $26. **90**

Saturated dark ruby with violet highlights. Aromatically distinctive with ripe aromas and distinctive woody accents. A rich entry leads a moderately full-bodied palate with a plush mouthfeel, and firm acidity. Well structured and intensely flavored.

1995 Cabernet Sauvignon, Windrow Vineyard, Walla Walla Valley $30. **86**

Deep red-violet. Moderately full-bodied. Highly extracted. Moderately tannic. Pepper, black fruits, earth. Generous and complex spice-accented aromas lead a supple, weighty mouthful of soft, fruity flavors that finish with some minerally intensity. Thick mouthfeel.

Scale: Superlative (96-100), Exceptional (90-95), Highly Recommended (85-89), Recommended (80-84), Not Recommended (Under 80)

1995 Cabernet Sauvignon-Merlot, Apogée, Pepper Bridge Vineyard, Walla Walla Valley $30.   93

Bright red-violet. Medium-bodied. Moderately extracted. Moderately tannic. Coconut, spice, crisp berry fruits. Exotic, spicy, high-toned aromas lead a vibrant mouthful of fruit flavors, with supple tannins and oak spice notes lingering. Very silky and stylish.

1996 Cabernet Sauvignon-Merlot, Seven Hills Vineyard, Walla Walla Valley $35.   86

Dark, saturated ruby-red hue. Full chocolate and dark fruit aromas with a distinctive, unusual note. A heavy entry leads a full-bodied palate with considerable weight and tart acids that make this angular and tough now.

1994 Merlot, Columbia Valley $22.   92

Deep ruby color. Medium-bodied. Moderately extracted. Moderately oaked. Moderately tannic. Reminiscent of black cherries, cedar, tobacco. Complex, deep nose. Rich, ripe fruity entry with complex toasty flavors and a minerally backbone through to a mild finish with grainy tannins. Very seductive and elegant.

1995 Merlot, Columbia Valley $24.   92

Very deep blackish ruby color. Medium-bodied. Balanced acidity. Moderately extracted. Moderately oaked. Mildly tannic. Brown spices, plums, dried herbs. Pleasantly aromatic and extremely flavorful, with a mile-long finish. The lush, inviting palate has a velvety texture and unobtrusive structure. Classic fruit and herbal flavors are intertwined with the judicious use of oak to make a complex and harmonious wine.

1996 Merlot, Columbia Valley $25.   88

Bright ruby red with a slight fade. Intense cedar and spice aromas show a dominant wood accent. A lush attack leads a moderately full-bodied palate with chunky, velvety tannins. Flavorful, spicy finish. Somewhat overpowered by its sweet wood flavors, but tasty nonetheless. Drink within five years.

Leonetti

1994 Cabernet Sauvignon, Columbia Valley $45.   93

Saturated dark black-cherry hue with purple highlights. Moderately full-bodied. Highly extracted. Moderately tannic. Toasted oak, dill, plums, earth, smoke. Full smoky, toasty oak nose has rich black fruit accents that follow through well on the palate. Rich, extracted flavors expand on the midpalate through a firm, deliciously toasty finish.

1995 Cabernet Sauvignon, Columbia Valley $45.   90

Saturated dark ruby hue. Richly aromatic with generous black fruit and marked oak spice. A silky entry leads a full-bodied palate with deep and complex flavors that persist through a long finish. Drink now.

Matthews

1996 Cabernet Sauvignon, Elerding Vineyard, Yakima Valley $35.   94

Saturated dark ruby hue. Moderately full-bodied. Highly extracted. Moderately tannic. Mint, chocolate, dark fruits. Broad, chocolatey aromas lead a concentrated, dry palate showing a core of lush fruit flavors, with firm Cabernet tannins clamping down on the finish. This needs more cellar time.

1995 Yakima Valley Red, Washington $28.   88

Bright cherry red. Medium-bodied. Moderately extracted. Mildly tannic. Vanilla, toasted oak, cherries. Inviting toasty nose. Straightforward crisp cherry flavors expand on the palate, with toasty oak flavors taking over on the finish. Well balanced and drinking nicely now.

1996 Cabernet Sauvignon-Cabernet Franc-Merlot, Yakima Valley Red, Washington $35.   84

Deep ruby-red hue. Intense, unusual anise and mineral aromas carry a marked oak accent. A crisp entry leads to a spicy, medium-bodied palate with firm acidity and lean tannins. Angular, zesty finish. Unusual but interesting. Drink now.

Mountain Dome

NV Brut Rosé, Washington $16.   86

Deep salmon color. Full-bodied. Full acidity. Highly extracted. Cream, red fruits, toast. Attractive aromatics show complexity throughout. Ripe, racy, and intense in the mouth, with a firm structure and vibrant carbonation. A sturdy, weighty style.

1993 Brut, Columbia Valley $16.   87

Bright yellow-gold. Medium-bodied. Pears, yeast. Distinctive, mature aromas follow through on a leesy palate, with broad, very marked yeasty flavors that dominate through the finish.

Patrick M. Paul

1994 Cabernet Sauvignon, Columbia Valley $12.   88

Deep red brick color. Medium-bodied. Highly extracted. Moderately tannic. Black cherries, brown spice, toasted oak. Very dry oaky nose follows through on the palate. Compact and tightly wound, with solid astringency and very pronounced oak flavors complemented by rich black fruit accents. Not everyone's style.

1993 Merlot, Conner Lee Vineyards, Columbia Valley $12.   90

Deep cherry red. Moderately full-bodied. Highly extracted. Heavily oaked. Moderately tannic. Reminiscent of oak, black tea, black fruits. Very distinctive oak-accented aromas. The palate is concentrated and tightly wound, with a long, dry spicy finish. A very individualistic style that will appeal to those who like strong oak flavors.

Portteus

1995 Cabernet Sauvignon, Yakima Valley $30.   92

Saturated, opaque blood red. Moderately full-bodied. Highly extracted. Moderately tannic. Black fruits, chocolate, minerals. Outstanding spiced aromas lead a fleshy dark fruit entry that reveals plenty of supple, earthy flavors that linger through the finish. Very complex, with a fine expression of terroir.

1994 Cabernet Sauvignon, Reserve, Yakima Valley $26.   90

Opaque blood red with a purple rim. Moderately full-bodied. Highly extracted. Moderately tannic. Earth, oak spice, tar, coffee, black fruits. Rich oaky, brown spice aromas follow through on the palate. Has a nice rich center of dark fruits and earth, with oak coming through strongly on the finish. A generous style.

1994 Merlot, Yakima Valley $16.   89

Deep, dark red. Medium-bodied. Moderately extracted. Moderately oaked. Moderately tannic. Reminiscent of blackberries, brown spice. A ripe berry fruit nose leads an imposingly rich fruity entry with adequate firm tannins on the lengthy finish giving this solid appeal.

1995 Merlot, Yakima Valley $16.   90

Deep blackish ruby hue to the rim. Medium-bodied. Balanced acidity. Moderately extracted. Moderately oaked. Mildly tannic. Minerals, red fruits, cedar. Very well balanced, with a big range of complex flavors. Well-integrated, lush finish. Quite tasty.

1995 Merlot, Reserve, Yakima Valley $29.   91

Very deep blackish ruby hue. Medium-bodied. Balanced acidity. Moderately extracted. Heavily oaked. Mildly tannic. Pencil shavings, coffee, black fruits. Quite aromatic and largely wood driven, though quite attractive. Features a lush and harmonious core of flavors on the palate. Extremely well balanced through the lengthy finish.

1997 Syrah, Yakima Valley $20.   83

Bright garnet red with a slight fade. Pungent stewed fruit, herb, and mineral aromas. A soft attack leads a medium-bodied palate, with drying tannins. Tough, rather edgy finish. An unusual mix of very ripe flavors allied to an austere frame. Drink now.

Scale: Superlative (96-100), Exceptional (90-95), Highly Recommended (85-89), Recommended (80-84), Not Recommended (Under 80)

Powers

1996 Chardonnay, Columbia Valley $10.   **82**

1996 Fumé Blanc, Columbia Valley $7.50.   **82**

1996 Cabernet Sauvignon, Washington $12.   **86**

Medium-dark violet red. Medium-bodied. Moderately extracted. Moderately tannic. Cassis, minerals. Fleshy black fruit aromas. Wonderfully wrought, with plump fruit flavors and generous fine-grained tannins not masking the pleasure.

1995 Cabernet Sauvignon, Mercer Ranch Vineyard, Columbia Valley $18.   **90**

Opaque red-purple. Moderately full-bodied. Highly extracted. Quite tannic. Minerals, black fruits. Lush, fruity entry. Austere and tough, it has dense, fine-grained tannins drying the finish. Shows fine weight, though the tannins are clamping down now.

1996 Cabernet-Merlot, Washington $12.   **86**

Deep red-purple. Moderately full-bodied. Highly extracted. Moderately tannic. Black fruits. Big-shouldered and generous, with fleshy dark fruit flavors and chunky tannins. No shy wallflower. Firm tannins will need some meaty accompaniment.

1995 Merlot, Columbia Valley $16.   **87**

Deep ruby hue with a garnet cast and brilliant clarity. Moderately light-bodied. Balanced acidity. Moderately extracted. Moderately oaked. Mildly tannic. Sweet herbs, red fruits, vanilla. Pleasantly aromatic, with a lighter-styled though lush mouthfeel. Red fruit flavors are accented by light oak accents and an herbal streak. Complex lingering finish.

1996 Pinot Noir, Columbia Valley $9.   **80**

Preston Premium

1998 Gamay Beaujolais Rosé, Columbia Valley $8.   **82**

1994 Cabernet Sauvignon, Reserve, Columbia Valley $21.   **89**

Dark brick red. Medium-bodied. Moderately extracted. Moderately oaked. Mildly tannic. Dill, bright red fruits, oak spice. American oak nose. Concentrated bright red fruit flavors on entry follow through to a lengthy powdery finish showing fine dry tannins. Good structure. Though drinking well now, this will be more attractive in a few years.

1995 Cabernet Sauvignon, Reserve, Columbia Valley $21.   **86**

Saturated, opaque brick red. Moderately full-bodied. Highly extracted. Moderately tannic. Brown spice, black fruits. Strong impression of oak on the nose. Remarkably intense and focused, with very elegant black fruit flavors and persistence on the finish. Powdery tannins leave a dry sensation.

1994 Merlot, Preston Vineyard, Columbia Valley $10.   **85**

Garnet cherry color. Medium-bodied. Moderately extracted. Mildly tannic. Reminiscent of red currants, dried herbs. Soft berry fruit flavors with mild tannins through the finish make this easygoing and very drinkable.

1993 Merlot, Reserve, Columbia Valley $18.99.   **89**

Deep garnet cherry color. Medium-bodied. Moderately extracted. Moderately oaked. Moderately tannic. Reminiscent of cherries, black tea, brown spice. An angular style with forward cherry fruit on entry and some tight tannins on the finish. Nice now but could withstand some short-term (1–2 years) cellaring.

1994 Merlot, Reserve, Columbia Valley $21.   **90**

Deep blackish red with a garnet cast. Medium-bodied. Balanced acidity. Moderately extracted. Heavily oaked. Mildly tannic. Chocolate, cedar, coffee. Couldn't be more aromatic and flavorful, but the flavors are largely wood driven. Nonetheless, this wine is well balanced and lush, with a very lengthy finish. Quite seductive in its own way.

1995 Merlot, Western White Oak, Columbia Valley $16.   **87**

Very deep ruby red to the rim. Medium-bodied. Balanced acidity. Moderately extracted. Moderately oaked. Mildly tannic. Red fruits, minerals, bacon. Still a little tight, with a youthful character on the palate. Well balanced, with a juicy note of acidity to the finish. Should open up quite nicely with near-term cellaring.

Quilceda Creek

1994 Cabernet Sauvignon, Washington $42.   91

Opaque violet red. Medium-bodied. Moderately extracted. Moderately tannic. Black fruits, chocolate. Rich black fruit aromas lead a firm mouthful of flavors, with rich, dry tannins featured on the finish. Concentrated, displaying sound structure and length.

1995 Cabernet Sauvignon, Washington $45.   93

Saturated violet-purple hue. Vanilla oak aromas have an oaky accent with cassis richness showing. A bright entry leads to a full-bodied palate with lively acids and dry, powdery tannins on the finish. Drink now or later.

Seth Ryan

1996 Cabernet Franc, Yakima Valley $14.81.   80

1994 Cabernet Sauvignon, Yakima Valley $25.93.   87

Opaque red-garnet hue. Moderately full-bodied. Highly extracted. Quite tannic. Black fruits, oak spice. Aromas show a heavy wood influence. Tough, severe, dry tannins on the finish make it hard to drink now. This has some rustic charm, and will develop in the course of a few years.

1996 Jessica's Meritage, Columbia Valley $32.41.   85

Deep ruby hue with a violet rim. Medium-bodied. Balanced acidity. Moderately extracted. Cherries, mineral, spice. Toasty, ripe, fruity aromas lead a bright, rounded palate with tart flavors and a spicy oak finish that lingers.

Seven Hills

1995 Cabernet Sauvignon, Columbia Valley $20.   88

Dark ruby red. Medium-bodied. Balanced acidity. Moderately extracted. Mildly tannic. Black fruits, sour cherry, oak spice. Supple, fleshy, and very well balanced, with the finish showing soft tannins.

1995 Cabernet Sauvignon, Walla Walla Valley $24.   89

Bright cherry red with violet highlights. Medium-bodied. Highly extracted. Moderately tannic. Pencil shavings, cassis, minerals. Classic, Claret-like aromas lead a bright, flavorsome mouthful with piercing fruit flavors and mineral snap.

1995 Cabernet Sauvignon, Klipsun Vineyard, Columbia Valley $24.   90

Opaque red-violet. Moderately full-bodied. Highly extracted. Quite tannic. Black fruits, mineral, spice. Reserved, dark fruit aromas lead a tightly wound, well-stuffed palate, with considerably dry, fine-grained tannins giving an assertive finish.

1994 Merlot, Columbia Valley $20.   85

Deep reddish purple. Medium-bodied. Moderately extracted. Moderately tannic. Reminiscent of red fruits, black tea. Brooding fruity aromas reveal a tightly wound center with concentrated flavors. This needs more time or good aeration.

1995 Merlot, Columbia Valley $20.   86

Very deep ruby red to the rim. Medium-bodied. Balanced acidity. Moderately extracted. Mildly tannic. Cherries, black pepper, minerals. Fruit-driven aromatics lead a lighter-styled palate showing vibrant acidity. Still a bit compact, with tannins that grip down on the finish.

1994 Merlot, Seven Hills Vineyard, Walla Walla Valley $24.   90

Opaque purplish black hue. Moderately full-bodied. Highly extracted. Heavily oaked. Moderately tannic. Reminiscent of black fruits, cedar, minerals. Heavily oak-accented nose. Solid and tight on the palate, showing fine extraction and focus, but a little attenuated on the finish. Needs more time in the cellar for optimum enjoyment.

Scale: Superlative (96-100), Exceptional (90-95), Highly Recommended (85-89), Recommended (80-84), Not Recommended (Under 80)

248

1995 Merlot, Seven Hills Vineyard, Walla Walla Valley $24.   **90**

Deep ruby with a slight purplish cast and brilliant clarity. Moderately full-bodied. Balanced acidity. Highly extracted. Moderately oaked. Moderately tannic. Black fruits, dried herbs, minerals. Big and rich in style, showing a chunky, youthful texture. Complex and flavorful, with a wave of velvety tannins on the palate. Well balanced and finely extracted, this is a solid candidate for mid-term (3–6 years) to long-term (7–10 years) cellaring.

1995 Merlot, Klipsun Vineyard, Columbia Valley $24.   **93**

Deep, opaque blackish ruby hue with a purple cast. Full-bodied. Full acidity. Highly extracted. Heavily oaked. Quite tannic. Red fruits, vanilla. From its color to its flavor profile, this wine is solidly New World. Aromatic, with a rush of big oak-driven flavors and a dense core of ripe fruit. Despite its weight it is well balanced, and though the tannins are considerable, they have been finely extracted. Long-term cellaring should mellow it and bring out some complexity. A show wine, not for near-term drinking.

Silver Lake

1997 Chardonnay, Columbia Valley $11.99.   **84**

Brilliant yellow-gold. Ripe yellow apple aromas. A pure, fruity attack leads a medium-bodied palate that has rounded, concentrated fruit flavors with subtle oak notes. A very well-balanced, harmonious style. Drink now.

1997 Chardonnay, Reserve, Columbia Valley $15.99.   **83**

Full gold. Lean appley aromas. A firm attack leads a full-bodied palate with weighty mouthfeel and deeply oaky flavors. Finishes with a degree of alcohol warmth. Powerful, intense style.

1995 Cabernet Sauvignon, Columbia Valley $12.99.   **84**

Bright ruby hue with a subtle fade. Generously oak accented aromas. A crisp entry leads to a medium-bodied palate with bright berry fruits and lingering vanilla and oak spice. Very straightforward, lighter style.

1995 Cabernet Sauvignon, Reserve, Columbia Valley $17.99.   **87**

Saturated dark ruby hue. Fragrantly aromatic with a vanilla oak and cassis character. A firm entry leads to a full-bodied palate with well-integrated, silky tannins that linger on the finish. Rather well structured and well extracted, this will need some time.

1994 Cabernet Sauvignon, Hervé, Cuvée Selipsky,
Columbia Valley $24.99.   **83**

Bright garnet hue. Unusual, mature forest and stewed fruit aromas show a spicy oak accent. A firm entry leads to a full-bodied palate with big chewy tannins. Rich, intense finish. Unusual but interesting. Drink within five years.

1995 Merlot, Columbia Valley $12.99.   **81**

1995 Merlot, Reserve, Columbia Valley $17.99.   **83**

Rich garnet red. Generous cedar, red fruit, and mineral aromas. A lush attack leads a medium-bodied palate with austere tannins that provide grip. The finish is angular, though. Drink within five years.

Staton Hills

1997 Chardonnay, Washington $12.95.   **84**

Full yellow-gold. Very ripe, generously fruity aromas of peach and apple. A lush attack leads a full-bodied palate with tropical fruit flavors and well-balanced oak. The mouthfeel is opulent and the finish is smooth. Drink now.

1996 Fumé Blanc, Yakima Valley $8.95.   **83**

Bright pale straw hue. Medium-bodied. Balanced acidity. Moderately extracted. Dried herbs, lemons. Aromatically reserved, revealing a straightforward and delicate palate through to a warm finish.

1994 Cabernet Sauvignon, Columbia Valley $16.   89

Dark ruby red hue. Generous spicy, oak accented aromas. A lean entry leads a
moderately full-bodied palate with rich oak dominated flavors. Finishes in an angular
manner with firm tannins and complex spicy flavors.

1995 Cabernet Sauvignon, Columbia Valley $15.95.   88

Bright red-violet. Medium-bodied. Highly extracted. Moderately tannic. Black fruits,
oak spice. Lush, fruity flavors with gentle oak spice and some fine-grained tannins giving
authority to the finish. Probably better in a few years.

Ste. Chapelle

1997 Chardonnay, Reserve, Idaho $15.   83

Pale straw hue. Elegant, smoky aromas. A juicy attack leads a medium-bodied palate
with piercing acids and oak flavors coming to the fore. Interesting though not elegant
cool climate Chardonnay style. Drink now.

1998 Johannisberg Riesling, Idaho $6.   83

Pale platinum-straw hue. Muted aromas of minerals and citrus zest. A crisp attack leads a
medium-bodied palate, with dry, zesty flavors and minerally firmness through the finish.
Drink now.

1998 Dry Johannisberg Riesling, Idaho $6.   86

Medium yellow-gold. Fresh aromas of crisp apples and herbs. A bright attack leads a
medium-bodied palate, with crisp fruit flavors persisting on the finish. Very refreshing.
Drink now.

Tefft

1994 Cabernet Sauvignon, Yakima Valley $25.   87

Full crimson red. Medium-bodied. Moderately extracted. Mildly tannic. Black tea, cassis,
cherries. Bright entry reveals a concentrated, angular palate with a firm finish. Still a little
tightly wound; should be better in a few years.

1995 Cabernet Sauvignon, Yakima Valley $21.99.   89

Opaque brick red. Moderately full-bodied. Highly extracted. Moderately tannic. Black
fruits, minerals, spice. Dusty, spiced fruit aromas lead a full-flavored palate that has a
degree of firmness and intensity that lingers through the finish. Still structured, though
it is drinkable now.

NV Merlot, Columbia Valley $15.   87

Deep ruby with a subtle garnet cast and brilliant clarity. Moderately full-bodied. Balanced
acidity. Moderately extracted. Heavily oaked. Mildly tannic. Brown spices, red fruits, dill
pickle. Quite aromatic, with a big oak overlay on the core of fruit flavors. Chewy on the
palate, with some dusty tannins and a lengthy finish.

1994 Merlot, Winemakers Reserve, Yakima Valley $25.   92

Deep reddish purple. Moderately full-bodied. Highly extracted. Quite tannic.
Reminiscent of minerals, black fruit, tea. Dense, brooding aromatics. An imposing,
slightly austere, but well-structured style with a solid minerally backbone and some
warmth on the finish. Should evolve with cellaring.

Paul Thomas

1995 Chardonnay, Washington $7.   83

Pale straw cast. Moderately full-bodied. Full acidity. Moderately extracted. Citrus,
minerals. Crisp and reserved in a lean and racy style. Clean and refreshing through
the finish.

1995 Cabernet Sauvignon, Reserve, Washington $14.99.   86

Bright violet-ruby color. Medium-bodied. Moderately extracted. Mildly tannic. Red fruits,
minerals, dried herbs. Well balanced, with bright, juicy acids and supple yet dry tannins
lingering on the finish.

1996 Cabernet Sauvignon, Reserve, Columbia Valley $17. 84

Pale ruby hue with a subtle fade. Lighter attractive aromas show a oak accent. A supple entry leads a medium-bodied palate with spicy oak flavors that are well integrated. Harmonious and lengthy. Drink now.

1995 Merlot, Washington $10.50. 84

Bright reddish purple. Medium-bodied. Moderately extracted. Moderately oaked. Mildly tannic. Reminiscent of herbs, red fruits, brown spice. Lively, crisp red fruit palate with an attractive toasty finish. Quite fresh and forward in style.

1997 Riesling, Reserve, Columbia Valley $7. 81

Crimson Rhubarb Wine, Washington $5.99. 87

Brilliant faded pink. Moderately full-bodied. Full acidity. Highly extracted. Yeast, minerals, toast. Extremely fragrant, with a forward yeasty overtone that is almost Champagne-like. Full and round in the mouth, with a continuation of the yeasty flavors and vibrant acidity through the drying finish. Exotic.

Dry Bartlett Pear, Washington $7.99. 83

Bright yellow-straw cast. Moderately full-bodied. Low acidity. Moderately extracted. Minerals, stone fruits. Rather reserved in style, with a lush mouthfeel that lacks a bit of grip. Turns angular on the finish.

Raspberry Wine, Washington $7.99. 86

Bright ruby-garnet cast. Medium-bodied. Full acidity. Highly extracted. Raspberries, minerals. Extremely aromatic and quite pure, with a definite raspberry accent to the flavors throughout. Surprisingly firm on the palate, with sturdy acidity that makes for a lean, drying finish.

Walla Walla Vintners

1996 Washington State Red Cuvée, Washington $18. 87

Bright ruby with a subtly fading rim. Elegant oaky aromas with ripe berry fruit accents. A supple entry leads a medium-bodied palate with harmonious well-fruited flavors and a chocolatey, vanilla-accented finish. Supple and well balanced. Drink now.

Washington Hills

1997 Chardonnay, Columbia Valley $9.99. 83

Bright yellow-gold. Crisp yellow apple aromas. A bright attack leads a medium-bodied palate with clean fruity flavors and very subtle oak. Drink now.

1998 Gewürztraminer, Columbia Valley $6. 80

1996 Semillon-Chardonnay, Columbia Valley $7.99. 84

Bright yellow-gold. Medium-bodied. Full acidity. Moderately extracted. Dried herbs, kiwi. High-toned tropical aromas have an herbal twist leading juicy, vibrant flavors in a clean, fresh style.

1995 Cabernet Sauvignon, Columbia Valley $9.99. 86

Cherry-brick red with a slight fade on the rim. Medium-bodied. Moderately extracted. Moderately tannic. Berry fruits, minerals. Bright and juicy aromas follow through on the palate, with a fruit-forward entry that builds through the midpalate. Dry mineral and spice notes persist on the finish.

1997 Cabernet-Merlot, Columbia Valley $10. 81

1995 Merlot, Columbia Valley $12.99. 80

1997 Merlot, Varietal Select, Columbia Valley $11. 81

1998 Late Harvest White Riesling, Columbia Valley $8/375 ml. 88

Brilliant yellow-gold. Sweet peach and apricot aromas. A ripe, sweet entry leads a medium-bodied palate with off-dry, lush primary fruit flavors following through on the finish. Pure and quite concentrated. Drink now.

Waterbrook

1997 Chardonnay, Columbia Valley $10.   83

Bright yellow-straw hue. Mild yellow apple aromas. A juicy entry leads a medium-bodied palate with straightforward, clean fruity flavors and very subtle oak nuances. The finish is clean. Drink now.

1997 Sauvignon Blanc, Columbia Valley $13.   86

Medium straw cast. Moderately full-bodied. Balanced acidity. Moderately extracted. Mildly oaked. Vanilla, smoke, citrus. Subtle toasty oak aromas lead a generous mouthfeel, with bright smoky citrus flavors and a spicy warm finish. Has stuffing and character.

1997 Viognier, Columbia Valley $18.   86

Bright golden hue. Full-bodied. Balanced acidity. Highly extracted. Pears, apples, minerals. Pearlike aromas. Full, though lean and angular on the finish, with some powdery dryness.

1995 Cabernet Sauvignon, Columbia Valley $24.   92

Dark ruby red with violet highlights. Medium-bodied. Highly extracted. Moderately tannic. Cassis, spice, vanilla. Youthful, oak spice-dominated aromas lead a brisk, tightly wound palate displaying intense black fruit flavors and dusty, dry tannins.

1994 Merlot, Columbia Valley $19.99.   93

Opaque purple. Moderately full-bodied. Highly extracted. Moderately oaked. Moderately tannic. Reminiscent of plums, currants, toasted oak. Rich, ripe aromas. Deep, extracted fruity flavors with a firm minerally backbone to the palate give this length and structure in a feminine style. Drinkable now, it should cellar well.

1996 Merlot, Columbia Valley $22.   86

Bright garnet red. Generous spice aromas belie a wood-dominated character. A rounded attack leads a medium-bodied palate with crisp acidity and mild tannins. The finish is lush and spicy. A mellow, rounded, but well-balanced style. Drink now.

1995 Merlot, Reserve, Columbia Valley $32.   92

Deep blackish ruby color. Moderately full-bodied. Balanced acidity. Moderately extracted. Moderately oaked. Mildly tannic. Black fruits, brown spices, minerals. Pleasantly aromatic and relatively firm in style, with an angular presence on the palate. Fleshes out toward the lengthy finish. A tad restrained, but quite elegant.

Whidbey

1990 Port, Washington $12.99.   90

Black ruby hue with brick rim. Moderately full-bodied. Balanced acidity. Highly extracted. Moderately tannic. Medium sweetness. Reminiscent of mocha, dried plums, grenadine. Intensely concentrated and still youthful, with a lengthy palate of sweet-tasting fruit enlivened by tangy spice notes. Shows nice grip in the finish.

Andrew Will

1994 Cabernet Sauvignon, Washington $30.   90

Garnet-blood red. Medium-bodied. Highly extracted. Moderately tannic. Earth, brown spice, black fruits, cedar. Earthy, oak-accented nose. The rich, chewy black fruit palate has exotic toasty notes, with a lengthy dry finish. Austere and full flavored, with sound angular structure.

1996 Cabernet Sauvignon, Washington $32.   90

Opaque, saturated dark purple hue. Deep, brooding aromas of dark ripe fruits and vanilla oak. A rich entry leads a full-bodied palate with fabulous fruit intensity and soft, supple tannins that coat the mouth. Extravagantly generous and concentrated, though very approachable. Drink now.

1994 Cabernet Sauvignon, Reserve, Washington $40.   **91**

Opaque dark blood red. Moderately full-bodied. Highly extracted. Quite tannic. Black tea, earth, tart plums, minerals. Full earthy, oaky nose. A big dry palate with assertive grainy tannins make this wine very tight through the finish. Impressively structured. Needs time.

1995 Cabernet Sauvignon, Reserve, Washington $40.   **93**

Saturated violet purple. Moderately full-bodied. Highly extracted. Quite tannic. Cherry fruits, vanilla, minerals. Expressively aromatic, in a very youthful manner. Follows through as expected on the palate; very focused and tight, with bright cherry fruit flavors and astringent tannins through the finish. Impressively structured, it needs time.

1995 Sorella, Washington $40.   **94**

Deep violet red with an opaque cast. Moderately full-bodied. Balanced acidity. Moderately extracted. Moderately oaked. Moderately tannic. Black cherries, minerals, spice. Deep, minerally aromas follow through on a lush mouthfeel with mineral-rich flavors. Shows great grip and balance.

1996 Sorella, Washington $38.   **92**

Saturated purple-violet hue. Richly fruity aromas show ripe berry fruit and cassis character. Mouthfilling and fruit-forward flavors on entry lead a moderately full-bodied palate with softer, supple tannins on the finish. Big, fruity, and supple. Drink now or later.

1994 Merlot, Washington $25.   **90**

Very deep cherry red. Moderately full-bodied. Highly extracted. Quite tannic. Reminiscent of dried herbs, black fruit, toasted oak, minerals. Glycerous notes on the mouthfeel. The concentrated palate is focused by fine acidity and lengthy tannins, all of which give this real cellaring potential.

1995 Merlot, Washington $28.   **90**

Very deep blackish ruby hue. Moderately full-bodied. Balanced acidity. Moderately extracted. Moderately oaked. Mildly tannic. Leather, black fruits, chocolate. Fully flavored and rich, with an accent on oak. The core of flavors is dense and the finish is quite firm. A bit compact, it could use near-term to mid-term (3–6 years) aging to mellow it out a bit.

1996 Merlot, Washington $26.   **86**

Deep purple-red with a slight haze. Generous dill pickle and red fruit aromas show what seems to be a big American oak accent. A crisp attack is followed by a medium-bodied palate with juicy acidity and a bright finish. Somewhat light in style but tasty. Drink now.

1997 Merlot, Ciel du Cheval, Washington $30.   **92**

Deep, opaque purple-red. Restrained, embryonic black fruit, mineral, and spice aromas. A soft attack leads a moderately full-bodied palate with firm tannins. Big, tannic finish. A stuffed, extracted style that needs quite a bit more time. Good for long-term cellaring.

1996 Merlot, Klipsun, Washington $28.   **90**

Deep, opaque purple-red to the rim. Perfumed spice, chocolate, and red fruit aromas show a toasty oak accent. A lush entry leads a medium-bodied palate with fine grip and velvety tannins. Persistent, flavorful finish. Rounded and inviting. Drink now.

1997 Merlot, Klipsun, Washington $30.   **90**

Dark, opaque violet-red to the rim. Restrained spice and black fruit aromas show a subtle oak accent. A firm attack leads a moderately full-bodied, lush palate with robust, chunky tannins. Buoyant acidity makes for a vibrant, flavorful finish. Lots of stuffing—should open with age. Good for long-term cellaring.

1997 Merlot, Pepper Bridge, Washington $30.   **91**

Dark, opaque violet-red to the rim. Intense, perfumed floral red fruit aromas. A lean attack leads a medium-bodied palate with angular tannins. Vibrant, flavorful finish.

Exotically flavored, with excellent grip and style. Good for long-term cellaring.

1994 Merlot, Reserve, Washington $28.   **91**

Reddish garnet cast. Medium-bodied. Highly extracted. Heavily oaked. Quite tannic. Reminiscent of red fruits, herbs, minerals. An oak-accented nose leads a tightly wound, compact palate with some grainy tannins on the long, dry finish. Well stuffed, this should resolve further with time in the cellar.

1995 Merlot, Reserve, Washington $32.   **96**

Very deep blackish ruby hue. Moderately full-bodied. Balanced acidity. Moderately extracted. Moderately oaked. Mildly tannic. Black fruits, vanilla, minerals. This one is all about mouthfeel. Supple, velvety, and dense, yet perfectly balanced. Features a very precise core of complex fruit flavors buttressed by a firm but unobtrusive structure and well-integrated oak accents. Very attractive now and will improve with age.

1997 Merlot, Seven Hills, Walla Walla Valley $30.   **90**

Deep, opaque ruby red to the rim. Subdued, brooding spice and mineral aromas. A lush attack leads a moderately full-bodied palate with rich, velvety tannins, followed by a deep, rounded finish. Shows beautiful structure and extract, and should open quite well. Drink now or later. Can improve with more age.

Wilridge

1996 Cabernet Sauvignon, Klipsun Vineyards, Yakima Valley $38.   **84**

Saturated dark ruby hue. Richly fruity aromas show black cherry and cassis aromas with moderate oak accents. A rich entry leads a medium-bodied palate with fruit-forward flavors that fill the mouth. Tannins are supple and harmonious through the finish. Drink now or later.

1996 Melange, Yakima Valley $19.   **86**

Bright ruby-violet hue. Floral, violet scented aromas. A light entry leads to a medium-bodied palate with crisp fruit flavors and juicy fruit flavors. Very supple and juicy through the finish. Drink now.

1994 Merlot, Crawford Vineyard, Columbia Valley $19.   **87**

Opaque reddish purple. Moderately full-bodied. Moderately extracted. Moderately tannic. Reminiscent of red berries, dried herbs, minerals. Bright, lively red fruit entry with fine acidity, carrying through the midpalate into the finish. A very focused fruit-accented style with fine integrated tannins.

1994 Merlot, Klipsun Vineyards, Columbia Valley $19.   **85**

Opaque purple. Moderately full-bodied. Highly extracted. Moderately tannic. Reminiscent of cherry, tea, spice. Huge ripe berry aromas. Dense and concentrated berry fruit on the palate, with well-integrated soft tannins.

1996 Merlot, Klipsun Vineyards, Yakima Valley $32.   **82**

Woodward Canyon

1997 Chardonnay, Columbia Valley $30.   **87**

Deep yellow-straw cast. Moderately full-bodied. Balanced acidity. Highly extracted. Orange blossom, bread, minerals. Ripe and rounded, with subdued flavors and a weighty yet well-structured palate. The finish is firm and brightly acidic.

1997 Chardonnay, Reserve, Columbia Valley $35.   **89**

Brilliant yellow-gold. Rich buttery, fruity aromas are very stylish. A lush entry leads a moderately full-bodied palate with bright fruity flavors and a buttery mouthfeel. The finish is lengthy, with a touch of alcohol heat. Drink now.

1997 Riesling, Walla Walla County $9.   **86**

Bright pale golden hue. Aromas show a tropical, pithy character. Sweet and juicy on entry, with a medium bodied palate and an herbal note to the sweet flavors that linger on the finish. Features fine varietal character. Try with fresh fruit.

1995 Cabernet Sauvignon, Artist Series, Canoe Ridge Vineyard, Washington $28.   93

Bright ruby red. Moderately light-bodied. Moderately extracted. Moderately tannic. Brown spice, minerals. Minerally, spicy aromas lead a firm mouthful of black fruit flavors heightened by bright acids. A degree of minerally intensity that showcases terroir.

1996 Cabernet Sauvignon, Artist Series, Canoe Ridge Vineyard, Columbia Valley $40.   88

Saturated dark ruby hue. Generously aromatic with ripe fruit and chocolate notes. Oak spice is very evident. A rich entry leads a moderately full-bodied palate with rich berry fruit flavors and supple, silky tannins. Very harmoniously balanced. Drink now.

1994 Cabernet Sauvignon, Captain Z.K. Straight, Columbia Valley $35.   92

Dark garnet red. Medium-bodied. Highly extracted. Moderately tannic. Plums, tobacco, cedar, earth, bitter chocolate. Solid, extracted black fruit flavors have many complex overtones. Assertive and full flavored, with a dry, well-defined finish showing some astringent tannins. Good structure.

1995 Cabernet Sauvignon, Old Vines, Columbia Valley $45.   99

Dark, opaque ruby cast. Moderately full-bodied. Moderately extracted. Quite tannic. Exotic spice, black fruits. Distinctively spicy aromas follow through on a concentrated palate showing precision and intensity. Very deep flavors are matched by supple but abundant tannins through the finish.

1994 Merlot, Columbia Valley $28.   91

Bright reddish purple. Moderately full-bodied. Moderately extracted. Moderately oaked. Moderately tannic. Reminiscent of raspberry, plum, tobacco. Rich, inviting aromatics lead a bright entry with a rich mouthfeel and chewy, supple tannins through the fine finish.

1995 Merlot, Columbia Valley $30.   95

Deep blackish ruby hue. Moderately full-bodied. Balanced acidity. Highly extracted. Mildly oaked. Moderately tannic. Chocolate, minerals, black fruits. Deeply flavored, with a brooding, complex core. Big and rich in texture, yet it maintains a sense of lightness. Well balanced and quite skillfully made, with a long finish. The velvety tannins will mellow with age.

1997 Merlot, Columbia Valley $30.   90

Medium ruby red with a fading rim. Very oak-accented aromas with bright fruity accents. A rich entry leads a moderately full-bodied palate with tightly wound fruit flavors and firm, dry tannins. Acids are bright.

Yakima River

1997 Lemberger, Sof Lem, Yakima Valley $9.   85

Pale ruby purple. Attractive spice and red fruit aromas carry a Rhone-like herbal overtone. A crisp entry leads a peppery, medium-bodied palate with a snappy, flavorful character. Soft through the finish. Drink now.

1994 Cabernet Sauvignon, Yakima Valley $15.   87

Cherry red with brick overtones and a pale rim. Medium-bodied. Moderately extracted. Mildly tannic. Tomato leaves, red fruits, dried herbs. Quite distinctive high-toned aromas lead a bright and juicy palate, but with solid astringency running through the finish. Leaning toward austerity, with clean acids keeping it lively.

1994 Cabernet Sauvignon, Winemakers Reserve, Yakima Valley $24.99.   88

Dark red with a subtle garnet cast. Medium-bodied. Highly extracted. Quite tannic. Black fruits, oak spice. Aromas show a degree of development, with very prominent oak spice. Bright black-fruit flavors are deluged under a wall of spice and tannins. Still hard edged, but well stuffed.

1997 Cabernet-Merlot, Yakima Valley $9.49.   81

1994 Merlot, Yakima Valley $15.   89

Deep ruby to the rim with a slight garnet cast. Moderately full-bodied. Balanced acidity. Highly extracted. Moderately oaked. Mildly tannic. Plums, minerals, licorice. Pleasantly aromatic, with a lush, mouthfilling character and good balance. Velvety tannins emerge at the finish.

1994 Merlot, Winemaker's Reserve, Yakima Valley $28.   90

Deep ruby with a garnet cast. Full-bodied. Full acidity. Highly extracted. Heavily oaked. Quite tannic. Cherry cordial, cinnamon, sweet herbs. Full throttled in every way, this is a firmly structured wine with big flavors to match. Fairly well balanced, with some drying tannins at the finish; it may dry out with age. In the meantime, it is a very interesting wine; attractive but not for everyday quaffing.

1995 Johns Vintage Port, Yakima Valley $16.   83

Deep ruby-garnet cast. Full-bodied. Full acidity. Highly extracted. Brown spices, black fruits, minerals. Carries a distinctive toasty oak note throughout. Quite flavorful, though full-throttled and somewhat fierce, with a marked hot quality. Drying through the finish, with very slight sweetness.

Scale: Superlative (96-100), Exceptional (90-95), Highly Recommended (85-89), Recommended (80-84), Not Recommended (Under 80)

three

The Wines
of Oregon

An Introduction: The Wines of Oregon

Oregon's wine industry is small and convivial. It is a cottage industry where the largest winery would be one of the Napa Valley's smaller operations on Highway 29. To put it into perspective there are single wineries in California that produce as much wine as all producers in the state of Oregon combined do. Unlike in France, however, Napoleon is not to blame for the way in which the industry has developed. There, in Burgundy, egalitarian succession laws introduced by the famous (or infamous depending on your particular cultural perspective) emperor led to the subdivision of the great wine estates among all heirs, not just the eldest male. Thus instead of a single Clos de Vougeot property of 124 acres, today there are no less than 77 proprietors of Clos de Vougeot, offering a bewildering array of labels.

Luckily, the situation in Oregon is actually the reverse. Pioneers such as David Lett of Eyrie, along with families like the Ponzis, Blossers, Eraths, and Adelsheims came along in the '60s and early '70s with idealistic dreams of cultivating fine wines in what was then very much a virgin territory. On a shoestring budget, their operations necessarily started small and have grown with widening public acclaim. The year 1979 ushered in a new age for the industry as Eyrie's 1975 Pinot Noir triumphed over several famous Burgundies in a Paris tasting sponsored by Gault-Millau. This so incensed the respected Burgundian negociant Robert Drouhin, that he restaged the tasting the following year in Beaune, with the same result.

Eighteen years later Mr. Drouhin's wine is at the head of the class, his Willamette Valley cuvée, Domaine Drouhin that is. The Drouhin's investment in what they believe to be Oregon's potential was followed by international vintners such as Laurent-Perrier and Brian Croser of Australia's Petaluma Winery. These investments have in turn opened several Californians' eyes to the possibilities, and suddenly Oregon is as dynamic and bustling with the exchange of ideas as any of the world's new viticultural regions. As the cross-pollination continues and new viticultural practices are translated to the vineyard, Oregon's wines will continue to improve. The embodiment of this is the International Pinot Noir Festival, held each summer in Oregon, where the world's producers get together to exchange ideas and information about the world's most fickle grape.

That grape is, indisputably, Oregon's signature varietal, and when people used to talk only of potential, they are now tasting the results. Oregon is unique in that, unlike any other potential Pinot Noir sites in the New World (but very much like Burgundy), it is possessed of a cool climate in which the warmer sites are sought out for viticulture. California and Australia, on the other hand, have warmer climates in which the coolest spots are sought out for the planting of Pinot Noir. In California, that coolness is usually provided by a blanket of fog from the Pacific Ocean, without which the production of Pinot Noir and many other grapes would be impossible. There is relative certainty in these areas that the fog will come, and in between the sun will shine, year in and year out. Very few of these vintages will ever be completely "washed out" by bad weather.

Oregon, however, is far more marginal, where it can be a genuine struggle to get the grapes ripe enough. Rain at harvest is a constant fear, and the vines themselves labor under a great deal of stress. In short, it is Pinot Noir heaven, and so enter the masochists. While Oregon will never be able to achieve great consistency in terms of the wine being very similar year in and year out, its highs such as those achieved in vintage years such as 1992 and 1994, for example, will be very high indeed. In off years, just as in Burgundy, it will be left to the individual producer to craft better wines than the vintage conditions might otherwise suggest. This can already be seen in the excellent wines produced by Oregon's top vintners in 1993 or 1995.

To the Pinot Noir fanatic this wide fluctuation in vintage is not all bad. To the contrary, each vintage is expressed quite differently, which in competent hands brings wines that are not better or worse but just different, and that difference can be half the fun. While the best 1993s are all silk and polish—a delight to drink now—the powerful 1994s are candidates for the cellar. Oregon most certainly does not display the sort of monotony in its vintages that some other regions have been accused of.

If it all sounds disarmingly like Burgundy, it is, and more than any other region in the United States, Oregon has the best chance of becoming America's "Golden Slope." As Robert Drouhin says when tasting Domaine Drouhin's wines, he wants to be able to say "if it is not Côte-de-Nuits, not Côte-de-Beaune, it must be Oregon." In somewhat cantankerous reference to the hundred or so producers of Pinot Noir in Oregon today, a certain producer sniffed that today only "20 or 30" were making truly serious wines. However, if Burgundy itself had only 20 or 30 producers to whom you could point to unknowingly on a shelf and say that the wine therein would be good, a number of wine writers would be put out of business.

Oregon at a Glance

Wines Reviewed:

235

Producers/Brands Represented:

61

Top 25 Oregon Pinot Noir Cuvées

Pinot Noir only ripens consistently (particularly in "off" vintages) in the most favorably situated Oregon vineyards. In such a climate, vineyard and cuvée designations on labels become very meaningful. Different vineyard locations—or microclimates—bring with them a range of factors such as slope, facing, or soil drainage that will result in fruit ripening at different times, or some vineyards being better able to cope with rain than others. Although buying Oregon Pinot Noir is not quite as fraught with peril as in Burgundy, it pays to know your cuvée designations. Below is a list of the top 25 Oregon Pinot Noir cuvées. These specific wines can usually be regarded as the best that Oregon will offer in Pinot Noir—year in and year out.

Adelsheim: *Elizabeth's Reserve*
Adelsheim: *Seven Springs Vineyard*
Bethel Heights: *Flat Block Reserve*
Beaux Frères: *Beaux Frères*
Chehelam: *Ridgecrest Vineyard*
Chehelam: *Rion Reserve*
Cristom: *Marjorie Vineyard*
Domaine Drouhin: *Laurene*
Domaine Serene: *Evanstead Reserve*
Elk Cove: *La Boheme*
Erath: *Weber Vineyard Reserve*
Evesham Wood: *Cuvée "J"*
Evesham Wood: *Temperence Hill Vineyard*
Oak Knoll: *Vintage Reserve*
Panther Creek: *Bednarik Vineyard*
Panther Creek: *Freedom Hill*
Ponzi: *Reserve*
St. Innocent: *Temperance Hill Vineyard*
St. Innocent: *Freedom Hill Vineyard*
St. Innocent: *O'Connor Vineyard*
Silvan Ridge: *Visconti Vineyard*
Silvan Ridge: *Eola Springs Vineyard*
Sokol Blosser: *Redland*
Willamette Valley Vineyards: *OVB*
Ken Wright Cellars: *Canary Hill*

Reviews

Adelsheim

1995 Pinot Noir, Oregon $18.99.   90

Full crimson hue to a cherry-red rim. Medium-bodied. Moderately extracted. Moderately oaked. Moderately tannic. Jammy, earthy aromas. Smooth and harmonious, with great integration of flavors and depth on the palate. Very well balanced, with judicious tannins.

1994 Pinot Noir, Seven Springs Vineyard, Polk County $30.   90

Cherry red appearance. Medium-bodied. Moderately extracted. Moderately tannic. Reminiscent of berries, tar, dried herbs. Ripe berry fruit nose. Juicy berry fruit entry leads a firm finish with good tannins. A little dry on the finish, though this should resolve with further age.

Amity

1994 Pinot Noir, Willamette Valley $16.   86

Deep red color. Medium-bodied. Moderately extracted. Moderately oaked. Mildly tannic. Reminiscent of berries, raspberries, vanilla. Ripe, juicy style with vanilla oak flavors through the finish. Attractive and very drinkable.

1995 Pinot Noir, Oregon $12.   82

1995 Pinot Noir, Willamette Valley $16.   82

1995 Pinot Noir, Sunnyside Vineyard, Willamette Valley $18.   86

Pale pinkish red. Moderately light-bodied. Moderately extracted. Mildly oaked. Mildly tannic. Subtle floral aromas lead a crisp but lively palate of red fruits and minerals, with some richness on the midpalate and a subtle toasty finish.

1993 Pinot Noir, Winemakers Reserve, Willamette Valley $35.   90

Full dark red. Medium-bodied. Highly extracted. Moderately oaked. Moderately tannic. Rich black fruit with aromas of leather and earth. Full dry palate presence reveals tart black cherry flavors, with firm dry tannins throughout and a hint of toasty oak on a dry finish. Impressive structure. Needs some time.

Archery Summit

1996 Pinot Noir, Premier Cuvée, Oregon $35.   81

1996 Pinot Noir, Arcus Estate, Oregon $59.   86

Pale ruby cast. Medium-bodied. Full acidity. Moderately extracted. Moderately oaked. Mildly tannic. Sweet oak, minerals, red fruits. Forward aromas show generous sweet oak flavors. Light and lean in the mouth with racy acidity. Tasty and direct.

1996 Pinot Noir, Red Hills Estate, Oregon $59.   84

Pale dark ruby cast. Moderately full-bodied. Full acidity. Moderately extracted. Moderately oaked. Mildly tannic. Vanilla, minerals. Forward aromas carry a pleasant woody overtone. Light and lean in the mouth with a tight, minerally quality.

1996 Pinot Noir, Archery Summit Estate, Oregon $75.   84

Deep pale ruby cast. Moderately light-bodied. Full acidity. Subtly extracted. Mildly oaked. Moderately tannic. Minerals, brown spices. Aromatically reserved, showing a lean and minerally overtone. Light in the mouth with unyielding linear tannins in the finish.

Argyle

1994 Brut, Knudsen Vineyards, Willamette Valley $19.50.   89

Pale yellow-gold. Medium-bodied. Full acidity. Bread, citrus. Toasty, bready aromas have a firm citrus accent that follows well on the palate, with brisk, long citrus flavors that veer toward the lean side. The fine persistence is impressive.

Ashland

1995 Merlot, Rogue Valley $12.49.   86

Deep blackish ruby color. Medium-bodied. Full acidity. Moderately extracted. Mildly
oaked. Mildly tannic. Red fruits, minerals. Flavorful and quite crisp in style, with acidity
to the fore. Well balanced, with an angular, minerally finish.

Autumn Wind

1994 Pinot Noir, Reserve, Oregon $30.   90

Opaque dark red. Moderately full-bodied. Highly extracted. Moderately oaked.
Moderately tannic. Reminiscent of black cherries, vanilla, licorice. Quite rich and chewy,
with well-integrated, soft tannins through the finish. Generously proportioned style.

1996 Pinot Noir, Estate Reserve, Oregon $29.99.   80

Beaux Frères

1995 Pinot Noir, Yamhill County $50.   90

Dark crimson purple with an even fade. Moderately full-bodied. Highly extracted.
Moderately oaked. Moderately tannic. A seductive monster. Very polished and rounded,
with lots of supple tannins giving this great texture. Cherries, red plums, chocolate
flavors up front. Approachable now, but best to cellar it for a few years.

1996 Pinot Noir, Yamhill County $54.   82

Benton Lane

1996 Pinot Noir, Oregon $15.   86

Bright cherry red. Medium-bodied. Moderately extracted. Mildly oaked. Mildly tannic.
Earthy, brambly aromas lead a palate with black cherry flavors, and a peppery, spicy
finish. Some dry tannins are evident, but are well balanced. Drinking nicely now.

1994 Pinot Noir, Reserve, Oregon $28.50.   90

Deep reddish purple. Moderately full-bodied. Highly extracted. Quite tannic.
Reminiscent of brown spice, red fruits, minerals. A full and powerful style with a
dense center of fruit and weighty tannins through the finish. Needs more time to
resolve its big components and fine acidity.

1996 Pinot Noir, Reserve, Oregon $28.   90

Full ruby red with a light rim. Medium-bodied. Moderately extracted. Moderately oaked.
Mildly tannic. Rounded, ripe cherry aromas lead a rich, glycerous mouthfeel that imparts
a sense of smoothness through the finish. Herbal tea notes add complexity. Generous
and balanced.

Bethel Heights

1996 Chardonnay, Reserve, Willamette Valley $17.   81

1994 Pinot Noir, Flat Block Reserve, Willamette Valley $24.   89

Deep reddish purple. Medium-bodied. Moderately extracted. Mildly tannic. Reminiscent
of cherries, minerals, brown spice. Elegant nose, with a balanced and solidly structured
palate through an oak-spice-accented finish.

1996 Pinot Noir, Flat Block Reserve, Willamette Valley $28.   83

Bright ruby purple. Medium-bodied. Full acidity. Moderately extracted. Mildly oaked.
Mildly tannic. Vanilla, red fruits. Forward aromas carry a sweet oak accent. Lean and
lively in the mouth, with subdued red fruit flavors. Crisp through the finish.

1995 Pinot Noir, Wadenswil Block Reserve, Willamette Valley $24.   85

Dark cherry red. Medium-bodied. Highly extracted. Moderately oaked. Moderately
tannic. Roasted, medicinal nose. Distinctly austere, earthy notes lead a solid palate with
black fruit hints and supple but dry tannins throughout. Austere style.

Bridgeview

1997 Chardonnay, Oregon $5.99.   84

Bright pale straw hue. Moderately light-bodied. Balanced acidity. Moderately extracted. Yellow apples. Simple fruity aromas lead a straightforward tart mouthful with a clean finish.

1997 Chardonnay, Blue Moon, Oregon $9.99.   80

1997 Pinot Gris, Oregon $9.99.   86

Dark straw color with a slight copper cast. Moderately full-bodied. Full acidity. Moderately extracted. Bananas, minerals. Quite aromatic, with a very ripe nose. Full and rich on the palate with lean acidity lending vibrancy to the rounded smoky finish.

1996 Merlot, Black Beauty, Paso Robles $17.   87

Very deep purplish ruby hue with brilliant clarity. Medium-bodied. Balanced acidity. Moderately extracted. Heavily oaked. Mildly tannic. Chocolate, red fruits, sweet herbs. Quite aromatic, with complex flavors and a supple entry. Turns a little more angular and austere on the palate. Pleasant finish with good grip.

1995 Pinot Noir, Oregon $7.99.   84

Cherry red with purple highlights. Medium-bodied. Moderately extracted. Mildly oaked. Mildly tannic. Reminiscent of ripe cherries, vanilla. Perfumed aromas. Bright cherry fruit and soft tannins make this forward and supple, though without great sophistication. Very quaffable.

1996 Pinot Noir, Oregon $10.99.   85

Brilliant dark purple. Medium-bodied. Moderately extracted. Moderately tannic. Bright black fruit aromas lead a blackberry-flavored palate, with some dry tannins clamping down on the finish. Best with richer foods.

1997 Pinot Noir, Oregon $9.99.   81

1995 Pinot Noir, Reserve, Oregon $15.99.   87

Bright pinkish red. Medium-bodied. Moderately extracted. Moderately oaked. Moderately tannic. Vanilla and black cherry aromas lead maraschino cherry flavors on the palate, with attractive vanilla oak on the finish. Some astringent tannins dry the finish.

Broadley

1995 Pinot Noir, Reserve, Oregon $18.   88

Bright reddish purple. Medium-bodied. Highly extracted. Moderately oaked. Moderately tannic. Full earthy aromas are quite powerful. Tightly wound red fruit flavors of cherry and raspberry up front. A strong mineral underlay keeps this dry and lean through the finish.

Callahan Ridge

1998 White Zinfandel, Umpqua Valley $7.   85

Brilliant pale pink. Subdued mineral and candied berry aromas. A crisp entry leads a medium-bodied palate showing mild sweetness and a firm acidic cut. Tart, juicy finish. Drink now.

Chateau Benoit

1995 Chardonnay, Estate Reserve, Willamette Valley $18.   80

1996 Chardonnay, Dijon Clone Reserve, Willamette Valley $35.   88

Bright green-straw hue. Medium-bodied. Full acidity. Moderately extracted. Moderately oaked. Brown spice, citrus. Spicy, lemony aromas lead an angular yet concentrated palate with a lengthy finish. Quite structured and austere in nature.

1995 Pinot Noir, Estate, Willamette Valley $15.   80

1994 Pinot Noir, Estate Reserve, Willamette Valley $25.   **92**

Opaque deep red. Moderately full-bodied. Highly extracted. Moderately oaked. Moderately tannic. Reminiscent of black cherries, minerals. Rich fruity entry with concentrated mineral notes follows through to a dry tannic finish. Very impressively proportioned, although a bit backward now for some palates. Has the stuffing to cellar.

1995 Pinot Noir, Estate Reserve, Willamette Valley $22.   **81**

1996 Sweet Marie, Willamette Valley $15/375 ml.   **84**

Brilliant bronze hue. Minerally aromas with a tropical fruit accent. A lush entry leads a very sweet, medium-bodied palate. Clean through the finish. Drink now.

Chehalem

1996 Pinot Gris, Reserve, Ridgecrest Vineyards, Willamette Valley $19.   **83**

Bright golden cast. Moderately full-bodied. Full acidity. Moderately extracted. Smoke, dried herbs. Quite aromatic, with full smoky flavors on the palate. Rich texture, though racy acidity balances the dry, flavorful finish.

1995 Pinot Noir, Three Vineyard, Willamette Valley $15.   **87**

Pale cherry red with a light rim. Moderately light-bodied. Moderately extracted. Moderately oaked. Mildly tannic. Lightly perfumed aromas of toasted oak and crisp red fruits. Elegant and lively mouthfeel. Slightly chocolatey flavors through the finish. Well balanced, drinking nicely now.

1996 Pinot Noir, Three Vineyard, Willamette Valley $18.   **85**

Bright pale ruby cast. Medium-bodied. Balanced acidity. Moderately extracted. Moderately oaked. Mildly tannic. Brown spices, red fruits. Forward aromas carry a hefty wood accent and a core of velvety berry flavors. Tasty, but lacks a bit for grip on the finish.

1995 Pinot Noir, Ridgecrest Vineyard, Willamette Valley $22.   **86**

Medium ruby red with a garnet cast . Medium-bodied. Moderately extracted. Moderately oaked. Mildly tannic. Full oak-accented aromas. An oaky palate with black cherry nuances and a crisp character. Some fruit persistence on the lingering toasty finish. Drinking nicely now.

1995 Pinot Noir, Rion Reserve, Willamette Valley $34.   **89**

Pale ruby red to a graduated light rim. Medium-bodied. Moderately extracted. Moderately oaked. Mildly tannic. Smoky cherry aromas lead a smooth, silky mouthfeel that reveals concentrated flavors and a rich texture. The tannins are mild but green tasting. This will be better with some bottle age.

1996 Pinot Noir, Rion Reserve, Ridgecrest Vineyard, Willamette Valley $38.   **83**

Pale ruby-garnet cast. Moderately full-bodied. Low acidity. Moderately extracted. Moderately oaked. Mildly tannic. Brown spices, dried herbs, red fruits. Subdued aromas feature an herbal overtone and a generous oak accent. Lush and supple in the mouth, but low acidity makes for a flat finish.

Cooper Mountain

1997 Chardonnay, Willamette Valley $14.75.   **85**

Pale straw color. Medium-bodied. Full acidity. Moderately extracted. Apple, sweet lemon. Apple aromas lead a lively, juicy mouthful of flavors, with a clean finish that has some grip. Fresh, lively, and cleansing.

1996 Chardonnay, Reserve, Willamette Valley $19.75.   **88**

Bright gold-straw color. Moderately full-bodied. Full acidity. Highly extracted. Lemon, green apple, minerals. Attractive yeasty aromas. Bright acids bolster austere citrus flavors that grip the palate through the finish. Drinking well, with some mature notes.

Scale: Superlative (96-100), Exceptional (90-95), Highly Recommended (85-89), Recommended (80-84), Not Recommended (Under 80)

264

1997 Pinot Gris, Willamette Valley $14.75.   86

Bright straw hue. Medium-bodied. Full acidity. Moderately extracted. Minerals, flint. Lean, crisp, and racy, with a sharp and tangy mouthfeel. Fleshes out with a bit of richness through the finish. Will cut rich foods well.

1994 Pinot Noir, Estate, Willamette Valley $15.75.   87

Medium ruby color. Medium-bodied. Moderately extracted. Moderately tannic. Reminiscent of tart cherries, minerals. Very firm acidity with some decent fruit extraction gives this a firm palate presence. Although not hugely proportioned, it is well balanced, and the acidity should allow it to improve further.

1995 Pinot Noir, Willamette Valley $13.   80

1994 Pinot Noir, Estate Reserve, Willamette Valley $29.75.   91

Dark red. Moderately full-bodied. Highly extracted. Moderately tannic. Reminiscent of red fruits, brown spice, earth. A firm, structured style with a concentrated plummy, fruity palate and impressive tannins through the finish. Tight, focused, and in need of cellar age.

1995 Pinot Noir, Reserve, Willamette Valley $25.   88

Bright crimson purple. Medium-bodied. Moderately extracted. Moderately oaked. Mildly tannic. Toasty black cherry aromas. Dried cherry flavors show some concentration. Quite tight right now, this has some stuffing, although it is not particularly tannic.

Cristom

1996 Pinot Noir, Louise Vineyard, Willamette Valley $32.   88

Deep ruby-garnet cast. Moderately full-bodied. Balanced acidity. Moderately extracted. Heavily oaked. Mildly tannic. Dried herbs, sandalwood, dill pickle. An aggressively herbal nose leads a lush mouthfeel with a hefty oak accent. Supple though firm. Features a lingering flavorful finish.

1994 Pinot Noir, Marjorie Vineyard, Willamette Valley $27.   92

Dark reddish purple. Moderately full-bodied. Highly extracted. Reminiscent of briar fruits, minerals, earth. Chunky, concentrated fruit-accented style. Quite rich, with a distinctive mineral note on the palate. Short- to medium-term cellaring should benefit this.

1995 Pinot Noir, Marjorie Vineyard, Willamette Valley $27.   89

Bright crimson with a very subtle purple fade to the rim. Medium-bodied. Moderately extracted. Mildly oaked. Moderately tannic. Herbal, earthy black fruit aromas play out well on the palate, with dry, fine-grained tannins providing some grip through the finish. Nice structure, suggesting it should develop well over the near term.

1996 Pinot Noir, Marjorie Vineyard, Willamette Valley $32.   90

Bright deep ruby hue. Moderately full-bodied. Balanced acidity. Moderately extracted. Moderately oaked. Mildly tannic. Red fruits, minerals, vanilla. Ripe and lush, with an aromatic interplay between fruit and wood flavors. Supple and generous in the mouth. Lingering spicy finish.

1994 Pinot Noir, Mt. Jefferson Cuvée, Willamette Valley $17. 89

Ruby color. Medium-bodied. Moderately extracted. Mildly tannic. Reminiscent of violets, black fruits, brown spices. A quite seductive, accessible style characterized by good mouthfeel and nice concentrated black fruit on the palate. There is some mild astringency on the finish. Drinking well now.

1995 Pinot Noir, Mt. Jefferson Cuvée, Willamette Valley $17. 85

Pale cherry red. Moderately light-bodied. Moderately extracted. Mildly oaked. Mildly tannic. Faint earthy, meaty, barnyard aromas lead a delicate dry palate of dried red fruit flavors through a finish with balanced fine-grained tannins. Quite a light style.

1996 Pinot Noir, Mt. Jefferson Cuvée, Willamette Valley $20. 82

1994 Pinot Noir, Reserv7e, Willamette Valley $27.   92

Bright red at the center with a purple-tinged rim. Moderately full-bodied. Highly extracted. Heavily oaked. Moderately tannic. Reminiscent of cranberry, leather, vanilla. Big leathery red fruit nose. Good center of red fruits well balanced by generous toasted oak flavors though the lengthy finish. Structured, generous, and drinking well now.

1995 Pinot Noir, Reserve, Willamette Valley $27.   88

Dark crimson, with an even fade on the rim. Medium-bodied. Moderately extracted. Moderately oaked. Mildly tannic. Green herbs and black cherry aromas lead a dark fruit entry with a bright character and lively acids. Some meaty notes linger through the finish, with fine-grained tannins. Well balanced, drinking nicely now.

1996 Pinot Noir, Reserve, Willamette Valley $30.   84

Pale ruby cast. Medium-bodied. Full acidity. Moderately extracted. Moderately oaked. Moderately tannic. Minerals, red fruits, spice. Aromatic yet lean, with a fragrant spicy quality and an angular mouthfeel. Finishes on the tough side.

Domaine Drouhin

1994 Pinot Noir, Oregon $30.   89

Bright reddish purple. Medium-bodied. Moderately extracted. Moderately oaked. Moderately tannic. Dry. Reminiscent of red fruits, minerals, cinnamon. Full, fruity aromatics lead a rich palate with rounded, mouthfilling flavors complemented by a minerally backbone through to a lengthy toasty finish. Approachable, though this has the structure to age.

1995 Pinot Noir, Oregon $28.   88

Deep ruby hue with a purple rim. Moderately full-bodied. Highly extracted. Moderately oaked. Moderately tannic. Reminiscent of red fruits, minerals, spice. A structured style with big balanced components, though it is rather closed and tight at present. Needs more time to come together.

1996 Pinot Noir, Oregon $33.   86

Pale ruby cast. Medium-bodied. Balanced acidity. Moderately extracted. Mildly oaked. Moderately tannic. Dried herbs, minerals, vanilla. Shows an attractive herbal edge throughout. Light in the mouth but balanced, with a lean finish that has grip.

1997 Pinot Noir, Oregon $33.   81

1994 Pinot Noir, Laurene, Willamette Valley $42.   94

Deep red with a bright purple rim. Moderately full-bodied. Highly extracted. Mildly oaked. Moderately tannic. Reminiscent of red fruits, vanilla, sweet herbs. A little closed aromatically but with dark, brooding aromas. Densely extracted flavors on the palate, with amazing focus and length. Extraordinary integration of flavors in this wine bodes well for its future.

1995 Pinot Noir, Laurene, Willamette Valley $45.   91

Dark crimson hue with an even fade. Medium-bodied. Moderately extracted. Moderately oaked. Moderately tannic. Undeveloped nose at present. Smooth, rich palate of soft red cherry flavors, with a toasty mocha note on a finish that shows good tannic grip.

1996 Pinot Noir, Laurene, Willamette Valley $48.   89

Bright ruby purple. Moderately full-bodied. Balanced acidity. Moderately extracted. Moderately oaked. Moderately tannic. Vanilla, red fruits. Attractive aromas are forward and clean, with ripe red fruits and a sweet oak accent. Shows some richness in the mouth and is finely balanced. Lean and angular through the flavorful finish.

Domaine Serene

1994 Pinot Noir, Reserve, Willamette Valley $20.   90

Bright reddish purple. Moderately full-bodied. Highly extracted. Moderately tannic. Reminiscent of ripe cherries, dried herbs, minerals. Bright, lively, lush fruit-accented style with a lengthy fruity finish complemented by soft tannins. Very elegant and long on the palate.

1994 Pinot Noir, Evenstad Reserve, Willamette Valley $30.   **91**

Dense reddish purple. Moderately full-bodied. Highly extracted. Reminiscent of brown spice, red fruits, oak. A bright, lively, concentrated palate with lots of ripe red fruits. Quite structured but very accessible.

1995 Pinot Noir, Evenstad Reserve, Willamette Valley $33.   **93**

Pale crimson hue. Moderately light-bodied. Moderately extracted. Mildly oaked. Mildly tannic. Perfumed, floral aromas. Crisp and lively red fruit flavors have a juicy black cherry character, with a faintly sweet vanilla oak note lingering on the finish.

Duck Pond

1997 Chardonnay, Fries' Family Cellars, Columbia Valley $9.99.   **84**

Bright straw cast. Moderately full-bodied. Full acidity. Highly extracted. Apples, pears, yeast. Forward aromas carry a firmly defined fruit quality and a yeasty accent. Full and ripe in the mouth with spritzy acidity through the finish.

1997 Cabernet Sauvignon, Fries' Desert Wind Vineyard,
Columbia Valley $12.   **81**

1995 Pinot Noir, Willamette Valley $8.   **89**

Pale ruby hue with a light rim. Medium-bodied. Moderately extracted. Mildly oaked. Moderately tannic. Reminiscent of smoke, cranberries, ferrous minerals. Tart fruit palate with some astringent notes. Good acidity gives this some backbone through the minerally finish.

1996 Pinot Noir, Willamette Valley $8.   **80**

1994 Pinot Noir, Fries, Family Reserve, Willamette Valley $25.   **91**

Deep ruby color. Moderately full-bodied. Moderately extracted. Heavily oaked. Moderately tannic. Reminiscent of black fruits, raspberries, new oak. Big oaky presence on the palate giving flavors that are matched by dense and finely extracted fruit through the lengthy finish.

Elk Cove

1995 Pinot Noir, Yamhill County $17.   **80**

1994 Pinot Noir, Estate Reserve, Willamette Valley $25.   **89**

Pale ruby color. Medium-bodied. Moderately extracted. Mildly oaked. Moderately tannic. Reminiscent of oriental spice, cola, red cherries. Mouthfilling bright fruit with a touch of leanness through to a mildly astringent finish.

1994 Pinot Noir, La Boheme Vineyard, Willamette Valley $35.   **90**

Ruby red with a subtle haze. Moderately full-bodied. Highly extracted. Mildly oaked. Moderately tannic. Reminiscent of earth, oriental spices, red fruits. Big, with a racy mouthfilling character and excellent fruit definition carried by brisk acidity. A little young for current drinking but should do well in the cellar.

1996 Pinot Noir, Roosevelt, Oregon $40.   **86**

Bright dark ruby cast. Moderately full-bodied. Full acidity. Moderately extracted. Moderately oaked. Moderately tannic. Black fruits, minerals. Forward aromas feature a spicy overtone and a core of red fruit flavors. Lean and quite angular in the mouth, with a firm finish.

Eola Hills

1996 Chardonnay, Oregon $12.   **88**

Medium green-straw cast. Medium-bodied. Balanced acidity. Moderately extracted. Green apples, citrus fruits. Bright, crisp aromas lead a rounded, fruity mouthful with clean flavors persisting through the finish.

1996 Pinot Noir, Reserve, Oregon $20.   **84**

Pale ruby-garnet cast. Medium-bodied. Low acidity. Highly extracted. Mildly oaked. Moderately tannic. Minerals, wood, red fruits. Shows a slight green overtone in the nose. Firm and unyielding in the mouth, with an angular finish.

NV Late Harvest Sauvignon Blanc, Vin D'Or, Willamette Valley $15.   **85**

Bronzed golden hue. Full-bodied. Full acidity. Highly extracted. Dried herbs, citrus. Sweet citrus aromas, with an amazingly sweet, viscous, and acidic palate. Impressive, but perhaps a bit much—only for the true sugar junkie.

Erath

1996 Chardonnay, Reserve, Willamette Valley $20.   **80**

1997 Chardonnay, Reserve, Willamette Valley $20.   **82**

1996 Chardonnay, Reserve, Niederberger Vineyard, Willamette Valley $50.   **88**

Bright gold-straw color. Moderately full-bodied. Full acidity. Mildly oaked. Citrus, vanilla, brown spice. Rich, spicy aromas lead an impressively concentrated spicy mouthful of flavors, with a lingering, persistent finish. Has the structure to improve with a few more years of age.

1997 Chardonnay, Reserve, Niederberger Vineyard, Willamette Valley $50.   **84**

Bright gold-straw color. Medium-bodied. Balanced acidity. Moderately extracted. Mildly oaked. Ripe apples, brown spice. Rounded and juicy, with clean, ripe Chardonnay fruit flavors accented by a hint of oak spice. Very forward and generous in character.

1997 Pinot Gris, Willamette Valley $12.   **82**

1996 Pinot Noir, Willamette Valley $13.   **82**

1993 Pinot Noir, Reserve, Willamette Valley $20.   **89**

Medium ruby color with a garnet cast. Medium-bodied. Moderately extracted. Moderately oaked. Mildly tannic. Reminiscent of spice, ferrous minerals, mild raspberries. Rather dry, with pronounced wood flavors and lean, high-toned fruit through the finish. The sum of the parts is a subtle but acquired taste that works well with food.

1996 Pinot Noir, Reserve, Willamette Valley $27.   **84**

Deep ruby red with a slight fade. Medium-bodied. Balanced acidity. Moderately extracted. Moderately oaked. Mildly tannic. Brown spices, minerals, red fruits. Forward aromas carry a big spicy overtone. Full in the mouth, though quite lean and structured. Flavorful through the finish.

1995 Pinot Noir, Vintage Select, Willamette Valley $19.   **86**

Bright ruby red with a gradually lightening rim. Medium-bodied. Moderately extracted. Moderately oaked. Mildly tannic. Runs the gamut from smooth, harmonious pie cherry flavors with a mildly bitter edge, to chocolate and cinnamon flavors that linger through the finish.

1994 Pinot Noir, Weber Vineyard Reserve, Willamette Valley $25.   **91**

Ruby color. Medium-bodied. Moderately extracted. Moderately oaked. Moderately tannic. Reminiscent of blackberries, earth, chocolate. Solid, rich black fruit palate with generous toasty flavors well integrated through to the lengthy finish. Drinking well now.

1997 Late Harvest White Riesling, Willamette Valley $9.   **83**

Pale gold luster. Bright apple and mineral aromas. An off-dry attack leads a medium-bodied palate displaying smooth, pure fruity flavors. Acids are quite soft through the finish. Drink now.

1997 Late Harvest, Gewürztraminer, Willamette Valley $18/375 ml.   **93**

Very deep copper-straw hue. Exotic aromas show an enticing, honeyed, bready quality. A rich entry leads a medium-bodied palate, with lots of sweetness and a lush, harmonious quality. Seems to have seen a good deal of botrytis. Very enticing. Drink now.

Evesham Wood

1994 Pinot Noir, Temperance Hill Vineyard, Willamette Valley $24.   **91**

Deep cherry red. Moderately full-bodied. Highly extracted. Reminiscent of blackberry, licorice, brown spice. Intense and deeply aromatic. A structured, big-shouldered style with impressive tannins through the finish. Nice oak notes are well balanced. Needs further cellar age.

Eyrie

1995 Pinot Noir, Willamette Valley $19.   **88**

Very pale garnet red. Moderately light-bodied. Moderately extracted. Moderately oaked. Moderately tannic. Perfumed, earthy, oriental spice box nose. A crisp, juicy palate shows soft red fruit flavors that are delicate though persistent through the finish. Lovely mouthfeel. Nice now.

1996 Pinot Noir, Willamette Valley $14.   **81**

Fiddlehead

1994 Pinot Noir, Willamette Valley $32.   **88**

Deep purplish red. Medium-bodied. Highly extracted. Moderately tannic. Reminiscent of raspberry, dried herbs. Bright youthful appearance. Concentrated berry fruit flavors on the palate give this a forward, fruit-driven character.

1995 Pinot Noir, Willamette Valley $32.   **88**

Medium cherry red. Medium-bodied. Moderately extracted. Moderately oaked. Mildly tannic. Sweet black fruit aromas reveal some jammy qualities on the palate. Cinnamon and chocolate flavors linger nicely on the finish.

Firesteed

1995 Pinot Noir, Oregon $9.99.   **87**

Pale cherry red with a light rim. Medium-bodied. Moderately extracted. Mildly tannic. Reminiscent of merde, dark fruits. Slightly Burgundian nose showing dark fruit. Rounded, elegant mouthfeel with a core of good red fruit through to a lengthy, fruity finish. Very accessible style.

1996 Pinot Noir, Oregon $9.99.   **81**

Flynn

1994 Pinot Noir, Estate, Willamette Valley $14.   **87**

Deep cherry red. Moderately full-bodied. Highly extracted. Moderately oaked. Moderately tannic. Reminiscent of cherries, black tea. A finely extracted, concentrated cherry fruit palate is well balanced by good astringent tannins through the finish. Impressive, but a little backward and tight at present.

Foris

1994 Cabernet Sauvignon, Klipsun Vineyard, Yakima Valley $19.   **88**

Opaque red-purple. Full-bodied. Highly extracted. Quite tannic. Black fruits. Dense, stuffed, and tightly wound at present. This has all the structural elements to age well, though is hard to appreciate now.

Girardet

1994 Pinot Noir, Barrel Select, Umpqua Valley $18.   **88**

Rich ruby appearance. Moderately full-bodied. Highly extracted. Moderately oaked. Moderately tannic. Reminiscent of briar fruits, vanilla. Pleasant aromas complement a clean, very concentrated berry palate with some mild astringency on the finish.

Henry Estate

1996 Chardonnay, Umpqua Valley $15.   89

Bright yellow-straw hue. Moderately full-bodied. Full acidity. Moderately oaked. Lime, vanilla, citrus. Spicy, oak-accented aromas lead a bright, racy mouthful, with concentrated flavors and impressive persistence through the finish.

1998 Gewürztraminer, Umpqua Valley $10.   84

Brilliant platinum hue. Subdued mineral and citrus aromas. A racy entry leads a medium-bodied palate, with aggressive acidity balancing ample richness. Clean, stylish finish. Drink now.

1998 Muller Thurgau, Umpqua Valley $8.   85

Bright straw hue. Ripe, spicy fruit cocktail aromas are quite generous. A sharp entry leads a light-bodied palate featuring tart acidity and a hint of sweetness. Intense and concentrated. Very clean, precise finish. Drink now.

1998 White Riesling, Umpqua Valley $8.   84

Very pale straw hue. Yellow apple aromas. A juicy entry leads a moderately light-bodied palate, with a good concentration of fruit flavors persisting through the finish. Drink now.

1997 Henry the IV, Umpqua Valley $20.   84

Brilliant purple-red hue. Lean earth, mineral, and black fruit aromas show a slight reductive note. A sharp attack leads to a moderately light-bodied palate with firm astringent tannins. Angular finish. A firm and austere style. Drink within five years.

1997 Merlot, Umpqua Valley $15.   82

1993 Pinot Noir, Barrel Select, Umpqua Valley $18.   87

Pale ruby hue. Medium-bodied. Moderately extracted. Mildly tannic. Rounded, balanced mouthfeel with some good glycerous notes. Though slightly lean in fruit flavors, it is a nice, relatively subtle style.

1994 Pinot Noir, Barrel Select, Umpqua Valley $24.   89

Dark cherry red with a purple cast. Medium-bodied. Moderately extracted. Moderately oaked. Moderately tannic. Vanilla oak and raspberry aromas are well expressed on the palate, with some intensity of fruit flavors and enough tannic grip to match.

1995 Pinot Noir, Barrel Select, Umpqua Valley $20.   86

Bright ruby purple. Moderately full-bodied. Balanced acidity. Moderately extracted. Moderately oaked. Mildly tannic. Carries a distinct hint of overripeness throughout. Ripe and flavorful in the mouth with a sense of richness. Sweet vanilla oak nuances play out in the finish.

1995 Pinot Noir, Umpqua Cuvée, Umpqua Valley $10.   85

Pale cherry red with purple highlights. Medium-bodied. Subtly extracted. Mildly oaked. Mildly tannic. Reminiscent of red berries, vanilla. A lighter style, with high-toned bright fruit and a balanced, mildly astringent finish. Highly quaffable.

1996 Pinot Noir, Umpqua Cuvée, Umpqua Valley $10.   80

1997 Pinot Noir, Umpqua Cuvée, Umpqua Valley $11.   81

Hinman

1998 Riesling, Willamette Valley $6.99.   81

1994 Pinot Noir, Oregon $10.99.   86

Bright reddish purple. Medium-bodied. Moderately extracted. Reminiscent of vanilla, cranberries, raspberries. Tart, lively palate with plenty of crisp fresh fruit and good astringency through the finish. Well integrated, with a seamless character.

1995 Pinot Noir, Oregon $11.   84

Bright reddish purple. Medium-bodied. Moderately extracted. Mildly oaked. Mildly tannic. Mild smoke and leather aromas. Simple but bright red cherry flavors have some fine-grained tannic grip through the finish.

Scale: Superlative (96-100), Exceptional (90-95), Highly Recommended (85-89), Recommended (80-84), Not Recommended (Under 80)

Honeywood

NV Niagara, Oregon $7.50.   80

Grande Cranberry Wine, $7.50.   87

Brilliant pale red with a pinkish cast. Moderately full-bodied. Full acidity. Highly extracted. Cranberries. Extremely fragrant, with a pure cranberry flavor throughout. Full and intense on the palate, with sturdy acidity and a definite bitter note that balances the sweetness. Fine.

Grande Peach Wine, $7.50.   88

Deep straw cast. Moderately full-bodied. Balanced acidity. Moderately extracted. Peaches. Extremely aromatic, with a pungent nose that is pure peach essence. The flavors are well translated onto the palate, and finish with some gentle sweetness. Pure and well crafted.

Red Currant Wine, Oregon $7.50.   88

Bright ruby-garnet cast. Moderately full-bodied. Full acidity. Highly extracted. Red fruits, dried herbs, wood. Quite aromatic, with distinctive herbal overtones. The palate is full throttled, with marked sweetness offset by a tart, juicy quality. Intense.

King Estate

1996 Chardonnay, Oregon $14.   81

1996 Chardonnay, Reserve, Oregon $18.   88

Medium yellow-gold. Smoky oak aromas. A vibrant attack leads a medium-bodied palate with crisp, well-defined fruit flavors and rich oaky accents that persist through the finish. Very well balanced, with good acid verve. This could improve over time. Drink now or later.

1996 Pinot Gris, Oregon $13.   90

Bright yellow-straw cast. Moderately full-bodied. Full acidity. Moderately extracted. Oranges, minerals, spice. Features a ripe nose, with a spicy accent to the fruit flavors. Full and rich with vibrant acidity through the rounded, smoky finish.

1996 Pinot Gris, Reserve, Oregon $18.   82

1994 Cabernet Sauvignon, Oregon $30.   86

Bright ruby red hue. Generous sweet herb and red fruit aromas. A lean entry leads to a medium-bodied palate with firm astringent tannins and a pronounced acidic cut. Intense, structured finish. A clean and precise structure suggests a useful wine at the table. Drink within five years.

1995 Pinot Noir, Oregon $18.   86

Pale ruby-garnet cast. Medium-bodied. Balanced acidity. Moderately extracted. Mildly oaked. Mildly tannic. Vanilla, red fruits, minerals. Generous aromas feature a spicy oak accent. Seamless and supple in the mouth, with a crisp finish.

1994 Zinfandel, Oregon $20.   87

Deep blackish ruby hue. Medium-bodied. Full acidity. Moderately extracted. Moderately oaked. Mildly tannic. Brown spices, red fruits. Toasty oak aromas, with a core of vibrant fruit flavors. Lighter on the palate, with sturdy acidity. Excellent grip and intensity, with a balance that makes for easy drinking.

Kramer

1993 Pinot Noir, Estate, Willamette Valley $18.   84

Cherry red with a garnet cast. Moderately light-bodied. Subtly extracted. Mildly tannic. Rather light in style with some dry wood notes through the finish. Certainly for current drinking.

1992 Pinot Noir, Reserve, Willamette Valley $22.   85

Medium ruby red with a subtle garnet cast. Medium-bodied. Moderately extracted. Reminiscent of red fruits, green tea, minerals. Has a solid center of crisp, mildly tart fruit, with some astringent tannins through the finish.

La Garza

1996 Cabernet Sauvignon, Umpqua Valley $15.   84

Bright ruby purple. Medium-bodied. Full acidity. Moderately extracted. Mildly tannic. Cherries, minerals. Crisp and tart, with a lighter-styled palate and an unusual note to the flavors. Clipped, zesty finish.

1995 Cabernet Sauvignon, Reserve, Umpqua Valley $25.   82

Lange

1997 Chardonnay, Willamette Valley $16.   81

1996 Chardonnay, Reserve, Willamette Valley $20.   84

Pale straw hue. Medium-bodied. Full acidity. Moderately extracted. Citrus, minerals. Subtly oxidized aromas. Crisp, bright, austere citrus flavors emerge, though the mouthfeel is generous. Finishes on a lean, minerally note.

1994 Pinot Noir, Willamette Valley $18.   90

Deep red, nearly opaque appearance. Moderately full-bodied. Highly extracted. Moderately oaked. Moderately tannic. Reminiscent of bing cherries, licorice, minerals. Floral-scented nose. Generous and well-integrated flavors on the palate, with a creamy texture and a harmonious character. Very approachable now.

1996 Pinot Noir, Estate, Willamette Valley $40.   81

1994 Pinot Noir, Reserve, Willamette Valley $40.   93

Deep ruby color. Medium-bodied. Moderately extracted. Reminiscent of black fruits, earth, sweet herbs. Intriguing and complex earthy nose. Rich center of dark fruits with complex earthy flavors that are well integrated through the lengthy finish. Refined and graceful. Drinking nicely now but should be cellared for optimum pleasure.

1996 Pinot Noir, Reserve, Willamette Valley $20.   82

LaVelle

1996 Pinot Gris, Winter's Hill Vineyard, Oregon $13.   86

Deep yellow-straw cast. Moderately full-bodied. Full acidity. Moderately extracted. Tropical fruits, cream, minerals. Quite ripe and aromatic, with a sense of richness to the flavors. Vibrant acidity lends a cleansing note to the palate. Good grip and fine length on the finish.

1997 Riesling, Susan's Vineyard, Willamette Valley $8.   86

Medium gold luster. Classic Riesling aromas of petrol and tropical fruits. A lush entry leads a medium-bodied palate, with a fine glycerous mouthfeel and generous sweet fruit flavors. The finish has an oily note. A comparatively soft, medium-sweet style. Drink now.

Lorane Valley

1996 Pinot Noir, Oregon $10.   81

McKinlay

1995 Pinot Noir, Special Selection, Willamette Valley $32.50. 89

Dark crimson with an even fade to the rim. Medium-bodied. Moderately extracted. Moderately oaked. Mildly tannic. Herbaceous, with smooth red berry fruits. Good persistence of fruit flavors, with dried herbal notes lingering on the finish. Easy going and supple. Drinking well now.

Montinore

1996 Chardonnay, Winemaker's Reserve, Willamette Valley $17.99. 83

Bright straw cast. Medium-bodied. Full acidity. Moderately extracted. Minerals, citrus. Aromatically reserved, with a crisp and lively palate feel. Vibrant and zesty through the finish.

Scale: Superlative (96-100), Exceptional (90-95), Highly Recommended (85-89), Recommended (80-84), Not Recommended (Under 80)

1997 Pinot Gris, Willamette Valley $9.99.   **86**

Platinum hue with a bright copper cast. Medium-bodied. Full acidity. Highly extracted. Blanched almonds, pears. Distinctive aromas lead an austere palate showing taut acids through a dry finish. Quite an assertive style that should partner with foods.

1995 Pinot Noir, Willamette Valley $10.   **83**

Pale cherry red. Moderately light-bodied. Moderately extracted. Mildly oaked. Moderately tannic. Reminiscent of green herbs, tart cherries, earth. A lighter style, with some astringent tannins on the midpalate through the finish. Would suit those who like subtler, leaner styles.

1994 Pinot Noir, Winemaker's Reserve, Willamette Valley $14.   **88**

Deep cherry red. Medium-bodied. Moderately extracted. Moderately oaked. Moderately tannic. Reminiscent of cherry fruit, earth, dried herbs. Quite solid on the palate, with ample acids, fruit, and tannins. Though a bit closed, it should resolve with some further age.

1995 Pinot Noir, Winemaker's Reserve, Willamette Valley $17.99.   **87**

Bright pinkish red. Medium-bodied. Moderately extracted. Moderately oaked. Moderately tannic. Tart red cherry aromas have sage and thyme nuances. Focused, crisp cherry and raspberry flavors are supported by bright acids and mild but dry tannins, with subtle oak influences on the finish. Plenty of primary fruit flavors.

Mystic Mountain

1997 Chardonnay, Willamette Valley $16.   **82**

Oak Knoll

1996 Chardonnay, Willamette Valley $14.   **86**

Green-straw color. Medium-bodied. Balanced acidity. Moderately extracted. Lemon, apples. Zesty aromas lead a full-flavored palate with bright fruity flavors that finish with a note of sourness, making for an assertive style.

1996 Pinot Gris, Willamette Valley $13.   **84**

Bright straw cast. Medium-bodied. Full acidity. Moderately extracted. Citrus zest, minerals. Bright, fresh, and racy in style with zesty acidity. Clean and crisp, if a tad unyielding in flavors. This does leave the palate refreshed.

1996 Pinot Gris, Vintage Reserve, Willamette Valley $17.   **93**

Deep straw cast. Moderately full-bodied. Full acidity. Highly extracted. Flowers, oranges, minerals. Perfumed, pungent aromas reveal a wave of complex and exotic flavors. Extremely vibrant and zesty on the palate, with a lean, cleansing finish that is quite assertive.

1995 Pinot Noir, Willamette Valley $15.   **87**

Pale cherry red with a light rim. Moderately light-bodied. Moderately extracted. Mildly tannic. Pungent leathery, earthy aromas. Lively, savory red cherry flavors have a meaty character that lingers through the finish. Well balanced, drinking nicely now.

1994 Pinot Noir, Silver Anniversary Reserve, Willamette Valley $20.   **90**

Reddish purple. Medium-bodied. Moderately extracted. Moderately tannic. Reminiscent of red fruits, brown spice, vanilla. Bright concentrated fruit on the entry, with impressive full tannins through the finish. Quite angular and structured, it needs more time.

1994 Pinot Noir, Vintage Reserve, Willamette Valley $34.   **91**

Dark black-cherry red. Medium-bodied. Highly extracted. Moderately oaked. Moderately tannic. Rich bramble fruit aromas lead a rich, flavorsome palate with a dry earthy backbone. Good tannic grip through the finish. Chewy and substantial, this has the structure to age well.

Frambrosia Raspberry Wine, Oregon $10/375 ml.   **87**

Bright ruby-garnet cast. Medium-bodied. Full acidity. Moderately extracted. Raspberries. Pungent aromas of raspberries are translated well to the palate. Flavorful, though firmly structured, with vibrant acidity making for a lean finish with the slightest hint of sweetness.

Panther Creek

1994 Pinot Noir, Bednarik Vineyard, Willamette Valley $35.　　　92

Opaque blackish red with a full-colored rim. Full-bodied. Highly extracted. Heavily oaked. Quite tannic. Reminiscent of plums, black cherries, tar. Deep, brooding nose. Hugely thick, rich, and textured, with plenty of rich, heavy, well-integrated tannins. This has all the components in big proportions and should be cellared long term. Exotic.

1995 Pinot Noir, Bednarik Vineyard, Willamette Valley $27.99.　　　88

Full crimson hue to a graduated, lightening rim. Medium-bodied. Moderately extracted. Moderately oaked. Moderately tannic. Full, aromatic earth and black cherry nose. A solid dry palate shows plenty of toasty oak character and dry berry and pomegranate fruit flavors. Needs a little time to come together.

1995 Pinot Noir, Freedom Hill Vineyard, Willamette Valley $27.99.　　　90

Dark crimson purple. Moderately full-bodied. Highly extracted. Moderately oaked. Quite tannic. Earthy, bright red fruit aromas. Solid, tightly wound, austere, and dry through the tannic finish. Some generous red cherry flavors are lurking. Structurally impressive, this needs cellar time.

1995 Pinot Noir, Shea Vineyard, Willamette Valley $27.99.　　　87

Dark crimson with very subtle purple hints. Medium-bodied. Moderately extracted. Moderately oaked. Moderately tannic. Full, rich earthy nose. A solid dry palate with an austere black fruit accent, and earth and licorice through the finish. Sound structure, though this needs some time to soften.

1996 Pinot Noir, Winemaker's Cuvée, Oregon $33.　　　83

Bright ruby cast. Medium-bodied. Full acidity. Moderately extracted. Mildly oaked. Moderately tannic. Minerals, brown spices, red fruits. Aromatic and spicy, with a lean and intense mouthfeel. Angular and grippy, with a mildly astringent finish.

Ponzi

1994 Pinot Noir, Willamette Valley $18.　　　89

Deep cherry red fading to a purple rim. Moderately full-bodied. Highly extracted. Moderately tannic. Reminiscent of raspberry, vanilla, minerals. Highly extracted palate with a dense center of fruit, and impressive tight tannins through the finish. Needs more cellar time to resolve its big components.

1996 Pinot Noir, Willamette Valley $16.　　　82

1993 Pinot Noir, Reserve, Willamette Valley $26.99.　　　92

Deep ruby hue with slight fade to the rim. Medium-bodied. Moderately extracted. Mildly tannic. Reminiscent of minerals, red fruits, black tea. Quite aromatic and delicate in style, with a feminine grace. Well balanced and lengthy through the refined finish. This wine is attractive now and shows wonderful complexity.

1994 Pinot Noir, Reserve, Willamette Valley $35.　　　92

Nearly opaque reddish purple. Moderately full-bodied. Highly extracted. Moderately tannic. Reminiscent of red fruits, brown spices, minerals. Big, complex oak spice nose. A dense, firm style with well-integrated tannins and a tightly concentrated midpalate. Excellent lengthy finish. Needs more cellar time.

1995 Pinot Noir, 25th Anniversary Reserve, Willamette Valley $50.　　　90

Medium crimson hue to a pale garnet rim. Medium-bodied. Moderately extracted. Moderately oaked. Mildly tannic. A toasty nose leads caramelized cherry flavors, with mocha and spice notes through the finish. Quite angular, with bright acids. Well balanced and drinking nicely now.

Redhawk

1994 Pinot Noir, Vintage Select, Willamette Valley $15.　　　84

Ruby colored with a slight garnet cast. Medium-bodied. Moderately extracted. Mildly oaked. Moderately tannic. Reminiscent of earth, forest floor, tar. Earthy flavors with supple tannins on a lush, rounded palate.

Scale: Superlative (96-100), Exceptional (90-95), Highly Recommended (85-89), Recommended (80-84), Not Recommended (Under 80)

1994 Pinot Noir, Estate Reserve, Willamette Valley $25. 91

Deep red. Moderately full-bodied. Highly extracted. Moderately oaked. Moderately tannic. Reminiscent of black fruits, pepper, tar. Very aromatic black fruit with a hint of wood. Rich, ripe, chewy style with unusual but nice roasted meat flavors. Quite complex, with impressive extraction.

Rex Hill

1994 Pinot Noir, Willamette Valley $10.99. 87

Deep reddish purple. Moderately full-bodied. Highly extracted. Moderately oaked. Moderately tannic. Reminiscent of raspberries, vanilla, brown spice. Juicy fruit-accented style emphasizes generous layered red and black fruits through the toasty finish, with ample soft tannins. Very accessible now.

1996 Pinot Noir, Kings Ridge, Oregon $12.50. 81

1996 Pinot Noir, Limited Selection, Willamette Valley $18. 82

Siduri

1995 Pinot Noir, Oregon $30. 92

Deep ruby color. Moderately full-bodied. Moderately extracted. Moderately oaked. Mildly tannic. Reminiscent of vanilla, chocolate, black fruits. Rich textured style with well-integrated ripe tannins. Very supple but substantial through the finish. Generous oak flavors are well matched by impressive extraction.

1996 Pinot Noir, Oregon $34. 85

Cherry red with a pinkish purple cast. Medium-bodied. Moderately extracted. Moderately tannic. Soft and supple, with sweet cherry flavors and a lovely toasty accent throughout that gives this a very appealing mocha character. Very much defined by its toasty character. Drinking nicely now.

1997 Pinot Noir, Oregon $28. 82

Silvan Ridge

1995 Chardonnay, Oregon $13. 83

Brilliant yellow-gold. Oak-accented aromas show a bright fruity underlay. A vibrant attack leads a moderately full-bodied palate with crisp acids and short fruity flavors that finish with spicy, blanched almond notes. Showing early signs of age. Drink now.

1996 Chardonnay, Carolyn's Cuvée, Willamette Valley $22. 83

Full golden yellow. Very aromatic with a full oaky, nutty character. A rich entry leads a full-bodied palate with broad nutty flavors that finish quickly. This is showing mature character already. Drink now.

1996 Pinot Gris, Oregon $13. 84

Pale golden hue. Moderately full-bodied. Balanced acidity. Highly extracted. Minerals, earth, blanched almonds. Aromatically reserved, with a rich though lean palate feel. Features a mildly bitter note through the lengthy, nutty finish.

1996 Merlot, Rogue Valley $19.75. 81

1995 Merlot, Seven Hills Vineyard, Walla Walla Valley $28. 80

1994 Pinot Noir, Willamette Valley $19. 88

Dense, bright reddish purple. Moderately full-bodied. Highly extracted. Moderately tannic. Reminiscent of raspberries, cherries, vanilla. Ripe cherry fruit in the nose. Chewy, fruity style with plenty of integrated soft tannins on the palate through the finish. Could use short- to medium-term cellaring.

1995 Pinot Noir, Willamette Valley $19. 88

Bright purple-red. Medium-bodied. Moderately extracted. Moderately oaked. Moderately tannic. Toasty oak and bright fruity aromas lead an elegant, crisp red fruit and pomegranate palate with some intensity of flavors. Dry, oak-influenced finish. Needs a little time to come together.

1996 Pinot Noir, Eola Springs Vineyard, Willamette Valley $26.   85

Bright blackish ruby cast. Medium-bodied. Low acidity. Subtly extracted. Mildly tannic. Minerals, cherry cola. Aromatically reserved, with a very light palate feel. Crisp and zesty through the finish.

1995 Pinot Noir, Hoodview Vineyard, Willamette Valley $22.   85

Dark black-cherry red with purple highlights. Moderately full-bodied. Highly extracted. Moderately oaked. Moderately tannic. Floral, ripe aromas. Dry and vibrant, with tight red fruit flavors on the midpalate. Fine-grained tannins make the finish dry.

1994 Pinot Noir, Visconti Vineyard, Willamette Valley $26.   88

Bright cherry red. Medium-bodied. Moderately extracted. Moderately oaked. Moderately tannic. Reminiscent of black cherry, oak toast, brown spice. Bright cherry fruit nose. Bright fruit-accented entry with lively acidity and good toasty oak flavors through the finish. Approachable now but further time will allow the acids to settle.

1997 Gewürztraminer, Ice Wine, Bing Vineyard, Umpqua Valley $16/375 ml.   89

Deep yellow-gold. Exotic tropical fruit and sweet melon aromas jump from the glass. A lush entry leads a full-bodied, viscous palate with tons of sweetness. Rich, intense finish. Drink now.

1998 Early Muscat, Semi-Sparkling, Oregon $13.   82

Sineann

1996 Zinfandel, Old Vine, The Pines Vineyard, Columbia Valley $25.   84

Bright blackish purple. Medium-bodied. Full acidity. Moderately extracted. Moderately oaked. Mildly tannic. Green herbs, minerals, pepper. Quite aromatic, with an herbal complexity and toasty oak accents. Lighter styled and angular on the palate, with zesty acidity through an intense finish.

Sokol Blosser

1998 Muller-Thurgau, $14.95.   85

Brilliant green-straw hue, with a slight spritz. Ripe pear and fruit aromas. A crisp entry leads a light-bodied palate, with vibrant acidity and a hint of sweetness. Clean and well balanced. Drink now.

1994 Pinot Noir, Willamette Valley $17.   89

Bright cherry red. Medium-bodied. Moderately extracted. Mildly oaked. Mildly tannic. Reminiscent of red fruits, earth, mushrooms. Aromatically quite complex. Rich and balanced in the mouth. Well proportioned, with a fine lengthy finish. Very approachable now.

1995 Pinot Noir, Willamette Valley $15.   87

Medium cherry red with purple hints at the rim. Medium-bodied. Full acidity. Moderately extracted. Moderately oaked. Mildly tannic. Reminiscent of cranberries, cherries, vanilla. High-toned toasty cherry nose. Markedly high acidity on the palate give this wine presence and carries through the finish. Should be enough stuffing to cellar for a year and resolve the acidity.

1996 Pinot Noir, Willamette Valley $15.   80

1993 Pinot Noir, Redland, Willamette Valley $25.   88

Impressive deep cherry red. Medium-bodied. Moderately extracted. Moderately oaked. Moderately tannic. Reminiscent of brown spice, black fruits. Dry brown-spice scent in the nose. Well extracted and fairly weighty palate presence, although there are plenty of dry assertive flavors through the finish. This needs rich foods.

1994 Pinot Noir, Redland, Willamette Valley $35.   92

Deep, nearly opaque appearance. Medium-bodied. Highly extracted. Moderately oaked. Moderately tannic. Reminiscent of raspberries, cherries, spice cupboard. Hugely aromatic with spicy oak in the nose. Well extracted, lush, spicy palate with more finesse than power. Suitably high tannins and acidity for cellaring.

Scale: Superlative (96-100), Exceptional (90-95), Highly Recommended (85-89), Recommended (80-84), Not Recommended (Under 80)

276

1995 Pinot Noir, Redland, Yamhill County $35.   86

Dark crimson hue with a purple cast. Medium-bodied. Highly extracted. Moderately oaked. Moderately tannic. Mildly leathery, bright plum aromas. A tart, minerally palate shows vibrant acids and intriguing austerity through the finish. Some tightly wound red fruit flavors might evolve with time.

St. Innocent

1995 Pinot Noir, Freedom Hill Vineyard, Willamette Valley $24.99.   91

Dark crimson purple with an even fade to the rim. Medium-bodied. Highly extracted. Moderately oaked. Moderately tannic. Full complex aromas of earth, black cherries, plums. Outstanding long finish, with juicy black fruit flavors lingering through a solid earthy persistence. Quite dry, with fine-grained tannins in evidence. Nice now, but better in a few years.

1994 Pinot Noir, O'Connor Vineyard, Willamette Valley $32.50.   89

Deep black cherry appearance. Moderately full-bodied. Highly extracted. Quite tannic. Reminiscent of bramble fruit, bacon, dry oak. Intense, chunky palate with impressive dry tannins through the finish. Quite complex and maybe too tough for some, but cellaring should resolve this.

1995 Pinot Noir, O'Connor Vineyard, Willamette Valley $19.99.   90

Crimson with a purple-red fading rim. Medium-bodied. Moderately extracted. Moderately oaked. Moderately tannic. Floral violet hints. Bright brambly cherry flavors with full toasty brown spice accents through the finish. Still rather youthful and vigorous.

1996 Pinot Noir, O'Connor Vineyard, Willamette Valley $20.   85

Pale dark ruby cast. Medium-bodied. Balanced acidity. Moderately extracted. Heavily oaked. Moderately tannic. Toasted coconut, minerals, sweet herbs. Quite aromatic, with a dominant sweet oak note. Light in style, yet quite firm, with an angular, minerally backbone.

1994 Pinot Noir, Seven Springs Vineyard, Willamette Valley $28.50.   90

Deep reddish purple, nearly opaque. Moderately full-bodied. Highly extracted. Quite tannic. Reminiscent of brown spice, tar, roses. The Barolo of Willamette Valley Pinot Noirs. Dense and concentrated, with strapping tannins that clamp down on the finish. Difficult now but could well be worth the wait.

1994 Pinot Noir, Temperance Hill Vineyard, Willamette Valley $32.50.   92

Deep, bright reddish purple. Medium-bodied. Moderately extracted. Moderately tannic. Reminiscent of blackberries, brown spice, leather. Brooding dark aromas. Very juicy black fruit with good clean astringent character through the very complex, lengthy finish. Much more forward than the O'Connor and Seven Springs bottlings.

Torii Mor

1995 Pinot Noir, Yamhill County $19.   88

Pale cherry red. Medium-bodied. Moderately extracted. Reminiscent of tart raspberries, chocolate, toasted oak. Spicy fruit aromas lead a bright entrance with crisp, clean acidity carrying through the toasty finish.

1994 Pinot Noir, Reserve, Yamhill County $28.   93

Deep reddish purple. Moderately full-bodied. Balanced acidity. Moderately extracted. Moderately oaked. Mildly tannic. Reminiscent of brown spice, black fruits, charred wood. Deep, finely extracted, and focused on the palate, with great acidity through a lengthy finish. Great finesse, elegance, and complexity.

Tualatin

1997 Riesling, Willamette Valley $8.50.   82

1994 Pinot Noir, Estate Reserve, Willamette Valley $20.   90

Bright red with purple highlights. Moderately full-bodied. Full acidity. Highly extracted. Mildly oaked. Moderately tannic. Reminiscent of sweet cherries, herbs, pine. Sweet fruit aromas. Ripe, juicy fruit on entry, with ample soft tannins well integrated with forceful acidity carrying through to the finish. Should resolve with cellaring.

1995 Pinot Noir, Oregon $12.50.　　　　　　　　　　　　　　85

Ruby appearance. Medium-bodied. Moderately extracted. Moderately oaked. Mildly tannic. Reminiscent of cherries, oak, toast. Pleasant fruity nose, with bright juicy fruit on the entry and soft tannins lingering through the finish.

1995 Pinot Noir, Founders' Reserve, Oregon $18.　　　　　　　89

Bright cherry red with purple highlights. Medium-bodied. Moderately extracted. Moderately oaked. Mildly tannic. Nice cherry-berry aromas with toasty oak notes. A substantial, textured mouthfeel reveals full bramble fruit and toasty oak flavors through the finish.

1996 Pinot Noir, Founders' Reserve, Oregon $28.　　　　　　83

Pale ruby cast. Medium-bodied. Balanced acidity. Subtly extracted. Mildly oaked. Mildly tannic. Dried herbs, minerals, spice. Aromatically subdued, with a slight herbal bent. Light in the mouth, with a crisp, angular finish.

1994 Pinot Noir, OVB, Oregon $30.　　　　　　　　　　　　89

Deep reddish purple. Medium-bodied. Highly extracted. Moderately oaked. Mildly tannic. Reminiscent of black cherries, chocolate. Ripe, brooding dark fruit aromas. Juicy fruit with integrated tannins and toasty oak flavors through the finish. Very approachable, but will probably cellar well for a few years.

1996 Pinot Noir, Whole Berry Fermented, Oregon $12.50.　　　80

1997 Pinot Noir, Whole Cluster Fermented, Oregon $14.99.　　81

1994 Pinot Noir Port, Quinta Reserva, Oregon $18.　　　　　80

1997 Gewürztraminer, Late Harvest, Willamette Valley $12/375 ml.　82

1997 Semi-Sparkling Muscat, Willamette Valley $14.　　　　　80

Tyee

1993 Pinot Noir, Willamette Valley $13.50.　　　　　　　　　85

Cherry red appearance. Medium-bodied. Moderately extracted. Moderately tannic. Reminiscent of raspberries, vanilla. Crisp and juicy fruit on entry through to a brief finish. Very quaffable.

1996 Pinot Noir, Willamette Valley $17.95.　　　　　　　　　83

Pale ruby cast. Medium-bodied. Full acidity. Moderately extracted. Mildly oaked. Moderately tannic. Vanilla, red fruits, minerals. High-toned fruity aromas feature a sweet woody accent. Crisp and zesty in the mouth, with vibrant acidity making for a piercing finish.

Valley View

1994 Anna Maria Reserve, Rogue Valley $20.　　　　　　　　86

Pale ruby-garnet cast. Medium-bodied. Full acidity. Moderately extracted. Moderately oaked. Mildly tannic. Spice, minerals. Features a hefty overlay of oak seasoning. Crisp, lean, and zesty in the mouth. Acidity provides an angular, juicy finish.

1995 Anna Maria Reserve, Rogue Valley $20.　　　　　　　　81

1995 Merlot, Anna Maria, Rogue Valley $25.　　　　　　　　83

Bright ruby red with a slight fade. Generous spice and cedar aromas show a dominant wood accent. A crisp attack leads a light-bodied palate with lean tannins. The finish is racy, with oak notes. A tasty quaffer. Drink now.

Van Duzer

1994 Pinot Noir, Eola Selection, Oregon $12.50.　　　　　　87

Deep cherry red. Medium-bodied. Moderately extracted. Moderately oaked. Moderately tannic. Reminiscent of raspberries, vanilla. Big raspberry-vanilla nose leads a ripe, chewy palate with attractive toasted oak flavors through the finish. Very accessible style.

1997 Pinot Noir, Oregon $18.　　　　　　　　　　　　　　82

Scale: Superlative (96-100), Exceptional (90-95), Highly Recommended (85-89), Recommended (80-84), Not Recommended (Under 80)

278

Willamette Valley Vineyards

1997 Chardonnay, Oregon $12.75. **86**

Pale straw hue. Elegant vanilla and lemon aromas show a judicious oak influence. A lean entry is followed by a medium-bodied palate with crisp acidity. Delicate and well balanced through the finish. Drink now.

1996 Chardonnay, Founders' Reserve, Oregon $14.99. **88**

Deep straw hue. Opulent cream, butter, and toast aromas carry a generous oak accent. A lush entry leads a moderately full-bodied palate with firm acidity. Full and flavorful, with admirable balance between wood and fruit. Drink now.

1996 Chardonnay, Estate, Dijon Clone, Oregon $21.99. **90**

Yellow-straw color. Medium-bodied. Balanced acidity. Moderately extracted. Vanilla, pine, apples. Bright and juicy, with a rounded mouthfeel and fruit-centered flavors showing a subtle hint of oak seasoning. Complex and distinctive, with yeasty flavors lingering.

Witness Tree

1995 Pinot Noir, Willamette Valley $17. **88**

Bright cherry red. Medium-bodied. Moderately extracted. Moderately oaked. Mildly tannic. Roasted walnut aromas. Smooth vanilla oak flavors with cherry pie accents through the finish. Lovely textured mouthfeel. Nice intensity and persistence.

Ken Wright Cellars

1995 Pinot Noir, Willamette Valley $18.49. **83**

Medium crimson red with a pinkish cast. Moderately light-bodied. Moderately extracted. Moderately oaked. Mildly tannic. Straightforward dry cherry flavors with raspberry accents. Vanilla oak hints come through on the finish.

1995 Pinot Noir, Canary Hill Vineyard, Willamette Valley $24.99. **90**

Bright cherry pink. Medium-bodied. Moderately extracted. Moderately oaked. Mildly tannic. Plenty of vanilla oak character complements sweet cherry flavors on the midpalate. Drinking nicely now, though tightly wound, with a lighter frame.

1995 Pinot Noir, Carter Vineyard, Willamette Valley $24.99. **88**

Bright crimson pink. Medium-bodied. Moderately extracted. Mildly oaked. Mildly tannic. Straightforward bright cherry flavors expand on the palate and linger through a supple finish. This shows some youthful vigor.

four

The Wines
of New York State

An Introduction: The Wines of New York State

New York State has actually been an important center of wine production since the earlier days of the Republic. People might be surprised to hear that it always ranks near the top of the states (though still well behind California) in volume production. Much of that production comes from the western part of the state near Buffalo, on the eastern shore of Lake Erie in particular. Most of these wines are destined to become inexpensive "ports" or sparkling wines, the latter a New York State specialty with national recognition since the mid-19th century. As for premium table wines, however, production is far more limited and centered largely on the Finger Lakes or Long Island—two very different and distinctive wine regions that should not be lumped together.

The Finger Lakes

The Finger Lakes is the longer established of the two, and is centered on a series of thin, deep, long lakes in the west-central part of the state. The moderating influence of these waters and the warmth provided by east-facing hills allows the fragile grapevines to survive the region's harsh winters and to ripen grapes in the summer. As it is a cool grape-growing region, it is only fitting that it should specialize in white wines. Riesling in particular is where the Finger Lakes are beginning to establish a very solid reputation, but high quality, sophisticated sparkling wines are also appearing with more regularity.

Just as in Germany, where Riesling reaches its apex, the grapes struggle to ripen in the cool Finger Lakes climate and the hillsides and rivers make viticulture possible. It should not come as a surprise that German winemakers have been drawn here and winery names such as Wiemer or Frank attest to the fact. As the fortunes of Riesling have waned in the Chardonnay-besotten United States, it is abroad that many of these wines are leaving a mark. I was recently at a dinner with a large Belgian wine buyer in the French countryside when he amazed me by asking not about the latest glamour winery in Napa, but rather what my opinion was of Finger Lakes Riesling. He then proceeded to list all the best producers from the top of his head and retreated to his hotel room to procure a sample bottle he had been toting all around the Mosel the previous weekend (to bemused admiration, apparently).

U.S. consumers will eventually catch on to Riesling, and when they do the Finger Lakes will be shown to be the nation's finest Riesling appellation. At present, the wines are a steal, with some great bottles going for $10 and sometimes less. As with fine Riesling anywhere, these wines also age well, and I have been delighted by five- to ten-year-old examples that have developed that inimitable "petrolly" note that is the hallmark of a fine Riesling with some age. Though availability is somewhat limited, the best retailers around the country will carry some of the best examples. As a "house" wine, Finger Lakes Rieslings are astonishing values, particularly at a half or a third the price of many innocuous Chardonnays.

Long Island

As for Long Island, the peninsula that extends over a hundred miles from New York City east, into the Atlantic, the atmosphere and style of the wines couldn't be different. Centered near the end of the peninsula on the North Fork, about two hours from Times Square (traffic permitting), the twenty odd Long Island wineries bask in the relative warmth of the Atlantic Ocean and the Gulf Stream. This moderate climate makes it possible to ripen reds, and it is with red varietals that most of the wineries are expending much of their efforts.

Though warmer than the Finger Lakes, it is still fairly cool, and the resultant wines are not nearly as alcoholic or thick as their California cousins can be. Bordeaux lies just on the other shore and the geographic similarities between the regions have not gone unnoticed. Unlike Bordeaux, however, Long Island has a very young industry, having really only been founded in the '70s. As with any new wine industry, there is a learning curve where vintners must adapt to the peculiarities of the local climate and settle on styles and varietals.

The understandable desire to make "world class wines" in a hurry meant that a number of examples were over-made. Some wine makers confused full extract and hard tannins combined with inky colors and the concept of ageability as equating with greatness. However, much as the approach has lightened up in California, so it has also in Long Island. The pendulum is swinging back and most of the better Long Island wineries are finally beginning to hone in on a style that is more appropriate to the climate: balance and elegance, with moderate alcohol and sound acidity. Exciting examples of Merlot and Cabernet are to be found, with even the odd successful Pinot Noir. Chardonnay leads the way with whites, just as in every other corner of the world. Long Island's versions tend to be somewhat lighter in style, due to the climate, but oak is certainly in vogue. Long Island is certainly a region on the rise.

New York at a Glance

Wines Reviewed:

169

Producers/Brands Represented:

33

Reviews

Bauer
1998 Vidal Blanc, Niagara County $8.99.   80

Bedell
1995 Chardonnay, North Fork of Long Island $11.99.   85

Deep, saturated straw hue. Generous mineral and cream aromas show a mature nutty accent. Supple and moderately full-bodied, with shy acidity. Lush finish. Drink now.

1995 Chardonnay, Reserve, North Fork of Long Island $14.99.   86

Deep yellow-straw hue. Complex, autolyzed, yeasty, smoky aromas. A firm attack leads a moderately full-bodied palate, with crisp acids. Firm and concentrated, with a phenolic edge to the finish. Drink now or later.

NV Main Road Red, New York $9.99.   84

Deep, saturated purple-red hue. Generous red fruit, spice, and mineral aromas. A supple entry leads a moderately full-bodied palate. A soft, flavorful quaffer. Drink now.

1995 Cabernet Sauvignon, North Fork of Long Island $21.50.   85

Dark, saturated ruby purple. Brooding black fruit, licorice, and lacquer aromas. A firm entry leads a full-bodied palate, with a wave of grainy tannins. Big and rich, but very tight and tannic. Perhaps time will help, perhaps not. Mid-term cellar candidate (3–6 years).

1994 Cupola, North Fork of Long Island $25.   88

Deep, saturated ruby red. Generous red fruit and mineral aromas. A firm attack leads a moderately full-bodied palate, with drying tannins. Reserved and balanced, with a hint of Bordeaux about it. Drink now.

1995 Cupola, North Fork of Long Island $27.50.   89

Dark, opaque ruby purple. Brooding mineral, black fruit, and smoke aromas carry a mild oak influence. A supple entry leads a full-bodied palate showing velvety tannins. Rich and flavor packed, but not tough. Drink now or later.

1995 Merlot, North Fork of Long Island $17.99.   86

Deep ruby purple to the rim. Generous black fruit and vanilla aromas show a marked wood accent. A firm entry leads a moderately full-bodied palate that has robust tannins. Full and rich, with an oaky finish. Drink now or later.

1995 Merlot, Reserve, North Fork of Long Island $27.50.   88

Opaque, saturated ruby purple. Powerful dark chocolate and black fruit aromas. A firm entry leads a brooding, full-bodied palate, with big, robust tannins. Thick and full-throttled. Needs time, but will probably always be aggressive. Mid-term cellar candidate (3–6 years).

NV Eis, New York $27.50/375 ml.   90

Deep, brilliant amber hue. Powerful butterscotch, pineapple, and tropical fruit aromas. A firm entry lead a sharp, full-bodied palate that has tons of acidity. Thick and rich, yet showing a firm acidic cut that keeps the wine from cloying. A big Eiswein. Drink now or later.

NV Raspberry Wine, New York $9.99.   91

Saturated dark ruby red. Powerful, generous chocolate and raspberry aromas. A firm entry leads a fairly sweet, full-bodied palate. Rich and intense, with tons of flavor and fine length.

Bidwell
1996 Chardonnay, North Fork of Long Island $14.99.   84

Bright, saturated yellow-straw hue. Lean mineral and citrus aromas carry a toasty accent. A firm entry leads a moderately full-bodied palate showing crisp acidity. Vibrant and elegant. Drink now.

Scale: Superlative (96-100), Exceptional (90-95), Highly Recommended (85-89), Recommended (80-84), Not Recommended (Under 80)

1996 Semi-Sweet Riesling, North Fork of Long Island $9.99.   **81**

1995 Cabernet Sauvignon, North Fork of Long Island $27.71.   **84**

Ruby-garnet hue with a slight fade. Cassis and chocolate aromas show an overripe note. A firm entry leads a moderately full-bodied palate, with drying tannins. Has convincing flavors on a lean frame. Drink now or later.

1995 Claret, North Fork of Long Island $34.99.   **85**

Ruby red with a slight fade. Shows cordial-like, overripe black fruit aromas. A firm entry leads a medium-bodied palate, with drying tannins. Very ripe, yet structured. Drink now or later.

1994 Merlot, North Fork of Long Island $19.99.   **80**

Casa Larga

1995 Cabernet Sauvignon, Finger Lakes $13.99.   **89**

Saturated red-purple. Moderately full-bodied. Highly extracted. Quite tannic. Ripe cherries, minerals, brown spice. Hints of overripe black fruits lead a firm palate of black fruit flavors with strong oak influences apparent. Hard-edged tannins clamp down on the finish.

1994 Pinot Noir, Finger Lakes $15.   **83**

Dark red. Medium-bodied. Moderately extracted. Mildly tannic. Austere herbaceous aromas with smoky tea accents. Dark fruit flavors are quite rich up front, with some dry tannin coming through on the finish.

Cayuga Ridge

NV Riesling, Cayuga Lake $9.50.   **83**

Very pale straw hue. Crisp aromas of tart peach and apple. A lively attack leads a medium-bodied palate, with juicy, tart peach flavors and a dry, minerally finish. Drink now.

Chateau Lafayette Reneau

1997 Chardonnay, Proprietor's Reserve, Finger Lakes $20.   **82**

1997 Johannisberg Riesling, Finger Lakes $9.99.   **81**

1997 Dry Riesling, Finger Lakes $9.99.   **84**

Very pale straw hue. Aromatically muted. A simple attack leads a moderately light-bodied palate, with attractive tart peach and herb flavors that linger on a fairly lengthy finish. Drink now.

1998 Pinot Noir Blanc, Finger Lakes $6.99.   **85**

Pale cherry-garnet hue with a slight spritz. Forward, pleasant berry aromas. A zesty entry leads a flavorful, medium-bodied palate. Crisp acids balance mild sweetness. Lengthy, clean, refreshing finish. Drink now.

1995 Cabernet Sauvignon, Finger Lakes $18.   **83**

Bright cherry red. Moderately light-bodied. Subtly extracted. Mildly tannic. Vanilla, red fruits. A lighter style, with bright acids and a quick finish. Shows very little typical Cabernet character, though tart acids and restrained balance make for a drinkable style.

1995 Cabernet Sauvignon, Owner's Reserve, Finger Lakes $20.   **86**

Bright cherry red with a pink rim. Medium-bodied. Highly extracted. Heavily oaked. Moderately tannic. Vanilla, cedar, red fruits. Aromas point to heavy use of oak, which is confirmed on the palate. Bright acids and astringency come through on the finish.

Duck Walk

1994 Merlot, Reserve, North Fork of Long Island $14.95.   **80**

1995 Merlot, Reserve, North Fork of Long Island $14.95.   **80**

1996 Blueberry Port, $12.95/375 ml.   **87**

Bright blackish purple. Moderately full-bodied. Balanced acidity. Moderately extracted. Mildly tannic. Black fruits, minerals, licorice. Pleasantly aromatic and fruit centered, with concentrated flavors on the palate, and a sense of lightness and balance throughout. Intense and clean, with an uplifting, angular finish.

Earle Estates

Blueberry Wine, $13.99.   **86**

Bright ruby purple. Medium-bodied. Full acidity. Moderately extracted. Blueberries, chocolate. Extremely aromatic, with a pure, fruit-accented quality. Exotically flavorful in the mouth, with vibrant acidity that lends a sense of balance to the sweetness in the finish.

Peach Perfection, $13.99.   **86**

Bright straw cast. Medium-bodied. Full acidity. Highly extracted. Peaches. Quite aromatic, with a forward, peachy quality. Sweet and round on the palate, with well-defined flavors. Spritzy acidity maintains a sense of balance and keeps the finish refreshing.

1996 Traditional Honey Mead, $13.99.   **80**

Chateau Frank

NV Celebre Cremant, Finger Lakes $10.   **83**

Bright green-straw cast. Moderately light-bodied. Full acidity. Citrus, tropical fruits. Forward fruity aromas lead a crisp and vibrant mouthfeel. Finishes with a touch of sweetness that will appeal to those who do not favor drier styles.

1991 Brut, Finger Lakes $15.   **88**

Medium straw color. Medium-bodied. Tropical fruits, citrus, smoke. Soft bready aromas. Elegant flavors have an impressively fruity center, with yeast complexity emerging on the finish.

1993 Blanc de Noirs, Finger Lakes $17.95.   **83**

Pale straw cast. Medium-bodied. Full acidity. Minerals, citrus peel. Aromatically reserved, with a lean and angular mouthfeel and plenty of citrus zest flavors through the crisp, vibrant finish.

Dr. Konstantin Frank

1997 Chardonnay, New York $10.95.   **82**

1998 Gewürztraminer, Limited Release, Finger Lakes $12.95.   **81**

NV Johannisberg Riesling, Salmon Run, New York $8.95.   **88**

Medium yellow-straw hue. Tropical fruit, ripe peach aromas. A flavorful attack leads a medium-bodied palate, with generous fruity flavors and a glycerous midpalate. Finishes smoothly with good persistence. Drink now.

1997 Semi-Dry Johannisberg Riesling, New York $9.95.   **84**

Medium yellow-straw hue. Pleasant aromas of minerals, apples, and herbs. A juicy, sweet entry leads a medium-bodied palate, with straightforward flavors and a hint of sour apple on the finish. An off-dry style. Drink now.

1997 Johannisberg Riesling, Dry, New York $9.95.   **82**

NV Cabernet, New York $14.95.   **83**

Bright violet-red. Medium-bodied. Moderately extracted. Mildly tannic. Violets, red berries, minerals. Floral, bright aromas lead a high-toned, fruity palate, with nice texture and a crisp, mineral-accented finish. Well balanced, drinking nicely now.

1995 Cabernet Sauvignon, Finger Lakes $22.   **86**

Full red-purple. Medium-bodied. Moderately extracted. Mildly tannic. Vanilla, minerals, red fruits. Primary fruit aromas indicate a fresh, youthful character that comes through on the palate. Finishes on the lean side; this is not built to age.

Scale: Superlative (96-100), Exceptional (90-95), Highly Recommended (85-89), Recommended (80-84), Not Recommended (Under 80)

1996 Cabernet Sauvignon, Old Vines, New York $22. **84**

Pale cherry red. Moderately light-bodied. Subtly extracted. Moderately oaked. Mildly tannic. Vanilla, red cherries. Candied fruit, floral aromas lead a lively vanilla-edged palate with a juicy finish. Crisp, lighter style.

1995 Pinot Noir, Finger Lakes $18.95. **86**

Medium cherry red. Medium-bodied. Moderately extracted. Mildly tannic. Faintly jammy red fruit aromas lead a crisp palate, with straightforward vague red fruit flavors through a mildly astringent finish. Nice weight and mouthfeel are a plus.

1996 Pinot Noir, Finger Lakes $18.95. **81**

1995 Johannisberg Riesling, Ice Wine, New York $29.95/375 ml. **90**

Brilliant amber hue. Generous caramel and spice aromas. A lush entry leads a viscous, full-bodied palate showing lean acids and lots of sweetness. Intense and stylish with great depth of flavor. Harmonious and pure. Drink now.

Glenora

1993 Blanc de Blancs, New York $12.99. **85**

Pale green-straw cast. Medium-bodied. Minerals, chalk, citrus zest. Reserved and elegant, with understated citrusy flavors. Balanced and lean, showing a judicious level of carbonation, a sense of roundness, and mild, sweet fruity notes on the finish.

NV Brut, New York $12.99. **86**

Pale gold. Moderately full-bodied. Ripe citrus, minerals. Full smoky, citrusy aromas lead a generously proportioned palate, with the accent on crisp fruit flavors. A substantial and rounded style.

1996 Chardonnay, Finger Lakes $13.99. **87**

Bright pale gold. Vibrant citrus aromas. Brightly acidic on the attack, with a medium-bodied palate and tart lemon flavors following cleanly through the finish. Impressively concentrated. A zesty, refreshing style that will work well with seafood. Drink now.

1996 Pinot Blanc, Finger Lakes $11.99. **80**

1998 Riesling, Finger Lakes $7.99. **83**

Pale straw hue. Mild aromas of minerals and stone fruits. A muted attack leads a moderately light-bodied palate showing straightforward fruit flavors that finish quickly. An off-dry style. Drink now.

1998 Dry Riesling, Finger Lakes $7.99. **84**

Pale straw hue. Perfumed aromas of yellow apples and herbs. A soft entry leads a medium-bodied palate, with crisp flavors and juicy acids on the finish. Drink now.

1995 Pinot Noir, North Fork of Long Island $11.99. **87**

Pinkish pale cherry red. Medium-bodied. Moderately extracted. Mildly tannic. Sweet raspberry aromas follow through on the palate, with lively acids to balance. Tannins are supple and balanced. An easy-drinking style.

1995 Cabernet Sauvignon, North Fork of Long Island $9.99. **83**

Deep cherry red with an even rim. Medium-bodied. Moderately extracted. Moderately oaked. Mildly tannic. Herbs, earth. Aromatically restrained, with an impression of austerity. Dry and earthy on the palate, with a minerally leanness that provides good grip on the finish, though faint bitterness persists.

1995 Cabernet Sauvignon, 20th Anniversary,
North Fork of Long Island $16.95. **83**

Bright cherry red with an even color to the rim. Medium-bodied. Moderately extracted. Moderately oaked. Moderately tannic. Minerals, black fruits. Austere aromas lead a juicy, bright palate, with black fruit flavors that turn very dry and lean through the finish. An angular style.

Goose Watch

1997 Merlot, Finger Lakes $16.50.   86

Bright violet red with a luminous cast. Bright, sweet, juicy aromas show violets and raspberries. A fresh, lively attack leads a medium-bodied palate with light but firm tannins. Very vibrant, fresh and youthful with zesty appeal. Drink now.

1997 Finale White Port, Finger Lakes $16.50/375 ml.   82

Gristina

1996 Chardonnay, North Fork of Long Island $11.99.   88

Rich yellow-straw hue. Forward tropical fruit and bread dough aromas. A supple entry leads a moderately full-bodied palate. Full yet crisp, with fine length. Drink now.

1995 Chardonnay, Andy's Field, North Fork of Long Island $21.99.   91

Rich yellow-straw hue. Fantastic tropical fruit and yeast aromas show a complex, leesy quality. A supple entry leads a full-bodied palate. Great intensity and complexity. Big, but well balanced. Drink now or later.

1997 Rosé of Cabernet, North Fork of Long Island $8.99.   85

Rich, brilliant raspberry pink. Reserved raspberry and bread dough aromas. A firm entry leads a full-bodied palate showing sharp acidity. Fruit centered, with a big bready finish. Drink now.

1996 Cabernet Sauvignon, North Fork of Long Island $15.99.   89

Deep ruby red with a slight fade. Generous cassis, mineral, and spice aromas show a gentle wood accent. A firm entry leads a moderately full-bodied palate, with drying tannins. Firm and intense, with a minerally finish. Drink now or later.

1993 Andy's Field Red, North Fork of Long Island $27.99.   90

Deep, saturated ruby purple. Powerful cassis, spice, and mineral aromas. A firm entry leads a full-bodied palate showing robust tannins. Highly extracted and intense. Accessible, but needs time. Mid-term cellar candidate (3–6 years).

1995 Merlot, North Fork of Long Island $14.99.   85

Dark, saturated ruby red. Black fruit and mineral aromas show a subtle oak accent. A firm entry leads a moderately full-bodied palate, with drying tannins. Sturdy and rich, with a tough-edged finish. Drink now or later.

1995 Pinot Noir, North Fork of Long Island $19.99.   86

Pale brick red. Powerful iron, spice, and red fruit aromas. A firm entry leads a medium-bodied palate, with drying tannins. Impressive aromatics; almost Burgundian. Drink now.

Hargrave

NV Chardonnay, Chardonette, North Fork of Long Island $6.99.   83

Bright straw hue. Lean mineral and melon aromas. A firm entry leads a crisp, medium-bodied palate. Zesty and angular. A clean, unoaked Chardonnay. Drink now.

1995 Chardonnay, Lattice Label, North Fork of Long Island $14.99.   85

Rich, saturated yellow-straw hue. Lean mineral and citrus aromas. A firm entry leads a moderately full-bodied palate that has crisp acidity. Firm and tight-fisted, with a phenolic edge to the finish. Drink now or later.

1997 Pinot Blanc, North Fork of Long Island $9.99.   84

Deep straw hue. Subdued melon, toast, and butter aromas. A supple entry leads a medium-bodied palate, with a lingering buttery finish. Clean and stylish, with Alsatian-type viscosity. Drink now.

1997 Cabernet Franc, North Fork of Long Island $14.99.   86

Bright cherry red with a slight fade. Generous herb, red fruit, and mineral aromas. A firm entry leads a medium-bodied palate, with drying tannins. Clipped, leafy finish. A lean Chinon style. Drink now.

1995 Pinot Noir, North Fork of Long Island $35.   90

Bright cherry-garnet hue with a slight fade. Powerful red fruit, mineral, and spice aromas show marked wood influence. A firm entry leads a moderately full-bodied palate, with drying tannins. Lengthy oak-tinged finish. Tasty and very stylish. Drink now or later.

Heron Hill

1997 Chardonnay, Ingle Vineyard, Proprietor's Reserve,
Finger Lakes $16.99.   83

Very pale straw hue. Smoky oak and citrus aromas. A zesty entry leads a medium-bodied palate with lean flavors that finish quickly with a note of oak spice. Rather shy on flavors, though clean and snappy. Drink now.

1996 Semi-Dry Riesling, Finger Lakes $8.49.   83

Pale straw hue. Lighter aroma of flowers and grapes. A crisp entry leads a light-bodied palate with brief mineral-accented flavors that finish quickly. A good match with shellfish. Drink now.

1997 Johannisberg Riesling, Ingle Vineyard, Finger Lakes $8.49.   83

Bright pale straw cast. Clean aromas of flowers and minerals. A juicy entry leads a medium-bodied palate, with white peach flavors that give way to a minerally finish. Lighter aperitif style. Drink now.

Hosmer

1997 Chardonnay, Cayuga Lake $12.   84

Bright straw cast. Medium-bodied. Full acidity. Highly extracted. Blanched almonds, minerals, butter. Aromatically reserved with a hint of oxidation that actually lends a sense of complexity. Ripe and rounded through the finish.

Raspberry Rhapsody, Finger Lakes $8.50.   83

Bright pale ruby cast. Medium-bodied. Balanced acidity. Moderately extracted. Red fruits. Rather reserved aromatically, with a lighter-styled though firmly structured palate feel. A hint of sweetness is balanced by angular acidity in the finish.

Hunt Country

1997 Seyval Blanc, Finger Lakes $6.99.   80

1997 Vidal Blanc, Ice Wine, Finger Lakes $24/375 ml.   85

Deep straw hue. Generous, earthy, honeyed melon aromas. A lean entry leads a sweet palate that has piercing acidity. Tart, intense finish. Drink now.

Jamesport

1997 Chardonnay, Cox Lane Vineyard, North Fork of Long Island $12.95.   81

Lamoreaux Landing

1997 Riesling, Dry, Finger Lakes $9.   82

1996 Cabernet Franc, Finger Lakes $14.   82

1995 Cabernet Sauvignon, Finger Lakes $18.   82

Laurel Lake

1996 Chardonnay, North Fork of Long Island $12.99.   85

Brilliant straw hue. Pleasant citrus, vanilla, and herb aromas. An acidic entry leads a crisp, moderately full-bodied palate. The finish is clipped and clean. Carries a bit of complexity, with a slight herbal edge. Drink now.

1995 Chardonnay, Reserve, North Fork of Long Island $13.99.   86

Luminous straw hue. Generous citrus, yeast, and mineral aromas. A firm entry leads a moderately full-bodied palate, with crisp acids. Firm and powerful, but restrained. Drink now.

NV Wind Song, North Fork of Long Island $7.99.   **81**

NV Lake Rosé, North Fork of Long Island $9.99.   **88**

Rich, saturated raspberry pink. Intense blackberry, citrus, and bread dough aromas. A firm entry leads a moderately full-bodied palate, with crisp acids and a dry finish. Shows some southern French overtones. Drink now.

1995 Cabernet Sauvignon, North Fork of Long Island $23.99.   **88**

Brilliant cherry-garnet hue with a slight fade. Forward herb, mineral, and cassis aromas. A firm entry leads a moderately full-bodied palate, with drying tannins, and a pure cassis note to the finish. Balanced and well made. Drink now or later.

1996 Merlot, North Fork of Long Island $12.99.   **85**

Bright cherry red with a slight fade. Subdued black cherry, dried herb, and mineral aromas. A firm entry leads a crisp, medium-bodied palate that has drying tannins. Light and stylish, and not overmade. Drink now.

Lenz

1992 "Cuvée" Sparkling Wine, North Fork of Long Island $19.99.   **86**

Rich straw hue with fine bubbles. Pleasant cream, mineral, and earth aromas. A firm entry leads a moderately full-bodied palate showing crisp acids. Rich and rounded, with a sense of ripeness. Drink now.

1996 Chardonnay, Vineyard Selection, North Fork of Long Island $9.99.   **85**

Rich yellow-straw hue. Subdued mineral, citrus, and butter aromas. A firm entry leads a moderately full-bodied palate, with crisp acids. Vibrant and restrained. Drink now.

1995 Chardonnay, Barrel Fermented, North Fork of Long Island $24.99.   **89**

Deep yellow-straw hue. Generous citrus, yeast, and butter aromas. A soft entry leads a moderately full-bodied palate. Rich, rounded, and leesy, with a creamy mouthfeel. Drink now.

1995 Gewürztraminer, North Fork of Long Island $10.99.   **88**

Brilliant yellow-straw hue. Pleasant, classic lychee and flower aromas. A soft entry leads a moderately full-bodied palate. Convincingly varietal, with an oily texture. Drink now.

1996 Blanc de Noir, North Fork of Long Island $7.99.   **80**

1995 Cabernet Sauvignon, Estate, North Fork of Long Island $24.99.   **90**

Deep ruby purple. Intense cassis, vanilla, and herb aromas. A supple entry leads a moderately full-bodied palate, with velvety, plush, rounded tannins. Solid yet supple, with fine balance. Drink now or later.

1997 Merlot-Cabernet, Vineyard Selection, North Fork of Long Island $16.99.   **86**

Deep, saturated ruby red. Pleasant red fruit and vanilla aromas carry a leafy accent. A soft entry leads a medium-bodied palate showing velvety tannins. Fruit centered, with mild oak accents. Drink now.

1995 Merlot, Estate, North Fork of Long Island $29.99.   **89**

Deep, saturated ruby red. Generous raspberry and vanilla aromas show an integrated oak accent. A supple entry leads a moderately full-bodied palate, with velvety tannins. A rounded, softly extracted, harmonious style. Drink now or later.

1995 Pinot Noir, Estate, North Fork of Long Island $14.99.   **84**

Bright ruby hue. Spice, mineral, and sour cherry aromas. A soft entry leads a moderately light-bodied palate that shows drying tannins. Snappy finish. A crisp, lighter style, with faint Pinot perfume. Drink now.

Macari

1997 Chardonnay, Stainless Steel, North Fork of Long Island $12.   **84**

Bright straw hue. Clean mineral, herb, and citrus aromas. A firm entry leads a moderately full-bodied palate that has crisp acidity. Vibrant, with a slightly green finish. Drink now.

Scale: Superlative (96-100), Exceptional (90-95), Highly Recommended (85-89), Recommended (80-84), Not Recommended (Under 80)

1996 Chardonnay, Barrel Fermented, North Fork of Long Island $14.   **88**

Deep yellow-straw hue. Forward spice, yeast, and banana aromas. A firm entry leads a moderately full-bodied palate. Full, lush, and complex, with a persistent yeasty finish. Drink now.

1997 Chardonnay, Barrel Fermented, North Fork of Long Island $17.   **93**

Deep yellow-straw hue. Fantastic vanilla, yeast, and cream aromas show an integrated oak influence. A supple entry leads a moderately full-bodied palate that features complex flavors. Lush, but powerful and lengthy. Drink now.

1997 Sauvignon Blanc, North Fork of Long Island $14.   **83**

Bright straw hue. Muted mineral and herb aromas. An acidic entry leads a medium-bodied palate, with crisp acidity. Zesty and straightforward. Drink now.

1997 Rosé d'Une Nuit, North Fork of Long Island $11.   **86**

Bright raspberry pink. Generous bread and red fruit aromas. A firm entry leads a moderately full-bodied palate, with a clean, lingering finish. Rich and rounded in a dry, Tavel-like style. Drink now.

1996 Merlot, North Fork of Long Island $20.   **90**

Bright ruby red. Pleasant dried herb, cedar, and cherry aromas show a generous wood accent. A supple entry leads a balanced, medium-bodied palate, with drying tannins. Lighter in style, but extremely flavorful and lengthy. Not overdone. Drink now.

Osprey's Dominion

NV Chardonnay, North Fork of Long Island $9.99.   **81**

1995 Chardonnay, North Fork of Long Island $11.99.   **83**

Rich straw hue. Mild citrus, vanilla, and butter aromas. A smooth entry leads a crisp, medium-bodied palate. Well balanced and clean through the finish. Drink now.

1996 Chardonnay, Reserve, North Fork of Long Island $25.   **84**

Deep yellow-straw hue. Generous apple, oak spice, and butter aromas. A firm entry leads a moderately full-bodied palate showing crisp acidity. Rich and full, with a lot of barrel influence. Drink now.

1997 Johannisberg Riesling, North Fork of Long Island $11.99.   **81**

1995 Cabernet Sauvignon, North Fork of Long Island $13.99.   **89**

Deep, saturated ruby red. Generous dried herb, mineral, and cassis aromas show mild oak influences. A soft entry leads a moderately full-bodied palate, with velvety tannins. Varietal and supple, with fine length. Drink now.

1996 Merlot, North Fork of Long Island $14.99.   **86**

Rich ruby hue with a slight fade. Generous raspberry and spice aromas. Medium-bodied, with silky tannins. Soft, smooth, and supple, with a lingering note of oak spice. Drink now.

1996 Pinot Noir, North Fork of Long Island $15.99.   **80**

NV Spice Wine, North Fork of Long Island $8.99.   **89**

Light garnet hue with a slight fade. Powerful cinnamon, spice, and berry aromas. A smooth entry leads a full-bodied palate, with a hint of sweetness and drying tannins. Rich, supple, extremely flavorful, and very tasty. Drink now.

Palmer

1997 Chardonnay, North Fork of Long Island $11.99.   **84**

Bright golden yellow. Mildly soured appley aromas. An angular attack leads a moderately full-bodied palate with crab apple flavors, but a generous mouthfeel. Rather awkward.

1996 Pinot Blanc, Estate, North Fork of Long Island $9.99.   **82**

**1995 Cabernet Franc, Proprietor's Reserve,
North Fork of Long Island $15.**   **80**

1995 Select Reserve Red, North Fork of Long Island $25.   84

Saturated purple-red. Medium-bodied. Highly extracted. Moderately tannic. Black cherry, licorice, earth. Solid black fruit-accented aromas lead a tightly wound palate with hard-edged tannins and lush, fruity flavors. Dry and angular through the finish, though not inaccessible now.

1995 Merlot, North Fork of Long Island $16.   82

1995 Merlot, Reserve, North Fork of Long Island $28.   89

Very deep blackish ruby hue. Moderately full-bodied. Balanced acidity. Highly extracted. Heavily oaked. Moderately tannic. Pencil shavings, cedar, black fruits, minerals. Oak driven on the nose, with a rich and extracted core of minerally fruit flavors. Firm in structure with grip to the tannins and a lengthy finish.

Paumanok

1997 Chardonnay, North Fork of Long Island $16.99.   86

Deep yellow-straw hue. Pleasant mineral, yeast, and bread aromas carry a toasty oak accent. A firm entry leads a moderately full-bodied palate. Rich and firmly structured. Should develop some complexities with a bit of age. Drink now or later.

1998 Chenin Blanc, North Fork of Long Island $12.   84

Rich yellow-straw hue. Pleasant citrus and mineral aromas. A firm entry leads a moderately full-bodied palate showing sharp acidity. The finish is firm and racy. Drink now.

1995 Cabernet Sauvignon, Grand Vintage, North Fork of Long Island $25.   90

Dark, saturated ruby purple. Generous cassis, mineral, and mint aromas. A firm entry leads a full-bodied palate, with moderate but big tannins. The finish is concentrated and powerful. Very varietal and intense. Drink now or later.

1995 Assemblage, North Fork of Long Island $24.   90

Deep, saturated ruby purple. Generous mint, black fruit, and vanilla aromas show modest wood influence. A firm attack leads a moderately full-bodied palate, with big, velvety tannins. Full, rich, deep, and packed with flavor. Drink now or later.

1995 Merlot, Grand Vintage, North Fork of Long Island $22.   88

Deep, saturated ruby purple. Forward black fruit, dried herb, and mint aromas. A firm entry leads a full-bodied palate showing robust tannins. Extracted and thick, with a leafy edge. Tannins clamp down on the finish. Needs time. Mid-term cellar candidate (3–6 years).

1997 Sauvignon Blanc, Late Harvest,
North Fork of Long Island $29/375 ml.   89

Rich straw hue. Attractive honey, tropical fruit, and citrus aromas. A firm entry leads a moderately full-bodied palate, with lots of sweetness offset by crisp acids. Botrytized yet clean, with a good snap to the finish. Drink now.

Peconic Bay

1995 Chardonnay, Rolling Ridge, North Fork of Long Island $18.99.   86

Deep straw cast. Moderately full-bodied. Balanced acidity. Highly extracted. Moderately oaked. Brown spices, bread, toast. Opulent and aromatic, with a big spicy overlay and a firm core of angular citric flavors. A big, intense style.

1996 Chardonnay, Sandy Hill, North Fork of Long Island $21.99.   82

1995 Merlot, North Fork of Long Island $19.99.   82

1995 Merlot, Epic Acre, North Fork of Long Island $24.99.   90

Deep blackish ruby hue. Moderately full-bodied. Balanced acidity. Highly extracted. Mildly oaked. Moderately tannic. Black fruits, minerals. Quite deep and focused, with a full-scaled structure supported by real density of flavor. Flavorful and rich through a firm, velvety finish.

Scale: Superlative (96-100), Exceptional (90-95), Highly Recommended (85-89), Recommended (80-84), Not Recommended (Under 80)

292

Pellegrini

1996 Chardonnay, North Fork of Long Island $12.99.   86

Bright golden cast. Medium-bodied. Balanced acidity. Moderately extracted. Pears, minerals, cream. Ripe and intense, with a rounded, creamy impression on the palate. Firm and flavorful through the finish.

1995 Cabernet Franc, North Fork of Long Island $23.   86

Brilliant ruby-red hue. Generous cedar, vanilla, and red fruit aromas. A crisp entry leads to a medium-bodied palate with firm, astringent tannins. Lean, angular finish. Rather tough at present, but should open with time. Drink within five years.

1995 Cabernet Sauvignon, North Fork of Long Island $15.99.   88

Deep, saturated purple-red hue. Intense vanilla and spice aromas show a dominant oak accent. A firm attack leads to a medium-bodied palate with grainy tannins. Lengthy, flavorful finish with solid acidic grip. Taut and stylish. Drink now or later.

1994 Encore, Vintner's Pride, North Fork of Long Island $23.99.   81

1995 Merlot, North Fork of Long Island $16.99.   88

Saturated dark ruby hue. Distinctive wood spice aromas. A firm attack leads a moderately full-bodied palate with firm, fine-grained tannins through a dry, lean finish. Shows underlying fruity character. Stylish and well balanced, with the stuffing and structure to improve over time.

Pindar

1994 Cuvée Rare Champagne, North Fork of Long Island $27.99.   88

Rich yellow-straw hue, with a fine, long-lasting bead. Generous mineral, white citrus, and dough aromas. A firm entry leads a crisp, moderately full-bodied palate. Lingering, vibrant finish. Rich and stylish, with a creamy texture. Drink now.

NV Long Island Winter White, North Fork of Long Island $7.99.   80

1997 Chardonnay, Peacock Label, North Fork of Long Island $10.99.   81

1996 Chardonnay, Reserve, North Fork of Long Island $12.99.   83

Rich, luminous straw hue. Generous mineral and dough aromas. A supple entry leads a medium-bodied palate. Lighter in style, with some richness to the finish. Drink now.

1996 Chardonnay, Sunflower Special Reserve,
North Fork of Long Island $16.99.   85

Deep yellow-straw hue. Generous mineral, cream, and dough aromas. A firm entry leads a moderately full-bodied palate showing crisp acids. Rich and firm, yet closed. Drink now or later.

1996 Viognier, North Fork of Long Island $19.99.   85

Deep yellow-straw hue. Unusual, sweaty, spicy aromas. A supple entry leads a medium-bodied palate. Shows some complexities, with a fat middle and a lean, minerally finish. Drink now.

1994 Cabernet Franc, North Fork of Long Island $12.99.   89

Light cherry red. Pleasant, perfumed sweet herb and spice aromas. A firm entry leads a medium-bodied palate, with drying tannins. Flavorful and angular, with good bite. Drink now or later.

1994 Cabernet Sauvignon, North Fork of Long Island $18.99.   85

Ruby red with a slight fade. Pleasant mineral, red fruit, and dried herb aromas. A firm entry leads a medium-bodied palate that shows drying tannins. Quite structured, with a lingering finish.

1993 Cabernet Sauvignon, Reserve, North Fork of Long Island $18.99.   86

Deep garnet hue. Mature and exotic forest, earth, and mineral aromas. A firm entry leads to a medium-bodied palate with lean, angular tannins. Sharp, flavorful finish. Showing lots of mature character on a very lean, somewhat austere frame. Will work well at the table. Drink now.

1994 Cabernet Sauvignon, Reserve, North Fork of Long Island $18.99.   **83**

Bright garnet hue. Generous cedar, herb, and mineral aromas show a degree of maturity and a marked oak accent. A soft attack leads to a medium-bodied palate with lean tannins. Angular, gripping finish. Interesting flavors, and not very intense. Drink now.

1995 Cabernet Sauvignon, Reserve, North Fork of Long Island $18.99.   **89**

Saturated, opaque ruby-purple hue. Reserved berry and mineral aromas. A firm entry leads to a moderately full-bodied palate with authoritative, lean tannins. Angular, cut finish. A tightly wound style that is rather ungenerous at present. Will always be austere, but should open with age. Drink now or later.

1997 Gamay, North Fork of Long Island $8.99.   **85**

Light cherry red with a slight fade. Sound mineral and red fruit aromas. A soft entry leads a moderately light-bodied palate that has crisp acids. Ripe, fruity, and generous. Drink now.

1993 Mythology, North Fork of Long Island $24.99.   **88**

Deep garnet-red hue. Perfumed brown spice, vanilla, and mineral aromas carry a marked oak accent. A lean attack leads to a medium-bodied palate with angular acidity and grippy tannins. Taut and well structured with an Italian-like edge. Firm, linear finish. Mature in flavor with a crisp structure that will work well at the table. Drink within five years.

1994 Mythology, North Fork of Long Island $24.99.   **88**

Full ruby red. Medium-bodied. Moderately extracted. Moderately tannic. Lead pencil, cranberries, earth. Attractive earthy nose has lead pencil qualities. The firm, dry, austere palate has great presence through a dry finish.

1995 Mythology, North Fork of Long Island $36.99.   **88**

Rich, saturated ruby red. Generous mineral, red fruit, and dried herb aromas. A firm entry leads a moderately full-bodied palate, with grainy tannins. Shows some leafy complexities. Finishes on a tough, lean note. Drink now or later.

1995 Merlot, North Fork of Long Island $18.99.   **84**

Deep, saturated ruby purple. Mild black fruit, mineral, and dried herb aromas. A firm entry leads a moderately full-bodied palate, with drying tannins. Firm and compact. A trifle mean through the finish. Drink now or later.

1995 Port, North Fork of Long Island $24.99.   **89**

Deep ruby red with a slight fade. Brooding berry and wood aromas carry a complex medicinal overtone. A firm entry leads a full-bodied, moderately sweet palate, with drying tannins. Full, rich, and ripe. Drink now or later.

**1996 Johannisberg Riesling, Eiswein,
North Fork of Long Island $35/375 ml.**   **86**

Deep yellow-straw hue. Generous tropical fruit, cream, and pineapple aromas. A supple entry leads a moderately full-bodied, sweet palate, with decent balancing acidity. Ripe and creamy. A tad fat. Drink now.

Prejean

1997 Gewürztraminer, Dry, Finger Lakes $12.   **80**
1997 Gewürztraminer, Semi-Dry, Finger Lakes $12.   **81**

Pugliese

1995 Blanc de Blanc Brut, North Fork of Long Island $15.99.   **80**
1995 Blanc de Noir, North Fork of Long Island $17.99.   **84**

Light pink, with a thin mousse and fine, long-lasting beads. Pleasant red fruit and mineral aromas. An acidic entry leads a sharp, medium-bodied palate. Steely and firm, with a quick fade. Drink now.

Scale: Superlative (96-100), Exceptional (90-95), Highly Recommended (85-89), Recommended (80-84), Not Recommended (Under 80)

294

1996 Sparkling Merlot, North Fork of Long Island $17.99.   81
1996 Chardonnay, Reserve, North Fork of Long Island $12.99.   80
1997 Cabernet Franc, North Fork of Long Island $13.99.   84
Bright ruby-garnet hue. Subdued mineral, red fruit, and herb aromas. A supple entry leads a medium-bodied palate, with velvety tannins. Flavorful and straightforward. Drink now.
1995 Merlot, Reserve, North Fork of Long Island $13.99.   80
1997 Sangiovese, North Fork of Long Island $13.99.   88
Bright raspberry pink. Intense, striking berry fruit and spice aromas. A supple entry leads a medium-bodied palate showing silky tannins. Generous, lush, and stylish. Lighter in style, but quite interesting. Drink now.
Port Bello, North Fork of Long Island $26.99.   80

Standing Stone
1997 Chardonnay, Finger Lakes $12.50.   82
1997 Cabernet Franc, Finger Lakes $15.50.   81
1996 Merlot, Finger Lakes $15.50.   80

Swedish Hill
1997 Cayuga White, Finger Lakes $6.99.   82
1997 Dry Riesling, Finger Lakes $9.99/.   84
Pale straw hue. Attractive aromas show peach and apricot character. A juicy, bright entry follows through on a medium-bodied palate, with tropical flavors well balanced by a citrus zest character on the finish. Drink now.
1997 Vidal Blanc, New York $7.99.   84
Very pale straw hue. Aromatically reserved, with tart citrus notes. A zesty entry leads a moderately light-bodied palate featuring clean flavors and a note of sweetness balanced by good acids. Drink now.

Ternhaven
1994 Cabernet Sauvignon, North Fork of Long Island $17.99.   88
Luminous garnet red with a slight fade. Pleasant black fruit, mineral, and spice aromas. A firm entry leads a medium-bodied palate that has drying tannins. A lighter style, but ripe, spicy, and very tasty through the finish. Drink now or later.
1995 Cabernet Sauvignon, North Fork of Long Island $15.99.   90
Dark, saturated ruby purple. Generous cassis, vanilla, and spice aromas show a hefty oak influence. A firm attack leads a moderately full-bodied palate, with drying tannins. Concentrated, persistent, and spicy. Drink now or later.
1994 Claret d'Alvah, North Fork of Long Island $18.99.   89
Bright ruby red with a slight fade. Pleasant red fruit, spice, and mineral aromas show a mild oak accent. A firm entry leads a medium-bodied palate, with drying tannins. The finish is well balanced, angular, and flavorful. Drink now or later.
1995 Claret d'Alvah, North Fork of Long Island $18.99.   90
Dark, saturated ruby purple. Generous cassis, mineral, and spice aromas carry a marked wood accent. A firm entry leads a moderately full-bodied palate that shows robust tannins. Lingering, spicy finish. Firm and grippy. Drink now or later.
1996 Claret d'Alvah, North Fork of Long Island $17.99.   85
Rich, saturated ruby red. Generous, unusual red fruit and dill pickle aromas show hefty (American?) oak influence. A firm entry leads a medium-bodied palate, with drying tannins. Intense and austere through the finish. Drink now or later.

1994 Merlot, North Fork of Long Island $18.99.   88

Luminous cherry red with a slight fade. Generous red fruit, mineral, and spice aromas show a fair amount of wood. A firm entry leads a medium-bodied palate, with drying tannins. Spicy and generous, with a tasty finish. Drink now.

1995 Merlot, North Fork of Long Island $19.99.   89

Dark, saturated ruby purple. Generous sweet, herb, black cherry, and spice aromas jump from the glass. Shows a hefty wood accent and a slightly unusual overtone. A firm entry leads a full-bodied mouthfeel, with velvety tannins. Concentrated and intense. Should improve. Mid-term cellar candidate (3–6 years).

Treleaven

1997 Chardonnay, Cayuga Lake $11.99.   89

Bright pale yellow. Interesting spicy, nutty aromas. A rich attack leads a medium-bodied palate with smooth texture and crisp apple flavors showing interesting spice through the finish. Rather distinctive.

Scale: Superlative (96-100), Exceptional (90-95), Highly Recommended (85-89), Recommended (80-84), Not Recommended (Under 80)

296

five

≈

The Wines
of Virginia

≈

An Introduction: The Wines of Virginia

Thomas Jefferson is one of this nation's better known wine-lovers. Never accused of turning down a good drink, he spent much of his time trolling around Europe, invariably sampling the local tipple. He brought back more than a passion for wine with him. An avid horticulturist, he set about trying to grow the great wine grapes of Europe in his back yard at Monticello. Today, modern-day residents of the Old Dominion have taken up the torch, and the state is a hot bed of wine production in the Mid-Atlantic. The most promising appellation? Monticello, the region around the bucolic town of Charlottesville with its Jefferson-designed university campus, which is nestled in the foothills of the Blue Ridge Mountains.

Though Virginian wines were well known in the early years of the 19th century, Prohibition was the final setback for an industry that had sputtered along for the previous hundred years. In recent times, however, the area has once again taken up winemaking, and it would seem that more and more new producers are jumping in with every passing year.

The notoriously long, hot summers are certainly capable of bringing all sorts of grapes to ripeness, but the intense humidity brings with it its own problems. This humidity is probably the biggest problem a modern-day Jeffersonian winemaker faces. It makes the region an attractive home to a number of bugs that like to munch on grapevines, but more seriously provides ideal conditions for rot in the vineyards—particularly later in the season when sugars have accumulated in the grapes. Virginia's viticulturists are a hardy lot, constantly combating nature's whims.

Given such difficulties, it may be surprising that Virginia actually makes some pretty good and occasionally outstanding wines. Reds are really its forte, with Bordeaux varietals seemingly the most popular. However, Virginia is also home to some of the nation's most experimental winemakers. Foremost among them would be Dennis Horton of Horton Vineyards, who has developed a national following for his Viognier and Rhône-style blends. The rapid-fire Mr. Horton seems to have just about every known grape variety planted, from Rkatsiteli, a little-known Eastern Mediterranean white, to a range of Portuguese table reds. If it's not there now it's because he's already tried it and ripped it out.

Then there is Barboursville, just down the road from Horton, an impressive estate owned by the Zonin family of Italy, one of that nation's larger wine producers. It would seem that Signore Zonin likes to fancy himself the country gentleman while riding around the property, surveying it on horseback, and no doubt cutting a dashing figure in the process. Less dashing perhaps, would be his winemaker Luca Paschina, an enologist from Alba in Piedmont who readily admits to being an awful horseman and who has come to look upon the owner's occasional visits with some trepidation because of it. Nonetheless, he is a better winemaker than equestrian, and has proceeded to add Italian specialties, such as Dolcetio and Pinot Grigio, to the line-up.

Scale: Superlative (96-100), Exceptional (90-95), Highly Recommended (85-89), Recommended (80-84), Not Recommended (Under 80)

What it all adds up to is an eclectic mix of young wineries that are each finding their own ways. As such, it is difficult to generalize about the wines, other than to say that they run the gamut. In some ways, that makes the region a lot of fun, as experimentation is sometimes rewarded. This makes it difficult to predict Virginia's future, but with characters like these, half the fun will no doubt be in getting there.

Reviews

Autumn Hill

1997 Chardonnay, Monticello $11.   81

1997 Chardonnay, Barrel Select,
Virginia $13.   81

1993 Cabernet Sauvignon,
Monticello $15.   84

Opaque saturated color. Medium-bodied. Highly extracted. Moderately tannic. Earth, minerals, brown spice. Tough and reserved, with dry, earthy flavors and an impression of black fruits. Finishes in a dry, forceful manner, though the acids are low.

Barboursville

1997 Chardonnay, Monticello $12.   81

1997 Chardonnay, Reserve,
Monticello $15.   83

Pale straw cast. Medium-bodied. Full acidity. Moderately extracted. Minerals, citrus. Lean, crisp, and zesty, with ripe citric flavors. A clean, easy-drinking style.

1997 Pinot Grigio, Monticello $13.   81

1997 Sauvignon Blanc, Monticello $11.   81

1995 Cabernet Sauvignon,
Monticello $15.   86

Blood red with an even fade to the rim. Medium-bodied. Moderately extracted. Moderately tannic. Mineral, vanilla, red fruits. A juicy, generous mouthfeel shows ripeness and tertiary flavors that are seamlessly woven with bright red fruits. Shows a nice acidic cut. Drinking well now.

1995 Cabernet Sauvignon, Reserve,
Monticello $20.   83

Bright pale ruby red with a fading rim. Moderately light-bodied. Moderately extracted. Mildly tannic. Cedar, red fruits, minerals. Crisp, minerally, and angular, with a wisp of dry tannins on the finish. A very tasty, rather lean style with a strong impression of new oak flavors.

Virginia at a Glance

Wines Reviewed:

94

Producers/Brands Represented:

26

1997 Dolcetto, Monticello $19.99.   84

Bright ruby cast. Moderately light-bodied. Full acidity. Moderately extracted. Mildly tannic. Dried herbs, earth, minerals. Shows distinctive and complex aromatics with a slight earthy edge. Lean and angular through the finish. Concentrated.

NV Octagon Red, Virginia $22.   84

Pale ruby red. Moderately light-bodied. Moderately extracted. Mildly tannic. Minerals, earth, cassis. Bright minerally aromas have a crisp fruity accent that follows through on the palate with a sense of elegance. The finish is bright, with an oak spice note. An Old World style.

1995 Pinot Noir, Monticello $14.99.   87

Dark red. Medium-bodied. Moderately extracted. Moderately oaked. Moderately tannic. Mildly herbaceous oak-accented aromas. Brisk, tart cherry flavors expand on the palate through a lingering, mildly astringent finish showing oak influence. Some substance, though short on finesse.

1997 Pinot Noir, Reserve, Monticello $19.99.   81

Breaux

1997 Chardonnay, Virginia $12.   82
1997 Chardonnay, Madeleine's, Virginia $15.   84

Bright yellow-straw cast. Medium-bodied. Balanced acidity. Moderately extracted. Pears, minerals, peaches. A fruit-forward style with ripe, generous flavors. Soft and lush in the mouth with just enough acidity to lend a sense of balance.

Chateau Morrisette

1997 Chardonnay, "M," Meadows of Dan, Virginia $14.   86

Bright yellow-gold. Clean yellow-apple aromas. A bright entry leads a medium-bodied palate with crisp citrus flavors that persist through the finish. No sign of oak. A very refreshing style.

Dashiell

1996 Chardonnay, Virginia $17.   86

Bright yellow-straw cast. Moderately full-bodied. Balanced acidity. Moderately extracted. Moderately oaked. Brown spices, citrus. Generous aromas feature ample wood seasoning and a zesty fruit component. Full but balanced and flavorful through the vibrant finish.

1997 Chardonnay, Virginia $17.   86

Bright yellow-gold. Clean aromas show subtle buttery and citrus notes and a slight nutty quality. A juicy entry leads a moderately full-bodied palate with fine texture and a smooth mouthfeel. Features clean citrus flavors with minimal oak influence. Drink now.

De Chiel

1997 Late Harvest Vidal Blanc, Montebello, Virginia $12/500 ml.   82

Dominion Wine Cellars

1996 Blackberry Merlot, Virginia $18.   82
1996 Raspberry Merlot, Virginia $19.   85

Deep ruby-garnet cast. Moderately full-bodied. Full acidity. Highly extracted. Mildly tannic. Stewed fruit. Carries a ripe fruit note to the flavors, and turns very puckering on the briskly tart berry finish.

Gray Ghost

1993 Cabernet Sauvignon, Virginia $25.   81

Scale: Superlative (96-100), Exceptional (90-95), Highly Recommended (85-89), Recommended (80-84), Not Recommended (Under 80)

300

Horton

Stonecastle White, Orange County $8. 82

1997 Chardonnay, Orange County $15. 83

Pale straw cast. Medium-bodied. Full acidity. Moderately extracted. Mildly oaked. Brown spices, minerals. Restrained aromatics carry a subtle hint of oak. Crisp and lively in the mouth with an angular finish.

1997 Chardonnay, Reserve, Orange County $18. 84

Bright yellow-straw cast. Moderately full-bodied. Balanced acidity. Moderately extracted. Tropical fruits, flowers, minerals. Forward flavors show an unusual aromatic varietal quality. Big but crisp in the mouth, with a balanced finish that has grip.

1996 Cabernet Franc, Virginia $12. 83

Pale ruby-garnet hue. Moderately light-bodied. Full acidity. Moderately extracted. Moderately oaked. Mildly tannic. Brown spices, cedar, minerals. Shows an obvious oak influence in the nose. Light and crisp in the mouth, with an angular finish.

1995 Malbec, Virginia $15. 81

1995 Mourvedre, Orange County $12.50. 81

1995 Cotes d'Orange, Orange County $14.75. 81

1994 Stonecastle Red, Orange County $11.50. 84

Bright garnet red. Generous herb, red fruit, and cedar aromas show a hefty oak accent. A soft attack leads a medium-bodied palate that shows bright acidity and tannic grip. Fine structure and balance. Lengthy, spicy finish. Drink now.

1995 Vintage Port, Orange County $20. 84

Opaque blackish ruby hue. Full-bodied. Balanced acidity. Highly extracted. Brown spices, licorice, earth. A pungent style, with complex, rather unusual aromatics. Rich, round, and full on the palate, with just a hint of sweetness.

Ingleside Plantation

1995 Cabernet Franc, Virginia $11.99. 84

Bright ruby red with a garnet rim. Medium-bodied. Full acidity. Moderately extracted. Mildly oaked. Mildly tannic. Vanilla, cherries, minerals. Aromatically reserved, but juicy and flavorful on the palate, with a lean and angular finish.

NV Cabernet Sauvignon, Chesapeake Claret, Virginia $8.99. 84

Pale ruby-garnet hue with a fading rim. Moderately light-bodied. Full acidity. Moderately extracted. Mildly tannic. Earth, minerals, tart red fruits. Mature, stewed aromas are showing through, with an angular, minerally palate and gripping acids through the finish.

1994 Cabernet Sauvignon, Virginia $17.99. 84

Blood-garnet red with a fading rim. Medium-bodied. Moderately extracted. Mildly tannic. Earth, stewed fruits. Soft, earthy aromas lead a soft, mature-tasting palate, with gentle tannins through the finish.

1994 Cabernet Sauvignon, Special Reserve, Virginia $19.99. 86

Blood red with a garnet cast. Medium-bodied. Moderately extracted. Moderately tannic. Vanilla, dill, red fruits. Earth and herbal aromas dominate, with a dusty accent. Dry and lean on the palate, with chunky tannins showing some age and softness. Nicely mature, drinking well now.

1995 Cabernet Sauvignon, Special Reserve, Virginia $17.99. 83

Pale ruby hue with a subtle garnet rim. Medium-bodied. Moderately extracted. Mildly tannic. Cherries, vanilla. Soft minerally notes with red fruit accents are conveyed on the palate. Finishes with gentle oak spice and soft tannins. Drinking well now.

1997 Merlot, Virginia $14.99. 86

Bright violet hue. Generous aromas of vanilla and raspberries. A crisp attack leads a medium-bodied palate that is fleshy and fruit centered and shows velvety tannins. A forward, supple style with good varietal character. Drink now.

Jefferson

1997 Chardonnay, Monticello $9.99.   83
Bright green-gold. Medium-bodied. Balanced acidity. Moderately extracted. Butter, citrus. Aromatically reserved, with subtle fruit nuances and a decided buttery note. Crisp and lean through the finish.

1997 Chardonnay, Fantaisie Sauvage, Monticello $22.   86
Bright yellow-gold. Moderately full-bodied. Full acidity. Moderately extracted. Mildly oaked. Cream, tropical fruits, toast. Forward aromas show a fine interplay between fruit and yeast flavors, with a judicious oak accent. The finish is crisp and balanced.

1997 Chardonnay, Signature Series Reserve, Monticello $20.   84
Bright yellow-gold. Moderately full-bodied. Balanced acidity. Moderately extracted. Butter, minerals. Ripe aromas belie a forward buttery character. Big, but showing some balance in the mouth, with linear acidity through the finish.

1997 Cabernet Franc, Monticello $15.   81

1995 Cabernet Sauvignon, Monticello $18.   85
Black cherry red. Medium-bodied. Highly extracted. Moderately tannic. Black cherries, black fruits, tea. Rich aromas lead a solid, proportioned palate with concentrated fruity flavors and a weighty mouthfeel. Finishes with textured tannins.

1995 Meritage, Monticello $26.   86
Bright purple-red. Moderately light-bodied. Moderately extracted. Mildly tannic. Cherries, black tea, minerals. A mineral-accented nose show bright cherry fruit notes. Quite compact and dry on the palate, with grainy tannins coming through on the finish. Well balanced.

1997 Meritage, Monticello $28.   86
Bright cherry red hue with a slight fade. Forward and attractive mineral, berry, and vanilla aromas show a judicious oak accent. A lean attack leads to a medium-bodied palate with angular tannins and crisp acidity. Austere, structured finish. A taut and well defined style. Drink within five years.

1997 Merlot, Monticello $19.   88
Pale ruby-violet hue. Clean minerally, red fruit aromas. A crisp attack leads a medium-bodied palate with light but dry, firm tannins. The finish is clean and has a minerally note. Drink now.

Linden

1998 Riesling-Vidal, Virginia $13.   83
Brilliant straw hue with a slight spritz. Subdued earth and mineral aromas. A crisp entry leads a moderately light-bodied, lean palate that has forward fruit flavors. Racy finish with a hint of sweetness. Drink now.

1994 Cabernet Sauvignon, Virginia $16.   88
Bright, deep brick red. Medium-bodied. Moderately extracted. Mildly tannic. Earth, red fruits, licorice, brown spice. Austere spicy nose leads a solid earthy palate, with mouthfilling dry flavors that linger through the finish. Has a fine gout de terroir. Elegant, though not fruity in the least.

1995 Cabernet Sauvignon, Virginia $17.   84
Saturated, opaque blackish ruby hue. Unusual, high-toned anise and mineral aromas. A lean attack leads to a medium-bodied palate with firm, grippy tannins and shy acidity. Clipped, woody finish. Drink now.

1997 Late Harvest Vidal, Virginia $18/375 ml.   84
Deep straw hue. Earthy, toasty, sweet citrus aromas. A vibrant entry leads a medium-bodied palate showing moderate sweetness. Elevated acidity makes for a crisp, clean finish. Drink now.

Montdomaine

1993 Cabernet Sauvignon, Virginia $13.50.   85

Pale reddish purple. Medium-bodied. Moderately extracted. Mildly tannic. Faint black fruits, brown spice. Clean, somewhat austere style, with crisp fruity flavors on entry and a lengthy astringent finish. Not a whole lot of varietal character, but it has a good mouthfeel.

1993 Heritage, Virginia $15.   89

Dark blackish red. Medium-bodied. Moderately extracted. Mildly tannic. Black fruits, tobacco, dried herbs. Full dark fruit aromas have exotic tobacco and herbal notes. Almost fleshy flavors expand on the palate, with dry powdery tannins lingering on the finish. A complex melange of flavors.

Naked Mountain

1997 Chardonnay, Virginia $15.   82

1998 Riesling, Virginia $13.   81

1997 Cabernet Franc, Virginia $12.   82

1996 Cabernet Sauvignon, Virginia $15.   86

Dark ruby red with a subtle fade on the rim. Medium-bodied. Moderately extracted. Moderately oaked. Mildly tannic. Vanilla, brown spice, black fruits. A rounded, soft, sweet fruit-centered palate with a cedary, spicy overlay. Minerally dryness emerges on the finish. Well balanced, and drinking well now.

Oakencroft

1995 Cabernet Sauvignon, Monticello $14.   86

Deep ruby red with a brightening rim. Medium-bodied. Moderately extracted. Mildly tannic. Red fruits, brown spices, peanut. Spicy, aromatic nose leads an elegant palate with a cedary, minerally profile and juicy acids. Mature Claret style.

Oasis

NV Brut, Virginia $28.   88

Pale straw hue. Medium-bodied. Full acidity. Citrus, smoke, toast. Zesty, yeasty aromas show a degree of complexity that follows through on the palate and the finish. Very bright and citrus accented.

NV Celebration 2000 Brut Cuvée D'Or, Virginia $50.   86

Pale straw hue. Medium-bodied. Full acidity. Bread, dried herbs, citrus. Curious yet complex yeasty aromas lead concentrated flavors outlined with cutting acids and fine-beaded carbonation. A very distinctive style that will not appeal to everyone.

1995 Chardonnay, Virginia $18.   81

1998 Dry Gewürztraminer, Virginia $18.   80

1997 Semi-Dry Riesling, Virginia $18.   88

Deep yellow-gold. Very aromatic, with a full apple and petrol character. A flavorful attack leads a moderately full-bodied palate that has classic oily Riesling qualities. A solid food wine. Drink now.

1995 Cabernet Franc, Virginia $18.50.   81

1995 Cabernet Sauvignon, Virginia $19.50.   80

1997 Cabernet Sauvignon, Reserve, Virginia $19.50.   81

1997 Meritage, Virginia $38.50.   84

Pale garnet hue. Subdued herb and cedar aromas show a subtle oak accent. A soft attack leads to a moderately light-bodied palate with angular tannins and crisp acidity. Lengthy, smoke-tinged finish. Quite light in style but tasty and well structured. Drink now.

1995 Merlot, Virginia $24.50.   80

Prince Michel

1995 The Prince's Brut, Virginia $20.   80

1997 Chardonnay, Virginia $13.95.   83

Bright pale straw. Mild aromas of apple and pear show a clean varietal character. A crisp entry leads a medium-bodied palate with bright, pure fruit flavors and a clean finish supported by crisp acids. A well-balanced, refreshing style. Drink now.

1997 Chardonnay, Barrel Select, Virginia $18.95.   88

Bright yellow-gold. Subtle oak aromas with ripe apple. A fruity attack leads a moderately full-bodied palate with bright acids and fresh fruity flavors. Judiciously oaked, with a lingering spicy finish. Drink now.

Rapidan River

1997 Gewürztraminer, Barrel Fermented, Virginia $18.95.   82

Rockbridge

1997 Chardonnay, Reserve, Virginia $15.   86

Deep yellow-gold. Ripe aromas show apple and butter. A bright entry leads a moderately full-bodied palate with a rounded buttery mouthfeel and concentrated flavors. Finishes with a note of alcohol warmth. A big, generous style. Drink now.

1997 St. Mary's Blanc, Virginia $8.   80

1997 Tuscarora White, Virginia $8.   83

Deep yellow-straw hue. Attractive candied pear and vanilla aromas. A rich entry leads a moderately full-bodied palate, with mild sweetness offset by sturdy acidity. Crisp, flavorful finish. Drink now.

1995 Cabernet, Virginia $14.   83

Bright violet-ruby hue. Medium-bodied. Moderately extracted. Mildly tannic. Spice, minerals. Dusty, minerally aromas. Plenty of oak spice flavors emerge on the palate, with light fruit flavors and a lean finish making for a more reserved style.

1996 Cabernet, Virginia $14.   84

Bright cherry red hue. Intense cranberry, cherry, and mineral aromas. A crisp attack leads to a moderately light-bodied, fruit centered palate with soft tannins. Bright finish. A straightforward quaffer. Drink now.

1997 Vidal Blanc, Late Harvest V d'Or, Virginia $15/375 ml.   80

Spotswood Trail

1997 Chardonnay, Ivy Creek, Monticello $15.   83

Bright yellow-gold. Moderately full-bodied. Balanced acidity. Moderately extracted. Moderately oaked. Brown spices, tropical fruits. Forward aromas have a high degree of ripeness and a hefty oak accent. Weighty and rich in the mouth with a hint of sweetness through the finish.

Swedenburg

1995 Cabernet Sauvignon, Virginia $14.   80

Tarara

1997 Chardonnay, Virginia $12.99.   83

Bright straw cast. Medium-bodied. Balanced acidity. Moderately extracted. Minerals, pears. Ripe, fruity aromas lead a straightforward, clean mouthfeel. The finish is soft.

1997 Sweet Vidal Blanc, Virginia $12.99/375 ml.   80

1997 Cabernet Franc, Virginia $13.99.   81

Scale: Superlative (96-100), Exceptional (90-95), Highly Recommended (85-89), Recommended (80-84), Not Recommended (Under 80)

White Hall Vineyards

1997 Chardonnay, Virginia $12.   80

1997 Chardonnay, Reserve, Virginia $18.   89

Bright green-gold cast. Moderately full-bodied. Full acidity. Moderately extracted. Moderately oaked. Smoke, brown spices, citrus. Ripe, forward aromas feature a generous oak accent. Full smoky flavors open up on the palate, backed by crisp acidity through a lengthy, flavorful finish.

1997 Cabernet Franc, Virginia $18.   84

Bright ruby with a garnet edge. Forward cedar and wood aromas. A firm entry leads to a medium-bodied palate with grippy, angular tannins. Lean, firm finish. Showing some substance. Drink now or later.

1997 Cabernet Sauvignon, Virginia $15.   81

NV Merlot, Lot 97, Virginia $12.99.   83

Medium ruby red with a subtle fade on the rim. Generous minerally, wood spice aromas. A supple attack leads a medium-bodied palate that has crisp acids and moderate, soft tannins. Drink now.

Williamsburg

NV Governor's White, American $6.49.   83

Bright straw hue. Reserved flower and mineral aromas. A lush entry leads a medium-bodied palate, with crisp acidity. Rounded, flavorful finish. Stylish. Drink now.

NV James River White, American $6.49.   80

1997 Chardonnay, Vintage Reserve, Virginia $21.   81

1993 Gabriel Archer Reserve, Virginia $21.   85

Pale cherry red. Medium-bodied. Moderately extracted. Mildly tannic. Red fruit, minerals, sun-dried tomatoes. Muted aromatics. The dry and dusty palate has some sweet cherry hints and a solid minerally backbone. Subtle bitter hints on the finish.

1995 Merlot, Reserve, Virginia $18.   82

Willowcroft

1997 Chardonnay, Reserve, Virginia $13.   81

1996 Cabernet Franc, Virginia $16.   84

Bright ruby hue with a slight fade. Medium-bodied. Full acidity. Moderately extracted. Heavily oaked. Mildly tannic. Menthol, minerals, brown spices. Quite aromatic, with oak-driven flavors riding a lean and angular frame. Finishes with some snap.

Wintergreen

Raspberry Wine, Virginia $11.97/375 ml.   84

Bright ruby-garnet cast. Medium-bodied. Full acidity. Moderately extracted. Dried herbs, minerals. Carries a big herbal note throughout. Lighter in style, with an angular finish and a hint of sweetness.

six

Other U.S. Wines

An Introduction: Other U.S. Wines

Grape growing and winemaking is actually practiced all around the United States—some places more probable than others—but it's a big country with lots and lots of microclimates that make wine production possible in a range of locales. The most important centers tend to be in the Midwest, on the Great Lakes, in Missouri, and in the Southwest.

The Heartland

In the Midwest, there are small wine industries all around the Great Lakes, but particularly along Lake Erie and Lake Michigan. Both Ohio and Michigan boast a number of family wineries, capable of producing surprisingly good wines. The vines are usually planted near the lakes, where the moderating climactic influence of the water allows the vines to survive the brutally cold winters. Nonetheless, summers can be short and cool, and it is with white wines that the best results are achieved. As for Missouri, the heat of the southern heartland comes more into play, and a wider range of wines is produced. The industry is centered on Augusta, midway between Kansas City and St. Louis, and was largely pioneered by German settlers. The area remains true to its German heritage to this day, and has become a popular tourist destination. Perhaps unsurprisingly, given the summer heat, the region has made a name for itself by the production of convincing port-styled wines. This is not to pigeonhole area vintners, however, as truly exciting reds and even some decent whites are known to pop up every now and again.

The Southwest

Finally, though it may sound like more Texan bravado, the Southwest—from west Texas through New Mexico and even into Arizona—is actually capable of producing decent wines. The Texans are centered in the famous Hill Country west of Austin. The dry, hot, arid climate is perfect for grapevines, with little threat of inopportune freezes, problematic humidity, or rain at harvest. This makes for big, ripe—the uncharitable would add occasionally roasted—wines. The industry has really just gotten going, and there's lots of land out there, so it's difficult to make generalizations, but there are some promising reds being produced. The ubiquitous Chardonnay makes an appearance as well, confirming its well-deserved moniker as the "weed" of the wine world.

Chipotle and Champagne

Northern New Mexico, being high desert (New Mexicans like to point out that their state would be bigger than Texas if similarly flattened out), actually has a more variable climate than the Texas Hill Country. Wineries tend to be far flung, but the wines on the whole are amazingly convincing. Gruet, a sparkling wine firm based in Albuquerque, and founded by two Frenchmen from Champagne no less, must surely be among the most improbable wineries in the country. While their fellow countrymen have made major investments in California, these brothers took a detour. As with many stories such as this, there seems to have been a woman involved. At any rate, Gruet is one of the finest producers of sparkling wine in the country, and a favorite of adventurous restaurants from coast to coast. Albuquerque is also home to one of my favorite wine festivals in

Scale: Superlative (96-100), Exceptional (90-95), Highly Recommended (85-89), Recommended (80-84), Not Recommended (Under 80)

the world. The New Mexico Wine Fair is usually held on Labor Day weekend, right around the Route 66 festival and one of many ballooning events. With the spectacular mountain scenery, the sophisticated southwestern cuisine, and a glass of Gruet Blanc de Blancs, it is a wine experience like no other in the world.

Reviews

Ackerman (Iowa)
Apricot Wine, $6.50.   **93**
Very deep yellow-gold. Full-bodied. Full acidity. Highly extracted. Apricots, spice, mint. Complex and pungent aromatics have a botrytis-like edge. Full and viscous in the mouth, with marked sweetness balanced by razor-sharp acidity. Structured almost like an ice wine.

Blackberry Wine, $6.50.   **85**
Bright garnet cast. Full-bodied. Balanced acidity. Highly extracted. Red fruits, minerals. Forward and unusual aromatics lead to a ripe and viscous mouthfeel. Quite sweet, though an edge of acidity lends a sense of balance to the finish. Fine length.

Alba (New Jersey)
Red Raspberry Wine, $9.99/500 ml.   **91**
Light ruby-garnet cast. Full acidity. Highly extracted. Dried herbs, red fruits. Rather unusual aromatics lead a lighter-styled palate feel, with an extremely tart finish.

Bartlett (Maine)
Sweet Raspberry Wine,
Maine $9.99/375 ml.   **91**
Deep ruby-garnet cast. Moderately full-bodied. Full acidity. Highly extracted. Raspberries. Pleasantly aromatic, with a wave of pure raspberry flavors. Full in the mouth, with an overtone of sweetness balanced by tart acidity. Chocolate, anyone?

Coastal Apple & Pear Wine, $8.99.   **87**
Bright straw cast. Medium-bodied. Full acidity. Moderately extracted. Green apples, minerals. Pleasantly aromatic, with a well-defined wave of appley flavors. Lush but crisp in the mouth, with a slight hint of sweetness balanced beautifully by vibrant acidity. Well balanced and intense.

Other
U.S. Wines
at a Glance

Wines Reviewed:

144

Producers/Brands
Represented:

39

Peach Wine, Semi-Dry, $11.99.   85

Deep yellow-gold. Moderately full-bodied. Full acidity. Highly extracted. Minerals, peaches. Features a rather unusual note on the nose that doesn't follow through to the palate. Firm and well-structured mouthfeel, with vibrant acidity balancing an overtone of sweetness and making for a dry finish.

Pear Wine, Dry, $9.99.   81

Pear Wine, French Oak Dry, $14.99.   90

Bright golden cast. Moderately full-bodied. Full acidity. Highly extracted. Mildly oaked. Pears, spices, minerals. Quite aromatic, with a very pure, pearlike note accented by well-integrated, spicy oak nuances. Mouthfilling and firm, with angular acidity and lengthy flavors. Intense and focused.

Wild Blueberry Wine, Oak Dry, $14.99.   87

Deep blackish ruby cast. Medium-bodied. Full acidity. Moderately extracted. Mildly tannic. Black fruits, dried herbs. Pleasantly aromatic, with a complex set of flavors. Firm and well structured in the mouth, with rather forceful acidity that makes for a drying finish. Flavorful and intense.

1994 Wild Blueberry Wine, Oak Dry, Winemakers Reserve, $21.99.   93

Very deep blackish ruby cast. Full-bodied. Balanced acidity. Highly extracted. Mildly oaked. Mildly tannic. Vanilla, cherry cordial, black fruits. Quite aromatic, with a distinctive spicy oak overlay to the deep core of dark fruit flavors. Firmly structured and well balanced, with a lengthy, intense finish.

Bell Mountain (Texas)

1995 Pinot Noir, Bell Mountain $12.   80

Biltmore (North Carolina)

NV Blanc de Blanc, North Carolina $16.99.   81

Chateau Biltmore 1995 Blanc de Blanc, North Carolina $24.99.   81

NV Chardonnay, American $14.99.   86

Bright straw cast. Medium-bodied. Balanced acidity. Moderately extracted. Mildly oaked. Vanilla, minerals, nuts. Forward aromas show an enticing leesy accent. Finishes in a lush and generous manner.

NV Merlot, American $13.99.   81

Cabernet Sauvignon, American $12.99.   86

Saturated brilliant red-purple. Medium-bodied. Highly extracted. Moderately oaked. Moderately tannic. Black cherries, minerals. Very expressive primary fruit aromas follow through on a lush entry that turns minerally and dry through the finish. Drinkable.

1997 Chateau Biltmore Cabernet Sauvignon, North Carolina $19.99. 89

Saturated purple. Moderately full-bodied. Highly extracted. Moderately tannic. Cassis, vanilla, licorice. Bright, spicy primary fruit aromas. Dense and saturated, with bright fruit flavors on entry that turn dry and lean through the finish. Better in a few years.

1997 Chateau Biltmore Vanderbilt Claret, North Carolina $19.99.

Boordy (Maryland)

1997 Seyval Blanc, Sur Lie Reserve, Maryland $8.50.   80

Cap Rock (Texas)

NV Sparkling Wine, American $12.99.   86

Bright yellow-straw hue. Medium-bodied. Tropical fruit, grass, minerals. Floral, grassy aromas follow through on the palate, with a decidedly grassy finish. Nonclassical flavors are refreshing and generous through the midpalate.

Scale: Superlative (96-100), Exceptional (90-95), Highly Recommended (85-89), Recommended (80-84), Not Recommended (Under 80)

1997 Chardonnay, Texas $8.99.   83

Bright straw cast. Moderately full-bodied. Full acidity. Moderately extracted. Minerals, citrus. Aromatically reserved, with a steely and angular mouthfeel. Crisp and vibrant through the finish.

1997 Topaz Royale White, Texas $6.99.   80

1996 Cabernet Sauvignon, Texas $7.99.   81

1996 Cabernet Sauvignon, Reserve, Newsom Vineyard,
Texas High Plains $12.99.   82

Cedar Creek (Wisconsin)

1998 Semi-Dry Riesling, American $7.   83

Very pale straw. Lean aromas show a minerally, floral note. A juicy entry leads a medium-bodied palate, with bright apple flavors that linger on the finish. Decent flavor concentration. Drink now.

1997 Semi-Dry Vidal Blanc, American $7.   81

NV Cranberry Blush, American $7.   87

Saturated pale pinkish garnet hue. Intense sweet berry aromas leap from the glass. A crisp entry leads a zesty, medium-bodied palate that shows great acidic cut and a touch of sweetness. Juicy, flavorful finish. Drink now.

Chaddsford (Pennsylvania)

1997 Chardonnay, Pennsylvania $10.   84

Pale straw cast. Moderately light-bodied. Full acidity. Moderately extracted. Dried herbs, minerals. Forward herbal aromas lead a clean and snappy mouthfeel. Crisp and linear through the finish.

1995 Chardonnay, Philip Roth Vineyard, Pennsylvania $26.   89

Bright straw cast. Medium-bodied. Balanced acidity. Moderately extracted. Moderately oaked. Toasted coconut, minerals, citrus. Forward oak-accented aromas merge with firm minerally flavors in the mouth. Crisp and austere on the palate, with fine grip and intensity through the finish.

1995 Chardonnay, Stargazers Vineyard, Pennsylvania $24.   84

Bright yellow-gold. Moderately full-bodied. Full acidity. Moderately extracted. Moderately oaked. Brown spices, citrus, minerals. Carries a generous oak accent to a core of lean citric flavors. The flavors are ripe, though snappy and crisp through the finish.

1996 Cabernet Franc, Pennsylvania $18.   86

Bright ruby hue with a slight purple cast. Medium-bodied. Full acidity. Moderately extracted. Mildly oaked. Mildly tannic. Green vegetables, vanilla. Carries a big spicy oak streak, and shows an underlying core of underripe flavors. The summary effect is a lighter-styled, interesting wine, with a Loire-like flavor profile.

1995 Merican Red, Pennsylvania $29.99.   83

Ruby red with a lightening rim. Medium-bodied. Moderately extracted. Moderately tannic. Brown spice, earth. Lean, herbal aromas follow through on the palate, with bright acids and a minerally character that lingers on the finish. A reserved style with some bitter elements.

1997 Johannisberg Riesling, Sweet Late Harvest Style $18.   83

Pale straw hue. Subdued mineral and talc aromas. A rich entry leads a sweet, medium-bodied palate that has sturdy acidic balance. Straightforward, woolly finish. Drink now.

Chalet Debonné (Ohio)

1998 Riesling, Lake Erie $8.49.   81

1998 Riesling, Reserve, Grand River Valley $8.49.   83

Bright pale straw hue. Crisp citrus zest aromas. A vibrant entry leads a moderately light-bodied palate, with clean, mineral-edged flavors through the finish. Drink now.

Chateau Elan (Georgia)
Georgian-Style Port, American $22. 83

Deep blackish garnet cast. Medium-bodied. Balanced acidity. Moderately extracted. Peaches, blackberries, minerals. Extremely fragrant, with an unusual, high-toned fruit quality throughout. Lighter on the palate, with a sense of brightness through the finish. Interesting.

Chateau Grand Traverse (Michigan)
1996 Chardonnay, Barrel Fermented, Old Mission Peninsula $12.49. 83

Deep straw cast. Medium-bodied. Full acidity. Moderately extracted. Minerals, citrus. Aromas show subtle vanilla notes. Clean and focused, with an angular minerally mouthfeel. Crisp and zesty finish.

1996 Chardonnay, Reserve, Old Mission Peninsula $13.99. 84

Bright straw cast. Moderately full-bodied. Balanced acidity. Moderately extracted. Mildly oaked. Minerals, toast, brown spices. Forward aromas carry a pleasant oaky accent. Ripe and lush in the mouth with a snappy finish.

1997 Dry Johannisberg Riesling, Michigan $9.99. 81

1997 Semi-Dry Johannisberg Riesling, Michigan $9.99. 82

1997 Late Harvest Johannisberg Riesling, Michigan $12.49. 83

Medium gold-straw hue. Pear and apple aromas have mild herbal overtones. A vibrant entry leads a medium-bodied palate, with mild sweetness, stone fruit flavors, and a drying finish. Drink now.

1997 Dry Johannisberg Riesling, Select Harvest,
Old Mission Peninsula $12.49. 84

Medium yellow-straw cast. Varietally pure aromas of wax and minerals. A crisp entry leads a medium-bodied palate, with tart acids and an angular finish that shows a good persistence of dry flavors. This would be a good foil for lighter foods. Drink now.

1995 Merlot, Reserve, Old Mission Peninsula $23.99. 80

1995 Pinot Noir, Limited Release, Old Mission Peninsula $13.49. 81

Dos Cabezas (Arizona)
1997 Chardonnay, Reserve, Cochise County $18. 88

Deep yellow-gold. Full-bodied. Full acidity. Highly extracted. Oranges, cream, spice. Full and ripe, with an intense, weighty mouthfeel. Spritzy acidity lends a sense of buoyancy to the finish. A rich, flavorful style.

1997 Pinot Gris, Cochise County $14.95. 87

Deep yellow-gold. Moderately full-bodied. Balanced acidity. Moderately extracted. Moderately oaked. Toasted coconut, minerals, smoke. Oak is readily apparent on the nose and is joined by an exotic spicy note on the palate. Full and ripe, with richness tempered by acidity through a weighty, smoky finish.

1997 Petite Sirah, Cochise County $15. 87

Saturated dark purple. Moderately full-bodied. Highly extracted. Moderately tannic. Prunes, herbs. Complex, savory herb and fleshy fruit aromas. A silky mouthfeel has inky, rich black fruit that stands up to the tannic structure. This is drinking well now. A touch overripe.

Elk Run (Maryland)
1997 Chardonnay, Liberty Tavern Reserve, Maryland $15. 84

Deep yellow-gold. Aromas show a heavy buttery quality. A rich entry leads a full-bodied palate with a thick, glycerous mouthfeel and full buttery flavors. Fruit flavors are more subdued, though acids are in balance. A rich style. Drink now.

1998 Gewürztraminer, American $13.25. 81

1998 Johannisberg Riesling, American $12. 81

Scale: Superlative (96-100), Exceptional (90-95), Highly Recommended (85-89), Recommended (80-84), Not Recommended (Under 80)

312

1997 Cabernet Franc, Maryland $15.   **82**

1997 Cabernet Sauvignon, Maryland $15.   **86**

Saturated ruby red hue. Intense, unusual anise and brown spice aromas show a big oak accent. A lean entry leads to a medium-bodied palate with firm grippy tannins and crisp acidity. Angular, flavorful finish. Drink now or later.

1997 Merlot, Maryland $18.   **84**

Saturated dark violet-ruby hue. Distinctively toasty aromas. A thick entry leads a moderately full-bodied palate with clunky, mean tannins. Rather inky and ungenerous through the finish. Drink now.

1997 Johannisberg Riesling, Vin de Jus Glacé, American $20/375 ml.   **80**

Fall Creek (Texas)

1997 Sauvignon Blanc, Texas $8.50.   **81**

1996 Meritus, Texas Hill Country $29.   **83**

Medium ruby red with a lightening rim. Medium-bodied. Moderately extracted. Moderately tannic. Cedar, red fruits, minerals. Very spicy, oak-driven aromas follow through on the palate, with a dry, lean character and a short finish.

Firelands (Ohio)

NV Riesling, Lake Erie $10.95.   **86**

Bright yellow-straw cast. Medium-bodied. Full acidity. Citrus, tropical fruits, minerals. Quite aromatic, with bright, Riesling-like flavors. Firm and frothy in the mouth, with refreshing acidity and a hint of sweetness to round things out.

1998 Gewürztraminer, Lake Erie $8.99.   **83**

Deep straw hue. Generous spicy aromas jump from the glass. A rich entry leads a fat, moderately full-bodied palate, with a bit of acidity through the finish that lends a sense of balance. Straightforward, tasty finish with a touch of sweetness. Drink now.

Fredericksburg Winery (Texas)

1997 Cabernet Sauvignon, Winecup, Texas $14.95.   **86**

Saturated dark ruby hue. Medium-bodied. Moderately extracted. Heavily oaked. Mildly tannic. Chocolate, spice, black fruits. Exotic toasted oak aromas show spicy complexity that comes through on the palate. Velvety, rich flavors are harmonious; despite the hefty oak accent, this does not turn too dry.

Good Harbor (Michigan)

1997 Semidry White Riesling, Leelanau Peninsula $8.   **88**

Rich golden hue. Deep, ripe tropical aromas. A rich entry leads a moderately full-bodied palate with a glycerous mouthfeel and a note of persistent fruit sweetness on the finish. Drink now.

Cherry Wine, Michigan $5.   **89**

Bright ruby red with a garnet tinge. Medium-bodied. Full acidity. Highly extracted. Black cherries. Pure and expressive aromatics are well translated onto the palate. Vibrant and racy, with tart acidity that balances a hint of sweetness in the finish. Flavorful and intense.

Grande River (Colorado)

1997 Chardonnay, Grand Valley $12.99.   **83**

Green-straw hue. Moderately full-bodied. Balanced acidity. Nuts, butter. Yeasty, faintly oxidized aromas. Soft nutty flavors emerge on a buttery mouthfeel with underlying lemon notes.

1996 White Meritage, Grand Valley $8.99.   **85**

Deep golden cast. Full-bodied. Low acidity. Moderately extracted. Vanilla, blanched almonds. Distinctive aromas lead a fat, viscous mouthfeel that concludes with marked dryness.

1996 Viognier, Grand Valley $19.99.   84

Bright golden hue. Moderately full-bodied. Balanced acidity. Moderately extracted. Minerals, oranges, flowers. Aromatically reserved, with delicate though complex flavors on the palate. Features fine length and intensity with solid grip.

1994 Grand Valley $12.99.   88

Deep brick red. Medium-bodied. Moderately extracted. Moderately tannic. Earth, brown spice, leather, mint. Generous earthy, spicy nose. Astringent, earthy palate has plenty of character and a mature flavor profile. Interesting and flavorful.

1995 Meritage, Grand Valley $12.99.   81

1996 Meritage, Grand Valley $12.99.   86

Bright cherry red hue. Perfumed spice, mineral, and red fruit aromas. A lean attack leads to a medium-bodied palate with angular, grippy tannins and sturdy acidity. Crisp, stylish finish. Drink now or later.

1996 Merlot, Grand Valley $11.99.   87

Bright ruby red to the rim. Powerful cedar, herb, and red fruit aromas show a big oak accent. A firm attack leads a medium-bodied palate with solid tannins. Mouthwatering, buoyant, flavorful finish. Well balanced and showing classic Merlot flavor complexities. Drink within five years.

1996 Syrah, Grand Valley $15.99.   84

Bright purple-red hue. Forward overripe red fruit and mineral aromas. A smooth attack leads a medium-bodied palate, with silky tannins. Supple, fruity finish. A pleasant quaffing style. Drink now.

Gruet (New Mexico)

NV Blanc de Noirs, New Mexico $14.   84

Pale straw cast with a slight copper tinge. Moderately full-bodied. Full acidity. Fruit, citrus, minerals. Carries a fruity overtone throughout. Lush and generous on the palate, with an ample mouthfeel. Well balanced and flavorful, this would partner well with food.

NV Brut, New Mexico $14.   83

Medium yellow-straw hue. Medium-bodied. Full acidity. Minerals, citrus. Refined and quite aromatic. Very full, fine-beaded carbonation with rounded, intense flavors that have a spicy, toasty quality persisting through the finish. Very distinctive flavors.

1994 Blanc de Blancs, New Mexico $20.   87

Bright green-straw cast. Moderately full-bodied. Full acidity. Highly extracted. Smoke, toast, minerals. Forward and attractive aromatics show a vibrant, toasty, smoky edge. Firm and aggressive in the mouth, with zesty carbonation and a racy finish.

1997 Chardonnay, New Mexico $13.   82

Henke (Ohio)

NV Riesling, American $10.37.   86

Bright pale gold hue. Oily, tropical fruit aromas. A flavorful attack leads a medium-bodied palate, with bright acids and classic oily, minerally Riesling flavors that linger on the finish. Drink now.

1997 Seyval, Ohio River Valley $9.   83

Deep yellow-straw hue. Powerful smoke and vanilla aromas show a hefty oak accent. A lush entry leads a medium-bodied palate that has a firm acidic edge. Rich. Rather like a flashy, oak-dominated Chardonnay. Drink now.

1997 Vidal Blanc, Ohio River Valley $8.49.   83

Pale green-straw hue. Quite aromatic, with a grassy, grapefruit-flavored character. A juicy entry leads a medium-bodied palate that has good flavor concentration and persistence through the finish. Drink now.

Hermannhof (Missouri)

1997 Vignoles, Missouri $13.99.   80

Indian Creek (Idaho)

1997 Chardonnay, Idaho $9.95.   86

Pale green-gold. Aromatically restrained with subtle oak spice and citrus fruits. A juicy attack leads a medium-bodied palate with crisp, subtle fruit flavors well balanced by oak. A light, precise, cool climate style. Drink now.

1998 White Riesling, Idaho $6.95.   84

Bright pale platinum hue. Ripe, sweet apple aromas. A juicy entry leads a medium-bodied palate with moderately sweet flavors of ripe apples and peaches. The finish is clean. A softer, sweeter style. Drink now.

Kokopelli (Arizona)

1996 Cabernet Sauvignon, Arizona $9.   80
1995 Pinot Noir, Arizona $9.   80

L. Mawby (Michigan)

NV Blanc de Blanc Brut, Michigan $15.   84

Bright yellow-gold. Moderately full-bodied. Full acidity. Highly extracted. Cream, toast, butter. Ripe and opulent aromas are unusual, but complex. Firm and intense in the mouth, with aggressive carbonation and a flavorful finish.

NV Cremant Brut, Leelanau Peninsula $18.   86

Deep pale gold hue. Medium-bodied. Minerals, biscuits. Aromatically reserved, but well balanced and flavorful on the palate, with a sense of biscuity richness. Crisp through the finish.

NV Talisman Brut, Leelanau Peninsula $22.   87

Bright pale gold cast. Moderately full-bodied. Full acidity. Yeast, cream. Forward aromas show yeast-accented complexity. Full and rounded in the mouth, with judicious carbonation, this shows fine length and intensity.

Lonz (Ohio)

3 Islands American Ruby Port, $6.50.   86

Deep ruby with brick rim. Moderately full-bodied. Balanced acidity. Moderately extracted. Heavily oaked. Medium sweetness. Reminiscent of dried orange peel, vanilla, raisins. Richly textured, firmly structured on the palate, and layered with distinctive sweet, woody nuances.

Meier's (Ohio)

No. 44 American Ruby Port, $6.95.   86

Deep brickish garnet hue. Medium-bodied. Balanced acidity. Moderately extracted. Medium sweetness. Reminiscent of nuts, earth, coffee, cherries. Well focused and firmly textured, with sweet fruit nuances that play into the finish. Surprisingly well integrated for a "Port" of this price.

No. 44 Cream Sherry, $7.49.   80

Messina Hof (Texas)

1995 Cabernet Sauvignon, Barrel Reserve, Texas $9.99.   87

Bright brick red. Medium-bodied. Moderately extracted. Mildly tannic. Leather, brown spice, earth, dried fruits. Very aromatic leathery, spicy aromas have baked accents. Rich, solid mouthful of earthy flavors has a smoothly textured mouthfeel and a subtle lingering finish showing supple tannins.

Mount Pleasant (Missouri)

1996 Chardonel, Augusta $14.   88

Bright straw hue. Attractive vanilla and spice aromas. A lush entry leads a medium-bodied palate with bright acidity and judicious oak. Rich, flavorful finish. Quite stylish. Drink now.

1997 Rayon d'Or, Missouri $14.   82

1994 Cabernet Sauvignon, Augusta $35.   83

Medium ruby red. Medium-bodied. Moderately extracted. Moderately oaked. Mildly tannic. Raspberry, cedar, toasted oak. Perfumed oak spice aromas follow through on a lighter-styled palate, with bright berry fruit flavors and mild tannins. Oak character is very prominent.

1994 Belle Yvonne, Missouri $50.   92

Bright cherry red. Medium-bodied. Moderately extracted. Mildly tannic. Dill, brown spice, cherries. Hugely toasty oak nose leads a smooth, mellow palate with an extravagant oak character that persists through a long chocolatey, spicy finish. Very elegant and distinctive, though maybe not for everyone.

1994 Merlot, Augusta $45.   85

Saturated dark ruby hue. Impressive chocolate and black fruit aromas show a heavy oak accent. A solid attack leads to a moderately full-bodied palate with dry gripping tannins and lively acids. Quite complex and chocolatey through the finish. The oak might be too much for some palates.

1994 Pinot Noir, Augusta $25.   83

Pale garnet orange. Moderately light-bodied. Subtly extracted. Mildly tannic. A minerally, dusty nose leads a crisp, lean mouthful of flavors with a brief, dry finish.

JRL's Barrel Select Port, Augusta $11.95.   85

Reddish brick hue with a distinctly browning rim. Medium-bodied. Highly extracted. Mildly tannic. Reminiscent of earth, dates, coffee. A caramelized coffee note runs through this. Though somewhat tawny in style, it still has plenty of stuffing.

1990 Port, Augusta, Missouri $18.   86

Opaque blackish garnet cast. Moderately full-bodied. Low acidity. Highly extracted. Charred yeast, smoke, treacle. Features an odd charred note in the nose that is hard to overlook. Lean and drying through the finish. Strange.

1996 White Port, Augusta Missouri $25/375 ml.   86

Deep straw cast. Moderately full-bodied. Balanced acidity. Moderately extracted. Blanched almonds, petrol, flowers. Quite aromatic and very traditional, with a touch of heat. Full, flavorful, and well balanced in the mouth, with a rounded, though not heavy, impression. Fresh, stylish, and convincing.

15 Barrel Tawny Port, Augusta $23.50.   88

Bright pale amber. Medium-bodied. Full acidity. Moderately extracted. Medium sweetness. Reminiscent of golden raisins, toffee, pralines. Thick, slightly syrupy textured fruit is countered by a pleasant, acidic snap. Assertive dried fruit notes last well into the finish, accompanied by a pleasant warmth.

Tawny Port, Library Vol. V, Augusta Missouri $28.   85

Bright orange-copper cast. Medium-bodied. Balanced acidity. Moderately extracted. Roasted nuts, caramel, brown spices. Pleasantly aromatic, with lush wood accents throughout. Rich and harmonious on the palate, with a well-balanced, lengthy finish.

1993 Vidal Blanc, Individual Berry Select, Augusta $30/375 ml.   85

Very deep, tawny amber hue. Unusual, pungent, raisiny aromas show a spicy, woody quality. A rich entry leads a silky, medium-bodied palate with lots of sweetness. Exceptionally flavorful and forceful, like a spice bomb, but a bit off center. A love it or hate it style. Drink now.

Scale: Superlative (96-100), Exceptional (90-95), Highly Recommended (85-89), Recommended (80-84), Not Recommended (Under 80)

Pend d'Oreille (Idaho)

1996 Chardonnay, Idaho $14.99. 81
1996 Cabernet Sauvignon, Idaho $15.99. 80

Sakonnet (Rhode Island)

1997 Chardonnay, Southeastern New England $15.95. 84

Pale yellow-straw hue. Lean citrus aromas. A bright attack leads a medium-bodied palate with pure citrus flavors and tart acids through the finish. Very fresh, pure style with no oak influence. Drink now.

1997 Gewürztraminer, Southeastern New England $14.95. 84

Bright yellow-straw hue. Aromatically subdued, with clean, minerally citrus flavors in the mouth. Medium-bodied and crisp, with vibrant acidity. Spicy, flavorful finish. Drink now.

1995 Pinot Noir, Southeastern New England $14.99. 81

St. Julian (Michigan)

1996 Chardonnay, Barrel Select, Michigan $12.95. 81
1997 Riesling, Michigan $11.99. 83

Pale green-straw hue. Crisp, tart fruit aromas. A vibrant entry leads a medium-bodied palate with white peach flavors and a note of glycerine on the mouthfeel. Finishes cleanly. Drink now.

1997 Seyval Blanc, Sweet Reserve, Lake Michigan Shore $6.50. 81
1997 Vidal Blanc, Sweet Reserve, Lake Michigan Shore $6.50. 83

Pale green-straw hue. Moderately aromatic with clean melon and citrus accents. A juicy entry leads a medium-bodied palate, with sweetness coming through on the finish. A straightforward off-dry style. Drink now.

1997 Vignoles, Michigan $9.50. 80
1995 Merlot, Lake Michigan Shore $20. 84

Deep blackish ruby hue. Medium-bodied. Full acidity. Highly extracted. Heavily oaked. Moderately tannic. Sour cherries, sweet herbs, vanilla. Aromatic, with a lean and austere palate feel that has up-front acidity. Mild astringency on the finish, but quite good length.

1995 Pinot Noir, Lake Michigan Shore $24. 86

Pale crimson hue. Moderately light-bodied. Moderately extracted. Mildly tannic. Vanilla oak aromas show crisp red berry accents with herbal nuances. Quite perfumed, with delicate flavors that have citrus acidity through the finish. Fresh style.

Catherman's Port, Michigan $12. 81
Solera Cream Sherry, Michigan $12. 88

Deep mahogany color with a slight greenish cast. Moderately full-bodied. Balanced acidity. Salted nuts, caramel, toffee. Shows attractive and authentic aromatics, with genuine complexity. Lush and sweet in the mouth, with a lengthy finish. Impressive.

Raspberry Champagne, Michigan $8.50. 88

Bright ruby-garnet cast with a slight fade. Medium-bodied. Full acidity. Highly extracted. Red fruits, minerals. Pleasantly aromatic, with gentle fruit overtones. Fully sparkling on the palate, with spritzy acidity balanced by a hint of sweetness. Flavorful and intense.

Ste. Chapelle (Idaho)

NV Brut, Idaho $7.99. 81
NV Johannisberg Riesling, Sparkling, Idaho $7.99. 84

Pale platinum cast. Moderately full-bodied. Full acidity. Highly extracted. Citrus peel, minerals. Pleasantly aromatic, with a firm and tart impression on the palate. Bright, angular, and citrusy through the finish.

1996 Chardonnay, Idaho $9.   86

Bright pale straw hue. Medium-bodied. Full acidity. Moderately extracted. Toasted oak, citrus. Austere minerally aromas lead a lean, angular palate punctuated by tart acidity. The mouthfeel has a rounded character, with a touch of smoky oak for complexity.

1996 Chardonnay, Canyon, Idaho $8.   84

Pale straw color. Moderately light-bodied. Balanced acidity. Moderately extracted. Tart apple, citrus. Faintly grassy, appley aromas lead straightforward, clean citrus flavors that linger on the finish.

1996 Fumé Blanc, Idaho $8.   84

Pale green-straw color Medium-bodied. Balanced acidity. Highly extracted. Grass, minerals, lemons. A very grassy, herbal nose reveals a flavorful palate that does not show primary fruit flavors. Finishes with authority.

1995 Cabernet Sauvignon, Washington $8.   89

Brick red. Medium-bodied. Moderately extracted. Moderately oaked. Moderately tannic. Candied red fruits, vanilla. Lean and taut, with elegant fruit flavors and drying tannins. A tougher style that is not built for cellaring, it will show best with food.

1995 Cabernet Sauvignon, Sagemoor's Dionysus Vineyard, Washington $12.99.   86

Deep brick red. Medium-bodied. Moderately extracted. Moderately tannic. Black tea, earth, coconut. Dry and austere, this features drying tannins through the finish, with much primary fruit sensation.

Ste. Genevieve (Texas)

NV Sauvignon Blanc, Texas $4.99.   86

Pale yellow-gold, brilliant clarity. Medium-bodied. Balanced acidity. Moderately extracted. Lemons, limes, minerals. Smoky, citrusy aromas lead a fresh, lively palate that has fine flavors on the midpalate and good grip through the finish.

NV White Zinfandel, American $4.99.   82
NV Pinot Noir, Texas $8.99/1.5 L.   83

Bright violet red. Medium-bodied. Moderately extracted. Mildly tannic. Sweet cherries, blueberries. Attractive candied fruit aromas lead a ripe, fruity mouthful with the softest of tannins on the finish. Easy drinking, attractive.

Stone Hill (Missouri)

1997 Seyval, Missouri $9.99.   82
1997 Seyval, Barrel Fermented, Missouri $11.99.   82
1994 Estate Bottled Port, Hermann $23.99.   83

Saturated black cherry color. Moderately full-bodied. Highly extracted. Mildly tannic. Reminiscent of black cherries, earth, minerals. Expressive fruity aromas. Rich black fruit entry gives way to a solid minerally finish.

1997 Late Harvest Vignoles, Missouri $19.99/375 ml.   85

Deep copper hue. Exotic apricot and nutty nuances. A sweet entry leads a medium-bodied palate, with generous flavors and lean acidity. The finish is clean. Stylish and well balanced. Drink now.

Valley Vineyards (Ohio)

1997 Seyval, Ohio River Valley $7.75.   86

Bright straw hue. Generous spice and vanilla aromas. A rich entry leads a rounded, buttery palate that has balanced acidity. Harmonious and showy. Drink now.

1997 Semi-Sweet Vidal Blanc, Ohio River Valley $7.75.   81

Scale: Superlative (96-100), Exceptional (90-95), Highly Recommended (85-89), Recommended (80-84), Not Recommended (Under 80)

1997 Vidal Blanc, Ice Wine, Ohio River Valley $22/375 ml.   **85**

Bright yellow-straw hue. Toasty, buttery, honeyed aromas. A lush entry leads a medium-bodied palate featuring lots of sweetness. Spicy, rounded finish. Supple. Drink now.

Westport Rivers (Massachusetts)

1994 Brut RJR Cuvée, Southeastern New England $24.95.   **82**

1994 Blanc de Noir, Southeastern New England $28.95.   **87**

Very pale copper cast. Full-bodied. Full acidity. Highly extracted. Cream, yeast, toast. Attractive yeasty aromas lead a rich, ripe, racy palate feel. Intense and flavorful through the finish, showing excellent grip and length.

1992 Blanc de Blanc, Southeastern New England $34.95.   **84**

Bright yellow-straw cast. Medium-bodied. Full acidity. Lime zest, minerals. Aromatically reserved, with firm, zesty flavors and a steely mouthfeel. The finish is angular and flavorful.

1995 Chardonnay, Silver Label, Southeastern New England $14.95.   **81**

1997 Chardonnay, Silver Label, Southeastern New England $15.95.   **86**

Bright yellow-straw hue. Crisp citrus aromas. A very bright attack leads a medium-bodied palate with vibrant acids and tart fruit flavors. The oak influence is very subtle. Taut, pure, clean style that would be good with seafood. Drink now.

Wollersheim (Wisconsin)

NV White Riesling, American $7.   **84**

Pale straw hue. Mild aromas of apples and minerals. A sweet fruit attack leads a moderately light-bodied palate. Mild flavors finish quickly, leaving a subtle herbal impression. Drink now.

NV Dry Riesling, American $8.   **84**

Very pale straw hue. Clean, bright aromas of white peach and herbs. A juicy entry leads a medium-bodied palate, with juicy acids lingering on the finish. Very refreshing. Drink now.

NV Seyval Blanc, Prairie Fumé, American $8.   **83**

Bright platinum-straw hue. Lean, minerally aromas. A crisp entry leads a medium-bodied palate, with tart acidity offsetting a hint of sweetness. Finishes on an aggressive phenolic note. Shows some clean intensity. Drink now.

NV Seyval Blanc, River Gold, American $6.50.   **80**

1998 White Marechal Foch, Prairie Blush, Wisconsin $7.50.   **90**

Pale cherry hue with a slight fade and a gentle spritz. Generous berry, herb, and toast aromas. A crisp entry leads a medium-bodied palate that has lots of flavor and lean, mouthwatering acidity. Snappy, tasty finish. Very refreshing. Drink now.

1997 Pinot Noir, Cuvée 961, American $12.   **84**

Pale cherry red. Moderately light-bodied. Subtly extracted. Mildly tannic. Crisp fruits, minerals. Subtle tart berry aromas follow through to a crisp yet flavorful palate, with hints of oak spice lingering.

seven

≈

The Wines
of Canada

≈

An Introduction: The Wines of Canada

Canada actually had a reasonably early start in North American winemaking. Sources claim Johann Schiller as being the father of the Canadian wine industry. Schiller was a German émigré who fought in the British army and took up winemaking on his discharge. Count Justin M. de Courtenay purchased his estate in 1864. De Courtenay, a man of letters, was certainly one of the earliest advocates of Canadian wines. He considered it feasible to produce Canadian wine the equal of, if not better than, those of Burgundy, and he told government ministers and officials of this view in his many letters. From his vineyards in Ontario he sent wine to be evaluated at a Paris exposition. The French tasters pronounced it to be similar to Beaujolais of that era, and commended it as worthy and *solide*, being of 13% alcohol in strength. Unfortunately this was not sufficient for the government to maintain his grant, so he ceased operation in 1878.

Subsequent to these early trials, indigenous "foxy" table grape varietals formed the backbone of grapes crushed for wine production in Canada until recently. Furthermore, World War I and 11 years of Prohibition have left a legacy of provincial control of alcoholic beverages that persists to this day. This Canadian wine of the past was frequently of dubious quality, often adulterated and fortified, and historically protected by steep tariffs.

Since the early '80s, Canadian winemaking has undergone a renaissance and small estate wineries are now creating a stir domestically and abroad. Canada, and particularly Ontario, has made international waves with its Icewines, and is producing serious table whites and reds from classic varieties and hybrids. In a short period of time Canada has developed a quality-minded commercial wine industry. The northerly location of Canada's wine-growing regions, the most important of which is the Niagara Peninsula, necessitates a preponderance of white varietals, which ripen more easily than reds.

As for popular whites, lean crisp Chardonnays are typical, though richer barrel fermented styles are also produced. Riesling is the most widely planted aromatic varietal and it renders a crisp lively style of wine. Gewürztraminer, Pinot Blanc, and sturdy hybrid varietals, are also widely planted.

Canada is not yet attracting international attention with its dry white wines in the manner that it is with its dessert wines. Because of its marginal climate, pioneering winemakers are still establishing its best vineyard locations. Very little dry white Canadian table wine is exported to the United States. Nonetheless, much palatable wine is produced, and it is well received on their domestic market. As things continue to improve and the industry continues to mature, certain sites and varietals will no doubt come to the fore, and Canadian whites will no doubt be seen with more regularity south of the border.

Dessert Styles

As for those dessert styles, Canada has slowly but surely been building a reputation as one of the world's most abundant and consistent producers of Icewine, a style of wine most closely associated with Germany. In Germany, Icewine is produced in miniscule quantities at astronomical prices; and even then, only in favorable years.

Scale: Superlative (96-100), Exceptional (90-95), Highly Recommended (85-89),
Recommended (80-84), Not Recommended (Under 80)

322

Most of Canada's Icewine is produced on the Niagara Peninsula, a cool growing region that can always count on a sustained cold spell in January to freeze Riesling or Vidal grapes on the vine. These grapes, when pressed in their frozen state, produce extraordinarily concentrated sweet wines with enough acidity to keep them fresh and uncloying. Given Canada's northerly latitude, other regions, particularly the Okanagan Valley in British Columbia, are also proving able to make outstanding Icewines. U.S. consumers have not yet been urged to seek these gems by the mainstream media; hence, these wines are not in widespread distribution. Devotees and enthusiasts will have to look to specialist wineshops in major markets.

Ontario and B.C.:
The Canadian Wine Country

Ontario provides 85% of Canadian wine, and is by far the most important province for wine production in Canada. All the growing regions are within hailing distance of a climate-moderating body of lake water. The three designated viticultural areas are Pelee Island, Lake Erie North Shore, and the Niagara Peninsula.

Ontario is a cool climate growing region with an abundance of microclimates whose potential is still being explored and realized. As with the Finger Lakes in New York State, there is still a valid place for hybrid varietals such as Vidal and Seyval. It is a tricky business to get noble varietals such as Chardonnay to ripen consistently in every vintage. Further, reliable ripening of the classic red varietals is by no means guaranteed. Consequently, white varietals account for the bulk of plantings. However, excellent Merlots, Pinot Noirs, and some Cabernets can be produced in years such as 1991 and 1995 when these varietals do fully ripen. The vagaries of vintage are not at all unlike some European regions.

The conventional wisdom seems to be that, stylistically, Ontario winemakers are not seeking to, and indeed cannot, emulate full-blown Californian wines. They do, however, have an eye on subtlety and elegance. The pace is being set by boutique wineries in these regions, in marked contrast to the former pre-

Canada
at a Glance

Wines Reviewed:

153

Producers/Brands
Represented:

29

eminence of the old, long-established volume wine producers. The present emphasis is on quality as the provincial liquor board no longer has the liberty to protect Canadian wines by excessively marking up imported wines—a consequence of GATT protestations by European trade ministers.

The Okanagan Valley

British Columbia has four designated viticultural regions, of which the most important is the Okanagan Valley. Planted vineyard acreage is approximately a seventh of that in Ontario.

The Okanagan Valley is 100 miles long from north to south and is situated inland in the central southern part of B.C., north of the increasingly famous Columbia Valley in Washington State. Like much of Washington, the climate is great for the production of red wines toward the southern part, where conditions are semi-arid and irrigation is required. These distinct climactic conditions exist for about 15 miles at the very southern point of the valley. Germanic white varieties predominate toward the northern part of the valley where the nearby presence of lake water moderates the climate.

Virtually all wine production is consumed within the province, but the potential indicated by the best Merlots and Pinot Noirs from the Okanagan Valley is very promising in these early days of Canada's revamped wine industry, and already seem to at least rival the best reds produced in Ontario.

Reviews

Calona

1996 Chardonnay, Artist Reserve Series, Okanagan Valley $8.50.　　　　**82**
1997 Chardonnay, Artist Series, Okanagan Valley $8.25.　　　　**86**
Brilliant yellow-straw cast. Generous pleasant spice and vanilla aromas belie hefty wood treatment. A supple attack leads to a medium-bodied palate with balanced acidity through a persistent oaky finish. A clean, flavorful, oaky style. Drink now.

1995 Chardonnay, Private Reserve, Okanagan Valley $12.　　　　**83**
Pale yellow-straw hue. Medium-bodied. Moderately extracted. Moderately oaked. Clean, simple apple and tart peach flavors have a nutty edge through the finish. Quite fresh, though not showing great concentration.

1996 Artist Reserve Series, Sovereign Opal, Okanagan Valley $6.25.　　　　**80**

1996 Pinot Blanc, Artist Reserve Series Burrowing Owl Vineyard, Okanagan Valley $7.10.　　　　**83**
Pale yellow. Medium-bodied. Moderately extracted. Sweet and tangy, with simple, light, floral fruit salad flavors. Quite juicy through the finish. Clean aperitif style.

1997 Pinot Blanc, Artist Series, Okanagan Valley $7.61.　　　　**83**
Pale yellow straw. Clean, buttery aromas with a note of ripe citrus fruits. A bright entry leads a medium-bodied palate with a broad texture and attractive citrus flavors through the finish. Well balanced. Drink now.

1997 Pinot Gris, Artist Series, Okanagan Valley $6.97.　　　　**83**
Very pale platinum-straw hue. Mild aromas show a hint of smoke and a note of citrus zest. Brightly acidic on the attack, leading a medium-bodied palate with clean flavors and minerally accent through the finish. Drink now.

Scale: Superlative (96-100), Exceptional (90-95), Highly Recommended (85-89),
Recommended (80-84), Not Recommended (Under 80)

1997 Fumé Blanc, Private Reserve, Okanagan Valley $9.50.   85

Pale brilliant straw hue. Subtle, clean bread dough and citrus aromas. Subtle wood treatment is apparent. A soft attack leads to a medium-bodied palate with balanced acidity. Smooth in character. Lingering flavorful finish. An ideal match for sole or delicate fish. Drink now.

1996 Semillon, Private Reserve, Burrowing Owl Vineyard, Okanagan Valley $10.70.   86

Medium straw color. Medium-bodied. Moderately extracted. Heavily oaked. Smoky vanilla aromas are very pronounced. The palate shows a heavy layer of toast and smoke, with supporting rounded citrus oil flavors. Quite exotic. Good with smoked foods, maybe.

1995 Optima, Private Reserve, Late Harvest, Botrytis Affected, Okanagan Valley $12.50/375 ml.   86

Brilliant yellow-gold. Medium-bodied. Moderately extracted. Nice floral, botrytized aromas lead a subtly sweet, almost grapey palate that concludes with a complex spicy finish.

1995 Ehrenfelser, Private Reserve, Late Harvest Botrytis Affected, Canada $21/375 ml.   90

Full orange-gold. Full-bodied. Low acidity. Pure honeyed apple aromas lead a thick, nectarous palate, with enormous concentration and sweetness making this a spectacular but cloying dessert in its own right.

Carriage House

1997 Chardonnay, Okanagan Valley $14.   84

Brilliant yellow-straw hue. Subdued cream and pear aromas. A firm attack leads to a medium-bodied palate with crisp acidity. Rich, rounded finish. Clean and refreshing, with a round character and no overt signs of oakiness. Drink now.

Cave Spring

1996 Chardonnay, Niagara Peninsula $9.95.   84

Pale straw cast. Moderately light-bodied. Moderately extracted. Moderately oaked. Aromas of pears and apples. Smooth, with a mildly glycerous mouthfeel and a buttery note. Some nutty nuances come through on the finish.

1997 Chardonnay, Niagara Peninsula $11.99.   81
1996 Dry Riesling, Niagara Peninsula $9.95.   80
1997 Riesling, Off Dry, Niagara Peninsula $7.99.   81
1997 Gamay, Niagara Peninsula $8.99.   84

Bright purple-red hue to the rim. Lean mineral and cranberry aromas. A sharp attack leads to a light-bodied palate with vibrant acidity. Clean, snappy finish. A refreshing quaffer. Drink now.

1997 Riesling, Indian Summer, Niagara Peninsula $16.99/375 ml.   88

Pale straw hue. Intense pineapple, ripe pear, and citrus aromas. A crisp attack leads to a medium-bodied palate with vibrant acidity and moderate sweetness. Finishes in a clean, citric manner. Refreshing. Drink now.

1997 Riesling, Icewine, Niagara Peninsula $48.99/375 ml.   95

Rich old gold hue. Generous butter, toffee, and tropical fruit aromas. A lush attack leads to a full-bodied palate with a lot of sweetness. Flavorful, lengthy, viscous finish. Opulent and intense. An impressively rich style of icewine. Drink now.

Cedar Creek

1995 Chardonnay, Okanagan Valley $13.95.   83

Pale silver-straw hue. Moderately light-bodied. Moderately extracted. Mildly oaked. Clean and fresh, with focused citrus flavors and a minerally backbone. Very straightforward and quaffable.

1995 Chardonnay, Reserve, Okanagan Valley $22.95.   **88**

Very pale silver-straw hue. Medium-bodied. Moderately extracted. Moderately oaked. Clean new oak aromas have a perfumed note. The palate is crisp, with focused citrus fruit flavors showing great definition. Vanilla oak flavors taper through the finish.

1995 Merlot, Reserve, Okanagan Valley $24.95.   **83**

Dark ruby red. Medium-bodied. Moderately extracted. Moderately oaked. Mildly tannic. Rich aromas of black fruits, earth, and toasted oak are followed by similar flavors on the palate. Very flavorsome, though not hugely structured. Rather short finish.

1995 Pinot Noir, Okanagan Valley $15.95.   **82**

1995 Riesling, Icewine, Okanagan Valley $49.95/375 ml.   **89**

Pale golden luster. Full-bodied. Hugely sweet and thick. Supersweet pear and apple flavors turn butterscotch-like on the finish. This is impressively sweet.

1995 Chardonnay, Reserve Icewine, Okanagan Valley $59.95/375 ml.   **90**

Pale golden luster. Full-bodied. Toasty, honeyed aromas. A smoky oak component adds complexity to the superrich apple and pear flavors that have a butter and caramel quality through the finish.

Colio

1995 Chardonnay, Lily Sparkling Wine, Ontario $8.   **83**

Pale yellow-straw cast. Medium-bodied. Moderately extracted. Mildly toasty nose with zesty notes leads a lemon zest palate with subtly toasty yeast flavors. Carbonation gives a frothy mouthfeel.

1996 Chardonnay, Lake Erie North Shore $8.   **81**

1996 Riesling-Traminer, Ontario $6.   **84**

Medium yellow-gold. Medium-bodied. Moderately extracted. Peach and grapefruit aromas follow through on a palate distinguished by a rounded mouthfeel with some weight.

1996 Vidal, Icewine, Ontario $20/375 ml.   **85**

Bright yellow. Medium-bodied. Aromas of sweet pears and apples follow through on a pure and concentrated palate with impressive levels of sweetness, though this is not a full-throttled style.

Gray Monk

1996 Gewürztraminer, Reserve, Okanagan Valley $10.95.   **87**

Very pale silver-straw cast. Medium-bodied. Moderately extracted. Perfumed faint lychee aromas are varietally suggestive. Lightly flavored palate, with simple floral accents and a clean finish. Delicate style with faithful aromatics.

1995 Pinot Auxerrois, Okanagan Valley $9.95.   **84**

Pale yellow-gold. Medium-bodied. Moderately extracted. Sweet peach blossom aromas lead a smooth, mildly glycerous mouthfeel, with stone fruit flavors lingering through the finish. Uncomplicated, clean, and easy drinking.

1995 Siegerrebe, Okanagan Valley $10.   **86**

Pale yellow-straw color. Medium-bodied. Moderately extracted. Attractively sweet lychee nut aromas play out on a smooth, rounded palate with a lingering sweet, spicy finish. Fruit cocktail. Highly quaffable.

1995 Pinot Blanc, Okanagan Valley $9.95.   **82**

1995 Pinot Gris, Okanagan Valley $10.95.   **80**

Harrow Estates

1996 Cabernet Franc, Lake Erie North Shore $7.   **81**

Hawthorne Mountain Vineyards

1996 Chardonnay, Okanagan Valley $9.95.   **81**

Scale: Superlative (96-100), Exceptional (90-95), Highly Recommended (85-89), Recommended (80-84), Not Recommended (Under 80)

326

1996 Muscat-Ottonel, Okanagan Valley $7.95.   **81**

1996 Riesling, Okanagan Valley $7.95.   **80**

Hester Creek

1996 Pinot Blanc, Okanagan Valley $7.80.   **82**

1996 Pinot Blanc, Grand Reserve, Okanagan Valley $9.25.   **86**

Very pale straw hue. Medium-bodied. Moderately extracted. Floral tangerine aromas lead a crisp and spritzy palate, with an impression of faintly sweet fruit that lingers through the finish. Light but fresh, excellent as an aperitif or a shellfish accompaniment.

1996 Pinot Blanc, Signature Release, Okanagan Valley $10.50.   **84**

Pale yellow-straw cast. Medium-bodied. Moderately extracted. Mildly oaked. Faintly toasty, smooth, malolactic mouthfeel has no rough edges. Nice crisp lemon flavors through the finish, with well-integrated oak notes.

1997 Cabernet Franc, Okanagan Valley $13.   **84**

Bright pale brick-red hue. Forward herb and wood aromas show a marked oak influence. A firm attack leads to a medium-bodied palate with lean, drying tannins. Finish is rather oaky and tannic. Interesting flavors but seems to be drying out. Drink within five years.

1997 Merlot, Okanagan Valley $15.   **82**

1997 Cabernet-Merlot, Okanagan Valley $14.   **84**

Deep garnet-red hue. Forward iron, red fruit, and spice aromas show a generous oak accent. A crisp attack leads to a medium-bodied palate with grippy tannins and zesty acidity through a clean flavorful finish. A lively, clean, fruit-forward style.

1996 Late Harvest Trebbiano, Grand Reserve,
Okanagan Valley $12.80/375 ml.   **88**

Brilliant golden luster. Moderately full-bodied. Moderately extracted. Rich tropical, spicy aromas have a honeyed quality. The palate shows juicy, sweet nectarine and peach flavors in abundance. Very well balanced, with no cloying character.

1997 Trebbiano, Reserve Late Harvest, Okanagan Valley $18/375 ml.   **83**

Bright old gold hue. Subdued pear and apple aromas. A crisp attack leads to a medium-bodied palate with mild sweetness and zesty acidity through a clean, fruity finish. Straightforward and racy. Drink now.

1996 Pinot Blanc, Grand Reserve Icewine,
Okanagan Valley $28.50/375 ml.   **89**

Brilliant yellow-gold. Medium-bodied. Full acidity. Sweet, crisp apple aromas lead a razor-sharp palate of green apple flavors with impressive sugar and acid levels. This might be better in a year or so when the acids have settled. Classic ice wine structure.

Hillebrand

1997 Trius Barrel Aged Icewine, Niagara Peninsula $50/375 ml.   **86**

Rich old gold hue. Intense citrus, butter, and tropical fruit aromas. A lush attack leads to a moderately full-bodied palate with marked sweetness and just enough acidity to prevent this from excessive cloying through a plush, sweet finish. A very sweet style. Drink now.

Inniskillin Okanagan

1995 Merlot-Cabernet Franc, Dark Horse Vineyard,
Okanagan Valley $13.95.   **85**

Bright ruby red. Moderately light-bodied. Moderately extracted. Mildly tannic. Black currant aromas lead crisp, high-toned cherry and licorice flavors that expand on the palate, with just a hint of tannin on the finish. Very easy drinking, with some classic flavors.

1995 Dark Horse Vineyard Meritage, Okanagan Valley $17.85.   **86**

Full ruby red. Medium-bodied. Moderately extracted. Moderately oaked. Oak and black cherry aromas are well expressed on the palate through to a lingering dry finish. Shows enough structure to allow this to work with richer foods.

Jackson-Triggs

1997 Gewürztraminer, Proprietors' Reserve, Okanagan Valley $6.89. **86**

Brilliant greenish straw hue. Generous lychee, pineapple, and spice aromas. A brisk attack leads to a moderately light-bodied palate with crisp acidity. Persistent flavorful finish. Well balanced and racy in a lighter style. Drink now.

1997 Pinot Blanc, Proprietors' Reserve, Okanagan Valley $6.90. **82**

1996 Dry Riesling, Proprietors' Reserve, Okanagan Valley $6.90. **86**

Luminous yellow-straw hue. Muted clean mineral and slate aromas. A firm attack leads to a medium-bodied palate with crisp acidity. Angular in character with a lingering flavorful finish. Showing the beginnings of a classic petrolly development. Drink now.

1997 Dry Riesling, Proprietors' Reserve, Okanagan Valley $6.90. **82**

1997 Proprietors' Reserve Blanc de Noir, Okanagan Valley $6.46. **86**

Brilliant raspberry-pink hue. Clean berry and mineral aromas. A crisp attack leads to a moderately light-bodied palate with zesty acidity. Sharp flavorful finish. A stylish dry Rosé. Drink now.

1996 Merlot, Proprietors' Reserve, Okanagan Valley $11.30. **86**

Brilliant ruby red hue to the rim. Generous red fruit and mineral aromas carry a spicy oak accent. A firm attack leads to a medium-bodied palate with grippy, lean tannins. Angular, flavorful finish. A focused, well-cut style. Drink now or later. Can improve with more age.

1996 Riesling, Proprietors' Grand Reserve Ice Wine,
Okanagan Valley $44.07/375 ml. **95**

Dark old gold hue. Powerful, complex honey, nut, and tropical fruit aromas. A ripe attack leads to a full-bodied palate with marked sweetness and angular acidity. Persistent, clean, complex finish. Well balanced and showing a range of flavors beyond the pineapple norm. Drink now or later. Can improve with more age.

1997 Riesling, Proprietors' Grand Reserve Ice Wine,
Okanagan Valley $44.07/375 ml. **94**

Dark yellow-golden hue. Intense pineapple and honey aromas. A lush entry leads to a full-bodied palate with powerful sweetness balanced by piercing acidity. Sweet, zesty finish. Viscous and very sweet yet tart. A classic Icewine structure. Drink now.

1997 Riesling, Proprietors' Reserve Ice Wine,
Okanagan Valley $31.50/375 ml. **89**

Dark golden-yellow hue. Pleasant tropical fruit and pineapple aromas. A viscous attack leads to a full-bodied palate with outrageous levels of sweetness. Thick, cloying finish. Hedonistic, but only for those with a real sweet tooth. Drink now.

Konzelmann

1996 Riesling, Niagara Peninsula $9.65. **82**

1995 Dry Riesling, Late Harvest, Niagara Peninsula $10.95. **85**

Bright yellow-gold. Medium-bodied. Full acidity. Highly extracted. Nice faintly petrol-accented nose shows good varietal character. The rich, rounded mouthfeel contrasts with the full, assertive tart citrus flavors that have a sense of depth.

1996 Vidal, Icewine, Niagara Peninsula $45.55/375 ml. **90**

Dark gold. Moderately full-bodied. Highly extracted. Heavy, rich, honeyed aromas lead a tropical fruit palate, with a juicy character on entry that turns a little syrupy through the finish. Impressive, though only for drinking in small quantities.

Lake Breeze

1996 Pinot Blanc, British Columbia $9. **82**

1996 Semillon, British Columbia $9.50. **81**

Scale: Superlative (96-100), Exceptional (90-95), Highly Recommended (85-89), Recommended (80-84), Not Recommended (Under 80)

328

Lang

1996 Gewürztraminer, Naramata $8.10. 86

Bright yellow-straw hue. Medium-bodied. Moderately extracted. Some weight and texture evident. If this is not varietally pure, it at least has some spicy character, with a juicy mouthfeel and nutty notes on the finish.

1995 Riesling, Icewine, British Columbia $33/375 ml. 89

Bright pale yellow. Medium-bodied. Moderately extracted. Honeyed pear and apple aromas lead a fresh, racy palate with plenty of sweet but pure flavors. Very clean on the finish. Acids are well matched to the sugar levels.

Magnotta

NV Moscato Superiore, $6. 83

Pale straw hue. Typical varietal aromas show a floral, fruity quality. A frothy, well carbonated entry leads a light-bodied palate with bright acids cutting through the residual sweetness. A crisp, quite dry style that remains fresh through the finish.

NV Rossana Blanc de Blancs, Canada $10. 85

Medium straw color. Medium-bodied. Highly extracted. Mildly oaked. Full smoky yeast and nutty, oaky aromas. Quite full-blown on the nose and palate, with some green apple fruit flavors in the background. Complex and interesting.

1997 Chardonnay, Barrel Fermented, Ontario $12. 86

Rich golden-yellow hue. Forward spice and vanilla aromas belie generous wood treatment. A firm attack leads to a moderately full-bodied palate and a lingering buttery finish. A rich but well-balanced style. An ideal match for lobster, crab, or any rich white fish. Drink now.

1997 Chardonnay, Chile International Series, Maipo Valley-Niagara $5. 81

1997 Chardonnay, Limited Edition, Ontario $9. 81

1995 Gewürztraminer, Limited Edition, Ontario $8.93. 88

Light yellow. Medium-bodied. Moderately extracted. Peach and apricot aromas lead a nutty, lychee-flavored palate that tapers to a lingering finish. Nice texture and mouthfeel give this extra appeal.

1996 Gewürztraminer, Limited Edition, Ontario $9. 83

Brilliant yellow-straw hue. Subtle clean mineral and citrus zest aromas. A crisp attack leads to a medium-bodied palate with firm acidity through a vibrant phenolic finish. Well structured but lacks somewhat for flavor intensity. Drink now.

1995 Gewürztraminer, Medium Dry, Ontario $6.39. 83

Medium straw color. Medium-bodied. Mildly sweet lychee and peach flavors give a fruit salad impression. Straightforward off-dry style.

1996 Gewürztraminer, Medium-Dry, Limited Edition, Ontario $9. 86

Brilliant green-gold hue. Clean and intense citrus zest and spice aromas. A soft attack leads to a moderately full-bodied palate with zesty acidity. Racy flavorful finish. Refreshing and varietally intense. Drink now.

1996 Pinot Gris, Special Reserve, Canada $7.10. 80

1997 Sauvignon Blanc, Chile International Series, Niagara-Maipo Valley $5. 81

1996 Sauvignon Blanc, Limited Edition, $9. 83

Deep, brilliant yellow-straw hue. Intense powerful dried herb and citrus aromas. A firm attack leads to a moderately full-bodied palate with crisp acidity. Quite lively through a clipped clean finish. Shows excellent varietal character but lacks a bit for intensity. Drink now.

1997 Cabernet Sauvignon, Chile International Series, Maipo Valley-Niagara $5. 81

1996 Cabernet Sauvignon, Limited Edition, Ontario $13. 82

1994 Cabernet Sauvignon, Special Reserve, Canada $7.10.   **83**

Dark cherry red. Medium-bodied. Moderately extracted. Mildly tannic. Good, varietally expressive black currant aromas lead a bright, dry, fruity palate with a minerally backbone that is highlighted by racy acids.

1997 Merlot, Chile International Series, Maipo Valley-Niagara $5.   **84**

Pale ruby-red hue with a fade to the rim. Unusual earth, herb, and mineral aromas. A firm attack leads to a moderately light-bodied palate with drying tannins through a clipped, crisp finish. Shows a particular (sulfur?) note to the nose that seems to blow off with aeration.

1991 Merlot, Limited Edition, Canada $12.50.   **87**

Cherry red with a subtly browning rim. Medium-bodied. Moderately extracted. Moderately oaked. Moderately tannic. Mature, developed aromas show great integration of oak and black fruits that are similarly expressed on the palate. The dry, lingering finish shows some earthy tannins and brown spice notes.

1995 Merlot, Limited Edition, Ontario $11.   **82**

1993 Merlot, Special Reserve, Canada $7.10.   **85**

Bright blood red. Medium-bodied. Moderately extracted. Mildly tannic. Crisp, bright acids carry flavors of cherries and red berry fruits through a minerally finish.

1994 Gran Riserva Red, Ontario $17.   **80**

1994 Gran Riserva Red, Canada $17.86.   **84**

Bright blood red. Medium-bodied. Moderately extracted. Moderately oaked. Moderately tannic. Plenty of concentrated crisp red cherry and berry fruit flavors dominate the palate, with a veneer of toasty oak that dries out the finish.

1991 Cabernet-Merlot, Limited Edition, Canada $11.07.   **82**

1995 Cabernet-Merlot, Limited Edition, Ontario $12.   **81**

1996 Millennium Red, Ontario $20.   **86**

Deep, opaque garnet-red hue. Powerful chocolate and spice aromas show a hefty oak influence. A supple attack leads to a moderately full-bodied palate with plush grippy tannins. Flavorful, well-structured finish. Stylish, weighty, and well balanced. Drink now or later. Can improve with more age.

1995 Syrah, Special Reserve, Canada $7.10.   **83**

Bright pale pinkish red. Moderately light-bodied. Moderately extracted. Mildly oaked. Crisp black and red fruit aromas lead a lively, fresh palate, with a juicy character and a hint of blackberries through a soft finish. Vanilla oak notes are well balanced. Easy-drinking style.

1994 Pinot Noir, Niagara Peninsula $7.10.   **85**

Cherry red center with a pale rim. Moderately light-bodied. Moderately extracted. A toasty, mature nose leads a very well-integrated palate with developed flavors of black cherries, earth, and leather. Quite supple and drinking well now.

1991 Pinot Noir, Limited Edition, Canada $11.79.   **87**

Medium brick-cherry red. Medium-bodied. Moderately extracted. Mildly tannic. Full, aromatic cherry and berry aromas lead a crisp, fruity palate showing good concentration of flavors, with great integration through a lingering finish.

1995 Pinot Noir, Limited Edition, Ontario $13.   **83**

Medium garnet-red hue with a slight fade. Restrained herb and red fruit aromas. A firm attack leads to a moderately light-bodied palate with lean tannins and crisp acidity through the sharp, clean finish. On the green side of the Pinot Noir spectrum, but refreshing. Drink now.

1995 Pinot Noir, Special Reserve, Canada $7.10.   **84**

Medium bright cherry red. Moderately light-bodied. Moderately extracted. Crisp, focused, juicy red cherry flavors on the palate taper to a fruity finish with soft, rounded tannins.

Scale: Superlative (96-100), Exceptional (90-95), Highly Recommended (85-89), Recommended (80-84), Not Recommended (Under 80)

330

Passito Del Santo, Ontario $11.95/500 ml.　　　　　　　　80

Framboise, Fortified Raspberry Dessert Wine, Ontario $11/500 ml.　　91

Opaque ruby-red hue to the rim. Powerful cassis and raspberry aromas. A lush attack leads to a full-bodied palate with moderate sweetness and a hint of tannin. Flavorful, grippy finish. Balanced to drink by itself. Excellent for fireplace contemplation. Drink now.

1997 Vidal, Late Harvest, Niagara Peninsula $9/375 ml.　　　　　83

Rich old gold hue. Subdued, unusual hay, honey, and smoke aromas. A crisp attack leads to a medium-bodied palate with zesty acidity and marked sweetness. Sharp, flavorful finish. Solid, but lacks somewhat for intensity. Drink now.

1994 Vidal, Select Late Harvest, Ontario $10.70/375 ml.　　　　86

Bright golden orange. Medium-bodied. Highly extracted. Faintly nutty, oxidized aromas lead sweet mandarin orange and apple flavors that are focused by crisp acids, keeping this fresh on the palate. Showing some maturity.

1997 Vidal, Icewine, Limited Edition, Niagara Peninsula $40/200ml.　89

Deep, brilliant copper-gold hue. Powerful honey, date, and citrus aromas. A racy attack leads to a moderately full-bodied palate with hefty sweetness offset by piercing acids. Persistent, flavorful, and sweet finish. Intense and well structured, this nectarous wine shows admirable balance. Excellent with fruit. Drink now or later. Can improve with more age.

1996 Vidal, Limited Edition Icewine, Niagara Peninsula $19.95/375 ml.　90

Dark golden luster. Full-bodied. Full acidity. Full pear and apple aromas lead a palate with impressive sweet fruit flavors and razor-sharp acidity to balance. This has a forceful presence on the palate. Well structured.

1996 Vidal, Sparkling Icewine, Ontario $50/375 ml.　　　　　91

Bright amber-gold hue with finely beaded, long lasting bubbles and a thin mousse. Powerful pineapple, honey, and citrus aromas. A zesty attack leads to a moderately full-bodied palate with marked sweetness shining through brisk carbonation. Flavorful, sweet, well-balanced finish. An exciting, well-crafted, and very tasty oddity. Excellent with chocolate. Drink now.

Mission Hill

1997 Chardonnay, Grand Reserve, Okanagan Valley $12.　　　　84

Luminous golden-yellow hue. Subtle, clean spice and citrus aromas. A crisp attack leads to a medium-bodied palate with racy acidity through a snappy, vibrant finish. A clean and racy Chard with the slightest hint of wood-derived flavors. Drink now.

1997 Chardonnay, Private Reserve, Bin 88, Okanagan Valley $6.　　83

Brilliant golden-yellow hue. Pleasant spice and vanilla aromas belie mild wood treatment. A firm attack leads to a full-bodied palate with aggressive acidity. Clean sharp finish. Well structured and youthful. Drink now or later. Can improve with more age.

1997 49 North White, Okanagan Valley $5.55.　　　　　　81

1997 49 North Red, Okanagan Valley $5.55.　　　　　　　82

1996 Pinot Noir, Grand Reserve, Okanagan Valley $11.　　　　82

1997 Pinot Noir, Private Reserve, Okanagan Valley $7.　　　　86

Bright garnet-red hue to the rim. Subdued berry and mineral aromas. A firm attack leads to a medium-bodied palate with lean, drying tannins. Clipped, clean finish. Rather ungenerous, but refreshing. Drink now.

Pelee Island Winery

1996 Gewürztraminer, Ontario $6.99.　　　　　　　　80

1995 Pinot Gris, Ontario $7.99.　　　　　　　　　　85

Pale gold. Medium-bodied. Moderately extracted. The rounded mouthfeel has nice texture. Crisp flavors of tart peach and lemon fill the palate. This has some depth and a lingering finish.

1996 Seyval Blanc, Ontario $5.99.   80

Peller Estates

1996 Chardonnay, Okanagan Valley $11.99.   84

Very pale straw hue. Moderately light-bodied. Moderately extracted. Mildly oaked. Smooth vanilla oak aromas lead a clean citrus palate, with faint orange blossom notes lingering on the finish. Some oak accents are a plus. Very quaffable.

1997 Chardonnay, Founder's Series, Niagara Peninsula $10.   88

Dark golden-yellow hue. Subtle vanilla, cream, and spice aromas belie mild wood treatment. A soft attack leads to a medium-bodied palate with gentle acidity. Rich harmonious finish. Elegant and well balanced. Drink now.

1996 Pinot Blanc, Okanagan Valley $11.99.   85

Pale yellow-gold. Medium-bodied. Moderately extracted. Peach and melon aromas follow through well on a crisp, well-defined palate. Tart tropical fruit on the lingering finish. Smooth mouthfeel is a plus.

1996 Late Harvest Vidal, Limited Edition Founder's Series,
Ontario $15/375 ml.   83

Brilliant golden-yellow hue. Powerful pineapple, honey, and citrus aromas. A soft attack leads to a medium-bodied palate with angular acidity and mild sweetness through a clean, vibrant finish. Tasty, but lacks real intensity. Drink now.

1997 Vidal, Icewine, Limited Edition Founder's Series,
Niagara Peninsula $45/375 ml.   91

Deep old gold hue. Intense honey, smoke, and tropical fruit aromas. A luxuriant attack leads to a moderately full-bodied palate with marked sweetness and just enough acidity for balance. Rich, opulent, rounded finish. Well made and exotic. Drink now.

Pillitteri

1997 Chardonnay, Niagara Peninsula VQA $7.77.   83

Deep old gold hue. Powerful butter and spice aromas belie generous wood treatment. A soft attack leads to a full-bodied palate with adequate acidity through a lingering buttery finish. Rather blowsy but tasty. Drink up.

1997 Merlot, Niagara Peninsula VQA $11.97.   83

Bright ruby-red hue to the rim. Forward dried herb and mineral aromas. A crisp attack leads to a medium-bodied palate with lean tannins through a crisp, angular finish. Rather ungenerous, but refreshing. Drink now.

1997 Vidal Icewine, Niagara Peninsula VQA $29.97/375 ml.   98

Rich copper-gold hue. Powerful date, honey, and tropical fruit aromas. A lush attack leads to a moderately full-bodied palate with marked sweetness and balanced acidity. Sweet, lengthy, flavorful finish. Plush, well balanced, and hedonistic. Drink now.

1996 Vidal, Icewine, Niagara Peninsula $38/375 ml.   86

Brilliant deep gold. Moderately full-bodied. Full, ripe aromas are reminiscent of overripe pears. Sweet and nectarous, with a thick mouthfeel that gives a honeyed quality. Impressive, though a tad cloying.

Quails' Gate

1994 Chardonnay, Family Reserve, Okanagan Valley $15.   86

Bright yellow-straw hue. Medium-bodied. Moderately extracted. Heavily oaked. Rich, complex nutty aromas. Plenty of oak and mature yeasty flavors dominate the palate, though this is not hugely fruity. Smoky and complex, it will appeal to some palates and not to others.

1995 Old Vines Foch, Okanagan Valley $14.   91

Opaque dark purple. Medium-bodied. Highly extracted. Heavily oaked. Exotic, toasty new oak aromas lead a concentrated palate of chocolatey black fruit, with very smoky oak flavors that dominate through the finish. Tannins are quite soft but textured.

Scale: Superlative (96-100), Exceptional (90-95), Highly Recommended (85-89), Recommended (80-84), Not Recommended (Under 80)

1995 Pinot Noir, Okanagan Valley $12. 80
1995 Pinot Noir, Family Reserve, Okanagan Valley $15. 85
Dark ruby red. Medium-bodied. Moderately extracted. Moderately oaked. Mildly tannic.
Rich toasty vanilla oak aromas lead a concentrated palate with red cherry flavors and
plenty of vanilla oak notes throughout.

Reif Estate
1996 Late Harvest Riesling, Niagara Peninsula $8.40. 85
Pale yellow-gold. Medium-bodied. Moderately extracted. Sweet, faintly petrol-like aromas
lead a mildly sweet peach and nectarine palate with a faint herbal backnote. Textured
mouthfeel gives a sense of depth.
1996 Vidal, Late Harvest, Ontario $7.50. 80
1995 Cabernet Sauvignon, Niagara Peninsula $12.80. 80
1996 Vidal, Select Late Harvest, Ontario $13.60/375 ml. 80
1996 Vidal, Icewine, Niagara Peninsula $35.60/375 ml. 91
Deep golden luster. Moderately full-bodied. Full acidity. Highly extracted. Strong
botrytis aromas lead a bright, high-toned palate of juicy sweet apple and apricot flavors.
A forceful balance between acids and sugars gives this a classic Icewine structure.
Distinguished by a long finish.

Southbrook Farms
NV Cassis, Canada $15/375 ml. 96
Deep purplish red. Moderately full-bodied. Big, pure sweet cassis aromas. The palate is
packed with pure black currant flavors, with natural levels of sweetness and acidity giving
this a mouthwatering finish. An outstanding example that has obvious dessert-matching
potential.
NV Framboise, Canada $15/375 ml. 93
Deep raspberry red. Moderately full-bodied. Rich, heavy berry fruit aromas. Sensuous
and silky, the sweet, fruity palate is just on the right side of cloying. Should provide
outstanding pairings with chocolate desserts.

St. Hubertus
1996 Gamay Noir, Okanagan Valley $8.50. 82
1996 Pinot Meunier, Oak Bay Vineyard, Okanagan Valley $10.95. 80

Stoney Ridge
1995 Chardonnay, Lenko Vineyard, Niagara Peninsula $13.95. 86
Pale yellow-straw cast. Medium-bodied. Moderately extracted. Moderately oaked. Lovely
nutty, toasty, yeasty aromas play out on a crisp, elegant palate, with a rounded, textured
mouthfeel and a lingering toasty yeast finish.
1996 Vidal, Puddicombe Vineyard, Select Late Harvest,
Niagara Peninsula $14.25/375 ml. 91
Brilliant yellow-gold. Moderately full-bodied. Full acidity. An intense style, with great
concentration of sweet, caramelized apple flavors that expand on the palate. Finishes
with a persistent toffeelike note. Verging on cloying, but hugely impressive as a sipping
dessert wine.
1996 Riesling-Traminer, Zimmerman Vineyard, Select Late Harvest,
Niagara Peninsula $14.25/375 ml. 88
Brilliant yellow-gold. Medium-bodied. Moderately extracted. Honeyed tropical fruit
aromas lead a silky smooth palate of sweet, juicy peach and apricot flavors. Very pure
and focused flavors through the finish. Glycerous, textured mouthfeel.
1995 Gewürztraminer, Icewine, Niagara Peninsula $35.95/375 ml. 90
Bright golden yellow. Moderately full-bodied. Highly extracted. Spicy aromas of nutmeg
and tropical fruits follow through on an exotically flavored palate, with a juicy sweet
character through the finish. Shows exotic complexity of flavors.

1996 Vidal, Icewine, Niagara Peninsula $28.95/375 ml.   88

Deep golden yellow. Full-bodied. Honeyed pear aromas lead a sweet and syrupy palate, with juicy fruit flavors on entry that turn thick through the finish. Nectarous, but only for drinking in small quantities.

1996 Riesling-Traminer, Icewine, Niagara Peninsula $35.95/375 ml.   90

Bright yellow-gold. Moderately full-bodied. Rich, sweet, honeyed aromas lead a succulently sweet palate of apple and apricot flavors through the finish. Aromatic varietal character is well defined and complemented by some spicy quality.

Strewn

1996 Chardonnay, Niagara Peninsula $9.95.   83

Very pale straw hue. Moderately light-bodied. Moderately extracted. Moderately oaked. A distinctive rich, yeasty nose comes through on the palate with a sense of weight. Quite substantial. Clean citrus flavors.

1996 Vidal, Icewine, Niagara Peninsula $45/375 ml.   90

Deep golden luster. Full-bodied. Rich honeyed aromas lead a viscous palate, with caramelized apple and peach flavors through the finish. Racy acids keep this from cloying. Classic Icewine structure.

Sumac Ridge

1993 Steller's Joy Brut, Okanagan Valley $12.95.   89

Pale straw cast. Medium-bodied. Moderately extracted. Rich Pinot Noir aromas lead a full, rounded mouthfeel with ripe flavors on a crisp palate. Has a similar flavor profile to a Pinot-rich Champagne. Soft bready notes add depth.

1996 Gewürztraminer, Private Reserve, Okanagan Valley $8.50.   83

Pale silver-straw hue. Medium-bodied. Moderately extracted. Tart and sweet citrus aromas, with a juicy, sweet lime zest palate. Long juicy finish. Shows some concentration and depth, though is not overburdened with varietal character.

1996 Pinot Blanc, Private Reserve, Okanagan Valley $9.95.   82

1995 Merlot, Okanagan Valley $11.95.   83

Dark ruby red. Medium-bodied. Moderately extracted. Mildly tannic. Decent rounded mouthfeel. Flavors of black fruits, licorice, oak spice, and earth that linger on the finish. Drinking well now.

1995 Pinot Noir, Private Reserve, Okanagan Valley $10.95.   80

1996 Pinot Blanc, Icewine, Okanagan Valley $19.95/375 ml.   94

Pale gold. Full-bodied. Full acidity. Superrich apple and tropical pineapple flavors are well focused through the finish by some piercing acids that give razor-sharp definition. This has the structure to develop further in the cellar.

Sunnybrook Farm

1997 Golden Peach Wine, Niagara $5.25.   81

1996 Spiced Apple Wine, Niagara $5.85.   80

Tinhorn Creek

1995 Merlot, Okanagan Valley $15.95.   80

1996 Pinot Noir, Okanagan Valley $13.95.   86

Bright cherry red with purple highlights. Moderately light-bodied. Moderately extracted. Moderately oaked. Mildly tannic. Racy, crisp cherry and blackberry flavors show good concentration, with bright acids highlighting the finish. Has a veneer of toasty oak.

1996 Kerner, Icewine, Okanagan Valley $39.50/375 ml.   89

Pale gold hue. Medium-bodied. Full acidity. Tinned fruit salad and honeyed apple flavors expand on the palate. Almost cloying on the finish, though juicy on the entry.

Scale: Superlative (96-100), Exceptional (90-95), Highly Recommended (85-89), Recommended (80-84), Not Recommended (Under 80)

Best Canadian Producers

Canadian Red Wines

Premier Canadian Red Producers (***)
- Inniskillin Okanagan (Meritage)
- Jackson-Triggs (Merlot)
- Stoney Ridge
  (Cabernet Sauvignon, Merlot)
- Tinhorn Creek (Pinot Noir, Merlot)

Great Canadian Red Producers (**)
- Cedar Creek
  (Pinot Noir, Reserve Merlot)
- Lang Vineyards (Foch)
- Magnotta (Limited Edition Series)
- Sumac Ridge (Merlot)

Dependable Canadian Red Producers (Recommended)
Some producers placed in this third tier are new (or new to us) and may merit a higher placement in subsequent vintages. These producers are offset by an asterisk.
- Harrow Estates (Cabernet Franc)
- *Hawthorne Mountain (Merlot)
- *Hester Creek
  (Merlot, Cabernet Sauvignon)
- Mission Hill (Pinot Noir)
- *Pillitteri (Merlot)
- *Quails Gate (Foch, Pinot Noir)
- *Reif (Merlot)
- *St. Hubertus
- *Vineland (Pinot Noir)

Canadian White Wines

Premier Canadian White Producers (***)
- Stoney Ridge (Chardonnay)

Great Canadian White Producers (**)
- Calona (Chardonnay, Semillon)
- Cedar Creek (Chardonnay)
- Colio
- Jackson-Triggs
  (Gewürztraminer, Riesling)
- Konzelmann (Riesling)
- Mission Hill (Riesling)
- Peller Estates (Chardonnay)

Dependable Canadian White Producers (Recommended)

Some producers placed in this third tier are new (or new to us) and may merit a higher placement in subsequent vintages. These producers are offset by an asterisk.
- *Carriage House (Chardonnay)
- *Gray Monk (Gewürztraminer)
- *Lake Breeze (Semillon, Pinot Blanc)
- Magnotta (Limited Edition)
- Mission Hill (Chardonnay)
- Quails' Gate (Chardonnay)
- *Strewn (Chardonnay)
- Sumac Ridge (Gewürztraminer)

Canadian Dessert Wines

Premier Canadian Dessert Wine Producers (***)
- Calona (Late Harvest & Icewines)
- Jackson-Triggs (Grand Reserve Icewine)
- Magnotta (Limited Edition Icewine &
  Sparkling Icewine)
- Stoney Ridge
  (Select Late Harvest & Icewines)

Great Canadian Dessert Wine Producers (**)
- Cedar Creek (Icewine)
- Colio (Icewine)
- Hester Creek (Icewine)
- Hillebrand (Icewine)
- Jackson-Triggs
  (Proprietor's Reserve Icewine)
- Lang (Late Harvest & Icewines)
- Peller Estates (Icewine)
- Pillitteri (Icewine)
- Strewn Winery (Icewine)
- Sumac Ridge (Icewine)
- Tinhorn Creek (Icewine)

Dependable Canadian Dessert Wine Producers (Recommended)

Some producers placed in this third tier are new (or new to us) and may merit a higher placement in subsequent vintages. These producers are offset by an asterisk.
- *Cave Spring (Icewine)
- *Inniskillin (Icewine)
- *Kittling Ridge (Icewine)
- *Konzelmann (Icewine)
- *London Winery
  (Late Harvest & Icewines)
- *Mission Hill (Late Harvest & Icewines)
- *Reif Estate (Icewine)
- *Stonechurch (Icewine)
- *Strewn Winery (Icewine)
- *Vineland (Icewine)

Section Two:
North America's
Most Popular
Varietals

eight

❧

The Importance
of the
Appellation
to the Consumer

❧

U.S. Wines: Why Is the Appellation (AVA) Important to the Consumer?

What does it mean to rate and review wines? A funny question one might think for people who engage in the effort on a daily basis, but an important one nonetheless. The point of such an exercise should be to provide the consumer with a frame of reference so that you can make informed buying decisions. On the face of it, this sounds simple enough, but the reality of the situation is a bit trickier.

On a monthly basis BTI produces the industry's largest and most comprehensive reviews of U.S. wines on a varietal by varietal basis. Five hundred Chardonnays, 500 Cabernets, 250 Merlots, and the list goes on. Confronted with page after page of names and numbers, the average consumer sets out to buy a bottle of Chardonnay. How is the decision made? I'll have an 89? Give me an 84? Hopefully some information can be gleaned from the tasting notes so that if one style of Chardonnay is preferred over another you will be steered in the right direction, but let's face it; the sheer number of choices has become bewildering.

Additionally, there just isn't that much truly bad wine being produced anymore. The rapid spread of modern winemaking technologies and their ready availability means that even at the least expensive end of the scale, very few wines will be deeply flawed or unpalatable. So then, gone are the early days of wine criticism, when I told you that wine A was bad, wine B was good, and therefore I recommend wine B. The reality is that in today's market the world is full of wine Bs.

We thus have to do more than provide a big list of ratings. We must describe what the wines in question are like in a way that will make sense to you. In order to do that they have to make sense to us first. This is why large categories such as Chardonnay require further subdivisions so that the information becomes more manageable and effective at the same time.

In U.S. categories, where we review over 200 wines of a specific varietal for a report, we taste the wines according to their geographic areas of origin and list them as such. We have been researching U.S. appellations in this manner since 1996 and believe that it is high time American wines were looked at through this rather European perspective. A number of factors have brought us to this conclusion.

It was only a short 20 years ago that the California wine industry was still coping with the devastating after-effects of Prohibition, trying to convince the world that it was an area capable of producing world-class wines. This was often done by holding comparative tastings between the best California wines and benchmarks from Bordeaux or Burgundy. So it was in the '80s as younger industries in Oregon, Washington, and even the East Coast struggled for public recognition by looking to have their wines compared with what had become California benchmarks. We think that at this point few will argue that wine-producing regions in such states as Oregon, Washington, New York, and Virginia are capable of producing world-class wines and sometimes do.

Whether we prefer this Willamette Valley Pinot Noir to that Carneros Pinot Noir might even be irrelevant, because these regions produce two very different versions of the varietal. There are differences between producers within these regions to be sure, but it is a fact that in general terms wines from the two areas just taste differently. If I prefer the style of wine produced in the Willamette and you prefer the style produced in Carneros, my preference becomes largely irrelevant for you. That's where the descriptive part comes in. We prefer to compare apples to apples, oranges to oranges, and then try to tell you what oranges and apples are like.

We attempt to give you more information, so that you can make your own decisions. This is done by highlighting key regions for specific varietals, making generalizations when we can, telling you when we can't, and trying to explain what makes the given area special. It is a long process, and one that has taken several hundred years in Burgundy or Bordeaux for instance, but what we should all be left with down the road is a better appreciation for the art of American viticulture. We will celebrate the differences, for it is these differences that make the world of wine interesting to begin with.

In order to facilitate this, we look at U.S. varietals as a whole according to their AVAs or American Viticultural Areas. The AVA system was adopted by the United States in the early '80s, in hopes of giving the consumer added information along the lines of the French AOC or Italian DOCG systems. Unlike these examples, however, an AVA comes without dictates about which varietals can be planted, yields, or even quality. Every bottle of American wine wears an AVA that tells the consumer where the grapes from which the wine was made came from.

If grapes were blended from various parts of California, the AVA would be California, and the bottle would reflect that. A blend of Napa and Sonoma grapes would be labeled North Coast. A blend of Sonoma AVAs, such as Dry Creek and Russian River Valley, would be labeled Sonoma County, while a wine coming solely from the Russian River will be labeled as such. Certainly the differences between larger or better-established appellations will be that much greater, but we also address the differences, for instance, between subregions within the Napa Valley, and what they might mean to you.

In the following chapters on North American wine styles the most popular varietals—Cabernet Sauvignon, Merlot, Pinot Noir, Zinfandel, and Chardonnay—contain extensive introductions and AVA information. These sections indicate those areas that particularly stand out for the given varietal, followed by a listing of highly recommended wines from that region, which are contained in this book. This means that instead of just looking for that 89-point Chardonnay with the tasting note that sounded intriguing, you might look for an Anderson Valley wine because you like Chardonnay that has firm acidity and makes an excellent aperitif, or maybe the area just sounds interesting. Either way it will be a more informed decision, and hopefully it will increase the chances that you will get what you are looking for.

nine

North American Cabernet Sauvignon and Red Meritage

An Introcuction: American Cabernet Sauvignon and Red Bordeaux Varietal Blends

In many respects the cradle of the resurgence of the American wine industry in the late 20th century was the Napa Valley. The decades of the '60s and '70s saw the rise of the boutique producers in the valley, and a worldwide reputation was rapidly achieved. The varietal with which that reputation was achieved was Cabernet Sauvignon. For years the measuring stick for world-class wine lay in the vineyards of Bordeaux, and as such it was with nothing short of shock that the wine world received the news that a California Cabernet had bested some of these Bordeaux benchmarks in Steven Spurrier's famous 1976 tasting. The revolution was launched, and in turn Napa served as a beacon for other emerging American wine regions. For many the concept of success in producing a great wine was synonymous with producing great Cabernet Sauvignon, and Napa itself had become a benchmark in this country.

Today the wine industries outside the North Coast, not only outside California but in other areas of the state as well, are maturing. They are discovering that producing world-class Cabernet no longer means trying to imitate Napa's wines, and instead they are learning how to deal with their own unique viticultural circumstances. To be sure, regional distinctions are emerging, and other areas are developing their own distinct reputations. Nonetheless, Napa still has much to offer in the way of trends.

Cabernet's Second Coming

Napa Cabernets have lightened up in recent years. After a period in the '70s and early '80s where many vintners thought the bigger the better, today's wine-makers have learned that wines don't need to be inaccessible in youth in order to age. Indeed, wines that are out of balance in youth don't magically come into balance with age. This realization has put Napa's vintners in the forefront with gentler winemaking techniques that emphasize the extraction of softer fruit tannins as opposed to harsh tannins. This has proven to be a real revolution. While critics were enamored of Napa's 1985 vintage, for instance, the tannic structure of many of those wines remains imposing to this day. Many of the wines were out of balance and it was assumed that the tannins would moderate with age. While it is true that the tannins have receded so have the other components in the wines. They are still by and large out of balance, as in many instances thick impressive tannic wines have merely turned into leaner, meaner tannic wines.

This decade has, so far, produced a string of great Cabernet vintages. The use of physiological ripeness and balance as guidelines, as opposed to high sugar levels alone, has made for a radical departure in style. Today's Napa Cabernets are still full-bodied, yet far better balanced than in years past. They are accessible in youth, yet show every indication of aging well. Time will tell, but in the meantime, regions such as the Santa Cruz Mountains and Washington State have followed Napa's lead and are applying these new vinification methods with zeal. The resultant wines are better than ever before, with only one caveat, price. While the quality is in the bottle, prices have jumped at amazing rates, and the best wines have become scarcer than ever. For the Cabernet collector, this

Scale: Superlative (96-100), Exceptional (90-95), Highly Recommended (85-89), Recommended (80-84), Not Recommended (Under 80)

may be good news, but for the Cabernet consumer, much of the category has unfortunately been taken off the everyday table.

Best U.S. Cabernet Producers

Premier U.S. Cabernet and Red Meritage Producers (***)

- S. Anderson (Richard Chambers Vineyard)
- Arrowood (Reserve Speciale)
- Beaulieu (Georges de la Tour)
- Beringer (Private Reserve and Single Vineyard Bottlings available only at the winery)
- Bernardus (Marinus)
- Cakebread (Reserve, Benchland, and Three Sisters)
- Cardinale
- Caymus (Napa Valley and Special Selection)
- Chimney Rock (Napa Valley, Reserve, and Elevage)
- Clos du Val (Reserve)
- Clos Pegase (Hommage)
- BR Cohn (Olive Hill)
- Cosentino (M. Coz Meritage)
- DeLille (Chaleur Estate)
- DeLoach (OFS)
- Diamond Creek (Volcanic Hill, Gravelly Meadow, Red Rock Terrace, and Lake)
- Dominus
- Dry Creek Vineyard (Reserve)
- Far Niente
- Ferrari Carano (Tresor)
- Fisher (Wedding and Lamb Vineyards)
- Flora Springs (Trilogy, Cypress Ranch, and Rutherford Reserve)
- Gallo Sonoma (Northern Sonoma Estate)
- Girard (Napa Valley and Reserve)
- Grace Family
- Grgich Hills (Napa Valley and Yountville Selection)
- Heitz (Martha's Vineyard)
- Hess Collection
- W. Hogue (The Terraces)
- Jarvis (Napa Valley, Reserve, and Lake William)
- Kathryn Kennedy (Santa Cruz Mountains)
- La Jota
- Laurel Glen
- L'Ecole No. 41 (Columbia Valley)
- Le Ducq (Meritage)
- Leonetti
- Merryvale (Profile and Reserve)
- Robert Mondavi (Reserve)

Cabernet at a Glance

Wines Reviewed:

941

Producers/Brands Represented:

397

Median Price:

$24

- Chateau Montelena (The Montelena Estate)
- Mount Veeder Winery (Napa Valley and Reserve)
- Niebaum-Coppola (Rubicon)
- Opus One
- Pahlmeyer
- Peju Province (Napa Valley and HB Estate)
- Joseph Phelps (Napa Valley, Backus, and Insignia)
- Pine Ridge (Stags Leap District, Howell Mountain, and Andrus)
- Plam
- Pride Mountain
- Quilceda Creek
- Ridge (Santa Cruz Mountains and Monte Bello)
- St. Clement (Howell Mountain and Orropas)
- St. Francis (Reserve)
- Chateau St. Jean (Reserve)
- Chateau Ste. Michelle (Horse Heaven, Cold Creek, and Artist Series Meritage)
- Shafer (Hillside Select and Stags Leap District)
- Signorello (Napa Valley and Founder's Reserve)
- Silverado (Limited Reserve)
- Silver Oak (Napa Valley and Alexander Valley)
- Spottswoode
- Stag's Leap Wine Cellars (Cask 23, Fay, and SLV)
- Stonestreet (Legacy)
- Waterbrook
- Whitehall Lane (Reserve)
- Andrew Will (Washington, Sorella, and Reserve)
- Woodward Canyon (Artist Series and Old Vines)

Great U.S. Cabernet and Red Meritage Producers (**)
- Adelaida (San Luis Obispo)
- Altamura
- S. Anderson (Stags Leap District)
- Anderson's Conn Valley Vineyards
- Apex
- Arrowood (Sonoma County)
- Barnard Griffin
- Barnett
- Benziger (Tribute, Reserve, and Sonoma County)
- Beringer (Knights Valley and Alluvium)
- Byington (Smith Reichel and Bates Ranch)
- Cain (Cain Five)
- Cakebread (Napa Valley)
- Canoe Ridge Vineyard
- Chapellet
- Cinnabar
- Clos du Val
- Clos LaChance
- Clos Pegase (Napa Valley)
- Columbia Winery (Red Willow and Otis)
- Conn Creek (Anthology)
- Cooper-Garrod (Proprietor's Reserve and Santa Cruz Mountains)
- Corison
- Cosentino (Reserve and The Poet Meritage)
- Robert Craig (Affinity)
- Cuvaison (Napa Valley)
- Dalla Valle
- Dehlinger
- DeLille (D2)
- deLorimier (Mosaic)
- Dry Creek Vineyard (Sonoma County and Meritage)
- Dunn
- Gary Farrell
- Ferrari Carano (Sonoma County)
- Fisher (Coach Insignia)
- Thomas Fogarty
- Forman
- Franciscan (Oakville Estate and Magnificat)
- Freemark Abbey (Bosché and Sycamore)
- Gallo Sonoma (Stefani, Barelli Creek, and Frei Ranch)
- Geyser Peak (Reserve, Reserve Alexandre)
- Groth
- Harrison
- Hartwell
- Hedges (Red Mountain Reserve and Three Vineyards)
- Heitz (Trailside Vineyard)
- Hendry
- Herzog (Special Reserve)
- Robert Keenan
- Kendall-Jackson (Grand Reserve and Buckeye Vineyard)
- Kenwood (Artist Series and

Jack London)
- Kathryn Kennedy (Lateral)
- Kiona (Reserve)
- Kunde
- Lambert Bridge
- Langtry
- Lewis
- Liparita
- Louis M. Martini
  (Monte Rosso and Reserve)
- Merryvale (Napa Valley)
- Peter Michael (Les Pavots)
- Robert Mondavi (Napa Valley and SLD)
- Mount Eden (Santa Cruz Mountains and Old Vine Reserve)
- Oakville Ranch (Napa Valley and Roberts Blend)
- Paradigm
- Pine Ridge (Rutherford)
- Portteus
- Chateau Potelle (VGS and Napa Valley)
- Ravenswood (Pickberry and Rancho Salina)
- Martin Ray (Diamond Mountain, Santa Cruz Mountains, and Saratoga Cuvee)
- Richardson (Synergy and Horne Vineyard)
- St. Clement (Napa Valley)
- St. Francis (Sonoma County)
- Chateau St. Jean (Cinq Cepages)
- Chateau Ste. Michelle (Columbia Valley)
- Seavey
- Sierra Vista (Five Star Reserve)
- Silverado (Napa Valley)
- Simi (Reserve)
- Soquel (Partner's Reserve)
- Staglin
- Stag's Leap Wine Cellars (Napa Valley)
- Stonestreet (Alexander Valley)
- Swanson
- Titus
- Truchard
- Tulocay
- Viader
- Villa Mt. Eden (Signature Series)
- Von Strasser
- Whitehall Lane (Napa Valley)
- ZD

Dependable U.S. Cabernet and Red Meritage Producers (Recommended)

Some producers placed in this third tier are new (or new to us) and may merit a higher placement in subsequent vintages. These producers are offset by an asterisk.

- *Adelaida (Calitage)
- Atlas Peak
- Belvedere
- WB Bridgman
- Burgess
- *Cafaro
- Carmenet
- Cedar Mountain
- Cloninger
- Columbia Crest
- Columbia Winery (Sagemoor and Reserve)
- *Cornerstone
- *Douglass Hill
- *Dunham
- Estancia
- Fetzer
- Gordon Brothers
- Guenoc
- Hanna
- *Havens
- Helena View
- Hogue
- Jordan
- *Judd's Hill
- Kendall-Jackson (Vintners Reserve)
- *Kestrel
- *L'Ecole No. 41 (Seven Hills, Apogee, and Windrow)
- *Livingston
- *Lokoya (Diamond Mountain, Mount Veeder, and Rutherford)
- Markham
- *Matthews (Elerding Vineyard)
- *Neyers
- Pindar
- Powers
- Quail Ridge
- *Quintessa
- *Rancho Sisquoc
- Raymond
- *Rocking Horse
- Rosenblum
- St. Supery
- V. Sattui
- Sequoia Grove

- *Seven Hills
- Seth Ryan
- Simi (Napa Valley)
- Smith & Hook
- Sonoma Creek
- Chateau Souverain
- *Spring Mountain Vineyard
- Stags' Leap Winery
- Staton Hills
- Tefft
- Turnbull
- Villa Mt. Eden (Grand Reserve)
- Windsor
- *Woodside
- Yakima River

Ten Key Regions for American Cabernet Sauvignon and Red Bordeaux Varietal Blends

Napa Valley
Wines Reviewed: **323**
Median Price: **$30.00**

Napa is the nation's "grand cru" appellation, and Napa vintners have been nothing if not successful in marketing the valley as America's wine Eden. Geographically, the Napa Valley is reasonably contiguous, being 34 miles in length and between one and four miles in width from the town of Napa in the south to that of Calistoga in the north. It is an easy region in which to ripen grapes and consistently produces ripe full wines. The cool air from the San Pablo Bay, just north of San Francisco, moves from south to north, thus giving the southern area cooler average temperatures.

An imprecise but useful generalization would be that the cooler southern end is more favorable to white varieties and Pinot Noir while the further north one gets, the more red varietals one will encounter as the temperatures increase, with emphasis on Cabernet. This simplification does not account for the vagaries of soil types, microclimates, and vintners throughout the valley, and as such there are many exceptions to the rule. Nine sub-appellations have been created since the inception of the Napa Valley AVA in 1983 and these go some way toward addressing the differences in climate between some parts of the valley. With the hugely significant exception of Carneros, these sub-appellations are of more relevance to Cabernet than Napa's other darling, Chardonnay.

The coolest area just to the north of Carneros includes Yountville and the Oak Knoll District where a few Cabernets are to be found. Indeed, much of this region is cool enough to produce sparkling wines. Nonetheless, some well-known vintners are here; not the least of which is Dominus. A Yountville style would be hard to pin down as there are relatively few Cabernets and the differences have more to do with winemaking, but a safe generalization would be that the wines are not nearly as thick as those produced up the valley, and that

Scale: Superlative (96-100), Exceptional (90-95), Highly Recommended (85-89), Recommended (80-84), Not Recommended (Under 80)

they show a sense of elegance. Still at this cooler end of the valley, yet just to the east of Yountville, lies an extremely prominent appellation for fine Cabernet, the Stags Leap District.

Wine lovers have known for some time that Stags Leap is a special area, as evidenced since the early '70s by the wines of Warren Winiarski at Stag's Leap Wine Cellars. It is cooler than areas to the north, as the ocean winds that move up from the San Pablo Bay act as an air conditioner and moderate the heat of the afternoon that builds up on the bare rocks of the eastern mountains, which allow for the greater ripening potential than Yountville to the west. Those rocks also feature in the very different soil composition of the area. Over 95% of the soil is derived from volcanic rocks, which makes for a gravelly, well-drained, and less fertile environment than that featured in the Rutherford Bench. These factors combine to draw out the ripening process, affording a longer growing season and the possibility of greater physiological maturity than other regions of the valley floor. This translates into a particularly flavorful and supple style of Cabernet, often marked by red berry overtones.

North of Yountville and Stags Leap is the "American Medoc" for Cabernet, the triumvirate of Oakville, Rutherford, and St. Helena, from coolest to warmest, respectively. The names and wines read like a who's who of the wine industry, and this narrow belt of this narrow valley has become world famous. In this area, all factors have come together to make an ideal growing climate for red Bordeaux varietals, with Cabernet Sauvignon at the fore. Furthest to the cooler southern end of the belt, Oakville produces Cabernets of great ripeness and richness with a certain restrained elegance. It is also quite common to see a distinctive minty quality intermixed with the red and black fruit flavors. Rutherford, just to the north, shows Cabernet of marginally greater weight, with considerable depth and remarkably consistent black fruit flavors, while St. Helena Cabernet adds just another layer of weight.

Finally, at the top of the valley and often a good 20 or even 30 degrees warmer than the extreme southern end lies Calistoga. As one might expect, Calistoga Cabernet is big, rich, and ripe, with huge levels of extract. Nonetheless, the wines usually avoid the jammy, porty notes that can sometimes interject themselves into such warm climate wines. Indeed, one of the most difficult factors facing the Calistoga winemaker is managing the abundance of tannins that come naturally to these wines. As such, advances in the management of tannins that have been made in the last decade have helped Calistoga's wines to a great degree.

Highly Recommended Napa Valley Cabernet Sauvignon and Red Meritage

Napa Valley (General)

98 • Jarvis (CA) 1994 Cabernet Sauvignon, Napa Valley. $58.

97 • Jarvis (CA) 1993 Reserve, Cabernet Sauvignon, Napa Valley. $75.

97 • Beringer (CA) 1994 Private Reserve, Cabernet Sauvignon, Napa Valley. $75.

96 • Merryvale (CA) 1994 Profile, Napa Valley. $55.

94 • The Terraces (CA) 1994 Cabernet Sauvignon, Napa Valley. $49.99.

94 • Pahlmeyer (CA) 1995 Red, Napa Valley. $60.

94 • Jarvis (CA) 1996 Lake William, Napa Valley. $48.

94 • Cosentino (CA) 1995 M. Coz Meritage, Napa Valley. $75.

94 • Cakebread (CA) 1995 Benchland Select, Cabernet Sauvignon, Napa Valley. $75.

93 • Silverado (CA) 1994 Limited Reserve, Cabernet Sauvignon, Napa Valley. $50.

93 • Signorello (CA) 1995 Founder's Reserve, Cabernet Sauvignon, Napa Valley. $55.

93 • Signorello (CA) 1994 Founder's Reserve, Cabernet Sauvignon, Napa Valley. $55.

93 • Robert Mondavi (CA) 1995 Reserve, Cabernet Sauvignon, Napa Valley. $75.

93 • Le Ducq (CA) 1994 Meritage, Napa Valley. $99.

93 • Jarvis (CA) 1993 Cabernet Sauvignon, Napa Valley. $55.

93 • Hendry (CA) 1993 Block 8, Cabernet Sauvignon, Napa Valley. $22.

93 • Grgich Hills (CA) 1995 Cabernet Sauvignon, Napa Valley. $45.

93 • Cakebread (CA) 1995 Three Sisters, Cabernet Sauvignon, Napa Valley. $75.

92 • Signorello (CA) 1996 Founder's Reserve, Cabernet Sauvignon, Napa Valley. $75.

92 • Signorello (CA) 1995 Cabernet Sauvignon, Napa Valley. $30.

92 • Quail Ridge (CA) 1993 Volker Eisele Vineyard Reserve, Cabernet Sauvignon, Napa Valley. $39.99.

92 • Philippe-Lorraine (CA) 1996 Cabernet Sauvignon, Napa Valley. $18.50.

92 • Le Ducq (CA) 1993 Meritage, Napa Valley. $91.

92 • Jarvis (CA) 1993 Lake William, Napa Valley. $45.

92 • Conn Creek (CA) 1995 Anthology, Napa Valley. $44.

91 • Silverado (CA) 1994 Cabernet Sauvignon, Napa Valley. $22.50.

91 • Signorello (CA) 1996 Cabernet Sauvignon, Napa Valley. $35.

91 • Robert Mondavi (CA) 1995 Cabernet Sauvignon, Napa Valley. $21.

91 • Merryvale (CA) 1995 Reserve, Cabernet Sauvignon, Napa Valley. $30.

91 • Merryvale (CA) 1995 Profile, Napa Valley. $66.

91 • Joseph Phelps (CA) 1996 Cabernet Sauvignon, Napa Valley. $30.

91 • Grgich Hills (CA) 1994 Cabernet Sauvignon, Napa Valley. $30.

91 • Fisher (CA) 1995 Coach Insignia, Cabernet Sauvignon, Napa Valley. $25.

91 • Cakebread (CA) 1994 Reserve, Cabernet Sauvignon, Napa Valley. $50.

91 • Altamura (CA) 1995 Cabernet Sauvignon, Napa Valley. $40.

90 • ZD (CA) 1993 Reserve, Cabernet Sauvignon, Napa Valley. $45.

90 • William Hill (CA) 1994 Reserve, Cabernet Sauvignon, Napa Valley. $27.

90 • Signorello (CA) 1994 Cabernet Sauvignon, Napa Valley. $30.

90 • Robert Craig (CA) 1994 Affinity, Napa Valley. $33.

90 • Peter Michael (CA) 1994 Les Pavots Red, Knights Valley. $35.

90 • Joseph Phelps (CA) 1995 Cabernet Sauvignon, Napa Valley. $27.

90 • Joseph Phelps (CA) 1994 Cabernet Sauvignon, Napa Valley. $24.

90 • Hendry (CA) 1995 Block 8, Cabernet Sauvignon, Napa Valley. $24.

90 • Cosentino (CA) 1994 The Poet Meritage, Napa Valley. $30.

90 • Cosentino (CA) 1994 Reserve, Cabernet Sauvignon, Napa Valley. $40.

90 • Cakebread (CA) 1995 Cabernet Sauvignon, Napa Valley. $30.

90 • Beaulieu (CA) 1994 Tapestry Reserve, Napa Valley. $20.

89 • Villa Mt. Eden (CA) 1995 Grand Reserve, Cabernet Sauvignon, Napa Valley. $20.

89 • Thomas Fogarty (CA) 1996 Cabernet Sauvignon, Napa Valley. $25.

89 • Rutherford Ranch (CA) 1993 Cabernet Sauvignon, Napa Valley. $12.

89 • Rust Ridge (CA) 1995 Cabernet Sauvignon, Napa Valley. $24.

89 • Robert Mondavi (CA) 1994 Reserve, Cabernet Sauvignon, Napa Valley. $75.

89 • Robert Craig (CA) 1995 Affinity, Napa Valley. $35.

89 • Page Mill (CA) 1995 Macaire, Napa Valley. $32.

89 • Mayacamas (CA) 1992 Cabernet Sauvignon, Napa Valley. $30.

89 • Markham (CA) 1994 Cabernet Sauvignon, Napa Valley. $15.49.

89 • Livingston (CA) 1995 Stanley's Selection, Cabernet Sauvignon, Napa Valley. $24.

Scale: Superlative (96-100), Exceptional (90-95), Highly Recommended (85-89), Recommended (80-84), Not Recommended (Under 80)

89 • Le Ducq (CA) 1995 Meritage, Napa Valley. $65.

89 • Le Ducq (CA) 1994 Sylviane, Cabernet Sauvignon, Napa Valley. $30.

89 • Judd's Hill (CA) 1995 Cabernet Sauvignon, Napa Valley. $28.

89 • Groth (CA) 1995 Cabernet Sauvignon, Napa Valley. $30.

89 • Freestone (CA) 1994 Cabernet Sauvignon, Napa Valley. $15.

89 • Cosentino (CA) 1995 The Poet Meritage, Napa Valley. $38.

89 • Chappellet (CA) 1995 Signature, Cabernet Sauvignon, Napa Valley. $24.

89 • Cafaro (CA) 1995 Cabernet Sauvignon, Napa Valley. $34.

89 • Beaulieu (CA) 1995 Tapestry Reserve, Napa Valley. $24.99.

88 • William Hill (CA) 1995 Reserve, Cabernet Sauvignon, Napa Valley. $27.

88 • Silverado (CA) 1995 Cabernet Sauvignon, Napa Valley. $25.

88 • Quail Ridge (CA) 1995 Volker Eisele Vineyard Reserve, Cabernet Sauvignon, Napa Valley. $40.

88 • Monticello (CA) 1994 Corley Reserve, Cabernet Sauvignon, Napa Valley. $35.

88 • Merryvale (CA) 1993 Profile, Napa Valley. $48.

88 • Markham (CA) 1995 Cabernet Sauvignon, Napa Valley. $19.

88 • Le Ducq (CA) 1995 Sylviane, Cabernet Sauvignon, Napa Valley. $30.

88 • Havens (CA) 1994 Bourriquot, Napa Valley. $28.

88 • Folie à Deux (CA) 1995 Reserve, Cabernet Sauvignon, Napa Valley. $22.

88 • Duckhorn (CA) 1994 Cabernet Sauvignon, Napa Valley. $35.

88 • Cosentino (CA) 1995 Reserve, Cabernet Sauvignon, Napa Valley. $40.

88 • Cakebread (CA) 1994 Cabernet Sauvignon, Napa Valley. $25.

88 • Beringer (CA) 1994 Cabernet Sauvignon, Knights Valley. $20.

87 • ZD (CA) 1994 Cabernet Sauvignon, Napa Valley. $30.

87 • Robert Mondavi (CA) 1994 Cabernet Sauvignon, Napa Valley. $22.

87 • Mirassou (CA) 1995 Harvest Reserve, Cabernet Sauvignon, Napa Valley. $17.95.

87 • Langtry (CA) 1994 Red Meritage, Napa Valley. $41.

87 • Folie á Deux (CA) 1995 Cabernet Sauvignon, Napa Valley. $18.

87 • Farella-Park (CA) 1994 Cabernet Sauvignon, Napa Valley. $28.

87 • Edgewood (CA) 1993 Cellarette Cuvée, Napa Valley. $22.50.

87 • Dunnewood (CA) 1994 Dry Silk, Cabernet Sauvignon, Napa Valley. $9.99.

87 • Clos du Val (CA) 1995 Cabernet Sauvignon, Napa Valley. $24.

87 • Clos du Val (CA) 1993 Cabernet Sauvignon, Napa Valley. $24.

86 • William Hill (CA) 1996 Cabernet Sauvignon, Napa Valley. $18.

86 • Vigil (CA) 1996 Valiente Claret, Napa Valley. $22.

86 • Vigil (CA) 1995 Valiente Claret, Napa Valley. $20.

86 • Stonegate (CA) 1995 Cabernet Sauvignon, Napa Valley. $18.

86 • Quail Ridge (CA) 1995 Cabernet Sauvignon, Napa Valley. $15.99.

86 • Monthaven (CA) 1995 Cabernet Sauvignon, Napa Valley. $9.99.

86 • Mirassou (CA) 1994 Harvest Reserve, Cabernet Sauvignon, Napa Valley. $17.95.

86 • Merryvale (CA) 1996 Hillside, Cabernet Sauvignon, Napa Valley. $18.

86 • Mayacamas (CA) 1993 Cabernet Sauvignon, Napa Valley. $38.

86 • Edgewood (CA) 1995 Cabernet Sauvignon, Napa Valley. $20.

86 • Beringer (CA) 1995 Appellation Collection, Cabernet Sauvignon, Knights Valley. $22.

86 • Beringer (CA) 1995 Alluvium Red, Knights Valley. $30.

85 • Stonehedge (CA) 1995 Cabernet Sauvignon, Napa Valley. $12.99.

85 • Ramspeck (CA) 1995 Cabernet Sauvignon, Napa Valley. $18.

85 • Quail Ridge (CA) 1994 Cabernet Sauvignon, Napa Valley. $14.99.

85 • Marcelina (CA) 1993 Cabernet Sauvignon, Napa County. $20.

85 • Hagafen (CA) 1995 Cabernet Sauvignon, Napa Valley. $20.

85 • Farella-Park (CA) 1995 Cabernet Sauvignon, Napa Valley. $32.

85 • Cosentino (CA) 1995 Cabernet Sauvignon, Napa Valley. $18.

Napa Valley (Calistoga)

95 • Fisher (CA) 1994 Lamb Vineyard, Cabernet Sauvignon, Napa Valley. $50.

93 • Cuvaison (CA) 1994 Cabernet Sauvignon, Napa Valley. $24.99.

93 • Clos Pegase (CA) 1994 Hommage Reserve, Cabernet Sauvignon, Napa Valley. $40.

92 • Fisher (CA) 1995 Lamb Vineyard, Cabernet Sauvignon, Napa Valley. $50.

92 • Chateau Montelena (CA) 1994 Montelena Estate, Cabernet Sauvignon, Napa Valley. $85.

90 • Chateau Montelena (CA) 1993 Montelena Estate, Cabernet Sauvignon, Napa Valley. $40.

89 • Guenoc (CA) 1995 Bella Vista Reserve, Cabernet Sauvignon, Napa Valley. $30.50.

89 • Clos Pegase (CA) 1995 Cabernet Sauvignon, Napa Valley. $22.99.

88 • Cuvaison (CA) 1995 Cabernet Sauvignon, Napa Valley. $.

87 • Chateau Montelena (CA) 1995 Calistoga Cuvée, Cabernet Sauvignon, Napa Valley. $18.

85 • Helena View (CA) 1995 Tradition, Cabernet Sauvignon, Napa Valley. $38.

85 • Guenoc (CA) 1994 Bella Vista Reserve, Cabernet Sauvignon, Napa Valley. $30.50.

Napa Valley (St. Helena)

94 • St. Clement (CA) 1996 Oroppas, Napa Valley. $35.

94 • Spottswoode (CA) 1993 Cabernet Sauvignon, Napa Valley. $42.

94 • Plam (CA) 1995 Vintner's Reserve, Cabernet Sauvignon, Napa Valley. $30.

94 • Beringer (CA) 1993 Private Reserve, Cabernet Sauvignon, Napa Valley. $65.

93 • Spottswoode (CA) 1994 Cabernet Sauvignon, Napa Valley. $45.

92 • Spottswoode (CA) 1995 Cabernet Sauvignon, Napa Valley. $55.

92 • Spottswoode (CA) 1992 Cabernet Sauvignon, Napa Valley. $39.

91 • Louis Martini (CA) 1994 Reserve, Cabernet Sauvignon, Napa Valley. $18.

91 • Forman (CA) 1995 Cabernet Sauvignon, Napa Valley. $40.

90 • Titus (CA) 1994 Cabernet Sauvignon, Napa Valley. $22.

90 • St. Clement (CA) 1995 Oroppas, Napa Valley. $35.

90 • St. Clement (CA) 1994 Cabernet Sauvignon, Napa Valley. $25.

90 • Seavey (CA) 1993 Cabernet Sauvignon, Napa Valley. $28.

90 • Raymond (CA) 1995 Generations, Cabernet Sauvignon, Napa Valley. $50.

90 • Plam (CA) 1994 Vintner's Reserve, Cabernet Sauvignon, Napa Valley. $30.

90 • Flora Springs (CA) 1995 Cypress Ranch, Cabernet Sauvignon, Napa Valley. $40.

90 • Anderson's Conn Valley Vineyards (CA) 1994 Estate Reserve, Cabernet Sauvignon, Napa Valley. $40.

89 • Neyers (CA) 1995 Cabernet Sauvignon, Napa Valley. $40.

89 • Newton (CA) 1995 Cabernet Sauvignon, Napa Valley. $36.99.

89 • Heitz (CA) 1992 Cabernet Sauvignon, Napa Valley. $20.

89 • Harrison (CA) 1994 Cabernet Sauvignon, Napa Valley. $33.

89 • Beaucanon (CA) 1994 Cabernet Sauvignon, Napa Valley. $14.

88 • Whitehall Lane (CA) 1996 Cabernet Sauvignon, Napa Valley. $22.

88 • V. Sattui (CA) 1995 Suzanne's Vineyard, Cabernet Sauvignon, Napa Valley. $22.50.

88 • Raymond (CA) 1994 Generations, Cabernet Sauvignon, Napa Valley. $35.

88 • Newlan (CA) 1995 Cabernet Sauvignon, Napa Valley. $20.

88 • Guenoc (CA) 1994 Beckstoffer IV Reserve, Cabernet Sauvignon, Napa Valley. $40.50.

88 • Forman (CA) 1994 Cabernet Sauvignon, Napa Valley. $38.

88 • Conn Creek (CA) 1994 Anthology, Napa Valley. $44.

87 • St. Clement (CA) 1995 Cabernet Sauvignon, Napa Valley. $26.

87 • Raymond (CA) 1996 Reserve, Cabernet Sauvignon, Napa Valley. $23.

87 • Merryvale (CA) 1994 Cabernet Sauvignon, Napa Valley. $27.

87 • Cecchetti Sebastiani (CA) 1993 Cabernet Sauvignon, Napa Valley. $30.

87 • Burgess (CA) 1994 Vintage Selection, Cabernet Sauvignon, Napa Valley. $22.

86 • Van Asperen (CA) 1994 Signature Reserve, Cabernet Sauvignon, Napa Valley. $28.

86 • Raymond (CA) 1995 Reserve, Cabernet Sauvignon, Napa Valley. $20.

86 • Raymond (CA) 1994 Reserve, Cabernet Sauvignon, Napa Valley. $20.

86 • Heitz (CA) 1994 Cabernet Sauvignon, Napa Valley. $25.

86 • Heitz (CA) 1993 Cabernet Sauvignon, Napa Valley. $21.

86 • Guenoc (CA) 1995 Beckstoffer IV Reserve, Cabernet Sauvignon, Napa Valley. $40.50.

86 • Burgess (CA) 1995 Vintage Selection, Cabernet Sauvignon, Napa Valley. $24.

86 • Beaucanon (CA) 1996 Reserve, Cabernet Sauvignon, Napa Valley. $14.

86 • Beaucanon (CA) 1995 Cabernet Sauvignon, Napa Valley. $14.

86 • Anderson's Conn Valley Vineyards (CA) 1995 Estate Reserve, Cabernet Sauvignon, Napa Valley. $48.

85 • V. Sattui (CA) 1994 Suzanne's Vineyard, Cabernet Sauvignon, Napa Valley. $20.

85 • Buehler (CA) 1995 Estate, Cabernet Sauvignon, Napa Valley. $35.

Napa Valley (Rutherford)

95 • Peju Province (CA) 1995 Estate Bottled, Cabernet Sauvignon, Napa Valley. $55.

95 • Lokoya (CA) 1995 Cabernet Sauvignon, Rutherford, Napa Valley. $100.

95 • Caymus (CA) 1994 Special Selection, Cabernet Sauvignon, Napa Valley. $110.

94 • Pine Ridge (CA) 1994 Andrus Reserve, Napa Valley. $85.

94 • Peju Province (CA) 1994 H.B. Vineyard, Cabernet Sauvignon, Napa Valley. $55.

93 • Peju Province (CA) 1995 Cabernet Sauvignon, Napa Valley. $28.

93 • Niebaum-Coppola (CA) 1995 Rubicon, Rutherford, Napa Valley. $65.

93 • Flora Springs (CA) 1995 Trilogy, Napa Valley. $40.

93 • Fetzer (CA) 1994 Reserve, Cabernet Sauvignon, Napa Valley. $28.

93 • Caymus (CA) 1995 Cabernet Sauvignon, Napa Valley. $65.

92 • Whitehall Lane (CA) 1994 Morisoli Vineyard Reserve, Cabernet Sauvignon, Napa Valley. $36.

92 • Staglin (CA) 1995 Cabernet Sauvignon, Rutherford, Napa Valley. $42.50.

92 • Niebaum-Coppola (CA) 1994 Rubicon, Rutherford, Napa Valley. $65.

92 • Freemark Abbey (CA) 1994 Bosché Estate, Cabernet Sauvignon, Napa Valley. $44.

92 • Freemark Abbey (CA) 1992 Bosché Estate, Cabernet Sauvignon, Napa Valley. $27.99.

92 • Caymus (CA) 1994 Cabernet Sauvignon, Napa Valley. $35.

92 • Beaulieu (CA) 1995 Georges de Latour Private Reserve, Cabernet Sauvignon, Rutherford. $59.99.

92 • Beaulieu (CA) 1994 Georges de Latour Private Reserve, Cabernet Sauvignon, Rutherford. $50.

91 • V. Sattui (CA) 1994 Rosenbrand Family Reserve, Cabernet Sauvignon, Napa Valley. $60.

91 • Pine Ridge (CA) 1995 Andrus Reserve, Napa Valley. $85.

91 • Niebaum-Coppola (CA) 1992 Rubicon, Rutherford, Napa Valley. $45.

91 • Heitz (CA) 1993 Trailside Vineyard, Cabernet Sauvignon, Napa Valley. $48.

90 • Whitehall Lane (CA) 1995 Morisoli Vineyard Reserve, Cabernet Sauvignon, Napa Valley. $40.

90 • St. Supéry (CA) 1994 Cabernet Sauvignon, Napa Valley. $15.75.

90 • Quintessa (CA) 1995 Red, Rutherford. $75.

90 • Pine Ridge (CA) 1996 Cabernet Sauvignon, Rutherford, Napa Valley. $25.

90 • Pine Ridge (CA) 1995 Cabernet Sauvignon, Rutherford, Napa Valley. $24.

90 • Helena View (CA) 1992 Cabernet Sauvignon, Napa Valley. $20.

90 • Freemark Abbey (CA) 1992 Sycamore Vineyard, Cabernet Sauvignon, Napa Valley. $26.49.

90 • Flora Springs (CA) 1996 Trilogy, Napa Valley. $45.

90 • Flora Springs (CA) 1994 Trilogy, Napa Valley. $30.

89 • V. Sattui (CA) 1995 Preston Vineyard, Cabernet Sauvignon, Napa Valley. $27.

89 • V. Sattui (CA) 1995 Morisoli Vineyard, Cabernet Sauvignon, Napa Valley. $25.

89 • St. Supéry (CA) 1994 Meritage, Napa Valley. $40.

89 • Sequoia Grove (CA) 1995 Reserve, Cabernet Sauvignon, Napa Valley. $35.

89 • Freemark Abbey (CA) 1993 Sycamore Vineyard, Cabernet Sauvignon, Napa Valley. $28.99.

89 • Corison (CA) 1994 Cabernet Sauvignon, Napa Valley. $35.

88 • Staglin (CA) 1994 Cabernet Sauvignon, Rutherford, Napa Valley. $37.

88 • St. Supéry (CA) 1995 Meritage Red, Napa Valley. $40.

88 • Rocking Horse (CA) 1994 Garvey Family Vineyard, Cabernet Sauvignon, Rutherford. $25.

88 • Freemark Abbey (CA) 1994 Cabernet Sauvignon, Napa Valley. $19.99.

87 • Heitz (CA) 1992 Trailside Vineyard, Cabernet Sauvignon, Napa Valley. $48.

87 • Freemark Abbey (CA) 1995 Cabernet Sauvignon, Napa Valley. $24.

86 • V. Sattui (CA) 1994 Morisoli Vineyard, Cabernet Sauvignon, Napa Valley. $25.

86 • Sequoia Grove (CA) 1995 Cabernet Sauvignon, Napa Valley. $22.99.

86 • Helena View (CA) 1994 Cabernet Sauvignon, Napa Valley. $32.50.

86 • Heitz (CA) 1993 Bella Oaks Vineyard, Cabernet Sauvignon, Napa Valley. $28.

86 • Bell (CA) 1994 Baritelle Vineyard, Cabernet Sauvignon, Rutherford. $50.

85 • V. Sattui (CA) 1994 Preston Vineyard, Cabernet Sauvignon, Napa Valley. $30.

Napa Valley (Oakville)

99 • Opus One (CA) 1995 Oakville, Napa Valley Red. $100.

97 • Opus One (CA) 1992 Oakville, Napa Valley Red. $65.

96 • Opus One (CA) 1993 Oakville, Napa Valley Red. $85.

94 • Opus One (CA) 1994 Oakville, Napa Valley Red. $90.

93 • Joseph Phelps (CA) 1995 Backus Vineyard, Cabernet Sauvignon, Napa Valley. $70.

93 • Joseph Phelps (CA) 1994 Insignia, Napa Valley. $70.

93 • Heitz (CA) 1992 Martha's Vineyard, Cabernet Sauvignon, Napa Valley. $68.

92 • Joseph Phelps (CA) 1995 Insignia, Napa Valley. $75.

92 • Joseph Phelps (CA) 1994 Backus Vineyard, Cabernet Sauvignon, Napa Valley. $70.

92 • Girard (CA) 1995 Cabernet Sauvignon, Napa Valley. $28.

91 • Oakville Ranch (CA) 1994 Robert's Blend, Napa Valley. $45.

91 • Girard (CA) 1994 Reserve, Cabernet Sauvignon, Napa Valley. $40.

91 • Franciscan (CA) 1994 Oakville Estate, Magnificat Meritage, Napa Valley. $25.

91 • Far Niente (CA) 1995 Cabernet Sauvignon, Napa Valley. $70.

90 • Silver Oak (CA) 1994 Cabernet Sauvignon, Napa Valley. $65.

90 • Silver Oak (CA) 1993 Cabernet Sauvignon, Napa Valley. $50.

90 • Girard (CA) 1994 Cabernet Sauvignon, Napa Valley. $25.

90 • Franciscan (CA) 1994 Oakville Estate, Cabernet Sauvignon, Napa Valley. $17.

90 • Far Niente (CA) 1994 Cabernet Sauvignon, Napa Valley. $55.

90 • Dalla Valle (CA) 1993 Cabernet Sauvignon, Napa Valley. $40.

89 • Oakville Ranch (CA) 1995 Robert's Blend, Napa Valley. $45.

89 • Oakville Ranch (CA) 1995 Cabernet Sauvignon, Napa Valley. $35.

89 • Franciscan (CA) 1995 Oakville Estate, Magnificat Meritage, Napa Valley. $30.

88 • Turnbull (CA) 1995 Cabernet Sauvignon, Napa Valley. $20.

88 • Turnbull (CA) 1994 Cabernet Sauvignon, Napa Valley. $22.

87 • Swanson (CA) 1995 Alexis, Napa Valley. $40.

87 • Saddleback (CA) 1996 Cabernet Sauvignon, Napa Valley. $32.

87 • Robert Mondavi (CA) 1995 Oakville, Cabernet Sauvignon, Napa Valley. $27.

87 • Robert Mondavi (CA) 1994 Oakville, Cabernet Sauvignon, Napa Valley. $28.

87 • Oakville Ranch (CA) 1994 Cabernet Sauvignon, Napa Valley. $30.

86 • Swanson (CA) 1994 Cabernet Sauvignon, Napa Valley. $24.

86 • Franciscan (CA) 1995 Oakville Estate, Cabernet Sauvignon, Napa Valley. $17.

85 • Volker Eisele (CA) 1996 Cabernet Sauvignon, Napa Valley. $30.

85 • Volker Eisele (CA) 1995 Cabernet Sauvignon, Napa Valley. $30.

Napa Valley (Stags Leap District)

97 • Stag's Leap Wine Cellars (CA) 1995 Cask 23, Napa Valley. $120.

96 • Stag's Leap Wine Cellars (CA) 1994 Cask 23, Cabernet Sauvignon, Napa Valley. $100.

95 • Shafer (CA) 1994 Hillside Select, Cabernet Sauvignon, Stags Leap District, Napa Valley. $85.

95 • S. Anderson (CA) 1994 Richard Chambers Vineyard, Cabernet Sauvignon, Stags Leap District. $54.

95 • Pine Ridge (CA) 1996 Cabernet Sauvignon, Stags Leap District, Napa Valley. $40.

94 • Stag's Leap Wine Cellars (CA) 1995 SLV, Cabernet Sauvignon, Napa Valley. $70.

94 • Stag's Leap Wine Cellars (CA) 1995 Fay, Cabernet Sauvignon, Napa Valley. $70.

94 • Stag's Leap Wine Cellars (CA) 1994 Fay, Cabernet Sauvignon, Napa Valley. $50.

94 • S. Anderson (CA) 1995 Richard Chambers Vineyard, Cabernet Sauvignon, Stags Leap District. $65.

94 • Hartwell (CA) 1995 Sunshine Vineyard, Cabernet Sauvignon, Stags Leap District. $80.

94 • Chimney Rock (CA) 1996 Cabernet Sauvignon, Napa Valley. $30.

94 • Chimney Rock (CA) 1995 Reserve, Cabernet Sauvignon, Stags Leap District. $50.

93 • Stag's Leap Wine Cellars (CA) 1994 SLV, Cabernet Sauvignon, Napa Valley. $50.

93 • Shafer (CA) 1995 Cabernet Sauvignon, Stags Leap District, Napa Valley. $30.

93 • Shafer (CA) 1993 Hillside Select, Cabernet Sauvignon, Stags Leap District, Napa Valley. $60.

93 • Pine Ridge (CA) 1995 Cabernet Sauvignon, Stags Leap District, Napa Valley. $37.50.

92 • Clos du Val (CA) 1994 Reserve, Cabernet Sauvignon, Napa Valley. $53.

91 • Clos du Val (CA) 1993 Reserve, Cabernet Sauvignon, Napa Valley. $50.

90 • Shafer (CA) 1994 Cabernet Sauvignon, Stags Leap District, Napa Valley. $28.

90 • Chimney Rock (CA) 1995 Elevage, Stags Leap District. $50.

90 • Chimney Rock (CA) 1994 Reserve, Cabernet Sauvignon, Stags Leap District. $50.

90 • Chimney Rock (CA) 1994 Elevage, Stags Leap District. $40.

89 • Stag's Leap Wine Cellars (CA) 1995 Cabernet Sauvignon, Napa Valley. $26.

89 • Shafer (CA) 1996 Cabernet Sauvignon, Stags Leap District, Napa Valley. $35.

88 • Robert Mondavi (CA) 1995 SLD, Cabernet Sauvignon, Napa Valley. $27.

88 • Chimney Rock (CA) 1994 Cabernet Sauvignon, Napa Valley. $26.

86 • Stags' Leap Winery (CA) 1995 Cabernet Sauvignon, Napa Valley. $30.

86 • Pine Ridge (CA) 1994 Cabernet Sauvignon, Stags Leap District, Napa Valley. $35.

85 • Hartwell (CA) 1994 Sunshine Vineyard, Cabernet Sauvignon, Stags Leap District. $45.

Napa Valley (Yountville)

95 • Dominus (CA) 1995 Napanook Vineyard, Cabernet Sauvignon, Napa Valley. $95.

95 • Dominus (CA) 1994 Napanook Vineyard, Napa Valley. $75.

93 • Grgich Hills (CA) 1994 Yountville Selection, Cabernet Sauvignon, Napa Valley. $85.

89 • Rosenblum (CA) 1995 Holbrook Mitchell Trio, Napa Valley. $35.

88 • Dominus (CA) 1992 Napanook Vineyard, Napa Valley. $50.

88 • Charles Krug (CA) 1994 Vintage Selection, Cabernet Sauvignon, Napa Valley. $47.

87 • Rosenblum (CA) 1996 Holbrook Mitchell Trio, Napa Valley. $35.

87 • Rosenblum (CA) 1995 Hendry Vineyard, Reserve, Cabernet Sauvignon, Napa Valley. $40.

86 • Trefethen (CA) 1994 Cabernet Sauvignon, Napa Valley. $24.

85 • Charles Krug (CA) 1994 Peter Mondavi Family, Generations, Napa Valley. $30.

Napa Mountains

Wines Reviewed: **45**

Median Price: **$34**

The Napa Valley is indeed a valley. This means that there are mountains to be found on either side of the valley, and in these mountains, intrepid vintners are to be found toiling away. Though home to a range of sub-appellations, including Atlas Peak, Diamond Mountain, Howell Mountain, Spring Mountain, and Mount Veeder, these Napa mountain districts are still entitled to use the term Napa Valley on their labels. This point serves to illustrate the occasionally silly inadequacies of the AVA system.

Mountain viticulture is quite different from that to be found on the valley floor and an altogether better solution would have been to lump the mountain ranges surrounding the Napa Valley into a Napa Mountains appellation. Nonetheless, these subdistricts, led by Howell Mountain, are making a name for themselves, and connoisseurs in particular are gravitating to these long-lived, imposingly structured wines. As a whole they tend to be quite concentrated with a reputation for backwardness. That may be changing, however, as within the last few years new tannin management techniques have paid enormous dividends. The current crop of wines has actually become approachable virtually on release, while retaining a solid sense of structure that belies their mountain origins. Separate and distinct from the Napa Valley proper, these difficult to farm appellations will never become commercially sizable, but will continue to be of great importance at the quality end of the spectrum for years to come.

Highly Recommended Napa Mountains Cabernet Sauvignon and Red Meritage

Napa Mountains (Atlas Peak)

89 • Tulocay (CA) 1996 Cliff Vineyard, Cabernet Sauvignon, Napa Valley. $21.

88 • Atlas Peak Vineyards (CA) 1994 Cabernet Sauvignon, Atlas Peak, Napa Valley. $18.

87 • Tulocay (CA) 1994 Cliff Vineyard, Cabernet Sauvignon, Napa Valley. $22.

Napa Mountains (Diamond Mountain)

93 • Martin Ray (CA) 1995 Cabernet Sauvignon, Diamond Mountain, Napa Valley. $45.

93 • Diamond Creek (CA) 1995 Volcanic Hill, Cabernet Sauvignon, Napa Valley. $75.

93 • Diamond Creek (CA) 1995 Red Rock Terrace, Cabernet Sauvignon, Napa Valley. $75.

90 • Von Strasser (CA) 1994 Cabernet Sauvignon, Diamond Mountain, Napa Valley. $32.

90 • Diamond Creek (CA) 1994 Volcanic Hill, Cabernet Sauvignon, Napa Valley. $50.

89 • Lokoya (CA) 1995 Cabernet Sauvignon, Diamond Mountain, Napa Valley. $100.

88 • Diamond Creek (CA) 1994 Red Rock Terrace, Cabernet Sauvignon, Napa Valley. $50.

87 • Von Strasser (CA) 1995 Cabernet Sauvignon, Diamond Mountain, Napa Valley. $36.

Napa Mountains (Howell Mountain)

97 • Pine Ridge (CA) 1996 Cabernet Sauvignon, Howell Mountain, Napa Valley. $40.

96 • La Jota (CA) 1996 15th Anniversary, Cabernet Sauvignon, Howell Mountain, Napa Valley. $58.

94 • Pine Ridge (CA) 1995 Cabernet Sauvignon, Howell Mountain, Napa Valley. $37.50.

93 • St. Clement (CA) 1995 Cabernet Sauvignon, Howell Mountain, Napa Valley. $45.

93 • La Jota (CA) 1995 Howell Mountain Selection, Cabernet Sauvignon, Howell Mountain, Napa Valley. $30.

92 • St. Clement (CA) 1994 Cabernet Sauvignon, Howell Mountain, Napa Valley. $45.

92 • Dunn (CA) 1993 Cabernet Sauvignon, Napa Valley. $35.

91 • Pine Ridge (CA) 1994 Cabernet Sauvignon, Howell Mountain, Napa Valley. $35.

91 • Cornerstone (CA) 1993 Beatty Ranch, Cabernet Sauvignon, Howell Mountain. $32.

89 • Viader (CA) 1993 Red, Napa Valley. $30.

87 • La Jota (CA) 1996 Howell Mountain Selection, Cabernet Sauvignon, Howell Mountain, Napa Valley. $34.

Napa Mountains (Mount Veeder)

95 • Mount Veeder Winery (CA) 1993 Reserve, Napa Valley. $40.

94 • Hess Collection (CA) 1993 Cabernet Sauvignon, Mount Veeder, Napa Valley. $20.

92 • Mount Veeder Winery (CA) 1995 Reserve, Napa Valley. $50.

92 • Hess Collection (CA) 1995 Cabernet Sauvignon, Mount Veeder, Napa Valley. $24.75.

92 • Chateau Potelle (CA) 1993 Cabernet Sauvignon, Mount Veeder, Napa Valley. $29.

91 • Mount Veeder Winery (CA) 1995 Cabernet Sauvignon, Napa Valley. $30.

91 • Hess Collection (CA) 1994 Cabernet Sauvignon, Mount Veeder, Napa Valley. $19.75.

89 • Chateau Potelle (CA) 1994 VGS, Cabernet Sauvignon, Mount Veeder, Napa Valley. $39.

87 • Lokoya (CA) 1995 Cabernet Sauvignon, Mount Veeder, Napa Valley. $100.

86 • Franus (CA) 1994 Cabernet Sauvignon, Napa Valley. $25.

Napa Mountains (Spring Mountain District)

98 • Pride Mountain (CA) 1996 Cabernet Sauvignon, Napa Valley. $29.99.

93 • Spring Mountain Vineyard (CA) 1993 Miravalle-Alba-Chevalier Red, Napa Valley. $28.

92 • Robert Keenan (CA) 1994 Hillside Estate, Cabernet Sauvignon, Spring Mountain District, Napa Valley. $24.

92 • Barnett (CA) 1995 Cabernet Sauvignon, Spring Mountain District, Napa Valley. $35.

91 • Cain (CA) 1994 Cain Five, Napa Valley. $50.

89 • Robert Keenan (CA) 1993 Hillside Estate, Cabernet Sauvignon, Spring Mountain District, Napa Valley. $23.

87 • Cain (CA) 1995 Cain Five, Napa Valley. $50.

87 • Barnett (CA) 1994 Cabernet Sauvignon, Spring Mountain District, Napa Valley. $35.

86 • Cain (CA) 1995 Cain Cuvee, Napa Valley. $22.

85 • Cain (CA) 1994 Cain Cuvee, Napa Valley. $19.

Sonoma County

Wines Reviewed: 159
Median Price: $24

Trying to pin down a "Sonoma County style" for Cabernet is virtually hopeless. That being said it is important to point out why. Sonoma County is a designation used as a catchall for wines from the far more precise sub-appellations of the Russian River, Dry Creek, Alexander, and Sonoma Valleys, with many further divisions among them. Each area is unique and distinctive. What many producers choose to do, however, is blend wines from the various regions within the county and label accordingly. This is not necessarily a bad thing.

Following the Australian model, it makes perfect sense that if one were trying to make a balanced and well-rounded wine year in and year out, the best solution might be to blend from vineyards that share complimentary qualities. Alexander Valley grapes for richness, Russian River for acidity, and Dry Creek for intensity of fruit perhaps? The resultant wines are quite good and may even be more consistent, but the blending tends to mitigate the notion of terroir, and it is dangerous to attempt to pigeonhole Sonoma County wines as a whole because they are bound to be blended from different regions, in different proportions, and for different reasons. Despite this fact, three regions in particular within Sonoma have become known for the production of high-quality Cabernet: the Alexander, Sonoma, and Dry Creek Valleys.

The Alexander Valley is one of the most notable of the AVAs within Sonoma County for Cabernet. It features one of the warmest climates in Sonoma County, and as such, it is ideally suited to Bordeaux varietals. Although it is only some 18 miles from the ocean, the maritime influence is not what it is in, say, the Russian River Valley, as it is shielded by north-south mountain ranges. Alexander Valley Cabernets tend to be relatively rich, though without the weight one associates with Napa bottlings. Additionally, the acidity levels seem a shade more prominent. In this way, it might be fairly said that Alexander Valley Cabernet is somewhat of a bridge in style between Napa and Sonoma, taking some of the better attributes of each, with a telltale, supple, plummy, fruit-driven quality.

As for the Sonoma Valley, it sits at the southern end of Sonoma County, abutting the Carneros. The valley proper runs between the Mayacamas Mountains, which form the border with Napa, and Sonoma Mountain. As the valley opens up past Sonoma Mountain at the town of Glen Ellen, the climate changes from that in the southern end. The area as a whole is filled with wild and precipitous hills, which afford the vineyards ideal exposures to the sun. This, in combination with a lengthy growing season, moderate temperatures afforded by the cooling breezes of San Pablo Bay and the Petaluma Gap, and fertile though well-drained soils have made for a vine growing Eden. Sonoma Valley Cabernet tends to be quite extracted with exotically deep colors and black fruit aromas. This intensity of fruit character is the wine's hallmark, and despite the unusual level of extract, generally pronounced acidity lends a measure of balance.

As for the Dry Creek Valley, though a stone's throw from the Russian River and Alexander Valleys, it is unique. As usual, Sonoma County's tortured and eternally confusing geography is to blame. The natural boundaries of the valley, however, makes this an exceptionally tight and well-defined appellation. The Dry Creek parallels the Alexander Valley on the western side and drains into the Russian River. From the point where the Dry Creek meets the Russian River, it is a distance of about 16 miles to the point to the northwest where the Dry Creek Valley abruptly ends. Surrounded by mountains on three sides, with the only opening at the Russian River, there is no outlet for wind as in the Alexander Valley. Additionally, what fog that does enter from the Russian River Valley often comes in at night and burns off quickly during the day. Hence, temperatures are far warmer than in the Russian River Valley, particularly at the northern end. The valley is only two miles wide at its widest point, and the valley floor itself is quite narrow. Benchlands and hillsides dominate the region, and in

Scale: Superlative (96-100), Exceptional (90-95), Highly Recommended (85-89), Recommended (80-84), Not Recommended (Under 80)

the warmer northern end of the valley, red wine is king.

The Dry Creek area was largely settled in the late 19th century by Italian families, and as in other parts of Sonoma County, Zinfandel was the favored grape, interspersed with the usual blend of black varieties. Cabernet has taken root, however, and the resultant wines have that signature Dry Creek stamp, an exotic briar fruit character with crisp acidity. The wines are lighter in body than those from the Alexander or Sonoma Valleys, yet are well balanced and eminently drinkable.

Highly Recommended Sonoma County Cabernet Sauvignon and Red Meritage

Sonoma County (General)

94 • Ferrari-Carano (CA) 1993 Tresor Reserve, Sonoma County. $55.

94 • Chateau St. Jean (CA) 1992 Reserve, Cabernet Sauvignon, Sonoma County. $45.

93 • Gallo Sonoma (CA) 1994 Estate, Cabernet Sauvignon, Northern Sonoma. $54.99.

92 • Fisher (CA) 1994 Wedding Vineyard, Cabernet Sauvignon, Sonoma County. $50.

92 • Arrowood (CA) 1994 Réserve Spéciale, Cabernet Sauvignon, Sonoma County. $50.

91 • Simi (CA) 1994 Reserve, Cabernet Sauvignon, Sonoma County. $46.67.

91 • Ferrari-Carano (CA) 1994 Cabernet Sauvignon, Sonoma County. $28.

91 • Ferrari-Carano (CA) 1992 Reserve Red, Sonoma County. $47.

90 • Gallo Sonoma (CA) 1993 Estate, Cabernet Sauvignon, Northern Sonoma. $45.

90 • Ferrari-Carano (CA) 1993 Cabernet Sauvignon, Sonoma County. $22.50.

90 • Benziger (CA) 1995 Cabernet Sauvignon, Sonoma County. $16.

90 • Arrowood (CA) 1995 Cabernet Sauvignon, Sonoma County. $35.

89 • Windsor (CA) 1995 Shelton Signature Series, Cabernet Sauvignon, Sonoma County. $22.

89 • Rodney Strong (CA) 1994 Reserve, Cabernet Sauvignon, Northern Sonoma. $35.

89 • Rodney Strong (CA) 1993 Reserve, Cabernet Sauvignon, Northern Sonoma. $30.

89 • Marietta (CA) 1996 Cabernet Sauvignon, Sonoma County. $17.

89 • Chateau St. Jean (CA) 1995 Cinq Cépages, Cabernet Sauvignon, Sonoma County. $24.

89 • Chateau St. Jean (CA) 1994 Cinq Cépages, Cabernet Sauvignon, Sonoma County. $24.

89 • Benziger (CA) 1996 Cabernet Sauvignon, Sonoma County. $17.

88 • Windsor (CA) 1995 Private Reserve Meritage, Sonoma County. $20.

88 • Windsor (CA) 1994 Shelton Signature Series, Cabernet Sauvignon, Sonoma County. $21.

88 • Rodney Strong (CA) 1993 Alexander's Crown Vineyard, Cabernet Sauvignon, Northern Sonoma. $22.

88 • Chateau St. Jean (CA) 1994 Reserve, Cabernet Sauvignon, Sonoma County. $60.

88 • Chalk Hill (CA) 1994 Cabernet Sauvignon, Chalk Hill, Sonoma County. $26.

88 • Canyon Road (CA) 1995 Reserve, Cabernet Sauvignon, Sonoma County. $18.

87 • Wellington (CA) 1994 Mohrhardt Ridge Vineyard, Cabernet Sauvignon, Sonoma County. $15.

87 • St. Francis (CA) 1995 Cabernet Sauvignon, Sonoma County. $10.99.

87 • Gallo Sonoma (CA) 1994 Cabernet Sauvignon, Sonoma County. $12.

87 • Davis Bynum (CA) 1994 Eclipse, Sonoma County. $28.

87 • Alderbrook (CA) 1996 Cabernet Sauvignon, Sonoma County. $16.

86 • Windsor (CA) 1993 Private Reserve Meritage, Sonoma County. $22.

86 • Rodney Strong (CA) 1995 Cabernet Sauvignon, Sonoma County. $13.

86 • Rodney Strong (CA) 1995 Alexander's Crown Vineyard, Cabernet Sauvignon, Northern Sonoma. $24.

86 • Gary Farrell (CA) 1995 Hillside Selection, Cabernet Sauvignon, Sonoma County. $24.

85 • Windsor (CA) 1994 Signature Series, Cabernet Sauvignon, Sonoma County. $25.

85 • Corbett Canyon (CA) 1995 Reserve, Cabernet Sauvignon, Sonoma County. $10.

Sonoma County (Alexander Valley)

92 • Silver Oak (CA) 1993 Cabernet Sauvignon, Alexander Valley. $38.

91 • Stonestreet (CA) 1995 Legacy, Alexander Valley. $65.

91 • Stonestreet (CA) 1994 Legacy, Alexander Valley. $50.

91 • Silver Oak (CA) 1994 Cabernet Sauvignon, Alexander Valley. $45.

91 • Murphy-Goode (CA) 1994 Brenda Block, Cabernet Sauvignon, Alexander Valley. $30.

91 • Herzog (CA) 1995 Special Reserve, Cabernet Sauvignon, Alexander Valley. $25.99.

91 • Herzog (CA) 1994 Special Reserve, Cabernet Sauvignon, Alexander Valley. $26.69.

91 • Estancia (CA) 1994 Red Meritage, Alexander Valley. $18.

90 • Stonestreet (CA) 1994 Cabernet Sauvignon, Alexander Valley. $35.

90 • Korbel (CA) 1994 Cabernet Sauvignon, Alexander Valley. $18.99.

90 • Hanna (CA) 1995 Cabernet Sauvignon, Alexander Valley. $20.

90 • Gallo Sonoma (CA) 1994 Barrelli Creek Vineyard, Cabernet Sauvignon, Alexander Valley. $20.

90 • de Lorimier (CA) 1994 Mosaic Meritage, Alexander Valley. $20.

90 • Chateau Souverain (CA) 1994 Winemaker's Reserve, Cabernet Sauvignon, Alexander Valley. $30.

89 • Windsor (CA) 1994 Private Reserve, Cabernet Sauvignon, Alexander Valley. $20.

89 • Simi (CA) 1994 Cabernet Sauvignon, Alexander Valley. $19.

89 • Murphy-Goode (CA) 1995 Cabernet Sauvignon, Alexander Valley. $20.

89 • Kendall-Jackson (CA) 1994 Buckeye Vineyard, Cabernet Sauvignon, Alexander Valley. $24.

89 • Geyser Peak (CA) 1995 Reserve, Cabernet Sauvignon, Alexander Valley. $24.99.

89 • de Lorimier (CA) 1995 Mosaic Meritage, Alexander Valley. $24.

89 • Chateau Souverain (CA) 1995 Cabernet Sauvignon, Alexander Valley. $16.50.

89 • Byington (CA) 1994 Smith Reichel Vineyard, Cabernet Sauvignon, Alexander Valley. $18.

88 • Venezia (CA) 1996 Meola Vineyards, Cabernet Sauvignon, Alexander Valley. $19.99.

88 • Stonestreet (CA) 1995 Cabernet Sauvignon, Alexander Valley. $37.

88 • Murphy-Goode (CA) 1994 Murphy Ranch, Cabernet Sauvignon, Alexander Valley. $25.

88 • Kendall-Jackson (CA) 1995 Buckeye Vineyard, Cabernet Sauvignon, Alexander Valley. $27.

88 • Jordan (CA) 1994 Cabernet Sauvignon, Alexander Valley. $34.

88 • Geyser Peak (CA) 1995 Reserve Alexandre Meritage, Alexander Valley. $24.99.

88 • Geyser Peak (CA) 1994 Reserve, Cabernet Sauvignon, Alexander Valley. $28.

88 • Geyser Peak (CA) 1994 Reserve Alexandre Meritage, Meritage, Alexander Valley. $28.

88 • Clos du Bois (CA) 1995 Winemaker's Reserve, Cabernet Sauvignon, Alexander Valley. $50.

87 • Venezia (CA) 1995 Meola Vineyards, Cabernet Sauvignon, Alexander Valley. $20.

87 • Simi (CA) 1995 Cabernet Sauvignon, Alexander Valley. $22.

86 • Pedroncelli (CA) 1995 Morris Fay Vineyard, Cabernet Sauvignon, Alexander Valley. $13.

Scale: Superlative (96-100), Exceptional (90-95), Highly Recommended (85-89), Recommended (80-84), Not Recommended (Under 80)

86 • Iron Horse (CA) 1994 T-T Vineyards, Cabernet Sauvignon, Alexander Valley. $20.

86 • Estancia (CA) 1995 Red Meritage, Alexander Valley. $22.

86 • Chateau Souverain (CA) 1995 Winemaker's Reserve, Cabernet Sauvignon, Alexander Valley. $35.

86 • Benziger (CA) 1995 Ash Creek Vineyards Reserve, Cabernet Sauvignon, Alexander Valley. $25.

86 • Alexander Valley Vineyards (CA) 1996 Cabernet Sauvignon, Alexander Valley. $17.50.

85 • Alexander Valley Vineyards (CA) 1995 Cabernet Sauvignon, Alexander Valley. $17.

Sonoma County (Dry Creek Valley)

94 • Dry Creek Vineyard (CA) 1995 Reserve, Cabernet Sauvignon, Dry Creek Valley. $27.

93 • Gallo Sonoma (CA) 1994 Frei Ranch Vineyard, Cabernet Sauvignon, Dry Creek Valley. $18.

93 • Dry Creek Vineyard (CA) 1996 Cabernet Sauvignon, Dry Creek Valley. $18.75.

92 • Lambert Bridge (CA) 1994 Crane Creek Cuvée, Dry Creek Valley. $28.

91 • Gallo Sonoma (CA) 1993 Frei Ranch Vineyard, Cabernet Sauvignon, Dry Creek Valley. $18.

90 • Windsor (CA) 1994 Private Reserve, Cabernet Sauvignon, Dry Creek Valley. $22.

90 • Michel-Schlumberger (CA) 1994 Cabernet Sauvignon, Dry Creek Valley. $20.

89 • Pezzi King (CA) 1995 Cabernet Sauvignon, Dry Creek Valley. $25.

89 • Belvedere (CA) 1995 Cabernet Sauvignon, Dry Creek Valley. $16.

89 • Belvedere (CA) 1994 Cabernet Sauvignon, Dry Creek Valley. $13.50.

88 • Peterson (CA) 1996 Bradford Mountain Vineyard, Cabernet Sauvignon, Dry Creek Valley. $25.

88 • Pedroncelli (CA) 1996 Three Vineyards, Cabernet Sauvignon, Dry Creek Valley. $12.

88 • Pedroncelli (CA) 1995 Three Vineyards, Cabernet Sauvignon, Dry Creek Valley. $12.50.

88 • Gallo Sonoma (CA) 1993 Stefani Vineyard, Cabernet Sauvignon, Dry Creek Valley. $18.

88 • Dry Creek Vineyard (CA) 1995 Meritage, Dry Creek Valley. $25.

86 • Michel-Schlumberger (CA) 1993 Schlumberger Reserve, Cabernet Sauvignon, Dry Creek Valley. $35.

86 • Michel-Schlumberger (CA) 1993 Cabernet Sauvignon, Dry Creek Valley. $19.50.

86 • Gallo Sonoma (CA) 1994 Stefani Vineyard, Cabernet Sauvignon, Dry Creek Valley. $18.

85 • Lambert Bridge (CA) 1995 Crane Creek Cuvée, Dry Creek Valley. $32.

Sonoma County (Russian River Valley)

92 • De Loach (CA) 1993 OFS, Cabernet Sauvignon, Russian River Valley. $25.

90 • De Loach (CA) 1994 OFS, Cabernet Sauvignon, Russian River Valley. $27.50.

88 • Dehlinger (CA) 1995 Cabernet Sauvignon, Russian River Valley. $28.

87 • Davis Bynum (CA) 1994 Hedin Vineyard, Cabernet Sauvignon, Russian River Valley. $24.

85 • Windsor (CA) 1994 River West Vineyard, Cabernet Sauvignon, Russian River Valley. $18.

Sonoma County (Sonoma Mountain)

92 • Louis Martini (CA) 1994 Monte Rosso Vineyard Selection, Cabernet Sauvignon, Sonoma Mountain. $30.

91 • Ravenswood (CA) 1995 Rancho Vineyards Red, Sonoma Mountain. $30.

91 • Benziger (CA) 1995 Tribute Red, Sonoma Mountain. $25.

90 • Ravenswood (CA) 1995 Pickberry Vineyards Red, Sonoma Mountain. $35.

90 • Laurel Glen (CA) 1995 Cabernet Sauvignon, Sonoma Mountain. $38.

90 • Laurel Glen (CA) 1994 Cabernet Sauvignon, Sonoma Mountain. $38.

90 • Benziger (CA) 1995 Reserve, Cabernet Sauvignon, Sonoma Mountain. $35.

89 • Sonoma Creek (CA) 1995 Van der Kamp Vineyard, Cabernet Sauvignon, Sonoma Mountain. $28.95.

88 • Benziger (CA) 1994 Tribute Red, Sonoma Mountain. $25.

Sonoma County (Sonoma Valley)

96 • St. Francis (CA) 1994 Reserve, Cabernet Sauvignon, Sonoma Valley. $30.

94 • Richardson (CA) 1996 Horne Vineyard, Cabernet Sauvignon, Sonoma Valley. $22.

94 • B.R. Cohn (CA) 1995 Olive Hill Vineyard, Cabernet Sauvignon, Sonoma Valley. $75.

93 • Kunde (CA) 1995 Cabernet Sauvignon, Sonoma Valley. $20.

92 • Sonoma Creek (CA) 1995 Reserve, Cabernet Sauvignon, Sonoma Valley. $17.95.

92 • Richardson (CA) 1996 Synergy, Sonoma Valley. $20.

92 • B.R. Cohn (CA) 1994 Olive Hill Vineyard, Cabernet Sauvignon, Sonoma Valley. $32.

91 • St. Francis (CA) 1995 Reserve, Cabernet Sauvignon, Sonoma Valley. $33.99.

91 • Sonoma Creek (CA) 1995 Rancho Salina Vineyard, Cabernet Sauvignon, Sonoma Valley. $28.95.

91 • Kenwood (CA) 1994 Jack London Vineyard, Cabernet Sauvignon, Sonoma Valley. $25.

91 • Carmenet (CA) 1993 Moon Mountain Estate Reserve Meritage, Sonoma Valley. $27.50.

90 • Kunde (CA) 1994 Cabernet Sauvignon, Sonoma Valley. $17.

90 • Kenwood (CA) 1995 Jack London Vineyard, Cabernet Sauvignon, Sonoma Valley. $25.

90 • Bartholomew Park (CA) 1996 Desnudos Vineyard, Cabernet Sauvignon, Sonoma Valley. $35.

89 • Sonoma Creek (CA) 1995 Meritage, Sonoma Valley. $17.95.

89 • Schug (CA) 1995 Heritage Reserve, Cabernet Sauvignon, Sonoma Valley. $40.

89 • Richardson (CA) 1995 Horne Vineyard, Cabernet Sauvignon, Sonoma Valley. $18.

89 • Ravenswood (CA) 1994 Rancho Salina Vineyards Red, Sonoma Valley. $30.

89 • Benziger (CA) 1995 Rancho Salina Vineyard, Cabernet Sauvignon, Sonoma Valley. $28.

88 • Kenwood (CA) 1995 Cabernet Sauvignon, Sonoma Valley. $18.

88 • Jessandra Vittoria (CA) 1995 Cabernet Sauvignon, Sonoma Valley. $30.

87 • Louis Martini (CA) 1995 Monte Rosso Vineyard Selection, Cabernet Sauvignon, Sonoma Valley. $35.

87 • Kenwood (CA) 1994 Cabernet Sauvignon, Sonoma Valley. $18.

87 • Gundlach Bundschu (CA) 1996 Rhinefarm Vineyards, Cabernet Sauvignon, Sonoma Valley. $24.

87 • Carmenet (CA) 1995 Moon Mountain Estate Reserve Meritage, Sonoma Valley. $40.

85 • Richardson (CA) 1994 Synergy, Sonoma Valley. $17.

85 • Kistler (CA) 1993 Kistler Vineyard, Cabernet Sauvignon, Sonoma Valley. $30.

Mendocino

Wines Reviewed: 12
Median Price: $18.50

Mendocino is the most northerly of California's wine-producing regions and as such it is far removed from the glamour and high society of the southern regions. It has four AVAs, of which Anderson Valley is the most significant and coolest, with its proximity to the coast giving a plentiful supply of cooling sea air along its length.

To the east of Anderson Valley runs the extreme northern section of the Russian

Scale: Superlative (96-100), Exceptional (90-95), Highly Recommended (85-89), Recommended (80-84), Not Recommended (Under 80)

362

River. It is along this stretch of water that the other vineyards of Mendocino County are to be found. Sea air does not have a significant impact in these inland regions and they do not exhibit the coolness found in the Anderson Valley.

Thus, it is here that red Bordeaux varietals are to be found. Though warmer than the coast, the region is still cool, and far cooler than the northern end of the Napa Valley, for instance. This makes for wines that, despite their deep color, feature flavors in the lighter red fruit spectrum of the grape. They are marked by well-balanced levels of acidity, and the tannins are by and large left in check.

Highly Recommended Mendocino Cabernet Sauvignon and Red Meritage

90 • Villa Mt. Eden (CA) 1995 Signature Series, Cabernet Sauvignon, Mendocino. $45.

90 • Villa Mt. Eden (CA) 1994 Signature Series, Cabernet Sauvignon, Mendocino. $50.

89 • Steele (CA) 1994 Cabernet Sauvignon, Anderson Valley. $28.

89 • Lolonis (CA) 1994 Private Reserve, Cabernet Sauvignon, Mendocino County. $25.

89 • Frey (CA) 1997 Butow Vineyards, Cabernet Sauvignon, Redwood Valley. $10.50.

88 • Yorkville (CA) 1995 Richard the Lion-Heart, Mendocino County. $20.

88 • Husch (CA) 1994 La Ribera Vineyard, Cabernet Sauvignon, Mendocino. $15.

86 • Windsor (CA) 1994 Private Reserve, Cabernet Sauvignon, Mendocino County. $22.

86 • Parducci (CA) 1995 Cabernet Sauvignon, Mendocino. $10.

86 • Husch (CA) 1996 Cabernet Sauvignon, Mendocino. $16.50.

Santa Cruz Mountains

Wines Reviewed: **30**

Median Price: **$25**

Santa Cruz is certainly one of California's more improbable, dare one say impractical regions. This craggy, imposing, conifer-peaked range of mountains nestles along the southwestern side of the San Francisco Bay, encompassing the San Andreas fault and some of the Golden State's finest vineyard locations.

Specifics of climate, and hence resulting wine styles, can vary with altitude and aspect of vineyards, making sweeping generalizations or even gradual variations in character impossible to extrapolate. Rainfall and average temperature vary significantly with altitude, and sunshine hours will be dependent upon the specific vineyard orientation, with east-facing slopes being considerably warmer. However, given the mountainous terrain and the poverty of the shale-like soil, yields are ungratifyingly low, and viticulture is labor intensive. These factors alone account for the lack of corporate money and presence in the Santa Cruz Mountains, notwithstanding the ownership of Ridge Vineyards by a Japanese financial services company. It is an outpost of devoted amateurs and occasional eccentrics seeking focused seclusion.

The region mostly falls solidly into Region I (the coolest viticultural climate) on the UC Davis heat summation scale, with the warmest areas achieving Region II status (on a par with Russian River Valley). This puts it in a class of its own in California, as few other Region I/II areas can satisfactorily ripen Cabernet Sauvignon to the level of intensity seen here. Impeccable canopy exposure and low yields certainly play their role, but long slow ripening with plenty of sunshine hours on favorable east-facing slopes certainly is a major factor. Thus, Santa Cruz is actually a warmer area than it would appear at face value.

The region's greatest and most historic winery is Ridge Vineyards, whose Monte Bello Vineyard, at an elevation of over 2,000 feet, first planted in 1885, was one of the first vineyards to be established here. This hallowed and somewhat inaccessible, though magnificently situated terraced vineyard, produces some of the world's most highly sought after and longest lived Cabernets. The style is always deep, firm, and rich, but focused, with a great clarity of fruit flavors that maturity does not seem to blur. Paul Draper's Zen-like stewardship of this winery since 1969 has seen its reputation, and price, match its celestial elevation of 2,660 feet.

Making world-class wine is a labor of love when done at altitude in the Santa Cruz Mountains and this philosophy is not likely to change, even with the currently inflated prices of top Californian Cabernets. Developing terraced vineyards in remote mountainous regions will always be an expensive proposition and, combined with miserly low yields, will always be a deterrence to all but the most far-sighted of investors. After all, even on the Côte-Rôtie in France it is still more rewarding for some farmers to grow artichokes than Syrah.

Highly Recommended Santa Cruz Mountains Cabernet Sauvignon and Red Meritage

96 • Ridge (CA) 1993 Monte Bello, Cabernet Sauvignon, Santa Cruz Mountains. $55.

95 • Ridge (CA) 1994 Monte Bello, Santa Cruz Mountains. $65.

95 • Kathryn Kennedy (CA) 1994 Cabernet Sauvignon, Santa Cruz Mountains. $75.

94 • Mount Eden (CA) 1993 Old Vine Reserve, Cabernet Sauvignon, Santa Cruz Mountains. $35.

94 • Kathryn Kennedy (CA) 1995 Cabernet Sauvignon, Santa Cruz Mountains. $110.

94 • Cinnabar (CA) 1994 Saratoga Vineyard, Cabernet Sauvignon, Santa Cruz Mountains. $25.

93 • Ridge (CA) 1995 Cabernet Sauvignon, Santa Cruz Mountains. $22.

93 • Cooper-Garrod (CA) 1995 Cabernet Sauvignon, Santa Cruz Mountains. $28.

92 • Ridge (CA) 1995 Monte Bello, Santa Cruz Mountains. $70.

91 • Soquel (CA) 1995 Partner's Reserve, Cabernet Sauvignon, Santa Cruz Mountains. $40.

91 • Soquel (CA) 1994 Partner's Reserve, Cabernet Sauvignon, Santa Cruz Mountains. $40.

91 • Byington (CA) 1994 Twin Mountains, Cabernet Sauvignon, Santa Cruz Mountains. $14.50.

90 • Woodside (CA) 1993 Cabernet Sauvignon, Santa Cruz Mountains. $25.

90 • Thomas Fogarty (CA) 1996 Cabernet Sauvignon, Santa Cruz Mountains. $25.

90 • David Bruce (CA) 1996 La Rusticana d'Orsa, Santa Cruz Mountains. $32.

90 • David Bruce (CA) 1994 Reserve, Cabernet Sauvignon, Santa Cruz Mountains. $20.

90 • Cooper-Garrod (CA) 1994 Cabernet Sauvignon, Santa Cruz Mountains. $25.

90 • Clos La Chance (CA) 1994 Cabernet Sauvignon, Santa Cruz Mountains. $22.

89 • Martin Ray (CA) 1995 Cabernet Sauvignon, Santa Cruz Mountains. $25.

89 • Cooper-Garrod (CA) 1995 Proprietor's Reserve, Cabernet Sauvignon, Santa Cruz Mountains. $35.

89 • Byington (CA) 1993 Bates Ranch, Cabernet Sauvignon, Santa Cruz Mountains. $20.

88 • Mount Eden (CA) 1995 Old Vine Reserve, Cabernet Sauvignon, Santa Cruz Mountains. $39.99.

88 • Mount Eden (CA) 1995 Cabernet Sauvignon, Santa Cruz Mountains. $20.

88 • Bargetto (CA) 1995 Cabernet Sauvignon, Santa Cruz Mountains. $18.

87 • Cinnabar (CA) 1995 Saratoga Vineyard, Cabernet Sauvignon,

Scale: Superlative (96-100), Exceptional (90-95), Highly Recommended (85-89), Recommended (80-84), Not Recommended (Under 80)

Santa Cruz Mountains. $25.

86 • Clos La Chance (CA) 1996 Cabernet Sauvignon, Santa Cruz Mountains. $22.

86 • Clos La Chance (CA) 1995 Cabernet Sauvignon, Santa Cruz Mountains. $21.

86 • Bargetto (CA) 1993 Bates Ranch, Cabernet Sauvignon, Santa Cruz Mountains. $18.

85 • Soquel (CA) 1994 Cabernet Sauvignon, Santa Cruz Mountains. $22.

Monterey

Wines Reviewed: **23**
Median Price: **$18**

Monterey has a considerable ocean breeze influence, giving it a distinctly cool growing climate at its closest point to the ocean in the Salinas Valley. Initial large plantings here during the 1970s in inappropriate locations gave this county a reputation for vegetal wines, as the vineyards exposed to the funneled sea breezes struggled to ripen red varietals. With more appropriate locations and a better understanding of microclimates, this region is now producing Chardonnay of the highest quality. Red wines have not been forgotten, however, just moved to more suitable locations.

First among these might be the Carmel Valley, although the Santa Lucia Highlands, in the form of the Smith & Hook Winery, is also showing promise. Though the Carmel Valley has similarly cool conditions as the rest of Monterey, it also has some very steep slopes that help in the ripening of Cabernet. The resultant wines are obviously cool climate in character, both lighter in body and lower in alcohol than their North Coast cousins are. Additionally, the wines often feature an herbal note that serves to add complexity when kept in check. Improved viticultural practices have now allowed vintners here to ripen red Bordeaux varietals with a certain measure of consistency, and the wines are showing continual improvement. Today, the Carmel Valley is producing Cabernet of outstanding quality, with the added benefit of having a very distinctive personality.

Highly Recommended Monterey Cabernet Sauvignon and Red Meritage

Monterey (General)

87 • Monterra (CA) 1996 Promise, Cabernet Sauvignon, Monterey County. $9.99.

87 • Lockwood (CA) 1994 Partners' Reserve, Cabernet Sauvignon, Monterey. $21.

87 • Jekel (CA) 1995 Sanctuary Estate Meritage, Monterey. $25.

87 • Cloninger (CA) 1994 Cabernet Sauvignon, Monterey. $13.

86 • Chateau Julien (CA) 1995 Private Reserve, Cabernet Sauvignon, Monterey County. $20.

85 • San Saba (CA) 1994 SSV, Cabernet Sauvignon, Monterey. $17.

85 • Mirassou (CA) 1993 Cabernet Sauvignon, Monterey County. $11.95.

Monterey (Carmel Valley)

91 • Bernardus (CA) 1994 Marinus, Carmel Valley. $28.

89 • Cloninger (CA) 1996 Quinn Vineyard, Cabernet Sauvignon, Carmel Valley. $14.

85 • Durney (CA) 1993 Cabernet Sauvignon, Carmel Valley. $20.

Monterey (Santa Lucia Highlands)

90 • Smith & Hook (CA) 1994 Masterpiece Edition, Cabernet Sauvignon, Santa Lucia Highlands. $35.

89 • Smith & Hook (CA) 1995 Cabernet Sauvignon, Santa Lucia Highlands. $18.

87 • Smith & Hook (CA) 1994 Cabernet Sauvignon, Santa Lucia Highlands. $18.

87 • Hahn Estates (CA) 1996 Red Meritage, Santa Lucia Highlands. $15.

86 • Smith & Hook (CA) 1995 Masterpiece Edition, Cabernet Sauvignon, Santa Lucia Highlands. $40.

Paso Robles

Wines Reviewed: **29**
Median Price: **$19**

Paso Robles is a large AVA without much ocean influence, making it a warm climate growing region, albeit with some cooler microclimates located toward the southwestern sector where sea air enters via the Templeton Gap. On the north it is bounded by Monterey County, with San Luis Obispo and Santa Barbara Counties to the south. Daytime temperatures are quite warm through the growing season and a high degree of ripeness is consistently achieved. These are conditions that emphatically make this red wine country, and Cabernet Sauvignon is the most widely planted varietal in the county.

Paso Robles Cabernet tends to be quite rich and ripe with deep berry and chocolate flavors. Occasionally the wines can veer into overripeness with some bottlings showing stewed flavors. As a younger region, Paso Robles is still in many respects finding its way, yet its unique physical attributes should continue to make for large-scaled, rustic leaning Cabernets with a greater sense of refinement in the years to come.

Highly Recommended Paso Robles
Cabernet Sauvignon and Red Meritage

89 • Martin Brothers (Renamed Martin & Weyrich, Spring 1999) (CA) 1995 Etrusco, Cabernet Sauvignon, Paso Robles. $18.

89 • Grey Wolf (CA) 1995 Barton Family Reserve Meritage, Paso Robles. $22.

88 • Justin (CA) 1994 Isosceles, Paso Robles. $32.50.

88 • Dover Canyon (CA) 1996 Ménage, Paso Robles. $28.

88 • Dover Canyon (CA) 1995 Ménage, Paso Robles. $22.

88 • Dark Star (CA) 1996 Cabernet Sauvignon, Paso Robles. $19.

87 • Grey Wolf (CA) 1994 Barton Family Reserve Meritage, Paso Robles. $19.

87 • Dark Star (CA) 1996 Ricordati, Paso Robles. $20.

86 • Pesenti (CA) 1996 Cabernet Sauvignon, Paso Robles. $15.

86 • Eberle (CA) 1996 Cabernet Sauvignon, Paso Robles. $20.

86 • Dover Canyon (CA) 1996 Cabernet Sauvignon, Paso Robles. $18.

86 • Castoro (CA) 1996 Cabernet Sauvignon, Paso Robles. $15.

86 • Carmody McKnight (CA) 1996 Cadenza, Paso Robles. $22.50.

85 • Castoro (CA) 1995 Cabernet Sauvignon, Paso Robles. $11.50.

Washington

Wines Reviewed: **123**
Median Price: **$23**

Washington State is a relative newcomer to the world of fine wines, but it has made as much progress in as little time as any region in the country. Luckily

Scale: Superlative (96-100), Exceptional (90-95), Highly Recommended (85-89), Recommended (80-84), Not Recommended (Under 80)

366

for the industry as a whole, two large wineries, Chateau Ste. Michelle and Columbia, have introduced consumers around the nation to the area's wines. Largely focusing on the production of high-quality wines at reasonable prices, the state's vintners have begun to firmly set their sights on the production of world-class products.

Geographically speaking, Washington is unlike any other viticultural area in the world. With virtually all the vineyards located in the rain shadow of the majestic Cascade Mountains, the area is in reality semi-arid. Only through irrigation with water from the mighty Columbia River and its tributaries can the area produce crops of any sort. Furthermore, virtually the entire Columbia Basin shares the same sand-based soil structure. This allows for something very rare in viticulture these days: vines planted on their own native rootstocks. Apparently, the root louse that causes *Phylloxera* doesn't travel very well in the sandy soils, and though it is endemic in some Washington vineyards, there is little alarm.

Eastern Washington is certainly a land of open skies and the region's volcanoes can be seen for hundreds of miles. This serves to illustrate the vastness of the region, and that region's potential. Of the possible vineyard sites, only a tiny fraction are actually planted. The biggest block to their development might be the brutal nature of the region's winters, which in February 1996 wiped out half of the state's production. Vines, however, are resilient things, and so are the area's vintners, who resumed full production in the 1997 harvest.

The AVA system in Washington is still underdeveloped, with a huge swath of land being entitled to use the Columbia Valley appellation. Smaller viticultural pockets such as the historic Yakima and Walla Walla Valleys should soon be augmented by the creation of new ones such as Canoe Ridge and Red Mountain.

Cabernet has been planted for some time in Washington, and in the last decade the region's winemakers have become quite adept at dealing with the varietal. Perhaps through their experience with Merlot, Washington winemakers have begun to ease up on the extraction of tannins, which so heavily marked bottlings from the mid '80s. Today, led by the boutique producers of the Walla Walla Valley, along with industry giants Chateau Ste. Michelle and Columbia, Washington Cabernet has taken on a new personality. Supple and brimming with character, the wines are still well structured with an emphasis on balanced acidity. Additionally, they tend to be a degree or two lower in alcohol than their California counterparts, making them quite a bit easier at the table. Today the top end of Washington Cabernet stands with California's best, and as production increases with the general level of quality, there is no doubt that Washington will earn a reputation not only in this country but also the world over.

Highly Recommended Washington Cabernet Sauvignon and Red Meritage

Washington/Columbia Valley (General)

99 • Woodward Canyon (WA) 1995 Old Vines, Cabernet Sauvignon, Columbia Valley. $45.

95 • Chateau Ste. Michelle (WA) 1995 Cold Creek Vineyard, Cabernet Sauvignon, Columbia Valley. $27.

94 • L'Ecole No. 41 (WA) 1995 Cabernet Sauvignon, Columbia Valley. $25.

94 • Kestrel (WA) 1995 Cabernet Sauvignon, Columbia Valley. $22.

94 • Chateau Ste. Michelle (WA) 1995 Horse Heaven Vineyard, Cabernet Sauvignon, Columbia Valley. $27.

94 • Chateau Ste. Michelle (WA) 1995 Artist Series Red Meritage, Columbia Valley. $50.

94 • Andrew Will (WA) 1995 Sorella, Washington. $40.

93 • Woodward Canyon (WA) 1995 Artist Series, Canoe Ridge Vineyard, Cabernet Sauvignon, Washington. $28.

93 • Quilceda Creek (WA) 1995 Cabernet Sauvignon, Washington. $45.

93 • Leonetti (WA) 1994 Cabernet Sauvignon, Columbia Valley. $45.

93 • Dunham (WA) 1995 Cabernet Sauvignon, Columbia Valley. $28.

93 • Andrew Will (WA) 1995 Reserve, Cabernet Sauvignon, Washington. $40.

92 • Woodward Canyon (WA) 1994 Captain Z.K. Straight, Cabernet Sauvignon, Columbia Valley. $35.

92 • Waterbrook (WA) 1995 Cabernet Sauvignon, Columbia Valley. $24.

92 • Hogue (WA) 1995 Genesis, Champoux Vineyard, Cabernet Sauvignon, Columbia Valley. $22.99.

92 • Andrew Will (WA) 1996 Sorella, Washington. $38.

91 • Quilceda Creek (WA) 1994 Cabernet Sauvignon, Washington. $42.

91 • Hedges (WA) 1994 Red Mountain Reserve, Columbia Valley. $30.

91 • Chateau Ste. Michelle (WA) 1994 Artist Series Red Meritage, Columbia Valley. $50.

91 • Barnard Griffin (WA) 1996 Cabernet Sauvignon, Columbia Valley. $16.95.

91 • Andrew Will (WA) 1994 Reserve, Cabernet Sauvignon, Washington. $40.

90 • Seven Hills (WA) 1995 Klipsun Vineyard, Cabernet Sauvignon, Columbia Valley. $24.

90 • Powers (WA) 1995 Mercer Ranch Vineyard, Cabernet Sauvignon, Columbia Valley. $18.

90 • Leonetti (WA) 1995 Cabernet Sauvignon, Columbia Valley. $45.

90 • L'Ecole No. 41 (WA) 1996 Cabernet Sauvignon, Columbia Valley. $26.

90 • L'Ecole No. 41 (WA) 1994 Cabernet Sauvignon, Columbia Valley. $24.

90 • Hedges (WA) 1995 Three Vineyards, Columbia Valley. $20.

90 • Chateau Ste. Michelle (WA) 1996 Cabernet Sauvignon, Columbia Valley. $16.

90 • Chateau Ste. Michelle (WA) 1995 Cabernet Sauvignon, Columbia Valley. $16.

90 • Chateau Ste. Michelle (WA) 1994 Ethos Red, Columbia Valley. $31.

90 • Canoe Ridge Vineyard (WA) 1995 Cabernet Sauvignon, Columbia Valley. $22.

90 • Apex (WA) 1994 Cabernet Sauvignon, Columbia Valley. $35.

90 • Andrew Will (WA) 1996 Cabernet Sauvignon, Washington. $32.

90 • Andrew Will (WA) 1994 Cabernet Sauvignon, Washington. $30.

89 • Ste. Chapelle (ID) 1995 Cabernet Sauvignon, Washington. $8.

89 • Staton Hills (WA) 1994 Cabernet Sauvignon, Columbia Valley. $16.

89 • Preston Premium (WA) 1994 Reserve, Cabernet Sauvignon, Columbia Valley. $21.

89 • Hedges (WA) 1995 Red Mountain Reserve, Columbia Valley. $30.

89 • Columbia Crest (WA) 1995 Reserve Red, Columbia Valley. $22.

89 • Columbia Crest (WA) 1994 Reserve Red, Columbia Valley. $20.

89 • Columbia Crest (WA) 1994 Estate Series, Cabernet Sauvignon, Columbia Valley. $17.

89 • Apex (WA) 1995 Cabernet Sauvignon, Columbia Valley. $35.

88 • Woodward Canyon (WA) 1996 Artist Series, Canoe Ridge Vineyard, Cabernet Sauvignon, Columbia Valley. $40.

88 • W.B. Bridgman (WA) 1994 Cabernet Sauvignon, Columbia Valley. $15.

88 • Staton Hills (WA) 1995 Cabernet Sauvignon, Columbia Valley. $15.95.

88 • Seven Hills (WA) 1995 Cabernet Sauvignon, Columbia Valley. $20.

88 • Patrick M. Paul (WA) 1994 Cabernet Sauvignon, Columbia Valley. $12.

88 • Matthews (WA) 1995 Yakima Valley Red, Washington. $28.

88 • Gordon Brothers (WA) 1996 Cabernet Sauvignon, Columbia Valley. $15.49.

88 • Gordon Brothers (WA) 1994 Tradition, Columbia Valley. $19.99.

Scale: Superlative (96-100), Exceptional (90-95), Highly Recommended (85-89), Recommended (80-84), Not Recommended (Under 80)

88 • E.B. Foote (WA) 1994 Cellar Reserve, Cabernet Sauvignon, Columbia Valley. $32.

88 • Columbia Winery (WA) 1994 Sagemoor Vineyard, David Lake Signature Series, Cabernet Sauvignon, Columbia Valley. $23.

88 • Columbia Crest (WA) 1995 Estate Series, Cabernet Sauvignon, Columbia Valley. $21.

88 • Caterina (WA) 1995 Wahluke Slope Vineyard Reserve, Cabernet Sauvignon, Columbia Valley. $32.

87 • W.B. Bridgman (WA) 1995 Cabernet Sauvignon, Columbia Valley. $13.99.

87 • Walla Walla Vintners (WA) 1996 Washington State Red Cuvée, Washington. $18.

87 • Silver Lake (WA) 1995 Reserve, Cabernet Sauvignon, Columbia Valley. $17.99.

87 • Kiona (WA) 1997 Cabernet Sauvignon, Washington. $17.99.

87 • Hogue (WA) 1994 Barrel Select, Cabernet Sauvignon, Columbia Valley. $14.

87 • E.B. Foote (WA) 1995 Cabernet Sauvignon, Columbia Valley. $15.

87 • Caterina (WA) 1995 Cabernet Sauvignon, Columbia Valley. $19.

87 • Barnard Griffin (WA) 1995 Cabernet Sauvignon, Washington. $16.95.

87 • Arbor Crest (WA) 1995 Cameo Reserve, Cabernet Sauvignon, Washington. $13.

86 • Washington Hills (WA) 1995 Cabernet Sauvignon, Columbia Valley. $9.99.

86 • W.B. Bridgman (WA) 1996 Cabernet Sauvignon, Columbia Valley. $14.

86 • Ste. Chapelle (ID) 1995 Sagemoor's Dionysus Vineyard, Cabernet Sauvignon, Washington. $12.99.

86 • Preston Premium (WA) 1995 Reserve, Cabernet Sauvignon, Columbia Valley. $21.

86 • Powers (WA) 1996 Cabernet-Merlot, Washington. $12.

86 • Powers (WA) 1996 Cabernet Sauvignon, Washington. $12.

86 • Paul Thomas (WA) 1995 Reserve, Cabernet Sauvignon, Washington. $14.99.

86 • Kiona (WA) 1996 Cabernet Sauvignon, Washington. $14.99.

86 • Hogue (WA) 1995 Reserve, Cabernet Sauvignon, Columbia Valley. $30.

86 • Covey Run (WA) 1996 Reserve, Cabernet Sauvignon, Columbia Valley. $24.

86 • Covey Run (WA) 1996 Cabernet Sauvignon, Columbia Valley. $12.99.

85 • Seth Ryan (WA) 1996 Jessica's Meritage, Columbia Valley. $32.41.

85 • Covey Run (WA) 1995 Cabernet Sauvignon, Columbia Valley. $12.99.

85 • Chateau Ste. Michelle (WA) 1994 Cabernet Sauvignon, Columbia Valley. $16.

Washington (Yakima Valley)

96 • DeLille (WA) 1996 Chaleur Estate, Yakima Valley. $38.

96 • DeLille (WA) 1994 Chaleur Estate, Yakima Valley. $32.

94 • Matthews (WA) 1996 Elerding Vineyard, Cabernet Sauvignon, Yakima Valley. $35.

94 • DeLille (WA) 1995 Chaleur Estate, Yakima Valley. $34.

93 • Columbia Winery (WA) 1994 Otis Vineyard, David Lake Signature Series, Cabernet Sauvignon, Yakima Valley. $23.

92 • Portteus (WA) 1995 Cabernet Sauvignon, Yakima Valley. $30.

92 • Kiona (WA) 1995 Reserve, Cabernet Sauvignon, Yakima Valley. $29.99.

92 • DeLille (WA) 1994 D2, Yakima Valley. $22.

91 • Columbia Winery (WA) 1994 Red Willow Vineyard, David Lake Signature Series, Cabernet Sauvignon, Yakima Valley. $23.

90 • Portteus (WA) 1994 Reserve, Cabernet Sauvignon, Yakima Valley. $26.

89 • Tefft (WA) 1995 Cabernet Sauvignon, Yakima Valley. $21.99.

89 • Columbia Winery (WA) 1995 Red Willow Vineyard, David Lake Signature Series, Cabernet Sauvignon, Yakima Valley. $29.

88 • Yakima River (WA) 1994 Winemakers Reserve, Cabernet Sauvignon, Yakima Valley. $24.99.

88 • Hyatt (WA) 1995 Reserve, Cabernet Sauvignon, Yakima Valley. $32.

88 • Foris (OR) 1994 Klipsun Vineyard, Cabernet Sauvignon, Yakima Valley. $19.

88 • Covey Run (WA) 1994 Whiskey Canyon Vineyard, Cabernet Sauvignon, Yakima Valley. $28.

88 • Columbia Winery (WA) 1995 Reserve, Cabernet Sauvignon, Yakima Valley. $15.

87 • Yakima River (WA) 1994 Cabernet Sauvignon, Yakima Valley. $15.

87 • Tefft (WA) 1994 Cabernet Sauvignon, Yakima Valley. $25.

87 • Seth Ryan (WA) 1994 Cabernet Sauvignon, Yakima Valley. $25.93.

87 • Hyatt (WA) 1994 Reserve, Cabernet Sauvignon, Yakima Valley. $32.

86 • Wilridge (WA) 1996 Melange, Yakima Valley. $19.

86 • DeLille (WA) 1996 D2, Yakima Valley. $24.

Washington (Walla Walla Valley)

93 • L'Ecole No. 41 (WA) 1995 Apogée, Pepper Bridge Vineyard, Cabernet Sauvignon-Merlot, Walla Walla Valley. $30.

89 • Seven Hills (WA) 1995 Cabernet Sauvignon, Walla Walla Valley. $24.

86 • L'Ecole No. 41 (WA) 1996 Seven Hills Vineyard, Cabernet Sauvignon-Merlot, Walla Walla Valley. $35.

86 • L'Ecole No. 41 (WA) 1995 Windrow Vineyard, Cabernet Sauvignon, Walla Walla Valley. $30.

Virginia

Wines Reviewed: 27
Median Price: $18

Thomas Jefferson's dreams of producing high quality *Vinifera* wines in his home state look to be becoming a reality. Even if his early efforts to establish vineyards around Charlottesville failed due to the intervention of the *Phylloxera* louse, his foresight in choosing suitable locations has been vindicated by the fact that this same area is at the forefront of the viticultural renaissance in the Old Dominion.

The vast majority of all vineyards are now in the service of *Vinifera* varietals such as Chardonnay and Cabernet Sauvignon. The state has six AVAs: Monticello, Northern Neck George Washington Birthplace, Shenandoah Valley, Eastern Shore, North Fork of Roanoke, and Rocky Knob, but the vintners themselves are still learning about the region's qualities, and the area as a whole is probably best dealt with in generalities. The newness of the industry makes it difficult to come to authoritative conclusions about differences in style among the various viticultural areas, however, the hotbed of production at the moment is centered around Charlottesville where the Monticello AVA resides.

To this point Virginia Cabernet has been somewhat variable, with solid efforts standing side by side with those that are still finding their way. Virginia presents a range of problems to the winegrower, not least among them the famous southern humidity, yet research and experience are allowing quality conscious producers to overcome these problems. As the process unfolds, some of the better efforts from producers such as Piedmont and Linden give reason to keep a careful eye on Virginia as an up-and-coming producer of quality Cabernet.

Highly Recommended Virginia Cabernet Sauvignon and Red Meritage

89 • Montdomaine (VA) 1993 Heritage, Virginia. $15.

88 • Linden (VA) 1994 Cabernet Sauvignon, Virginia. $16.

86 • Oakencroft (VA) 1995 Cabernet Sauvignon, Monticello. $14.

86 • Naked Mountain (VA) 1996 Cabernet Sauvignon, Virginia. $15.

86 • Jefferson (VA) 1997 Meritage, Monticello. $28.

86 • Jefferson (VA) 1995 Meritage, Monticello. $26.

Scale: Superlative (96-100), Exceptional (90-95), Highly Recommended (85-89), Recommended (80-84), Not Recommended (Under 80)

86 • Ingleside Plantation (VA) 1994 Special Reserve, Cabernet Sauvignon,
Virginia. $19.99.

86 • Barboursville (VA) 1995 Cabernet Sauvignon, Monticello. $15.

85 • Williamsburg (VA) 1993 Gabriel Archer Reserve, Virginia. $21.

85 • Montdomaine (VA) 1993 Cabernet Sauvignon, Virginia. $13.50.

85 • Jefferson (VA) 1995 Cabernet Sauvignon, Monticello. $18.

Long Island, New York
Wines Reviewed: **30**
Median Price: **$20.25**

When speaking about New York Cabernet, one is almost exclusively talking
about wines from Long Island. As an appellation, Long Island extends nearly
120 miles out into the Atlantic Ocean from New York City. Only 15 miles or so
wide, the island is split into two long fingers divided by the Peconic Bay near the
town of Riverhead, 70 miles from the East River. Known as the North and South
Forks, this end of the island is where viticulture has taken hold. The South Fork
is synonymous to many with the Hamptons, New York's answer to Malibu, and
the area is home to a few vineyards. The majority, however, are in the more rural
and pastoral North Fork, which at only five miles wide and 35 miles long is all
but surrounded by water.

At present there are about 20 wineries in the area, all but two of which are relatively small. It is still a very young industry with the earliest wineries dating from
the 1970s, but expansion has been swift as the area has a laundry list of natural
attributes. While the more established upstate New York viticultural areas have a
more extreme climate that favors white *Vinifera* varietals, Long Island has the
ability to ripen red varieties such as Cabernet and Merlot. The warmer climate
is a function of the more southerly latitude, the fact that the vineyards are nearly surrounded by the moderating influence of the Atlantic, and that they are
shielded from extreme freezes by warm moist winds that blow in from the
Carolinas in the fall and winter. Additionally, there is the enviable position of
being a stone's throw from one of the largest markets for fine wines in the world,
New York City.

As for Long Island Cabernet, many of the wines bear a resemblance to Bordeaux
or Washington, in that they feature more restrained levels of alcohol and higher acidity levels than their California counterparts. In many ways, today's wines
remind one of similar efforts from Washington ten or even 15 years ago. It may
just be that the area's winemakers are a bit behind in the winemaking curve that
California and Washington vintners have set, and Long Island will claim its place
in the upper echelon in the near future. As was the case with Washington (and
Oregon's Pinot Noir) in the 1980s, the potential is certainly there.

Highly Recommended Long Island
Cabernet Sauvignon and Red Meritage

90 • Ternhaven (NY) 1995 Claret d'Alvah, North Fork of Long Island. $18.99.

90 • Ternhaven (NY) 1995 Cabernet Sauvignon, North Fork of Long Island. $15.99.

90 • Paumanok (NY) 1995 Grand Vintage, Cabernet Sauvignon,
North Fork of Long Island. $25.

90 • Paumanok (NY) 1995 Assemblage, North Fork of Long Island. $24.

90 • Lenz (NY) 1995 Estate, Cabernet Sauvignon, North Fork of Long Island. $24.99.

90 • Gristina (NY) 1993 Andy's Field Red, North Fork of Long Island. $27.99.

89 • Ternhaven (NY) 1994 Claret d'Alvah, North Fork of Long Island. $18.99.

89 • Pindar (NY) 1995 Reserve, Cabernet Sauvignon, North Fork of Long Island. $18.99.

89 • Osprey's Dominion (NY) 1995 Cabernet Sauvignon, North Fork of Long Island. $13.99.

89 • Gristina (NY) 1996 Cabernet Sauvignon, North Fork of Long Island. $15.99.

89 • Bedell (NY) 1995 Cupola, North Fork of Long Island. $27.50.

88 • Ternhaven (NY) 1994 Cabernet Sauvignon, North Fork of Long Island. $17.99.

88 • Pindar (NY) 1995 Mythology, North Fork of Long Island. $36.99.

88 • Pindar (NY) 1994 Mythology, North Fork of Long Island. $24.99.

88 • Pindar (NY) 1993 Mythology, North Fork of Long Island. $24.99.

88 • Pellegrini (NY) 1995 Cabernet Sauvignon, North Fork of Long Island. $15.99.

88 • Laurel Lake (NY) 1995 Cabernet Sauvignon, North Fork of Long Island. $23.99.

88 • Bedell (NY) 1994 Cupola, North Fork of Long Island. $25.

86 • Pindar (NY) 1993 Reserve, Cabernet Sauvignon, North Fork of Long Island. $18.99.

86 • Lenz (NY) 1997 Vineyard Selection, Merlot-Cabernet, North Fork of Long Island. $16.99.

85 • Ternhaven (NY) 1996 Claret d'Alvah, North Fork of Long Island. $17.99.

85 • Pindar (NY) 1994 Cabernet Sauvignon, North Fork of Long Island. $18.99.

85 • Bidwell (NY) 1995 Claret, North Fork of Long Island. $34.99.

85 • Bedell (NY) 1995 Cabernet Sauvignon, North Fork of Long Island. $21.50.

Scale: Superlative (96-100), Exceptional (90-95), Highly Recommended (85-89), Recommended (80-84), Not Recommended (Under 80)

372

Top Wines

99 • Woodward Canyon (WA) 1995 Old Vines, Cabernet Sauvignon, Columbia Valley. $45.

99 • Opus One (CA) 1995 Oakville, Napa Valley Red. $100.

98 • Pride Mountain (CA) 1996 Cabernet Sauvignon, Napa Valley. $29.99.

98 • Jarvis (CA) 1994 Cabernet Sauvignon, Napa Valley. $58.

97 • Stag's Leap Wine Cellars (CA) 1995 Cask 23, Napa Valley. $120.

97 • Pine Ridge (CA) 1996 Cabernet Sauvignon, Howell Mountain, Napa Valley. $40.

97 • Opus One (CA) 1992 Oakville, Napa Valley Red. $65.

97 • Jarvis (CA) 1993 Reserve, Cabernet Sauvignon, Napa Valley. $75.

97 • Beringer (CA) 1994 Private Reserve, Cabernet Sauvignon, Napa Valley. $75.

96 • Stag's Leap Wine Cellars (CA) 1994 Cask 23, Cabernet Sauvignon, Napa Valley. $100.

96 • St. Francis (CA) 1994 Reserve, Cabernet Sauvignon, Sonoma Valley. $30.

96 • Ridge (CA) 1993 Monte Bello, Cabernet Sauvignon, Santa Cruz Mountains. $55.

96 • Opus One (CA) 1993 Oakville, Napa Valley Red. $85.

96 • Merryvale (CA) 1994 Profile, Napa Valley. $55.

96 • La Jota (CA) 1996 15th Anniversary, Cabernet Sauvignon, Howell Mountain, Napa Valley. $58.

96 • DeLille (WA) 1996 Chaleur Estate, Yakima Valley. $38.

96 • DeLille (WA) 1994 Chaleur Estate, Yakima Valley. $32.

95 • Shafer (CA) 1994 Hillside Select, Cabernet Sauvignon, Stags Leap District, Napa Valley. $85.

95 • S. Anderson (CA) 1994 Richard Chambers Vineyard, Cabernet Sauvignon, Stags Leap District. $54.

95 • Ridge (CA) 1994 Monte Bello, Santa Cruz Mountains. $65.

95 • Pine Ridge (CA) 1996 Cabernet Sauvignon, Stags Leap District, Napa Valley. $40.

95 • Peju Province (CA) 1995 Estate Bottled, Cabernet Sauvignon, Napa Valley. $55.

95 • Mount Veeder Winery (CA) 1993 Reserve, Napa Valley. $40.

95 • Lokoya (CA) 1995 Cabernet Sauvignon, Rutherford, Napa Valley. $100.

95 • Kathryn Kennedy (CA) 1994 Cabernet Sauvignon, Santa Cruz Mountains. $75.

95 • Fisher (CA) 1994 Lamb Vineyard, Cabernet Sauvignon, Napa Valley. $50.

95 • Dominus (CA) 1995 Napanook Vineyard, Cabernet Sauvignon, Napa Valley. $95.

95 • Dominus (CA) 1994 Napanook Vineyard, Napa Valley. $75.

95 • Chateau Ste. Michelle (WA) 1995 Cold Creek Vineyard, Cabernet Sauvignon, Columbia Valley. $27.

95 • Caymus (CA) 1994 Special Selection, Cabernet Sauvignon, Napa Valley. $110.

ten

North American Merlot

An Introduction: North American Merlot

Merlot is becoming a big business. In a very short period of time Cabernet's second sister has been introduced to the consuming public on a grand scale, and they like what they have seen so far. Easier to pronounce, made for earlier drinking, and softer than Cabernet Sauvignon, Merlot is quickly becoming the nation's red wine of choice. The news media has talked about the promise of Viognier and continues to trot out and dust off the "Rhône Rangers" as the perennial next big thing, but Merlot has quietly and systematically begun to break the tyranny of Cabernet. Someone hit the ignition switch a couple years back and no one seems to have noticed, except the buying public.

While all this may sound rosy, it poses certain problems when trying to assess the varietal on a regional basis. Quite frankly, with so many new Merlot vineyards coming on line, and the temptation for vintners to stretch yields to meet the seemingly insatiable demand, there is a certain sameness to much of the Merlot currently on the market. Until a vineyard reaches a certain age (purists would argue ten years or so at the least), it is hard to get a picture of what type of quality one might ultimately expect. Additionally, huge swaths of California's Central Valley and other areas that one generally wouldn't associate with Bordeaux varietals are being planted with the grape, largely to make wine to compete in the fighting varietal market.

Merlot has been produced for some time, however, in the cradle of California viticulture, Napa and Sonoma. It is here that, unsurprisingly, the best California Merlots are to be found, and correspondingly, some of the most suitable growing conditions. California, however, is not the entire story. For the last several years, Washington State has produced Merlots that stand with the best in the country, and in great years such as 1992 and 1994 has produced the *best* Merlots in the country. If you like Merlot and you haven't tried Washington's version, it's time for a quick trip to your favorite retailer. Often described as two-thirds Bordeaux, one-third California, Washington Merlot is supple and accessible, yet well structured and possessed of sound acidity with more subtle alcohol levels than many California wines. This makes them particularly successful with food while not overpowering when being consumed without. Finally, New York's Long Island has been working with Merlot for a decade or more and some early signs have been promising.

In the most general terms, Merlot of world-class quality is being produced in only a handful of areas such as these. Even the fickle Pinot Noir, despite what are theoretically far-greater growing restrictions, is planted in a wider range of locations. Much of this is probably due to the newness of many plantings, but with its rise in popularity, the varietal will certainly be planted in many more areas, some successfully and others not. For now, however, the consumer looking for the best Merlots in the nation should look to the wines from Napa, Sonoma, and Washington. Fortunately, as the benchmarks, these regions also have developed styles that are separate and distinct.

Scale: Superlative (96-100), Exceptional (90-95), Highly Recommended (85-89), Recommended (80-84), Not Recommended (Under 80)

376

Best U.S. Merlot Producers

Premier U.S. Merlot Producers (***)

- S. Anderson (Reserve)
- Arrowood
- Beringer (Bancroft Ranch)
- Chateau St. Jean (Reserve)
- Chateau Ste. Michelle
- Flora Springs (Windfall Vineyard)
- L'Ecole No. 41
- Leonetti
- Matanzas Creek
- Pahlmeyer
- Pine Ridge (Carneros)
- Plam
- Rutherford Hill (Reserve)
- Silverado
- St. Francis (Reserve)
- Stag's Leap Wine Cellars
- Waterbrook
- Whitehall Lane (Leonardini Reserve)
- Andrew Will
- Woodward Canyon

Great U.S. Merlot Producers (**)

- Apex
- Barnard Griffin
- Benziger
- Davis Bynum
- Cafaro
- Canoe Ridge Vineyard
- Chateau St. Jean (Sonoma County)
- Clos du Val
- Clos Pegase
- Columbia Crest
- Columbia Winery
- Cosentino
- Cuvaison
- Duckhorn
- Fisher
- Franciscan
- Gary Farrell
- Hyatt
- Lambert Bridge
- Lockwood
- MacRostie
- Newton
- Oakville Ranch
- Robert Pecota (Steven Andre Vineyard)
- Joseph Phelps

Merlot at a Glance

Wines Reviewed:

383

Producers/Brands Represented:

240

Median Price:

$20

- Philippe-Lorraine
- Pine Ridge (Crimson Creek)
- Portteus
- Preston Premium
- Rancho Sisquoc
- Rodney Strong
- Rosenblum
- Seven Hills
- Shafer
- St. Francis (Sonoma County)
- Swanson
- Ternhaven
- Whitehall Lane (Napa Valley)
- Wildhurst

Dependable U.S. Merlot Producers (Recommended)

Some producers placed in this third tier are new (or new to us) and may merit a higher placement in subsequent vintages. These producers are offset by an asterisk.

- *Antares
- Bargetto
- Bedell
- *Byington
- Caterina
- *Chappellet
- Cinnabar
- Covey Run
- Crichton Hall
- Estancia
- Farella-Park
- Ferrari-Carano
- *Fetzer (Bonterra)
- *Gainey
- Gallo-Sonoma
- Geyser Peak
- Gordon Brothers
- Havens
- Hogue
- *Jarvis
- Jekel
- Chateau Julien
- *Justin
- Kendall-Jackson
- Kenwood
- Kiona
- Kunde
- J. Lohr
- Lolonis

- *Macari
- Markham
- Merryvale
- Robert Mondavi
- *Monticello
- *Neyers
- *Niebaum Coppola
- Palmer
- *Fess Parker
- *Peju
- *Powers
- *Ravenswood
- Rombauer
- *Charles Shaw
- Robert Sinskey
- Chateau Souverain
- St. Clement
- Stags' Leap Winery
- Sterling
- Stonestreet
- *Tefft
- Voss
- *Wellington
- Wild Horse
- Windsor
- Yakima River

Scale: Superlative (96-100), Exceptional (90-95), Highly Recommended (85-89), Recommended (80-84), Not Recommended (Under 80)

Five Key Regions for American Merlot

Washington
Wines Reviewed: **99**
Median Price: **$21.50**

"Washington State is making world-class Merlot." So says Chateau Ste. Michelle winemaker Mike Januik, and his sentiments are being echoed not only by neighboring winemakers but by many in the news media as well. Since the 1992 vintage, the finest Washington Merlots have been competitive with the best in the country and in outstanding vintages such as 1994 they can be *the* best. How have Washington Merlots become this good?

Good vintages have surely helped, but the revolution has been fermenting for some time. Quite simply, the vineyards of eastern Washington are worlds apart from the established coastal appellations of California and Oregon. Separated from the ocean by two mountain ranges, including the towering Cascades, rainfall is sparse. Averaging six to ten inches a year, the landscape is semi-desert, with the mighty Columbia River providing the lifeblood, as with much agriculture in the West, water for irrigation. Precisely regulated drip irrigation serves for most producers, meaning water at regular intervals, in the right quantities, and at the right times. The arid climate also makes for long, hot, and sunny summer days with correspondingly cool night temperatures. This allows even and reliably ripened grapes in most years with a remarkably high level of acidity given the ripeness achieved.

Are there other factors, perhaps something even more obvious? "Yes," responds Januik, "Most of Washington's vineyards are planted on their own rootstocks, not grafted native rootstocks which are almost universally used elsewhere in the hopes of thwarting *Phylloxera*." This element further distinguishes the area from those to the south, and has long been rumored a great benefit for those lucky enough to possess such vineyards. The potential benefits also outweigh the risks, in that Washington's vineyards are not as densely packed as those in California, and the *Phylloxera* louse has difficulty navigating through Washington's largely sandy soils.

The 1992 vintage proved to be a turning point for high-end wines from this part of the world, but wineries such as Ste. Michelle, Columbia, and Hogue have been turning out high-quality wines that have flown off retailers' shelves for some time. It is probable that this initial commitment to quality *and* value, which generated a large and profitable industry, has come full circle and allowed the proliferating boutique wineries such as Leonetti, Waterbrook, and L'Ecole No. 41 to move right into a market that has already been cut out for the state's wines. They now reside on the shelves alongside their large-scaled neighbors who are increasingly setting their sights on making world-class wines; and, at the moment, Merlot is driving the bus.

The AVA system in Washington is still underdeveloped, with a huge swath of land entitled to use the Columbia Valley appellation, however, there are more precise areas that have shown some distinctive characteristics. As mentioned before, Washington Merlot is often thought of as being one-part California and two-parts Bordeaux, with the same lushness, yet firmer acidity than California versions, being a hallmark. Generally speaking, Yakima Valley Merlots tend to be a bit more structured than those from other areas, with a tendency to tougher tannins. This may be due in part to the tastes of the area's winemakers, but is a feature of the wines nonetheless. A subregion in the area, Red Mountain, shows wines that are even deeper, with high levels of extract, as exemplified by Kiona and Hedges.

On the opposite end of the scale is Walla Walla, with its string of boutique wineries. Lush and endearing with a heavy reliance on oak seasoning, the Merlots of Leonetti, Waterbrook, L'Ecole No. 41, Patrick M. Paul, and the like are highly coveted and eminently accessible. It must be noted that this also has much to do with winemaking, as many of these wineries' bottlings utilize grapes grown outside the vastly underdeveloped Walla Walla Valley.

Finally, further west down the Columbia River lies the micro-appellation of Canoe Ridge, a 1,000-foot hill rising from the riverbanks and looking out over the barren scrubland on the Oregon side. Named by the explorers Lewis and Clark during their famous 19th century expedition through the area, the hill resembles an overturned canoe. It is jointly owned, in its entirety, by Chateau Ste. Michelle, and the Canoe Ridge Winery, a member of the prestigious Chalone family of wineries. Planted only in the late '80s, it would be an understatement to say that the initial releases have shown promise. They are already some of the best Merlots in the state *and* the country. Lying somewhere between Yakima and Walla Walla in style, Canoe Ridge shows attractive fruit, while being relatively elegant and restrained. The wines are also blessedly devoid of harsh tannins.

The scary part of all this good news is that this is a young industry that is still feeling its way. The wines are going to get even better at the top end. More important, industry leaders such as Ste Michelle and Columbia have undergone aggressive and exhaustive research programs in conjunction with Washington universities. This has allowed them to answer many questions about the regional peculiarities of grape growing in Washington itself, as opposed to relying on information from the University of California at Davis, which is more often than not designed for the California industry. What they have learned is being shared with the state's other growers and promises a shoring up of quality from top to bottom. At the moment there is a high level of cooperation between vintners, as the market for Washington wines has so far seemed unlimited, and that bodes very well for the industry in the near future. In short, with regards Merlot, Washington is at present the most exciting spot in the country.

Highly Recommended Washington Merlot

96 • Chateau Ste. Michelle (WA) 1994 Chateau Reserve, Merlot, Columbia Valley. $40.

96 • Andrew Will (WA) 1995 Reserve, Merlot, Washington. $32.

95 • Woodward Canyon (WA) 1995 Merlot, Columbia Valley. $30.

93 • Waterbrook (WA) 1994 Merlot, Columbia Valley. $19.99.

93 • Seven Hills (WA) 1995 Klipsun Vineyard, Merlot, Columbia Valley. $24.

92 • Waterbrook (WA) 1995 Reserve, Merlot, Columbia Valley. $32.

92 • Tefft (WA) 1994 Winemakers Reserve, Merlot, Yakima Valley. $25.

92 • L'Ecole No. 41 (WA) 1995 Merlot, Columbia Valley. $24.

92 • L'Ecole No. 41 (WA) 1994 Merlot, Columbia Valley. $22.

92 • Chateau Ste. Michelle (WA) 1995 Chateau Reserve, Merlot, Columbia Valley. $42.

92 • Chateau Ste. Michelle (WA) 1994 Cold Creek Vineyard, Merlot, Columbia Valley. $28.

92 • Barnard Griffin (WA) 1994 Reserve, Merlot, Columbia Valley. $24.

92 • Apex (WA) 1995 Merlot, Columbia Valley. $40.

92 • Apex (WA) 1994 Merlot, Columbia Valley. $28.99.

92 • Andrew Will (WA) 1997 Ciel du Cheval, Merlot, Washington. $30.

91 • Woodward Canyon (WA) 1994 Merlot, Columbia Valley. $28.

91 • Portteus (WA) 1995 Reserve, Merlot, Yakima Valley. $29.

91 • Andrew Will (WA) 1997 Pepper Bridge, Merlot, Washington. $30.

91 • Andrew Will (WA) 1994 Reserve, Merlot, Washington. $28.

90 • Yakima River (WA) 1994 Winemaker's Reserve, Merlot, Yakima Valley. $28.

90 • Woodward Canyon (WA) 1997 Merlot, Columbia Valley. $30.

90 • St. Clement (WA) 1995 Merlot, Columbia Valley. $22.

90 • Seven Hills (WA) 1995 Seven Hills Vineyard, Merlot, Walla Walla Valley. $24.

90 • Seven Hills (WA) 1994 Seven Hills Vineyard, Merlot, Walla Walla Valley. $24.

90 • Preston Premium (WA) 1994 Reserve, Merlot, Columbia Valley. $21.

90 • Portteus (WA) 1995 Merlot, Yakima Valley. $16.

90 • Patrick M. Paul (WA) 1993 Conner Lee Vineyards, Merlot, Columbia Valley. $12.

90 • Hyatt (WA) 1994 Reserve, Merlot, Yakima Valley. $29.99.

90 • Columbia Winery (WA) 1995 Red Willow Vineyard, David Lake Signature Series, Merlot, Columbia Valley. $23.

90 • Columbia Winery (WA) 1994 Red Willow Vineyard, David Lake Signature Series, Merlot, Yakima Valley. $23.

90 • Columbia Crest (WA) 1995 Estate Series, Merlot, Columbia Valley. $22.

90 • Chateau Ste. Michelle (WA) 1995 Canoe Ridge Estate Vineyard, Merlot, Columbia Valley. $31.

90 • Chateau Ste. Michelle (WA) 1994 Indian Wells Vineyard, Merlot, Columbia Valley. $30.

90 • Canoe Ridge Vineyard (WA) 1994 Merlot, Columbia Valley. $18.

90 • Barnard Griffin (WA) 1995 Reserve, Merlot, Columbia Valley. $26.95.

90 • Andrew Will (WA) 1997 Seven Hills, Merlot, Walla Walla Valley. $30.

90 • Andrew Will (WA) 1997 Klipsun, Merlot, Washington. $30.

90 • Andrew Will (WA) 1996 Klipsun, Merlot, Washington. $28.

90 • Andrew Will (WA) 1995 Merlot, Washington. $28.

90 • Andrew Will (WA) 1994 Merlot, Washington. $25.

89 • Yakima River (WA) 1994 Merlot, Yakima Valley. $15.

89 • Preston Premium (WA) 1993 Reserve, Merlot, Columbia Valley. $18.99.

89 • Portteus (WA) 1994 Merlot, Yakima Valley. $16.

89 • Columbia Crest (WA) 1996 Merlot, Columbia Valley. $16.

89 • Caterina (WA) 1994 Merlot, Columbia Valley. $16.

89 • Canoe Ridge Vineyard (WA) 1995 Merlot, Columbia Valley. $18.

89 • Barnard Griffin (WA) 1997 Ciel du Cheval Vineyard, Merlot, Columbia Valley. $39.

88 • L'Ecole No. 41 (WA) 1996 Merlot, Columbia Valley. $25.

88 • Hyatt (WA) 1994 Merlot, Yakima Valley. $14.99.

88 • Covey Run (WA) 1994 Reserve, Merlot, Yakima Valley. $23.

88 • Columbia Winery (WA) 1994 Merlot, Columbia Valley. $14.

88 • Columbia Crest (WA) 1994 Estate Series, Merlot, Columbia Valley. $19.

88 • Chateau Ste. Michelle (WA) 1996 Merlot, Columbia Valley. $18.

88 • Chateau Ste. Michelle (WA) 1995 Horse Heaven Vineyard, Merlot, Columbia Valley. $31.

88 • Caterina (WA) 1996 Merlot, Columbia Valley. $18.

88 • Canoe Ridge Vineyard (WA) 1996 Merlot, Columbia Valley. $19.

87 • Wilridge (WA) 1994 Crawford Vineyard, Merlot, Columbia Valley. $19.

87 • Tefft (WA) NV Merlot, Columbia Valley. $15.

87 • Preston Premium (WA) 1995 Western White Oak, Merlot, Columbia Valley. $16.

87 • Powers (WA) 1995 Merlot, Columbia Valley. $16.

87 • Hogue (WA) 1994 Genesis, Merlot, Columbia Valley. $23.

87 • Gordon Brothers (WA) 1994 Merlot, Columbia Valley. $16.99.

87 • Chateau Ste. Michelle (WA) 1994 Merlot, Columbia Valley. $17.

87 • Barnard Griffin (WA) 1995 Merlot, Washington. $16.95.

87 • Apex (WA) 1996 Merlot, Columbia Valley. $35.

86 • Waterbrook (WA) 1996 Merlot, Columbia Valley. $22.

86 • Seven Hills (WA) 1995 Merlot, Columbia Valley. $20.

86 • Hogue (WA) 1994 Merlot, Columbia Valley. $15.

86 • Columbia Winery (WA) 1996 Red Willow Vineyard, David Lake Signature Series, Milestone Merlot, Yakima Valley. $24.

86 • Andrew Will (WA) 1996 Merlot, Washington. $26.

85 • Wilridge (WA) 1994 Klipsun Vineyards, Merlot, Columbia Valley. $19.

85 • W.B. Bridgman (WA) 1995 Merlot, Columbia Valley. $14.99.

85 • Seven Hills (WA) 1994 Merlot, Columbia Valley. $20.

85 • Preston Premium (WA) 1994 Preston Vineyard, Merlot, Columbia Valley. $10.

85 • Covey Run (WA) 1995 Reserve, Merlot, Yakima Valley. $23.

85 • Chateau Ste. Michelle (WA) 1995 Indian Wells Vineyard, Merlot, Columbia Valley. $31.

Napa Valley

Wines Reviewed: 81
Median Price: $26

In the Napa Valley Cabernet is king. So runs the conventional wisdom anyway, but the reality is much more complicated. When speaking of the Napa Valley for appellation purposes, one is talking about a very diverse region capable of producing a wide range of varietals. From the downright chilly southern end of the valley to the semi-tropical northern end, from the heights of the mountains to the fog-banked valley floor, the Napa Valley is capable of growing almost anything.

Cabernet, however, is what brought the valley into the international limelight some 20 years ago. Though grown successfully in a number of spots, many of the premier Cabernets come from a small area in the center of the valley known as the Rutherford Bench. This is important when thinking about the less-established Merlot varietal. Though introduced as a stand-alone by Sterling nearly 30 years ago, the grape until quite recently was used, as in Bordeaux, as a blending component to soften Cabernet, or as a more significant component of a Meritage-style blend.

With the explosion of popularity Merlot has enjoyed, Napa's vintners have rapidly reassessed the varietal. In Bordeaux, Merlot generally prefers slightly cooler conditions than Cabernet, and if one applies this lesson to the Napa Valley and follows the cooler temperature gradients south from the Rutherford Bench, you just might land smack in the middle of the Stags Leap District. By coincidence, or maybe it is not a coincidence at all, this is the home to what seems to be some of the more promising Merlot vineyards in the valley, with a disproportionate level of representation on the list of key producers.

S. Anderson, Silverado, Shafer, Stag's Leap Wine Cellars, Clos du Val: the names are a veritable who's who of great Merlot producers.

Wine lovers have known for some time that Stags Leap is a special area, as evidenced since the early '70s by the wines of Warren Winiarski at Stag's Leap Wine Cellars. It is cooler than areas to the north, as the ocean winds that move up from San Pablo Bay act as an air conditioner and moderate the heat of the afternoon, which builds up on the bare rocks of the eastern mountains. Those rocks also feature in the very different soil composition of the area. Over 95% of the soil is derived from volcanic rocks, which makes for a gravelly, well-drained, and less fertile environment than the Rutherford Bench. These factors combine to draw out the ripening process, affording a longer growing season and the possibility of greater physiological maturity than other regions of the valley floor.

This translates into a particularly flavorful and supple style of Merlot, often marked by subtle minty overtones. The prowess of the region's winemakers and the scarcity of poor vintages also make for consistent wines, which still manage to reflect the subtle differences from one growing season to the next. Saying that Stags Leap may be positioning itself as the Rutherford Bench of Merlot, however, is not to exclude many excellent Merlots from other parts of the valley, just as exceptional Cabernet is made in a range of areas within the overall appellation.

A primary example might be Howell Mountain. Since its recent introduction, Beringer's Bancroft Ranch bottling has generated a great deal of consumer and critical interest. Big, firm, ripe, deep, and rich, the adjectives pour forth, and belie the wine's mountain origins. Merlot, however, throws a new dimension into the traditional Howell Mountain equation: aging potential with earlier approachability. While the monumental Cabernets from Napa mountain producers such as Dunn, Diamond Creek, or Pahlmeyer are usually well balanced and age quite well, they are rarely if ever accessible in their youths. Indeed, a debate has raged for some time about how to soften the mountain fruit or whether one would want to at all, as fans of the style think the proposal to be sacrilege.

Beringer's Bancroft Ranch may portend an interesting compromise: full throttle depth and intensity indicative of mountain fruit, with the tannins naturally softened by a less tannic varietal. This could well lead to a growing sub-genre of Napa Merlot, just as with Cabernet, utilizing the region's distinctive mountain fruit. The results, however, might be even more spectacular, as the varietal may prove itself easier to keep in balance than Cabernet. Napa's various mountain vineyards, including examples in the western range exemplified by Newton and Hess, just might be where some of the most significant developments in Napa Merlot could be seen in the near future.

Highly Recommended Napa Valley Merlot

94 • S. Anderson (CA) 1996 Reserve, Merlot, Stags Leap District. $40.

94 • Silverado (CA) 1995 Merlot, Napa Valley. $22.50.

94 • Rutherford Hill (CA) 1996 Reserve, Merlot, Napa Valley. $44.

93 • Whitehall Lane (CA) 1995 Leonardini Vineyard Reserve, Merlot, Napa Valley. $36.

93 • Plam (CA) 1995 Vintner's Reserve, Merlot, Napa Valley. $25.

93 • Flora Springs (CA) 1995 Windfall Vineyard, Merlot, Napa Valley. $32.

92 • Whitehall Lane (CA) 1996 Leonardini Vineyard Reserve, Merlot, Napa Valley. $40.

92 • Niebaum-Coppola (CA) 1995 Francis Coppola Family Wines, Merlot, Napa Valley. $32.

92 • Flora Springs (CA) 1996 Windfall Vineyard, Merlot, Napa Valley. $40.

92 • Cosentino (CA) 1996 Reserve, Merlot, Napa Valley. $34.

92 • Beringer (CA) 1994 Bancroft Ranch, Merlot, Howell Mountain. $45.

91 • Swanson (CA) 1995 Merlot, Napa Valley. $24.

91 • Philippe-Lorraine (CA) 1996 Merlot, Napa Valley. $21.

91 • Neyers (CA) 1996 Merlot, Napa Valley. $28.

90 • Rutherford Hill (CA) 1995 Reserve, Merlot, Napa Valley. $40.

90 • Peju Province (CA) 1995 Merlot, Napa Valley. $35.

90 • Oakville Ranch (CA) 1995 Merlot, Napa Valley. $35.

90 • Monticello (CA) 1994 Corley Reserve, Merlot, Napa Valley. $28.

90 • Merryvale (CA) 1995 Reserve, Merlot, Napa Valley. $32.

90 • Le Ducq (CA) 1994 Sylviane, Merlot, Napa Valley. $30.

90 • Joseph Phelps (CA) 1995 Merlot, Napa Valley. $26.

90 • Duckhorn (CA) 1995 Merlot, Napa Valley. $28.

90 • Duckhorn (CA) 1993 Merlot, Howell Mountain, Napa Valley. $30.

90 • Cosentino (CA) 1996 Merlot, Oakville, Napa Valley. $60.

90 • Beringer (CA) 1995 Bancroft Ranch, Merlot, Howell Mountain. $50.

89 • Voss (CA) 1995 Merlot, Napa Valley. $20.

89 • S. Anderson (CA) 1995 Reserve, Merlot, Stags Leap District. $32.

89 • Shafer (CA) 1996 Merlot, Napa Valley. $32.

89 • Shafer (CA) 1995 Merlot, Napa Valley. $28.

89 • Robert Keenan (CA) 1996 Merlot, Napa Valley. $30.

89 • Pine Ridge (CA) 1996 Crimson Creek, Merlot, Napa Valley. $25.

89 • Niebaum-Coppola (CA) 1996 Merlot, Napa Valley. $32.

89 • Markham (CA) 1995 Reserve, Merlot, Napa Valley. $38.

89 • Joseph Phelps (CA) 1996 Merlot, Napa Valley. $30.

89 • Fisher (CA) 1996 RCF Vineyard, Merlot, Napa Valley. $30.

89 • Charles Krug (CA) 1994 Reserve, Merlot, Napa Valley. $21.50.

89 • Chappellet (CA) 1996 Merlot, Napa Valley. $22.

89 • Audubon (CA) 1996 Hopper Creek Vineyard, Merlot, Napa Valley. $20.

88 • Whitehall Lane (CA) 1996 Merlot, Napa Valley. $22.

88 • Whitehall Lane (CA) 1995 Merlot, Napa Valley. $20.

88 • Stag's Leap Wine Cellars (CA) 1994 Merlot, Napa Valley. $26.

88 • Markham (CA) 1995 Merlot, Napa Valley. $18.

88 • Farella-Park (CA) 1995 Merlot, Napa Valley. $24.

88 • Duckhorn (CA) 1996 Merlot, Napa Valley. $32.

88 • Cakebread (CA) 1995 Merlot, Napa Valley. $28.50.

88 • Cafaro (CA) 1995 Merlot, Napa Valley. $30.

87 • Stags' Leap Winery (CA) 1995 Merlot, Napa Valley. $28.

87 • St. Clement (CA) 1994 Merlot, Napa Valley. $24.

87 • Robert Pecota (CA) 1995 Steven Andre Vineyard, Napa Valley. $25.

87 • Robert Mondavi (CA) 1995 Merlot, Napa Valley. $26.

87 • Newton (CA) 1996 Merlot, Napa Valley. $32.

87 • Flora Springs (CA) 1995 Merlot, Napa Valley. $16.

86 • Sterling (CA) 1995 Merlot, Napa Valley. $14.

86 • Robert Pecota (CA) 1996 Steven Andre Vineyard, Merlot, Napa Valley. $29.

86 • Robert Mondavi (CA) 1996 Merlot, Napa Valley. $26.

86 • Merryvale (CA) 1996 Reserve, Merlot, Napa Valley. $32.

86 • Markham (CA) 1996 Merlot, Napa Valley. $19.

Scale: Superlative (96-100), Exceptional (90-95), Highly Recommended (85-89), Recommended (80-84), Not Recommended (Under 80)

86 • Le Ducq (CA) 1995 Sylviane, Merlot, Napa Valley. $30.
86 • Jarvis (CA) 1996 Merlot, Napa Valley. $46.
86 • Crichton Hall (CA) 1996 Merlot, Napa Valley. $26.
85 • Beaulieu (CA) 1994 Merlot, Napa Valley. $12.99.

Sonoma County Merlot
Wines Reviewed: **43**
Median Price: **$20**

As mentioned earlier, trying to pin down a "Sonoma County style" for Merlot is virtually hopeless. That being said it is important to point out why. Sonoma County is a designation used as a catchall for wines from the far more precise sub-appellations of the Russian River, Dry Creek, Alexander, and Sonoma Valleys, with many further divisions among them. Each area is unique and distinctive. What many producers choose to do, however, is blend wines from the various regions within the county and label accordingly. This is not necessarily a bad thing.

Aside from the Sonoma Valley, which is covered later, Merlots that specifically come from the Dry Creek and Russian River Valleys are of particular note. These regions are generally cool with the exception of the northern end of Dry Creek. Thus, within each valley, there is a band that has similar climactic conditions that allow for the ripening of high-quality Merlot. In the Russian River Valley, this band is to the east, further from the ocean and past some of the state's best Pinot Noir vineyards. In the Dry Creek Valley the prime locations are toward the southern cooler end of the valley. The wines themselves are marked by an abundant fruity quality and soft, lush personalities.

Finally, the Merlots that come from Sonoma Mountain at the southern end of the county deserve a special mention. Rising out of the Sonoma Valley, the Sonoma Mountain vineyards are over 1,000 feet off the valley floor, in wild and rugged terrain. Benziger's Merlot exemplifies the style and shares more in common with Napa's mountain Merlots than with those in the Sonoma Valley proper. The wines are rich, ripe, and rugged with perhaps more charisma than their seemingly better-behaved Napa mountain soul mates.

Highly Recommended Sonoma County Merlot

Sonoma County (General)
97 • Chateau St. Jean (CA) 1994 Reserve, Merlot, Sonoma County. $55.
92 • St. Francis (CA) 1996 Merlot, Sonoma County. $23.99.
92 • Benziger (CA) 1995 Reserve, Merlot, Sonoma County. $32.
90 • Windsor (CA) 1995 Shelton Signature Series, Merlot, Sonoma County. $23.50.
89 • St. Francis (CA) 1995 Merlot, Sonoma County. $18.
89 • Quatro (CA) 1996 Merlot, Sonoma County. $12.
89 • Kenwood (CA) 1995 Merlot, Sonoma County. $20.
89 • Byington (CA) 1995 Bradford Mountain, Merlot, Sonoma County. $20.
88 • Windsor (CA) 1996 Shelton Signature Series, Merlot, Sonoma County. $24.50.
88 • Rodney Strong (CA) 1996 Merlot, Sonoma County. $16.
88 • Lambert Bridge (CA) 1996 Merlot, Sonoma County. $20.
88 • Estancia (CA) 1996 Merlot, Sonoma County. $14.
88 • Chateau St. Jean (CA) 1996 Merlot, Sonoma County. $18.

87 • Gallo Sonoma (CA) 1996 Merlot, Sonoma County. $11.
86 • Windsor (CA) 1995 Private Reserve, Merlot, Sonoma County. $18.
86 • Gary Farrell (CA) 1995 Ladi's Vineyard, Sonoma County. $22.
85 • Fetzer (CA) 1995 Barrel Select, Merlot, Sonoma County. $13.99.

Sonoma County (Alexander Valley)
91 • Clos du Bois (CA) 1995 Selection, Merlot, Alexander Valley. $20.
89 • Hanna (CA) 1995 Merlot, Alexander Valley. $21.
89 • de Lorimier (CA) 1996 Merlot, Alexander Valley. $18.
88 • Geyser Peak (CA) 1996 Reserve, Merlot, Alexander Valley. $32.
86 • Clos du Bois (CA) 1996 Merlot, Alexander Valley. $20.
85 • Trentadue (CA) 1994 Merlot, Alexander Valley. $18.

Sonoma County (Dry Creek Valley) ·
88 • Belvedere (CA) 1996 Merlot, Dry Creek Valley. $16.
87 • Peterson (CA) 1996 Merlot, Dry Creek Valley. $22.50.
86 • Belvedere (CA) 1995 Preferred Stock, Merlot, Dry Creek Valley. $24.

Sonoma County (Russian River Valley)
91 • Gary Farrell (CA) 1996 Merlot, Russian River Valley. $22.
90 • Rosenblum (CA) 1995 Lone Oak Vineyard, Merlot, Russian River Valley. $20.
89 • Mietz (CA) 1995 Merlot, Sonoma County. $21.
89 • Davis Bynum (CA) 1995 Laureles Estate Vineyard, Merlot, Russian River Valley. $24.
88 • Louis Martini (CA) 1995 Reserve, Merlot, Russian River Valley. $18.

Sonoma Valley
Wines Reviewed: 11
Median Price: $25.00

"I ride over my beautiful ranch. Between my legs is a beautiful horse. The air is wine. The grapes on a score of rolling hills are red with autumn flame. Across Sonoma Mountain, wisps of sea fog are stealing. The afternoon sun smolders in the drowsy sky. I have everything to make me glad I am alive." So wrote Jack London of the vineyard that now bears his name and fruit for Kenwood Vineyards, in the Sonoma Valley. Little did he know that he might have been surveying what would become California's Pomerol, a tiny super-appellation with a brilliant affinity for Merlot.

As an appellation, Sonoma Valley sits at the southern end of Sonoma County, abutting the Carneros. The valley proper runs between the Mayacamas Mountains, which form the border with Napa, and Sonoma Mountain. As the valley opens up past Sonoma Mountain at the town of Glen Ellen, the climate changes from that in the southern end. It is here, and more precisely between the town of Kenwood and Santa Rosa, that a combination of factors has come together to make for a Merlot growing Eden. A lengthy growing season, moderate temperatures afforded by the cooling breezes of the San Pablo Bay and the Petaluma Gap, and fertile though well-drained soils are the area's hallmark.

Unlike virtually all other California sites, the valley's potential for Merlot was realized almost 30 years ago. As early as 1971, Joseph T. Martin, a furniture store owner, sold his share in that business and bought a 100-acre prune and walnut orchard near Kenwood. He established 90 acres of vineyards, including plantings of Merlot. Miller later went on to build the St. Francis Winery. St. Francis

Scale: Superlative (96-100), Exceptional (90-95), Highly Recommended (85-89),
Recommended (80-84), Not Recommended (Under 80)

was one of the varietal's earliest proponents, and produced a stand-alone Merlot bottling from the outset.

Today, other notable Merlot producers include Matanzas Creek, Kenwood, and Wellington, with others almost certain to follow their successes. Matanzas Creek in particular has drawn attention to the region with its Journey project, a stated attempt to produce no less than one of the world's greatest Merlots. Using draconian selection and impeccable vinification methods, they have certainly succeeded in producing a world-class wine. Is the wine worth the $155 price tag, however? The question is almost irrelevant, because it is made in such limited quantities, and there will always be collectors to snap such rarities up. Rather, the wine was produced to make a point, and that point has been duly noted. This part of the Sonoma Valley will be a force in American Merlot for years to come.

Sonoma Valley Merlot has overtones of tobacco with a slight herbal quality, which reminds one of the varietal's character as seen in Bordeaux. Complex and aromatic, the wines are not the blockbusters that some Napa Valley Merlots can be. Rather, there is a certain restraint, evidenced even by show wines such as the Journey. Balance and finesse take precedence over a core of red fruit flavors, which still evoke the wine's California origins. These qualities combine to make for a very intriguing style of Merlot indeed.

Highly Recommended Sonoma Valley Merlot

94 • Matanzas Creek (CA) 1994 Journey, Merlot, Sonoma Valley. $155.
94 • Bartholomew Park (CA) 1996 Alta Vista Vineyards, Merlot, Sonoma Valley. $32.
93 • St. Francis (CA) 1995 Reserve, Merlot, Sonoma Valley. $33.99.
93 • St. Francis (CA) 1994 Reserve, Merlot, Sonoma Valley. $29.
89 • Wellington (CA) 1995 Merlot, Sonoma Valley. $16.
89 • Kenwood (CA) 1995 Massara, Merlot, Sonoma Valley. $25.
89 • Kenwood (CA) 1995 Jack London Vineyard, Merlot, Sonoma Valley. $25.
89 • Gundlach Bundschu (CA) 1996 Rhinefarm Vineyards, Merlot, Sonoma Valley. $21.
88 • Matanzas Creek (CA) 1996 Merlot, Sonoma Valley. $47.
88 • Castle (CA) 1996 Merlot, Sonoma Valley. $18.
86 • Kunde (CA) 1997 Merlot, Sonoma Valley. $17.

Long Island, New York

Wines Reviewed: **20**
Median Price: **$19**

Long Island extends nearly 120 miles out into the Atlantic Ocean from New York City. Only 15 miles or so wide, the island is split into two long fingers divided by the Peconic Bay near the town of Riverhead, 70 miles from the East River. Known as the North and South Forks, this end of the island is where viticulture has taken hold. The South Fork is synonymous to many with the Hamptons, New York's answer to Malibu, and the area is home to a few vineyards. The majority, however, are in the more rural and pastoral North Fork, which at only five miles wide and 35 miles long is all but surrounded by water.

At present there are about 20 wineries in the area, all but two of which are relatively small. It is still a very young industry with the earliest wineries dating from the 1970s, but expansion has been swift as the area has a laundry list of natural attributes. While the more established upstate New York viticultural areas have a more extreme climate that favors white *Vinifera* varietals, Long Island has the ability to ripen red varieties such as Cabernet and Merlot. The warmer climate is a function of the more southerly latitude, the fact that the vineyards are nearly surrounded by the moderating influence of the Atlantic, and that they are shielded from extreme freezes by warm moist winds that blow in from the Carolinas in the fall and winter. Additionally, there is the enviable position of being a stone's throw from one of the largest markets for fine wines in the world, New York City.

As for Long Island Merlot, there is no doubt that the area's vintners can ripen the grapes, and that they are of sufficiently high quality to make very good wines. The winemaking in many instances, however, is still finding its way. The wines often tend to be quite tannic and extracted, bordering on toughness. It would be questionable whether many of the current releases would blossom with age. As California vintners have been learning since the 1980s, bigger doesn't always mean better, and wines that are out of balance in youth don't gain balance with age.

It is almost as if the area is still trying too hard to make world-class wines, instead of making world-class *Long Island* wines. It is hard to say what form Long Island Merlot will eventually evolve into. That being said, many of the wines do bear a resemblance to Bordeaux or Washington State, in that they feature more restrained levels of alcohol and higher acidity levels than their California counterparts. In many ways, today's wines remind one of similar efforts from Washington ten and 15 years ago. It may just be that the area's winemakers are a bit behind in the winemaking curve that California and Washington vintners have set, and Long Island will claim its place in the upper echelon in the near future. As was the case with Washington (and Oregon's Pinot Noir) in the 1980s, the potential is certainly there.

Highly Recommended Long Island Merlot

90 • Peconic Bay (NY) 1995 Epic Acre, Merlot, North Fork of Long Island. $24.99.
90 • Macari (NY) 1996 Merlot, North Fork of Long Island. $20.
89 • Ternhaven (NY) 1995 Merlot, North Fork of Long Island. $19.99.
89 • Palmer (NY) 1995 Reserve, Merlot, North Fork of Long Island. $28.
89 • Lenz (NY) 1995 Estate, Merlot, North Fork of Long Island. $29.99.
88 • Ternhaven (NY) 1994 Merlot, North Fork of Long Island. $18.99.
88 • Pellegrini (NY) 1995 Merlot, North Fork of Long Island. $16.99.
88 • Paumanok (NY) 1995 Grand Vintage, Merlot, North Fork of Long Island. $22.
88 • Bedell (NY) 1995 Reserve, Merlot, North Fork of Long Island. $27.50.
86 • Osprey's Dominion (NY) 1996 Merlot, North Fork of Long Island. $14.99.
86 • Bedell (NY) 1995 Merlot, North Fork of Long Island. $17.99.
85 • Laurel Lake (NY) 1996 Merlot, North Fork of Long Island. $12.99.
85 • Gristina (NY) 1995 Merlot, North Fork of Long Island. $14.99.

Top Wines

97 • Chateau St. Jean (CA) 1994 Reserve, Merlot, Sonoma County. $55.

96 • Chateau Ste. Michelle (WA) 1994 Chateau Reserve, Merlot, Columbia Valley. $40.

96 • Andrew Will (WA) 1995 Reserve, Merlot, Washington. $32.

95 • Woodward Canyon (WA) 1995 Merlot, Columbia Valley. $30.

94 • Silverado (CA) 1995 Merlot, Napa Valley. $22.50.

94 • S. Anderson (CA) 1996 Reserve, Merlot, Stags Leap District. $40.

94 • Rutherford Hill (CA) 1996 Reserve, Merlot, Napa Valley. $44.

94 • Pine Ridge (CA) 1996 Merlot, Carneros. $35.

94 • Matanzas Creek (CA) 1994 Journey, Merlot, Sonoma Valley. $155.

94 • Bartholomew Park (CA) 1996 Alta Vista Vineyards, Merlot, Sonoma Valley. $32.

93 • Whitehall Lane (CA) 1995 Leonardini Vineyard Reserve, Merlot, Napa Valley. $36.

93 • Waterbrook (WA) 1994 Merlot, Columbia Valley. $19.99.

93 • St. Francis (CA) 1995 Reserve, Merlot, Sonoma Valley. $33.99.

93 • St. Francis (CA) 1994 Reserve, Merlot, Sonoma Valley. $29.

93 • Seven Hills (WA) 1995 Klipsun Vineyard, Merlot, Columbia Valley. $24.

93 • Ridge (CA) 1996 Monte Bello Ridge, Merlot, Santa Cruz Mountains. $40.

93 • Plam (CA) 1995 Vintner's Reserve, Merlot, Napa Valley. $25.

93 • Flora Springs (CA) 1995 Windfall Vineyard, Merlot, Napa Valley. $32.

92 • Whitehall Lane (CA) 1996 Leonardini Vineyard Reserve, Merlot, Napa Valley. $40.

92 • Waterbrook (WA) 1995 Reserve, Merlot, Columbia Valley. $32.

92 • Tefft (WA) 1994 Winemakers Reserve, Merlot, Yakima Valley. $25.

92 • St. Francis (CA) 1996 Merlot, Sonoma County. $23.99.

92 • Niebaum-Coppola (CA) 1995 Francis Coppola Family Wines, Merlot, Napa Valley. $32.

92 • Lockwood (CA) 1995 Partners' Reserve, Merlot, Monterey County. $24.

92 • L'Ecole No. 41 (WA) 1995 Merlot, Columbia Valley. $24.

92 • L'Ecole No. 41 (WA) 1994 Merlot, Columbia Valley. $22.

92 • Flora Springs (CA) 1996 Windfall Vineyard, Merlot, Napa Valley. $40.

92 • Cosentino (CA) 1996 Reserve, Merlot, Napa Valley. $34.

92 • Chateau Ste. Michelle (WA) 1995 Chateau Reserve, Merlot, Columbia Valley. $42.

92 • Chateau Ste. Michelle (WA) 1994 Cold Creek Vineyard, Merlot, Columbia Valley. $28.

92 • Beringer (CA) 1994 Bancroft Ranch, Merlot, Howell Mountain. $45.

92 • Benziger (CA) 1995 Reserve, Merlot, Sonoma County. $32.

92 • Barnard Griffin (WA) 1994 Reserve, Merlot, Columbia Valley. $24.

92 • Apex (WA) 1995 Merlot, Columbia Valley. $40.

92 • Apex (WA) 1994 Merlot, Columbia Valley. $28.99.

92 • Andrew Will (WA) 1997 Ciel du Cheval, Merlot, Washington. $30.

eleven

❧

North American Pinot Noir

❧

An Introduction: American Pinot Noir

For many (admittedly mad) vintners in various remote locations around the world, Pinot Noir is the Holy Grail. No other wine is so ephemeral, such an enigma. Great Pinot combines an extraordinary bouquet of spice, fruits, and earth, with a sense of lightness, sometimes bordering on frailty, in the mouth. Pinot Noir can indeed be a sensuous if sometimes fleeting experience. While the Cabernet Sauvignon of Bordeaux is all power and weight, Pinot Noir is the epitome of grace and elegance. Accordingly, vignerons in Bordeaux tend to concern themselves with structure. If the wine feels right in the mouth, the bouquet, with time, will inevitably work itself out. In Burgundy, vignerons try to get that all-important bouquet, and having accomplished that, feel that the mouthfeel cannot help but follow suit. Frankly, Pinot Noir is a tougher proposition.

It seems almost fitting then, that Pinot Noir just might be the world's most difficult grape to grow. Maddening and often disheartening, Pinot Noir has been the ruin of more than a few well-intentioned vintners, and it may be just that legacy that has attracted a new breed of individualistic pioneers to relatively remote places like Oregon or California's South Central Coast. While Burgundy has long been the undisputed home of the world's great Pinot Noirs, no other location in the Old World has shown much promise with the grape. Despite some token success here and there, countries with centuries of grape growing tradition, such as Spain and Italy, have had very little success. The initial reason for this is climate. Pinot Noir will not make quality wines in warm climates. Indeed, on the widely recognized heat summation scale that vintners use, Pinot Noir will almost invariably need to be grown in the coolest climate. Still, cooler temperatures alone will not guarantee success, for the fickle grape reacts viciously to many other factors.

Thus, the regions in which the grape can even hope to be grown are very few indeed, and even then it is often on the margins, where all factors will need to come together frequently at precisely the right time for a vintage to be great. Burgundy has been the benchmark, yet Burgundians themselves can often expect no more than two "great" vintages a decade. While Chardonnay has turned into the world's darling, a chameleon of a grape that can make at least decent wines in a huge range of locations, Pinot Noir is the exact opposite. Yet, for the vintner, or wine drinker, who has caught the bug, nothing else will suffice.

I have a theory as to why people are prepared to spend such amazing sums, while often being disappointed, in the search for great Pinot Noir, whether they are making it or drinking it. Pinot Noir is like nirvana, the seventh chakra, and only the select few will ever get there. When one first develops an interest in wine, it is often through the introduction of something white or rosé that has a bit of sweetness such as White Zinfandel or Riesling. Then the tastes turn drier as the budding wine drinker finds that drier whites such as Chardonnay are better at the dinner table, and are viewed as being more "sophisticated." Once a taste for dryness is achieved, the next step is red, and for many the bigger the taste the better. The subtlety is not as important as the power and confidence that a Bordeaux or California Cabernet can engender. Many wine drinkers stop here, but sometimes the dedicated Cabernet fanatic has his interest piqued by something else: the exotic nature of a great Pinot Noir, its grace and finesse, and how

Scale: Superlative (96-100), Exceptional (90-95), Highly Recommended (85-89), Recommended (80-84), Not Recommended (Under 80)

difficult an experience it often is to repeat. The bug has bitten and the fanatic has been born, often looking down his nose a bit at his Bordeaux drinking cousins.

Needless to say, a driven core of New World winemakers have been bitten and are searching high and low for the new Cote d'Or. Unlike Chardonnay, which sometimes seems to be sprouting up in every corner of the country, Pinot Noir is successful in only a few pockets, as its failure was mercifully swift and unequivocal in other areas. When talking about terroir, or the factors that differentiate a wine from Carneros and a wine from Oregon's Willamette Valley, Pinot Noir is probably the world's best vehicle. It is the varietal that most readily reflects its origins in the way it tastes, smells, and looks. Though the race has just begun (most U.S. experience with Pinot Noir is less than twenty years old), it is already possible to discern regional distinctions, and possible even to look at our crystal ball to see what scenarios the future might bring for those brave few who have taken up the search for wine's Holy Grail.

Best U.S. Pinot Noir Producers

Premier U.S. Pinot Noir Producers (***)

- Adelsheim
- Au Bon Climat
- Beringer (Stanly Ranch)
- Bernardus
- Calera
- Carneros Creek
- David Bruce
- Dehlinger
- Domaine Drouhin
- Domaine Serene
- Gary Farell
- Panther Creek
- Ponzi
- Robert Mondavi (Reserve)
- Rochioli
- Sanford
- Signorello
- St. Innocent
- Williams Selyem

Pinot Noir at a Glance

Wines Reviewed:

417

Producers/Brands Represented:

196

Median Price:

$20

Great U.S. Pinot Noir Producers (**)

- Babcock
- Benton Lane
- Benziger
- Bouchaine
- Byington
- Byron
- Cambria
- Chalone
- Chimere
- Clos La Chance
- Cosentino
- Cristom
- Domaine Carneros
- Elkhorn Peak
- El Molino
- Etude
- Evesham Wood
- Fiddlehead
- Thomas Fogarty
- Foxen
- Gainey
- Hartford Court
- Kalin
- Macrostie
- Morgan
- Mount Eden
- Oak Knoll
- Paraiso Springs
- Stephen Ross
- Saintsbury
- Schug
- Sokol Blosser
- Steele
- Torii Mor
- Bethel Heights
- Castle
- Chateau St. Jean
- Chateau Souverain
- Claudia Springs
- Clos du Val
- Cooper Mountain
- Davis Bynum
- De Loach
- Edmeades
- Edna Valley Vineyard
- Erath
- Eyrie
- Fetzer
- *Foley
- *Hargrave
- Kendall-Jackson
- La Crema
- *Laetitia
- *Martinelli
- Meridian
- Newlan
- *Nichols
- Fess Parker
- *Siduri
- Silvan Ridge
- Rodney Strong
- Talley
- Tulocay
- Wild Horse
- Willamette Valley Vineyards
- *Ken Wright Cellars
- ZD

Dependable U.S. Pinot Noir Producers (Recommended)

Some producers placed in this third tier are new (or new to us) and may merit a higher placement in subsequent vintages. These producers are offset by an asterisk.

- Acacia
- Adelaida
- *Anderson's Conn Valley Vineyards
- Archery Summit
- Argyle
- Beaux Frères

Scale: Superlative (96-100), Exceptional (90-95), Highly Recommended (85-89), Recommended (80-84), Not Recommended (Under 80)

Five Key Regions for American Pinot Noir

Oregon

Wines Reviewed: 152
Median Price: **$22**

Oregon Pinot Noir has come as close as that of any region outside Burgundy to what purists adore about this tricky grape. Indeed, this grape variety alone has put Oregon on the international wine map through the efforts of small producers who have taken a similar challenge as vignerons in Burgundy. That challenge is to ripen these notoriously fickle red grapes in a cool climate.

Oregon offers a marginal climate for ripening red wine grapes. Its finest appellations are sandwiched between the Coast Ranges to the west and the Cascades to the east. These appellations are subjected to a marked maritime influence of low cloud and rain that flow over the green crests of the Coast Range mountains.

Unlike California, there are no swathes of vineyards carpeting valley floors and walls. In Oregon slopes have to be carefully chosen, if they are to have any chance of ripening Pinot Noir. Oregon's finest vineyards are dotted throughout the wine-producing areas on southeast- and southwest-facing slopes, to get the maximum of precious sunlight hours.

The three principal appellations of Oregon are the Willamette Valley, the Umpqua Valley, and the Rogue Valley, which are stretched from north to south between the mountains of the Coastal Ranges and Cascades. In these appellations, Burgundy's celebrated red grape variety is the mainstay of the Oregon wine industry. The Willamette Valley is the most important and largest appellation for Pinot Noir, and it grows the grapes for most of Oregon's finest wines.

Oregon Pinot Noir is generally richer than Burgundy—the grapes can often accumulate more sugar—but usually is lighter than California. At its best it comes closer to encapsulating the magical perfume and texture of Pinot Noir than does California, and of course, it is a great deal less heady, rarely exceeding 13% alcohol by volume.

Vintage variation is a fact of life in many great regions, and Oregon is no exception. When the weather gods are smiling, as they were in 1994, sumptuously rich Pinot Noirs can be produced by virtually all producers. The 1995, 1996, and 1997 vintages are more mixed in that all experienced some rain around the harvest, though those wineries that held their nerve, or were lucky, still triumphed in difficult conditions. The year 1998 has been proclaimed a potentially outstanding vintage for Oregon Pinot Noir and these wines are eagerly anticipated by devoted Pinotophiles.

Oregon Pinot Noir is not inexpensive, and weighs in at between $20 and $40 per bottle. Then again, no serious attempt to make Pinot Noir will come very cheaply.

Highly Recommended Oregon Pinot Noir

94 • Domaine Drouhin (OR) 1994 Laurene, Pinot Noir, Willamette Valley. $42.
93 • Torii Mor (OR) 1994 Reserve, Pinot Noir, Yamhill County. $28.

93 • Lange (OR) 1994 Reserve, Pinot Noir, Willamette Valley. $40.

93 • Domaine Serene (OR) 1995 Evenstad Reserve, Pinot Noir, Willamette Valley. $33.

92 • St. Innocent (OR) 1994 Temperance Hill Vineyard, Pinot Noir, Willamette Valley. $32.50.

92 • Sokol Blosser (OR) 1994 Redland, Pinot Noir, Willamette Valley. $35.

92 • Siduri (OR) 1995 Pinot Noir, Oregon. $30.

92 • Ponzi (OR) 1994 Reserve, Pinot Noir, Willamette Valley. $35.

92 • Ponzi (OR) 1993 Reserve, Pinot Noir, Willamette Valley. $26.99.

92 • Panther Creek (OR) 1994 Bednarik Vineyard, Pinot Noir, Willamette Valley. $35.

92 • Cristom (OR) 1994 Reserve, Pinot Noir, Willamette Valley. $27.

92 • Cristom (OR) 1994 Marjorie Vineyard, Pinot Noir, Willamette Valley. $27.

92 • Chateau Benoit (OR) 1994 Estate Reserve, Pinot Noir, Willamette Valley. $25.

91 • St. Innocent (OR) 1995 Freedom Hill Vineyard, Pinot Noir, Willamette Valley. $24.99.

91 • Redhawk (OR) 1994 Estate Reserve, Pinot Noir, Willamette Valley. $25.

91 • Oak Knoll (OR) 1994 Vintage Reserve, Pinot Noir, Willamette Valley. $34.

91 • Evesham Wood (OR) 1994 Temperance Hill Vineyard, Pinot Noir, Willamette Valley. $24.

91 • Erath (OR) 1994 Weber Vineyard Reserve, Pinot Noir, Willamette Valley. $25.

91 • Duck Pond (OR) 1994 Fries Family Reserve, Pinot Noir, Willamette Valley. $25.

91 • Domaine Serene (OR) 1994 Evenstad Reserve, Pinot Noir, Willamette Valley. $30.

91 • Domaine Drouhin (OR) 1995 Laurene, Pinot Noir, Willamette Valley. $45.

91 • Cooper Mountain (OR) 1994 Estate Reserve, Pinot Noir, Willamette Valley. $29.75.

90 • Tualatin (OR) 1994 Estate Reserve, Pinot Noir, Willamette Valley. $20.

90 • St. Innocent (OR) 1995 O'Connor Vineyard, Pinot Noir, Willamette Valley. $19.99.

90 • St. Innocent (OR) 1994 Seven Springs Vineyard, Pinot Noir, Willamette Valley. $28.50.

90 • Ponzi (OR) 1995 25th Anniversary Reserve, Pinot Noir, Willamette Valley. $50.

90 • Panther Creek (OR) 1995 Freedom Hill Vineyard, Pinot Noir, Willamette Valley. $27.99.

90 • Oak Knoll (OR) 1994 Silver Anniversary Reserve, Pinot Noir, Willamette Valley. $20.

90 • Lange (OR) 1994 Pinot Noir, Willamette Valley. $18.

90 • Ken Wright Cellars (OR) 1995 Canary Hill Vineyard, Pinot Noir, Willamette Valley. $24.99.

90 • Elk Cove (OR) 1994 La Boheme Vineyard, Pinot Noir, Willamette Valley. $35.

90 • Domaine Serene (OR) 1994 Reserve, Pinot Noir, Willamette Valley. $20.

90 • Cristom (OR) 1996 Marjorie Vineyard, Pinot Noir, Willamette Valley. $32.

90 • Benton Lane (OR) 1996 Reserve, Pinot Noir, Oregon. $28.

90 • Benton Lane (OR) 1994 Reserve, Pinot Noir, Oregon. $28.50.

90 • Beaux Freres (OR) 1995 Pinot Noir, Yamhill County. $50.

90 • Autumn Wind (OR) 1994 Reserve, Pinot Noir, Oregon. $30.

90 • Amity (OR) 1993 Winemakers Reserve, Pinot Noir, Willamette Valley. $35.

90 • Adelsheim (OR) 1995 Pinot Noir, Oregon. $18.99.

90 • Adelsheim (OR) 1994 Seven Springs Vineyard, Pinot Noir, Polk County. $30.

89 • Willamette Valley Vineyards (OR) 1995 Founders' Reserve, Pinot Noir, Oregon. $18.

89 • Willamette Valley Vineyards (OR) 1994 OVB, Pinot Noir, Oregon. $30.

89 • St. Innocent (OR) 1994 O'Connor Vineyard, Pinot Noir, Willamette Valley. $32.50.

89 • Sokol Blosser (OR) 1994 Pinot Noir, Willamette Valley. $17.

89 • Ponzi (OR) 1994 Pinot Noir, Willamette Valley. $18.

89 • McKinlay (OR) 1995 Special Selection, Pinot Noir, Willamette Valley. $32.50.

89 • Henry Estate (OR) 1994 Barrel Select, Pinot Noir, Umpqua Valley. $24.

89 • Erath (OR) 1993 Reserve, Pinot Noir, Willamette Valley. $20.

89 • Elk Cove (OR) 1994 Estate Reserve, Pinot Noir, Willamette Valley. $25.

89 • Duck Pond (OR) 1995 Pinot Noir, Willamette Valley. $8.

89 • Domaine Drouhin (OR) 1996 Laurene, Pinot Noir, Willamette Valley. $48.

89 • Domaine Drouhin (OR) 1994 Pinot Noir, Oregon. $30.

89 • Cristom (OR) 1995 Marjorie Vineyard, Pinot Noir, Willamette Valley. $27.

89 • Cristom (OR) 1994 Mt. Jefferson Cuvee, Pinot Noir, Willamette Valley. $17.

89 • Chehalem (OR) 1995 Rion Reserve, Pinot Noir, Willamette Valley. $34.

89 • Byington (CA) 1995 Pinot Noir, Willamette Valley. $20.

89 • Bethel Heights (OR) 1994 Flat Block Reserve, Pinot Noir, Willamette Valley. $24.

88 • Witness Tree (OR) 1995 Pinot Noir, Willamette Valley. $17.

88 • Torii Mor (OR) 1995 Pinot Noir, Yamhill County. $19.

88 • Sokol Blosser (OR) 1993 Redland, Pinot Noir, Willamette Valley. $25.

88 • Silvan Ridge (Or) 1995 Pinot Noir, Willamette Valley. $19.

88 • Silvan Ridge (OR) 1994 Visconti Vineyard, Pinot Noir, Willamette Valley. $26.

88 • Silvan Ridge (OR) 1994 Pinot Noir, Willamette Valley. $19.

88 • Panther Creek (OR) 1995 Bednarik Vineyard, Pinot Noir, Willamette Valley. $27.99.

88 • Montinore (OR) 1994 Winemaker's Reserve, Pinot Noir, Willamette Valley. $14.

88 • Ken Wright Cellars (OR) 1995 Carter Vineyard, Pinot Noir, Willamette Valley. $24.99.

88 • Girardet (OR) 1994 Barrel Select, Pinot Noir, Umpqua Valley. $18.

88 • Fiddlehead (OR) 1995 Pinot Noir, Willamette Valley. $32.

88 • Fiddlehead (OR) 1994 Pinot Noir, Willamette Valley. $32.

88 • Eyrie (OR) 1995 Pinot Noir, Willamette Valley. $19.

88 • Domaine Drouhin (OR) 1995 Pinot Noir, Oregon. $28.

88 • Cristom (OR) 1996 Louise Vineyard, Pinot Noir, Willamette Valley. $32.

88 • Cristom (OR) 1995 Reserve, Pinot Noir, Willamette Valley. $27.

88 • Cooper Mountain (OR) 1995 Reserve, Pinot Noir, Willamette Valley. $25.

88 • Broadley (OR) 1995 Reserve, Pinot Noir, Oregon. $18.

87 • Van Duzer (OR) 1994 Eola Selection, Pinot Noir, Oregon. $12.50.

87 • Sokol Blosser (OR) 1995 Pinot Noir, Willamette Valley. $15.

87 • Rex Hill (OR) 1994 Pinot Noir, Willamette Valley. $10.99.

87 • Panther Creek (OR) 1995 Shea Vineyard, Pinot Noir, Willamette Valley. $27.99.

87 • Oak Knoll (OR) 1995 Pinot Noir, Willamette Valley. $15.

87 • Montinore (OR) 1995 Winemaker's Reserve, Pinot Noir, Willamette Valley. $17.99.

87 • Henry Estate (OR) 1993 Barrel Select, Pinot Noir, Umpqua Valley. $18.

87 • Flynn (OR) 1994 Estate, Pinot Noir, Willamette Valley. $14.

87 • Firesteed (OR) 1995 Pinot Noir, Oregon. $9.99.

87 • Cooper Mountain (OR) 1994 Estate, Pinot Noir, Willamette Valley. $15.75.

87 • Chehalem (OR) 1995 Three Vineyard, Pinot Noir, Willamette Valley. $15.

87 • Bridgeview (OR) 1995 Reserve, Pinot Noir, Oregon. $15.99.

86 • Sokol Blosser (OR) 1995 Redland, Pinot Noir, Yamhill County. $35.

86 • King Estate (OR) 1995 Pinot Noir, Oregon. $18.

86 • Hinman (OR) 1994 Pinot Noir, Oregon. $10.99.

86 • Henry Estate (OR) 1995 Barrel Select, Pinot Noir, Umpqua Valley. $20.

86 • Erath (OR) 1995 Vintage Select, Pinot Noir, Willamette Valley. $19.

86 • Elk Cove (OR) 1996 Roosevelt, Pinot Noir, Oregon. $40.

86 • Domaine Drouhin (OR) 1996 Pinot Noir, Oregon. $33.

86 • Chehalem (OR) 1995 Ridgecrest Vineyard, Pinot Noir, Willamette Valley. $22.

86 • Benton Lane (OR) 1996 Pinot Noir, Oregon. $15.

86 • Archery Summit (OR) 1996 Arcus Estate, Pinot Noir, Oregon. $59.

86 • Amity (OR) 1995 Sunnyside Vineyard, Pinot Noir, Willamette Valley. $18.

86 • Amity (OR) 1994 Pinot Noir, Willamette Valley. $16.

85 • Willamette Valley Vineyards (OR) 1995 Pinot Noir, Oregon. $12.50.

85 • Tyee (OR) 1993 Pinot Noir, Willamette Valley. $13.50.

85 • St. Innocent (OR) 1996 O'Connor Vineyard, Pinot Noir, Willamette Valley. $20.

85 • Silvan Ridge (OR) 1996 Eola Springs Vineyard, Pinot Noir, Willamette Valley. $26.

85 • Silvan Ridge (OR) 1995 Hoodview Vineyard, Pinot Noir, Willamette Valley. $22.

85 • Siduri (OR) 1996 Pinot Noir, Oregon. $34.

85 • Kramer (OR) 1992 Reserve, Pinot Noir, Willamette Valley. $22.

85 • Henry Estate (OR) 1995 Umpqua Cuvee, Pinot Noir, Umpqua Valley. $10.

85 • Cristom (OR) 1995 Mt. Jefferson Cuvee, Pinot Noir, Willamette Valley. $17.

85 • Chehalem (OR) 1996 Three Vineyard, Pinot Noir, Willamette Valley. $18.

85 • Bridgeview (OR) 1996 Pinot Noir, Oregon. $10.99.

85 • Bethel Heights (OR) 1995 Wadenswil Block Reserve, Pinot Noir, Willamette Valley. $24.

California's South Central Coast

Wines Reviewed: **40**
Median Price: **$24.50**

As one drives south, and south, and south from San Francisco, logic would follow that the climate would be correspondingly warmer. In general terms this is true, but when you finally make it down to Santa Barbara you find out that the immediate area is, in fact, downright chilly. It has to do with a quirk of nature and California's tortured geology. Between Alaska and the Strait of Juan de Fuca at South America's southern tip, the coastal mountain ranges have a north-south orientation, effectively blocking the maritime influence of the Pacific, but for the few gaps to be found here and there.

The valleys and mountains around Santa Barbara, however, have an east-west orientation, which ushers in the cool Pacific air. Were it not for this, we would be discussing the area's affinity for Port. In several small valleys near the coast in San Luis Obispo and Santa Barbara Counties, however, the conditions have all come together for the production of world class Pinot Noir. Two vineyards in particular, "Bien Nacido" and "Sanford & Benedict," are among the very finest Pinot Noir sites in the state and supply many of the top producers. Additionally, since there are subtle differences again between fruit from the Edna, Arroyo Grande, and Santa Maria Valleys, it is quite common to see producers blend their Pinot Noirs with a range of sources.

Generally, however, the area produces wines that are exceedingly generous in their fruit characters, from lighter cherry to plum flavors, but rarely if ever with the overripe aspects common to warmer climates. The intriguing varietal characters that are found in Pinot Noir often complement this forcefulness of fruit. It is often described as a subtle stemminess or gamey quality that adds a tremendous amount of complexity to the bouquet and avoids the simple red cherry spectrum of the grape. In very broad terms and specific examples notwithstanding, it is this area that at the moment often produces the state's most complex examples of Pinot Noir.

Scale: Superlative (96-100), Exceptional (90-95), Highly Recommended (85-89), Recommended (80-84), Not Recommended (Under 80)

398

Highly Recommended
South Central Coast Pinot Noir

94 • Cambria (CA) 1996 Reserve, Pinot Noir, Santa Maria Valley. $42.

93 • Laetitia (CA) 1996 Laetitia Vineyard, Pinot Noir, San Luis Obispo County. $29.

93 • Byron (CA) 1996 Pinot Noir, Santa Maria Valley. $18.

92 • Au Bon Climat (CA) 1996 Piccho and Rincon, Pinot Noir,
   Arroyo Grande Valley. $40.

91 • Steele (CA) 1995 Bien Nacido Vineyard, Pinot Noir, Santa Barbara County. $34.

91 • Laetitia (CA) 1996 Les Galets Vineyard, Pinot Noir, San Luis Obispo County. $29.

90 • Sanford (CA) 1995 Pinot Noir, Santa Barbara County. $20.

90 • Nichols (CA) 1996 Cottonwood Canyon Vineyard, Pinot Noir,
   Santa Barbara County. $33.

90 • Fess Parker (CA) 1995 American Tradition Reserve, Pinot Noir,
   Santa Barbara County. $28.

90 • Au Bon Climat (CA) 1996 Sanford & Benedict Vineyard, Pinot Noir,
   Santa Ynez Valley. $35.

89 • Gainey (CA) 1996 Limited Selection, Pinot Noir, Santa Maria Valley. $28.

89 • Foxen (CA) 1995 Sanford & Benedict Vineyard, Pinot Noir, Santa Ynez Valley. $28.

89 • Foley (CA) 1997 Santa Maria Hills Vineyard, Pinot Noir, Santa Maria Valley. $32.

89 • Cambria (CA) 1995 Julia's Vineyard, Pinot Noir, Santa Maria Valley. $27.

89 • Babcock (CA) 1997 Pinot Noir, Santa Barbara County. $20.

88 • Whitcraft (CA) 1996 Bien Nacido Vineyard, Pinot Noir, Santa Maria Valley. $34.99.

88 • Meridian (CA) 1996 Coastal Reserve, Pinot Noir, Santa Barbara County. $20.

88 • Fetzer (CA) 1995 Bien Nacido Vineyard Reserve, Pinot Noir,
   Santa Barbara County. $24.

87 • York Mountain Winery (CA) 1994 William Cain Vineyard, Pinot Noir,
   San Luis Obispo County. $14.

87 • Stephen Ross (CA) 1996 Bien Nacido Vineyard, Pinot Noir, Santa Maria Valley. $24.

87 • Norman (CA) 1995 William Cain Vineyard, Pinot Noir, Paso Robles. $18.

87 • Gary Farrell (CA) 1996 Bien Nacido Vineyard, Pinot Noir,
   Santa Barbara County. $28.

87 • Foley (CA) 1996 Santa Maria Hills Vineyard, Pinot Noir, Santa Maria Valley. $25.

86 • Stephen Ross (CA) 1996 La Colline Vineyard, Pinot Noir, Arroyo Grande Valley. $20.

86 • Stephen Ross (CA) 1996 Edna Ranch, Pinot Noir, Edna Valley. $22.

86 • Laetitia (CA) 1996 Reserve, Pinot Noir, San Luis Obispo County. $18.

86 • Fess Parker (CA) 1996 American Tradition Reserve, Pinot Noir,
   Santa Barbara County. $26.

86 • Byron (CA) 1994 Reserve, Pinot Noir, Santa Barbara County. $24.

86 • Babcock (CA) 1996 Pinot Noir, Santa Ynez Valley. $30.

85 • Santa Rita Creek (CA) 1995 Pinot Noir, Paso Robles. $14.50.

85 • Meridian (CA) 1997 Pinot Noir, Santa Barbara. $14.

85 • Fess Parker (CA) 1996 Pinot Noir, Santa Barbara County. $18.

85 • Au Bon Climat (CA) 1996 La Bauge Au-Dessus, Pinot Noir,
   Santa Barbara County. $25.

Russian River Valley

Wines Reviewed: **30**
Median Price: **$29**

The Russian River Valley is an exceedingly beautiful part of Sonoma County, only miles from the cooling waters of the Pacific. It is carved by the Russian River as it flows south from Mendocino, through the Alexander Valley, and into the Pacific. Because of its proximity to the ocean and the natural funnels for sea air that are provided by the river and the Petaluma Gap to the south, the climate is frequently very chilly. In the western parts nearest the ocean, there is a sub-appellation, the Green Valley, in which conditions are so cool that some of California's most noted sparkling wines are produced there by Iron Horse, Gloria Ferrer, and Korbel.

The area has a long viticultural history and the Korbel Cellars in particular date to 1886. Pinot Noir has long been important to the region and most of the vineyards upon which the area's reputation has been made were planted in the early '70s. The Allen, Rochioli, and Olivet Lane vineyards are of particular distinction and their fruits have the good fortune of being vinified by some of the state's best winemakers. Gary Farrel, Rochioli, Dehlinger, and Williams Selyem all are making stunning Pinot Noirs with grapes from one or all of these vineyards.

Because of the coolness of the climate, the growing season is quite long with the early ripening Pinot Noir generally being harvested in mid-September. This, in combination with the well-established vineyards, the proclivity of the climate, and superior winemaking has resulted in some of the country's best Pinot Noirs to date.

There is indeed a very distinct Russian River style. It is marked by a penetrating depth of flavor. The wines tend to brooding and concentrated flavors that remind the taster of vibrant and piercing crushed raspberries or blackberries. They are exceedingly pure and direct with deep colors. The gamey leathery edge that one might find in the South Central Coast is less frequent here, but the wines are typically more concentrated, focused, and fruit driven. Additionally, the winemaking is more even, with a great consistency from top to bottom. If the South Central Coast at its best someday might emulate wines from the Côte-de-Nuits, the Russian River is already producing wine that has more than a passing resemblance to the Côte-de-Beaune. If you are a fan of exotically pure, fruit-driven Pinot Noir, look no further.

Highly Recommended
Russian River Valley Pinot Noir

92 • David Bruce (CA) 1995 Reserve, Pinot Noir, Russian River Valley. $26.

91 • Davis Bynum (CA) 1995 Limited Edition, Pinot Noir, Russian River Valley. $28.

90 • Stonestreet (CA) 1995 Pinot Noir, Russian River Valley. $30.

90 • Gary Farrell (CA) 1995 Allen Vineyard, Pinot Noir, Russian River Valley. $40.

90 • David Bruce (CA) 1996 Pinot Noir, Russian River Valley. $.

89 • Signorello (CA) 1996 Martinelli Vineyard, Pinot Noir, Russian River Valley. $45.

89 • Rochioli (CA) 1995 Pinot Noir, Russian River Valley. $34.99.

89 • Gary Farrell (CA) 1995 Rochioli Vineyard, Pinot Noir, Russian River Valley. $50.

89 • Cosentino (CA) 1996 Pinot Noir, Russian River Valley. $50.

88 • Signorello (CA) 1995 Martinelli Vineyard, Pinot Noir, Russian River Valley. $48.

88 • Martinelli (CA) 1996 Martinelli Vineyard, Pinot Noir, Russian River Valley. $25.

88 • Kenwood (CA) 1995 Olivet Lane, Pinot Noir, Russian River Valley. $22.

88 • Hartford Court (CA) 1996 Arrendell Vineyard, Pinot Noir, Russian River Valley. $42.

88 • Gary Farrell (CA) 1996 Pinot Noir, Russian River Valley. $22.50.

87 • Hartford Court (CA) 1995 Arrendell Vineyard, Pinot Noir, Russian River Valley. $34.

86 • Rochioli (CA) 1996 Pinot Noir, Russian River Valley. $35.

86 • Patz & Hall (CA) 1996 Pinot Noir, Russian River Valley. $30.

86 • Moshin (CA) 1995 Pinot Noir, Russian River Valley. $16.

86 • Davis Bynum (CA) 1996 Limited Edition, Pinot Noir Limited Edition, Russian River Valley. $28.

Carneros

Wines Reviewed: **52**
Median Price: **$26**

Carneros sits just north of the shores of San Pablo Bay, a northern extension of San Francisco Bay, and is divided between Napa and Sonoma Counties. The division is purely political, and from a viticultural standpoint Carneros stands alone, separate and distinct from Napa or Sonoma, and is one of California's most homogenous and best-conceived AVAs.

Like other areas that are showing promise for Pinot Noir, Carneros, or more properly Los Carneros, has a chilly climate. It is moderated by the waters of the bay, and the maritime fogs and winds. The late afternoon winds in particular, are notorious in their strength as they race from the bay and the Petaluma Gap to the warmer inland valleys. Indeed, recent research has shown that the winds may have an effect even beyond the temperature. It has been shown that in response to high winds a grapevine will slow or shut down the photosynthetic process in order to avoid dehydration. This additional stress coupled with the lengthy growing season should bode well for Pinot Noir.

The results, however, though competent, have not usually been as exciting as one might expect. Carneros Pinot Noir tends to wind up in the delicate red cherry-flavored end of the spectrum with little of the exotic notes that make great Pinot Noir so thrilling. To date, most of the wines have been very correct, but somehow lacking that extra dimension.

Suspicion has been directed to the clones of Pinot Noir that were originally planted. Mainly the product of UC Davis, these clones may be more suited to viticultural regions that don't share the more marginal climate of Carneros. These questions are being addressed, and Francis Mahoney of Carneros Creek has been in the forefront of research in this area. In a classic example of the maddening properties of Pinot Noir, Mahoney is in the final phase of a three-part clonal selection program that he began in 1975! With the arrival of *Phylloxera* in the area, perhaps the more unfortunate aspects of having to replant will be offset by a greater understanding of how new Pinot Noir clones will help to boost Carneros Pinot to the forefront. To be sure Pinot Noir from Mahoney and some other producers are beginning to show those added dimensions that have proven so elusive, and the next few years may see a revolution in Carneros Pinot Noir.

Highly Recommended Carneros Pinot Noir

93 • Beaulieu (CA) 1996 Reserve, Pinot Noir, Carneros. $30.

92 • Signorello (CA) 1995 Las Amigas Vineyard, Pinot Noir, Carneros. $48.

92 • Bouchaine (CA) 1994 Reserve, Pinot Noir, Carneros. $27.

91 • Signorello (CA) 1996 Los Amigas Vineyard, Pinot Noir, Carneros. $45.

91 • Saintsbury (CA) 1995 Reserve, Pinot Noir, Carneros. $28.

91 • MacRostie (CA) 1995 Reserve, Pinot Noir, Carneros. $25.

91 • Beringer (CA) 1995 Stanly Ranch, Pinot Noir, Los Carneros, Napa Valley. $30.

90 • Robert Mondavi (CA) 1996 Reserve, Pinot Noir, Napa Valley. $36.

90 • ZD (CA) 1995 Pinot Noir, Carneros. $24.

89 • Robert Mondavi (CA) 1995 Reserve, Pinot Noir, Napa Valley. $31.

89 • Schug (CA) 1995 Heritage Reserve, Pinot Noir, Carneros. $30.

89 • Richardson (CA) 1996 Sangiacomo Vineyard, Pinot Noir, Carneros. $19.

89 • Etude (CA) 1995 Pinot Noir, Carneros. $33.50.

89 • Chateau St. Jean (CA) 1995 Durell Vineyard, Pinot Noir, Carneros. $30.

89 • Castle (CA) 1997 Sangiacomo Vineyard, Pinot Noir, Los Carneros. $30.

89 • Buena Vista (CA) 1995 Grand Reserve, Pinot Noir, Carneros. $26.

88 • Robert Mondavi (CA) 1995 Pinot Noir, Napa Valley. $18.

88 • Robert Mondavi (CA) 1995 Pinot Noir, Carneros. $26.

88 • MacRostie (CA) 1995 Pinot Noir, Carneros. $17.75.

88 • Carneros Creek (CA) 1996 Pinot Noir, Carneros. $18.

87 • Domaine Chandon (CA) 1996 Pinot Noir, Carneros. $28.95.

87 • Cuvaison (CA) 1995 Eris, Pinot Noir, Carneros. $18.99.

87 • Crichton Hall (CA) 1995 Pinot Noir, Napa Valley. $25.

87 • Castle (CA) 1997 Durell Vineyard, Pinot Noir, Los Carneros. $30.

87 • Beaulieu (CA) 1995 Reserve, Pinot Noir, Carneros. $29.95.

87 • Acacia (CA) 1995 Pinot Noir, Carneros. $16.

86 • Saintsbury (CA) 1996 Reserve, Pinot Noir, Carneros. $34.

86 • Domaine Carneros (CA) 1995 Pinot Noir, Carneros. $20.

86 • Cosentino (CA) 1996 Pinot Noir, Carneros. $30.

85 • Clos du Val (CA) 1995 Pinot Noir, Carneros. $20.

Scale: Superlative (96-100), Exceptional (90-95), Highly Recommended (85-89),
Recommended (80-84), Not Recommended (Under 80)

California's Mount Harlan and Chalone

Wines Reviewed: **6**
Median Price: **$35**

Though not really in the same spirit as the aforementioned larger viticultural areas, it would be impossible to discuss the state of American Pinot Noir without addressing the extraordinary "micro-appellations" of Chalone and Mt. Harlan. Both appellations are in the Gavilan Mountain Range above and between the Monterey and San Benito AVAs east of Monterey. It is one of the few areas in California with limestone-based soils. Additionally, both are essentially single winery AVAs with extraordinary histories.

Mount Harlan is the home of Calera, the winery founded by California's current day Pinot Noir guru, Josh Jensen. His vineyards are at an altitude of 2,200 feet, and despite some reports to the contrary from journalists who have never actually been to the area, Mt. Harlan provides the cool temperatures and long growing season favored by Pinot Noir. Indeed, the average annual temperature is between 58 and 60 degrees Fahrenheit.

The vineyards were established in 1974 after an exhaustive search for the limestone soils that were similar to those Jensen remembered from working the 1970 vintage at Burgundy's Domaine de la Romanée-Conti. What the limestone means in Burgundy is good drainage, which is important in an area prone to inopportune rainfall. What it has meant on Mt. Harlan, an area with very little rainfall, is a draconian yield. This was especially true in the early days when Jensen was driving water up the side of Mt. Harlan by truck.

His winemaking philosophy is completely non-interventionist, with the centerpiece being an eight-story gravity flow winery, which allows him to go from grape to bottle without mechanical handling. Jensen relies on wild yeasts and never filters his wines. Additionally, being a true "terroirist" he has divided his Pinot Noir holdings into four separate and distinct vineyards. Reed, Jensen, Selleck, and Mills are vinified and bottled separately, providing a fascinating opportunity to taste and compare. The range is complemented by a pleasant, though quite different, Central Coast bottling, which allows him to stay in business.

To say the single vineyard Mt. Harlan Pinot Noirs are exotic would be an understatement. They are incredibly concentrated with outrageous bouquets, yet on the palate they display a sense of lightness. They are wines that are exceedingly difficult to compare to other Pinot Noirs, and one is left inevitably with the conclusion that they are not Côte-de-Nuits, not Côte-de-Beaune, but Mt. Harlan. If you are passionate about Pinot Noir, the wines of Calera cannot be missed.

As for Chalone, the vineyards are located some 30 miles as the crow flies further down the Gavilan Range, and are exceedingly remote. At about 1,650 feet they are above the fog line, and the vineyard is made all the more impressive by the dramatic backdrop of the jagged mountains of the Pinnacles National Monument.

The area was originally planted by a Frenchman in 1919, and the holdings were extended in 1946. Chalone's reserve Pinot Noir is crafted from these 1946 plantings and accordingly shows all the concentration one would expect. A tiny winery was constructed in 1960 by some amateur enthusiasts, and was subsequently purchased by Richard Graff, a Harvard music graduate who had been studying at UC Davis. The first release of Chalone was in 1969 and the property is now a publicly held corporation in a coalition with several wineries, including Carmenet, Acacia, and Canoe Ridge in Washington.

Chalone's Pinot Noirs are built for the long haul, and made in a very elegant and restrained style. Though not bursting at the seams with varietal intensity, their track record in the cellar is unquestionable. These are wines for contemplation, and are correspondingly difficult to evaluate in their youth. After several years of age the wines tend to open up with a minerally complexity accented by soft floral notes. Along with Calera, these wines stand out as being quite separate and distinct from the rest of California's Pinot Noirs, and deserve a place in any well-stocked cellar.

Highly Recommended Mount Harlan and Chalone Pinot Noir

95 • David Bruce (CA) 1996 Pinot Noir, Chalone. $32.

94 • David Bruce (CA) 1995 Pinot Noir, Chalone. $32.

91 • Calera (CA) 1995 Selleck, Twentieth Anniversary Vintage, Pinot Noir, Mount Harlan. $38.

88 • Chalone (CA) 1993 Reserve, Pinot Noir, Chalone . $35.

86 • Calera (CA) 1994 Mills, Pinot Noir, Mount Harlan. $35.

86 • Calera (CA) 1994 Jensen, Pinot Noir, Mount Harlan. $38.

Top Wines

95 • **David Bruce (CA) 1996 Pinot Noir, Chalone. $32.**

94 • **Domaine Drouhin (OR) 1994 Laurene, Pinot Noir, Willamette Valley. $42.**

94 • **David Bruce (CA) 1995 Pinot Noir, Chalone. $32.**

94 • **Cambria (CA) 1996 Reserve, Pinot Noir, Santa Maria Valley. $42.**

93 • **Torii Mor (OR) 1994 Reserve, Pinot Noir, Yamhill County. $28.**

93 • **Lange (OR) 1994 Reserve, Pinot Noir, Willamette Valley. $40.**

93 • **Laetitia (CA) 1996 Laetitia Vineyard, Pinot Noir, San Luis Obispo County. $29.**

93 • **Edmeades (CA) 1996 Pinot Noir, Anderson Valley. $20.**

93 • **Domaine Serene (OR) 1995 Evenstad Reserve, Pinot Noir, Willamette Valley. $33.**

93 • **Byron (CA) 1996 Pinot Noir, Santa Maria Valley. $18.**

93 • **Beaulieu (CA) 1996 Reserve, Pinot Noir, Carneros. $30.**

92 • **St. Innocent (OR) 1994 Temperance Hill Vineyard, Pinot Noir, Willamette Valley. $32.50.**

92 • **Sokol Blosser (OR) 1994 Redland, Pinot Noir, Willamette Valley. $35.**

92 • **Signorello (CA) 1995 Las Amigas Vineyard, Pinot Noir, Carneros. $48.**

92 • **Siduri (OR) 1995 Pinot Noir, Oregon. $30.**

92 • **Ponzi (OR) 1994 Reserve, Pinot Noir, Willamette Valley. $35.**

92 • **Ponzi (OR) 1993 Reserve, Pinot Noir, Willamette Valley. $26.99.**

92 • **Panther Creek (OR) 1994 Bednarik Vineyard, Pinot Noir, Willamette Valley. $35.**

92 • **David Bruce (CA) 1995 Reserve, Pinot Noir, Russian River Valley. $26.**

92 • **Cristom (OR) 1994 Reserve, Pinot Noir, Willamette Valley. $27.**

92 • **Cristom (OR) 1994 Marjorie Vineyard, Pinot Noir, Willamette Valley. $27.**

Scale: Superlative (96-100), Exceptional (90-95), Highly Recommended (85-89), Recommended (80-84), Not Recommended (Under 80)

404

92 • Chateau Benoit (OR) 1994 Estate
Reserve, Pinot Noir,
Willamette Valley. $25.

92 • Bouchaine (CA) 1994 Reserve,
Pinot Noir, Carneros. $27.

92 • Au Bon Climat (CA) 1996 Piccho and
Rincon, Pinot Noir,
Arroyo Grande Valley. $40.

91 • Steele (CA) 1995 Bien Nacido
Vineyard, Pinot Noir,
Santa Barbara County. $34.

91 • St. Innocent (OR) 1995 Freedom Hill
Vineyard, Pinot Noir,
Willamette Valley. $24.99.

91 • Signorello (CA) 1996 Los Amigas
Vineyard, Pinot Noir, Carneros. $45.

91 • Saintsbury (CA) 1995 Reserve,
Pinot Noir, Carneros. $28.

91 • Redhawk (OR) 1994 Estate Reserve,
Pinot Noir, Willamette Valley. $25.

91 • Oak Knoll (OR) 1994 Vintage
Reserve, Pinot Noir, Willamette
Valley. $34.

91 • Nichols (CA) 1996 Pisoni Vineyard,
Pinot Noir, Monterey County . $42.

91 • MacRostie (CA) 1995 Reserve,
Pinot Noir, Carneros. $25.

91 • Laetitia (CA) 1996 Les Galets
Vineyard, Pinot Noir, San Luis Obispo
County. $29.

91 • Evesham Wood (OR) 1994
Temperance Hill Vineyard,
Pinot Noir, Willamette Valley. $24.

91 • Erath (OR) 1994 Weber Vineyard
Reserve, Pinot Noir, Willamette
Valley. $25.

91 • Duck Pond (OR) 1994 Fries Family
Reserve, Pinot Noir,
Willamette Valley. $25.

91 • Domaine Serene (OR) 1994
Evenstad Reserve, Pinot Noir,
Willamette Valley. $30.

91 • Domaine Drouhin (OR) 1995
Laurene, Pinot Noir,
Willamette Valley. $45.

91 • Davis Bynum (CA) 1995 Limited
Edition, Pinot Noir,
Russian River Valley. $28.

91 • David Bruce (CA) 1996 Pinot Noir,
Central Coast. $16.

91 • David Bruce (CA) 1994 Estate
Reserve, Pinot Noir, Santa Cruz
Mountains. $35.

91 • Cooper Mountain (OR) 1994 Estate
Reserve, Pinot Noir, Willamette
Valley. $29.75.

91 • Claudia Springs (CA) 1996 Reserve,
Pinot Noir, Anderson Valley. $18.

91 • Calera (CA) 1995 Selleck, Twentieth
Anniversary Vintage, Pinot Noir,
Mount Harlan. $38.

91 • Beringer (CA) 1995 Stanly Ranch,
Pinot Noir, Los Carneros, Napa
Valley. $30.

twelve

❧

North American Zinfandel

❧

An Introduction: American Zinfandel

Old Vine Zinfandel: King of the California Reds?

The great wine-growing regions of the world tend to have one thing in common. Their reputations are often inextricably linked to a single varietal. Merlot and Cabernet in Bordeaux, Burgundian Pinot Noir, Tuscan Sangiovese, German Riesling, or Australian Shiraz—the pairings are evocative to wine lovers and often say something about the regions themselves. It is almost possible to taste the sunny Mediterranean character of Sangiovese, the elegance of Bordeaux, or the epic proportions and brash fruitiness of an Australian Shiraz. What then is the quintessential California wine?

The Ups and Downs of Zinfandel

The last quarter century has seen the renaissance of a wine industry that was decimated by Prohibition, and for most, the Holy Grail has been Cabernet Sauvignon. In a rush to show the world that California could once again produce world-class wines, winemakers looked to Europe for a measuring stick, and that stick was firmly planted in the great vineyards of Bordeaux. Meeting with critical acclaim, and, more important, consumer acceptance, vintners rushed to plant Cabernet, followed in short order by Chardonnay, Pinot Noir, and Merlot. Indeed, these are world-class wines, and well deserved of their growing international reputations, but they came at a price, and that price was often a very part of California's viticultural heritage.

For the previous hundred years, Zinfandel had been the king of California reds. In 1884 it accounted for 40 percent of all the state's grapevines, but the grand old vineyards increasingly fell victim to modern economics and changing trends. Replaced by more popular varietals, attacked by *Phylloxera*, or succumbing to senility and neglect, old Zinfandel vineyards have been under siege. Fortunately, a small band of dedicated producers, coupled with a near-fanatical cult following, have continued to hold out, and against all odds, the pendulum just might be poised to swing back.

Zinfandel Strikes Back

So just what is it about these old vineyards that is helping to put Zinfandel back on the map? The consensus seems to be that a vineyard reaches a qualitative peak between 25 and 50 years of age. Because of Prohibition, there are relatively few old vineyards in California. Of the state's 350,000 acres of *Vinifera*, fewer than three percent are over 50 years of age. The vast majority of these are devoted to Zinfandel. While the percentage of Cabernet vineyards exceeding even 25 years of age is minute, it is quite possible to sample the fruits of a fully mature Zinfandel vineyard, often at half the price.

In addition, old vineyards inherently produce less fruit. This factor provides a natural limit on the vine's tendency to overproduce. Though a problem if quantity is the ultimate goal, it is an essential factor in the production of high quality wines. Since the price of Cabernet has risen so precipitously in the last few years, it has once again become economical for vintners to produce wine from shy-yielding old Zinfandel vineyards, and winemakers are scouring the state looking for the odd parcel of vines. Also, the vintners have learned how well

Scale: Superlative (96-100), Exceptional (90-95), Highly Recommended (85-89), Recommended (80-84), Not Recommended (Under 80)

some of the old methods of pruning and farming these vineyards have worked, and are seeking to apply these principles to more and more new plantings.

Drink Your Zin!

When it comes to the appeal of Zinfandel, Paul Draper, winemaker and C.E.O. of Ridge Vineyards has summed it up best. He says, "From day one, Zinfandel has so much forward fruit that it's sensual to drink right away. Its appeal is immediate, whereas Cabernet needs time to develop. You can have a very sensual experience with Cabernet, but you can have a comparable experience with young Zinfandel, which is why, in a restaurant, I'd be more likely to order a Zinfandel than a Cabernet."

Sacrilegious though it may sound, the best releases of Zinfandel are flatly outperforming many of the more highly touted Cabernets. In our tastings of current release Zinfandel's high percentages are rated 90 points or above. This percentage is often shockingly high. Indeed, at this point on the market it is virtually impossible to find many bad bottles of Zinfandel. In addition to the renewed efforts of some of California's best winemakers, recent vintages have gone from strength to strength. More varied, more accessible, and often more interesting, the current crop of Zinfandel's are on a roll and less expensive than Cabernet to boot. So then, the quintessential California wine? If one could capture the essence of the Golden State in a glass, it would most certainly contain a hearty, warming, and self-assured measure of Zinfandel.

Best U.S. Zinfandel Producers

Premier U.S. Zinfandel Producers (***)

- Chateau Potelle (VGS)
- Cline
- De Loach (OFS)
- Gary Farrell
- Lamborn Family Vineyards
- Martinelli
- Ravenswood
- Ridge
- Rocking Horse
- Rosenblum

Zinfandel at a Glance

Wines Reviewed:

209

Producers/Brands Represented:

132

Median Price:

$18

- St. Francis
- Steele
- Storybook Mountain (Reserve)
- Turley
- Wellington

Great U.S. Zinfandel Producers (**)

- Adelaida
- Benziger
- Robert Biale
- Bogle
- David Bruce
- Castle
- Chateau Potelle
- Davis Bynum
- De Loach
- De Rose
- Edmeades
- Ferrari-Carano
- Franciscan
- Frog's Leap
- Gallo Sonoma
- Grgich Hills
- Hartford Court
- Hendry
- Hop Kiln
- Kenwood
- Kunde
- Lambert Bridge
- Limerick Lane
- Lolonis
- Marietta
- Nalle
- Portteus
- Renwood
- Richardson
- Saucelito Canyon
- Scheutz Oles
- Sierra Vista
- Signorello
- Sineann
- Sobon
- Storybook Mountain
- Truchard
- Windsor

Dependable U.S. Zinfandel Producers (Recommended)

Some producers placed in this third tier are new (or new to us) and may merit a higher placement in subsequent vintages. These producers are offset by an asterisk.

- Alderbrook
- Beringer
- Brutocao
- Burgess
- *Claudia Springs
- Clos du Val
- Creston
- *Deaver
- *Dickerson
- Dry Creek Vineyard
- Eberle
- *Edmunds St. John
- Fanucchi
- Fetzer
- Folie à Deux
- Green & Red
- *Grey Wolf
- Haywood
- Herzog
- *Jackson Valley Vineyards
- Karly
- Kendall-Jackson
- *Markham
- Louis M. Martini
- Martini & Prati
- McIlroy
- Meeker
- Meridian
- Mission View
- Newlan
- *Niebaum Coppola
- Oakville Ranch
- Pedroncelli
- Pesenti
- *Pezzi King
- Preston
- Rafanelli
- River Run
- Sonora
- *Sparrow Lane
- *Storrs
- Rodney Strong
- Joseph Swan
- *The Terraces
- Titus
- Topolos
- *Tria
- *Valley of the Moon
- Villa Mt. Eden
- Voss
- *Wildhurst

Five Key Regions for American Zinfandel

Sonoma Valley
Wines Reviewed: 16
Median Price: $23

Sonoma County is great Zinfandel country. That has long been the common wisdom, and by all measure of results that is the truth. Three of the top five appellations are all within Sonoma County, and each displays a distinct style. That fact is a testament to the diversity of growing regions within the county. The Sonoma, Russian River, and Dry Creek Valleys, however, each share a distinctive fruit-forward character about their Zins, which tends to separate them from other great Zin-producing areas such as the Napa Valley or Amador County. Of the three areas, the Sonoma Valley has played the most historic role.

As an appellation, Sonoma Valley sits at the southern end of Sonoma County, abutting the Carneros. The valley proper runs between the Mayacamas Mountains, which form the border with Napa and Sonoma Mountain. As the valley opens up past Sonoma Mountain at the town of Glen Ellen, the climate changes from that in the southern end. The area as a whole is filled with wild and precipitous hills that afford the vineyards ideal exposures to the sun. This, in combination with a lengthy growing season, moderate temperatures afforded by the cooling breezes of San Pablo Bay and the Petaluma Gap, and fertile though well-drained soils have made for a vine-growing Eden.

These attributes were not lost on 19th century author, Jack London, who owned a ranch in the area and commented that "the grapes on a score of rolling hills are red with autumn flame." Many of those vineyards, as was quite typical of the time, were planted with Zinfandel, and often accompanied by a field blend of Petite Sirah, Carignane, or even Alicante Bouchet. Some of the younger vineyards about which London wrote are even bearing fruit today, and that is a key to the greatness of Sonoma Valley Zinfandel. St. Francis, Wellington, Ravenswood, Kunde, and others have bottlings of Zin sourced all or in part from vineyards better than 100 years old, while many other vineyards are 50 years and older. Monte Rosso, Old Hill, Cooke, and Pagani: these and other famous Sonoma Valley Zinfandel vineyards read like pages from California's viticultural history; and now that Zinfandel is once again receiving its proper due, winemakers have begun to dote on these vineyards and there has been an explosion in rare vineyard-designated bottlings.

As for the overall style of Sonoma Valley Zin, the age of the vineyards and their composition once again figure prominently. Though varying from vintner to vintner, Sonoma Valley Zin tends to be rich, ripe, and heavily extracted with impressive coloring. Some of that coloring and extraction is often lent by the small percentages of Petite Sirah and other grapes that are common to the valley's Zin vineyards, while the age of these vineyards leads to smaller and more intense crops. Yields of one to two tons to the acre and sometimes less are not uncommon. The region's sunny climate, and the cool nights in particular, help to concentrate the fruit while retaining acidity for balance. This makes for wines such as the St. Francis Pagani Vineyard and others that may be upward of 15% alcohol, yet still maintain a sense of balance, and rarely come across as being overripe. This is a marked difference from the porty notes that are common to similarly scaled wines from warmer places such as Amador County. Finally, as for winemaking, though small barrel aging is common, it is quite rare to come across a wood dominated or even a heavily toasted "claret style" Zin, as is so often found in the Napa Valley to the east. Rich, deep, and brooding with dark fruit flavors, yet balanced and crisp, that's Sonoma Valley Zin in a nutshell.

Highly Recommended
Sonoma Valley Zinfandel

95 • St. Francis (CA) 1996 Pagani Vineyard Reserve, Zinfandel, Sonoma Valley. $28.

95 • Rosenblum (CA) 1996 Samsel Vineyard, Maggie's Reserve, Zinfandel, Sonoma Valley. $28.

95 • Ravenswood (CA) 1996 Monte Rosso, Zinfandel, Sonoma Valley. $24.

91 • Ridge (CA) 1995 Pagani Ranch, Late Picked 100 Year Old Vines, Zinfandel, Sonoma Valley. $22.

91 • Ravenswood (CA) 1996 Old Hill Vineyard, Zinfandel, Sonoma Valley. $26.

90 • Valley of the Moon (CA) 1995 Zinfandel, Sonoma Valley. $25.

87 • Haywood (CA) 1995 Rocky Terrace, Los Chamizal Vineyard, Zinfandel, Sonoma Valley. $25.

86 • Louis Martini (CA) 1993 Heritage Collection, Zinfandel, Sonoma Valley. $12.

86 • Kenwood (CA) 1995 Zinfandel, Sonoma Valley. $15.

86 • Kenwood (CA) 1995 Upper Weise Ranch, Zinfandel, Sonoma Valley. $20.

85 • Coturri (CA) 1996 P. Coturri Family Vineyards, Zinfandel, Sonoma Valley. $23.

Russian River Valley
Wines Reviewed: **18**
Median Price: **$20**

The Russian River Valley in Sonoma County has a long viticultural history and today it is known widely for world class Pinot Noir. This is understandable given the coolness of the climate. Accordingly, the production of fine Zinfandel's in the area might sound strange, as the grape is generally associated with much warmer climates such as Amador and the northern end of the Napa Valley. Such is the versatility of Zinfandel that it can produce great wines in a wide range of locations. Additionally, the Russian River bottlings tend to be quite distinctive in reflection of their cool climate origins.

Due to the cold, the growing season is extremely long with the Zinfandel harvest generally occurring in mid to late October. This extended "hang time" allows for an extreme degree of physiological ripeness that concentrates the region's typically vibrant fruit flavors. Meanwhile, the coolness of the climate keeps acidity levels up and balances the opulence of the fruit nicely. The wines, in a flavor profile not totally dissimilar to the region's Pinot Noirs, display a vibrant piercing crushed raspberry and blackberry flavor. They are quite pure and focused in character, even when they reach higher alcohol levels. Finally, as with the Sonoma Valley, most winemakers seem content to use oak seasoning judiciously, preferring to let that spectacularly pure Russian River fruit shine through.

Again like Sonoma Valley, the Russian River is well endowed with many turn-of-the-century vineyards, and attention has been refocused on them in the wake of Zinfandel's resurrection. No one is more indicative of this trend than De Loach. In 1995 they bottled five vineyard-designated Zins in addition to their regular bottlings. These vineyards were planted between 1895 and 1934. Best illustrating the changing economics and perceptions of Zinfandel, however, is the fact that the fruit from these vineyards was used to make De Loach's *white* Zinfandel until 1990. Today, the lucky consumer who is able to secure a few bottles will be rewarded with a fascinating tour of Russian River Zin.

Highly Recommended
Russian River Valley Zinfandel

96 • Martinelli (CA) 1996 Jackass Vineyard, Zinfandel, Russian River Valley. $25.

94 • Ravenswood (CA) 1996 Wood Road Belloni, Zinfandel, Russian River Valley. $24.

94 • De Loach (CA) 1996 Barbieri Ranch, Zinfandel, Russian River Valley. $20.

93 • De Loach (CA) 1996 Saitone Ranch, Zinfandel, Russian River Valley. $20.

93 • De Loach (CA) 1996 OFS, Zinfandel, Russian River Valley. $27.50.

91 • Martinelli (CA) 1997 Louisa & Giuseppe, Zinfandel, Russian River Valley. $18.

90 • Martini & Prati (CA) 1996 Reserve, Zinfandel, Russian River Valley. $18.

89 • Signorello (CA) 1996 Zinfandel, Russian River Valley. $25.

89 • De Loach (CA) 1996 Papera Ranch, Zinfandel, Russian River Valley. $20.

88 • Limerick Lane (CA) 1996 Collins Vineyard, Zinfandel, Russian River Valley. $24.

86 • Topolos (CA) 1995 Piner Heights, Zinfandel, Russian River Valley. $16.50.

86 • McIlroy (CA) 1996 Porter-Bass Vineyard, Zinfandel, Russian River Valley. $18.

86 • De Loach (CA) 1996 Zinfandel, Russian River Valley. $18.

86 • De Loach (CA) 1996 Pelletti Ranch, Zinfandel, Russian River Valley. $20.

Napa Valley

Wines Reviewed: **34**

Median Price: **$18**

When speaking of the Napa Valley for appellation purposes, one is talking about a very diverse region capable of producing a wide range of varietals. From the downright chilly southern end of the valley to the semi-tropical northern end, from the heights of the mountains to the fog-banked valley floor, the Napa Valley is capable of growing almost anything. Though Zinfandel can thrive, at least theoretically, in conditions as diverse as the Russian River Valley or Amador County, it should come as no surprise that its plantings in the Napa Valley are far more limited. Frankly, with the astronomical prices that Oakville, Rutherford, or St. Helena Cabernet have reached, why bother with Zinfandel?

These areas produce some of the world's best Cabernet and the vast majority of Zin vineyards that lasted into the Cabernet boom of the 1980s have long since been dug up and replanted with Cabernet. Nonetheless, Zinfandel continues to thrive in the mountain ranges on either side of the valley proper, and at the very northern tip of the valley in Calistoga. Additionally, with the second coming of Zinfandel in the last few years, it is starting to pop up again in the portfolios of many of the valley's better-known vintners, most of whom had retired the varietal, at least in its red manifestation, years ago. Unfortunately, many of these producers have been forced to source their fruit from newly established vineyards that are often outside the Napa Valley proper.

Some vintners, however, have continued to carry the torch. Ravenswood and Rosenblum, as in other areas of California, have been able to ferret out some spectacular vineyards, while wineries such as Lamborn, Sky, and Storybook Mountain have against all odds, and probably their bankers' advice, chosen to specialize in Napa Valley Zinfandel. Storybook Mountain is probably the best-known Napa estate Zin specialist, and deservedly so. Purchased as a long defunct winery in 1976 by Dr. J. Bernard Seps, a Stanford history professor otherwise known as Jerry, Storybook Mountain was re-established as a vineyard after lengthy consultations with the legendary enologist Andre Tchelistcheff, among others. Considering the clay loam soil and mountainside topography, it was most certainly red wine country, and Dr. Seps threw himself headlong into Zinfandel. Since then he has spent the last 20 years being not only the Napa Valley's foremost Zinfandel producer but also its most tireless promoter.

His wines are typical of the Napa Valley style; one that is separate and distinct from Sonoma's various appellations as well as Amador County. In short the Napa Valley seems to be the primary home of the often talked about "claret style" of Zinfandel. Napa's Zins tend to exhibit a certain restraint, with more tightly wound characters. Oak aging also tends to play a greater part in the wines, particularly when compared to Sonoma bottlings. Napa Valley Zins are often vinified in much the same manner as the valley's Cabernets—hence the claret moniker. Nonetheless, these wines are well made and would certainly appeal to the fan of California Bordeaux varietals. The wines are like well-behaved versions of other California Zins, where the outrageous fruit forward or porty characters of the grape are usually downplayed. Indeed, this may make Napa Zin easier to deal with at the table, but the real Zinfandel fanatic will often lament that claret style Zinfandels have had too much of their ebullient fruit characters, or "Zinniness" if you will, covered up and domesticated.

Highly Recommended Napa Valley Zinfandel

95 • Turley (CA) 1996 Hayne Vineyard, Zinfandel, Napa Valley. $35.

95 • Rosenblum (CA) 1996 White Cottage Vineyard, Zinfandel, Howell Mountain. $21.

94 • Rocking Horse (CA) 1996 Lamborn Vineyard, Zinfandel, Howell Mountain. $18.

93 • Lamborn Family (CA) 1995 The French Connection, Unfiltered, Zinfandel, Howell Mountain, Napa Valley. $22.50.

92 • Markham (CA) 1995 Zinfandel, Napa. $16.

91 • Ravenswood (CA) 1996 Dickerson Vineyard, Zinfandel, Napa Valley. $24.

91 • Chateau Potelle (CA) 1995 VGS, Zinfandel, Mount Veeder, Napa Valley. $35.

90 • Storybook Mountain (CA) 1995 Eastern Exposures, Zinfandel, Napa Valley. $19.50.

90 • Sparrow Lane (CA) 1996 Reserve, Beatty Ranch, Zinfandel, Howell Mountain. $25.

89 • V. Sattui (CA) 1995 Zinfandel, Howell Mountain, Napa Valley. $18.

89 • Hendry (CA) 1995 Block 7, Zinfandel, Napa Valley. $18.

88 • Signorello (CA) 1994 Zinfandel, Napa Valley. $25.

88 • Schuetz Oles (CA) 1996 Korte Ranch, Zinfandel, Napa Valley. $18.

88 • Rosenblum (CA) 1996 Reserve, Hendry Vineyard, Zinfandel, Napa Valley. $22.

88 • Ridge (CA) 1995 York Creek, Zinfandel, Spring Mountain. $22.

88 • Niebaum-Coppola (CA) 1996 Edizione Pennino, Zinfandel, Napa Valley. $26.

87 • Stonehedge (CA) 1995 Zinfandel, Napa Valley. $14.99.

87 • Signorello (CA) 1995 Zinfandel, Napa Valley. $25.

87 • Robert Mondavi (CA) 1996 Zinfandel, Napa Valley. $18.

87 • Monthaven (CA) 1995 Zinfandel, Napa Valley. $9.99.

86 • V. Sattui (CA) 1995 Suzanne's Vineyard, Zinfandel, Napa Valley. $16.75.

86 • Turley (CA) 1995 Moore "Earthquake" Vineyard, Zinfandel, Napa Valley. $35.

86 • Rust Ridge (CA) 1996 Zinfandel, Napa Valley. $18.

86 • Edgewood (CA) 1995 Zinfandel, Napa Valley. $14.

Scale: Superlative (96-100), Exceptional (90-95), Highly Recommended (85-89), Recommended (80-84), Not Recommended (Under 80)

414

Dry Creek Valley
Wines Reviewed: 12
Median Price: $16

The Dry Creek Valley, though a stone's throw from the Russian River and Alexander Valleys, is unique. As usual Sonoma County's tortured and eternally confusing geography is to blame. The natural boundaries of the valley, however, make this an exceptionally tight and well-defined appellation. The Dry Creek parallels the Alexander Valley on the western side and drains into the Russian River. From the point where the Dry Creek meets the Russian River, it is about 16 miles to the northwest where the Dry Creek Valley abruptly ends. Surrounded by mountains on three sides, with the only opening being at the Russian River, there is no outlet for wind as in the Alexander Valley. Additionally, what fog does enter from the Russian River Valley often comes in at night and burns off quickly during the day. Hence, temperatures are far warmer than in the Russian River Valley, particularly at the northern end. The valley is only two miles wide at its widest point, and the valley floor itself is quite narrow. Benchlands and hillsides dominate the region, and in the warmer northern end of the valley, red wine is king.

The Dry Creek area was largely settled in the late 19th century by Italian families, and as in other parts of Sonoma County, Zinfandel was the favored grape, interspersed with the usual blend of black varieties. First planted in the 1880s, some of these vineyards have miraculously survived to this day. None of Dry Creek's old vineyards are more famous than one, however. That vineyard (actually a collection of three vineyards) is known as Lytton Springs, and it is easily one of the greatest vineyards, of any varietal, in the country. The oldest sections of the vineyard are better than 100 years of age but the wine was first bottled by Ridge Vineyards in 1972. Since that time, the wine has enjoyed cult status, and stood defiantly through Zinfandel's darker days. It was this wine that opened the eyes of the world to the quality of Zinfandel from the Dry Creek Valley, and paved the way for Zin specialists such as Nalle. In 1991 and 1995, Ridge purchased two of the three parcels of vineyards that comprise the Lytton Springs bottling, and in 1993 dropped the word Zinfandel from the label altogether, in deference to the field blend that contains a significant dollop of Petite Sirah with a touch of Grenache. The resultant wines are beautifully balanced and complex, with a penetrating, though not overwhelming depth of flavor, the classic Dry Creek profile.

In describing a general style for Dry Creek Valley Zinfandel, it is probably easiest to first explain what it is not. Dry Creek's Zins are not as deep and extracted as Sonoma Valley's. They are not as racy or fruity as their Russian River neighbors are, nor are they as restrained or as oak influenced as examples from the Napa Valley. Finally, they are not as big and rustic as the wines from Amador. What's left, in a word, is balance. Dry Creek Zinfandel comes across as being almost elegant while retaining that beautiful core of brambly fruit without which a Zinfandel would be lost. Dry Creek Zins don't shout at you, but stand out as having a bit of everything, in a very enticing package. As such, they are wines of undeniably broad appeal.

Highly Recommended Dry Creek Valley Zinfandel

92 • Ridge (CA) 1996 Lytton Springs, Zinfandel, Dry Creek Valley. $25.

91 • Rosenblum (CA) 1996 Rockpile Vineyard, Zinfandel, Dry Creek Valley. $22.

91 • Lambert Bridge (CA) 1996 Zinfandel, Dry Creek Valley. $20.

90 • Pedroncelli (CA) 1996 Mother Clone, Special Vineyard Selection, Zinfandel, Dry Creek Valley. $12.

89 • Tria (CA) 1996 Zinfandel, Dry Creek Valley. $18.

86 • Pedroncelli (CA) 1996 Pedroni-Bushnell Vineyard, Single Vineyard Selection, Zinfandel, Dry Creek Valley. $13.

86 • Nalle (CA) 1996 Zinfandel, Dry Creek Valley. $20.

Amador County

Wines Reviewed: **21**

Mean Price: **$15**

Amador County is a historic part of California in the western foothills of the Sierra Mountains. It is here that the gold rush began in 1848 and by 1870 more than 100 wineries were operating in the area, servicing the miners' enological needs. Of those 100 wineries, only one has survived through the trials and tribulations of a century of California viticulture. That winery is now known as Sobon Estate. Luckily, several of the original plantings of Zinfandel fared better than the wineries and are bearing fruit today. Indeed, the Grand-Pere Vineyard, which was planted in 1868 and is currently bottled by Renwood, is reputed to be the oldest vineyard in the state. Since 1973, there has been a new influx of wineries, and the region's modern day reputation has been staked largely on Zinfandel, which accounts for two-thirds of Amador's plantings.

Climatically and physically, Amador County is miles away from the coastal appellations of California. It sits on the eastern edge of the great Central Valley, and the cooling influence of the ocean is only present in the form of afternoon breezes. This makes for a very warm climate, which is mitigated largely by planting at the higher elevations of the Sierra foothills. The principal AVA within Amador, the Shenandoah Valley, is planted around the 1,000 foot line, while another, Fiddletown, is between 1,500 and 2,500 feet. Nonetheless, daytime temperatures in the ripening season are consistently between 80 and 100 degrees Fahrenheit, and the resulting fruit tends to gather a great deal of tannin and intensity.

Amador County Zins tend to be big and rustic, often with a distinctive stewed fruit character that has port like overtones. The wines can divide tasters, and some find them overwhelming. Traditionalists and Zin fanatics, however, will see the wines' charms, and vineyard-designated bottlings from some of the historic plantings are rapidly becoming cult items. What can be said with certainty, however, is that Amador County Zinfandel is one of the nation's most distinctive and individual styles of wine.

Scale: Superlative (96-100), Exceptional (90-95), Highly Recommended (85-89),
Recommended (80-84), Not Recommended (Under 80)

416

Highly Recommended Amador County Zinfandel

93 • Sierra Vista (CA) 1996 Reeves Vineyard, Zinfandel, El Dorado. $15.

89 • Deaver (CA) 1994 Old Vines, Zinfandel, Amador County. $12.99.

87 • Folie à Deux (CA) 1996 Eschen Vineyard Old Vine, Zinfandel, Fiddletown. $22.

86 • Sierra Vista (CA) 1996 Herbert Vineyard, Zinfandel, El Dorado. $15.

86 • Shenandoah Vineyards (CA) 1996 Vintners Selection, Zinfandel, Shenandoah Valley. $15.

86 • Madroña (CA) 1996 Reserve, Zinfandel, El Dorado. $16.

86 • Granite Springs (CA) 1995 Zinfandel, El Dorado. $11.50.

86 • Folie à Deux (CA) 1996 Old Vine, Zinfandel, Amador County. $18.

86 • Deaver (CA) 1995 Zinfandel, Amador County. $15.

Top Wines

97 • Cline (CA) 1996 Big Break Vineyard, Zinfandel, Contra Costa County. $24.

96 • Martinelli (CA) 1996 Jackass Vineyard, Zinfandel, Russian River Valley. $25.

95 • Turley (CA) 1996 Hayne Vineyard, Zinfandel, Napa Valley. $35.

95 • Steele (CA) 1996 Catfish Vineyard, Zinfandel, Clear Lake. $18.

95 • St. Francis (CA) 1996 Pagani Vineyard Reserve, Zinfandel, Sonoma Valley. $28.

95 • Rosenblum (CA) 1996 White Cottage Vineyard, Zinfandel, Howell Mountain. $21.

95 • Rosenblum (CA) 1996 Samsel Vineyard, Maggie's Reserve, Zinfandel, Sonoma Valley. $28.

95 • Rosenblum (CA) 1996 Annette's Reserve, Rhodes Vineyard, Zinfandel, Redwood Valley. $20.

95 • Ridge (CA) 1996 Dusi Ranch, Zinfandel, Paso Robles. $25.

95 • Ravenswood (CA) 1996 Monte Rosso, Zinfandel, Sonoma Valley. $24.

95 • Cline (CA) 1996 Live Oak Vineyard, Zinfandel, Contra Costa County. $24.

94 • St. Francis (CA) 1996 Old Vines, Zinfandel, Sonoma County. $20.

94 • Rocking Horse (CA) 1996 Lamborn Vineyard, Zinfandel, Howell Mountain. $18.

94 • Ravenswood (CA) 1996 Wood Road Belloni, Zinfandel, Russian River Valley. $24.

94 • De Loach (CA) 1996 Barbieri Ranch, Zinfandel, Russian River Valley. $20.

93 • Steele (CA) 1996 Du Pratt Vineyard, Zinfandel, Mendocino. $20.

93 • Sierra Vista (CA) 1996 Reeves Vineyard, Zinfandel, El Dorado. $15.

93 • Lamborn Family (CA) 1995 The French Connection, Unfiltered, Zinfandel, Howell Mountain, Napa Valley. $22.50.

93 • De Loach (CA) 1996 Saitone Ranch, Zinfandel, Russian River Valley. $20.

93 • De Loach (CA) 1996 OFS, Zinfandel, Russian River Valley. $27.50.

92 • Turley (CA) 1996 Old Vines, Zinfandel, California. $30.

92 • Steele (CA) 1996 Pacini Vineyard, Zinfandel, Mendocino. $16.

92 • Ridge (CA) 1996 Lytton Springs, Zinfandel, Dry Creek Valley. $25.

92 • Ridge (CA) 1995 Geyserville, Zinfandel, Sonoma County. $22.

92 • Markham (CA) 1995 Zinfandel, Napa. $16.

91 • Rosenblum (CA) 1996 Rockpile Vineyard, Zinfandel, Dry Creek Valley. $22.

91 • Rosenblum (CA) 1996 Harris Kratka Vineyard, Zinfandel, Alexander Valley. $22.

91 • Ridge (CA) 1995 Pagani Ranch, Late Picked 100 Year Old Vines, Zinfandel, Sonoma Valley. $22.

91 • Ravenswood (CA) 1996 Old Hill Vineyard, Zinfandel, Sonoma Valley. $26.

91 • Ravenswood (CA) 1996 Dickerson Vineyard, Zinfandel, Napa Valley. $24.

91 • Martinelli (CA) 1997 Louisa & Giuseppe, Zinfandel, Russian River Valley. $18.

91 • Lambert Bridge (CA) 1996 Zinfandel, Dry Creek Valley. $20.

91 • Gary Farrell (CA) 1996 Old Vine Selection, Zinfandel, Sonoma County. $22.50.

91 • David Bruce (CA) 1995 Ranchita Canyon Vineyard, Zinfandel, Paso Robles. $15.

91 • Cline (CA) 1996 Bridgehead Vineyard, Zinfandel, Contra Costa County. $24.

91 • Chateau Potelle (CA) 1995 VGS, Zinfandel, Mount Veeder, Napa Valley. $35.

Scale: Superlative (96-100), Exceptional (90-95), Highly Recommended (85-89), Recommended (80-84), Not Recommended (Under 80)

thirteen

❧

North American Red Rhône Varietals

❧

Red Rhône Varietals at a Glance

Wines Reviewed:

132

Producers/Brands Represented:

87

Median Price:

$18

In Introduction: Who in the World Are the Rhône Rangers?

The Rhône Rangers are a hearty band of U.S. vintners who have been planting and promoting lesser-known varietals from France's Rhône Valley as opposed to the chocolate and vanilla of the wine world: Cabernet and Chardonnay. Instead, they sing the praises of wines such as Syrah, Mourvedre, Grenache, and Carignane. Syrah and Mourvedre tend to be full-bodied, rich, and flavorful reds while Grenache and Carignane tend to the lighter side of the spectrum. Additionally, we have included Petite Sirah. Although not technically a Rhône varietal (its origins are a matter of dispute), Petite Sirah, like Zinfandel, has become a California original. Often made from plots planted at the turn of the century, California's best Petite Sirahs often outperform the more hyped (but younger) plantings of Syrah. Rich, tannic, and dense, Petite Sirah is a real mouthful, and offers one of the best values in California wine today.

Best U.S. Red Rhône Producers

Premier U.S. Red Rhône Varietal Producers (***)
- Alban (Grenache, Syrah)
- Bonny Doon (Le Cigare Volant)
- David Bruce (Petite Sirah)
- Cambria (Syrah)
- Cline (Mourvedre, Carignane)
- Columbia Crest (Syrah)
- Dehlinger (Syrah)
- Edmunds St. John (Syrah)
- La Jota (Petite Sirah)
- Marietta (Blend, Syrah)
- Joseph Phelps (Le Mistral, Syrah)
- Ridge (Mataro, Petite Sirah)
- Stags' Leap Winery (Petite Sirah)
- Thackrey (Syrah, Petite Sirah)

Scale: Superlative (96-100), Exceptional (90-95), Highly Recommended (85-89), Recommended (80-84), Not Recommended (Under 80)

Great U.S. Red Rhône Varietal Producers (**)

- Bogle (Petite Sirah)
- Cline (Syrah)
- Columbia (Syrah)
- Concannon (Petite Sirah)
- Curtis (Syrah)
- Edmunds St. John (Mourvedre, Les Cotes Sauvages)
- Fess Parker (Syrah)
- Fife (Petite Sirah, Max Cuvee)
- Geyser Peak (Shiraz)
- McDowell (Syrah)
- Qupe (Syrah)
- Renwood (Syrah)
- Sierra Vista (Syrah)
- Stag's Leap Wine Cellars (Petite Sirah)
- Swanson (Syrah)

Dependable U.S. Red Rhône Varietal Producers (Recommended)

Some producers placed in this third tier are new (or new to us) and may merit a higher placement in subsequent vintages. These producers are offset by an asterisk.

- *Beaulieu (Ensemble, Syrah)
- *Bonterra (Syrah)
- WB Bridgman (Syrah)
- *Fetzer (Syrah, Petite Sirah)
- Foppiano (Petite Sirah)
- *Fox Hollow (Shiraz)
- Guenoc (Petite Sirah)
- *Hogue (Genesis)
- Horton (Stonecastle Red, Cotes d'Orange, Syrah, Mourvedre)
- Jory (Red Zeppelin, Mano Nera)
- *Kathryn Kennedy (Syrah)
- *LinCourt (Syrah)
- *McCrea (Syrah)
- *Orfila (Syrah)
- *Kent Rasmussen (Petite Sirah, Syrah)
- *Ravenswood (Icon)
- *Rockland (Petite Sirah)
- Rosenblum (Petite Sirah, Mourvedre, Carignane)
- *Santa Barbara Winery (Syrah)
- *Shooting Star (Grenache)
- *Signorello (Petite Sirah, Syrah)
- *Stillman Brown (Petite Sirah)
- *Tablas Creek (Tablas Hills Cuvée Rouge)
- Trentadue (Carignane)
- *Villa Mt. Eden (Syrah)
- *Voss (Syrah)
- *Wellington (Syrah, Alicante Bouschet)

Highly Recommended "Rhône Rangers"

Carignane
91 • Cline (CA) 1996 Ancient Vines, Carignane, Contra Costa County. $18.
89 • Windsor (CA) 1996 Carignane, Mendocino County. $10.
87 • Trentadue (CA) 1995 Carignane, Sonoma County. $12.
86 • River Run (CA) 1996 Wirz Vineyard, Carignane, Cienega Valley. $15.

Cinsault
86 • Castle (CA) 1997 Cinsault, Dry Creek Valley. $19.

Grenache
92 • Alban (CA) 1996 Alban Estate Vineyard, Grenache, Edna Valley. $29.

Mourvedre
95 • Cline (CA) 1996 Small Berry Vinyard, Mourvedre, Contra Costa. $28.
93 • Cline (CA) 1996 Ancient Vines, Mourvedre, Contra Costa County. $18.
88 • Ridge (CA) 1997 Bridgehead, Mataro, Contra Costa County. $.
86 • Wild Horse (CA) 1996 James Berry Vineyard, Mourvedre, Paso Robles. $16.
86 • Rosenblum (CA) 1997 Chateau La Paws, Côte du Bone, Mourvedre, Contra Costa County. $9.50.

Petite Sirah
92 • Bogle (CA) 1997 Petite Sirah, California. $10.
90 • Stags' Leap Winery (CA) 1995 Petite Sirah, Napa Valley. $22.
90 • Ridge (CA) 1996 York Creek, Petite Sirah, Spring Mountain, Napa Valley. $.
88 • Signorello (CA) 1996 110 Year Old Vines, Petite Sirah, Napa Valley. $25.
88 • Geyser Peak (CA) 1996 Winemaker's Selection, Petite Sirah, Alexander Valley. $20.
88 • David Bruce (CA) 1997 Petite Syrah, Central Coast. $16.
87 • Edmeades (CA) 1996 Eagle Point Vineyard, Petite Sirah, Mendocino. $20.
87 • Dos Cabezas (AZ) 1997 Petite Sirah, Cochise County. $15.
86 • Windsor (CA) 1996 Petite Sirah, North Coast. $12.
85 • David Bruce (CA) 1997 Ranchita Canyon, Petite Sirah, Paso Robles. $18.

Syrah
97 • Thackrey (CA) 1995 Orion, Old Vines Rossi Vineyard, Syrah, St. Helena, Napa Valley. $45.
95 • Thackrey (CA) 1996 Orion, Old Vines Rossi Vineyard, St. Helena, Napa Valley. $60.
95 • Thackrey (CA) 1993 Orion, Old Vines Rossi Vineyard, Syrah, St. Helena, Napa Valley. $30.
94 • Thackrey (CA) 1994 Orion, Old Vines Rossi Vineyard, St. Helena, Napa Valley. $30.
93 • Signorello (CA) 1996 Syrah, Napa Valley. $30.
93 • Kathryn Kennedy (CA) 1996 Maridon Vineyard, Syrah, Santa Cruz Mountains. $38.
93 • Edmunds St. John (CA) 1996 Syrah, California. $18.
92 • Qupé (CA) 1996 Bien Nacido Hillside Estate, Syrah, Santa Barbara County. $35.
92 • Beaulieu (CA) 1995 Signet Collection, Syrah, Dry Creek Valley. $25.
92 • Alban (CA) 1996 Reva Syrah, Edna Valley. $23.
91 • Glen Fiona (WA) 1997 Syrah, Walla Walla Valley. $35.
91 • Dehlinger (CA) 1996 Goldridge Vineyard, Syrah, Russian River Valley. $28.
91 • Dehlinger (CA) 1995 Syrah, Russian River Valley. $35.
91 • Bonterra (CA) 1996 Syrah, Mendocino County. $25.
90 • LinCourt (CA) 1996 Syrah, Santa Barbara County. $14.
90 • Columbia Crest (WA) 1996 Reserve, Syrah, Columbia Valley. $22.

Scale: Superlative (96-100), Exceptional (90-95), Highly Recommended (85-89), Recommended (80-84), Not Recommended (Under 80)

422

89 • Qupé (CA) 1996 Bien Nacido Reserve, Syrah, Santa Barbara County. $25.

89 • Marietta (CA) 1996 Syrah, California. $16.

89 • Kent Rasmussen (CA) 1996 Ramsay Reserve, Syrah, Napa Valley. $20.

89 • Fess Parker (CA) 1996 American Tradition Reserve, Rodney's Vineyard, Syrah, Santa Barbara County. $30.

89 • Cambria (CA) 1996 Tepusquet Vineyard, Syrah, Santa Maria Valley. $18.

89 • Alban (CA) 1996 Lorraine, Syrah, Edna Valley. $29.

88 • Zaca Mesa (CA) 1996 Zaca Vineyards, Syrah, Santa Barbara County. $20.

88 • W.B. Bridgman (WA) 1997 Syrah, Columbia Valley. $18.

88 • Voss (CA) 1995 Shiraz, Napa Valley. $16.

88 • Swanson (CA) 1996 Syrah. $40.

88 • Meridian (CA) 1996 Syrah, Paso Robles. $14.

88 • J. Lohr (CA) 1996 South Ridge, Syrah, Paso Robles. $14.

88 • Fess Parker (CA) 1996 Syrah, Santa Barbara County. $18.

87 • Geyser Peak (CA) 1996 Reserve, Shiraz, Sonoma County. $32.

87 • Curtis (CA) 1996 Ambassador's Vineyard, Syrah, Santa Ynez Valley. $18.

87 • Columbia Winery (WA) 1996 Red Willow Vineyard, Syrah, Yakima Valley. $29.

87 • Beaulieu (CA) 1996 Signet Collection, Syrah, North Coast. $25.

86 • Wild Horse (CA) 1996 James Berry Vineyard, Syrah, Paso Robles. $18.

86 • Seven Peaks (CA) 1996 Shiraz, Paso Robles 1.6% rs. $16.

86 • Richardson (CA) 1997 Syrah, Sonoma Valley. $22.50.

86 • R.H. Phillips (CA) 1996 EXP, Syrah, Dunnigan Hills. $12.

86 • Paraiso Springs (CA) 1996 Syrah, Santa Lucia Highlands. $22.50.

86 • Monterra (CA) 1996 Syrah, Monterey County. $9.99.

86 • Michel-Schlumberger (CA) 1996 Syrah, Coastal California. $20.

86 • Kendall-Jackson (CA) 1996 Vintner's Reserve, Syrah, California. $16.

86 • Kendall-Jackson (CA) 1995 Grand Reserve, Syrah, California. $20.

86 • Hogue (WA) 1996 Genesis, Syrah, Columbia Valley. $15.

86 • Geyser Peak (CA) 1996 Shiraz, Sonoma County. $16.

86 • Fox Hollow (CA) 1996 Shiraz, California. $8.99.

86 • Domaine de la Terre Rouge (CA) 1996 Sentinel Oak Vineyard, Pyramid Block, Syrah, Shenandoah Valley. $25.

86 • Cline (CA) 1996 Syrah, Caneros. $18.

85 • McDowell (CA) 1997 Syrah, Mendocino. $12.

85 • Chateau Ste. Michelle (WA) 1995 Reserve, Syrah, Columbia Valley. $28.

Rhône Varietal Blend

92 • Joseph Phelps (CA) 1996 Le Mistral, California. $25.

90 • Qupé (CA) 1996 Los Olivos Red Cuvee, Ibarra, Young, and Stolpman Vineyards, Santa Barbara County. $18/375 ml.

90 • Bonny Doon (CA) 1996 Le Cigare Volant, California. $22.

90 • Beaulieu (CA) 1996 Ensemble, Signet Collection, California. $25.

88 • Tablas Creek (CA) 1996 Tablas Hills Cuvée Rouge, Paso Robles. $19.99.

88 • Fife (CA) 1996 Max Cuvee, Napa Valley. $30.

87 • Beaulieu (CA) 1996 Beauzeaux, Signet Collection, California. $20.

86 • Thackrey (CA) NV Pleiades VII Old Vines Red, California. $28.

85 • Mount Palomar (CA) 1996 Rey Sol Le Mediterrane Old Vines Selection Red, South Coast. $10.

85 • Curtis (CA) 1997 Heritage, Old Vines Red, California. $10.

fourteen

≫

North American Red Italian Varietals

≫

An Introduction: What About These New-Wave Italian Varietals?

Red Italian Varietals at a Glance

Wines Reviewed:

49

Producers/Brands Represented:

42

Median Price:

$18

In the nineteenth century California had a great deal of Charbono and Barbera planted. This was in great part due to the Italian heritage of many of the area's winemakers. These men were no fools. They planted varietals that grew well in California's Italianesque climate, and made pleasant everyday wines. While today's producers of Barbera and Charbono are a direct link to that lineage, Italy's glamour grapes, Sangiovese and Nebbiolo, are being planted with ever increasing frequency

The beauty of Sangiovese in particular is its diversity. In its Tuscan home it produces not only simple Chianti but also powerful Brunellos and innovative "Super Tuscan" blends. With as much clonal diversity as Pinot Noir (quite a bit indeed), Sangiovese can be made into a wide variety of wines. From lighter-styled reds with a food friendly streak of edgy acidity, to Cabernet enhanced cellar candidates, California Sangiovese should offer a lot to vintner and consumer alike. Surprisingly, however, the results have so far been spotty.

As for Nebbiolo, the jury is still out. Notoriously difficult to grow, the wines produced thus far in California have ranged from brutal to decent but overpriced. At no time has Piedmont seemed in danger. There has, however, been signs of life on the horizon. Martin Brothers' 1994 Nebbiolo "Vecchio" from the Central Coast was the first Nebbiolo that we have tasted from California that was actually a dead ringer for a solid Barolo (it's all in the bouquet—that unmistakable yet rarely seen "tar and roses" aroma). A fluke perhaps, but Martin Brothers (renamed Martin & Weyrich in Spring '99) has been working with the grape since the mid '80s and has recently been finding more and more success with some of their other Italianesque bottlings, such as their now consistently excellent Moscato d'Asti knock-off, Allegro. Perhaps it's a bit early to say that Nebbiolo, like Sangiovese, is showing

Scale: Superlative (96-100), Exceptional (90-95), Highly Recommended (85-89), Recommended (80-84), Not Recommended (Under 80)

signs of taking off, but remember Sangiovese itself has come a long way in five years. After all, stranger things have happened.

Best U.S. Red Italian Varietal Producers

Premier U.S. Italian Varietal Producers (***)

• Altamura (Sangiovese)
• Chameleon (Barbera, Sangiovese)
• Ferrari Carano (Siena)
• Shafer (Firebreak)
• Staglin (Stagliano)
• Swanson (Sangiovese)
• Venge (Sangiovese)

Great U.S. Italian Varietal Producers (**)

• Adelaida (Sangiovese)
• Bella Vista (Dolcetto, Sangiovese)
• Cambria (Sangiovese)
• Castelletto (Sangiovese)
• Cosentino (Sangiovese, Nebbiolo)
• Eberle (Barbera)
• Estancia (Sangiovese)
• Montevina (Barbera, Sangiovese)
• Kent Rasmussen (Dolcetto)
• Renwood (Barbera)
• Venezia (Sangiovese)

Dependable U.S. Italian Varietal Producers (Recommended)

Some producers placed in this third tier are new (or new to us) and may merit a higher placement in subsequent vintages. These producers are offset by an asterisk.

• *Acorn (Dolcetto, Sangiovese)
• *Babcock (Sangiovese)
• Barboursville (Barbera)
• Beaulieu (Sangiovese)
• *Benziger (Sangiovese)
• *Bonterra (Sangiovese)
• *Byington (Nebbiolo)
• *Chappellet (Sangiovese)
• *Coturri (Sangiovese)
• *Duckhorn (Paraduxx)
• *Fife (Barbera, Charbono, Sangiovese)
• Flora Springs (Sangiovese)
• *Thomas Fogarty (Sangiovese)
• *Forest Glen (Sangiovese)
• Justin (Nebbiolo)
• Martin Brothers (Nebbiolo)
• Martini & Prati (Barbera)
• Robert Mondavi (Barbera, Sangiovese)
• *Pugliese (Sangiovese)
• Rabbit Ridge (Barbera)
• *Rutherford Hill (Sangiovese)
• Sebastiani (Barbera)
• *Silverado (Sangiovese)
• Trentadue (Sangiovese)

Highly Recommended American-Italian Reds

Barbera

89 • Chameleon (CA) 1996 Barbera, Amador County. $14.

87 • Terra d'Oro (CA) 1995 Montevina, Barbera, Amador County. $18.

87 • Louis Martini (CA) 1994 Heritage Collection, Barbera, Lake County. $12.

Dolcetto

87 • Acorn (CA) 1996 Alegria Vineyards, Dolcetto, Russian River Valley. $18.

Sangiovese

91 • Thomas Fogarty (CA) 1996 Estate Reserve, Sangiovese,
    Santa Cruz Mountains. $27.50.

91 • Rutherford Hill (CA) 1995 21st Anniversary, Sangiovese, Napa Valley. $30.

90 • Staglin (CA) 1996 Stagliano, Sangiovese, Rutherford, Napa Valley. $35.

90 • Altamura (CA) 1994 Sangiovese, Napa Valley. $28.

90 • Adelaida (CA) 1995 Sangiovese, San Luis Obispo County. $24.

89 • Trentadue (CA) 1995 Sangiovese, Alexander Valley. $18.

89 • Chappellet (CA) 1995 Sangiovese, Napa Valley. $22.

88 • Pugliese (NY) 1997 Sangiovese, North Fork of Long Island. $13.99.

88 • Chameleon (CA) 1996 Sangiovese, North Coast. $16.

87 • Terra d'Oro (CA) 1995 Montevina, Sangiovese, Amador County. $16.

87 • Obester (CA) 1995 20th Anniversary, Sangiovese, Mendocino County. $13.95.

87 • Forest Glen (CA) 1996 Sangiovese, California. $9.99.

87 • Amador Foothill Winery (CA) 1995 Sangiovese, Shenandoah Valley. $12.

86 • Venge (CA) 1996 Penny Lane Vineyard, Sangiovese, Oakville, Napa Valley. $20.

86 • Iron Horse (CA) 1995 T-bar-T Vineyards, Sangiovese, Alexander Valley. $16.

86 • Deaver (CA) 1996 Sangiovese, Amador County. $16.

86 • Cambria (CA) 1996 Tepusquet Vineyard, Sangiovese, Santa Maria Valley. $18.

86 • Atlas Peak Vineyards (CA) 1995 Reserve, Sangiovese, Atlas Peak, Napa Valley. $24.

86 • Albertoni (CA) 1996 Sangiovese, California. $13.99.

85 • Venezia (CA) 1996 Alegria Vineyards, Sangiovese, Russian River Valley. $19.99.

85 • Folie à Deux (CA) 1996 Sangiovese, Amador County. $16.

85 • Babcock (CA) 1996 Eleven Oaks, Sangiovese, Santa Ynez Valley. $18.

Italian Varietal Blends

93 • Duckhorn (CA) 1995 Paraduxx, Napa Valley. $20.

87 • Shafer (CA) 1995 Firebreak, Napa Valley. $27.

86 • Hidden Cellars (CA) 1996 Sorcery Red, Mendocino. $28.

86 • Ferrari-Carano (CA) 1995 Siena, Sonoma County. $28.

fifteen

❦

North American Cabernet Franc, Malbec, and Petit Verdot

❦

An Introduction: What about U.S. Cabernet Franc, Malbec, and Petit Verdot?

Cabernet Franc is very closely related to Cabernet Sauvignon and, indeed, it is widely presumed that Cabernet Franc is just a well-established mutation of Cabernet Sauvignon. It is ideally suited to cooler climates as it buds and ripens earlier than Cabernet Sauvignon. Additionally, it is less susceptible to poor weather during harvest. In the Medoc and Graves region of Bordeaux, where it typically constitutes about 15% of the final blend, it is seen as a measure of insurance against poor Cabernet Sauvignon or Merlot weather. Cabernet Franc used to be planted almost as widely as Cabernet Sauvignon in Bordeaux well into the '60s, but Cabernet Sauvignon had swung into such favor that 20 years later it had twice the acreage of Cabernet Franc. Cabernet Franc tends to be lighter in color and tannins than Cabernet Sauvignon, with an earlier maturing character. On Bordeaux's Right Bank, Cabernet Franc has a stronger foothold, and is best known as the dominant grape in the blend for the famed chateau, Cheval Blanc. In the Loire it is the most widely planted red varietal where it yields lighter wines, with distinct herbal overtones. U.S. Cabernet Francs are still largely in the experimental stage and there is a huge spectrum of interpretations, from heavy Napa wines to lighter styles from the East Coast.

Malbec is a rarely planted varietal in Bordeaux, which yields a wine of great color if sometimes it is somewhat short on flavor. It can be tricky to grow as it is susceptible to a range of vineyard diseases. Nonetheless, it has taken hold in Argentina, where it produces a rich rustic wine. In the United States there is very little planted, but some early efforts have proven to be promising.

Petit Verdot, on the other hand, can yield a wine of great depth and personality. It has fallen from favor in Bordeaux, however, as it ripens later than Cabernet Sauvignon and hence only in the best of years. This might

Cabernet Franc, Malbec, and Petit Verdot at a Glance

Wines Reviewed:

65

Producers/Brands Represented:

57

Median Price:

$18

bode well for the varietal in California, which has no such ripening problems, and indeed some of the early efforts with the grape have been surprisingly excellent, with solid structure, deep color, and exotic aromatics. Of all three varieties in California, Petit Verdot just may be the one to watch in the long run.

Best U.S. Cabernet Franc, Malbec, and Petit Verdot Producers

Premier U.S. Cabernet Franc, Malbec, and Petit Verdot Producers (***)

• Benziger Imagery Series (Cabernet Franc, Petit Verdot, & Malbec)
• Jarvis (Cabernet Franc)

Great U.S. Cabernet Franc, Malbec, and Petit Verdot Producers (**)

• Columbia Winery
  (Red Willow Cabernet Franc)
• Chateau Ste. Michelle (Cold Creek Vineyard Cabernet Franc)
• Helena View (Cabernet Franc)

Dependable U.S. Cabernet Franc, Malbec, and Petit Verdot Producers (Recommended)

Some producers placed in this third tier are new (or new to us) and may merit a higher placement in subsequent vintages. These producers are offset by an asterisk.

• Ahlgren (Cabernet Franc)
• Badger Mountain (Cabernet Franc)
• Barboursville (Cabernet Franc)
• Carmenet (Cabernet Franc)
• *Chappellet
• Clos du Bois (Cabernet Franc)
• Cosentino (Cabernet Franc)
• Gainey (Limited Selection Cabernet Franc)
• Geyser Peak (Cabernet Franc, Petit Verdot, & Malbec)
• Guenoc (Cabernet Franc & Petit Verdot)
• Horton (Cabernet Franc & Malbec)
• Jekel (Cabernet Franc, Petit Verdot, & Malbec)
• Justin (Cabernet Franc)
• Kendall-Jackson (Cabernet Franc)
• *Niebaum Coppola (Cabernet Franc)
• *Peju Province (Cabernet Franc & Petit Verdot)
• *Pride Mountain (Cabernet Franc)
• Quail Ridge (Cabernet Franc)
• *Signorello (Cabernet Franc)
• *Waterbrook (Cabernet Franc)

Highly Recommended Cabernet Franc, Malbec, and Petit Verdot

Cabernet Franc

93 • Jarvis (CA) 1996 Cabernet Franc, Napa Valley. $44.

90 • Signorello (CA) 1995 Cabernet Franc, Napa Valley. $35.

90 • Niebaum-Coppola (CA) 1996 Cabernet Franc, Napa Valley. $20.

89 • Pride Mountain (CA) 1996 Cabernet Franc, Sonoma County. $25.

89 • Pindar (NY) 1994 Cabernet Franc, North Fork of Long Island. $12.99.

89 • Benziger (CA) 1996 Imagery Series, Rancho Salina & Blue Rock Vineyards, Cabernet Franc, Sonoma County. $22.

89 • Ahlgren (CA) 1996 Bates Ranch, Cabernet Franc, Santa Cruz Mountains. $18.

88 • Cosentino (CA) 1996 Cabernet Franc, Napa Valley. $25.

87 • Midnight Cellars (CA) 1995 Crescent, Cabernet Franc, Paso Robles. $15.

87 • Hagafen (CA) 1996 Cabernet Franc, Napa Valley. $18.

86 • Yorkville (CA) 1996 Rennie Vineyard, Cabernet Franc, Mendocino County. $14.

86 • Pellegrini (NY) 1995 Cabernet Franc, North Fork of Long Island. $23.

86 • Kendall-Jackson (CA) 1995 Buckeye Vineyard, Cabernet Franc, Alexander Valley. $20.

86 • Hargrave (NY) 1997 Cabernet Franc, North Fork of Long Island. $14.99.

86 • Gainey (CA) 1996 Limited Selection, Cabernet Franc, Santa Ynez Valley. $20.

86 • Columbia Winery (WA) 1996 Red Willow Vineyard, David Lake Signature Series, Cabernet Franc, Yakima Valley. $19.

86 • Columbia Winery (WA) 1995 Red Willow Vineyard, David Lake Signature Series, Cabernet Franc, Yakima Valley. $20.99.

86 • Chappellet (CA) 1996 Cabernet Franc, Napa Valley. $24.

86 • Chaddsford (PA) 1996 Cabernet Franc, Pennsylvania. $18.

85 • Mission View (CA) 1995 Cabernet Franc, Paso Robles. $13.50.

85 • Hogue (WA) 1994 Genesis, Cabernet Franc, Columbia Valley. $15.

Malbec

85 • Geyser Peak (CA) 1996 Winemaker's Selection, Malbec, Alexander Valley. $20.

Petite Verdot

86 • Geyser Peak (CA) 1996 Winemaker's Selection, Petite Verdot, Alexander Valley. $20.

sixteen

North American Chardonnay

American Chardonnay

Chardonnay is the world's most recognized and requested white wine, so much so that it has effectively become a cliché. This popularity is further exaggerated in the United States where Chardonnay has become synonymous with white wine. Why is Chardonnay so popular? First and foremost, Chardonnay is not only capable of producing some of the world's greatest white wines, but also it grows virtually anywhere. It is a straightforward wine to produce.

Chardonnay is made at all price points but has also reached the pinnacle of quality in many nations and several continents, not only in its native France. Chardonnay simply has mass flavor appeal. Other varietals may present more distinctive personalities: Sauvignon Blanc with its aggressive herbal flavors and gripping acidity; Gewürztraminer filling the nose and palate with hints of rose-water and spice; or Viognier in its wildly exotic, unctuous manifestations. Chardonnay strikes the proverbial middle chord that translates to universal magnetism and a marketer's dream.

In the last decade or so Chardonnay has become the most popular white wine in the United States. This has led to massive plantings of the varietal, and there are now better than a thousand different bottlings produced in every vintage. From Massachusetts to Arizona, and most everywhere in between, Chardonnay has taken root. Differences in both style and price are as much, if not more, a product of winemaking decisions than of location. This is not to say that fruit from cool states such as Oregon does not differ from that of California's hot Central Valley. Chardonnay, perhaps more than any other variety, is the wine-maker's equivalent of a blank white canvas.

Left to its own devices, Chardonnay is simple, fresh, and clean with fruit ranging in flavors from apple and pear in cooler regions to tropical fruit notes in hot climates. The winemaker's decision to use oak or not greatly impacts both flavor and price. Oak barrels are very expensive. Chardonnay is often left on its lees, the sediment precipitated during fermentation. This imparts a toasty bread-like flavor. This process, which is sometimes indicated on the label as "Sur Lie," takes time and time equals money. A major contributor to flavor is the use of a secondary fermentation known technically as "malolactic fermentation." This secondary fermentation is bacteria-induced and creates no additional alcohol. Instead, it converts one kind of acid, *malic*, which is found in Granny Smith apples, to another softer acid, *lactic*, which is found in milk. In addition to acid conversion, malolactic fermentation creates a natural compound called diacetyl. Diacetyl is used by margarine producers to make their product taste like butter. It does the same for Chardonnay. Again this process takes time, which, as we know, in turn equals money. Chardonnay tends to ride out vintage difficulties fairly well, and outside of Oregon's notoriously fickle weather it usually offers a modicum of consistency, particularly in California. Recently, however, the West Coast has had some difficult Chardonnay vintages.

Difficult Vintages?

Craig Williams, the well-respected winemaker of Napa Valley stalwart Joseph Phelps refers to the challenging nature of the '96 harvest with mention of "heat spikes that rendered the sugar/acid/flavor balance between vineyards as highly variable." He goes on to say that "although many excellent wines have been produced from the '96 vintage, it was not a year where quality was consistent throughout." The results of our tastings of '96 Chardonnays from California bear this out. Through rigorous selection and a bit of luck, many producers made fine wines, while a number of others had difficulty maintaining acid levels. Across the board, the '96 Chardonnays are accessible in youth, with ripe and generous characters that won't take well to bottle age. The 1997s will be a definite step up in quality.

As for the Northwest, while 1994 was excellent and 1995 was sound in Oregon, 1996 and 1997 have proven to be even more difficult than California's '96. Combating rain and a lack of ripeness, better Oregon vintners were at least able to make attractive zesty wines, but we will have to wait for future vintages to see a repeat of the knockout 1994s. The 1998 vintage should be just the ticket, as vintners are talking about a replay of 1994. Luckily, Washington fared much better than Oregon in 1996, and a number of outstanding wines were produced.

What has all this meant for price? Not much, as prices are still creeping upward. Fortunately, the increases have been nowhere near the magnitude of those experienced in Cabernet, Merlot, or Pinot Noir, but the average bottle of U.S. Chardonnay will still set you back about $18.

Chardonnay and Food

In regards to pairing Chardonnay with food, pricey and flashy Chardonnay, from California glamour appellations, tends to be fat and rich, with plenty of oak, butter, and spice. On their own these wines are interesting, if heavy. With food they can be clumsy, dominating, and largely incompatible. Cooler climate Chardonnays are often more restrained, with clean fruit balanced by crisp acidity. These wines work with a great deal of dishes from fish to fowl. Crisp, "simplistic" Chardonnay also works well as an aperitif, stimulating the palate rather than drowning it.

Chardonnay at a Glance

Wines Reviewed:

599

Producers/Brands Represented:

376

Median Price:

$18

Best U.S. Chardonnay Producers

Premier U.S. Chardonnay Producers(***)

- Arrowood (Cuvée Michel Berthoud)
- Au Bon Climat (Various Bottlings)
- Beringer (Private Reserve and Sbragia)
- Chateau Potelle (VGS)
- Chateau Ste. Michelle (Reserve and Vineyard designated bottlings)
- Columbia Winery (Wyckoff and Otis Vineyards)
- Gary Farrell
- Ferrari-Carano (Alexander Valley, Reserve, and Tre Terre)
- Fisher (Whitney's Vineyard)
- Franciscan (Cuvée Sauvage)
- Gallo-Sonoma (Estate)
- Guenoc (Genevieve Magoon)
- Hanzell
- Jarvis
- Kistler
- Lewis Cellars
- Matanzas Creek
- Mer et Soleil
- Peter Michael
- Robert Mondavi (Reserve)
- Mount Eden Vineyards
- Newton
- Patz and Hall
- Joseph Phelps (Ovation)
- Qupe
- Ridge
- Rombauer
- San Saba Vineyard
- Shafer (Red Shoulder Ranch)
- Signorello (Founder's Reserve and Hope's Cuvée)
- Stag's Leap Wine Cellars (Reserve and Beckstoffer)
- Talbott

Great U.S. Chardonnay Producers(**)

- Adelaida
- Apex
- Arrowood (Sonoma County)
- Beaucanon
- Bernardus
- Beringer
- David Bruce (Estate Reserve)
- Byington
- Byron (Reserve)
- Calera
- Cambria
- Chalk Hill
- Chalone Vineyard
- Chateau Montelena
- Chateau Potelle
- Chateau St. Jean (Robert Young, Belle Terre, and Durell)
- Chateau Ste. Michelle
- Cinnabar
- Columbia Winery
- Cooper Mountain
- Crichton Hall
- Cronin
- Cuvaison
- Dehlinger
- De Loach (OFS)
- Domain Hill and Mayes
- Edmeades
- El Molino
- Eola Hills
- Far Niente
- Fisher (Coach Insignia)
- Thomas Fogarty (Estate Reserve)
- Franciscan (Napa Valley)
- Gainey
- Gallo-Sonoma (Stefani and Laguna Ranch)
- Grgich Hills
- Gristina (Andy's Field)
- Hess
- Jory (Lion Oaks Ranch)
- Kendall-Jackson
- La Crema
- Landmark
- Laurier
- L'Ecole No. 41
- J. Lohr
- Merryvale
- Robert Mondavi (Carneros, Napa Valley)
- Morgan
- Oakville Ranch
- Paraiso Springs
- Fess Parker
- Peju Province
- Joseph Phelps
- Plam
- Qupe

Scale: Superlative (96-100), Exceptional (90-95), Highly Recommended (85-89), Recommended (80-84), Not Recommended (Under 80)

- Rochioli
- Rosenblum
- Sanford
- Santa Barbara Winery
- Signorello (Napa Valley)
- Silverado
- Simi (Reserve)
- Sonoma-Cutrer
- Sonoma-Loeb
- St. Clement
- St. Francis (Reserve)
- Stag's Leap Wine Cellars
- Steele
- Swanson
- Mark West
- Wild Horse
- Wildhurst
- Woodward Canyon

Dependable U.S. Chardonnay Producers (Recommended)

Some producers placed in this third tier are new (or new to us) and may merit a higher placement in subsequent vintages. These producers are offset by an asterisk.

- Anapamu
- *Babcock
- Barnard Griffin
- Benziger
- *Burgess
- Byron
- Camelot
- Canoe Ridge Vineyard
- Carmenet
- *Chappellet
- Chateau Morrisette
- Chateau Woltner
- Clos La Chance
- Clos Pegase
- Cobblestone
- *Cristom
- *Curtis
- Dry Creek Vineyard (Reserve)
- Elkhorn Peak
- Gloria Ferrer
- Flora Springs
- *Foley
- Forest Glen
- Foxen

- Guenoc
- Harrison
- *Hartford Court
- Horton
- Joullian
- Kalin
- Robert Keenan
- *Kestrel
- *Lambert Bridge
- *Long
- *Macari
- MacRostie
- *Martinelli
- *Peter McCoy
- *McCrea
- McIlroy
- Meridian
- *Monticello
- Murphy-Goode
- *Neyers
- *Nichols
- *Niebaum-Coppola
- *Fess Parker
- *Pezzi King
- *Piedmont
- Pine Ridge
- *Ramey
- *Rancho Zabaco
- Martin Ray (Mariage)
- Stephen Ross
- Saintsbury
- Schug
- Sterling
- *Storrs
- Talley
- *Testarossa
- Marimar Torres
- Treleaven
- *Truchard
- *Venezia
- Villa Mt. Eden
- Waterbrook
- Willamette Valley Vineyards
- ZD

10 Key Regions for American Chardonnay

Napa Valley
Wines Reviewed: **90**
Median Price: **$22.00**

Napa is the nation's "grand cru" appellation, and Napa vintners have been nothing if not successful in marketing the valley as America's wine Eden. Geographically, the Napa Valley is reasonably contiguous, being 34 miles in length and between one and four miles in width from the town of Napa in the south to that of Calistoga in the north. It is an easy region in which to ripen grapes and consistently produces ripe full wines. The cool air from San Pablo Bay, just north of San Francisco, moves from south to north, giving the southern area cooler average temperatures.

An imprecise but useful generalization would be that the cooler southern end is more favorable to white varieties and Pinot Noir while the further north one gets the more red varietals one will encounter as the temperatures increase, with emphasis on Cabernet. This simplification does not account for the vagaries of soil types, microclimates, and vintners throughout the valley, and as such there are many exceptions to the rule. Nine sub-appellations have been created since the inception of the Napa Valley AVA in 1983, and these go some way toward addressing the differences in climate between some parts of the valley. With the hugely significant exception of Carneros, these sub-appellations are of more relevance to Cabernet than Chardonnay.

In style Napa Valley Chardonnays tend typically to be rich and ripe with an appealing fatness that makes them very accessible when young. They are generally made in relatively full-blown styles with more than a passing resemblance to Australian show wines, albeit with firmer structures. Though the winemaking runs the gamut, there is a definite tendency to endow the wines with a solid measure of oak. If you want a wine that will stand up to rich poultry or seafood dishes look no further, but those seeking a crisp aperitif style may want to look elsewhere. A number of wines listed here, however, may be sourced all or in part from the Napa subregion of Carneros. These wines tend to be in a lighter style (see Carneros, two sections forward). In the end, quality is universally high, and very few disappointing wines will carry the Napa AVA.

Highly Recommended Napa Valley Chardonnay
94 • Newton (CA) 1997 Chardonnay, Napa County. $25.
94 • Franciscan (CA) 1996 Oakville Estate, Cuvée Sauvage, Chardonnay, Napa Valley. $30.
94 • Ferrari-Carano (CA) 1995 Reserve, Chardonnay, 87% Napa County, 13% Sonoma County. $34.
94 • Beringer (CA) 1996 Sbragia-Limited Release, Chardonnay, Napa Valley. $35.
93 • Signorello (CA) 1997 Hope's Cuvée, Chardonnay, Napa Valley. $60.
92 • Robert Mondavi (CA) 1996 Reserve, Chardonnay, Napa Valley. $30.
92 • Peju Province (CA) 1997 Chardonnay, Napa Valley. $18.
92 • Cuvaison (CA) 1996 Reserve, Chardonnay, Napa Valley. $.
92 • Beringer (CA) 1997 Private Reserve, Chardonnay, Napa Valley. $36.
91 • Patz and Hall (CA) 1997 Chardonnay, Napa Valley. $30.
91 • Franciscan (CA) 1995 Oakville Estate, Cuvée Sauvage, Chardonnay, Napa Valley. $30.

Scale: Superlative (96-100), Exceptional (90-95), Highly Recommended (85-89), Recommended (80-84), Not Recommended (Under 80)

91 • Clos La Chance (CA) 1997 Chardonnay, Napa Valley. $17.

91 • Chappellet (CA) 1997 Signature Estate, Chardonnay, Napa Valley. $26.

90 • Stag's Leap Wine Cellars (CA) 1996 Reserve, Chardonnay, Napa Valley. $37.

90 • Signorello (CA) 1996 Hope's Cuvée, Chardonnay, Napa Valley. $60.

90 • Signorello (CA) 1996 Founder's Reserve, Chardonnay, Napa Valley. $45.

90 • Peter Michael (CA) 1996 "Clos du Ciel," Chardonnay, Napa County. $38.

90 • Peter McCoy (CA) 1996 Clos de Pierres, Chardonnay, Knights Valley. $39.

90 • Lewis Cellars (CA) 1997 Reserve, Chardonnay, Napa Valley. $34.99.

90 • Jarvis (CA) 1996 Reserve, Chardonnay, Napa Valley. $48.

90 • Jarvis (CA) 1996 Chardonnay, Napa Valley. $38.

90 • Beringer (CA) 1996 Private Reserve, Chardonnay, Napa Valley. $30.

89 • Venezia (CA) 1997 Regusci Vineyards, Chardonnay, Napa Valley. $20.

89 • Signorello (CA) 1997 Chardonnay, Napa Valley. $30.

89 • Peter Michael (CA) 1996 "Belle Côte," Chardonnay, Knights Valley. $42.

89 • Patz and Hall (CA) 1997 Carr Vineyard, Chardonnay, Mount Veeder. $42.

89 • Joseph Phelps (CA) 1996 Ovation, Chardonnay, Napa Valley. $40.

89 • Hess Collection (CA) 1996 Chardonnay, Napa Valley. $15.

89 • Elkhorn Peak (CA) 1997 Fagan Creek Vineyard, Chardonnay, Napa Valley. $18.

89 • Cosentino (CA) 1997 "The Sculptor" Reserve, Chardonnay, Napa Valley. $30.

89 • Chateau Potelle (CA) 1996 VGS, Chardonnay, Mount Veeder, Napa Valley. $38.

89 • Beaucanon (CA) 1997 Reserve, Chardonnay, Napa Valley. $12.

88 • Sterling (CA) 1997 Chardonnay, Napa Valley. $15.

88 • Raymond (CA) 1996 Generations, Chardonnay, Napa Valley. $27.

88 • Peju Province (CA) 1997 HB Vineyard, Chardonnay, Napa Valley. $26.

88 • Niebaum-Coppola (CA) 1997 Chardonnay, Napa Valley. $20.

88 • Monticello (CA) 1996 Wild Yeast Corley Reserve, Chardonnay, Napa Valley. $32.50.

88 • Grgich Hills (CA) 1997 Chardonnay, Napa Valley. $30.

88 • Flora Springs (CA) 1997 Reserve, Chardonnay, Napa Valley. $24.

88 • Edgewood (CA) 1997 Chardonnay, Napa Valley. $18.

88 • Crichton Hall (CA) 1996 Chardonnay, Napa Valley. $22.

88 • Chappellet (CA) 1997 Estate, Chardonnay, Napa Valley. $17.

87 • Robert Mondavi (CA) 1996 Chardonnay, Napa Valley. $19.

87 • Monthaven (CA) 1997 Chardonnay, Napa Valley. $9.99.

87 • Hagafen (CA) 1997 Reserve, Chardonnay, Napa Valley. $18.

87 • Cosentino (CA) 1997 Chardonnay, Napa Valley. $18.

87 • Beaucanon (CA) 1997 Jacques de Coninck, Chardonnay, Napa Valley. $30.

86 • William Hill (CA) 1997 Reserve, Chardonnay, Napa Valley. $20.

86 • William Hill (CA) 1997 Chardonnay, Napa Valley. $14.50.

86 • V. Sattui (CA) 1997 Carsi Vineyard, Chardonnay, Napa Valley. $18.

86 • Stags' Leap Winery (CA) 1997 Chardonnay, Napa Valley. $21.

86 • S. Anderson (CA) 1997 Chardonnay, Stags Leap District. $22.

86 • St. Supéry (CA) 1996 Dollarhide Ranch, Chardonnay, Napa Valley. $12.50.

86 • Pine Ridge (CA) 1997 Knollside Cuvée, Chardonnay, Napa Valley. $17.50.

86 • Parducci (CA) 1996 Carneros Bighorn Ranch, Reserve, Chardonnay, Napa Valley. $20.

86 • Franciscan (CA) 1997 Oakville Estate, Chardonnay, Napa Valley. $15.

86 • Far Niente (CA) 1997 Chardonnay, Napa Valley. $40.

86 • Chateau Montelena (CA) 1996 Chardonnay, Napa Valley. $29.

86 • Beringer (CA) 1996 Chardonnay, Napa Valley. $15.

86 • Atlas Peak Vineyards (CA) 1997 Chardonnay, Atlas Peak, Napa Valley. $16.

85 • Oakville Ranch (CA) 1996 ORV, Chardonnay, Oakville. $32.

85 • Merryvale (CA) 1996 Reserve, Chardonnay, Napa Valley. $30.

Sonoma County

Wines Reviewed: **99**
Median Price: **$20**

Sonoma County as an AVA is twice the size of the Napa Valley. It is generally cooler and somewhat more complex as a region than Napa, encompassing six major AVAs and their sub-appellations as well as the two large umbrella AVAs of Northern Sonoma and Sonoma Coast. These AVAs go some way toward defining the different styles of wine within the county. With the exception of Carneros, straddled across Napa Valley and Sonoma County, and with its own identity, it is difficult to easily determine a consistent style throughout the region. Most producers blend from different sub-appellations throughout the county and thus label with the Sonoma County designation.

The Russian River Valley is one of the most notable of the AVAs within Sonoma County. A distinctly maritime climate with cooling sea winds and the influence of the Russian River itself all combine to give cooler growing conditions that produce leaner styles of Chardonnay in general, as exemplified by Sonoma-Cutrer, Gary Farrell, and De Loach. An indication of the climactic leanings of the area is that much of the Chardonnay in Russian River is used in the production of sparkling wine. This will indicate wines that are very crisp and focused with solid acidity. Some Russian River bottlings, accordingly, are best when held for a year or two.

On the other hand, the Alexander Valley is one of the warmest climate AVAs in Sonoma County, and as such, much of its Chardonnay production is destined toward "county" designated blends. Although it is only some 18 miles from the ocean, the maritime influence is not what it is in the Russian River Valley, and the Alexander is actually a much more important producer of varietals such as Cabernet and even Zinfandel. At the high end of production, the style of Alexander Valley could be described as lush, rich, and tropical.

Overall, Sonoma County Chardonnay can reach great heights, and at the very top might be even more exciting than Napa bottlings, but the wines as a whole are much more variable. They tend to be higher in acidity than Napa Chardonnays, with firmer structures, and are accordingly less approachable in youth. Without question, high end Sonoma Chardonnay shows best at the table when paired with foods.

Highly Recommended Sonoma County Chardonnay

Sonoma County (General)

94 • Gallo Sonoma (CA) 1996 Estate, Chardonnay, Northern Sonoma. $38.

92 • Sonoma-Cutrer (CA) 1996 Les Pierres, Chardonnay, Sonoma County. $29.99.

92 • Arrowood (Ca) 1996 Réserve Spéciale, Cuvée Michel Berthoud, Chardonnay, Sonoma County. $38.

91 • St. Francis (CA) 1997 Reserve, Chardonnay, Sonoma County. $22.99.

91 • Sonoma-Cutrer (CA) 1996 The Cutrer, Chardonnay, Sonoma County. $27.99.

91 • Pezzi King (CA) 1997 Chardonnay, Sonoma County. $21.

91 • La Crema (CA) 1997 Cold Coast Vineyards, Chardonnay, Sonoma Coast. $19.

91 • Domaine Laurier (CA) 1996 Reserve, Chardonnay, Sonoma County. $16.

90 • Dry Creek Vineyard (CA) 1997 Reserve, Chardonnay, Sonoma County. $20.

89 • Paradise Ridge (CA) 1997 Barrel Select, Nagasawa Vineyard, Chardonnay, Sonoma County. $17.95.

89 • Hartford Court (CA) 1996 Seascape Vineyard, Chardonnay, Sonoma Coast. $35.

89 • Fisher (CA) 1997 Whitney's Vineyard, Chardonnay, Sonoma County. $40.

88 • Simi (CA) 1995 Reserve, Chardonnay, Sonoma County. $29.

88 • Laurier (CA) 1996 Chardonnay, Sonoma County. $15.

88 • Landmark (CA) 1996 Damaris Reserve, Chardonnay, Sonoma County. $32.

88 • Lambert Bridge (CA) 1997 Chardonnay, Sonoma County. $18.

87 • Rodney Strong (CA) 1996 Chalk Hill Vineyard Reserve, Chardonnay, Northern Sonoma. $24.

87 • Dry Creek Vineyard (CA) 1997 Chardonnay, Sonoma County. $16.

86 • Simi (CA) 1996 Chardonnay, Sonoma County. $17.

86 • Martinelli (CA) 1996 Charles Ranch, Chardonnay, Sonoma Coast. $30.

86 • Chalk Hill (CA) 1996 Chardonnay, Chalk Hill, Sonoma County. $28.

Sonoma County (Alexander Valley)

93 • Ferrari-Carano (CA) 1996 Chardonnay, Alexander Valley. $21.

92 • Chateau St. Jean (CA) 1996 Robert Young Vineyard, Chardonnay, Alexander Valley. $24.

90 • Geyser Peak (CA) 1996 Reserve, Chardonnay, Alexander Valley. $23.

89 • Murphy-Goode (CA) 1996 Island Block Reserve, Chardonnay, Alexander Valley. $24.

89 • Huntington (CA) 1997 Cairns Cuvée, Chardonnay, Alexander Valley. $16.

86 • Venezia (CA) 1996 Big River Ranch, Chardonnay, Alexander Valley. $19.99.

86 • de Lorimier (CA) 1996 Chardonnay, Alexander Valley. $16.

86 • Clos du Bois (CA) 1997 Calcaire Vineyard, Chardonnay, Alexander Valley. $18.

Sonoma County (Dry Creek Valley)

88 • Pedroncelli (CA) 1997 F. Johnson Vineyard, Chardonnay, Dry Creek Valley. $13.

86 • Gallo Sonoma (CA) 1996 Stefani Vineyard, Chardonnay, Dry Creek Valley. $18.

Sonoma County (Russian River Valley)

95 • Martinelli (CA) 1996 Gold Ridge, Chardonnay, Russian River Valley. $20.

94 • Gary Farrell (CA) 1996 Allen Vineyard, Chardonnay, Russian River Valley. $28.

93 • Rochioli (CA) 1995 Estate, Chardonnay, Russian River Valley. $25.

92 • Zabaco (CA) 1996 Chardonnay, Russian River Valley. $14.

89 • Murphy-Goode (CA) 1996 J&K Murphy Vineyard Reserve, Chardonnay, Russian River Valley. $24.

89 • Mark West (CA) 1996 Chardonnay, Russian River Valley. $15.

89 • Joseph Swan (CA) 1997 Estate Vineyard, Chardonnay, Russian River Valley. $22.50.

88 • Gallo Sonoma (CA) 1997 Chardonnay, Russian River Valley. $14.

87 • Gallo Sonoma (CA) 1996 Laguna Ranch Vineyard, Chardonnay, Russian River Valley. $20.

87 • Chateau Souverain (CA) 1996 Winemaker's Reserve, Chardonnay, Russian River Valley. $20.

86 • Windsor (CA) 1996 Preston Ranch, Private Reserve, Chardonnay, Russian River Valley. $14.

86 • Windsor (CA) 1996 Barrel Fermented, Private Reserve, Chardonnay, Russian River Valley. $15.

86 • Herzog (CA) 1996 Special Reserve, Chardonnay, Russian River Valley. $19.99.

85 • Windsor (CA) 1996 Private Reserve Estate, Chardonnay, Russian River Valley. $20.

85 • Rutz (CA) 1996 Dutton Ranch, Chardonnay, Russian River Valley. $30.

Sonoma County (Sonoma Valley)

94 • Matanzas Creek (CA) 1995 Journey, Chardonnay, Sonoma Valley. $95.

88 • Steele (CA) 1996 Parmlee-Hill Vineyard, Chardonnay, Sonoma Valley. $26.

88 • Matanzas Creek (CA) 1996 Chardonnay, Sonoma Valley. $30.

87 • Kunde (CA) 1996 Wildwood Vineyard, Chardonnay, Sonoma Valley. $20.

86 • Kunde (CA) 1996 Kinneybrook Vineyard, Chardonnay, Sonoma Valley. $20.

Carneros

Wines Reviewed: **40**

Median Price: **$24**

Carneros has an identity quite distinct from either the Napa Valley or Sonoma County. The cool and windy climate has a strong maritime influence with winds racing from the San Pablo Bay and through the Petaluma Gap on the Sonoma Coast. Cool foggy mornings are the norm here.

Arguably, typical Carneros Chardonnay is among the easier styles of California wines to pick out in blind tastings. The style is characterized by lean, tart, crisp apple flavors and many are quite understated when young. These wines are often not at their best in extreme youth and better examples can develop tertiary nutty qualities with some bottle age. A sizable proportion of the region's Chardonnay, as much as a third, is used for high-quality sparkling wine production.

Carneros is not the home to many wineries, but supplies grapes to wineries outside its boundaries. Indeed, most Chardonnays from wineries in the Napa Valley proper are produced with Carneros fruit. This is further testament to the fact that this district produces some of the nation's best examples of the varietal.

Highly Recommended Carneros Chardonnay

94 • Shafer (CA) 1997 Red Shoulder Ranch, Chardonnay, Carneros, Napa Valley. $35.

93 • Shafer (CA) 1996 Red Shoulder Ranch, Chardonnay, Carneros, Napa Valley. $30.

92 • Patz & Hall (CA) 1997 Hyde Vineyard, Chardonnay, Carneros. $36.

91 • Truchard (CA) 1996 Chardonnay, Carneros, Napa Valley. $24.

91 • Steele (CA) 1996 Durell Vineyard, Chardonnay, Carneros. $26.

91 • Ramey (CA) 1996 Hyde Vineyard, Chardonnay, Carneros, Napa Valley. $45.

89 • St. Clement (CA) 1997 Abbots Vineyard, Chardonnay, Carneros, Napa Valley. $20.

89 • Cuvaison (CA) 1997 Chardonnay, Carneros. $.

88 • Chateau St. Jean (CA) 1996 Durell Vineyard, Chardonnay, Carneros. $24.

87 • Stag's Leap Wine Cellars (CA) 1996 Beckstoffer Ranch, Chardonnay, Napa Valley. $30.

87 • Rombauer (CA) 1997 Chardonnay, Carneros. $25.75.

87 • Adastra (CA) 1996 Chardonnay, Carneros, Napa Valley. $22.

86 • Schug (CA) 1997 Chardonnay, Carneros. $18.

86 • Schug (CA) 1996 Heritage Reserve, Chardonnay, Carneros. $25.

86 • Salmon Creek (CA) 1996 Chardonnay, Los Carneros, Sonoma County. $16.

86 • Foxridge (CA) 1997 Chardonnay, Carneros. $9.99.

86 • Ehlers Grove (CA) 1997 Winery Reserve, Chardonnay, Carneros, Napa Valley. $30.

86 • Bouchaine (CA) 1996 Chardonnay, Carneros. $18.

86 • Benziger (CA) 1996 Chardonnay, Carneros. $13.

86 • Anderson's Conn Valley Vineyards (CA) 1996 Fournier Vineyard, Chardonnay, Carneros. $40.

Scale: Superlative (96-100), Exceptional (90-95), Highly Recommended (85-89), Recommended (80-84), Not Recommended (Under 80)

85 • Neyers (CA) 1997 Chardonnay, Carneros. $27.99.

85 • Liparita (CA) 1997 Chardonnay, Carneros. $24.

Monterey

Wines Reviewed: **33**

Median Price: **$16**

Surprise, Surprise...In several of the last few vintages the highest percentage of outstanding Chardonnay within any given area in the country has come from Monterey and its surrounding appellations.

Monterey has a considerable ocean breeze influence, giving it a distinctly cool growing climate at its closest point to the ocean in the Salinas Valley. Initial large plantings here during the 1970s in inappropriate locations gave this county a reputation for vegetal wines, as the vineyards exposed to the funneled sea breezes struggled to ripen red varietals. With more appropriate locations and a better understanding of microclimates, this region is now producing Chardonnay of the highest quality. Our tastings reveal that Monterey often turns in the highest proportion of 'excellent' Chardonnays, and although this is hardly a scientific measurement, it is clearly a sign that something very exciting is happening with Chardonnay in this region.

The most notable of the sub-appellations farther from the coast are Arroyo Secco, Chalone, and the Santa Lucia Highlands. Most producers are choosing to use the Monterey designation on their bottlings, but it is reasonable to assume that in time these AVAs will gain stronger identities in their own right, as more producers will choose to use the more specific AVA designation on their label. The style of top-notch Monterey Chardonnay is not a statement of outright power but more often ripeness of flavors allied to balance and refinement with excellent acidity. Mirassou exemplifies the style perfectly with their consistently excellent but value-conscious Chardonnays that are made with fruit sourced from the Arroyo Secco AVA. These are wines that can be enjoyed by themselves or right through the meal.

Highly Recommended Monterey Chardonnay

93 • San Saba (CA) 1997 Chardonnay, Monterey. $20.

91 • Talbott (CA) 1996 Cuvée Cynthia, Chardonnay, Monterey. $45.

91 • Morgan (CA) 1996 Reserve, Chardonnay, Monterey. $25.

91 • J. Lohr (CA) 1997 Riverstone, Chardonnay, Monterey. $14.

90 • Talbott (CA) 1995 Diamond T Estate, Chardonnay, Monterey. $45.

89 • Paraiso Springs (CA) 1997 Chardonnay, Santa Lucia Highlands. $16.

89 • Chalone (CA) 1996 Reserve, Chardonnay, Chalone. $45.

88 • Joullian (CA) 1996 Chardonnay, Monterey. $15.50.

88 • Chalone (CA) 1997 The Pinnacles, Chardonnay, Chalone. $31.

88 • Chalone (CA) 1996 Chardonnay, Chalone. $27.

88 • Bernardus (CA) 1996 Chardonnay, Monterey County. $18.

87 • Testarossa (CA) 1996 Chardonnay, Chalone Appellation, Monterey County. $29.

86 • Wente (CA) 1996 Riva Ranch Reserve, Chardonnay, Arroyo Secco, Monterey. $16.

86 • Shale Ridge (CA) 1997 Chardonnay, Monterey. $9.99.

86 • Raymond (CA) 1997 Chardonnay, Monterey. $13.

86 • Monterra (CA) 1997 San Bernabé Ranch, Chardonnay, Monterey County. $8.99.

86 • Lockwood (CA) 1997 Chardonnay, Monterey. $14.99.

86 • Heartswood (CA) 1995 Private Reserve, Chardonnay, Monterey. $9.99.

86 • Guglielmo (CA) 1997 Private Reserve, Chardonnay, Monterey County. $14.
85 • Jekel (CA) 1997 FOS Reserve, Chardonnay, Monterey. $22.
85 • Kendall-Jackson (CA) 1996 Paradise Vineyard, Chardonnay, Arroyo Seco. $18.

California's South Central Coast
Wines Reviewed: **54**
Median Price: **$20**

The southerly location of the South Central Coast and the associated heat is mitigated in pockets with cooler microclimates created by the access of cool sea air through river valleys leading to the ocean. With coolness being dictated by access to sea air, it follows that a variety of different growing conditions exist. The more northerly county of San Luis Obispo is divided into four AVAs: Paso Robles, York Mountain, Edna Valley, and Arroyo Grande. Paso Robles is a large AVA without much ocean influence, making it a warm climate growing region with some cooler microclimates located toward the southwestern sector where the sea air enters via the Templeton Gap. Edna Valley and Arroyo Secco are further south and closer to the ocean, giving them cooler maritime climates and a more natural association overall with the Chardonnay vines that dominate both appellations. Indeed, both AVAs are also a source of premium sparkling wine grapes supplied to a number of wineries.

Santa Barbara has a cool climate for grape growing thanks to the cool ocean air that moves along the Santa Maria Valley. Just how cool a given area might be is dictated by its distance along the valley from the ocean. This region produces some of the finest Chardonnays of the South Central Coast as exemplified by bottlings from Au Bon Climat. At their best these wines have the richness of Napa but with more finesse and fine acidity to match. The style of winemaking, however, is often quite flashy, with a heavy reliance on toasty oak. These are wines, like Napa's, which pair well with richer dishes.

A little further southwards in Santa Barbara the Santa Ynez Valley provides slightly warmer growing conditions, but westwards along the river toward the ocean are some excellent cooler microclimates that are ideally suited to Burgundian varietals such as Pinot Noir and Chardonnay. Longoria and Babcock are two such wineries that produce fine Santa Ynez bottlings.

Highly Recommended South Central Coast Chardonnay

98 • Foley (CA) 1997 Barrel Select, Chardonnay, Santa Barbara County. $28.
95 • Foley (CA) 1997 Bien Nacido Vineyard, Chardonnay, Santa Maria Valley. $24.
94 • Foley (CA) 1996 Barrel Select, Chardonnay, Santa Barbara County. $25.
93 • Villa Mt. Eden (CA) 1996 Signature Series, Bien Nacido Vineyard, Chardonnay, Santa Maria Valley. $30.
93 • Qupé (CA) 1997 Bien Nacido Vineyard, Chardonnay, Santa Barbara County. $18.
93 • Au Bon Climat (CA) 1997 Alban Vineyard, Chardonnay, Edna Valley. $35.
91 • Steele (CA) 1996 Bien Nacido Vineyard, Chardonnay, Santa Barbara County. $26.
90 • Stephen Ross (CA) 1997 Bien Nacido Vineyard, Chardonnay, Santa Maria Valley. $20.
90 • Seven Peaks (CA) 1997 Reserve, Chardonnay, Edna Valley. $16.
90 • Santa Barbara Winery (CA) 1996 Reserve, Chardonnay, Santa Ynez Valley. $24.
90 • Qupé (CA) 1996 Bien Nacido Reserve, Chardonnay, Santa Barbara County. $25.
89 • Meridian (CA) 1996 Coastal Reserve, Chardonnay, Edna Valley. $15.
89 • LinCourt (CA) 1997 Chardonnay, Santa Barbara County. $14.

Scale: Superlative (96-100), Exceptional (90-95), Highly Recommended (85-89), Recommended (80-84), Not Recommended (Under 80)

446

89 • Fess Parker (CA) 1997 American Tradition Reserve, Marcella's Vineyards, Chardonnay, Santa Barbara County. $24.

89 • Baileyana (CA) 1997 Chardonnay, Edna Valley. $17.

89 • Au Bon Climat (CA) 1997 Chardonnay, Santa Barbara County. $18.

89 • Au Bon Climat (CA) 1996 Le Bouge D'à Côte, Chardonnay, Santa Barbara County. $19.

88 • Villa Mt. Eden (CA) 1997 Grand Reserve, Bien Nacido Vineyard, Chardonnay, Santa Maria Valley. $18.

88 • Stephen Ross (CA) 1997 Edna Ranch, Chardonnay, Edna Valley. $18.50.

88 • McKeon-Phillips (CA) 1996 Reserve, Chardonnay, Santa Barbara County. $21.33.

88 • Fess Parker (CA) 1997 American Tradition Reserve, Chardonnay, Santa Barbara County. $22.

88 • Cambria (CA) 1996 Reserve, Chardonnay, Santa Maria Valley. $36.

87 • Talley (CA) 1997 Chardonnay, Arroyo Grande Valley. $22.

87 • Nichols (CA) 1996 Paragon Vineyard, Chardonnay, Edna Valley. $32.

87 • Gainey (CA) 1996 Limited Selection, Chardonnay, Santa Barbara County. $28.

87 • Fess Parker (CA) 1997 Chardonnay, Santa Barbara County. $16.

86 • Rosenblum (CA) 1997 Chardonnay, Edna Valley. $23.

86 • Nichols (CA) 1997 Edna Ranch Vineyard, Chardonnay, Edna Valley. $32.

86 • Laetitia (CA) 1996 Reserve, Chardonnay, San Luis Obispo County. $18.

86 • Justin (CA) 1997 Reserve, Chardonnay, Paso Robles. $18.

86 • Cottonwood Canyon (CA) 1994 Barrel Select, Chardonnay, Santa Barbara County. $29.

86 • Adelaida (CA) 1996 Chardonnay, San Luis Obispo County. $21.

85 • Testarossa (CA) 1997 Chardonnay, Santa Maria Valley. $26.

85 • Sanford (Ca) 1997 Chardonnay, Santa Barbara County. $18.

85 • Kendall-Jackson (CA) 1996 Camelot Vineyard, Chardonnay, Santa Maria Valley. $19.

85 • Harmony (CA) 1997 Chardonnay, San Luis Obispo County. $14.50.

Mendocino

Wines Reviewed: 14

Median Price: $18

Mendocino is the most northerly of California's wine-producing regions and as such it is far removed from the glamour and high society of the southern regions. It has four AVAs, of which Anderson Valley is the most significant and coolest with its proximity to the coast giving a plentiful supply of cooling sea air along its length. As is so often the pattern this is also sparkling wine country with Roederer Estate and Scharfenberger sourcing their Chardonnay from here. Unblended Chardonnays from this region show all the character of cool climate wines with bright acidity bolstering clean styles without heavy oak treatment. These wines are the Chablis of California—an ideal way to start a meal or quaff without food.

To the east of Anderson Valley runs the extreme northern section of the Russian River. It is along this stretch of water that other vineyards of Mendocino County are associated. Sea air does not have a significant impact on the other growing areas of Mendocino that are farther inland and hence they do not exhibit the coolness found in the Anderson Valley. Fetzer has a major presence along the Russian River in Mendocino and produces consistently reliable Chardonnay from their extensive plantings in the region.

Highly Recommended Mendocino Chardonnay

89 • Jepson (CA) 1996 Chardonnay, Mendocino County. $15.

89 • Edmeades (CA) 1996 Chardonnay, Anderson Valley. $18.

88 • Lolonis (CA) 1996 Private Reserve, Chardonnay, Redwood Valley, Mendocino. $25.

88 • Indigo Hills (CA) 1997 Chardonnay, Mendocino County. $11.

88 • Fetzer (CA) 1996 Reserve, Chardonnay, Mendocino County. $20.

87 • Husch (CA) 1996 Special Reserve, Chardonnay, Anderson Valley. $22.

86 • Steele (CA) 1996 Du Pratt Vineyard, Chardonnay, Mendocino County. $26.

Washington

Wines Reviewed: **42**

Median Price: **$14.50**

The AVA system in Washington is still underdeveloped, with a huge swath of land being entitled to use the Columbia Valley appellation. Smaller viticultural pockets such as the historic Yakima and Walla Walla Valleys should soon be augmented by the creation of new ones, such as Canoe Ridge and Red Mountain. With Chardonnay it makes more sense to treat Washington in general terms, but with varietals that show more stylistic variation, such as Merlot and Cabernet, there is more variation within the state, and hence more in-depth coverage in those chapters.

As for Chardonnay, it is certainly a widely planted and produced varietal. Washington Chardonnay tends to be well structured with solid acidity, due to the very cool desert nights and a lengthy growing season. Winemaking, though variable, tends to be a bit lighter handed with regard to oak treatment, allowing for a harmonious style built on finesse. There are exceptions, and some winemakers in the Walla Walla area have a tendency to swing for the fences. When Washington Chardonnay is good, it is very good, but quality on the whole can still be somewhat variable, as would be expected of such a new region. Nonetheless, it is one of the nation's most exciting viticultural areas and developments should prove quite interesting.

Highly Recommended Washington Chardonnay

93 • Kestrel (WA) 1996 Chardonnay, Columbia Valley. $22.

92 • Chateau Ste. Michelle (WA) 1996 Indian Wells Vineyard, Chardonnay, Columbia Valley. $26.

91 • Columbia Winery (WA) 1996 Otis Vineyard, Chardonnay, Yakima Valley. $19.

90 • Columbia Winery (WA) 1996 Wyckoff Vineyard, Chardonnay, Yakima Valley. $19.

90 • Chateau Ste. Michelle (WA) 1996 Cold Creek Vineyard, Chardonnay, Columbia Valley. $26.

90 • Apex (WA) 1997 Chardonnay, Columbia Valley. $17.99.

89 • Woodward Canyon (WA) 1997 Reserve, Chardonnay, Columbia Valley. $35.

89 • Hogue (WA) 1997 Genesis, Sunnyside Vineyard, Chardonnay, Yakima Valley. $19.99.

89 • Chateau Ste. Michelle (WA) 1996 Reserve, Chardonnay, Columbia Valley. $31.

88 • Columbia Crest (WA) 1997 Estate Series, Chardonnay, Columbia Valley. $14.

88 • Columbia Crest (WA) 1996 Reserve, Chardonnay, Columbia Valley. $18.

88 • Chateau Ste. Michelle (WA) 1996 Canoe Ridge Estate Vineyard, Chardonnay, Columbia Valley. $28.

88 • Canoe Ridge Vineyard (WA) 1997 Chardonnay, Columbia Valley. $14.

88 • Bookwalter (WA) 1997 Vintner's Select, Chardonnay, Washington. $18.

88 • Barnard Griffin (WA) 1997 Chardonnay, Washington. $12.95.

Scale: Superlative (96-100), Exceptional (90-95), Highly Recommended (85-89), Recommended (80-84), Not Recommended (Under 80)

87 • Woodward Canyon (WA) 1997 Chardonnay, Columbia Valley. $30.

87 • L'Ecole No. 41 (WA) 1997 Chardonnay, Washington. $19.50.

87 • Claar (WA) 1997 Chardonnay, Columbia Valley. $10.99.

86 • W.B. Bridgman (WA) 1997 Chardonnay, Columbia Valley. $10.99.

86 • Hogue (WA) 1997 Chardonnay, Columbia Valley. $13.95.

86 • Covey Run (WA) 1996 Celilo Vineyard, Chardonnay, Washington. $25.

86 • Columbia Crest (WA) 1997 Chardonnay, Columbia Valley. $9.

86 • Chateau Ste. Michelle (WA) 1996 Chardonnay, Columbia Valley. $14.

86 • Caterina (WA) 1997 Chardonnay, Columbia Valley. $15.

86 • Bookwalter (WA) 1997 Chardonnay, Columbia Valley. $8.

86 • Barnard Griffin (WA) 1996 Reserve, Chardonnay, Columbia Valley. $17.95.

Oregon

Wines Reviewed: **24**
Median Price: **$17.50**

Though sometimes lumped together with Washington, its neighbor to the north, Oregon is in fact as different from that area as is possible. In diametrical opposition, Oregon's vineyards are largely planted in the cool and rainy river valleys south of Portland. There is a considerable marine influence, and consequently a reliance on cool climate varietals such as Chardonnay, Pinot Noir, and Pinot Gris. Furthermore, it is largely a cottage industry, with over a hundred tiny producers, and no huge winery to bring forth the message.

Pinot Noir has already achieved greatness in many Oregon vineyards, but, confusingly, Chardonnay seems to have lagged behind somewhat. Lately many Oregon winemakers have come to the realization that this may be in large part due to the fact that most of the Chardonnay vineyards were planted with a clone of the grape imported from California, and better adapted to that state's much hotter climate. Oregon's climate shares more in common with that of Burgundy and growers are rushing to experiment with a greater variety of Burgundian clones. Early results have been promising.

The resulting wines can be quite complex with high levels of acidity and solid structures. Due to its marginal climate, Oregon, unlike California, has wide vintage swings. In some ways, this makes things more interesting as a particular vineyard's wine will have a markedly different character from year to year. The year 1994 was among the best, if not the best, Oregon vintage in the last decade, and the Pinot Noirs in particular are stunning. Subsequent vintages have been somewhat more problematic, but 1998 appears to be a fantastic vintage waiting in the wings. Though still quite youthful, Oregon is beginning to come into its own for Chardonnay and clonal improvements should help to paint a very different picture in years to come.

Highly Recommended Oregon Chardonnay

90 • Willamette Valley Vineyards (OR) 1996 Estate, Dijon Clone, Chardonnay, Oregon. $21.99.

89 • Henry Estate (OR) 1996 Chardonnay, Umpqua Valley. $15.

88 • Willamette Valley Vineyards (OR) 1996 Founders' Reserve, Chardonnay, Oregon. $14.99.

88 • King Estate (OR) 1996 Reserve, Chardonnay, Oregon. $18.

88 • Erath (OR) 1996 Reserve, Niederberger Vineyard, Chardonnay, Willamette Valley. $50.

88 • Eola Hills (OR) 1996 Chardonnay, Oregon. $12.
88 • Cooper Mountain (OR) 1996 Reserve, Chardonnay, Willamette Valley. $19.75.
88 • Chateau Benoit (OR) 1996 Dijon Clone Reserve, Chardonnay,
    Willamette Valley. $35.
86 • Willamette Valley Vineyards (OR) 1997 Chardonnay, Oregon. $12.75.
86 • Oak Knoll (OR) 1996 Chardonnay, Willamette Valley. $14.
85 • Cooper Mountain (OR) 1997 Chardonnay, Willamette Valley. $14.75.

New York
Wines Reviewed: **34**
Median Price: **$13**

The wine regions of New York State are all toward the cooler end of the spectrum in climactic terms. With the state's cold winters the moderating presence of water is a necessity for the successful growing of vinifera grapes. The two regions of significance in this respect are the Finger Lakes and the North Fork of Long Island.

The Finger Lakes, south of Lake Ontario, are comprised of a series of narrow but very deep lakes. The most important are Cayuga Lake, Seneca Lake, and Keuka Lake. The vineyards are situated on hills by the lakes that angle the sun's warmth onto the grapes. With the severity of winter always posing a risk to the noble grape varieties, hybrid varieties such as Seyval Blanc and Vignoles are also grown in abundance here.

Much of the Chardonnay goes toward the production of premium sparkling wine. The styles of Chardonnay tend toward the delicate and lean end of the spectrum. The finest examples display a European sense of refinement and elegance and make natural partners to shellfish and seafood. Such wines often carry the label of Dr. Konstantin Frank, one of the region's top producers, founded by a Russian immigrant who was one of the first to exploit the potential of the area for quality wine production.

As for Long Island, the North Fork of Long Island AVA perfectly describes its location in its own title. It is markedly warmer than the Finger Lakes. The principal factors behind this are its more southerly location, the surrounding waters of the Atlantic Ocean, and the warm air that moves up from southern states during the winter. Vinifera varieties grow more easily here, even Cabernet Sauvignon and Merlot. Relative to the Finger Lakes, the Chardonnay styles are a tad richer although they are as yet more variable. Long Island is still a very new region, but early signs have been encouraging, and further developments should prove to be quite interesting.

Highly Recommended New York Chardonnay
93 • Macari (NY) 1997 Barrel Fermented, Chardonnay, North Fork of Long Island. $.
91 • Gristina (NY) 1995 Andy's Field, Chardonnay, North Fork of Long Island. $21.99.
89 • Treleaven (NY) 1997 Chardonnay, Cayuga Lake. $11.99.
89 • Lenz (NY) 1995 Barrel Fermented, Chardonnay, North Fork of Long Island. $24.99.
88 • Macari (NY) 1996 Barrel Fermented, Chardonnay, North Fork of Long Island. $14.
88 • Gristina (NY) 1996 Chardonnay, North Fork of Long Island. $11.99.
87 • Glenora (NY) 1996 Chardonnay, Finger Lakes. $13.99.
86 • Pellegrini (NY) 1996 Chardonnay, North Fork of Long Island. $12.99.
86 • Peconic Bay (NY) 1995 Rolling Ridge, Chardonnay,
    North Fork of Long Island. $18.99.

86 • Paumanok (NY) 1997 Chardonnay, North Fork of Long Island. $16.99.

86 • Laurel Lake (NY) 1995 Reserve, Chardonnay, North Fork of Long Island. $13.99.

86 • Bedell (NY) 1995 Reserve, Chardonnay, North Fork of Long Island. $14.99.

85 • Pindar (NY) 1996 Sunflower Special Reserve, Chardonnay,
   North Fork of Long Island. $16.99.

85 • Lenz (NY) 1996 Vineyard Selection, Chardonnay, North Fork of Long Island. $9.99.

85 • Laurel Lake (NY) 1996 Chardonnay, North Fork of Long Island. $12.99.

85 • Hargrave (NY) 1995 Lattice Label, Chardonnay, North Fork of Long Island. $14.99.

85 • Bedell (NY) 1995 Chardonnay, North Fork of Long Island. $11.99.

Virginia

Wines Reviewed: **25**

Median Price: **$15**

Thomas Jefferson's dreams of producing high-quality vinifera wines in his home state look to be becoming a reality. Even if his early efforts to establish vineyards around Charlottesville failed due to the intervention of the *Phylloxera* louse, his foresight in choosing suitable locations has been vindicated by the fact that this same area is at the forefront of the viticultural renaissance in the Old Dominion.

The styles of Chardonnay emerging in Virginia seem much more rooted in Europe than the West Coast of the United States, with higher acidity levels and a pleasant affinity for the table. Use of oak varies from subtle to occasionally overbearing. In Virginia Chardonnay is usually more competent than exciting. It is with red wines, particularly Bordeaux varietals, that Virginia is making its clearest statements so far.

Highly Recommended Virginia Chardonnay

89 • White Hall Vineyards (VA) 1997 Reserve, Chardonnay, Virginia. $18.

88 • Prince Michel (VA) 1997 Barrel Select, Chardonnay, Virginia. $18.95.

86 • Rockbridge (VA) 1997 Reserve, Chardonnay, Virginia. $15.

86 • Jefferson (VA) 1997 Fantaisie Sauvage, Chardonnay, Monticello. $22.

86 • Dashiell (VA) 1997 Chardonnay, Virginia. $17.

86 • Dashiell (VA) 1996 Chardonnay, Virginia. $17.

86 • Chateau Morrisette (VA) 1997 "M," Meadows of Dan, Chardonnay, Virginia. $14.

Top American Chardonneys

98 • Foley (CA) 1997 Barrel Select,
Chardonnay,
Santa Barbara County. $28.

95 • Martinelli (CA) 1996 Gold Ridge,
Chardonnay,
Russian River Valley. $20.

95 • Foley (CA) 1997 Bien Nacido
Vineyard, Chardonnay,
Santa Maria Valley. $24.

94 • Shafer (CA) 1997 Red Shoulder
Ranch, Chardonnay, Carneros,
Napa Valley. $35.

94 • Newton (CA) 1997 Chardonnay,
Napa County. $25.

94 • Mer et Soleil (CA) 1993 Chardonnay,
Central Coast. $30.

94 • Matanzas Creek (CA) 1995 Journey,
Chardonnay, Sonoma Valley. $95.

94 • Gary Farrell (CA) 1996 Allen
Vineyard, Chardonnay,
Russian River Valley. $28.

94 • Gallo Sonoma (CA) 1996 Estate,
Chardonnay, Northern Sonoma. $38.

94 • Franciscan (CA) 1996 Oakville Estate,
Cuvée Sauvage, Chardonnay,
Valley. $30.

94 • Foley (CA) 1996 Barrel Select,
Chardonnay,
Santa Barbara County. $25.

94 • Ferrari-Carano (CA) 1995 Reserve,
Chardonnay, 87% Napa County,
13% Sonoma County. $34.

94 • Beringer (CA) 1996 Sbragia-Limited
Release, Chardonnay,
Napa Valley. $35.

93 • Villa Mt. Eden (CA) 1996 Signature
Series, Bien Nacido Vineyard,
Chardonnay, Santa Maria Valley. $30.

93 • Storrs (CA) 1997 Ben Lomond
Mountain, Chardonnay, Santa Cruz
Mountains. $24.

93 • Signorello (CA) 1997 Hope's Cuvée,
Chardonnay, Napa Valley. $60.

93 • Shafer (CA) 1996 Red Shoulder
Ranch, Chardonnay, Carneros, Napa
Valley. $30.

93 • San Saba (CA) 1997 Chardonnay,
Monterey. $20.

93 • Rochioli (CA) 1995 Estate,
Chardonnay,
Russian River Valley. $25.

93 • Qupé (CA) 1997 Bien Nacido
Vineyard, Chardonnay,
Santa Barbara County. $18.

93 • Mer et Soleil (CA) 1995 Chardonnay,
Central Coast. $35.

93 • Mer et Soleil (CA) 1994 Chardonnay,
Central Coast. $31.99.

93 • Macari (NY) 1997 Barrel Fermented,
Chardonnay, North Fork of Long
Island.

93 • Kestrel (WA) 1996 Chardonnay,
Columbia Valley. $22.

93 • Ferrari-Carano (CA) 1996
Chardonnay, Alexander Valley. $21.

93 • Au Bon Climat (CA) 1997 Alban
Vineyard, Chardonnay,
Edna Valley. $35.

92 • Zabaco (CA) 1996 Chardonnay,
Russian River Valley. $14.

92 • Sonoma-Cutrer (CA) 1996 Les
Pierres, Chardonnay,
Sonoma County. $29.99.

92 • Robert Mondavi (CA) 1996 Reserve,
Chardonnay, Napa Valley. $30.

92 • Ridge (CA) 1996 Chardonnay, Santa
Cruz Mountains. $25.

92 • Peju Province (CA) 1997 Chardonnay,
Napa Valley. $18.

92 • Patz & Hall (CA) 1997 Hyde
Vineyard, Chardonnay, Carneros. $36.

92 • Mer et Soleil (CA) 1996 Chardonnay,
Central Coast. $34.99.

92 • Guenoc (CA) 1997 "Unfiltered"
Reserve, Genevive Magoon Vineyard,
Chardonnay, Guenoc Valley. $30.

92 • Cuvaison (CA) 1996 Reserve,
Chardonnay, Napa Valley.

92 • Chateau Ste. Michelle (WA) 1996
Indian Wells Vineyard, Chardonnay,
Columbia Valley. $26.

92 • Chateau St. Jean (CA) 1996 Robert
Young Vineyard, Chardonnay,
Alexander Valley. $24.

92 • Beringer (CA) 1997 Private Reserve,
Chardonnay, Napa Valley. $36.

92 • Arrowood (Ca) 1996 Réserve
Spéciale, Cuvée Michel Berthoud,
Chardonnay, Sonoma County. $38.

Scale: Superlative (96-100), Exceptional (90-95), Highly Recommended (85-89),
Recommended (80-84), Not Recommended (Under 80)

seventeen

❧

Sauvignon Blanc, White Meritage, and Semillon

❧

Sauvignon Blanc at a Glance

Wines Reviewed:
102

Producers/Brands Represented:
89

Median Price:
$10

White Meritage at a Glance

Wines Reviewed:
15

Producers/Brands Represented:
15

Median Price:
$16

Semillon at a Glance

Wines Reviewed:
11

Producers/Brands Represented:
10

Median Price:
$10

What Is American Sauvignon Blanc?

Sauvignon Blanc is widely planted in the United States, and produces a wine in two broadly different styles following two different examples. In France (from whence the varietal emigrated) it is grown widely in the Loire and Bordeaux. In Bordeaux it is barrel fermented and produces a ripe, rich wine that is not unlike a Chardonnay with a bit more snap. The vast majority of U.S. wines are vinified in this style. In the Loire, however, Sauvignon is often left out of barrel and the varietal is allowed to show its aggressive herbal side and brisk acidity. One of the world's great wine styles, Sancerre (and more recently New Zealand, which has "out Sancerred" Sancerre) can be a shock to the uninitiated, but many who do try it are smitten. Thus, U.S. wineries have tended to shy away from this latter manifestation, though some such as Voss, have made it into a specialty. Rumblings are being heard that more producers may choose to follow the latter path. Only time will tell.

Best U.S. Sauvignon Blanc Producers

Premier U.S. Sauvignon Blanc Producers (***)
- Cain (Musque)
- Chalk Hill
- Ferrari Carano (Reserve)
- Murphy-Goode (The Deuce & Reserve)
- Matanzas Creek
- Robert Mondavi (I-Block)
- Rochioli
- Spottswoode
- Voss

Great U.S. Sauvignon Blanc Producers (**)
- Benziger
- Cakebread
- Chateau St. Jean (La Petite Etoile)
- Duckhorn
- Ferrari Carano
- Gainey (Limited Selection)

Scale: Superlative (96-100), Exceptional (90-95), Highly Recommended (85-89), Recommended (80-84), Not Recommended (Under 80)

- Grgich Hills
- Iron Horse
- Kendall Jackson
- Merryvale
- Robert Mondavi (Fumé Blanc Reserve)
- Murphy Goode
- Sanford
- Stag's Leap Wine Cellars
- Waterbrook

Dependable U.S. Sauvignon Blanc Producers (Recommended)

Some producers placed in this third tier are new (or new to us) and may merit a higher placement in subsequent vintages. These producers are offset by an asterisk.

- Beringer
- *Calaghan
- DeLoach
- *Dos Cabezas
- Dry Creek Vineyards
- *Estancia
- *Foley
- William Hill
- Kenwood (Reserve)
- Markham
- *Peter Micheal (L'Apres-Midi)
- Morgan
- Robert Pepi
- Chateau Ste. Michelle
- Simi
- St. Clement

Highly Recommended Blanc Sauvignon

95 • Voss (CA) 1997 Sauvignon Blanc, Napa Valley. $12.50.

94 • Estancia (CA) 1996 Pinnacles, Fumé Blanc, Monterey County. $10.

94 • Cain (CA) 1996 Musque, Ventana Vineyard, Sauvignon Blanc, Monterey. $16.

93 • Murphy-Goode (CA) 1996 The Deuce, Fumé II, Alexander Valley. $24.

93 • Foley (CA) 1996 Sauvignon Blanc, Santa Barbara County. $14.

93 • Chalk Hill (CA) 1996 Sauvignon Blanc, Chalk Hill, Sonoma County. $19.

92 • Robert Mondavi (CA) 1995 To-Kalon Vineyard I Block, Fumé Blanc, Napa Valley. $50.

92 • Murphy-Goode (CA) 1996 Reserve, Fumé, Alexander Valley. $16.50.

91 • St. Supéry (CA) 1997 Dollarhide Ranch, Sauvignon Blanc, Napa Valley. $9.90.

91 • Peter Michael (CA) 1996 L' Apres-Midi, Sauvignon Blanc, Napa County. $20.

91 • Matanzas Creek (CA) 1996 Sauvignon Blanc, Sonoma County. $18.

90 • Cakebread (CA) 1996 Sauvignon Blanc, Napa Valley. $14.

90 • Beringer (CA) 1996 Sauvignon Blanc, Napa Valley. $9.

90 • Benziger (CA) 1996 Fumé Blanc, Sonoma County. $10.

89 • Spottswoode (CA) 1996 Sauvignon Blanc, Napa Valley. $18.

89 • Robert Mondavi (CA) 1994 To-Kalon Vineyard Reserve, Fumé Blanc, Napa Valley. $20.

89 • Merryvale (CA) 1996 Sauvignon Blanc, Napa Valley. $17.

89 • Chateau Potelle (CA) 1996 Sauvignon Blanc, Napa Valley. $11.

88 • Stonegate (CA) 1996 Sauvignon Blanc, Napa Valley. $9.50.

88 • Husch (CA) 1996 La Ribera Vineyard, Sauvignon Blanc, Mendocino. $10.50.

88 • Chateau St. Jean (CA) 1996 La Petite Etoile Vineyard, Fumé Blanc, Russian River Valley. $13.

87 • Robert Mondavi (CA) 1995 To-Kalon Vineyard Reserve, Fumé Blanc, Napa Valley. $22.

87 • Renaissance (CA) 1997 Sauvignon Blanc, North Yuba. $10.

87 • Grgich Hills (CA) 1996 Fumé Blanc, Napa Valley. $18.

87 • Dry Creek Vineyard (CA) 1996 Reserve, Fumé Blanc, Dry Creek Valley. $15.75.

87 • Domaine Napa (CA) 1996 Fumé Blanc, Napa Valley. $9.99.

86 • Waterbrook (WA) 1997 Sauvignon Blanc, Columbia Valley. $13.

86 • Ste. Genevieve (TX) NV Sauvignon Blanc, Texas. $4.99.

86 • Rutherford Vintners (CA) 1995 Barrel Select, Fumé Blanc, North Coast. $8.99.

86 • Rochioli (CA) 1997 Sauvignon Blanc, Russian River Valley. $16.

86 • Raymond (CA) 1996 Valley Reserve, Sauvignon Blanc, Napa Valley. $11.

86 • Murphy-Goode (CA) 1997 Fumé Blanc, Sonoma County. $11.50.

86 • Kenwood (CA) 1996 Reserve, Sauvignon Blanc, Sonoma Valley. $15.

86 • Dunnewood (CA) 1996 Coastal Series, Vintner's Select, Sauvignon Blanc, Mendocino. $5.99.

86 • Covey Run (WA) 1996 Fumé Blanc, Columbia Valley. $8.

86 • Columbia Crest (WA) 1996 Estate Series, Sauvignon Blanc, Columbia Valley. $9.

86 • Canyon Road (CA) 1997 Sauvignon Blanc, California. $6.99.

86 • Arbor Crest (WA) 1996 Sauvignon Blanc, Washington. $7.25.

85 • Temecula Crest (CA) 1997 Sauvignon Blanc, Temecula. $9.95.

85 • Page Mill (CA) 1997 French Camp Vineyard, Sauvignon Blanc, San Luis Obispo. $11.

85 • Morgan (CA) 1997 Sauvignon Blanc, Sonoma-Monterey. $13.

85 • Calona (Canada) 1997 Private Reserve, Fumé Blanc, Okanagan Valley. $9.50.

What Is White Meritage?

Meritage was the term (chosen in a contest...no kidding) given to U.S. wines made from a traditional blend of Bordeaux style varietals that can vary from year to year. The red meritage category, a blend of Cabernet Sauvignon, Merlot, Cabernet Franc, etc. is better known, as wines such as Opus One and Dominus have caught the public's fancy. There is a white side to the meritage coin, however. White Meritage refers to a blend of Sauvignon Blanc and Semillon, which is then barrel fermented. The rich rounded flavors of Semillon are used to round out the snappy and vibrant Sauvignon, while the barrel aging adds

a layer of oaky complexity. The resultant wines are a bit like Chardonnays that are not quite as round in the mouth and tend to be more firmly structured with a sturdy vibrant finish.

Best U.S. White Meritage Producers

Premier White Meritage Producers (***)

• Carmenet (Paragon Vineyard)
• Yorkville (Eleanor of Aquitaine)

Great White Meritage Producers (**)

• Benziger (Tribute)
• Cardinale (Royale)
• Cosentino (The Novelist)
• Flora Springs (Soliloquy)
• Guenoc (Langtry)
• Merryvale (Vignette)
• Venezia

Dependable White Meritage Producers (Recommended)

Some producers placed in this third tier are new (or new to us) and may merit a higher placement in subsequent vintages. These producers are offset by an asterisk.

• Beringer (Alluvium)
• Concannon (Assemblage)
• deLorimier (Spectrum)
• Hidden Cellars (Alchemy)
• Simi (Sendal)

Highly Recommended Meritage

93 • Merryvale (CA) 1996 Vignette, Napa Valley. $22.

91 • Cardinale (CA) 1996 Royale, California. $20.

91 • Benziger (CA) 1995 Tribute White, Sonoma Mountain. $17.

87 • Langtry (CA) 1996 White Meritage, Guenoc Valley. $21.

86 • Yorkville (CA) Eleanor of Aquitaine, Randle Hill Vineyard, Mendocino. $16.

Scale: Superlative (96-100), Exceptional (90-95), Highly Recommended (85-89), Recommended (80-84), Not Recommended (Under 80)

86 • Carmenet (CA) 1996 Reserve White Meritage, Paragon Vineyard, Edna Valley. $15.

85 • Simi (CA) 1995 Sendal, Sonoma County. $20.

85 • Grande River (CO) 1996 White Meritage, Grand Valley. $8.99.

What Is American Semillon?

Semillon is best known as the blending grape used with Sauvignon Blanc in Bordeaux. It is bottled alone however in Australia, and increasingly in the United States. Several Washington vintners in particular seem to have shown interest in the varietal. In the United States it produces a medium-bodied, lush wine that has distinctive figgy flavors and often features a yeasty note. It tends to be fairly rich and lower in acidity. As such, it makes a good match with poultry or rich seafood dishes. The best examples are seriously underpriced and make for excellent value.

Best U.S. Semillon Producers

Premier Semillon Producers (***)
• Brutocao
• Signorello
• Yorkville

Great Semillon Producers (**)
• Clos du Val
• Columbia Winery
• Kendall Jackson
• L'Ecole No. 41
• Windsor

Dependable Semillon Producers (Recommended)

Some producers placed in this third tier are new (or new to us) and may merit a higher placement in subsequent vintages. These producers are offset by an asterisk.

• Amador Foothill Winery
• Columbia Crest
• *Rosenblum
• Chateau Ste. Michelle

Highly Recommended Semillon

89 • Fenestra (CA) 1996 Semillon, Livermore Valley. $9.50.

87 • Signorello (CA) 1996 Semillon, Napa Valley. $20.

87 • L'Ecole No. 41 (WA) 1996 Semillon, Washington. $13.50.

86 • Hogue (WA) 1996 Semillon, Columbia Valley. $8.

86 • Calona (Canada) 1996 Private Reserve, Burrowing Owl Vineyard, Semillon, Okanagan Valley. $10.70.

86 • Amador Foothill Winery (CA) 1996 Semillon, Shenandoah Valley. $9.

eighteen

Riesling, Gewürztraminer, and Chenin Blanc

Riesling at a Glance

Wines Reviewed:
64

Producers/Brands Represented:
48

Median Price:
$9

Gewürztraminer at a Glance

Wines Reviewed:
38

Producers/Brands Represented:
33

Median Price:
$10

Chenin Blanc at a Glance

Wines Reviewed:
11

Producers/Brands Represented:
9

Median Price:
$9

What about American Riesling?

Riesling is widely grown throughout the United States. Indeed, most regions sport at least some bottlings of this noble German variety. U.S. Riesling is uniformly inexpensive, often representing good value. In general character these wines are cheerful, trading on their fresh, exuberant tropical flavors and absence of oak seasoning. Cooler California climates such as Monterey, Washington, Oregon, and the Finger Lakes in New York tend to supply the best examples of U.S. Riesling. These wines are rarely earthy, nor do they show the classic "petrol" aromas and vibrant acidity that characterizes German Rieslings. Rather, they tend to be early drinking quaffers, and a good alternative to those tiring of Chardonnay.

Best U.S. Riesling Producers

Premier U.S. Riesling Producers (***)
- Jekel
- Mirassou
- Paraiso Springs
- Hermann J. Wiemer

Great U.S. Riesling Producers (**)
- Argyle
- Concannon
- Covey Run
- Fetzer
- Dr. Konstantin Frank
- Gainey
- Glenora
- Hogue
- Indian Creek
- Kiona
- J. Lohr
- Kendall-Jackson
- Peconic Bay
- Standing Stone
- Ventana
- Washington Hills

Scale: Superlative (96-100), Exceptional (90-95), Highly Recommended (85-89), Recommended (80-84), Not Recommended (Under 80)

Dependable U.S. Riesling Producers (Recommended)

Some producers placed in this third tier are new (or new to us) and may merit a higher placement in subsequent vintages. These producers are offset by an asterisk.

- *Amity
- Bonny Doon
- Chateau St. Jean
- Chateau Ste. Michelle
- Columbia Crest
- Columbia Winery
- Durney
- Eola Hills
- Firestone
- Freemark Abbey
- Geyser Peak
- *Good Harbor
- LaVelle
- *Fess Parker
- V. Sattui
- St. Julian
- Windsor

Highly Recommended Riesling

90 • Paraiso Springs (CA) 1997 Riesling, Santa Lucia Highlands. $9.

89 • Firestone (CA) 1997 Riesling, Santa Barbara County 1.67% rs. $7.

88 • Oasis (VA) 1997 Semi-Dry Riesling, Virginia 2% rs. $18.

88 • Good Harbor (MI) 1997 Semidry White Riesling, Leelanau Peninsula 2% rs. $8.

88 • Fetzer (CA) 1997 Johannisberg Riesling, California 2.93% rs. $6.99.

88 • Dr. Konstantin Frank (NY) NV Salmon Run, Johannisberg Riesling, New York. $8.95.

86 • Woodward Canyon (WA) 1997 Riesling, Walla Walla County. $9.

86 • V. Sattui (CA) 1998 Dry Johannisberg Riesling, Napa Valley. $11.25.

86 • Ste. Chapelle (WA) 1998 Dry Johannisberg Riesling, Idaho. $6.

86 • LaVelle (OR) 1997 Susan's Vineyard, Riesling, Willamette Valley 2.4% rs. $8.

86 • Kendall-Jackson (CA) 1997 Vintner's Reserve, Johannisberg Riesling, California 2.42% rs. $11.

86 • Jackson-Triggs (Canada) 1996 Proprietors' Reserve, Dry Riesling, Okanagan Valley 1.26% rs. $6.90.

86 • Henke (OH) NV Riesling, American 1.75% rs. $10.37.

86 • Hagafen (CA) 1998 Johannisberg Riesling, Napa Valley 2.6% rs. $12.

85 • Reif Estate (Canada) 1996 Late Harvest Riesling, Niagara Peninsula 4% rs. $8.40.

85 • Konzelmann (Canada) 1995 Late Harvest, Dry Riesling, Niagara Peninsula. $10.95.

85 • Concannon (CA) 1997 Johannisberg Riesling, Arroyo Seco-Monterey 3% rs. $9.95.

What about American Gewürz?

Gewürztraminer is most closely associated with Alsace, where it reaches its enological apex in late harvest form— in styles that vary from dry to very sweet. U.S. Gewürztraminer rarely achieves the intensity of varietal character found in wines from Alsace, nonetheless there are numerous delicious dry examples to be found.

Cooler regions in California often yield the best results for Gewürztraminer, in circumstances where this variety can ripen late and produce distinctive clove and lychee-like varietal flavors. Cool climate Oregon and even the Finger Lakes of New York also have a number of producers of good dry Gewürztraminer that will often be characterized by fresh acidity and a leaner style.

Best U.S. Gewürztraminer Producers

Premier U.S. Gewürztraminer Producers (***)
- Adler Fels

Great U.S. Gewürztraminer Producers (**)
- Alderbrook
- Bouchaine

- Cosentino
- De Loach
- Thomas Fogarty
- Stonestreet
- Windsor

Dependable U.S. Gewürztraminer Producers (Recommended)

Some producers placed in this third tier are new (or new to us) and may merit a higher placement in subsequent vintages. These producers are offset by an asterisk.

- Apex
- Bargetto
- Chateau St. Jean
- *Claiborne & Churchill
- Concannon
- Dr. Konstantin Frank
- *Eola Hills
- Fetzer
- Geyser Peak
- Handley
- Husch
- Lazy Creek
- *Lenz
- *Martinelli
- Montinore
- *Mosby
- Navarro
- *Joseph Phelps
- *Chateau Ste. Michelle
- Snoqualmie
- *Treleaven

Highly Recommended Gewürztraminer

93 • Martinelli (CA) 1997 Gewürztraminer, Russian River Valley. $12.

92 • Adler Fels (CA) 1997 Gewürztraminer, Sonoma County. $11.

89 • Thomas Fogarty (CA) 1997 Gewürztraminer, Monterey. $12.50.

88 • Stonestreet (CA) 1997 Gewürztraminer, Anderson Valley. $16.

88 • Magnotta (Canada) 1995 Limited Edition, Gewürztraminer, Ontario. $8.93.

88 • Lenz (NY) 1995 Gewürztraminer, North Fork of Long Island. $10.99.

87 • Paraiso Springs (CA) 1997 Gewürztraminer, Santa Lucia Highlands. $9.

87 • Gray Monk (Canada) 1996 Reserve, Gewürztraminer, Okanagan Valley. $10.95.

86 • Magnotta (Canada) 1996 Medium-Dry, Limited Edition, Gewürztraminer, Ontario 2% rs. $9.

86 • Lang (Canada) 1996 Gewürztraminer, Naramata 1.1% rs. $8.10.

86 • Jackson-Triggs (Canada) 1997 Proprietors' Reserve, Gewürztraminer, Okanagan Valley 1.18% rs. $6.89.

86 • Husch (CA) 1998 Gewürztraminer, Anderson Valley. $11.

86 • Forest Ville (CA) 1997 Gewürztraminer, California 2.88% rs. $5.99.

86 • Columbia Winery (WA) 1998 Gewürztraminer, Yakima Valley 3% rs. $6.

85 • Covey Run (WA) 1997 Celilo Vineyard, Gewürztraminer, Washington. $12.

What about American Chenin Blanc?

Chenin Blanc is almost as widely planted in California as Chardonnay, but most of these vines are confined to the Central Valley where they produce undistinguished generic white wines from high yielding vineyards. The typical U.S. style of Chenin is rather fruitier and lacking the "sweaty" note that characterizes many French Loire examples. Only a handful of producers in California persist with making world-class dry Chenin Blancs from low yielding vines in prime vineyard locations that have not yet been planted with ubiquitous Cabernet and Chardonnay vines. The best, however, can offer fine value for money.

Scale: Superlative (96-100), Exceptional (90-95), Highly Recommended (85-89), Recommended (80-84), Not Recommended (Under 80)

Best U.S. Chenin Blanc Producers

Premier U.S. Chenin Blanc Producers (***)
- Chappellet (Old Vine Cuvée)
- Chalone
- Ventana

Great U.S. Chenin Blanc Producers (**)
- Chappellet
- Covey Run
- Dry Creek Vineyard
- Husch
- Kiona
- William Wheeler

Dependable U.S. Chenin Blanc Producers (Recommended)
Some producers placed in this third tier are new (or new to us) and may merit a higher placement in subsequent vintages. These producers are offset by an asterisk.

- *Arciero
- *Columbia Winery
- *Durney
- Pine Ridge

Highly Recommended Chenin Blanc

88 • Chappellet (CA) 1997 Old Vine Cuvée, Special Select White Wine, Napa Valley. $14.

86 • Weinstock (CA) 1998 Contour, Clarksburg. $8.95.

85 • Chappellet (CA) 1997 Dry Chenin Blanc, Napa Valley. $11.

84 • Robert Pecota (CA) 1998 Dry Chenin Blanc, Monterey County. $11.

84 • Paumanok (NY) 1998 Chenin Blanc, North Fork of Long Island. $12.

84 • Husch (CA) 1998 Chenin Blanc, Mendocino 2% rs. $8.50.

84 • Chalone (CA) 1996 Reserve, Chenin Blanc, Chalone. $20.

83 • Kendall-Jackson (CA) 1997 Vintner's Reserve, Chenin Blanc, California 2.1% rs. $11.

83 • Callaway (CA) 1998 Chenin Blanc, California. $7.50.

82 • Weinstock (CA) 1997 Contour, Clarksburg. $8.95.

81 • Bookwalter (WA) 1998 Chenin Blanc, Washington 3.3% rs. $6.

nineteen

North American New Wave Whites: Viognier, Pinot Gris, and Pinot Blanc

An Introduction: New Tastes in U.S. Whites?

Quibble not, Chardonnay is the nation's most popular white wine. It is, in fact, synonymous with white wine, having officially supplanted the misused term "chablis" (lower case intended) some time ago. Like its red counterpart Cabernet, however, there are some rumblings. As they say, familiarity breeds contempt, and while the world of white wine has as yet to find its Merlot in shining armor (nor even a Pinot Noir or Syrah for that matter), there are growing indications that the "cutting edge" of the wine consuming public is proving ever more receptive to at least the occasional Chardonnay alternative. Some of the hottest white wines, for both winemakers and consumers, include Viognier, Pinot Gris, and Pinot Blanc. Viognier in particular has taken off not only in the United States, but in many areas around the world. Where plantings were once confined to a small corner of the northern Rhône Valley, the grape can now be found in Australia, South Africa, Chile, the Languedoc, and Virginia to name but a few. As winemakers in emerging areas try to figure out what goes best and where, Viognier, in a remarkably short period of time, has been added to the arsenal.

The winemaking behind Viognier is a topic of debate, and as expected, wineries have embraced a wide range of vinification techniques. Viognier, in its Condrieu manifestation, is fat and lush, with a honeyed, tropical fruit-accented bouquet and lower levels of acidity. As such, it does not age well and is almost always best consumed within two or three years of the vintage. In the United States, unlike Condrieu, some Viogniers are being made like Chardonnays, with a heavy reliance on oak. Unfortunately, the varietal usually doesn't possess the structure of Chardonnay, and as a result the oak can become overwhelming. Those versions that have largely been fermented in stainless steel seem to better preserve the grape's natural attributes—a lush mouthfeel and an exotic natural bouquet. Oaked or not, U.S. Viognier, like Condrieu, is best consumed early, as some of the better releases from the last year or two have already begun to fall apart. For all its richness, this can still be a wine for many seasons. Its lighter manifestations are ideal as summer wines, consumed as aperitifs, or served with seafood, while heftier versions can ward off winter's chill.

Certain areas have chosen to take a pass on Viognier and chart new directions (some but not all dictated by climate), For instance, savvy marketers have taken an Austrian leaning white from the cooler northern alpine vineyards of Italy and created a sensation. Clean, crisp, and vibrant, that wine is Italian Pinot Grigio, made from a varietal that has accordingly gained an unexpected measure of cachet. Vintners in Oregon have taken notice, and while their Pinot Gris (the French and English synonym) was originally thought of as a "cash flow" wine that simply had an affinity for their chilly climate, it has begun to take on a life of its own. Some Oregon producers have reported that the demand for Pinot Gris has outstripped that for their Chardonnays, and it has been confirmed that the variety as a whole is selling briskly. The Pacific Northwest is an area of the country awash with regional pride and Pinot Gris has been looked on locally with a great deal of affection, following the success of Oregon Pinot Noir and the Bordeaux varietals of Washington.

Finally, though associated with Alsace, the "Pinot Blanc" often planted in the United States, and more specifically in California, is actually believed to be

Scale: Superlative (96-100), Exceptional (90-95), Highly Recommended (85-89), Recommended (80-84), Not Recommended (Under 80)

Melon (may-lon). Melon's origins actually lie in Burgundy where it was seen as a lesser alternative to Chardonnay. However, it is now more prevalent in the Loire, where it is bottled as Muscadet. Many U.S. Pinot Blancs have the flinty attributes of Muscadet, especially when they are fermented in stainless steel (no malolactic) and without wood aging. Others, however, use the full treatment, with some or full malolactic and lots of oak. This style is prevalent in the wines of Monterey in particular. On the whole, U.S. Pinot Blancs range from tart orchard fruit flavors with crisp acidity and racy mouth feels, to those with more lushness and viscosity. Pinot Blanc works well at the table in its "Chardonnay-like" Monterey versions, while lighter U.S. Pinot Blancs, like Muscadets, work well as an aperitif or with shellfish. As always, tasting notes will provide a good indication of the style in which the wine was made.

Best U.S. New Wave White Producers

Premier U.S. New Wave White Producers (***)
• Alban (Viognier, Roussanne)
• Cline (Marsanne)
• Joseph Phelps (Viognier)

Great U.S. New Wave White Producers (**)
• Beringer (Viognier)
• Bonterra (Viognier)
• Calera (Viognier)
• Chalone (Pinot Blanc)
• Chateau St. Jean (Pinot Blanc)
• Eberle (Viognier)
• Eyrie (Pinot Gris)
• Hinman (Pinot Gris)
• Horton (Viognier, Marsanne)
• Kunde (Viognier)
• Laetitia (Pinot Blanc)
• Lockwood (Pinot Blanc)
• J. Lohr (Pinot Blanc)
• Mirassou (Pinot Blanc)
• Oak Knoll (Pinot Gris)
• Paraiso Springs (Pinot Blanc)
• Fess Parker (Viognier)
• Silvan Ridge (Pinot Gris)
• Steele (Pinot Blanc)
• Twin Brook (Pinot Gris)

New Wave Whites at a Glance

Wines Reviewed:

69

Producers/Brands Represented:

59

Median Price:

$14

Dependable U.S. New Wave White Producers (Recommended)

Some producers placed in this third tier are new (or new to us) and may merit a higher placement in subsequent vintages. These producers are offset by an asterisk.

- *Bell (Viognier)
- Benziger (Viognier, Pinot Blanc)
- *Bernardus (Marsanne)
- Byron (Pinot Gris)
- Cooper Mountain (Pinot Gris)
- *DeRose (Viognier)
- *Dos Cabezas (Pinot Gris)
- *Eola Hills (Pinot Gris)
- Iron Horse (Viognier)
- *Karly (Marsanne)
- King Estate (Pinot Gris)
- McDowell (Viognier)
- *La Famiglia di Robert Mondavi (Pinot Gris)
- *Morgan (Marsanne)
- Mount Palomar (Rousanne, Viognier)
- Preston (Viognier)
- Renwood (Viognier)
- *Rosenblum (Viognier)
- Saddleback (Pinot Blanc)
- *Smith & Hook (Viognier)
- Sobon (Viognier, Roussanne)
- *Sunstone (Viognier)
- Villa Mt. Eden (Pinot Blanc)
- Wild Horse (Pinot Blanc)

Highly Recommended New Wave Whites

Pinot Blanc

88 • Laetitia (CA) 1996 Reserve, Pinot Blanc, San Luis Obispo County. $17.

88 • Laetitia (CA) 1996 La Colline Vineyard Designated Reserve, Pinot Blanc. $25.

87 • Byron (CA) 1996 Pinot Blanc, Santa Maria Valley. $16.

86 • Saddleback (CA) 1997 Pinot Blanc, Napa Valley. $13.50.

86 • Hester Creek (Canada) 1996 Grand Reserve, Pinot Blanc, Okanagan Valley. $9.25.

85 • Peller Estates (Canada) 1996 Pinot Blanc, Okanagan Valley. $11.99.

85 • Murphy-Goode (CA) 1996 Pinot Blanc, Sonoma County. $13.50.

Pinot Gris

93 • Oak Knoll (OR) 1996 Vintage Reserve, Pinot Gris, Willamette Valley. $17.

90 • King Estate (OR) 1996 Pinot Gris, Oregon. $13.

88 • Martini & Prati (CA) 1996 Vino Grigio, California. $12.50.

87 • Dos Cabezas (AZ) 1997 Pinot Gris, Cochise County. $14.95.

87 • Bargetto (CA) 1997 Pinot Grigio, Central Coast. $15.

86 • Montinore (OR) 1997 Pinot Gris, Willamette Valley. $9.99.

86 • LaVelle (OR) 1996 Winter's Hill Vineyard, Pinot Gris, Oregon. $13.

86 • La Famiglia di Robert Mondavi (CA) 1996 Pinot Grigio, California. $16.

86 • Cooper Mountain (OR) 1997 Pinot Gris, Willamette Valley. $14.75.

86 • Callaway (CA) 1997 Pinot Gris, Temecula. $12.

86 • Bridgeview (OR) 1997 Pinot Gris, Oregon. $9.99.

85 • Pelee Island Winery (Canada) 1995 Pinot Gris, Ontario. $7.99.

85 • Columbia Winery (WA) 1996 Pinot Gris, Yakima Valley. $10.99.

Viognier

91 • Rosenblum (CA) 1997 Viognier, Santa Barbara County. $15.

91 • Fess Parker (CA) 1996 Viognier, Santa Barbara County. $22.

90 • Joseph Phelps (CA) 1996 Vin du Mistral, Viognier, Napa Valley. $28.

89 • De Rose (CA) 1996 Viognier, Cienega Valley. $15/375 ml.

87 • Smith & Hook (CA) 1996 Viognier, Arroyo Seco. $18.

87 • Glen Ellen (CA) 1995 Expressions, Viognier, San Benito County. $11/375 ml.

87 • Beringer (CA) 1996 Viognier, Napa Valley. $25.

86 • Waterbrook (WA) 1997 Viognier, Columbia Valley. $18.

86 • Iron Horse (CA) 1997 Viognier, Alexander Valley. $18.

Scale: Superlative (96-100), Exceptional (90-95), Highly Recommended (85-89), Recommended (80-84), Not Recommended (Under 80)

85 • Pindar (NY) 1996 Viognier,
North Fork of Long Island. $19.99.

85 • Calera (CA) 1997 Viognier,
Mount Harlan. $30.

Other Whites

93 • Mount Palomar (CA) 1996
Castelletto, Cortese, Temecula. $16.

91 • Cline (CA) 1996 Marsanne,
Los Carneros. $20.

89 • La Famiglia di Robert Mondavi (CA)
1996 Tocai Friulano, California. $18.

88 • Mount Pleasant (MO) 1996
Chardonel, Augusta. $14.

88 • Robert Pepi (CA) 1997 Malvasia
Bianca, Central Coast. $14.

87 • Mount Palomar (CA) 1997
Rey Sol Le Mediterrane Blanc,
Temecula. $16.

86 • Rosenblum (CA) 1996 Semillon-
Chardonnay, Livermore Valley. $11.

86 • Zaca Mesa (CA) 1996 Zaca Vineyards,
Roussanne, Santa Barbara County.
$16.50.

86 • Mount Palomar (CA) 1997 Rey Sol,
Roussane, Temecula. $18.

86 • Hogue (WA) 1996 Semillon-
Chardonnay, Columbia Valley. $8.

85 • Windsor (CA) 1998 Late Harvest,
Murphy Ranch, Muscat Canelli,
Alexander Valley 4.2% rs. $13.50.

85 • Sokol Blosser (OR) 1998
Muller-Thurgau. $14.95.

85 • Henry Estate (OR) 1998 Muller
Thurgau, Umpqua Valley 2% rs. $8.

twenty

North American Sparkling Wines

An Introduction: What about American Bubbly?

Ahh sparkling wines. At the base of many a party, sparkling wines are seen as an indispensable celebratory ingredient. In recent years, however, the French original, Champagne, has become dauntingly expensive. Enter the U.S. alternative. At the very top end of the quality spectrum U.S. bubbly has become good enough to compete with mass market Champagne, and often at a fraction of the price. U.S. sparklers tend to be fruitier in flavor and feature less of the complex yeasty notes that belie a quality Champagne. The very best producers offer wines in the $20 range and even less, making them exceptional value when compared to comparable Champagnes.

Best U.S. Sparkling Wine Producers

Premier U.S. Sparkling Wine Producers (★★★)
• Argyle
• Domaine Carneros (Le Rêve)
• Equinox
• Iron Horse
• J. Wine Co.
• Roederer Estate
• Scharffenberger
• Schramsberg

Great U.S. Sparkling Wine Producers (★★)
• S. Anderson
• Domaine Carneros
• Domaine Chandon
• Codorniu
• Gloria Ferrer
• Glenora
• Gruet
• Handley
• Mumm Cuvée Napa
• Piper-Sonoma

Sparkling Wines at a Glance

Wines Reviewed:

86

Producers/Brands Represented:

46

Median Price:

$19

Dependable U.S. Sparkling Wine Producers (Recommended)

Some producers placed in this third tier are new (or new to us) and may merit a higher placement in subsequent vintages. These producers are offset by an asterisk.

- *Falconer
- Chateau Frank
- Robert Hunter
- Jepson
- *Laetitia
- L. Mawby
- *Maxus
- Mountain Dome
- *Paradise Ridge
- Pindar
- Domaine Ste. Michelle
- Tribaut
- Wente
- Westport Rivers
- Windsor

Highly Recommended Sparkling Wines

Brut

93 • Roederer Estate (CA) 1992 L'Ermitage, Anderson Valley. $35.

92 • Iron Horse (CA) 1989 Brut LD, Sonoma County Green Valley. $45.

92 • Gloria Ferrer (CA) 1989 Carneros Cuvée Brut, Carneros. $28.

91 • Schramsberg (CA) 1992 J.Schram, Napa Valley. $65.

91 • Maxus (CA) 1991 English Cuvée, California. $29.99.

91 • Domaine Carneros (CA) 1993 Brut, Carneros. $19.

90 • Maxus (CA) 1991 Brut, California. $19.99.

90 • J Wine Co. (CA) 1994 J Brut, Sonoma County. $28.

90 • Iron Horse (CA) 1993 Brut, Sonoma County. $23.50.

90 • Equinox (CA) NV Harmony Cuvée Brut, Santa Cruz Mountains. $27.

89 • Roederer Estate (CA) NV Brut, Anderson Valley. $17.

89 • Iron Horse (CA) 1993 Vrais Amis, Sonoma County. $28.

89 • Iron Horse (CA) 1993 Russian Cuvée, Sonoma County. $23.50.

89 • Domaine Chandon (CA) 1998 25th Anniversary Reserve Cuvée, Napa County. $24.

89 • Argyle (OR) 1994 Brut, Knudsen Vineyards, Willamette Valley. $19.50.

88 • Pindar (NY) 1994 Cuvée Rare Champagne, North Fork of Long Island. $27.99.

88 • Oasis (VA) NV Brut, Virginia. $28.

88 • Laetitia (CA) 1993 Elegance Brut, California. $23.

88 • Gloria Ferrer (CA) 1990 Royal Cuvée Brut, Vintage Reserve, Carneros. $20.

88 • Domaine Chandon (CA) NV Brut Cuvée, Napa County. $18.

88 • Chateau Frank (NY) 1991 Brut, Finger Lakes. $15.

87 • Piper Sonoma (CA) NV Brut, Sonoma. $14.

87 • Mumm Cuvée Napa (CA) NV Brut Prestige, Napa Valley. $15.95.

87 • Mountain Dome (WA) 1993 Brut, Columbia Valley. $16.

86 • Oasis (VA) NV Celebration 2000 Brut Cuvée D'Or, Virginia. $50.

86 • Lenz (NY) 1992 "Cuvée" Sparkling Wine, North Fork of Long Island. $19.99.

86 • Glenora (NY) NV Brut, New York. $12.99.

86 • Cap Rock (TX) NV Sparkling Wine, American. $12.99.

85 • Folie à Deux (CA) 1993 Fantaisie Brut, Napa Valley. $18.

Blanc de Blancs

93 • Domaine Carneros (CA) 1992 Le Reve, Blanc de Blancs, Carneros. $35.

92 • Schramsberg (CA) 1994 Blanc de Blancs, Napa Valley. $26.

92 • Iron Horse (CA) 1990 Blanc de Blancs LD, Sonoma County, Green Valley. $45.

92 • Equinox (CA) 1992 Cuvée de Chardonnay, Blanc de Blanc, Santa Cruz Mountains. $33.

91 • Iron Horse (CA) 1991 Blanc de Blancs, Sonoma County. $30.

90 • Falconer (CA) 1983 Blanc de Blancs RD, San Luis Obispo County. $19.95.

Scale: Superlative (96-100), Exceptional (90-95), Highly Recommended (85-89), Recommended (80-84), Not Recommended (Under 80)

474

87 • Gruet (NM) 1994 Blanc de Blancs,
   New Mexico. $20.

86 • Tribaut (CA) NV Blanc de Blancs
   Brut, California. $9.

85 • Glenora (NY) 1993 Blanc de Blancs,
   New York. $12.99.

Blanc de Noirs

91 • Schramsberg (CA) 1992 Blanc de
   Noirs, Napa Valley. $27.

90 • Piper Sonoma (CA) NV Blanc de
   Noir, Sonoma. $15.

88 • Mumm Cuvée Napa (CA) NV Blanc
   de Noir, Napa Valley. $15.95.

87 • Westport Rivers (MA) 1994
   Blanc de Noir, Southeastern
   New England. $28.95.

86 • Gloria Ferrer (CA) NV Blanc de
   Noirs, Carneros. $15.

86 • Domaine Chandon (CA) NV Blanc de
   Noirs, Carneros. $18.

85 • Robert Hunter (CA) 1992 Brut de
   Noirs, Sonoma Valley. $25.

Brut Rosé

92 • Roederer Estate (CA) NV Brut Rosé,
   Anderson Valley. $21.

90 • Maxus (CA) 1991 Midnight Cuvée,
   California. $19.99.

90 • Iron Horse (CA) 1993 Brut Rosé,
   Sonoma County. $28.

87 • Laetitia (CA) 1993 Elegance Brut
   Rosé, San Luis Obispo County. $23.

86 • Mountain Dome (WA) NV Brut Rosé,
   Washington. $16.

Other Sparkling Wines

89 • Sumac Ridge (Canada) 1993 Steller's
   Joy Brut, Okanagan Valley. $12.95.

87 • L. Mawby (MI) NV Talisman Brut,
   Leelanau Peninsula. $22.

86 • L. Mawby (MI) NV Cremant Brut,
   Leelanau Peninsula. $18.

86 • Firelands (OH) NV Riesling, Lake
   Erie. $10.95.

85 • Magnotta (Canada) NV Rossana
   Blanc de Blancs, Canada. $10.

twenty-one

❧

North American Rosé

❧

An Introduction: What about American Rosé?

U.S. Rosés cover a multitude of variations on a subtle theme. Colors vary from barely perceptible pink tinges to full blown cranberry hues. They are rarely vinified with the lavish expense of premium wines, and they can be made from a wide array of red grape varieties. By definition they are not usually very varietally expressive, and as such can be made from almost any grape that can add some color. A favorite is Zinfandel, which for many years has been the mainstay of California blush wines. At the lower end of the spectrum, Rosés, frequently bearing the White Zinfandel tag, can have rather faint flavors, sometimes obvious sweetness, and an occasional lack of acidity. At their best, U.S. Rosés made from noble varietals are fresh and fruity, sporting much more character and color than French Rosés. Italian and Rhône varietals often yield the best results in California, sometimes even with a touch of oak seasoning.

Best U.S. Rosé Producers

Premier U.S. Rosé Producers (***)
• Paraiso Springs (Baby Blush)
• Swanson (Rosato of Sangiovese)

Great U.S. Rosé Producers (**)
• Cosentino (Tenero Rosa)
• McDowell (Grenache Rosé)
• Pedroncelli (Zinfandel Rosé)
• Joseph Phelps (Vin du Mistral Rosé)
• Sanford (Vin Gris de Pinot Noir)
• Sobon (Rhone Rosé)
• Wollersheim (Prairie Blush)
• Les Vieux Cepages (Ronfleur)

Dependable U.S. Rosé Producers (Recommended)
Some producers placed in this third tier are new (or new to us) and may merit a higher placement in subsequent vintages. These producers are offset by an asterisk.

• *Beaulieu (Solaris & Pinot Noir de Vin Gris)
• *Beringer (Rosé de Saignee)
• Cakebread (Rosé)

Rosé at a Glance

Wines Reviewed:
43

Producers/Brands Represented:
40

Median Price:
$7.50

- Concannon (Righteously Rosé)
- *Curtis (Syrah Rosé)
- De Loach (White Zinfandel)
- *La Famiglia di Robert Mondavi (Rosato Sangiovese)
- *Peju (Provence)
- Preston (Gamay Rosé)
- *Thornton (Grenache Rosé)
- *Treleaven (Saumon Blush)

Highly Recommended Rosé Wines

92 • Pedroncelli (CA) 1998 Vintage Selection, Zinfandel Rosé, Sonoma County. $8.

90 • Wollersheim (WI) 1998 Prairie Blush, White Marechal Foch, Wisconsin 1.8% rs. $7.50.

90 • Thornton (CA) 1998 Collins Ranch, Grenache Rosé, Cucamonga Valley 1.45% rs. $7.99.

89 • Beringer (CA) 1997 Rosé de Saignée, California. $16.

88 • Sobon (CA) 1997 Rhone Rose, Shenandoah Valley. $9.

88 • Laurel Lake (NY) NV Lake Rosé, North Fork of Long Island. $9.99.

88 • Curtis (CA) 1997 Syrah Rosé, Santa Ynez Valley. $8.

87 • Swanson (CA) 1998 Rosato, Sangiovese, Napa Valley. $14.

87 • Cedar Creek (WI) NV Cranberry Blush, American 2.9% rs. $7.

86 • Peju Province (CA) 1997 Provence-A California Table Wine, California 1.1% rs. $16.50.

86 • Montevina (CA) 1997 Rosato, Nebbiolo, Amador County 1.7% rs. $7.50.

86 • Macari (NY) 1997 Rosé d 'Une Nuit, North Fork of Long Island. $11.

86 • Jackson-Triggs (Canada) 1997 Proprietors ' Reserve Blanc de Noir, Okanagan Valley 1.15% rs. $6.46.

85 • Yakima River (WA) 1997 Sof Lem, Lemberger, Yakima Valley. $9.

85 • Gristina (NY) 1997 Rosé of Cabernet, North Fork of Long Island. $8.99.

85 • Chateau Lafayette Reneau (NY) 1998 Pinot Noir Blanc, Finger Lakes 2.5% rs. $6.99.

85 • Callahan Ridge (OR) 1998 White Zinfandel, Umpqua Valley 4% rs. $7.

Scale: Superlative (96-100), Exceptional (90-95), Highly Recommended (85-89), Recommended (80-84), Not Recommended (Under 80)

twenty-two

North American Fortified Wines

An Introduction: American Fortified Wines

Fortified wines, those inevitable after dinner elixirs, have been a part of the American wine industry since its inception. Indeed, the early American taste for fortified wines was well documented, as the signing of the declaration of independence was toasted with a round of Madeira, and it, along with Port and Sherry, was the preferred drink of the Eastern aristocracy well into our own century. That the native industry should strive to compete for this market was only natural.

As in much of the wine-producing New World, vintners took a run at Sherry (and do to this day), but the results on the whole pale, often quite literally, to the Spanish original. Port, however, has been an altogether more satisfying experience. While the climate and soil of Jerez have not been duplicated elsewhere, the broiling heat and unique winemaking practices of the Douro have proven much easier to replicate, perhaps nowhere more so than in California's Amador County and San Joaquin Valley.

Beyond California, Port-style wines are being made in much of the country. As might be expected a certain measure of heat helps, and the most successful examples have come from warm states such as Missouri. As the saying goes a little residual sugar can cover up a multitude of sins, but the Missouri Ports of producers such as Stone Hill and Mount Pleasant truly stand on their own merits, and have proven as consistently competent as many California versions.

Best U.S. Fortified Wine Producers

Premier U.S. Fortified Wine Producers (***)
• Beaulieu (Muscat)
• Bonny Doon (Cassis, Framboise)
• Cedar Mountain (Port)
• Guenoc (Port)
• Ficklin (Port)
• Quady (Muscat, Port)

Fortified Wines at a Glance

Wines Reviewed:

61

Producers/Brands Represented:

43

Median Price:

$18

Great U.S. Fortified Wine Producers (**)

- Beringer (Port)
- Geyser Peak (Port)
- Mount Pleasant (Port)
- Pindar (Port)
- Stone Hill (Port)
- Whidbey (Port)
- Windsor (Port)

Dependable U.S. Fortified Wine Producers (Recommended)

Some producers placed in this third tier are new (or new to us) and may merit a higher placement in subsequent vintages. These producers are offset by an asterisk.

- *Duck Walk (Port)
- Horton (Port)
- Justin (Port)
- Pesenti (Port)
- *Prager (Port)
- Rosenblum (Muscat, Port)
- *St. Amant (Port)
- St. Julian (Sherry)
- Sonora (Port)
- Trentadue (Port)
- *Twin Hills (Port)

Highly Recommended Fortified Wines

93 • Quady (CA) 1990 Vintage Starboard, Amador County 10.6% rs. $21.50.

92 • Ficklin (CA) 10 Year Old Tawny Port, California 9.5% rs. $22.

92 • Cedar Mountain (CA) 1996 Vintage Port, Amador County 10% rs. $19.50.

91 • Quady (CA) 1993 LBV Port, Amador County 8.18% rs. $12.

91 • Ficklin (CA) 1988 Vintage Port, California 9% rs. $25.

90 • Whidbey (WA) 1990 Port, Washington 9.8% rs. $12.99.

90 • Quady (CA) 1989 Frank 's Vineyard Vintage Starboard, California 10.4% rs. $19.

89 • Twin Hills (CA) Zinfandel Port, Lot XCII, Paso Robles 5% rs. $25.

89 • Quady (CA) Batch 88 Starboard, California 11.1% rs. $11.50.

89 • Quady (CA) 1990 Frank 's Vineyard Vintage Starboard, California 10.2% rs. $19.

89 • Prager Winery & Port Works (CA) Noble Companion 10 Year Old Tawny Port, Napa Valley 8.4% rs. $45.

89 • Pindar (NY) 1995 Port, North Fork of Long Island. $24.99.

88 • Trentadue (CA) 1994 Petite Sirah Port, Alexander Valley 8.6% rs. $20.

88 • St. Julian (MI) Solera Cream Sherry, Michigan 17% rs. $12.

88 • Prager Winery & Port Works (CA) 1993 Royal Escort LBV Port, Petite Sirah, Napa Valley 5.5% rs. $38.50.

88 • Mount Pleasant (MO) 15 Barrel Tawny Port, Augusta 8.5% rs. $23.50.

88 • Beringer (CA) 1994 Port of Cabernet Sauvignon, Napa Valley 10.29% rs. $20.

87 • Guenoc (CA) 1994 Vintage Port, California 9.7% rs. $25.

87 • Geyser Peak (CA) 1995 Henry 's Reserve Shiraz Port, Alexander Valley. $15/375 ml.

87 • Duck Walk (NY) 1996 Blueberry Port 10% rs. $12.95/375 ml.

86 • Sonora Winery & Port Works (CA) 1994 Vintage Port, Sierra Foothills 8.5% rs. $16/500 ml.

86 • Mount Pleasant (MI) 1996 White Port, Augusta Missouri 10.5% rs. $25/375 ml.

86 • Mount Pleasant (MI) 1990 Port, Augusta, Missouri 11.1% rs. $18.

86 • Meier 's (OH) No. 44 American Ruby Port 8.3% rs. $6.95.

86 • Lonz (OH) 3 Islands American Ruby Port 9.9% rs. $6.50.

86 • Justin (CA) 1996 Obtuse, Paso Robles 15% rs. $22.50.

86 • Ficklin (CA) Tinta Port, California 8.5% rs. $12.

85 • Windsor (CA) Rare Port, California 11.9% rs. $13.

85 • St. Amant (CA) 1995 Vintage Port, Amador County 7% rs. $28.

85 • Mount Pleasant (MO) JRL 's Barrel Select Port, Augusta 6.75% rs. $11.95.

Scale: Superlative (96-100), Exceptional (90-95), Highly Recommended (85-89), Recommended (80-84), Not Recommended (Under 80)

484

85 • Mount Pleasant (MI) Tawny Port,
  Library Vol. V, Augusta Missouri
  10.9% rs. $28.

85 • Dominion Wine Cellars (VA) 1996
  Raspberry Merlot,
  Virginia 18.5% rs. $19.

twenty-three

❧

North American Dessert Wines

❧

An Introduction: American Dessert Wines

Most American dessert wines are late harvest or botrytised styles, which means that the sugars are concentrated in the grapes allowing for a sweet and often viscous wine. These methods are applied to many varietals around the country, but broadly speaking, there are two major styles. The first involves Sauvignon Blanc and/or Semillon and is modeled on the famous sweet wines from the Sauternes district of Bordeaux. Most are botrytised and then aged in oak barrels to add an overlay of luxuriant oaky flavors. Semillon achieves a rich, figgy sort of personality while Sauvignon tends to have a bit more acidity and comes across as being not quite so lush. They are sometimes bottled individually but often work best in combination for this style of wine.

Beyond the Sauternes style, U.S. producers make late harvest or "Icewines" from aromatic varietals such as Riesling, Gewürztraminer, Chenin Blanc, and Muscat. These wines often emulate classic European styles such as Piemontese Moscato, German Trockenbeerenausleses, and Alsatian Vendange Tardives. California provides the vast majority of the late harvest dessert wines, blessed as it is with a dry, lengthy harvesting season. Washington State has a suitable climate for making high-quality Icewine from naturally frozen late harvested grapes, as does New York and other northern tier states. With a labor-intensive production process, these wines will always be more expensive then dry table wines, but they often represent considerable value when compared to imported French and German alternatives.

Canada has slowly but surely been building a reputation as one of the world's most abundant and consistent producers of Icewine, a style of wine most closely associated with Germany. In Germany, Icewine is produced in miniscule quantities at astronomical prices; and even then, only in favorable years. Most of Canada's Icewine is produced on the Niagara Peninsula, a cool growing region that can always count on a sustained cold spell in January to freeze Riesling or Vidal grapes on the vine. These grapes when pressed in their frozen state produce extraordinarily concentrated sweet wines with enough acidity to keep them fresh and uncloying. Given Canada's northerly latitude, other regions, namely, the Okanagan Valley in British Columbia, are also proving able to make outstanding Icewines. U.S. consumers have not yet been urged to seek these gems by the mainstream media; hence, these wines are not in widespread distribution. Devotees and enthusiasts will have to look to specialist wineshops in major markets. A separate list of Canadian Best Producers for dessert wines is on page 335.

Best U.S. Dessert Wine Producers

Premier U.S. Dessert Wine Producers (***)
• Beringer (Special Select Johannisberg Riesling & Nightingale)
• Callaway (Sweet Nancy)
• Chappellet (Moelleux Chenin Blanc)
• Dolce
• Freemark Abbey (Edelwein Gold)
• Grgich Hills (Violetta)
• Swanson (Late Harvest Semillon)

❧

Dessert Wines at a Glance

Wines Reviewed:

107

Producers/Brands Represented:

78

Median Price:

$30 ($15/375ml. Bottles)

❧

Great U.S. Dessert Wine Producers (**)

- Alderbrook (Late Harvest Muscat de Frontignan)
- Bonny Doon (Vin de Glacière)
- Chateau St. Jean (Belle Terre Vineyards, Special Select Riesling)
- De Loach (Late Harvest Gewürztraminer)
- de Lorimier (Lace)
- Elk Cove (Ultima Riesling)
- J. Lohr (Late Harvest Johannisberg Riesling)
- Joseph Phelps (Eisrebe)
- Martin Brothers (Moscato Allegro)
- Newlan (Late Harvest Johannisberg Riesling)
- Quady (Orange Muscat & Black Muscat)
- Silvan Ridge (Various Late Harvest and Icewines)

Dependable U.S. Dessert Wine Producers (Recommended)

Some producers placed in this third tier are new (or new to us) and may merit a higher placement in subsequent vintages. These producers are offset by an asterisk.

- Amity (Select Cluster Riesling)
- *Apex (Icewine)
- *Bedell (Eis)
- *Chalk Hill (Botrytised Semillon)
- *Chateau Grand Traverse (Icewine)
- Chateau Ste. Michelle (Late Harvest/Icewine Riesling)
- Elk Cove (Ultima Gewürztraminer)
- Ferrari-Carano (Eldorado Gold)
- *Dr. Konstantin Frank (Riesling Icewine)
- Geyser Peak (Late Harvest Riesling)
- Jekel (Late Harvest Riesling)
- *Kendall-Jackson (Late Harvest Chardonnay)
- *Martinelli (Muscat Alexandria)
- *Navarro (Late Harvest Cluster Select Riesling)
- Robert Pecota (Moscato d'Andrea)
- Renaissance (Late Harvest Riesling)
- *Santa Barbara Winery (Late Harvest Sauvignon Blanc)
- *Voss (Botrytis Sauvignon Blanc)

Scale: Superlative (96-100), Exceptional (90-95), Highly Recommended (85-89), Recommended (80-84), Not Recommended (Under 80)

Outstanding Dessert Wines

97 • Dolce (CA) 1995 Late Harvest Dessert Wine, Napa Valley 10% rs. $50/375 ml. Cellar Selection.

95 • Beringer (CA) 1994 Nightingale, Private Reserve, Botrytized Sauvignon Blanc-Semillon, Napa Valley 17.1% rs. $22/375 ml.

93 • Erath (OR) 1997 Late Harvest, Gewürztraminer, Willamette Valley 19.5% rs. $18/375 ml.

93 • Ackerman (IA) Apricot Wine 9% rs. $6.50. Best Buy.

92 • Chateau St. Jean (CA) 1995 Belle Terre Vineyards, Special Select Late Harvest, Johannisberg Riesling, Alexander Valley 18.1% rs. $25/375 ml.

92 • Apex (WA) 1997 Ice Wine, Gewürztraminer, Columbia Valley 16.7% rs. $35/375 ml.

91 • Stoney Ridge (Canada) 1996 Puddicombe Vineyard, Select Late Harvest, Vidal, Niagara Peninsula 13.5% rs. $14.25/375 ml.

91 • Magnotta (Canada) Framboise, Fortified Raspberry Dessert Wine, Ontario 18% rs. $11/500 ml.

91 • Bartlett (ME) Sweet Raspberry Wine, Maine 11% rs. $9.99/375 ml.

91 • Alba (NJ) Red Raspberry Wine 13% rs. $9.99/500 ml.

90 • Martinelli (CA) 1997 Jackass Hill, Muscat Alexandria, Russian River Valley. $18/375 ml.

90 • Grgich Hills (CA) 1995 Violetta, Late Harvest, Napa Valley 11% rs. $40/375 ml.

90 • Dr. Konstantin Frank (NY) 1995 Ice Wine, Johannisberg Riesling, New York 22% rs. $29.95/375 ml.

90 • Claar (WA) 1997 Botrytisized Ice Wine, Riesling, Columbia Valley 23% rs. $29.99/375 ml.

90 • Calona (Canada) 1995 Private Reserve, Late Harvest Botrytis Affected, Ehrenfelser, Canada. $21/375 ml.

90 • Bonny Doon (CA) 1997 Muscat Vin de Glacière, California 19.3% rs. $15/375 ml.

90 • Bedell (NY) NV Eis, New York. $27.50/375 ml.

90 • Beaulieu (CA) NV Muscat de Beaulieu, California 12% rs. $10.99/375 ml.

Icewine

98 • Pillitteri (Canada) 1997 Vidal Icewine, Niagara Peninsula VQA 19.8% rs. $29.97/375 ml.

95 • Jackson-Triggs (Canada) 1996 Proprietors' Grand Reserve Ice Wine, Riesling, Okanagan Valley 26.4% rs. $44.07/375 ml.

95 • Cave Spring (Canada) 1997 Icewine, Riesling, Niagara Peninsula 21% rs. $48.99/375 ml.

94 • Sumac Ridge (Canada) 1996 Icewine, Pinot Blanc, Okanagan Valley 26.75% rs. $19.95/375 ml. Cellar Selection.

94 • Jackson-Triggs (Canada) 1997 Proprietors' Grand Reserve Ice Wine, Riesling, Okanagan Valley 24.9% rs. $44.07/375 ml.

91 • Reif Estate (Canada) 1996 Icewine, Vidal, Niagara Peninsula 19.5% rs. $35.60/375 ml.

91 • Peller Estates (Canada) 1997 Icewine, Limited Edition Founder's Series, Vidal, Niagara Peninsula 20% rs. $45/375 ml.

91 • Magnotta (Canada) 1996 Sparkling Icewine, Vidal, Ontario 18% rs. $50/375 ml.

90 • Strewn (Canada) 1996 Icewine, Vidal, Niagara Peninsula 20% rs. $45/375 ml.

90 • Stoney Ridge (Canada) 1996 Icewine, Riesling-Traminer, Niagara Peninsula 19.5% rs. $35.95/375 ml.

90 • Stoney Ridge (Canada) 1995 Icewine, Gewürztraminer, Niagara Peninsula 21% rs. $35.95/375 ml.

90 • Magnotta (Canada) 1996 Limited Edition Icewine, Vidal, Niagara Peninsula 19% rs. $19.95/375 ml.

90 • Konzelmann (Canada) 1996 Icewine, Vidal, Niagara Peninsula 18.5% rs. $45.55/375 ml.

90 • Cedar Creek Estate (Canada) 1995 Reserve Icewine, Chardonnay, Okanagan Valley 32% rs. $59.95/375 ml.

twenty-four

❧

North American
Fruit Wines

❧

An Introduction: American Fruit Wines

We have extolled the virtues of traditionally made American fruit wines for some years now, and this year shall be no different, as the category is full of well-made and downright excellent wines. Perhaps most surprising is the fact that some of the best wines are actually made in dry table styles.

"It's about time dry fruit wines got some attention," declares winemaker Bob Bartlett happily. Indeed, Bartlett's blueberry wines, made from Maine berries, continue to be quite a rarity. Unlike the sweet dessert styles made by most fruit wine producers, Bartlett's top blueberry cuvée is dry and aged up to 18 months in 100% new French oak. Deep and exotic, with an extraordinary fragrance and a supple structure, this wine has proven to be one of the nation's great wine secrets, year after year. Those looking for fruity blueberry juice need not apply. It resembles sweet, fresh blueberries about as much as Cabernet resembles sweet, fresh grapes.

New French oak for fruit wines is rare because it is both risky and expensive, but Bartlett believes his wines are worth it. Hand-picked low bush blueberries, which are smaller and juicier than the high bush blueberries found in supermarkets, are crushed in a conventional grape crusher, then cold fermented on the skins. The wines are also from a single patch (Bartlett's Blueberry Monopole?). Some sugar must be added to bring alcohol levels up, but there is no residual sweetness in the final product.

Bartlett has often had to fight to get his products released. When he and his wife started making fruit wines in 1981, new state legislation had to be written to allow them to sell from their winery. Bartlett wrote that law and got it sponsored. He has also tried to get permission to put vintage dates on his labels (the fruit for his wines is often from a single vintage, and yes there is vintage variation). An implacable BATF won't allow it, however, ruling that vintages can only apply to grapes.

Fruit Wines at a Glance

Wines Reviewed:

21

Producers/Brands Represented:

9

Median Price:

$9

"What about vintage cars?" laughs Bartlett, amused but also angered by the pointless restriction.

Bartlett makes only fruit wines, some of which are sweet, but his dry wines are his pride and joy. In addition to the blueberry wines, he produces white pear and apple wines, and has introduced a mead. The dry table wines are, like most grape-based wines, often at their best with food. "It's really exciting to match these wines with food," Bartlett says, "because there's no history, no precedent." He suggests serving the blueberry wine with Italian dishes or grilled lamb, and the pear wine with smoked fish. A tasty thought indeed.

Best U.S. Fruit Wine Producers

Premier U.S. Fruit Wine Producers (***)
• Bargetto (Chaucer's)
• Bartlett
• St. Julian (Raspberry Champagne)

Great U.S. Fruit Wine Producers (**)
• Hosmer
• Paul Thomas

Dependable U.S. Fruit Wine Producers (Recommended)
Some producers placed in this third tier are new (or new to us) and may merit a higher placement in subsequent vintages. These producers are offset by an asterisk.

• *Ackerman
• *Alba
• *Bedell
• Earle Estates
• *Good Harbor
• *Honeywood
• Hoodsport
• Nashoba Valley Winery
• Wildwood Cellars
• *Wintergreen

Highly Recommended Fruit Wines

96 • Southbrook Farms (Canada) NV Cassis, Canada 16% rs. $15/375 ml.

93 • Southbrook Farms (Canada) NV Framboise, Canada 16% rs. $15/375 ml.

93 • Bartlett (ME) 1994 Wild Blueberry Wine, Oak Dry, Winemakers Reserve. $21.99.

91 • Bedell (NY) NV Raspberry Wine, New York. $9.99.

90 • Bartlett (ME) Pear Wine, French Oak Dry. $14.99.

89 • Good Harbor (MI) Cherry Wine, Michigan. $5. Best Buy.

88 • Honeywood (OR) Red Currant Wine, Oregon. $7.50. Best Buy.

88 • Honeywood (OR) Grande Peach Wine. $7.50. Best Buy.

87 • Paul Thomas (WA) Crimson Rhubarb Wine, Washington 1.2% rs. $5.99. Best Buy.

87 • Honeywood (OR) Grande Cranberry Wine. $7.50. Best Buy.

87 • Bartlett (ME) Wild Blueberry Wine, Oak Dry. $14.99.

87 • Bartlett (ME) Coastal Apple & Pear Wine 1.4% rs. $8.99.

86 • Paul Thomas (WA) Raspberry Wine, Washington 3.6% rs. $7.99. Best Buy.

86 • Earle Estates (NY) Peach Perfection 5% rs. $13.99.

86 • Earle Estates (NY) Blueberry Wine 3% rs. $13.99.

85 • Bartlett (ME) Peach Wine, Semi-Dry 4.5% rs. $11.99.

Scale: Superlative (96-100), Exceptional (90-95), Highly Recommended (85-89), Recommended (80-84), Not Recommended (Under 80)

496

Part Two: Imported Wines

twenty-five

❧

France
Alsace

❧

Alsace Market Overview

Alsace may be France's premier wine region, and is almost certainly its most consistent. This may seem a heretical statement to those legions of collectors with cellars full of fearfully expensive wine from Bordeaux and Burgundy. Indeed, American wine drinkers have not yet been persuaded of the relative merits of the great white wines of Alsace, despite the good value that the region currently offers. Could those Belgians and Swiss be onto something good?

The greatness of any region is ultimately a reflection of the climactic potential and aspect of vineyards. Many harvests in France's classic wine regions are compromised by the arrival of rain before the grapes are optimally ripe. This is less of a problem in Alsace thanks to the location of vineyards along a narrow strip stretching 60 miles north to south along the eastern foothills of the Vosges Mountains. The Vosges Mountains act as rain shelter from the moist Atlantic air, allowing for a long, balmy ripening season with harvest in late September to early October. Washout harvests are rarer in Alsace than Bordeaux or Burgundy and this is directly reflected in the quality of the wines produced in this corner of France.

In a wine store, buying an Alsatian wine could not be simpler as bottles from the region all carry a varietal name, a producer name and, if applicable, a Grand Cru designation (which in practice serves as a vineyard designation). The labeling regulations in Alsace represent an ideal combination of the French and German approach. However, the currency of Grand Cru is not quite as valuable in Alsace as in other French regions: critics have rightly pointed out that 54 Grand Cru vineyards is an excessive number.

Key Varietals & Styles

The noble varieties of Alsace are (Tokay) Pinot Gris, Muscat, Riesling, and Gewürztraminer. Other grape varieties grown include Sylvaner, Pinot Blanc (you might encounter Klevner and Pinot Auxerrois: These are cousins of Pinot Blanc and often show more finesse), and Pinot Noir.

Pinot Gris can come in a dry or off-dry form. At its best it is highly aromatic, intense, and powerful with a notably thick mouthfeel. Alsatian produces the most intense, rich versions of this grape that often stand in stark contrast to the Pinot Gris of Veneto or Northern Italy. Alsace Pinot Gris will often be softer and richer than Riesling, though *Vendanges Tardives* (late harvest) examples can cellar very well.

Riesling is usually vinified in a dry style. When mature, it shares the distinctive petrol aromas of its German counterparts, but has more body and earthier characteristics, and is generally much drier. Grand Cru Alsace Rieslings can be long-lived; indeed, they only develop their true character after a period of cellaring. Riesling in a Vendanges Tardives style will have residual sweetness, though it will often be countered by bright acidity.

Gewürztraminer is the most characterful and pugnacious of varieties in Alsace. It displays inimitable "lychee-like" varietal character that is rarely matched anywhere else in the world. Non-late harvest Gewürztraminer can be made in

Scale: Superlative (96-100), Exceptional (90-95), Highly Recommended (85-89), Recommended (80-84), Not Recommended (Under 80)

a bone dry or off-dry style while Vendanges Tardives wines are generally appreciably sweet.

Muscats are generally bone dry and characterized by floral aromas and tropical fruit flavors. Muscat is not widely planted in Alsace though the finest examples can be among the best dry Muscats in the world.

Pinot Blanc is not a noble variety in Alsace and will never carry a Grand Cru designation. Generally, it is clean, fresh, and medium- to full-bodied. It can produce very good results from lesser vineyards, but rarely will it produce great wine.

Sylvaner is an acidic varietal, which can make pleasant varietally labeled wine and is often used for blending in Edelzwicker (rarely seen outside Alsace), the local wine made from a melange of varieties.

Pinot Noir makes the only red wine of Alsace. It is generally not a wine of note and quenches the local thirst for a light red wine, though some producers do try to fashion something rather more serious.

Sweetness

Alsace is a region of predominantly dry white wines. Sweetness only becomes a serious factor with Vendanges Tardives wines, which can vary from off dry to markedly sweet depending on the vintage character. In exceptional years nectarous *Selection de Grains Nobles* are fashioned from individually selected, *Botrytis*-affected berries. SGNs are dessert wine rarities and can be extraordinarily expensive.

Consumer confusion can arise in discerning whether a Gewürztraminer (and occasionally a Pinot Gris) not labeled as late-harvest is dry or off dry—a factor that will be influenced by the winemaker's preference and the vintage character. Unfortunately, there is no helpful indication on the label in this instance, though dry styles are becoming more prevalent in Alsace.

Alsace at a Glance

Wines Reviewed:

269

Producers/Brands Represented:

39

Value Rating:

Good

In Focus: Alsace with Food

Wines from Alsace transcend French regional chauvinism in that they will be found on most restaurant lists throughout the Gallic nation. This is an acknowledgement that Alsatian wines compliment a wide variety of foods. To look at the table possibilities one need look no further than the gastronomy of Alsace. Pork based dishes are a central theme in a region that gave the world *choucroute*, an unpromising sounding but outstanding combination of cabbage and pork sausage. Alsatian wines are not limited to pork and Alsatian Riesling; anywhere where a white wine might work Alsace will come up with a convincing alternative. An alternative to Grand Cru white Burgundy? Try Alsace Grand Cru Pinot Gris. Looking for a seafood partner? How about a crisp, clean Alsatian Pinot Blanc. A foie gras starter? Dust down an off dry Alsatian Gewürztraminer. Using Alsatian wines at the table is often an intuitive task, as they are not marked by the use of oak maturation (extremely rare in Alsace) and retain fresh malic acids unlike many Chardonnays whose malic acidity has been rendered soft and buttery by conversion to lactic acid.

Recent Vintages

1995

1995 was a good vintage, producing big, rich wines though without the general precision and clarity of flavors seen in the tauter wines from 1996. Riesling and Pinot Gris were generally more successful than Gewürztraminer. Yields were kept naturally low due to flowering problems in the spring; hence there are a good number of concentrated wines. Conditions produced plenty of noble rot and the Vendanges Tardives and SGNs were of impressive proportions and of excellent quality.

1996

1996 produced tight, firm, and racy wines with fine acidic structures that will bode well for the future. Cool, dry conditions at the end of the ripening season kept the grapes' acidity very fresh in most cases. These wines are likely to have long term keeping potential. *Botrytis* was minimal and late harvest wines will not be showing much honeyed character.

1997

1997 was a vintage of warm and dry weather, producing wines with flattering levels of acidity and a generosity of fruit flavors that will yield earlier drinking pleasure than 1996. All three major varietals were successful. However, wines from 1996 showed brighter acids and in many cases were ideally structured for cellaring.

Scale: Superlative (96-100), Exceptional (90-95), Highly Recommended (85-89), Recommended (80-84), Not Recommended (Under 80)

Best Producers: Alsace

Premier Alsatian Producers (***)

- Leon Beyer (Comtes d'Eguisheim)
- Josmeyer (L'Exception)
- Albert Mann
- Domaine Ostertag
- Schoffit
- Trimbach (Clos Ste. Hune)
- Domaine Weinbach
- Zind Humbrecht

Great Alsatian Producers (**)

- Lucien Albrecht
- Francois Baur
- Jean Becker
- Leon Beyer
- Boeckel
- Bott Freres
- Bott-Geyl
- Marcel Deiss
- Dopff et Irion
- Jerome Geschickt
- Hartweg
- Hugel
- Josmeyer
- Marc Kreydenweiss
- Kuentz-Bas
- Gustave Lorentz
- Arthur Metz
- Julien Meyer
- Rene Mure
- Pfaffenheim
- Riefle
- Francois Schwach
- Schlegel Boeglin
- Schlumberger
- Pierre Sparr
- Trimbach
- Cave Vinicole de Kientzheim-Kayersberg

Dependable Alsatian Producers (Recommended)

These producers have impressed us. Some are new. Some are older but improving steadily. Some have done well in the past but we have not tasted enough vintages to classify them as Premier or Great yet.

- Domaine Barmes Buecher
- Charles Baur
- Jean-Pierre Bechtold
- Bennwihr
- Jean-Marc Bernhard
- Bestheim
- Fleith
- Clos du Letzenberg
- Mader
- Les Viticulteurs Reunis a Sigolsheim
- Scherer
- Charles Schleret

Reviews

Lucien Albrecht

Riesling, Pfingstberg Grand Cru, Alsace 1995 $20.   **89**

Deep straw-yellow. Moderately full-bodied. Balanced acidity. Minerals, citrus peel, cream. Aromatically reserved. Full and rounded mouthfeel. Angular and ripe through the finish.

Tokay Pinot Gris, Alsace 1997 $14.   **83**

Barmes Buecher

Gewürztraminer, Rosenberg, Alsace 1996 $16.50.   **83**

Pinot Blanc, Rosenberg, Alsace 1996 $16.   **84**

Riesling, Rosenberg, Alsace 1996 $18.   **86**

Bright yellow-gold. Medium-bodied. High acidity. Herbs, lemons. Lean, tart, and angular at present. Time may soften the acids. Best suited to shellfish.

Charles Baur

Gewürztraminer, Pfersigberg Grand Cru, Alsace 1995 $15.   **83**

Gewürztraminer, Pfersigberg Grand Cru, Alsace 1996 $15.   **84**

Gewürztraminer, Fronenberg, Alsace 1997 $14.   **88**

Brilliant green-gold. Moderately full-bodied. Balanced acidity. Lychee, mineral. Intensely spicy and pungent, with similar intensity in the flavors. Very long and concentrated. An extraordinary varietal expression.

Pinot Blanc, Alsace 1996 $8.50.   **86**

Brilliant straw-yellow. Moderately full-bodied. High acidity. Highly extracted. Minerals, citrus zest. Aromatically reserved. Lean, firm, zesty mouthfeel. Clean and weighty in the mouth. This would make a versatile wine at the table.

Pinot Blanc, Alsace 1997 $8.50.   **84**

Riesling, Alsace 1996 $10.   **81**

Riesling, Alsace 1997 $11.   **88**

Brilliant yellow-gold. Medium-bodied. Balanced acidity. Apple, melon. Juicy, pure aromas follow through on the palate. Sensational mouthfeel and textural elegance point to real class.

Sylvaner, Alsace 1997 $6.99.   **84**

Francois Baur

Gewürztraminer, Brand Grand Cru, Vendange Tardive, Alsace 1996 $43.   **93**

Deep gold. Moderately full-bodied. Balanced acidity. Honey, tropical fruit, lychee. Rich, honeyed aromas. Deep, flavorful palate, with glycerous richness and mild sweetness that lingers on the finish. Very generous and stylish.

Riesling, Brand Grand Cru, Alsace 1995 $18.   **88**

Bright straw. Moderately full-bodied. High acidity. Highly extracted. Minerals, citrus, petrol. Aromatically reserved. Weighty and firm mouthfeel. Ripe and rounded through the finish.

Riesling, Brand Grand Cru, Alsace 1996 $18.   **83**

Riesling, Brand Grand Cru, Vendange Tardive, Alsace 1995 $31.   **91**

Deep straw hue. Moderately full-bodied. Balanced acidity. Highly extracted. Honey, citrus zest, petrol. Outrageously aromatic. Full and round mouthfeel. Underlying acidic backbone. Ripe and complex through to the finish. Drinkable now, but structured for the long haul.

Tokay Pinot Gris, Herrenweg, Cuvée Prestige, Alsace 1995 $31.   **86**

Deep yellow-gold. Full-bodied. Balanced acidity. Highly extracted. Spice, butter. Intriguingly aromatic. Rounded, lush, and viscous mouthfeel. Opulent, complex flavors. Extraordinarily long finish. Exotic.

Tokay Pinot Gris, "Domaine Langehald," Alsace 1996 $22.   **83**

Jean Becker

Gewürztraminer, Sonnenglanz Grand Cru, Alsace 1995 $19.   **84**

Pinot Gris, Froehn Vendanges Tardives,
Grand Cru, Alsace 1996 $29/500 ml.   **87**

Bright pale gold. Medium-bodied. High acidity. Smoke, orange blossom, glycerin. Mild smoky aromas. Ripe, glycerous style with piquant acids. Juicy through the finish.

Scale: Superlative (96-100), Exceptional (90-95), Highly Recommended (85-89), Recommended (80-84), Not Recommended (Under 80)

Riesling, Schoenenbourg Grand Cru, Alsace 1996 $19.   88
Bright straw. Medium-bodied. High acidity. Moderately extracted. Talc, citrus, minerals.
Pleasantly aromatic. Delicate throughout. Vibrant and crisp through the finish.

Jean-Pierre Bechtold

Gewürztraminer, Collection Robert Beltz, Alsace 1996 $13.   83
Gewürztraminer, Engelberg Grand Cru, Alsace 1996 $23.   83
Gewürztraminer, Engelberg Grand Cru, Alsace 1997 $21.   84
Riesling, Engelberg Grand Cru, Alsace 1996 $19.   90
Bright yellow-gold. Moderately full-bodied. Full acidity. Petrol, tropical fruits. Rich
aromas. Exotic ripeness on the expansive palate. Full-throttled style. Concentrated
tropical flavors and fine acids will allow this to develop further.

Riesling, Engelberg Grand Cru, Alsace 1997 $19.   86
Bright straw-yellow. Moderately full-bodied. High acidity. Sweet apples, honey. Ripe,
honeyed aromas. Juicy, sweet, fruity palate. Attractive character invites drinking now.
Will develop with more age. Concentrated.

Tokay Pinot Gris, "E," Alsace 1996 $14.   86
Bright straw. Medium-bodied. High acidity. Moderately extracted. Minerals, smoke.
Muted aromatics. Lean and brisk mouthfeel. Sharp and vigorous through the finish.

Tokay Pinot Gris, "E," Alsace1997 $15.   83

Jean-Marc Bernhard

Pinot Blanc, Bouquet de Printemps, Alsace 1997 $9.   86
Brilliant straw-yellow. Moderately full-bodied. High acidity. Highly extracted. Blanched
almonds, flint, cream. Generous, complex aromas. Rounded and soft in the mouth,
with enough acidity to lend a sense of balance. Drinking well now.

Riesling, Alsace 1996 $12.   81

Bestheim

Gewürztraminer, Marckrain Grand Cru, Alsace 1997 $15.   84
Muscat, Bollenberg, Alsace 1997 $8.50.   83
Pinot Blanc, Tulipes des Vignes, Alsace 1997 $8.   82
Riesling, Rebgarten, Alsace 1996 $10.   84

Leon Beyer

La Cuvée, Alsace 1997 $9.95.   84
Brilliant greenish straw. Medium-bodied. High acidity. Highly extracted. Spice, citrus
peel, sweet herbs. Generous Muscat-like aromatics. Crisp and bone dry on the palate,
with zesty acidity through the clean finish. Excellent with shellfish.

Gewürztraminer, Alsace 1995 $15.99.   90
Straw color. Golden highlights. Moderately full-bodied. Lychee, tropical fruits, minerals.
Classic spicy aromas. Oily mouthfeel. Bone-dry palate and finish with pure varietal flavors.
Its dryness should make this an outstanding food match with pork-based dishes.

Gewürztraminer, Alsace 1997 $14.95.   83
Gewürztraminer, Cuvée des Comtes d'Eguisheim, Alsace 1996 $33.95.   90
Deep yellow-gold. Full-bodied. Balanced acidity. Highly extracted. Butter, spice, minerals.
Powerful aromatics. Rich and oily mouthfeel. Intense and persistent. Bright acids bode
well for aging potential.

Gewürztraminer, Cuvée des Comtes d'Eguisheim, Alsace 1997 $33.95.   89
Highly saturated yellow-gold. Full-bodied. High acidity. Highly extracted. Spice, minerals,
flowers. Pleasantly aromatic. Full and intense on the palate. Approachable now. Will
probably improve with near-term cellaring.

Gewürztraminer, Vendanges Tardives, Alsace 1997 $59.95.   84

Pinot Blanc de Blancs, Alsace 1995 $12.99.   80

Riesling, Alsace 1995 $14.99.   83

Riesling, Alsace 1997 $13.95.   84

Riesling, "Les Ecaillers," Alsace 1997 $19.95.   88

Bright greenish straw. Medium-bodied. High acidity. Flowers, talc. Clean aromas. Bright citric acid flavors. Austere style that will show best with food.

Riesling, Comtes d'Eguisheim, Alsace 1995 $34.95.   98

Brilliant yellow-gold. Moderately full-bodied. High acidity. Honey, lemon. Ripe aromas. Citrus zest accent on the lively, dry palate. Intense acids evident on the finish. Mid-term cellaring is recommended.

Riesling, Comtes d'Eguisheim, Alsace 1996 $34.95.   87

Brilliant pale straw. Medium-bodied. High acidity. Lemon, mineral. Youthful, reserved aromas. Concentrated, dry palate. Evident structure and bright acids highlight the austere finish. Further bottle age recommended.

Riesling, Comtes d'Eguisheim, Alsace 1997 $33.95.   92

Bright pale straw color. Medium-bodied. Full acidity. Flint, green apples. Very precise, minerally, linear palate and finish. Elegant style. Very racy and somewhat delicate.

Tokay Pinot Gris, Alsace 1995 $14.99.   85

Tokay Pinot Gris, Alsace 1997 $13.95.   84

Tokay Pinot Gris, Comtes d'Eguisheim, Alsace 1995 $32.95.   92

Deep yellow-gold. Moderately full-bodied. High acidity. Highly extracted. Minerals, citrus peel, spice. Aromatically reserved. Concentrated and intense in the mouth. Tightly wound flavors. Firm and austere structure. Impressive now, but should develop further with age.

Tokay Pinot Gris, Comtes d'Eguisheim, Alsace 1996 $32.95.   92

Deep green-gold cast. Full-bodied. High acidity. Highly extracted. Minerals, citrus. Aromatically reserved. Firm and intense palate feel. Minerally backbone. Impressive, but not very user-friendly now. Cellaring is recommended.

Tokay Pinot Gris, Comtes d'Eguisheim, Alsace 1997 $32.95.   92

Bright straw cast. Moderately full-bodied. Balanced acidity. Highly extracted. Spice, orange blossom, minerals. Subtle aromatics. Deeply flavored and full in the mouth. Oily and extremely ripe through the finish. Almost approachable, but will develop with age.

Tokay Pinot Gris, Sélection de Grains Nobles, Alsace 1997 $89.95.   91

Brilliant yellow-straw color. Full-bodied. High acidity. Highly extracted. Smoke, ranges, honey. Pleasantly aromatic. Ripe and rounded mouthfeel. Still quite youthful, with marked sweetness and zesty acidity punctuating the finish. Mid-term cellaring is recommended.

Boeckel

Edelzwicker, Alsace 1996 $12.75.   88

Pale yellow straw. Medium-bodied. Balanced acidity. White citrus, dough. Yeasty, doughy nose. Smooth and silky on the palate. Mildly flavored. Texture and mouthfeel are the keynotes.

Gewürztraminer, Réserve, Alsace 1996 $18.   86

Brilliant green yellow. Medium-bodied. High acidity. Spice, mineral. Spicy, exotic nose. Dry, austere palate with a strong mineral accent through the finish. A lean style.

Gewürztraminer, Zotzenberg Grand Cru, Alsace 1995 $23.   89

Bright pale gold. Medium-bodied. Balanced acidity. Spice, mineral. Clean, yeasty, spicy aromas. Angular, minerally palate with austere flavors. Not for keeping.

Pinot Blanc, Réserve, Alsace 1997 $19.75.   NR

Riesling, Réserve, Alsace 1996 $13.75.   85

Scale: Superlative (96-100), Exceptional (90-95), Highly Recommended (85-89), Recommended (80-84), Not Recommended (Under 80)

504

Riesling, Wibelsberg Grand Cru, Alsace 1993 $20.   87
Brilliant gold. Moderately full-bodied. Balanced acidity. Petrol, mineral. Assertive petrol
and marked spice aromas. Very attractive mature Riesling character throughout.

Bott Frèrcs

Pinot Blanc, Sélection, Alsace 1997 $7.   84
Pinot Gris, Réserve Personnelle, Alsace 1996 $13.   86
Brilliant greenish straw. Moderately full-bodied. High acidity. Highly extracted. Minerals,
citrus peel. Precise and crisp aromas. Lean palate feel with piercing acidity. Taut and
zesty through the finish.

Riesling, Cuvée Exceptionnelle, Alsace 1996 $10.   88
Bright yellow-gold. Medium-bodied. High acidity. Citrus, fusel. Fine, petrol-edged
aromas are youthful and vibrant. Palate follows through with citrus and mineral
qualities that linger.

Riesling, Réserve Personelle, Alsace 1996 $12.   89
Bright yellow straw. Medium-bodied. High acidity. Petrol, mineral, tart peach.
Fine, petrol-accented nose. Racy, elegant flavors. Intense finish.

Bott-Geyl

Tokay Pinot Gris, Sonnenglanz Grand Cru, Alsace 1995 $26.   93
Brilliant gold hue. Moderately full-bodied. Full acidity. Smoke, yeast, tropical fruits.
Pungently aromatic, with generous, spicy accents. Great depth of flavor, with a juicy
fruit and balancing acids.

Clos du Letzenberg

Gewürztraminer, Alsace 1996 $12.   84
Gewürztraminer, Vendanges Tardives, Alsace 1996 $18/500 ml.   93
Bright gold. Full-bodied. Balanced acidity. Wax, tropical fruit. Intense aromas.
Concentrated palate, with warming alcohol through the finish. Mildly sweet.

Riesling, Alsace 1997 $11.50.   NR
Tokay Pinot Gris, Alsace 1997 $12.   81
Tokay Pinot Gris, Vendanges Tardives, Alsace 1996 $20/500 ml.   91
Brilliant gold color. Moderately full-bodied. Balanced acidity. Smoke, ripe apples, tropical
fruits. Pungently smoky, intense aromas. Lush, sweet mouthful of fruit flavors. Exotic.

Pinot Noir, Alsace 1996 $15.   NR

Marcel Deiss

Pinot Noir, Burlenberg, Vieille Vigne, Alsace 1995 $40.   83
Altenberg Bergheim Grand Cru, Alsace 1995 $35.   89
Brilliant yellow-gold. Full-bodied. High acidity. Highly extracted. Orange blossom, spice,
honey. Powerful aromas. Rounded mouthfeel with definitive sweetness. Botrytis flavors.
Long, rich finish.

Gewürztraminer, Bergheim, Alsace 1995 $14.   NR
Gewürztraminer, Bergheim, Alsace 1996 $15.   NR
Gewürztraminer, Saint Hippolyte, Alsace 1996 $22.   87
Bright yellow-gold. Moderately full-bodied. High acidity. Highly extracted. Butter, spice,
minerals. Pleasantly aromatic. Firm, slightly austere palate feel. Crisp and dry finish.

Gewürztraminer, "Burg," Vendanges Tardives, Alsace 1995 $40.   85
Pinot Gris, Bergheim, Alsace 1995 $14.   87
Bright straw-yellow. Moderately full-bodied. High acidity. Highly extracted. Minerals,
citrus zest. Aromatically reserved. Slight minerally, oxidized note on the palate. Crisp,
rich finish.

Pinot Gris, Bergheim, Alsace 1996 $15.   **88**

Bright gold. Full-bodied. High acidity. Highly extracted. Citrus peel, minerals, spice. Rather reserved aromatically. Full-throttled and aggressive palate. Hearty extraction. Vibrant acidity. Finishes with marked sweetness. Built for long-term aging.

Tokay Pinot Gris, Altenberg de Bergheim Grand Cru,
Sélection de Grains Nobles, Alsace 1995 $80.   **NR**

Riesling, "Engelgarten," Alsace 1995 $20.   **94**

Brilliant yellow-gold. Moderately full-bodied. High acidity. Petrol, mineral, fusel. Earthy, mineral nose is very pronounced. Assertive mineral flavors, with austere citrus character. A solid, well-structured wine that will blossom with a bit of aging.

Riesling, "Saint Hippolyte," Alsace 1995 $20.   **86**

Bright yellow-gold. Medium-bodied. High acidity. Herb, mineral, citrus. Fresh, lean, and uncomplicated. Straightforward character. Lively acids. Minerally grip on finish.

Riesling, "Burg," Vendanges Tardives, Alsace 1995 $44.   **88**

Bright golden yellow. Medium-bodied. Full acidity. Wax, honey, sweet peach. Honeyed, inviting aromas. Youthful fruit flavors balanced with juicy acidity. Accessible.

Riesling, Schoenenbourg Grand Cru, Vendanges Tardives, Alsace 1995 $45. **NR**

Riesling, Altenberg de Bergheim Grand Cru, Vendanges Tardives,
Alsace 1995 $58.   **89**

Pale yellow. Medium-bodied. Balanced acidity. Peach, apple. Fresh, juicy, and very drinkable. Open-knit fruit salad flavors. Very appealing style.

Riesling, Altenberg de Bergheim Grand Cru, Alsace 1996 $38.   **83**

Gewürztraminer, Altenberg de Bergheim Grand Cru,
Sélection de Grains Nobles, Alsace 1995 $80.   **87**

Brilliant yellow-gold. Moderately full-bodied. Balanced acidity. Minerals, tropical fruits. Concentrated. Silky mouthfeel. Subdued sweetness. Lean, minerally finish.

Gewürztraminer, Altenberg de Bergheim Grand Cru,
Sélection de Grains Nobles, Alsace 1996 $85.   **88**

Bright gold. Moderately full-bodied. Balanced acidity. Citrus zest, lychee, mineral. Pure aromas with a zesty edge. Juicy mouthful of flavors. Varietal character manifests itself on the spicy finish. Elegant style.

Dopff & Irion

Pinot Noir, La Cuvée Rene Dopff, Alsace 1996 $NA.   **84**

Crustacés, Alsace 1997 $9.   **83**

Gewürztraminer, "Domaines du Château de Riquewihr, Les Sorcières,"
Alsace 1996 $23.   **NR**

Gewürztraminer, Sporen Grand Cru, Alsace 1996 $27.   **81**

Gewürztraminer, Sélection de Grains Nobles, Alsace 1994 $59.   **95**

Deep gold. Full-bodied. Balanced acidity. Lychee, butter, tropical fruits. Round, juicy, and full. Lovely buttery presence on the palate. Tropical fruit and spice flavors. Silky feel. Drinking well now.

Gewürztraminer, Alsace 1997 $14.   **NR**

Gewürztraminer, Vendanges Tardives, Alsace 1994 $67.   **89**

Bright yellow-gold. Full-bodied. Low acidity. Highly extracted. Petrol, spice, tropical fruits. Perfumed and exotic, with a late-harvest overtone. Rich and oily in the mouth, with a viscous quality. Very flavorful through the velvety finish.

Muscat, Alsace 1997 $11.   **86**

Rich straw-yellow. Moderately full-bodied. High acidity. Highly extracted. Spice, orange blossom, peach skin. Generous, complex and unusual aromas. Full and rounded in the mouth. Lean, dry finish.

Scale: Superlative (96-100), Exceptional (90-95), Highly Recommended (85-89), Recommended (80-84), Not Recommended (Under 80)

506

Pinot Blanc, Alsace 1997 $11. **86**
Medium straw. Medium-bodied. High acidity. Moderately extracted. Butter, minerals, toast. Pleasantly aromatic. Firm and lean palate feel. Long, clean finish.

Riesling, Alsace 1997 $12. **83**

Riesling, "Les Murailles," Domaines du Château de Riquewihr 1995 $20. **84**

Riesling, Schoenenbourg Grand Cru, Alsace 1994 $27. **89**
Bright yellow green. Medium-bodied. High acidity. Moderately extracted. Apples, citrus. Elegant floral, petrol aromas. Crisp, minerally palate with a clean finish. Well balanced. Drinking nicely now.

Riesling, Vendanges Tardives, Alsace 1994 $69. **92**
Bright yellow-gold. Moderately full-bodied. Balanced acidity. Peach, apple. Tropical, petrol-like nose. Subtly sweet, weighty palate with a glycerous mouthfeel. Generous. Beginning to develop. Drinking well now. Will hold for a few years.

Tokay Pinot Gris, Alsace 1997 $13. **87**
Pale straw. Medium-bodied. Balanced acidity. Moderately extracted. Minerals, citrus peel, yellow apple. Aromatically reserved. Lean and crisp mouthfeel. Vibrant and angular through the finish.

Tokay Pinot Gris, Domaines du Château de Riquewihr,
"Les Maquisards," Alsace 1996 $22. **86**
Bright greenish straw. Medium-bodied. High acidity. Moderately extracted. Citrus, minerals. Aromatically reserved. Crisp and minerally mouthfeel. Vibrant, refreshing, and straightforward.

Fleith

Klevner, Alsace 1997 $8. **83**

Riesling, Alsace 1995 $9. **NR**

Riesling, Alsace 1997 $10. **83**

Tokay Pinot Gris, Réserve, Alsace 1996 $10. **89**
Deep yellow-gold. Moderately full-bodied. High acidity. Moderately extracted. Oranges, spice, minerals. Pleasantly aromatic. Rich and full mouthfeel balanced by vibrant acidity. Zesty through the finish.

Tokay Pinot Gris, Furstentum Grand Cru, Alsace 1996 $19/500 ml. **95**
Very deep yellow-gold. Full-bodied. Balanced acidity. Moderately extracted. Honey, tropical fruits, smoke. Exotically aromatic, with a ripe and glycerous mouthfeel. Rich and flavorful, with enough acidity to lend a sense of balance. Intense and fairly sweet through the finish. Drinking well, but should improve.

Jerome Geschickt & Fils

Gewürztraminer, Kaefferkopf, Alsace 1997 $15. **84**

Riesling, Kaefferkopf, Vendanges Tardives, Alsace 1996 $24/500 ml. **89**
Deep straw-yellow. Moderately full-bodied. Balanced acidity. Moderately extracted. Spice, citrus, lychee. Complex and forward aromas. Rich and oily mouthfeel. Firm acidic structure. Very long finish. Further cellaring recommended.

Hartweg

Pinot Gris, Vendanges Tardives, Alsace 1996 $29. **90**
Pale gold color. Medium-bodied. Balanced acidity. Mineral oil, smoke, sweet peach. Intense and concentrated. High alcohol evident on the finish. Powerful, though approachable now.

Riesling, Alsace 1996 $10. **83**

Riesling, Mandelberg Grand Cru, Alsace 1996 $19. **89**
Bright pale straw. Medium-bodied. High acidity. Green apples, citrus. Ripe, fruity aromas. Juicy fruit flavors. Concentrated, intense finish. Complex.

Hugel

Gentil, Alsace 1995 $8.99.   88

Medium straw. Medium-bodied. Moderately extracted. Apples, lemon grass. Forward zesty aromas. Crisp, clean style. Some viscosity on the palate.

Gewürztraminer, Jubilee, Alsace 1995 $24.   84

Tokay Pinot Gris, Jubilee, Réserve Personnelle, Alsace 1995 $25.   89

Bright straw-yellow. Full-bodied. Balanced acidity. Highly extracted. Smoke, minerals. Deeply aromatic, with a lush and exotic smoky quality. Rounded and full in the mouth, with a generous oily texture. Rich finish.

Josmeyer

Gewürztraminer, Alsace 1996 $20.   81

Gewürztraminer, L'Exception, Alsace 1995 $65.   94

Deep gold. Full-bodied. Balanced acidity. Highly extracted. Butter, spice, citrus peel. Outrageously aromatic. Profoundly ripe and generous palate. Unctuous and viscous, with an intense, oily mouthfeel. A sweet hint comes out on the finish.

Pinot Blanc, Alsace 1996 $11.99.   84

Riesling, Alsace 1996 $17.   86

Bright yellow-gold. Medium-bodied. High acidity. Lemon, minerals. Youthful, intense aromas. Angular and concentrated on the palate. Gripping acids. Bone-dry finish. Further bottle age recommended.

Riesling, L'Exception, Alsace 1995 $65.   97

Bright yellow-gold. Moderately full-bodied. Balanced acidity. Peach, green apple. Rich, glycerous aromas. Plenty of sweet, tropical, juicy flavors, with fine intensity and length. A pity to drink this now, though it is very approachable. Luxurious.

Tokay Pinot Gris, Alsace 1996 $20.   83

Tokay Pinot Gris, L'Exception, Alsace 1995 $65.   98

Deep greenish gold. Full-bodied. Balanced acidity. Highly extracted. Petrol, tropical fruits, spice. Extraordinarily aromatic and complex. Ripe and full mouthfeel marked by sweetness. Balanced by vibrant acids. Intense finish. This is drinking wonderfully now, but is in no danger of fading.

Cave Vinicole de Kientzheim-Kayersberg

Gewürztraminer, Furstentum Grand Cru 1996 $20.   86

Bright straw. Medium-bodied. Balanced acidity. Moderately extracted. Orange peel, spice, minerals. Pleasantly aromatic. Fruit-accented, supple palate feel. Rounded through the finish, with enough acidity to lend a sense of balance.

Riesling, Schlossberg Grand Cru, Alsace 1996 $15.   89

Bright yellow. Moderately full-bodied. High acidity. Paraffin, green apples. Intense varietal expression on nose and palate. Forceful concentration of flavors linger on a finish punctuated by acids. Structure and balance suggest that further aging will be rewarded.

Tokay Pinot Gris, Réserve, Alsace 1997 $14.   89

Bright straw. Medium-bodied. Balanced acidity. Moderately extracted. Oranges, smoke, minerals. Aromatically reserved. Fat and ripe in the mouth, with a touch of sweetness and full flavors.

Marc Kreydenweiss

Gewürztraminer, Kritt, Alsace 1997 $NA.   83

Pinot Blanc, Kritt, Alsace 1997 $NA.   83

Pinot Gris, Moenchberg Grand Cru, Alsace 1997 $NA.   83

Pinot Gris, "Clos Rebberg," Alsace 1997 $NA.   83

Scale: Superlative (96-100), Exceptional (90-95), Highly Recommended (85-89), Recommended (80-84), Not Recommended (Under 80)

Riesling, Kastelberg Grand Cru, Alsace 1997 $NA.   **86**

Pale straw. Medium-bodied. Balanced acidity. Sweet apples. Attractive, fruity flavors with a touch of sweetness. Very approachable style.

Riesling, Wiebelsberg Grand Cru, Alsace 1997 $NA.   **83**

Gustave Lorentz

Gewürztraminer, Reserve, Alsace 1995 $14.99.   **86**

Medium straw-yellow. Medium-bodied. Moderately extracted. Citrus zest, grapefruit, spice. Vibrant aromas. Bright fruity palate with forward acidity. Very fresh through the finish. Aperitif style.

Gewürztraminer, Réserve, Alsace 1996 $16.   **NR**

Gewürztraminer, Rotenberg, Alsace 1995 $20.   **84**

Gewürztraminer, Altenberg de Bergheim Grand Cru, Alsace 1993 $35.   **83**

Muscat, Domaine Lorentz, Alsace 1995 $16.99.   **88**

Pale straw. Medium-bodied. Moderately extracted. Grapefruit, citrus, rose water. Attractive floral perfumed nose. Fresh, zesty style. Not a heavyweight. Great aromatic complexity. Best suited to aperitif use.

Pinot Blanc, Réserve, Alsace 1997 $10.   **84**

Riesling, Reserve, Alsace 1995 $14.99.   **89**

Pale straw. Medium-bodied. Moderately extracted. Flowers, apricots, citrus. Delicate and refreshingly balanced palate. Clean finish. Versatile enough for use as an aperitif or with lighter foods.

Riesling, "Rotenberg," Alsace 1995 $20.   **83**

Riesling, Réserve, Alsace 1996 $16.   **84**

Riesling, Altenberg de Bergheim Grand Cru, Alsace 1993 $35.   **95**

Luminous yellow-gold. Medium-bodied. Balanced acidity. Petrol, peach, lemon zest. Very rich aromas and flavors. Crisp acids give structure and focus. Drinkable now or later.

Riesling, Kanzlerberg Grand Cru, Alsace 1993 $35.   **86**

Medium yellow-gold. Medium-bodied. Balanced acidity. Petrol, spice, minerals. Mineral- and petrol-dominated aromas. Oily richness on the palate. Finishes quickly. Drinking nicely now.

Tokay Pinot Gris, Reserve, Alsace 1995 $14.99.   **89**

Pale straw. Medium-bodied. Moderately extracted. Citrus peel, peach, spice. Floral aromatics. Bright fruity palate with elegance and balance. Clean flavors through the finish.

Tokay Pinot Gris, Réserve, Alsace 1996 $16.   **84**

Albert Mann

Gewürztraminer, Steingrubler Grand Cru, Alsace 1995 $23.   **91**

Deep gold-straw cast. Full-bodied. Balanced acidity. Moderately extracted. Spice, orange peel, lychee. Richly aromatic with generous, spicy complexity. Round and full in the mouth, with an acidic backbone that keeps it in fine balance.

Gewürztraminer, Furstentum Grand Cru, Alsace 1995 $23.   **89**

Bright greenish gold. Full-bodied. High acidity. Highly extracted. Honey, spice, citrus. Opulent late-harvest aromas. Emphatically dry on the palate. Big, round, and ripe, with excellent balance. Should keep.

Gewürztraminer, Steingrubler Grand Cru, Alsace 1996 $22.   **86**

Bright greenish gold. Moderately full-bodied. High acidity. Highly extracted. Cream, sweet herbs, citrus. Very aromatic. Weighty and generous mouthfeel. Zesty acidity through the finish. Youthful.

Gewürztraminer, Furstentum Grand Cru, Alsace 1996 $22.   **84**

Pinot Auxerrois, Vieilles Vignes, Alsace 1995 $14.99.   **84**

Riesling, Schlossberg Grand Cru, Alsace 1995 $22.   **87**

Bright yellow-gold. Moderately full-bodied. High acidity. Highly extracted. Mineral, fusel, citrus. Developed, mildly honeyed aromas. Minerally, dry palate with an austere character. Persistent through the finish. Forceful and structured, this needs food.

Riesling, Schlossberg Grand Cru, Alsace 1996 $21.   **86**

Bright pale yellow. Medium-bodied. High acidity. Apples, minerals. Lean and tart, with a green character that will make this better suited to pairing with shellfish.

Riesling, Furstentum Grand Cru, Alsace 1995 $24.   **91**

Bright yellow-gold. Medium-bodied. Full acidity. Fusel, honey, apple. Petrol and honey aromas. Mouthfilling flavors with a fine acid cut through to the finish.

Riesling, Furstentum Grand Cru, Alsace 1996 $23.   **93**

Bright yellow-gold. Medium-bodied. Full acidity. Minerals, citrus. Fresh aromas. Vibrant acids balance the palate. High-toned and youthful. Viscous texture and rich fruit on the palate and finish.

Riesling, "Rosenberg (Pleck)," Vendanges Tardives, Alsace 1995 $45.   **93**

Bright golden yellow. Moderately full-bodied. Balanced acidity. Petrol, fusel, peach. Complex, developed aromas. Very aromatic. Juicy and full flavored, with great persistence. Very enjoyable now, but further cellaring is warranted.

Riesling, "Cuvée Antoine," Alsace 1995 $75/500 ml.   **99**

Deep yellow-gold. Moderately full-bodied. High acidity. Honey, peach, lemon. Spicy, honeyed aromas. Full-throttled palate. Residual sweetness, but underlying acidity gives a drier sensation. Long, spiced finish. Rich, extravagantly textured mouthfeel. Although delicious now, this should be cellared to reveal its full potential.

Tokay Pinot Gris, Furstentum Grand Cru, Alsace 1995 $20.   **87**

Rich straw-yellow. Moderately full-bodied. Balanced acidity. Moderately extracted. Smoke, honeysuckle, yeast. Extremely aromatic. Full and rounded mouthfeel. Ripe and smoky, with flavorful tropical notes through the finish.

Tokay Pinot Gris, Furstentum Grand Cru, Alsace 1996 $21.   **88**

Bright straw-yellow. Full-bodied. Balanced acidity. Highly extracted. Dried herbs, minerals. Ripe and complex in the mouth, with a thick palate feel and extravagant flavors that are very individual. Herbal note through to finish.

Tokay Pinot Gris, Hengst Grand Cru, Alsace 1995 $25.   **94**

Deep yellow-gold. Full-bodied. Balanced acidity. Highly extracted. Smoke, citrus zest, orange blossom. Complex, vibrant aromatics. Ripe, rounded mouthfeel. Intense. Long finish.

Tokay Pinot Gris, Hengst Grand Cru, Alsace 1996 $22.   **92**

Deep yellow-gold. Moderately full-bodied. Balanced acidity. Highly extracted. Smoke, orange blossom, citrus. Exotically aromatic. Luscious, rounded mouthfeel. Rich and ripe through to the finish.

Tokay Pinot Gris, Vendanges Tardives, Alsace 1996 $45.   **94**

Deep yellow-straw hue. Full-bodied. Balanced acidity. Highly extracted. Earth, spice, citrus. Ripe, full, and rounded, with a big, generous palate feel. Shows great depth and intensity through to the finish.

Tokay Pinot Gris, Altenbourg, Sélection de Grains Nobles, Alsace 1996 $75.   **94**

Deep gold. Moderately full-bodied. High acidity. Honey, peach. Juicy, honeyed aromas. Intensely flavorful palate, with pure, primary fruit expression kept very lively by juicy acids. Very hedonistic. Drinking well now.

Julien Meyer

Klevner Pinot Blanc, Les Pierres Chaudes, Alsace 1995 $9.59.   **83**

Riesling, "Grittermatte," Alsace 1995 $28.   **84**

Scale: Superlative (96-100), Exceptional (90-95), Highly Recommended (85-89), Recommended (80-84), Not Recommended (Under 80)

Riesling, Muenchberg Grand Cru, Alsace 1995 $28.   90

Deep yellow-gold. Moderately full-bodied. Balanced acidity. Highly extracted. Lanolin, spice, citrus. Pleasantly aromatic. Warm, exotic spice on the palate. Full, rounded, and luscious. Dry finish.

Tokay Pinot Gris, Cuvée Fanny Elisabeth, Alsace 1995 $21.   88

Deep straw-yellow. Full-bodied. Balanced acidity. Highly extracted. Honey, butter, smoke. Opulent, forward aromatics. Full and lush in the mouth. Velvety richness through the finish.

Rene Muré

Gewürztraminer, Vorbourg Grand Cru, "Clos St. Landelin," Alsace 1996 $23.   91

Bright yellow-gold. Full-bodied. Balanced acidity. Highly extracted. Spice, butter, bananas. Very aromatic. Ripe and weighty on the palate. Complex finish. Seamless and elegant, with extraordinary texture.

Riesling, Vorbourg Grand Cru, "Clos St. Landelin," Alsace 1996 $20.   89

Bright straw-yellow. Medium-bodied. High acidity. Lemons, minerals. Tightly wound, tart flavors with assertive acids. Dry finish. Youthful. Serious weight and structure. Needs time.

Tokay Pinot Gris, Vorbourg Grand Cru, "Clos St. Landelin,"
Sélection de Grains Nobles, Alsace 1996 $105.   92

Bright golden yellow. Moderately full-bodied. Full acidity. Honey, peach. Rich peach and tropical fruit flavors fill the mouth. Delicious youthful fruit flavors linger on the finish. Hedonistic.

Ostertag

Gewürztraminer, Fronholz, Alsace 1995 $27.   91

Luminous golden yellow. Full-bodied. High acidity. Highly extracted. Spice, citrus peel, cream. Generous smoky aromas. Yeasty character on the palate. Structured, tightly wound palate feel. Opens toward the finish, with richness and spicy intensity. Exotic and complex.

Gewürztraminer, Vignoble D'Epfig, Alsace 1997 $23.   82

Pinot Blanc, Barriques, Alsace 1997 $14.   89

Medium straw. Moderately full-bodied. Balanced acidity. Highly extracted. Butter, flint, green herbs. Pleasantly aromatic. Complex array of flavors. Full and firm in the mouth. Lean, long finish.

Pinot Gris, Fronholz, Alsace 1996 $29.   92

Deep yellow-gold. Full-bodied. High acidity. Highly extracted. Yeast, citrus peel, minerals. Exotically aromatic, with a distinctive yeasty note. Firm, intense, and minerally on the palate. Great concentration. Further bottle age is recommended.

Pinot Gris, Muenchberg Grand Cru, Alsace 1996 $43.   95

Vibrant yellow-gold. Full-bodied. High acidity. Highly extracted. Flowers, yeast, citrus peel. Ripe and extremely exotic aromas that could be mistaken for barrel aging. Intense and deep on the palate, with very firm acids. Complex and persistent. Built for long-term aging.

Riesling, "Heissenberg," Alsace 1995 $26.   86

Pale gold. Medium-bodied. Balanced acidity. Apples, mineral, yeast. Rich, buttery, yeasty aromas. Straightforward flavors. Generous mouthfeel. Long finish.

Riesling, Muenchberg Grand Cru, Alsace 1995 $30.   93

Bright golden straw hue. Moderately full-bodied. Balanced acidity. Spice, tropical fruit, mineral. Intense ripe fruit and spice aromas. Luscious, juicy mouthfeel with an oily character. Very classy and attractive now, though this is in no danger of fading.

Riesling, Muenchberg Grand Cru, Vendanges Tardives, Alsace 1995 $54.   **94**

Brilliant golden straw hue. Moderately full-bodied. High acidity. Tropical fruit, peach. Tropical hints on the nose. Weighty and sweet, with corresponding bright acids. Not showing its best paces now. Though attractive, this will need more time.

Riesling, "Vignoble D'Epfig," Alsace 1997 $24.   **84**

Pfaffenheim

Pinot Noir, Alsace 1997 $10.   **86**

Light ruby with a slight fade. Moderately full-bodied. Balanced acidity. Moderately extracted. Mildly oaked. Mildly tannic. Plums, spice, dried herbs. Pleasantly aromatic. Surprisingly full and structured mouthfeel. Rich and zesty finish.

Pinot Noir, Grande Réserve, Cuvée des Dominicains, Alsace 1996 $19.   **84**

Gewürztraminer, Alsace 1997 $10.   **92**

Brilliant gold color. Moderately full-bodied. Balanced acidity. Lychee, tropical fruits. Rich, glycerous spice aromas. Thick, rounded palate with a streak of acid on the finish. Weighty, powerful style. Impressively long finish.

Gewürztraminer, Cuvée Bacchus, Grande Réserve, Alsace 1994 $19.   **91**

Brilliant yellow-gold. Moderately full-bodied. Balanced acidity. Lychee nuts, spice. Abundant, pure varietal aromas. Surprisingly dry palate. Concentrated and nectarlike. Drinking very well now.

Gewürztraminer, Goldert Grand Cru, Gueberschwihr, Alsace 1994 $20.   **89**

Bright yellow-gold. Moderately full-bodied. Balanced acidity. Lychee nuts, lanolin. Spicy aromas and flavors. Appealing fat, glycerous texture. Very drinkable now.

Gewürztraminer, Zinnkoepfle Grand Cru, Westhalten, Alsace 1996 $20.   **86**

Bright yellow-gold. Moderately full-bodied. High acidity. Lychee, minerals. Varietally expressive aromas. Rounded mouthfeel. Oily character enlivened with fine acids. Will improve with more bottle age.

Muscat, Alsace 1997 $10.   **84**

Pinot Blanc, Schneckenberg, Alsace 1995 $11.   **91**

Highly saturated yellow-gold. Moderately full-bodied. High acidity. Highly extracted. Honey, vanilla bean, lime. Pleasantly aromatic. Complex array of flavors. Full and well structured in the mouth. Firm finish. Drink with rich foods.

Pinot Blanc, Cuvée Chevalier, Alsace 1997 $10.   **84**

Riesling, Alsace 1997 $9.   **86**

Brilliant yellow-gold. Medium-bodied. High acidity. Moderately extracted. Peach, apples. Waxy tropical aromas are fully expressed on the palate. Concentration and purity bodes well for the next few years.

Riesling, Rebgarten Grand Cru, Gueberschwihr, Alsace 1995 $13.   **93**

Vibrant yellow-gold. Medium-bodied. Balanced acidity. Fusel, minerals, apples. Complex aromas. Oily but dry palate with fine texture and concentration. Powerful now. Lively acidity. Time will enhance the desirable petrol-like qualities.

Riesling, Steinert Grand Cru, Alsace 1993 $22.   **89**

Brilliant yellow-gold. Moderately full-bodied. Balanced acidity. Yellow apples, fusel, petrol. Ripe and intense aromas and flavors. Oily, rich mouthfeel. This is showing some development. Drink now.

Riesling, Grande Réserve, Cuvée Jupiter, Alsace 1994 $19.   **93**

Bright yellow-gold. Medium-bodied. Full acidity. Moderately extracted. Mineral, fusel, citrus. Petrol aromas are developing. Pure varietal flavors. Mineral backbone. Already nice, this can only improve with further maturity.

Riesling, Goldert Grand Cru, Gueberschwihr, Alsace 1995 $22.   **88**

Bright yellow-gold. Medium-bodied. Balanced acidity. Minerals, ripe citrus. Lean, yet well concentrated, with minerally presence through the finish. Assertive and flavorsome now. This should continue to develop well.

Scale: Superlative (96-100), Exceptional (90-95), Highly Recommended (85-89), Recommended (80-84), Not Recommended (Under 80)

Riesling, Zinnkoepfle Grand Cru, Westhalten, Alsace 1996 $22.   88

Brilliant green yellow. Medium-bodied. Balanced acidity. Moderately extracted. Green apples, fusel. Fresh, lively aromas have a waxy note. Crisp, cutting acids give this presence and structure. Approachable now, but will improve with a few more years in bottle.

Tokay Pinot Gris, Cuvée Rabelais, Alsace 1997 $14.50.   86

Deep straw. Medium-bodied. High acidity. Talc, smoke, orange blossom. Full, forceful, high-toned aromatics. Ripe and full in the mouth. Underlying crisp, lean edge. Long finish.

Tokay Pinot Gris, "Cuvée Rabelais" Grande Réserve, Alsace 1995 $19.   93

Deep golden straw. Moderately full-bodied. Balanced acidity. Highly extracted. Minerals, spice, citrus. Pleasantly aromatic. Full and rounded mouthfeel. Crisp, well-balanced acidity. Long finish.

Tokay Pinot Gris, Steinert Grand Cru, Alsace 1994 $22.50.   91

Deep yellow-gold. Full-bodied. Balanced acidity. Highly extracted. Petrol, spice, smoke, oranges. Pungent and complex. Concentrated, powerful palate feel. Intense finish.

Tokay Pinot Gris, Cuvée Ste Catherine, Vendanges Tardives, Alsace 1992 $46.   89

Deep yellow-gold. Full-bodied. Low acidity. Moderately extracted. Butter, smoke, orange blossom. Opulent and showy, with a range of complex flavors. Full and rounded in the mouth. Low acidity levels leaving a distinctly fat impression. Long, full finish. Delicious, but not for the long haul.

Gewürztraminer, Sélection de Grains Nobles, Alsace 1994 $65/500 ml.   94

Luminescent yellow-gold. Full-bodied. Balanced acidity. Lychee, spice. Pure, intense, spicy varietal aromas. Remarkable concentration. Acids are restrained, with a bit of alcohol showing on the finish. Delicious now.

Riefle

Pinot Noir, Côte de Rouffach, Alsace 1996 $16.99.   85

Gewürztraminer, Steinert Grand Cru, Alsace 1995 $19.99.   86

Brilliant gold. Moderately full-bodied. Balanced acidity. Lychee, spice, oil. Intense, varietally expressive aromas. Oily character on the palate. Bold and dry through the finish.

Gewürztraminer, "Côte de Rouffach," Bergweingarten de Pfaffenheim, Alsace 1997 $22.99.   88

yellow-gold. Moderately full-bodied. Balanced acidity. Tropical fruits, lychee nuts. Honeyed, spicy aromas. Sweet, fat, generous palate. Warming alcohol and lingering spice on the finish.

Riesling, Côte de Rouffach, "Gaentzbrunnen de Pfaffenheim," Alsace 1995 $14.99.   87

Deep yellow-gold. Moderately full-bodied. Balanced acidity. Moderately extracted. Flowers, grappa, dried herbs. Extremely aromatic. Complex array of flavors. Full and firm on the palate. Angular finish. Intense.

Riesling, Steinert Grand Cru, Alsace 1996 $23.99.   89

Rich yellow-gold. Moderately full-bodied. High acidity. Moderately extracted. Honey, lime zest, minerals. Jubilant aromatics. Firm and flavorful on the palate. Rounded, ripe, and exotic through the finish. Intense and concentrated. Will benefit from bottle age.

Tokay Pinot Gris, Steinert Grand Cru, Alsace 1996 $23.99.   89

Bright yellow-gold. Medium-bodied. Balanced acidity. Apples, sweet lemon. Zesty, rich aromas. Sweet, ripe fruit flavors balanced with gripping acids. Long, intense finish.

Scherer

Tokay Pinot Gris, Vieilles Vignes, Alsace 1996 $16.99.   85

Schlegel Boeglin

Gewürztraminer, Zinnkoepfle Grand Cru, Alsace 1996 $13. 88

Bright greenish yellow. Moderately full-bodied. Balanced acidity. Highly extracted. Spice, citrus peel, minerals. Very aromatic. Lean palate. Firm and flavorful through the spicy, dry finish.

Riesling, Zinnkoepfle Grand Cru, Alsace 1996 $12.50. 89

Deep yellow-gold. Moderately full-bodied. High acidity. Highly extracted. Honey, pear skin, yeast, spice. Extremely aromatic. Lush and exotic mouthfeel. Rich and ripe on the palate. Full, long finish.

Tokay Pinot Gris, Vendanges Tardives, Alsace 1996 $26/500 ml. 88

Dark yellow-gold. Moderately full-bodied. Balanced acidity. Plastic, tropical fruits. Rich, fat, spicy aromas. Thick and glycerous on the palate, with low acids accentuating generosity. Some sweetness evident. Drinking very well now.

Charles Schleret

Gewürztraminer, Herrenweg, Alsace 1996 $15.99. 82

Schlumberger

Gewürztraminer, Kessler Grand Cru, Alsace 1994 $32. 93

Bright yellow-gold. Full-bodied. Low acidity. Moderately extracted. Honey, spice, minerals. Classic varietal aromas with a late-harvest accent. Opulent and complex palate. Fat and weighty in the mouth, with a dry finish.

Pinot Gris, Alsace 1995 $19.50. 87

Deep yellow-gold. Moderately full-bodied. High acidity. Highly extracted. Apple, coconut, minerals. Bright and slightly bracing. Richly flavored. Intense finish. Needs time to allow acids to settle.

Pinot Gris, "Les Princes Abbes," Alsace 1996 $19.50. 86

Rich straw-yellow. Moderately full-bodied. Balanced acidity. Moderately extracted. Minerals, citrus, smoke. Crisp aromatics. Full and rounded mouthfeel. Oily and rich through the long finish.

Pinot Gris, Kitterle Grand Cru, Alsace 1996 $32. 89

Rich straw-yellow. Moderately full-bodied. Balanced acidity. Highly extracted. Spice, smoke, oranges. Pleasantly aromatic. Ripe and rounded mouthfeel. Rich and flavorful, with a touch of sweetness buttressed by vibrant acidity.

Sylvaner, Alsace 1995 $12. 87

Pale yellow-gold. Moderately full-bodied. High acidity. Highly extracted. Honey, fig, slate. Aromatic, botrytis-influenced nose. Lightly flavored. Lean and angular on the palate. Tightly wound. Needs time.

Schoffit

Chasselas, Cuvée Caroline, Vieilles Vignes, Alsace 1997 $16.99. 86

yellow-gold. Moderately full-bodied. Balanced acidity. Peach, talc, spice. Generous spicy, floral nose follows through on a rich palate. Gingery spice notes linger on the finish. Exotic.

Gewürztraminer, Harth, Cuvée Alexandre, Alsace 1997 $25/500 ml. 94

Deep yellow-gold. Full-bodied. Balanced acidity. Highly extracted. Spice, cream, tropical fruits. Pleasantly aromatic. Rich, unctuous mouthfeel. Gripping acidity on the finish. Needs time to mellow.

Gewürztraminer, Rangen de Thann Grand Cru, "Clos Saint-Theobald," Alsace 1996 $45. 86

Bright yellow-gold. Full-bodied. Balanced acidity. Highly extracted. Spice, minerals. Exotic, spicy aromas and flavors. Ripe and lush in the mouth, with solid weight and intensity. Well balanced.

Scale: Superlative (96-100), Exceptional (90-95), Highly Recommended (85-89), Recommended (80-84), Not Recommended (Under 80)

514

Gewürztraminer, Rangen de Thann Grand Cru, "Clos Saint-Theobald," Alsace 1997 $45. 89
Deep yellow-gold. Full-bodied. Low acidity. Moderately extracted. Bananas, tropical fruits, spice. Pleasantly aromatic. Lush and generous mouthfeel. Oily and exotic. Intense finish.

Gewürztraminer, Rangen de Thann Grand Cru, "Clos Saint-Theobald" Vendanges Tardives, Alsace 1995 $60/500 ml. 98
Brilliant yellow-gold. Full-bodied. Balanced acidity. Highly extracted. Petrol, honey, apricots. Outrageously aromatic, with a distinctive late-harvest accent. Oily, rich, and seamless in the mouth, with a hint of sweetness offset by zesty acidity. Perfectly and harmoniously balanced. This is drinking wonderfully now and has a long future.

Muscat, Cuvée Alexandre, Alsace 1997 $25. 88
Brilliant greenish straw. Moderately full-bodied. Balanced acidity. Moderately extracted. Spice, lychee, orange blossom. Intense aromas. Weighty palate with a hint of sweetness. Rich and persistent finish.

Pinot Blanc, Cuvée Caroline, Alsace 1997 $16.99. 86
Rich yellow. Moderately full-bodied. Balanced acidity. Moderately extracted. Honey, cream, spice. Very aromatic, with a late-harvest accent. Full and rounded in the mouth. Hint of sweetness balanced by crisp acidity.

Riesling, Cuvée Alexandre, "Harth," Alsace 1997 $25. 88
Bright straw. Moderately full-bodied. Balanced acidity. Moderately extracted. Cream, zest, talc. Pleasantly aromatic. Glycerous, rounded mouthfeel. Crisp and vibrant through the finish.

Riesling, Rangen de Thann Grand Cru, "Clos Saint-Theobald," Alsace 1995 $40. 94
Brilliant yellow-gold. Moderately full-bodied. High acidity. Stones, minerals, lemons, fusel. Honeyed, vibrant nose. Racy, tart palate. Acidic and awkward now. Richness lurks behind the structure. This needs time to soften the very impressive frame.

Riesling, Rangen de Thann Grand Cru, "Clos Saint-Theobald," Alsace 1996 $40/500 ml. 89
Brilliant yellow-gold. Medium-bodied. High acidity. Honey, apples, minerals. Ripe, late-harvest aromas. Vibrant, spicy palate with a minerally backbone. Drinking well now. Will improve with cellar age.

Riesling, Rangen de Thann Grand Cru, "Clos Saint-Theobald," Alsace 1997 $40. 91
Bright yellow-gold. Moderately full-bodied. High acidity. Mineral, apples. Intense minerally nose. Strong mineral streak through the palate. Weighty and concentrated. A generous wine that will improve over the near to middle term.

Riesling, Rangen de Thann Grand Cru, "Clos Saint-Theobald," Vendanges Tardives, Alsace 1997 $55. 87
Brilliant yellow-gold. Medium-bodied. Balanced acidity. Apple, herbs, minerals. Lean, herbal nose is at odds with the color. Softly flavored. Open-knit character invites earlier drinking.

Tokay Pinot Gris, Cuvée Alexandre, Vieilles Vignes, Alsace 1995 $25/500 ml. 93
Rich yellow-gold. Moderately full-bodied. Balanced acidity. Honey, tropical fruits, smoke. Hedonistic aromas. Broad palate with sweet, tropical flavors. Finishes with a dry, minerally note. Concentrated and serious.

Tokay Pinot Gris, Cuvée Alexandre, Vieilles Vignes, Alsace 1996 $25. 86
Bright yellow-gold. Moderately full-bodied. High acidity. Moderately extracted. Smoke, mineral oil. Ripe fruit aromas. Sweet, zesty mouthful of flavors. Lively finish. Very drinkable.

Tokay Pinot Gris, Rangen de Thann Grand Cru,
"Clos Saint-Theobald," Alsace 1995 $45.   **95**

Brilliant yellow-gold. Moderately full-bodied. High acidity. Honey, smoke, tropical fruits. Abundant, honeyed aromas with a citric backnote. Opulent flavors lifted with bright acidity. One to keep, though exceptional now.

Tokay Pinot Gris, Rangen de Thann Grand Cru,
"Clos Saint-Theobald," Alsace 1996 $45.   **95**

Bright yellow-gold. Moderately full-bodied. Full acidity. Honey, peach, smoke. Pungent, high-toned aromas. Bright acids and concentrated flavors on the palate. Impressive and youthful at present, this is one for the cellar.

Tokay Pinot Gris, Rangen de Thann Grand Cru, "Clos Saint-Theobald,"
Sélection de Grains Nobles, Alsace 1995 $95/500 ml.   **94**

Rich yellow-gold. Full-bodied. High acidity. Tropical fruits, apple pie spice, lemon. Forceful, spicy nose has a botrytis character. Extremely thick and unctuous mouthfeel, with vibrant acids and heavy tropical fruit flavors vying for attention. Structured for cellaring.

Tokay Pinot Gris, Rangen de Thann Grand Cru, "Clos Saint-Theobald,"
Sélection de Grains Nobles, Alsace 1996 $90/500 ml.   **87**

Brilliant yellow-gold. Moderately full-bodied. High acidity. Honey, peach. Rich, honeyed aromas are very impressive. Sensational flavors burst on the palate. Tropical flavors elevated by juicy acids. Delightful now.

Francois Schwach & Fils

Gewürztraminer, Vendanges Tardives, Alsace 1997 $18/500 ml.   **89**

Bright gold. Moderately full-bodied. Balanced acidity. Tropical fruits, spice. Soft and oily mouthfeel, with copious amounts of spice and sugar. Very smooth and drinkable. A dessert style for near-term drinking.

Riesling, "Muehlforst," Alsace 1997 $11.50.   **83**
Riesling, Cuvée Clement, Alsace 1997 $12.50.   **84**
Riesling, Rosacker Grand Cru, Alsace 1997 $15.   **90**

Pale emerald-yellow. Medium-bodied. Balanced acidity. Flowers, sweet citrus. Attractive, ripe aromas. Juicy mouthful of fruit flavors. User-friendly, easy-drinking style with a faint hint of sweetness. Clean finish. Has the structure to age further.

Pierre Sparr

Pinot Noir, Sparr Prestige, Alsace 1996 $19.90.   **84**
Cuvée d'Alsace, Alsace 1997 $8.99.   **83**
Gewürztraminer, Réserve, Alsace 1996 $11.99.   **87**

Bright yellow-gold. Moderately full-bodied. Balanced acidity. Butter, minerals, spice. Buttery, fat aromas follow through on the palate. Rich, round, and generous, with grip and structure.

Gewürztraminer, Réserve, Alsace 1997 $13.99.   **86**

Brilliant yellow-gold. Moderately full-bodied. Balanced acidity. Nuts, mineral, spice. Sweet, juicy aromas have a fine varietal expression. Lush, textured mouthfeel with well-balanced acids.

Gewürztraminer, Brand Grand Cru, Alsace 1996 $24.   **88**

Bright yellow-gold. Medium-bodied. Balanced acidity. Lychee, minerals. Crisp, dry style, with an oily texture moderated by lively acids. Drinking well now. Serve with food.

Gewürztraminer, Sporen Grand Cru, Alsace 1996 $25.   **88**

Bright yellow-gold. Moderately full-bodied. Balanced acidity. Lychee, butter. Rich, spicy aromas. Weighty palate, with broad flavors and a warm finish. Classic oily, spiced character.

Scale: Superlative (96-100), Exceptional (90-95), Highly Recommended (85-89), Recommended (80-84), Not Recommended (Under 80)

Pinot Blanc, Réserve, Alsace 1996 $8.99. 83

Pinot Blanc, Réserve, Alsace 1997 $9.90. 88

Brilliant greenish straw. Medium-bodied. High acidity. Moderately extracted. Minerals, citrus. Pleasantly aromatic. Crisp and zesty mouthfeel. Lean and clean through the finish. An excellent shellfish wine.

Pinot Gris, Réserve, Alsace 1996 $11.99. 86

Deep straw-yellow. Moderately full-bodied. High acidity. Moderately extracted. Minerals, citrus. Aromatically reserved. Ripe and full mouthfeel buttressed by racy acidity. Taut, firm, tightly wound finish.

Pinot Gris, Prestige, Alsace 1996 $19.90. 88

Deep straw-yellow. Moderately full-bodied. Balanced acidity. Moderately extracted. Minerals, flowers, spice. Pleasantly aromatic. Rounded but firm mouthfeel. Finishes with a slight hint of sweetness.

Pinot Gris, Brand Grand Cru, Alsace 1996 $27. 89

Deep straw-yellow. Full-bodied. Balanced acidity. Moderately extracted. Smoke, orange blossom, spice. Pleasantly aromatic. Ripe and rounded mouthfeel. Very concentrated. Lush and seamless through the weighty, flavorful finish.

Riesling, Réserve, Alsace 1996 $12.99. 83

Riesling, Réserve, Alsace 1997 $12.99. 88

Pale straw. Medium-bodied. High acidity. Lemon, minerals. Intense, citrus-dominated aromas. Generous on the mid-palate. Finishes with a persistent bitter-lemon note. Further age may soften the acids.

Riesling, Brand Grand Cru, Alsace 1996 $23. 94

Bright yellow-gold. Moderately full-bodied. High acidity. Citrus, minerals, flint. Youthful, vibrant, mineral-edged aromas. Solid, structured palate. Tightly wound flavors bolstered by vibrant acids. Impressive, but not user-friendly now; cellaring recommended.

Riesling, Mambourg Grand Cru, Alsace 1996 $24. 91

Brilliant golden yellow. Medium-bodied. Full acidity. Fusel, petrol, tart peach. Ripe fruit and stony aromas. Piercing, rich flavors. Very concentrated and intense palate and finish. Already nice, this will get better.

Riesling, Schoenenbourg Grand Cru, Alsace 1996 $24. 92

Bright golden yellow. Medium-bodied. Full acidity. Tart peach, fusel. Oily, rich aromas. Youthful, angular acids complement rich flavors, with mineral grip throughout. This needs time for the angular, intense structure to soften.

Trimbach

Pinot Blanc, Alsace 1995 $9. 83

Pinot Gris, Réserve, Alsace 1995 $15. 86

Deep straw. Moderately full-bodied. Balanced acidity. Moderately extracted. Minerals, apples. Aromatically reserved. Full but angular mouthfeel. Lean and minerally through the finish.

Weinbach

Gewürztraminer, "Clos des Capucins," Cuvée Laurence, Alsace 1996 $35.99. 89

Deep straw-yellow. Full-bodied. Balanced acidity. Highly extracted. Minerals, citrus peel, spice. Pleasantly aromatic. Full and rounded palate feel. Lush and generous through the finish. Well balanced.

Muscat, "Clos des Capucins" Réserve, Alsace 1996 $26.99. 84

Pinot Blanc, "Clos des Capucins" Réserve, Alsace 1996 $16.99. 86

Rich straw-yellow. Moderately full-bodied. Balanced acidity. Moderately extracted. Butter, citrus. Aromatically reserved. Full palate, cut by zesty acidity. Lingering, crisp finish.

Riesling, "Clos des Capucins," Réserve Personnelle, Alsace 1996 $16.99. 84

Riesling, "Clos des Capucins," Cuvée Theo, Alsace 1996 $23.99. **86**
Bright straw-yellow. Medium-bodied. Balanced acidity. Apple, minerals. Brash, fruity flavors drop off quickly on a slightly bitter finish. Not a long-term keeper.

Riesling, Schlossberg Grand Cru, "Clos des Capucins," Alsace 1996 $29.99. **89**
Bright yellow-gold. Medium-bodied. High acidity. Green apples, tart peach. Linear, pure, and focused, with lemony intensity that persists through a long finish. Concentrated, intense and acidic. Needs time to soften.

Riesling, "Clos des Capucins," Cuvée Ste Catherine, Alsace 1996 $35.99. **91**
Bright yellow-gold. Moderately full-bodied. High acidity. Tart peach, apple, mineral. Classic varietal aromatics. Opulent flavors balanced with zesty youthful acidity. Intense finish. Built to last.

Riesling, Schlossber Grand Cru, "Clos des Capucins," Cuvée Ste Catherine, Alsace 1996 $39.99. **93**
Brilliant yellow-gold. Moderately full-bodied. High acidity. Spice, lemon, green apple. Aromatically reserved. Weighty and forceful on the palate. Long, mineral finish. Austere and intense now. Long-term cellar prospect.

Tokay Pinot Gris, Cuvée Laurence, "Clos des Capucins," Alsace 1996 $39.99. **91**
Brilliant yellow-gold. Full-bodied. High acidity. Highly extracted. Smoke, oranges, yeast. Powerful and exotic aromas. Full, ripe palate. Rich and rounded. Concentration balanced by racy acidity. Drinking well now, but should continue to improve.

Zind Humbrecht

Gewürztraminer, Hengst Grand Cru, Alsace 1996 $52. **92**
Bright yellow-gold. Full-bodied. High acidity. Highly extracted. Minerals, spice, citrus peel. Intense aromas. Richly flavored. Generous mouthfeel. Hefty and full-throttled. Further cellaring is recommended.

Gewürztraminer, Goldert Grand Cru, Alsace 1996 $52. **94**
Brilliant yellow-gold. Full-bodied. High acidity. Highly extracted. Honey, smoke, citrus. Very aromatic. Richly flavored with balancing zesty acidity. Intense finish. This has all the prerequisites for mid-term cellaring.

Pinot Gris, "Heimbourg," Turckheim, Alsace 1996 $42. **92**
Bright yellow-gold. Full-bodied. High acidity. Highly extracted. Minerals, smoke, spice. Subtle aromas. Complex and flavorful on the palate. Tightly wound, with very firm acidity and a dry finish. Built to last.

Pinot Gris, "Clos Windsbuhl," Hunawihr, Alsace 1996 $47. **93**
Bright yellow-gold. Full-bodied. High acidity. Highly extracted. Honey, baked apples, minerals. Intense aromas. Very flavorful palate. Distinct sweetness offset by piercing acidity. Long finish. Needs time to show its true colors.

Pinot Gris, Rangen de Thann Grand Cru, "Clos Saint Urbain," Alsace 1996 $56. **98**
Bright yellow-gold. Full-bodied. High acidity. Highly extracted. Tropical fruits, spice, minerals. Very aromatic. Flavorful and oily in texture. Marked sweetness and vibrant acidity. Rather sweet. Impressive by itself or with carefully chosen dishes. Should age well.

Riesling, "Clos Hauserer," Alsace 1996 $29. **95**
Brilliant yellow-gold. Moderately full-bodied. High acidity. Mineral, lemon. Beautiful varietal aromas and flavors beginning to show. Bright, angular, and concentrated. Impressive framework. Needs time to soften and develop.

Scale: Superlative (96-100), Exceptional (90-95), Highly Recommended (85-89), Recommended (80-84), Not Recommended (Under 80)

twenty-six

❦

France
Bordeaux

❦

Bordeaux Market Overview

Bordeaux is like no other wine region in the world. To be more precise, Cru Classé Bordeaux is sold like no other wine in the world. Americans do not actually drink all that much Bordeaux wine—about the same volume as many small European countries. In the U.S. wine trade Bordeaux is synonymous with Cru Classé wines, although they only represent the tip of the iceberg of the vast amount of wine produced in the Gironde Department of Southwestern France. The bulk of unclassified wine from humble producers is sold at modest prices for everyday consumption.

Opaque, impossibly tannic wines are a thing of the past in Bordeaux. Winemaking styles are far from homogenous, but Bordeaux wines are increasingly of the deeply colored, softer, riper mold—particularly at the top level. Even first growths are much more approachable on release than they were twenty years ago. Modern vineyard management and winery techniques are permitting the Bordelaises to produce ever more attractive young wines. There seems little doubt that the French have taken a look at the manner in which Australian, Chilean, and Californian wines have threatened their markets and acted accordingly to raise their technical game.

Distinctly non-traditional technology is allowing the well-funded chateaux to combat their occasionally unfriendly climate. Many of the top growths now have must concentrators, devices that allow the removal of excess water from the grape must. These devices were called into action in the Médoc during the 1998 harvest and could well be the reason that many top estates showed wines with little evidence of rain dilution.

Key Varietals

Red wines

Cabernet Sauvignon

Cabernet Sauvignon is the world's most popular premium red wine grape due to the quality of the red wines it produces in the Médoc, where it forms anywhere from 60–90% of the blend of a typical wine. It forms a lesser though still dominant proportion of Graves blends and a minority (with a few exceptions) of Saint-Emilion and Pomerol blends. Its late ripening accounts for the later harvest in the Médoc. It is strongly associated with the flavors of black currants when ripe and when unripe it can be herbaceous and display unpleasant tannins.

Cabernet Franc

Cabernet Franc is an earlier ripening relative of Cabernet Sauvignon. When ripe it has a spicy, olivey character, though it can be overtly herbaceous when unripe. It is generally used in small amounts to add complexity to Médoc and Graves blends. In Saint-Emilion and Pomerol it can form as much as 50% of a blend.

Merlot

Merlot is the perfect blending counterpart to Cabernet Sauvignon as it produces softer, fleshier wines with more supple tannins that can soften the sometimes tough, austere nature of Cabernet Sauvignon. It rarely dominates a Médoc or Graves blend; though frequently it does so in Saint-Emilion and is used almost exclusively in Pomerol. Significantly, Merlot ripens earlier than Cabernet Sauvignon.

Petit Verdot

Petit Verdot is a minor variety in Bordeaux whose principal contribution is color and backbone supplied from its thick, tannin-rich skin. However, it rarely ripens in Bordeaux. When unripe it produces harsh blending wine. If used it will be in the very small quantities of 1–5%.

White Wines

Sauvignon Blanc and Semillon

Sauvignon Blanc is the most widely planted white variety in Bordeaux, where, under the guise of Bordeaux Sec it typically produces cheap, pleasant white wines of no great distinction. Large appellations such as Entre-deux-mers are synonymous with value priced, clean Sauvignon Blanc. Nowhere in Bordeaux does Sauvignon Blanc reach the varietal intensity of examples from the Loire. However, in the Graves, Sauvignon Blanc is rendered in its finest form, often with some oak influence and a small proportion of Semillon, the other white grape of Bordeaux. Indeed, this is the basis of Pessac-Léognan, a sub-appellation of the Graves. Here, new oak and low yields produce rich, succulent white wines that have the capacity to age.

Semillon's ability to rot in a noble fashion, concentrating sugars within the grape, in the communes of Sauternes and Barsac is, of course, the basis for the great sweet wines of Bordeaux. Sauvignon Blanc plays a minor, supporting role in Bordeaux's sweet wines.

Bordeaux at a Glance

Wines Reviewed:

432

Producers/Brands Represented:

264

Value Rating:

Poor

Key Appellations

The Left Bank: The Médoc

The Médoc, on the left bank of the Gironde estuary, is a long narrow strip of flat monoculture devoted to the production of red wine. The gravelly well-drained areas of the Médoc are well suited to the ripening of Cabernet Sauvignon, the dominant grape variety planted here.

The Médoc contains four great communes that host all of its great estates. These sub-appellations, extending from south to north, are: Margaux, Saint-Julien, Pauillac, and Saint-Estèphe. The wines from each of these communes has been assigned classic characteristics through centuries of intellectual deconstruction by connoisseurs, though it is not always possible to easily discern the difference between, for example, a Saint-Julien and a Margaux in a blind tasting. In a nutshell these characteristics are: Firm, austere wines with "pencil shaving" aromas in Pauillac; Softer, fruitier, and more supple wines from Margaux; Inky, solid, leaner wines from Saint Estèphe; Saint-Julien falls somewhere between the firmness of Pauillac and the suppleness of Margaux.

The Médoc has plenty of vineyards outside its four classic commune appellations. Cru Bourgeois, which can rival the quality of Cru Classé estates but rarely the price, present the consumer with the possibility of good Médoc wine at reasonable prices. Cru Bourgeois chateaux from the sub-appellations of Moulis and Listrac in the Médoc, as well as from the "big four" appellations, are more than ever a counterpoint to the high prices of the leading Châteaux wines.

The Graves

The Graves, on the outskirts of Bordeaux, is close enough to urban life to allow the incongruity of graffiti covered walls enclosing the finest vineyards in the region. Starting where the Médoc finishes, it skirts the western limits of the city of Bordeaux and continues parallel to the Gironde down to the southern extremity of the Bordeaux region. The Graves is the region that has seen the most dramatic improvements in quality in recent years despite the fact that it has been home to one of the region's most highly rated Château for 200 years. Frequently, the finest wines produced in the entire region hail from the unattractive, partly urbanized northern Graves appellation of Pessac-Léognan— home to Château Haut-Brion and La Mission Haut-Brion. The character of the Cabernet Sauvignon from the gravelly soils of the Graves is, to the student of Bordeaux wines, quite distinct when compared to the Cabernet of the Médoc: Deep, tannic, and frequently opaque in appearance with pure black fruits and a distinct nose of tobacco, cedar, and smoke. Haut-Brion and La Mission excepted, the red wines of Pessac-Léognan have never been as fashionable as those from the Médoc, yet they are now often every bit as good and can represent better value.

Pessac-Léognan also produces Bordeaux's finest dry white wine, from Sauvignon Blanc and Semillon. Pessac white wines are barrel fermented and oak aged and can often benefit from some years of cellaring. At their best these wines are concentrated, showing melon, citrus, and fig aromas and flavors which deepen with age.

Sauternes and Barsac

The southwest of France, as far as scenery goes, has a little bit of the U.S. Deep South in the communes of Sauternes and Barsac. The phenomenon of micro-climate that renders this part of Bordeaux largely unfit for conventional wine-making also encourages the growth of sub-tropical vegetation in addition to nobly rotting the grapes on the vines. With little more than a glass of sweet wine per vine produced at the highest level, the more justifiable record high prices for Sauternes and Barsac have encouraged great improvements in the region through infusion of money and expertise. Good Bordeaux sweet wine can now be made far more frequently than even ten years ago.

The Right Bank: Saint-Emilion, Pomerol, and Beyond

The Right Bank of Bordeaux, due east of the city, encompasses the ancient town of Saint-Emilion and the nearby commune of Pomerol. The vineyards of both communes are planted heavily to Merlot and Cabernet Franc, which favors the cooler, often richer soils found here as opposed to those in the Médoc. Saint-Emilion is a complex region with many soil variations within a small area. Nonetheless, with the Médoc as a frame of reference, the character of Right Bank wines can be said to be a degree richer in alcohol, and more fruit-centered, with supple, quicker maturing tannins: All traits which have endeared these wines to modern wine drinkers. Pomerol is a much smaller and more compact appellation, about the size of Margaux. Its wines are often more consistent in a given vintage and bargains are few among these sought-after wines.

Bargain seekers should pay particular attention to the outlying Saint-Emilion satellite appellations, recognizable by having their commune names hyphenated before Saint-Emilion on the label. The right bank proper also encompasses Fronsac, Côte de Bourg, and Côtes de Blaye, all of whose wines attract far less media interest and carry much lower price tags.

Merlot on the Right Bank is harvested, on average, two weeks earlier than the Cabernet Sauvignon of the Left Bank. This simple fact makes generalizations about the character of a vintage in Bordeaux difficult to encapsulate by assign-ing a number to a vintage in "Bordeaux." Vintages like 1992 and 1993 were poor in the Médoc and much more successful on the Right Bank. Early indications are that 1998 will be an outstanding Right Bank vintage and a merely fair to good Left Bank one. In both cases getting the grapes in before the rain was the dif-ference in quality between Left and Right Bank, and this is no small matter in a region that often gives estate managers anxiety attacks as rain clouds darken the sky when vines are heavy with almost ripe grapes.

The phenomenon of the Saint-Emilion *garagiste*, the small scale winemaker with little more than a garage and a plot of vines, has grabbed the attention of the fine wine world with deeply concentrated, tiny production wines that command hefty prices. Garagistes have been providing much of the buzz of excitement in the region in recent years and their wines continue to set new price records in the fine wine world.

In Focus: The Futures Market

Bordeaux Cru Classé wine is the closest thing that the wine world has to a tradable commodity and it has a highly developed futures market. The prices offered by the Bordeaux negociants every year are a factor of controlled supply, the world economy, and perceived quality. Occasionally, as with markets, pricing seems to defy common sense. Consequently, Bordeaux has seen cyclical crashes, or readjustments, in pricing throughout its history.

After the excellent 1990 vintage, a series of difficult vintages from 1991–1994 resulted in peak demand for wine from the good 1995 vintage. Futures prices were offered at record high levels. 1996, though not generally thought as strong across the board as 1995, brought yet new record prices for the first offerings of futures. 1997, a mediocre year, saw another price hike; though few buyers were convinced. This sequence of vintages had brought Bordeaux Cru Classé prices to an astronomical high point, aided by the increased interest in fine wine from Japan and Asia. The up to 20% decreases announced for the 1998 futures offerings still leave classed growth Bordeaux at glaringly high levels. It remains to be seen whether they are sustainable. The top echelons of Bordeaux are not currently rich pickings for bargain hunters and may not offer quick profits for speculators either.

Recent Vintages

1995

1995 broke the run of poor to disappointing vintages from 1991-1994. An excellent ripening season with a touch of rain in September resulted in great quality from the Cabernet Sauvignon in the Médoc and the Merlot on the Right Bank. The Cabernet and Merlot of the Graves were also impressive. A huge crop throughout the region produced ripe-styled wines with impressive tannins and structures. This is a vintage for red wines where uniformity of high quality applies. The dry whites of the Graves and the sweet whites of Sauternes and Barsac are of generally sound but unexciting quality. Those who purchased futures of 1995 have made some quick profits, given the escalating prices since this vintage.

1996

1996 witnessed a normal summer until heavy rain in August, though wind and dry conditions dried the vineyards out. It was a fine year for Cabernet Sauvignon in the Médoc, producing rich, concentrated wines with great cellaring potential and impressive flavor concentration. The Right Bank appellations of St Emilion and Pomerol were a great deal less consistent than in 1995, though top estates produced some good to great wines. The red Graves were of a very good quality while the white Graves were more rain affected and lacked a ripe Semillon component, showing a greener Sauvignon Blanc character—they may not be the best cellaring wines. Sauternes and Barsac produced their finest sweet wines since 1990. 1996 was a year of record price increases of 50-100% on the opening futures offerings of 1995.

Scale: Superlative (96-100), Exceptional (90-95), Highly Recommended (85-89), Recommended (80-84), Not Recommended (Under 80)

1997

1997 was an unusual vintage in Bordeaux. On paper it was one of the hottest, driest ripening seasons on record. However, the ripening was very uneven, with heat and humidity hampering the process. The Cabernet Sauvignon-based left bank wines were very uneven and a big step down from 1996 or 1995. Low acidity was a general theme and notes of over-ripeness were often seen, though wines were far from fruitless. The Right Bank Merlot-based wines of St Emilion and Pomerol were considerably better, with many potentially very good wines, though there was a measure of inconsistency. The red Graves farced better than the Médoc reds, while the dry whites from Graves and Pessac-Léognan had a few disappointments but equally some outstanding wines. The minuscule production of Sauternes and Barsac in 1997 was outstandingly rich and concentrated. Overall in the region, the biggest problem was the astronomical price being asked for wines of average quality.

1998

The 1998 vintage in Bordeaux will be more memorable for the right reasons on the Merlot-dominated Right Bank (St-Emilion, Pomerol) than the Cabernet-rich Left bank (Médoc). As has been the case with other recent vintages in Bordeaux, rain partly spoiled the party in the Médoc during the late September-early October harvest. The early indications are that many Médoc wines will have more tannic stuffing than they did in 1997, though some estates did struggle to get ripe Cabernet Sauvignon, hence quality is not uniform. The Right Bank largely harvested before the rains and managed to produce a potentially classic vintage of the highest quality with many outstanding wines sure to be seen when this vintage is released. The red Graves are of good potential, better and more uniform than the reds of the Médoc, while the dry whites from the Graves were ripe and softer and will offer good early-drinking pleasure. The first take on Sauternes and Barsac is that it will not be a classic year for sweet wines. Many of the young wines sampled lacked acidity and persistence for long-term cellaring, while others seemed rather heavy. Prices for the 1998's are still higher than 1995 or 1996. There will be few bargains among Cru Classé wines from this vintage.

Reviews

d'Agassac
1998 Cru Bourgeois, Haut-Médoc $NA.   **90-95**

Saturated bright purple hue. Perfumed, high-toned flower and red berry aromas jump from the glass. A lush entry leads to a medium-bodied palate with rounded tannins. Supple and fruit forward. Very tasty and pure with a silky finish. Drink now or later.

Aile d'Argents
1997 Bordeaux Blanc $NA.   **84**

l'Angelus
1998 St. Emilion $NA.   **90-95**

Deep saturated purple hue. Intensely fragrant earth, berry, and mineral aromas. A lush entry leads to a rounded, medium-bodied palate with velvety tannins. Soft and generous with lowish acidity. Drink now or later.

d'Angludet
1997 Margaux $NA.   NR
1998 Margaux $NA.   85-89
Very dark, opaque blackish purple hue. Brooding, subdued mineral and licorice aromas. A rich entry leads to a thick, full-bodied mouthfeel with big ripe tannins. A note of acidity maintains a sense of balance through the finish, but rather monolithic at present. Long-term cellar.

d'Arche
1998 Cru Bourgeois, Haut-Médoc $NA.   85-89
Deep, saturated ruby with slight purple overtones. Rich black fruit aromas show a slight funky edge. A supple entry leads to a firm, moderately full-bodied palate with robust grippy tannins. A bruiser. Deeply flavored, but needs time. Midterm cellar candidate.
1998 Sauternes $NA.   90-95
Bright yellow-straw hue. Attractive honeyed pear and brown spice aromas. A rich entry leads to a full-bodied palate with lots of sweetness and balanced acidity. Impressively botrytised with good intensity. Drink now or later.

d'Arcins
1998 Haut-Médoc $NA.   90-95
Dark, opaque ruby-purple hue. Pleasant cassis and mineral aromas have a cedary accent. A soft entry leads to a moderately full-bodied palate with ripe, velvety tannins. Lush, supple, and refined in a hedonistic style. Drink now.

d'Armilhac
1997 Pauillac $NA.   84
1998 Pauillac $NA.   85-89
Deep, saturated purple hue. Classic lead pencil and mineral aromas are already beginning to emerge. A firm entry leads to a full-bodied palate with a wave of chewy, drying tannins. Rather shy in acidity with a tough finish. Will need time. Midterm cellar candidate.

d'Arsac
1998 Cru Bourgeois, Margaux $NA.   8084
Deep ruby-garnet hue. Lean minerally aromas show an herbal overtone, but emerge as velvety red fruit flavors in the mouth. A firm entry leads to a lush, medium-bodied palate with grippy tannins. Nice length. Drink now or later.

d'Aurilhac
1998 Cru Bourgeois, Haut-Médoc $NA.   80-84

Andron Blanquet
1998 Cru Bourgeois, St. Estèphe $NA.   85-89
Brilliant, saturated purple hue. Bright candied red fruit aromas carry an unusual pickled aspect. A lush entry leads to a medium-bodied palate with rounded, silky tannins. Harmonious, lush mouthfeel. Perhaps the nose is just in an awkward stage. Stylish. Drink now or later.

Aney
1998 Cru Bourgeois, Haut-Médoc $NA.   NR

Arnauld
1998 Cru Bourgeois, Haut-Médoc $NA. **85-89**

Deep, saturated ruby-purple hue. Meaty, spicy aromas show a reductive edge which should blow off with aeration. A rich entry leads to a supple, moderately full-bodied palate with good flavor intensity. Rounded, generous finish.

Artigues
1998 Cru Bourgeois, Pauillac $NA. **80-84**

La Bahans du Château Haut-Brion
1997 Rouge, Pessac-Léognan $NA. **85-89**

Deep ruby-purple. Medium-bodied. Low acidity. Moderately extracted. Mildly tannic. Minerals, earth, black fruits. Pleasantly aromatic, with a lush and generous palate feel. Lacks a bit for intensity and grip, but should provide pleasant near-term drinking.

1998 Rouge, Pessac-Léognan $NA. **85-89**

Very deep blackish ruby hue with a purple edge. Brooding aromas show a deeply fruited core with a generous vanilla overlay. Ripe but lean, with very firm tannins through the finish. A tad austere, but intense. Midterm cellar candidate.

Balestard la Tonnelle
1997 St. Emilion $NA. **80-84**
1998 St. Emilion $NA. **85-89**

Deep, saturated purple hue. Aromatically subdued, but shows a firm core of chocolate and black fruit flavors in the mouth. A ripe entry leads to a moderately full-bodied palate with sturdy, grippy tannins. Well structured, if a bit four square. Drink now or later.

Barateau
1998 Cru Bourgeois, Haut-Médoc $NA. **80-84**

Barreyres
1998 Cru Bourgeois, Haut-Médoc $NA. **NR**

Bastor-Lamontagne
1997 Sauternes $NA. **85-89**

Bright yellow-gold. Medium-bodied. Full acidity. Moderately extracted. Honey, citrus. Rather reserved aromatically, with a racy, vibrant palate feel. Does not appear heavily botrytized. More closely resembles the vibrancy and high acidity typical of a Germanic style. Well structured, and should cellar quite well.

1998 Sauternes $NA. **85-89**

Deep yellow golden hue. Subdued pineapple and tropical fruit aromas. A rich entry leads to a fat, moderately full-bodied palate with shy acidity and lots of sweetness. Rich, rounded, flavorful finish. Drink now or later.

Beau-Sejour Becot
1997 St. Emilion $NA. **90-95**

Bright blackish ruby hue with a purple rim. Medium-bodied. Balanced acidity. Moderately extracted. Mildly tannic. Red fruits, spice, chocolate. Aromatic and extremely flavorful, with a lighter frame. Almost feminine, with silky, attractive flavors. Well-balanced, with fine grip and length.

1998 St. Emilion $NA. **90-95**

Very deep, saturated purple hue. Aromatically subdued but showing a rich core of black fruit and mineral flavors. A lush entry leads to a concentrated, full-bodied palate with good grip through the lengthy tobacco accented finish. Ripe but complex. Drink now or later.

Beau-Site
1998 Cru Bourgeois, St. Estèphe $NA.   85-89

Saturated, opaque blackish purple hue. Forward, jammy black fruit and spice aromas show slight overripe qualities. A rich entry leads to a lush and opulent, moderately full-bodied mouthfeel with robust silky tannins. A fat but hedonistic early drinker. Drink now.

Beaumont
1997 Haut-Médoc $NA.   85-89

Blackish ruby hue with a slight fade. Medium-bodied. Balanced acidity. Moderately extracted. Mildly tannic. Minerals, black fruits. High-toned aromas follow through nicely on the palate. Lighter in style, with mild tannins and a touch of greenness to the finish. Well-balanced.

1998 Haut Médoc $NA.   80-84

Beauregard
1997 Pomerol $NA.   80-84

1998 Pomerol $NA.   90-95

Brilliant, vibrant purple hue. Perfumed cedar, flower, and black fruit aromas. A rich entry leads to a moderately full-bodied palate with great depth of flavor and grippy tannins. Acidity helps to balance out the fatness through the very lengthy finish. Very stylish and seductive. Drink now or later.

Beausejour
1998 St. Emilion $NA.   80-84

Bel Air
1998 Cru Bourgeois, Haut-Médoc $NA.   80-84

Belair
1998 St. Emilion $NA.   85-89

Bright ruby with a slight purple edge. Vibrant, high-toned candied berry fruit and mineral aromas. A lean entry leads to a medium-bodied palate with grippy tannins and an attractive spice accent. Well-balanced in a lighter style, but quite tasty. Drink now or later.

Belgrave
1997 Haut-Médoc $NA.   85-89

Deep ruby-purple. Medium-bodied. Balanced acidity. Moderately extracted. Moderately tannic. Red berries, vanilla. Some ripeness evident in the nose, with a high-toned fruit accent. Firm in structure, with bright acids and solid, textured tannins. Firm but well-balanced.

1998 Haut-Médoc $NA.   85-89

Saturated, vibrant, opaque purple hue. Generous aromas show a core of red fruit and anise with a flashy oak vanillin overlay. A firm entry leads to a moderately full-bodied palate with gripy tannins and good acidity. Showy and youthful. Needs time. Midterm cellar candidate.

1998 Médoc $NA.   85-89

Dark, opaque saturated ruby-purple hue. Forward cassis and vanilla aromas. A smooth entry leads to a moderately full-bodied palate with rounded, velvety tannins. Big and chunky with a lingering finish. Round and soft with hedonistic appeal. Drink now.

Bernadotte
1998 Cru Bourgeois, Haut-Médoc $NA.   80-84

Scale: Superlative (96-100), Exceptional (90-95), Highly Recommended (85-89),
Recommended (80-84), Not Recommended (Under 80)

Beychevelle

1997 St. Julien $NA.   85-89

Bright ruby-purple. Medium-bodied. Low acidity. Moderately extracted. Mildly tannic.
Spice, red fruits. Rather full in the mouth, though it maintains a sense of lightness.
Lacks a bit for structure, but attractive.

1998 St. Julien $NA.   90-95

Very deep, saturated vibrant purple hue. Firm mineral, black fruit, and tobacco aromas.
A firm entry leads to a rich, full-bodied palate with lots of stuffing and grippy tannins.
Intense and concentrated. Needs time. Long-term cellar.

Blaignan

1998 Médoc $NA.   NR

Le Boscq

1998 Cru Bourgeois, St. Estèphe $NA.   90-95

Opaque ruby-purple hue. Fancy, exotic ginger, flower, red fruit, and vanilla aromas.
A lush entry leads to a moderately full-bodied palate with very supple, velvety tannins
and lots of flavor. Soft, but perfectly balanced and very stylish. Drink now.

Bouscaut

1997 Blanc, Pessac-Léognan $NA.   80-84

1998 Blanc, Pessac-Léognan $NA.   NR

1997 Rouge, Pessac-Léognan $NA.   NR

1998 Rouge, Pessac-Léognan $NA.   NR

Branaire-Ducru

1997 St. Julien $NA.   80-84

1998 St. Julien $NA.   85-89

Saturated, opaque ruby-purple hue. Restrained minerally aromas. A lean entry leads to a
medium-bodied palate with angular tannins. Taut and edgy through the finish. Compact.
Midterm cellar candidate.

Brane-Cantenac

1997 Margaux $NA.   NR

1998 Margaux $NA.   80-84

La Bridane

1998 Cru Bourgeois, St. Julien $NA.   90-95

Vibrant, saturated purple hue. Intense, exotic lead pencil, mineral, and vanilla aromas.
A lush entry leads to a rich, moderately full-bodied palate with big, supple tannins. Fleshy
and deeply flavored. Very stylish with complex flavors. Drink now or later.

Broustet

1997 Barsac $NA.   85-89

Very deep gold. Moderately full-bodied. Full acidity. Moderately extracted. Earth, honey.
Very earthy/funky in aroma. Viscous and rich in the mouth, with focused, concentrated
acidity. Quite sweet, with good length.

1998 Barsac $NA.   80-84

La Cabanne

1997 Pomerol $NA.   90-95

Saturated blackish ruby hue. Medium-bodied. Balanced acidity. Highly extracted.
Moderately tannic. Black fruits, flowers, vanilla. Fruit-forward, high-toned aromas lead
a concentrated palate with good grip and persistence. Fine intensity and structure.

1998 Pomerol $NA.   85-89

Deep, brilliant purple hue. A lush entry leads to a ripe, medium-bodied palate with grippy tannins. Compact and structured. Needs time. Long-term cellar.

Caillou
1997 Barsac $NA.   90-95

Bright golden cast. Full-bodied. Low acidity. Moderately extracted. Honey, yeast, earth. Quite aromatic and flavorful, with an extremely fat and rich palate. Very heavily botrytized, with extremely persistent flavors and a very lengthy finish.

1998 Barsac $NA.   80-84

Cambon La Pelouse
1998 Cru Bourgeois, Haut-Médoc $NA.   85-89

Saturated vibrant purple hue. Stylish, modern vanilla and red fruit aromas already show an oak accent, but a core of fruit flavors helps to balance it out. A firm entry leads to a moderately full-bodied palate with robust, grippy tannins. Closes down on the tough finish. Highly extracted. Needs time, but will probably always be on the tough side. Long-term cellar.

Camensac
1997 Haut-Médoc $NA.   85-89

Bright ruby-purple. Medium-bodied. Balanced acidity. Moderately extracted. Moderately tannic. Vanilla, black fruits. Ripeness evident on the nose. Features a solid mouthfeel with good grip and structure. Finishes with sturdy tannins and ripe Cabernet character.

1998 Haut-Médoc $NA.   85-89

Brilliant, vibrant purple hue. Unusual, high-toned mineral and flower aromas lead to a concentrated bright fruit palate. Medium-bodied and rich with grippy tannins and a solid acidic cut. Taut. Drink now or later.

Canon
1997 St. Emilion $NA.   85-89

Bright blackish ruby hue. Medium-bodied. Balanced acidity. Moderately extracted. Mildly tannic. Brown spices, black fruits. Aromatic and flavorful, with a soft, lighter-styled palate. Rather delicate, but quite tasty.

1998 St. Emilion $NA.   80-84

Canon-La-Gaffelliere
1997 St. Emilion $NA.   85-89

Opaque blackish hue. Full-bodied. Balanced acidity. Highly extracted. Quite tannic. Dried herbs, black fruits. Shows a slight herbal note to the nose. Dense, thick, and very full, with a big frame. Finishes with chunky tannins and a hint of bitterness. Rather awkward and perhaps a bit out of balance, but may come around with time.

1998 St. Emilion $NA.   90-95

Deep, opaque purple hue. Aromatically subdued, but shows a dense core of black fruit and chocolate flavors. A concentrated entry leads to a full-bodied palate with robust, velvety tannins. Shows solid grip through the finish. Rich and dense in a fat, hedonistic style. Long-term cellar.

Cantemerle
1998 Haut-Médoc $NA.   NR

Cantenac Brown
1997 Margaux $NA.   NR

Scale: Superlative (96-100), Exceptional (90-95), Highly Recommended (85-89), Recommended (80-84), Not Recommended (Under 80)

1998 Margaux $NA.   **85-89**

Very deep ruby-purple hue. Aromatic, generous black fruit and cassis aromas.
A lush entry leads to a medium-bodied palate with rounded tannins and a minerally
undercurrent. Fairly well-balanced. Needs time. Midterm cellar candidate.

Cap de Mourlin

1997 St. Emilion $NA.   **85-89**

Bright blackish ruby hue with a purple cast. Medium-bodied. Balanced acidity.
Moderately extracted. Mildly tannic. Minerals, red fruits. Rather reserved aromatically,
with a flavorful, lighter-framed palate. Pleasant, if a tad straightforward, showing good
grip on the finish.

1998 St. Emilion $NA.   **90-95**

Deep, opaque purple hue. Intensely aromatic and flashy with generous vanilla and black
fruit aromas. A lush entry leads to a moderately full-bodied palate with solid tannic grip
and a measure of acidity that lends a sense of balance. Deep and firm. Long-term cellar.

Carbonnieux

1997 Blanc, Pessac-Léognan $NA.   **NR**

1998 Blanc, Pessac-Léognan $NA.   **85-89**

Bright greenish straw hue. Generous spice and grapefruit aromas jump from the glass.
A rich entry leads to a full-bodied palate with creamy acidity. Stylish. Drink now or later.

1997 Rouge, Pessac-Léognan $NA.   **80-84**

1998 Rouge, Pessac-Léognan $NA.   **80-84**

La Cardonne

1998 Médoc $NA.   **90-95**

Deep ruby-purple hue. Complex, elegant pencil shaving and cassis aromas. A smooth
entry leads to a medium-bodied palate with a wave of velvety tannins. Lush, rounded,
and mouthfilling with softer acids. Persistent through the finish with impressive depth.
Drink now or later.

Les Carmes-Haut-Brion

1997 Rouge, Pessac-Léognan $NA.   **85-89**

Bright blackish purple. Medium-bodied. Low acidity. Moderately extracted. Mildly tannic.
Tobacco, earth, chocolate. Quite aromatic, with a classic Graves flavor profile. Lighter in
structure, with a ripe, fat palate feel. Lacking somewhat for grip, but seductive.

1998 Rouge, Pessac-Léognan $NA.   **90-95**

Brilliant neon purple hue. Attractive brown spice and tobacco aromas. A rich entry
leads to a medium-bodied palate with grippy tannins. Extremely flavorful with a wave
of complex flavors that accelerates through the finish. Midterm cellar candidate.

Carruades de Lafite Rothschild

1997 Pauillac $NA.   **85-89**

Deep ruby cast. Medium-bodied. Low acidity. Moderately extracted. Mildly tannic. Black
fruits, licorice. Pleasantly aromatic, with a full and generous palate feel. Low acidity levels
make for a fat impression through the finish. Drink up.

1998 Pauillac $NA.   **85-89**

Very deep, opaque purple hue with a color that paints the side of the glass. Generous
and very ripe black fruit and mineral aromas. A lean entry leads to a full-bodied palate
with firm, grippy tannins. Taut through the finish. Compact.

du Cartillon
1998 Cru Bourgeois, Haut-Médoc $NA.   85-89

Deep, bright ruby hue. Forward, high toned flower, spice, and mineral aromas. A lush entry leads to a medium-bodied palate with firm, grippy tannins. Structured. Needs time. Midterm cellar candidate.

Castera
1998 Médoc $NA.   NR

Chambert-Marbuzet
1998 Cru Bourgeois, St. Estèphe $NA.   85-89

Bright ruby-purple hue. Vibrant, high-toned berry aromas show an almost Pinot Noir-like purity of expression and a slight hint of overripeness. A lush entry leads to a medium-bodied palate with soft rounded tannins. Supple and easy-going. Drink now.

de Chantegrive
1997 Blanc, Graves $NA.   85-89

Deep straw cast. Medium-bodied. Balanced acidity. Moderately extracted. Mildly oaked. Dried herbs, yeast, minerals. Quite aromatic, with a green edge. Full but quite clean, with an angular finish.

1998 Blanc, Graves $NA.   85-89

Brilliant yellow-straw hue. Forward tropical aromas carry an oaky, toasted coconut accent. A lush entry leads to a generous, moderately full-bodied palate with rounded but balanced acidity. Flavorful finish. Drink now or later.

1997 Rouge, Graves $NA.   80-84
1998 Rouge, Graves $NA.   85-89

Deep ruby-purple hue. Forward vanilla and black fruit aromas. A lush entry leads to a rich, medium-bodied palate with rounded tannins. Silky and stylish with a subtle herbal influence. Drink now or later.

Chantelys
1998 Médoc $NA.   80-84

La Chapelle de la Mission Haut-Brion
1997 Rouge, Pessac-Léognan $NA.   80-84
1998 Rouge, Pessac-Léognan $NA.   90-95

Very deep ruby with a slight purple edge. Generous black fruit and mineral aromas. A lush entry leads to a moderately full-bodied palate with lean tannic grip. Angular, firm, and very precise. Ripe, intense, and well structured. Midterm cellar candidate.

Chasse-Spleen
1997 Moulis $NA.   NR
1998 Moulis $NA.   90-95

Very deep brilliant purple hue. Generous, luscious red fruit and vanilla aromas. A lush entry leads to a moderately full-bodied palate with rounded tannins. Supple and extremely well-balanced. Hedonistic. Drink now or later.

Cheval Blanc
1997 St. Emilion $NA.   90-95

Saturated dark ruby-purple. Full-bodied. Balanced acidity. Moderately extracted. Mildly tannic. Plums, spice, black cherries. Extremely aromatic and flavorful, with a rich, generous palate feel. Quite deep and darkly flavored, with sound grip and powdery tannins through the finish. Should age gracefully in the mid-term. Hedonistically attractive.

1998 St. Emilion $NA.   96-100

Deep, saturated ruby-purple hue. Complex, intense tobacco, black fruit, and mineral aromas show fine complexity. A firm entry leads to a lush, moderately full-bodied, beautifully balanced palate with rounded tannins. Supple, but intense and quite flavorful. Drink now or later.

Cissac

1998 Haut-Médoc $NA.   90-95

Bright, deep ruby-purple hue. Forward toasted oak and black fruit aromas. A smooth entry leads to a moderately full-bodied palate with grainy tannins and a firm finish. Impressively concentrated with lots of stuffing and grip. Midterm cellar candidate.

Citran

1997 Médoc $NA.   80-84

1998 Haut-Médoc $NA.   85-89

Brilliant, deep neon purple hue. Flashy vanilla aromas already show a hefty oak accent. A lean entry leads to a medium-bodied palate with firm, aggressive tannins. Concentrated fruit flavors define the finish. Needs time. Long-term cellar.

La Clare

1998 Médoc $NA.   80-84

Clarke

1997 Listrac $NA.   80-84

1998 Listrac $NA.   85-89

Very deep, saturated ruby-purple hue. Generous mineral, lead pencil, and cassis aromas show style and breed. A lush entry leads to a moderately full-bodied palate with rounded, ripe tannins. Big, but complete and well-balanced. Should develop nicely. Midterm cellar candidate.

Clement-Pichon

1998 Cru Bourgeois, Haut-Médoc $NA.   90-95

Deep, opaque ruby-purple hue. Intense, perfumed spice, licorice, and black fruit aromas. A lush entry leads to a ripe, rounded, moderately full-bodied palate. Supple and silky with elegant tannins. Great length. Very, very tasty. Drink now or later.

Clerc Millon

1997 Pauillac $NA.   86

Very deep, saturated ruby hue. Aromatically subdued with a firm black fruit and mineral undertone. A soft entry leads a moderately full-bodied palate with velvety tannins. Quite forward, but shows a bit of structure to the finish. Drink now.

1998 Pauillac $NA.   90-95

Saturated, opaque blackish purple hue. Enticing cassis and black fruit aromas show a sweet oak accent. A firm entry leads to a full-bodied palate with very firm, robust tannins. Very ripe with lower levels of acidity, but structured. Needs time. Long-term cellar.

Clinet

1998 Pomerol $NA.   96-100

Deep, opaque saturated purple hue. Forward berry, coffee, and mineral aromas jump from the glass and show a very pure and intense expressiveness in the mouth. A rich entry leads to a moderately full-bodied palate with robust velvety tannins. Shows great complexity and style with a very lengthy finish. Hedonistic. Drink now or later.

Clos Fourtet
1997 St. Emilion $NA.   85-89

Opaque blackish purple color. Moderately full-bodied. Low acidity. Moderately extracted. Mildly tannic. Black fruits. Intensely fruit driven, with very dark and deep flavors. Rich, but rather at a loss for structure. Good, but falls a bit short.

1998 St. Emilion $NA.   85-89

Deep, brilliant purple hue. Aromatically reserved with rich black fruit flavors coming through in the mouth. A ripe entry leads to a chunky, moderately full-bodied palate with rounded tannins. Fat and rich. Drink now or later.

Clos Haut-Peyraguey
1997 Sauternes $NA.   80-84

1998 Sauternes $NA.   90-95

Very deep yellow-straw hue. Pungent honey, smoke, and yeast aromas. An intense entry leads to a medium-bodied palate with good sweetness and solid balancing acidity. Stylish, complex, and well-balanced. Should develop. Midterm cellar candidate.

Colombier Monpelou
1998 Cru Bourgeois, Pauillac $NA.   80-84

La Conseillante
1997 Pomerol $NA.   85-89

Deep blackish ruby hue with a slight fade to the rim. Medium-bodied. Balanced acidity. Moderately extracted. Mildly tannic. Licorice, minerals, black fruits. High-toned aromas feature a distinctive leafy streak. Juicy and crisp on the palate, with decent acidity. Soft through the finish.

1998 Pomerol $NA.   96-100

Brilliant ruby hue. Perfumed berry and flower aromas jump from the glass. A ripe entry leads to a medium-bodied palate with great interplay between grippy tannins and buoyant acidity. Shows great depth and purity of flavor. Complex and stylish, but not the least bit ponderous. Drink now or later.

Cos Labory
1997 St. Estèphe $NA.   NR
1998 St. Estèphe $NA.   90-95

Deep, opaque vibrant purple hue. Aromatically subdued with a firm backbone of mineral and red fruit flavors. A lean entry leads to a moderately full-bodied palate with firm tannins. Intense, concentrated, and stuffed. Needs time. Long-term cellar.

Coufran
1997 Haut-Médoc $NA.   80-84
1998 Haut-Médoc $NA.   90-95

Bright ruby-purple hue. Generous, stylish red fruit and vanilla aromas. A lean entry leads to a lush, medium-bodied palate with grippy tannins and solid acidic grip. Well-balanced with a fine cut. Should age well. Midterm cellar candidate.

Coutelin Merville
1998 Cru Bourgeois, St. Estèphe $NA.   NR

Coutet
1997 Barsac $NA.   90-95

Bright yellow-gold. Moderately full-bodied. Balanced acidity. Moderately extracted. Apricots, honey, citrus. Exceptionally aromatic and flavorful, with pure and focused flavors. Well-balanced, with excellent interplay between sweetness and acidity.

Scale: Superlative (96-100), Exceptional (90-95), Highly Recommended (85-89), Recommended (80-84), Not Recommended (Under 80)

1998 Barsac $NA.   85-89

Brilliant yellow-straw hue. Lush toasted coconut and honeyed citrus aromas. A rich
entry leads to a supple, medium-bodied palate with lots of sweetness and rounded
acidity. Flavorful and supple, but not cloying. Fairly well-balanced. Drink now.

Le Crock
1998 Cru Bourgeois, St. Estèphe $NA.   90-95

Saturated vibrant purple hue. Opulent, pure ripe berry and mineral aromas jump from
the glass. A lush entry leads to a medium-bodied palate with silky tannins. Intense and
generously fruited with good fruit acids. Should age nicely over the mid-term. Drink
now or later.

de La Croix
1998 Médoc $NA.   85-89

Deep ruby-purple hue. Generous cassis and mineral aromas. A smooth attack leads to a
moderately full-bodied palate with thick, rich tannins and a good concentration of fruit.
Persistent, flavorful finish. Lush and quite ripe. Drink now or later.

La Croix de Gay
1997 Pomerol $NA.   85-89

Deep ruby red to the rim. Medium-bodied. Balanced acidity. Moderately extracted.
Mildly tannic. Red fruits, violets. Lighter in style, with a juicy attack and an angular,
mildly tannic finish. High-toned and fairly well-balanced.

1998 Pomerol $NA.   85-89

Deep brilliant purple hue. Exotic, stylish coffee, spice cabinet, and black fruit aromas. A
lush entry leads to a thick, full-bodied palate with rounded tannins. Rich, but somewhat
shy of acidity. Shows an interesting gamey note through the finish. Drink now or later.

Croizet-Bages
1997 Pauillac $NA.   80-84
1998 Pauillac $NA.   80-84

Dassault
1997 St. Emilion $NA.   90-95

Deep blackish ruby hue with a purple cast. Moderately full-bodied. Low acidity.
Moderately extracted. Mildly tannic. Licorice, vanilla, black fruits. Aromatic and flavorful,
with a big, chewy, fruit-centered palate. Lacks a bit for acidity, but quite seductive, with
supple tannins and enough grip to the finish to lend a sense of balance.

1998 St. Emilion $NA.   80-84

Dauzac
1997 Margaux $NA.   NR
1998 Margaux $NA.   90-95

Very deep, opaque purple hue. Intense black fruit and mineral aromas. A fat entry leads
to a lush, full-bodied palate with big silky tannins and good grip through the finish.
Forward and stylish. Very tasty. Drink now or later.

David
1998 Médoc $NA.   NR

Deyrem Valentin
1998 Cru Bourgeois, Margaux $NA.   90-95

Deep ruby hue. Intense, generous flower and red fruit aromas. A lush entry leads to a moderately full-bodied palate with firm but rounded tannins. Silky, seductive finish. Very stylish. Drink now or later.

Dillon
1998 Cru Bourgeois, Haut-Médoc $NA.   80-84

Doisy-Daene
1997 Barsac $NA.   85-89

Deep yellow-gold. Full-bodied. Low acidity. Moderately extracted. Honey, smoke. Extremely fat and rich, with a big, viscous quality. Large-framed, honeyed flavors are very sweet. Impressive, but could use a bit more grip. Almost cloying.

1998 Barsac $NA.   80-84

Doisy-Vedrines
1997 Barsac $NA.   90-95

Bright yellow-gold. Moderately full-bodied. Balanced acidity. Moderately extracted. Coconut, tropical fruits, cream. Extraordinarily aromatic, with a wave of complex flavors on the palate. Exquisitely balanced, with wonderful tension between acidity, sweetness, and viscosity. Fine length.

1998 Barsac $NA.   NR

Domaine de Chevalier
1997 Blanc, Pessac-Léognan $NA.   85-89

Bright green-gold hue. Medium-bodied. Full acidity. Highly extracted. Minerals. Rather reserved aromatically, with a tightly wound palate feel. Firm and concentrated. Should develop with time.

1998 Blanc, Pessac-Léognan $NA.   80-84
1997 Rouge, Pessac-Léognan $NA.   80-84
1998 Rouge, Pessac-Léognan $NA.   85-89

Deep ruby-purple hue. Aromatically reserved, but shows firm mineral and red fruit flavors. A firm entry leads to a full-bodied palate with tough, austere tannins. Rather mean. Needs lots of time. Long-term cellar.

La Dominique
1997 St. Emilion $NA.   85-89

Very dark blackish ruby hue. Moderately full-bodied. Low acidity. Moderately extracted. Moderately tannic. Chocolate, plums, brown spice. Extremely ripe and rich, with a generous if somewhat low-acid palate feel. Rich finish, with chunky tannins. Should drink well early.

1998 St. Emilion $NA.   80-84

Duhart-Milon Rothschild
1998 Pauillac $NA.   90-95

Very deep opaque purple hue. Exotic smoke, tobacco, and black fruit aromas are quite generous. A lush entry leads to a moderately full-bodied palate with rounded, velvety tannins and a firm minerally undercurrent. Already quite stylish with lots of complexity, but structured to age. Midterm cellar candidate.

Duplessis
1998 Moulis $NA.   85-89
Deep ruby-purple hue. Generous flower, cherry, and vanilla aromas. A soft entry leads to a medium-bodied palate with velvety tannins. Soft, supple, and delicate with a lingering flavorful finsh. Stylish and elegant. Drink now.

l'Evangile
1997 Pomerol $NA.   85-89
Opaque blackish ruby hue with a purple cast. Medium-bodied. Balanced acidity. Moderately extracted. Moderately tannic. Mint, flowers, black fruits. Quite perfumed, with a rich though supple palate feel. Concentrated, with soft tannins and fine depth. Finishes with a hint of bitterness.

La Fagotte
1998 Cru Bourgeois, Haut-Médoc $NA.   85-89
Saturated, opaque deep purple hue. Attractive, generous blackberry, flower, and vanilla aromas jump from the glass. A lush entry leads to a medium-bodied palate with great purity of fruit flavors. Grippy tannins and buoyant acidity through the finish. Very tasty, but not quite with the depth or intensity for greatness. Drink now or later.

Ferrande
1998 Blanc, Graves $NA.   NR
1998 Rouge, Graves $NA.   85-89
Brilliant deep purple hue. Intensly aromatic cedar and tobacco aromas carry a slight green edge. A lush entry leads to a medium-bodied palate with silky, harmonious tannins. Very flavorful and exceptionally well-balanced. Drink now or later.

Ferriere
1998 Margaux $NA.   90-95
Deep blackish purple hue. Exotic spice cabinet, black fruit, and flower aromas are attractive and complex. A rich entry leads to a silky, full-bodied mouthfeel with lush velvety tannins. Lengthy finish. Very skillful and extremely well-balanced. Harmonious. Drink now or later.

Fieuzal
1997 Blanc, Pessac-Léognan $NA.   90-95
Bright straw with a green cast. Moderately full-bodied. Full acidity. Moderately extracted. Dried herbs, minerals, citrus. Aromatic and clean, with a full and vibrant mouthfeel. Well structured and flavorful.

1998 Blanc, Pessac-Léognan $NA.   90-95
Deep, greenish yellow-straw hue. Intense grapefruit, mineral, and vanilla aromas. A rich entry leads to a moderately full-bodied palate with firm structural acidity. Varietal, stylish, and well-balanced. Drink now or later.

1997 Rouge, Pessac-Léognan $NA.   85-89
Saturated bright blackish purple. Moderately full-bodied. Balanced acidity. Moderately extracted. Moderately tannic. Black fruits, tea. Aromatic and fruit centered, with a rich, full, low-acid palate. Chunky tannins rear up on the finish. Rather tough at present, but has the extract to stand up to the tannins.

1998 Rouge, Pessac-Léognan $NA.   85-89
Opaque blackish purple hue. Brooding black fruit and licorice aromas carry a hefty oak accent. A tough entry leads to a full-bodied palate with big, aggressive tannins and chewy flavors. Impressive but rather tough. Certainly needs time. Long-term cellar.

Figeac
1997 St. Emilion $NA.   **90-95**

Bright blackish ruby hue to the rim. Moderately full-bodied. Low acidity. Moderately extracted. Mildly tannic. Licorice, black fruits. Quite flavorful and aromatic, with a ripe and seductive mouthfeel. Fat, but shows enough grip through the finish to maintain balance. Will drink well early, but balanced for age. Seductive.

1998 St. Emilion $NA.   **85-89**

Deep ruby with a slight purple overtone. Rich berry and mineral aromas are already showing a flashy wood accent. A firm entry leads to a moderately full-bodied palate with big, grippy tannins. Shows depth and concentration, but rather mean through the finish. Will need lots of time. Long-term cellar.

Filhot
1997 Sauternes $NA.   **80-84**

1998 Sauternes $NA.   **NR**

La Fleur Peyrabon
1998 Cru Bourgeois, Pauillac $NA.   **NR**

Fonbadet
1998 Cru Bourgeois, Pauillac $NA.   **NR**

Fonplegade
1997 St. Emilion $NA.   **90-95**

Bright blackish ruby color. Medium-bodied. Balanced acidity. Moderately extracted. Mildly tannic. Black fruits, minerals. Aromatic and flavorful, with a high-toned, lighter-styled palate. Silky, though well structured, with some grip to the finish. Should drink well early.

1998 St. Emilion $NA.   **NR**

Fonreaud
1997 Listrac $NA.   **NR**

1998 Listrac $NA.   **80-84**

Fontis
1998 Médoc $NA.   **80-84**

Les Forts de Latour
1997 Pauillac $NA.   **90**

Very deep ruby hue. Intense, almost pungent cedar and pencil-shaving aromas. A lush entry leads a medium-bodied palate with lean tannins and good grip. Harmonious, balanced, and drinking well now. Drink now.

1998 Pauillac $NA.   **85-89**

Very deep purple hue. Brooding, subdued black fruit and mineral aromas. A rich entry leads to a full-bodied palate with big chunky tannins. Round and lush with lower levels of acidity. Full and rich. Midterm cellar candidate.

Fourcas-Dupré
1997 Listrac $NA.   **80-84**

1998 Listrac $NA.   **80-84**

Fourcas-Hosten
1997 Listrac $NA.   **NR**

1998 Listrac $NA.   **NR**

Franc-Mayne

1997 St. Emilion $NA.   85-89

Blackish ruby hue with a purple edge. Moderately full-bodied. Low acidity. Moderately extracted. Mildly tannic. Vanilla, black fruits. Aromatic and flavorful, with a big, rich palate feel coming across as slightly fat on the entry. Turns a little more angular, showing some grip on the finish. Solid.

1998 St. Emilion $NA.   90-95

Deep, saturated purple hue. Generous black fruit and vanilla aromas. A rich entry leads to a moderately full-bodied palate with grippy tannins and decent acidity. Well-balanced and deeply flavored with fine length. Should age beautifully, but precocious. Drink now or later.

de France

1997 Blanc, Pessac-Léognan $NA.   NR
1998 Blanc, Pessac-Léognan $NA.   90-95

Brilliant yellow green hue. Intense, opulent ginger, herb, and cream aromas are pungent and complex. A rich entry leads to a full-bodied palate with rounded, but firm acidity. Very big and very fancy. Drink now or later.

1997 Rouge, Pessac-Léognan $NA.   80-84
1998 Rouge, Pessac-Léognan $NA.   85-89

Deep ruby-purple hue. Subdued spice and mineral aromas. A thick entry leads to a lush, full-bodied palate with chewy, drying tannins. Lots of velvety extract with a bit of an edge to the finish. Needs time. Midterm cellar candidate.

La Gaffeliere

1998 St. Emilion $NA.   85-89

Brilliant, vibrant purple hue. A lush entry leads to a full-bodied, rounded palate with grippy tannins and sturdy balancing acidity. Fat, but fairly well-balanced. Needs time. Midterm cellar candidate.

Gazin

1997 Pomerol $NA.   85-89

Opaque blackish ruby cast. Moderately full-bodied. Balanced acidity. Highly extracted. Moderately tannic. Red fruits, black tea. Full aromas reveal a fruit-centered palate with big, strapping tannins. Large-scaled, with a rich and chunky finish.

1998 Pomerol $NA.   NR

Giscours

1997 Margaux $NA.   80-84
1998 Margaux $NA.   96-100

Very deep, saturated purple hue. Generous mint, chocolate, and black fruit aromas are complex and attractive. A ripe entry leads to a moderately full-bodied palate with supple, rounded tannins. Very hedonistic and well-balanced with outstanding length. Drink now or later.

du Glana

1998 Cru Bourgeois, St. Julien $NA.   90-95

Deep, opaque purple hue. Very attractive licorice, berry, and spice aromas jump from the glass. A rich entry leads to a lush, medium-bodied palate with silky tannins and lovely flavors. Harmonious and very stylish. Drink now or later.

La Gorre

1998 Médoc $NA.   NR

Grand-Mayne

1997 St. Emilion $NA.   90-95

Blackish ruby hue with a purple cast. Medium-bodied. Balanced acidity. Moderately extracted. Moderately tannic. Minerals, black fruits. Aromatic and flavorful, with a full though well-structured and lean mouthfeel. Astringent tannins rear up on the finish, but this wine is well-balanced overall. Should be a keeper.

1998 St. Emilion $NA.   85-89

Opaque, saturated purple hue. Unusual, generous herb, anise, and jammy briar fruit aromas. A rich entry leads to a medium-bodied palate with lean tannins. Lighter in style, but shows an extremely lengthy and attractive chocolate-edged finish. Drink now or later.

Grand-Puy-Ducasse

1997 Pauillac $NA.   85-89

Bright blackish ruby hue. Medium-bodied. Balanced acidity. Moderately extracted. Mildly tannic. Minerals, black fruits. Full and flavorful, with a well-structured palate that has a sense of angularity. Shows decent grip.

1998 Pauillac $NA.   85-89

Deep, saturated neon purple hue. A rich entry leads to a moderately full-bodied palate with big grippy tannins. Rounded, but showing a slight green edge and a firm structure. Compact finish. Needs time. Long-term cellar.

Grandis

1998 Cru Bourgeois, Haut-Médoc $NA.   NR

Les Grands Chénes

1998 Médoc $NA.   85-89

Dark, opaque ruby-purple hue. Sound black fruit and mineral aromas. A firm entry leads to a moderately full-bodied palate with big grainy tannins. Firmly structured with a lingering tannic finish. A solid, stuffed Cabernet-dominant style. Needs time. Midterm cellar candidate.

Greysac

1997 Médoc $NA.   NR
1998 Médoc $NA.   85-89

Saturated, opaque blackish purple hue. Forward, attractive black fruit, mineral, and cassis aromas are clean and pure. A lean entry leads to a medium-bodied palate with grippy, angular tannins. Fine intensity, and well-balanced through the finish. Drink now or later.

Griviere

1998 Médoc $NA.   90-95

Dark, saturated ruby-purple hue. Generous, intense black fruit and toasted oak aromas. A smooth entry leads to a moderately full-bodied palate with plentiful velvety tannins. Rich and lush with a lingering flavorful finish. Attractive and stylish. Drink now or later.

Gruaud Larose

1997 St. Julien $NA.   90-95

Opaque blackish ruby hue. Moderately full-bodied. Balanced acidity. Moderately extracted. Mildly tannic. Mint, black fruits, minerals. Quite aromatic, with real complexity of flavor. Solid and rich, with excellent balance and fine length. Will drink early, but should also keep. Intense.

1998 St. Julien $NA.   85-89

Deep, opaque blackish purple hue. Lean, high-toned anise and briar aromas. A taut entry leads to a medium-bodied palate with grippy tannins and good cut. Lighter in style—lacking real depth—but tasty. Drink now.

Guiraud
1997 Sauternes $NA.   85-89

Bright golden cast. Moderately full-bodied. Low acidity. Moderately extracted. Earth, honey, apricots. Has an earthy overtone to the complex flavors. Thick and lush on the palate, with low levels of acidity. Moderate sweetness maintains a sense of balance.

1998 Sauternes $NA.   80-84

La Gurgue
1998 Cru Bourgeois, Margaux $NA.   NR

Hanteillan
1998 Cru Bourgeois, Haut-Médoc $NA.   80-84

Haut-Bages-Liberal
1997 Pauillac $NA.   80-84
1998 Pauillac $NA.   85-89

Deep, opaque vibrant purple hue. Subdued cedar and lead pencil aromas. A rich entry leads to a full-bodied palate with shy acidity and robust, angular tannins. Closes down on the finish. Needs time. Long-term cellar.

Haut-Bages-Monpelou
1998 Cru Bourgeois, Pauillac $NA.   NR

Haut-Bailly
1997 Rouge, Pessac-Léognan $NA.   85-89

Very bright blackish purple. Moderately full-bodied. Low acidity. Moderately extracted. Mildly tannic. Minerals, red fruits. Somewhat reserved aromatically, with some mineral flavor nuances. Lighter in style with an austere finish, but showing some snap.

1998 Rouge, Pessac-Léognan $NA.   90-95

Brilliant dark neon purple hue. Intense, brooding black fruit, tobacco, and mineral aromas. A rich entry leads to a big, full-bodied palate with firm grippy tannins. Well balanced for its size. Needs time. Impressive and immense. Long-term cellar.

Haut-Beausejour
1998 Cru Bourgeois, St. Estèphe $NA.   80-84

Haut-Bergey
1997 Blanc, Pessac-Léognan $NA.   85-89

Bright green-straw cast. Medium-bodied. Full acidity. Moderately extracted. Lemon zest, minerals. Aromatically serious, but reserved. Firm and tight on the palate, with a zesty attack and a tough, minerally finish. Lacks charm at present, but should develop with time.

1998 Blanc, Pessac-Léognan $NA.   80-84
1997 Rouge, Pessac-Léognan $NA.   NR
1998 Rouge, Pessac-Léognan $NA.   85-89

Dark, opaque neon purple hue. Generous black fruit and spice aromas. A rich entry leads to a velvety, full-bodied palate with big supple tannins. Weighty, with lower acid levels, but very deep and flavorful. Should be approachable early. Drink now or later.

Haut-Breton-Larigaudiere
1998 Cru Bourgeois, Margaux $NA.   85-89

Vibrant purple hue. Aromatically subdued, but shows a nice intensity of red berry and vanilla flavors in the mouth. A firm entry leads to a medium-bodied palate with grainy tannins. Shows fine length with an exceptionally attractive finish. Drink now or later.

Haut-Brion

1998 Blanc, Pessac-Léognan $NA.   **90-95**

Very deep yellow-straw hue with a greenish cast. Ripe, forward citrus and cream aromas. A lush entry leads to a big, full-bodied, creamy mouthfeel. Weighty and lush with good balancing acidity. An opulent style which should be approachable young but hold. Drink now or later.

1997 Rouge, Pessac-Léognan $NA.   **90-95**

Deep ruby-purple. Moderately full-bodied. Low acidity. Moderately extracted. Mildly tannic. Minerals, tobacco, black fruits. Quite aromatic, with a soft, lush palate feel. Lower acidity levels make for a fat impression, but has enough structure to maintain a sense of balance. Finishes with a mild bitter note.

1998 Rouge, Pessac-Léognan $NA.   **96-100**

Very deep blackish ruby hue. Closed, brooding mineral and black fruit aromas. A rich entry leads to a full-bodied palate with lean, angular tannins. Quite firmly structured, but explodes with minerally flavor through the finish. Intense, but needs lots of time. Long-term cellar.

Haut-Canteloup

1998 Médoc $NA.   **80-84**

Haut-Madrac

1998 Cru Bourgeois, Haut-Médoc $NA.   **85-89**

Deep ruby hue with a slight fade. Generous spice and red fruit aromas. A soft entry leads to a velvety, medium-bodied palate with supple but firm tannins. Well-balanced and flavorful. Should develop nicely. Drink now or later.

Haut-Maurac

1998 Médoc $NA.   **85-89**

Deep, saturated ruby-purple hue. Generous toasted oak and ripe cassis aromas. A smooth entry leads to a moderately full-bodied palate with big thick tannins. Soft and lush with a fine texture. Lingering, flavorful finish. A rich, rounded style that will drink well early. Drink now.

Kirwan

1997 Margaux $NA.   **80-84**
1998 Margaux $NA.   **90-95**

Opaque blackish purple hue. Generous, flashy aromas show a hefty oak influence and a core of ripe red fruits. A lush entry leads to a medium-bodied palate with supple tannins. Rounded, hedonistic, and very stylish. Ripe, supple finish. Midterm cellar candidate.

Labegorce

1997 Margaux $NA.   **NR**
1998 Margaux $NA.   **85-89**

Deep, saturated blackish purple hue. Aromatically subdued with a sweet red fruit undercurrent. A lush entry leads to a medium-bodied palate with rounded, supple tannins. Lighter, but well-balanced and tasty. Drink now or later.

Lafaurie-Peyraguey

1997 Sauternes $NA.   **85-89**

Deep golden hue. Moderately full-bodied. Balanced acidity. Moderately extracted. Brown spices, tropical fruits. Aromatic and flavorful, with hefty botrytis flavors. Thick and quite viscous, with just enough acidity to maintain a sense of balance through the finish.

1998 Sauternes $NA.   **80-84**

Scale: Superlative (96-100), Exceptional (90-95), Highly Recommended (85-89), Recommended (80-84), Not Recommended (Under 80)

Lafite Rothschild

1997 Pauillac $NA.   90-95

Deep ruby-purple. Moderately full-bodied. Balanced acidity. Highly extracted. Mildly tannic. Lead pencil, red fruits, cedar. Pleasantly aromatic, and already quite forward in flavor. Shows fine generosity, with an inherent silky quality. Decent acidity and supple tannins lend structure to the finish.

1998 Pauillac $NA.   96-100

Very deep, opaque purple hue. Generous, lush spice, black fruit, and mineral aromas are attractive and opulent. A firm entry leads to a moderately full-bodied palate with lush, velvety tannins. Already showing some complexities and finishes for a mile. Very classy...and delicious. Should age beautifully, if you can keep your hands off it. Long-term cellar.

Lafon

1998 Médoc $NA.   85-89

Dark opaque purple hue. Intense black fruit and vanilla aromas. A smooth entry leads to a medium-bodied palate with drying tannins and a forward oak accent. An aromatic, flavorful, modern style. Drink now.

Lafon-Rochet

1997 St. Estèphe $NA.   80-84
1998 St. Estèphe $NA.   90-95

Very deep, vibrant purple hue. Intense, fragrant cedar, mineral, and red fruit aromas. A taut entry leads to a moderately full-bodied palate with lean, grippy tannins. Stylish and intense. Midterm cellar candidate.

Lagrange

1997 St. Julien $NA.   80-84
1998 St. Julien $NA.   85-89

Brilliant purple hue. Unusual anise and mineral aromas seem to be at an awkward stage. A lean entry leads to a rich, supple, and stylish finish. Rounds out toward the lengthy finish with fine grained tannins. Harmonious. Midterm cellar candidate.

de Lamarque

1998 Haut-Médoc $NA.   80-84

Lamothe

1997 Sauternes $NA.   85-89

Deep golden hue. Moderately full-bodied. Full acidity. Moderately extracted. Honey, citrus, yeast. Quite rich and sweet, with a flavorful, viscous mouthfeel. Well-balanced, with a lingering finish. Just enough acidity to maintain a sense of balance.

1998 Sauternes $NA.   80-84

Lamothe-Bergeron

1998 Cru Bourgeois, Haut-Médoc $NA.   80-84

Lamothe-Cissac

1998 Cru Bourgeois, Haut-Médoc $NA.   85-89

Deep saturated ruby hue with a slight purple overtone. Attractive, perfumed red fruit, licorice, and vanilla aromas. A soft entry leads to a moderately full-bodied palate with rounded, but firm tannins. Big and weighty, with a good structure. Should develop. Midterm cellar candidate.

Lamothe-Guignard
1997 Sauternes $NA.   80-84
1998 Sauternes $NA.   80-84

Landat
1998 Cru Bourgeois, Haut-Médoc $NA.   NR

Langoa-Barton
1997 St. Julien $NA.   85-89
Bright ruby-purple. Medium-bodied. Low acidity. Moderately extracted. Mildly tannic.
Red fruits, spice. Pleasantly aromatic, with a fruit accent throughout. Fleshy on the
palate, with a lighter frame. Powdery tannins. Tasty.

1998 St. Julien $NA.   90-95
Opaque vibrant purple hue. Generous aromas jump from the glass and show an
attractive oak accent. A firm entry leads to a big, full-bodied palate. Has lots of stuffing
and intensity, yet well-balanced. Should age beautifully. Long-term cellar.

Larcis Ducasse
1997 St. Emilion $NA.   80-84
1998 St. Emilion $NA.   85-89
Brilliant blackish ruby hue with a slight purple overtone. Generous flower, berry, and
chocolate aromas. A lush entry leads to a lighter-styled, medium-bodied palate with silky
tannins. Lacks somewhat for grip, but tasty. Drink now.

Larmande
1997 St. Emilion $NA.   90-95
Very deep and saturated blackish ruby color. Moderately full-bodied. Balanced acidity.
Highly extracted. Moderately tannic. Black fruits. Quite aromatic, with a big, firm, highly
structured, though chewy mouthfeel. Excellent concentration and grip, with good length
and sturdy tannins.

1998 St. Emilion $NA.   90-95
Very deep, vibrant opaque purple hue. Flashy, oaky vanillin aromas already jump
from the glass with a core of very ripe mineral and berry flavors. A rich entry leads to
a full-bodied palate with firm tannins and decent structural acidity. Very big, but well
balanced. A quintessential show wine. Lots of flash, but with the substance to back it up.
Long-term cellar.

Larose-Trintaudon
1998 Cru Bourgeois, Haut-Médoc $NA.   80-84

Larrivet-Haut-Brion
1997 Blanc, Pessac-Léognan $NA.   85-89
Bright yellow-straw color. Moderately full-bodied. Balanced acidity. Moderately extracted.
Butter, dried herbs, citrus. Generous aromas have an herbal edge. Full and rich on
the palate, with a sturdy mouthfeel. Lacks a bit of acidity, but has decent structure.
Attractive now.

1998 Blanc, Pessac-Léognan $NA.   90-95
Bright greenish golden hue. Opulent vanilla, tropical fruit, and cream aromas already
carry an oaky accent. A rich entry leads to a blowsy, full-bodied palate with rounded
acidity. Fat and weighty, but tasty. Drink now.

1997 Rouge, Pessac-Léognan $NA.   85-89
Bright blackish purple. Medium-bodied. Low acidity. Moderately extracted. Mildly
tannic. Licorice, minerals. Pleasantly aromatic, with a lighter-styled though rich and
supple frame. Rather low in acidity, but flavorful and pleasant. Should drink well early.

1998 Rouge, Pessac-Léognan $NA.   80-84

Lascombes

1997 Margaux $NA.   80-84

1998 Margaux $NA.   80-84

Latour

1997 Pauillac $NA.   94

Deep, brilliant ruby hue. Intense and exotic cedar, mineral, and walnut aromas. A firm entry leads a moderately full-bodied palate with big, gripping tannins. Attractive, but well structured. Should age quite nicely. Very successful. Long-term cellar candidate.

1998 Pauillac $NA.   90-95

Deep, opaque purple hue. Deep, brooding black fruit and mineral aromas. A firm entry leads to a full-bodied palate with very big, ripe tannins. Rich and chunky with lower acidity levels. Will need lots of time. Long-term cellar.

Latour-Martillac

1997 Blanc, Pessac-Léognan $NA.   85-89

Bright yellow-straw cast. Medium-bodied. Balanced acidity. Moderately extracted. Minerals, citrus. Aromatically reserved. Full in the mouth, but lacking generosity in flavors. Sound acidity and structure. May open with time.

1998 Blanc, Pessac-Léognan $NA.   85-89

Bright yelllow straw hue. Generous herb aromas feature a leesy accent and a forceful Sauvignon character. A crisp entry leads to a medium-bodied palate with vibrant acidity. Racy and flavorful. Drink now or later.

1997 Rouge, Pessac-Léognan $NA.   80-84

1998 Rouge, Pessac-Léognan $NA.   85-89

Deep, opaque blackish purple hue. Aromatically subdued, with a brooding mineral and licorice undercurrent. A firm entry leads to a big, full-bodied palate with edgy tannins. Extracted but closed. Will need lots of time. Long-term cellar.

La Lauzette

1998 Listrac $NA.   80-84

Laville Haut-Brion

1998 Blanc, Pessac-Léognan $NA.   85-89

Brilliant yellow-straw hue. Forward tropical fruit and lanolin aromas show lots of ripeness. A lush entry leads to a moderately full-bodied palate with vibrant acidity through the finish. Big, but carries its ripeness well. Drink now or later.

Lavillotte

1998 Cru Bourgeois, St. Estèphe $NA.   NR

Léoville Barton

1997 St. Julien $NA.   90-95

Deep blackish purple. Moderately full-bodied. Balanced acidity. Moderately extracted. Mildly tannic. Flowers, minerals, spice. Quite aromatic, with real complexity to the flavors. Rather thick, but has acceptable structure. Fine length and intensity.

1998 St. Julien $NA.   90-95

Opaque, saturated blackish purple hue. Brooding mineral and black fruit aromas. A firm entry leads to a full-bodied palate with big, grippy tannins. An absolute monster, but still balanced. Will need lots of time. Long-term cellar.

Léoville-Poyferre
1997 St. Julien $NA.   NR
1998 St. Julien $NA.   85-89

Saturated, opaque blackish purple hue. Generous berry and mineral aromas. A fat, lush entry leads to a full-bodied palate with shy acidity and a green edge to the tannin. Hedonistic, but not really deep. Drink now or later.

Lilian Ladouys
1998 Cru Bourgeois, St. Estèphe $NA.   85-89

Saturated, opaque ruby hue. Generous chocolate and red fruit aromas. A rich entry leads to a moderately full-bodied palate with ripe, lush tannins and lots of flavor intensity. Well-balanced and supple. Drink now or later.

Liversan
1998 Cru Bourgeois, Haut-Médoc $NA.   80-84

Loudenne
1997 Médoc $NA.   80-84
1998 Médoc $NA.   85-89

Deep, opaque ruby-purple hue. Rich black fruit and smoke aromas. A smooth entry leads to a moderately full-bodied palate with ripe, thick tannins. Rather four square at present, with impressive weight and fleshy flavors. Should improve. Drink now or later.

Lousteauneuf
1998 Médoc $NA.   NR

La Louviere
1997 Blanc, Pessac-Léognan $NA.   90-95

Bright green-straw cast. Medium-bodied. Balanced acidity. Moderately extracted. Ripe lemons, brown spice, minerals. Aromatically forward. Excellent grip and intensity, with a persistent, flavorful finish. Fine structure. Attractive now, but should develop.

1998 Blanc, Pessac-Léognan $NA.   85-89

Brilliant greenish straw hue. Subdued mineral and herb aromas. A lean entry leads to a medium-bodied palate with crisp acidity and a kiss of oak. Well-cut finish. Drink now or later.

1997 Rouge, Pessac-Léognan $NA.   NR
1998 Rouge, Pessac-Léognan $NA.   85-89

Deep ruby-purple hue. Subdued mineral and black fruit aromas. A firm entry leads to a big, full-bodied palate with a wave of drying tannins. Closes down on the finish, but complex Graves-like flavors sneak through. Needs lots of time. Long-term cellar.

Lynch-Bages
1997 Pauillac $NA.   90-95

Light blackish ruby color. Moderately full-bodied. Balanced acidity. Moderately extracted. Mildly tannic. Minerals, lead pencil, cassis. Classically aromatic, with a firm, slightly angular palate feel. Well structured, with sound grip.

1998 Pauillac $NA.   90-95

Opaque blackish ruby hue. Brooding red fruit, lead pencil, and chocolate aromas. A rich entry leads to a massive, full-bodied palate with waves of extract and thick, robust tannins. Way too much at present, but seems stuffed and built to age. Long-term cellar.

Scale: Superlative (96-100), Exceptional (90-95), Highly Recommended (85-89), Recommended (80-84), Not Recommended (Under 80)

Lynch-Moussas

1997 Pauillac $NA. 90-95

Lighter ruby-purple color. Medium-bodied. Balanced acidity. Moderately extracted. Mildly tannic. Minerals, cassis. Aromatic, with a solid Cabernet flavor profile. Well structured, with good grip to the finish and fine length.

1998 Pauillac $NA. 80-84

Magdelaine

1998 St. Emilion $NA. 90-95

Deep, brilliant purple hue. Forward, lifted, berry fruit aromas carry a generous vanilla oak accent. A lush entry leads to a supple, medium-bodied palate with gentle velvety tannins and bright fruit acids. Lush and hedonistic. Drink now or later.

Malartic-Lagraviere

1997 Blanc, Pessac-Léognan $NA. 85-89

Bright yellow-straw cast. Low acidity. Moderately extracted. Smoke, butter, apples. Forward aromas lead a soft, generous attack. Lacking some acidity, but finishes with authority.

1998 Blanc, Pessac-Léognan $NA. 80-84

Deep greenish yellow hue. Aromatically subdued with a buttery overtone. A lush entry leads to a fat, moderately full-bodied palate with rounded acidity. Lacks somewhat for grip. Drink now.

1997 Rouge, Pessac-Léognan $NA. NR

1998 Rouge, Pessac-Léognan $NA. 90-95

Brilliant ruby-purple hue. Extravagant cedar, tobacco, and mineral aromas are lush and exotic. A rich entry leads to a full-bodied palate with robust velvety tannins that bite down on the finish. Very, very stylish. Midterm cellar candidate.

Malescasse

1997 Haut-Médoc $NA. 85-89

Deep ruby hue. Medium-bodied. Balanced acidity. Moderately extracted. Mildly tannic. Minerals, cassis. Fragrant and stylish, with a softer palate feel. Has some grip to balance the finish.

1998 Cru Bourgeois, Haut-Médoc $NA. 85-89

Deep, saturated ruby hue. Forward licorice and jammy fruit aromas. A rich entry leads to a moderately full-bodied palate with firm but velvety tannins. Lots of flavor, but needs a bit of time to soften. Midterm cellar candidate.

Malescot Saint Exupery

1997 Margaux $NA. 80-84

1998 Margaux $NA. 80-84

de Malle

1997 Sauternes $NA. 96-100

Very deep golden hue. Full-bodied. Balanced acidity. Highly extracted. Honey, apricots, vanilla. Aromatic and flavorful, with an extremely rich and luxuriant mouthfeel. Quite heavily botrytized and very fine, with an extremely lengthy finish. Intense.

1998 Sauternes $NA. 90-95

Brigt yellow golden hue. Attractive smoke, yeast, and honeyed pear aromas. A rich entry leads to a moderately full-bodied palate with generous sweetness balanced by good acidic grip. Honeyed and rich but well-balanced. Stylish. Drink now or later.

de Malleret
1998 Cru Bourgeois, Haut-Médoc $NA.   80-84

Château Margaux
1997 Margaux $NA.   92

Deep, brilliant ruby-purple. Enticing spice and berry aromas jump from the glass. A lush entry leads a moderately full-bodied, flavorful palate with velvety tannins. Fades toward the finish. Forward, stylish, and well-balanced. Drink now.

1998 Margaux $NA.   96-100

Very deep, saturated purple hue. Enticing, brooding black fruit and mineral aromas with very pure flavors in the mouth. A concentrated entry leads to a full-bodied palate with excellent acidic and tannic grip. Very firm, but well-balanced and deep. Taut and dense, but showing no signs of bitterness or overextraction. Long-term cellar.

Marquis de Terme
1997 Margaux $NA.   85-89

Bright purple. Moderately full-bodied. Low acidity. Moderately extracted. Mildly tannic. Red fruits. Forward, fruity aromas lead to a high-toned, fleshy palate with dry tannins. Still quite fat, but persistent.

1998 Margaux $NA.   90-95

Deep, brilliant purple hue. Attractive, intense red fruit, cassis, and mineral aromas already carry a sweet oak accent. A lush entry leads to a moderately full-bodied palate with silky tannins and solid acidic grip. Shows fine length and harmony. Well-balanced. Drink now or later.

Marsac Seguineau
1998 Cru Bourgeois, Margaux $NA.   85-89

Deep, saturated ruby with a purple overtone. Subdued red fruit aromas show a touch of heat. A lush entry leads to a medium-bodied palate with grainy tannins and a kiss of oak. Fairly lengthy finish. Drink now or later.

Martinens
1997 Margaux $NA.   NR

Maucaillou
1997 Moulis $NA.   NR
1998 Moulis $NA.   80-84

Maucamps
1998 Haut-Médoc $NA.   85-89

Dark, opaque ruby-purple hue. Generous, forward cherry and mineral aromas. A soft entry leads to a moderately full-bodied palate with silky tannins and lush, rounded fruit. Supple and flavorful. Will be very good on release. Drink now.

Meyney
1998 Cru Bourgeois, St. Estèphe $NA.   85-89

Deep, saturated ruby with a slight purple overtone. Lean mineral and red fruit aromas show an herbal accent. A lush entry leads to a medium-bodied palate with grippy tannins through the finish. Ripe and stylish. Midterm cellar candidate.

Le Meynieu
1998 Cru Bourgeois, Haut-Médoc $NA.   NR

Scale: Superlative (96-100), Exceptional (90-95), Highly Recommended (85-89), Recommended (80-84), Not Recommended (Under 80)

Meyre
1998 Cru Bourgeois, Haut-Médoc $NA. **90-95**

Deep, saturated purple hue. Intense, exotic flower, spice, and mineral aromas. A rich entry leads to a supple, rounded palate with elegant and perfectly balanced tannins. Like drinking liquid silk. Very enticing. Drink now or later.

La Mission Haut-Brion
1997 Rouge, Pessac-Léognan $NA. **85-89**

Deep ruby-purple. Moderately full-bodied. Balanced acidity. Highly extracted. Moderately tannic. Black fruits, tobacco, earth. Quite aromatic, with a complex array of flavors on the palate. Firm and quite angular, with a rather unyielding quality. Finishes on an astringent note. Perhaps it will open with time.

La Mission Haut-Brion
1998 Rouge, Pessac-Léognan $NA. **96-100**

Very deep blackish ruby hue with a purple edge. Brooding mineral, tobacco, and black fruit aromas. A rich entry leads to a very full-bodied palate with robust velvety tannins. Firm through the finish. Carries tons of extract and concentration, without being over-extracted. Will need time, but shows all the signs of developing in a profound manner. Long-term cellar.

Les Moines
1998 Médoc $NA. **80-84**

Monbrison
1997 Margaux $NA. **85-89**

Bright ruby cast. Moderately full-bodied. Low acidity. Moderately extracted. Mildly tannic. Red fruits. High-toned red fruit aromas lead a firm palate. Finishes with some dry, fine-grained tannins. Has some structure, but still very forward.

1998 Margaux $NA. **85-89**

Deep, saturated blackish purple hue. Generous berry fruit and mineral aromas jump from the glass. A rich entry leads to a supple, moderately full-bodied palate with ripe tannins. Carries a slightly bitter edge through the finish. Midterm cellar candidate.

Montrose
1997 St. Estèphe $NA. **90-95**

Bright ruby-purple. Medium-bodied. Balanced acidity. Moderately extracted. Mildly tannic. Vanilla, black fruits, minerals. Features a fragrant, perfumed, floral nose with ripeness evident. A soft and rounded attack features some mild yet adequate tannins that kick in on the midpalate. Lighter framed, but showing solid structure and grip.

Moulin de la Rose
1998 Cru Bourgeois, St. Julien $NA. **85-89**

Vibrant, bright purple hue. Generous, high-toned berry and mineral aromas. A rich entry leads to a moderately full-bodied palate with robust velvety tannins. Flavors accelerate through the coffee-accented finish. Chunky. Midterm cellar candidate.

Moulin Riche
1998 Cru Bourgeois, St. Julien $NA. **85-89**

Deep, saturated brilliant purple hue. Forward licorice, mineral, and flower aromas stand out. A lush entry leads to a medium-bodied palate with very pure fruit-centered flavors, lush tannins, and uplifting fruit acidity. Crisply flavored. Drink now or later.

du Moulin Rouge
1998 Cru Bourgeois, Haut-Médoc $NA.   **90-95**

Deep ruby hue with slight purple highlights. Attractive, perfumed flower, red fruit, and vanilla aromas. A lush entry leads to an extremely flavorful and supple, medium-bodied palate with a wave of grainy tannins through the finish. Reminiscent of a baby Cheval Blanc. Drink now or later.

Mouton Rothschild
1997 Pauillac $NA.   **92**

Very deep, opaque purple. Brooding black fruit and mineral aromas are rather reserved. A firm entry leads a full-bodied, rich mouthfeel with gripping tannins. Shows good grip and intensity, but almost approachable already. Should drink well over the next decade. Drink now or later.

1998 Pauillac $NA.   **90-95**

Very deep purple hue. Brooding black fruit, mineral, and lead pencil aromas. A rich entry leads to a full-bodied palate with big, chunky tannins. Quite weighty, with a firm but rounded tannic structure. Softer acidity. Needs time. Long-term cellar.

Muret
1998 Cru Bourgeois, Haut-Médoc $NA.   **NR**

de Myrat
1997 Sauternes $NA.   **90-95**

Bright golden hue. Full-bodied. Balanced acidity. Moderately extracted. Honey, oranges, spice. Extremely aromatic and flavorful, with a full though well-balanced mouthfeel. Shows good complexity of flavor and solid grip on the finish.

1998 Sauternes $NA.   **NR**

Nairac
1997 Barsac $NA.   **85-89**

Very deep yellow-gold. Full-bodied. Full acidity. Moderately extracted. Honey. Quite rich and viscous, with vibrant acidity. Impressively structured, but lacking somewhat in complexity. Perhaps it will come with age.

1998 Barsac $NA.   **80-84**

Noaillac
1998 Médoc $NA.   **80-84**

Olivier
1997 Blanc, Pessac-Léognan $NA.   **80-84**
1998 Blanc, Pessac-Léognan $NA.   **80-84**
1997 Rouge, Pessac-Léognan $NA.   **80-84**
1998 Rouge, Pessac-Léognan $NA.   **80-84**

Les Ormes de Pez
1997 St. Estèphe $NA.   **80-84**

Les Ormes de Pez
1998 St. Estèphe $NA.   **85-89**

Brilliant purple hue. Aromatically subdued, with a high-toned berry and anise note. A lush entry leads to a moderately full-bodied palate with astringent tannins. Very ripe, yet showing a green edge. Lenghty, flavorful finish. Drink now or later.

Scale: Superlative (96-100), Exceptional (90-95), Highly Recommended (85-89), Recommended (80-84), Not Recommended (Under 80)

550

Palmer

1997 Margaux $NA.   90-95

Deep ruby-purple. Moderately full-bodied. Low acidity. Highly extracted. Moderately tannic. Brown spices, black fruits. Shows a spicy quality throughout. Thick and rich in the mouth, with textured tannins. Chewy, forward, and generous, but retains some structural integrity.

Paloumey

1998 Cru Bourgeois, Haut-Médoc $NA.   85-89

Bright, vibrant purple hue. Generous, complex lead pencil, spice, and game aromas. A lush entry leads to a soft, medium-bodied palate with silky tannins. Lighter in style, but harmonious and very tasty. Drink now.

Pape Clement

1997 Blanc, Pessac-Léognan $NA.   90-95

Full green-straw cast. Moderately full-bodied. Balanced acidity. Moderately extracted. Yeast, ripe lemons, smoke. A forward, smoky nose leads a full and rounded palate with some mineral grip to the finish. Showing quite well already.

1998 Blanc, Pessac-Léognan $NA.   85-89

Brilliant, saturated greenish yellow cast. Aromatically subdued, with waxy nuances and an oaky undertone beginning to emerge. A rich entry leads to a full-bodied palate with clean, rounded acidity. Intense, if rather subdued at present. Drink now or later.

1997 Rouge, Pessac-Léognan $NA.   80-84
1998 Rouge, Pessac-Léognan $NA.   90-95

Opaque blackish purple hue. Intense spice and tobacco aromas show lots of breed and are already quite Graves-like. A rich entry leads to a moderately full-bodied palate with grippy tannins and tons of flavor. Exotic and powerful. Midterm cellar candidate.

Patache d'Aux

1998 Médoc $NA.   80-84

Pauillac (Latour's third label)

1997 Pauillac $NA.   85-89

Deep blackish ruby color. Medium-bodied. Balanced acidity. Moderately extracted. Mildly tannic. Minerals, black fruits. Rather green in aromatics, with a firm, minerally palate. Clean and well-balanced.

1998 Pauillac $NA.   80-84

Paveil de Luze

1998 Cru Bourgeois, Margaux $NA.   80-84

Pavie

1997 St. Emilion $NA.   90-95

Bright blackish ruby hue with a purple cast. Moderately full-bodied. Balanced acidity. Moderately extracted. Mildly tannic. Red fruits, minerals. Aromatic and fruit centered, with a lighter-styled though supple and elegant mouthfeel. Well-balanced, with good grip to the finish.

1998 St. Emilion $NA.   90-95

Brilliant deep purple hue. Intense, exotic coffee, spice, and black fruit aromas. A rich entry leads to a full-bodied palate with grippy tannins and solid balancing acidity. Very big and firmly structured, with good depth and intensity of flavor. Long-term cellar.

Pavie Decesse

1997 St. Emilion $NA.   85-89

Dense, opaque blackish purple hue. Full-bodied. Low acidity. Highly extracted. Quite tannic. Black fruits. Reserved aromatically, with a very dense, tightly wound palate. Big and very well extracted, if lacking some acidity. Big, chunky tannins through the finish. Will require cellaring. Perhaps over the top.

1998 St. Emilion $NA.   96-100

Very deep, vibrant purple hue. Intense vanilla, black fruit and mineral aromas. A flashy but firm entry leads to a moderately full-bodied palate with angular tannins and buoyant acidity. Shows great intensity of flavor in the mouth. Concentrated and balanced. Very stylish and pure. Midterm cellar candidate.

Pavillon Rouge du Château Margaux

1997 Margaux $NA.   85-89

Deep ruby cast. Medium-bodied. Low acidity. Moderately extracted. Mildly tannic. Dried herbs, red fruits. Features a decided herbal streak throughout. Soft and lush in the mouth, with a supple, almost fat finish.

1998 Margaux $NA.   90-95

Deep brilliant purple hue. Attractive vanilla and spice aromas turn to a firm core of mineral and black fruit flavors. A rich entry leads to a full-bodied palate with big grippy tannins. Taut finish. Well structured and balanced. Should develop well. Concentrated and ripe. Long-term cellar.

Le Petit Cheval

1998 St. Emilion $NA.   85-89

Deep, brilliant ruby hue. Subdued mineral and red fruit aromas. A firm entry leads to a moderately full-bodied palate with lean, grippy tannins that bite down on the finish. Carries an interesting minerally overtone throughout. Midterm cellar candidate.

Le Petit Mouton

1997 Pauillac $NA.   89

Very deep ruby-purple. Attractive Cassis aromas show a sweet vanilla oak accent. A soft entry leads a rounded, medium-bodied palate with supple, velvety tannins. Gentle and harmonious. Drinking beautifully now.

Petit-Village

1997 Pomerol $NA.   90-95

Deep blackish ruby hue. Medium-bodied. Balanced acidity. Moderately extracted. Mildly tannic. Brown spices, chocolate, cedar. Quite aromatic, with a soft and flavorful palate. Supple and tasty, with enough grip to lend a sense of balance.

1998 Pomerol $NA.   80-84

Peyrabon

1998 Cru Bourgeois, Haut-Médoc $NA.   80-84

de Pez

1998 Cru Bourgeois, St. Estèphe $NA.   85-89

Deep, opaque ruby hue. Forward, opulent spice box, black fruit, and mineral aromas. A lush entry leads to a moderately full-bodied palate with velvety tannins. Supple and hedonistic with very good flavor intensity. Grippy finish. Drink now or later.

Phelan-Segur

1997 St. Estèphe $NA.   NR

Scale: Superlative (96-100), Exceptional (90-95), Highly Recommended (85-89), Recommended (80-84), Not Recommended (Under 80)

552

1998 St. Estèphe $NA.   90-95

Opaque blackish purple hue. Restrained spice and mineral aromas. A concentrated entry leads to a big, full-bodied palate with firm tannins and solid grip. Shows lots of intensity and extract, yet well-balanced. Midterm cellar candidate.

Picard

1998 Cru Bourgeois, St. Estèphe $NA.   80-84

Pichon-Baron

1997 Pauillac $NA.   90-95

Bright saturated blackish ruby hue. Moderately full-bodied. Low acidity. Moderately extracted. Mildly tannic. Red fruits, briar fruits. Quite aromatic and flavorful, with a hefty fruit accent. Well-structured finish. Sturdy, hedonistic, and ripe.

1998 Pauillac $NA.   85-89

Very deep brilliant purple hue. Classic lead pencil aromas jump from the glass and show fine breed. A rich entry leads to a medium-bodied palate with rounded tannins and a touch of bitterness. Interesting, but rather shy of acidity and grip. Midterm cellar candidate.

Pichon-Lalande

1997 Pauillac $NA.   85-89

Bright ruby-purple. Moderately full-bodied. Low acidity. Moderately extracted. Mildly tannic. Black fruits. Rather thick in the mouth, and lacking a bit for grip. Full and flavorful finish without any greenness. Drinkable early.

1998 Pauillac $NA.   80-84

Picque-Caillou

1997 Blanc, Pessac-Léognan $NA.   NR

1998 Blanc, Pessac-Léognan $NA.   80-84

1997 Rouge, Pessac-Léognan $NA.   85-89

Bright blackish purple. Medium-bodied. Low acidity. Moderately extracted. Mildly tannic. Black fruits, tobacco. Quite aromatic, with a soft, lush, ripe palate feel. Flavorful and supple. Will provide pleasant early drinking.

1998 Rouge, Pessac-Léognan $NA.   90-95

Deep, saturated blackish purple hue. Generous, ripe black fruit and mineral aromas. A rich entry leads to a thick, full-bodied palate with big velvety tannins. Shows a range of terroir derived flavors through the finish. Long-term cellar.

Plantey

1998 Cru Bourgeois, Pauillac $NA.   80-84

La Pointe

1997 Pomerol $NA.   85-89

Blackish ruby hue with a slight fade. Medium-bodied. Low acidity. Moderately extracted. Moderately tannic. Earth, black fruits. Pleasantly aromatic, with a core of dark fruit flavors in the mouth. Lighter in style. Rather soft, with a finish that falls a bit short.

1998 Pomerol $NA.   85-89

Brilliant, vibrant purple hue. Flashy aromas carry a big vanillin oak influence and a ripe berry core. A lush entry leads to a rounded, moderately full-bodied palate with rich tannins and decent acidity. Will be rather oak dominated, but shows very pure and exotic fruit. Drink now or later.

Pomys
1998 Cru Bourgeois, St. Estèphe $NA.   80-84

Pontet-Canet
1997 Pauillac $NA.   85-89

Bright ruby-purple. Moderately full-bodied. Low acidity. Moderately extracted. Mildly tannic. Brown spices, black fruits. Full, thick, and chunky, with a big, ripe character. No greenness, but a tad hot. Lacks a bit for grip.

1998 Pauillac $NA.   85-89

Deep, brilliant purple hue. Very stylish lead pencil and mineral aromas. A rich entry leads to a moderately full-bodied palate with grippy tannins. Rather shy of acidity. Lush, yet austere at the same time. Well-balanced and showing some complexities. Should develop. Midterm cellar candidate.

Poujeaux
1997 Moulis $NA.   NR
1998 Moulis $NA.   85-89

Deep, opaque blackish purple hue. Subdued black fruit and plum aromas. A lush entry leads to a full-bodied, fleshy palate with big rounded tannins and a firm minerally undercurrent. Stylish. Should develop well. Drink now or later.

Preuillac
1998 Médoc $NA.   85-89

Dark, saturated ruby-purple hue. Generous, intense black cherry and vanilla aromas. A smooth entry leads to a moderately full-bodied palate with drying tannins. Concentrated, stylish, and supple. Should drink well early. Drink now or later.

Prieure-Lichine
1997 Margaux $NA.   80-84
1998 Margaux $NA.   85-89

Opaque, saturated blackish purple hue. Subdued aromas hint at brooding black fruits. A ripe entry leads to a fat, full-bodied palate with lean undertones. Slightly green through the finish. Midterm cellar candidate (3–6 years).

Rabaud-Promis
1997 Sauternes $NA.   90-95

Bright yellow-gold. Moderately full-bodied. Balanced acidity. Moderately extracted. Apricots, citrus, honey. Racy and bright in structure, with a perfumed quality. Well structured, with excellent balance between sweetness and acidity. Intense and lengthy, with a long life ahead of it.

1998 Sauternes $NA.   90-95

Deep yellow golden hue. Intense, clean pear and honey aromas. A rich entry leads to a full-bodied palate with moderate sweetness and balanced acidity. Shows good intensity and cut. Will develop nicely. Midterm cellar candidate.

Rahoul
1997 Blanc, Graves $NA.   85-89

Bright straw with a greenish cast. Medium-bodied. Balanced acidity. Moderately extracted. Citrus, smoke. Aromatic and flavorful, with a crisp and vibrant mouthfeel. Rounded, clean finish. Good snap.

1998 Blanc, Graves $NA.   80-84
1997 Rouge, Graves $NA.   80-84

Scale: Superlative (96-100), Exceptional (90-95), Highly Recommended (85-89), Recommended (80-84), Not Recommended (Under 80)

554

1998 Rouge, Graves $NA.   85-89

Deep, bright violet-red hue. Subdued mineral and cedar aromas. A lush entry leads to a medium-bodied palate with silky tannins. Harmonious, forward, soft, and well-balanced. Should drink well early. Drink now or later.

Ramafort

1998 Médoc $NA.   85-89

Dark, saturated ruby-purple hue. Deep, brooding black fruit aromas. A smooth entry leads to a moderately full-bodied palate with thick tannins. Good weight and flesh with softer acids. A rich, broad style. Drink now.

Ramage La Batisse

1998 Haut-Médoc $NA.   85-89

Deep, saturated ruby-purple hue. Forward cassis and vanilla aromas. A smooth entry leads to a moderately full-bodied palate with thick, robust tannins. Rich, with good weight and flavor intensity. Minerally tannins close down on the finish. Needs time. Midterm cellar candidate.

Rausan-Segla

1997 Margaux $NA.   85-89

Bright ruby-purple. Medium-bodied. Balanced acidity. Moderately extracted. Mildly tannic. Vanilla, black fruits. A toasty nose leads a palate that features enough acidity to lend a sense of balance. High-toned flavors have solid persistence.

1998 Margaux $NA.   90-95

Brilliant, saturated ruby hue with a subtle purple overtone. Generous black fruit and vanilla aromas are ripe and stylish. A lush entry leads to a supple, medium-bodied palate with rounded tannins. Very well-balanced. Forward and lush. Drink now or later.

Rauzan-Gassies

1997 Margaux $NA.   85-89

Bright purple. Medium-bodied. Low acidity. Moderately extracted. Mildly tannic. Red berries. Rich, round, and thick, with fruity, high-toned flavors. Soft and supple tannins emerge on the finish to lend some structure. Very forward.

1998 Margaux $NA.   85-89

Brilliant ruby hue with a slight purple cast. Ripe red fruit and chocolate aromas. A lush entry leads to a moderately full-bodied palate with supple tannins. Rounded and elegant with a well-balanced finish. Will age gracefully. Midterm cellar candidate.

Rayne-Vigneau

1997 Sauternes $NA.   80-84

1998 Sauternes $NA.   85-89

Deep yellow-straw hue. Intense pineapple and smoke aromas. A rich entry leads to a sweet, moderately full-bodied palate with decent acidity. Rather straightforward but should develop a bit. Drink now or later.

Reysson

1998 Cru Bourgeois, Haut-Médoc $NA.   80-84

Rieussec

1997 Sauternes $NA.   90-95

Very deep golden hue. Full-bodied. Low acidity. Moderately extracted. Browned butter, smoke, tropical fruits. Quite aromatic and flavorful, with deep, complex flavors. Extremely rich, thick, and viscous. Impressive and heavy. Should drink well early.

1998 Sauternes $NA.   **90-95**

Very deep yellow golden hue. Luscious pineapple and apricot aromas show a good degree of botrytis and a smoky accent. A lush entry leads to a fat, rounded, full-bodied palate with creamy acidity. Big, opulent, and very rich. A bit four square. Will be approachable in youth. Drink now or later.

Rollan de By
1998 Médoc $NA.   **90-95**

Dark, saturated ruby-purple hue. Powerful spice and rich cassis aromas explode from the glass. A smooth entry leads to a full-bodied palate with a wave of velvety tannins. Voluptuous and beautifully textured with a persistent, flavorful finish. Shows serious concentration and depth. Very stylish. Drink now or later.

Romer du Hayot
1997 Sauternes $NA.   **90-95**

Very deep golden hue. Full-bodied. Full acidity. Moderately extracted. Citrus, butter, smoke. Quite bright in structure, with vibrant acidity and citric flavors. Rich and luxuriant through the finish, with a lengthy, rounded mouthfeel.

Saint-Aubin
1998 Médoc $NA.   **NR**

Château Saint-Estèphe
1998 Cru Bourgeois, St. Estèphe $NA.   **NR**

Saint-Paul
1998 Cru Bourgeois, Haut-Médoc $NA.   **85-89**

Opaque ruby hue with purple highlights. Closed down aromatically with a solid core of brooding black fruit and mineral flavors in the mouth. A firm entry leads to a full-bodied palate with big, chunky tannins. Deep, but monolithic. Solid extract bodes well for the aging required. Long-term cellar.

Segur de Cabanac
1998 Cru Bourgeois, St. Estèphe $NA.   **80-84**

Senejac
1998 Cru Bourgeois, Haut-Médoc $NA.   **80-84**

Senilhac
1998 Cru Bourgeois, Haut-Médoc $NA.   **80-84**

Sigalas-Rabaud
1997 Sauternes $NA.   **85-89**

Bright yellow-gold. Moderately full-bodied. Low acidity. Moderately extracted. Citrus, honey. Very citric in aroma and flavor. Of moderate weight, but quite fat. Lacking acidity, but a modest level of sweetness keeps it from cloying.

1998 Sauternes $NA.   **80-84**

Sigognac
1998 Médoc $NA.   **NR**

Siran
1997 Margaux $NA.   **NR**

1998 Margaux $NA.   90-95

Deep, saturated brilliant purple hue. Exotic ginger, spice, and red fruit aromas. A lush entry leads to a rich, full-bodied palate with waves of velvety tannins. Very forward and supple with lots of fruit intensity. Lengthy finish. Will be approachable early. Drink now or later.

Smith-Haut-Lafitte

1997 Blanc, Pessac-Léognan $NA.   90-95

Bright yellow-straw cast. Moderately full-bodied. Balanced acidity. Moderately extracted. Dried herbs, citrus, minerals. Developed herbal aromas lead to a rich, rounded palate. Has fine acids for balance. Refined, with good length and intensity.

1998 Blanc, Pessac-Léognan $NA.   90-95

Bright greenish yellow hue. Intense cream, yeast, and citrus aromas show an attractive oak accent. A rich entry leads to a moderately full-bodied palate with firm acids. Rich and showy with a great deal of style. Drink now or later.

1997 Rouge, Pessac-Léognan $NA.   80-84

1998 Rouge, Pessac-Léognan $NA.   90-95

Brilliant ruby-purple hue. Extravagant, classic cedar, tobacco, and black fruit aromas. A ripe entry leads to a lush, full-bodied palate with rounded, velvety tannins. Big, but well-balanced and harmonious. Should age beautifully. Midterm cellar candidate.

Soudars

1998 Haut-Médoc $NA.   85-89

Deep ruby red hue. Generous red fruit and mineral aromas. A soft entry leads to a medium-bodied palate with drying tannins. Well gripped, with a classic austere finish and a firm minerally backbone. Drink now or later.

Le Souley Ste. Croix

1998 Cru Bourgeois, Haut-Médoc $NA.   85-89

Deep ruby hue with slight purple highlights. Fragrant berry and licorice aromas. A lush entry leads to a medium-bodied palate with a rush of velvety tannins. Supple, but rather closed through the finish. Should develop. Midterm cellar candidate.

Suau

1997 Barsac $NA.   80-84

1998 Barsac $NA.   85-89

Very deep yellow golden hue. Rich butter, cream, and honey aromas. A rich entry leads to a moderately full-bodied palate with racy pineapple flavors, good acidity, and balanced sweetness. Clean finish. Drink now or later.

Suduiraut

1997 Sauternes $NA.   96-100

Very deep yellow-gold. Moderately full-bodied. Balanced acidity. Moderately extracted. Honey, citrus, spice. Aromatic and flavorful, with a pure, well-structured palate feel. Showing great intensity and length. Complex and fine.

1998 Sauternes $NA.   80-84

Talbot

1997 St. Julien $NA.   85-89

Deep ruby-purple. Moderately full-bodied. Low acidity. Moderately extracted. Mildly tannic. Black fruits, minerals. Rather reserved aromatically, with a big, rich, chunky palate feel. Lacking grip, but should drink well early.

1998 St. Julien $NA. 90-95
Opaque blackish purple hue. Generous spice, earth, and anise aromas are rather unusual. A lush entry leads to a moderately full-bodied palate with good grip and supple tannins. Flavorful and intense with a chocolatey finish. Drink now or later.

Le Temple
1998 Médoc $NA. 80-84

Terrey Gros Cailloux
1998 Cru Bourgeois, St. Julien $NA. 80-84

Tour Blanche
1998 Médoc $NA. 85-89
Dark, opaque ruby-purple hue. Fantastic toasted oak and cassis aromas jump from the glass. A smooth entry leads to a thick, moderately full-bodied palate with plush tannins and softer acids. Lingering, flavorful finish. Lush and ripe. Drink now.

La Tour Blanche
1997 Sauternes $NA. 90-95
Deep golden hue. Moderately full-bodied. Balanced acidity. Moderately extracted. Tropical fruits, honey, cream. Aromatic and flavorful, with very ripe and complex flavors. Elegant and well-balanced through the finish.

1998 Sauternes $NA. 90-95
Very deep old-gold hue. Intense, generous smoke, tropical fruit, and yeast aromas. A rich entry leads to a rounded, moderately full-bodied palate with good, yet balanced sweetness. Smoky, complex finish. Very stylish. Drink now or later.

La Tour de By
1997 Médoc $NA. 80-84
1998 Médoc $NA. 80-84

La Tour Carnet
1997 Haut-Médoc $NA. 80-84
1998 Haut-Médoc $NA. NR

La Tour Figeac
1997 St. Emilion $NA. 80-84
1998 St. Emilion $NA. 90-95
Deep, saturated ruby-purple hue. Generous chocolate, black fruit, and spice aromas. A lush entry leads to a moderately full-bodied palate with velvety tannins. Shows fine grip and lots of depth. Very lengthy finish. Stylish. Long-term cellar.

La Tour Haut-Brion
1998 Rouge, Pessac-Léognan $NA. 90-95
Very deep, opaque ruby-purple hue. Generous spice and black fruit aromas. A rich entry leads to a moderately full-bodied palate with lush, velvety tannins. Rounded and harmonious, with excellent balance and solid acidic grip. May be approachable young but should develop beautifully. Drink now or later.

Tour du Haut-Moulin
1998 Cru Bourgeois, Haut-Médoc $NA. 85-89
Bright ruby-purple hue. Generous vanilla and berry aromas. A lush entry leads to a rounded, moderately full-bodied palate with velvety tannins. Flavorful and harmonious with a firm smoky finish. Drink now or later.

La Tour de Mons
1998 Cru Bourgeois, Margaux $NA.   80-84

Tour de Pez
1998 Cru Bourgeois, St. Estèphe $NA.   85-89

Deep, saturated ruby hue. Subdued aromas show a brooding black fruit, licorice, and earth undertone. A rich entry leads to a lush, medium-bodied palate with supple tannins. Rounded, flavorful finish. Stylish. Drink now.

Tour des Termes
1998 Cru Bourgeois, St. Estèphe $NA.   85-89

Opaque ruby-purple hue. Pure, high-toned berry and flower aromas. A lush entry leads to a medium-bodied palate with rounded tannins and a bit of an edge to the finish. Stylish, with an uplifting finish. Drink now or later.

Tronquoy Lalande
1998 Cru Bourgeois, St. Estèphe $NA.   85-89

Deep, opaque purple hue. Intense, lush red fruit and vanilla aromas. A rich entry leads to a stylish, medium-bodied palate with supple tannins. Good grip through the finish. Very strylish. Midterm cellar candidate.

Troplong-Mondot
1998 St. Emilion $NA.   85-89

Deep, opaque purple hue. Generous vanilla and black fruit aromas show great persistence. A rich entry leads to a full-bodied palate with thick, velvety tannins. Rather fat and chunky with shy acidity. Somewhat ponderous. Drink now.

Trottevielle
1998 St. Emilion $NA.   90-95

Very deep blackish purple hue. Deep, brooding mineral, licorice, and black fruit aromas. A firm entry leads to a full-bodied palate with a big wave of velvety tannins. Shows lots of intensity and richness with acidity providing uplifting flavors through the finish. Very tasty. Midterm cellar candidate.

Vieux Château Certan
1997 Pomerol $NA.   90-95

Deep blackish purple hue. Moderately full-bodied. Balanced acidity. Moderately extracted. Moderately tannic. Sweet herbs, red fruit. Full and forward aromas follow through quite well on the palate. Ripe and rich, with soft, rounded tannins. Very attractive early drinking.

1998 Pomerol $NA.   80-84

Vieux Robin
1998 Médoc $NA.   85-89

Dark, brilliant ruby-purple hue. Pleasant vanilla and red fruit aromas are quite generous. A smooth attack leads to a medium-bodied palate with velvety tannins. Fruit forward in an impressive modern style. Drink now or later.

de Villambis
1998 Cru Bourgeois, Haut-Médoc $NA.   85-89

Bright ruby-purple hue. Generous vanilla and red fruit aromas. A lush entry leads to a velvety, medium-bodied palate with big but supple tannins. Rich, fullish finish. Drink now or later.

Villegeorge
1998 Cru Bourgeois, Haut-Médoc $NA. NR

Villemaurine
1997 St. Emilion $NA. 85-89

Bright ruby hue. Medium-bodied. Balanced acidity. Moderately extracted. Mildly tannic. Red fruits, brown spices, minerals. Aromatic and quite flavorful, with real complexity. Lighter in style, though very well-balanced, with grip to the finish.

1998 St. Emilion $NA. 85-89

Deep, brilliant purple hue. Forward, high-toned tobacco, herb, mineral, and flower aromas. A rich entry leads to a medium-bodied palate with lush velvety tannins. Finishes on an herbaceous spicy note. Rather shy of acidity but interesting. Drink now.

d'Yquem
1994 Sauternes $NA. 98

Deep, exotic yellow golden hue. Intense apricot, honey, and vanilla aromas jump from the glass and show tremendous complexity. A viscous entry leads to a full-bodied palate with lots of sweetness and solid balancing acidity. A real mouthful at present, but already showing amazing complexity. Attractive, but far better with lots of age. Try in a decade or two. Long-term cellar.

twenty-seven

≈

France
Burgundy

≈

Burgundy Market Overview

Burgundy is a complex region due to both human and geographical factors. The elusive nature of the pursuit of perfection with Pinot Noir and Chardonnay on Burgundy's "golden" slopes may well make the rewards of success so much sweeter for the many collectors in the United States who pay large sums for wines of miniscule production.

The market for Burgundy is currently at an all-time high with prices having been pushed up by demand for a very successful, large vintage in 1996. Small harvests in 1997 and 1998 have caused another bout of price hikes. The increase in prices has not been uniform. Many négociants, who had to purchase fruit at very inflated prices demanded by the growers, will have to raise prices more than the estate producers will. The position for the négociants is thus worse than that for the top domaines. The latter will probably sell their wines with little effort in 1999 and 2000 whereas the former may well encounter problems with passing on inflated prices for the 1997 and 1998 wines. The only thing that may help to offset the significant cost of Burgundy will be a weakening euro and a strengthening dollar and the decision by some large concerns to sell at a loss.

There is an increasing number of younger, quality-minded producers in Burgundy these days but it is still too easy for mediocre Burgundy producers to sell their production from glamorous appellations at high prices not warranted by the quality of the wine. To avoid becoming the unwitting recipient of expensive, pale, and flavor-challenged wine from a producer pumping out (by fair means or foul) more wine than conscience or law should permit, it is very important to have a strong grasp of which producers are quality minded and which are not. If this sounds like a lot of hard work and commitment: welcome to the world of the Burgundy collector!

Key Varietals

Pinot Noir

Pinot Noir is the red wine grape of Burgundy that is most intensively planted in the northern Côte de Nuits half of the Côte d'Or. It is a tricky grape to ripen properly, not least in Burgundy. In the right hands and in the right vineyards it can produce sumptuous wines that uplift the soul. Conversely, in the wrong hands and in less favorable vineyards it will produce wine that is a shadow of its potential.

Chardonnay

Chardonnay is the white wine grape of Burgundy. It is exclusively planted in Chablis and takes over from Pinot Noir immediately south of Beaune, in the Côte de Beaune section of the southern Côte d'Or. It can produce anything from hedonistically rich wines (in Chassagne-Montrachet) and minerally, lean wines (in Chablis) to unchallenging, simple, everyday wines (in the Mâconnais) depending on the specific vineyard and how it is handled in the winery. Compared to Pinot Noir, Chardonnay is a more malleable grape in the winery. It is also easier to grow and more commercially rewarding for the grower.

Scale: Superlative (96-100), Exceptional (90-95), Highly Recommended (85-89), Recommended (80-84), Not Recommended (Under 80)

Minor varieties

Miniscule amounts of Gamay are planted in some parts of the Côte d'Or where it produces a refreshing wine for local consumption called Bourgogne-Passetoutsgrains—a more rustic version of Beaujolais. The white varieties Pinot Blanc and Pinot Gris are also planted in insignificant quantities. Both may be used to blend with Chardonnay.

Key Appellations & Styles (from North to South)

Chablis

Although part of Burgundy, Chablis is almost halfway to Paris from the Côte d'Or and is a cooler, more northerly appellation. Chablis produces Chardonnay-based wines that have the reputation of being steely, concentrated, and firm—with an ability to age. This character is best seen in the wines from the seven impressive southerly exposed Grand Cru vineyards. There are 40 individual Premier Cru vineyards, though only 17 of these vineyard names are generally used on labels. A large quantity of generic Chablis Village wine is produced, much of it from different soils than those which made Chablis famous. Such wines may be drinkable but are not classic.

Côte de Nuits

Gevrey-Chambertin

Gevrey-Chambertin is the largest of the great appellations of the Côte de Nuits and contains the lion's share of the Grand Crus, nine, and 26 Premier Crus. As personified by the leading Grand Cru of Chambertin, the style of Gevrey's wines is full, solid, and rich. At the humbler end relatively good value can be found in a good Gevrey-Chambertin Village wine, although these wines will often be toward the lighter side. In attributing a character to Gevrey one must first point out some of the pitfalls that await anyone that blindly buys a bottle of Gevrey. The Village appellation boundaries extend further east from the

Burgundy at a Glance

Wines Reviewed:

298

Producers/Brands Represented:

34

Value Rating:

Poor

base of the slope than some might consider decent. Quality and character can vary widely and it is still depressingly easy to find an under-performing Village wine from what should be a good vintage.

Morey-Saint-Denis

Morey could be said to bridge the gap in style as well as geography between Chambolle and Gevrey. Its reputation is upheld by four Grand Cru vineyards and 20 rather small Premier Crus—the latter will challenge the expert to recall. Morey is eternally damned to be described in relation to its illustrious neighbors Chambolle and Gevrey—less structured than the latter and not quite as fruity as the former.

Chambolle-Musigny

Chambolle-Musigny is an appellation whose wines are among the easier to spot in a blind tasting, possessing as they do fruit-centered, supple characters that set them apart from the more muscular wines of Vosne-Romanée or Gevrey. Although Chambolle has two Grand Crus, it has 23 Premier Crus and a generous amount of Village acreage. By virtue of its compactness and keeping of vineyards behind the accepted eastern threshold of the Dijon-Beaune road, even a humble Chambolle-Musigny Village should carry a delightful, pure Pinot-fruit appeal. At its best, the wines of the Grand Cru, Le Musigny, strike an extraordinarily hedonistic balance that many critics consider to be close to the Holy Grail of Pinot Noir pleasure.

Vougeot

Clos-de-Vougeot, the dominating grand Cru vineyard of Vougeot, is a magic name that confers instant respectability on any bottle graced with its name. Unfortunately, as anyone who has ever cast their eyes upon the sizable walled vineyard with the Chateau de Vougeot in it midst can vouch, it is singularly unimpressive in parts with hollows that see little sun and poorly drained lower sections that are not exactly located on dizzying slopes. Extensive tastings of Clos Vougeot often fail to produce wines that are worthy of their price and pomp. Given the sum asked for Grand Cru Burgundy, this appellation should carry with it a Caveat Emptor (buyer beware) warning. The vineyard is sub-divided among at least 80 owners, some with much better situations than others. The best examples are impressive: rich and full, with less tannic structure than Vosne-Romanée Grand Crus and not as aromatic and opulent as wines from Le Musigny. Well-vinified plots on less favorable sections can also yield fine wine. Vougeot also has very small amounts of Village wine and very modest amounts of Premier Cru vineyards.

Vosne-Romanée & Flagey-Echézeaux

Price and expectations, if not outright quality, reach their peak with the wines of Vosne-Romanée and Flagey-Echézeaux. The latter's vineyards are so limited and contiguous with those of Vosne that it is often referred to in the same breath. Four of the eight Grand Cru vineyards are monopoles (owned exclusively by a single producer). The wines of Vosne have probably consumed more critics' ink over the years than most of the rest of the region put together. The finest are silky and powerful with a degree of minerality matched by austere dark fruit

Scale: Superlative (96-100), Exceptional (90-95), Highly Recommended (85-89), Recommended (80-84), Not Recommended (Under 80)

564

flavors; they are classic cellaring wines. The general style holds well throughout the Premier Crus and even the Village wines. Not many bargains will be found bearing Vosne-Romanée or Echézeaux on the label.

Nuits-Saint-Georges

The (gentler) slopes have not conferred any Grand Crus upon the Nuits-Saint-Georges appellation though it boasts 27 Premier Crus. The finest examples display a robust, solidly flavorful character with minerality and dark fruit flavors. Poor examples are lightly colored and vapid in flavor but the name will always guarantee that they will not be very cheap. In past vintages surely more wine bearing the name Nuits-Saint-Georges emerged from négociants or English wine merchants' cellars than the vineyards could conceivably produce. The name has a magical ability to sell bottles, as it became the darling of the English. Today, not everything has changed. Poor examples await anyone who buys on the appellation name alone. It pays to be picky about wines from this commune.

Côte de Beaune

Corton: Ladoix, Aloxe-Corton, and Pernand-Vergellesses

Just north of Beaune, the gentle slope of the Côte d'Or complicates matters by folding over to produce a hill that has south, east, and westerly exposures that look down on Aloxe, Ladoix, and Pernand respectively. The *mont* (hill) of Corton has given its name to the Grand Cru vineyards that wrap around its sloping section. Rather more excitement is generated, and higher prices paid, for white Corton than for red. Replanting with Chardonnay is diminishing the importance of red Corton and it is fair to say that more spectacular whites emerge from the hill of Corton than do reds. Due to differing sunlight exposure, white Corton will have a rich, full, and deeply colored character from the eastern and southern side (where the Grand Cru sub-appellation of Corton-Charlemagne is used) and will tend toward a (relatively) leaner style in the western aspects.

Beaune

The gentle slopes of Beaune's vineyards contain a whopping 44 Premier Crus, most of which are planted to Pinot Noir. It is a good source of hearty, solid Pinot Noir with a small amount of full-bodied white produced. Being a large appellation by Burgundian standards, the quality and character of its red wines will vary, sometimes showing the guts and muscle of neighboring Pommard and other times displaying the perfume and delicacy of Volnay. Beaune Premier Cru and Village wines rarely receive the acclaim of either of the two more celebrated Côte de Beaune red wine communes and are a good source of volume wine for the négociants of Beaune.

Pommard

The very name seems to suggest muscularity and depth: Pommard is where the biggest, toughest red wines of the Côte de Beaune are to be found. The style is a factor of soil type. Looking at a typical glass of dark, foursquare Pommard and ruby, perfumed wine from next-door Volnay is a stark reminder of how specific location in a geographically small area can make such a dramatic difference to the style of Pinot Noir in Burgundy. Pommard contains no Grand Crus but has 28 Premier Crus and also produces a relatively large amount of Village wine.

Volnay

The most elegant and delicately perfumed Pinot Noirs in Burgundy come from the small commune of Volnay, sandwiched between Meursault to the south and Pommard to the north. The many small producers in Volnay maintain an impressive quality level across the board and the fragrant style applies to wines throughout the appellation—at least when compared to the bigger wines of its neighbor, Pommard. Volnay produces more Premier Cru wine than Village wine—a factor that may help explain its high average quality level.

Meursault

Meursault marks the geographical transition from red wines to white wines in the Côte de Beaune. Reds produced within its boundaries come from the Volnay side of the appellation and are labeled as Volnay, with red Meursault being a very rare exception. The character of Meursault has been classically associated with hazelnuts, peaches, and cream. Certainly it is softer, more buttery, and rounder in the mouth than typical wines from Puligny or Chassagne. These classical traits are more easily identifiable in Premier Cru wines than they are in Village production. Meursault is a large commune by Burgundian standards, though as with all white Burgundy, it is very fashionable and easily sells the two million odd bottles of white wine that it produces annually.

Puligny-Montrachet

The sleepy town of Puligny-Montrachet can lay claim to being the spiritual home of Chardonnay, being host or part host (some overlap into neighboring Chassagne) to four Grand Cru vineyards and 23 Premier Cru vineyards. Chardonnay can reach an extraordinary level of ripeness and concentration from the Grand Cru vineyards, and none more so than Le Montrachet can. These rare and highly expensive wines have set the benchmark for power, intensity, finesse, and longevity that so many New World Chardonnays have aimed to emulate in spirit.

Puligny-Montrachet Premier Cru is a more affordable, though increasingly pricey proposition. The style of wine will vary, but it will generally have more minerality and taut citrus character than richer wines from neighboring Chassagne. The bulk of the appellation produces Village wine which can be of excellent quality from good producers and disappointing quality from lesser négociants and producers.

Chassagne-Montrachet

Chassagne produces both white and red wine. Its whites are far more impressive expositions of Chardonnay than its reds are of Pinot Noir. The Chassagne white style is full and rich, yet firmer than neighboring Meursault and less citrus and mineral-accented than Puligny. This rule of thumb will have many exceptions. Chassagne-Montrachet is a big commune producing as much Village wine as it does Premier Cru wine; though the former is predominantly red while the later is mainly white. Chassagne shares the Grand Cru vineyard of Le Montrachet with Puligny and is host to two other Grand Cru vineyards.

The Mâconnais

The Mâconnais is a sprawling region and is the southerly outpost of white Burgundy, containing numerous appellations. It is almost entirely devoted to the production of cheaper Chardonnay wines, often unoaked. Pouilly-Fuissé is the most highly regarded and expensive of the Mâconnais appellations, producing clean, fuller-bodied wines that occasionally see new oak barrels. The best of the rest will come bearing a Mâcon-Village appellation and can sometimes aspire to the quality levels of more illustrious appellations from the Côte de Beaune. The relatively few quality-minded producers in the Mâconnais can produce wines of the best value in the region.

Vintage Overview

1994: Red & White

1994 will be a vintage that will fade into obscurity. Rain almost washed out the vintage throughout the region and gray rot was a common affliction. Not many great wines were produced and a great many very poor wines with coarse, dilute flavors and weak colors were in evidence. Without good buying advice consumers should be cautious about any stocks of 1994 still on sale. Even some good domaines produced poor wine in such trying conditions.

1995: Reds

1995 was a significant improvement from 1994, though ripening was late due to late flowering in the spring. Harvesting conditions were complicated by rain storms that brought on rot. The 1995 reds are not of uniformly high quality though there were many good wines produced, exhibiting good concentration and firm tannins though lacking the freshness of 1993 or 1996. The best will have medium-term cellaring potential.

1995: Whites

1995 was a good year for white Burgundies on the Côte de Beaune. After a problematic flowering, a warm dry ripening season with some late rain resulted in concentrated, ripe fruit that produced thicker, lower acid wines in many cases. Many of the 1995s will be drinking well now and do not require cellaring.

1996: Reds

1996 reds from the Côte de Beaune and Côte de Nuits will be classic cellaring wines with bright acids and firm tannins. Dry conditions with warm days and cool nights allowed for intense flavors and high natural acidity. In most cases the 1997s will be drinking better than the equivalent 1996s, as the nature of the tannins is firmer in the latter case. Most producers turned large harvests, though demand will see to it that most of these wines are snapped up by collectors.

1996: Whites

1996 is an excellent vintage for stocking the cellar with white Burgundy. A warm dry ripening season featured cool nights that allowed the grapes to retain fresh acids. From Chablis to the Côte de Beaune the character of the whites was fresh and firm, with pure fruit flavors. Some greenness was occasionally noted from those that picked too soon or were not selective at harvest, but the finest wines will be long-term cellaring candidates.

1997: Reds

Coming after 1996, a big vintage producing classic cellaring wines with high acidity, the contrast was striking when the 1997s were tasted side-by-side. From 1997 expect to see ripe, rounded wines with lower acids and less tannic grip than wines from 1996. As a factor of lower concentration of acidity in the red wines of 1997, the colors were often less intense than the deep, purple-tinged wines of 1996. Aggressive tannins, quite typical for youthful Pinot Noir from Burgundy, where conspicuous by their absence. The reds will be attractive to drink young and from an investment point of view will probably always suffer in comparison to those more classic, tighter wines from 1996.

1997: Whites

The whites from the Côte de Beaune have broadly followed the same pattern as the reds in the Côte de Nuits, being subject to similar ripening and harvesting conditions. Do not expect lean, tight wines that will need cellaring. Grapes were harvested at high natural sugars, occasionally exceeding 14% potential alcohol. Acidity was generally markedly lower than 1996. Expect fatter, well colored, ripe wines that will be very pleasing from the outset. A number of fat, blowsy wines were tasted. We think it fair to say that these wines will not need much cellaring, and in most cases will be lovely on release and quite unlike the tauter, structured wines from 1996.

Best Producers: Burgundy, Cote d'Or

Premier Côte d'Or Producers (***)

- Bonneau du Martray
- Coche-Dury
- Marquis D'Angerville
- Domaine Dujac
- Louis Jadot (Premier & Grand Cru Côte d'Or Bottlings)
- Henry Jayer
- Comtes Lafon
- Domaine Leflaive
- Domaine Leroy
- Ramonet
- Romanée-Conti
- Aromand Rousseau
- Comtes George de Vogüe

Great Côte d'Or Producers (**)

- Arlot
- Auvenay
- JM Boillot
- Daniel Chopin
- J.J. Confuron
- Rene Engel
- Henri Gouges
- Grivot
- Louis Jadot
- Lafarge
- Louis Latour
- Olivier Leflaive
- Maison Leroy
- Meo-Camuzet
- Thomas Moillard
- Mongeard-Mugneret
- J. Frederic Mugnier
- H. de Montille
- Denis Mortet
- Michel Niellon
- Ponsot
- Pousse d'Or
- Remoissenet
- Georges Roumier
- Etienne Sauzet
- Christian Serafin

Dependable Côte d'Or Producers (Recommended)

These producers have impressed us. Some are new. Some are older but improving steadily. Some have done well in the past but we have not tasted enough vintages to classify them as Premier or Great yet.

- Robert Ampeau
- Robert Arnoux
- Denis Bachelet
- Ghislaine Barthod-Noëllat
- Michel Bouzereau
- Alain Burguet
- Louis Carillon
- Sylvain Cathiard
- Jean Chauvenet
- Robert Chevillon
- Bruno Clair
- Bruno Clavelier
- Jacky Confuron-Conteditot
- Joseph Drouhin
- Claude Dugat
- Bernard Dugat-Py
- Andre Esmonin
- Faiveley
- Jean-Noel Gagnard
- Gagnard-Delegrange
- Robert Groffier
- Anne Gros
- Alain Hudelot-Noëllat
- Patrick Javillier
- Francois Jobard
- Matrot
- Prince Florent de Merode
- Pierre Morey
- Albert Morot
- Philippe Naddef
- Daniel Rion
- Joseph Roty

Reviews: 1997 Vintage

Amiot-Servelle

Chambolle-Musigny, 1997 $NA. (SR)   90

Brilliant pale ruby hue. Fragrant, jammy red fruit and spice aromas. Judicious oak accent. Medium-bodied palate with rounded tannins. Supple and perfumed with a sense of richness through the finish. Eminently attractive. Drink now or later.

Chambolle-Musigny "Les Charmes," Premier Cru 1997 $52. (SR)   91

Brilliant cherry-red. Perfumed red fruit and spice aromas show generous wood influence. Medium-bodied palate with rounded tannins. Lush and attractive with a bit of weight through the finish. Drink now or later.

Chambolle-Musigny "Derriere-la-Grange," Premier Cru 1997 $66. (SR)   95

Brilliant purple. Perfumed flower, red fruit, and mineral aromas jump from the glass. Velvety palate with soft tannins. Voluptuous, but enlivened by bright acidity. A hedonistic, spicy, supple Chambolle. Drinking beautifully. Drink now or later.

Chambolle-Musigny "Les Amoureuses," Premier Cru 1997 $90. (SR)   93

Saturated brilliant ruby hue. Intense red fruit, mineral, and flower aromas are classic and seductive. Medium-bodied palate with rounded, supple tannins. Bright acidity through to the finish. A stylish, accessible wine that should develop. Mid-term cellar candidate.

Clos Vougeot, Grand Cru 1997 $78. (SR)   89

Pale ruby-red. Spicy four-square aromas accent a hearty red fruit backbone. Medium-bodied palate with ripe flavors. Fades toward the finish. Tasty, but lacking some of the grip and intensity of the Domaine's Chambolles. Drink now.

l'Arlot

Nuits St. Georges Blanc, 1997 $NA. (SR)   86

Bright straw hue. Subdued mineral and toast aromas show a subtle leesy accent. A rounded entry leads to a medium-bodied, lush palate. Very shy on the oak with solid varietal flavors. Clean and stylish. Drink now.

Nuits St. Georges "Clos des Forets" Blanc, Premier Cru 1997 $NA. (SR)   89

Brilliant yellow-straw hue. Aromatically subdued, but ripe citric flavors take on a slight tropical accent in the mouth. A rich entry leads to a moderately full-bodied palate with rounded acidity. Lush and stylish, with oak firmly in the background. Drink now.

Côtes de Nuits Villages "Clos du Chapeau," 1997 $24. (SR)   84

Beaune "Greves," Premier Cru 1997 $NA. (SR)   86

Pale ruby-red. Forward spice, earth, and mineral aromas. Medium-bodied palate with lean, angular tannins. A lighter, softer style, showing some maturity. Drink now.

Nuits St. Georges, Jeuene Vignes de "Clos des Forets" 1997 $NA. (SR)   88

Bright, highly saturated ruby-red. Powerful red fruit, mineral, and oak aromas. Rich, moderately full-bodied palate. Low in acidity but framed by firm tannins. Has the structure and concentration to develop. Mid-term cellar candidate.

Nuits St. Georges "Clos de l'Arlot," Premier Cru 1997 $47. (SR)   89

Pale ruby hue. Generous fruit, mature spice, and forest aromas. Medium-bodied palate with gripping tannins. Light in style, with delicate, elegant flavors through to the finish. Very supple and attractive. Drink now.

Vosne Romanée "Les Suchots," Premier Cru 1997 $NA. (SR)   91

Pale ruby hue. Forward red fruit, a mineral undercurrent, and a gentle oak influence mark the aromas and flavors. Medium-bodied palate with gripping tannins. Lean and flavorful. Intense, focused, and well balanced. Drink now or later.

Scale: Superlative (96-100), Exceptional (90-95), Highly Recommended (85-89), Recommended (80-84), Not Recommended (Under 80)

Nuits St. Georges "Clos des Forets," Premier Cru 1997 $50. (SR)   93
Bright, saturated ruby hue. Aromatically subdued. A core of red fruit flavors emerges on the palate. Firm mineral structure. Moderately full-bodied with gripping tannins. Long, flavorful finish. Approachable but firm. Should develop nicely. Drink now or later.

Romanée St. Vivant, Grand Cru 1997 $NA. (SR)   93
Brilliant ruby with purple highlights. Attractive flower and mineral aromas. Medium-bodied palate with lean tannins. Very elegant and complex with a taut structure. Long, perfumed finish, with a subtle taste of oak. Delightful. Drink now or later.

Côte de Nuits Villages "Clos du Chapeau," 1998 $24. (SR)   90-95
Bright, saturated purple hue. Generous sweet berry and vanilla aromas jump from the glass. A rich entry leads to a moderately full-bodied palate with chunky tannins. Very stylish, showing power, yet already approachable. Drink now or later.

Nuits St. Georges "Clos des Forets," Premier Cru 1998 $50. (SR)   90-95
Saturated bright purple hue. Forward sweet berry and mineral aromas. A rich entry leads to a moderately full-bodied palate with grippy tannins. Shows good concentration and snap through the finish. Defined by its very ripe, sweet fruit. Midterm cellar candidate.

Bonneau du Martray

Corton-Charlemagne, Grand Cru 1997 $100. (SR)   92
Bright straw hue. Aromatically restrained. Intense sea spray, mineral, and citrus flavors emerge in the mouth. Firm and structured with a steely backbone. Almost austere at present. Long-term cellar candidate.

Le Corton, Grand Cru 1997 $60. (SR)   89
Brilliant ruby-purple. Intense flower and red fruit aromas jump from the glass. Medium-bodied palate with subtle tannins. Lighter in style and elegant, but lacking real depth. A sensual, accessible wine. Forward. Drink now or later.

Bouchard Pére et Fils

Bourgogne Blanc, La Vignee 1997 $11.99. (SR)   80
Puligny-Montrachet, 1997 $51. (SR)   83
Beaune Blanc, Premier Cru 1997 $NA. (SR)   85
Meursault "Genevrieres," Premier Cru 1997 $88. (SR)   90
Brilliant straw-yellow. Attractive, forward nut and cream aromas are classic Meursault. Moderately full-bodied palate with solid balancing acidity. Flavorful and stylish with a long finish. Drink now or later.

Chevalier-Montrachet, Grand Cru 1997 $264. (SR)   92
Straw-yellow. Exotic, generous ginger, coconut, and tropical fruit aromas jump from the glass. Full-bodied mouthfeel with richness and intensity. Approachable now but should hold and develop well over the next few years. Drink now or later.

Bourgogne Rouge, La Vignee 1997 $11.99. (SR)   83
Gevrey-Chambertin, 1997 $38. (SR)   86
Saturated ruby hue. Subdued mineral and berry aromas. Medium-bodied palate with lush tannins and ripe fruit. Rounded, supple finish. Drink now.

Beaune "Clos de la Mousse," 1997 $40. (SR)   85
Volnay "Caillerets," Premier Cru 1997 $55. (SR)   88
Saturated ruby-purple. Attractive, high-toned anise and mineral aromas. Moderately light-bodied palate with crisp tannins and attractive fruit flavors. Feminine and stylish. Drink now.

Nuits-St.-Georges "Clos St. Marc," Premier Cru 1997 $67. (SR)   87
Deeply saturated ruby-red. Generous black fruit, vanillin, and mineral aromas. Medium-bodied palate with chunky tannins. Shows some richness, but overall rather clean and correct. Drink now or later.

Le Corton, Grand Cru 1997 $88. (SR)   **88**

Deeply saturated ruby hue. Earth, baking spice, subtle fruit. Full-bodied palate with big tannins. Chunky and four-square. Needs time. Long-term cellar candidate.

Michel Bouzereau

Meursault "Les Grands Charrons," 1997 $45. (SR)   **87**

Brilliant straw-yellow. Lean mineral aromas. Medium-bodied palate. Crisp acidity. Forward and stylish with a soft finish. Drink now.

Meursault "Les Tessons," 1997 $50. (SR)   **89**

Brilliant straw-yellow. Forward smoky and subtle vanilla aromas. Medium-bodied palate. Balanced acidity. Light and delicate style. Drink now or later.

Meursault "Charmes," Premier Cru 1997 $65. (SR)   **90**

Brilliant yellow. Exotic fruits, sweet vanilla, and clean yeasty aromas with a sweet vanilla accent. Medium-bodied palate. Richness buoyed by zesty acidity. Very long finish. Hedonistic, but clean, pure, and well balanced. Drink now.

Bourgogne Blanc, 1998 $14.99. (SR)   **80-84**

Meursault "Les Grands Charrons," 1998 $45. (SR)   **85-89**

Bright, pale yellow-gold. Expressive pear and citrus nose. Moderately full-bodied with firm acids and a minerally backbone. Well gripped with a steely finish. Drink now or later.

Meursault "Les Tessons," 1998 $55. (SR)   **85-89**

Brilliant yellow-straw hue. Clean, rich aromas of butter, pears, and apples. A generous, round entry leads to a moderately full-bodied palate. Showing a good crisp, citric backbone, but quite forward. Drink now or later.

Puligny-Montrachet "Champ-Gain," Premier Cru 1998 $60. (SR)   **85-89**

Bright yellow-straw hue. Ripe citrus and yeast dominated aromas. Moderately full-bodied with a very ripe, almost fat mouthfeel. Quite forward. Drink now.

Meursault "Genevrieres," Premier Cru 1998 $65. (SR)   **90-95**

Deep, golden yellow hue. Baked pear and nut aromas are very ripe, forward, and expressive. Moderately full-bodied, with lots of weight, and clean yeasty flavors lending complexity through the finish. Forward, but with the acidic structure to age. Drink now or later.

Meursault "Charmes," Premier Cru 1998 $65. (SR)   **90-95**

Bright yellow-straw hue. Firm minerally aromas show a concentrated citric undertone. Unevolved on the moderately full-bodied palate, with lots of grip and structure. Shows lots of stuffing. Bodes well for aging. Midterm cellar candidate.

Louis Carillon

Puligny-Montrachet, 1997 $48.50. (SR)   **90**

Brilliant straw-yellow. Forward, vibrant sea spray, yeast, and citrus aromas. Medium-bodied palate with racy acidity. Shows lots of character and complexity. Drink now or later.

Puligny-Montrachet "Les Champs-Canet," Premier Cru 1997 $68.50. (SR)   **90**

Brilliant straw-yellow. Vibrant lemon cream, mineral, and toast aromas. Moderately full-bodied palate with gripping acidity. Fresh, complex finish. Drink now or later.

Puligny-Montrachet "Les Combettes," Premier Cru 1997 $73.50. (SR)   **91**

Brilliant straw-yellow. Fresh, aromatic mineral, sea spray, and citrus aromas. Medium-bodied palate with racy acidity. Crisp, stylish finish. Drink now or later.

Puligny-Montrachet "Les Perrieres," Premier Cru 1997 $63.50. (SR)   **93**

Brilliant yellow. Tremendous nut, cream, and mineral aromas. Moderately full-bodied palate with rounded acidity. Weighty but very fresh and delicate in flavor. Drink now or later.

Scale: Superlative (96-100), Exceptional (90-95), Highly Recommended (85-89), Recommended (80-84), Not Recommended (Under 80)

Puligny Montrachet "Les Referts," Premier Cru 1997 $NA. (SR) 92

Brilliant yellow. Very aromatic, featuring fresh, spicy ginger and citrus. Medium-bodied palate with stylish, delicate flavors. Long finish. Drink now or later.

Bienvenues-Batard-Montrachet, Grand Cru 1997 $165. (SR) 94

Deep straw-yellow. Fantastic toasted coconut, ginger, and spice aromas. Moderately full-bodied palate. High acidity. Already showing some complexity, but very well structured. Attractive now. Should develop beautifully in the bottle. Drink now or later.

Yves Chaley

Hautes Côtes de Nuits Rouge, "Cuvee de la Tour Saint Denis"
Vieilles Vignes 1997 $NA. (SR) 89

Brilliant ruby-purple hue. Magnificent flower, mineral, and red fruit aromas. A lean entry leads to a medium-bodied palate with grippy tannins. Shows great cut. Very stylish and taut with a flash of wood through the finish. Drink now or later.

Hautes Côtes de Nuits Blanc, Clonal Selection 1998 $NA. (SR) 85-89

Deep yellow-straw hue. Very generous cream, mineral, and ripe fruit aromas. A lush entry leads to a medium-bodied palate with sharp acidity. Rounded, yet firm. Drink now or later.

Hautes Côtes de Nuits Blanc, Selection Masale 1998 $NA. (SR) 85-89

Deep yellow-straw hue. Aromatically reserved, with a firm minerally array of flavors. A lean entry leads to a medium-bodied palate with sharp acidity, and a touch of nuttiness to the finish. Stylish. Drink now or later.

Chartron et Trebuchet

Bourgogne Blanc, Vieilles Vignes, Cuvee de Jean Chartron 1997 $18. (SR) 88

Bright straw hue. Generous, leesy, creamy aromas. A lush entry leads to a weighty, moderately full-bodied palate with rounded acidity. Quite flavorful, with crisp acidity through the finish. Drink now.

Pouilly-Fuisse, Domaine de la Chapelle 1997 $NA. (SR) 85

Rich straw-yellow. Lean, flinty, mineral aromas. Rounded, medium-bodied mouthfeel with creamy acidity. Buttery finish. Drink now.

Rully "La Chaume," 1997 $22. (SR) 90

Deep straw hue. Generous toasty aromas carry a sweet vanilla accent. A crisp entry leads to a medium-bodied palate with a solid acidic cut. Crisp and stylish with a lengthy finish. Drink now or later.

Saint-Romain, 1997 $NA. (SR) 85

Pale straw hue. Aromatically reserved, with subdued minerally undertones. A lean entry leads to a medium-bodied palate with a rounded mouthfeel. Lacks somewhat for intensity of flavor. Drink now.

Saint-Aubin "La Chatoniere," Premier Cru 1997 $30. (SR) 87

Pale straw hue. A crisp entry leads to a lean, medium-bodied palate with vibrant acidity. Steely, wood accented finish. May open with a little further age. Drink now or later.

Meursault, 1997 $45. (SR) 89

Pale straw-yellow. Aromatically reserved. Structured richness and breadth in the mouth. Moderately full-bodied with creamy acidity. Rich finish. Hint of sweet wood. Should open. Drink now or later.

Chassagne-Montrachet "Morgeots," Premier Cru 1997 $65. (SR) 92

Bright straw-yellow. Attractive yeast, citrus, and vanilla aromas. Medium-bodied palate. Bright structural acidity. Expands in the mouth as the flavors accelerate through the finish. Fine grip and intensity. Drink now or later.

Puligny-Montrachet "Les Pucelles," Premier Cru 1997 $80. (SR)   **89**
Bright straw-yellow. Classic pear, peach, and sweet oak aromas. Moderately full-bodied palate with rounded acidity. Weighty and creamy. Should develop over the near term, but lacks taut structure. Attractive nonetheless. Drink now.

Puligny-Montrachet "Clos du Caillerets," Premier Cru 1997 $85. (SR)   **92**
Straw-yellow. Generous fruit aromas. Oak and leesy accents. Moderately full-bodied palate. Precise. Well structured and intense. Should open with age. Mid-term cellar candidate.

Chevalier-Montrachet "Clos des Chevaliers," Grand Cru 1997 $225. (SR)   **91**
Brilliant yellow-gold. Reserved vanilla and mineral aromas. Weighty, full-bodied mouthfeel. Rich in style with a touch of viscosity. Impressive, but on the fat side. Drink now or later.

Corton-Charlemagne, Grand Cru 1997 $NA. (SR)   **95**
Brilliant straw hue. Fresh, classic citrus, sea spray, and toast aromas. Full-bodied mouthfeel with racy acids. Well structured. Power and grace. Enticing now and already developing complexity, but will age beautifully. Drink now or later.

Bourgogne Rouge, Vieilles Vignes, Cuvee des Jean Chartron 1997 $NA. (SR) **80**
Mercurey, 1997 $NA. (SR)   **87**
Brilliant ruby-purplepurple hue. Attractive minerally red fruit and toast aromas. A lean entry leads to a medium-bodied mouthfeel. Subtle tannins, but really great acidity which makes for an intense, flavorful finish. Very stylish and well balanced. Drink now.

Pommard, 1997 $NA. (SR)   **84**
Aloxe-Corton, 1997 $NA. (SR)   **88**
Brilliant, saturated ruby-red. Subdued red fruit and mineral aromas. Flavorful, medium-bodied palate. Gripping tannins and juicy acidity. Lighter in style but intensely flavored. Drink now.

Chassagne-Montrachet "Les Benoites," Rouge 1997 $NA. (SR)   **89**
Brilliant ruby-purple. Intense, forward black cherry and vanilla aromas. Moderately full-bodied palate with lean tannins and crisp acidity. Deeply flavored, with a mouthwatering, flavorful finish. Lively. Drink now or later.

Gevrey-Chambertin, 1997 $NA. (SR)   **85**
Mazis-Chambertin, Grand Cru 1997 $NA. (SR)   **93**
Brilliant ruby-purple. Opulent flower and red fruit aromas jump from the glass. Moderately full-bodied. Intensely flavored palate. Angular tannins. Extremely long, but rather delicate. Chambolle-like. Drink now or later.

Bourgogne Blanc, Vieilles Vignes, Cuvee Jean Chartron 1998 $NA. (SR)   **85-89**
Brilliant yellow-straw hue. Leesy, yeasty aromas. A crisp entry leads to a medium-bodied palate with racy acids. Showing some old vine intensity and lots of flavor. Drink now.

Saint-Aubin "Murget," Premier Cru 1998 $NA. (SR)   **80-84**
Meursault, 1998 $NA. (SR)   **85-89**
Deep straw hue. Smoky, toasty aromas. A firm entry leads to a moderately full-bodied palate with racy acids. A lean style, may reveal more with time. Midterm cellar candidate.

Chassagne-Montrachet, 1998 $NA. (SR)   **90-95**
Brilliant yellow-straw hue. Intense, leesy, citric aromas. A racy entry leads to a moderately full-bodied, lively palate with fresh flavors and crisp structure. Very agreeable. Drink now or later.

Puligny-Montrachet, 1998 $NA. (SR)   **85-89**
Pale straw hue. Subdued minerally aromas. A taut entry leads to a medium-bodied palate with vibrant acidity. Carries a slight nutty nuance. Will need time. Midterm cellar candidate.

Puligny Montrachet "Cailleret," Premier Cru 1998 $NA. (SR)   96-100

Deep yellow-straw hue. Exotic, opulent ginger, spice, and fresh fruit aromas. A lush entry leads to a moderately full-bodied palate with intense, racy flavors. Already quite complex. Midterm cellar candidate.

Puligny Montrachet "Les Pucelles," Premier Cru 1998 $NA. (SR)   90-95

Deep straw hue. Intense, jazzy grapefruit, vanilla, and ginger aromas. A racy entry leads to a moderately full-bodied palate with crisp acids. Full and rich with great weight and intensity of flavor. Drink now or later.

Puligny Montrachet "Folatieres," Premier Cru 1998 $NA. (SR)   96-100

Deep golden straw hue. Exotic, amazingly intense butterscotch, vanilla, and tropical fruit aromas. Great ripeness allied to a firm, zesty structure. Big, intense, and stylish with great length and complexity. Midterm cellar candidate.

Puligny Montrachet "Referts," Premier Cru 1998 $NA. (SR)   90-95

Brilliant yellow-straw hue. Forward, complex vanilla, citrus, and pear aromas. A firm entry leads to a vibrant, medium-bodied palate with powerful acidity. Firm, well-structured finish. Long-term cellar.

**Chevalier-Montrachet "Clos des Chevaliers,"
Grand Cru 1998 $NA. (SR)**   96-100

Brilliant pale golden hue. Outrageous oriental spice, tropical fruit, and mineral aromas jump from the glass. A rich entry leads to a full-bodied palate with complexity and great intensity of flavor. Extremely powerful and stylish. A real mouthful. Drink now or later.

Batard-Montrachet, Grand Cru 1998 $NA. (SR)   90-95

Deep yellow-straw hue. Intense tropical fruit and butter aromas. A weighty entry leads to a full-bodied, flashy mouthfeel. Big and almost fat with a sense of viscosity. Vibrant acidity lends a sense of balance. Midterm cellar candidate.

Bruno Clair

Marsannay Blanc, 1997 $29.99. (SR)   81

Morey-St.-Denis Blanc "En la rue de Vergy," 1997 $57.99. (SR)   84

Corton-Charlemagne, Grand Cru 1997 $117.50. (SR)   90

Bright straw-yellow. Attractive, fresh toasted coconut and citrus aromas. Moderately full-bodied palate with refreshing acidity. Stylish and flavorful. Drink now.

Marsannay Rouge "Grasses-Tetes," 1997 $29. (SR)   88

Brilliant purple hue. Jammy, ripe black fruit and flower aromas jump from the glass. A rich entry leads to a medium-bodied palate with supple tannins and decent acidic cut. Absolutely stuffed with flavor. Drink now.

Marsannay Rouge "Longeroies," 1997 $29. (SR)   85

Chambolle-Musigny "Les Veroilles," 1997 $47.99. (SR)   87

Brilliant, saturated ruby hue. Subtle violet, oak, and mineral aromas. Medium-bodied palate with lean tannins. Delicate, flavorful, feminine finish. Drink now.

Morey-St.-Denis "En la rue de Vergy," 1997 $49. (SR)   86

Deeply saturated ruby hue. Intense jammy aromas. Moderately full-bodied palate with lean, gripping tannins. Firm, structured finish. Needs time. Mid-term cellar candidate.

Savigny-les-Beaune "La Dominode," Premier Cru 1997 $57. (SR)   85

Gevrey-Chambertin "Clos du Fonteny," Premier Cru 1997 $78. (SR)   90

Deep ruby-red. Big, ripe jammy aromas with a likable floral accent. Moderately full-bodied palate with breadth and richness. Supple tannins. Stylish, flavorful finish. Drink now or later.

Gevrey-Chambertin "Cazetiers," Premier Cru 1997 $101. (SR)   90

Brilliant ruby-purple. Generous ripe black fruit and hefty oak aromas. Moderately full-bodied palate with gripping tannins. Forward and attractive. Intensity of flavor on finish. Drink now or later.

Clos de Beze, Grand Cru 1997 $149. (SR) 92

Saturated ruby hue. Perfumed red fruit, vanillin, and mineral aromas. Moderately full-bodied, structured palate with gripping tannins. Reserved at present. Needs time. Mid-term cellar candidate.

Comte Georges de Vogue

Le Musigny "Vieilles Vignes," Grand Cru 1997 $230. (SR) 100

Bright ruby-purple. Enticing, perfumed flower, mineral, and berry aromas jump from the glass. Medium-bodied palate with vibrant tannins and juicy acidity. Soft texture with a backdrop of power. Explodes with typical Musigny flowery flavors through the long finish. Approachable now, but should drink beautifully for another decade. Sensual and elegant in an intense way. Drink now or later.

Comtes Lafon

Meursault, 1997 $63. (SR) 90

Rich straw-yellow. Generous nut and cream aromas. Moderately full-bodied palate that explodes with flavor. Taut structure with undercurrent of acidity. Will develop wonderfully. Drink now or later.

Meursault "Desiree," 1997 $68. (SR) 88

Straw-yellow. Lush pear and tropical fruit aromas. Medium-bodied palate with soft acidity. Varietally expressive and accessible. Drink now.

Meursault "Clos de la Barre," 1997 $68. (SR) 92

Brilliant yellow-gold. Complex, leesy, yeasty vanilla aromas fill the air. Moderately full-bodied palate with sturdy acidity. Drink now or later.

Meursault "Gouttes d'Or," Premier Cru 1997 $68. (SR) 95

Deep yellow-gold. Rich, nutty, creamy aromas. Full-bodied, viscous palate. Big and impressive. Balanced with an underpinning of acidity. Drink now or later.

Meursault "Genevrieres," Premier Cru 1997 $68. (SR) 95

Bright yellow-gold. Exotic yeast, ginger, and toast aromas. Medium-bodied palate with outstanding acidic grip. Waves of classic nutty flavors mark the finish. Very attractive now, but structured to age. Drink now or later.

Meursault "Charmes," Premier Cru 1997 $99. (SR) 93

Vibrant golden yellow. Exotic, leesy aromas with an attractive nutty accent. Weighty. Moderately full-bodied palate offset by firm structural acidity. Fresh, complex finish. Needs time. Mid-term cellar candidate.

Meursault "Perrieres," Premier Cru 1997 $105. (SR) 93

Bright yellow-gold. Forward cream and yeast aromas. Moderately full-bodied palate with rounded acidity. Smoky, supple finish. An attractive, flashy style. Drink now or later.

Puligny Montrachet "Champs Gain," Premier Cru 1997 $99. (SR) 94

Deep yellow-gold. Fresh yeast, citrus, and sea spray aromas are delicate and complex. Medium-bodied palate. Intense finish. Classic. Drink now or later.

Le Montrachet, Grand Cru 1997 $500. (SR) 98

Brilliant, highly saturated yellow-gold. Absolutely exotic ginger, tropical fruit, and spice aromas jump from the glass. Big, viscous, full-bodied palate. Complex flavors accelerate in the mouth and expand at the finish. Outrageously intense and lush, but structured to keep. Luscious...14.5% alcohol naturally, and carries it effortlessly. Long-term cellar candidate.

Volnay "Champans," Premier Cru 1997 $NA. (SR) 92

Brilliant ruby-purple. Exotic floral and red fruit aromas jump from the glass. Medium-bodied palate with gripping tannins and tingling acidity. Deeply flavored and very stylish. Drink now or later.

Scale: Superlative (96-100), Exceptional (90-95), Highly Recommended (85-89), Recommended (80-84), Not Recommended (Under 80)

Volnay "Santenots," Premier Cru 1997 $NA. (SR)   **90**

Brilliant ruby-purple. Still quite youthful, and somewhat closed. A brace of red fruit flavors emerges on the palate. Weighty for a Volnay. Moderately full-bodied, with firm tannins. Lots of stuffing, but needs long-term cellaring.

Meursault "Charmes," Premier Cru 1998 $NA. (SR)   **90-95**

Bright straw hue. Crisp, lean, and stylish. A vibrant entry leads to a medium-bodied palate with a big acidic cut. Four square. Will need time. Long-term cellar.

Meursault "Perrieres," Premier Cru 1998 $NA. (SR)   **90-95**

Vibrant yellow-straw hue. Forawrd ripe aromas. A rich entry leads to a full-bodied palate with lots of stuffing. Rich and rounded. Should be accessible earlier. Midterm cellar candidate.

Volnay "Santenots," Premier Cru 1998 $NA. (SR)   **90-95**

Very deep ruby-purple hue. Firm and intense with a full-bodied palate and grippy tannins. Powerful, but backwards. Should develop beautifully. Long-term cellar.

Joseph Drouhin

St. Veran, 1997 $NA. (SR)   **86**

Deep straw cast. Moderately full-bodied. Balanced acidity. Moderately extracted. Mildly oaked. Minerals, cream. Pleasantly aromatic with gentle oak overtones. Rounded and almost fat through the finish.

Rully, 1997 $20. (SR)   **84**

Montagny, 1997 $NA. (SR)   **88**

Deep straw cast. Moderately full-bodied. Full acidity. Moderately extracted. Mildly oaked. Brown spice, citrus. Redolent of oak in the nose. Features a clean and racy palate feel with solid grip. Finishes with lengthy toasted oak nuances.

Chablis, Domaine de Vaudon 1997 $NA. (SR)   **90**

Bright straw cast. Moderately full-bodied. High acidity. Highly extracted. Mildly oaked. Minerals, citrus zest, vanilla. Fairly aromatic with a subtle suggestion of oak treatment. Clean, fresh, and racy in the mouth with solid grip.

Saint Aubin, 1997 $NA. (SR)   **81**

Chassagne Montrachet, 1997 $NA. (SR)   **86**

Bright yellow-gold. Moderately full-bodied. High acidity. Highly extracted. Mildly oaked. Minerals, citrus zest. Rather reserved aromatically with a crisp mineral palate. Clean and steely through the finish.

Meursault, 1997 $NA. (SR)   **89**

Bright yellow-gold. Full-bodied. High acidity. Highly extracted. Mildly oaked. Yeast, smoke. Distinctive smoky note on the nose. Starts off full and rich. Angular finish.

Puligny-Montrachet, "Folatieres" Premier Cru 1997 $NA. (SR)   **91**

Bright greenish gold. Full-bodied. High acidity. Highly extracted. Mildly oaked. Lemon cream, sea breeze. Quite aromatic and flavorful with a full, pure, and expressive personality. Well balanced and intense with a clean, racy finish.

Corton-Charlemagne, Grand Cru 1997 $NA. (SR)   **94**

Brilliant yellow-gold. Full-bodied. Balanced acidity. Highly extracted. Moderately oaked. Vanilla, minerals, cream. Rather muted aromas and flavors at present. Full, fat, lush and opulent texture. Should open nicely with near to mid-term cellaring.

Dujac

Morey St. Denis, 1997 $NA. (SR)   **86**

Bright ruby hue. Powerful cinnamon, red fruit, and mineral aromas show classic Pinot Noir elegance. Moderately light-bodied palate with gripping tannins. Delicate, flavorful finish. Stylish and drinking well. Drink now.

Chambolle-Musigny, 1997 $NA. (SR)   **85**

577

Chambolle-Musigny "Le Gruenchers," Premier Cru 1997 $NA. (SR)   **90**

Bright ruby-red. Exotic flower, mineral, and spice aromas are beguiling and complex. Medium-bodied palate with velvety tannins. Shows fine balance and structure with great length through the finish. Drink now.

Gevrey-Chambertin "Aux Combottes," Premier Cru 1997 $NA. (SR)   **89**

Bright ruby-red with a slight fade. Powerful berry and mineral aromas carry a sweet oak accent. Moderately full-bodied palate with well-structured tannins. Intense, gripping finish. Could use some time to round out. Drink now or later.

Charmes-Chambertin, Grand Cru 1997 $NA. (SR)   **93**

Bright ruby hue with a purple edge. Highly perfumed with exotic floral nuances, mineral red fruits, and sweet oak. Moderately full-bodied palate with crisp, structured tannins. The flavors expand considerably in the mouth and intensify further on the finish. Powerful, but balanced. Drink now or later.

Clos St. Denis, Grand Cru 1997 $NA. (SR)   **92**

Bright ruby-red. Opulent spice and red fruit aromas are generous and complex. Medium-bodied palate with rounded tannins. A delicate style with elegant flavors. Generous. Well structured. Drink now.

Clos de la Roche, Grand Cru 1997 $NA. (SR)   **93**

Brilliant ruby hue. Moderately full-bodied palate. Big, structured tannins. A firm, intense style with sturdy flavor extraction and solid structure. Should open nicely with age. Mid-term cellar candidate.

Echézeaux, Grand Cru 1997 $NA. (SR)   **89**

Pale ruby-purple. Perfumed flower, spice, and mineral aromas. Medium-bodied palate with a green edge to the tannins. A leaner style. Tasty but lacks depth at the moment.

Bonnes Mares, Grand Cru 1997 $NA. (SR)   **92**

Pale ruby hue. Subdued mineral and red fruit aromas. Moderately full-bodied palate with rich tannins. Flavors open and intensify in the mouth. Well balanced and concentrated. Should open nicely. Long-term cellar candidate.

Rene Engel

Vosne-Romanée, 1997 $NA. (SR)   **85**

Vosne-Romanée "Les Brulees," Premier Cru 1997 $NA. (SR)   **87**

Pale ruby hue. Distinct strawberry and herb aromas. Forward and intense flavors. Medium-bodied. Lean tannins. Shows a viney character throughout. Crisp finish. Drink now.

Echézeaux, Grand Cru 1997 $NA. (SR)   **89**

Saturated ruby-red. Distinct herb and candied red fruit aromas and flavors. Moderately full-bodied. Lean, gripping tannins. Not fully expressive now. Needs time. Mid-term cellar candidate.

Clos Vougeot, Grand Cru 1997 $NA. (SR)   **88**

Pale ruby hue. Forward herb and candied red fruit aromas. Medium-bodied palate. Soft tannins. Ripe, flavorful finish. Tasty, but lacks real depth. Drink now or later.

Henri Gouges

Nuits St. Georges, 1997 $39.99. (SR)   **88**

Deep ruby with purple highlights. Aromatically subdued. Firm, viney Pinot Noir flavors emerge in the mouth, with a backbone of black fruit and minerals. A rich, four-square, moderately full-bodied style with velvety tannins. Supple. Drink now or later.

Nuits St. Georges "Les Pruliers," Premier Cru 1997 $6357.99. (SR)   **90**

Deep ruby-purple. Intense mineral, black fruit, and licorice aromas. Moderately full-bodied palate with supple tannins. A big style. Should develop beautifully. Mid-term cellar candidate.

Nuits St. Georges "Vaucrains," Premier Cru 1997 $69. (SR)   **92**

Brilliant ruby-purple. Perfumed, exotic ripe jammy fruit and flower aromas. Broad, moderately full-bodied palate with lush tannins. Enlivened through to the finish by bright acidity. Ripe and forward, yet showing sturdy structure. Mid-term cellar candidate.

A.F. Gros

Bourgogne Rouge, 1998 $NA. (SR)   **80-84**

Chambolle-Musigny, 1998 $NA. (SR)   **85-89**

Bright cherry-red with purple highlights. Generous flower, herb, and mineral aromas. A lean entry leads to a medium-bodied palate with crisp tannins. Lighter in style with a sense of delicacy buttressed by a taut structure. Drink now or later.

Vosne-Romanée, 1998 $NA. (SR)   **85-89**

Brilliant pale purple hue. Restrained mineral and berry aromas. A firm entry leads to a medium-bodied palate with lean tannins. Quite closed at present with a firm structure. Will need time to open. Midterm cellar candidate.

Clos Vougeot, Grand Cru 1998 $NA. (SR)   **90-95**

Brilliant purple hue. Restrained mineral, red fruit, and vanilla aromas. A lush entry leads to a moderately full-bodied palate with supple tannins. Shows richness throughout with a sense of depth. Powerful but restrained. Will need time to blossom. Long-term cellar.

Richebourg, Grand Cru 1998 $NA. (SR)   **90-95**

Brilliant dark purple hue. Deep mineral and red fruit aromas are brooding and subdued. A powerful entry leads to a moderately full-bodied palate with firm tannins. Finely structured and rich, but not showing much at present. Shows all the signs of developing well. Long-term cellar.

Louis Jadot

Pouilly Fuisse, 1997 $20. (SR)   **87**

Deep straw-yellow. Opulent cream and toast aromas. Moderately full-bodied, ripe palate with vibrant acidity. Supple and drinking beautifully. Drink now.

Meursault, 1997 $41. (SR)   **89**

Bright straw-yellow. Forward toast and nut aromas. Moderately full-bodied palate with racy acids. Rounded, lush finish. Already approachable but should develop further complexity with age. Mid-term cellar candidate.

Corton-Charlemagne, Grand Cru 1997 $128. (SR)   **92**

Bright straw-yellow. Aromatically subdued. Fresh yeast and vibrant fruit flavors emerge on the palate. Moderately full-bodied palate with sturdy acidity. Expansive finish. Will open beautifully with age. Long-term cellar candidate.

Chevalier-Montrachet "Les Demoiselles," Grand Cru 1997 $234. (SR)   **95**

Deep straw cast. Forward pear and subtle sweet vanilla oak aromas. Full-bodied palate with solid structural acidity. Ample and weighty in the mouth with very impressive concentration. Already attractive. Drink now or later.

Le Montrachet, Grand Cru 1997 $NA. (SR)   **97**

Highly saturated bright yellow-gold. Forward tropical fruit and oak aromas are opulent and enticing. Full-bodied palate with solid acidity. Powerful. Viscous texture. Perfumed and exotic. Big yet exquisitely balanced. Drink now or later.

Savigny-les-Beaune "Clos de Guettes," Premier Cru 1997 $NA. (SR)   **87**

Opaque purple hue. Subdued black fruit and mineral aromas. A firm entry leads to a rich, extracted palate. Four-square with a big, rich character. Rather monolithic at present. Should develop with time. Long-term cellar.

Beaune "Clos des Ursules," Premier Cru 1997 $NA. (SR)   **93**

Deep purple. Exotic, plummy, jammy aromas with a spicy oak accent. Big, ripe, moderately full-bodied palate with brawny tannins. Complex flowery finish. Extravagant. Almost approachable, but structure dictates long-term cellaring.

Clos Vougeot, Grand Cru 1997 $NA. (SR)   **96**

Rich ruby-purple. Intense, exotic, flowery and jammy aromas. Moderately full-bodied palate with gripping tannins. Extremely long finish. Opulent, complex, and exciting. Mid-term cellar candidate.

Echézeaux, Grand Cru 1997 $NA. (SR)   **93**

Rich purple. Intensely fragrant violet, mineral, and red fruit aromas. Medium-bodied palate with gripping tannins, acidic cut, and precision. A lush, feminine style. Supple and enticing. Drink now or later.

Grands Echézeaux, Grand Cru 1997 $NA. (SR)   **97**

Saturated brilliant purple. Exotic berry fruit and flower aromas are extraordinary. Medium-bodied palate with angular tannins and explosive flavors. Elegant, yet powerful. A very pure expression of Vosne-Romanée. Long-term cellar candidate.

Musigny, Grand Cru 1997 $NA. (SR)   **100**

Vibrant deep purple. Extravagantly fragrant flower and mineral aromas are enticing and exotic. Palate explodes with flavor. Medium-bodied with gripping tannins and vibrant acids. Amazingly complex and buoyant. Narcissus. Perfection. Drink now or later.

Clos de Beze, Grand Cru 1997 $NA. (SR)   **96**

Deeply saturated purple. Powerful mineral and black fruit aromas. Moderately full-bodied palate with robust, fine-grained tannins. Rich and intense with great depth. Weighty, but elegant. Long-term cellar candidate.

Bonnes Mares, Grand Cru 1997 $NA. (SR)   **98**

Deeply saturated purple. Perfumed red fruit, spice, and flower aromas are seductive and elegant. Moderately full-bodied palate with an explosion of flavors and lean tannins. Exotic and intense, with a long, opulent finish. Mid-term cellar candidate.

Puligny Montrachet "Clos de la Garenne," Duc de Magenta,
Premier Cru 1998 $NA. (SR)   **85-89**

Deep yellow-straw hue. Subdued banana and mineral aromas carry a leesy accent. A rich entry leads to a moderately full-bodied palate with vibrant acids. Rich and round. Midterm cellar candidate.

Meursault "Genevrieres," Premier Cru 1998 $NA. (SR)   **90-95**

Deep yellow-straw hue. Forward leesy aromas. A rich entry leads to a creamy, full-bodied palate with racy acids. Rich and round. Midterm cellar candidate.

Chassagne Montrachet "Cailleret," Premier Cru 1998 $NA. (SR)   **85-89**

Deep yellow-straw hue. Subdued minerally aromas. A rich entry leads to a moderately full-bodied palate with racy acids. Big and dense. Needs lots of time. Long-term cellar.

Corton-Charlemagne, Grand Cru 1998 $NA. (SR)   **96-100**

Deep yellow-golden hue. Opulent tropical fruit, sea spray, and toasted coconut aromas are complex and enticing. A rich entry leads to a full-bodied palate with great generosity. Outstanding. Long-term cellar.

Chevalier-Montrachet "Les Demoiselles," Grand Cru 1998 $NA. (SR)   **96-100**

Deep yellow-golden hue. Intense, yeasty, biscuity aromas. A rich entry leads to a full-bodied palate with zesty acidity, great concentration, and intensity. Already showing complexity. Power allied to delicacy. Long-term cellar.

Bienvenues-Batard-Montrachet, Grand Cru 1998 $NA. (SR)   **90-95**

Deep yellow-golden hue. Subdued mineral and cream aromas. A weighty entry leads to a robust palate with vibrant acids. Powerful and rich. Needs lots of time. Long-term cellar.

Le Montrachet, Grand Cru 1998 $NA. (SR)   **96-100**

Dark golden hue. Opulent citrus, tropical fruit, and bread aromas. A big entry leads to a full-bodied palate with prominent acidity. Rich and powerful but almost austere through the finish. Very deep and concentrated. Will require extended cellaring to appreciate. Long-term cellar.

Scale: Superlative (96-100), Exceptional (90-95), Highly Recommended (85-89), Recommended (80-84), Not Recommended (Under 80)

580

Musigny, Grand Cru 1998 $NA. (SR)   96-100

Brilliant dark purple hue. A potpourri of flower and exotic fruit aromas scream from the glass. Exotically aromatic. An intense entry leads to an unbelieveably flavorful palate with grippy tannins and buoyant acidity. Very Musigny. One of the greatest young Burgundies I have ever tasted. Could be perfection. Long-term cellar.

Clos Vougeot, Grand Cru 1998 $NA. (SR)   96-100

Saturated ruby-purple hue. Exotic, jammy, floral aromas are complex and decadent. A firm entry leads to a full-bodied palate with rough and tumble tannins. Lots of grip and intensity. Quite tough, but already amazingly flavorful. Tons of extract. Needs a long time. Long-term cellar.

Michel Lafarge

Meursault, 1997 $NA. (SR)   92

Deep straw-yellow. Showy nut, yeast, and tropical fruit aromas. Flavorful, moderately full-bodied palate. Bright acidity. Extraordinarily intense in flavor and well structured. Drink now or later.

Meursault, Vendange Selectionne 1997 $NA. (SR)   92

Highly saturated yellow. Powerful nut and cream aromas. Moderately full-bodied palate. Sharp acidity. Reserved at present. Highly extracted. Will evolve gracefully. Mid-term cellar candidate.

Bourgogne, Passetoutgrains 1997 $NA. (SR)   85

Bourgogne Rouge, 1997 $26. (SR)   83

Volnay, 1997 $55. (SR)   88

Deep ruby hue. Subdued mineral and red fruit aromas. Medium-bodied palate with lean tannins and clean, precise flavors. Elegant. Drink now or later.

Volnay, Vendange Selectionne 1997 $62. (SR)   91

Deep ruby-red. Subtle aromatics. Deep mineral and floral flavors on the moderately full-bodied palate. High acidity. Gripping tannins. Impressively structured. Long finish. Mid-term cellar candidate.

Volnay, Premier Cru 1997 $NA. (SR)   92

Brilliant ruby-purple. Jazzy red fruit and flower aromas are feminine and seductive. Medium-bodied palate. Balancing acidic cut. Crisp finish. Exceptionally stylish and tasty. Drink now or later.

Beaune "Greves," Premier Cru 1997 $82.50. (SR)   89

Bright garnet cast. Early-maturing aromas carry an earthy, forest-note edge. Moderately full-bodied palate. Lean mineral backbone and powerful grip. Lighter style. Well structured. Firm tannic finish. Drink now or later.

Volnay "Clos du Chateau des Ducs," Premier Cru 1997 $103.50. (SR)   93

Brilliant ruby hue. Attractive mineral and red fruit aromas. Expansive flavors. Medium-bodied palate with angular tannins. Gripping. High flavor intensity. Delightful. Drink now or later.

Volnay "Clos des Chenes," Premier Cru 1997 $110. (SR)   93

Deep ruby. Brooding mineral and ripe red fruit aromas. Moderately full-bodied. Intense mouthfeel. Gripping tannins. Pure Pinot. Should develop nicely. Mid-term cellar candidate.

Louis Latour

Saint-Veran, Les Deux Moulins 1997 $12. (SR)   84

Pouilly-Fuisse, 1997 $22. (SR)   83

Santenay, 1997 $20. (SR)   85

Beaune Blanc, 1997 $31. (SR)   85

Chassagne-Montrachet, 1997 $54. (SR)   **88**

Brilliant straw-yellow. Citrus, spice, and yeast aromas and flavors. Medium-bodied palate with fine acidity. Delicate. Complex. Very stylish. Drink now.

Meursault "Charmes," Premier Cru 1997 $74. (SR)   **87**

Brilliant straw-yellow. Generous toast and mineral aromas and flavors. Nutty finish. Medium-bodied with a solid acidic cut. Weighty but taut. Needs time. Mid-term cellar candidate.

Puligny-Montrachet "Les Folatieres," Premier Cru 1997 $70. (SR)   **90**

Deep straw-yellow. Generous allspice, cream, and vanilla aromas. Moderately full-bodied palate with rounded acidity. Rich and stylish. Well balanced and drinking beautifully. Drink now or later.

Corton-Charlemagne, Grand Cru 1997 $120. (SR)   **93**

Bright straw-yellow. Reserved but elegant mineral and toast aromas are complex, fresh, and stylish. Concentrated in the mouth. Moderately full-bodied. Defining acidic cut. Very long finish. Rather impressive now, but will hold beautifully. Drink now or later.

Marsannay, 1997 $17. (SR)   **83**

Olivier Leflaive

Bourgogne Blanc, Les Setilles 1997 $16.50. (SR)   **85**

Rully, Premier Cru 1997 $23.49. (SR)   **84**

Saint-Aubin "En Remilly," Premier Cru 1997 $33.50. (SR)   **86**

Deep yellow-straw hue. Unusual toast and smoke aromas. A crisp entry leads to a flavorful, medium-bodied palate. Rich and lush, though with an edge to the finish. Drink now or later.

Chassagne-Montrachet, 1997 $49.99. (SR)   **87**

Brilliant straw-yellow. Generous citrus and yeast aromas. Medium-bodied palate. Taut with acidity. Lean structure with ripe flavors. Well balanced. Drink now.

Meursault, 1997 $49.49. (SR)   **89**

Brilliant yellow-gold. Classic Meursault nut and toast aromas and flavors. Rich mouthfeel. Balanced acidity. Long finish. Stylish. Drink now.

Puligny-Montrachet, 1997 $53.49. (SR)   **90**

Deep straw-yellow. Exotic fresh cream, vanilla, and yeast aromas. Medium-bodied palate. Balanced acidity. Delicate, elegant, and flavorful. Drink now.

Meursault "Narvaux," Premier Cru 1997 $NA. (SR)   **89**

Brilliant yellow. Reserved cream and nut aromas. Medium-bodied palate. Firm structural acidity. Stylish. Could use a bit more time to open. Mid-term cellar candidate.

Chassagne-Montrachet "Chaumées," Premier Cru 1997 $62.50. (SR)   **88**

Rich straw-yellow. Youthful, reserved aromatics and flavors. Firm mineral backbone. Medium-bodied palate. Taut acidic structure. Lean and firm. May blossom with time. Mid-term cellar candidate.

Meursault "Charmes," Premier Cru 1997 $68.49. (SR)   **91**

Bright straw-yellow. Aromatically reserved. Broad creamy quality on the palate. Moderately full-bodied. Balanced acidity. A lush style. Attractive now, but should develop nicely. Drink now or later.

Puligny Montrachet "Champs Gain," Premier Cru 1997 $68.49. (SR)   **93**

Bright straw-yellow. Gorgeous aromas of coconut, citrus, and minerals. Medium-bodied palate. Defining acidic grip. Explodes with flavor through the finish. Exotic and stylish. Very hedonistic. Drink now or later.

Corton-Charlemagne, Grand Cru 1997 $109.99. (SR)   **92**

Brilliant straw-yellow. Reserved fresh toast and citrus aromas. Full-bodied palate. Well-balanced acidity. Intense finish. Lush and forward but should develop nicely. Drink now or later.

Scale: Superlative (96-100), Exceptional (90-95), Highly Recommended (85-89), Recommended (80-84), Not Recommended (Under 80)

Bourgogne Rouge 1997 $NA. (SR)   81

Santenay 1997 $NA. (SR)   80

Monthelie, Premier Cru 1997 $NA. (SR)   80

Pommard, 1997 $NA. (SR)   83

Volnay "Clos des Angles," Premier Cru 1997 $NA. (SR)   85

Brilliant, saturated ruby hue. Ripe berry and slight earthy aromas. Medium-bodied palate with supple tannins. Clean, feminine finish. Drink now.

Pommard "Charmots," Premier Cru 1997 $NA. (SR)   88

Brilliant, saturated ruby-purple. Forward berry, mineral, and vanilla aromas. Medium-bodied palate with gripping tannins. Spicy intensity. Long, flavorful finish. Drink now or later.

Matrot

Bourgogne Blanc, 1997 $16.50. (SR)   87

Brilliant straw hue. Generous vanilla and lemon cream aromas. A crisp entry leads to a medium-bodied palate with great acidic grip. Fresh in flavor with a crisp, well balanced finish. Drink now.

Meursault, 1997 $33.99. (SR)   89

Brilliant straw-yellow. Subdued mineral aromas hint at origin. Medium-bodied, angular palate with taut acidity. Tightly wound and reserved. Structured to age over the long term.

Meursault "Blagny," Premier Cru 1997 $51. (SR)   89

Brilliant straw-yellow. Taut, reserved, mineral aromas with a subtle vanilla accent. Medium-bodied palate with crisp acids. Tightly wound and lean. Needs time. Long-term cellar candidate.

Meursault "Charmes," Premier Cru 1997 $55.99. (SR)   90

Brilliant straw-yellow. Aromatically reserved. Grapefruit flavors. Moderately full-bodied palate. Taut structure. Mouthwatering acidity. Intense finish. Needs time to blossom. Long-term cellar candidate.

Meursault "Perrieres," Premier Cru 1997 $NA. (SR)   92

Brilliant yellow. Exotic lemon cream, ginger, and spice aromas. Moderately full-bodied palate with a wave of complex flavors bolstered by vibrant acidity. Already showing a lot, but will develop beautifully. Mid-term cellar candidate.

Volnay "Santenots," Premier Cru 1997 $41.50. (SR)   86

Bright ruby-purple. Prominent raspberry and mineral aromas. Medium-bodied palate with firm gripping tannins. Well flavored, but austere. Needs time to round itself out. Mid-term cellar candidate.

Blagny "La Piece sous le Bois," Premier Cru 1997 $41.50. (SR)   84

Meo-Camuzet

Hautes Côtes de Nuits, Blanc 1997 $28.50. (SR)   90

Deep straw hue. Extravagant yeast and toast aromas show a judicious oak accent. A rich entry leads to a moderately full-bodied palate with excellent balancing acidity. Firm and substantive, but flashy, with a big leesy note and a clean finish. Drink now or later.

Nuits St. Georges, 1997 $49. (SR)   88

Brilliant purple. Attractive black fruit, licorice, and subtle oak spice aromas. Moderately full-bodied palate. Lean tannins. A richer, weightier style with firm structure and an underlying note of complex, mineral terroir. Approachable now, but should develop well. Mid-term cellar candidate.

Vosne Romanée "Les Chaumes," Premier Cru 1997 $85. (SR)   **93**

Brilliant purple. Perfumed flower, mineral, and spice aromas. Judicious oak accent. Silky, medium-bodied palate with supple tannins. Opulent and delicate. Chambolle-like flowery, charming character. Elegant and drinking beautifully, but structured to hold over the mid-term. Drink now or later.

Nuits St. Georges "Murgers," Premier Cru 1997 $96. (SR)   **92**

Rich ruby-purple color is quite dark for the vintage. Brooding mineral, licorice, and black fruit and oak aromas and flavors. Chunky, moderately full-bodied palate with gripping tannins. Intense finish. A big style. Mid-term cellar candidate.

Nuits St. Georges, 1998 $NA. (SR)   **85-89**

Brilliant, deep purple hue. Firm mineral and black fruit aromas. A rich entry leads to a chunky, moderately full-bodied palate with grippy tannins. A chunky, four square style. Midterm cellar candidate.

Nuits St. Georges "Murgers," Premier Cru 1998 $NA. (SR)   **90-95**

Deep, saturated ruby-purple hue. Brooding mineral and black fruit aromas. A rich entry leads to a full-bodied palate with firm tannins. A big, chunky style. Rather monolithic at present, but very well extracted. Should develop beautifully, but needs time. Long-term cellar.

Vosne Romanée "Les Chaumes," Premier Cru 1998 $NA. (SR)   **90-95**

Deep, saturated purple hue. Attractive, flowery, red fruit and mineral aromas. A rich entry leads to a moderately full-bodied palate with lush tannins. Big, but accessible and quite stylish. Fairly hedonistic. Drink now or later.

Thomas Moillard

Savigny-les-Beaune, 1997 $21.99. (SR)   **85**

Hautes Côtes de Nuits, 1997 $16.99. (SR)   **NR**

Savigny-les-Beaune, 1997 $19.99. (SR)   **83**

Beaune "Greves," Premier Cru 1997 $33.99. (SR)   **88**

Rich ruby hue. Intense, jammy black fruit and subtle oak aromas. Weighty, moderately full-bodied mouthfeel. Supple, rounded finish. Drink now or later.

Nuits St. Georges "Clos de Thorey," Premier Cru 1997 $44.99. (SR)   **90**

Bright ruby-red. Generous spice and very ripe fruit aromas. Moderately full-bodied palate with rounded tannins. Supple and rich in style. Chunky, but should develop nicely. Mid-term cellar candidate.

Vosne Romanée "Malconsorts," Premier Cru 1997 $49.99. (SR)   **92**

Bright purple. Attractive berry, mineral, and sweet oak aromas. Medium-bodied palate with ripe tannins. Harmonious and supple. Strikes a great balance between wood and fruit. Forward, but structured to develop. Drink now or later.

Clos Vougeot, Grand Cru 1997 $74.99. (SR)   **89**

Saturated ruby hue. Intense licorice, black fruit, and subtle oak aromas. Hint of overripeness. Full-bodied palate with gripping tannins. Firm and intense. Rather reserved at present, but should develop nicely. Mid-term cellar candidate.

Moillard-Grivot

Hautes Côtes de Nuits Blanc, 1997 $16.99. (SR)   **82**

Meursault, 1997 $42.99. (SR)   **87**

Brilliant straw cast. Generous oak spice and citrus aromas show an attractive oak accent. Medium-bodied palate with well-integrated acidity. Ripe, nutty finish. Very attractive. Drink now.

Rully, 1997 $16.99. (SR)   **81**

Bourgogne Rouge, Cent Cinquante Ans 1997 $13.99. (SR)   **85**

Saint-Aubin, 1997 $18.99. (SR)   **80**

Scale: Superlative (96-100), Exceptional (90-95), Highly Recommended (85-89), Recommended (80-84), Not Recommended (Under 80)

Chorey-les-Beaune, 1997 $19.99. (SR) **81**
Morey St. Denis, 1997 $31.99. (SR) **84**
Pernand Vergelles "Fichots," Premier Cru 1997 $24.95. (SR) **85**

Denis Mortet
Bourgogne Rouge, 1997 $24. (SR) **81**
Marsannay "Les Longeroies," 1997 $35. (SR) **86**
Bright purple hue. Generous, forward aromas show intense ripe berry qualities and a lash of new oak. A firm entry leads to a moderately full-bodied palate with structured tannins. A weighty, rich, ripe style. Drink now or later.

Gevrey-Chambertin, 1997 $48. (SR) **90**
Highly saturated purple. Brooding, sultry aromas. Moderately full-bodied palate with rich tannins. A big, extracted style. Weighty through to the finish. Mid-term cellar candidate.

Gevrey Chambertin "En Motrot," 1997 $54. (SR) **91**
Bright ruby-purple. Ripe berry, mineral, and flower aromas. Moderately full-bodied palate with velvety tannins. Powerful, yet showing finesse. Mid-term cellar candidate.

Gevrey Chambertin "Combes Dessus," 1997 $54. (SR) **89**
Bright purple. Restrained, brooding aromas. Moderately full-bodied palate with grainy tannins. A powerful, weighty style with attractive gamey overtones. Mid-term cellar candidate.

Gevrey-Chambertin "Au Velle," 1997 $54. (SR) **89**
Highly saturated ruby-purple. Aromatically subdued. Full-bodied palate with a big tannic smack through to the finish. Very firmly structured, with lots of extract to match. An impressive style, but lacks a bit of finesse at present. Long-term cellar candidate.

Gevrey-Chambertin "En Champs," 1997 $60. (SR) **90**
Saturated purple. Forward berry and mineral aromas with a generous new oak accent. Full-bodied palate with velvety tannins. Supple and weighty with great ripeness. A flashy style. Drink now.

Chambolle-Musigny "Les Beaux-Bruns," Premier Cru 1997 $70. (SR) **93**
Bright purple. Forward, perfumed flower and red fruit aromas. Medium-bodied palate with gripping tannins. Extremely long finish with a wave of exotic, ephemeral flavors. A weighty Chambolle, but very stylish. Drink now or later.

Gevrey-Chambertin "Les Champeaux," Premier Cru 1997 $70. (SR) **90**
Deep ruby-purple. Forward aromas of new wood, red fruit, and mineral flavors. Moderately full-bodied palate with firm tannins. Lots of structure. Reserved. Needs time. Mid-term cellar candidate.

Gevrey-Chambertin "Lavaux St. Jacques," Premier Cru 1997 $70. (SR) **92**
Saturated purple. Big, brooding game, mineral, and red fruit aromas. Full-bodied palate. Ripeness offset by lean mineral undertones and firm tannins. Extracted and rich with lots of flavor intensity and new oak. Long-term cellaring will help.

Clos Vougeot, Grand Cru 1997 $99. (SR) **93**
Deep purple. Deep black fruit and mineral aromas. Moderately full-bodied palate. Long, expressive finish with complex mineral and flower nuances. Very stylish. Drink now or later.

Le Chambertin, Grand Cru 1997 $144. (SR) **96**
Highly saturated purple. Powerful black fruit and mineral aromas. Full-bodied palate with big rich tannins. Depth of flavor supported by classic structure. Intense finish. Attractive now, but should really gain complexity over the next decade. Long-term cellaring recommended.

Mugneret-Gibourg

Vosne-Romanée, 1997 $NA. (SR)   88

Brilliant, saturated ruby-purple. Generous perfume and red fruit aromas. Medium-bodied palate. Tannic cut. Delicate, but sharp and focused through the finish. Drink now or later.

Chambolle-Musigny "Les Feusselottes," Premier Cru 1997 $70. (SR)   91

Brilliant ruby-purple. Flowers, ripe red fruit, and gentle oak aromas. Medium-bodied palate. Buttressed by vibrant acidity. Generous flavors intensify on the finish. Stylish. Drink now.

Echézeaux, Grand Cru 1997 $90. (SR)   94

Brilliant ruby hue. Old vine, jammy, black fruit aromas with a mineral undercurrent. Full-bodied palate. Big but supple tannins. Ample and rich, with balancing acidic cut. Seductive. Drink now or later.

Ruchottes-Chambertin, Grand Cru 1997 $110. (SR)   89

Pale ruby-red. Distinctive mineral and herb aromas with a subtle oak accent. Medium-bodied palate. Vibrant acidity. Soft tannins. Atypical style. Very forward and attractive. Drink now.

Clos Vougeot, Grand Cru 1997 $120. (SR)   90

Saturated ruby hue. Forward mineral, licorice, and red fruit aromas. Distinctive sense of terroir. Forward flavors. Lean, racy palate. Well balanced. Lighter in style but very attractive. Drink now.

JF Mugnier

Chambolle-Musigny, 1997 $55. (SR)   88

Brilliant purple. Restrained mineral and red fruit aromas. Moderately light-bodied palate with crisp acids and subtle tannins. Delicate Chambolle flavors emerge on the finish. Lighter and elegant. Drink now.

Chambolle-Musigny "Les Fuées," Premier Cru 1997 $82.50. (SR)   89

Bright ruby hue. Delicate red fruit, mineral, and vanillin aromas. Medium-bodied palate with gripping tannins. Stylish and quite flavorful through the finish with a balancing cut. Drink now or later.

Chambolle-Musigny "Les Amoureuses," Premier Cru 1997 $124.50. (SR)   91

Pale ruby-red. Enticing herb and red fruit aromas are classic Pinot Noir. Medium-bodied palate with gripping tannins. Light in body. Lush, with flowery flavors that intensify at the finish. A delicate, flavorful style. Drink now.

Bonnes Mares, Grand Cru 1997 $124.50. (SR)   92

Rich ruby to garnet. Attractive berry, mineral, and flower aromas are restrained at first but open beautifully in the mouth. Medium-bodied palate with gripping tannins. Powerful yet delicate. Concentrated. Well balanced. Intense finish.

Les Musigny, Grand Cru 1997 $162. (SR)   95

Brilliant pale purple. Restrained red fruit, mineral, and flower aromas are classic Musigny. Medium-bodied palate with soft tannins and bright acidity. Perfumed and showy, with delicacy allied to a touch of power. Drinking beautifully, but structured to age. Sensually exciting. Mid-term cellar candidate.

Michel Niellon

Chassagne-Montrachet "Maltroie," Premier Cru 1997 $60. (SR)   NR
Chassagne-Montrachet "Champ-Gain," Premier Cru 1997 $60. (SR)   89

Brilliant yellow-gold. Subdued citrus, mineral, and leesy aromas. Medium-bodied palate with racy acidity. Well balanced. Harmonious. Flavorful finish. Drink now or later.

Chassagne-Montrachet "Clos St. Jean," Premier Cru 1997 $60. (SR)   91

Rich straw-yellow. Aromatically reserved. Firm mineral, leesy, and oak flavors. Medium-bodied. Vibrant, defining acidity. Stylish. Already attractive, but should develop. Drink now or later.

Chassagne-Montrachet "Chaumées," Premier Cru 1997 $60. (SR)   86

Brilliant straw-yellow. Muted mineral and ripe apple aromas. Medium-bodied palate with zesty acidity. Lighter in style and refreshing. Drink now or later.

Chassagne-Montrachet "Vergers," Premier Cru 1997 $60. (SR)   93

Brilliant straw-yellow. Forward melon, apple, and honey aromas are pure and varietally intense. Concentrated, moderately full-bodied palate. Balancing acidic grip. Pure and very intense finish. Drink now or later.

Chevalier-Montrachet, Grand Cru 1997 $210. (SR)   96

Brilliant straw-yellow. Aromatically subdued. Forward and complex flavors of honey, spice, and tropical fruit. Full-bodied palate. Acidic grip. Intense and long finish. A very hedonistic wine. Drink now or later.

Chassagne-Montrachet, 1998 $NA. (SR)   85-89

Bright yellow-straw hue. Ripe, biscuity apple and mineral aromas. A lean entry leads to a rich, medium-bodied palate with solid acidity. Shows good concentration through the finish. Midterm cellar candidate.

Batard-Montrachet, Grand Cru 1998 $NA. (SR)   90-95

Brilliant yellow-golden hue. Very forward apple, honey, and pear aromas are exotically pure and varietally intense. Lots of richness and amazing purity. A great expression of Chardonnay fruit. Drink now or later.

Chevalier-Montrachet, Grand Cru 1998 $NA. (SR)   96-100

Brilliant yellow-straw hue. Intense, exotic honey, pear, and spice aromas. A crisp entry leads to a medium-bodied palate with racy acidity. Very pure and expressive, with a taut structure. Finishes with a lengthy, leesy accent. Very complex. Intellectual. Midterm cellar candidate.

Ponsot

Gevrey-Chambertin, 1997 $47.50. (SR)   90

Saturated ruby hue. Enticing red fruit and mineral aromas and flavors. Moderately full-bodied palate. Lush tannins. Acidic grip. Intense finish. Drink now or later.

Chambolle-Musigny "Les Charmes," Premier Cru 1997 $79. (SR)   93

Brilliant ruby hue. Aromatically reserved. Attractive, floral, red fruit flavors. Medium-bodied. Hedonistic mouthfeel. Rounded tannins. Enticing and supple. Classic Chambolle. Delicious. Drink now or later.

Griottes-Chambertin, Grand Cru 1997 $173.99. (SR)   94

Deep ruby-red. Ripe, forward red fruit aromas. Full-bodied palate. Gripping tannins. Powerful and rich. A little closed at present. Needs long-term cellaring.

Chapelle-Chambertin, Grand Cru 1997 $173.99. (SR)   92

Rich ruby hue. Forward, jammy aromas. Moderately full-bodied palate. Supple tannins. Big, weighty style. Deeply flavored. A little closed at present. Needs time. Mid-term cellar candidate.

Clos de La Roche, Vieilles Vignes, Grand Cru 1997 $200. (SR)   96

Rich ruby hue. Intense red fruit, mineral, and flower aromas and flavors. Moderately full-bodied palate with supple tannins. Elegant, powerful, silky, and flavorful. Intense finish. Outstanding. Almost approachable, but will keep. Drink now or later.

Pousse d'Or

Santenay "Gravieres" Blanc, Premier Cru 1997 $NA. (SR)   **90**

Deep yellow-straw hue. Generous yeast and citrus aromas. A rich entry leads to a weighty, moderately full-bodied palate with good acidity. A big, weighty style showing lots of complexity. Drink now or later.

Santenay "Gravieres" Rouge, Premier Cru 1997 $NA. (SR)   **87**

Brilliant cherry garnet hue. Subdued mineral and red fruit aromas. A lean entry leads to a silky, medium-bodied palate with supple tannins. A soft, feminine style, which shows lots of flavor through the finish. Drink now.

Santenay "Clos des Tavannes," Premier Cru 1997 $NA. (SR)   **86**

Saturated garnet hue. Aromatically subdued with firm minerally red fruit flavors emerging in the mouth. A soft entry leads to a medium-bodied palate with supple tannins. Crisp through the finish. Tasty, but lacks a bit for grip. Drink now.

Volnay "En Caillerets," Premier Cru 1997 $NA. (SR)   **87**

Saturated garnet hue. Aromatically subdued. Mineral red fruit flavors. Slight note of maturity in the mouth. Soft and rounded texture. Moderately light-bodied. Gentle tannins. Drink now.

Volnay "Clos de l'Audignac," Premier Cru 1997 $NA. (SR)   **89**

Brilliant ruby to garnet. Forward red fruit, mineral, and flower aromas. Medium-bodied. Soft but edgy tannins. Moderate acidity. Flavorful. Drinking beautifully now.

Volnay "Clos des 60 Ouvrées," Premier Cru 1997 $NA. (SR)   **91**

Deep ruby hue. Aromatically subdued. Red fruit flavors with and a firm mineral backbone. Moderately full-bodied. Crisp acids. Angular tannins. Intense finish with emphasis on oak flavors. Well proportioned. Drink now or later.

Volnay "Clos de la Bousse d'Or," Premier Cru 1997 $NA. (SR)   **90**

Saturated ruby-red. Mineral aromas. Moderately full-bodied. Gripping tannins. Soft acidity. Not revealing much now. Well structured. A weighty Volnay. Lacks acidic cut for long-term keeping, but will develop in the near term. Mid-term cellar candidate.

Pommard "Les Jarolieres," Premier Cru 1997 $NA. (SR)   **88**

Rich ruby hue. Subdued mineral, earth, and red fruit aromas. Moderately full-bodied. Big tannins. Attractive flavors emerge on the finish. In need of cellaring. Lean and angular at present. Mid-term cellar candidate.

Jacques Prieur

Meursault "Clos de Mazeray," 1997 $48. (SR)   **90**

Bright yellow. Rich, creamy, nutty aromas. Moderately full-bodied palate. Very edgy acidity. Lean structure. Needs time. Mid-term cellar candidate.

Beaune "Champs Pimont," Premier Cru 1997 $48. (SR)   **88**

Brilliant golden straw hue. Fresh, complex mineral and sea salt aromas. A lean entry leads to a medium-bodied palate with very crisp acids. Lengthy minerally finish. Outstanding shellfish choice. Drink now or later.

Puligny-Montrachet "Les Combettes," Premier Cru 1997 $75. (SR)   **93**

Brilliant yellow. Exotic yeast, mineral, and spice aromas. Moderately full-bodied palate. Underlying acidic grip. Intense and rich, showing something now, but structured to develop beautifully with long-term cellaring.

Beaune "Clos de la Feguine," Premier Cru 1997 $52. (SR)   **83**

Chevalier-Montrachet, Grand Cru 1997 $250. (SR)   **92**

Highly saturated yellow-gold. Very rich vanilla, butterscotch, and tropical fruit aromas indicate lots of ripeness and a hefty oak accent. Full-bodied palate with shy acidity and a high level of flavor intensity. A big, flashy, almost Californian style. Hedonistic. Drink now.

     Scale: Superlative (96-100), Exceptional (90-95), Highly Recommended (85-89), Recommended (80-84), Not Recommended (Under 80)

Corton-Charlemagne, Grand Cru 1997 $115. (SR) 97

Vibrant yellow. Exotic, fresh sea spray, ginger, and spice aromas jump from the glass. Very ripe, full-bodied palate buoyed by vibrant acidity. Outstanding length and intensity. Extreme finish. A very ripe, rich Corton. Drink now or later.

Le Montrachet, Grand Cru 1997 $400. (SR) 95

Bright yellow-gold. Complex, brooding mineral, cream, and honey aromas. Full-bodied palate with well-integrated acidity. The finish goes on for a mile, with a haunting minty, honeyed overtone. Exotic. Drink now or later.

Meursault "Clos de Mazeray" Rouge, 1997 $40. (SR) 89

Deep ruby-purple hue. Intense black fruit, cassis, and mineral aromas are big and ripe. A firm entry leads to a moderately full-bodied palate with rounded tannins. Lush and stylish with a deeply fruited finish. Drink now or later.

Beaune "Champs Pimont," Premier Cru 1997 $42. (SR) 88

Brilliant purple. Subdued black fruit and flower aromas. Medium-bodied palate with aggressive floral fruit flavors and lean, gripping tannins. A clean, modern, tasty, forward style. Drink now or later.

Beaune "Gréves," Premier Cru 1997 $42. (SR) 89

Deep, brilliant ruby with purple highlights. Moderately full-bodied palate with gripping tannins. Deeply fruited finish with sweet oak accents. Should keep beautifully. Drink now or later.

Volnay "Clos des Santenots," Premier Cru 1997 $62. (SR) 92

Brilliant ruby-purple. Elegant flower, mineral, and red fruit aromas. Moderately full-bodied palate with lean tannins. Delicate in style (full for Volnay). Long finish. Modern and attractive. Mid-term cellar candidate.

Corton-Bressandes, Grand Cru 1997 $105. (SR) 93

Highly saturated purple. Deep, brooding mineral and black fruit aromas. Full-bodied palate with big, firm tannins. Oak tones dominate the finish. High levels of extraction, but a little closed at present. Impressive, but needs time. Very deep. Long-term cellar candidate.

Echézeaux, Grand Cru 1997 $120. (SR) 92

Rich ruby hue. Mineral and black fruit aromas. Full-bodied palate with big, aggressive tannins. Weight and intensity. Long-term cellar candidate.

Le Musigny, Grand Cru 1997 $150. (SR) 92

Brilliant purple. Exotic chocolate and red fruit aromas. Medium-bodied palate with velvety tannins. Richly flavored. A chunky Musigny, atypical but impressive. Mid-term cellar candidate.

Hervé Roumier

Hautes Côtes de Nuits Rouge, 1997 $NA. (SR) 80

Chambolle-Musigny, 1997 $NA. (SR) 88

Brilliant pale purple. Attractive flower and mineral aromas. Medium-bodied palate with defining acidic cut. Lean, but stylish and flavorful. Drink now.

Chambolle-Musigny "Amoureuses," Premier Cru 1997 $NA. (SR) 90

Brilliant pale purple. Attractive, feminine, flowery and red fruit aromas. Medium-bodied palate with defining acidity. Well balanced and very flavorful. Elegant. Drink now or later.

Clos Vougeot, Grand Cru 1997 $NA. (SR) 92

Brilliant ruby-purple. Exotically spicy and very aromatic, with a core of ripe fruit flavors. Medium-bodied. Gripping tannins and balancing acidity. Lighter in style, but shows great intensity of flavor. Very attractive already. Drink now or later.

Bonnes Mares, Grand Cru 1997 $NA. (SR) 90

Brilliant deep ruby-red. Aromatically subdued. Opens on the palate with a core of red fruit flavors. Moderately full-bodied. Gripping tannins and acidity. Needs time, but promising. Mid-term cellar candidate.

Armand Rousseau

Gevrey-Chambertin, 1997 $NA. (SR)   87

Bright ruby-purple. Subdued jammy red fruit aromas. Medium-bodied palate with soft tannins. Structured but feminine in style. Drink now.

Gevrey-Chambertin "Cazetiers," Premier Cru 1997 $NA. (SR)   88

Bright ruby-purple. Subtle aromatics. Medium-bodied palate with rounded tannins. Rather subdued at present, but well balanced and supple in style.

Charmes-Chambertin, Grand Cru 1997 $NA. (SR)   90

Bright ruby-purple. Generous red fruit, spice, and mineral aromas. Medium-bodied palate with vibrant tannins. A clean and flavorful style. Very attractive. Drink now.

Mazis-Chambertin, Grand Cru 1997 $NA. (SR)   90

Bright ruby hue. Aromatically subdued. Moderately full-bodied palate with gripping tannins. Light for the appellation, and rather closed at present, but it shows promising structure. Should develop nicely. Mid-term cellar candidate.

Clos de la Roche, Grand Cru 1997 $NA. (SR)   93

Bright ruby-purple. Jammy red fruit and mineral aromas with a spicy wood accent. Moderately full-bodied palate with gripping tannins. Ripe fruit flavors intensify through the finish. Classy. Drink now or later.

Ruchottes-Chambertin, Grand Cru 1997 $NA. (SR)   91

Saturated ruby hue. Restrained aromas. Moderately full-bodied palate with rich tannins. Rather subdued, but showing powerful structure. Should develop nicely. Long-term cellar candidate.

Gevrey Chambertin "Clos St. Jacques," Premier Cru 1997 $NA. (SR)   89

Bright ruby-red. Perfumed, forward flower and red fruit aromas. Medium-bodied palate with gripping tannins. Lighter in style with obvious oak tannins on the finish. Very attractive already. Drink now.

Clos de Beze, Grand Cru 1997 $NA. (SR)   93

Bright saturated ruby-red. Jammy fruit and mineral aromas. Moderately full-bodied palate with firm tannins, a gamey edge, and attractive wood spice. Powerful but already attractive. Long-term cellaring recommended.

Le Chambertin, Grand Cru 1997 $NA. (SR)   93

Saturated ruby hue. Full-bodied palate with big tannins. Youthful and closed, but showing promising power and depth. Very solid. Should develop nicely. Long-term cellar candidate.

Serafin

Gevrey-Chambertin, Vieilles Vignes 1997 $45. (SR)   90

Saturated ruby-purple. Generous spice, mineral, and anise aromas and flavors. Full-bodied. Gripping tannins. Concentrated and intense but rather closed at present. Long-term cellar candidate.

Gevrey-Chambertin "Les Corbeaux," 1997 $52. (SR)   91

Saturated purple. Intensely fragrant. Meaty, mineral berry and oak aromas. Moderately full-bodied palate. Gripping tannins. Full and intense with a distinctive sense of terroir. Long-term cellar candidate.

Gevrey-Chambertin "Fonteny," Premier Cru 1997 $58. (SR)   93

Deep ruby-red. Brooding black fruit, mineral, and licorice aromas. Full-bodied palate. Big tannins. Concentrated and intense. Well structured. Should develop beautifully with long-term cellaring.

Gevrey-Chambertin "Cazetiers," Premier Cru 1997 $70. (SR)   94

Brilliant ruby-red. Perfumed flower, oak spice, and red fruit aromas. Medium-bodied palate. Supple tannins. Attractive, feminine flavors. Delicate style. Long finish. Drink now or later.

Charmes-Chambertin, Grand Cru 1997 $100. (SR)   95

Scale: Superlative (96-100), Exceptional (90-95), Highly Recommended (85-89), Recommended (80-84), Not Recommended (Under 80)

Saturated ruby hue. Smoky, spicy aromas. Weighty, full-bodied palate. Lush, rounded tannins. Mouthfilling. Forward, with complex fruit flavors through to the finish. Supple and hedonistic. Mid-term cellar candidate.

Chambolle-Musigny "Les Baudes," Premier Cru 1997 $52. (SR)   **90**

Brilliant ruby hue. Attractive, flowery red fruit and mineral aromas carry a mineral accent. Medium-bodied. Crisp acids. A lighter, delicate style. Stylish and very drinkable. Drink now.

Morey St. Denis "Les Millandes," Premier Cru 1997 $52. (SR)   **91**

Saturated ruby hue. Delicate oak spice and red fruit aromas. Moderately full-bodied palate. Gripping tannins. Flavors intensify on the finish. Strikes a nice balance between wood and intense fruit flavors. Drink now or later.

twenty-eight

❧

France
Champagne

❧

Champagne Market Overview

Champagne is much more than a drink. The region, located 90 miles northeast of Paris, still produces most of the world's finest sparkling wines and still manages to command a significantly higher price for them than rival wines from the Old and New World. Champagne began promoting itself as a regional brand before the modern concept of brand was understood. Such a good marketing job has been done that many consumers, particularly American ones, no longer consider Champagne as a wine, but as something special requiring a sense of occasion. Champagne is a wine of course; a sparkling wine that has gained its bubbles by a secondary fermentation of still wine in the bottle in which it is sold. Champagne certainly deserves to be drunk more uniformly throughout the year as a fine wine in its own right. Relative to European drinkers, Americans still have a long way to go before they could confidently consider drinking Champagne (or sparkling wine) with a meal or routinely as an aperitif.

Grape Varieties

Three grape varieties are legally used in Champagne and all three are generally used in a Non-Vintage or Vintage wine.

Pinot Noir (37% of planted acreage)

Pinot Noir produces a rich, fruity, and broad style when it is used as the majority of a blend. Black grapes produce white wine, as the juice is not allowed to remain in contact with the skins.

Pinot Meunier (37% of planted acreage)

Pinot Meunier, a black grape with genetic links to Pinot Noir, adds softness and an early maturing element when it is used in a Champagne blend. It is generally considered a less noble variety though it is widely used in Non-Vintage blends.

Chardonnay (26% of planted acreage)

Chardonnay adds a racy, fruity character and gives a wine acidic backbone to age, as well as a distinctive piercing fruit flavor. In the Champagne region Blanc de Blancs are made entirely from Chardonnay.

Champagne Styles

Sweetness

At the bottling stage Champagne is nearly always sweetened by the addition of a small sweetened dose of wine, called the dosage. The vast bulk of Champagne (including all Vintage releases) is of the "Brut" level of dryness: Dry to the palate though very lightly sweetened. The exact level of dryness in a brut style will vary from producer to producer. The indicators of sweetness that you can find on a Non-Vintage label are as follows:

Extra Brut: Un-sweetened. Acidity is too much for most people at this level of dryness.

Brut: Lightly dosaged to be dry to the palate.

Extra Dry: An off-dry style.

Scale: Superlative (96-100), Exceptional (90-95), Highly Recommended (85-89), Recommended (80-84), Not Recommended (Under 80)

Demi Sec: Perceptible sweetness is evident.

Doux: Markedly sweet.

Non-Vintage

Non-Vintage Brut is the most important category of Champagne. The vast bulk of Champagne is Non-Vintage and the healthy sales of this category are what keeps the francs flowing in the region. A typical Non-Vintage cuvée will be composed of wine from two of the most recent vintages blended together, with very small amounts of older vintages. The demanding task of a Champagne blender is to maintain a typical house style by blending many different batches of wine. Quality does vary, consistent at least from year to year if not batch to batch. A succession of good vintages will result in great Non-Vintage Champagne with inverse consequences from a run of lesser years.

Vintage

Vintage Brut Champagnes are the product of a single vintage. Champagne houses may decide to not produce a Vintage Brut if the quality of the vintage is poor and good inventory of a better vintage allows them to meet demand for their vintage wine.

Blanc de Blancs

Blanc de Blancs are made from 100% Chardonnay. The style is typified by a brilliant green-gold hue, concentrated apple flavors, and racy acidity. In time the best of such wines take on a nutty character much like fine Burgundy. Only the finest Chardonnay fruit from Champagne can successfully be used for Blanc de Blancs and it will generally be from the Côte de Blancs region.

Rosé

Rosé Champagne generally gets its color from a proportion of red wine, conventionally made from Pinot Noir, being added to the blend. The more difficult method involves allowing the must to remain in contact with the skins for just long enough to get a pink hue. In style expect anything from a pink, bright, fruity wine up to copper-hued, rich, and faintly Burgundian styles.

Champagne at a Glance

Wines Reviewed:

207

Producers/Brands Represented:

56

Value Rating:

Poor to Average

Tête de Cuvée

The Tête de Cuvée is the ultimate expression of a Champagne house and it is usually expensive and lavishly packaged. Overall the Champenois maintain an outstanding quality at this level, particularly from the fine vintages of 1988, 1989, or 1990. Tête de Cuvées may be Rosés or Blanc de Blancs, or a conventional blend of Pinot Meunier, Pinot Noir, and Chardonnay

In Focus: Beyond Leading Brands

Growers and Grand Crus

Champagne has only one appellation: Champagne. Nonetheless, the region does have a highly developed Cru system that rates each vineyard for its potential quality. The appellation of Champagne is composed of five sub-regions, which contain communes rated as Grand Cru, Premier Cru, or bearing no Cru designation. The Champagne from big-name producers that most consumers are familiar with is generally a highly blended product made from fruit sourced from many of Champagne's sub-regions. Such Champagnes may contain significant amounts of Grand Cru fruit, particularly in the more prestigious cuvées. When one sees "Grand Cru" on a label, the name of the commune will also be marked. Such Champagne is invariably a *grower* Champagne from a small producer who owns holdings in one commune.

For the connoisseur that is prepared to seek out quality and character, grower Champagnes are well worth tracking down. A grower Champagne has been vinified by the owner of the vines, often on a very small scale, by a family concern. Only a handful of the hundreds produced make it through to the U.S. market, but they can often be found in good wine specialty stores. Serge Mathieu and Jacques Selosse are examples of particular grower labels that are noteworthy for rivaling and exceeding the big name brands in quality. The most prestigious grower Champagnes come from the exclusively Chardonnay-planted Côte de Blancs sub-region of Champagne. Grand Cru communes such as Avize, Chouilly, Crammant, Le Mesnil-sur-Oger, and Vertus supply the region's most sought-after grapes and are the source of the finest grower Champagne.

Aging Champagne

Many U.S. drinkers of Champagne are missing a lot of its potential pleasure and complexity by drinking it too young. Most good Champagne can age respectably, even Non-Vintage cuvées. Exactly how old one should drink any wine is a matter of individual taste. Indeed, most houses are releasing wines with respectable bottle age, so the yeast in the bottle has *autolyzed* to produce some bready, biscuity aromas and flavors, and the acids have softened. It can certainly do no harm to purchase newly released, Non-Vintage Champagne and allow this maturation to progress for another six months to a year. Some of the better Non-Vintage cuvées can cellar for far longer than this. Good, cool cellaring conditions are essential, as Champagne is particularly sensitive to heat—more so than most still wine.

Scale: Superlative (96-100), Exceptional (90-95), Highly Recommended (85-89), Recommended (80-84), Not Recommended (Under 80)

Vintage Overview

Declaring vintage years is the prerogative of the Champagne houses—when they feel that the quality of the harvest merits it, and occasionally, when dwindling stocks of vintage wines mandate it. The major producers generally, though not always, declare the same vintages. Thus, 1990 will be universally declared, while 1984 was not declared by any of the grand marque houses.

1982. A big, rich vintage with ripe character. Top Vintage Bruts and Tête de Cuvées such as Krug will still be showing well.

1983. A good year with good acid levels to give long cellar life; also a record harvest, yielding 300 million bottles. Blanc de Blancs Tête de Cuvées are particularly fine; the best will still be going strong now.

1985. A small harvest produced ripe but balanced wine. Spring frost killed many of the vines, resulting in a small yield of 151 million bottles. Top Vintage Bruts and Tête de Cuvées are drinking well now.

1986. Following a disastrous 1984 and a small 1985, this was widely declared, though quality was not uniformly high. Yields were high, with total production at 258 million bottles. Some good Tête de Cuvées were produced, notably excellent were Pol Roger Cuvée de Winston Churchill, Pol Roger Blanc de Blancs, and Dom Pérignon Rosé.

1988. A classic cellaring vintage declared by most houses. Firm, dry wines have a solid structure that will reward those with patience. Total production: 221 million bottles.

1989. This harvest produced big, ripe, voluptuous wines that are drinking well now—in most cases. Weather throughout the harvest was excellent, so much so that a second harvest was possible well into October. Most houses declared this quick-maturing vintage. Drink these while waiting for the 1988s to mature.

1990. Much lauded as a classic vintage, with warm ripening conditions persisting well into October. Big, ripe wines with structure and balance are drinking very well on release in many cases. Several will be worth cellaring. Total yield: 288 million bottles.

1991. A decent vintage, though not a classic. It was not widely declared, as most houses were well stocked with the '90 vintage. Total production: 274 million bottles.

1992. By many accounts, a mediocre vintage with dilution and low alcohol levels not uncommon. This vintage accounted for the dip in quality of many a Non-Vintage blend in which it was used, and it was not widely declared as a vintage. This was the year that regulations banning the use of second pressings came into effect, though the top houses never practiced this economy. Total production: 288 million bottles.

1993. Rain at harvest severely affected concentration and ripeness. It seems unlikely to be a great vintage year; although some houses doubtless will keep quality adequate by severe selection. It is too early to make a definitive judgment.

1994. Rain arrived a few days before the 1994 harvest could be picked on September 15. Quality will be affected at all levels and it seems that most of the wine from this vintage will go into the Non-Vintage blending vat. Few 1994s have been released yet. Total harvest equaled 244 million bottles.

1995. A good though not outstanding vintage is in prospect for 1995. Given the run of less than great 1990s vintages this will doubtlessly be declared by some houses to maintain stocks of vintage wines after and in the run-up to the millennium celebrations. The summer saw hot spells in June and July, though rain showers in August and September will mean the best results will come from the most severe selection of grapes.

1996. Early harvest report indicators are that 1996 will be a classic vintage of high quality. The harvest stretched over a long period allowing for the picking of ripe grapes. It seems likely that it will be very widely declared for vintage wines to be released from 2002 onwards.

Scale: Superlative (96-100), Exceptional (90-95), Highly Recommended (85-89), Recommended (80-84), Not Recommended (Under 80)

Best Producers: France, Champagne

What Is Champagne?

Champagne is a sparkling wine, but not all sparkling wines are Champagne. The name refers to a small district in the North of France which transformed their rather thin and acidic wines into a worldwide phenomenon. The crisp, bubbly, effervescent, and refreshing character of sparkling Champagne is now widely emulated throughout the world. At the top end however, nothing beats great Champagne. The down side? The Champenois know it and charge accordingly. Nonetheless, it is perhaps the world's most jovial splurge wine.

Premier Champagne Producers (***)

- Bollinger
- Gosset
- Krug
- Moët & Chandon (Dom Pérignon)
- Philipponnat (Clos des Goisses & Grand Blanc)
- Louis Roederer
- Pol Roger (Cuvée Sir Winston Chuchill)
- Ruinart
- Salon
- Jacques Selosse
- Taittinger (Comtes de Champagne)

Great Champagne Producers (**)

- Henri Abèle (Sourire de Reims)
- Ayala
- Beaumont de Crayères
- Billecart Salmon
- Bricout
- Charles de Cazanove
- René Collard
- de Méric
- de Saint Gall
- de Venoge
- Delamotte
- Deutz
- Drappier
- Duval Prétrot
- Nicolas Feuillatte (Cuvée Palme d'Or)
- Pierre Gimonnet
- Alfred Gratien (Cuvée Paradis)
- Charles Heidsieck
- Heidsieck Monopole
- J. Lassalle
- Joseph Perrier
- Laurent Perrier
- Serge Mathieu
- Moët & Chandon
- Oudinot
- Bruno Paillard
- Palmer
- Philipponnat
- Ployez Jacquemart
- Pol Roger
- Taittinger
- Veuve Clicquot
- Vilmart

Dependable Champagne Producers (Recommended)

These producers have impressed us. Some are new. Some are older but improving steadily. Some have done well in the past but we have not tasted enough vintages to classify them as Premier or Great yet.

- Henri Abèle
- Cattier
- Duval Leroy
- Nicolas Feuillatte
- Alfred Gratien
- Henriot
- Lanson
- Guy Larmandier
- Mumm
- Montaudon
- Pannier
- Perrier-Jouet
- Piper-Heidsieck
- Pommery
- Vranken

Reviews

Henri Abèle

NV Brut Champagne $25.   83

1986 Le Sourire de Reims Champagne $85.   91

Brilliant yellow-gold. Moderately full-bodied. Highly extracted. Complex, developed aromas lead a mouth-filling, assertive style, showing baked pear flavors and plenty of vigor. Maturity is evident in the nutty, spicy notes that linger. Very traditional, connoisseur's style.

Ayala

NV Brut Champagne $24.99.   90

Bright pale yellow-straw. Medium-bodied. Moderately extracted. Stone fruit, apricot. Elegant toasty aromas. The palate reveals an austere character yet the stone fruit flavors are quite concentrated and lengthy on the finish. Elegant and balanced, this shows some finesse.

Paul Bara

1989 Special Club, Bouzy Grand Cru Champagne $50.   90

Deep golden yellow. Moderately full-bodied. Balanced acidity. Highly extracted. Exotic, mature aromas show honey and almond notes. Rich, rounded mouthfeel with an assertive set of flavors that finish in a mildly bitter manner. Very flavorful, traditional style that will go best with food.

Beaumont des Crayères

NV Cuvée de Prestige Brut Champagne $28.   90

Bright pale straw appearance. Medium-bodied. Moderately extracted. Well integrated spicy nose with subtle toasty yeast. Well-rounded palate with fruity flavors to the fore with a lingering nutty note through the finish. This shows some elegance.

NV Cuvée de Réserve Brut Champagne $32.   88

Deep straw cast. Moderately full-bodied. Full acidity. Highly extracted. Ripe and toasty on the nose. In the mouth, this is forceful in style, with a firm and vibrant palate feel. Weighty and full through the finish. Very generous, with a fine mousse.

1994 Cuvée de Prestige Champagne $34.   85

Bright yellow-straw. Medium-bodied. Moderately extracted. Lighter, bready aromas with fruity accents. Shows a lighter touch in the mouth, with soft, creamy yeast flavors and fine-beaded bubbles.

NV Cuvée Rosé Privilege Champagne $36.   89

Full salmon hue. Moderately light-bodied. Moderately extracted. Subtle, toasty aromas, with bright red fruit accents. Youthful, undeveloped aromas have a zesty, red fruit accent. Vibrant and bright on the palate, with firmness through the finish.

1990 Cuvée Spéciale, Nostalgie Brut Champagne $44.   91

Full golden luster. Medium-bodied. Moderately extracted. Stone fruits, lemons. Very rich, ripe aromas with smoky accents. Somewhat obvious with rich fruity flavors that are supported by good acid levels and a weighty mouthfeel. Quite unctuous in an almost buttery sense.

Billecart-Salmon

NV Brut Réserve Champagne $23.99.   85

Bright pale straw. Medium-bodied. Moderately extracted. Generous berry-like black grape aromas lead a flavorsome, fruity palate with very subtle toasty yeast coming through on the finish. Not hugely complex but very fruity.

Scale: Superlative (96-100), Exceptional (90-95), Highly Recommended (85-89), Recommended (80-84), Not Recommended (Under 80)

NV Brut Rosé Champagne $47.99.   88

Pale orange-gold color. Medium-bodied. Highly extracted. orange, lemons, minerals. Harmonious toasty yeasty aromas are quite high-toned. Very bright and lively on the palate with orange and cherry flavors. This has plenty of flavor and lively acids that dominate on the palate.

1988 Blanc de Blancs Champagne $62.   93

Deep golden yellow. Full-bodied. Highly extracted. Smoke, roasted coffee. Aromas of roasted coffee and smoke have a rich, oily theme conveyed on the palate with viscous texture and pronounced burnt notes through the finish. A very distinguished, mature and powerful style.

Bollinger

NV Special Cuvée Brut Champagne $30.   90

Deep yellow-straw cast. Full-bodied. Full acidity. Highly extracted. Nutty, blanched-almond aromas. Showing maturity in both color and flavor, with forward aromas hinting at a degree of maderization. Curiously youthful and vibrant in the mouth, however, with a racy finish. A style best suited to the table.

1988 Brut Rosé Champagne $60.   92

Brilliant orange. Moderately full-bodied. Full acidity. Highly extracted. Mature, smoky aromas. Angular and lean, with tart acids and austere flavors that grip the palate. Very tightly wound and intense through the finish, though it opens markedly with aeration. This is substantial and food-friendly.

1989 Grande Année Champagne $70.   94

Full yellow-gold. Moderately full-bodied. Highly extracted. Very developed, toasty aromas of baked bread and nutmeg lead a rich, rounded palate with opulent flavors that persist through the finish. Decadent, drinking very well now, though this should not fade anytime soon.

1990 Grande Année Champagne $70.   91

Brilliant bright golden luster. Moderately full-bodied. Balanced acidity. Highly extracted. Rich, bready aromas show maturity in a caramelized, maderized note. Sumptuous mouthfeel with broad flavors showing. Powerful shellac-like character emerges with aeration; may be overwhelming for sensitive souls. Drinking very well now.

1985 R.D. Extra Brut Champagne $132.   92

Bright yellow-gold luster. Moderately full-bodied. Highly extracted. Outstanding rich smoky character carries through the finish. This has considerable weight and tartness with strong acids taking over on the finish. Hugely impressive roasted, burnt yeast toasty yeast. A food wine.

1989 Vieilles Vignes Françaises Blanc de Noirs Brut Champagne $180.   97

Deep straw. Full-bodied. Reminiscent of earth, dried herbs, citrus. Intense earthy, herbal aromas lead into a phenomally intense and extracted palate with lingering nutty complexity on the long finish. Still tight and youthful with great structure, but peversely showing some developed flavors. Quite unusual. Certainly a connoisseur's wine.

Bricout

1989 Premier Cru Brut Champagne $26.   94

Straw color. Moderately full-bodied. Balanced acidity. Reminiscent of smoke, stone fruits, toast. Smokey, integrated, and complex aromas reveal a sumptuous and creamy palate showing great finesse and some good mature yeasty notes that linger through the finish. Drinking well now. A great buy.

1991 Premier Cru Brut Champagne $26.   86

Pale yellow-straw color. Moderately light-bodied. Moderately extracted. lemon, minerals, smoke. High toned subtly smoky, spicy nose leads a crisp focused lemony palate with a fine smoky yeast overlay. Mouthfeel and balance are good, though this is a light accessible style.

Cattier

NV Brut Antique, Premier Cru Champagne $36.95.　　　　**86**

Deep straw cast. Medium-bodied. Full acidity. Moderately extracted. Distinctive pear and black-grape aromas point to the rich pinot-noir domination of this wine. Broad and flavorful, with generous fruity character that will give this a wide appeal.

Charles de Cazanove

NV Magenta Brut Champagne $24.99.　　　　**86**

Bright pale yellow-straw. Medium-bodied. Moderately extracted. Tart peach, lemons, minerals. Clean briskly fruity style with bright lemony acids and tart peach flavors on the palate and subtle lingering yeasty notes on the finish.

NV Brut Azur Champagne $25.99.　　　　**89**

Straw color. Moderately full-bodied. Reminiscent of citrus, stone, dried herbs. Pronounced nutty smokey aromas lead into a full-flavored palate with a rich mouthfeel. Finishes with lingering complexity.

1990 Brut Champagne $29.99.　　　　**87**

Brilliant yellow-gold appearance. Medium-bodied. Moderately extracted. Citrus, stone fruit. Focused roasted, yeasty aromas leads a crisp well-balanced palate that finishes cleanly. Drinking well now, though more time would increase the toasty yeast complexity.

NV Brut Rosé Champagne $29.99.　　　　**87**

Bright pale metallic orange color. Moderately light-bodied. Moderately extracted. White peach, ripe citrus fruits. Mildly toasty, bready aromas. Juicy appealing citrus and peach flavors have a mouthwatering finish. Very rounded and balanced. A lighter more delicate style, feminine even.

1989 Stradivarius Champagne $49.99.　　　　**92**

Straw color. Moderately full-bodied. Full acidity. Reminiscent of toast, flowers, orchard fruits. Very zesty aromas precede a vibrant palate with strong citrus tones and some pleasing toasty mature notes present on the mid-palate through the finish. A big angularly styled Champagne.

Charbaut

NV Brut Champagne $27.　　　　**83**

René Collard

NV Carte d'Or Brut Champagne $34.95.　　　　**85**

Medium yellow-straw appearance. Medium-bodied. Moderately extracted. Smoky, nutty nose with mildly oxidized nuances. Highly concentrated dry fruity flavors are quite austere. A very traditional style that may not be everyone's cup of tea.

1969 Carte d'Or Brut Champagne $79.95.　　　　**93**

Deep golden straw color. Medium-bodied. Moderately extracted. brown spice, Outrageous almondy, Fino sherried nose. Austere oxidized palate has plenty of lean stone fruit character. Still plenty of life giving acidity in this. Very distinctive and certainly alive and kicking. This will appeal to those who like aged Champagnes.

1975 Carte D'Or Champagne $69.95.　　　　**87**

Bright pale yellow-straw. Medium-bodied. Balanced acidity. Very oxidized, spicy nose has aromas of roasted almonds. Vigorous acids and zesty qualities are overwhelmed by nutty, oxidized flavors that dominate the finish. Still very much alive and vigorous, with great mousse.

1985 Carte D'Or Champagne $49.95.　　　　**93**

Bright golden luster. Medium-bodied. Moderately extracted. Honeyed, almondy aromas. Lively and vigorous on the palate, with a velvety mouthfeel and a honeyed character that gives way to an elegant, spicy finish. The mousse is impressively lively and elegant.

1985 Brut Rosé Champagne $59.95.　　　　　　　　　　　　　　　91

Pale golden orange color. Medium-bodied. Moderately extracted. Limes, minerals, roasted coffee. Sherry-like aromas with pronounced toasty yeast aromas. The flavors are lean with bright lime acids and with a maderized note through a long nutty finish. This will met the approval of those that like mature Champagne.

Comte Audoin de Dampierre

1985 Champagne de Grand Cru $89.95.　　　　　　　　　　　　87

Straw color. Full-bodied. Balanced acidity. Reminiscent of rubber, green herbs, tropical fruit. Outrageous complexity on the aromatics translates well on the palate. Shows good maturity and development. Mouthfeel is creamy and rich through finish. For the connoissers of petits Champagnes.

Delamotte

NV Brut Champagne $26.　　　　　　　　　　　　　　　　　89

Bright straw cast. Moderately full-bodied. Full acidity. Moderately extracted. Fine smoky, toasty aromas lead a stylish, complex range of flavors. Mouthfilling, rich flavors turn crisp and lively through the finish.

1990 Blanc de Blancs Champagne $40.　　　　　　　　　　　　90

Brilliant golden yellow. Full-bodied. Balanced acidity. Highly extracted. Ripe, rich aromas have a smoky accent. The flavors have a tropical richness, with apple and peach notes conveyed by softer acids. Exceptionally generous and rich, this is for those who like rich, fruity wines.

Demilly De Baere

NV Brut Champagne $19.99.　　　　　　　　　　　　　　　84

Very pale straw appearance. Medium-bodied. Full acidity. Moderately extracted. Spicy nose is unusual. Fine concentration of citrus and apple flavors with razor sharp acids giving this focus through a lingering finish. Seems quite young right now.

NV Brut Blanc de Blancs Champagne $19.99.　　　　　　　　　80

Deutz

NV Brut Classic Champagne $29.　　　　　　　　　　　　　88

Bright yellow-straw cast. Full-bodied. Full acidity. Highly extracted. Forward buttery, toasty aromatics. Big and racy in the mouth, with weight and intensity. A generous, mouth-filling style with rich flavors.

NV Cuvée Marie-Demarisse, Brut Rosé Champagne $35.　　　91

Bright pale metallic orange color. Medium-bodied. Moderately extracted. Berry fruits, autolysed yeast, lemons. Impressive roasted nose. Full berry fruit flavors with some assertive dryness and fine lemony acids through the finish. Robust and hearty style that will partner foods well.

1990 Brut Champagne $40.　　　　　　　　　　　　　　　90

Brilliant bright yellow-gold appearance. Medium-bodied. Moderately extracted. Stone fruits, apples, toasty yeast. Generous black grape-inspired aromas with toasty yeast notes lead a robustly flavorsome palate with broad fruity appeal and a lingering fruity finish. Generous style, drinking nicely now.

1990 Brut Rosé Champagne $40.　　　　　　　　　　　　　91

Full salmon hue. Moderately full-bodied. Full acidity. Highly extracted. Smoky, dried red fruit aromas. Big shouldered and angular, with vibrant acids and a strong, minerally underlay. Not a shy, retiring flower, this is a powerhouse style that could use more age.

1989 Blanc de Blancs Brut Champagne $45.　　　　　　　　94

Brilliant yellow-gold appearance. Medium-bodied. Moderately extracted. Green apples, white peach, minerals, toasted nuts. Outstandingly complex, well-developed aromas show nutty, toasty accents. The palate is fresh and lively with green apple and white peach flavors, and more complex nutty notes lingering on the finish.

1993 Blanc de Blancs Champagne $45.   **83**

1988 Cuvée William Deutz Brut Champagne $85.   **92**

Bright yellow-gold luster. Moderately full-bodied. Highly extracted. Brioche-like nose. Rich rounded mouthfeel has great presence and plenty of pinot character. Very long and rich with a chalky, creamy feel. This is a classy food wine and can only improve with more age.

1990 Cuvée William Deutz Brut Champagne $85.   **87**

Bright yellow-gold. Moderately full-bodied. Balanced acidity. Moderately extracted. Nutty, spicy aromas lead a substantial mouthfeel with smooth, supple character. The flavors do not fill the mid-palate as one would wish, though this has stuffing and persistence.

Drappier

NV Carte Blanche Brut Champagne $34.   **85**

Very pale straw. Moderately light-bodied. Moderately extracted. Anise, white citrus. Subtly toasty nose has an herbal, anise accent making for complex aromas. Bright snappy palate has a minerally edge that comes through on the finish.

NV Brut Carte D'Or Champagne $34.   **87**

Deep straw cast. Medium-bodied. Full acidity. Moderately extracted. Forward, biscuity aromas show an impressive degree of maturity. Supple and well-balanced in the mouth, with a yeasty character, a refreshing finish, and fine length.

NV Signature Blanc de Blancs Brut Champagne $42.   **90**

Bright pale yellow-straw color. Medium-bodied. Moderately extracted. nuts, peach, green apples. High toned fruity aromas. Packed with bright Chardonnay flavors of peach and green apples that conclude with a honeyed nutty finish that distinguishes this.

NV Val des Demoiselles Rosé Brut Champagne $42.   **84**

Bright reddish gold appearance. Medium-bodied. Moderately extracted. Sour cherry, vanilla. Fruity, though faintly undeveloped vanilla accented nose. Good mouthfeel and general structure with sour cherries flavors. Six months to a year in bottle should see this showing even better.

1990 Carte D'Or Brut Champagne $47.   **91**

Full medium golden straw luster. Medium-bodied. Moderately extracted. stone fruits, apricot, ripe apples, roasted coffee. Well integrated smoky, roasted toasty yeast is confirmed on the palate showing a fine mouthfeel. Mild astringency on the finish gives this youthful character. Great balance and finesse, though a few more years would help this.

1989 Grande Sendrée Champagne $80.   **93**

Bright yellow-gold appearance. Moderately full-bodied. Highly extracted. smoke, nuts, orchard fruits. Fine roasted coffee notes on the nose comes through well on the finish. This shows great concentration and complexity with smoky orchard fruit flavors. Showing some maturity now, but the acids would suggest that this has further to go.

1990 Grande Sendrée Champagne $85.   **89**

Bright yellow-straw. Moderately full-bodied. Rich, rounded, and mildly sweet through the finish. This has a bready, tropical note and could use more age to develop further complexity. The dosage seems a tad high.

Duval Prétrot

1994 Brut Champagne $39.95.   **88**

Bright yellow-straw. Moderately full-bodied. Highly extracted. Yeasty, toasty aromas show fine development. Rich and rounded, with a generous peach-apple accent throughout. This is showing considerable ripeness and weight.

Duval-Leroy

NV Brut Champagne $24.50.   85

Mid straw. Medium-bodied. Reminiscent of citrus, flowers, lees. Attractive aromatics lead into a bright and refreshing palate showing good concentration of fruit flavors. An assertive but refreshing aperitif style.

1990 Blanc de Blancs Champagne $49.50.   86

Straw with gold highlights. Medium-bodied. Balanced acidity. Reminiscent of tropical fruits, citrus, minerals. Good fruity aromas lead into a slightly austere style with a hint of yeasty complexity through the minerally finish. A refined and elegant style with very precise fruit flavors.

Nicolas Feuillatte

NV Brut Premier Cru Champagne $24.99.   83

NV Premier Cru Rosé Champagne $27.99.   86

Reddish orange tint. Moderately light-bodied. Moderately extracted. Red berry fruits, strawberries, yeast. Berry fruit nose has bready hints that are confirmed on the palate. Bright fruity strawberry flavors up front finish cleanly.

1994 Rosé Millesime Champagne $30.   86

Bright samon-pink. Moderately full-bodied. Moderately extracted. Bright, primary red fruit aromas lead a fruity, creamy mouthfeel. Delicate, spicy finish is carried by bright acids. Friendly, though this is not showing much maturity.

1988 Cuvée Spéciale, 1er Cru Brut Champagne $37.99.   92

Full bright golden appearance. Medium-bodied. Moderately extracted. Apple, apricots, Creamy nutty mouthfeel with lush fruit flavors and a fairly assertive toasty finish. This is developing lovely biscuity character. Moderately rich, elegant style. This could probably mature further.

1990 Cuvée Palmes d'Or Brut Champagne $97.   90

Pale bright yellow-gold. Medium-bodied. Balanced acidity. Highly extracted. Lemons, apples, minerals. Very tight, with bright acids and zesty lemon and apple flavors. Impressively structured, though this is not yet showing mature complexity.

Georges Gardet

NV Brut Special Champagne $35.99.   84

Pale yellow-straw. Medium-bodied. Moderately extracted. Green apples, pears, cinnamon. Somewhat rustic and and vinous. This has plenty of green apple and pear fruit flavors and some structure but has not quite come together yet.

Pierre Gimonnet

1992 Grand Cru Chardonnay, Special Club, Brut Champagne $33. 88

Brilliant yellow-straw. Moderately full-bodied. Balanced acidity. Mature aromas lead a rich, rounded mouthfeel, with a creamy texture and apple flavors that finish in a spicy manner. Drinking well now; this needs no further cellaring.

Gosset

NV Excellence Brut Champagne $33.99.   83

NV Grande Réserve Brut Champagne $44.99.   91

Deep straw cast. Full-bodied. Full acidity. Highly extracted. Bready, creamy aromas with forward, complex flavors. Though this is full and rich in the mouth, it has an underlying firmness and solidity that will allow it to improve with age.

1988 Grand Rosé Champagne $57.99.   92

Bright orange-gold. Moderately full-bodied. Full acidity. Toasty, citrus-edged aromas lead a vibrant, leaner style showing dried cherry notes, with taut acids and firm, minerally accents through the finish. A powerful, artisanal style that will work well with food.

1985 Grand Millesime Champagne $81.99.   **95**

Yellow gold luster. Moderately full-bodied. Full acidity. Highly extracted. Mature, evolved aromas have nutty, toasty richness that follows through on the palate with a silky, yet powerful character showing great maturity. Aristocratic, artisanal style that opens up spectacularly with aeration. Drink with food.

1989 Grand Millesime Champagne $81.99.   **88**

Brilliant pale straw. Full acidity. Highly extracted. Nutty, reserved aromas. This has a deep core of minerally character, with tart, tropical flavors lingering through the finish. Seems a tad backward now, though this should blossom in the cellar.

1990 Celebris Champagne $108.99.   **90**

Yellow gold. Full-bodied. Highly extracted. Rich, doughy aromas follow through on the palate. Very deep, intense and flavorful, with great persistence through the finish. This is still youthful, though impressive. A markedly traditional style.

Alfred Gratien

NV Brut Classique Champagne $40.   **89**

Bright straw cast. Medium-bodied. Full acidity. Moderately extracted. Complex aromas, yet reserved in flavor, with a nutty, spicy nuance throughout. Light and racy in the mouth, yet well-balanced. Shows fine length and intensity.

Charles Heidsieck

NV Brut Réserve Champagne $34.   **89**

Deep yellow-straw cast. Moderately full-bodied. Full acidity. Highly extracted. Good nutty maturity; complex, with generous bready flavors and a weighty, yet well-balanced mouthfeel. Zesty and intense through the finish. Very stylish.

1990 Brut Champagne $48.   **90**

Medium straw appearance. Medium-bodied. Moderately extracted. Roasted coffeee, stone fruits, apples. Aromas hint of roasted coffee. Fine mouthfeel with a rich, well balanced character. The flavors and finish do not yet seem developed. This is in a youthful stage and two–three years will see this showing better.

1985 Brut Rosé Champagne $55.   **92**

Brilliant bright orange-gold. Moderately full-bodied. Full acidity. Outstandingly developed, mature nose shows full, yeasty development. In the mouth, this is still vibrant, with rich, nutty flavors persisting through the finish. Very sophisticated; fully mature now.

1985 Blanc des Millenaires Champagne $70.   **99**

Brilliant yellow-green. Moderately full-bodied. Full acidity. Highly extracted. Extraordinarily intense, fruit-driven, burnt-coffee aromas follow through on the palate, with pure Chardonnay fruit flavors that show a terrific, nutty accent throughout. The mouthfeel is substantial, even decadent, with a mile-long finish not unlike a mature Burgundy.

Heidsieck Monopole

NV Blue Top Brut Champagne $28.   **85**

Bright straw cast. Moderately full-bodied. Full acidity. Moderately extracted. Aromatically reserved, with a youthful, aggressive palate feel showing a green apple character. Lean and austere through the finish, with a subtle, bready overtone.

1988 Diamant Rosé Champagne $60.   **98**

Brilliant golden-orange hue. Moderately full-bodied. Full acidity. Mature, burnt aromas point to exotic development. Shows some caramelized notes on the palate, with a marked burnt-coffee note on the finish. Very aristocratic and mature, with little primary fruit character. A connoisseur's style.

Scale: Superlative (96-100), Exceptional (90-95), Highly Recommended (85-89), Recommended (80-84), Not Recommended (Under 80)

1989 Diamant Bleu Champagne $60.   **89**

Brilliant yellow-gold. Moderately full-bodied. Highly extracted. Mature aromas have a very nutty accent. Mouthfeel is rounded and generous, with caramelized accents on the gripping finish. A well-endowed, powerful style that is quite evolved now.

NV Diamant Blanc Champagne $100.   **94**

Bright straw. Moderately full-bodied. Highly extracted. Outstanding roasted-coffee aromas follow through on the palate to give this a powerful yeasty component. An assertive, flavorful style with honeyed notes. This is drinking well now.

Krug

Grande Cuvée Champagne $100.   **95**

Bright yellow-straw. Full-bodied. Highly extracted. Honeyed, spicy aromas lead a full-flavored mouthful, with nutty richness pervading the palate. This bottling has more than a touch of sherried character, and is drinking wonderfully now.

1985 Brut Champagne $120.   **97**

Full golden straw. Full-bodied. Highly extracted. Carmelized apple, fino. Roasted nuts and faint sherried accents on the nose. Rich weighty mouthfeel has great viscosity and depth of flavors. It is very approachable now, and showing some maturity, but it has years to go before it reveals its potential.

1989 Brut Champagne $120.   **96**

Full golden luster. Full-bodied. Outstanding vinous nose follows through on a richly flavored palate, showing an oily texture and powerful spicy, nutty flavors through the finish. Drinking very well now, though this will develop much more complexity.

Rosé Champagne $150.   **95**

Bright orange color. Full-bodied. Highly extracted. Amontillado Sherry, mocha, strawberries. Rich maderized aromas have plenty of coffee notes. Mature Sherry flavors come through on the palate with hints of dried berry fruits. Quite subtle in its rosé character with mocha and strawberry hints. Complex and relatively mature. This is not losing any of its vigor and connoisseurs of aged Champagne could cellar this further.

1976 Collection Champagne $210.   **100**

Deep straw colored with amber highlights. Full-bodied. Balanced acidity. Reminiscent of lychee, roasted nuts, Amontillado Sherry. Big elegant and roasted aromas lead into an sublimely complex and elegant palate with big rounded nutty flavors. The mouthfeel is rich and creamy through to an extraordinarily long finish. Quite exceptional and distinctive with plenty of sparkle left.

1985 Clos du Mesnil Champagne $210.   **95**

Bright yellow-gold luster. Full-bodied. Full acidity. Highly extracted. Assertive toasty, nutty aromas. Very concentrated tight racy stone fruit flavors have a huge minerally underlay. Extraordinarily structured and powerful with an assertive finish. This is certainly best suited to drinking with food though extensive cellaring is really required.

1989 Clos du Mesnil Champagne $210.   **100**

Deep bright golden luster. Honeyed, buttery, opulent aromas that follow through on a rich, thick palate with strikingly well-developed flavors that assault the palate. Other-worldly in its power and persistence. This is approachable now, yet will certainly become richer and more honeyed with age. Possibly the most forward vintage ever of Clos du Mesnil.

Lanson

NV Black Label Champagne $17.99.   **85**

Bright straw cast. Moderately full-bodied. Full acidity. Moderately extracted. Showing some maturity, with bright, yeasty flavors. Crisp, lean, and racy in the mouth, with vibrant citrus-peel flavors and a refreshing finish.

Guy Larmandier

NV Cramant Grand Cru, Blanc de Blancs Champagne $36.   86

Bright pale straw. Medium-bodied. Full acidity. Racy and elegant, with a light touch throughout. Clean Chardonnay fruit flavors have a lime-like purity. Nervous and feminine in style.

J. Lassalle

NV 1er Cru Brut Rosé Champagne $35.99.   89

Bright orange with subtle amber highlights. Medium-bodied. Moderately extracted. Bread, roasted nuts, strawberries. Generous bready nose leads a rounded generous mouthfeel. The palate shows strawberry and mild roasted nuts flavors with some lingering yeasty notes persisting.

NV 1er Cru Brut Champagne $38.99.   88

Full golden straw appearance. Moderately full-bodied. Moderately extracted. Bread dough, ripe pears. Well developed nose. Rich full-flavored palate asserts itself with complex distinctive flavors of bread dough and pears. Rounded mouthfeel with a lingering flavorful finish. This would work with food.

Laurent-Perrier

NV Brut L.P. Champagne $28.99.   85

Bright greenish straw cast. Medium-bodied. Full acidity. Moderately extracted. Fragrant and forward, with a distinctive green edge and a touch of smoke. Lighter in the mouth, but quite flavorful, with a lean finish.

NV Cuvée Rosé Brut Champagne $49.99.   89

Bright red salmon hue. Medium-bodied. Balanced acidity. Moderately extracted. Generously bready, fruity aromas. A delicate style showing dried strawberry notes with a silky mouthfeel. This is pure, hedonistic delight that will seduce anyone.

1990 Brut Champagne $58.99.   89

Pale yellow-gold. Moderately full-bodied. Full acidity. Smoke, tart tropical fruits. Smokey aromas lead an extravagant mouthfeel, with rounded, almost tropically rich flavors that are kept in check by citrus acids. Still lively and young, though drinking well now.

1988 Grand Siècle Champagne $99.99.   92

Bright pale yellow-straw. Moderately full-bodied. Full acidity. Highly extracted. Elegant nutty, spicy aromas. Wonderful, developed, Chardonnay-rich mouthfeel with pure, fruit-driven flavors buoyed by fine acids. Quite intense, this will cellar well to gain more nutty complexity.

Serge Mathieu

NV Brut Rosé Champagne $34.99.   90

Full reddish orange tint. Medium-bodied. Moderately extracted. Cherries, roasted coffee, yeast. Complex aromas of bread and roasted coffee show great integration. Full flavored and harmonious with berry fruit flavors to the fore and a delicate lingering finish with a yeasty accent. Delicious, very attractive style that should find broad appeal.

NV Cuvée Prestige Brut Champagne $34.99.   85

Bright pale yellow-gold appearance. Medium-bodied. Moderately extracted. Stone fruits, citrus fruits, minerals. Mildly toasty nose leads a bright fruity palate with a clean finish. Not showing much yeast complexity yet, though this is well-balanced.

NV Cuvée Tradition Blanc de Noirs Brut Champagne $34.99.   84

Brilliant bright yellow-gold color. Medium-bodied. Moderately extracted. Coconut, mineral, stone fruits. Mildly smoky, fruity nose with coconut nuances. Brash, full fruity flavors expand on the palate. Very rounded, weighty mouthfeel. Youthful.

1990 Brut Millesime Champagne $38.99.   **89**

Straw color. Moderately full-bodied. Balanced acidity. Reminiscent of citrus, roasted nuts, minerals. Harmonious aromas reveal a well-integrated and flavorsome palate with a nicely textured mouthfeel. The texture and mouthfeel are the hallmarks of class.

1991 Brut Millesime Champagne $39.99.   **88**

Bright yellow-gold. Medium-bodied. Moderately extracted. Toasted coffee, apricots, limes, minerals. Aromas hint at toasty, spicy toasty yeast with almond notes. Rounded, weighty mouthfeel. Excellent lingering finish shows a classy toasty note. Still too young and vibrant to show its full potential, this should be cellared.

NV Tête de Cuvée Select Brut Champagne $39.99.   **86**

Very bright pale gold. Medium-bodied. Moderately extracted. roasted coffee, stone fruits, tart apple. Generous smoky nose shows fine toasty yeast. Concentrated tart apple and stone fruit flavors are accented by bold acids. This has the structure to improve with further age.

Champagne de Méric

NV Brut Selection Champagne $29.95.   **86**

Bright greenish straw cast. Moderately full-bodied. Full acidity. Highly extracted. Aromatically reserved, with a sturdy and forceful mouthfeel revealing citrus peel and mineral flavors. Crisp and linear, with precise flavors through the finish.

NV Blanc de Blancs Champagne $34.95.   **91**

Straw with gold highlights. Moderately full-bodied. Balanced acidity. Reminiscent of grapefruit, dried herbs, nuts. Mature aromas reveal a rich creamy palate in a traditional style with good extract and a lengthy finish. A hefty wine and a natural food partner.

NV Brut Rosé Champagne $37.95.   **87**

Bright cherry-red appearance. Moderately full-bodied. Highly extracted. Cherries, berry fruits, minerals, bread. Powerful aromatics show fruity character with well-integrated bready notes. Assertive berry fruit flavors up front turn dry through the finish. Quite robust and hearty with plenty of character.

1988 Brut Selection Champagne $39.95.   **86**

Yellow gold. Medium-bodied. Highly extracted. Very spicy, developed aromas. Flavorful and long, with a rich, nutty accent that lingers through the finish. A more austere, firmly traditional style that is still very vibrant.

NV Cuvée Prestige Catherine de Medicis Champagne $59.95.   **95**

Deep straw color. Full-bodied. Reminiscent of tropical fruit, toasted nuts. Deeply toned mature aromatics showing yeast complexity. Pleasant entry and a rich and creamy mid-palate with some good acidity to lift the finish. A good food wine.

Moët & Chandon

NV Demi-Sec Champagne $38.   **86**

Pale straw color. Moderately full-bodied. Balanced acidity. Reminiscent of stone fruits, dried herbs. Inviting aromatics reveal a sumptuous and reasonably complex palate with a lingering full-flavored finish. Sweetness gives some extra body and is balanced by a good concentration of flavors.

NV Nectar Imperial Champagne $38.   **86**

Very pale straw appearance. Medium-bodied. Moderately extracted. Peaches, honey, grapes. Sweet tropical fruit nose with peach and honey follows through onto the palate. Attractive and creamy with no edges or evident dryness on the finish.

NV Brut Imperial Champagne $40.   **84**

Pale greenish straw cast. Medium-bodied. Balanced acidity. Moderately extracted. Aromatically reserved, showing a mildly toasty note with a supple, yet crisp mouthfeel. Well balanced, with a sweet note to the finish. Very rounded and fruity, though in a more lightweight style.

NV Brut Rosé Champagne $40.   83

1992 Brut Imperial Champagne $48.   87

Bright yellow-gold. Medium-bodied. Moderately extracted. Smoky aromas betray a note of unripeness, though this still has plenty of smoky yeast character. Finish is curiously rough, though the mouthfeel is quite refined.

1992 Brut Imperial Rosé Champagne $53.   81

1990 Cuvée Dom Pérignon Champagne $110.   94

Bright medium straw. Moderately full-bodied. Balanced acidity. Honeysuckle, smoke aromas. Silky, rich mouthfeel, with generously biscuity, fruity flavors and vibrant mousse stretching into the finish. Very polished. Drinking nicely now, although this should have considerable longevity in the cellar.

1986 Cuvée Dom Pérignon Rosé Champagne $200.   94

Deep orange-gold. Moderately full-bodied. Extravagant, smoky, mature aromas show full yeast development. Supple, textured mouthfeel conveys harmonious elegance, with developed, smoky, Pinot Noir character in evidence. Perfect now, this is the epitome of sophistication in rosé Champagne.

Montaudon

NV Chardonnay Premier Cru Champagne $32.   84

Brilliant pale yellow-straw. Medium-bodied. Full acidity. Youthful, high-toned citrus and herbal aromas lead a bright, juicy, mouthwatering set of flavors through a tart finish. Very effervescent and youthful. Ideally this needs more bottle age.

1993 Brut Millesime Champagne $35.   NR

NV Brut Champagne $35.   84

Bright straw cast. Moderately full-bodied. Full acidity. Highly extracted. Markedly high-toned citrus aromas lead to a lean and lively palate feel. Angular and austere through the finish. This is quite a weighty wine with leaner flavors. More bottle age should help.

Mumm

NV Carte Classique, Extra Dry Champagne $23.   NR

NV Cordon Rouge Champagne $25.   81

NV Mumm de Cramant, Blanc de Blancs Champagne $42.   86

Bright yellow-gold. Medium-bodied. Bright, lively and dry through the finish, with an herbal streak to the citrus flavors. Carbonation is very frothy: quite a distinctive feature. A fine seafood or aperitif style.

Oudinot

NV Brut Champagne $19.99.   83

NV Brut 1er Cru Champagne $24.   92

Medium straw with a golden cast. Medium-bodied. Moderately extracted. Roasted coffee, crème brûlée ripe, apples, Rich developed roasted coffee and crème brûlée aromatics show assertive toasty yeast. Full flavored and mouthfilling with satisfying richness and a hint of sweetness on the mid-palate.

Bruno Paillard

NV Brut Première Cuvée Champagne $35.   89

Deep yellow-straw hue. Moderately full-bodied. Balanced acidity. Moderately extracted. Forward creamy, vanilla aromas are complex and show a degree of toasty maturity. Ripe and supple in the mouth, with excellent balance and an angular finish.

Scale: Superlative (96-100), Exceptional (90-95), Highly Recommended (85-89), Recommended (80-84), Not Recommended (Under 80)

NV Brut Rosé Première Cuvée Champagne $45. **86**

Pale orange-gold. Moderately full-bodied. Highly extracted. Elegant and vibrant, with a strong citrus streak through the finish. Still seems rather youthful and structured, with dry sensations clamping down on the finish.

Palmer

NV Brut Champagne $28.99. **85**

Medium straw with a pale gold cast. Medium-bodied. Moderately extracted. Lemons, ripe apples, minerals. Mildly toasty, yeasty nose. Flavors on the palate are well extracted with ripe apple and citrus accents through a minerally feel on the finish.

NV Brut Rosé Champagne $33.99. **90**

Medium dark golden luster with an orange tint. Medium-bodied. Moderately extracted. Dough, vanilla, lemon, minerals. Mildly roasted doughy toasty yeast on the nose. Soft creamy mouthfeel with generous yeasty character complemented by some lemony acids and a minerally feel through the finish.

1988 Blanc de Blancs Brut Champagne $39.99. **89**

Bright yellow-gold appearance. Medium-bodied. Moderately extracted. Apple tart, toast, mild smoke. Aromas have a strong impression of brown spice with a nutty accent that follows through well on the finish. Well structured, and vibrant enough to cellar further if one should so wish.

1989 Brut Champagne $39.99. **89**

Pale bright yellow-gold. Medium-bodied. Moderately extracted. Rather distinctive toasty, spiced aromas lead a bright crisp palate of tart fruit flavors through to a lingering spicy finish. Quite elegant and racy.

Pannier

NV Selection Brut Champagne $23.99. **86**

Pale bright yellow-straw. Medium-bodied. Moderately extracted. Zesty, mildly yeasty aromas lead a bright palate of lemon, lime flavors with toasty hints that linger through the mildly astringent finish.

NV Cuvée Louis Eugène Brut Champagne $32.99. **85**

Pale yellow-gold appearance. Medium-bodied. Moderately extracted. Vinous aromas seem youthful. Has some nutty richness with a nicely textured mouthfeel. Some astringency comes through on the finish. This should be better in 12 months.

1990 Cuvée Egerie Brut Champagne $36.99. **84**

Very bright golden straw appearance. Medium-bodied. Moderately extracted. Butterscotch, apples, lemon cream. Mild butterscotch and toast aromas lead apple and lemon cream flavors. Well balanced and with good length though this seems to have a fairly youthful character with a hint of astringency on the finish. More time would probably help.

Joseph Perrier

NV Cuvée Royale Brut Champagne $19. **86**

Pale bright straw color. Moderately light-bodied. Full acidity. Moderately extracted. Lemon, tart peach, minerals. Subtle spicy overtones on the nose lead a youthful, vivacious and vibrant palate with bright flavors and a clean finish showing a hint of astringency. Although light-bodied, this has the structure to age further in bottle. Perfect with shellfish or as an aperitif.

NV Cuvée Royale Blanc de Blancs Brut Champagne $39. **90**

Full medium straw luster. Moderately light-bodied. Moderately extracted. Brioche, lemon zest, toast, minerals. Complex aromas of zest and brioche are quite high toned. Bright and zesty flavors are enhanced by a lovely mouthfeel and very long flavorful finish. Quite a light-bodied style but packed with flavor.

1989 Cuvée Royale Brut Champagne $40.   91

Brilliant yellow appearance. Moderately light-bodied. Moderately extracted. Zesty, smoky aromas follow through on the palate. Quite light in style, with very precise flavors and clean acids dominating the palate, through to a lingering burnt note on the finish. Drinking well now.

NV Cuvée Royale Brut Rosé Champagne $45.   92

Bright orange-gold appearance. Medium-bodied. Moderately extracted. Berry fruits, lemons, minerals. Spectacular mature nose has maderized notes that come through well on the palate which displays a solid steely backbone with berry fruit nuances. This has seen some generous bottle age that has given it a character that will delight lovers of mature flavors. Try with food.

1985 Cuvée Joséphine Brut Champagne $96.   90

Brilliant yellow-straw color. Medium-bodied. Highly extracted. Tart green apples, burnt autolysis. Deep bready, biscuity nose. Elegant, concentrated mouthfeel with flavors of tart green apples. Amazingly persistent finish has plenty of rich biscuity character. Still vigorously fruity despite its age. Nowhere near fading at this point.

Perrier-Jouet

NV Grand Brut Champagne $28.   81

1989 Fleur de Champagne $94.99.   86

Bright yellow-gold. Moderately full-bodied. Moderately extracted. Lemons, minerals, ripe apples. Rounded and quite weighty with ripe apple and lemon flavors. Not overly complex though this does have a fine mouthfeel.

1990 Fleur de Champagne $85.   88

Bright yellow-gold. Moderately full-bodied. Balanced acidity. Highly extracted. Ripe and rounded, showing a generous mouthfeel. Though this has little flavor complexity, it does convey a ripe, generous impression and a degree of textural elegance. Drinking nicely now.

1988 Fleur de Champagne Brut Rosé Champagne $104.99.   88

Pale orange-gold color. Medium-bodied. Moderately extracted. roasted coffee, lemons, dried berry fruits. Mild roasted coffee aromas. Hints of dried berry fruits come through on the palate. Clean direct style with a lingering finish. Distinguished by a good mouthfeel.

1989 Fleur de Champagne, Brut Rosé Champagne $105.   88

Pale salmon. Moderately full-bodied. Balanced acidity. Subdued, smoky aromas. Nice, rounded mouthfeel shows an angular texture through the finish. Flavors do not show much complexity or development, with mineral dominance on the finish.

Philipponnat

NV Brut Royale Réserve Champagne $25.99.   83

NV Réserve Rosé Champagne $35.99.   94

Pale salmon. Medium-bodied. Vinous aromas follow through on the palate. Fine, mature style, with creamy, toasty, yeast flavors lingering on the finish. A complex style, but still tight on the finish; this could use 1–2 years cellaring.

NV Le Reflet Brut Champagne $39.99.   88

Pale yellow-straw. Medium-bodied. Moderately extracted. Nice bready nose. Rich stone fruit flavors expand on the palate, making for a very accessible appealing style with a lingering chalky, fruity finish.

1986 Grand Blanc Brut Champagne $49.99.   95

Straw color. Moderately full-bodied. Balanced acidity. Reminiscent of pine nuts, stone fruits, dried herbs. Marked mature and complex aromas lead into a rich palate showing strong tertiary character. Finish is lenghty and assertive. A rich food partner made in an artisanal style.

Scale: Superlative (96-100), Exceptional (90-95), Highly Recommended (85-89), Recommended (80-84), Not Recommended (Under 80)

612

1988 Grand Blanc Brut Champagne $49.99.	93

Bright yellow-gold color. Medium-bodied. Moderately extracted. Very refined smoky lemon cream aromas follow through well on the palate with racy Chardonnay flavors throughout. Amazingly long finish with bright peachy acids persisting. Harmonious and elegant.

1989 Grand Blanc Brut Champagne $49.99.	97

Rich yellow-gold. Moderately full-bodied. Balanced acidity. Mature, smoky, ripe aromas point to fine development. This is rounded and nutty in the mouth, with flavors of ripe apples and a hint of dryness on the finish. Drinking very well now.

1988 Clos des Goisses Champagne $99.	94

Bright pale straw. Moderately full-bodied. Full acidity. Highly extracted. Green apples, lemons, minerals. Exotic floral nose hints at green apples and lemons. Impressively concentrated fruit flavors, well-structured with a tight assertive finish. This is not showing its best yet but is very impressive. Three to five years in cellar.

Piper-Heidsieck

NV Extra Dry Champagne $20.	87

Deep greenish golden color. Moderately full-bodied. Balanced acidity. Moderately extracted. Full, bready, mature aromas. Quite complex, with a forward, generous character and a restrained sweetness that make for a very rounded style.

NV Cuvée Brut Champagne $28.	84

Pale yelow straw. Medium-bodied. Balanced acidity. Bread and pear aromas follow through on the palate with full fruity accent and a vigorous mousse with medium-sized beads. Rather straightforward, but very flavorsome with a high degree of black grape flavors.

NV Brut Rosé Champagne $48.	88

Deep orange salmon. Moderately full-bodied. Balanced acidity. Highly extracted. Mature aromas of dried red fruits and smoke lead an austere but bright palate, with dry minerally flavors that grip the finish. A substantial, structured wine that will best accompany food.

1988 Rare Champagne $65.	90

Mid straw color. Medium-bodied. Full acidity. Reminiscent of citrus, stone fruits. High-toned stone-fruit aromas translates onto a very lively and structured palate with a distinct minerally finish. Quite assertive in style and could probably age well in the cellar.

Ployez-Jacquemart

NV Brut Champagne $26.	87

Deep greenish straw cast. Moderately full-bodied. Full acidity. Highly extracted. Pear and black-grape aromas have a toasty, smoky, yeast component that comes through on the palate. Rich and weighty in the mouth, with forceful carbonation and fine length.

Pommery

NV Brut Royal Champagne $22.99.	85

Bright straw cast. Moderately light-bodied. Balanced acidity. Moderately extracted. Aromatically reserved, with a crisp and zesty palate feel and subtle mineral and apple flavors. Refreshing and lively, in a lighter style.

NV Brut Royal Apanage Champagne $29.99.	85

Deep straw cast. Medium-bodied. Full acidity. Moderately extracted. High-toned aromas have a crisp, green-apple accent. Lean and zesty in the mouth, with a straightforward, minerally finish.

1988 Louise Tête de Cuvée Champagne $95.	89

Bright yellow-straw. Moderately full-bodied. Full acidity. Highly extracted. Smoky, developed aromas lead an assertive, smoky mouthful of flavors, with burnt, yeasty flavors lingering on the finish. A powerful, weighty style lacking a little for refinement, though further cellar age may soften some edges.

Louis Roederer

NV Carte Blanche Champagne $40. 87

Bright pale yellow-straw. Moderately full-bodied. Moderately extracted. Nice sweet toasty nose. Rich and mouthfilling with a succulent mouthfeel that has a sweet fruity character allied to a rich toasty finish. Pair with fruit-based desserts.

NV Extra Dry Champagne $40. 90

Full golden straw appearance. Moderately full-bodied. Moderately extracted. Roasted nuts, toast, lychee, allspice. Rich roasted, nutty nose. Assertively flavored with mature complex character showing lychee-like flavors through a very lengthy finish. This comes across as being quite dry. A good food partner.

NV Brut Premier Champagne $42. 87

Deep straw cast. Moderately full-bodied. Full acidity. Moderately extracted. Biscuity, toasty aromas show a degree of complexity. Crisp and intense on the palate, with forceful, finely beaded bubbles. Flavorful and yeasty, yet elegant and well-balanced.

1990 Brut Champagne $54. 90

Yellow gold. Moderately full-bodied. Highly extracted. Intensely bright, with piercing acids and a sense of reserved tightness. Finish clamps down with dry, gripping character. Very impressive, though this needs more time to reveal its potential.

1993 Blanc de Blancs Champagne $55. 90

Bright yellow-straw. Medium-bodied. Full acidity. Bready, citrus aromas. Racy, persistent citrus flavors betray a touch of toughness on the finish. Mouthfeel and carbonation are quite elegant. Quite youthful; further time will help this.

1991 Brut Rosé Champagne $56. 90

Pale golden with a very subtle amber tint. Medium-bodied. Moderately extracted. Dough, mocha, strawberry, lemons, minerals. Full doughy nose indicates generous yeasty character with lots of complex rich aromas. Palate is tight and reined-in with lemon and strawberry flavors. Well structured, this will take some time to show its paces.

1993 Brut Rosé Champagne $56. 93

Pale salmon. Medium-bodied. Full acidity. Youthful aromas have a brisk, citrus edge, with pinot-skin nuances. Very elegant mouthfeel, with dried strawberry flavors lingering through the finish. Nice now, though this could develop more yeast complexity.

1990 Cristal Champagne $149. 91

Brilliant yellow-gold. Moderately full-bodied. Moderately extracted. Distinguished by a very long finish, with tart fruit persistence. Silky mouthfeel, with very supple texture. Shows lime-like intensity, with fine, smoky accents throughout. This has a great future.

Pol Roger

NV Brut Champagne $35. 86

Deep yellow-straw cast. Moderately full-bodied. Full acidity. Moderately extracted. Smoky, blanched-almond aromas. Ripe, but linear in the mouth, with a zesty, firm finish. A firm, solid style that should improve with further bottle age.

NV Brut Extra Cuvée de Réserve Champagne $40. 88

Bright yellow-gold color. Medium-bodied. Highly extracted. Bitter lemon, minerals, smoke. Somewhat smoky nose. Rich, well-structured wine with bitter lemon flavors through a long assertive finish. This has an impressive presence on the palate. Quite tight and austere.

1988 Vintage Brut Champagne $49.99. 94

Mid straw color. Medium-bodied. Full acidity. Reminiscent of stone fruits, bread, brown spice. Striking smoky nose leads into a slightly tight and focused palate with classy smokey overtones through the finish. A big classy wine that needs further bottle age to appreciate its full potential.

Scale: Superlative (96-100), Exceptional (90-95), Highly Recommended (85-89), Recommended (80-84), Not Recommended (Under 80)

1988 Brut Rosé Champagne $58.   91

Bright orange-gold. Moderately full-bodied. Full acidity. Highly extracted. Smoke, spice, roasted coffee. Complex rather traditional nose. Bright acids and tight structure. Strong roasted coffee and toasty flavors linger on the finish. For lovers of austere and powerful styles.

1990 Brut Rosé Champagne $58.   90

Pale salmon. Moderately full-bodied. Full acidity. Highly extracted. Distinctively smoky, mature aromas. Expansive, rich mouthfeel shows pedigree and youthful structure. Very rich and classy. This could use further cellaring.

1988 Brut Chardonnay Champagne $62.   89

Pale straw color. Medium-bodied. Full acidity. Reminiscent of stone fruits, green apple, dried herbs. Focused and crisp in style. Rather youthful structure, though still showing some yeasty complexity. Needs cellar age to show its true class.

1990 Brut Chardonnay Champagne $65.   89

Bright pale gold. Moderately full-bodied. Highly extracted. Exceptional length and mouthfeel, with smoky yeast notes already well-developed. This is still reserved, yet firm, with some grip on the finish. Very nice now, though it will be better in 2–3 years.

1986 Cuvée Sir Winston Churchill Champagne $125. 97

Mid straw color. Moderately full-bodied. Full acidity. Reminiscent of apricots, lacquer, spices. Rather complex spicy aromas. On the palate, elegant yet still structured with some good concentration of flavors, focused and still quite tight. Finish is long and flavorsome. This will cellar for years, gaining further tertiary character.

1988 Cuvée Sir Winston Churchill Champagne $130. 94

Brilliant yellow-gold. Moderately full-bodied. Full acidity. Highly extracted. Broad, biscuity aromas lead an expansive, rich mouthful of tart peach and citrus flavors. Wonderfully weighty and rich, this is drinking well, though the finish is still quite dry. One to cellar for as long as you can keep your hands off it.

Ruinart

NV Brut Champagne $33.   87

Bright straw cast. Moderately full-bodied. Full acidity. Moderately extracted. Shows a degree of complexity, with a forward, very "telltale Ruinart" smoky quality. Firm and zesty in the mouth, yet well-balanced and flavorful through the finish.

1990 Brut Champagne $45.49.   94

Mid straw. Moderately full-bodied. Full acidity. Reminiscent of smoke, toast, yeast, tropical fruit. Striking burnt aromas reveal a full-throttle palate, with a textured mouthfeel and big leesy flavors through the finish. Certainly should develop more complexity with cellar age although it is drinking nicely now.

1992 Brut Champagne $50.   85

Pale straw. Medium-bodied. Pungent, burnt nose leads a lighter-styled palate with an elegant mouthfeel. Rather dominated by its yeasty, mature flavors. Has all the imprints of house style that will please Ruinart fans, albeit in a lighter frame.

NV Brut Rosé Champagne $70.   94

Bright orange hue. Moderately full-bodied. Highly extracted. Fine-developing smoky, burnt nose. Weighty and rich on the palate, with an almost glycerous mouthfeel and subdued carbonation. Silky texture, with fruity flavors making for a hedonistic style.

1988 Dom Ruinart, Blanc de Blancs Champagne $97. 93

Dark golden straw. Moderately full-bodied. Balanced acidity. Powerful, mature aromas strike an oily, burnt note. Rich and extravagantly textured, with deep, nutty flavors and a long, complex finish. An assertive style that will work well with food. Mature, though this is in no danger of fading.

1986 Dom Ruinart, Brut Rosé Champagne $112.   95

Orange-salmon hue. Full-bodied. Highly extracted. Distinctive, charred aromas are a turn-on (or -off, depending on your persuasion). Plenty of dried, red fruit flavors with a strong accent on smoky yeast flavors that dominate the finish. Classic, powerful style. Showing a mature character; outstanding.

Champagne de Saint Gall

1990 Blanc de Blancs, Premier Cru Champagne $50.   89

Rich golden yellow. Moderately full-bodied. Full acidity. Nutty, yeasty aromas indicate some maturity. The palate reveals an extraordinarily apple-like mouthful of flavors that tapers to a spicy finish. This is extremely ripe and generous up front, though the finish is a tad brief.

1988 Cuvée Orpale Grand Cru Champagne $85.   87

Bright yellow-straw. Moderately full-bodied. Full acidity. Highly extracted. Bright, lemony nose with a smoky yeast accent leads a vibrant, citrus-centered mouthful of flavors and a clean, zesty finish. This has picked up some mature notes, but is still jarringly youthful in its acids.

Salon

1988 Blanc de Blancs Champagne $100.   97

Bright pale golden luster. Moderately full-bodied. Highly extracted. Broad, rich, nutty flavors show great richness and length, with a buttery mouthfeel. This has developed great nutty complexity that follows through on a powerful finish. An outstanding wine, this begs for food.

Jacques Selosse

NV Grand Cru Brut Champagne $34.99.   90

Bright golden straw luster. Moderately full-bodied. Highly extracted. Pear, apples, earth, nuts. Outstanding sherried nose has perfumed accents. Rich oxidized flavors lead a mouthfilling silky palate with pear and apple flavors and a distinctive *gout de terroir.* This could accompany richer food.

1989 Blanc de Blanc, Grand Cru Brut Champagne $49.99.   90

Deep golden appearance. Moderately full-bodied. Moderately extracted. Cinnamon, apples, stone fruit, minerals. Hints of oak in the nose. Very distinctive brown spice aromas come through on the palate and linger through the long finish. Rich full Chardonnay flavors have some nutty qualities. This is well-structured and should improve in the cellar.

Taittinger

NV Brut La Française Champagne $37.99.   88

Deep straw cast. Medium-bodied. Full acidity. Moderately extracted. Crisp, citrusy aromas show a subtle, toasty note. Displays an elegant and balanced impression on the palate, with lively mousse. Crisp and flavorful through the finish.

NV Cuvée Prestige Rosé Champagne $47.99.   84

Bright, king salmon hue. Medium-bodied. Full acidity. Minerally, citrus aromas. Bright and snappy, with a vibrant character and subdued, dried raspberry flavors. Rather on the lean side.

1991 Brut Millesime Champagne $51.99.   89

Bright pale yellow-straw color. Medium-bodied. Moderately extracted. Lemon cream, toast, spice. Mild toasted nose. Soft rounded, almost creamy palate with a full fruity mid-palate that has a tight finish showing some astringency that leaves a dry, minerally impression. Quite flavorsome. This needs a little more time to come together.

1992 Brut Millesime Champagne $51.99.   **86**

Bright yellow-straw. Medium-bodied. Full acidity. Moderately extracted. Lean, crisp aromas show some yeasty complexity. A lighter style with brisk citrus flavors, though this has fine-beaded carbonation and a sense of elegance.

1989 Comtes de Champagne Blanc de Blancs Champagne $112.99.   **91**

Brilliant pale yellow-straw color. Medium-bodied. Highly extracted. Apples, toasted nuts, citrus zest. Full smoky, nutty nose. Bright full lively mouthful of Chardonnay flavors expand on the middle with a tapering, long finish of toasted nuts and citrus zest. Nice now.

1990 Comtes de Champagne Blanc de Blancs Champagne $112.99.   **92**

Deep green straw. Moderately full-bodied. Highly extracted. Toasty, nutty aromas lead a bright, fruit-centered mouthful of Chardonnay flavors with a rich, nutty accent. Rounded, rich, decadent mouthfeel. Drinking very nicely now.

1991 Comtes de Champagne Rosé Champagne $149.99.   **90**

Bright pink highlights. Moderately full-bodied. Full acidity. Reminiscent of berry fruit, minerals, yeast. Impressively extracted with a hint of astringency on the finish. Full acidity is well-balanced by big flavor components. This has excellent structure and a youthful character. Should be stashed in the cellar.

1993 Comtes de Champagne Rosé Champagne $162.99.   **91**

Pale salmon pink. Moderately full-bodied. Highly extracted. Youthful, vinous nose shows red fruit accents and broad, bready notes that come through on the palate. This has not developed much tertiary complexity yet, though it has bright enough acids and weight to cellar.

Champagne de Venoge

NV Brut Cordon Bleu Champagne $27.   **88**

Bright pale yellow-straw. Medium-bodied. Moderately extracted. Burnt rubber, tart peach, smoke. Very characterful yeasty aromas give this an assertive nose that carries through the palate. Distinguished by a fine mouthfeel with tart stone fruit flavors and a smoky note through the finish.

1990 Blanc de Blancs Brut Champagne $35.   **86**

Deep golden straw color. Moderately full-bodied. Highly extracted. Ripe apples, stone fruits, toasted nuts. Nutty-accented aromas lead a rich, full-flavored palate with ripe Chardonnay flavors of stone fruits and apples, and a creamy mouthfeel. This is showing some development. Drinking very well now.

NV Princesse Rosé Champagne $35.   **83**
1990 Cuvée des Princes Brut Champagne $79.   **91**

Deep golden straw color. Moderately full-bodied. Highly extracted. Roasted nuts, green apples, stone fruits. Rich roasted aromas show complexity in well-integrated nutty nuances. Very forward stone fruit and green apple flavors expand on the palate showing a textured mouthfeel. This is drinking very well now, though should benefit from some cellaring.

Veuve Clicquot

NV Yellow Label Brut Champagne $28.   **89**

Pale greenish straw cast. Moderately full-bodied. Full acidity. Moderately extracted. Yeasty, yet youthful aromas lead a rounded mouthfeel, with a sense of weight and bready generosity; this retains youthful character in its steely finish.

1989 Vintage Réserve Champagne $30.   **87**

Pale golden luster. Moderately full-bodied. Highly extracted. Developed smoky, toasty aromas. Rounded and generous, with broad, fat flavors that seem very harmonious now. Drinking very well, with a full complement of biscuity character.

1989 Rosé Réserve Brut Champagne $50.   **89**

Bright pale salmon. Moderately full-bodied. Full acidity. Highly extracted. Distinguished smoky aromas show a roasted-coffee note. Very long, persistent flavors show rich Pinot Noir flavors and broad, biscuity accents. Very lush mouthfeel makes for a generous style.

1989 La Grande Dame Champagne $75.   **92**

Bright yellow-gold. Moderately full-bodied. Balanced acidity. Juicy, tart, citrus-centered palate, with rounded texture and a fine, smoky accent running through the finish. Weight and mouthfeel are the keynotes. This is drinking very well now.

1988 La Grande Dame Rosé Champagne $180.   **90**

Deep orange-gold. Full-bodied. Highly extracted. Vinous, mature aromas lead a powerful, tight mouthful of flavors, with angularity on the finish. Very dry and flavorful, with a very long finish. This will best complement food, and may well blossom with more cellar age.

Vilmart

NV Blanc de Blancs Champagne $25.   **85**

Bright yellow-gold. Medium-bodied. Moderately extracted. Curiously mature, with a subtle note of oxidation that follows through with a vinous, complex character and a persistent finish. A very distinctive, artisanal style that will appeal to connoisseurs of grower Champagne.

NV Grand Cellier Champagne $30.   **86**

Deep straw cast. Medium-bodied. Full acidity. Moderately extracted. Mature aromas. Very distinctive, with a forward, yet unusual range of flavors. Lively and racy in the mouth, with a hint of oxidation that lingers on the lengthy finish. Interesting, rustic style.

1991 Coeur de Cuvée Champagne $55.   **93**

Pale yellow-straw. Moderately full-bodied. Highly extracted. Toasty, yeasty, leesy aromas lead a very spicy, cider-like palate that shows artisanal character. The mouthfeel is quite refined, with a lingering finish. Very impressive and powerful; a markedly complex style.

Vranken

NV Demoiselle Grande Cuvée Brut Champagne $28.   **82**

1989 Demoiselle Tête de Cuvée Brut Champagne $40.   **89**

Full pale golden . Medium-bodied. Moderately extracted. Pear, apples, toast. Well integrated toasty nose has fine character. Rich, ripe toasty mouthful of flavors shows great development through a complex toasty finish that is not overly long. Drinking nicely now.

1990 Demoiselle Tête de Cuvée Brut Champagne $45.   **86**

Bright pale straw. Moderately full-bodied. Subtly smoky aromas. The mouthfeel is very rich, though the flavors do not follow in the same proportions. Finishes dryly; this impresses with its weight.

NV Demoiselle Tête de Cuvée Brut Rosé Champagne $45.   **NR**

1990 Premiers Crus Tête de Cuvée Brut Champagne $60.   **87**

Pale yellow-gold. Medium-bodied. Moderately extracted. Pears, apples, smoky yeasts. Mildly smoky aromas. Concentrated apple and pear flavors have a clean, lean character through a lengthy finish. This is starting to show some nutty character, though is still a little tight on the finish.

Demoiselle Cuvée 21 Champagne $100.   **91**

Bright yellow-straw. Moderately full-bodied. Smoked, almost tropically rich aromas show a developed yeasty note. Sumptuous, rounded mouthfeel is complemented by ripe, generous, fruit-centered flavors, with good, biscuity complexity.

Scale: Superlative (96-100), Exceptional (90-95), Highly Recommended (85-89), Recommended (80-84), Not Recommended (Under 80)

Outstanding Champagne by Type

Brut NV
92 • Oudinot NV Brut 1er Cru, Champagne $24.
91 • Gosset NV Grande Réserve Brut, Champagne $44.99.
90 • Jacques Selosse NV Grand Cru Brut, Champagne $34.99.
90 • Bollinger NV Special Cuvée Brut, Champagne $30.
90 • Beaumont des Crayères NV Cuvée de Prestige Brut, Champagne $28.
90 • Ayala NV Brut, Champagne $24.99.

Brut Vintage
94 • Ruinart 1990 Brut, Champagne $45.49.
94 • Pol Roger 1988 Vintage Brut, Champagne $49.99.
94 • Bricout 1989 Premier Cru Brut, Champagne $26.
93 • René Collard 1985 Carte D'Or, Champagne $49.95.
92 • Nicolas Feuillatte 1988 Cuvée Spéciale, 1er Cru Brut, Champagne $37.99.
91 • Joseph Perrier 1989 Cuvée Royale Brut, Champagne $40.
91 • Drappier 1990 Carte D'Or Brut, Champagne $47.
91 • Beaumont des Crayères 1990 Cuvée Spéciale, Nostalgie Brut, Champagne $44.
90 • Paul Bara 1989 Special Club, Bouzy Grand Cru, Champagne $50.
90 • Louis Roederer 1990 Brut, Champagne $54.
90 • Deutz 1990 Brut, Champagne $40.
90 • Charles Heidsieck 1990 Brut, Champagne $48.

Blanc de Blancs
97 • Philipponnat 1989 Grand Blanc Brut, Champagne $49.99.
95 • Philipponnat 1986 Grand Blanc Brut, Champagne $49.99.
94 • Deutz 1989 Blanc de Blancs Brut, Champagne $45.
93 • Philipponnat 1988 Grand Blanc Brut, Champagne $49.99.
93 • Billecart-Salmon 1988 Blanc de Blancs, Champagne $62.
91 • Champagne de Méric NV Blanc de Blancs, Champagne $34.95.
90 • Louis Roederer 1993 Blanc de Blancs, Champagne $55.
90 • Joseph Perrier NV Cuvée Royale Blanc de Blancs Brut, Champagne $39.
90 • Jacques Selosse 1989 Blanc de Blanc, Grand Cru Brut, Champagne $49.99.
90 • Drappier NV Signature Blanc de Blancs Brut , Champagne $42.
90 • Delamotte 1990 Blanc de Blancs, Champagne $40.

Brut Rosé
98 • Heidsieck Monopole 1988 Diamant Rosé, Champagne $60.
95 • Ruinart 1986 Dom Ruinart, Brut Rosé, Champagne $112.
95 • Krug Rosé, Champagne $150.
94 • Ruinart NV Brut Rosé, Champagne $70.
94 • Philipponnat NV Réserve Rosé, Champagne $35.99.
94 • Moët & Chandon 1986 Cuvée Dom Pérignon Rosé, Champagne $200.
93 • Louis Roederer 1993 Brut Rosé, Champagne $56.
92 • Joseph Perrier NV Cuvée Royale Brut Rosé, Champagne $45.
92 • Gosset 1988 Grand Rosé, Champagne $57.99.
92 • Charles Heidsieck 1985 Brut Rosé, Champagne $55.
92 • Bollinger 1988 Brut Rosé, Champagne $60.
91 • Taittinger 1993 Comtes de Champagne Rosé, Champagne $162.99.
91 • René Collard 1985 Brut Rosé, Champagne $59.95.

91 • Pol Roger 1988 Brut Rosé, Champagne $58.

91 • Deutz NV Cuvée Marie-Demarisse, Brut Rosé, Champagne $35.

91 • Deutz 1990 Brut Rosé, Champagne $40.

90 • Veuve Clicquot 1988 La Grande Dame Rosé, Champagne $180.

90 • Serge Mathieu NV Brut Rosé, Champagne $34.99.

90 • Pol Roger 1990 Brut Rosé, Champagne $58.

90 • Palmer NV Brut Rosé, Champagne $33.99.

90 • Louis Roederer 1991 Brut Rosé, Champagne $56.

Tête de Cuvée

100 • Krug 1989 Clos du Mesnil, Champagne $210.

100 • Krug 1976 Collection, Champagne $210.

99 • Charles Heidsieck 1985 Blanc des Millenaires, Champagne $70.

97 • Salon 1988 Blanc de Blancs, Champagne $100.

97 • Pol Roger 1986 Cuvée Sir Winston Churchill, Champagne $125.

97 • Krug 1985 Brut, Champagne $120.

97 • Bollinger 1989 Vieilles Vignes Françaises Blanc de Noirs Brut, Champagne $180.

96 • Krug 1989 Brut, Champagne $120.

95 • Krug Grande Cuvée, Champagne $100.

95 • Krug 1985 Clos du Mesnil, Champagne $210.

95 • Gosset 1985 Grand Millesime, Champagne $81.99.

95 • Champagne de Méric NV Cuvée Prestige Catherine de Medicis, Champagne $59.95.

94 • Pol Roger 1988 Cuvée Sir Winston Churchill, Champagne $130.

94 • Philipponnat 1988 Clos des Goisses, Champagne $99.

94 • Moët & Chandon 1990 Cuvée Dom Pérignon, Champagne $110.

94 • Heidsieck Monopole NV Diamant Blanc, Champagne $100.

94 • Bollinger 1989 Grande Année, Champagne $70.

93 • Vilmart 1991 Coeur de Cuvée, Champagne $55.

93 • Ruinart 1988 Dom Ruinart, Blanc de Blancs, Champagne $97.

93 • René Collard 1969 Carte d'Or Brut, Champagne $79.95.

93 • Drappier 1989 Grande Sendrée, Champagne $80.

92 • Veuve Clicquot 1989 La Grande Dame, Champagne $75.

92 • Taittinger 1990 Comtes de Champagne Blanc de Blancs, Champagne $112.99.

92 • Laurent-Perrier 1988 Grand Siècle, Champagne $99.99.

92 • Deutz 1988 Cuvée William Deutz Brut, Champagne $85.

92 • Charles de Cazanove 1989 Stradivarius, Champagne $49.99.

92 • Bollinger 1985 R.D. Extra Brut, Champagne $132.

91 • Vranken Demoiselle Cuvée 21, Champagne $100.

91 • Taittinger 1989 Comtes de Champagne Blanc de Blancs, Champagne $112.99.

91 • Louis Roederer 1990 Cristal, Champagne $149.

91 • Henri Abèle 1986 Le Sourire de Reims, Champagne $85.

91 • Champagne de Venoge 1990 Cuvée des Princes Brut, Champagne $79.

91 • Bollinger 1990 Grande Année, Champagne $70.

90 • Taittinger 1991 Comtes de Champagne Rosé, Champagne $149.99.

90 • Piper-Heidsieck 1988 Rare, Champagne $65.

90 • Nicolas Feuillatte 1990 Cuvée Palmes d'Or Brut, Champagne $97.

90 • Joseph Perrier 1985 Cuvée Joséphine Brut, Champagne $96.

90 • Gosset 1990 Celebris, Champagne $108.99.

Extra Dry

90 • Louis Roederer NV Extra Dry, Champagne $40.

Scale: Superlative (96-100), Exceptional (90-95), Highly Recommended (85-89), Recommended (80-84), Not Recommended (Under 80)

twenty-nine

France
Loire

Loire Overview

The wines of the Loire valley have not ignited the passions of US wine drinkers or critics in recent years. Although the Loire produces some red wines, it is whites that are the mainstay. It would seem that the Chardonnay, Cabernet, Syrah, and Merlot varietal bandwagon that has propelled the interest of U.S. drinkers has largely passed the Loire by. Maybe it is the lack of toasty, barrel-fermented, thick wines or the fact that the flavors of Sauvignon Blanc and Chenin Blanc—the two most important grape varieties in the Loire—are not fashionable today. Regardless, consumers who want to really discover a true expression of either of the aforementioned grape varieties should get to grips with the wines of the Loire. Having done so, the ripe, oaky manifestations of Sauvignon Blanc, or even Chenin Blanc, from California may never have quite the same appeal again.

The Loire is a long, drawn-out wine region, and not a distinct entity. Following as it does the river Loire from Nantes on the Atlantic coast some hundreds of miles inland, it encompasses dozens of sub-regions and appellations. Naturally, many of the appellations of the Loire do not see U.S. retail shelves and will be of more interest to the tourist than of relevance to the average U.S. consumer.

Key Grape Varieties and Their Appellations

Sauvignon Blanc

Facing each other on opposite sides of the river Loire, Pouilly-Fumé and Sancerre produce the classic styles of Sauvignon Blanc in the Loire, though a host of other appellations, such as Menetou-Salon and Touraine, also use the grape variety. In a good vintage, the best Loire Sauvignons show brilliant yellow straw hues and exhibit classic herbaceous "black currant" leaf and tropical fruit aromas. In less ripe vintages Loire Sauvignon can take on a sweaty, "wet wool" character, which is not utterly pejorative unless it is overwhelming. With very few exceptions, new oak is not a factor in making these wines, and Loire Sauvignons should not be aged more than a year or two before their lively fruits and acids are dulled.

Chenin Blanc

Chenin Blanc is greatly under-appreciated in the United States as a high-quality wine grape. However, it unquestionably makes the Loire's finest wines of both the dry and sweet variety, south of the river at Angers in the appellations of Savennières and Coteaux du Layon. Anjou Blanc, copiously produced though rarely seen in the United States, is also produced from Chenin Blanc. When pushed to its full ripeness by top producers, Chenin produces stunningly rich, concentrated dry wines that can age for upwards of a decade, becoming deep, honeyed, and earthy in the instance of a mature Savennières.

In a couple of vintages per decade, typically, outstanding dessert wines are produced from grapes afflicted with noble rot. Such wines can last for many decades. The principal sweet wine appellations—in routine vintages they produce dry and demi-sec wines—are Vouvray, Bonnezeaux, and Coteaux du Layon.

Fully sweet dessert styles from these appellations carry the word Moelleux (sweet) on the label.

Cabernet Franc

Despite its northerly location, the Loire has pockets of vineyards that can ripen red grape varieties. The grape of favor is the early-ripening minor Médoc variety, Cabernet Franc, although a small amount of Cabernet Sauvignon is also planted. The latter is a difficult proposition to ripen in all but the most exceptional years. Loire reds are of a herbaceous nature and often display crisp acids, vegetal overtones, and tart fruit flavors that can stop the regular consumers of ripe, fruity New World wines dead in their tracks. The weightiest of these wines come from the appellations of Bourgueil and Chinon, located to the west of Tours. Bourgueil can be lean and tough, though rich and cellar-worthy in exceptional vintages. Neighboring Chinon generally produces wines of more finesse—often of a lighter, raspberry-fruited nature—though in exceptional vintages dense, cellar-worthy wines are made. Often the most silky and raspberry-scented reds of all come from the vineyards around the picturesque town of Saumur, and carry the appellation of Saumur-Champigny.

The Loire is, or certainly was, famous for its off-dry rosé from Anjou, Rosé d'Anjou, which is made from Cabernet Franc. This style of rosé has fallen out of fashion among contemporary drinkers, though good examples are still delightful and fruity. Bad examples, unfortunately, are all too common.

Muscadet/Melon de Bourgogne

Muscadet is one of the few appellations that carries the name of the grape cultivated within its boundaries. The Muscadet grape is also known by the synonym Melon de Bourgogne. The Pays Nantais region from which it comes produces a vast amount of cheap, acidic white wine destined for local consumption. The best wines, and generally the only ones exported to the United States, come from the strip of land between the Loire tributaries of Sèvre-Nantaise and Maine, and it is called

Loire
at a Glance

Wines Reviewed:
52

Producers/Brands Represented:
30

Value Rating:
Average to Good

Muscadet de Sèvre-et-Maine. Look for the words "Sur Lie" on the label, indicating that the wine has been aged on its lees, giving it some extra yeasty character. With very few exceptions Muscadet does not age well and is best drunk in its youth, with its natural partner, shellfish.

Vintages

1995 produced good whites across the board, and particularly fine sweet wines. Although the Sauvignon Blancs should all have been consumed by now, good dry Chenins should be going strong, and sweet wines from Bonnezeaux, Vouvray, and Coteaux du Layon are all set to be fine cellaring wines, though not as unctuous as the sweet wines from 1990. The reds from 1995 are a little on the lean side.

1996 was another particularly fine year for Sauvignon Blanc and dry Chenin from the classic appellations, and produced fine Moelleux wines, albeit with mild *Botrytis* affection. They should have good cellar lives in front of them, though they are not as rich as sweet wines from 1990. Reds are of good quality and the best from Bourgueil and Chinon will be candidates for the cellar.

1997 is a step down from the riper whites of 1995 and 1996. Leaner, racier wines are much in evidence, and Sancerre and Pouilly-Fumé show leaner, herbal qualities. Savennières and Vouvray both produced less impressive wines than in either 1995 or 1996. Few Moelleux wines were made in 1997.

1998 is another disappointment for the Loire as rain affected the harvest, after a period of drought. Expect variable wines from 1998, with overall quality not reaching anywhere near the levels of 1995 or 1996. It seems unlikely that the red from Chinon or Bourgueil will offer much charm.

Reviews

Bernard Blanchet
Pouilly-Fumé, Les Champs des Plantes 1995 $14.99.   86
Pale straw appearance. Medium-bodied. Moderately extracted. Chalk, citrus, grapefruit. Fresh, mildly tart style with a mineral backbone that persists through the finish. Quite austere on the palate.

Marc Brédif
Chinon, 1996 $16.   81
Vouvray, 1996 $16.   83

Alain Cailbourdin
Pouilly-Fumé, Les Cornets 1996 $14.   83

Pierre Chainier
Vouvray, Domaine Chainier Meloterie 1996 $5.99.   84

Jean-Claude Chatelain
Pouilly-Fumé, 1996 $16.99.   90
Bright pale yellow. Moderately full-bodied. Balanced acidity. Moderately extracted. Green grass, lemon zest. Ripe and fruity aromas. Rounded and generous, with ripe tropical flavors through to the finish. Classic.

Pouilly-Fumé, Les Charmes Chatelain 1995 $15.99.   88

Bright pale straw color. Moderately full-bodied. Moderately extracted. Grapefruit, lemon grass. Full ripe varietal aromas. Concentrated and full-flavored palate with rich notes through the finish.

Cherrier
Sancerre, 1997 $18.99.   89

Pale yellow-straw. Medium-bodied. Balanced acidity. Moderately extracted. Citrus, minerals, herbs. Herbaceous, generous aromas. Bright, concentrated, juicy style with ripe citrus flavors filling the palate. Finishes cleanly.

Clos Paradis
Sancerre, 1996 $14.   89

Bright yellow-gold. Moderately full-bodied. Balanced acidity. Moderately extracted. Grapefruit, fresh herbs. Generous fruit aromas follow through on the palate, with rich flavors and glycerous texture. Very appealing color, weight, and ripeness. Near-term drinking recommended.

Domaine du Closel
Savenniéres, Cuvée Speciale 1995 $13.99.   87

Pale straw color. Medium-bodied. Balanced acidity. Moderately extracted. Reminiscent of citrus, grapefruit, honey. Elegant, perfumed aromas reveal a rounded mouth feel with fine acidity stretching out an impressive finish. Very approachable.

Comte LaFond
Sancerre, 1996 $27.50.   92

Pale straw. Medium-bodied. Balanced acidity. Moderately extracted. Pink grapefruit, minerals, fresh herbs. Rich, varietally expressive aromas follow through on the palate with great flavor depth that continues through the finish. Structured and concentrated, this will improve with a year or two of cellaring.

Jean Dabin
Muscadet, Domaine du Ventois 1995 $8.99.   NR

Didier Dagueneau
Pouilly-Fumé, 1995 $17.99.   90

Medium straw color. Moderately full-bodied. Balanced acidity. Moderately extracted. Melon, ripe citrus fruits, minerals. Ripe fruit aromas. Concentrated, varietally pure expressions of flavors through to the finish. Rich and forward style.

Pouilly-Fumé, Silex 1994 $50.   90

Bright gold color. Moderately full-bodied. Highly extracted. Mildly oaked. Citrus, vanilla, exotic spice. Mild toasty aromas. Piercing citrus acidity makes this hard to evaluate at present. Has the structure for cellaring.

Vincent Delaporte
Sancerre, 1997 $23.49.   88

Bright yellow-gold. Moderately full-bodied. Balanced acidity. Moderately extracted. Citrus, lemon oil. Very aromatic, fruit-centered nose. Generous, rounded mouthfeel. Ripe citrus flavors and citrus oil notes through the finish.

Jean Douillard
Muscadet de Sèvre et Maine, Domaine de la Fruitière 1995 $7.99.   85

Philippe Foreau
Vouvray, Clos Naudin, Demi-Sec 1994 $17.99.   84
Vouvray, Clos Naudin, Sec 1994 $14.99.   80

Fouassier
Sancerre, Clos Paradis 1995 $17.99.   88

Medium straw with gold highlights. Medium-bodied. Moderately extracted. Fresh herbs, tart peach, minerals. Restrained, subtle aromas. More assertive on entry with well-extracted flavors on the palate. Long expressive finish.

Sancerre, Les Romains 1995 $14.99.   90

Bright yellow. Moderately full-bodied. Highly extracted. Black currant leaf, wet wool, tart peach. Rich, oily-textured mouth feel that has great persistence through the finish. Classic varietal aromas and flavors. Classy wine.

Denis Gaudry
Pouilly-Fumé, 1995 $16.99.   82

Château de la Genaiserie
Anjou Gamay, 1996 $9.   84
Coteaux du Layon Chaume, Les Tetuères 1995 $25.   92

Deep golden hue. Moderately full-bodied. Balanced acidity. Highly extracted. Honey, peaches, spice. Honeyed, botrytis-affected aromas lead a thick, glycerous mouthful of sweet flavors. Delicious now, though will doubtlessly improve.

Coteaux du Layon Saint-Aubin, Les Simonnelles 1995 $25.   93

Deep golden yellow. Moderately full-bodied. Balanced acidity. Highly extracted. Honey, tropical fruits. Spicy aromas have a honeyed note, but are quite reserved. Lush mouthfeel with plenty of glycerin and concentrated flavors, though this may need further cellaring to show its best.

Coteaux du Layon Saint-Aubin,
Sélection de Grains Nobles 1993 $23.99/500 ml.   93

Rich deep golden luster. Full-bodied. Highly extracted. Reminiscent of honey, nuts, apricots. Botrytis affected nose leads a honeyed rich palate with an unctuous character through the finish. Very attractive now though it has fine acidity and should cellar well.

Pascal Jolivet
Pouilly-Fumé, 1997 $17.   84
Pouilly-Fumé, Domaine La Loge aux Moines 1996 $23.   85
Pouilly-Fumé, La Grande Cuvée 1994 $44.   92

Bright straw appearance. Moderately full-bodied. Highly extracted. Peaches, grapefruit, minerals. Assertive and complex aromas. Full flavored and austere with great persistence. Structured to develop further in bottle but accessible now.

Sancerre, 1997 $17.   83

de Ladoucette
Pouilly-Fumé, 1996 $29.   86

Brilliant yellow-gold. Medium-bodied. Balanced acidity. Moderately extracted. Fresh herbs, grapefruit. Classic varietal aromas are ripe and generous. Lush, rounded mouthfeel. Bright acids give a juicy character.

Pouilly-Fumé, Baron de Ladoucette 1992 $65.   89

Medium straw color. Moderately full-bodied. Highly extracted. Minerals, citrus, grass. Weighty palate with firm acidity and a solid mineral backbone that carries through to the finish. Would probably show best with food.

Scale: Superlative (96-100), Exceptional (90-95), Highly Recommended (85-89), Recommended (80-84), Not Recommended (Under 80)

Château Moncontour
Vouvray, 1993 $9.99.   88

Pale straw with platinum highlights. Medium-bodied. Moderately extracted. Mild sweetness. Reminiscent of oil, herbs, minerals. Astringent aromas lead a crisp minerally palate with complex flavors that persist through the finish. Slight sweetness is well balanced by full acidity.

Vouvray, Demi-Sec 1995 $16.   84
Vouvray, Moelleux 1995 $28.   88

Bright yellow gold. Medium-bodied. Balanced acidity. Highly extracted. Spice, tropical fruits. Abundant, spicy, sweet aromas lead a juicy, tropical palate with a firm, minerally backbone. Even though acids are not elevated, this seems well structured and firm.

Vouvray, Tête de Cuvée Brut 1994 $16.   82

Le Peu de la Moriette
Vouvray, 1997 $14.99.   88

Bright pale gold cast. Medium-bodied. Balanced acidity. Moderately extracted. Sweet citrus, minerals. Flavorful and juicy, with a strong sweet-citrus flavor profile. Finishes with a flinty note that lends personality.

Michel Picard
Vouvray, 1996 $11.99.   86

Bright pale golden cast. Medium-bodied. Full acidity. Moderately extracted. Melon, citrus. Full, sweaty, tropical aromas lead a generous palate of fruit flavors, with juicy acids persisting through the finish.

La Poussie
Sancerre, Blanc 1996 $25.   86

Bright yellow-gold. Medium-bodied. Balanced acidity. Moderately extracted. Herb, citrus. Bright, leafy, zesty aromas. Straightforward flavors finish quickly, with a dry sensation.

Sancerre, Rouge 1995 $27.   NR

Château de la Ragotière
Muscadet Sèvre et Maine, Black Label 1996 $12.99.   88

Pale yellow gold. Medium-bodied. Balanced acidity. Moderately extracted. Lemons, minerals. Delightful, zesty aromas. Crisp and lively, without being overly acidic. Juicy, clean style with a citrus zest finish.

Château de la Roche-aux-Moines
Savennières, Becherelle 1995 $19.99.   90

Bright golden straw color. Moderately full-bodied. Highly extracted. Reminiscent of dill, herbs, dried peach, apricot. Complex heavy aromatics lead an oily rich palate with intensity and great length. Very drinkable now but will undoubtedly gain more character with bottle age.

Savennières, Becherelle 1996 $26.   90

Bright pale gold. Medium-bodied. Balanced acidity. Moderately extracted. Earth, ripe citrus, minerals. Earthy nose. Firm and bone-dry, with a long, mineral-dominated finish. This will show best with richer foods. Firmness, length, and track record support extended cellaring.

Savennières, Clos de la Bergerie 1994 $25.99.   88

Deep golden straw appearance. Moderately full bodied. Highly extracted. Reminiscent of yeast, minerals, ripe citrus. Quite rich with ripe flavors on entry and a minerally mid-palate with an oily note through the finish. This is relatively more restrained only when compared to Joly's other two Savennières tasted.

Savennières, Clos de la Bergerie 1995 $32.   **93**

Bright golden yellow. Moderately full-bodied. Full acidity. Highly extracted. Citrus, minerals. Powerful mineral aromas. Flavor-packed, bone-dry palate with rich, yet austere flavors that make this particularly easy to pair with richer foods. Solid structure and intensity suggest further cellaring.

Savennières, Clos de la Coulée de Serrant 1994 $40.99.   **97**

Intense straw with deep golden cast. Full bodied. Highly extracted. Reminiscent of earth, ripe tropical fruits, Heavy complex aromas with mild botrytis notes. Rich oily, viscous palate reveals layers of complex flavors through the impressively lengthy finish. Seems a little closed, although this is very drinkable at present.

Savennières, Clos de la Coulée de Serrant, Moelleux 1995 $75.   **89**

Deep golden yellow. Moderately full-bodied. Full acidity. Highly extracted. Spice, minerals. Rich, spicy aromas. Full-throttled, late-harvest style in terms of texture, though showing only a touch of residual sweetness. Botrytis influence is marked throughout. Surprisingly, this is not particularly sweet.

Jean-Max Roger

Menetou-Salon Morogues, Le Petit Clos 1995 $12.99.   **88**

Pale yellow with gold highlights. Medium bodied. Balanced acidity. Moderately extracted. Reminiscent of grass, gooseberries, citrus fruits. Varietally pure aromatics reveal an elegant, seamless palate with a hint of grassy back notes through the finish.

Sancerre, Cuvée G.C. 1996 $17.99.   **89**

Medium straw. Moderately full-bodied. Balanced acidity. Moderately extracted. Green leaves, grapefruit. Ripe, varietally expressive aromas. Silky mouthfeel. Long finish.

Domaine de la Rossignole

Sancerre, Cuvée Vieilles Vignes 1997 $13.99.   **83**

Moulin des Sablons

Chinon, 1996 $9.99.   **85**

Jean Baptiste Thibault

Pouilly-Fumé, La Chesnaie 1997 $15.99.   **86**

Medium straw cast. Medium-bodied. Balanced acidity. Moderately extracted. Citrus, leafy, dusty. Broad, citrus palate. Dry, minerally note. Crisp and refreshing.

Sancerre, La Duchesne 1997 $14.99.   **88**

Medium straw color. Medium-bodied. High acidity. Moderately extracted. Citrus, minerals. Mineral-dominated nose follows through to a zesty, straightforward palate. Snappy, crisp style

thirty

France
The Rhône,
Provence, and
the Sunny South

Rhône Market Overview

The Rhône is no longer a completely undiscovered region of France among U.S. wine consumers. The top wines from this geographically diverse part of France fetch impressively large sums, and are keenly sought after. However, being a large region with localized climates, diverse grape varieties, and hugely varied soil types, the Rhône still has plenty of value and originality to offer the neophyte and connoisseur alike, though it may not come from the increasingly pricey top appellations of the northern Rhône.

The Rhône is becoming fashionable again and collectors are now willing to fork out ever larger amounts for top wines, particularly Syrah-based wines from the north. Gone are the days when such gems could be purchased at a fraction of the cost of Bordeaux cru classées. At current market prices, some Rhône wines are already among the most expensive in the world. Happily, the Rhône will always be a source of good value wines from its more expansive tracts of southern vineyards.

The two Rhônes

There are really two Rhônes, the north and the south, which should be thought of as two regions with differing climates, producing distinctively different wines from different grape varieties. In the cooler north, vineyards only prosper on dramatically steep slopes and the wines they produce are among the most concentrated and exotic in the world. Bottlings from appellations such as Côte-Rôtie, Hermitage, and Condrieu can command high prices and are in short supply. It is these appellations that supply the Rhône's most sought-after wines.

Directly south, two hour's drive along the highway from the northernmost Côte-Rôtie sector of the Rhône valley, the onset of the southern Rhône heralds a change in climate and the graduation to the more dramatic and colorful southern French landscape. Here, the sprawling Côte-du-Rhône vineyards and highly distinctive "rock desert" vineyards of Châteauneuf-du-Pape produce large volumes of wine of much more variable quality. Potentially, the southern Rhône offers the best possibilities to the selective, value-conscious consumer looking for everyday affordability. Unfortunately (or fortunately for the producers) in recent years sharp price increases have been seen in Châteauneuf-du-Pape, the most glamorous of the southern Rhône's sub-regions, and these estate wines are often not quite the bargain they were a few short years ago.

Key Grape Varieties

Syrah

Syrah is one of the trinity of French noble red grape varieties—the others being Cabernet Sauvignon and Merlot. It prospers on the slopes of Hermitage and Côte-Rôtie in the northern Rhône. It is a thick-skinned grape producing deeply colored wines with lavish dark fruit flavors that can be accented by tarred, meaty, or medicinal (a positive feature!) notes. Typically Syrahs have abundant, softer tannins than Cabernet Sauvignon, and are often a little easier to drink in youth, which is not to say that they cannot be extraordinarily long-lived and firmly tannic when young.

Scale: Superlative (96-100), Exceptional (90-95), Highly Recommended (85-89), Recommended (80-84), Not Recommended (Under 80)

Viognier

Viognier is a delicate grape that only prospers in the Rhône on the slopes of Condrieu (and the adjacent monopole appellation of Château Grillet). The acreage devoted to it is minuscule in relation to its fame. In good years Viogniers (read Condrieu) throw-up exotic perfumes of apricot, peach, and honeysuckle and deliver rich, unctuous textures that make them a standout. Generally, Viognier does not age well, and should be drunk within a year or two of the vintage.

Grenache

Grenache is the workhorse grape of the southern Rhône and accounts for the majority of plantings in the south. In the Rhône, Grenache-based wines are rarely deeply colored, have ripe strawberry and red fruit aromas, are soft on the palate, and rarely show aggressive tannins. A feature of Grenache is that it ages quickly and is best drunk in youth. Most Côte-du-Rhônes are Grenache-based, and Châteauneuf-du-Pape usually has a good proportion of this versatile variety.

Mourvèdre

Mourvèdre is a thick-skinned grape variety that is generally blended with Grenache to produce wines with more color, backbone, and tannic structure. Used in high proportions in Châteauneuf-du-Pape it can produce very dark red-hued wines that have an elegant minerality and firm structures. By itself—which is a rare occurrence in the Rhône—Mourvèdre has an inky, dark character that takes years to evolve into something more complex and friendly.

Other Grape Varieties

The southern Rhône is host to many grape varieties, both red and white, that have unfamiliar names. For example, Châteauneuf-du-Pape is permitted to use thirteen different grape varieties. However, in practice, few producers use all of the permissible grapes, and the more obscure ones will only form a tiny fraction of the overall blend.

The Rhône at a Glance

Wines Reviewed:

238

Producers/Brands Represented:

79

Value Rating:

Average to Good

Key Appellations

Northern Rhône

Côte-Rôtie

Côte-Rôtie (literally: roasted slope) lies at the extreme northern end of the Rhône Valley wine region. This is a small appellation planted on back-breakingly steep, terraced, southeasterly slopes that stretch for five miles alongside the river Rhône. In successful vintages, Côte-Rôtie produces Syrah wines in their most aromatic and intensely flavorful form. In poor vintages rain at harvest can result in weakly colored, lighter wines. Producers widely use a small dose (1–3%) of Viognier to enhance the perfume of Côte-Rôtie.

Condrieu

Immediately south of Côte-Rôtie, Condrieu produces some of France's rarest white wines from the steep, terraced, granite slopes where Viognier is exclusively planted. Though relatively expensive to buy, it is still not commercially very rewarding for many growers, considering the hand labor required and the low yields. Great Condrieu is unctuously rich, with low acidity and a delicate perfume of peach and citrus blossom. It is a wine to be drunk young and it inspires devotion from people who fall under its spell.

St. Joseph

St. Joseph starts where Condrieu ends and stretches 40 miles southwards along the West Bank of the Rhône, taking in vineyard sites with varying potential for quality production. Syrah within St. Joseph can produce anything from rather weak reds to serious, deeply hued, and richly flavored ones, depending on the specific producer and vineyard. Marsanne and Roussanne produce similarly variable whites. Most St. Joseph is consumed locally.

Cornas

Cornas starts at the southern tip of St. Joseph and its vines occupy the granite-soiled slopes facing the town of Cornas. The Syrah based wines from this less glamorous appellation have a deserved reputation for rusticity and longevity, though the best examples achieve some of the elegance of Hermitage. If the clamor for Syrah from the north's finite slopes continues, Cornas could realize its true potential by becoming fashionable and, of course, more expensive.

Hermitage

Located on the east bank, an hour's drive southwards from Côte-Rôtie along the river Rhône, the hill of Hermitage are the most famous in the wine world. South-facing vineyards on varying soils produce the most famous of Syrah wines. Smaller quantities of long-lived white Hermitage is produced from Marsanne and Roussanne grape varieties. The finest red Hermitages from such producers as Jaboulet, Chave, Chapoutier, and Delas are deeply hued, featuring very ripe black fruit flavors and rich tannins. Red Hermitage from a good vintage is a classic cellaring wine that evolves slowly into something that connoisseurs liken to a mature Cabernet Sauvignon. White Hermitage, a less fashionable wine, can also evolve over many years to become a distinctively nutty, honeyed nectar.

Scale: Superlative (96-100), Exceptional (90-95), Highly Recommended (85-89), Recommended (80-84), Not Recommended (Under 80)

Crozes-Hermitage

Crozes-Hermitage vineyards encompass the less favorable northern slope of the Hermitage hill and outlying land that makes "Crozes" much more abundant than Hermitage. Syrah produces red wines that have some of the character of red Hermitage but always in a lighter, less intense style. Very rarely do they have the capacity to age. Floral, moderately full-bodied, white Crozes-Hermitage is made from Marsanne and Roussanne. Well-chosen red or white Crozes-Hermitage is one of the northern Rhône's great buys.

Southern Rhône

Châteauneuf-du-Pape

Châteauneuf-du-Pape is in the geographical heart of the large southern Rhône sector. It produces the finest and most expensive wine from the southern Rhône. Legally it can be a blend of thirteen different grape varieties, though practically one can consider the red varieties of Grenache Noir, Mourvèdre, Syrah, and Cinsault as being the only ones of real significance. The character of wines from Châteauneuf-du-Pape can vary considerably. Negociant Châteauneuf-du-Pape wines are often lighter, easy drinking wines. Styles will even vary among quality-minded estates, due to the differing proportions of grape varieties in use. Producers who use significant amounts of Syrah and Mourvèdre in the blend will produce wines of deeper color, richer tannins, and fuller body than will those with a very high proportion of Grenache. Small amounts of white varieties are commonly used to add perfumed aromas. In short, Châteauneuf-du-Pape comes in all sorts of hues, with delicate red fruit to deeper black fruit flavors and varying amounts of spiciness. These wines are generally less fleshy, rich or long-lived than the northern Syrah-based wines. However, they more readily show a deep minerality that appropriately reflects the barren, rock-strewn landscape from which they come.

Côtes-du-Rhône

The Côtes-du-Rhône appellation produces about 30 million cases of red and white wine per year—nearly all of it in the cheap and cheerful category. The vineyards that use this appellation stretch from the edge of the northern Rhône in a 50-mile swathe that runs for 100 miles southwards. Some 50 villages are entitled to label their output as Côtes-du-Rhône Villages, a nominally superior appellation.

Grenache rules supreme here among the red varieties and much of the highly commercial wine produced with it is light and fruity. Serious, quality-minded producers use proportions of Syrah and Mourvèdre to give their wines more stuffing and richness. The floral white wines of the Côtes-du-Rhône are medium to moderately full-bodied, generally unoaked, and typically use Grenache Blanc, with better examples incorporating Marsanne and Roussanne. Many of the best Côte-du-Rhônes emerge from large northern negociants such as Guigal, Chapoutier, and Jaboulet.

Gigondas & Vacqueyras

Gigondas and Vacqueyras are two adjacent appellations contained within the Côtes-du-Rhône region. Sandy soils and moderate slopes help create the full-bodied, generous wines that are typical of both appellations. Traditionally, lighter Grenache-based wines were in vogue, but use of new oak barrels in conjunction with Syrah and Mourvèdre has given greater appeal to wines from more forward-thinking producers.

Vintages

1994 was the best vintage in the southern Rhône since 1990. Those that did not wait for extreme maturity avoided the heavy rains of mid-September 1994 and made structured, concentrated red wines with good color. In the north, 1994 was a weak year in Côte-Rôtie and Hermitage, which were marked by rain and difficult ripening conditions for Syrah, though good producers did make aromatic, pleasant wines of an early-drinking, lighter nature.

1995 produced a few problems with rain throughout the region, though there was plenty of opportunity to pick ripe grapes after the early September rains had passed. Tough tannins and high acidity will give the red wines of the northern appellations a long potential cellar life. On balance the southern Rhône may have fared better with reds overall, producing ripe, well-balanced wines, the best of which will have some aging potential. It is a particularly fine vintage for CdP.

Overall, the whites in the southern Rhône did not fare so well, tending towards the leaner, acidic side. The finest cellar-worthy, whites came from Hermitage, which produced powerful and brightly acidic wines that will age well. Condrieu did not produce classically rich wines and, regardless, should have been consumed by now.

1996 was a cellaring vintage in the northern Rhône, producing tart, dense, and concentrated red wines in Côte-Rôtie and Hermitage. The best producers made long-lived wines with tough tannins and high acids. In the southern Rhône, lighter and softer reds were produced in Châteauneuf-du-Pape and Côte-du-Rhône. In general, 1996 will not be a keeping vintage for Châteauneuf-du-Pape reds or whites.

1997 will be an outstanding vintage for wines from Côte-Rôtie—all of which should be attractive on release. Tasted from barrel, these wines promise something special. The story will be similar for Hermitage, though the opulent vintage character will probably be better worn by the wines of Côte-Rôtie. A precursor to the later released northern reds will be the delicious Côte-du-Rhônes from 1997 and the generous Châteauneuf-du-Papes.

The north produced more memorable whites than the south in 1997. Expect rich Hermitage and very good Condrieu. The whites from Châteauneuf-du-Pape will probably not be for cellaring, being of the fatter, softer style.

Scale: Superlative (96-100), Exceptional (90-95), Highly Recommended (85-89), Recommended (80-84), Not Recommended (Under 80)

Reviews – The Rhône Valley

Daniel et Denis Alary

Côtes-du-Rhône Rouge, La Font d'Estevenas, "Cairanne" 1995 $17.   84

Earl Barruol

Gigondas, Château de Saint Cosme, "Valbelle" 1995 $23.   89

Deep ruby-garnet cast. Moderately full-bodied. Balanced acidity. Moderately extracted. Moderately oaked. Mildly tannic. Brown spices, minerals, dried herbs. Hefty, spicy oak overlay. Flavorful, well-integrated palate feel. Lush, though firmly structured and well balanced through the finish.

Gigondas, Château de Saint Cosme, "Valbelle" 1996 $22.   86

Deep blackish-garnet hue. Moderately full-bodied. Balanced acidity. Highly extracted. Moderately oaked. Mildly tannic. Spice, minerals. Quite aromatic, with a big, spicy, mature edge to the flavors. Ripe and full, with a well-balanced, rich finish.

Coudoulet de Beaucastel

Côtes-du-Rhône Rouge, 1995 $21.   88

Deep ruby cast. Moderately full-bodied. Balanced acidity. Highly extracted. Mildly oaked. Mildly tannic. Brown spices, berry fruits, minerals. Engagingly spicy, fruity aromas, balanced with toasty oak. Firm and flavorful, with a lengthy, fruity finish.

Côtes-du-Rhône Rouge, 1996 $21.   86

Bright ruby with a slight purple cast. Medium-bodied. Full acidity. Moderately extracted. Mildly tannic. Red fruits, minerals. Crisp and lean, with vibrant acidity. Fragrant and fruit centered through to the finish. Lively, fresh style.

Beaucastel

Châteauneuf-du-Pape Rouge, 1995 $42.   91

Deep ruby to the rim. Moderately full-bodied. Balanced acidity. Highly extracted. Mildly oaked. Mildly tannic. Plums, blackberries, minerals. Firmly structured through the finish, with a deep core of fleshy black fruits. Approachable now, but this is built to age.

Châteauneuf-du-Pape Rouge, 1996 $40.   89

Deep ruby to the rim. Moderately full-bodied. Balanced acidity. Highly extracted. Mildly oaked. Mildly tannic. Minerals, ripe berry fruits, earth. Youthful and intense, with a lean and angular impression on the palate, buoyed by firm acidity. Crisp and flavorful finish shows minerally length.

Châteauneuf-du-Pape Blanc, 1997 $45.   91

Bright straw cast. Full-bodied. Balanced acidity. Highly extracted. Bread dough, tropical fruits, yeast. Extraordinarily aromatic, with great complexity and richness. Fat and opulent, yet with the requisite structure to lend a sense of balance. A ripe and generous style.

Belle

Crozes-Hermitage Blanc, 1997 $NA. (SR)   85

Hermitage Blanc, 1995 $38.   86

Bright yellow-straw luster. Moderately full-bodied. Balanced acidity. Moderately extracted. Menthol, banana, ripe citrus. Marked menthol aromas follow through on the palate, with ripe citrus flavors in support. Unusual, very distinctive set of flavors. Classic texture. Moderately long finish.

Hermitage Blanc, 1996 $NA. (SR)   88

Brilliant pale straw hue. Generous mineral and citrus aromas show a slight vanillin quality. Round and full with evident acidity. Taut and stylish. Drink now or later.

Crozes-Hermitage Rouge, Cuvée Louis Belle 1995 $20.   92

Bright ruby with a purple hue. Moderately full-bodied. Moderately extracted. Moderately tannic. Black and red fruits, minerals. Generous, classic, slightly medicinal, ripe fruit aromas. Solid, well-extracted palate of similar fruit flavors. Finishes with a layer of dry tannins. Nice now. Better in a few years.

Crozes-Hermitage Rouge, Cuvée Louis Belle 1996 $NA. (SR)   92

Deep, saturated purple. Intense and profound aromas of game, herbs de Provence, and ripe fruit with toasty vanillin. Full-bodied palate with lots of tannic and acidic grip. Intense finish. Tasty, but needs time. Long-term cellar candidate.

Crozes-Hermitage Rouge, Les Pierrelles 1996 $NA. (SR)   90

Deep, brilliant purple. Exotic roasted game, red fruit, and spice aromas and flavors. Rich entry. Firm and full-bodied with intensity, concentration, and cut. Gripping tannins and long finish. Mid-term cellar candidate (3–6 years).

Hermitage Rouge, 1995 $50.   91

Saturated red-purple. Moderately full-bodied. Balanced acidity. Highly extracted. Moderately tannic. Red and black berry fruits. Intense old-vine character. Youthful primary aromas indicate a fleshy richness which is confirmed on the palate. Tightly wound. Extravagantly fruity. Softly textured tannins. A very plush style.

Hermitage Rouge, 1996 $NA. (SR)   90

Deep, saturated purple. Aromatics dominated by ripe fruit and new wood. A firm entry leads a full-bodied palate with robust, velvety tannins. Intense and concentrated with a drying finish. Marked by its wood at present. Should develop with time. Long-term cellar candidate.

Bois de Boursan

Châteauneuf-du-Pape Rouge, 1994 $25.   83

Bosquet des Papes

Châteauneuf-du-Pape Rouge, 1995 $28.   86

Deep ruby with a garnet edge. Full-bodied. Balanced acidity. Moderately extracted. Moderately oaked. Moderately tannic. Chocolate, minerals, exotic spices. Quite aromatic, with a firm, rich palate feel. The flavors have a rustic charm, with spice and minerals lingering on the finish.

Henry Bouachon

Châteauneuf-du-Pape Rouge, La Tiare du Pape 1996 $18.   86

Full ruby red. Medium-bodied. Balanced acidity. Moderately extracted. Moderately tannic. Black fruits, tar. Generous black fruit flavors are supported by oak tannins that grip, especially on the finish. Rounded, generous mouthfeel is a plus.

Côte-Rôtie, Prince de Montvert 1995 $28.   88

Deep blackish-ruby cast. Medium-bodied. Balanced acidity. Highly extracted. Mildly oaked. Mildly tannic. Black fruits, licorice, minerals. Full and rounded palate, with fleshy flavors up front. This turns rather lean through the finish, making for a firm style.

Brusset

Gigondas, Les Hauts de Montmirail 1995 $25.   86

Deep ruby-purple. Moderately full-bodied. Balanced acidity. Highly extracted. Mildly oaked. Mildly tannic. Black fruits, minerals, vanilla. Aromatic and flavorful, with a firm and intense palate feel. Modern in style. Rich, ripe, and weighty, with a firm structure.

Cabrieres
Châteauneuf-du-Pape Rouge, 1995 $18.   87
Pale ruby red. Medium-bodied. Moderately extracted. Mildly tannic. Vanilla, red fruits, mineral. Sweet woody aromas lead a juicy mouthful of mineral flavors. A delicate, elegant style, drinking well now.

du Caillou
Châteauneuf-du-Pape Rouge, Vieilles Vignes Réserve 1995 $34.   94
Bright cherry red. Medium-bodied. Moderately extracted. Moderately oaked. Moderately tannic. Red fruits, tobacco, vanilla. Oak-accented aromas. Vibrant, racy style with a strong streak of new oak. Well-delineated underlying flavors. Very modern, bright, and delicate. Well balanced. Long finish.

Les Cailloux
Châteauneuf-du-Pape Blanc, 1996 $25.   84
Châteauneuf-du-Pape Rouge, 1995 $28.   92
Deep ruby-garnet hue. Moderately full-bodied. Balanced acidity. Moderately extracted. Mildly oaked. Mildly tannic. Brown spices, minerals, red fruits. Firm and complex palate with a solid integration of wood and fruit notes.

Cave de Tain l'Hermitage
Hermitage Blanc, Les Nobles Rives 1996 $29.   86
Bright yellow-gold. Moderately full-bodied. Balanced acidity. Moderately extracted. Apricot, apple. Pleasant floral nose leads a straightforward, juicy palate with clean acids. Crisp and youthful, with an estery character. Further age should round this out.
Cornas, Les Nobles Rives 1995 $20.   87
Deep ruby-purple. Moderately full-bodied. Balanced acidity. Moderately extracted. Mildly tannic. Minerals, dark berry fruits. Aromatically reserved, with a firm and minerally palate feel. Lighter in style, with a slight herbal note.
Hermitage Rouge, Les Nobles Rives 1995 $28.   91
Saturated cherry-purple hue. Moderately full-bodied. Moderately extracted. Heavily oaked. Moderately tannic. Toasted oak, baking spice, dark fruits. Powerful, oak-dominated aromas follow through on the palate with an overwhelming sensation of oak that may not please all, though this has a solid core of black fruit flavors.
St. Joseph Rouge, Les Nobles Rives 1996 $15.   83

Caves des Papes
Cornas, Les Reillots 1995 $15.   89
Bright ruby-purple. Full-bodied. Balanced acidity. Highly extracted. Mildly oaked. Moderately tannic. Brown spices, earth, red fruits. Aromatic, with a full and grainy palate feel characterized by a rich, ripe mouthfeel and firm tannins through the finish.
Côte-Rôtie, Boucharey 1996 $30.   93
Deep blackish-ruby cast. Full-bodied. Full acidity. Highly extracted. Moderately oaked. Moderately tannic. Dried herbs, oriental spices, black fruits. Exotically aromatic, with a spicy range of flavors. Rich and thick in the mouth, though quite firmly structured. Tannins bite down on the finish. Needs time.
Hermitage Rouge, Les Echalas 1995 $30.   88
Saturated ruby-purple. Moderately full-bodied. Moderately extracted. Moderately tannic. Black fruits, minerals, spice. Bright black fruit aromas lead a firm, well-structured palate with fine primary fruit flavors. Ripe, medium-weight style that should improve with further cellaring.

St. Joseph Rouge, Les Chailles 1996 $21.   **86**

Deep ruby-purple. Moderately full-bodied. Balanced acidity. Highly extracted.
Mildly tannic. Mint, black fruits, minerals. Pleasantly aromatic, with a firm and
angular mouthfeel. Lean and well structured through the flavorful finish.

du Cayron
Gigondas, 1995 $21.   **82**

Chapoutier
Châteauneuf-du-Pape Blanc, La Bernardine 1996 $NA. (SR)   **82**
Condrieu, 1997 $NA. (SR)   **92**

Bright straw hue. Enticing, perfumed flower and tropical fruit aromas jump from the
glass. A rich entry leads a full-bodied, viscous palate. Ripe and intense with a very lengthy
finish. Drink now.

Côtes-du-Rhône Blanc, Belleruche 1997 $NA. (SR)   **80**
Crozes-Hermitage Blanc, Les Meysonniers 1997 $NA. (SR)   **87**

Deep yellow-gold. Aromatically subdued, with a slightly earthy, honeyed overtone.
A rich entry leads a rounded, moderately full-bodied palate with creamy acidity. Rather
subdued, but rich. Drink now or later.

Crozes-Hermitage Blanc, Petite Ruche 1997 $NA. (SR)   **85**
Hermitage Blanc, Chante-Alouette 1996 $NA. (SR)   **92**

Brilliant golden yellow. Attractive mineral and honey aromas are framed by a touch of
oaky vanillin. A firm entry leads a full-bodied palate that is well rounded with acidity.
Creamy and very rich. Drink now or later.

Ermitage Blanc, De la O'ree 1996 $NA. (SR)   **94**

Deep golden yellow. Exotic flower and honey aromas show a flash of oak. Very full-bodied
palate with excellent balancing acidity. Very big but well framed. A little closed in at
present. Should develop nicely. Long-term cellar candidate.

St. Joseph Blanc, Deschants 1997 $NA. (SR)   **89**

Vibrant yellow-gold. Subdued earth and mineral aromas. A lush entry leads a rich,
full-bodied palate with a touch of viscosity. Shows firm acidic grip. Big, but rather
closed at present. Mid-term cellar candidate (3–6 years).

St. Joseph Blanc, Les Granits 1996 $NA. (SR)   **92**

Deep golden yellow. Exotic honey and tropical fruit aromas jump from the glass.
A rich entry leads a very full-bodied palate with a viscous quality, kept in balance
by sturdy acidity. Exceptionally flavorful with a creamy finish. Drink now or later.

Châteauneuf-du-Pape Rouge, La Bernardine 1996 $NA. (SR)   **84**
Châteauneuf-du-Pape Rouge, Barbe Rac 1996 $NA. (SR)   **94**

Deep ruby-purple. Opulent vanilla and black fruit aromas. Full-bodied, rounded palate
with lush tannins. Exotic gamey flavors emerge in the mouth. Intense, complex, and very
stylish. Harmonious and well balanced enough to drink now or later.

Cornas, 1997 $NA. (SR)   **88**

Deep, brilliant purple. Generous fruit, smoke and mineral aromas carry a roasted,
meaty edge. Rich, full-bodied mouthfeel. Lean in structure with a kiss of wood through
the finish. Mid-term cellar candidate (3–6 years).

Côte-Rôtie, 1995 $36.   **88**

Bright blackish-ruby cast. Moderately full-bodied. Balanced acidity. Moderately extracted.
Moderately oaked. Mildly tannic. Vanilla, black fruits, sweet herbs. Pleasantly aromatic,
with a range of flavors. Light in the mouth. Well balanced with firm acidity. Finishes on
a slight herbal note.

Côte-Rôtie, 1996 $NA. (SR)   **85**

Scale: Superlative (96-100), Exceptional (90-95), Highly Recommended (85-89),
Recommended (80-84), Not Recommended (Under 80)

Côte-Rôtie, La Mordorée 1996 $NA. (SR)   89

Opaque blackish purple. Opulent aromas show a lash of new oak and a deep core of jammy, black fruit and anise nuances. Very, very ripe. Full-bodied palate with very gripping, drying tannins. Carries an impression of overripeness with a tough edge to the finish. Will it come around? Mid-term cellar candidate (3–6 years).

Côtes-du-Rhône Rouge, Belleruche 1997 $NA. (SR)   85

Côtes-du-Rhône Villages Rouge, Rasteau 1996 $NA. (SR)   80

Crozes-Hermitage Rouge, Les Meysonniers 1996 $NA. (SR)   88

Very deep ruby-purple. Deep, brooding mineral and black fruit aromas carry an herbal edge and a touch of vanillin. Moderately full-bodied palate with angular tannins and taut acidity. Lean and firm, with good depth and intensity. Should develop. Mid-term cellar candidate (3–6 years).

Crozes-Hermitage Rouge, Les Varonniers 1995 $49.99.   92

Deep purple. Medium-bodied. Balanced acidity. Moderately extracted. Moderately tannic. Vanilla, red berries. Sweet, oak-scented aromas lead a bright, almost grapey entrance, with lush mouthfeel and generous soft tannins through the finish. Very stylish; better in a few years.

Crozes-Hermitage Rouge, Petite Ruche 1997 $NA. (SR)   88

Deep ruby-purple. Enticing, forward tar, mineral, and black fruit aromas. Moderately full-bodied palate with lush tannins. Shows good intensity of flavor through the finish. Stylish. Drink now or later.

Hermitage Rouge, Monier de la Sizeranne 1996 $NA. (SR)   84

Ermitage Rouge, Pavillon 1996 $NA. (SR)   90

Very deep purple. Intense meat, mineral, and black fruit aromas. Full-bodied palate with mouth-searing tannins. Lean as opposed to rich or rounded, with a firm acidic edge. Not a wine to cuddle up to but may come around with time—lots of it. Intense and very highly extracted. Long-term cellar candidate.

Gigondas, 1996 $NA. (SR)   83

St. Joseph Rouge, Deschamps 1996 $NA. (SR)   90

Deep, brilliant purple. Enticing, intense blackberry and mineral aromas. Moderately full-bodied palate with a firm acidic edge and gripping tannins. Intense, but requires cellaring. Mid-term cellar candidate (3–6 years).

Charvin

Châteauneuf-du-Pape Rouge, 1995 $28.   91

Rich ruby red. Medium-bodied. Highly extracted. Moderately tannic. Leather, mineral, tar. Deep, brooding aromas follow through on the somewhat austere palate. Well structured, with a persistent mineral note on the finish. A solid traditional style.

J.C. Chassagne

Gigondas, Domaine du Pourra 1995 $12.   84

Chaume-Arnaud

Côtes-du-Rhône Villages Rouge, Cuvée Massif d'Uchaux 1996 $12.   NR

Bernard Chave

Crozes-Hermitage Rouge, Domaine de la Burge 1995 $25.   86

Ruby red with a gentle fade to the rim. Medium-bodied. Balanced acidity. Moderately extracted. Moderately tannic. Blackberries, earth, and medicinal aromas follow through with bright acids and well-defined flavors. Firm, gripping finish.

Hermitage Rouge, 1994 $44. 87

Ruby with a garnet fade. Medium-bodied. Moderately extracted. Moderately tannic. Dark berries, earth, mineral. Distinctively rustic aromas. An herbal streak runs through the palate, with red fruit accents and lean astringency through the finish. For near-term drinking.

JL Chave

Hermitage Blanc, 1995 $65. 94

Golden luster. Moderately full-bodied. Balanced acidity. Highly extracted. Honey, peach. Rich, honeyed, waxy aromas. Lush, rounded palate with unctuous flavors and texture. Drinking beautifully now, with low acids accentuating the richness. No need to cellar this.

Hermitage Rouge, 1994 $53.99. 94

Bright purplish-ruby hue. Medium-bodied. Highly extracted. Mildly tannic. Blackberry, tar, eucalyptus, dried herbs. Exotically aromatic with medicinal notes. Lush and forward palate with fine balancing acidity through the finish. Drinking nicely now.

Clape

Côtes-du-Rhône Rouge, Cuvée Spéciale 1995 $18. 89

Bright ruby-purple. Medium-bodied. Balanced acidity. Moderately extracted. Moderately oaked. Mildly tannic. Vanilla, tar, boysenberry, and mint. Aromatic and flavorful, with a firm, linear palate feel and an impressive degree of concentration. Long finish. Carries a hefty oak influence throughout.

Clusel Roch

Condrieu, 1997 $NA. (SR) 86

Brilliant yellow-straw hue. Restrained banana, tropical fruit, and pear aromas. Fat, full-bodied palate with shy acidity and a touch of spritz through the finish. Lots of weight. Stylish, but won't hold beyond a year or two. Drink now.

Côte-Rôtie, Cuvée Classique 1994 $38. 88

Bright ruby-garnet cast. Moderately full-bodied. Balanced acidity. Highly extracted. Mildly oaked. Moderately tannic. Bacon, blackberry, baking spice, and minerals. Exotically aromatic, with a forward quality and evident complexity. Firm and compact on the palate, with vibrant acidity. Intense.

Côte-Rôtie, Cuvée Classique 1995 $40. 89

Deep blackish-ruby cast. Moderately full-bodied. Balanced acidity. Moderately extracted. Mildly oaked. Moderately tannic. Vanilla, black fruits, mint. Firm, youthful, and tightly wound, with an emphasis on primary flavors. Tannins clamp down on the finish. Impressive constituents, though this will need some time to show its best.

Côte-Rôtie, Cuvée Classique 1996 $NA. (SR) 83

Côte-Rôtie, Cuvée Classique 1997 $NA. (SR) 85-89

Deep, brilliant purple hue. Exotic game, smoke, and black fruit aromas. A lush entry leads to a medium-bodied palate with very complex flavors and grippy tannins. Enlivened by sturdy acidity. Somewhat lighter in style, but very stylish. Drink now or later.

Côte-Rôtie, Cuvée Classique 1998 $NA. (SR) 80-84

Côte-Rôtie, Les Grandes Places 1994 $50. 89

Deep blackish-ruby hue. Full-bodied. Balanced acidity. Highly extracted. Heavily oaked. Moderately tannic. Vanilla, mint, black fruits. Oak dominated, with a generous array of flavors. Still quite young, but aeration begins to reveal more exotic qualities. Firmly structured and cellarable.

Côte-Rôtie, Les Grandes Places 1995 $60. 90

Deep blackish-ruby hue. Moderately full-bodied. Balanced acidity. Highly extracted. Moderately oaked. Mildly tannic. Mint, licorice, black fruits. Powerful aromatics lead a rich, ripe, firm palate feel. Quite youthful, but already showing complexity. This has all the stuffing and structure to cellar well.

Scale: Superlative (96-100), Exceptional (90-95), Highly Recommended (85-89), Recommended (80-84), Not Recommended (Under 80)

Côte-Rôtie, Les Grandes Places 1996 $NA. (SR) **90**

Very deep purple. Concentrated, complex spice, smoke, dark berry and tar aromas. Medium-bodied palate with excellent flavor intensity and gripping tannins. Very stylish, with classic Côte-Rotie flavors. Drink now or later.

Côte-Rôtie, Les Grandes Places 1997 $NA. (SR) **90-95**

Very deep blackish purple hue. Spice, blackberry, and game aromas are brooding, deep, and complex. A rich entry leads to a deeply flavored, stuffed, full bodied palate with big grippy tannins. Impressive if rather closed at present. Will develop beautifully. Long-term cellar.

Côte-Rôtie, Les Grandes Places 1998 $NA. (SR) **90-95**

Very deep purple hue. Deep, rich game, black fruit, and tar aromas. A lush entry leads to a full bodied palate with big, robust tannins and great depth of flavor. Firm, structured finish. Quite powerful. Will need time. Long-term cellar.

du Colombier

Crozes-Hermitage Rouge, 1996 $15. **89**

Bright purple-red. Medium-bodied. Balanced acidity. Moderately extracted. Mildly tannic. Black fruits, tar. Excellent varietal expression. Mouthfilling primary fruit. Softer tannins are apparent on the finish.

Crozes-Hermitage Rouge, Cuvée Gaby 1996 $15. **87**

Bright purple. Medium-bodied. Balanced acidity. Moderately extracted. Mildly tannic. Dried herbs, red fruits. Bright, vigorously youthful aromas follow through on the palate. Supple texture. Best appreciated in its youth.

Hermitage Rouge, 1995 $35. **89**

Saturated ruby red. Moderately full-bodied. Highly extracted. Quite tannic. Mineral, black fruits. Subtle aromas. Weighty palate. This is rather austere and structured at present. Cellar age should tame the firmness.

Jean-Luc Colombo

Cornas, Les Ruchets 1995 $50. **87**

Deep ruby-purple. Moderately full-bodied. Balanced acidity. Moderately extracted. Mildly tannic. Horse, earth, chocolate, and berry jam. Shows complex, earthy, funky aromatics throughout. Rich and lush on the palate, with a lengthy, firm finish.

La Crau de Ma Mère

Châteauneuf-du-Pape Rouge, 1995 $20. **89**

Bright ruby red. Moderately full-bodied. Balanced acidity. Moderately extracted. Mildly tannic. Charred wood, leather, red fruits. Meaty, leathery aromas. Supple, fruity character. Rounded texture. Moderately long finish.

Delas

Condrieu, Clos Boucher 1997 $NA. (SR) **87**

Deep yellow-gold. Opulent honey and tropical fruit aromas with a slight vanilla oak accent. Full-bodied palate with light acidity. Wood has tamed some of the fruit's exuberance. Drink now.

Condrieu, La Galopine 1997 $NA. (SR) **89**

Brilliant yellow-gold. Perfumed tropical fruit, spice, and lychee aromas jump from the glass. Rounded, moderately full-bodied palate. Fat and weighty. Drink now.

Côtes-du-Rhône Blanc, Val Muzols 1997 $NA. (SR) **80**

Crozes-Hermitage Blanc, Les Launes 1997 $NA. (SR) **80**

Hermitage Blanc, Marquise de la Tourette 1997 $NA. (SR) **90**

Deep golden straw hue. Generous cream and butter aromas with a subdued oak accent. Full-bodied palate balanced by moderate acidity. Fat and supple, but still structured. Drink now or later.

St. Joseph Blanc, Les Challeys 1996 $NA. (SR)   84

Châteauneuf-du-Pape Rouge, Les Calcerniers 1996 $NA. (SR)   83

Cornas, Chante-Perdrix 1996 $NA. (SR)   89

Very deep, saturated ruby-purple. Big, exotic, roasted game and herbs de Provence aromas. Rich and full-bodied palate with big, rustic tannins and a wave of olive flavors. Long-term cellar candidate.

Côte-Rôtie, Seigneur de Maugiron 1996 $NA. (SR)   90

Brilliant deep purple. Enticing, aromatic red fruit, flower, and game aromas. Medium-bodied palate with supple tannins. Light style. Complex. Drink now or later.

Côteaux du Tricastin Rouge, Escarlate 1997 $NA. (SR)   80

Côtes-du-Rhône Rouge, Domaine du Chatelain 1996 $NA. (SR)   87

Deep ruby hue. Raspberry jam, earth, and spice aromas. Moderately full-bodied palate with gripping tannins. Structured, rich, and showing some complexity. Drink now or later.

Côtes-du-Rhône Rouge, Saint-Esprit 1997 $NA. (SR)   87

Deep ruby-purple. Ripe forest, berry, and tar aromas show a distinctive old-vine note. Medium-bodied palate with old-vine intensity of flavor. Angular through the finish. Solid. Drink now or later.

Côtes-du-Rhône Rouge, Val Muzols 1997 $NA. (SR)   84

Côtes du Ventoux Rouge, Escarlate 1998 $NA. (SR)   82

Crozes-Hermitage Rouge, Cuvée Tour d'Albon 1995 $NA. (SR)   90

Deep ruby hue. Opulent aromas with a complex, spicy, roasted edge. Moderately full-bodied palate with robust velvety tannins. Deep and rich through the finish. Drink now or later.

Crozes-Hermitage Rouge, Les Launes 1997 $NA. (SR)   84

Gigondas Rouge, Les Reinages 1997 $NA. (SR)   83

Hermitage Rouge, Les Bessards 1994 $65.   94

Ruby with a subtle garnet cast. Medium-bodied. Balanced acidity. Moderately extracted. Moderately tannic. Red berries, minerals. Very aromatic and appealing. Dusty aromas indicate early onset of mature flavors. Vibrant red fruit flavors on entry yield to a bright, astringent finish, giving an angular character. Very appealing now.

Hermitage Rouge, Les Bessards 1996 $NA. (SR)   95

Very deep, saturated ruby hue. Exotic, enticing game, chocolate, and ripe berry aromas. Full-bodied palate with big, supple, velvety tannins. Very long and expressive finish. Accessible, but will keep.

Hermitage Rouge, Marquise de la Tourette 1996 $NA. (SR)   91

Deep ruby-purple. Generous chocolate and black fruit aromas. Big frame, and a supple mouthfeel with great flavor intensity. Very harmonious and hedonistic. Drinking well now. Cellarable.

St. Joseph Rouge, Cuvée François de Tournon 1996 $NA. (SR)   82

St. Joseph Rouge, Les Challeys 1996 $NA. (SR)   83

St. Joseph Rouge, Sainte-Epine 1996 $NA. (SR)   87

Brilliant, deep ruby-purple. Generous game and black fruit aromas. Moderately full-bodied palate with supple tannins. Round, harmonious, and flavorful. Drink now.

Vacqueyras Rouge, Domaine des Genets 1996 $NA. (SR)   85

Lucien Deschaux

Châteauneuf-du-Pape Rouge, Le Vieux Abbé 1994 $14.99.   82

Scale: Superlative (96-100), Exceptional (90-95), Highly Recommended (85-89), Recommended (80-84), Not Recommended (Under 80)

Desmeures

Hermitage Rouge, Cuvée Emilie 1995 $35.   91

Saturated red-purple. Moderately full-bodied. Highly extracted. Moderately tannic. Cinnamon, vanilla, sweet dark fruits. Forward aromas. Solid and tight on the palate, with tightly wound flavors. Fine persistence, with deep, fruity flavors lingering. Well structured, this will develop further in the cellar.

des Entrefaux

Crozes-Hermitage Rouge, 1995 $20.   88

Bright ruby red. Medium-bodied. Balanced acidity. Moderately extracted. Mildly tannic. Black fruits, minerals. Bright berry aromas follow through on a juicy, open-knit palate. Supple, fruity flavors and a hint of dry tannin on the finish. Drinking very well now.

Ferraton

Crozes-Hermitage Rouge, La Matiniere 1995 $18.   87

Ruby with a fade to the rim. Medium-bodied. Balanced acidity. Moderately extracted. Moderately tannic. Horse saddle, black fruits, earth. Earthy aromas follow through on the palate, with an emphasis on dry flavors that make for an assertive, angular style.

Hermitage Rouge, La Cuvée des Miaux 1995 $35.   91

Bright pale ruby hue. Medium-bodied. Moderately extracted. Mildly tannic. Herbs, bacon fat, minerals. Expressive and classic aromas follow through on the palate. Very crisp and vibrant, with a mineral theme and mild tannins on the finish. Drinking well now.

Font de Michelle

Châteauneuf-du-Pape Rouge, 1996 $17.   85

Châteauneuf-du-Pape Rouge, Cuvée Etienne Gonnet 1996 $25.   89

Ruby red with a fading rim. Moderately full-bodied. Moderately extracted. Mildly tannic. Red fruits, leather, brown spice. Very aromatic, with dusty, spicy aromas. Bright, juicy, and flavorful. This is drinking well now.

Pierre Gaillard

Côte-Rôtie, Côte Brune et Blonde 1996 $36.   89

Bright ruby-purple. Medium-bodied. Balanced acidity. Moderately extracted. Mildly oaked. Mildly tannic. Red fruits, sweet herbs, minerals. Lighter style, with pretty berry flavors. Lean and firm through the finish. Very youthful, but approachable.

Côte-Rôtie, Rosé Pourpre 1996 $55.   90

Bright blackish-ruby cast. Moderately full-bodied. Balanced acidity. Moderately extracted. Moderately oaked. Mildly tannic. Vanilla, briar fruits. Buoyant, fruit-centered personality and a hefty oak overlay. Still youthful, with dominant primary flavors. Should develop complexity with bottle age.

St. Joseph Rouge, Clos de Cuminaille 1996 $20.   89

Bright purple. Moderately full-bodied. Full acidity. Highly extracted. Mildly oaked. Mildly tannic. Vanilla, minerals, sage, berry fruit. Firm, minerally palate feel. Crisp and lean through the finish.

St. Joseph Rouge, Les Pierres 1996 $25.   92

Bright purple. Moderately full-bodied. Balanced acidity. Highly extracted. Mildly oaked. Mildly tannic. Vanilla, black fruits, minerals. Sultry fruit. Generous oak. Firm and intense. Ripe tannins. Long finish.

Les Galets Blonds

Châteauneuf-du-Pape Rouge, 1995 $18.99.   89

Ruby red with a garnet cast. Medium-bodied. Highly extracted. Moderately oaked. Mildly tannic. Mineral, leather, blackberry. Dry, austere mouthful of flavors with the accent on traditional character, as evidenced by the elegant mineral character that persists.

Henri et Philippe Gallet
Côte-Rôtie, 1994 $32.   89

Deep ruby-garnet with a fading rim. Moderately full-bodied. Balanced acidity. Moderately extracted. Mildly oaked. Mildly tannic. Baking spice, bacon, earth. Attractively aromatic. Light in the mouth and early maturing. Well balanced and captivating.

Gangloff
Condrieu, 1998 $NA. (SR)   90-95

Brilliant yellow golden hue. Ripe tropical fruit and cream aromas. An explosive entry leads to a full bodied palate with great richness and intensity. Rich, but showing fine cut through the finish. Drink now.

Côte-Rôtie, 1995 $54.   97

Bright blackish-ruby cast. Full-bodied. Balanced acidity. Moderately extracted. Mildly oaked. Mildly tannic. Roasted coffee, brown spices, black fruits. Compelling aromatics. Exotic, complex flavors. Firm and well balanced, with fine length and intensity. This strikes a classic balance between power and finesse, with exceptionally complex aromas.

Côte-Rôtie, 1996 $NA. (SR)   96

Deep, opaque purple. Intense, exotic smoke, mineral, and game aromas. Taut, full-bodied palate. Very intense. Built for the long haul. Finishes with a wave of tannin. Impressive, but needs long-term cellaring.

Côte-Rôtie, 1997 $NA. (SR)   98

Deep, opaque purple. Complex smoke, game, and spice aromas jump from the glass. Full-bodied palate with great cut and outrageous intensity. The finish goes on and on. Great balance and opulence, with an exotic bacon fat quality to the finish. Drink now or later.

Côte-Rôtie, 1998 $NA. (SR)   96-100

Deep, saturated purple hue. Exotic game, smoke, and berry aromas. A rich entry leads to a full bodied palate with great grip and depth. Very stylish and intense with an enchanting, luxuriously perfumed quality throughout. Outrageously deep. Drink now or later.

Côte-Rôtie, Barbarine 1995 $39.   95

Bright ruby cast. Moderately full-bodied. Balanced acidity. Moderately extracted. Mildly oaked. Mildly tannic. Earth, brown spices, red fruits. Earthy, spicy aromas. Firm and angular palate feel. Tight and youthful, with a clipped finish. Very solidly structured, with exotic flavors that flourish with aeration. Further cellaring recommended.

Côte-Rôtie, Barbarine 1996 $NA. (SR)   93

Very deep ruby with subtle purple highlights. Intense spice, mineral, and game aromas. Intense, moderately full-bodied palate with outstanding length and a fine acidic cut. Perfumed. Mid-term cellar candidate (3–6 years).

Côte-Rôtie, Barbarine 1997 $NA. (SR)   94

Very deep purple. Outrageous game, spice, and black fruit aromas. Full-bodied and rich in the mouth with big, grainy tannins. Opulent, intense, and perfumed. Drink now or later.

Côte-Rôtie, Barbarine 1998 $NA. (SR)   90-95

Deep, brilliant purple hue. Exotic, intense game and smoke aromas. A rich entry leads to a moderately full bodied palate. Rounded, supple, and harmonious. Drink now or later.

Marie-Claude Lafoy et Vincent Gasse
Côte-Rôtie, Cuvée Vieilles Vignes 1994 $NA.   84

Les Goubert
Gigondas, 1995 $20.   83

Gigondas, Cuvée Florence 1994 $35.   89

Deep ruby cast. Medium-bodied. Balanced acidity. Moderately extracted. Moderately oaked. Mildly tannic. Exotic spices, forest floor. Powerful, mature aromatics. Firmly structured palate with some lush fruit. Turns lean toward the finish. Pleasant, but drying—drink up.

Alain Graillot

Crozes-Hermitage Rouge, 1996 $15.   92

Saturated red-purple. Moderately full-bodied. Highly extracted. Moderately tannic. Ripe sweet boysenberry and blackberry fruit with typical tarry and earthy aromas and flavors. Impressive and dense. Tight palate with some tough edges. Underlying generosity showing through. This will be better in a few years.

Crozes-Hermitage Rouge, La Guiraude 1996 $19.   93

Saturated red-purple. Medium-bodied. Moderately extracted. Mildly tannic. Herbs, dark berry fruits. Old-vine character is evident in the color and intense herb-tinged aromas. On the palate, the juicy flavors open up, concluding with a mineral finish. Drinking very well now.

Grand Veneur

Châteauneuf-du-Pape Blanc, La Fontaine 1995 $NA.   93

Rich yellow-gold. Moderately full-bodied. Balanced acidity. Highly extracted. Mildly oaked. Yeast, bread dough, spices. Generously aromatic, with an opulent yeasty note that follows through on the palate. Rich, ripe, and generous in the mouth, with a lengthy, exotic finish.

Guigal

Condrieu, 1997 $NA. (SR)   91

Deep golden yellow. Expressive, perfumed flower, tropical fruit, and mineral aromas. Moderately full-bodied. Honeyed palate with creamy acidity. Lush and fat. Drink now.

Condrieu, La Doriane 1997 $NA. (SR)   94

Deep yellow-gold. Exotic honey and tropical fruit aromas jump from the glass. Full-bodied, viscous mouthfeel. Extremely weighty, yet firmly structured from time in barrel. Finishes with a rounded buttery quality and an attractive vanillin oak accent. Drink now.

Côtes-du-Rhône Blanc, 1997 $10.   86

Bright straw cast. Moderately full-bodied. Full acidity. Highly extracted. Bread dough, minerals. Soft aromas, with a rounded and firm mouthfeel. This has a sound palate presence, though flavors are neutral enough to allow versatility.

Hermitage Blanc, 1994 $NA. (SR)   89

Deep golden hue. Attractive leesy aromas show a nutty, tertiary quality and a pleasant oak accent. Moderately full-bodied palate with a firm acidic edge. Weighty. Balanced with acidic cut. Already blossoming, but should develop nicely. Drink now or later.

Châteauneuf-du-Pape Rouge, 1995 $25.   89

Bright ruby red. Medium-bodied. Moderately extracted. Moderately oaked. Moderately tannic. Vanilla, red fruits, spice. Scented, wood-influenced aromas. Firm, dry palate. A modern style. Drinking well now, but better in a few years.

Châteauneuf-du-Pape Rouge, 1996 $NA. (SR)   83

Côte-Rôtie, Château d'Ampuis 1995 $NA. (SR)   93

Deep, saturated purple. Exotic vanilla, spice, and black fruit aromas. Rich, full-bodied mouthfeel with big but ripe tannins. Youthful and primary with a hefty new oak influence. Beautiful and intense. Wait for complexity. Long-term cellar candidate.

Côte-Rôtie, Côte Brune et Blonde 1994 $32.   **93**

Deep blackish-ruby hue. Moderately full-bodied. Balanced acidity. Moderately extracted. Mildly oaked. Mildly tannic. Game, brown spices, roasted earth. Richly aromatic, with a firm, well-balanced, flavorful mouthfeel. Still quite youthful, this wine should develop well over the next decade, but is approachable now.

Côte-Rôtie, Côte Brune et Blonde 1995 $NA. (SR)   **88**

Deep, saturated ruby hue. Still quite youthful and aromatically subdued with attractive bacon fat and black fruit nuances. Full-bodied palate with lean, gripping tannins. Rather tough at present. Needs time. Mid-term cellar candidate (3–6 years).

Côte-Rôtie, La Landonne 1994 $150.   **98**

Deep blackish-ruby hue. Full-bodied. Balanced acidity. Highly extracted. Mildly oaked. Moderately tannic. Coffee, roasted earth, black fruits. Exotically aromatic, with a rich and opulent mouthfeel. Rich and velvety in texture, though quite firm, with serious intensity through the finish. Approachable, but will cellar beautifully.

Côte-Rôtie, La Landonne 1995 $NA. (SR)   **97**

Dark, opaque purple. Deep and brooding aromas show a core of anise, black fruit, and mineral nuances. Full-bodied palate with gripping tannins to match. Shows amazing depth and intensity, but closes down entirely on the finish. Needs lots of time. Try in a decade, but should hold for the long haul.

Côte-Rôtie, La Mouline 1995 $NA. (SR)   **100**

Deep, saturated purple. Exotic and amazingly intense jasmine, oriental spice, and black fruit aromas fill the air. Mindbogglingly intense. Medium-bodied palate with a rush of supple tannins. Hedonistic and stylish. Amazingly complete and already drinking beautifully. Drink now or later.

Côte-Rôtie, La Turque 1994 $150.   **96**

Deep blackish purple. Full-bodied. Balanced acidity. Highly extracted. Moderately oaked. Mildly tannic. Oriental spices, black fruits, sweet herbs. Exotically aromatic, with a firm and well-structured mouthfeel. Has fine intensity and length, with excellent grip through the finish. Despite the extraordinarily developed aromas, this has fine cellaring potential.

Côte-Rôtie, La Turque 1995 $NA. (SR)   **97**

Brilliant purple. Opulent and outrageously intense sweet coconut, oriental spice, and black fruit aromas. Full-bodied palate that finishes with a wave of thick, velvety tannins. Amazingly deep, but very well balanced and rich. Approachable, but will develop beautifully. Enticing. Mid-term cellar candidate (3–6 years).

Côte-Rôtie, La Turque 1996 $NA. (SR)   **96-100**

Very deep purple hue. Exotic spice, anise, and black fruit aromas. A lush entry leads to a full bodied palate with ripe and rounded tannins. Supple and almost approachable already. Harmonious and very complete. Should be drinking beautifully on release. Drink now or later.

Côtes-du-Rhône Rouge, 1996 $NA. (SR)   **86**

Brilliant ruby hue. Attractive berry and spice aromas become jammy in the mouth. Medium-bodied palate with drying tannins. Stylish. Drink now.

Gigondas, 1996 $NA. (SR)   **81**

Hermitage Rouge, 1994 $32.   **89**

Bright ruby red. Moderately full-bodied. Highly extracted. Moderately tannic. Leather, black fruits, earth. Spicy aromas follow through on the palate, with a silky mouthfeel giving way to moderate astringency on the finish. Nice now, this will cellar over the medium term.

Hermitage Rouge, 1995 $NA. (SR)   **92**

Deep ruby hue with a slight purple cast. Generous black fruit and vanilla aromas with an exotic smoky edge. Full-bodied palate with robust grainy tannins. Big and structured. Approachable, but really meant to age. Long-term cellar candidate.

Scale: Superlative (96-100), Exceptional (90-95), Highly Recommended (85-89), Recommended (80-84), Not Recommended (Under 80)

Jaboulet

Côtes-du-Rhône Blanc, Parallèle 45 1997 $NA. (SR)　　　　　80

Crozes-Hermitage Blanc, Mule Blanche 1997 $NA. (SR)　　　　89

Deep straw hue. Intense mineral, citrus, and tropical fruit aromas with a touch of vanilla. Medium-bodied, ripe, rich, and stylish with a lean acidic cut through the finish. Drink now or later.

Hermitage Blanc, Chevalier de Sterimberg 1997 $NA. (SR)　　　91

Deep golden hue. Taut mineral and citrus aromas with a vanillin wood accent. Medium-bodied and luscious with a very firm acidic cut. Big and rich. Drink now or later.

St. Joseph Blanc, 1997 $NA. (SR)　　　　90

Deep golden hue. Subdued butterscotch, honey, and mineral aromas. Fat, full-bodied mouthfeel with luscious flavors and a touch of viscosity. Rich, hedonistic, and supple. Drink now.

Châteauneuf-du-Pape Rouge, Les Cèdres 1997 $NA. (SR)　　　84

Cornas, 1997 $NA. (SR)　　　　90

Very deep, opaque ruby-purple. Roasted game, meat, and mineral aromas. Full-bodied, rich, and rustic with big, drying tannins. Chunky and intense. Drink now or later.

Côte-Rôtie, 1997 $NA. (SR)　　　　92

Very deep, opaque ruby-purple. Exotic game, roasted meat, and chocolate aromas. Full-bodied palate with velvety tannins. Explosively flavored and complex. Drink now or later.

Côtes-du-Rhône Rouge, Parallèle 45 1997 $NA. (SR)　　　82

Crozes-Hermitage Rouge, Domaine de Thalabert 1996 $25.　　87

Saturated dark ruby hue. Moderately full-bodied. Full acidity. Highly extracted. Moderately tannic. Black fruits, minerals. Youthful and angular on the palate, with oak spice and vibrant acids on the finish. Well structured. Better balance in a few years.

Crozes-Hermitage Rouge, Domaine Raymond Roure 1996 $29.　　88

Saturated, opaque ruby-red. Moderately full-bodied. Highly extracted. Moderately tannic. Black fruits, chocolate, earth. Very toasty, oak-influenced aromas lead a dry, mouthfilling palate, with a veneer of dry tannins that will need a few years to settle.

Crozes-Hermitage Rouge, Domaine Raymond Roure 1997 $NA. (SR)　　92

Very deep, saturated ruby hue. Intense black fruit and mineral aromas are quite extravagant. Opulent, with an explosion of fruit in the mouth and a rich chocolate accent. Full-bodied and robust with velvety tannins. Drink now or later.

Crozes-Hermitage Rouge, Les Jalets 1997 $NA. (SR)　　　86

Deep ruby-purple. Generous black fruit, tar, and mineral aromas. Moderately full-bodied with firm, gripping tannins. Concentrated. Solid structure. Drink now or later.

Hermitage Rouge, La Chapelle 1995 $75.　　　　94

Saturated, opaque ruby red. Full-bodied. Highly extracted. Quite tannic. Red fruits, minerals, earth. Solid and well-proportioned, with tough tannins not obscuring generous fruit flavors. This is too backward for current consumption. A long-term cellar wine with great potential.

Hermitage Rouge, La Chapelle 1996 $NA. (SR)　　　94

Deep, opaque blackish-ruby hue. Brooding black fruit and mineral aromas. Full-bodied palate with big, chunky tannins. Very deep and intense. High extract and concentration. Rather unapproachable at the moment. Should drink well in 10 to 12 years, while holding for 20-plus.

Hermitage Rouge, La Pied La Côte 1996 $NA. (SR)　　　90

Deep, saturated ruby hue. Brooding blackberry and chocolate aromas. Full-bodied palate with firm tannins and balancing acidic cut. Very stylish, complete, and harmonious. Drink now or later.

St. Joseph Rouge, 1996 $NA. (SR)   87

Very deep ruby with a slight purple overtone. Intense black fruit and mineral aromas. Moderately full-bodied palate with acidic cut and sturdy tannins. Taut and closed through the finish. Mid-term cellar candidate (3–6 years).

Muscat de Beaumes de Venise, 1996 $22.   93

Deep yellow-straw hue. Full-bodied. Balanced acidity. Highly extracted. Orange blossom, honey. Outrageously aromatic, with a rounded, viscous palate feel. Ripe and generous, with fine length and a touch of warmth to the finish. Well balanced and impressive, this will be best in its youth.

Jamet

Côte-Rôtie, 1995 $35.   92

Deep blackish-ruby hue. Full-bodied. Balanced acidity. Highly extracted. Mildly oaked. Moderately tannic. Roasted meats, earth, black fruits. Quite aromatic, and beginning to develop complexity despite its firm, youthful character. Weighty, but quite tight in the mouth, with firm tannins. Needs time.

Côte-Rôtie, 1996 $NA. (SR)   89

Very deep brilliant purple. Opulent blackberry, game, and mineral aromas. Firm, moderately full-bodied palate with gripping tannins. Taut through the finish. Rather austere and closed in the mouth, but concentrated. Needs time. Long-term cellar candidate.

Côte-Rôtie, 1997 $NA. (SR)   96-100

Brilliant purple hue. Exotic, enticing flower and mineral aromas. A lean entry leads to a moderately full bodied palate which shows a firm supporting structure. Grippy tannins and vibrant acidity enliven the complex flavors. Finishes with a powerful, deep fruit accent. Midterm cellar candidate (3–6 years).

Côte-Rôtie, 1998 $NA. (SR)   90-95

Brilliant, deep purple hue. Exotic tar, earth, and game aromas. A rich entry leds to a full bodied palate with already supple tannins. Weighty but forward with great, roasted, old vine fruit intensity. Complex and very stylish. Drink now or later.

de la Janasse

Châteauneuf-du-Pape Rouge, 1995 $24.99.   88

Bright ruby red. Medium-bodied. Moderately extracted. Moderately oaked. Moderately tannic. Dill, red fruits, vanilla. Very clean and aromatic, with an oaky accent that comes through on the palate. Wood accents and primary red fruit flavors make this a modern style.

Châteauneuf-du-Pape Rouge, Chaupin 1995 $29.99.   NR
Châteauneuf-du-Pape Rouge, Vieilles Vignes 1995 $34.99.   91

Saturated red-purple. Medium-bodied. Highly extracted. Moderately tannic. Red fruit, minerals, vanilla. Youthful aromas. Fruit-accented style confirmed on the palate. Weighty and generous, with an opulent core. Drinkable now, but cellarable.

Jasmin

Côte-Rôtie, 1995 $35.   90

Bright blackish-ruby color. Full-bodied. Balanced acidity. Highly extracted. Moderately oaked. Moderately tannic. Bacon, earth, black fruits. Powerful aromas are complex and exotic. Ripe and firm in the mouth, with fine length and intensity. Approachable now, but should continue to develop.

Côte-Rôtie, 1996 $NA. (SR)   89

Brilliant ruby with a slight purple accent. Enticing spice and mineral aromas are very pure. Moderately full-bodied palate with excellent grip and depth. Firm and concentrated in an angular style. Mid-term cellar candidate (3–6 years).

Scale: Superlative (96-100), Exceptional (90-95), Highly Recommended (85-89), Recommended (80-84), Not Recommended (Under 80)

Côte-Rôtie, 1997 $NA. (SR)   **90**

Very deep brilliant purple. Enticing, high-toned flower and mineral aromas are quite exotic. Medium-bodied palate with gripping tannins. Very elegant and stylish, with great flavor complexity and a very taut finish. Lean in structure. Should develop well. Mid-term cellar candidate (3–6 years).

Côte-Rôtie, 1998 $NA. (SR)   **85-89**

Deep, brilliant purple hue. Aromatically reserved, with very firm minerally flavors. A taut entry leads to a full bodied palate with a wave of robust, lean tannnins. Lots of stuffing, but quite austere. Needs lots of time. Long-term cellar.

Gabriel Liogier

Côtes-du-Rhône Rouge, Domaine de la Taladette 1996 $8.99.   **84**

Châteauneuf-du-Pape Rouge, Montjoie 1995 $17.99.   **88**

Bright ruby red. Medium-bodied. Balanced acidity. Moderately extracted. Moderately tannic. Leather, sage, brown spice. Generous black fruit and leather aromas lead a crisp mouthful of flavors, with grainy tannins through the finish. A rustic style with plenty of flavor.

de Marcoux

Châteauneuf-du-Pape Rouge, 1995 $20.   **89**

Ruby red with lightening at the rim. Medium-bodied. Moderately extracted. Moderately tannic. Vanilla, spice, black fruits. Appealing nose and palate delve beyond primary fruit into secondary aromas and flavors. Elegant and flavorful, with great length and nuance through the finish.

Thomas Moillard

Côtes-du-Rhône Rouge, Les Violettes 1997 $8.99.   **83**

Crozes-Hermitage Rouge, 1996 $11.99.   **84**

Mommessin

Châteauneuf-du-Pape Rouge, 1995 $17.99.   **84**

Châteauneuf-du-Pape Rouge, Clos des Brusquières 1995 $18.99.   **86**

Bright ruby-garnet cast. Medium-bodied. Balanced acidity. Moderately extracted. Mildly oaked. Mildly tannic. Brown spices, earth, dried herbs. Pleasantly aromatic, with a firm and complex palate feel. Lean and angular through the finish.

Côtes-du-Rhône Rouge, Château de Domazan 1997 $7.99.   **81**

du Monteillet

Condrieu, 1996 $NA.   **86**

Bright pale gold. Medium-bodied. Balanced acidity. Moderately extracted. Citrus, minerals. Thick palate; glycerous richness provides balancing contrast to zesty citrus and chalky flavors. A clean, lean style.

Mont-Redon

Châteauneuf-du-Pape Rouge, 1995 $25.   **91**

Bright ruby red. Medium-bodied. Balanced acidity. Moderately extracted. Mildly tannic. Leather, red fruits, minerals. Developed aromas. Rich, complex flavors with a traditional accent. Earthy, meaty note through the finish.

Châteauneuf-du-Pape Rouge, 1996 $25.   **84**

de la Mordorée

Châteauneuf-du-Pape Rouge, Cuvée de la Reine des Bois 1996 $26.   93

Saturated blackish-ruby hue. Moderately full-bodied. Balanced acidity. Highly extracted. Moderately oaked. Moderately tannic. Black fruits, vanilla, minerals. Concentrated and rich, with dense, fruity flavors and rich tannins. Although this is nice now, it will repay keeping. Very modern winemaking evident, with new oak in abundance.

Yves & Catherine Nativelle

Muscat de Beaumes de Venise, Domaine de Coyeux 1994 $19.   83

La Nerthe

Châteauneuf-du-Pape Blanc, 1996 $23.   86

Bright green-straw cast. Moderately full-bodied. High acidity. Highly extracted. Tropical fruits, citrus, minerals. Generous aromatics are complex and unusual. Rich and ripe in the mouth. Firm and angular finish.

Châteauneuf-du-Pape Rouge, 1995 $28.   93

Deeply saturated ruby hue. Moderately full-bodied. Balanced acidity. Highly extracted. Moderately oaked. Mildly tannic. Red fruits, vanilla. Ripe, round, and rich, with a generous aromatic character. Full and sturdy in a modern, fruit-centered style, with complementary chunky tannins.

Michel Ogier

Côte-Rôtie, 1994 $34.   86

Dark ruby-garnet color. Moderately full-bodied. Full acidity. Highly extracted. Moderately oaked. Mildly tannic. Earth, minerals, brown spices, red fruits. Showing early signs of maturity in both color and flavor. Still quite complex, with a firm and angular mouthfeel. Acidity plays a prominent role.

Reine Pédauque

Côtes-du-Rhône Blanc, Les Rigaudes 1997 $9.   82

Châteauneuf-du-Pape Rouge, Fontchaillou 1995 $17.   82

Châteauneuf-du-Pape Rouge, Les Bories, Cuvée Prestige 1995 $24.   82

Côtes-du-Rhône Rouge, Les Bouffons de la Reine 1996 $9.   NR

Côtes-du-Rhône Rouge, Les Rigaudes 1996 $9.   NR

Crozes-Hermitage Rouge, Chantoiselle 1995 $12.   89

Ruby red. Medium-bodied. Balanced acidity. Moderately extracted. Moderately tannic. Black fruit, bacon fat, minerals. Smoky aromas. Clean, mineral-accented palate with an austere character and grainy tannins through the finish. A lighter style, but very individual and drinkable.

du Pegau

Châteauneuf-du-Pape Rouge, Cuvée Réservée 1995 $50.   94

Dark ruby hue. Medium-bodied. Moderately extracted. Moderately tannic. Plums, spice. Deep aromas follow through on the palate with some angular, fine-grained tannins on the finish. Youthful and tough, this needs more time, but the underlying depth and concentration is evident.

Châteauneuf-du-Pape Rouge, Cuvée Réservée 1996 $38.   87

Ruby red with a subtle purple cast. Medium-bodied. Highly extracted. Quite tannic. Black fruits, tea. Youthful fruit. Slightly meaty aromas. Fleshy entry, with dry tannins gripping the finish. Rather reserved now, this will need more time in the cellar.

Scale: Superlative (96-100), Exceptional (90-95), Highly Recommended (85-89), Recommended (80-84), Not Recommended (Under 80)

André Perret

Condrieu, Côteau de Chery 1996 $34.99.   86

Bright pale gold. Moderately full-bodied. Balanced acidity. Moderately extracted. Ripe apricot, white pepper, dried herbs and flowers. Lush and soft, with enough acidity to remain juicy through the finish.

Perrin

Côtes-du-Rhône Blanc, Réserve 1997 $10.49.   86

Bright straw cast. Moderately full-bodied. Full acidity. Moderately extracted. Tropical fruits, dough, minerals. Pleasant aromatics feature a note of complexity. Full and firm in the mouth, with a sense of richness and an angular finish.

Châteauneuf-du-Pape Rouge, Les Sinards 1996 $25.   83

Côtes-du-Rhône Rouge, Réserve 1996 $10.49.   84

Gigondas, 1995 $23.   83

Muscat de Beaumes de Venise, 1996 $14.   86

Bright straw cast. Medium-bodied. Balanced acidity. Moderately extracted. Minerals, citrus, tropical fruits. Pleasantly aromatic, with a decided fruit accent. Crisp and lively on the lighter-styled palate, with a clean, flavorful finish.

Michel Picard

Châteauneuf-du-Pape Rouge, 1996 $23.   86

Bright ruby red. Balanced acidity. Moderately extracted. Moderately tannic. Mineral, dried red fruits. A lighter style with some dried fruit flavors and a mineral theme through the firm finish.

Côtes-du-Rhône Rouge, 1996 $10.99.   NR

Pichon

Condrieu, 1995 $NA.   92

Bright golden straw. Moderately full-bodied. Low acidity. Highly extracted. Smoke, dill, citrus zest, white peach. Extravagant aromas. Very distinctive and exotic. Unctuous, oily mouthfeel. Drink in the near term.

Domaine Raspail-Ay

Gigondas, 1995 $20.   86

Deep ruby cast. Moderately full-bodied. Balanced acidity. Moderately extracted. Mildly oaked. Mildly tannic. Strawberries, earth, licorice, spice. A range of warm, rustic flavors. Rich and chunky in the mouth, with a lush finish.

Rayas

Châteauneuf-du-Pape Blanc, Réserve 1995 $65.   96

Bright yellow-gold. Full-bodied. Full acidity. Highly extracted. Yeast, hazelnuts, smoke. Opulent and exotic aromatics are rich and enormously complex. Rich and flavorful through the finish. Not unlike an exotic White Burgundy. Great depth and intensity.

des Relagnes

Châteauneuf-du-Pape Rouge, 1995 $20.   84

La Roquette

Châteauneuf-du-Pape Blanc, Clos la Roquette 1997 $28.   81

Châteauneuf-du-Pape Rouge, 1996 $25.   91

Deep ruby red to the rim. Full-bodied. Balanced acidity. Highly extracted. Moderately oaked. Mildly tannic. Vanilla, black fruits, earth. Extraordinarily aromatic, with a solid interplay between fruit and wood nuances. Firm and rich in the mouth, with a sense of opulence that makes for an attractive, youthful style.

René Rostaing
Condrieu, La Bonnette 1996 $60.   84

Joseph Sabon
Côtes-du-Rhône Rouge, Cuvée Spéciale, Vieilles Vignes 1996 $18.   84

Domaine Saint Benoît
Châteauneuf-du-Pape Rouge, 1995 $15.   86

Saturated dark ruby red. Moderately full-bodied. Highly extracted. Moderately tannic.
Earth, red fruits. Impressive, earthy aromas. Rich, sumptuous mouthfeel has a degree of
fruity softness and ripeness that make for a hedonistic style.

Châteauneuf-du-Pape Rouge, La Truffière 1995 $30.   92

Saturated ruby-garnet hue. Moderately full-bodied. Highly extracted. Quite tannic.
Mineral, earth, game. A very traditional style with mature qualities. Well structured.
Concentrated. Solid, earthy palate. Long finish.

Domaine Santa Duc
Gigondas, 1995 $20.   85

des Senechaux
Châteauneuf-du-Pape Rouge, 1995 $20.   84

Marc Sorrel
Crozes-Hermitage Rouge, 1995 $NA.   84
Hermitage Rouge, Le Greal 1995 $40.   90

Bright ruby red to the rim. Moderately full-bodied. Highly extracted. Moderately tannic.
Red berries, minerals, earth. Bright, mineral-accented aromas. Lean, elegant palate with
great mineral length. Excellent balance and a succinct expression of origin.

Tardieu Laurent
Châteauneuf-du-Pape Rouge, 1995 $40.   87

Deep ruby cast. Full-bodied. Balanced acidity. Highly extracted. Mildly tannic. Horse,
minerals, earth. Quite aromatic, with a full and rounded texture. Earthy, rustic flavors
make more impression than primary fruit accents, making for a traditional style.

Raymond Usseglio
Châteauneuf-du-Pape Rouge, Cuvée Impériale 1995 $26.   92

Deep ruby hue with a slight fade. Moderately full-bodied. Balanced acidity. Moderately
extracted. Moderately oaked. Mildly tannic. Red fruits, cedar, minerals. Perfumed quality.
Intense, rich, and ripe in the mouth. Well structured with a firm, long finish.

Daniel et Roland Vernay
Côte-Rôtie, Grand' Place 1994 $35.   83

La Vieille Ferme
Rhône Valley Blanc, 1997 $7.49.   83
Rhône Valley Rouge, 1996 $7.49.   84

Le Vieux Donjon
Châteauneuf-du-Pape Rouge, 1995 $25.   90

Deep ruby cast. Moderately full-bodied. Full acidity. Moderately extracted. Moderately
tannic. Pepper, red fruits, minerals. Lean and firm. Impressive minerally depth and
persistence. A traditional style in the best sense of the word.

Scale: Superlative (96-100), Exceptional (90-95), Highly Recommended (85-89),
Recommended (80-84), Not Recommended (Under 80)

du Vieux Lazaret
Châteauneuf-du-Pape Rouge, 1995 $17.   81

Vieux Mas des Papes
Châteauneuf-du-Pape Blanc, 1996 $NA.   89

Bright green-gold cast. Moderately full-bodied. Full acidity. Highly extracted. Lacquer, blanched almonds, honey. Carries an unusual oxidized note, with a clean palate and excellent snap to the green finish. Almost like a fresh Fino Sherry. Interesting and individualistic, to say the least.

Châteauneuf-du-Pape Rouge, 1996 $24.   86

Pale ruby with a fading rim. Moderately light-bodied. Moderately extracted. Moderately tannic. Mineral, dried red fruits. Dry and lean style with a stony, austere character. Not built for extensive cellaring.

Vieux Télégraphe
Châteauneuf-du-Pape Blanc, La Crau 1997 $32.   89

Bright straw cast. Moderately full-bodied. Full acidity. Moderately extracted. Minerals, toast, nuts. Generously aromatic, with a firm and linear palate feel. Youthful and tight, with a firm, minerally backbone through the finish. Rather reserved now, but a year or two should reveal more nutty charm.

Châteauneuf-du-Pape Rouge, La Crau 1996 $35.   91

Deep ruby hue with a slight garnet cast. Full-bodied. Balanced acidity. Highly extracted. Moderately oaked. Mildly tannic. Cedar, black fruits, minerals. Aromatic and rich, with a full and rounded mouthfeel. Ripe and generously fruity center, with firm tannins giving grip on the finish. Rich and fleshy, this is very drinkable now.

Provence and the Sunny South

The Languedoc and Provence contain some of the most exciting vineyards in France. This sunny southern country produces red wines that have a robustness that comes from dry vineyards where vines have to dig deep for water. In terms of cost, it seems unlikely that the estate wines from southern France will ever reach the dizzying heights of Bordeaux and Burgundy. Indeed, these wines can be France's best buys for those who are prepared to step off the beaten path and explore the southern appellations. A $20 bill can buy something with far more complexity and personality than it ever could in Bordeaux or Burgundy.

One needs to coin certain terms when describing the wines of the south. They seem to smell of sunshine, olives, and the dried-up scrub bush that is characteristic of Provence. Well, all of this is a bit of a mouthful to say each time, and the French have obliged us with a nice little term: "garrigue." It encapsulates all the smells of the south, particularly of Provence, that seem—regardless of whether it can be scientifically proven—to emanate from southern French wines.

Provence and the Sunny South at a Glance

Wines Reviewed:

46

Producers/Brands Represented:

30

Value Rating:

Good to Excellent

Key Varietals and Appellations

Syrah

The grape of the northern Rhône has been one of the key "improvers" in the Languedoc-Roussillon where it can add flesh, richness, and complexity to tougher, traditional varieties like Carignan. It has found a particular affinity in the Languedoc, where in appellations such as Coteaux de Languedoc, Minervois, and Corbières it is responsible for distinctively northern Rhône-like wines. Note that Syrah is not a mandated grape variety in any of these appellations, and it is still the exception and not the rule for a cuvée to contain an abundance of it.

Mourvèdre

Mourvèdre can be found all over the south of France, but it is particularly abundant in Provence. It is used almost exclusively in the small southern Provençal appellation of Bandol where it produces famously inky, dark red wines that are tough and chewy in youth but that blossom with some bottle age. Some traditional producers of Bandol still persevere with old-fashioned wines that will need to be bequeathed to your grandchildren, but there are more friendly examples that can be enjoyed in relative youth.

Bordeaux Varietals: Cabernet and Merlot

The Bordelaises jealously guard their right to champion Cabernet Sauvignon, and the political powers that govern appellation rules have been slow to let newer appellations exploit this, the most famous of French grape varieties. One appellation that does produce Cabernet-dominated bottlings is Coteaux d'Aix en Provence, about an hour north of Marseille. Here the sunny south transforms the Cabernet-Merlot blend into something rounded, fruity, and often showing a dash of new oak. (Syrah and Mourvèdre are also exploited in this appellation, and are often used together in cuvées to produce olivey, Rhône-like wines.)

Other Varieties: Carignan and Cinsault

Carignan is the traditional grape of the south of France and left to its own devices it will produce large amounts of highly colored, tannic, and charmless wine. Modern viticulture and, particularly, modern winemaking have tamed this variety. With cooler fermentations and removal of stems, it can be made to produce fleshier, fruitier wines. Indeed, it is still the backbone of the Languedoc appellations of Fitou, Corbières, and Minervois. However, it still needs the support of varieties like Syrah or Cinsault to produce wines of interest to overseas consumers. The latter, traditional, variety is widely planted in the appellations of the south, though rarely used to form a majority of an estate blend.

Reviews – Provence and the Sunny South

Domaine de Baruel
Vin de Pays des Cévennes, Rouge 1994 $14.   82

Domaine des Béates
Coteaux d'Aix en Provence, Les Matines 1996 $8.99.   84
Bright blackish ruby cast. Moderately full-bodied. Balanced acidity. Moderately extracted. Mildly tannic. Black fruits, provençal herbs, roasted meat. Quite aromatic, with complex, classically Mediterranean flavors. Lighter in the mouth, but quite well structured, with vibrant acidity. Crisp through the lengthy finish.
Coteaux d'Aix en Provence, 1994 $17.   81

Domaine Borie de Maurel
Syrah, Minervois 1997 $8.   82
Minervois, Cuvée Sylla 1996 $17.   97
Deep blackish ruby hue. Full-bodied. Balanced acidity. Moderately extracted. Mildly tannic. Olives, provençal herbs, black fruits. Features a wonderfully expressive and complex nose, with a wave of chunky flavors on the palate that remind one of old-vine Syrah. Rich and thick in the mouth, with fine length and intensity. Supple, though well structured.

Château les Bouysses
Cahors, 1994 $11.   80

Comte André de Monpezat
Cahors, 1994 $7.50.   NR

Comte Cathare
Saint-Chinian, Château de Combebelle Prestige 1995 $9.   80
Minervois, Château Maris 1995 $9.   84
Bright ruby with a slight garnet edge. Moderately full-bodied. Balanced acidity. Moderately extracted. Moderately tannic. Minerals, dried herbs. Aromatically reserved, with a lean, firm palate feel. Crisp and angular through the taut finish.
Saint-Chinian, Château de Combebelle 1995 $15.   84
Bright ruby-purple cast. Moderately full-bodied. Balanced acidity. Moderately extracted. Moderately tannic. Dried herbs, minerals, black fruits. Features an herbal edge throughout, with a ripe, though lean palate feel. Firm tannins bite down on the finish.

Minervois, Château Maris Prestige 1995 $15. 84

Deep ruby with a slight fade. Moderately full-bodied. Balanced acidity. Moderately extracted. Mildly tannic. Brown spices, chocolate, earth. Pleasantly aromatic, with a complex array of flavors. Full and firm, yet well balanced on the palate, with a sense of lushness through the finish.

Lucien Deschaux

Côtes de Duras, Blanc de Blancs 1995 $5.99. 81

Coteaux du Languedoc, Bresson 1995 $5.99. 82

Destavel

Côtes du Roussillon Villages, 1994 $9.99. 84

Deep reddish purple. Medium bodied. Highly extracted. Mildly tannic. Reminiscent of black fruits. vanilla, cola. Spicy fragrant nose. Chewy and mouthfilling with black fruits flavors and some rich tannins. Good mouthfeel and balance. Robust style.

Domaine Arretxea

Irouléguy, 1996 $15. 89

Bright blackish ruby cast. Medium-bodied. Balanced acidity. Moderately extracted. Mildly tannic. Provençal herbs, red fruits. Pleasantly aromatic, with a distinctive flavor profile. Lighter in the mouth, with a crisp and angular quality to the finish. Solid grip and intensity.

Irouléguy, Cuvée Haitza 1995 $20. 89

Deep blackish purple hue. Moderately full-bodied. Balanced acidity. Highly extracted. Mildly tannic. Black fruits, licorice, mint. Quite aromatic, with complex flavors throughout. Full-framed and well structured, with an angular, lengthy finish. Well balanced and structured to age.

Château Dona Baissas

Côtes du Roussillon Villages, 1994 $7.99. 83

Château de Haute-Serre

Cahors, 1993 $16. 89

Bright reddish purple. Medium-bodied. Full acidity. Moderately extracted. Moderately oaked. Mildly tannic. Bright lively red fruit flavors are enlivened by tart acids through the finish. The firm minerally backbone gives this some presence on the palate, with restrained tannins making it quite drinkable now, though quite austere in fruit flavors.

Impernal

Cahors, 1994 $9. 86

Opaque blackish purple. Full-bodied. Highly extracted. Moderately oaked. Quite tannic. Chocolate, blackberries. Bitter chocolate and black berry fruits fill the palate with tightly wound, astringent, and dry mouthcoating tannins giving this an impressive palate presence. A very traditional, somewhat rustic style that will need some cellar age to soften.

Château des Lanes

Corbières, 1994 $8.99. 85

Bright reddish purple. Medium bodied. Moderately extracted. Moderately tannic. Reminiscent of raspberries, dried herbs, earth. Austere aromatic hint of dried herbs. Full earthy palate with a minerally richness through the finish. A solid presence on the palate with some subtlety of flavors.

Château de Lastours

Corbières, 1993 $9.   88

Brick red with a light rim. Medium bodied. Moderately extracted. Mildly tannic. Reminiscent of brown spice, leather, earth, licorice. Earthy caramelized aromas show some mature character. Smooth harmonious palate show fine integration of flavors with some spicy notes on the finish.

Corbières, Futs de Chène 1993 $14.   89

Ruby center with a right cherry rim. Medium bodied. Moderately extracted. Moderately oaked. Mildly tannic. Reminiscent of vanilla, oak spice, berry fruits. Full oak-spiced aromas follow through well on the palate with rounded fruity flavors through a pronounced oak finish. This has some weight and persistence.

Mas de Daumas Gassac

Vin de Pays de L'Hérault Blanc, Haute Vallée du Gassac 1996 $25.   87

Deep yellow golden cast. Full-bodied. Full acidity. Moderately extracted. Tropical fruits, cream, coconut. Quite aromatic, with a full and flavorful palate feel. Spritzy acidity lends a sense of balance to what is otherwise a very weighty wine. Finishes with a slight impression of sweetness.

Vin de Pays de L'Hérault Rouge, Haute Vallée du Gassac 1995 $25.   86

Bright blackish ruby cast. Medium-bodied. Balanced acidity. Moderately extracted. Moderately tannic. Spice, red fruits. Aromatically reserved, with a lean, firmly structured palate. Tannins bite down on the finish.

Mas de Gourgonnier

Les Baux de Provence Rouge, 1995 $9.   86

Bright blackish ruby cast. Medium-bodied. Balanced acidity. Highly extracted. Mildly tannic. Tar, earth, red fruits. Pleasantly aromatic, with a rounded, though firm and angular palate. Quite lean through the finish, with a hint of bitterness.

Mas de la Dame

Les Baux de Provence, Cuvée de la Stele 1995 $NA.   86

Deep ruby cast. Moderately full-bodied. Balanced acidity. Moderately extracted. Mildly tannic. Chocolate, spice, earth. Generous aromas lead to a fully flavored, rich palate feel. Complexity comes with a rustic edge. Ripe and firm through the finish.

Château de Mercues

Cahors, Cuvée Prestige 1994 $14.   85

Full magenta purple hue. Medium-bodied. Highly extracted. Moderately oaked. Moderately tannic. Red fruits, dried herbs. Faintly herbal red fruit aromas. Fine, minerally mouthfeel has delicacy and elegance, though character is dry and austere. Not overly generous, but this has classy, minerally feel through the finish.

Château Milhau-Lacugue

Saint Chinian, 1994 $7.99.   85

Full cherry red with purple accents. Medium bodied. Moderately extracted. Moderately tannic. Reminiscent of red fruits, black tea, blackberry, clove. Vanilla and berry fruit aromas lead a bright and full-flavored palate with some dry tannins through the finish. Drinking nicely now for matching with robust foods.

Château Moulin de Carsac

Corbières, 1994 $8.99.   84

Deep bright purple. Medium bodied. Moderately extracted. Mildly tannic. Reminiscent of raspberry, vanilla. Bright fruity entry shows a youthful but very accessible character. Highly drinkable and distinguished by a rounded mouthfeel.

Château Revelette

Coteaux d'Aix en Provence, 1995 $10.　　　　　　　　　　　　81
Coteaux d'Aix en Provence, Le Grand Rouge de Revelette 1995 $19.　　　84

Deep ruby hue. Medium-bodied. Full acidity. Moderately extracted. Mildly oaked. Moderately tannic. Brown spices, minerals, red fruits. Pleasantly aromatic, with a subtle, spicy, wood-influenced quality. Deeply flavored, though lighter in body, with a firm, racy structure. Crisp through the finish.

Domaine Richeaume

Côtes de Provence, Cuvée Tradition 1996 $17.　　　　　　　　　89

Deep ruby-purple cast. Moderately full-bodied. Balanced acidity. Highly extracted. Moderately oaked. Moderately tannic. Vanilla, black fruits. Almost like an Australian Shiraz, with a hefty overlay of oak seasoning and a ripe core of fruit-centered flavors. Ripe and well balanced, with firm tannins through the finish.

Côtes de Provence, Cuvée Columelle 1996 $22.　　　　　　　　91

Deep blackish purple cast. Moderately full-bodied. Balanced acidity. Highly extracted. Mildly tannic. Black fruits, mint. Aromatically reserved, with a tightly wound, youthful palate feel. Features a core of dark, fruit-centered flavors. Crisp and firm through the finish. Well balanced and age-worthy.

Seigneurs du Périgord

Bergerac Blanc, 1995 $7.　　　　　　　　　　　　　　　87

Pale golden appearance. Medium-bodied. Moderately extracted. Melons, flowers, citrus fruits. Lovely fresh floral aromas have melony accents. Lively acids are balanced with bright crisp fruity flavors that conclude cleanly on the lingering finish. For all its easily enjoyable character, this has some complexity.

Bergerac Rouge, 1996 $7.　　　　　　　　　　　　　　84

Bright cherry red with purple highlights. Moderately light-bodied. Moderately extracted. Mildly tannic. Berry fruits, dried herbs. Fresh-berry accented aromas lead a crisp palate full of red fruit flavors with a subtle herbal note pervading the finish. Fresh and lively, with a lovely crisp bite that is appealing in its simplicity.

Domaine Sorin

Bandol, 1994 $21.　　　　　　　　　　　　　　　　93

Deep blackish ruby cast. Moderately full-bodied. Balanced acidity. Highly extracted. Mildly tannic. Vanilla, tar, black fruit, minerals. Quite aromatic, with a hefty oak overlay and a ripe core of fruit flavors. Rich and full style, with expressive black fruit flavors through the finish.

Domaine Tempier

Bandol, 1995 $25.　　　　　　　　　　　　　　　　86

Bright ruby-purple cast. Medium-bodied. Full acidity. Moderately extracted. Mildly tannic. Red fruits, minerals, dried herbs. Pleasantly aromatic, with a zesty, fruit-centered quality. Crisp and zesty through the finish, with fine grip. Should pair well with food.

Bandol, Cuvée Spéciale 1995 $27.　　　　　　　　　　　89

Bright ruby-purple cast. Medium-bodied. Full acidity. Moderately extracted. Mildly tannic. Provençal herbs, olives, red fruits. Pleasantly aromatic, with a wave of complex and harmonious flavors. Lighter in the mouth, though well balanced, with fine length and intensity. Finishes with a sense of crispness.

Bandol, Cuvée Spéciale, La Migoua 1994 $29.　　　　　　　88

Bright blackish ruby cast with a fade to the rim. Moderately full-bodied. Balanced acidity. Moderately extracted. Mildly tannic. Earth, olives, minerals. Quite aromatic, with an unusual, earthy flavor profile. Rich and well balanced in the mouth, with a crisp finish.

Château Tournelles
Buzet, Cuvée Prestige 1994 $8.   85

Bright cherry red . Medium-bodied. Moderately extracted. Mildly tannic. Raspberry, blackcurrant, dried herbs. Fruity mildly herbaceous aromas. Bright raspberry and blackcurrant flavors fill the palate with lively acids and very fine-grained astringent tannins lingering on the finish.

Domaine de Trevallon
Vin de Pays des Bouches du Rhône, 1995 $32.   94

Deep red-purple cast. Moderately full-bodied. Highly extracted. Quite tannic. Olives, grilled meat. Brooding aromas show Provençal character. Concentrated, tightly wound flavors and firm tannins grip the palate and finish. This is youthful, but impressive at present. Three to four years of cellaring will allow this to show its paces.

Val d'Orbieu
Vin de Pays d'Oc, Cuvée Mythique 1995 $15.   88

Bright blackish ruby cast. Medium-bodied. Full acidity. Highly extracted. Moderately oaked. Mildly tannic. Brown spices, red fruits. Pleasantly aromatic, with an attractive toasty-oak overlay. Lighter in style on the palate, though quite firmly structured, with a racy quality through the finish. Angular.

Château Val Joanis
Côtes du Lubéron, 1995 $8.69.   84

Medium straw appearance. Medium bodied. Balanced acidity. Moderately extracted. Reminiscent of apples, dried herbs, minerals. Mild floral accents on the aromas. Clean and crisp with a solid mouthfeel and some minerally length on the finish.

Côtes du Lubéron, 1993 $8.69.   87

Medium cherry red appearance. Medium bodied. Moderately extracted. Mildly tannic. Reminiscent of mint, earth, blackfruits, licorice. Attractive full aromas lead an open knit accessible palate with minty qualities through the lingering finish. Beautifully balanced. Drinking nicely now.

Côtes du Lubéron, Les Griottes 1992 $14.99.   NR

Château Valmoure
Coteaux du Languedoc, Vigne Antique 1996 $8.99.   93

Deep blackish purple hue. Moderately full-bodied. Full acidity. Highly extracted. Mildly tannic. Provençal herbs, tar, bacon fat. Outrageously aromatic and complex, with a full, though well-structured and lean palate feel. Angular and crisp through the finish, with fine length and intensity.

thirty-one

France
Vin de Pays

The Vin de Pays: Fighting Varietals

In the 1980s and 1990s the popularity in countries such as the United States and Britain of user-friendly, inexpensive, varietally labeled wines created the demand for a category of wine that the French were not meeting. This challenge was taken up in what was the heartland of "vin ordinaire," that part of France historically called the Midi that covers the Languedoc and Roussillon departments. Languedoc-Roussillon has planted much of its vineyards with classic varieties such as Cabernet Sauvignon, Syrah, Merlot, Sauvignon Blanc, Chardonnay, and even Viognier. These wines, labeled as Vin de Pays d'Oc, have been a notable export success in the nineties, an era when France has lost export market share to New World regions. Frequently priced at around $10, these wines often deliver what they promise, without any of the baggage associated with overpriced, mediocre, or downright poor wine from one of France's more glamorous appellations.

Vin de Pays and Appellations

Vin de Pays are regional wines that are not subject to the complex, restrictive laws that govern appellations. A low minimum yield, strict maximum production limits, mandated grape varieties, and stipulations about typicity are out. Instead Chardonnay, Sauvignon Blanc, Merlot, and Cabernet Sauvignon can grow in relative proximity to each other. The producers can make their wines to meet the demands of the market, choosing to have low yields or to oak age. Most important, Vin de Pays can be labeled with the grape variety or blend of grape varieties from which they are made.

A disappointing Vin de Pays is merely a poor generic wine. A bad Appellation Contrôlée wine that is supposedly typical of its appellation is often little more than a sham for which the consumer often pays too much. Self-regulated "typicity" of wines from glamour appellations is what allows poor producers to prosper in "big name" appellations.

Generally, France's appellation system prohibits varietal labeling, Alsace excepted. Thus a Sancerre is not labeled as a Sauvignon Blanc, nor is a Médoc wine labeled as Cabernet Sauvignon. However, some large producers in Bordeaux and even Burgundy have taken to having it both ways by labeling their basic generic appellation wines with varietal labels. Technically, this is forbidden, but the authorities have not enforced the letter of the law.

Key Vin de Pays Designations

Although the Pays d'Oc is the best known of France's regional wines, it is far from the only one. There are 100 Vin de Pays designations. The large departmental Vin de Pays regions each have a multitude of smaller Vin de Pays sub-regions, and the vast majority of the latter will never see the shores of the United States.

Vin de Pays d'Oc

The Vin de Pays d'Oc encompasses the Languedoc and Roussillon regions that take in a huge swathe of vineyards from the Rhône Valley all the way to the Pyrenees on the Spanish border. This vast region borders the Mediterranean, which provides cooling influences during the warm southern French summers and moderated temperatures during the winter. The Vin de Pays d'Oc designation is responsible for 80% of Vin de Pays production in France, and only the very best of this is ever exported. The region is best known through the portfolios of major brands like Fortant de France, Georges Duboeuf, and most recently Vichon (owned by Robert Mondavi). All of France's classic varieties are grown in this region.

Vin de Pays de l'Hérault

Vin de Pays de l'Hérault is a sub-region located in the central section of the Vin de Pays d'Oc and many Hérault varietal wines carry the Pays d'Oc designation. Nonetheless, it still has a high profile in its own right. The most expensive Vin de Pays of France comes from this large region: Mas de Daumas-Gassac. Aimé Guibert purchased an old farmhouse and its estate near the small town of Aniane in 1970, initially having no plans for vineyards or wine production until a Bordeaux enologist informed him that it was a "God-given terroir" for winemaking. Since then it has risen to become one of France's better estate wines and has not been slowed by having to bear a Vin de Pays label.

Vin de Pays de l'Ardèche

This region covers the Ardèche, to the south of the Rhône Valley wine region. It seems to have become one of the regions of choice for Burgundy negociants who wish to diversify into cheaper varietal wines. The prime example is Beaune negociant Louis Latour, who own extensive Chardonnay and Pinot Noir plantings for their highly successful range of varietal Vin de Pays wines. In addition to these varieties Syrah does well here. However, the Ardèche is probably best known as the home to the $10 Viognier that actually tastes like a Viognier. This is where Georges Duboeuf decided to plant the largest holdings of Viognier in the world.

Vin du Pays du Jardin de la France

Literally, the garden of France, this is the large multi-departmental Vin de Pays that covers the entire Loire region and beyond. Being a cool, northerly region, it is known for white wines. Good-value Loire-styled Sauvignon Blanc in particular is produced here.

Vin de Pays at a Glance

Wines Reviewed:

83

Producers/Brands Represented:

25

Value Rating:

Average to Good

Reviews

La Baume
1996 Syrah, Vin de Pays d'Oc $6.99.   **86**
Deep ruby-purple cast. Moderately full-bodied. Balanced acidity. Moderately extracted. Mildly tannic. Black fruits, minerals, tar. Pleasantly aromatic, with a pure presentation of varietal flavors. Lighter in style, but shows flavor intensity in a sturdy, angular finish.
1995 Merlot, Vin de Pays d'Oc $6.99.   **84**
1996 Chardonnay, Vin de Pays d'Oc $6.99.   **83**
1995 Cabernet Sauvignon, Vin de Pays d'Oc $6.99.   **82**

Borie-Manoux
1997 Le Birdie, Merlot, Vin de Pays d'Oc $10.   **83**

Domaine Capion
1995 Merlot, Vin de Pays d'Oc $7.   **NR**

Domaine La Chevalière
1995 Première Cuvée Blanc, Vin de Pays d'Oc $12.99.   **88**
Deep greenish gold. Moderately full-bodied. Full acidity. Highly extracted. Mildly oaked. Vanilla, toast, citrus. Ripe and aromatic, with generous, rounded flavors. A weighty mouthfeel is offset by vibrant acidity, making for a clean finish.
1996 Viognier, Vin de Pays d'Oc $12.99.   **83**
1996 Réserve, Syrah, Vin de Pays d'Oc $9.99.   **NR**

Couleur Volant
1996 Merlot, Vin de Pays d'Oc $8.   **88**
Deep blackish-ruby hue. Moderately full-bodied. Full acidity. Moderately extracted. Mildly oaked. Mildly tannic. Red fruits, minerals, cedar. Pleasantly aromatic, with a taut, linear palate feel. Clean and well defined on the palate, with bright acidity through the finish.
1996 Sauvignon Blanc, Vin de Pays d'Oc $8.   **83**
1996 Syrah, Vin de Pays des Coteaux de L'Ardèche $8.   **NR**
1996 L'Aude, Chardonnay, Vin de Pays d'Oc $8.   **NR**

Delas
1996 Merlot, Vin de Pays d'Oc $7.   **83**
1996 Viognier, Vin de Pays de la Drôme $10.   **NR**

Lucien Deschaux
1996 Chardonnay, Vin de Pays d'Oc $6.99.   **82**
1996 Syrah, Vin de Pays d'Oc $6.99.   **81**
1996 "Charnay les Mâcon," Cabernet Sauvignon, Vin de Pays d'Oc $6.99.   **NR**
1996 Merlot, Vin de Pays d'Oc $6.99.   **NR**

Georges Duboeuf
1997 Merlot, Vin de Pays d'Oc $5.99.   **86**
Bright ruby purple to the rim. Moderately full-bodied. Balanced acidity. Moderately extracted. Mildly oaked. Mildly tannic. Red fruits, vanilla, minerals. Pleasantly aromatic, with a firm yet generous palate feel. Shows excellent grip and fine length through the finish.

1997 Viognier, Vin de Pays de L'Ardèche $9.　　　　　　　86

Pale yellow-straw luster. Medium-bodied. Moderately extracted. Nutmeg, flowers, citrus oil. Floral, spicy aromas lead a rounded, glycerous palate with textural elegance and a spicy note on the finish. An excellent varietal expression at this price.

1997 Sauvignon Blanc, Vin de Pays du Jardin de la France $5.99.　　84

1997 Chardonnay, Vin de Pays d'Oc $6.99.　　　　　　　83

1997 Syrah, Vin de Pays d'Oc $5.99.　　　　　　　81

1997 Cabernet Sauvignon, Vin de Pays d'Oc $5.99.　　　　NR

Fortant de France

1995 Sauvignon Blanc, Vin de Pays d'Oc $7.49.　　　　　85

1996 Merlot, Vin de Pays d'Oc $7.49.　　　　　　　84

1995 Cabernet Sauvignon, Vin de Pays d'Oc $7.49.　　　　82

Gallerie

1996 Sauvignon Blanc, Vin de Pays de L'Hérault $7.99.　　　86

Medium straw appearance. Medium-bodied. Moderately extracted. Black currant leaves, grass, and grapefruit on the nose. These racy varietal markers are evident on the palate as well, all wrapped up into a silky, glycerous mouthfeel.

1994 Pinot Noir, Vin de Pays de L'Hérault $7.99.　　　　85

1996 Chardonnay, Vin de Pays de L'Hérault $6.99.　　　　85

1995 Merlot, Vin de Pays de L'Hérault $6.99.　　　　　84

1995 Cabernet Sauvignon, Vin de Pays de L'Hérault $6.99.　　84

1994 Syrah, Vin de Pays de L'Hérault $7.99.　　　　　NR

Jaja de Jau

1996 Syrah-Grenache, Vin de Pays d'Oc $7.　　　　　86

Bright raspberry red with violet highlights. Moderately light-bodied. Moderately extracted. Mildly tannic. Violets, jammy fruit, and pepper aromas. Sweet fruit flavors on the palate are balanced with a counterpoint of acidity. Attractive peppery note lasts through to the finish. Serve at room temperature or slightly chilled.

1996 Cabernet-Merlot, Vin de Pays d'Oc $7.　　　　　84

1996 Cabernet-Merlot, Vin de Pays d'Oc $6.　　　　　84

1996 Syrah-Grenache, Vin de Pays d'Oc $6.　　　　　84

Jenard

1996 Sauvignon Blanc, Vin de Pays d'Oc $7.99.　　　　83

1996 Caves des Papes, Merlot, Vin de Pays d'Oc $7.99.　　　83

1997 Caves des Papes, Chardonnay, Vin de Pays d'Oc $7.99.　　83

1996 Caves des Papes, Cabernet Sauvignon, Vin de Pays d'Oc $7.99.　82

1996 Caves des Papes, Syrah, Vin de Pays d'Oc $7.99.　　　NR

W. Klug

1996 Chardonnay-Sauvignon Blanc, Vin de Pays d'Oc $7.　　83

1996 Chardonnay, Vin de Pays d'Oc $8.　　　　　　83

1996 Merlot, Vin de Pays d'Oc $8.　　　　　　　82

1995 Cabernet Sauvignon-Merlot, Vin de Pays d'Oc $8.　　80

Marquise de Lassime

1997 Chardonnay, Vin de Pays du Jardin de la France $4.99.　　83

Louis Latour

1996 Grand Ardèche, Chardonnay, Vin de Pays des Coteaux de L'Ardèche $13. **87**

Bright pale gold. Moderately full-bodied. Full acidity. Highly extracted. Moderately oaked. Vanilla, smoke, yeast. Quite aromatic, with a toasty oak accent and yeasty flavors throughout. Full and rich, yet crisp through the finish.

1996 "Domaine de Valmoissine," Pinot Noir, Vin de Pays des Coteaux du Verdon $17. **87**

Pale ruby cast. Medium-bodied. Balanced acidity. Highly extracted. Mildly oaked. Cinnamon, red fruits, dried herbs. Pleasantly aromatic, with a full and flavorful palate. Well balanced. Excellent varietal intensity all the way through to the finish.

1996 Chardonnay, Vin de Pays des Coteaux de L'Ardèche $8. **NR**

Henri Miquel

1996 "Domaine Miquel," Viognier, Vin de Pays d'Oc $12.99. **86**

Bright yellow-gold. Medium-bodied. Balanced acidity. Moderately extracted. Herbs, minerals, peach. Generous aromas show fine varietal character. Rounded texture is complemented by acidity that leaves the mouth refreshed.

Louis Mousset

1997 "Le P'Tit Bistro" Blanc, Vin de Pays du Gard $4.99. **84**

1997 "Le P'Tit Bistro" Rouge, Vin de Pays du Gard $4.99. **NR**

l'Orval

1996 Merlot, Vin de Pays d'Oc $5.99. **82**

1996 Chardonnay-Chasan, Vin de Pays d'Oc $6.99. **82**

1996 Chardonnay, Vin de Pays d'Oc $6.99. **81**

1996 Cabernet Sauvignon, Vin de Pays d'Oc $5.99. **NR**

1996 Syrah, Vin de Pays d'Oc $5.99. **NR**

Michel Picard

1996 Syrah, Vin de Pays d'Oc $9.99. **88**

Bright ruby purple. Moderately full-bodied. Balanced acidity. Moderately extracted. Mildly oaked. Mildly tannic. Minerals, black fruits, spice. Pleasantly aromatic. Rich, viscous mouthfeel. Intense right through to the lingering finish.

1996 Chardonnay, Vin de Pays d'Oc $9.99. **86**

Bright golden cast. Moderately full-bodied. Balanced acidity. Moderately extracted. Cream, toast, minerals. Ripe and rounded in style, with enough acidity to lend a sense of balance. Nicely textured and flavorful.

1996 Merlot, Vin de Pays d'Oc $9.99. **84**

1996 Cabernet Sauvignon, Languedoc-Roussillon, Vin de Pays $9.99. **82**

Réserve St. Martin

1996 Cabernet Sauvignon, Vin de Pays d'Oc $7. **84**

1996 Viognier, Vin de Pays d'Oc $10. **84**

1996 Chardonnay, Vin de Pays d'Oc $7. **82**

Richemont

1995 Réserve, Syrah, Vin de Pays d'Oc $7. **88**

Deep blackish-ruby hue. Moderately full-bodied. High acidity. Highly extracted. Mildly oaked. Moderately tannic. Boysenberry, mocha, and vanilla. Flavorful and crisp in the mouth, with a racy edge to the finish.

Scale: Superlative (96-100), Exceptional (90-95), Highly Recommended (85-89), Recommended (80-84), Not Recommended (Under 80)

1995 Réserve, Merlot, Vin de Pays d'Oc $7.	85
1996 Réserve, Chardonnay, Vin de Pays d'Oc $7.	NR

Domaine de Triennes

1996 Viognier, Vin de Pays du Var $12.99.	90

Deep yellow-straw cast. Full-bodied. Balanced acidity. Highly extracted. Tropical fruits, sweet herbs. Outrageously aromatic, with a wave of pure and varietally intense flavors. Rich and lush in the mouth, with fine length and intensity.

1995 Syrah, Vin de Pays du Var $9.99.	85
1995 Cabernet Sauvignon, Vin de Pays du Var $9.99.	84
1996 Chardonnay, Vin de Pays du Var $12.99.	81

Vichon

1996 Mediterraean, Cabernet Sauvignon, Vin de Pays d'Oc $10.	86

Bright ruby hue. Medium-bodied. High acidity. Moderately extracted. Mildly tannic. Minerals, red fruits. Forward aromas lead a lighter-styled, angular mouthfeel. Crisp and lean. Flavorful, with a gripping finish.

1996 Viognier, Vin de Pays d'Oc $10.	83
1996 Mediterranean, Chardonnay, Vin de Pays d'Oc $10.	83
1996 Mediterranean, Chasan, Vin de Pays d'Oc $10.	81
1996 Merlot, Vin de Pays d'Oc $10.	NR

Virginie

1996 Viognier, Vin de Pays d'Oc $5.99.	86

Medium gold luster. Medium-bodied. Moderately extracted. Citrus zest, grapefruit, floral. Aromas are well expressed on the palate. Pleasant lingering finish shows floral accents. Silky mouthfeel adds appeal.

1995 Merlot, Vin de Pays d'Oc $5.99.	80
1996 Chardonnay, Vin de Pays d'Oc $5.99.	NR

Yvon Mau

1996 Merlot, Vin de Pays des Côtes de Gascogne $6.	82
1996 Cabernet Sauvignon, Vin de Pays des Côtes de Gascogne $6.	NR

thirty-two

Italy
Piedmont

Positively Piedmont

Piedmont, the Italian province situated in the northwest corner of the country, in the shadow of the Alps, is one of the world's greatest wine regions. The Piemonteses make a wide range of styles and, refreshingly, nearly all are unique to the region. At the top of Piedmont's wine hierarchy lie Barolo and Barbaresco, majestic wines that are coveted the world over for their intoxicating perfumes—referred to traditionally as the smell of "tar and roses." Beyond these spectacular wines however, there is a wine for virtually any occasion, from aperitif to dessert. Piedmont's major regions and styles include:

Barolo

Barolo, often referred to as the king of Italian reds, is produced in limited quantities from the fickle Nebbiolo grape. The grape itself takes its name from the fog (nebbia) which frequently envelops this hilly terrain just south of the Alps. This is indicative of an area which is blessed, (and also cursed), with a marginal climate in which conditions only occasionally lend themselves to producing what is thought of as "classic" Barolo. In this way, it shares more in common with Burgundy than perpetually sunny California or Australia. In a great vintage the full potential of the Nebbiolo is realized and the resultant wines are among the most concentrated, aromatic, and age-worthy reds on Earth. In the last decade 1988, 1989, and 1990 were great vintages as will be the upcoming trio of 1995 through 1997. With better winemaking technology however, more difficult vintages such as 1991 through 1994 are capable of producing solid wines, with the added bonus that most are drinkable upon release. Of these "lighter" vintages, 1993 was most successful followed by 1991. While waiting for the release of the upcoming "collectible" wines from 1995–1997, an appropriate strategy would be to invest in the 1993s, as they will make for excellent drinking over the next decade.

Barbaresco

Barbaresco has long been in the shadow of its famous neighbor, Barolo. Like Barolo, it is a dry, complex, and aromatic red capable of long-term aging. In general terms, however, Barbaresco tends to be somewhat softer and earlier maturing. Like Barolo, it is made from the Nebbiolo grape and in Piedmont's marginal climate there may be only three truly great vintages of Barbaresco in any given decade. In a vintage pattern similar to Barolo, over the last ten years, 1988, 1989, and 1990 were all great years, while the same can be said of the upcoming 1995 through 1997 trio. As for 1991 through 1994, these are of the earlier drinking, accessible type, with 1994 seeming to have a shade more grip than 1993…a situation that is the inverse of Barolo.

Barbera

Barbera is a grape native to Piedmont. It tends to produce fragrant wines of moderate weight with sharp acidity. As such, they work quite well at the table. Most Barberas will be labeled either Barbera d'Alba or Barbera d'Asti. Barbera from Alba is grown in the same general region as Barolo and Barbaresco, and the wines tend to have more power and weight than those grown in neighboring Asti do. Additionally, they tend to share some of the same aromatic features as their more famous cousins, with a greater tendency toward the fruit spectrum of flavors. Earlier ripening than Nebbiolo, Barbera is planted in the parts of the vineyard that can't ripen Nebbiolo: generally lower elevations and north facing slopes. While Barbaresco and Barolo are special occasion wines, Barbera can be viewed as a wine for all occasions and an excellent introduction to the style of the region.

Dolcetto

Dolcetto is also native to Piedmont. While Barolo and Barbaresco can take many years of cellaring to drink at their best, Dolcetto is very different. It is a fresh grapey wine released soon after the harvest and meant to be consumed in its youth. Dolcettos are Piedmont's answer to Beaujolais, though somewhat firmer of structure and with higher acidity. Fresh, clean, and crisp, Dolcetto makes a fantastic quaffer.

Whites in Piedmont

While it is true that Piedmont is noted primarily for its great red wines, there are also a handful of whites produced. Two white grapes in particular are indigenous to the region and produce unique wines: Arneis and Cortese. While an Arneis will be labeled as such, a Cortese will actually be labeled after the town around which production is centered, Gavi. Arneis is a crisp, racy, high acid white that makes an excellent aperitif or accompaniment to shellfish. Gavi on the other hand tends to have a fuller impression in the mouth. The Italians tend to liken it to Chardonnay, but even the best examples tend to be rather neutral in flavor. Contrary to popular opinion, Arneis is probably the more interesting of the two. Finally, as in all other parts of the world, Chardonnay and Sauvignon Blanc are beginning to pop up here and there. Not surprisingly, as the region's climate is well suited to these international varietals, the initial releases have been quite competent. One would be excused for asking however, why a region with such a wealth of unique varietals would feel the need to jump on the Chardonnay bandwagon?

Piedmont at a Glance

Wines Reviewed:

565

Producers/Brands Represented:

246

Value Rating:

Average

671

Moscato d'Asti or Asti Spumante, What's the Difference?

While most consumers recognize Asti Spumante instantly, few have heard of a related though very different wine, Moscato d'Asti. Asti Spumante refers to a fully sparkling wine with straightforward sweet and fruity flavors, which can be quite enjoyable as a dessert selection. Moscato d'Asti on the other hand, is one of the world's great wine styles. It is a low alcohol semi-sparkling wine with about half the carbonation of a typical sparkling wine, and is released very soon after the vintage to preserve its uniquely fresh character. It is extremely aromatic with a famously complex perfume, and generally has a mild level of sweetness that is counterbalanced by vibrant acidity. Moscato d'Asti makes an exceptional dessert wine but is also versatile enough to have as an aperitif. Served alone, it is one of the most refreshing wines in the world, and one would be hard pressed to find something better for a hot summer day. One final note... Moscato d'Asti is always best consumed within two years of the vintage on the label.

Best Producers: Piedmont, Barbaresco

Premier Barbaresco Producers (***)
• Gaja
• Bruno Giacosa
• Moccagatta
• Vietti (Masseria)

Great Barbaresco Producers (**)
• Castello di Neive
• Ceretto
• Pio Cesare
• Michele Chiarlo
• Cigliuti
• Contratto
• Marchese di Gresy
• Pelissero
• Prunotto
• Albino Rocca
• Vietti

Dependable Barbaresco Producers (Recommended)
Some producers placed in this third tier are new (or new to us) and may merit a higher placement in subsequent vintages. These producers are offset by an asterisk.

• *Fratelli Barale
• *Bel Colle
• *Ca' del Baio
• *Cantina del Parocco di Neive
• *Cantina della Porta Rossa
• *Cascina Ballarin
• *Cascina Luisin Minuto
• *Giuseppe Cortese
• *Fontanabianca
• Fontanafredda
• Fratelli Giacosa
• *Fratelli Grasso
• *Clemente Guasti
• *Gianluigi Lano
• *Ugo Lequio
• *La Licenziana
• *Giuseppe Negro
• *Pasquero Elia di Paitin
• *Palladino
• Armando Piazzo
• Poderi Colla
• Produttori del Barbaresco
• *Bruno Rocca
• *Rocca Giancarlo Ronchi
• Scarpa
• *Sottimano
• *La Spinetta
• Terre da Vino
• Torregiorgi
• *Rino Varaldo
• Virna

Scale: Superlative (96-100), Exceptional (90-95), Highly Recommended (85-89), Recommended (80-84), Not Recommended (Under 80)

Reviews

Enrico e Luigi Abbona

Dolcetto di Dogliani, Vigna Munta, La Fusina 1998 $NA. (SR)   **89**

Saturated, bright purple hue. Generous flower, mineral, and berry aromas. A lush entry leads to a velvety, medium-bodied palate which explodes with flavor. Ripe, stylish, and intense. Drink now.

Fratelli Abrigo

Barbera d'Alba, La Galupa 1997 $NA. (SR)   **89**

Deep, saturated ruby-purple hue. Forward vanilla and berry aromas jump from the glass and show a marked oak influence. A rich entry leads to a supple, medium-bodied palate. Quite modern, but well balanced and ripe. Drink now or later.

Ada Nada

Barbaresco "Valeirano," 1996 $NA. (SR)   **85**

Brilliant garnet hue. Forward, meaty, reductive aromas. A lush entry leads to a taut, moderately full-bodied palate with firm, grippy tannins. Rich and intense in the mouth: The nose may come around with aeration or bottle age. Worth a try and may merit a higher rating in the future. Mid-term cellar candidate (3–6 years).

Barbaresco "Vigneto Cichin," 1996 $NA. (SR)   **90**

Brilliant garnet hue. Intense, complex saddle leather, game, and smoke aromas jump from the glass. A rich entry leads to a moderately full-bodied palate with a firm, taut structure and angular tannins. Big and stylish with great flavor intensity. Drink now or later.

Dolcetto d'Alba, Autinot 1998 $NA. (SR)   **85**

Saturated, brilliant ruby-purple hue. Generous fresh berry aromas. A lush entry leads to a rich palate with fine cut and intensity. Light-bodied, but really flavorful with slight tannins. Drink now.

Langhe, La Bisbetica 1996 $37.   **82**

Marco e Vittorio Adriano

Barbera d'Alba, 1997 $NA. (SR)   **82**

Crissante Alessandria

Barolo "Otin Capalot," 1995 $NA. (SR)   **88**

Brilliant garnet hue. Traditional leather, forest, and spice aromas are fairly evolved. A rich entry leads to a firm, moderately full-bodied palate with powerful tannic grip. Lots of intensity, but closes down on the finish. Needs time. Mid-term cellar candidate (3–6 years).

Fratelli Alessandria

Barolo "Monvigliero," 1995 $NA. (SR)   **89**

Deep, saturated ruby hue. Subdued mineral aromas lead to a brooding core of red fruit flavors. A rich entry leads to a rounded, full-bodied palate with a sturdy fruit emphasis. Big and showy. Needs time.

Gianfranco Alessandria

Barolo "San Giovanni," 1995 $NA. (SR)   **86**

Brilliant blackish-garnet hue. Forward spice and mineral aromas. A rich entry leads to a weighty, rounded, full-bodied palate. Thick and chunky in style without the usual taut definition, but should develop nicely. Mid-term cellar candidate (3–6 years).

Giovanni Almondo
Roero Rosso, Bric Valdiana 1996 $NA. (SR)　　　　　　85
Brilliant ruby-garnet hue. Forward spice and berry aromas. A crisp entry leads to a lean, medium-bodied palate with a subtle wood accent. Finishes with a nice cut and angular tannins. Drink now.

Elio Altare
Barolo, 1995 $NA. (SR)　　　　　　90
Deep ruby hue. Attractive spice, anise, and dried flower aromas show a mild oak accent. A soft entry leads to a spicy, moderately full-bodied palate with lean tannins. A harmonious, modern-leaning style. Drink now or later.
Barolo "Arborina," 1993 $39.99.　　　　　　94
Bright blackish-ruby hue with a slight fade. Medium-bodied. Balanced acidity. Highly extracted. Heavily oaked. Moderately tannic. Black fruits, vanilla, minerals. Quite modern with a hefty oak accent, supple extraction, and velvety tannins. More fruit centered in flavor with a relatively firm finish. Well made and well balanced in a more international style.
Barolo "Arborina," 1995 $NA. (SR)　　　　　　92
Deep ruby-garnet hue. Exotic sandalwood and leather aromas jump from the glass. A firm entry leads to a moderately full-bodied palate with a sturdy tannic structure. Shows complexity and intensity of flavor. Drink now or later.

Anselma
Barbera d'Alba, 1995 $14.　　　　　　NR

Antichi Poderi dei Gallina
Barbaresco "Gallina," Vigneto 'I Ciaciaret 1996 $NA. (SR)　　　　　　81

Giacomo Ascheri
Barolo "Sorano," 1995 $NA. (SR)　　　　　　91
Brilliant deep garnet hue. Opulent, spicy leather, dried fruit, and earth aromas jump from the glass. A lush entry leads to a supple, moderately full-bodied palate with a broad texture. Weighty and rich but shows lots of extract. Needs time. Mid-term cellar candidate (3–6 years).
Barolo "Vigna dei Poia," 1995 $NA. (SR)　　　　　　96
Deep ruby-garnet hue. Generous brown spice and berry aromas hint at a modern style. A soft, rounded entry leads to a full-bodied palate with exceptional fruit intensity and a judicious oak accent. Modern-styled, but still very much a Barolo in character. Exotically stylish and hedonistic. Drink now or later.
Dolcetto d'Alba, Vigna Nirane 1998 $NA. (SR)　　　　　　87
Brilliant pale purple hue. Generous fresh berry aromas jump from the glass. A crisp entry leads to a medium-bodied palate with great intensity of fruit and an intriguing chocolate quality. Stylish. Drink now.

Banfi
Gavi, Principessa Gavia 1996 $12.　　　　　　83
Dolcetto d'Acqui, Argusto 1995 $14.　　　　　　88
Bright ruby hue. Moderately light-bodied. Full acidity. Subtly extracted. Heavily oaked. Mildly tannic. Vanilla, red fruits, brown spices. Quite redolent of oak and very nontraditional, with some signs of barrel maturity. Almost Rioja-like, with a very aromatic quality and a juicy sense of lightness. Quite tasty, with fine length.

Barale
Barolo "Castellero," 1995 $NA. (SR) 83

Sergio Barale
Barbera d'Alba, Preda 1997 $NA. (SR) 80

Pietro Barbero
Barbera d'Asti, Bricco Verlenga 1996 $19.99. 84
Bright ruby-garnet hue. Forward spice and leather aromas show a big oak accent. A lean entry leads to a medium-bodied palate with firm acids. Angular through the finish. Tasty, if somewhat austere. Drink now.

Barbera d'Asti, La Vignassa 1995 $34.95. 86
Brilliant ruby-garnet hue. Generous spice and berry aromas show a hefty oak accent. A lean entry leads to a medium-bodied palate with vibrant acidity. Stylish, with a flashy wood component. Drink now.

Batasiolo
Moscato d'Asti, Bosc della Rei 1998 $NA. (SR) NR
Chardonnay, Langhe 1994 $25. NR
Gavi, 1995 $11. 84
Pale gold. Moderately full-bodied. Full acidity. Highly extracted. Green apples, lanolin, lacquer. Quite aromatic and not unlike a young Hunter Valley Semillon. Full in the mouth, with a firm structure and some bitterness toward the finish. A tad overextracted, but very interesting.

Gavi di Gavi, Granee 1995 $14. NR
Barbaresco, 1993 $20. NR
Barbaresco, 1996 $NA. (SR) 89
Deep, saturated garnet hue. Powerful cherry and dried flower aromas show a toasty vanilla accent. A lean entry leads to a rich, moderately full-bodied palate with angular tannins and good intensity of flavor. Shows both modern and traditional nuances. Complex, lengthy finish. Drink now or later.

Barolo, 1995 $NA. (SR) 82
Dolcetto d'Alba, 1995 $12. NR

Cocconato Bava
Monferrato, Alteserre Bianco 1997 $29. 88
Deep yellow-straw hue. Attractive pineapple and tropical fruit aromas. A rich entry leads a ripe, supple mouthfeel. Fairly concentrated, with a good intensity of flavor. Sort of like a pure, high-end, unwooded Chardonnay. Drink now.

Barbara d'Asti Superiore, Arbest 1994 $25. 85
Brilliant garnet hue. Subdued, leathery, spicy aromas. A crisp entry leads a lighter-styled, medium-bodied palate. Well balanced and stylish. A fine effort given a difficult vintage. Drink now.

Bel Colle
Arneis, Roero 1998 $NA. (SR) 87
Bright greenish-straw hue. Fresh, lean dried herb and mineral aromas. A crisp entry leads to a clean, rounded, moderately light-bodied palate with attractive creamy flavors. Ripe, but zesty. Drink now.

Barbaresco, 1996 $NA. (SR) 89
Deep, saturated ruby-garnet hue. Forward berryish aromas jump from the glass and show an integrated vanilla oak accent. A lush entry leads to a very ripe, moderately full-bodied palate with buoyant acidity and lean tannins. A well balanced, modern leaning style with excellent cut. Lengthy, oak kissed finish. Drink now or later.

Barolo, 1995 $NA. (SR)   **86**

Deep, saturated garnet hue. Exotic spice and leather aromas. A rich entry leads to a rounded, moderately full-bodied palate. Softer in style but finishes with considerable tannic grip. Intense and flavorful, but needs time. Mid-term cellar candidate (3–6 years).

Barolo "Monvigliero," 1995 $NA. (SR)   **88**

Deep garnet hue. Exotic Indian spice and sandalwood aromas jump from the glass. A rich entry leads to a weighty, full-bodied palate offset by solid acidity and big, lean tannins. Shows excellent intensity of flavor. Should develop nicely. Mid-term cellar candidate (3–6 years).

Roero Rosso, Monvije 1996 $NA. (SR)   **82**

Bella
Piemonte, Spumante NV $5.99.   **NR**

Fratelli Bera
Asti, Cascina Palazzo Spumante NV $15.   **NR**

Moscato d'Asti, 1998 $NA. (SR)   **82**

Moscato d'Asti, Su Reimond 1998 $NA. (SR)   **86**

Very pale straw hue with a decent frothy mousse. Faint green apple and citrus aromas. A vibrant entry leads to a medium-bodied palate with moderate sweetness and crisp acids. Shows very pure and intense flavors. Well balanced, but could use some more aromatic intensity. Drink now.

Dolcetto d'Alba, 1998 $NA. (SR)   **NR**

Bersano
Gavi di Gavi, 1996 $11.99.   **NR**

Barbaresco "Mantico," 1996 $NA. (SR)   **80**

Barbaresco, 1993 $29.99.   **87**

Bright ruby-garnet hue. Medium-bodied. Full acidity. Moderately extracted. Mildly tannic. Red fruits, dried herbs, minerals. Pleasantly aromatic and mouthfilling with solid grip on the palate. Straightforward with solid length.

Barolo "Badarina," 1995 $NA. (SR)   **91**

Bright ruby-garnet hue. Subdued mineral and berry aromas lead to a broad spicy palate with a solid core of fruit flavor. Moderately full-bodied, rich, and supple with rounded tannins. Quite generous and well structured and should develop nicely with time. Drink now or later.

Barolo, 1993 $34.99.   **81**

Bianchi
Gattinara, 1993 $21.99.   **82**

Boasso
Barbera d'Alba, 1996 $NA. (SR)   **NR**

Angelo Boffa
Barbera d'Alba, 1997 $NA. (SR)   **81**

Fratelli Boffa
Barbera d'Alba, 1997 $NA. (SR)   **88**

Deep blackish-ruby hue. Intense toasted coconut and vanilla aromas scream new barrique. A rich entry leads to a medium-bodied, rounded palate. Lush and enticing. A rather wood-dominated Super-Barbera style, but interesting. If you like oak, you won't be disappointed. Drink now.

Scale: Superlative (96-100), Exceptional (90-95), Highly Recommended (85-89), Recommended (80-84), Not Recommended (Under 80)

Dolcetto d'Alba, Sori Parisio 1998 $NA. (SR)   **88**

Deep brilliant purple hue. Generous, rich chocolate and black fruit aromas. A lush entry leads to a rounded, supple, moderately light-bodied palate. Ripe and quite harmonious. Drink now.

Enzo Boglietti

Barbera d'Alba, 1996 $17.   **87**

Bright ruby with a garnet cast. Medium-bodied. Balanced acidity. Moderately extracted. Mildly oaked. Mildly tannic. Red fruits, dried herbs, vanilla. Rather subdued aromatically, firm and angular on the palate. Nice core of fruit flavor and a lingering oak-tinged finish. Well balanced and tasty.

Barolo, Vigna delle Brunate 1993 $44.   **89**

Deep ruby with a slight garnet cast. Moderately full-bodied. Balanced acidity. Moderately extracted. Heavily oaked. Moderately tannic. Black fruits, brown spices, minerals. Firmly modern with hefty oak influence and supple character with velvety tannins. Decidedly fruit forward, with good structure. Lacks the astringent edge of most Barolos. Well crafted for this kind of style.

Barolo "Case Nere," 1995 $NA. (SR)   **93**

Bright ruby-garnet hue with a slight fade. Intense, exotic brown spice, leather, and dried flower aromas. A soft entry leads to a ripe, moderately full-bodied palate with great flavor intensity. Rich, but well gripped and angular through the finish. Drink now or later.

Dolcetto d'Alba, Tiglineri 1996 $18.   **86**

Bright saturated purple hue. Moderately light-bodied. Full acidity. Highly extracted. Mildly tannic. Black fruits, minerals. A little reined in aromatically, but opens up on the palate with juicy acidity and ripe mineral-tinged flavors. Finishes on a slightly chalky tannic note.

Bompre

Moscato d'Asti, 1998 $NA. (SR)   **82**
Moscato d'Asti, Aureum 1998 $NA. (SR)   **87**

Brilliant yellow-straw hue with a slight mousse. Attractive peach and apple aromas. A vibrant entry leads to a moderately sweet palate with ripe flavors. Crisp, refreshing, flavorful finish. Drink now.

Borgogno

Barbera d'Alba, 1996 $13.   **NR**
Barolo, Virna 1993 $29.95.   **NR**

Giacomo Borgogno

Barolo, Classico 1995 $NA. (SR)   **91**

Deep garnet hue. Forward spice and mineral aromas. A rich entry leads to an intense, oak accented palate. Full-bodied and weighty with lots of flavor intensity. A showy wine with a firm structure and good cut. Should develop beautifully. Mid-term cellar candidate (3–6 years).

Serio e Battista Borgogno

Barolo "Cannubi," 1995 $NA. (SR)   **84**

Brilliant garnet hue. Lean anise, orange peel, and brown spice aromas. A soft entry leads to a rounded, medium-bodied palate. Acidity pops up in the finish, but lacks somewhat for grip. Tasty anyway. Drink now.

Dolcetto d'Alba, 1998 $NA. (SR)   **81**

Lodovico Borgognot Borgogno
Barolo "Preda-Sarmassa," 1995 $NA. (SR)　　　　　　　　　　NR

Francesco Boschis
Dolcetto di Dogliani, Pianezzo 1997 $NA. (SR)　　　　　　　89

Brilliant purple-red hue to the rim. Intense vanilla and red fruit aromas show a fair amount of wood. A smooth entry leads a medium-bodied palate with shy acidity and velvety tannins. Round and rich with a fine cut to the finish. Very modern. Drink now or later.

Dolcetto di Dogliani, Pianezzo 1998 $NA. (SR)　　　　　　　86

Brilliant deep purple hue. Luscious fresh fruit and mineral aromas jump from the glass. Velvety and rounded with a moderately light body. Generous. Drink now.

Oscar Bosio
Moscato d'Asti, La Bruciata 1998 $NA. (SR)　　　　　　　　92

Brilliant greenish-straw hue with a thin mousse. Attractive, ripe peach, flower, and sweet citrus aromas are forward and generous. A ripe entry leads to a medium-bodied palate with moderate sweetness. Exquisitely balanced and explosive in flavor. Drink now.

Giacomo Brezza
Barolo "Cannubi," 1995 $NA. (SR)　　　　　　　　　　　　93

Deep ruby-garnet hue. Exotic sandalwood, leather, and dried flower aromas carry a judicious oak influence. A rich entry leads to a big, full-bodied palate with solid flavor intensity. Well flavored and complex with a wild olive quality through the finish. Drink now or later.

Bricco del Prete
Roero Rosso, Val de Prete 1996 $NA. (SR)　　　　　　　　　NR

Fratelli Brovia
Barolo "Villero," 1995 $NA. (SR)　　　　　　　　　　　　85

Bright ruby-garnet hue. Lean, earthy, mineral aromas. A firm entry leads to a lighter styled, medium-bodied palate. Well flavored, with nice grip to the finish. Drink now or later.

Buganza
Arneis, Roero 1998 $NA. (SR)　　　　　　　　　　　　　　82
Barbera d'Alba, 1997 $NA. (SR)　　　　　　　　　　　　　81

Piero Busso
Barbaresco "Vigna Borgese," 1996 $NA. (SR)　　　　　　　NR

Ca'Bianca
Gavi di Gavi, Castello La Centuriona 1997 $10.99.　　　　90

Brilliant greenish-straw hue. Elegant, complex yeast, mineral, and biscuit aromas. An angular entry leads to a medium-bodied palate with a rich, rounded quality. Balanced by lean acidity. Drink now.

Barbera d'Asti, 1997 $11.99.　　　　　　　　　　　　　　83

Ca' del Baio
Barbaresco "Asili," 1996 $NA. (SR)   92

Deep, inky ruby hue. Forward berry and vanilla aromas show a marked oak influence. A lush, rounded entry leads to a moderately full-bodied palate with supple, velvety tannins. Stylish and very modern. Approachable in youth, but structured to develop. Drink now or later.

Ca' del Re
Brachetto Piemonte, 1998 $NA. (SR)   83

Cabutto
Barolo "Vigna la Volta," 1995 $NA. (SR)   84

Bright garnet hue. Unusual, meaty, citrusy aromas. A soft entry leads to a rounded, medium-bodied palate. Supple and approachable. Better in the mouth than on the nose. Finishes with velvety tannins. Drink now or later.

Cagliero
Barbera d'Alba, 1997 $NA. (SR)   82
Barolo "Ravera," 1995 $NA. (SR)   94

Brilliant orange-garnet hue. Exotic saddle leather, sandalwood, and black tea aromas form a perfumed melange. A rich entry leads to a full-bodied, rounded palate. Shows marked oak influences, but has much more to go with it. Harmonious and intense. Drink now or later.

Vincenzo Calorio
Arneis, Roero 1998 $NA. (SR)   NR

Cantina del Glicine
Barbaresco "Cura," 1996 $NA. (SR)   82

Cantina del Parocco di Neive
Barbaresco "Gallina," 1996 $NA. (SR)   91

Deep, saturated ruby hue. Gorgeous, complex aromas of sandalwood, earth, and leather jump from the glass. A rich entry leads to a moderately full-bodied palate. Lots of richness, but showing fine cut and grippy tannins that bite down on the finish. Needs time, but should become quite exotic with age. Long-term cellar.

Cantina della Porta Rossa
Barbaresco, 1996 $NA. (SR)   92

Pale cherry-garnet hue. Attractive spice, leather, and forest aromas show an exotic perfumed quality. A lean entry leads to a medium-bodied palate with complex flavors and a taut structure. Angular and very well balanced with a clean finish. Showing well now, but well structured and will gain further complexity with moderate age. Mid-term cellar candidate (3–6 years).

Barolo "Bricco Ambroggio," 1995 $NA. (SR)   90

Deep, saturated garnet hue. Forward herb and mineral aromas. A firm entry leads to a medium-bodied palate with angular tannins and good intensity of flavor. Traditional and taut, this needs time. Mid-term cellar candidate (3–6 years).

Dolcetto di Diano d'Alba, Superiore 1997 $NA. (SR)   80

Cantina Terrenostre
Dolcetto d'Alba, Vitevecchia 1998 $NA. (SR)   80

Capetta
Brachetto Piemonte, 1998 $NA. (SR) NR
Moscato d'Asti, Corte dei Balbi Soprani 1998 $NA. (SR) NR

Cascina Ballarin
Barbera d'Alba, Giuli 1996 $25. 90
Brilliant ruby hue. Perfumed spice and leather aromas. A lean entry leads to a medium-bodied palate with juicy acidity and complex flavors. Well balanced, with complex flavors and a great mouthfeel. Very stylish.

Barolo, 1995 $45.99. 86
Brilliant ruby-garnet hue. Perfumed sandalwood and dried fruit aromas. A lean entry leads to a firm, medium-bodied palate with grippy tannins and forceful acidity. Needs time, but not overly concentrated. Drink now or later.

Barolo "Bussia," 1995 $NA. (SR) 90
Deep garnet hue. Attractive sandalwood and leather aromas jump from the glass. A rich entry leads to a supple, rounded, medium-bodied mouthfeel. Softer, but showing fine complexity with good grip through the finish. An early maturing style. Drink now or later.

Langhe, Ballarin 1996 $26.99. 90
Deep ruby-garnet hue. Complex tobacco, mineral, and earth aromas are quite generous. A rich entry leads to a rounded, full-bodied palate with grippy tannins. Extremely flavorful and individual. Fine length. Should be amazing with earthy dishes. Drink now or later.

Cascina Bruni
Barolo, Vigna Batistot 1993 $46. NR

Cascina Ca'Rossa
Roero Rosso, Vigna Audinaggio 1996 $NA. (SR) 90
Deep ruby-garnet hue. Exotic leather, earth, and berry aromas jump from the glass. A rich entry leads to a rounded, supple intensely flavored palate. Moderately full-bodied with soft acidity and velvety tannins. Approachable early and already showing complexity. Drink now.

Cascina Casanova
Dolcetto d'Alba, Madonna Como 1998 $NA. (SR) 81

Cascina Chicco
Arneis, Roero 1997 $15.99. NR
Barbera d'Alba, Bric Loira 1996 $24.99. 89
Saturated, inky ruby-purple hue. Intense licorice, vanilla, and black fruit aromas explode from the glass. A lean entry leads to a firm, moderately full-bodied palate. Has lots of stuffing in an international style. Well gripped finish. Drink now or later.

Roero Rosso, Valmaggiore 1996 $24.99. 88
Brilliant ruby hue. Exotic, perfumed flower and sandalwood aromas. A lean entry leads to a medium-bodied palate with rich flavors and grippy tannins. A bit strange, but shows tons of character. Drink now or later.

Cascina Luisin Minuto
Barbaresco "Rabaja," 1996 $NA. (SR) 92
Deep ruby-garnet hue. Powerful sandalwood, forest, and leather aromas jump from the glass. A lush entry leads to a moderately full-bodied palate with a fine cut. Complex in flavor, with a sturdy, angular finish. Drink now or later.

Scale: Superlative (96-100), Exceptional (90-95), Highly Recommended (85-89), Recommended (80-84), Not Recommended (Under 80)

Barbaresco "Sori Paolin," 1996 $NA. (SR)   86

Deep, saturated blackish-garnet hue. Exotic spice, saddle leather, and black fruit aromas. A lush entry leads to a fat, weighty, full-bodied palate with shy acidity. Grippy tannins support the finish. Great flavors, but could just use a little better cut to be top drawer. Drink now or later.

Cascina Morassino

Barbaresco "Ovello," 1996 $NA. (SR)   NR

Cascinetta

Moscato d'Asti, di Forno Ermanno 1998 $NA. (SR)   80

Fratelli Casetta

Arneis, Roero 1998 $NA. (SR)   82
Barbaresco "Vigna Magallo," 1996 $NA. (SR)   NR
Barbaresco "Vigna Magallo," 1995 $12.10.   NR
Barbera d'Alba, 1997 $NA. (SR)   NR
Barbera d'Alba, Vigna Suri 1995 $18.   80
Barolo "Case Nere," 1995 $NA. (SR)   NR
Barolo "Case Nere," 1993 $11.50.   NR
Dolcetto d'Alba, 1998 $NA. (SR)   NR
Colline Saluzzesi, Pelaverga 1996 $19.99.   NR
Roero Rosso Superiore, Vigna Pioiero 1996 $NA. (SR)   80

Castello di Neive

Arneis, Langhe 1996 $13.50.   88

Bright platinum hue. Moderately light-bodied. Full acidity. Moderately extracted. Cream, sweet herbs, yeast. Light, delicate and racy in style, with an expansive array of champagnelike flavors on the palate. Crisp acidity makes for a clean finish.

Barbaresco, Santo Stefano 1993 $29.   85

Bright garnet hue. Medium-bodied. Balanced acidity. Moderately extracted. Moderately tannic. Red fruits, minerals. Somewhat lighter in style with a slightly overripe quality. Firm and compact with some mild astringency. Fairly successful given the difficult vintage.

Barbera d'Alba, Mattarello 1997 $NA. (SR)   86

Deep ruby hue. Oak tinged vanilla and spice aromas jump from the glass. A lean entry leads to a medium-bodied palate with edgy tannins. Stylish and flavorful. Drink now or later.

Dolcetto d'Alba, Basarin 1998 $NA. (SR)   81

Castello di Verduno

Barbaresco "Rabaja," 1996 $NA. (SR)   82
Barolo "Massara," 1995 $NA. (SR)   89

Deep, evolved brickish-garnet hue. Classic tar and roses aromas jump from the glass. A rich entry leads to a big, full-bodied palate with lots of traditional flavors and grippy tannins. Full and intense, but not exactly cut. Drink now or later.

Castelvero

Barbera, Piemonte 1996 $9.   81
Barbera d'Asti, 1996 $11.   87

Bright ruby-red to the rim. Medium-bodied. Full acidity. Moderately extracted. Mildly tannic. Red fruits, minerals. Pure and expressive, with razor-sharp red fruit flavors brought into focus by an edge of acidity. Well balanced, and quite modern.

Barbera d'Asti, 1995 $13.   **84**

Bright blackish ruby with a slight fade to the rim. Medium-bodied. Full acidity.
Moderately extracted. Mildly oaked. Mildly tannic. Vanilla, red fruits. Oak influence
on the nose. Straightforward and focused on the palate though a trifle dilute.
Well-structured acidity with dusty tannins and a mildly astringent note to the finish.

Caudrina

Asti, La Selvatica 1998 $NA. (SR)   **90**

Pale greenish-straw hue with a thick white mousse. Pure peach, mineral, and citrus
flavors. A crisp entry leads to a vibrant, stylish palate with great intensity of flavor and
mild sweetness. Very well balanced. A serious, stylish Asti. Drink now.

Moscato d'Asti, La Caudrina, Romano Dogliotti 1998 $NA. (SR)   **92**

Brilliant greenish-straw hue. Lean mineral, peach, and green apple aromas. A frothy
entry leads to a rich, but moderately light-bodied palate with mild sweetness. Well
balanced, clean, and very refreshing. Sweetness is very well balanced. Drink now.

Moscato d'Asti, La Galeisa, Romano Dogliotti 1998 $NA. (SR)   **89**

Bright greenish-straw hue with a thin mousse. Fragrant orange blossom, peach, and
flower aromas. A crisp entry leads to a moderately light-bodied palate with mild sweetness
offset by crisp acids. Concentrated, lengthy, and fresh. Drink now.

Fratelli Cavallotto

Barolo "Bricco Boschis," 1995 $NA. (SR)   **88**

Deep ruby-garnet hue. Intense anise aromas jump from the glass. A lean entry leads to
a medium-bodied palate with angular tannins and a berryish quality through the finish.
Sturdy and well balanced. Should develop nicely. Drink now or later.

Ceretto

Moscato di Santo Stefano, 1998 $NA. (SR)   **90**

Brilliant greenish-straw hue with a slight effervescence. Fantastic white citrus, flower, and
pear aromas. A crisp entry leads to a racy, light-bodied palate with a hint of sweetness.
Very stylish, with great balance. The ultimate summer drink. Drink now.

Arneis, Langhe 1998 $NA. (SR)   **87**

Brilliant greenish-straw hue. Lean herb and citrus aromas. A crisp entry leads to a
moderately light-bodied palate with a firm acidic cut. Taut and refreshing. A solid
shellfish wine. Drink now.

Chardonnay, Langhe 1997 $NA. (SR)   **85**

Deep yellow-golden hue. Opulent toasted oak and cream aromas. A lean entry leads
to an angular, medium-bodied palate. Crisp, but doesn't quite deliver what the nose
promises. Drink now.

Barbaresco "Asij," 1993 $17.99.   **82**

Barbaresco "Asij," 1996 $NA. (SR)   **81**

Barbaresco "Bricco Asili," 1993 $51.99.   **89**

Bright garnet hue. Balanced acidity. Highly extracted. Quite tannic. Dried herbs, earth,
minerals. Showing early signs of maturity with developed aromas and flavors. Quite firm
with a full mouthfeel that shows a good level of grip. Quite tannic through the finish.
Fairly complex but will always be tough.

Barbaresco "Bricco Asili," 1996 $NA. (SR)

Deep ruby-garnet hue. Opulent, spicy leather, tobacco, and mineral aromas. A firm entry
leads to a lean, moderately full-bodied palate with grainy, drying tannins. Concentrated,
but fairly closed. Needs time. Mid-term cellar candidate (3–6 years)

Barolo "Brunate," 1995 $NA. (SR)   **92**

Brilliant garnet hue. Exotic, attractive sandalwood, spice, and leather aromas. A firm
entry leads to a weighty, moderately full-bodied palate with lean, drying tannins and
complex, intense flavors. Needs time. Mid-term cellar candidate (3–6 years)

Scale: Superlative (96-100), Exceptional (90-95), Highly Recommended (85-89),
Recommended (80-84), Not Recommended (Under 80)

Barolo "Prapo," 1995 $NA. (SR)   93

Very deep garnet hue. Intense, generous tobacco, earth, and dried flower aromas. A rich entry leads to a weighty, full-bodied palate. Closed in at present through the finish, but shows great intensity. Will need lots of age, but should blossom beautifully. Long-term cellar.

Barolo "Zonchera," 1995 $NA. (SR)   85

Brilliant garnet hue. Attractive olive and dried fruit aromas. A lush entry leads to a rounded, medium-bodied palate. Almost supple in style with firm tannins through the finish. Accessible. Drink now.

Barolo "Brunate, Bricco Rocche," 1993 $50.   88

Bright garnet hue with a fade to the rim. Medium-bodied. Balanced acidity. Moderately extracted. Mildly oaked. Quite tannic. Chocolate, black tea, earth. Showing some maturity in the aromatics. The palate is quite lean and finishes with a wave of astringency. Nice flavors, but will always be tough.

Cabernet Sauvignon, Langhe 1996 $NA. (SR)   89

Saturated, inky ruby-purple hue. Forward lead pencil, mineral, and black fruit aromas. A firm entry leads to a moderately full-bodied palate with firm, angular tannins. Shows some weight, but well structured. Needs time. Mid-term cellar candidate (3–6 years).

Monsordo, Piemonte 1996 $NA. (SR)   85

Deep, saturated inky purple hue. Generous black pepper and mineral aromas. A rich entry leads to a lean, medium-bodied palate. Shows good cut. On the austere side, but flavorful. Drink now or later.

Pinot Nero, Langhe 1996 $NA. (SR)   80

Moscato di Santo Stefano, Passito 1996 $NA/375 ml. (SR)   90

Deep yellow-golden hue. Exotic ginger, vanilla, and oriental spice aromas show a complex rancio edge. A rich entry leads to a supple, moderately full-bodied palate with moderate sweetness. Well balanced, with very intense flavors. Drink now.

Pio Cesare

Cortese di Gavi, 1996 $20.   86

Pale straw hue. Medium-bodied. Full acidity. Moderately extracted. Citrus, minerals. Clean, racy, and modern in style. Somewhat subdued in flavor with a slightly rounded mouthfeel. Well balanced and intense.

Barbaresco, 1996 $NA. (SR)   86

Deep blackish-garnet hue. Unusual earth and licorice aromas. A firm entry leads to a moderately full-bodied palate with lean, stroppy tannins. Shows some weight in the mouth, but leaves an overriding impression of rusticity in the end. Tough through the finish. Time may help, but??? Mid-term cellar candidate (3–6 years).

Barbera d'Alba, 1994 $17.   80

Barolo, 1993 $39.   89

Bright garnet color. Moderately full-bodied. Balanced acidity. Moderately extracted. Mildly oaked. Moderately tannic. Red fruits, dried herbs, minerals. Pleasantly aromatic with a round sense of lushness to the palate. Judicious use of wood creates a softened presence on the palate. Well balanced, and a nice compromise between modern and traditional styles.

Barolo, 1995 $NA. (SR)   90

Deep, saturated ruby-garnet hue. Generous, perfumed cedar, brown spice, and mineral aromas. A rich entry leads to a supple, moderately full-bodied palate with a firm tannic edge. Shows fine grip and intensity. Drink now or later.

Barolo "Ornato," 1995 $NA. (SR)   94

Deep, saturated ruby-red hue is quite modern. Generous berry and vanilla aromas signal a forward oak influence and confirm modernist leanings. A rich entry leads to a supple, rounded palate with velvety tannins. A very well-made and flavorful Barolo in the modern, international style. Some bottle age should bring out a bit more traditional Nebbiolo character, but this is delicious in its own right. Drink now or later.

Barolo "Ornato," 1993 $92.   **93**

Bright ruby hue with a slight fade. Medium-bodied. Balanced acidity. Highly extracted. Moderately oaked. Moderately tannic. Black fruits, minerals, vanilla. Oak flavors on the nose are well-integrated with classic Barolo flavors throughout. Firm, focused, and highly structured, the wine is very well balanced and should age gracefully.

Ceste

Arneis, Roero 1997 $NA. (SR)   **88**

Pale yellow-golden hue. Generous vanilla and orange aromas show a smoky oak influence. An angular entry leads to a firm, medium-bodied palate. Rounded and flavorful, yet shows clean acidity through the finish. Drink now.

Barbera d'Alba, 1997 $NA. (SR)   **86**

Deep, inky purple hue. Intense, cordial-like black fruit and vanilla aromas. A rich entry leads to an extracted, medium-bodied palate with nervy acidity and grippy tannins. Could use a couple years to soften. Drink now or later.

Cherubin

Dolcetto d'Alba, 1998 $NA. (SR)   **87**

Brilliant saturated purple hue. Lean, attractive flower, mineral, and pepper aromas. A taut entry leads to a firm, medium-bodied palate with angular tannins, a solid acidic cut, and fine intensity of flavor. Drink now.

Michele Chiarlo

Moscato d'Asti, Nivole 1996 $8.99/375 ml.   **84**

Bright straw cast. Moderately light-bodied. Full acidity. Subtly extracted. Tropical fruits, citrus. Light, fresh, and extremely fruity with an outrageously aromatic character. Comes across as being sweet, but zippy carbonation saves it from becoming overly cloying.

Gavi, 1996 $13.99.   **NR**

Barbaresco "Asili," 1995 $76.99.   **87**

Bright ruby color. Medium-bodied. Full acidity. Moderately extracted. Mildly oaked. Moderately tannic. Red fruits, minerals, dried herbs. Quite aromatic with vibrant, mouthfilling character. Flavors accelerate through the firm finish and feature fine length. A tad one dimensional, lacking a little grip at present, but will gain complexity with age.

Barbaresco "Asili," 1996 $NA. (SR)   **91**

Deep, saturated brilliant ruby hue. Carries a wave of perfumed smoky brown spice aromas. A lush entry leads to a moderately full-bodied palate with velvety tannins and a hefty oak accent to the flavors. A very modern style, with a mellow, rounded finish. Drink now or later.

Barolo, 1993 $32.99.   **82**

Barolo, Vigna Rionda di Serralunga 1993 $63.99.   **88**

Bright garnet hue. Medium-bodied. Balanced acidity. Moderately extracted. Mildly oaked. Moderately tannic. Sweet herbs, vanilla, minerals. Complex in aromatics, with an angular impression on the palate that rounds out in the mouth. Lacking some of the intensity expected through the finish, but quite pleasant.

Barolo "Cerequio," 1993 $76.99.   **92**

Bright ruby with a slight garnet cast. Moderately full-bodied. Balanced acidity. Moderately extracted. Moderately tannic. Flowers, brown spices, minerals. Quite aromatic. Firm and angular on the palate. Mouthfilling and flavorful with good intensity and fine length. Opens with aeration currently and should reward mid-term to long-term cellaring.

Barolo "Cerequio," 1995 $NA. (SR)   **92**

Deep, brilliant ruby-red hue with a slight purple cast. Forward berry and spice aromas show some exotic leathery overtones. A rich entry leads to a rounded, full-bodied palate with a solid tannic cut. Lean and intense through the finish. Modern, but taut. Mid-term cellar candidate (3–6 years).

Scale: Superlative (96-100), Exceptional (90-95), Highly Recommended (85-89), Recommended (80-84), Not Recommended (Under 80)

Monferrato, Countacci 1995 $35.99.   90

Bright saturated blackish-ruby hue. Moderately full-bodied. Balanced acidity. Moderately extracted. Mildly oaked. Mildly tannic. Cassis, minerals, brown spices. Pleasantly aromatic, with a very pure and expressive palate feel. Lean and angular through the finish with excellent grip and intensity.

Chionetti

Dolcetto di Dogliani, San Luigi 1996 $17.   82
Dolcetto di Dogliani, Briccolero 1996 $19.   85

Bright purple color. Moderately light-bodied. Full acidity. Moderately extracted. Mildly tannic. Black fruits, minerals. Quite aromatic with an accent on forward primary fruit flavors. Crisp, clean, and angular through the finish.

Fratelli Cigliuti

Barbaresco, Serraboella 1993 $42.99.   89

Deep blackish-ruby with a garnet cast. Medium-bodied. Balanced acidity. Moderately extracted. Moderately tannic. Earth, game, truffles. Quite aromatic with a sense of lushness. Shows early maturity and lacks some grip, but quite complex and flavorful overall. Should drink nicely over the next four or five years.

Domenico Clerico

Barolo "Ciabot Mentin Ginestra," 1993 $33.49.   89

Bright blackish-garnet hue. Medium-bodied. Balanced acidity. Moderately extracted. Moderately tannic. Earth, brown spices, minerals. Relatively aromatic with a lush mouthfeel showing good integration of wood and classic Barolo flavors. Supple in extraction with some drying tannins. Not overly intense, but should age gracefully.

Barolo "Ciabot Mentin Ginestra," 1994 $NA. (SR)   81
Barolo "Pajana," 1995 $NA. (SR)   91

Deep blackish-garnet hue. Brooding, traditional aromas of earth, smoke, and leather. A rich entry leads to a weighty, intense palate with lots of chocolate extract buttressed by a good acidic cut and velvety tannins. Softer, but showing fine intensity. Lengthy finish. Drink now or later.

Elvio Cogno

Barbera d'Alba, Bricco dei Merli 1997 $NA. (SR)   88

Saturated, inky blackish-purple hue. Pronounced vanilla aromas show a dominant oak influence. A rich entry leads to a moderately full-bodied palate with firm, grainy tannins. A well balanced, flavorful, modern style. Drink now or later.

Barolo "Ravera," 1995 $NA. (SR)   89

Very deep ruby-garnet hue. Brooding dusty cherry and mineral aromas. An angular entry leads to a big, moderately full-bodied palate with a wave of firm tannins. Rich, but needs time. Long-term cellar.

Aldo Conterno

Barolo, 1993 $89.99.   93

Bright brownish garnet hue. Medium-bodied. Balanced acidity. Moderately extracted. Moderately tannic. Earth, dried herbs, minerals. Fiercely traditional, without overt wood notes. Classic aromas and flavors play out on a lighter, delicately styled palate. Well balanced and complex, finishing with mild astringency.

Barolo "Cicala," 1995 $NA. (SR)   92

Brilliant blackish-garnet hue. Restrained mineral, leather, and dried flower aromas show a measure of complexity. A firm entry leads to a ripe, but well structured palate with excellent acidic cut. Taut and intense. Should develop and open beautifully. Mid-term cellar candidate (3–6 years).

Az. Agr. Conterno (Cascina Sciulun)

Barbera d'Alba, Vigna Pugnane 1997 $NA. (SR)   84

Brilliant, saturated ruby-purple hue. Aromatically subdued, but richly flavored. Medium-bodied, with a fresh, fruity palate and solid acidity. Lush and ripe. Drink now.

Barolo, Bussia Munie 1995 $NA. (SR)   84

Bright ruby-garnet hue. Lean mineral and leather aromas. A lighter entry leads to a reserved, medium-bodied palate with firm tannins. Taut and crisp but not overly complex. Drink now or later.

Dolcetto d'Alba, Vigna Bussia 1997 $NA. (SR)   82

Giacomo Conterno

Barolo "Cascina Francia," 1993 $89.99.   94

Bright garnet hue. Medium-bodied. Full acidity. Moderately extracted. Moderately tannic. Dried herbs, minerals, earth. Quite traditional with wonderfully complex Barolo aromatics. Rich and beautifully extracted with depth and great complexity. Shows great texture, good balance, with fine length and intensity. Almost approachable now but should cellar beautifully.

Barolo "Cascina Francia," 1995 $NA. (SR)   92

Brilliant garnet hue. Exotic anise and mineral aromas. A rich entry leads to an intense, rounded, moderately full-bodied palate with a rounded texture and firm finish. This will blossom with time. Mid-term cellar candidate (3–6 years).

Barolo "Cascina Francia," 1996 $NA. (SR)   96-100

Deep, saturated ruby-garnet hue. Fantastic ripe fruit, mineral, and leather aromas. A weighty entry leads to a full, rich palate with great intensity. Exquisite and already quite complex. A magnificent wine that should age spectacularly, but already showing very well. Drink now or later, if you can keep your hands off it.

Barolo "Monfortino," 1993 $NA. (SR)   94

Deep ruby-garnet hue. Exquisite leather, spice, and mineral aromas. A rich entry leads to a massive, full-bodied palate with outrageous intensity. Very full and opulent with a drying finish. Has lots of stuffing to blossom with age. Long-term cellar.

Paolo Conterno

Barolo "Ginestra," 1995 $NA. (SR)   86

Deep ruby-garnet hue. Toasty, smoky aromas show a mineral, berryish undercurrent. A rich entry leads to a supple, moderately full-bodied palate with velvety tannins. Softer in style, but still fairly well structured. Drink now or later.

Contratto

Asti, De Miranda 1995 $25.99.   85

Bright straw hue. Moderately light-bodied. Full acidity. Moderately extracted. Citrus, green apples. Pleasantly aromatic with a flavorful palate feel. Frothy and clean in the mouth with exquisite balance and fine grip. Quite lengthy through the refreshing finish.

Moscato D'Asti, Tenuta Gilardino 1997 $15.99.   90

Deep straw cast. Moderately light-bodied. Full acidity. Subtly extracted. Citrus, white pepper, bread dough. Complex in aromatics and quite flavorful, with a highly carbonated, almost bracing palate feel. Finishes with a decided note of sweetness.

Chardonnay, Piemonte 1996 $26.   NR

Gavi di Gavi, Le Arnelle 1998 $15.99.   85

Brilliant straw hue with a slight spritz. Pure mineral and citrus peel aromas. A lean entry leads to a medium-bodied palate with firm acids. Rounded, bready finish. Clean. Drink now.

Scale: Superlative (96-100), Exceptional (90-95), Highly Recommended (85-89), Recommended (80-84), Not Recommended (Under 80)

Barbera d'Asti, Panta Rei 1997 $13.99.   **90**

Bright, brilliant ruby hue. Intense fresh berry and flower aromas jump from the glass.
A crisp entry leads to a medium-bodied palate. Quite ripe, but buoyed by vibrant acidity.
Clean, varietal, and pure. Great fruit. Drink now.

Barbera d'Asti, Pian Del Re 1994 $16.99.   **NR**

Barbera d'Asti, Solus Ad 1994 $37.99.   **82**

Barbera d'Asti, Solus Ad 1996 $44.99.   **86**

Brilliant ruby-garnet hue. Subdued spicy aromas belie a generous oak accent. A lean
entry leads to a firm, high acid, medium-bodied palate. Lighter in style with an angular
finish. Drink now.

Barolo, Cerequio, Tenuta Secolo 1993 $43.99.   **90**

Bright ruby-garnet color. Medium-bodied. Full acidity. Moderately extracted. Moderately
oaked. Moderately tannic. Vanilla, red fruits, minerals. Fairly modern in style with a discernible oak influence in flavor and texture. Relatively supple extraction has softened the
palate feel. Flavorful, classy, and well balanced with fine intensity and length.

Barolo, Cerequio, Tenuta Secolo 1995 $75.   **92**

Brilliant ruby-garnet hue. Perfumed sandalwood and spice aromas suggest a generous
oak accent. A lean entry leads to an angular, well-cut, moderately full-bodied palate
showing precise flavors and firm structure that are the hallmarks of real pedigree.
Drink now or later.

Coppo

Chardonnay, Piemonte 1996 $15.50.   **80**

Gavi, La Rocca 1997 $18.   **86**

Brilliant straw hue. Forward citrus and flower aromas. A zesty entry leads to a moderately
light-bodied palate with racy acids. Piercing and pure. Drink now.

Barbera d'Asti, Avvocata 1996 $11.   **90**

Bright ruby hue. Moderately light-bodied. Full acidity. Moderately extracted. Mildly
tannic. Red fruits, minerals. Aromatic and light in style though quite well balanced.
Mineral-tinged fruit flavors are pure and expressive. Sharp acidity lends brightness
throughout. Fine length on the clean finish.

Barbera d'Asti, Camp du Rouss 1995 $17.   **89**

Bright ruby with a fade to the rim. Medium-bodied. Balanced acidity. Highly extracted.
Mildly oaked. Mildly tannic. Spice, green herbs, earth, minerals. Pleasantly aromatic and
full. Earthy throughout with a rounded mouthfeel supported by solid acidity. Barrel
influences play an important role in flavor and the rounded structure. Heavy extraction
lends mild bitterness to the finish.

Barbera d'Asti, Camp du Rouss 1996 $17.   **85**

Brilliant garnet hue. Subdued licorice and earth aromas. A lean entry leads to a
moderately light-bodied palate with nervous acidity. Angular, but flavorful. Drink now.

Piemonte, Mondaccione 1995 $28.   **86**

Bright saturated ruby color with brilliant clarity. Moderately full-bodied. Full acidity.
Moderately extracted. Moderately oaked. Mildly tannic. Red fruits, minerals, brown
spices. Quite aromatic, with a lighter-styled palate feel. Well structured, with zesty
acidity and a sense of delicacy throughout. Clean and snappy finish.

Corino

Barolo, Vigna Giachini 1994 $NA. (SR)   **86**

Deep, saturated brick red. Generous wood, earth, and mineral aromas. A firm entry
leads a moderately full-bodied palate with linear tannins. Lingering finish. Shows some
generosity despite its lean structure. Drink now or later.

Cornarea
Arneis, Roero 1996 $18.   NR

Matteo Correggia
Barbera d'Alba, 1997 $NA. (SR)   91

Inky, opaque violet-red hue. Generous blueberry and chocolate aromas. A firm entry leads a moderately full-bodied palate with velvety tannins. Lengthy oak-tinged finish. Rich, round, and very modern. California cum Piedmont. Drink now or later.

Roero Rosso, Roche d'Ampse 1996 $NA. (SR)   89

Very deep, saturated blackish-ruby hue. Powerful vanilla and berry aromas point to marked oak influence. A rich entry leads to a moderately full-bodied palate with grippy tannins and a good intensity of flavor. Well made in a modern style, but needs time. Mid-term cellar candidate (3–6 years).

Giuseppe Cortese
Barbaresco "Rabaja," 1996 $NA. (SR)   87

Deep, saturated ruby hue with a slight fade. Generous vanilla and mineral aromas show an integrated oak accent. A lush entry leads to a moderately full-bodied, weighty palate. Decent acidity keeps everything in check. Lacks somewhat for grip. Needs some time to develop complexity. Mid-term cellar candidate (3–6 years).

Dolcetto, Trifolera 1996 $12.   83

Costa di Bussia
Barolo "Campo dei Buoi," Tenuta Arnulfo 1995 $NA. (SR)   84

Deep blackish-garnet hue. Intense anise and mineral aromas. A rich entry leads to a powerful, moderately full-bodied palate. Chunky and earthy, with drying tannins through the finish. Needs time. Mid-term cellar candidate (3–6 years).

Barolo, Tenuta Arnulfo 1995 $NA. (SR)   84

Brilliant garnet hue. Rustic forest, anise, and mineral aromas jump from the glass. A lush entry leads to a medium-bodied palate with grippy tannins. Lean and reserved through the finish. Drink now or later.

Ermanno Costa
Roero Rosso "San Deferente," Cascina Spagnolo 1996 $NA. (SR)   NR

Rinaldo Costa
Arneis, Roero 1998 $NA. (SR)   83
Barbera d'Alba, Zoanni 1996 $NA. (SR)   86

Saturated ruby hue with a slight purple edge. Forward spice and licorice aromas show a marked wood influence. A crisp entry leads to a medium-bodied palate with racy acids. Lots of wood, but well cut. Drink now or later.

Armando Cuniberto
Arneis, Roero 1998 $NA. (SR)   88

Bright yellow-straw hue. Lean mineral and cream aromas. A tart entry leads to an intense, medium-bodied palate with very firm acidity. Well cut. Should develop nicely over the next year. A shellfish foil. Drink now or later.

Barbera d'Alba, Bric Muntvada 1996 $NA. (SR)   80

Damilano
Barolo, 1995 $NA. (SR)   89

Very deep garnet hue. Pronounced anise and mineral aromas. A soft entry leads to a rich, rounded, full-bodied palate. Has lots of stuffing balanced by lean tannins. Great cut to the finish. Should develop nicely, but will be approachable early. Drink now or later.

Scale: Superlative (96-100), Exceptional (90-95), Highly Recommended (85-89), Recommended (80-84), Not Recommended (Under 80)

Del Cavaliere
Barbera d'Alba, 1996 $NA. (SR)   82

Deltetto
Arneis, Roero 1996 $13.99.   90

Pale straw hue. Medium-bodied. Full acidity. Highly extracted. Green apples, minerals, cream. Extremely aromatic and well translated onto the palate with a purity to the flavors. Racy acidity lends a clean and intense finish. Well balanced and stylish.

Roero Rosso, Braja 1996 $NA. (SR)   89

Bright ruby-garnet hue. Forward spice and berry aromas show a marked oak accent. A lush entry leads to a rounded, supple, medium-bodied palate with velvety tannins. Well flavored, with crisp acids keeping everything in check through the finish. Stylish. Drink now.

Mario Devalle
Dolcetto di Dogliani, Vigna Bric sur Pian 1998 $NA. (SR)   80

Luigi Drocco
Barbera d'Alba, 1997 $NA. (SR)   NR

Ecco Domani
Barbera d'Alba, 1997 $10.   NR

Erbaluna
Barolo "Vigna Rocche," 1995 $NA. (SR)   NR

Stefano Farina
Barolo, 1995 $NA. (SR)   89

Deep, saturated ruby-garnet hue. Generous earth, spice, and jammy berry aromas. A rich entry leads to a ripe, moderately full-bodied palate with big, velvety tannins. Powerful and well balanced with good cut to the finish. Drink now or later.

Giacomo Fenocchio
Barolo "Bussia," 1995 $NA. (SR)   82
Barolo "Villero," 1995 $NA. (SR)   80

Marisa Fenocchio
Barbera d'Alba, 1997 $NA. (SR)   81
Dolcetto di Diano d'Alba, 1998 $NA. (SR)   NR

Ferdinando Giordano
Barbera d'Alba, 1997 $NA. (SR)   89

Bright ruby-purple hue. Forward brown spice and cedar aromas show a marked oak influence. A lean entry leads to a firm, medium-bodied palate with rounded tannins and good cut. Flavorful and rich through the finish. Drink now or later.

Barolo, 1995 $NA. (SR)   85

Deep garnet hue. Subdued, smoky, mineral aromas. A lean entry leads to a firm, medium-bodied palate. Lean tannins and crisp acids make for an angular finish. Taut and well balanced. Straightforward. Drink now or later.

Figini
Gavi di Gavi, 1996 $15.   86

Deep yellow-straw hue. Rich, generous butter and pineapple aromas. A lean entry leads to a crisp, medium-bodied palate with zesty acidity. Lean finish. Drink now.

Domenico Filippino
Barbera d'Alba, 1997 $NA. (SR)   91

Deep, saturated inky purple hue. Rich, brooding chocolate and black fruit aromas.
A ripe entry leads to a medium-bodied palate with great intensity and delicious flavors.
Finishes with a fine acidic cut. Drink now or later.

Firesteed
Barbera d'Asti, 1995 $8.99.   NR

Ettore e Livia Fontana
Barolo, 1993 $50.   82
Barolo "Villero," 1995 $NA. (SR)   83

Fontanabianca
Barbaresco "Sori Burdin," 1996 $NA. (SR)   90

Deep blackish-garnet hue. Perfumed sandalwood, leather, and spice aromas. A lush
entry leads to a rich, rounded, moderately full-bodied palate. Unusually harmonious
and forward at this stage with softer acidity, but shows nice grip to the finish. Should
develop nicely over the mid-term. Drink now or later.

Fontanafredda
Moscato d'Asti, Le Fronde 1998 $NA. (SR)   83
Chardonnay, Langhe 1996 $15.   91

Pale straw hue. Moderately light-bodied. Full acidity. Moderately extracted. Moderately
oaked. Vanilla, citrus, minerals. A light touch of wood is apparent on the nose. Racy and
crisp in style with vibrant acidity. Well-integrated and balanced, it is not unlike a wooded
Chablis.

Barbaresco, 1996 $NA. (SR)   84

Rich orange-garnet hue. Subdued forest, mineral, and leather aromas. A taut entry leads
to a lean, medium-bodied palate with a mature edge to the flavors. Already showing some
complexity. A no holds barred traditional style with a firm edge to the finish. Drink now
or later.

Barbaresco "Coste Rubin," 1993 $23.   84

Bright garnet hue. Moderately light-bodied. Full acidity. Moderately extracted. Mildly
tannic. Sandalwood, forest, earth. Quite light in style though pleasantly aromatic.
Vibrant acidity makes for a racy palate feel. Clean and precise on the tapering finish.
Straightforward but tasty.

Barbaresco "Coste Rubin," 1996 $NA. (SR)   88

Deep garnet hue. Enticing sandalwood, anise, and leather aromas jump from the glass.
A soft entry leads to a medium-bodied palate with grippy tannins and an angular finish.
Already showing some complexities, but should continue to develop. Drink now or later.

Barolo, Galarey 1995 $NA. (SR)   89

Brilliant orange-garnet hue. Opulent spice, cedar, and roasted game aromas show a
toasted oak accent. A firm entry leads to a lean, moderately full-bodied palate with good
intensity. Shows good cut, but grippy tannins bite down on the finish. Needs time. Mid-
term cellar candidate (3–6 years).

Barolo, Serralunga d'Alba 1995 $NA. (SR)   90

Brilliant orange-garnet hue. Exotic cinnamon, sandalwood, and leather aromas jump
from the glass. A rich entry leads to a moderately full-bodied palate with firm tannins.
Flavorful, rich, and powerful in a traditional mold. Drink now or later.

Scale: Superlative (96-100), Exceptional (90-95), Highly Recommended (85-89),
Recommended (80-84), Not Recommended (Under 80)

Barolo, Serralunga D'Alba 1993 $32. **85**

Bright garnet hue. Medium-bodied. Balanced acidity. Moderately extracted. Mildly tannic. Red fruits, minerals. Relatively forward in style with a rounded mouthfeel and fine grained tannins. Not overly complex and lacking a bit for intensity, but drinking very nicely. Would make an excellent introduction to the traditional style of Barolo.

Barolo, Galarey 1993 $35. **90**

Bright garnet hue. Medium-bodied. Full acidity. Moderately extracted. Mildly oaked. Mildly tannic. Earth, vanilla, dried herbs. Quite forceful in aromatics, with classic Barolo flavors lightly accented by an oak note. Lighter in style on the palate, with a racy vibrant character and a slight hint of oxidation. Fine intensity and length.

Barolo, Vigna La Rosa 1993 $35. **88**

Bright garnet hue. Moderately light-bodied. Balanced acidity. Moderately extracted. Moderately tannic. Minerals, earth. Quite youthful with reined-in aromatics that open up on the palate. Almost delicate in the mouth, with an angular, well-structured, though lighter-styled finish. Should gain in complexity with mid-term aging.

Barolo, Vigna Lazzarito 1993 $35. **88**

Bright garnet hue. Moderately light-bodied. Full acidity. Moderately extracted. Mildly tannic. Earth, dried herbs, minerals. Lighter in style with a hint of maturity to the aromatics. Lean and almost delicate on the palate. Well structured through the finish. Should gain in complexity with mid-term aging.

Dolcetto d'Alba, Treiso 1998 $NA. (SR) **NR**

Dolcetto di Diano d'Alba, Vigna La Lepre 1998 $NA. (SR) **88**

Deep, saturated ruby-purple hue. Aromatically reserved, but explodes with fresh red fruit and mineral flavors in the mouth. Medium-bodied and weighty, but well cut, with very firm definition. Drink now or later.

Fratelli Sperone Funtanin

Roero Rosso, Bricco Barbisa Superiore 1996 $NA. (SR) **86**

Brilliant deep ruby hue. Attractive fresh berry and chocolate aromas. A taut entry leads to a lean, medium-bodied palate with a nervous edge of acidity. Clean, vibrant finish with good fruit intensity. Drink now or later.

Gianni Gagliardo

Barbera d'Alba, La Matta 1995 $15. **87**

Bright purple-ruby to the rim. Medium-bodied. Full acidity. Moderately extracted. Mildly tannic. Black fruits, minerals. A little subdued aromatically, but opens up on the palate with a wave of flavor. Firmly structured acidity lends vibrancy to the clean, precise finish. Fine length.

Barolo, Preve 1995 $NA. (SR) **NR**

Piemonte, Batie 1993 $34.95. **NR**

Gagliassi

Barolo, 1993 $35. **90**

Bright ruby with a garnet edge. Medium-bodied. Full acidity. Moderately extracted. Mildly oaked. Moderately tannic. Cedar, minerals, red fruits. Complex in aromas and flavors, with a well-structured and lean palate feel. Clean and elegant through the finish, with some mild astringency. Excellent grip and intensity.

Mario Gagliasso

Dolcetto d'Alba, 1998 $NA. (SR) **87**

Bright ruby-purple hue. Forward anise and mineral aromas. A rich entry leads to a medium-bodied palate with a velvety texture and ripe fruit. A rich Dolcetto. Drink now.

Gaja

Chardonnay, Piemonte 1996 $50.   89

Pale golden hue. Moderately full-bodied. Balanced acidity. Highly extracted. Mildly oaked. Tropical fruits, vanilla, yeast. Pleasantly aromatic with a leesy accent to the tropical fruit flavors. Well-integrated oak accents in the finish. Complex and firmly structured, although relatively angular. May reward mid-term aging by opening up more on the palate.

Barbaresco, 1994 $80.   89

Deep blackish-garnet hue. Moderately full-bodied. Full acidity. Moderately extracted. Mildly oaked. Moderately tannic. Dried herbs, chocolate, minerals. Lighter style with some early maturing classic aromas. Oak accents are well-integrated given the lighter vintage. Well balanced and relatively soft, it should drink well over the next five years.

Barbaresco, 1995 $NA.   90

Saturated ruby-garnet hue. Extravagantly spicy aromas point to a hefty oak influence. A lean entry leads to a rich, moderately full-bodied palate with firm tannins. Although very oaky, this also shows nice fruit flavor intensity. Youthful now, this will come together with some age. Mid-term cellar candidate (3–6 years).

Barolo, Sperss 1993 $110.   88

Bright blackish-ruby hue. Medium-bodied. Balanced acidity. Moderately extracted. Heavily oaked. Moderately tannic. Vanilla, black fruits, minerals. Aromatically reined in with a hint of oak that intensifies in the finish. Lean and angular on the palate, but well balanced. Should gain some tertiary complexities with mid-term aging.

Barolo, Sperss 1994 $NA.   89

Deep ruby-garnet hue. Exotic black fruit aromas show a gamey accent and judicious oak. A firm entry leads to a moderately full-bodied palate with a fleshy quality. Firm tannins bite into the finish. Stylish. Mid-term cellar candidate (3–6 years).

Giacinto Gallina

Moscato d'Asti, Farfarello 1998 $NA. (SR)   88

Pale greenish-straw hue with a thin mousse. Attractive, delicate peach and flower aromas. A racy entry leads to a medium-bodied palate with moderate sweetness and generous flavors. A fairly intense, well balanced, and refreshing style. Drink now.

Antonio Gallino

Arneis, Roero 1998 $NA. (SR)   86

Brilliant pale straw hue. Attractive bread dough and citrus aromas. A ripe entry leads to a rounded, medium-bodied palate. Generous and clean. Drink now.

Filippo Gallino

Roero Rosso Superiore, 1996 $NA. (SR)   NR

Fausto Gemme

Gavi di Gavi, La Merlina 1996 $13.99.   NR

Ettore Germano

Barolo "Cerretta," 1995 $NA. (SR)   88

Brilliant blackish-garnet hue. Enticing sandalwood, spice, and mineral aromas jump from the glass. A rich entry leads to a full-bodied palate with a broad, weighty texture. Excellent intensity of flavor with big chunky tannins. Needs time, but has lots of stuffing to keep. Mid-term cellar candidate (3–6 years).

Barolo "Prapo," 1995 $NA. (SR)   86

Brilliant garnet hue. Generous sandalwood and leather aromas. A firm entry leads to a full-bodied palate. Intense, with big grainy tannins that take over on the finish. Certainly needs time, but will probably always be a bit tough. Long-term cellar.

Scale: Superlative (96-100), Exceptional (90-95), Highly Recommended (85-89), Recommended (80-84), Not Recommended (Under 80)

Attilio Ghisolfi

Barbera d'Alba, 1996 $15.99. 87

Brilliant, saturated ruby hue. Generous spice and berry aromas. A rich entry leads to a ripe, medium-bodied palate with velvety tannins. Lush and supple with grippy acids adding buoyancy to the finish. Drink now.

Barolo "Bricco Visette," 1994 $32.99.

Barolo "Bricco Visette," 1995 $NA. (SR) 89

Brilliant blackish-garnet hue. High-toned, reserved forest and mineral aromas. A firm entry leads to a rich, moderately full-bodied palate with good flavor intensity. Tannins provide a nice framework cut to the finish. Should develop. Drink now or later. 80

Bruno Giacosa

Arneis, Roero 1997 $22. 82

Barbaresco "Santo Stefano," 1993 $69.99. 86

Bright blackish-garnet hue. Moderately full-bodied. Balanced acidity. Highly extracted. Quite tannic. Game, leather, forest. Quite mature aromatically, lush and flavorful on the palate. Finishes on an astringent tannic note with some complexity. Will always be fairly tough.

Barbaresco "Santo Stefano," 1996 $NA. (SR) 91

Deep brilliant garnet hue. Perfumed oriental spice, leather, and earth aromas jump from the glass. A lush entry leads to a rich, full-bodied palate with drying tannins through the finish. Shows lots of extract and flavor, but needs time. Powerful. Mid-term cellar candidate (3–6 years).

Barolo "Falletto," 1995 $NA. (SR) 84

Brilliant orange-garnet hue. Distinctive olive, spice, and jammy red fruit aromas. A soft entry, leads to a supple, rounded, medium-bodied palate with shy acidity. Could use a bit more grip, but has some merit. A softer wood-accented style. Drink now.

Carlo Giacosa

Barbaresco, Narin 1993 $26. NR

Barbera d'Alba, Vigna Mucin 1996 $14. 80

Dolcetto d'Alba, Vigna Cuchet 1996 $14. 84

Very deeply saturated purple. Moderately full-bodied. Full acidity. Highly extracted. Moderately tannic. Minerals, black fruits. Full and almost muscular for a Dolcetto, with a sense of richness and good extraction. Quite firmly structured and a little closed in at present.

Fratelli Giacosa

Arneis, Roero 1998 $NA. (SR) 83

Barbaresco "Rio Sordo," 1996 $NA. (SR) 86

Brilliant cherry-garnet hue. Subdued mineral and spice aromas. A lush entry leads to a rich, medium-bodied palate. A ripe, straightforward style with a decent edge to the finish. Will need some time to develop complexity, but not structured to age for the long term. Mid-term cellar candidate (3–6 years).

Barbera d'Alba, Mario Giona 1997 $NA. (SR) 86

Bright ruby-purple hue. Licorice and spice aromas jump from the glass and show a marked wood influence. A lush entry leads to a rounded, medium-bodied palate with velvety tannins and harmonious acidity. Almost supple in style. Drink now.

Barolo "La Mandorla," 1995 $NA. (SR) 92

Deep blackish-garnet hue. Generous cedar and spice aromas carry a complex earthy undercurrent. A firm entry leads to a rich, full-bodied palate with great flavor intensity. Lengthy, flavorful finish. Could use some time. Mid-term cellar candidate (3–6 years).

Tomasso Gianolio
Dolcetto d'Alba, 1998 $NA. (SR)   83

Gigi Rosso
Barbera d'Alba, Cascina Rocca-Giovino 1996 $13.50.   83
Barolo "Arione," 1993 $55.   89
Deep brick hue with orange highlights. Ripe dried fruit and spice aromas. A lean entry leads a medium-bodied palate with fine cut. Flavorful and lengthy with great grip. Drink now or later.
Barolo "Arione," 1995 $NA. (SR)   86
Brilliant deep garnet hue. Forward, jammy black fruit and chocolate aromas. A rich entry leads to a full-bodied palate with a broad texture and rounded tannins. A big, chunky style, but shows good cut to the finish. Drink now or later.
Barolo "Castelletto," 1995 $NA. (SR)   88
Brilliant orange-garnet hue. Powerful, complex tobacco, cedar, and spice aromas jump from the glass. A lush entry leads to a moderately full-bodied palate with fine acidic cut and fine grained tannins. Doesn't quite deliver what the nose promises, but solid. Drink now or later.
Barolo, Riserva 1993 $NA. (SR)   83
Dolcetto di Diano d'Alba, Moncolombetto 1998 $NA. (SR)   86
Brilliant, saturated purple hue. Generous blueberry, chocolate, and anise aromas. A lush entry leads to a firm, medium-bodied palate with fine cut and intensity. Very ripe, but well structured. Drink now.
Dolcetto di Diano d'Alba, Moncolombetto 1997 $11.99.   83

Francesco Gili
Arneis, Roero 1998 $NA. (SR)   80
Barbera d'Alba, 1997 $NA. (SR)   80

Giribaldi
Arneis, Roero 1998 $NA. (SR)   86
Very pale straw hue. Aromatically subdued with faint mineral qualities. An angular entry leads to a clean, rounded, moderately light-bodied palate. Fairly stylish, with a creamy accent. Drink now.

Giuseppe Veglio
Barolo, Bricco Rosso 1992 $32.99.   85
Bright blackish-garnet hue. Medium-bodied. Balanced acidity. Moderately extracted. Mildly tannic. Red fruits, dried herbs, minerals. Restrained in flavor but very nicely structured with vibrant acidity and mild astringency. Well balanced, and should develop some tertiary character with mid-term aging.

Elio Grasso
Barolo "Ginestra Casa Mate," 1995 $NA. (SR)   90
Deep garnet hue. Exotic saddle leather, cinnamon, and earth aromas are forward and complex. A rich entry leads to a taut, moderately full-bodied palate with grippy tannins and fine cut. Has a lot of extract, but needs time to round out. Mid-term cellar candidate (3–6 years).

Fratelli Grasso

Moscato d'Asti, 1998 $NA. (SR)   NR

Barbaresco "Sori Valgrande," 1996 $NA. (SR)   93

Deep ruby-garnet hue. Forward leather and roasted game aromas jump from the glass. A rich entry leads to a big, mouthfilling palate with excellent balancing acidity and angular, grippy tannins. Full throttle with tons of extract and structure, but rather tough at present. Should blossom wonderfully. Long-term cellar.

Dolcetto d'Alba, 1998 $NA. (SR)   86

Bright purple hue. A rich entry leads to a medium-bodied palate with excellent fruit intensity and rounded acids. Shows a rich, chocolate blueberry note through the finish. Drink now.

Silvio Grasso

Barbera d'Alba, 1997 $NA. (SR)   90

Saturated, opaque violet-red hue. Generous chocolate, black fruit, and earth aromas. A firm entry leads a moderately full-bodied palate with robust tannins. Persistent, flavorful finish. Big and extracted with a lean, firm structure. Mid-term cellar candidate (3–6 years).

Barolo, 1993 $25.99.   80

Barolo "Ciabot Manzoni," 1993 $32.99.   84

Bright ruby with a slight fade. Medium-bodied. Balanced acidity. Moderately extracted. Moderately tannic. Toasted coconut, minerals. Toasty new oak on the nose dominates the flavor profile in the mouth. Lighter styled with a clean and angular mouthfeel that is a bit shy of intensity. Tasty but a tad one dimensional.

Barolo "Bricco Luciani," 1995 $NA. (SR)   94

Deep, saturated ruby hue. Exotic tobacco and brown spice aromas are perfumed and enticing. A rich entry leads to a moderately full-bodied palate with generous chunky tannins. Shows lots of weight and extract. Should develop nicely. Mid-term cellar candidate (3–6 years).

Dolcetto d'Alba, 1997 $NA. (SR)   88

Bright, saturated ruby-purple hue. Generous flower and red fruit aromas. A firm entry leads a moderately light-bodied palate with crisp acidity. Lingering, fruity finish. Lively and buoyant with good depth of flavor. Drink now.

Grimaldi

Barolo "San Biagio," 1995 $NA. (SR)   NR

Clemente Guasti

Moscato d'Asti, 1998 $NA. (SR)   83

Barbaresco, 1996 $NA. (SR)   89

Brilliant cherry-garnet hue. Attractive spice and leather aromas. A lean entry leads to a taut, medium-bodied palate with grippy tannins. Shows complex, earthy flavors with a slight jammy edge to the fruit. Angular finish. Drink now or later.

Barolo, 1995 $NA. (SR)   83

Icardi

Moscato d'Asti, La Rosa Selvatica 1997 $15.   80

Chardonnay, Piemonte 1996 $20.   84

Pale straw hue. Medium-bodied. Balanced acidity. Moderately extracted. Pears, grapefruit, bread dough. Light, delicate, and angular in style with subtle flavors. Rounds out in the mouth towards the finish. No overt oaking: straightforward and clean.

Barbera d'Alba, Suri di Mu 1995 $19. 88

Bright ruby with a slight fade to the rim. Medium-bodied. Full acidity. Highly extracted. Moderately oaked. Mildly tannic. Anise, vanilla, minerals. Oak flavors up front mix with an extracted core of spice and mineral-tinged fruit flavors. Angular, with firm acidity and a note of bitterness to the finish.

Dolcetto d'Alba, Rousori 1996 $16. 82

Nebbiolo, Langhe 1995 $19. 87

Bright saturated ruby to the rim. Medium-bodied. Full acidity. Moderately extracted. Mildly oaked. Mildly tannic. Minerals, black fruits. Aromatic, with a pure, focused, fruit-centered palate feel. Firmly structured and angular, with fine grip and intensity.

Il Falchetto

Moscato d'Asti, Tenuta del Fant 1998 $NA. (SR) NR

Dolcetto d'Alba, Souli Braida 1998 $NA. (SR) 84

Brilliant saturated purple hue. Brooding mineral and berry aromas show a slight reductive quality. A crisp entry leads to a medium-bodied palate with nervous acidity. Well extracted, but very youthful. May come around in a few months time? Drink now or later.

Il Vignale

Gavi, Vigne Alte 1996 $14.99. NR

La Ca' Nova

Barbaresco "Montestefano," 1996 $NA. (SR) NR

Barbaresco, Bric Mentina 1993 $36. 80

Barbaresco, Bric Mentina 1995 $40. 80

La Licenziana

Barbaresco, 1996 $NA. (SR) 94

Deep cherry-garnet hue. Exotically perfumed with a wave of oriental spice, leather, and bitter cherry aromas. A lean entry leads to a moderately full-bodied palate that shows great complexity and intensity of flavor. Full, but very well cut, and certainly in the traditional mold. Should develop beautifully, so try in a few years time. Mid-term cellar candidate (3–6 years).

Barbera d'Alba, 1997 $NA. (SR) 83

La Meirana

Gavi di Gavi, Broglia 1997 $18. 81

La Pergola

Brachetto Piemonte, 1998 $NA. (SR) 85

Deep raspberry-pink hue with a thin mousse. Exotic fresh berry and cranapple aromas. A rich entry leads to a medium-bodied palate with moderate sweetness offset by a zesty effervescence. A great chocolate wine. Drink now.

La Sera

Barbera, Piemonte 1996 $7.99. 82

Barbera del Monferrato, 1997 $11.99. 85

Deep, saturated ruby-purple hue. Intriguing, complex black fruit and mineral aromas. A firm entry leads to a moderately light-bodied palate with racy acids. Finishes on a pleasant pure fruit note. Drink now.

Scale: Superlative (96-100), Exceptional (90-95), Highly Recommended (85-89), Recommended (80-84), Not Recommended (Under 80)

Barbera d'Alba, Il Cielo 1997 $15.99.   89

Saturated ruby-purple hue. Deep, brooding chocolate and black fruit aromas. A rich entry leads to a ripe, luscious, medium-bodied palate. Shows great intensity of fruit flavors, enhanced by a backbone of racy acidity. Should develop. Drink now or later.

La Spinetta

Barbaresco "Gallina," 1996 $NA. (SR)   97

Deep, saturated blackish-garnet hue. Exotically aromatic with a wave of oriental spice, leather, and chocolate aromas. A rich entry leads to a full-bodied, highly flavored palate with firm tannins and a sturdy tannic edge. Perfumed, lengthy, and explosively flavored with great grip. Mid-term cellar candidate (3–6 years).

Barbaresco "Starderi," 1996 $NA. (SR)   89

Deep, saturated blackish-garnet hue. Enticing sandalwood, leather, and game aromas jump from the glass. A rich entry leads to a weighty, full-bodied palate with shy acidity. Very ripe and flavorful with firm tannins through the finish. Rather monolithic at present, but very stylish. Drink now or later.

Barbera d'Asti, Ca' di Pian 1997 $NA. (SR)   88

Saturated, opaque ruby-purple hue. Generous red fruit and vanilla aromas show a hefty oak accent. A firm entry leads a medium-bodied palate with velvety tannins. Lingering, oaky finish. Very modern, extracted, and rich, with a sturdy structural backbone. Drink now or later.

La Spinona

Barbaresco "Faset," 1996 $NA. (SR)   81

Gianluigi Lano

Barbaresco, 1996 $NA. (SR)   89

Deep, saturated ruby-garnet hue. Forward anise, mineral, and flower aromas jump from the glass. A lean entry leads to a rich, medium-bodied palate with lean grippy tannins. Stylish and flavorful with a good cut to the finish. Drink now or later.

Barbera d'Alba, 1997 $NA. (SR)   90

Brilliant inky purple hue. Brooding chocolate and blueberry aromas. A rich entry leads to a weighty, medium-bodied palate with good intensity of flavor and a sense of richness. Should develop nicely. Drink now or later.

Dolcetto d'Alba, 1998 $NA. (SR)   84

Brilliant pale purple hue. Attractive flower, mineral, and berry aromas. A lean entry leads to a supple, medium-bodied palate with a tannic edge. Ripe and weighty. Drink now.

Le Strette

Barbera d'Alba, 1997 $NA. (SR)   80

Ugo Lequio

Barbaresco "Gallina," 1996 $NA. (SR)   93

Deep, saturated blackish-ruby hue with a slight fade. Perfumed spice and berry aromas jump from the glass. A rich entry leads to a moderately full-bodied palate with great richness and intensity. Big and full, but well structured with a firm tannic veil that bites into the finish. Should develop beautifully. Mid-term cellar candidate (3–6 years).

Malabaila

Roero Rosso, Bric Volta Superiore 1996 $NA. (SR)   84

Brilliant, saturated ruby hue with a slight purple overtone. Interesting leather, berry, and mineral aromas. A taut entry leads to a lean, medium-bodied palate with firm acidity. Vibrant finish, with a wrap of mildly astringent tannins. Drink now or later.

Malvira

Arneis, Roero 1996 $18.   80

Arneis, Roero 1996 $18.   89

Pale golden hue. Medium-bodied. Full acidity. Moderately extracted. Cream, sweet herbs, minerals. Quite aromatic with a clean and angular presence on the palate. Expands on the finish. Well balanced and well crafted.

Roero Rosso Superiore, 1996 $NA. (SR)   87

Brilliant dark ruby hue. Brooding, attractive chocolate and berry aromas. A rich entry leads to a firm, moderately full-bodied palate. A flavorful spicy style, with firm tannins through the finish. Needs time. Mid-term cellar candidate (3–6 years).

Roero, Riserva 1995 $30.   80

Giovanni Manzone

Barolo "La Gramolere Vigna Bricat," 1995 $NA. (SR)   88

Deep garnet hue. Aromatically subdued. A rich entry leads to a firm, full-bodied palate with a wave of tannin. Big and powerful, but austere. Will need lots of time. Long-term cellar.

Manzoni

Barbera d'Alba, La Serra 1994 $NA. (SR)   88

Deep, saturated ruby-red with a slight fade. Subdued red fruit, mineral, and wood aromas. A firm entry leads a moderately full-bodied palate with drying tannins. Lingering, flavorful finish. Rather modern and well balanced, with a fruit accent and a kiss of oak. Drink now or later.

Marcarini

Barolo, Brunate 1993 $32.99.   87

Bright ruby-garnet hue. Medium-bodied. Full acidity. Moderately extracted. Mildly oaked. Moderately tannic. Vanilla, red fruits, minerals. Oak treatment is apparent on the nose and rounds out the mouthfeel. Not overly complex but quite tasty with solid structural tannins at the finish. Approachable now but will hold.

Marchesi di Barolo

Barbera d'Alba, Paiagal 1995 $24.99.   NR

Marchesi di Barolo

Arneis, Roero 1995 $16.99.   NR

Gavi , Le Lune 1996 $12.99.   NR

Barbera d'Alba, Ruvei 1997 $NA. (SR)   83

Barolo, 1993 $28.99.   NR

Barolo, 1995 $NA. (SR)   90

Deep garnet hue. Subdued earth and mineral aromas. A rounded entry leads to a spicy, full-bodied palate with lean tannins. Well flavored and rich. Should develop nicely. Drink now or later.

Dolcetto d'Alba, Madonna di Como 1998 $NA. (SR)   85

Bright, saturated purple hue. Lean mineral, licorice, and pepper aromas. A structured entry leads to a medium-bodied palate with fine grained tannins. Weighty and firm in style. Drink now.

698

Scale: Superlative (96-100), Exceptional (90-95), Highly Recommended (85-89), Recommended (80-84), Not Recommended (Under 80)

Marchesi di Gresy

Barbaresco "Camp Gros Martinenga," 1996 $NA. (SR)　　　　　86

Brilliant, saturated garnet hue. Classic spice, leather, and dried flower aromas are complex and perfumed. A lush entry leads to a flavorful, full-bodied palate with a ripe, glycerous texture. Almost fat, with rounded acidity. Flashes grippy tannins on the finish. Should develop nicely in the mid-term, but lacks the acidity for serious aging. Drink now or later.

Barbaresco "Gaiun Martinenga," 1996 $NA. (SR)　　　　　85

Deep cherry red hue. Sweet toasted coconut and vanilla aromas are oak dominated at present. A lush entry leads to a ripe, fat, moderately full-bodied palate. Glycerous and rounded, but some structure pops up on the finish. A modern, early drinking style, but rather one dimensional at present. Drink now.

Aldo Marenco

Dolcetto di Dogliani, Parlapa 1998 $NA. (SR)　　　　　89

Deep, saturated purple hue. Brooding black fruit and licorice aromas. A rich entry leads to a weighty, moderately full-bodied palate. Full and chocolate. Very big, with grainy tannins. Needs time. Mid-term cellar candidate (3–6 years).

Dolcetto di Dogliani, Suri 1998 $NA. (SR)　　　　　88

Deep, saturated purple hue. Exotic pepper, spice, and dried flower aromas are quite generous. A rich entry leads to a firm, medium-bodied palate with lots of weight and intensity. Fairly big, could probably use two or even three years of bottle age. Drink now or later.

Carlo Marenco

Barbera d'Alba, 1997 $NA. (SR)　　　　　82

Barbera d'Alba, Vigna Sesto 1997 $NA. (SR)　　　　　90

Brilliant purple hue. Enticing vanilla and toasted coconut aromas carry a sweet oak note. A crisp entry leads to a medium-bodied palate with ripe fruit flavors. Markedly oaky, but still fresh and well balanced. Drink now or later.

Barolo, 1995 $NA. (SR)　　　　　88

Brilliant garnet hue. Elegant, evolved tar and dried flower aromas. A lean entry leads to a medium-bodied palate with lean acids and angular, but not hard tannins. A delicate, flavorful, traditional style. Drink now or later.

Mario Marengo

Barolo "Brunate," 1995 $NA. (SR)　　　　　85

Brilliant garnet hue. Unusual black tea, mineral, and forest aromas are forward and complex. A lush entry leads to a full-bodied, forceful palate with solid tannic grip. The flavors are left of center throughout, but very intriguing. Some will love it, some will hate it. Drink now or later.

Beppe Marino

Moscato d'Asti, 1998 $NA. (SR)　　　　　80

Marsaglia

Roero Rosso Superiore, San Servesio 1996 $NA. (SR)　　　　　83

Franco Martinetti

Barbera d'Asti, Montruc 1995 $20.　　　　　81
Barbera d'Asti, Bric dei Banditi 1996 $22.　　　　　83

Piemonte, Sul Bric 1995 $48.   88

Deeply saturated ruby hue. Medium-bodied. Full acidity. Moderately extracted.
Moderately oaked. Mildly tannic. Brown spices, cassis. Oak on the nose combines with
pure fruit driven flavors on the palate. Firmly structured with angular acidity and a lean
finish. Quite clean and modern with good grip and intensity.

Martini & Rossi
Asti, Spumante NV $12.   83

Bartolo Mascarello
Barolo, 1995 $NA. (SR)   92

Brilliant orange-garnet hue. Exotic, mature forest and spice aromas jump from the glass.
A rich entry leads to a full-bodied palate with complex, generous flavors. Quite stylish.
Drink now or later.

Giuseppe Mascarello
Barolo "Monprivato," 1995 $NA. (SR)   87

Deep, saturated ruby-garnet hue. Subdued mineral and leather aromas. A taut entry
leads to a lean, medium-bodied palate. Very firm tannins rear up and clamp down on
the finish. Rather tough at present. Needs time. Mid-term cellar candidate (3–6 years).

Massolino
Barolo "Margheria," Vigna Rionda 1995 $NA. (SR)   90

Deep ruby-garnet hue. Generous spice, earth, and leather aromas. A weighty entry leads
to a rich, full-bodied palate with great flavor intensity. Supple and full, yet well balanced,
with chunky structural tannins. Needs time to develop complexity. Mid-term cellar candidate (3–6 years).

Barolo "Parafada," Vigna Rionda 1995 $NA. (SR)   92

Deep blackish-garnet hue. Generous mineral, brown spice, and sandalwood aromas.
A lush entry leads to a rich, full-bodied palate with a broad, weighty texture. Big and
rounded with firm tannins through the finish. Needs time. Mid-term cellar candidate
(3–6 years).

Dolcetto, Barilot 1996 $14.50.   80

Moccagatta
Barbaresco "Bric Balin," 1996 $NA. (SR)   96

Deep blackish-garnet hue. Smoky, spicy aromas jump from the glass and show an exotic,
mineral, earthy accent. A lush entry leads to a rich, full-bodied palate with tons of flavor
intensity and great grip. Generous, intense finish. A real flavor bomb. Drink now or later.

Molino
Barbera d'Alba, Castellinaldo 1997 $NA. (SR)   80
Barolo, Vigna Conca 1993 $NA. (SR)   80

Monchiero
Barbera d'Alba, 1997 $NA. (SR)   90

Deep, inky blackish purple hue. Generous earth, leather, and black fruit aromas. A rich
entry leads to a complex, moderately full-bodied palate with velvety tannins. Well gripped
and flavorful. Drink now or later.

Barolo "Roere," 1995 $NA. (SR)   92

Brilliant garnet hue. Enticing saddle leather and dried flower aromas show breed and
complexity. A ripe entry leads to a forceful, full-bodied palate with firm tannic grip. Fine
cut and intensity. A solid traditional style. Mid-term cellar candidate (3–6 years).

Scale: Superlative (96-100), Exceptional (90-95), Highly Recommended (85-89),
Recommended (80-84), Not Recommended (Under 80)

Dolcetto d'Alba, 1998 $NA. (SR)   87

Deep, saturated brilliant purple hue. Lovely chocolate, blueberry, and flower aromas. A lush entry leads to a supple, rounded, medium-bodied palate. Finishes with a little edge of tannin, but really flavorful. Drink now.

Monchiero Carbone

Arneis, Roero 1998 $13.99.   84

Brilliant, pale yellow-straw hue. Lean mineral and citrus aromas. A crisp entry leads to a medium-bodied palate with fresh acidity. Rounds out toward the finish. Clean. Drink now.

Barbera d'Alba, Mon Birone 1996 $21.95.   87

Very deep blackish-ruby hue. Generous chocolate and black fruit aromas. A lean entry leads to a medium-bodied palate with firm acids. Well flavored with a touch of oak. Grippy, austere finish. Drink now.

Roero Rosso Superiore, 1995 $24.95.   85

Brilliant garnet hue. Subdued spice and leather aromas. A lean entry leads to a medium-bodied palate with mildly astringent tannins. Flavorful and well structure, showing signs of maturity. Drink now.

Roero Rosso Superiore, Srü 1996 $24.95.   80

Mondoro

Asti, Spumante NV $14.   89

Bright platinum cast. Moderately light-bodied. Full acidity. Subtly extracted. Moderately tannic. Tropical fruits, citrus, chalk. Extremely aromatic with very pure Moscato flavors. Light, racy, and clean, with sweetness nicely counterbalanced by the acidity.

Monfalletto

Barolo "Villero Enrico VI," 1995 $NA. (SR)   93

Deep blackish-garnet hue. Generous, spicy cedar and sandalwood aromas. A rich entry leads to a moderately full-bodied, rounded palate with great flavor intensity. Well cut and precise through the finish. Very stylish. Drink now or later.

Stefanino Morra

Arneis, Roero 1998 $NA. (SR)   80

Barbera d'Alba, Castellinaldo 1997 $NA. (SR)   89

Deep, inky blackish-purple hue. Perfumed spice and black fruit aromas jump from the glass. A rich entry leads to a ripe, rounded, medium-bodied palate. Lush and stylish with an integrated oak influence. Drink now or later.

Roero Rosso Superiore, 1996 $NA. (SR)   91

Deep ruby hue with a slight garnet overtone. Generous leather, spice, and berry aromas jump from the glass. A lean entry leads to a firm, medium-bodied palate with a solid acidic cut and angular, but unobtrusive tannins. Shows excellent intensity of flavor and a measure of complexity on a lighter frame. Drink now or later.

Fiorenzo Nada

Barbaresco, 1996 $NA. (SR)   85

Deep, saturated blackish-ruby hue. Generous spice and saddle leather aromas. A rich entry leads to a weighty, full-bodied palate with soft acidity. Round and ripe but shows decent cut with a tannic bite through the finish. Could just use some more acidic grip. Drink now or later.

Giuseppe Nada

Barbaresco "Casotto," 1996 $NA. (SR)   81

Angelo Negro

Arneis, Roero 1998 $NA. (SR) NR

Roero Rosso, Prachiosso 1996 $NA. (SR) 85

Brilliant, saturated ruby-purple hue. Forward, jammy red fruit and vanilla aromas show an overripe accent. A lush entry leads to a medium-bodied palate with rounded tannins. Supple and soft in style with generous flavors. Drink now.

Roero Rosso, Sodisfa 1996 $NA. (SR) 89

Deep, brilliant purple hue. Generous toasted coconut aromas jump from the glass and show a marked oak influence. A rich entry leads to a medium-bodied palate with lush tannins and a broad, supple texture. A well-made international style. Drink now.

Giuseppe Negro

Barbaresco "Piancavallo," 1996 $NA. (SR) 93

Deep garnet hue. Attractive sandalwood and leather aromas. A firm entry leads to a taut, mineral palate with great intensity and a firm structure. A solid, intense, traditional style that will develop beautifully with age. Long-term cellar.

Nervi

Gattinara, Vigneto Molsino 1990 $28. 87

Deep blackish-garnet color. Medium-bodied. Balanced acidity. Moderately extracted. Moderately tannic. Earth, chocolate, minerals, overripe red fruits. Aromatic and flavorful with real complexity. Relatively lush and round with firm tannins on the finish. Approachable now and should continue to mellow with long-term cellaring.

Aurelio Nota

Dolcetto d'Alba, 1998 $NA. (SR) 80

Ranieri Oberti

Dolcetto di Diano d'Alba, Sori Parisa 1998 $NA. (SR) 82

Andrea Oberto

Barbera d'Alba, Giada 1995 $30. 89

Bright blackish ruby to the rim. Moderately full-bodied. Balanced acidity. Highly extracted. Heavily oaked. Moderately tannic. Vanilla, black cherries, minerals. Modern international style with hefty oak influences and extraction. Wood dominates the nose. Full, rounded palate with a nice core of fruit flavors and crisp acidity through the finish. Features mildly astringent, dusty tannins.

Barolo "Vigneto Rocche," 1993 $36. 86

Bright garnet cast. Medium-bodied. Balanced acidity. Highly extracted. Heavily oaked. Moderately tannic. Leather, cedar, minerals. Heavy wood influence dominates. Quite full in the mouth with a rounded character that finishes on an angular note with some mild astringency.

Barolo "Vigneto Rocche," 1995 $NA. (SR) 90

Bright ruby-garnet hue. Generous spice, mineral, and red fruit aromas. A rich entry leads to a moderately full-bodied palate with good intensity of flavor. A powerful wine. Needs time, as stroppy tannins bite down on the finish. Mid-term cellar candidate (3–6 years).

Dolcetto d'Alba, Vigneto Vantrino Albarella 1996 $18. 87

Bright purple color. Moderately light-bodied. Full acidity. Highly extracted. Mildly tannic. Dried herbs, minerals, earth. Quite minerally and clean with an extracted character on the palate. A little tight at present with some mild astringency on the flavorful finish.

Scale: Superlative (96-100), Exceptional (90-95), Highly Recommended (85-89), Recommended (80-84), Not Recommended (Under 80)

Fratelli Oddero

Barolo, Vigna Rionda 1995 $NA. (SR)   85

Deep, saturated ruby hue. Brooding chocolate, earth, and brown spice aromas are quite enticing. A rich entry leads to a thick, roasted, full-bodied mouthfeel with a wall of aggressive tannins. Impressive but a bit overdone perhaps. Try it in the cellar, but it will probably always be tough. Long-term cellar.

Barolo, 1993 $28.99.   80

Barolo, Mondoca di Bussia Soprana 1993 $37.49.   81

Pietro Olivero

Arneis, Roero 1998 $NA. (SR)   80

Opici

Asti, Spumante NV $11.99.   83

Pasquero Elia di Paitin

Barbaresco "Sori Paitin," 1995 $NA. (SR)   84

Brick red with a slight fade. Muted forest and herb aromas. A firm entry leads a medium-bodied palate with drying tannins. Clipped, lean finish. Interesting aromatically, but rather ungenerous. Drink now or later.

Barbaresco "Sori Paitin," 1996 $NA. (SR)   89

Deep, opaque blackish-ruby hue with a slight fade. Powerful, complex aromas of spice, chocolate, and black fruits. A rich entry leads to a weighty, supple palate with great flavor intensity, vibrant acidity, and firm grippy tannins. A bruiser, but should develop well. Drink now or later.

Palladino

Barbaresco, 1996 $NA. (SR)   91

Pale cherry-garnet hue. Extraordinarily fragrant with bitter cherry, spice, and leather aromas showing lots of complexity. A lush entry leads to a medium-bodied palate with a ripe, glycerous texture. Weighty, yet almost delicate with fine balance and cut. Very stylish. Drink now or later.

Barolo "Vigna Broglio," 1995 $NA. (SR)   87

Bright ruby hue with a garnet edge to the rim. Exotic anise, spice, and leather aromas jump from the glass. Lighter in style and medium-bodied with a sense of delicacy, soft tannins, and a crisp finish. Drink now or later.

Parusso

Barolo, Vigna Munie 1994 $NA. (SR)   86

Brick red hue with a fading rim. Intense forest, truffle, and leather aromas. A firm entry leads a medium-bodied palate with lean acidity and drying tannins. Lingering, flavorful finish. Mature, bright, and lean. Drink now.

Barolo, Bussia Vinga Rocche 1993 $38.99.   85

Bright garnet hue. Medium-bodied. Balanced acidity. Moderately extracted. Quite tannic. Minerals, dried herbs. Quite traditional and youthful with reined-in aromatics and a tightly wound palate feel. Tannins are quite astringent. Should open up further with age, but will probably always be a little tough.

Patrizi

Arneis, Roero 1998 $NA. (SR)   88

Brilliant pale straw hue. Lean mineral and citrus aromas. A taut entry leads to a moderately light-bodied palate with some creamy overtones. Stylish, clean, and flavorful. Drink now.

Dolcetto di Dogliani, 1998 $NA. (SR) 80

Fratelli Pecchenino
Dolcetto di Dogliani, Siri d'Jermu 1996 $18. 88

Deep blackish-ruby hue with a purple cast. Medium-bodied. Full acidity. Moderately extracted. Mildly tannic. Black fruits, vanilla, minerals. Aromatic and richly flavored in a precise and expressive manner with a cordial-like intensity. Very clean and angular with a crisp finish and fine length.

Dolcetto di Dogliani, Siri d'Jermu 1997 $18. 91

Deep, saturated, opaque blackish-purple hue. Extravagant chocolate, mineral, and blueberry aromas jump from the glass. A lush entry leads to a deep, brooding, intense mouthfeel. Moderately full-bodied and velvety with a rich finish. Highly extracted. A Super-Dolcetto. Drink now or later.

Pelissero
Barbaresco, Vanotu 1995 $45. 90

Deep blackish-ruby color. Moderately full-bodied. Balanced acidity. Highly extracted. Heavily oaked. Moderately tannic. Brown spices, minerals. Quite modern with big oak-driven flavors. Round, firm, and well balanced, with dusty tannins and solid grip. Tasty, though perhaps a tad one dimensional.

Barbaresco, 1996 $NA. (SR) 91

Brilliant garnet hue. Exotic sandalwood, oriental spice, and smoked game aromas jump from the glass. A rich entry leads to a weighty, full-bodied palate with great intensity of flavor and solid grip. Full and ripe, but fairly well balanced. Drink now or later.

Barbera d'Alba, Piani 1996 $18.50. 83
Dolcetto d'Alba, Munfrina 1998 $NA. (SR) 89

Very deep, inky purple hue. A rich entry leads to a lush, medium-bodied palate with fine weight and velvety tannins. Ripe and full with a rounded, chocolate quality. A big Dolcetto. Drink now or later.

Nebbiolo, Langhe 1996 $20. 87

Bright ruby to the rim with a slight fade. Medium-bodied. Full acidity. Moderately extracted. Mildly oaked. Moderately tannic. Red fruits, chocolate, minerals. Pleasantly aromatic with a ripe, well-structured character. Angular and quite focused through the finish, with a lash of astringency. Well balanced, and though approachable now, it should develop with near-term cellaring.

Elio Perrone
Moscato d'Asti, Sourgal 1997 $19. 86

Bright straw cast. Moderately light-bodied. Full acidity. Moderately extracted. Stone fruits, minerals. Quite clean and crisp in style with a racy, highly carbonated palate feel. Zesty acidity combines with the carbonation to offset the sweetness. Very refreshing finish.

Elvio Pertinace
Chardonnay, Langhe 1996 $15.99. NR
Chardonnay, Langhe 1996 $22.99. 80
Barbaresco "Vigneto Marcarini," Cantina Vignaioli 1996 $NA. (SR) 80
Dolcetto d'Alba, Cantina Vignaioli 1998 $NA. (SR) 80

Scale: Superlative (96-100), Exceptional (90-95), Highly Recommended (85-89), Recommended (80-84), Not Recommended (Under 80)

Armando Piazzo
Moscato d'Asti, 1998 $NA. (SR)   **80**
Barbaresco "Suri Fratin," 1996 $NA. (SR)   **88**

Deep garnet hue. Forward leather, earth, and spice aromas hint at a degree of maturity. A rich entry leads to a full-bodied palate with a round, glycerous texture offset by stroppy tannins. Weighty through the finish with a core of ripe berry flavors. Needs time. Mid-term cellar candidate (3–6 years).

Barbera d'Alba, Mugiot 1997 $NA. (SR)   **82**
Barolo, 1995 $NA. (SR)   **83**
Dolcetto d'Alba, 1998 $NA. (SR)   **80**

E. Pira & Figli
Barolo "Cannubi," 1995 $NA. (SR)   **90**

Deep garnet hue. Pungent anise, cedar, and spice aromas. A soft entry leads to a big, full-bodied, rounded palate. Somewhat dominated by its oak at present. A very modern style. Should develop more complexity with age and has the stuffing to do so. Long-term cellar.

Giorgio Pira
Barolo, 1993 $40.   **88**

Deep ruby-garnet hue. Richly aromatic with a deep, gamey, black fruit core. A ripe entry leads to a lush, supple, moderately full-bodied palate. Complex in flavor, with a fleshy quality. Fruit acidity balances the chocolate finish. On the fat side, but quite good. Drink now.

Giovanni Pira
Dolcetto di Dogliani, Cascina Bergamino 1998 $NA. (SR)   **NR**

Poderi Colla
Barbaresco "Tenuta Roncaglia," 1996 $NA. (SR)   **86**

Brilliant garnet hue. Perfumed sandalwood, spice, and dried flower aromas are classic and enticing. A lush entry leads to a rounded, medium-bodied palate with shy acidity. Great flavor, but lacks somewhat for grip or structure. Drink over the near term. Drink now.

Barbera d'Alba, 1997 $NA. (SR)   **85**

Deep, saturated ruby-red hue. Generous brown spice, leather, and berry aromas are pronounced and complex. A lean entry leads to a medium-bodied palate with grippy tannins. A taut, modern style, but rather reliant on oak. Drink now.

Barolo "Bussia Dardi Le Rose," 1995 $NA. (SR)   **94**

Brilliant orange-garnet hue. Generous earth, mineral, and leather aromas jump from the glass. A lush entry leads to a stylish, very flavorful palate with great spicy complexity and fine cut. Exhibits great length. Well balanced with grainy tannins. Finishes for a mile. Drink now or later.

Dolcetto di Diano d'Alba, Sori du Rabin 1998 $NA. (SR)   **89**

Brilliant purple hue. Attractive flower and fresh berry aromas explode in the mouth. Moderately light-bodied with racy acids and an angular structure. Vibrant and intense. Drink now.

Poderi la Collina
Arneis, Langhe 1997 $20.   **86**

Deep straw hue. Generous aromas have a forceful, ripe, herbal overtone-not unlike a varietal Sauvignon. A crisp entry leads to a moderately light-bodied, high acid palate. Lengthy, snappy finish. A dead ringer for a high quality Sauvignon. Drink now.

Dolcetto di Dogliani, Vigneto Castiglia 1996 $21.   81
Dolcetto di Dogliani, Labbra di Giada 1996 $25.   86

Brilliant, saturated ruby hue. Enticing spicy aromas point to oak maturation. A crisp entry leads to a lighter-styled medium-bodied palate. Berryish flavors explode with a spicy, herbal accent through the finish. Stylish. Drink now.

Langhe, Primo Solo Rosso 1995 $30.   89

Brilliant garnet hue. Attractive sandalwood and leather aromas. A lean entry leads to a medium-bodied palate with juicy acidity. Well balanced and vibrant with a complex olive, gamey note to the finish. Drink now.

Piemonte, Primassolo 1994 $30.   89

Deep ruby with a slight fade to the rim. Moderately full-bodied. Full acidity. Moderately extracted. Heavily oaked. Mildly tannic. Brown spices, earth, minerals, red fruits. Up-front oak flavors join a core of earthy red fruit on the palate. Vibrant and zesty acidity lends buoyancy to the flavorful finish. Good grip, with solid length and intensity.

Portinale
Roero Rosso Superiore, Giacu Mus 1996 $NA. (SR)   83

Ferdinando Principano
Barolo "Boscareto," 1995 $NA. (SR)   94

Deep, saturated ruby-garnet hue. Opulent leather, earth, and spicy berry aromas jump from the glass. A rich entry leads to a moderately full-bodied palate with a broad, rounded texture. Generous and weighty, with the extract to develop beautifully. Drink now or later.

Prinsi
Barbaresco "Gallina," 1996 $NA. (SR)   NR
Barbaresco "Prinsi," 1996 $NA. (SR)   83

Produttori del Barbaresco
Barbaresco, 1996 $NA. (SR)   80
Barbaresco, 1994 $26.   80
Nebbiolo, Langhe 1997 $16.   NR

Prunotto
Barbaresco "Bric Turot," 1996 $NA. (SR)   80
Barbaresco, Classico 1996 $NA. (SR)   80
Barbera d'Asti, Fiulot 1996 $11.   85

Bright blackish ruby to the rim. Medium-bodied. Full acidity. Moderately extracted. Mildly oaked. Mildly tannic. Black fruits, minerals. Quite austere and tightly wound with a compact minerally character. Sharp and angular acidity makes for a very precise finish. Fruit and oak nuances linger. Well balanced and focused.

Barolo "Bussia," 1995 $NA. (SR)   89

Deep, saturated modern ruby-red hue. Generous berry and vanilla aromas show a marked oak influence. A lush entry leads to a rounded, moderately full-bodied palate. Stylish, and lengthy, but has as yet to develop any Barolo complexities. With time perhaps. Drink now or later.

Barolo "Cannubi," 1995 $NA. (SR)   86

Deep ruby-garnet hue. Forward berry, spice, and mineral aromas. A soft entry leads to a fruit accented, medium-bodied palate with pronounced acidity. A very modern style, but not overly intense. Drink now.

Scale: Superlative (96-100), Exceptional (90-95), Highly Recommended (85-89), Recommended (80-84), Not Recommended (Under 80)

Barolo, Classico 1995 $NA. (SR)   86

Deep, saturated, modern ruby hue. Generous earth, mineral, and black fruit aromas. A rich entry leads to a weighty, full-bodied palate with firm tannins. Strikes a slightly reductive note throughout which should blow with age. Needs time, but may come around quite nicely, justifying a higher rating in the future. Mid-term cellar candidate (3–6 years).

Dolcetto d'Alba, 1996 $14.50.   84

Bright purple. Moderately light-bodied. Full acidity. Moderately extracted. Mildly tannic. Minerals, anise, black fruits. Crisp, clean and direct, with a focused quality on the palate. Angular through the mildly tart finish.

Punset

Barbaresco, 1996 $NA. (SR)   90

Saturated brilliant ruby hue. Subdued berry and mineral aromas. A firm entry leads to a moderately full-bodied palate with drying tannins. Taut and stylish with a great structure. Should develop nicely with age. Long-term cellar.

Barbaresco "Campo Quadro," 1996 $NA. (SR)   NR

Dolcetto d'Alba, 1996 $12.99.   88

Bright purple. Medium-bodied. Full acidity. Moderately extracted. Mildly tannic. Black fruits, black pepper. Quite aromatic and flavorful with a rounded and lush palate feel. Structural acidity buoys a crisp, clean finish.

Renato Ratti

Barbera, Piemonte 1995 $13.49.   NR

Barolo, 1993 $40.   83

Barolo "Marcenasco," 1993 $48.   90

Bright garnet hue. Medium-bodied. Balanced acidity. Moderately extracted. Quite tannic. Minerals, dried herbs, red fruits. Quite focused and pure with an expressive, precise mouthfeel. Still a little reined in aromatically, but beautifully structured and intense. Well balanced, and best left to cellar for the middle to long term.

Barolo "Marcenasco," 1995 $NA. (SR)   84

Garnet-browning hue with a fade to the rim. Generous forest, spice, and mineral aromas. A soft entry leads to a rounded, supple palate. Turns a little lean on the finish. Lacks real depth, but sturdy. Drink now or later.

Barolo "Rocche," 1993 $68.   92

Bright ruby-garnet hue. Medium-bodied. Balanced acidity. Moderately extracted. Quite tannic. Minerals, dried herbs. Complex in aromatics with a firm and precise palate feel. Exhibits fine intensity and grip with astringent tannins on the finish. Well balanced, this should cellar beautifully for the long term.

Barolo "Rocche," 1995 $NA. (SR)   94

Brilliant garnet hue. Exotic spice, leather, and sandalwood aromas jump from the glass. A rich entry leads to a powerful, full-bodied palate with a very firm tannic grip. Shows great intensity, with the stuffing and extract to age. Fortunate, because the tannins require it. Long-term cellar.

Dolcetto d'Alba, 1998 $NA. (SR)   82

Piemonte, I Cedri 1995 $33.   88

Blackish ruby with a slight fade and brilliant clarity. Medium-bodied. Balanced acidity. Moderately extracted. Moderately oaked. Moderately tannic. Brown spices, minerals, black fruits. Quite aromatic, with a pleasant interplay between wood and fruit driven flavors. Lean and angular in the mouth with a very focused and precise palate feel. Well balanced with good grip. Should develop nicely with mid-term cellaring.

Eraldo Revelli

Dolcetto di Dogliani, 1998 $NA. (SR)　　　　90

Deep, saturated ruby-purple hue. Exotic bacon fat, berry, and sweet herb aromas. A rich entry leads to a supple, rounded, medium-bodied palate with explosive flavors and a wonderful texture. Very, very stylish and harmonious. Drink now or later.

Fratelli Revello

Barolo "Vigna Giachini," 1995 $NA. (SR)　　　　90

Deep ruby-garnet hue. Generous spice and anise aromas. A rich entry leads to a moderately full-bodied palate with lots of richness and a kiss of oak. Firm tannins define the finish. Should develop Barolo complexities with age. A rich, modern style. Mid-term cellar candidate (3–6 years).

Francesco Rinaldi

Barolo "Cannubio," 1995 $NA. (SR)　　　　89

Deep, saturated ruby-garnet hue. Exotic roasted game, demi-glace, and tar aromas. A rich entry leads to a big, full-bodied palate. Ripe and intense with rounded acidity and firm tannins. Would be fantastic with highly seasoned roasted meats. Drink now or later.

Giuseppe Rinaldi

Barbera d'Alba, 1996 $16.　　　　90

Bright ruby with a slight fade to the rim. Moderately light-bodied. Full acidity. Moderately extracted. Mildly tannic. Red fruits, sweet herbs, minerals. Pleasantly aromatic with complex flavors through the finish. Light and delicate with an ephemeral quality. Well structured acidity lends sharpness and focus to the palate. Fine length and good balance.

Barolo "Brunate," 1992 $36.　　　　88

Bright garnet hue. Medium-bodied. Full acidity. Moderately extracted. Moderately tannic. Flowers, tar, minerals. Extremely classic with a delicate bouquet. Although lighter in style, it is focused and pure with good acidity and a clean finish. Oak accents are emphatically absent. Well balanced and expressive in a difficult vintage.

Barolo "Brunate," Le Coste 1993 $35.　　　　90

Bright ruby-garnet hue. Medium-bodied. Balanced acidity. Moderately extracted. Quite tannic. Anise, flowers, minerals. Very traditional with complex aromatics that lead to a precise, focused, and austere palate feel. Delicate, yet powerful and well balanced, this should age quite well.

Barolo "Brunate," Le Coste 1995 $NA. (SR)　　　　95

Brilliant, intense garnet hue. Intense sandalwood, spice, and leather aromas. A rich entry leads to a flavorful, moderately full-bodied, well cut palate. Shows great intensity of flavor and fine balance. A very stylish wine. Powerful but almost showing a sense of delicacy Drink now or later.

Fratelli Rivetti

Arneis, Langhe 1996 $15.　　　　81

Barbera d'Alba, Cairel, Vigneto Caveia 1997 $NA. (SR)　　　　80

Barbera d'Alba, Cairel, Vigneto Caveia 1996 $13.　　　　82

Barolo, Cairel 1993 $24.　　　　84

Bright ruby-garnet hue. Medium-bodied. Balanced acidity. Moderately extracted. Moderately tannic. Dried herbs, minerals, red fruits. Pleasantly aromatic and relatively straightforward with a fruit centered palate. Rounded mouthfeel with some angular acidity and mildly astringent tannins. Well balanced, if a touch simple.

Dolcetto d'Alba, Cairel, Vigneto del Mandorlo 1997 $14.　　　85

Brilliant ruby hue. Reserved aromas show gentle spicy overtones. A lean entry leads to a moderately light-bodied palate with rounded tannins. Soft and supple, but balanced by crisp acids through the finish. Drink now.

Dolcetto d'Alba, Cairel, Vigneto del Mandorlo 1998 $NA. (SR)　　　86

Very deep brilliant purple hue. Exotic spice, berry, and mineral aromas jump from the glass. A lean entry leads to a moderately light-bodied palate with crisp acids. Well flavored, with a sturdy acidic cut. Drink now.

Nebbiolo d'Alba, Cairel, Vigneto Raine 1995 $16.　　　80

Albino Rocca

Barbaresco "Bric Ronchi," 1995 $NA. (SR)　　　89

Bright, luminescent ruby hue. Forward mineral, red fruit, and leather aromas. A firm entry leads a medium-bodied palate with drying tannins. Lighter in style but well gripped. Drink now or later.

Barbaresco "Bric Ronchi," 1996 $NA. (SR)　　　88

Deep, saturated ruby hue. Forward anise and cherry aromas. A lush entry leads to a full-bodied, glycerous palate with big stroppy tannins. A rich, weighty style. Needs time to develop complexity. Youthful. Mid-term cellar candidate (3–6 years).

Barbaresco "Vigneto Loreto," 1996 $NA. (SR)　　　90

Deep, saturated ruby hue. Brooding mineral and black fruit aromas. A rich entry leads to a rounded, full-bodied palate with fine weight and a sturdy tannic grip. Big and stylish, but needs time to develop tertiary complexities. Mid-term cellar candidate (3–6 years).

Barbera d'Alba, Gepin 1996 $NA. (SR)　　　91

Saturated dark ruby hue. Rich game and black fruit aromas. A smooth entry leads a moderately full-bodied palate with crisp acidity and velvety tannins. Focused and aromatic with great grip. Drink now or later.

Dolcetto d'Alba, Vinalunga 1997 $NA. (SR)　　　89

Saturated purple hue. Ripe black cherry aromas. A lush entry leads a medium-bodied palate with crisp acidity and soft tannins. Chunky and rich with an assertive wood note. Drink now or later.

Bruno Rocca

Barbaresco "Rabaja," 1996 $NA. (SR)　　　88

Deep, saturated blackish-ruby hue. Generous spice and anise aromas jump from the glass. A rich entry leads to a full-bodied, supple palate. A weighty, ripe style with a big flavorful core. Spicy finish, with lean tannins. Almost on the fat side, but tasty. Drink now or later.

Rocche Costamagna

Barbera d'Alba, Annunziata 1995 $17.　　　88

Bright ruby to the rim. Medium-bodied. Full acidity. Moderately extracted. Mildly tannic. Minerals, red fruits. Holds its cards close to the vest. Tightly wound, firmly structured with a dense core of flavor. Well balanced with some richness offset by angular acidity. Opens up with aeration, suggesting it as a near-term cellar candidate.

Barbera d'Alba, Annunziata 1997 $NA. (SR)　　　90

Bright ruby-purple hue. Attractive, high-toned dried flower and berry aromas. A lean entry leads to a harmonious, moderately light-bodied palate. Lighter in style, but harmonious and exceptionally flavorful. Well cut through the finish. Drink now or later.

Barolo, Rocche dell'Annunziata 1995 $NA. (SR)　　　94

Brilliant garnet hue. Expressive spice, mineral, and anise aromas jump from the glass. A rich entry leads to a full-bodied palate with powerful, well-extracted flavors and firm tannins. Carries an intense, and highly distinctive mineral note. This will need time to show its best. Long-term cellar.

Barolo, Vigna Francesca 1995 $NA. (SR)   **92**

Brilliant garnet hue. Intense, exotic smoke, mineral, and leather aromas. A rich entry leads to a weighty, full-bodied palate with solid extract. Full and sturdy. Tannins clamp down on the finish. Needs time. Long-term cellar.

Barolo, Rocche dell'Annunziata 1993 $32.   **90**

Bright ruby-garnet hue. Medium-bodied. Balanced acidity. Moderately extracted. Quite tannic. Red fruits, dried herbs, minerals. Extremely firm and focused in a traditional style without overt wood accents. Subtle aromatics but the palate opens up with great flavor intensity. Quite angular through the finish. Well balanced and should cellar quite nicely.

Barolo, Vigna Francesco 1993 $38.   **89**

Deep ruby-garnet hue. Medium-bodied. Balanced acidity. Moderately extracted. Mildly oaked. Moderately tannic. Brown spices, minerals, red fruits. Oak flavors are apparent upfront, but not aggressive and are well-integrated on the palate. Somewhat rounded in the mouth with an angular finish. Good intensity and length.

Rocca Giancarlo Ronchi
Barbaresco, 1996 $NA. (SR)   **89**

Deep, saturated ruby hue with a garnet edge. Generous berry and anise aromas carry a spicy edge. A lush entry leads to a moderately full-bodied palate with lean tannins. Quite ripe, with a sense of richness. Well gripped finish. Could use time to develop some tertiary complexities, but promising. Mid-term cellar candidate (3–6 years).

Salvano
Barbera d'Alba, Maestrale 1996 $NA. (SR)   **NR**

San Biagio
Barolo, 1993 $35.   **85**

Brilliant brick hue. Reserved mineral and licorice aromas. A lean entry leads to a taut, medium-bodied palate. Rather austere, with firm acidity that bites into the finish. May need time, but lighter in style. Drink now or later.

Barolo, 1994 $35.   **87**

Brilliant brickish-orange hue. Lean mineral and sandalwood aromas. A lush entry leads to a weighty, rounded palate with vibrant acidity. Flavorful and well balanced. Shows fine grip to the finish. Drink now or later.

San Michelle
Barbaresco "Gallina," 1996 $NA. (SR)   **83**

Sandrone
Barolo, La Vigne 1993 $45.99.   **92**

Bright blackish-ruby hue with a garnet cast. Medium-bodied. Balanced acidity. Moderately extracted. Heavily oaked. Mildly tannic. Vanilla, black fruits, minerals. Extremely modern with new oak flavors combined with a very supple mouthfeel and velvety tannins. Round and well balanced with a fruit-centered palate. This is a very well-made international style.

Santini
Asti, Spumante NV $7.   **NR**

Giorgio Scarzello
Barolo, 1995 $NA. (SR)   **82**

Scale: Superlative (96-100), Exceptional (90-95), Highly Recommended (85-89), Recommended (80-84), Not Recommended (Under 80)

Paolo Scavino

Barbera d'Alba, Affinato in Carati 1996 $NA. (SR) 91

Saturated ruby-purple hue. Powerful game, truffle, and chocolate aromas. A firm entry leads a moderately full-bodied palate with crisp acids and drying tannins. Lingering, flavorful finish. Intense and concentrated in a New World vein. Drink now or later.

Barolo, 1995 $NA. (SR) 91

Saturated garnet red. Intense game, wood, and earth aromas. A firm entry leads a moderately full-bodied palate with big grainy tannins. Quite intense with a firm structure. Shows wood in the finish, but not blatantly modern. An attractive compromise. Mid-term cellar candidate (3–6 years).

Barolo, Bric Del Fiasc 1995 $NA. (SR) 90

Deep, saturated garnet hue with a slight fade. Lean mineral, chocolate, and leather aromas. A firm entry leads a moderately light-bodied palate with astringent tannins. Clipped finish. Lighter in style and quite lean, but stylish and firm. Mid-term cellar candidate (3–6 years).

Barolo, Cannubi 1995 $NA. (SR) 94

Rich garnet red with a slight fade. Generous earth, chocolate, and mineral aromas. A firm entry leads a full-bodied palate with mildly astringent tannins. Persistent and intense. A real mouthful. Needs time. Long-term cellar candidate.

Barolo, 1993 $37.99. 89

Bright ruby-garnet hue. Medium-bodied. Balanced acidity. Moderately extracted. Moderately tannic. Minerals, red fruits. Pleasantly aromatic and rounded on the palate with a very slight oak accent that is well-integrated with classic Barolo flavors. Lean and angular through the finish, though well balanced, this should age gracefully.

Dolcetto d'Alba, Vigneto del Fiasc 1997 $NA. (SR) 89

Rich ruby-purple hue to the rim. Generous vanilla and red fruit aromas show a brush of oak. A soft entry leads a moderately full-bodied palate with velvety tannins. Very modern and ripe, with a thick rounded finish. Drink now or later.

Seghesio

Barolo, Vigneto La Villa 1994 $NA. (SR) 80

Enrico Serafino

Arneis, Roero 1998 $NA. (SR) 86

Very pale straw hue. Austere, flinty, mineral aromas. A vibrant entry leads to a crisp, moderately light-bodied palate with focused flavors. Solid acidity. A little Chablis-like. Drink now.

Barbera d'Alba, 1997 $NA. (SR) 88

Brilliant purple hue with a touch of spritz. Exotic mineral, flower, and anise aromas. A crisp entry leads to a lean, medium-bodied palate with great flavor intensity. Lighter in style, but refreshing, pure, and delicious. Drink now.

Aurelio Settimo

Barolo "Rocche," 1995 $NA. (SR) NR

Sigillo dell'Abate

Barolo, 1993 $36. 85

Bright ruby-garnet hue. Moderately full-bodied. Balanced acidity. Moderately extracted. Heavily oaked. Mildly tannic. Red fruits, vanilla, minerals. Quite modern in style with a heavy wood influence, a supple palate, and lush tannins. Round and flavorful with an angular finish. Solid but perhaps lacks a bit intensity.

Dolcetto d'Alba, 1996 $17. NR

Giovanni Sordo
Barolo, 1994 $28.   88

Pale brickish-orange hue. Exotic spice, earth, and olive aromas. A soft entry leads to a rounded, medium-bodied palate. Complex and well flavored with surprising richness. A fine effort for a tough vintage. Drink now.

Sottimano
Barbaresco "Pajore," Vigna Lunetta 1995 $NA. (SR)   NR
Barbaresco "Vigna del Salto," 1996 $NA. (SR)   94

Deep, saturated ruby-garnet hue. Exotic spice, roasted game, and chocolate aromas. A rich entry leads to a lean, full-bodied palate with an assertive angular structure to balance the richness. A real mouthfull, with great flavor intensity. Chewy tannins bite down on the finish. Needs time. Mid-term cellar candidate (3–6 years).

Oreste Stroppiana
Barolo "Vigna San Giacomo," 1995 $NA. (SR)   93

Brilliant garnet hue. Attractive toasty oak aromas define the nose. A rich entry leads to a firm, moderately full-bodied palate with solid intensity. Rather closed in at present, with big tannins, but should develop nicely. Mid-term cellar candidate (3–6 years).

Tenuta Carretta
Arneis, Roero 1998 $NA. (SR)   85

Brilliant greenish-straw hue. Lean mineral, toast, and citrus aromas. A crisp entry leads to a moderately light-bodied palate with piercing acidity. Taut and clean. Drink now.

Arneis, Roero 1996 $15.   80
Barbaresco, Cascina Bordino 1993 $20.   NR
Barolo, Cannubi 1992 $18.   NR
Dolcetto d'Alba, 1996 $12.   NR
Roero Rosso Superiore, Bric Paradiso 1996 $NA. (SR)   87

Bright cherry-garnet hue. Forward herb and berry aromas. A lean entry leads to a firm, medium-bodied palate with a fine acidic cut. Shows good ripeness and intensity of flavor in the mouth. Very stylish. Drink now.

Teo Costa
Roero Rosso, Batajot 1996 $NA. (SR)   80

Terre da Vino
Gavi di Gavi, La Rocca del Forte 1997 $11.99.   80
Barbaresco "La Casa in Collina," 1995 $22.99.   NR
Barbaresco "La Casa in Collina," 1996 $NA. (SR)   92

Deep, saturated ruby hue. Forward anise and red fruit aromas. A lush entry leads to a rounded, moderately full-bodied palate. Supple and stylish with a rounded texture, but a very traditional quality to the brisk, taut red fruit flavors. Drink now or later.

Barbera d'Asti, La Luna e i Falo 1995 $11.99.   NR
Barolo, Paesi Tuoi 1995 $NA. (SR)   88

Deep blackish-garnet hue. Restrained anise and mineral aromas. A rich entry leads to a big, supple, moderately full-bodied mouthfeel. Crisp through the finish. Well extracted, and should develop nicely. Drink now or later.

Barolo, Poderi Parussi 1995 $NA. (SR)   90

Deep, saturated ruby-red hue. Generous vanilla aromas point to oak influence and a modern style. A lush entry leads to a rounded, medium-bodied palate with velvety tannins. Will need time to develop complexity, but balanced and supple. Drink now or later.

Scale: Superlative (96-100), Exceptional (90-95), Highly Recommended (85-89),
Recommended (80-84), Not Recommended (Under 80)

Terre del Barolo
Barbera d'Alba, 1997 $NA. (SR)   80
Barolo, 1995 $NA. (SR)   85
Deep garnet hue. Subdued earth and mushroom aromas. A firm entry leads to a lean, medium-bodied palate with angular tannins. On the rustic side, but well cut. Drink now or later.

Dolcetto di Diano d'Alba, 1998 $NA. (SR)   84
Saturated, brilliant ruby-purple hue. Lean mineral and berry aromas. A taut entry leads to a firm, stylish palate. Richly fruited with an attractive spicy nuance and fine cut. Drink now.

Tonnelli
Asti, Spumante $11.99.   84
Pale yellow-straw cast. Floral, sweet fruit aromas. Carbonation is fine beaded and creamy with sweet fruity flavors and a lingering finish. Shows some finesse.

Moscato d'Asti, 1997 $8.99.   NR

Tosti
Asti, Spumante NV $8.99.   82

Travaglini
Gattinara, 1994 $11.   NR
Gattinara, Riserva 1993 $19.50.   80
Gattinara, 1993 $17.   NR

GD Vajra
Langhe Bianco, 1997 $NA. (SR)   84
Brilliant golden straw hue. Lean mineral and citrus aromas. A crisp entry leads to a medium-bodied palate with a lean cut. Finishes with a hint of interesting petrolly Riesling character. Drink now or later.

Barbera d'Alba, 1997 $NA. (SR)   88
Bright ruby with a slight fade. Generous vanilla and berry aromas belie a flashy wood accent. A rich entry leads to a rounded, medium-bodied palate with excellent acidic grip. Focused and very pure in style. Drink now.

Barolo "Bricco delle Viole," 1995 $NA. (SR)   89
Bright, modern ruby hue. Forward toast and berry aromas show a modern accent. A firm entry leads to a lean, medium-bodied palate. Acidity provides a nice cut to the finish. Straightforward at present, but should develop complexity with age. Well structured and clean. Mid-term cellar candidate (3–6 years).

Dolcetto d'Alba, Coste & Fassati 1998 $NA. (SR)   86
Brilliant purple hue. Aromatic, perfumed spice, blueberry, and mineral aromas. A crisp entry leads to a medium-bodied palate with waves of luscious fruit. Ripe and rounded. Very pure and stylish with a touch of tannin to the finish. Drink now.

Nebbiolo, Langhe 1998 $NA. (SR)   83

Valdinera
Barbera d'Alba, Ca'Rusa 1997 $NA. (SR)   90
Bright ruby-purple hue. Generous, enticing saddle leather and spice aromas. A rich entry leads to a firm, medium-bodied palate with good weight. Flavorful, stylish, and well balanced. The oak is nicely integrated. Drink now or later.

Roero Rosso, 1996 $NA. (SR)   84

Brilliant pale purple hue. Crisp berry and mineral aromas. A taut entry leads to a moderately light-bodied palate with crisp acidity. Straightforward and clean with a nice cut. Drink now.

Valditerra
Gavi, 1996 $18.   88

Pale straw hue. Medium-bodied. Full acidity. Moderately extracted. Minerals, citrus, toast. Pleasantly aromatic with a rounded presence on the palate. An unusual interpretation of the style. Good acidity with some fullness without any bitterness. Clean, delicate, and well balanced with a lingering finish. Subtle but far from simple.

Rino Varaldo
Barbaresco "Bricco Libero," 1996 $NA. (SR)   93

Deep, saturated blackish-garnet hue. Intense anise, sandalwood, and brown spice aromas jump from the glass. A firm entry leads to a moderately full-bodied palate with good grip and intensity of flavor. Lean and structured through the finish. Should develop beautifully. Drink now or later.

Barbaresco "Sori Loreto," 1996 $NA. (SR)   80
Barolo "Vigna di Aldo," 1995 $NA. (SR)   85

Brilliant garnet hue. Forward, pronounced earth and leather aromas. A soft entry leads to a firm, moderately full-bodied palate. Big, but rather lacking in grip through the finish. Drink now or later.

Giovanni Veglio
Dolcetto di Diano d'Alba, 1998 $NA. (SR)   87

Brilliant, saturated purple hue. Attractive flower and red fruit aromas jump from the glass. A ripe entry leads to a rich, medium-bodied palate with lots of fruit intensity, grippy tannins, and a firm acidic cut. Very fresh. Drink now.

Mauro Veglio
Barolo "Vigneto Arborina," 1995 $NA. (SR)   80

Romano e Lorenzo Veglio
Barbera d'Alba, Elisa 1997 $NA. (SR)   87

Deep ruby-purple hue. Enticing, smoky licorice and red fruit aromas. A lush entry leads to a ripe, moderately full-bodied palate. Quite flavorful and pure in style. Drink now.

Giovanni Viberti
Barolo, 1995 $NA. (SR)   95

Deep, saturated ruby-garnet hue. Outrageous sandalwood, leather, and earth aromas race from the glass. A rich entry leads to an exotically flavored, full-bodied palate with great intensity and cut. Has tons of traditional complexity with a wave of rich olive-like flavors. Long-term cellar.

Giacomo Vico
Barbera d'Alba, 1997 $NA. (SR)   87

Brilliant purple hue. Unusual flower, mineral, and fresh red fruit aromas show a perfumed quality. A crisp entry leads to a medium-bodied palate. Ripe and showing nice complexity. Edgy finish. A fun wine. Drink now.

Vietti

Barbaresco "Masseria," 1996 $NA. (SR)   **90**

Deep cherry red hue with a slight fade. Candied red fruit and vanilla aromas carry a marked oak influence. A firm entry leads to a lean, medium-bodied palate with grippy tannins. A perfumed, delicate style with a firm structure. Drink now or later.

Barbera d'Alba, Tre Vigne 1996 $16.95.   **84**

Bright ruby with a slight fade to the rim. Medium-bodied. Full acidity. Moderately extracted. Mildly tannic. Earth, red fruits, minerals. Rustic Old World aromas lead a zingy, sharp presence on the palate. Austere through the clean finish. A solid food wine.

Barolo "Lazzarito," 1995 $NA. (SR)   **NR**

Barolo "Rocche," 1993 $44.99.   **90**

Bright garnet hue. Medium-bodied. Full acidity. Moderately extracted. Mildly tannic. Earth, minerals, dried herbs. Forcefully aromatic and quite flavorful with earthy terroir notes on the nose. Sense of lushness and roundness throughout. Soft extraction results in a supple wine. Angular finish, but with good structure. Drinkable now but should hold.

Barolo "Rocche," 1995 $NA. (SR)   **83**

Dolcetto d'Alba, Tre Vigne 1996 $15.95.   **90**

Bright blackish-purple cast. Medium-bodied. Full acidity. Moderately extracted. Mildly tannic. Black fruits, minerals. Classic and extremely well-made Dolcetto. Fruit centered, aromatic, and quite flavorful with a lush and rounded palate feel buttressed by structural acidity in the finish. Well balanced with fine length.

Antonio Viglione

Arneis, Roero 1998 $NA. (SR)   **82**

Villa Ile

Barbaresco, 1996 $NA. (SR)   **80**

Villa Rosa

Gavi di Gavi, Black Label 1996 $12.99.   **82**

Villa Sparina

Gavi di Gavi, 1996 $15.   **88**

Pale straw hue. Moderately light-bodied. Full acidity. Moderately extracted. Bananas, minerals, citrus. Pleasantly aromatic with delicate and pure flavors. Clean, racy and vibrant, with some spritz. Well balanced and well-made without the bitterness the varietal often acquires.

Villadoria

Barbaresco, 1994 $19.99.   **NR**

Barbera d'Alba, 1995 $12.99.   **NR**

Barolo, Vendemmia 1993 $21.99.   **82**

Barolo, Riserva 1991 $29.99.   **82**

Virna

Barbaresco, 1995 $29.95.   **86**

Deep brickish-ruby hue. Attractive cedar and dried fruit aromas. A rich entry leads to a moderately full-bodied palate with grippy tannins. Flavorful and ripe with pleasant length. Drink now or later.

Nebbiolo d'Alba, 1995 $13.95.   **83**

Gianni Voerzio

Barolo "La Serra," 1995 $NA. (SR)   94

Deep, saturated ruby hue. Extremely intense smoke, mineral, and dried flower aromas show great complexity. A rich entry leads to a ripe, moderately full-bodied palate with great focus and intensity. Powerful and opulent. Should develop beautifully. Mid-term cellar candidate (3–6 years).

Dolcetto d'Alba, Rochettevino 1998 $NA. (SR)   89

Brilliant, saturated purple hue. Attractive red fruit and mineral aromas show a good degree of ripeness. A rich entry leads to a flavorful, medium-bodied palate with a juicy, mouthwatering quality. Well cut and intense. Drink now.

Roberto Voerzio

Chardonnay della Langhe, 1996 $36.   87

Pale golden hue. Medium-bodied. Full acidity. Moderately extracted. Mildly oaked. Yeast, minerals, citrus, dried herbs. Racy, clean, and vibrant in style with a delicate character on the palate. Flavors are subtle but complex. Yeast and oak nuances are well-integrated. Finishes with snap.

Barolo "Cerequio," 1995 $NA. (SR)   90

Brilliant garnet hue. Intense, exotic saddle leather, brown spice, and sweet herb aromas. A rich entry leads to a rich, full-bodied mouthfeel. Quite flavorful and stylish. Rounded, but shows grippy tannins through the finish. Drink now or later.

Zonin

Asti, Spumante NV $13.   84

Yellow-straw hue. Sweet floral and grape and sweet citrus aromas. Medium-bodied, simple, frothy, and mildly sweet, with a good streak of tart acidity. Drink now.

Scale: Superlative (96-100), Exceptional (90-95), Highly Recommended (85-89), Recommended (80-84), Not Recommended (Under 80)

thirty-three

❧

Italy
Tuscany

❧

Tuscany 2000: An Embarrassment of Riches

As the millennium arrives, the beautiful Italian province of Tuscany is producing some of the world's best wines. Buzzing with enthusiasm and riding the winds of change, the region's winemakers have put themselves at the forefront of experimentation and charted a bold new course for Tuscan wine. With a run of good to fantastic vintages (1995–1997) poised for release, the next few years should prove to be their coming out party. Rooted in tradition, yet looking to the future, Tuscany has probably become the world's most dynamic and fluid wine region. How and when did it all happen? The story begins with the region's workhorse, Chianti.

The New Chianti

While Chianti may still conjure images of red checkered tablecloths and straw bottles, the truth is that Chianti has reinvented itself in the last decade. The new Chianti is one of the world's great wines. Made primarily from Sangiovese, Chianti lies somewhere in style between Pinot Noir and Cabernet Sauvignon. It is weightier than Pinot but features excellent acidity and a sort of rustic "Mediterranean" perfume. Chiantis drink well in youth, yet hold well with mid-term aging. Additionally, the wines that are just coming onto the market are great, showing generous and forward characters. Indeed, 1995 and 1997 will prove to be the best vintages in most of Italy since 1990. This is not to belittle the 1994 and 1993 riservas that are still on the market, however, as another advantage of Chianti is that the wines are generally quite pleasant in "lesser" vintages.

The Second Tuscan Renaissance

How did the transformation from straw bottle to great red take place? The Chianti production zone between Florence and Sienna has had a reputation for exceptional wines since the 13th century. For centuries the area has been planted to Sangiovese along with Canaiolo, Trebbiano, Malvasia, and several lesser-known varietals. It was not until 1872, however, that the modern formula for Chianti was devised after decades of experimentation. This recommended that Chianti be based on Sangiovese with the addition of small amounts of Canaiolo to soften the wine. Additionally, if the wine was meant to be drunk young it could be further softened with a dollop of the white grape, Malvasia.

Difficult economic conditions in post-war Italy saw many producers try to stretch these guidelines in order to increase production. Furthermore, as vineyards were replanted in the 1960s and 1970s a different clone of Sangiovese, Sangiovese di Romagna was widely used. This grape was known for producing wine in great quantity, yet the end product was often dilute and undistinguished. The end result was an overall lowering of the quality of the wines between 1965 and 1980, precisely the period in which the United States was enjoying a wine boom and tastes and opinions were being formed. Chianti's reputation had been tarnished in the eyes of many U.S. consumers.

As the decline in quality served to exasperate the difficult economic conditions, important growers began to redress the problems that had beset Chianti. The 1980s saw a tightening of regulations and an emphasis on quality instead of quantity as being the key to the region's comeback. The growers' consortium even sponsored a program, still underway, called Chianti 2000, which aims to figure out which clones of Sangiovese are best for which sites, and what vinification

Scale: Superlative (96-100), Exceptional (90-95), Highly Recommended (85-89), Recommended (80-84), Not Recommended (Under 80)

techniques are most appropriate. It is perhaps the most comprehensive viticultural program for a single wine region that the world has ever seen.

Finally, following the dark days, a number of maverick producers started experimenting with Cabernet, Merlot, and other foreign varietals as well as non-traditional vinification techniques such as new oak barrels. While this circumvented the regulations at the time, it served to reenergize both the producers' and the area's sagging reputations. Things have come full circle, and the experience gained with these "Super-Tuscans" has benefited Chianti as well. Adjustments to the very regulations that these wines were made to circumvent have allowed the addition of Cabernet, Merlot, or even Syrah to the Sangiovese base of Chianti. Though this practice is still somewhat controversial (many fear that some of the resultant wines have lost too much of their typical "Chianti" character) there is no denying that today's Chianti is better than ever before. Meanwhile, the Super Tuscan phenomenon shows no signs of slowing.

Just What Is a Super Tuscan?

Many, but not all Super Tuscan wines originate from the Chianti Classico region. The first Super Tuscan was Sassicaia, although the term was not in use at the time. This wine appeared commercially in 1968, even though the original vineyards were planted as early as 1944. Sassicaia caused a stir as a non-traditional blend of the French grapes Cabernet Sauvignon and Cabernet Franc. It is located outside the Chianti Classico region, equidistant from Sienna and Florence with vineyards on slopes that are only four and a half miles from the sea at their closest point in the Bolgheri region. Thus, it benefits from a true maritime climate that has given it great consistency of quality from vintage to vintage. Many others have followed Sassicaia's lead and Bolgheri has become one of the hottest areas for viticultural investment in all of Italy. Even Piedmont's favorite native son, Angelo Gaja, has gotten into the act with the purchase of his new Pieve di Santa Restituta estate.

Tuscany at a Glance

Wines Reviewed:

384

Producers/Brands Represented:

150

Value Rating:

Average to Good

Inspired by Sassicaia, Piero Antinori and his winemaker created Tignanello in the early seventies. This Cabernet Sauvignon and Sangiovese blend was designed to demonstrate the true potential of inventive combinations that DOCG composition regulations would not permit. The rules were circumvented by labeling it not as a "Chianti," but as Vino da Tavola, or "table wine," even though the pricing was that of a premium wine. This opened the floodgates, and now virtually all major Chianti producers have a Super Tuscan label in their portfolio. The fashion has spread to unblended Cabernet, Merlot, Syrah and even Sangiovese, all of which must bear the Vino da Tavola designation. A significant feature of the production of Super Tuscan wines is aging in small French barriques, a global fashion adopted for most modern premium wines that is now being adopted more frequently for Chianti Classico Riserva bottlings. In this manner and many others, the emergence of Super Tuscan labels has served to greatly increase the quality of Chianti Classico through cross-fertilization of modern techniques to more traditional wines. Additionally, Tuscany can now be looked to for some of the world's most exciting and innovative super-premium wines. There is, however, another Tuscan star that sometimes gets lost in all the hoopla about the Super Tuscan movement, Brunello di Montalcino.

Don't Forget About Brunello

Montalcino, one of Italy's premier wine towns, produces one of Italy's most expensive wines: Brunello di Montalcino. Brunello is famous for its austerity and extraordinary aging potential, but in recent years vinification techniques have lightened up and today's Brunellos are more notable for their rich, ripe, and generally attractive qualities. The Biondi Santi family originally put the region on the map with their consistent efforts dating from 1842, when Brunello was first noted as a distinct subspecies of Sangiovese in the family vineyards in Greppo, southeast of Montalcino. Much of the reputation of these powerful wines is built upon the extraordinary cellaring ability demonstrated by Biondi Santi's wines over the ages.

Vineyards are typically located on reasonably steep slopes ranging up to 1500 feet, giving the Brunello slow ripening conditions essential for its sturdy character. Extended wood aging is an essential part of the wines' character, with three and a half years being obligatory. Some critics have asserted that in weaker vintages this time spent in wood dries out the wine prematurely, reducing its ability to age. Nonetheless, the best producers of Brunello consistently produce some of Italy's finest wines, and Brunello is widely recognized as one of the world's greats. Brunello, however, has an alter ego produced only miles away, Vino Nobile di Montepulciano.

Scale: Superlative (96-100), Exceptional (90-95), Highly Recommended (85-89), Recommended (80-84), Not Recommended (Under 80)

...and Vino Nobile di Montepulciano

The town of Montepulciano in the southeast of Tuscany is host to one of the region's most ancient wines, Vino Nobile di Montepulciano, and was also Italy's first DOC region elevated to DOCG status, in 1983.

In style one might say that the best Vino Nobile is a combination of the grace and finesse of fine Chianti Riservas and the power of Brunello. They are certainly muscular wines that can require patient cellaring. Sangiovese in the guise of Prugnolo Gentile forms the bulk of the typical blend here, and many producers chose to ignore the optional white varieties that traditionally have been used, but are no longer mandated. Softer red blending grapes are used to reduce the toughness of Prugnolo in its youth. Vineyards are mostly planted on gentle southeast facing slopes that become rather steeper around the town itself.

Vino Nobile is shaking off some of the more recent bad press that afflicted it as recently as the early eighties when the wines did not meet universal acclaim. With prices and quality now matching that of the best Chianti Riservas, these wines represent a quality alternative to pricey Brunello.

The Tuscan White: Vernaccia di San Gimignano

Vernaccia di San Gimignano is Tuscany's premier white wine. It comes from the famous and ancient village of San Gimignano whose renaissance towers (one was measured by the height of one's tower, so to speak) were the skyscrapers of their day. The wine is made from a local grape called Vernaccia and tends to be soft and full with pleasant complimentary acidity. Though not as accomplished as Tuscany's reds, Vernaccias are not overly expensive, and will at least offer a measure of respite from another evening of Chardonnay.

Reviews

Vincenzo Abbruzzese
Brunello di Montalcino, Riserva, Madonna del Piano 1993 $NA. (SR)   **94**
Very deep, dark ruby-garnet hue. Roasted game, dried fruit, and chocolate aromas are explosive and exotic. A rich entry leads to a weighty, full-bodied palate with intense sweet fruit flavors. Ripe and glycerous with big grainy tannins. Very powerful. Drink now or later.

Aia della Macina
Morellino di Scansano, Vigneto Roggetone 1997 $35.   **86**
Dark ruby-red hue. Exotic berry and spice aromas. Vibrant, lush berry flavors on the attack, leading a moderately full-bodied palate with zesty acids and exotic herbal nuances. Very fresh and delicious now. Drink now.

Ambra
Carmignano Riserva, 1995 $NA. (SR)   **87**
Bright ruby hue. Generous black fruit, iron, and spice aromas. A firm entry leads a moderately full-bodied palate with drying tannins. Generous and deep though well structured, with a lean acidic cut. Drink now or later.

Antinori

Toscana, Galestro 1997 $8.50.   **80**

Toscana, Villa Bianco 1998 $9.   **82**

Chianti Classico, Villa Antinori Riserva 1996 $19.   **83**

Chianti Classico, Tenute Marchese Antinori Riserva 1994 $33.   **91**

Deep blackish-ruby cast. Moderately full-bodied. Full acidity. Moderately oaked. Mildly tannic. Brown spices, earth, black fruits. Quite firm and tightly wound, with a core of dark flavors and a hefty oak overlay. Rich and well structured on the palate, with a lengthy, lingering finish. Should open further with mid-term aging.

Chianti Classico, Tenute Marchesi Antinori Riserva 1995 $33.   **90**

Deep ruby-garnet hue. Complex, brooding smoky, gamey, olive aromas. A rich entry leads to a moderately full-bodied palate with excellent flavor intensity and a velvety texture. Quite ripe, but balanced by decent acidity. Lengthy finish. Stylish and complex.

Sangiovese, Toscana 1997 $9.   **83**

Bolgheri, Guado al Tasso, Tenuta Belvedere 1994 $51.   **94**

Opaque blackish-ruby cast. Moderately full-bodied. Full acidity. Moderately extracted. Heavily oaked. Mildly tannic. Mint, sweet herbs, chocolate. Outrageously aromatic, with an exotic, spicy, herbal edge. Lighter in style, but extremely well balanced on the palate, with an angular quality. Vibrant acidity enlivens the lengthy, flavorful finish. Excellent grip and intensity.

Bolgheri, Guado al Tasso, Tenuta Belvedere 1995 $52.   **87**

Deep blackish-ruby hue. Exotic dill pickle and mineral aromas rush from the glass, showing a hefty oak accent. A lean entry leads to a firm, moderately full-bodied palate. Finishes with drying tannins. Dominated by its wood at present. May come around, but lighter in style. Drink now or later.

Toscana, Tignanello 1994 $51.   **93**

Deep blackish-ruby cast. Medium-bodied. Balanced acidity. Moderately extracted. Mildly oaked. Mildly tannic. Red fruits, minerals, cedar. Pleasantly aromatic, with real complexity to the range of flavors. Lighter on the palate and rather soft, but well balanced and harmonious, with a very lengthy finish. Drinking beautifully now.

Toscana, Tignanello 1996 $65. (SR)   **97**

Saturated, inky ruby-purple hue. Exquisite perfumes of fresh berries, oriental spice, and minerals are absolutely explosive. A lush entry leads to a firm, full-bodied palate with a wave of intense flavors. Oak certainly plays a role, but only in support of what is a monumental Sangiovese. Finishes for a mile with a lengthy dried fruit and flower quality. Structured with drying tannins. Delicious already, but will develop. Drink now or later.

Toscana, Solaia 1994 $90.   **93**

Opaque blackish-purple hue. Moderately full-bodied. Balanced acidity. Highly extracted. Heavily oaked. Mildly tannic. Vanilla, black fruits, minerals. Quite aromatic, with a big overlay of toasty oak accents and a deep, brooding core of dark flavors. Mouth filling and rich, though well structured, with a lush and flavorful finish. Well balanced, with tannins that bite down on the finish, suggesting that mid-term aging should be handsomely rewarded.

Toscana, Solaia 1995 $90.   **93**

Dark, saturated ruby-purple hue. Extraordinarily exotic lead pencil, tobacco, and mineral aromas share much in common with a top flight Graves. A rich entry leads to an opulent, chewy, full-bodied palate. Explosively flavored with grippy tannins on the finish. Should age beautifully, but this has enough wild and exotic character to drink right now. Drink now or later.

Vin Santo di Toscana, Tenute Marchese Antinori 1993 $29.   **87**

Bright copper cast. Medium-bodied. Balanced acidity. Moderately extracted. Biscuits, orange peel, caramel. Reserved aromatically, with a subtle roasted overtone. Lighter on the palate, with a racy, flavorful finish.

Scale: Superlative (96-100), Exceptional (90-95), Highly Recommended (85-89), Recommended (80-84), Not Recommended (Under 80)

Argiano
Brunello di Montalcino, 1993 $45.   94
Saturated dark ruby-red. Moderately full-bodied. Highly extracted. Heavily oaked. Plenty of oak spice on the nose. Rich palate shows dry, powdery tannins through the finish. Rather restrained on the finish at present. Luxuriously proportioned.

Avignonesi
Chardonnay, Toscana 1998 $28.   81
Pinot Nero, Toscana 1995 $28.   89
Bright ruby-garnet cast. Medium-bodied. Full acidity. Moderately extracted. Heavily oaked. Mildly tannic. Game, cedar, dried herbs. Extremely aromatic, with an oak-driven personality accented by gamey fruit flavors. Lighter in the mouth but still rather full and round, with a well-structured, flavorful finish.
Cabernet di Toscana IGT, Grifi 1995 $45.   87
Deep blackish-ruby hue. Unusual forest and dried fruit aromas. A firm entry leads to a full-bodied palate with a wave of grainy tannins that clamp down on the finish. Quite tough at present, but has lots of stuffing. Long-term cellar.
Vino Nobile di Montepulciano, 1995 $28.   85
Deep ruby-garnet hue. Enticing earth and saddle leather aromas. A rich entry leads to a moderately full-bodied palate with firm tannins. Rich, but highly structured. Closes down on the finish. Could use time. Mid-term cellar candidate (3–6 years).

Badia a Coltibuono
Toscana, Cetamura Bianco 1997 $13.   NR
Chianti Classico, Roberto Stucchi Signature 1997 $21.   NR
Sangiovese di Toscana, Cancelli 1996 $11.   80

Badia a Passignano
Chianti Classico, 1996 $12.50.   83
Chianti Classico, Riserva 1993 $36.   90
Deep blackish-ruby cast. Moderately full-bodied. Balanced acidity. Moderately extracted. Heavily oaked. Mildly tannic. Brown spices, earth, minerals. Quite aromatic, with a hefty oak overlay and a lush, generous palate feel. Firm and weighty in the mouth, with a well-structured finish.
Chianti Classico, Riserva 1995 $36.   89
Bright ruby-garnet hue. Generous brown spice aromas show a marked barrique accent. A lush entry leads to a supple, rounded, medium-bodied palate. Finishes with drying tannins. A richer style with lots of wood. Drink now.

Barone Ricasoli
Chianti Classico, Brolio 1995 $11.99.   86
Blood red. Medium-bodied. Balanced acidity. Moderately extracted. Moderately tannic. Leather, earth, black fruits. Solid, chewy mouthful of dark fruit flavors, with some chunky dry tannins on the finish. Flavorsome and richly textured.
Chianti Classico, Rocca Guicciarda, Riserva 1994 $16.99.   87
Deep blackish-ruby cast. Medium-bodied. Full acidity. Moderately extracted. Mildly oaked. Mildly tannic. Dried herbs, black fruits, spice. Reserved aromatically, with a full and rich palate feel. Well structured, with a lean and austere finish.
Sangiovese, Toscana 1996 $14.   83

Lucia Sanjust Bazzocchi
Toscana, Terre di Galatrona 1996 $38.   81

Beato
Brunello di Montalcino, 1994 $NA. (SR)   86

Deep ruby-garnet hue. Enticing dried fruit and cedar aromas. A lush entry leads to a rounded, medium-bodied palate with grippy tannins and crisp acids. Lighter in style, with lots of wood influence, but tasty. Drink now.

Biondi-Santi
Brunello di Montalcino, 1994 $65.   91

Brilliant orange-garnet hue. Lean mineral aromas show a complex floral overtone. A taut entry leads to a firm, medium-bodied palate with drying tannins. Hard to appreciate at this stage. However, a sample left half emptied for two weeks developed magnificently, with an awakening of exotic aromas and flavors and no sign of a drop off in structure. Seemingly indestructible, if not exactly a wine to cuddle up to. Either decant 48 hours before drinking, or put it in the cellar and leave it to the kids. Long-term cellar.

Rosso di Montalcino, 1995 $30.   90

Brilliant orange-garnet hue. Lean flower, orange rind, and earth aromas. A taut entry leads to a firm, flavorful, medium-bodied palate with grippy tannins. Flavorful and well cut with solid acidity. Well balanced, and a fine foil for food. Drink now or later.

Borgo Salcetino
Chianti Classico, Salcineto 1996 $25.   86

Deep, brilliant ruby hue. Extravagant spicy aromas jump from the glass. A lean entry leads to a moderately light-bodied palate with juicy acidity and buoyant fruitiness. Very zesty finish. A great quaffer. Drink now.

Chianti Classico, Lucarello, Riserva 1996 $40.   87

Brilliant ruby hue. Reserved, mineral, meaty aromas. A lean entry leads to a firm, medium-bodied palate with vibrant acidity. A little restrained at present. Should blossom with time. Drink now or later.

Brolio
Toscana, Vin Santo 1988 $26.   89

Deep orangeish-copper cast. Medium-bodied. Balanced acidity. Moderately extracted. Toffee, caramel, toast. Pleasantly aromatic, with overtones of rancio. Lighter in style, with biscuity flavors and a hint of sweetness in the finish. Fully mature and exotic.

Camigliano
Brunello di Montalcino, 1994 $NA. (SR)   88

Saturated ruby hue with a garnet edge to the rim. Subdued aromas show a modest brown spice quality. A lean entry leads to a firm, full-bodied palate with structured tannins and a brooding core of mineral and berry flavors. Well extracted, but will need lots of time to open. Long-term cellar.

Brunello di Montalcino, Riserva 1993 $NA. (SR)   89

Saturated ruby-red hue. Enticing vanilla and berry aromas belie a modern style with generous oak influence. A lean entry leads to a rich, moderately full-bodied palate with drying tannins. Quite stylish. Drink now or later.

Rosso di Montalcino, 1997 $NA. (SR)   NR

Canalicchio di Sopra
Brunello di Montalcino, 1994 $NA. (SR)   89

Deep, brilliant garnet hue. Subdued black fruit and spice aromas. A lush entry leads to a roasted, medium-bodied palate. Well flavored and supple. A ripe, lush wine. Drinking well. Drink now or later.

Scale: Superlative (96-100), Exceptional (90-95), Highly Recommended (85-89), Recommended (80-84), Not Recommended (Under 80)

Brunello di Montalcino, 1993 $45.   88

Deep garnet red. Moderately full-bodied. Highly extracted. Moderately oaked.
Moderately tannic. Leathery, rich aromas. The palate shows a broad array of earth
and black fruit flavors, with chewy tannins coating the mouth. Substantial, with a
lovely mouthfeel.

Cantina di Montalcino

Brunello di Montalcino, 1994 $NA. (SR)   90

Dark, saturated ruby hue with a garnet edge. Brooding oriental spice and licorice
aromas. A rich entry leads to a moderately full-bodied palate with rounded tannins.
Very generous and firm. Drink now or later.

Brunello di Montalcino, 1993 $45.   83
Chianti, 1997 $8.99.   83
Chianti, Riserva $18.99.   87

Deep ruby hue. Brooding minerally aromas show an herbal undertone. A lean entry
leads a medium-bodied palate with crisp acids. Flavorful, fruit-centered finish. Drink now.

Rosso di Montalcino, 1997 $NA. (SR)   80
Toscana, Poggio del Sasso 1996 $9.99.   83
Toscana, Villa di Corsano 1996 $12.50.   87

Deep, saturated blackish-ruby hue. Generous black fruit and vanilla aromas are quite
modern. A rich entry leads a moderately full-bodied palate with lush, velvety tannins.
Ripe and rounded with a supple finish. Quite stylish. Drink now.

Cantina Vini Tipici dell'Aretino

Bianco Toscano, Arezio 1997 $7.   80
Chianti Colli Aretini, Vasari 1997 $10.   85

Deep ruby hue. Intense, attractive berry and mineral aromas. A lush entry leads to a
medium-bodied palate with angular acidity. Well balanced and flavorful. Drink now.

Rosso Toscano, Arezio 1997 $7.   NR

Capanna

Brunello di Montalcino, Fattoi 1994 $NA. (SR)   91

Deep, saturated garnet hue. Forward, earthy, leathery aromas. A firm entry leads to
a lush, moderately full-bodied palate. Quite rich, with good intensity of flavor and big,
rounded tannins. Drink now or later.

Brunello di Montalcino, Fattoi 1993 $45.   92

Deep, saturated ruby-garnet hue. Intense brown spice and smoke aromas show gamey,
foresty overtones. A lean entry leads to a forceful, moderately full-bodied palate. Quite
flavorful, with a drying, grippy finish. Needs rich foods. Drink now or later.

Rosso di Montalcino, Fattoi 1997 $23.   90

Brilliant ruby hue. Reserved berryish aromas show an earthy, exotically gamey character.
Very ripe in the mouth, with jammy fruit flavors. Medium-bodied with acidity making for
a buoyant finish. Drink now.

Caparzo

Chardonnay-Trebbiano, Toscana 1995 $9.   80
Brunello di Montalcino, 1994 $NA. (SR)   87

Deep, saturated ruby-garnet hue. Shows distinctive, earthy, leathery aromas. A lean entry
leads to a rich, moderately full-bodied palate with rounded flavors. Supported by angular
tannins, but somewhat softer in style. Herb-tinged throughout. Drink now or later.

Brunello di Montalcino, La Casa 1994 $NA. (SR)   **93**

Deep, saturated ruby-garnet hue. Enticing, exotic brown spice, fresh berry, and leather aromas jump from the glass. A rich entry leads to a firm, moderately full-bodied palate with angular tannins and an enlivening acidic cut. Quite intense. Should develop with time. Mid-term cellar candidate (3–6 years).

Brunello di Montalcino, 1993 $49.99.   **91**

Full blood red. Medium-bodied. Balanced acidity. Moderately extracted. Mildly oaked. Minerals, red fruits, brown spice. Intense, minerally, with concentrated red fruit flavors that give a classy sense of austerity. Solid grip, though a lighter style that is very approachable now.

Brunello di Montalcino, Riserva 1993 $NA. (SR)   **94**

Deep saturated ruby hue. Generous wood spice and berry aromas jump from the glass. A lush entry leads to a weighty, full-bodied palate with chunky tannins. Powerful and still quite youthful. Should develop beautifully with time. Mid-term cellar candidate (3–6 years).

Rosso di Montalcino, 1997 $NA. (SR)   **88**

Brilliant cherry-garnet hue. Attractive red-cherry and mineral aromas carry a pleasant spicy accent. A rich entry leads to a supple, moderately full-bodied palate with fine cut and intensity. Well balanced and lean finish. Drink now or later.

Rosso di Montalcino, Vigna La Caduta 1996 $NA. (SR)   **85**

Bright ruby hue with a slight fade. Attractive mineral and bitter cherry aromas. A lean entry leads to a firm, medium-bodied palate with angular tannins. Ripe, but taut and well structured. Drink now or later.

Capezzana

Sangiovese, Toscana 1994 $9.   **82**

Toscana, Conti Contini Bonacossi, Ghiaie Della Furba 1995 $48.   **97**

Deep blackish-garnet cast. Moderately full-bodied. Balanced acidity. Moderately extracted. Moderately oaked. Mildly tannic. Cedar, dried herbs, black fruits. Quite aromatic, with a complex melange of flavors well beyond its relative youth. Ripe and supple in the mouth, showing great similarities to a top-class St. Emilion. Quite lengthy, with excellent grip to the finish.

Federico Carletti

Vino Nobile di Montepulciano, 1995 $20.99.   **89**

Deep ruby-red. Moderately full-bodied. Moderately extracted. Moderately tannic. Red cherries, vanilla. Rich, fruit-centered aromas. Starts with a fruity splash, turning dry and angular on the palate, with solid tannins through the finish. Youthful and very structured.

Carobbio

Chianti Classico, Riserva 1993 $31.99.   **93**

Deep blackish-ruby cast. Full acidity. Moderately extracted. Moderately oaked. Mildly tannic. Vanilla, black fruits. Quite aromatic, with a hefty overlay of oak and a solid core of wild, fruit-centered flavors. Deep and quite intense on the palate, with a firm structure and an angular, minerally finish.

Carpineto

Brunello di Montelcino, 1993 $42.99.   **86**

Bright cherry red. Medium-bodied. Full acidity. Moderately extracted. Moderately oaked. Mildly tannic. Perfumed aromas. Exotically aromatic nose. Supple, juicy, and almost open-knit palate, with very soft tannins through the finish. Drinking nicely now.

Chianti Classico, 1996 $15.99. 91

Ruby with a slight purple cast. Medium-bodied. Balanced acidity. Moderately extracted. Mildly oaked. Violets, red cherries. Ripe and fleshy, with a generous red fruit center. Soft, supple tannins on the finish with a touch of vanilla oak. Classy winemaking; lots of Sangiovese character.

Chianti Classico, Riserva 1994 $19.99. 90

Bright blackish-purple cast. Moderately full-bodied. Full acidity. Moderately extracted. Mildly oaked. Mildly tannic. Black fruits, brown spices. Still quite youthful, with a tightly wound, focused character. Attractive oak accents meet a ripe core of fruit flavors on a well-structured and firm palate. Well balanced and intense, this needs a few years.

Casaloste

Chianti Classico, 1995 $25. 84

Bright brickish-garnet hue. Pleasant, leathery, spicy aromas. A taut entry leads to a moderately light-bodied palate. Fades toward the finish. A well-flavored, softer style. Drink now.

Chianti Classico, Riserva 1994 $40. 90

Brilliant garnet hue. Enticing tobacco and brown spice aromas. A rich entry leads to a supple, rounded, moderately full-bodied palate. Quite ripe, with an inherent sweetness to the fruit. Very stylish. Drinking nicely now.

Casanova di Neri

Brunello di Montalcino, 1994 $NA. (SR) 88

Deep ruby-garnet hue. Attractive roasted game and spice aromas. A lush entry leads to a rounded, medium-bodied palate with soft tannins. Generous and supple. Drink now or later.

Brunello di Montalcino, Tenuta Nuova 1993 $52. 91

Saturated blood red. Moderately full-bodied. Highly extracted. Moderately oaked. Moderately tannic. Brown spice, black fruits, earth. Angular, spicy aromas lead a dry, flavorsome, rich palate with vibrant character and firm tannins. Plenty of stuffing, though this will be better with more bottle age.

Rosso di Montalcino, 1995 $16. 81

Rosso di Montalcino, 1996 $16. 88

Dark red-purple. Medium-bodied. Moderately extracted. Mildly tannic. Briar fruits, licorice. Aromatic dark berry aromas. Inky, textured palate with succulent dark fruit flavors that persist through the finish.

Casisano-Colombaio

Brunello di Montalcino, Vigneto dei Cottimelli 1994 $NA. (SR) 86

Brilliant orange-garnet hue. Forward, mature cedar and dried flower aromas. A soft entry leads to a moderately light-bodied palate with sweet fruit flavors and lush tannins. Lighter, but attractively flavored. Drink now.

Rosso di Montalcino, 1997 $NA. (SR) 80

Castelgiocondo

Brunello di Montalcino, 1993 $47. 83

Castelli del Grevepesa

Chianti Classico, Clemente VIII 1997 $13. 85

Brilliant brickish-garnet hue. Reserved mineral and leather aromas. A rich entry leads to a supple, rounded, medium-bodied palate with velvety tannins. Quite ripe, but shows nice grip to the finish. Drink now.

Chianti Classico, Castello di Bibbione 1995 $20.   87

Brilliant brickish-garnet hue. Generous saddle leather and red fruit aromas. A ripe
entry leads to a lush, medium-bodied palate with mildly astringent tannins. Lighter,
but showing some complexity. Drink now.

Chianti Classico, Vigna Elisa 1995 $20.   86

Brilliant garnet hue. Reserved, dusty cherry and vanilla aromas show a sense of
refinement. A firm entry leads to a medium-bodied palate with grippy tannins and
solid flavor intensity. Sturdy. Drink now or later.

Toscana, Gualdo al Luco 1994 $36.   94

Opaque blackish-ruby hue. Moderately full-bodied. Balanced acidity. Highly extracted.
Moderately oaked. Moderately tannic. Brown spices, minerals, cassis. Shows plenty of
oak accents on the nose, and a core of lean minerally flavors. Taut and firmly structured
through the finish.

Toscano, Gualdo al Luco 1995 $38.   90

Very deep blackish-ruby hue. Perfumed sweet vanilla and black fruit aromas. A ripe entry
leads to a moderately full-bodied palate with grippy tannins. Chocolatey and full with
solid flavor intensity. Lots of wood. Drink now or later.

Toscano, Coltifredi 1995 $38.   84

Brilliant ruby-garnet hue. Attractive sandalwood and brown spice aromas show a
generous oak accent. A lean entry leads to a medium-bodied palate with grainy tannins.
Lighter in style, but flavorful. Drink now.

Castello Banfi

Pinot Grigio-Chardonnay, Toscana 1997 $9.   NR

Pinot Grigio, Toscana 1997 $13.   86

Bright yellow-gold. Medium-bodied. Balanced acidity. Moderately extracted. Mildly
oaked. Citrus zest, vanilla. Well balanced, with a touch of oak evident in the nose and
the finish.

Chardonnay, Sant'Antimo 1996 $18.   82

Brunello di Montalcino, 1993 $38.   86

Deep blood red. Medium-bodied. Balanced acidity. Moderately extracted. Dried red
fruits, minerals. Austere, dusty aromas follow through as expected on the palate. Taut
and well structured, with an impression of lush dried berry fruits and softly extracted tannins. A modern style.

Brunello di Montalcino, 1994 $38.   90

Deep, saturated ruby-garnet hue. Attractive brown spice and mineral aromas. A firm
entry leads to a moderately full-bodied palate with grippy tannins. Rich and stylish in
a modern leaning fashion. Should develop. Drink now or later.

Brunello di Montalcino, Poggio all'Oro Riserva 1993 $125.   97

Deep, saturated ruby-garnet hue. Powerful chocolate, dried fruit, and leather aromas
show great complexity. A rich entry leads to a weighty, full-bodied palate with great
intensity of fruit. Shows amazing persistence and length. Chunky tannins envelop the
finish. Delicious now, but better in time. Mid-term cellar candidate (3–6 years).

Rosso di Montalcino, 1995 $21.   88

Deep ruby-red. Medium-bodied. Moderately extracted. Mildly tannic. Vanilla, red berry
fruits, dried herbs. Generous fruit-accented aromas lead a lively, vibrant, berry-centered
palate with an herbal note and a taut finish. Supple, ripe flavors.

Rosso di Montalcino, 1997 $NA. (SR)   91

Saturated, modern ruby-purple hue. Opulent vanilla and red fruit aromas jump from
the glass. A rich entry leads to a moderately full-bodied palate with ripe, plummy flavors.
Quite generous, but supported by firm tannins on the finish. Drink now or later.

Sangiovese-Cabernet, Toscana 1996 $9.   NR

Scale: Superlative (96-100), Exceptional (90-95), Highly Recommended (85-89),
Recommended (80-84), Not Recommended (Under 80)

Cabernet Sauvignon, Montalcino 1994 $25.　　　　　　89

Deep blackish-garnet cast. Moderately full-bodied. Balanced acidity. Moderately extracted. Mildly oaked. Mildly tannic. Minerals, cassis. Rather reserved aromatically, though featuring a solid core of fruit-centered flavors on the palate. Lean and firmly structured through the finish.

Cabernet Sauvignon, Toscana IGT 1995 $33.　　　　　88

Deep, saturated ruby-garnet hue. Generous game, spice, and dried fruit aromas. A rich entry leads to a supple, moderately full-bodied palate. Shows fine intensity of flavor with grippy tannins through the finish. Drink now or later.

Merlot, Toscana 1995 $33.　　　　　　　　　　　85

Deep blackish-garnet hue. Generous smoke, mineral, and brown spice aromas. A rich entry leads to a lush, medium-bodied palate. On the fat side, with a rounded finish. Drink now.

Pinot Noir, Sant'Antimo 1996 $33.　　　　　　　　80

Syrah, Sant'Antimo 1996 $33.　　　　　　　　　　89

Deep, saturated blackish-ruby hue. Powerful brown spice and sandalwood aromas show a hefty oak accent. A lean entry leads to a lush, medium-bodied palate with supple tannins. Tasty, but largely wood-driven. Drink now or later.

Montalcino, Summus 1994 $40.　　　　　　　　　　91

Deep blackish-garnet cast. Moderately full-bodied. Balanced acidity. Moderately extracted. Moderately oaked. Mildly tannic. Cedar, cassis, minerals. Pleasantly aromatic, with a flavorful mouthfeel. Soft on the entry, with some mild astringency through the lengthy finish.

Toscana, Summus 1995 $47.　　　　　　　　　　　90

Deep brilliant ruby hue. Reserved mineral and black fruit aromas. A rich entry leads to a supple, moderately full-bodied palate with velvety tannins. Rather shy at present, but well balanced with lots of stuffing. Should open with time. Mid-term cellar (3–6 years).

Toscana, Excelsus 1995 $50.　　　　　　　　　　　92

Deep, saturated blackish-ruby hue. Enticing leather, black fruit, and chocolate aromas. A rich entry leads to a chewy, full-bodied palate. Round and supple through the finish. Has lots of density, but rather closed. Needs time. Mid-term cellar candidate (3–6 years).

Castello dei Rampolla

Toscana, Sammarco 1994 $65.　　　　　　　　　　91

Opaque blackish-ruby cast. Full-bodied. Balanced acidity. Highly extracted. Moderately oaked. Moderately tannic. Cassis, earth, lead pencil. Quite aromatic, with complex, brooding flavors on the palate. Rich and very deep, with a real sense of weight. Finishes with a big wave of tannins that bite into the finish; well balanced nonetheless. This may reward long-term aging, but is rather tough at present.

Castello di Brolio

Chianti Classico, Riserva 1994 $17.　　　　　　　　86

Deep blackish-ruby hue. Medium-bodied. Full acidity. Moderately extracted. Moderately oaked. Mildly tannic. Vanilla, black fruits, minerals. Aromatic, with a generous, oak-accented palate. Lighter in the mouth, with a flavorful character and zesty acidity through the finish.

Toscana, Casalferro 1995 $27.　　　　　　　　　　89

Opaque blackish-ruby hue. Moderately full-bodied. Balanced acidity. Moderately extracted. Moderately oaked. Mildly tannic. Cedar, cassis, minerals. Quite aromatic, with a decided oak accent and ripe, fruit-centered flavors. Supple, round, and rich through the lengthy finish. Well balanced and intense.

Castello di Farnetella

Sauvignon Blanc, Toscana 1996 $20.   88

Pale straw. Medium-bodied. Balanced acidity. Moderately extracted. Grass, green apple. Expressive aromas. Juicy, fresh flavors. Shows some Sauvignon Blanc varietal character.

Chianti Colli Senesi, 1995 $12.   88

Bright ruby-red. Medium-bodied. Balanced acidity. Moderately extracted. Mildly tannic. Red berries. Generous fruity aromas follow through well on the palate, with a gamey hint. Soft tannins provide some grip on the finish. Well balanced.

Castello di Gabbiano

Chianti, 1996 $9.   81

Chianti Classico, Titolato Gabbiano 1995 $11.   86

Garnet red. Medium-bodied. Balanced acidity. Moderately extracted. Mildly tannic. Leather, earth, red fruits. Mature, spicy, earthy aromas. Flavorful, soft palate has clean acids and a fine layer of dusty tannins on the finish. Rustic but tasty.

Chianti Classico, Riserva 1994 $15.   84

Deep garnet cast. Medium-bodied. Full acidity. Moderately extracted. Mildly oaked. Mildly tannic. Spice, minerals, dried herbs. Reserved aromatically, but shows an earthy core of flavors on the lean and focused palate. Austere through the finish. A solid table wine.

Chianti Classico, Riserva, Gold Label 1993 $24.   83

Toscana, Per Ania 1993 $38.   90

Deep blackish-ruby hue. Subdued, rich spice and black fruit aromas. A firm entry leads a big, supple, moderately full-bodied palate. Harmonious and well extracted with fine grip. Accessible, but should develop. Drink now or later.

Castello di Nipozzano

Chianti Rufina, Riserva 1994 $20.   89

Bright blackish-garnet cast. Medium-bodied. Full acidity. Moderately extracted. Moderately oaked. Mildly tannic. Brown spices, red fruits, dried herbs. Quite aromatic, with pleasant wood overtones that meet a core of complex flavors. Well structured and lean in the mouth, with excellent grip and a lengthy finish.

Castello di Querceto

Chianti, 1997 $7.99.   82

Chianti Classico, 1996 $10.99.   86

Bright garnet hue. Attractive spicy aromas have a pipe tobacco-like accent. A firm entry leads to a lean, medium-bodied palate. Well flavored with a drying finish. Drink now.

Chianti Classico, Riserva 1995 $16.99.   85

Brilliant deep ruby-garnet hue. Attractive spice and licorice aromas jump from the glass. A lush entry leads to a medium-bodied palate with a firm acidic edge. Lighter in style with a juicy finish. Drink now.

Chianti Classico, Riserva, Il Picchio 1993 $26.99.   84

Deep brickish-ruby hue. Subdued mineral aromas have mature overtones. A firm entry leads to a medium-bodied palate with edgy acidity. Tannins bite down on the finish. Drink up.

Toscana, La Corte 1993 $26.99.   86

Deep blackish-garnet cast. Medium-bodied. Full acidity. Moderately extracted. Mildly oaked. Mildly tannic. Dried herbs, minerals, red fruits. Reined in aromatically, with a firm and unyielding palate feel. Softer in style on the entry, with solid grip to the finish. A trifle mean.

Toscana, Il Quericolaia 1991 $32.99.   **86**

Deep blackish-garnet cast. Moderately full-bodied. Full acidity. Moderately extracted. Mildly oaked. Mildly tannic. Earth, black fruits, spice. Pleasantly aromatic, with hints of maturity to the flavors throughout. Firmly structured and intense, with sound grip and a lengthy finish.

Castello di Verrazzano

Chianti Classico, 1996 $18.   **87**

Saturated blood red. Medium-bodied. Balanced acidity. Moderately extracted. Mildly tannic. Black cherries, minerals. Full, ripe, complex aromas. A fleshy, rounded, expressive core of black fruit flavors that expand through the midpalate, and linger through the long, long finish. Very hedonistic.

Toscana, Sassello 1995 $50.   **84**

Bright blackish-ruby cast. Medium-bodied. Balanced acidity. Moderatcly extracted. Mildly tannic. Red fruits, earth. Quite aromatic, with a slightly left-of-center flavor profile. Surprisingly light on the palate, with a forward berryish quality and a high-toned, angular finish.

Castello di Volpaia

Toscana, Bianco Val d'Arbia 1997 $11.99.   **86**

Pale straw hue. Intense, heavily smoked, herb-tinged aromas. A crisp entry leads to a lush rounded palate, with an oily, ripe texture. Rich, but clean. Drink now.

Chianti Classico, 1996 $17.99.   **85**

Deep garnet hue. Attractive smoke, tobacco, and leather aromas. A lush entry leads to a ripe, medium-bodied palate that show a degree of richness. Rounded, with good grip to the finish. Drink now.

Chianti Classico, Riserva 1995 $24.99.   **89**

Deep, saturated ruby-garnet hue. Extravagant brown spice, leather, and dried fruit aromas. A rich entry leads to a moderately full-bodied palate with firm grippy tannins. A solid, weighty style. Should develop. Mid-term cellar candidate (3–6 years).

Toscana, Coltassala 1994 $35.99.   **88**

Bright blackish-ruby cast. Moderately full-bodied. Full acidity. Moderately extracted. Mildly oaked. Mildly tannic. Minerals, red fruits, licorice. Quite aromatic, with a lighter-styled, well-balanced palate feel. Lean and crisp through the finish, with solid acidity providing a juicy quality.

Toscana, Balifico 1993 $31.49.   **90**

Deep blackish-garnet cast. Moderately full-bodied. Full acidity. Moderately extracted. Moderately oaked. Mildly tannic. Red fruits, cassis, lead pencil. Pleasantly aromatic, with a well-structured, fruit-centered core of flavors and a well-integrated oak accent. Lean and taut in the mouth, with a lengthy finish.

Toscana, Balifico 1994 $37.99.   **92**

Deep, saturated ruby-garnet hue. Attractive saddle leather, spice, and chocolate aromas jump from the glass. A rich entry leads to a supple, moderately full-bodied palate with a lush, velvety mouthfeel. Seductive and lengthy. Drink now or later.

Castello La Leccia

Chianti Classico, 1997 $16.   **88**

Dark ruby-garnet hue. Intense brown spice, licorice, and red fruit aromas. A rich entry leads to a rounded, supple, medium-bodied palate. Grippy tannins structure the finish. Ripe and flavorful. Drink now.

Chianti Classico, Riserva 1995 $30.   **92**

Deep ruby-garnet hue. Perfumed berryish aromas feature an attractive vanilla accent. A firm entry leads to a medium-bodied palate with great intensity of flavor. Stylish and elegant with a lengthy finish. Drink now or later.

Toscana, Bruciagna 1996 $35.   93

Deep ruby-garnet hue. Extravagant chocolate and brown spice aromas point to a heavy barrique influence. A lush entry leads to a big, ripe, full-bodied palate with chunky tannins. Intense and youthful with great depth. Flavorful finish. Should develop with further age. Drink now or later.

Cecchi

Chianti Classico, 1996 $12.   84

Pale ruby-red. Moderately light-bodied. Balanced acidity. Subtly extracted. Juicy red fruit flavors follow through a crisp, clean finish with a mineral accent.

Chianti Classico, Messer Pietro di Teuzzo Riserva 1993 $27.   88

Brilliant garnet hue. Mature, mushroom, earthy aromas. A lush entry leads to a rounded, medium-bodied palate. Shows lots of tertiary complexity. Grippy finish. A fine effort in a difficult vintage. Drink now.

Morellino di Scansano, Valle delle Rose Estate 1997 $15.   86

Deep, saturated ruby hue. Intense, high-toned mineral and red fruit aromas have an attractive oak accent. A lean entry leads to a ripe, medium-bodied palate with classic dusty cherry flavors. Angular finish. Crisp. Drink now.

Morellino di Scansano, Vale delle Rose Estate Riserva 1996 $20.   82

Sangiovese, Toscana 1996 $9.   81

Toscana, Spargolo 1993 $38.   84

Bright blackish-garnet hue. Moderately full-bodied. Balanced acidity. Highly extracted. Heavily oaked. Moderately tannic. Cedar, pine, minerals. Extremely aromatic, with a wood-dominated flavor profile. Firm and highly structured with some astringency to the finish. Rather tough at present, but quite stylish with great length.

Toscana, Spargolo 1995 $38.   89

Bright ruby-purple cast. Moderately full-bodied. Full acidity. Moderately extracted. Heavily oaked. Mildly tannic. Vanilla, briar fruits. Extremely aromatic and modern in style, with a big overlay of sweet oak flavors and a forward, berry fruit quality on the palate. Flavorful throughout, with a lighter-styled, well balanced mouthfeel. Bright, intense, lengthy finish. Not overwhelmingly deep, just hedonistically tasty.

Vino Nobile di Montepulciano, 1995 $15.   83

Luigi Cecchi

Chianti Classico, Villa Cerna, Riserva 1993 $17.   92

Bright pale red. Medium-bodied. Balanced acidity. Moderately extracted. Heavily oaked. Oak-accented aromas follow through on a toasty, juicy, red fruit palate with a lingering smoky, spicy finish. Quite exotic.

Cennatoio

Chardonnay, Toscana 1996 $26.   83

Chianti Classico, 1996 $22.   90

Bright ruby-purple. Medium-bodied. Highly extracted. Moderately oaked. Black cherries, vanilla, mushrooms. Classy, expensive, toasted-oak aromas. Bright red fruit flavors have an overlay of oak dryness that lingers through the finish.

Chianti Classico, 1997 $22.   88

Brilliant garnet hue. Attractive spice and leather aromas jump from the glass. A ripe entry leads a lush, medium-bodied palate with supple tannins. Rounded, soft, and flavorful. Drink now.

Scale: Superlative (96-100), Exceptional (90-95), Highly Recommended (85-89), Recommended (80-84), Not Recommended (Under 80)

Chianti Classico, Riserva 1996 $35. 91

Deep ruby-garnet hue. Generous, elegant brown spice aromas. A rich entry leads a moderately full-bodied palate with juicy, vibrant acidity. Classic Sangiovese dusty cherry fruit emerges on the palate and rushes through the finish. Well balanced, with excellent grip and length. Drink now.

Chianti Classico, Riserva, O'Leandro 1995 $48. 94

Deep blackish-purple cast. Moderately full-bodied. Full acidity. Moderately extracted. Moderately oaked. Mildly tannic. Vanilla, red fruits, minerals. Quite aromatic, with a hefty overlay of oak seasoning and a core of ripe flavors. Well balanced in the mouth, with a harmonious quality and a lean, intense, flavorful finish. Should gain in complexity with mid-term aging...similar to a well-made young super Tuscan.

Sangiovese, Toscana 1996 $19. 86

Ruby purple. Medium-bodied. Balanced acidity. Moderately extracted. Black cherries, licorice. Full, rich mouthfeel turns quite dry on the finish. A solid, somewhat inky wine showing some tannic structure at present.

Sangiovese Toscana, E, All'Omo il Vino 1997 $20. 87

Brilliant ruby-garnet hue. Attractive, mineral, leathery aromas. A firm entry leads to a moderately full-bodied palate with drying, grippy tannins. Rather closed at present, but well stuffed. Needs time. Mid-term cellar candidate (3–6 years).

Cabernet Sauvignon, Toscana 1995 $55. 96

Deep blackish-ruby cast. Moderately full-bodied. Balanced acidity. Moderately extracted. Moderately oaked. Mildly tannic. Cassis, minerals, brown spices. Aromatic and extremely flavorful, with a hedonic edge to the fruit-driven flavors. Rich, ripe, and intense, with supple tannins through the finish. A very modern style.

Toscana, Mammolo 1994 $55. 93

Deep blackish-ruby hue. Moderately full-bodied. Balanced acidity. Moderately extracted. Heavily oaked. Mildly tannic. Pickle barrel, cassis, black fruits. Quite aromatic, with a hefty overlay of oak seasoning and a sturdy core of ripe fruit flavors. Supple and richly flavored in the mouth, with a lean and intense finish.

Toscana, Mammolo 1995 $60. 84

Deep, saturated ruby-garnet hue. Intense aromas have a marked herbal accent. A lean entry leads to a firm, medium-bodied palate. Lighter through the finish. Not overly deep. Drink now.

Sangiovese Toscana, Etrusco 1995 $60. 89

Saturated red-purple. Medium-bodied. Balanced acidity. Highly extracted. Moderately oaked. Vanilla, oak spice, red fruits. Dense oak-accented aromas. A solid, tightly wound palate shows impressive flavor concentration and a dry finish. Structured enough to improve with some cellar age.

Sangiovese Toscana, Etrusco 1996 $60. 93

Inky blackish-ruby hue. Extravagant brown spice and black fruit aromas belie barrique maturation. A supple entry leads to a rich, rounded, moderately full-bodied palate. Full and ripe, but buoyed by solid acidity. Has a wonderfully harmonious mouthfeel. Drink now or later.

Toscana, Arcibaldo 1995 $60. 97

Deep blackish-ruby cast. Moderately full-bodied. Balanced acidity. Moderately extracted. Heavily oaked. Mildly tannic. Cedar, lead pencil, black fruits. Extremely aromatic, with a hefty dose of oak seasoning and a ripe core of fruit flavors. Supple, rich, and flavorful on the palate, with mild tannins and a lengthy finish. A very New World style.

Toscana, Arcibaldo 1996 $60. 94

Inky blackish-ruby hue. Powerful spice and vanilla aromas show a lash of new oak. A rich entry leads a supple, full-bodied palate with great depth of flavor. Chewy and lush with great density. Compelling and tasty now, but balanced to develop over the long haul. Drink now or later.

Vin Santo del Chianti Classico, Occhio di Pernice,
Rosso di Caratello 1991 $30/375 ml.   88

Deep brilliant amber hue. Intense salted pecan and Sherried, honeyed aromas jump from the glass. A rich entry leads to a medium-bodied palate with just a hint of sweetness. Subdued, nutty, biscuity finish. Doesn't quite follow through. Drink now.

Vin Santo del Chianti Classico, Uvae 1991 $30/375 ml.   80

Centolani

Rosso di Montalcino, Tenuta Friggiali 1997 $NA. (SR)   83

Cerbaiona

Brunello di Montalcino, 1994 $NA. (SR)   84

Saturated blackish-garnet hue. Exotic brown spice and leather aromas. A rich entry leads to a powerful, moderately full-bodied palate with sweet fruit flavors, big tannins, and pronounced acidity. Lots of stuffing, but needs time. A little left of center. Mid-term cellar candidate (3–6 years).

Giovanni Ciacci

Brunello di Montalcino, Campo della Spinaia 1993 $36.99.   84

Blood red. Moderately full-bodied. Balanced acidity. Highly extracted. Moderately tannic. Black berry fruits, sweaty leather, minerals. Old leathery aromas follow through on the palate. Bright and vibrant, with decent structure and length through the finish. Rather muted.

Rosso di Montalcino, Campo della Spinaia 1996 $18.   89

Saturated red-purple. Medium-bodied. Moderately extracted. Mildly tannic. Violets, red fruits. Floral, high-toned aromas lead a bright, fruity palate showing no great depth. Very modern, early-drinking style. Quite stylish.

Ciacci Piccolomini d'Aragona

Brunello di Montalcino, Vigna di Pianrosso 1994 $NA. (SR)   83
Rosso di Montalcino, Vigna della Fonte 1997 $NA. (SR)   81
IGT Toscana, Ateo 1996 $NA. (SR)   93

Saturated ruby-garnet hue. Generous black fruit and violet aromas. A smooth entry leads a crisp, moderately full-bodied palate with lush, velvety tannins. Extraordinarily floral with a rich yet juicy character. Very complex and highly drinkable. Drink now or later.

Col d'Orcia

Brunello di Montalcino, 1993 $35.   91

Deep, saturated garnet hue. Exotic, sweet fruit cake and Christmas spice aromas jump from the glass. A robust, rounded entry leads to a supple, full-bodied palate. Big, but not tough, yet shows real density of flavor. This could be drunk now, but it should develop further with cellaring. Drink now or later.

Brunello di Montalcino, 1994 $NA. (SR)   89

Deep, saturated ruby-garnet hue. Complex dried flower, mineral, and leather aromas. A lush entry leads to a medium-bodied palate with rounded tannins and generous flavors. Shows fine intensity through the finish. Fairly approachable. Drink now or later.

Brunello di Montalcino, Riserva, Poggio al Vento 1993 $NA. (SR)   88

Deep, saturated blackish-garnet hue. Opulent game and chocolate aromas. A rich entry leads to a full-bodied palate that closes down with a rush of chunky, aggressive tannins. Certainly needs time, but will probably always be tough despite the formidable levels of extract. Long-term cellar.

Scale: Superlative (96-100), Exceptional (90-95), Highly Recommended (85-89), Recommended (80-84), Not Recommended (Under 80)

Rosso di Montalcino, 1997 $NA. (SR)   **87**

Bright saturated ruby hue. Attractive black fruit and fresh berry aromas jump from the glass. A rich entry leads to a moderately full-bodied palate with good richness and lean, grippy tannins. Quite approachable, harmonious, and flavorful. Drink now or later.

Colle dei Bardellini

Pigato Riviera Ligure di Ponente, Bianco 1997 $19.   **80**

Colle Santa Mustiola

Sangiovese Toscana, Poggio ai Chiari 1994 $25.   **85**

Deep, saturated ruby hue. Generous vanilla and black fruit aromas show a modest oak accent. A rich entry leads to a firm, medium-bodied palate with velvety tannins. Shows some substance with a chunky finish. Drink now.

Collemattoni

Brunello di Montalcino, 1994 $NA. (SR)   **NR**

Collosorbo

Brunello di Montalcino, 1994 $NA. (SR)   **81**

Rosso di Montalcino, 1997 $NA. (SR)   **88**

Brilliant ruby-garnet hue. Attractive, spicy leather and red fruit aromas. A lush entry leads to a supple, medium-bodied palate with lean tannins. Rich, stylish, and flavorful with an angular finish. Drink now or later.

Donatella Cinelli Colombini

Brunello di Montalcino, 1994 $NA. (SR)   **85**

Brilliant ruby-garnet hue. Lean herb, berry, and mineral aromas. A firm entry leads to a medium-bodied palate with grippy tannins. Lighter in style. Fades a bit at the finish, but well balanced. Drink now.

Brunello di Montalcino, Prime Donne 1994 $NA. (SR)   **89**

Deep, saturated modern ruby hue. Attractive brown spice and vanilla aromas accent a lush core of berry flavors. A rich entry leads to a ripe, medium-bodied palate with juicy acidity and rounded tannins. Somewhat lighter in style, but very tasty. Drink now or later.

Corte Pavone

Brunello di Montalcino, 1994 $NA. (SR)   **91**

Deep, saturated ruby-garnet hue. Toasty brown spice aromas jump from the glass suggesting generous wood influences. A lean entry leads to a medium-bodied palate with bright acidity. Shows great cut and intensity of flavor while striking a balance between wood and fruit notes. Stylish. Drink now or later.

Crocedimezzo di Vannoni Fiorella

Brunello di Montalcino, 1994 $NA. (SR)   **83**

Rosso di Montalcino, 1997 $NA. (SR)   **86**

Deep, saturated ruby-garnet hue. Attractive spice and red fruit aromas. A ripe, rounded entry leads to a moderately full-bodied palate with supple tannins and good bite. Well balanced and harmonious, with pronounced acidity. Drink now or later.

Dattilo di Roberto Cerando

Lipuda IGT, Amineo Rosso 1997 $22.95.   **80**

Dei

Rosso di Montepulciano, 1997 $NA. (SR)   81

Toscana IGT, Santa Catharina 1996 $NA. (SR)   88

Saturated ruby-red. Muted pepper, meat, and earth aromas. A smooth entry leads a medium-bodied palate with velvety tannins. Rounded and ripe, with grip. Drink now.

Vino Nobile di Montepulciano, 1996 $NA. (SR)   86

Saturated, deep ruby-red. Generous overripe red fruit, chocolate, and wood aromas. A firm entry leads a moderately full-bodied palate with drying tannins. Big and rich with a sense of thickness to the finish. Drink now.

Del Falegname

Chianti Colli Senesi, 1996 $9.99.   82

Dievole

Chianti Classico, 1996 $13.50.   89

Bright reddish purple. Medium-bodied. Moderately extracted. Cherries, vanilla, lead pencil. Ripe, fleshy aromas. Generous, juicy red fruit flavors hint at some Cabernet Sauvignon. Well structured; a little reserved right now.

Chianti Classico, Riserva 1995 $16.99.   89

Very deep, saturated blackish-ruby hue. Brooding chocolate and black fruit aromas show a solid degree of ripeness. A firm entry leads a rich, medium-bodied palate. Fleshy, but supported by juicy, mouthwatering acidity. Should develop beautifully with bottle age. Mid-term cellar candidate (3–6 years).

Toscana, Rinascimento 1995 $15.99.   89

Deep blackish-ruby cast. Medium-bodied. Full acidity. Moderately extracted. Mildly tannic. Minerals, anise, earth. Somewhat unyielding aromatically, with a firm and focused palate feel. Well balanced, with a taut, angular finish. Should open with near-term cellaring.

Toscana, Broccato 1995 $22.50.   89

Deep blackish-ruby hue. Moderately full-bodied. Full acidity. Moderately extracted. Mildly oaked. Mildly tannic. Red fruits, brown spices. Pleasantly aromatic, with ripe cherry flavors and well-integrated oak accents. Well structured and lean, with an angular, lengthy finish. Eminently drinkable.

Ecco Domani

Sangiovese di Toscana, 1997 $10.   82

Riccardo Falchini

Vernaccia di San Giminano, Vigna a Solatio 1998 $8.99.   84

Pale straw hue. Tart apple and mineral aromas, with a note of blanched almonds. Crisp on the attack with a medium-bodied palate and taut flavors that show a note of oxidation. Drink now.

Vernaccia di San Gimignano, Vinea Doni 1997 $15.99.   88

Pale straw hue. Fresh citrus zest and mineral aromas. A smooth entry leads a medium body with some oily richness and an austere finish. Drink now.

Chianti Colli Senesi, Colombaia 1997 $8.99.   83

Toscana, Paretaio 1995 $19.99.   89

Bright blackish-ruby cast. Moderately full-bodied. Balanced acidity. Moderately extracted. Mildly oaked. Mildly tannic. Red fruits, dried herbs, minerals. Quite aromatic, with an herb-tinged, fruit-centered quality on the palate. Full and flavorful, yet lean in structure, with an angular finish. Forceful and intense.

Toscana, Paretaio 1996 $19.99.   **86**

Brilliant, saturated ruby hue. Lean pepper and mineral aromas. A crisp entry leads to a medium-bodied palate with firm acids. Lighter in style with a slight green streak. Drink now.

Toscana, Campora 1994 $54.99.   **92**

Deep, saturated ruby-garnet hue. Enticing chocolate and brown spice aromas jump from the glass. A lush entry leads to a ripe, moderately full-bodied palate with big, supple tannins. Flavorful and complex, but light on its feet. Drink now or later.

Toscana, Vin Santo di Caratello 1993 $15.99/500 ml.   **80**

Fattoria Carpineta Fontalpino

Chianti Colli Senesi, Gioia 1995 $14.   **81**

Fattoria dei Barbi

Brunello di Montalcino, Colombini 1994 $NA. (SR)   **80**

Brunello di Montalcino, Colombini Riserva 1993 $NA. (SR)   **92**

Brilliant garnet hue. Complex saddle leather, spice, and dried fruit aromas. A rich entry leads to a rounded, medium-bodied palate with lush tannins. Powerful, but generous. Drink now or later.

Rosso di Montalcino, 1997 $NA. (SR)   **89**

Deep, saturated ruby-garnet hue. Enticing chocolate and berry aromas. A rich entry leads to a firm, moderately full-bodied palate with grippy tannins. Lush and weighty with good intensity. Could use some time to develop complexity. Mid-term cellar candidate (3–6 years).

Toscana, Brusco dei Barbi 1996 $13.99.   **82**

Fattoria di Ambra

Chianti Riserva, La Bigattiera 1995 $NA. (SR)   **NR**

Fattoria di Felsina

Chianti Classico, Berardenga 1996 $18.   **87**

Red-purple. Medium-bodied. Balanced acidity. Moderately extracted. Moderately tannic. Red fruits, minerals. Fine weight and mouthfeel, with bright cherry and raspberry flavors making for a clean, fruit-centered style.

Chianti Classico, Berardenga, Riserva 1994 $27.   **88**

Deep blackish-ruby cast. Moderately full-bodied. Balanced acidity. Highly extracted. Mildly oaked. Mildly tannic. Chocolate, minerals, earth. Deep, brooding aromatics lead to a rich, earthy palate feel. Firm and well structured through the finish.

Chianti Classico, Berardenga, Rancia Riserva 1994 $34.   **90**

Deep blackish-ruby cast. Moderately full-bodied. Balanced acidity. Highly extracted. Moderately oaked. Mildly tannic. Chocolate, earth, spice. Quite aromatic, with pleasant wood overtones to the core of deep, earthy flavors. Full, rich, and brooding, in a muscular style. A little ungenerous now, but should show a bit more with mid-term aging.

Toscana, Fontalloro 1994 $45.   **93**

Opaque blackish-ruby cast. Moderately full-bodied. Full acidity. Moderately extracted. Moderately oaked. Mildly tannic. Cedar, red fruits, minerals. Quite aromatic, with a hefty overlay of exotic wood nuances and a core of complex flavors. Firm and quite linear on the palate, with excellent grip and fine length.

Toscana, Berardenga Vin Santo 1988 $80/500 ml. **98**

Deep orange-copper cast. Full-bodied. Full acidity. Highly extracted. Roasted and salted nuts, treacle, brown spices. Outrageously aromatic, with a full-throttled, viscous palate feel balanced by vibrant acidity. Shows intense rancio, Amontillado-like flavors throughout. Finishes with excellent grip and intensity. Attractive now, but still youthfully structured. Should develop for decades.

Fattoria di Manzano

Toscana, Podere di Fontarca 1996 $22. **86**

Bright yellow-gold. Medium-bodied. Balanced acidity. Moderately extracted. Minerals, citrus, yeast. Distinctive, yeasty aromas follow through on the palate with a minerally feel through the finish. Flavorful style with no shortage of character.

Toscana, Podere Il Vescovo 1996 $40. **85**

Bright blackish-purple cast. Moderately full-bodied. Balanced acidity. Moderately extracted. Moderately oaked. Mildly tannic. Black fruits, vanilla. Quite aromatic in a New-World style with supple fruit flavors and a hefty oak accent. Soft and lush on the palate, with a lingering, flavorful finish.

Fattoria di S. Angelo

Rosso di Montalcino, Lisini 1996 $12. **87**

Bright ruby-purple. Medium-bodied. Moderately extracted. Mildly oaked. Mildly tannic. Black berry fruits. Generous, fleshy, fruity aromas follow through well on the palate, with very elegant, finely wrought flavors. Sound, juicy and drinking nicely now.

Fattoria di Montemaggio

Toscano, Montemaggio II 1996 $14.90. **NR**
Chianti Classico, Riserva 1996 $29.90. **89**

Brilliant garnet hue. Reserved, mineral, smoky aromas. A rich entry leads to a weighty, moderately full-bodied palate with excellent acidic grip. Rather closed at present, but has lots of stuffing. Should open with time. Mid-term cellar candidate (3–6 years).

Fattoria Ormanni

Chianti Classico, 1997 $18. **80**
Chianti Classico, Riserva 1995 $24.99. **89**

Dark, saturated ruby-garnet hue. Intense brown spice and vanilla aromas suggest extended barrique aging. A lean entry leads to a firm, moderately full-bodied palate with solid intensity of flavor. Well cut finish. Could use a bit more time. Drink now or later.

Colli della Toscana Centrale, Julius 1997 $32.99. **87**

Deep, saturated blackish-ruby hue. Intense lead pencil, black fruit, and cassis aromas. A rich entry leads to a thick full-bodied palate. Lower in acidity. Fat through the finish with tough, drying tannins. Needs time, but rather shy of acidity. Mid-term cellar candidate (3–6 years).

Fazi Battaglia

Rosso di Montepulciano, Fassati Selcaia 1996 $9.50. **81**
Vino Nobile di Montepulciano, Fassati 1993 $15. **83**

Fontodi

Chianti Classico, 1996 $18. **86**

Bright red-purple. Medium-bodied. Full acidity. Moderately extracted. Mildly oaked. Moderately tannic. Sour cherries, minerals. Rich and flavorsome, with a chewy mouthfeel and a center of bitter cherry flavors. Fine, minerally length. Very solid.

Chianti Classico, Vigna del Sorbo, Riserva 1994 $32. **87**

Deep blackish-ruby cast. Moderately full-bodied. Full acidity. Highly extracted. Moderately oaked. Mildly tannic. Chocolate, earth, minerals. Quite aromatic, with a deep core of complex, earthy flavors. Firm and rich on the palate, with a lean, focused finish.

Pinot Nero, Toscana 1995 $38. **86**

Bright saturated ruby cast. Moderately full-bodied. Low acidity. Moderately extracted. Mildly oaked. Mildly tannic. Red fruits, vanilla. Pleasantly aromatic, with a distinctly modern melange of fruit and wood flavors. Lush and round in the mouth, with lower levels of acidity. Mildly astringent tannins provide some grip through the finish.

Syrah, Toscana 1995 $42. **84**

Opaque blackish-purple hue. Full-bodied. Balanced acidity. Highly extracted. Mildly oaked. Moderately tannic. Black pepper, dried herbs, earth. Aromatic, with a peppery, herbal quality that shares more in common with Northern Rhône examples than New World ones. Full and quite firm in the mouth, with an angular, highly structured finish.

Toscana, Flaccianello della Pieve 1995 $46. **86**

Deep blackish-ruby cast. Moderately full-bodied. Moderately extracted. Moderately oaked. Mildly tannic. Chocolate, earth, black fruits. Quite aromatic, with a decided earthy accent. Lush and supple in the mouth, with a rounded quality and velvety tannins through the finish, which shows fine grip.

Friggiali

Brunello di Montalcino, 1994 $NA. (SR) **90**

Dark, saturated ruby-garnet hue. Enticing brown spice, leather, and dried fruit aromas jump from the glass. A lean entry leads to a firm, moderately full-bodied palate with angular tannins. Showing some complexity and richness, but rather tough at present. Needs time. Mid-term cellar candidate (3–6 years).

Fuligni

Brunello di Montalcino, Vigneti dei Cottimelli 1994 $NA. (SR) **89**

Deep, saturated ruby-garnet hue. Subdued mineral, herb, and dried red fruit aromas. A firm entry leads to a well flavored, moderately full-bodied palate buoyed by crisp acids. Tannins are lean and structured. Well balanced. Drink now or later.

Brunello di Montalcino, Riserva, Vigneti dei Cottimelli 1993 $NA. (SR) **94**

Very deep, saturated ruby hue with a garnet rim. Exotic coffee, chocolate, and ripe black fruit aromas race from the glass. A rich entry leads to a weighty, full-bodied palate with tremendous richness and intensity of flavor. Great concentration. Should develop beautifully, if you can wait. Drink now or later.

Gattavecchi

Vino Nobile di Montepulciano, 1994 $17. **80**

Geografico

Vernaccia di San Gimignano, 1998 $9.99. **NR**

Chianti Colli Senesi, 1997 $9.99. **NR**

Chianti Classico, 1996 $13.99. **84**

Brilliant, saturated cherry hue. Ripe red fruit aromas. A lush entry leads to a medium-bodied, cheerful, fruit-centered palate. Ripe, but well cut on the finish. Straightforward and tasty. Drink now.

Toscana, Capitolare di Biturica 1995 $25.95. **88**

Deep, saturated ruby hue. Enticing, spicy, gamey aromas. A rich entry leads to a firm, moderately full-bodied palate with grippy tannins and vibrant acidity. Angular, juicy finish. Drink now or later.

Vin Santo del Chianti, 1994 $24.95. **83**

Ghibello
Chianti dei Colli Fiorentini, $9.99.   NR

Il Greppone Mazzi
Brunello di Montalcino, 1994 $NA. (SR)   81

Il Palagetto
Vernaccia di San Gimignano, 1997 $10.   83
Vernaccia di San Gimignano, Riserva 1996 $20.   89

Bright yellow-straw hue. Perfumed and exotically complex with oily, subtlety and yeasty aromas. Smokey oak is also evident. Rich on the attack, with a moderately full-bodied palate and a lush rounded finish featuring lemony acids. Drink now.

Rosso Toscano, Sottobosco 1996 $25.   89

Dark, saturated ruby hue. Generous brown spice aromas jump from the glass and suggest barrique maturation. A rich entry leads to a powerful, full-bodied palate with concentrated, tightly-wound fruit flavors. Intense and youthful with firm acidity and grippy tannins. Should develop. Mid-term cellar candidate (3–6 years).

Il Poggiolo
Brunello di Montalcino, 1994 $NA. (SR)   NR
Brunello di Montalcino, Sassello 1994 $NA. (SR)   80

Il Poggione
Brunello di Montalcino, 1994 $NA. (SR)   86

Deep blackish-garnet hue. Reserved mineral and licorice aromas. A firm entry leads to a rich, moderately full-bodied palate with good intensity of flavor. Firm tannins bite down on the finish. Needs time. Mid-term cellar candidate (3–6 years).

Brunello di Montalcino, Riserva 1993 $NA. (SR)   91

Deep, saturated ruby-garnet hue. Explosive dried fruit, chocolate, and leather aromas are complex and inviting. A rich entry leads to a full-bodied, supple, and harmonious palate. Framed by drying tannins, but has terrific fruit extract. Should develop beautifully. Mid-term cellar candidate (3–6 years).

Rosso di Montalcino, 1997 $NA. (SR)   82
Toscana, San Leopoldo 1995 $34.   89

Very deep blackish-garnet cast. Moderately full-bodied. Balanced acidity. Highly extracted. Mildly oaked. Mildly tannic. Minerals, black fruits, pepper. Unyielding aromatically, with a firm, brooding character. Lean and intense through the finish. Sturdy and perhaps a bit tough at present.

Isole e Olena
Syrah, Toscana 1994 $25.   82

La Doccia
Chianti Classico, Riserva 1995 $32.   82

La Fornace
Brunello di Montalcino, 1994 $NA. (SR)   82
Rosso di Montalcino, 1997 $NA. (SR)   88

Deep, saturated ruby-garnet hue. Generous spice, cedar, and leather aromas jump from the glass. A rich, supple entry leads to a medium-bodied palate with fine intensity of flavor and a lush texture. Lengthy, flavorful finish. Drink now or later.

Scale: Superlative (96-100), Exceptional (90-95), Highly Recommended (85-89), Recommended (80-84), Not Recommended (Under 80)

La Fortuna

Brunello di Montalcino, 1994 $NA. (SR)   92

Deep ruby-garnet hue. Enticing, smoky, leathery aromas jump from the glass. A rich entry leads to a ripe, full-bodied palate with complex herbal flavors and a judicious oak accent. Complex and almost approachable with admirable generosity. Drink now or later.

Rosso di Montalcino, 1997 $NA. (SR)   89

Brilliant cherry red hue. Generous, modern red fruit and vanilla aromas. A lush entry leads to a supple, medium-bodied palate with fine grained tannins. Harmonious and well balanced. Drink now or later.

La Macioche

Rosso di Montalcino, 1997 $NA. (SR)   NR

La Palazzetta

Brunello di Montalcino, 1994 $NA. (SR)   91

Dark blackish-ruby hue. Rich chocolate, mineral, and black fruit aromas carry a distinctive peppery quality. A lush entry leads to a rounded, moderately full-bodied palate with great fruit intensity. Finishes with firm, ripe tannins. A well done, modern leaning style that should develop further complexity with age. Drink now or later.

Rosso di Montalcino, 1997 $NA. (SR)   90

Brilliant ruby-purple hue. Generous vanilla and red fruit aromas show a hefty oak influence and belie a modern style. A lean entry leads to a spicy, medium-bodied palate with excellent fruit intensity. Crisp, angular finish. Very stylish. Drink now or later.

Rosso di Montalcino, 1995 $14.   87

Saturated red-purple. Medium-bodied. Moderately extracted. Mildly tannic. Red berries, vanilla, mushrooms. Succulent aromatics. Bright, juicy palate with an open-knit structure and easy fruity flavors. A very textured, modern style.

La Torre

Brunello di Montalcino, 1994 $NA. (SR)   85

Brilliant brick hue. Forward, earthy, bretty aromas. A lean entry leads to a rich, moderately full-bodied palate with grainy tannins. Exceptionally flavorful with a richness that accelerates through the finish. A softer (though still fairly tannic) style. Drink now or later.

Rosso di Montalcino, 1997 $NA. (SR)   84

Brilliant garnet hue. Enticing earth and leather aromas show a degree of rusticity. A rich entry leads to a firm, moderately full-bodied palate with lush tannins. Flavorful, but not really deep. Drink now or later.

Lagerla

Brunello di Montalcino, 1994 $NA. (SR)   88

Deep ruby hue with a garnet edge. Attractive dried fruit and brown spice aromas jump from the glass. A rich entry leads to a firm, moderately full-bodied palate. Generous and well structured, but rather closed at present. Needs time. Mid-term cellar candidate (3–6 years).

Brunello di Montalcino, Riserva 1993 $NA. (SR)   82

Lamole di Lamole

Chianti Classico, 1994 $15.99.   86

Bright ruby-garnet cast. Medium-bodied. Full acidity. Moderately extracted. Mildly tannic. Earth, mushrooms, dried herbs. Aromatic in a more traditional vein, with complex earthy flavors. Lighter in structure, but well balanced and intense, with solid grip to the finish.

Chianti, Vigneto di Campolungo, Riserva 1990 $29.99. **86**

Deep blackish-garnet cast. Medium-bodied. Full acidity. Moderately extracted. Mildly oaked. Mildly tannic. Brown spices, earth, minerals. Pleasantly aromatic, with a flavorful and intense mouthfeel. Firmly structured, with mild astringency through the finish.

Le Macioche

Brunello di Montalcino, 1994 $NA. (SR) **83**
Brunello di Montalcino, 1993 $49.99. **88**

Deep, saturated ruby-garnet hue. Generous spice, licorice, and chocolate aromas jump from the glass. A rich entry leads to a big, full-bodied palate with firm tannins. Buoyed by vibrant acidity. Lots of flavor intensity, but tough at present. Needs time. Long-term cellar.

Rosso di Montalicino, 1996 $21.99. **NR**

Le Miccine

Chianti Classico, 1996 $17. **88**

Bright garnet hue. Exotic, earthy, olive aromas. A supple entry leads to a medium-bodied palate with velvety tannins. Rich, rounded finish. Drink now.

Chianti Classico, da Gino 1997 $19. **86**

Brilliant ruby-garnet hue. Lean, spicy, mineral aromas. An angular entry leads to a lighter-styled, moderately light-bodied palate. Grippy finish with an attractive chocolate overtone. Drink now.

Chianti Classico, 1997 $22. **88**

Brilliant ruby-purple hue. Lovely, ripe chocolate and berry aromas. A rich entry leads to a supple, velvety, moderately full-bodied palate. Rounded finish with grippy tannins. Drink now.

Rosso di Toscano, da Gino 1996 $17. **83**

Le Presi

Pinot Noir, Brunello di Montalcino 1994 $NA. **83**
Brunello di Montalcino, 1994 $NA. (SR) **83**
Brunello di Montalcino, Riserva 1993 $NA. (SR) **86**

Brilliant garnet hue. Generous, earthy, leathery aromas. A lean entry leads to a rounded, medium-bodied palate with supple tannins. Shows a nice intensity of sweet fruit, but lighter in style. Drink now.

Luce

Toscana, La Vite Lucente 1995 $25. **90**

Deep blackish-ruby cast. Moderately full-bodied. Balanced acidity. Moderately extracted. Mildly oaked. Mildly tannic. Lead pencil, minerals, black fruits. Reserved aromatically, but quite flavorful on the palate. Firmly structured and intense, with a sense of leanness through the finish.

Toscana, La Vite Lucente 1996 $27. **87**

Deep, saturated ruby hue. Attractive red fruit and spice aromas. A lean entry leads to a medium-bodied palate, with crisp acidity and grippy tannins. Well-flavored and approachable. Drink now.

Toscana, Luce della Vite 1994 $52. **91**

Deep blackish-ruby cast. Moderately full-bodied. Balanced acidity. Highly extracted. Moderately oaked. Mildly tannic. Brown spices, earth, black fruits. Quite aromatic, with a generous, spicy oak accent and a deep core of earth-tinged flavors. Round and ripe on the palate, with velvety tannins and a lush, lengthy finish. Well balanced.

Toscana, Luce della Vite 1995 $55.   **90**

Inky blackish-ruby hue. Rich spice and chocolate aromas. A rich entry leads to a chewy, full-bodied palate with lots of fruit density. The tannins bite down hard on the finish. Impressively concentrated, but needs lots of time. Long-term cellar.

Luiano
Chianti Classico, 1996 $11.99.   **84**

Medium ruby hue. Moderately light-bodied. Balanced acidity. Moderately extracted. Mildly tannic. Violets, red fruits. Quite aromatic, with a lively, juicy palate showing bright sour cherry flavors and a lingering minerally finish that belies its lighter style.

Chianti Classico, Riserva 1993 $17.99.   **83**

Marchesato degli Aleramici
Brunello di Montalcino, 1994 $NA. (SR)   **92**

Deep, saturated brick-garnet hue. Forward herb and mineral aromas. A rich entry leads to a firm, moderately full-bodied palate with grippy tannins. Shows a good intensity of dried fruit flavors. Lean through the finish. A sturdy, traditional style that will need time. Mid-term cellar candidate (3–6 years).

Rosso di Montalcino, 1997 $NA. (SR)   **92**

Brilliant, saturated ruby-garnet hue. Enticing mineral, berry, and spice aromas. A rich entry leads to a weighty, moderately full-bodied palate with good intensity of flavor. Ripe and full. Tannins bite down on the finish. Could actually use some time. Mid-term cellar candidate (3–6 years).

Marchesi de Frescobaldi
Pomino, Bianco 1997 $17.   **84**

Bright golden yellow. Medium-bodied. Full acidity. Moderately extracted. Citrus, minerals. Expressive, pure fruit aromas that follow through on the palate. Fresh, lively acids.

Pomino, Benefizio 1995 $26.   **NR**

Pomino, Rosso 1995 $22.   **86**

Bright blackish-ruby cast. Medium-bodied. Full acidity. Moderately extracted. Mildly tannic. Red fruits, dried herbs, minerals. Exotically aromatic, with real complexity of flavor. Carries a sense of lightness on the palate, with a firm, linear finish. Solid grip and intensity.

Cabernet Sauvignon, Toscana 1995 $42.   **87**

Opaque blackish-ruby cast. Full-bodied. Balanced acidity. Highly extracted. Moderately oaked. Moderately tannic. Cassis, minerals, earth. Youthful and quite closed at present, with a thick and firmly structured palate feel. Immense and unyielding, though quite well balanced, showing the propensity for at least a decade of cellaring, if not two or three. Impressive if you can afford the wait.

Merlot, Toscana 1995 $42.   **89**

Opaque blackish-ruby cast. Medium-bodied. Balanced acidity. Moderately extracted. Mildly oaked. Mildly tannic. Earth, black fruits. Reserved aromatically, with powerful, brooding flavors on the palate. Well structured and firm on the palate, with chunky tannins. Well balanced. Should develop nicely with mid-term to long-term aging.

Martini di Cigala
Chianti Classico, San Giusto a Rentennano 1996 $NA. (SR)   **86**

Bright ruby-red to the rim. Generous dried herb and mineral aromas. A firm entry leads a medium-bodied palate with drying tannins. Perfumed and flavorful with a lean edge. Drink now.

Mastrojanni

Brunello di Montalcino, 1994 $NA. (SR) 93

Saturated brickish-garnet hue. Exotic sandalwood and saddle leather aromas are powerful and complex. A ripe entry leads to a lush, moderately full-bodied palate with rounded, supple tannins. Extremely flavorful, and already approachable. Drink now or later.

Brunello di Montalcino, Riserva 1993 $NA. (SR) 92

Deep, saturated ruby-garnet hue. Brooding chocolate and black fruit aromas. A rich entry leads to a full-bodied palate with a glycerous texture to the fruit. Firm tannins clamp down on the finish. Powerful, but tough. Needs lots of time to reveal its true potential, and may warrant a higher rating in the future. Long-term cellar.

Toscana, San Pio 1993 $28. 88

Deep blackish-ruby hue. Moderately full-bodied. Balanced acidity. Highly extracted. Moderately oaked. Mildly tannic. Earth, black fruits, minerals. Pleasantly aromatic and quite flavorful throughout, with a firm, focused palate feel. Rich and lengthy through the finish.

Melini

Chianti Classico, Laborel, Riserva 1995 $15.99. 81

Chianti Classico, "La Selvanella," Riserva 1993 $20. 84

Deep garnet hue. Rich leathery aromas. A supple entry leads to a medium-bodied palate with rounded tannins and crisp acidity. Quite lean through the finish. Drink now.

Mocali

Brunello di Montalcino, 1994 $NA. (SR) 87

Dark, saturated ruby-garnet hue. Brooding saddle leather, flower, and dried fruit aromas show fine complexity. A firm entry leads to a rich, full-bodied palate with a wave of chewy tannins. Well extracted. Drink now or later.

Brunello di Montalcino, Riserva 1993 $NA. (SR) 89

Deep ruby-garnet hue. Enticing licorice, mineral, and brown spice aromas. A lush entry leads to a rounded, moderately full-bodied palate with grainy tannins. Fairly tough through the finish. Powerful. Needs time. Long-term cellar.

Rosso di Montalcino, 1997 $NA. (SR) 82

Monsanto

Chianti Classico, Riserva 1994 $16.99. 88

Pale garnet, fading rim. Moderately light-bodied. Balanced acidity. Moderately extracted. Mildly tannic. Spice, leather. Dusty, leathery aromas. Faded, mature palate has a nice linear progression, with subtlety the key point. Not much primary flavor to grab attention.

Monte Vertine

Toscana, Le Pergole Torte 1994 $45. 87

Bright blackish-garnet cast. Medium-bodied. Balanced acidity. Moderately extracted. Moderately oaked. Mildly tannic. Earth, leather, minerals. Quite aromatic, with a rustic, earthy edge. Lighter on the palate and quite soft on the entry, with a velvety quality. Astringent tannins bite down on the finish.

Montegiachi

Chianti Classico, Cinughi de Pazzi, Riserva 1995 $21. 84

Brilliant garnet hue. Chocolatey, earthy aromas carry a marked, but not off-putting, Brett influence. A lean entry leads to a moderately light-bodied palate with juicy acidity and mild tannins. Rustic, but showing lots of flavor and character. Drink now.

Scale: Superlative (96-100), Exceptional (90-95), Highly Recommended (85-89), Recommended (80-84), Not Recommended (Under 80)

Mormoraia

Toscana, Ostrea 1996 $23.   86

Golden straw. Moderately full-bodied. Balanced acidity. Moderately extracted. Moderately oaked. Brown spice, vanilla, tropical fruits. Oak-accented aromas follow through on a generously toasty palate with rounded mouthfeel and ripe character. Chardonnay-like winemaking.

Nozzole

Chardonnay, Toscana 1997 $13.   86

Very pale straw hue. Generous pear and stone fruit aromas. A lean entry leads to a moderately light-bodied palate. Crisp and clean with a slight buttery note to the finish. Stylish. Drink now.

Chianti Classico, Riserva 1994 $21.   NR

Toscana IGT, Il Pareto 1995 $49.   85

Deep, saturated ruby-garnet hue. Extravagant sweet brown spice aromas are oak dominated. A rich entry leads to a moderately full-bodied palate with drying wood tannins. Concentrated, with a supple mouthfeel, but the oak is out of control and masks any other aspect of the wine. If you like wood, you'll love this. Drink now.

Tenuta dell Ornellaia

Sauvignon Blanc, Toscana 1997 $22.   90

Brilliant deep straw hue. Generous apricot aromas suggest a degree of overripeness or even a hint of Botryitis. A rich entry leads to a concentrated, medium-bodied palate with firm acidity and a varietal herbal accent. A very ripe, intensely flavored Sauvignon with a clean finish. Drink now.

Toscana IGT, Le Volte 1997 $20.   86

Brilliant ruby hue. Perfumed herb, mineral, and berry aromas. A crisp entry leads to a lighter-styled, medium-bodied palate. Straightforward and tasty with a slight green streak. Drink now.

Bolgheri, Ornellaia 1994 $50.   91

Deep blackish-ruby cast. Moderately full-bodied. Balanced acidity. Moderately extracted. Mildly oaked. Mildly tannic. Minerals, black fruits, dried herbs. Rather closed aromatically, but full and flavorful on the palate. Firmly structured, with tannins that clamp down on the finish. Overall balance suggests this wine will open nicely with mid-term to long-term aging.

Guido Padelletti

Brunello di Montalcino, Riserva 1993 $NA. (SR)   91

Brilliant, saturated garnet hue. Exotic mineral, dried fruit, and leather aromas. A rich entry leads to a supple, moderately full-bodied palate with explosive flavors. Harmonious, rounded, and complex. Drink now or later.

Palazzetti

Brunello di Montalcino, 1993 $49.99.   89

Very dark blackish-garnet hue. Exotic roasted game, tobacco, and fruitcake aromas explode from the glass and show intense ripeness. A rich entry leads a chewy, moderately full-bodied palate with tons of flavor. Walks the wild side of rustic street, but interesting. Doesn't quite deliver what the nose promises. Mid-term cellar candidate (3–6 years).

Pian di Macina

Rosso di Montalcino, 1997 $NA. (SR)   80

Piccini

Chianti, 1997 $6.49.	83
Chianti Classico, 1996 $10.99.	84

Full cherry red. Medium-bodied. Balanced acidity. Moderately extracted. Mildly tannic. Ripe red berries. Fleshy, berry-scented aromas. Rounded palate showing some glycerous mouthfeel and ripe flavors. Fruit-centered style. A dusting of dry tannin gives this some grip on the finish.

Chianti Classico, Riserva 1994 $14.99.	81

Pietrafitta

Vernaccia di San Gimignano, La Costa, Riserva 1995 $16.99.	80
Chianti Colli Senesi, 1996 $9.99.	NR

Pietroso

Brunello di Montalcino, 1994 $NA. (SR)	89

Brilliant brickish-garnet hue. Rustic leather, earth, and dried herb aromas. A lean entry leads to a firm, moderately full-bodied palate with good depth of flavor. Angular through the finish with fine intensity. Drink now or later.

Pieve Santa Restituta

Brunello di Montalcino, Rennina 1994 $80.	91

Brilliant garnet hue. Roasted, gamey, dried fruit and cedar aromas. A lush entry leads to a ripe, rounded, medium-bodied palate. Lighter in style, but showing great intensity of flavor with a sweet fruit core. Very tasty. Drink now or later.

Poggio Capponi

Chianti, 1997 $8.99.	80

Poggio San Polo

Brunello di Montalcino, 1994 $NA. (SR)	90

Deep, saturated ruby hue with a garnet rim. Brooding, subdued chocolate and dried fruit aromas. A rich entry leads to a firm, full-bodied palate with lots of richness and extract. Quite weighty, but rather closed. Needs time. Mid-term cellar candidate (3–6 years).

Rosso di Montalcino, 1997 $NA. (SR)	91

Brilliant, saturated ruby-garnet hue. Generous berry and spice aromas have a complex leathery accent. A rich entry leads to a firm, medium-bodied palate with pronounced acidity and excellent cut. Earthy and distinctive, with great concentration. Needs time. Mid-term cellar candidate (3–6 years).

Poliziano

Vino Nobile di Montepulciano, 1995 $23.	91

Deep ruby with purple highlights. Medium-bodied. Balanced acidity. Moderately oaked. Moderately tannic. Vanilla, tart cherries. New-oak accents on the nose follow though on the concentrated palate, with a dose of dry tannin and oak dryness on the finish. Austere and reined in.

Giuseppi Rigoli

Carmignano, Ambra, Vigna di Santa Cristina 1995 $15.	82
Carmignano, Ambra 1996 $NA. (SR)	85

Bright ruby-red. Mineral and red fruit aromas. A firm entry leads a crisp, medium-bodied palate with drying tannins. Linear and well gripped. Bright, youthful, and tight. Drink now or later.

Scale: Superlative (96-100), Exceptional (90-95), Highly Recommended (85-89),
Recommended (80-84), Not Recommended (Under 80)

Riguardo

Brunello di Montalcino, 1993 $37.49.   87

Saturated ruby-garnet hue. Enticing dried fruit and leather aromas. A firm entry leads to a rich, moderately full-bodied palate with chunky tannins. Firm finish. Big and extracted. Needs time. Mid-term cellar candidate (3–6 years).

Rivera

Castel del Monte, Il Falcone, Castel del Monte Riserva 1995 $11.99.   84

Brilliant, saturated garnet hue. Enticing dried fruit, sandalwood, and licorice aromas. A ripe entry leads to a lean, medium-bodied palate. Angular through the lighter-styled finish. Drink now.

Rocca delle Macie

Chianti Classico, 1996 $11.   84

Blood red. Moderately light-bodied. Balanced acidity. Moderately extracted. Mildly oaked. Mildly tannic. Earth, red fruits. Mildly stewed nose. Light, minerally style with an austere character through the finish. Fine finish has some grip.

Rocca di Castagnoli

Chianti Classico, 1995 $19.99.   83

Ruffino

Chardonnay-Pinot Grigio, Toscana 1996 $12.   83
Chianti Classico, Tenuta Santedame 1995 $18.   84

Pale ruby color. Moderately light-bodied. Balanced acidity. Moderately extracted. Faint leather and berry aromas. Juicy and lively on the palate, with a minerally finish.

Chianti Classico, Riserva Ducale 1994 $20.   89

Deep blackish-ruby hue. Moderately full-bodied. Full acidity. Moderately extracted. Mildly oaked. Mildly tannic. Red fruits, chocolate, minerals. Attractive, forward aromatics, with a slight hint of overripeness. Rich and supple in the mouth, with a well-structured, angular finish.

Chianti Classico, Riserva Ducale, Gold Label 1990 $30.   91

Deep blackish-garnet cast. Medium-bodied. Full acidity. Moderately extracted. Black fruits, tea, earth. Stewed, ripe, red fruit aromas follow through on the palate. Very soft, ripe, generous flavors show the vintage character. Complex, with enough soft, chewy tannins to give authority through the finish.

Sangiovese, Toscana 1996 $14.   81

Salvioni

Brunello di Montalcino, 1994 $85.   93

Deep ruby-garnet hue. Exotic dried fruit and chocolate aromas are quite pronounced, showing a touch of wood. Weighty and rich in the mouth with a ripe, full-bodied palate and dusty, drying tannins. Quite flavorful through the finish. Opens up with lots of aeration, boding well for long term cellaring, otherwise a bit tough at present. Long-term cellar.

Rosso di Montalcino, 1997 $40.   86

Brilliant ruby-garnet hue with a slight fade. Brooding date and chocolate aromas. A rich entry leads to a weighty, rounded palate with tons of extract and density. Sweet fruit flavors are supported by grainy tannins. Acidity is on the softer side leaving a heavy, forceful impression. At 14% natural alcohol, it is showing the extreme ripeness of this freakish vintage in spades. Drink now or later.

San Fabiano Calcinaia

Chianti Classico, 1996 $12.99.   88

Bright ruby-red. Medium-bodied. Full acidity. Moderately extracted. Mildly tannic. Lead pencil, cherries, herbs. High-toned, faintly herbal aromas follow through on the palate. Juicy red fruit flavors have an herbal edge, with bright acids rearing up on the finish. Very characterful.

Chianti, Chianti Classico 1994 $19.99.   89

Blood red. Medium-bodied. Balanced acidity. Moderately extracted. Moderately oaked. Moderately tannic. Brown spice, vanilla, red fruits. Quite aromatic, with soft, fleshy fruit flavors and plenty of new-oak influence coming through on the finish. Softer, velvety tannins.

Rosso di Toscana, Cerviolo 1995 $21.   89

Deep blackish-ruby cast. Moderately full-bodied. Balanced acidity. Moderately extracted. Mildly oaked. Mildly tannic. Minerals, black fruits, earth. Quite aromatic, with a complex, earth-tinged character throughout. Firm and very well structured in the mouth, with a firm, angular finish. Fine grip and intensity.

Toscana IGT, Cerviolo 1996 $34.99.   90

Inky blackish-ruby hue. Enticing mint, vanilla, and black fruit aromas are brooding and complex. A rich entry leads to a big, full-bodied palate framed by firm tannins. Dense and deeply flavored, though this closes down on the finish. Needs time to develop and come together. Long-term cellar.

San Vincenti

Chianti Classico, 1995 $14.99.   89

Garnet red. Medium-bodied. Balanced acidity. Moderately extracted. Moderately tannic. Cherries, minerals. Austere aromas. Quite structured, with solid tannins through the finish. Not a fruit-forward style, but it shows intensity of earthy flavors with fine length. Nice now, though this should age well for a few years.

Chianti Classico, Riserva 1994 $19.99.   NR

Angelo Sassetti

Brunello di Montalcino, 1992 $37.   91

Blood red with a garnet cast. Moderately full-bodied. Full acidity. Highly extracted. Quite tannic. Green herbs, minerals, tart red fruits. Very aromatic, with a spicy, herbal accent. Fruit flavors are carried with bright, juicy acids. Very angular, racy, and exciting. Shows thoroughbred pedigree.

Livio Sassetti

Brunello di Montalcino, 1994 $NA. (SR)   91

Bright brickish-ruby hue. Generous leather and mineral aromas. A lean entry leads a moderately full-bodied palate with crisp acidity and drying tannins. Round and supple, but showing traditional cut. Drink now or later.

Rosso di Montalcino, 1996 $NA. (SR)   85

Bright ruby-red. Pleasant red fruit and mineral aromas. A lean entry leads a medium-bodied palate with drying tannins and firm acidic grip. Quite bright, with a good, clean, minerally persistence. Drink now.

IGT Toscana, Fili di Seta 1996 $NA. (SR)   86

Bright ruby with a brickish cast. Brown spice and red fruit aromas. A supple entry leads a medium-bodied palate with lush tannins. Rich and meaty in an early-maturing style. Drink now.

Scale: Superlative (96-100), Exceptional (90-95), Highly Recommended (85-89), Recommended (80-84), Not Recommended (Under 80)

Michele Satta

Toscana, Costa di Giulia 1997 $15. 84

Pale yellow-gold. Medium-bodied. Full acidity. Moderately extracted. Citrus zest, smoke, minerals. Elegant smoky aromas. Zesty, angular style with good acidic cut and some glycerous mouthfeel.

Sangiovese, Toscana 1995 $42. 87

Deep blackish-garnet cast. Moderately full-bodied. Balanced acidity. Highly extracted. Moderately oaked. Mildly tannic. Chocolate, red fruits, dried herbs. Quite aromatic, with a sturdy oak overlay to the core of ripe flavors. Firm and lean in structure, though with a sense of richness. Lengthy and intense through the finish.

Bolgheri Rosso, Piastraia 1995 $45. 97

Bright blackish-garnet cast. Moderately full-bodied. Full acidity. Moderately extracted. Moderately oaked. Mildly tannic. Cedar, earth, dried herbs, black fruits. Extremely aromatic, with a complex melange of flavors that play out on the palate. Well structured, though quite round and ripe, with a supple quality through the lengthy finish.

Silvio Nardi

Brunello di Montalcino, 1993 $34.99. 86

Bright ruby-red. Medium-bodied. Full acidity. Moderately extracted. Moderately tannic. Earth, minerals, red fruits. Traditional style with leathery aromas. Angular and minerally, with high-toned red fruit flavors. A sturdy wine.

Brunello di Montalcino, Riserva 1993 $NA. (SR) 90

Very deep blackish-garnet hue. Intense, brooding saddle leather, black fruit, and mineral aromas. A rich entry leads to a full-bodied palate with sweet fruit and drying tannins through the finish. Powerful. Could really use more time. Mid-term cellar candidate (3–6 years).

Brunello di Montalcino, 1994 $NA. (SR) 84

Deep, saturated ruby-garnet hue. Brooding dried herb, mineral, and licorice aromas. A lush entry leads to a lean, medium-bodied palate with a good cut. Somewhat lighter in style, but shows great acidity. Drink now or later.

Rosso di Montalcino, 1996 $16.99. 84

Saturated reddish-purple. Medium-bodied. Moderately extracted. Mildly oaked. Vanilla, black cherries. Generous aromas show ripe berry fruit accents that are revealed on the palate. Generous and forward, for near-term drinking.

Rosso di Montalcino, 1997 $NA. (SR) 90

Very deep blackish-ruby hue. Exotic mineral, licorice, and black fruit aromas jump from the glass. A rich entry leads to a weighty palate with excellent concentration of flavor. Full-bodied, with a firm, ripe structure. Drink now or later.

Spalletti

Vernaccia di San Gimignano, 1996 $9.99. 86

Bright pale gold. Medium-bodied. Balanced acidity. Moderately extracted. Apples, peach skins. Fresh and fruity, with a clean, glycerous mouthfeel. Finishes with a touch of phenolic dryness. Very versatile style.

Chianti Rufina, Riserva, Poggio Reale 1993 $20. 89

Brilliant garnet hue. Forward brown spice and leather aromas show a toasty oak accent. A supple entry leads to a rounded, medium-bodied palate. Lush and harmonious with a velvety finish. Drink now.

Giovannella Stianti

Chianti Classico, Castello di Volpaia, Riserva 1994 $22.49. 84

Bright blackish-garnet cast. Medium-bodied. Full acidity. Moderately extracted. Mildly oaked. Mildly tannic. Brown spices, earth, dried herbs. Aromatic, with spicy oak nuances and a rustic core of earthy flavors. Well structured and lean in the mouth, with a firm, linear finish.

Strozzi

Toscana, Millanni 994 1994 $56.   95

Opaque blackish-ruby hue. Moderately full-bodied. Balanced acidity. Moderately extracted. Mildly oaked. Mildly tannic. Black fruits, earth, minerals. Quite aromatic, with deep, brooding, earth-tinged flavors. Rich, supple, and round in the mouth, with solid flavor intensity and a firm finish. Well balanced; should gain in complexity with mid-term aging.

Talenti

Brunello di Montalcino, Podere Pian di Conte 1994 $NA. (SR)   81
Brunello di Montalcino, Riserva, Podere Pian di Conte 1993 $NA. (SR)   83
Rosso di Montalcino, Podere Pian di Conte 1997 $NA. (SR)   80

Tenuta del Terriccio

Toscana, Tassinaia 1996 $60.   94

Deep, brilliant ruby hue. Exotic mint and black fruit aromas. A chewy entry leads to a full-bodied palate with supple tannins. Dense flavors accelerate through the lengthy finish. Complex, delicious and quite rich. Drink now or later.

Tenuta di Ghizzano

Toscana, Veneroso 1994 $35.   88

Opaque blackish-ruby hue. Moderately full-bodied. Balanced acidity. Moderately extracted. Moderately oaked. Mildly tannic. Smoke, cedar, chocolate. Quite aromatic, with an exotic, distinctive smoky quality. Lush and quite ripe in the mouth, with chunky tannins through the lengthy finish.

Tenuta di Sesta

Brunello di Montalcino, 1994 $NA. (SR)   92

Deep, saturated garnet hue. Exotic, powerful saddle leather, dried fruit, and spice aromas. A lush entry leads to an extremely flavorful palate with fine cut and persistence. Moderately full-bodied with grippy tannins. Acidity enlivens the finish. Intense and quite stylish in a traditional fashion. Drink now or later.

Tenuta La Poderina

Brunello di Montalcino, 1994 $NA. (SR)   90

Very deep modern ruby hue with a slight fade to the rim. Generous vanilla and berry aromas point to a pronounced oak influence. A rich entry leads to a lush, rounded, moderately full-bodied palate. Stylish. Should develop further complexity with age. Drink now or later.

Brunello di Montalcino, Riserva 1993 $NA. (SR)   95

Deep, modern blackish-ruby hue. Enticing plum and black fruit aromas carry an oaky vanilla accent. A lush entry leads to a rich, full-bodied palate with waves of flavor and chewy tannins. An extremely impressive modern style. Should develop further complexity with time. Mid-term cellar candidate (3–6 years).

Rosso di Montalcino, 1997 $NA. (SR)   92

Deep, saturated ruby-purple hue. Attractive black fruit and vanilla aromas jump from the glass and belie a modern style. A rich entry leads to a full-bodied, supple palate. Intense and generous with fine length and grainy tannins. A very good wine, but not of the exotic, roasted and traditional Brunello mold. Drink now or later.

Tenuta San Guido
Bolgheri, Sassicaia 1994 $70.   94

Deep blackish-ruby cast. Moderately full-bodied. Balanced acidity. Moderately extracted. Moderately oaked. Mildly tannic. Spice, minerals, cassis. Exotically aromatic, with a complex melange of spicy flavors that meet a deep core of fruit on the palate. Well structured and firm, though round and quite generous. Fine length and intensity. Showing well now, but has the balance for long-term aging.

Terrabianca
Toscana, Scassino 1995 $15.   85

Bright ruby cast. Medium-bodied. Full acidity. Moderately extracted. Mildly tannic. Red fruits, dried herbs. Reserved aromatically, with a lighter-styled, lean palate feel. Finishes with some mildly astringent tannins. Unyielding.

Terreno
Chianti Classico, 1996 $16.   86

Ruby with purple highlights. Medium-bodied. Balanced acidity. Moderately extracted. Mildly oaked. Moderately tannic. Cherries, minerals, vanilla. Bright, precise, and focused red fruit flavors with solid tannins giving grip on the finish.

Uccelliera
Brunello di Montalcino, 1994 $NA. (SR)   89

Deep, saturated ruby-garnet hue. Lean herb-tinged aromas. An angular entry leads to a firm, medium-bodied palate. Assertive dried berry and flower flavors open up through the finish. Fairly rich and intense in a traditional manner. Drink now or later.

Rosso di Montalcino, 1997 $NA. (SR)   86

Brilliant, saturated garnet hue. Lean mineral and berry aromas show an attractive spicy accent. A firm entry leads to a medium-bodied palate with a lean tannic cut. Stylish. Drink now or later.

Vagnoni
Vernaccia di San Gimignano, 1998 $13.   84

Metallic pale straw appearance. Crisp, fresh aromas of tart apples and melon. Smooth on the entry, with a medium body and a soft finish with some lingering oiliness. Drink now.

Chianti Colli Senesi, 1996 $12.   88

Bright ruby-purple. Medium-bodied. Full acidity. Moderately extracted. Mildly oaked. Mildly tannic. Plums, red fruits, minerals. Reserved aromatically but quite flavorful on the palate, with a burst of ripe red fruit flavors. Well structured and austere, with a focused, lean finish. Excellent grip and intensity.

Chianti Colli Senesi, Riserva 1995 $13.   84

Bright garnet hue. Generous leathery aromas. A lean entry leads to a firm, medium-bodied palate with angular acidity. Lighter in style. Fades somewhat toward the finish. Drink now.

Val di Suga
Brunello di Montalcino, Vigna del Lago 1993 $85.   92

Dark, blackish-ruby hue with a garnet edge. Extravagant chocolate and ripe black fruit aromas show an attractive spicy edge. A rich entry leads to a weighty, full-bodied palate with chewy tannins and a dense structure. Very flavorful with firm tannins. Opens well with extended aeration, but best in time. Long-term cellar.

Valdicava
Brunello di Montalcino, 1994 $NA. (SR)   NR

Valiano

Chianti Classico, 1997 $11.99.   83

Chianti Classico, Casarossa 1996 $19.99.   86

Bright ruby-red. Moderately light-bodied. Balanced acidity. Moderately extracted. Mildly tannic. Red berries, herbs. Bright and berry scented. Juicy flavors on a lush entry reveal a solid minerally underlay that follows through on the finish. Fine grip.

Chianti Classico, Poggio Teo 1996 $19.99.   88

Full ruby-red. Medium-bodied. Balanced acidity. Moderately extracted. Mildly tannic. Minerals, red berries. Lively, high-toned red fruit flavors burst on the front of the palate, with juicy acids and mild tannins through the finish. Fresh, clean.

Chianti Classico, Riserva 1994 $19.99.   86

Bright ruby-garnet cast. Medium-bodied. Full acidity. Moderately extracted. Mildly oaked. Mildly tannic. Brown spices, minerals. Pleasantly aromatic, with a spicy oak quality throughout. Firm and lean in the mouth, with a focused, austere finish.

Chianti Classico, Riserva 1995 $19.99.   84

Mature garnet hue. Generous brown spice and tobacco aromas jump from the glass. A lean entry leads to a medium-bodied palate with aggressive acidity. Quite firm. May come around a bit with time. Drink now or later.

Verbena

Brunello di Montalcino, 1994 $NA. (SR)   92

Deep, saturated blackish-garnet hue. Rich chocolate and dried fruit aromas are quite enticing. A ripe entry leads to a weighty, rounded, moderately full-bodied palate with harmonious tannins. Supple, balanced, and very generous. Already approachable but should hold beautifully. Drink now or later.

Rosso di Montalcino, 1997 $NA. (SR)   82

Villa Alberti

Chianti, 1998 $12.   80

Villa Cafaggio

Chianti Classico, 1996 $15.99.   84

Cherry center, faint purple rim. Moderately light-bodied. Balanced acidity. Subtly extracted. Mildly tannic. Vin nouveau aromas. Candied fruit flavors on entry turn quite dry and minerally through the finish.

Chianti Classico, 1997 $16.99.   90

Deep, saturated ruby-purple hue. Attractive chocolate, mineral, and pure red fruit aromas. A rich entry leads to a lush, moderately full-bodied palate with velvety tannins. Ripe, supple, and stylish with a complex herbal edge. Drink now.

Chianti Classico, Riserva 1995 $27.99.   90

Deep blackish-ruby cast. Moderately full-bodied. Full acidity. Highly extracted. Moderately oaked. Mildly tannic. Black fruits, vanilla. Quite firm and youthful, with a tightly wound, deeply flavored personality. Well structured with an angular finish and excellent ripeness. Bodes well for mid-term cellaring.

Chianti Classico, Riserva 1996 $28.99.   88

Very deep blackish-ruby hue. Subdued mineral and red fruit aromas show a soft spicy accent. A firm entry leads to a rounded, medium-bodied palate with angular acidity. Taut finish, with brooding dark fruit flavors.

Chianti Classico, Solatio Basilica, Riserva 1995 $42.   93

Very deep blackish-ruby hue. Opulent vanilla and berry aromas. A rich entry leads to a big, moderately full-bodied palate with wonderfully pure Sangiovese flavors and an impressive, judiciously oak accent that comes through on the lengthy finish. More of a super-Tuscan style. Drink now or later.

Scale: Superlative (96-100), Exceptional (90-95), Highly Recommended (85-89), Recommended (80-84), Not Recommended (Under 80)

Toscano, San Martino 1995 $42.   **95**
Deep blackish-purple cast. Moderately full-bodied. Full acidity. Moderately extracted.
Moderately oaked. Mildly tannic. Black fruits, minerals, vanilla. Extremely aromatic and
quite flavorful throughout, with a well-crafted interplay between oak and fruit nuances.
Lean and well structured on the palate, with excellent ripeness and a very lengthy, juicy
finish. Intense and focused.

Toscana, San Martino 1996 $42.   **92**
Deep, saturated blackish-ruby hue. Reserved, elegant mineral and black fruit aromas.
A ripe entry leads to a rich, thick, full-bodied palate with vibrant acidity. Youthful and
closed. Should develop with time. Long-term cellar.

Toscano, Cortaccio 1995 $45.99.   **91**
Opaque blackish-ruby cast. Moderately full-bodied. Balanced acidity. Moderately
extracted. Moderately oaked. Mildly tannic. Cassis, vanilla, minerals. Pleasantly aromatic,
with a deep, intense core of flavors. Firm and elegantly wrought, with an angular,
focused finish. Accessible now, but should improve with age.

Villa di Geggaino
Chianti Classico, Riserva 1990 $28.   NR

Vistarenni
Toscana, Codirosso 1993 $23.99.   NR

thirty-four

≈

Italy
The Provinces

≈

Unexplored Italy: Diversity and Value

When a wine is required do you find yourself reaching for a coin, tossing it in the air and calling, "heads for Cabernet and tails for Chardonnay?" If so, you're in a rut and in desperate need of the stylish and flavorful regional wines of Italy. Italy is wine. The flavors and textures of Italian wines vary widely—everything from lean, intense, aromatic whites to rustic reds that are as much of a chew as they are a drink. No other country offers the sheer volume—roughly 20% of the world's output—or variety of wines that Italy does. The nation is covered with vines, from its cool Alpine districts in the north, to the near desert-like conditions of Sicily. Every one of Italy's twenty provinces has vineyards. While Piedmont and Tuscany receive the lion's share of notoriety, huge swathes of the Italian countryside are producing interesting wines, often at very attractive prices. Some of the key regions and varietals to watch for include:

Amarone

Amarone is one of the world's most distinctive and unusual wine styles. It is produced in the same northern Italian region that creates Valpolicella and is a product of the indigenous Corvina grape. When harvested, select lots of grapes are set out on mats to dry, thereby concentrating their sugars and flavors. The resultant wine is thick and rich with alcohol levels around 15% quite common. Flavorwise, the wines have distinctive porty overtones, though they are generally dry. Paired with game or other rich dishes, Amarone can be a revelation, though the style of the wine is certainly not for everyone.

Montepulciano d'Abruzzo

Montepulciano d'Abruzzo today is one of the world's best values in dry red wines. Grown in the central Italian province of Abruzzi, a mountainous region with a long coastline on the Adriatic, Montepulciano yields a dark, rich, and flavorful wine with excellent balancing acidity. It is often described as having a distinctive gamey note, though some of the best examples are now being aged in oak barrels. Amazingly, the vast majority of these consistently pleasing reds can be had for less than ten dollars—a bargain indeed.

Pinot Grigio

While U.S. consumers have chosen Chardonnay as the nation's house white, "nuovo" Italians might be accused of having chosen Pinot Grigio as theirs. Pinot Grigio is the Italian synonym for Pinot Gris, a rather neutral white varietal that generally only reaches rarefied heights in Alsace (though it is also being pushed as the next big thing in Oregon). Grown all over northern Italy, Pinot Grigio can be depended on for crisp, high acid, refreshing white wines. The genre's success has as much to do with marketing as quality, but in the hands of the very best producers Pinot Grigio can offer at least a measure of complexity. Nonetheless, with all those fancy bottles and print ads to pay for, you are likely to pay rather more for a Pinot Grigio than quality would otherwise dictate. Caveat emptor!

Tocai Friulano

Tocai Friulano is the Tocai variety from Friuli situated in Northeast Italy. Tocai is a wonderful and complex wine demonstrating a unique merging of fruity, floral,

Scale: Superlative (96-100), Exceptional (90-95), Highly Recommended (85-89),
Recommended (80-84), Not Recommended (Under 80)

and herbal aromas. The palate is washed with silky, soft tropical fruit flavors and buoyed by a firm edge of acidity. They are not unlike powerful Rieslings in structure. Several sub-districts of Tocai Friulano exist, and some of them fetch a handsome price. At the moment, values exist and should be enjoyed whenever the opportunity presents itself. Tocai can age, but is best enjoyed with all of its youthful fruit intact.

Orvieto

Orvieto is one of Italy's most famous white wines, produced around the medieval town of the same name in the province of Umbria, about an hour north of Rome. Trebbiano is the grape that forms the base of the wine, with another minor varietal, Grechetto, forming much of the rest. Orvietos tend to be rather rich and weighty, but as is often the case with Italian whites, is accused of being fairly neutral. In the hands of the best producers, however, Orvieto can make for a flavorful and distinctive white. It is also not all that unusual to see an example with a hint of sweetness, though most are dry. At its best, Orvieto is a fine match for rich seafood and poultry dishes.

Soave

Soave is the most common dry white wine from the Veneto region in northeast Italy, near Venice. It is made primarily from an indigenous varietal, Garganega, and blended with up to 30 percent Chardonnay, Pinot Blanc, or Trebbiano. Though widely regarded as a simple quaffer, in the hands of the best and most conscientious producers, Soave can become a rich, flavorful, and delicious white. Many of these producers have also taken to oak aging for the wines. The result can be a tasty and distinctive alternative to Chardonnay.

But What to Eat?

All Italian varietals are ideal food companions, so while there may be "ideal" combinations, don't sweat the details. This is because they are very rarely overly alcoholic and they tend to have zesty levels of acidity. Both factors are essential if a wine is to complement food as opposed to competing with it or even overshadowing it.

The Italian Provinces at a Glance

Wines Reviewed:

363

Producers/Brands Represented:

143

Value Rating:

Good to Excellent

Reviews

Albola
Pinot Grigio, Umbria 1995 $10. 83

Serego Alighieri
Valpolicella, Bianco di Garganega E Sauvignon 1996 $16. 84

Pale straw. Medium-bodied. Balanced acidity. Moderately extracted. Flowers, ripe citrus fruits. Clean, faintly aromatic nose. Good rounded mouthfeel with some glycerous character well supported by juicy acids.

Amistani di Guarda
Merlot, Montello e Colli Asolani 1997 $NA. (SR) 80
Della Marca Trevigiana, Centaro Rosso Gran Riserva IGT 1994 $NA. (SR) 81

Antinori
Chardonnay, Umbria 1997 $11.50. 82
Orvieto Classico, Campogrande 1997 $9. NR
Umbria, Cevaro della Sala 1997 $28. 92

Brilliant yellow-golden hue. Yeasty, brown spice aromas point to oak maturation. A crisp entry leads a lush, rounded, medium-bodied palate balanced by vibrant acidity. Richly flavored and concentrated with a complex finish. New World flavors married to Italian structure. Drink now or later.

Sauvignon, Umbria 1997 $11.50. 82
Botrytised Sauvignon, Umbria 1995 $30/375 ml. 86

Brilliant yellow-golden hue. Generous pineapple and honey aromas. A rich entry leads a moderately full-bodied, mildly viscous palate with moderate sweetness. Ripe rounded finish. Drink now.

Antonelli
Montefalco Rosso, 1995 $11.99. 84

Bright garnet cast. Medium-bodied. Full acidity. Moderately extracted. Mildly oaked. Mildly tannic. Overripe red fruits, minerals. Quite aromatic with a subtle portlike overtone. Light on the palate and quite lean, with a clean and vibrant finish.

Sagrantino di Montefalco, 1994 $21.99. 84

Deep blackish-ruby cast. Moderately full-bodied. Balanced acidity. Highly extracted. Moderately tannic. Black pepper, earth, tar. Aromatic with distinctive earthy overtones. Big, ripe, and lush in the mouth with a wave of powdery tannins that bite into the finish. Tough at present.

Argiolas
Isola dei Nuraghi IGT, Perdera 1996 $10. 86

Deep, saturated ruby-garnet hue. Lean spicy aromas. A ripe entry leads to a rich, full-bodied palate with grippy tannins. Robust, drying finish. Shows rustic overtones and lots of character. Drink now or later.

Isola dei Nuraghi IGT, Costera 1996 $13. 88

Dark ruby-garnet hue. Intense licorice and roasted game aromas show a hint of overripeness. A weighty entry leads to a full-bodied palate with big supple tannins. Well balanced for its size with good grip to the finish. Drink now or later.

Albino Armani

Chardonnay, Valdadige 1995 $23.   81

Pinot Grigio, Valdadige 1996 $20.   83

Sauvignon di Piccola Botte, Veneto 1997 $21.   90

Bright straw hue with a slight spritz. Outstanding, varietal herb and gooseberry aromas. A crisp entry leads to a rich, ripe, moderately full-bodied palate. Flavorful, creamy finish. A very stylish Sauvignon. Drink now.

Italy, Corvara 1994 $26.   85

Bright blackish-purple cast. Medium-bodied. Full acidity. Moderately extracted. Mildly tannic. Minerals, black fruits. Rather reserved aromatically, with a firmly structured though flavorful mouthfeel. Lean and angular with a precise finish.

Bagnoli

Pinot Grigio, Friuli 1996 $12.99.   NR

Merlot, Friuli 1996 $10.99.   82

Baltieri

Amarone della Valpolicella, Sortilegio 1994 $NA. (SR)   90

Brilliant cherry hue. Exotic berry and game aromas jump from the glass. A ripe entry leads to a supple, full-bodied palate with sweet fruit flavors and a drying finish. Rich and stylish with good depth. Drink now or later.

Valpolicella, La Romensa 1998 $NA. (SR)   83

Valpolicella Superiore, Monte Paradisio 1994 $NA. (SR)   87

Bright cherry-garnet hue. Exotic cordial and berry aromas jump from the glass. A ripe entry leads to a rich, medium-bodied palate with grippy tannins. Quite concentrated, and drinking well. On the rustic side. Drink now or later.

Banfi

Brachetto d'Acqui, Dolce Sparkling 1996 $19.   88

Bright cherry color with a garnet cast. Moderately light-bodied. Full acidity. Subtly extracted. Red fruits, dried herbs, cream. Pleasantly aromatic with some real complexity to the flavors that are well translated to the palate. A hint of sweetness on the finish with cleansing acidity. Good intensity and length.

Piemonte, Brut Metodo Classico NV $20.   NR

Barone Fini

Pinot Grigio, Valdadige 1996 $8.99.   NR

Merlot, Trentino 1996 $8.99.   89

Bright cherry red. Medium-bodied. Balanced acidity. Moderately extracted. Mildly tannic. Black cherries, herbs, earth. Herbaceous cherry notes follow through on the palate. Generous, but showing grip through the finish. Classic cool-climate Merlot character.

Bartolomeo Beato

Pinot Grigio Superiore, Breganze 1998 $NA. (SR)   86

Brilliant platinum hue. Lovely, perfumed, talc aromas. A crisp entry leads to a lean, medium-bodied palate with crisp acidity. Clean, flavorful finish. Drink now.

Pinot Nero Superiore, Breganze 1997 $NA. (SR)   80

Bepi

Montepulciano d'Abruzzo, 1995 $6.99.   NR

Bertani

Recioto della Valpolicella Amarone, Classico Superiore 1988 $60.   91

Deep blackish-garnet cast. Full-bodied. Balanced acidity. Highly extracted. Mildly tannic. Chocolate malt, stewed fruits, leather. Outrageously aromatic with a melange of complex flavors. Rich and ripe on the palate yet very well balanced, with a fine cut of acidity. Solid grip and intensity with exceptional length. Showing signs of maturity, yet still quite youthful in structure.

Bigi

Orvieto Classico, Secco 1996 $5.99.   84

Pale green-straw hue. Medium-bodied. Balanced acidity. Moderately extracted. Citrus, pear. Muted aromas lead clean, fresh flavors on the palate. The finish is clean though short.

Est!Est!!Est!!! di Montefiascone, Graffiti 1997 $5.99.   86

Pale brilliant straw hue Moderately light-bodied. Full acidity. Moderately extracted. Apples, grass. Grassy high-toned aromas lead a juicy, rounded palate with clean flavors and a touch of dryness on the finish. Intense and pure.

Boccadigabbia

Rosso Piceno, 1996 $NA. (SR)   86

Ruby-red with a fading rim. Forward, meaty, minerally aromas. An acidic entry leads a crisp, medium-bodied palate with drying tannins. Juicy and clean with a stylish, well-gripped finish. Drink now.

Rosso Piceno, Saltapicchio 1995 $NA. (SR)   90

Saturated ruby hue. Generous chocolate, earth, and black fruit aromas. A smooth entry leads a moderately full-bodied palate with velvety tannins. Gamey, lush, and rich. Very varietally suggestive, like a good Chianti. Drink now or later.

Rosso Piceno, Villamaggio 1996 $NA. (SR)   83

Bolla

Soave Classico, Tufaie Castellaro 1996 $14.   82

Amarone Classico della Valpolicella, 1990 $32.   84

Deep blackish-ruby with a slight garnet cast. Moderately full-bodied. Balanced acidity. Moderately extracted. Mildly tannic. Black fruits, earth. Aromatic, with earthy overtones throughout. Fat and ripe on the palate with mature flavors through the finish. A mouth-filling wine, though it could use a bit more grip.

Cabernet Sauvignon, Veneto 1991 $27.   93

Deep blackish-garnet cast. Moderately full-bodied. Balanced acidity. Moderately extracted. Moderately oaked. Mildly tannic. Black fruits, brown spices. Very aromatic with a hefty overlay of oak seasoning and a lean core of minerally fruit flavors. Intense and focused in the mouth with a lean finish.

Merlot, Venezie 1996 $14.   88

Deep ruby-red. Medium-bodied. Balanced acidity. Moderately extracted. Mildly oaked. Red plums, sweet herbs. Generous fleshy aromas do not disappoint on the palate. Rich and supple, with ripe flavors and sweet herbal overtones through the finish. Drinking nicely now.

Valoplicella Classico, Le Poiane Jago 1994 $14.   81

Bollini

Chardonnay, Trentino 1997 $10.99.   NR

Pinot Grigio, Trentino 1998 $10.99.   85

Pale straw hue. Subdued appley aromas carry a honeyed accent. A crisp entry leads to a medium-bodied palate with an oily texture offset by zesty acidity. Clean, rounded finish. Drink now.

Scale: Superlative (96-100), Exceptional (90-95), Highly Recommended (85-89), Recommended (80-84), Not Recommended (Under 80)

760

Pinot Grigio, Grave del Friuli 1996 $15.99.   **88**

Brilliant yellow-straw hue. Intense mineral, earth, and orange blossom aromas. A vibrant entry leads to a concentrated, tightly-wound palate. Angular, well structured finish. Great structure-should open with a bit of age. Drink now or later.

Merlot, Trentino 1997 $10.99.   **89**

Deep, saturated ruby hue. Ripe berry and chocolate aromas. A rich entry leads to a moderately full-bodied, ripe, fruit-centered palate. Supple and harmonious with a fine finish. Drink now.

Merlot, Trentino 1995 $18.99.   **87**

Deep, saturated ruby-garnet hue. Enticing brown spice and leather aromas point to oak maturation. A rich entry leads to a lush, medium-bodied palate. Rounded, elegant, and flavorful with velvety tannins. Drink now.

Borgo Magredo

Pinot Grigio, Grave del Friuli 1998 $8.99.   **83**

Pinot Grigio, Friuli 1998 $9.99.   **NR**

Cabernet Sauvignon, Friuli 1997 $8.99.   **84**

Brilliant ruby-garnet hue. Subdued herb and red fruit aromas. A firm entry leads to a medium-bodied palate with bright acidity. Crisp finish with mild tannins. A quaffer. Drink now.

Merlot, Friuli 1997 $8.99.   **89**

Bright cherry-purple hue. Tart berry fruit, herb aromas. Crisp on the attack, with a smooth medium-bodied palate and supple tannins. A softly herbaceous style with clean acidity. Very stylish.

Josef Brigl

Pinot Grigio, Alto Adige 1997 $9.99.   **83**

Merlot, Alto Adige 1995 $9.99.   **82**

Ca' del Bosco

Franciacorta, Cuvee Annamaria Clementi 1991 $71.   **97**

Deep golden hue. Full-bodied. Full acidity. Highly extracted. Yeast, vanilla, cream. Opulent aromas, with a yeasty, Champagne-like flavor profile. Rich and quite round in the mouth with an excellent persistence of bubbles. May have seen a touch of oak as vanilla nuances rear up in the finish.

Rosso del Sebino, Maurizio Zanella 1995 $82.   **97**

Deep blackish-purple hue. Moderately full-bodied. Full acidity. Highly extracted. Moderately oaked. Moderately tannic. Lead pencil, minerals, cassis. Generous aromas follow through with complex flavors. Firm and highly structured with excellent balance and grip. Still rather tough on the finish, but should develop beautifully with age.

Ca' del Monte

Amarone della Valpolicella Classico, 1993 $34.99.   **92**

Deep, saturated ruby-garnet hue. Concentrated, brooding chocolate and black fruit aromas. A lush entry leads to a big, full-bodied palate with tons of flavor intensity and waves of supple tannins. Not very evolved, but structured to age beautifully. A dense, solid style. Long-term cellar.

Valpolicella Classico Superiore, Vigneto Scaiso 1993 $17.99.   **90**

Deep, saturated ruby-garnet hue. Exotic chocolate, soy, and dried fruit aromas are forceful and complex. A lush entry leads to a weighty, moderately full-bodied palate with lots of fruit sweetness but a dry palate. Framed by supple tannins. A monster Valpolicella. Drink now or later.

Ca' Montini

Veneto, Prosecco Superiore di Cartizze NV $19.99.   84

Pale straw cast. Medium-bodied. Full acidity. Moderately extracted. Citrus, tropical fruits. Quite aromatic, with a fruit-centered personality. Light and racy on the palate, with a decided note of sweetness through the finish. Straightforward and very drinkable.

Chardonnay-Pinot Grigio, Veneto 1997 $10.   84

Very pale straw hue. Moderately light-bodied. Balanced acidity. Moderately extracted. Flowers, minerals, citrus. Elegant floral, citrusy nose follows through on a clean, juicy palate with delicious freshness through the finish.

Amarone Classico della Valpolicella, 1995 $24.99.   81

Ca'Rugate

Soave Classico, 1996 $11.99.   83

Soave Classico, Monte Alto 1996 $13.99.   87

Full gold-yellow. Moderately full-bodied. Balanced acidity. Moderately extracted. Cheese, asparagus, spice. Distinctive minerally, sweaty aromas show complexity. Rounded, fat, juicy flavors with a weighty mouthfeel. Light and quite clean on the finish with very subtle spicy notes.

Recioto di Soave, La Perlara 1995 $18.99/500 ml.   87

Bright orange-gold. Medium-bodied. Balanced acidity. Moderately extracted. Figs, yeast, herbs. Figgy, herbal aromas come through on the palate. Very marked complex aromas follow through well on the palate, with very restrained and balanced sweetness.

Michele Calo

Alezio, Mjère Rosso 1996 $21.   84

Brick-red hue. Mature, dusty aromas. Lean on the attack, with a medium-bodied palate, dried red fruits, and plenty of dry tannins gripping the finish. Rather rustic. Drink now.

Salento, Vigna Spano 1993 $35.   91

Deep blackish-garnet cast. Moderately full-bodied. Balanced acidity. Highly extracted. Moderately oaked. Mildly tannic. Brown spices, black fruits, leather. Expressively aromatic, with a decided oak accent and a big core of complex, fruit-centered flavors. Well structured and firm on the palate, with an intense and flavorful finish.

Campanile

Pinot Grigio, Friuli 1997 $11.   84

Deep straw cast. Moderately full-bodied. Full acidity. Moderately extracted. Cheese, earth, minerals. Forward aromatics are unusual but distinctive, with a rounded, earthy, flavorful palate feel. Concentrated and intense through the smoky finish.

Cantina di Cortaccia

Pinot Grigio, Alto Adige 1997 $9.99.   NR

Cantina La Vis

Chardonnay, Trentino 1998 $9.99.   NR

Merlot, Trentino 1997 $9.99.   83

Pinot Nero, Trentino 1997 $10.99.   83

Cantina Sociale Valpolicella

Amarone della Valpolicella, Domini Veneti 1995 $NA. (SR)   80

Valpolicella Classico Superiore, Domini Veneti 1997 $NA. (SR)   NR

Caravaglio

Salina Rosso, NV $14.   86

Bright blackish purple. Moderately light-bodied. Full acidity. Subtly extracted. Mildly tannic. Red fruits, minerals. Pleasantly aromatic with a light-styled, fruit-forward personality. Crisp and delicate in the mouth with a racy finish.

Casa di Pescatori

Sicilia, White 1997 $5.99.   83

Sicilia, Rosso 1998 $5.99.   83

Casal Bordino

Montepulciano d'Abruzzo, Collegiata 1996 $8.99.   81

Montepulciano d'Abruzzo, Colimoro 1994 $9.99.   82

Michele Castellani

Amarone della Valpolicella Classico, i Castei 1993 $34.99.   90

Very deep blackish-garnet hue. Rich game, pepper, and dark black fruit aromas. A lush entry leads to a big, full-bodied palate with supple tannins. Big and intense. Despite its massive proportions, this slides down smoothly. Drink now or later.

Recioto della Valpolicella Classico, i Castei 1995 $29.99.   90

Semi-sparkling with a deep, saturated ruby hue. Profound, brooding chocolate, wild game, and dark fruit aromas. A rich entry leads to a full-bodied, slightly frizante palate. Intense and opulent with great depth of flavor. Rather like a wild sparkling Shiraz with an underlying hint of sweetness.

Castelvecchio

Carso, Turmino 1995 $20.49.   86

Pale ruby hue. Lean, dusty aromas. Bright and juicy on the attack, with a medium-bodied palate showing vibrant red fruits and subdued mineral tannins through the finish. Elegant. Drink now.

Cavit

Merlot, Trentino 1996 $8.99.   NR

Gerardo Cesari

Chardonnay, Venezie 1997 $NA. (SR)   84

Deep straw hue. Attractive spice and mineral aromas show a slight oak accent. Ripe and rounded with solid acidity through the finish. Drink now.

Pinot Grigio, Venezie 1998 $NA. (SR)   83

Amarone Classico della Valpolicella, 1993 $22.99.   82

Amarone della Valpolicella, 1995 $NA. (SR)   86

Saturated ruby hue. Generous plum and brown spice aromas show a touch of the exotic. Ripe and intense in the mouth with an attractive fruit sweetness and a drying finish. Stylish. Drink now or later.

Amarone della Valpolicella, Il Prosco 1995 $NA. (SR)   90

Brilliant ruby-garnet hue. Intense saddle leather, game, and ripe berry aromas. A ripe entry leads to a lush, moderately full-bodied palate. Concentrated, harmonious, and very flavorful. Already drinking beautifully. Drink now or later.

Merlot, Venezie 1997 $NA. (SR)   86

Brilliant pale ruby-purple hue. Generous berry and spice aromas. A lush entry leads to a supple, rounded palate with grippy tannins. Stylish, with a mineral accent to the finish. Drink now or later.

Valpolicella, Mara, Vino di Ripasso 1995 $NA. (SR)   82
Vino di Ripasso Valpolicella, Mara, Classico Superiore 1995 $15.99.   NR

Umberto Cesari
Chardonnay, Emilia 1996 $12.99.   85

Brilliant, deep straw hue. Forward, spicy aromas show an unusual, curried, basil-like quality. A lush entry leads to a rich, moderately full-bodied palate with tons of flavor. Rounded finish. Walks the line—rather bizarre but has lots of character. Drink now.

Sangiovese-Cabernet Sauvignon, Emilia 1995 $14.99.   89

Brilliant, saturated ruby hue. Enticing brown spice and sandalwood aromas show an attractive wood accent. A rich entry leads to a rounded, ripe, moderately full-bodied palate with supple tannins. Drink now.

Sangiovese di Romagna, Il Poggio, Superiore 1997 $6.99.   83
Sangiovese di Romagna, Riserva 1995 $10.99.   86

Brilliant ruby-garnet hue. Attractive leather and mineral aromas. A lush entry leads to a supple, medium-bodied palate with classic dusty cherry flavors. Rounded finish with grippy tannins. Drink now.

Professor Cescon
Sauvignon, Veneto 1998 $NA. (SR)   87

Deep straw hue. Attractive floral aromas jump from the glass. A crisp entry leads to a taut, moderately light-bodied palate with firm acids. Well cut and tart. Great with shellfish. Drink now.

Veneto, Raboso Rosso 1997 $NA. (SR)   85

Brilliant pale cherry hue with purple highlights. Attractive bitter cherry and licorice aromas. A lean entry leads to a moderately light-bodied palate with grippy acids. Straightforward and stylish. Drink now.

Cielo
Pinot Grigio, Veneto 1996 $5.99.   81
Merlot, Veneto 1996 $5.99.   NR

Concilio
Chardonnay, Trentino 1997 $7.99.   81
Pinot Grigio, Trentino 1997 $11.99.   88

Medium yellow-gold. Bright, attractive apple and smoke aromas. Lively on the attack, leading a medium-bodied palate with crisp, tart acids and a fine apple fruit intensity though the finish. Drink now.

Sauvignon, Trentino 1997 $7.99.   81
Cabernet Sauvignon, Trentino 1994 $11.99.   86

Deep, saturated blackish-ruby hue. Intense herb and spice aromas point to extended oak aging. A lean entry leads a firm, medium-bodied palate with drying tannins. Complex in flavor (on the herbal side of Merlot) with good cut. Drink now.

Merlot, Trentino 1996 $11.99.   86

Ruby-brick red hue. Plummy, red berry aromas. A flavorful attack leads a medium-bodied palate with succulent fruit flavors and fine texture. Acids frame the soft tannins on the finish. Drink now.

Merlot, Trentino 1997 $7.99.   81

Consorzio Produttori Vini di Velletri
Velletri, Rosso 1994 $8.99.   81

Scale: Superlative (96-100), Exceptional (90-95), Highly Recommended (85-89), Recommended (80 84), Not Recommended (Under 80)

Contadi Castaldi

Franciacorta, Brut NV $17.99.   82

Terre di Franciacorta, Bianco 1997 $9.99.   92

Brilliant greenish-straw hue. Intense, biscuity, mineral aromas are quite complex and show a leesy undertone. A lean entry leads to a ripe but crisp, medium-bodied palate that finishes in an elegant, minerally manner. Very stylish, like a fine Chablis. Drink now.

Conte Alessandro Piovene

Sauvignon, Colli Berici 1998 $NA. (SR)   84

Pale straw hue. Lean mineral and dried herb aromas. A rich entry leads to a lush, rounded palate. Lean acidity maintains a sense of balance, but quite ripe. More of a Chardonnay style. Drink now.

Cabernet, Colli Berici 1997 $NA. (SR)   89

Deep, saturated ruby-purple hue. Intense cedar, mineral, and berry aromas have a flashy Cabernet Franc quality. A rich entry leads to a rich, supple, moderately full-bodied palate. Ripe and flavorful. Needs time. Midterm cellar candidate (3–6 years).

Tocai Rosso, Colli Berici 1998 $NA. (SR)   82

Conte Collalto

Pinot Grigio, Colli Trevigiani 1997 $NA. (SR)   84

Pale straw hue. Lean mineral and herb aromas. A lush entry leads to a ripe, rounded medium-bodied palate. Supple, flavorful finish. Drink now.

Cabernet, Vini del Piave 1994 $NA. (SR)   88

Saturated blackish-ruby hue. Brooding smoked meat and berry aromas. A rich entry leads to a weighty, full-bodied palate with grainy tannins. Quite robust. Needs time. Midterm cellar candidate (3–6 years).

Cabernet, Vini del Piave 1997 $NA. (SR)   84

Deep, saturated ruby hue. Intense smoke and herb aromas show a marked Franc imprint. A lush entry leads to a rounded, medium-bodied plate with supple tannins. Quite tasty. Drink now.

Colli di Conegliano, Rosso 1995 $NA. (SR)   89

Brilliant ruby-purple hue. Flashy spice and berry aromas show an attractive wood accent. A supple entry leads to a full-bodied palate with big grippy tannins. Stylish and harmonious with a lengthy finish. Midterm cellar candidate (3–6 years).

Incrocio Manzoni 2.15, Colli Trevigiani 1997 $NA. (SR)   84

Bright cherry-garnet hue. Lean mineral and berry aromas have an interesting floral overtone. A ripe entry leads to a lush, rounded, medium-bodied palate. Supple and approachable. Drink now.

Conte d'Attimis-Maniago

Pinot Grigio, Colli Orientali del Friuli 1997 $14.95.   NR

Conti Brandolini d'Adda

Merlot, Friuli 1995 $16.50.   86

Full cherry red. Medium-bodied. Balanced acidity. Moderately extracted. Mildly oaked. Pencil lead, dried herbs, red fruits. Lean classic aromas lead a tight minerally palate showing concentration, and a certain oaky leanness of style. Finishes with fine minerally austerity. Very Bordelaise in its style.

Conti Zecca

Salice Salentino, Cantalupi 1992 $10.   83

Corte Sant'Alda

Amarone della Valpolicella, 1992 $34.99.　　　　　　　　　　93

Deep blackish-ruby cast. Full-bodied. Balanced acidity. Highly extracted. Mildly tannic. Brown spices, black fruits, chocolate. Extremely aromatic with a melange of oak-tinged complex flavors. Fat, full, and ripe on the palate, with an overtone of sweetness through the rich finish.

Valpolicella, 1996 $11.99.　　　　　　　　　　81
Valpolicella, Superiore 1994 $14.99.　　　　　　　　　　83
Recioto della Valpolicella, 1995 $15.99/375 ml.　　　　　　　　　　86

Deep blackish-ruby hue. Moderately full-bodied. Balanced acidity. Moderately extracted. Mildly tannic. Overripe black fruits, earth. Quite aromatic, with a distinctive Porty note and a lush, flavorful mouthfeel. Finishes with some mild sweetness.

Valpolicella, Mithas, Superiore 1994 $19.99.　　　　　　　　　　88

Deep blackish-purple hue. Medium-bodied. Full acidity. Moderately extracted. Mildly tannic. Stewed fruits, chocolate, minerals, flowers. Quite aromatic, with classic, slightly overripe flavors. Youthful and vibrant on the full but lighter-styled palate. Buoyant acidity lends some real grip to the finish.

Fabio Coser

Pinot Grigio, Collio 1997 $16.05.　　　　　　　　　　88

Bright yellow-gold hue. Aromatically intense, showing smoke, lime zest character. Very flavorful and rich on the attack, with a moderately full-bodied palate and a lingering finish. Rich and buttery, yet acids come though on the finish.

Alessandro de Conciliis

Cilento, Donnaluna 1997 $14.99.　　　　　　　　　　90

Brilliant straw hue. Exotic pineapple and honey aromas jump from the glass. A lean entry leads to a medium-bodied palate with outstanding intensity of flavor. Angular acidity provides a sense of balance. Intense. Drink now.

Della Scala

Merlot, Piave 1995 $7.99.　　　　　　　　　　NR

Di Meo

Greco di Tufo, Bianco 1996 $19.99.　　　　　　　　　　83
Fiano di Avellino, Bianco 1996 $22.99.　　　　　　　　　　84

Brilliant greenish-straw hue. Exotic, spicy, cheesy aromas jump from the glass. A lean entry leads to a crisp, moderately light-bodied palate. Doesn't quite deliver what the nose promises. Lively, clean finish. Interesting. Drink now.

Taurasi, Rosso 1994 $24.99.　　　　　　　　　　86

Brilliant garnet hue. Aromatically austere with mineral, earth, and pepper nuances. Firm on the attack, with a medium-bodied palate and lean, smoky flavors that conclude with mineral dryness. Interesting. Drink now.

Doro Princic

Tocai Friulano, Collio 1997 $19.　　　　　　　　　　85

Brilliant platinum-straw hue. High-toned grapefruit, flower, and spice aromas jump from the glass. A lean entry leads to a medium-bodied palate with a ripe, oily texture. Acidity maintains balance through the finish. Drink now.

Dotto Lidio

Colli Euganei, Bianco 1998 $NA. (SR)　　　　　　　　　　81

Scale: Superlative (96-100), Exceptional (90-95), Highly Recommended (85-89), Recommended (80-84), Not Recommended (Under 80)

Cabernet, Colli Euganei 1997 $NA. (SR)   88

Deep, saturated ruby hue. Extravagant herb and black fruit aromas show a definitive Franc influence. A supple entry leads to a rounded, medium-bodied palate with mouthwatering acidity. Quite ripe, and drinking very well. Drink now.

Duca di Salaparuta

Sicily, Duca Enrico 1993 $60.   95

Deep blackish-ruby cast. Full-bodied. Full acidity. Highly extracted. Moderately oaked. Mildly tannic. Black fruits, vanilla, dried herbs. Very aromatic with an oak accent that meets a deep core of herb-tinged fruit flavors on the palate. Highly structured, with great grip and intensity through the lengthy finish.

Ecco Domani

Pinot Bianco delle Venezie, 1996 $10.   86

Brilliant greenish-straw hue. Lean stone fruit and mineral aromas have a woolly overtone. A crisp entry leads to a medium-bodied palate with a honeyed richness. Zesty, flavorful finish. May have a hint of overripeness, but adds a level of complexity. Drink now.

Pinot Grigio delle Venezie, 1997 $10.   80
Merlot delle Venezie, 1995 $10.   83
Pinot Nero delle Venezie, 1997 $10.   NR

Enrico & Renato Facchin

Colli Euganei, Bianco 1998 $NA. (SR)   80
Cabernet, Colli Euganei 1997 $NA. (SR)   81
Colli Euganei, Fior d'Arancio Vino Spumante Dolce NV $NA. (SR)   88

Pale straw hue with a thin mousse. Generous flower and orange blossom aromas. A crisp entry leads to a medium-bodied palate with forward citrus flavors. Well balanced and very refreshing. Drink now.

Falesco

Est!Est!!Est!!! di Montefiascone, Poggio dei Gelsi 1997 $12.   80
Umbria, Vitiano Rosso 1998 $10.   92

Dark, brilliant ruby-purple hue. Intense vanilla and berry aromas are very New World-like. A lush entry leads to a very ripe, medium-bodied palate with supple tannins. Has a wonderful mouthfeel and a very lengthy, flavorful finish. Drink now or later.

Fantinel

Pinot Grigio, Grave Friuli 1997 $10.   NR
Pinot Grigio, Collio 1997 $18.   89

Bright yellow-gold hue. Sensational oily, smoky aromas. A rich attack leads a moderately full-bodied palate with concentrated flavors and a smooth, oily mouthfeel with a very ripe personality through the finish. Very stylish.

Cabernet Sauvignon, Friuli 1997 $18.   NR
Merlot, Grave 1997 $10.   81

Fattoria Coroncino

Verdicchio dei Castelli di Jesi Classico Superiore, Il Coroncino 1997 $14.99. 90

Brilliant yellow-straw hue. Enticing, delicate orange blossom and mineral aromas. A vibrant entry leads to an intensely flavored, medium-bodied palate. Features a lengthy, complex finish. Quite stylish.

Fattoria la Valentina
Montepulciano d'Abruzzo, 1994 $7.99.   84

Deep blackish ruby hue. Moderately full-bodied. Balanced acidity. Moderately extracted. Mildly oaked. Cinnamon, chocolate, black fruits. Very aromatic, with a pleasant wood accent to the core of ripe fruit flavors. Soft and lush palate with a solid dose of acidity at the finish.

Fazi-Battaglia
Verdicchio dei Castelli Jesi, Classico 1996 $8.99.   NR
Sangiovese delle Marche, Vino de Tavola 1995 $8.99.   85

Bright ruby cast with a slight fade. Moderately light-bodied. Balanced acidity. Moderately extracted. Bitter cherries, minerals. Bright fruity aromas lead a lush, ripe mouthfeel. Finishes with a zesty note of acidity.

Feudi di San Gregorio
Avellino, Albente 1997 $12.   88

Bright golden hue. Exotic lanolin and mineral aromas. A rich entry leads to a moderately full-bodied palate with angular acidity. On the richer side. Very interesting, with a clean finish. Drink now.

Italy, Rubrato 1997 $16.   86

Brilliant ruby-garnet hue. Fresh, high-toned, licorice aromas show a fresh fruit accent. A ripe entry leads to a medium-bodied palate with chewy tannins. Finishes with a sweet red fruit quality. Quite rich. Drink now or later.

Firriato
Catarratto-Chardonnay, Sicilia 1998 $NA.   86

Brilliant golden hue. Attractive brown spice and citrus peel aromas. A lean entry leads to a moderately full-bodied palate with rich flavors. Angular acidity provides a firm structure. Has lots of character. Drink now.

Grillo-Chardonnay, Sicilia 1998 $10.99.   87

Deep straw hue. Intense lanolin and flower aromas. A crisp entry leads to a lean, angular, medium-bodied palate with concentrated flavors. Well structured with a vibrant finish. Drink now.

Nero D'Avola-Syrah, Sicilia 1997 $NA.   91

Bright purple-red hue. Exotic aromas show a spicy, toasty oak accent. Almost charred. Crisp on the attack, with a medium body and taut, gripping tannins with lush, toasty oak flavors overwhelming ripe, plummy fruit. Exotic now, the oak should settle with some age. Drink now or later.

Nero d'Avola-Cabernet Sauvignon, Sicilia 1997 $10.99.   89

Deep, saturated ruby-purple hue. Intense vanilla and cassis aromas strike a very modern accent. A rich entry leads to a ripe, jammy palate with abundant fruit flavors. Full-bodied with drying tannins. Bears more than a passing resemblance to an old vine California Zinfandel. Drink now or later.

Fontana Candida
Frascati, Superiore 1996 $7.49.   83
Pinot Grigio, Delle Venezie 1997 $7.49.   NR

Fossmarai
Italy, Prosecco Sparkling NV $11.99.   81

Scale: Superlative (96-100), Exceptional (90-95), Highly Recommended (85-89), Recommended (80-84), Not Recommended (Under 80)

Frecciarossa

Pinot Nero, Oltrepo Pavese 1993 $26. 84

Bright ruby-garnet cast. Medium-bodied. Full acidity. Moderately extracted. Mildly oaked. Mildly tannic. Dried herbs, red fruits, brown spices. Pleasantly aromatic with a distinctive wood accent to the core of complex Pinot flavors. Lean and well structured through the finish. Features excellent grip and intensity.

Oltrepo' Pavese, Villa Odero Reserva 1990 $40. 90

Deep blackish-ruby hue. Moderately full-bodied. Full acidity. Highly extracted. Heavily oaked. Mildly tannic. Vanilla, black fruits, minerals. Rich aromas reveal a modern style with effusive wood and fruit flavors. Purely Italian in structure however, with excellent grip, racy acidity, and a lean finish.

Oltrepo' Pavese, Villa Odero Reserva 1991 $26. 83

Furlan

Friuli Venezia Giulia, Castelcosa Grigio 1996 $12.99. 84

Bright yellow-gold. Medium-bodied. Balanced acidity. Moderately extracted. Minerals, flowers. Minerally nose with a floral note. Weighty, firm palate has dry flavors through the finish. Quite full, structured and austere, with acids accentuating the dryness.

Friuli Venezia Giulia, Castelcosa Tai 1994 $15.99. 87

Golden straw. Moderately full-bodied. Balanced acidity. Moderately extracted. Earth, sweet herbs, mint. Rich expressive aromas show an oily, aromatic varietal character. Round and ripe flavors have an herbal edge through a lengthy finish. Very solid, concentrated.

Merlot, Friuli Venezia Giulia 1994 $14.99. 80

Gancia

Piemonte, Spumante Rosso NV $9.49. NR

Il Falcone

Val di Cornia Suvereto, Falcobianco 1997 $9.99. NR
Val di Cornia Suvereto, Falcorosso 1997 $9.99. NR

Illuminati

Chardonnay, Controguerra 1997 $10. NR
Controguerra, Costalupo 1997 $8. 86

Pale green-straw hue. Medium-bodied. Balanced acidity. Moderately extracted. Zest, tropical fruits. Bright, clean fruit salad aromas follow through on the palate. Plenty of aromatic varietal character.

Montepulciano d'Abruzzo, Riparosso 1997 $9. 82
Montepulciano d'Abruzzo Vecchio, Zanna 1993 $22. 91

Deep blackish-ruby hue. Full-bodied. Balanced acidity. Moderately extracted. Moderately oaked. Mildly tannic. Cinnamon, black fruits, chocolate. Very aromatic, with attractive spicy oak accents and a core of ripe fruit flavors. Thick and rich though well balanced with excellent grip and intensity.

Montepulciano d'Abruzzo, Zanna 1994 $23. 90

Deep, saturated blackish-ruby hue. Generous chocolate, dried fruit, and forest aromas are exotic and complex. A rich entry leads a ripe, chunky, moderately full-bodied palate with velvety tannins. Well balanced, with a great mouthfeel and tons of flavor intensity. Drink now or later.

Montepulciano d'Abruzzo, Lumen 1994 $40.   **95**

Deep blackish-ruby hue. Full-bodied. Balanced acidity. Highly extracted. Mildly oaked. Mildly tannic. Chocolate, black fruits, spices. Very aromatic, with a melange of dark and brooding flavors. Deep and quite rich on the palate with a sense of thickness buoyed by solid acidity and tannins that rear up on the finish.

La Colombaia

Pinot Grigio, Valdadige 1996 $9.99.   **80**

Merlot, Veneto 1996 $9.99.   **86**

Solid cherry red. Medium-bodied. Balanced acidity. Moderately extracted. Heavily oaked. Brown spice, vanilla, red fruits. Pronounced toasted oak aromas. Soft fleshy fruit defers to a huge dose of toasted oak flavors. Good mouthfeel and soft finish suggest that this is not for keeping.

La Monacesca

Verdicchio di Matelica, 1996 $13.   **80**

La Montecchia

Chardonnay, Colli Euganei 1998 $NA. (SR)   **84**

Deep greenish-straw hue. Generous banana and tropical fruit aromas. A lean entry leads to a ripe, medium-bodied palate. Straightforward, with a clean finish. Drink now.

Cabernet, Colli Euganei 1996 $NA. (SR)   **85**

Bright cherry-garnet hue. Mature cedar and tobacco aromas jump from the glass. A lean entry leads to a medium-bodied palate with rounded tannins. Lighter and showing some maturity. Drink now.

Merlot-Cabernet, Colli Euganei 1996 $NA. (SR)   **88**

Bright garnet hue. Generous cedar and herb aromas. A lush entry leads to a rounded, medium-bodied palate with soft flavors. Harmonious with grippy tannins through the finish. Drink now.

Lamberti

Recioto Della Valpolicella Amarone, Corte Rubini 1993 $22.99.   **81**

Le Terrazze

IGT Marche, Chaos 1997 $NA. (SR)   **90**

Saturated violet-ruby hue. Intense chocolate and black fruit aromas show a generous oak accent. A smooth entry leads a full-bodied palate with thick robust tannins. Highly structured, voluptuous, and rich, with a heavyweight Shiraz-like character. Mid-term cellar candidate (3–6 years).

Rosso Conero, 1997 $NA. (SR)   **90**

Saturated ruby-purple hue. Intense game, leather, and black fruit aromas. A smooth entry leads a moderately full-bodied palate with velvety tannins. Attractive and rich with mild oak influences and a solid structure. Drink now or later.

Leone de Castris

Salice Salentino, Riserva 1995 $8.99.   **84**

Deep blackish ruby hue with a slight fade. Medium-bodied. Balanced acidity. Moderately extracted. Earth, chocolate, black fruits. Very aromatic, with a complex array of flavors. Quite rich and ripe, but carries a sense of lightness on the palate. Linear acidity makes for a clean finish. Well balanced.

Librandi

Cirò, Rosso Classico 1997 $9.   **NR**

Scale: Superlative (96-100), Exceptional (90-95), Highly Recommended (85-89), Recommended (80-84), Not Recommended (Under 80)

Lis Neris

Picol-Sauvignon, Isonzo del Friuli 1997 $17.   84

Brilliant platinum-straw hue. Complex, restrained herb, spice, and mineral aromas.
A zesty entry leads to a moderately light-bodied palate with a glycerous undertone.
Quite ripe, with a crisp finish. Drink now.

Livio Felluga

Pinot Grigio, Esperto 1996 $14.   85

Bright straw cast. Moderately full-bodied. Full acidity. Moderately extracted. Green herbs,
earth, minerals. Subtle aromas, yet the flavors are complex, with a nuanced character.
Ripe and round in the mouth with a solid edge of acidity through the finish.

Pinot Grigio, Friuli 1996 $18.50.   82

Tocai Friulano, Friuli 1996 $18.50.   90

Lustrous golden straw. Moderately full-bodied. Balanced acidity. Highly extracted.
Asparagus, sweet herbs, minerals. Wonderfully ripe, sweet herbal aromas. Weighty, oily
textured, full palate is complex and dry, with excellent grip through the finish. Very
expressive, powerful style.

Merlot, Friuli 1994 $32.   88

Deep red with a purple rim. Moderately full-bodied. Balanced acidity. Highly extracted.
Moderately oaked. Moderately tannic. Brown spice, black tea, black fruits. Plenty of
toasty new oak aromas. Backward, structured palate has imposing drying tannins on
the astringent finish. Seems well structured, with plenty of oak influence.

Merlot, Friuli 1995 $22.50.   83

Lizzano

Tarantino, Primitivo 1995 $9.   86

Bright blackish ruby cast. Moderately full-bodied. Full acidity. Moderately extracted.
Mildly tannic. Briar fruits, minerals. Aromatic, with a deeply flavored, fruit-centered
palate. Lush and rich in the mouth, with vibrant acidity through the finish.

Tarantino, Il Taurus 1993 $11.   84

Deep garnet cast. Medium-bodied. Full acidity. Moderately extracted. Mildly oaked.
Mildly tannic. Leather, prunes. Extremely aromatic in a very Old World, rustic manner.
Light on the palate with vibrant acidity and a lean, flavorful finish.

Malvira

Piemonte, Birbet NV $15.   87

Pale ruby with brilliant clarity. Moderately light-bodied. Full acidity. Moderately extracted.
Red fruits, fresh herbs. Forcefully aromatic with vibrant, fruit centered flavors. Light and
zesty with about half the carbonation of a traditional sparkling wine. Sweetness is nicely
balanced by acidity. Clean and refreshing through the flavorful finish.

Marega

Chardonnay, Collio 1996 $12.99.   82

Friuli Venezia Giulia, Holbar Bianco 1992 $19.99.   91

Deep golden yellow. Moderately full-bodied. Balanced acidity. Highly extracted.
Petrol, minerals. Petrol aromas are outstanding. Rich, rounded, and oily, this has the
character of a mature Mosel wine. The long dry finish is quite clean. Wonderfully
mature, displaying tertiary character.

Pinot Bianco, Collio 1996 $14.99.   84

Bright pale gold. Medium-bodied. Balanced acidity. Moderately extracted. Mineral,
citrus. Fresh aromas lead a clean, citric palate with a mineral edge through the finish.
A very clean, easy-drinking style.

Pinot Grigio, Collio 1996 $12.99.   80

Tocai Friulano, Collio 1996 $12.99.   80
Friuli Venezia Giulia, Holbar Rosso 1993 $19.99.   82

Danieli Marina
Italy, Faralta Vino Rosso da Tavola 1992 $16.99.   82

Masi
Soave Classico Superiore, 1997 $7.99.   NR
Amarone Classico della Valpolicella, 1994 $32.   NR
Campofiorin, Veronese 1994 $17.   84
Bright garnet cast. Medium-bodied. Full acidity. Highly extracted. Mildly oaked. Moderately tannic. Brown spices, black fruits, sweet herbs. Pleasantly aromatic with a clean and vibrant palate feel. Lighter in style and racy through the finish.
Valpolicella Classico, Superiore 1996 $7.99.   81

Masottina
Merlot, Piave 1998 $NA. (SR)   83
Colli di Conegliano, Rosso 1996 $NA. (SR)   89
Brilliant, saturated ruby-purple hue. Intense vanilla and spice aromas show a dominant oak accent. A ripe entry leads to a lush, rounded, full-bodied palate. Very rich, supple mouthfeel. Lengthy. Drink now or later.

Mastroberardino
Lacryma Christi del Vesuvio, Bianco 1996 $15.   90
Bright yellow-gold. Moderately full-bodied. Balanced acidity. Moderately extracted. White melon, honey. Grassy, complex aromas. Rounded, weighty palate has a fine mouthfeel. Flavors develop through the long, long finish.
Greco di Tufo, 1995 $20.   89
Deep old gold hue. Moderately full-bodied. Full acidity. Highly extracted. Cheese, honey. Mature nose has some buttery notes. Rich and mouthfilling with considerable depth and roundness. Crisp finish. Distinctive and unusual style.
Fiano di Avellino, Radici 1994 $26.   NR
Irpinia, Lacrimarosa, Dry Rosé 1995 $14.99.   83
Lacryma Christi del Vesuvio Rosso, 1996 $15.   81
Taurasi, Radici 1994 $22.50.   91
Bright blackish-ruby cast. Moderately full-bodied. Balanced acidity. Moderately extracted. Moderately oaked. Mildly tannic. Vanilla, dried herbs, red fruits. Extremely aromatic with a complex range of oak-accented flavors. Well balanced and harmonious in the mouth, with a lengthy, angular finish. An enticing marriage of modern vinification and Old World terroir.

Mazzi
Valpolicella Classico Superiore, 1996 $NA. (SR)   84
Pale ruby-red. Bright anise, red fruit, and mineral aromas. A lean entry leads a moderately light-bodied palate with crisp acidity. Vibrant finish. Quite aromatic, in a "clean" rustic style.

Mezzacorona
Pinot Grigio, Trentino 1997 $7.99.   82
Merlot, Trentino 1997 $7.99.   86
Red-purple hue. Primary aromas of tart berry fruits. Vibrant on the attack, leading a medium-bodied palate with taut acids and tart berry flavors. Tannins are mild. Drink now.

Moletto

Veneto, Colmello Bianco 1991 $19.99.　　　　87

Deep golden straw. Moderately full-bodied. Balanced acidity. Moderately extracted. Rancio, earth, yeast. Profoundly aromatic, oily, ripe. Complex yeasty notes with rancio-like maturity. Full, rich mouthfeel has excellent texture, with a fine old Riesling-like mouthfeel. Complex earthy finish.

Pinot Grigio, Piave 1997 $9.99.　　　　83

Cabernet Franc, Lison Pramaggiore 1995 $11.99.　　　　85

Bright blackish ruby cast. Medium-bodied. Full acidity. Highly extracted. Mildly tannic. Mint, dried herbs, minerals. Pungent, with an array of herbal, almost medicinal aromas. Light in style though well structured on the palate, with a firm, extremely flavorful finish. An attention-grabbing style that may not appeal to all.

Veneto Orientale, Colmello Rosso 1991 $19.99.　　　　86

Bright ruby-garnet cast. Medium-bodied. Full acidity. Highly extracted. Mildly oaked. Mildly tannic. Minerals, brown spices. Spicy, mature aromas lead a firm and austere palate feel. Lean, focused, and flavorful finish. This is drinking well now.

Molon Ornella Traverso

Vite Bianca, Veneto 1995 $NA. (SR)　　　　90

Deep golden hue. Exotic yeast and mineral aromas show a great leesy accent. A rich entry leads to a ripe, flavorful palate with rounded acidity. A big, lushly styled wine with complex, yeasty accents through the finish. Drink now.

Sauvignon, Veneto 1997 $NA. (SR)　　　　89

Deep greenish golden hue. Attractive gooseberry and mineral aromas show a big varietal accent. A firm entry leads to a ripe, moderately full-bodied palate with intense flavors. Supported by solid acidity. Drink now.

Merlot, Piave 1995 $NA. (SR)　　　　90

Brilliant ruby-garnet hue. Attractive cedar and berry aromas show a lush wood accent. A ripe entry leads to a rounded, medium-bodied palate with lush, intense fruit flavors. Supple and generous. Drink now.

Veneto, Vite Rossa 1995 $NA. (SR)　　　　89

Deep cherry-garnet hue. Attractive, exotic spice and berry aromas. A lush entry leads to a supple, moderately full-bodied palate. Harmonious and intense. Drink now or later.

Monarco

Esino Bianco, Terrazzo 1997 $7.99.　　　　81

Esino Rosso, Terrazzo 1996 $7.99.　　　　84

Full crimson-ruby hue. Austere aromas of dried cherries and flowers. Crisp on the attack, with a medium-bodied palate showing fine acids, concentrated red fruits, and a mineral finish. Drink now or later.

Montesel

Prosecco di Conegliano Valdobbiadene, Extra Dry Sparkling Wine 1997 $16.　　　　86

Pale straw hue. Lean, mineral, floral aromas. A crisp attack leads a moderately light-bodied palate with apple flavors lingering through the finish. Carbonation is fine beaded and frothy. Clean and refreshing style.

Sergio Nardin

Chardonnay, Lison Pramaggiore 1998 $NA. (SR)　　　　82

Pinot Grigio, Lison Pramaggiore 1998 $NA. (SR)   86

Deep greenish-straw hue. Exotic smoke and mineral aromas. A firm entry leads to a weighty, moderately full-bodied palate with very robust flavors. Should open with a bit of time. Drink now or later.

Cabernet Sauvignon, Lison Pramaggiore 1997 $NA. (SR)   87

Deep ruby-garnet hue. Intense herb and cedar aromas jump from the glass. A ripe entry leads to a rounded, medium-bodied palate. Exceptionally flavorful with good acidic cut to the finish. Drink now or later.

Lison Pramaggiore, Vigna Melonetto, Merum Rosso 1996 $NA. (SR)   90

Deep saturated purplish-ruby hue. Forward dill and spice aromas show a hefty oak accent. A ripe entry leads to a lush, moderately full-bodied palate. Rounded, but with grippy tannins. Very attractive but should be better over the next few years. Drink now or later.

Nino Negri

Valtellina Superiore, Inferno 1995 $10.99.   84

Pale ruby-red. Austere, mineral aromas. Crisp on the attack, with tart red berry flavors and a medium body. Finishes with fine mineral grip. Drink now.

Vincentini Orgnani

Pinot Grigio, Friuli 1997 $14.80.   88

Bright yellow hue. Tart apple and mineral aromas. Crisp on the attack, leading a medium-bodied palate with fine acid cut and good intensity of tart fruit flavors through a persistent finish. Very flavorful. Drink now.

Ottella

Lugana, Bianco 1998 $NA. (SR)   85

Pale straw hue. Attractive, subdued almond and mineral aromas. A rounded entry leads to a ripe, medium-bodied palate with zesty acidity. Rich and stylish, but refreshing, with an apricot accented finish.

Lugana, Bianco Le Creete 1998 $NA. (SR)   86

Brilliant straw hue. Lean mineral and herb aromas. A crisp entry leads to a firm, medium-bodied palate with edgy acidity and fine concentration. Fairly intense. An excellent accompaniment to shellfish. Drink now.

Rosso Veronese, Campo Sireso, IGT 1996 $NA. (SR)   89

Brilliant pale purple hue. Attractive vanilla aromas show an enticing oak accent. A lush entry leads to a rounded, medium-bodied palate with grippy tannins. Exceptionally flavorful and lengthy. Drink now or later.

Rosso Veronese, Rosso Ottella IGT 1998 $NA. (SR)   85

Brilliant pale purple hue. Attractive, ripe berry, mineral, and pepper aromas jump from the glass. A lean entry leads to a moderately light-bodied palate with fruit accented flavors and bright acidity. Drink now.

Palama

Rosso Salento, Metiusco 1997 $13.95.   89

Bright ruby-red. Deeply fruity aromas of ripe cherries and spice. Concentrated cherry flavors lead a moderately full-bodied palate with fine acids, polished tannins, and amazing length. Drinkable now, though this will improve with age.

Paternoster

Aglianico del Vulture, 1995 $21.   NR

774

Scale: Superlative (96-100), Exceptional (90-95), Highly Recommended (85-89), Recommended (80-84), Not Recommended (Under 80)

Pecorari
Gris Pinot Grigio, Italy 1996 $22.51.   **90**

Bright yellow hue. Intense on the nose with apple and smoke and a nutty character. Flavors are similarly intense on the moderately full-bodied palate with citrus acidity keeping a firm grip on the finish. Impressive flavor concentration. Rather distinctive. Drink now.

Pichierri
Primitivo di Manduria, Terrarossa 1996 $15.   **82**

Pighin
Pinot Grigio, Grave del Friuli 1998 $13.   **81**
Pinot Grigio, Collio 1997 $20.   **89**

Brilliant straw hue. Lean mineral and lanolin aromas. A vibrant entry leads to a medium-bodied palate with crisp acids. Concentrated and intense. Exotic—not unlike a powerful, unoaked, Australian Semillon. Should develop. Drink now or later.

Pino
Salento, Rosso 1996 $8.99.   **81**

Pisani
Merlot, Basilicata 1996 $10.99.   **NR**

Pra'di Pradis
Tocai Friulano, Collio 1994 $13.99.   **89**

Deep straw cast. Moderately full-bodied. Full acidity. Highly extracted. Flowers, citrus zest, green herbs. Extremely aromatic, with complex flavors. The mouthfeel is full and rounded yet well balanced by vibrant acidity. Shows fine length and concentration through the finish.

Pravini
Merlot, Trentino 1997 $9.99.   **83**

Remo Farina
Soave Classico Superiore, 1996 $7.99.   **NR**
Amarone della Valpolicella Classico, 1995 $30.99.   **88**

Deep, saturated ruby-garnet hue. Aromatically reserved with a subtle spicy overtone. A weighty entry leads to a robust, full-bodied palate with chewy tannins. Ample, but rather restrained at present. Should open with time. Midterm cellar candidate (3–6 years).

Valpolicella Classico Superiore, 1996 $9.99.   **84**

Brilliant garnet hue. Lean mineral aromas. A firm entry leads to a medium-bodied palate with rounded tannins. Shows some richness, but not overly flavorful. Drink now or later.

Luigi Righetti
Soave Classico Superiore, Campochiaro 1997 $9.99.   **NR**
Valpolicella Classico Superiore, Campolietti 1995 $NA.   **87**

Deep, saturated ruby-garnet hue. Generous, spicy red fruit and mineral aromas. A rich entry leads a moderately full-bodied palate. Robust flavors are enlivened by sturdy acidity. Harmonious and well balanced with a clean finish. Drink now.

Riunite
Merlot, delle Venezie 1995 $6.   **NR**
Lambrusco, Emilia NV $5.   **82**

Lancellota, Emilia NV $5.   86

Deep blackish purple. Moderately light-bodied. Full acidity. Moderately extracted.
Raspberries, minerals. Aromatic and deeply flavored with a cordial-like intensity to
the flavors. Light and racy with a hint of sweetness to the semi-sparkling finish.

Rivera

Castel del Monte, Rupicolo di Rivera 1996 $6.99.   NR
Castel del Monte, Terre al Monte, Aglianico Rosso 1996 $10.99.   88

Deep ruby-red hue. Floral, dried red cherry aromas. Firm on the attack, with a
moderately full-bodied palate with concentrated ripe cherry flavors and a rich texture
through the finish. Drink now.

Bernarda Rocca

Pinot Grigio, Colli Orientali del Friuli 1997 $14.99.   89

Bright yellow hue. Distinctive aromas of green tea, smoke, and citrus fruits. Fresh and
lively on the attack, leading a medium-bodied palate showing crisp, ripe fruit flavors and
a clean, mineral finish featuring subtle smoky nuances. Drink now.

Tocai Friulano, Colli Orientali del Friuli 1997 $13.99.   82

Roccadoro

Orvieto Classico, Secco 1995 $8.   81

Rotari

Trento, Brut Arte Italiana NV $10.99.   86

Bright yellow-straw hue. Complex aromas show a mature, yeasty character. A rich
entry leads a medium-bodied palate with concentrated flavors and a long finish
revealing nutty character.

San Valentino

Colli di Rimini, Eclissi di Sole 1997 $15.95.   84

Saturated dark purple hue. Strong aromas of crisp red fruits and minerals. Bright and
lemony on the attack, leading a moderately full-bodied palate with tart cherry flavors
and dense grainy tannins clamping down on the finish. Drink now or later.

Santi

Pinot Grigio, Trentino 1998 $11.99.   83

Savese

Primitivo di Manduria, Terrarossa 1996 $15.   81

Scarlatta

Trebbiano d'Abruzzo, 1995 $4.25.   82
Pinot Grigio, Veneto 1996 $4.75.   83
Cabernet, Veneto 1996 $4.75.   86

Bright blackish ruby cast. Medium-bodied. Full acidity. Moderately extracted. Mildly
tannic. Dried herbs, red fruits. Pleasantly aromatic with a distinctive herbal bent to the
core of fruit flavors. A light style with a lean and intense finish.

Merlot, Veneto 1996 $4.75.   82
Montepulciano d'Abruzzo, 1996 $4.25.   83
Sangiovese, Terre di Chieti 1996 $4.25.   NR

Scale: Superlative (96-100), Exceptional (90-95), Highly Recommended (85-89),
Recommended (80-84), Not Recommended (Under 80)

Sella & Mosca

Vermentino di Sardegna, La Cala 1997 $9.50.   NR

Cannonau di Sardegna, Riserva 1993 $11.99.   84

Bright ruby-garnet cast. Medium-bodied. Full acidity. Highly extracted. Moderately oaked. Moderately tannic. Minerals, brown spices, dried herbs. Pleasantly aromatic with an intense and flavorful entry. Lean, well structured and quite focused through the finish.

Alghero, Tanca Farra' 1990 $17.50.   89

Bright blackish-garnet cast. Moderately light-bodied. Full acidity. Highly extracted. Mildly tannic. Tea, sweet herbs, mushrooms. Outrageously aromatic with a huge wave of mature, earthy flavors. Lean and firmly structured on the palate with an angular, mildly astringent finish. Engaging style, though very distinctive.

Soletta

Cannonau di Sardegna, Firmadu 1996 $15.   83

Italy, Dolce Valle 1996 $23/500 ml.   93

Full copper-orange cast. Moderately full-bodied. Full acidity. Highly extracted. Orange blossom, caramel. Pungent, almost medicinal Moscato aromas. Dry on the palate with a caramelized character and a thick mouthfeel that is kept in check by fine acids. Sweetness is quite restrained.

Soraval

Chardonnay, Trentino 1997 $13.49.   83

Pinot Grigio, Valdadige 1997 $10.99.   86

Bright yellow hue. Classic smoky aromas. A weighty attack leads a medium-bodied palate with a fine mouthfeel and smoky flavors that finish with a note of citrus acidity and mineral austerity. Drink now.

Merlot, Trentino 1996 $10.99.   NR

Stival

Chardonnay, Veneto 1995 $11.99.   91

Bright gold. Moderately full-bodied. Full acidity. Highly extracted. Cheese, hazelnuts, tropical fruits. Extremely aromatic with a complex melange of aromas that follow through on the palate. Full and tightly wound on the palate with vibrant acidity through the finish.

Merlot, Veneto 1995 $11.99.   NR

Taurino

Rosso del Salento, Notarpanaro 1993 $14.   84

Deep, saturated ruby-garnet hue. Exotic game, dried fruit, and leather aromas. A rich entry leads to a velvety, full-bodied palate. Drying finish, but lots of character. Drink now.

Salice Salentino, Riserva 1995 $11.   85

Brilliant garnet hue. Restrained sweet vanilla and berry aromas. A lean entry leads to a crisp, medium-bodied palate. Shows rustic nuances, but elegant overall. Drying finish. Drink now.

Tenuta Cocci Grifoni

Falario dei Colli Ascolani, Vigneti San Basso 1998 $9.99.   80

Rosso Piceno Superiore, 1997 $9.99.   83

Rosso Piceno Superiore, Vigna Messieri 1997 $13.99.   86

Dark ruby-red. Impressively deep, fruit-laden aromas of black fruits. Concentrated, deeply fruity flavors on the attack, with a moderately full-bodied palate and fine-grained tannins gripping the finish. Drink now or later.

Terlano

Alto Adige, Terlaner Classico 1998 $11.99.   83

Alto Adige, Terlaner Nova Domus 1996 $30.   88

Bright yellow-gold. Medium-bodied. Balanced acidity. Moderately extracted. Mildly oaked. Peach, vanilla. Faintly smoky oak nose leads a juicy forward palate with oak spices in the background emerging on the finish.

Alto Adige, Terlaner Nova Domus 1997 $26.99.   90

Brilliant greenish-straw hue. Smoky, spicy aromas hint at barrel age. A rich entry leads to a concentrated, medium-bodied palate with good flavor intensity supported by crisp acids. Lengthy, buttery, oak-tinged finish. Drink now.

Sauvignon, Alto Adige 1996 $30.   84

Bright yellow-straw hue. Medium-bodied. Balanced acidity. Moderately extracted. Guava, grass. Crisp and high toned, with a grassy, herbal character and plenty of citrus fruit flavors. A fresh, lively style with a solid mouthfeel.

Gewürztraminer, Alto Adige 1997 $30.99.   91

Deep yellow-straw hue. Forceful, honeyed spice, lychee, and pineapple aromas are classic Gewurz with a hint of overripeness. An oily entry leads to a full-bodied, textured palate with explosive flavors and a drying finish. Very complex, and varietally expressive. Drink now.

Pinot Bianco, Alto Adige 1988 $41.   91

Deep yellow-gold. Moderately full-bodied. Balanced acidity. Moderately extracted. Honey, exotic spice, glycerin. Honeyed, ripe aromas need time to develop in the glass. Rich, rounded, and wonderfully textured in the mouth. Finishes with a touch of spice and dryness.

Pinot Bianco, Alto Adige 1995 $16.50.   86

Bright yellow. Medium-bodied. Balanced acidity. Moderately extracted. Citrus, minerals. Clean, bright, and faintly tropical. Good concentration and mouthfeel, and a surprisingly long, pure finish. A very drinkable and refreshing style.

Pinot Bianco, Alto Adige 1996 $15.99.   88

Brilliant deep straw hue. Reserved mineral and stone fruit aromas. A tart entry leads to a medium-bodied palate with edgy acidity. Quite nervous, but opens up with a buttery quality and a firm mineral undertone through the finish. May continue to open over the next few years. Drink now or later.

Pinot Grigio, Alto Adige 1995 $14.99.   89

Brilliant yellow-gold. Moderately full-bodied. Full acidity. Highly extracted. Citrus, herbs. Zesty, fragrant aromas have a smoky note. Sensational acidity and concentration of flavors play out on a long, long finish. Racy, generous style.

Pinot Grigio, Alto Adige 1996 $11.49.   88

Bright gold. Moderately full-bodied. Full acidity. Highly extracted. Dried herbs, smoke, minerals. Subtle but complex aromas play out with great intensity on the firm palate. Firm acidity makes for a clean finish with a hint of dryness. Concentrated and tightly wound style.

Pinot Grigio, Alto Adige 1997 $15.99.   90

Pale straw hue. Glycerous aromas show a distinct mineral character. A weighty entry leads a moderately full-bodied palate with classy, austere mineral flavors that persist through the finish. The mouthfeel displays a very good texture. Drink now.

Pinot Grigio, Alto Adige 1998 $11.99.   88

Pale straw hue. Aromas show a fresh, zesty character with a mineral accent. Vibrant on the attack, leading a medium-bodied palate with a racy, clean finish. Impressive intensity of citrus flavors. Very refreshing.

Scale: Superlative (96-100), Exceptional (90-95), Highly Recommended (85-89), Recommended (80-84), Not Recommended (Under 80)

Porphyr, Lagrein, Riserva 1995 $16.   89

Deep blackish-ruby cast. Moderately full-bodied. Full acidity. Highly extracted.
Moderately oaked. Mildly tannic. Vanilla, earth, black fruits. Reserved aromatically, with
a firm and austere palate feel. Lean and very angular through the firm finish. This has
the structure to age nicely.

Tommasi

Pinot Grigio, Valdadige 1998 $9.95.   NR
Amarone della Valpolicella Classico, 1993 $34.95.   94

Deep, saturated ruby-garnet hue. Extraordinary date, dried fruit, and chocolate aromas
jump from the glass. A rich entry leads to a massive, full-bodied palate with outrageous
flavor intensity. Finishes with big but supple tannins and an intense sweet fruit note.
Drink now or later.

Tonnelli

Malvasia, Spumante NV $11.99.   81
Italy, Malvasia Daunia 1997 $8.99.   NR

Torre Rosazza

Pinot Grigio, Colli Orientali del Friuli 1997 $12.99.   84

Bright yellow hue. Zesty, mildly smoked aromas. Bright citrus flavors on the attack,
with a medium-bodied-palate and a snappy, acidic finish. A clean and refreshing style.
Drink now.

Cabernet Sauvignon, Colli Orientali del Friuli 1996 $14.99.   87

Deep blackish-ruby hue. Enticing black fruit and mineral aromas have a sweet oak
accent. A rich entry leads to a firm, full-bodied palate, with big tannins. Ripe, but
austere in structure. Could use time. Midterm cellar candidate (3–6 years).

Merlot, Colli Orientali del Friuli 1994 $24.99.   85

Bright ruby-red with a lightening rim. Aromas of plums, earth and oak spice. A firm
attack leads a medium-bodied palate with mineral, grippy tannins and brisk acids giving
this a tough character. Drink now.

Torresella

Chardonnay, Veneto 1996 $7.99.   87

Deep straw cast. Moderately full-bodied. Balanced acidity. Moderately extracted.
Lacquer, blanched almonds, oranges. Quite aromatic with a distinctive and complex
array of flavors on the palate. Round and ripe with a linear note of acidity through
the flavorful finish.

Pinot Grigio, Veneto 1996 $7.99.   NR
Cabernet, Veneto 1996 $7.99.   NR
Merlot, Veneto 1996 $8.99.   NR

Trexenta

Cannonau di Saroegna, Rosso 1994 $14.99.   83
Italy, Tanca su Conti, Barricato Rosso 1993 $23.99.   90

Brilliant brickish-garnet hue. Mature forest and earth aromas. A lush entry leads to a
rich, rounded, moderately full-bodied palate. Chewy, but harmonious, with a great
mouthfeel. Supple finish. Drink now or later.

Umani Ronchi

Verdicchio dei Castelli di Jesi Classico Riserva, Plenio 1995 $10.99.   88

Brilliant yellow-golden hue. Exotic, opulent, honeyed aromas suggest a very ripe wine. A rich, oily entry confirms this impression and leads to a moderately full-bodied palate marked by a hint of oak spice. Drying, crisp finish. A very solid wine to be sure, but partial oak treatment may have actually served to dull some of this wine's intensely ripe, varietal character. Drink now or later.

Verdicchio dei Castelli di Jesi Classico Superiore, CaSal di Serra 1997 $10.99.   81

Montepulciano d'Abruzzo, Jorio 1996 $11.99.   84

Saturated blackish-ruby hue. Unusual herbal aromas jump from the glass. A rich entry leads to a moderately full-bodied palate with grainy tannins and firm acidity. Turns a bit tough on the finish. Needs time. Midterm cellar candidate (3–6 years).

Marche, Pelago 1994 $44.99.   97

Deep blackish-ruby cast. Moderately full-bodied. Balanced acidity. Moderately extracted. Moderately oaked. Mildly tannic. Earth, mint, vanilla. Exotically aromatic with a wave of deep and complex flavors on the palate. Well structured and lush, with a lengthy, flavorful finish. This is drinking spectacularly well now.

Marche, Pelago 1995 $49.99.   94

Dark, inky blackish-garnet hue. Elegant brown spice aromas. A robust entry leads to a rich, moderately full-bodied palate with chewy tannins. Rounded and intense, with a lovely structure that bodes well for the future. Accessible, but age-worthy. Drink now or later.

Rosso Conero, 1996 $6.99.   86

Bright blackish ruby hue. Medium-bodied. Moderately extracted. Mildly oaked. Mildly tannic. Minerals, red fruits, vanilla. Engagingly aromatic in a modern fashion, with well-integrated fruit and wood flavors. Lean and crisp in the mouth,with a sturdy, angular finish.

Rosso Conero, San Lorenzo 1995 $8.99.   84

Bright, saturated blackish ruby hue. Moderately full-bodied. Balanced acidity. Moderately extracted. Mildly oaked. Mildly tannic. Black fruits, minerals, vanilla. Pleasantly aromatic, with a well-structured, flavorful mouthfeel. Lean and firm through the finish, showing solid grip and intensity.

Sangiovese, Marche 1997 $8.99.   84

Deep, saturated ruby-garnet hue. Brooding chocolate and ripe black fruit aromas. A rich entry leads to a medium-bodied palate with crisp acids. Rounded, but vibrant through the finish, with an herbal overtone. Drink now.

Umberto Cesari

Albana di Romagna, Colle del Re Passito 1993 $24.99/500 ml.   91

Brilliant autumn gold. Moderately full-bodied. Balanced acidity. Highly extracted. Toasted oak, honey, peaches. Honeyed, spicy, toasty nose. Exotically smoky palate has delicious caramelized flavors that linger through the smoky finish.

Vallone

Brindisi, Vigna Flaminco Rosso, Riserva 1994 $9.99.   NR

Italy, Graticciaia 1993 $38.49.   89

Very deep, saturated blackish-ruby hue. Exotic dried fruit and chocolate aromas jump from the glass. A thick, supple entry leads to a full-bodied palate showing waves of dark fruit flavors that come across with a touch of sweetness. Finishes with big tannins. Amarone-like. Drink now or later.

Salice Salentino, Vereto Rosso Riserva 1995 $8.99.   89
Brilliant garnet hue. Opulent spice, saddle leather, and tobacco aromas. A rich entry leads to a supple, rounded palate. Stylish and flavorful, with velvety tannins. Pleasant, lingering finish. Drink now.

Venegazzu

Colli Trevigiani, Loredan Gasparini Capo di Stato IGT 1996 $NA. (SR)   89
Brilliant cherry hue. Generous lead pencil and mineral aromas hint at a classic Bordeaux accent. A ripe entry leads to a medium-bodied, concentrated palate. Firm and austere through the finish. Should age well. Midterm cellar candidate (3–6 years).

Colli Trevigiani, Loredan Gasparini IGT 1996 $NA. (SR)   82

Villa Bellini

Amarone della Valpolicella Classico, 1993 $NA. (SR)   88
Brilliant cherry-garnet hue. Exotic leather, dried fruit, and chocolate aromas jump from the glass. A lush entry leads to a ripe, rounded, moderately full-bodied palate. Flashes firm tannins. Could use more time. Midterm cellar candidate (3–6 years).

Amarone della Valpolicella Classico, 1994 $NA. (SR)   89
Brilliant cherry-garnet hue. Exotic saddle leather and chocolate aromas jump from the glass. A rich entry leads to a chewy, soft, medium-bodied palate. Finishes with mild tannins, vibrant acidity, and an attractive bittersweet chocolate note. Drink now or later.

Valpolicella Classico, Il Brolo 1998 $NA. (SR)   81
Valpolicella Classico Superiore, Taso 1995 $NA. (SR)   82
Valpolicella Classico Superiore, Taso 1996 $NA. (SR)   88
Brilliant cherry-garnet hue. Attractive leather and spice aromas. A ripe entry leads to a rounded, supple palate. Quite ripe, but not overbearing. Flavor with elegance. Drink now or later.

Villa Brunesca

Chardonnay, Piave 1998 $NA. (SR)   85
Brilliant greenish-straw hue. Attractive, toasty, smoky aromas show an oak accent. A lean entry leads to a medium-bodied palate with crisp acids. Straightforward finish. Drink now.

Pinot Grigio, Piave 1998 $NA. (SR)   88
Deep straw hue. Subdued toast and vanilla aromas show an oak accent. A lush entry leads to a rounded, medium-bodied palate. Generous and quite stylish. Drink now.

Incroce Manzone 6.0.13, Veneto 1998 $NA. (SR)   83
Sauvignon, Veneto 1998 $NA. (SR)   86
Brilliant straw hue. Intense herb and mineral aromas show a pronounced varietal accent. A rich entry leads to a firm, medium-bodied palate with a lean acidic cut. Clean, racy finish. Drink now.

Cabernet, Piave 1996 $NA. (SR)   83
Merlot, Piave 1997 $NA. (SR)   87
Deep, saturated ruby-garnet hue. Enticing dill and spice aromas show a wood accent. A lush entry leads to a rounded, moderately full-bodied palate with supple tannins. Ripe, flavorful finish. Drink now or later.

Refosco, Veneto IGT 1997 $NA. (SR)   82

Villa Frattina

Pinot Grigio, Lison-Pramaggiore 1997 $12.   86
Pale yellow-straw hue. Citrus and mineral aromas. A zesty attack leads a medium-bodied palate with lemony flavors showing fine intensity. Racy acids lift the smoky, subtly herbal finish. Drink now.

Merlot, Lison-Pramaggiore 1997 $12.   **84**

Bright cherry red hue. Tart aromas of minerals, herbs, and cherries. Crisp and vibrant on the attack, leading a medium-bodied palate with light tannins and juicy acids through the finish. Shows a subtle oak spice note that comes though on the finish. Drink now.

Villanova

Pinot Grigio, Collio 1996 $14.99.   **88**

Clear, bright yellow-gold. Medium-bodied. Full acidity. Moderately extracted. Citrus, minerals. Tart, zesty aromas follow through well on the palate. Clean minerally finish with bright acidity.

Viviani

Valpolicella Classico Superiore, 1995 $16.   **82**

Volpe Pasini

Pinot Grigio, Colli Orientali del Friuli 1997 $17.99.   **80**

Elena Walch

Gewürztraminer, Alto Adige 1997 $12.   **80**
Pinot Bianco, Alto Adige 1997 $12.   **85**

Deep greenish-straw hue. Reserved biscuit and orange blossom aromas are quite attractive. A crisp entry leads to a racy, medium-bodied palate with vibrant acidity. Clean, citrusy finish. Drink now.

Pinot Grigio, Alto Adige 1997 $12.   **87**

Bright yellow hue. Exotic aromas of mineral, smoke and peach skin. A rich attack leads a moderately full-bodied palate with impressive mouthfeel and fine intensity of flavors through the mineral finish. This has enough weight to work with richer foods.

Merlot, Alto Adige 1996 $20.   **88**

Brick red hue. Developed oak accented aromas. Toasty on the attack, leading a medium-bodied palate with rounded tannins, plum fruit flavors and a smooth, oaky finish. Drinking well now.

Zenato

Lugana, San Benedetto 1997 $12.   **80**
Pinot Grigio delle Venezie, 1998 $9.   **82**
Valpolicella Classico Superiore, 1995 $11.   **81**

Zeni

Soave Classico, 1998 $NA. (SR)   **80**
Soave Classico, Vignealte 1998 $NA. (SR)   **86**

Pale straw hue. Lean mineral and herb aromas. A crisp entry leads to a firm, medium-bodied palate with zesty acidity. Concentrated and mineral with a clean finish. Drink now.

Valpolicella Classico Speriore, 1997 $NA. (SR)   **82**
Amarone della Valpolicella Classico, 1995 $NA. (SR)   **90**

Brilliant ruby-garnet hue. Elegant plum, mineral, and brown spice aromas. A rich entry leads to a medium-bodied, but richly textured palate. A lighter style of Amarone, but flavorful and stylish. Drink now or later.

Amarone della Valpolicella Classico, Barriques 1995 $NA. (SR)   **90**

Deep, saturated ruby hue. Forward spice and berry aromas show lots of ripeness and a dash of wood. A rich entry leads to a weighty, full-bodied palate with great fruit richness and a drying finish. Drink now or later.

Amarone della Valpolicella Classico, Vignealte 1995 $NA. (SR)   88

Deep, brilliant ruby hue. Attractive, generous roasted game, spice, and black fruit aromas. A rich entry leads to a moderately full-bodied palate with fantastic cut. Exceptionally flavorful, and very well balanced. Drink now or later.

Valpolicella Classico Superiore, Vignealte 1997 $NA. (SR)   83

Fratelli Zeni

Vino Rosso Veronese, Cruino 1995 $NA. (SR)   90

Dark ruby-garnet hue. Exotic roasted game and brown spice aromas jump from the glass. A rich entry leads to a full-bodied palate with outrageously smoky flavors. Very interesting indeed. This one walks on the wild side. Drink now or later.

Zonin

Pinot Grigio, dell Umbria 1996 $8.99.   NR

White Merlot, Veneto 1996 $7.99.   NR

Amarone della Valpolicella, 1994 $10.99.   85

Bright ruby-garnet hue. Moderately full-bodied. Low acidity. Subtly extracted. Mildly tannic. Black fruits, tar, dried herbs. Aromatically reserved, with a fat and ripe mouthfeel. Turns rather linear toward the finish, showing solid grip.

Montepulciano d'Abruzzo, 1996 $7.99.   81

Merlot-Cabernet, Veneto 1996 $6.99.   NR

Venezia Giulia, Berengario 1993 $22.   82

thirty-five

❧

Spain
Rioja

❧

Rioja: Textbook Mediterranean Reds

The buzz for all things Mediterranean shows no signs of subsiding. New and interesting are in, stodgy and staid out. Rusticity, authenticity, and value for money are all-important buzzwords, and in many instances, just as can be the case with certain Italian wines, the wines of Spain fit the bill. Perhaps none more so than Spain's most marketable and recognizable red—Rioja.

What is Rioja?

Rioja is Spain's most prestigious viticultural region containing her oldest wine estates, partly a tribute to producers from Bordeaux who moved there in the late 1800s when *Phylloxera* was ravaging France. Current figures indicate that as much as 40% of all Spanish wine exports to the U.S. are Rioja reds. The Rioja region is situated in the far north of Spain, mainly in Basque country. Despite its nearness to the ocean, Rioja is insulated from chilly maritime influences by mountain ranges. Coolness of vineyard site is largely governed by height above sea level. Rioja contains three sub regions, Rioja Alta, Rioja Alavesa, and Rioja Baja. The first two lie to the west of the region, while the latter, the hottest and driest of the three, occupies the eastern sector.

Tempranillo is the principal black grape of Rioja, although Garnacha is also widely planted, along with a number of other minor varieties. Although fruity nouveau style wines are produced in Rioja, these are seldom seen outside the region. Rioja is strongly associated with oak aged wines. The reason for this might be that Tempranillo is very resistant to oxidation, and would develop very slowly if traditionally vinified and bottled without some form of prior maturation in oak casks. Small American oak barrels are still the most favored maturation vessel, although French oak is also used by some bodegas (wine producers). The former often imparts a telltale sweet vanilla aroma.

Rioja at a Glance

Wines Reviewed:

97

Producers/Brands Represented:

39

Value Rating:

Good

Scale: Superlative (96-100), Exceptional (90-95), Highly Recommended (85-89), Recommended (80-84), Not Recommended (Under 80)

Regulations stipulate the time that different categories of Rioja must remain in cask: "crianza" and "reserva" wines spend one-year minimum, while "gran reservas" spend a minimum of two years. The wine undergoes further mandatory aging in bottle or tank before being released: crianza wines receive one year, reserva wines two years, and gran reservas three years. Some estates may well exceed these minimums and often do. Most Rioja reds are in principal ready for drinking when released, but many of the best can be cellared for years longer, if not decades, a tribute as to how deceptively gracefully Tempranillo ages. Another useful consequence of extended barrel aging is that Rioja wines rarely throw any sediment in bottle, having already left their sediment in the barrel. Decanting is not necessary.

Winemaking techniques, and consequently wine styles, vary widely in Rioja. Marques de Caceres and Martinez Bujanda are two producers that have adopted a very modern approach to their winemaking, eschewing the traditional procedure of extended oak aging in order to try to capture fresher, more fruit-driven, "international" flavors. Most, however, like the revered Bodegas of Marques de Murrietta or La Rioja Alta still produce wines that reflect a more traditional outlook.

As such, most wines, and particularly those labeled reserva or gran reserva, will be soft and mellow, with oak tinged flavors. Additionally, these wines usually retain a certain sharpness of acidity. It is the combination of these qualities that make these wines so perfect at the table. They are flavorful, unique, ready to drink, easy to pair with a wide range of foods, and fairly inexpensive to boot!

Reviews

Abel Mendoza
Jarrarte, Rioja 1995 $15. **89**
Deep ruby cast. Moderately full-bodied. Full acidity. Moderately extracted. Moderately oaked. Mildly tannic. Red fruits, vanilla, sweet herbs. Forward aromas carry an attractive oak accent. Rich and intense in the mouth with a powerful core of fruit flavors. Unusually full, though admirably balanced by bright acidity through the finish.

Artadi
Viñas de Gain, Crianza, Rioja 1995 $16. **83**

Baron de Ley
Blanco, Rioja 1997 $7.99. **NR**
El Meson, Seleccion Especial, Rioja NV $8.99. **82**
Reserva, Rioja 1994 $13.99. **89**
Brickish ruby hue with a gentle fade. Medium-bodied. Full acidity. Moderately extracted. Moderately oaked. Mildly tannic. Leather, spice, earth. Traditional in style, with a fragrant, woody character and a light, lean palate feel. Angular and flavorful through the finish.

Baron de Ona
Reserva, Rioja Alavesa 1992 $13.99. **86**
Full ruby red. Medium-bodied. Highly extracted. Big earthy, black fruit aromas have an herbal accent and lead a ripe blackberry-like palate with dry fine-grained tannins. Seems to be very Cabernet-like in flavors and structure.

Berberana
Tempranillo, Rioja 1995 $10.   83
Reserva, Rioja 1990 $13.   81

Bodegas Bilbainas
Viña Pomal, Rioja 1993 $11.   84

Bodegas Bretón
Loriñon, Reserva, Rioja 1994 $16.   87

Very deep ruby cast. Medium-bodied. Full acidity. Moderately extracted. Mildly oaked. Mildly tannic. Vanilla, red fruits. Quite modern in style with a saturated color and wood accented, bright, fruity flavors. Lighter in the mouth with a youthful vibrance that enlivens the finish.

Campo Viejo
Crianza, Rioja 1995 $8.99.   NR
Reserva, Rioja 1990 $11.   83
Gran Reserva, Rioja 1988 $19.99.   90

Garnet ruby. Medium-bodied. Moderately extracted. Mildly tannic. Earthy, leathery aromas. Quite concentrated on the palate with some dry tannins still giving this grip and authority through the finish and making for a drier, austere style.

J. Garcia Carrion
Solar de Carrion, Rioja 1996 $7.99.   NR

Bodegas Consejo de la Alta
Alta Rio, Cosecha, Rioja 1997 $9.   81
Alta Rio, Crianza, Rioja 1995 $12.   83
Alta Rio, Reserva, Rioja 1994 $20.   81

Contino
Crianza, Rioja 1995 $23.99.   89

Deep ruby cast. Medium-bodied. Full acidity. Moderately extracted. Heavily oaked. Mildly tannic. Toasted coconut, chocolate, black fruits. Attractive aromatics show a big sweet oak accent and a rich core of fruit flavors. Ripe and flavorful, yet zesty, with acidity lending a sense of vibrance through the finish.

Bodegas Corral
Don Jacobo, Rioja 1995 $8.50.   82
Don Jacobo Reserva, Rioja 1994 $12.50.   84

Cosme Palacio y Hermanos
Rioja 1996 $11.   84

CVNE
Monopole Blanco Seco, Rioja 1996 $12.99.   87

Pale yellow. Medium-bodied. Balanced acidity. Oak spice, vanilla. Prominently oaky, spicy aromas. Crisp, vibrant flavors show a heavy overlay of vanilla and spice. Fruit flavors are very mild.

Clarete, Rioja 1995 $10.99.   83
Viña Real, Rioja 1995 $12.99.   84
Reserva, Rioja 1994 $18.99.   84

Scale: Superlative (96-100), Exceptional (90-95), Highly Recommended (85-89), Recommended (80-84), Not Recommended (Under 80)

Imperial Reserva, Rioja 1991 $26.99.   91

Deep brick cast with a slight fade to the rim. Medium-bodied. Full acidity. Moderately extracted. Heavily oaked. Mildly tannic. Brown spices, sandalwood, minerals. Perfumed aromas show an exotic spicy quality. Silky and mellow in the mouth with an extremely lengthy finish. Very traditional and very good.

Viña Real, Gran Reserva, Rioja 1990 $29.99.   89

Bright brick hue with a fade to the rim. Medium-bodied. Balanced acidity. Moderately extracted. Heavily oaked. Mildly tannic. Sandalwood, cedar, spice. Perfumed and silky with an exotic melange of wood-tinged flavors. Lighter in the mouth with a silky, flavorful palate feel.

Imperial Gran Reserva, Rioja 1989 $32.50.   90

Pale ruby with a fading rim. Moderately full-bodied. Moderately extracted. Mildly tannic. Bright red cherry aromas have a spicy cinnamon accent. Rich black fruit flavors finish with a somewhat smoky, charred wood note. Silky mouthfeel. This still has plenty of vigor, although it is drinking well now.

Imperial Gran Reserva, Rioja 1990 $34.99.   92

Deep ruby with a garnet rim. Medium-bodied. Full acidity. Moderately extracted. Moderately oaked. Mildly tannic. Spice, leather, red fruits. Dusty, spicy aromas portend a mellow, complex, and flavorful character. Supple and generous in the mouth with acidity enlivening the finish. Fine length.

Fernando Remirez de Ganuza

Ganuza, Rioja 1994 $50.   87

Dark blackish ruby hue. Full-bodied. Full acidity. Highly extracted. Mildly oaked. Moderately tannic. Tea, earth, minerals. Unusual aromas lend an air of complexity throughout. Large framed and rich in the mouth, with crisp acidity lending a sense of buoyancy through the finish. Should open with age.

Bodegas Faustino Martinez

Faustino VII, Rioja 1996 $8.99.   80

Faustino V, Reserva, Rioja 1993 $13.99.   86

Deep ruby cast. Medium-bodied. Full acidity. Moderately extracted. Mildly oaked. Mildly tannic. Red fruits, spices, minerals. Aromatically reserved, with a bright and youthful quality on the palate. Lean and crisp through the finish. Straightforward and clean.

Faustino I, Gran Reserva, Rioja 1991 $23.99.   88

Deep ruby with a slight fade. Medium-bodied. Full acidity. Moderately extracted. Moderately oaked. Mildly tannic. Chocolate, spice, minerals. High-toned, fragrant aromatics lead to a lean and racy palate feel. Crisp and vibrant through the finish.

Finca Allende

Rioja 1995 $15.   88

Deep blackish ruby cast with purple highlights. Full-bodied. Full acidity. Highly extracted. Moderately oaked. Moderately tannic. Vanilla, minerals, black fruits. Brooding aromas portend a ripe and extracted palate feel. Dark, rich flavors emerge from a shroud of firm tannins through the finish. Structured for a lengthy stay in the cellar.

Bodegas Franco-Españolas

Bordon Crianza, Rioja 1995 $7.99.   83

Bordon Reserva, Rioja 1991 $12.99.   89

Pale orange-brick cast. Medium-bodied. Full acidity. Moderately extracted. Heavily oaked. Mildly tannic. Brown spices, tea, leather. Very traditional Rioja with light color and body that belies a mellow, oak-dominated character. Spicy, gamey flavors linger through the finish.

Bordón Gran Reserva, Rioja 1991 $32.99.   88

Bright brick hue. Moderately light-bodied. Full acidity. Moderately extracted. Moderately oaked. Mildly tannic. Anise, flowers, brown spices. Bright, high-toned aromas lead to a surprisingly light palate feel. Crisp and zesty through the finish.

Bodegas Herencia Lasanta

Crianza, Rioja 1994 $10.99.   84

Riserva, Rioja 1991 $14.99.   90

Bright cherry red with subtle purple highlights. Medium-bodied. Moderately extracted. Moderately oaked. Moderately tannic. Ripe fruity cherry and raspberry aromas lead a palate with concentrated and expansive fruity flavors that follow the aromas. Has a nice overlay of vanilla oak and supple tannins on the finish. Squeaky clean, modern style.

La Rioja Alta

Viña Ardanza Blanco Reserva, Rioja 1990 $14.99.   87

Bright golden yellow. Medium-bodied. Highly extracted. Moderately oaked. Full, smoky, mature aromas. Weighty mouthfeel shows plenty of oak character and brown spice with lemony acids. Will please lovers of traditional white Rioja.

Viña Alberdi Reserva, Rioja 1994 $13.99.   90

Medium cherry red. Medium-bodied. Moderately extracted. Moderately oaked. Mildly tannic. Pronounced earthy aromas lead a full flavored, complex palate with dried herbs, black fruits, earth, and toasted oak flavors lingering through a persistent finish showing bittersweet chocolate. Ripe style with a great mouthfeel.

Viña Arana Reserva, Rioja 1991 $17.99.   89

Fading red orange. Medium-bodied. Moderately extracted. Heavily oaked. Very aromatic leathery, spicy aromas. Concentrated dried berry flavors with dry oaky, spicy components that dominate the finish. Seems quite mature now, and high-toned acids make this austere and lively.

Viña Ardanza Reserva, Rioja 1989 $23.99.   89

Full cherry red with an orange cast. Medium-bodied. Moderately extracted. Heavily oaked. Moderately tannic. Mature faintly stewed spicy aromas are complex and developed. High-toned spicy cherry-berry flavors are crisp through a toasty oak finish. Acids are commendably brisk. This is nice now, but could get more interesting.

Gran Reserva 904, Rioja 1987 $39.99.   87

Garnet brown. Medium-bodied. Moderately extracted. Heavily oaked. Mildly tannic. Full leather and dusty spice aromas lead an very bright palate lifted by juicy citrus-like acidity with dried red fruit flavors and faded rustic tannins lingering on the finish. A lighter vintage, but well balanced.

Bodegas Lan

Vina Lanciano Reserva, Rioja 1991 $17.   90

Dark ruby-purple. Medium-bodied. Moderately extracted. Moderately oaked. Moderately tannic. Generous black fruit and dried herb aromas. Rounded velvety tannins are well integrated giving a textured mouthfeel through a lingering sweet herbal finish.

Viña Lanciano, Reserva, Rioja 1994 $18.   89

Deep ruby cast. Medium-bodied. Full acidity. Moderately extracted. Heavily oaked. Mildly tannic. Vanilla, licorice, red fruits. Attractive aromas feature a big oak accent and merge with a core of deep fruit flavors in the mouth. Full and rich though well balanced, with zesty acidity making for a snappy finish.

Marques de Arienzo

Crianza, Rioja 1994 $12.   83

Reserva, Rioja 1992 $14.99.   84

Scale: Superlative (96-100), Exceptional (90-95), Highly Recommended (85-89), Recommended (80-84), Not Recommended (Under 80)

790

Gran Reserva, Rioja 1989 $24.99.   87

Deep brick hue. Medium-bodied. Full acidity. Moderately extracted. Heavily oaked. Mildly tannic. Pipe tobacco, vanilla, cedar. An extravagantly spicy and generous bouquet leads to a lighter-styled, lean palate feel. Crisp and angular with fine intensity to the finish.

Marques de Caceres

Dry White, Rioja 1997 $6.99.   NR

Satinela Blanco, Rioja 1997 $6.99.   NR

Dry Rosé, Rioja 1997 $6.99.   80

Vendimia Seleccionada, Rioja 1995 $7.99.   85

Reserva, Rioja 1991 $17.99.   88

Deep ruby cast. Moderately full-bodied. Balanced acidity. Moderately extracted. Moderately oaked. Mildly tannic. Vanilla, red fruits. Shows a hefty oak overtone and a core of ripe fruit flavors. Very modern in style and quite well made. Rich and flavorful through the finish.

Gran Reserva, Rioja 1987 $24.99.   86

Brick ruby with a fade to the rim. Medium-bodied. Balanced acidity. Moderately extracted. Moderately oaked. Mildly tannic. Brown spices, pepper, leather. Quite fragrant with a mature and spicy bouquet. Lighter in the mouth with a lean, juicy quality to the finish.

Gran Reserva, Rioja 1989 $23.99.   88

Saturated ruby with a slight fade. Moderately full-bodied. Full acidity. Moderately extracted. Moderately oaked. Mildly tannic. Anise, chocolate, spice. High-toned spicy aromatics lead to a rich and supple palate feel. Lush and generous with solid grip through the finish.

Marques de Griñon

Rioja 1997 $10.   86

Pale ruby cast. Medium-bodied. Full acidity. Moderately extracted. Moderately oaked. Mildly tannic. Brown spices, toasted oak, red fruits. Forward aromas are attractive and spicy. Crisp and stylish in the mouth with a zesty quality through the flavorful finish.

Coleccion Personal, Reserva, Rioja 1993 $19.   NR

Marques de Murrieta

Ygay, Coleccion 2100 Blanco, Rioja 1996 $9.49.   82

Ygay, Coleccion 2100, Rioja 1996 $10.99.   NR

Ygay, Reserva, Rioja 1994 $18.99.   84

Castillo Ygay, Gran Reserva Especial, Rioja 1989 $34.99.   92

Deep ruby with a slight fade. Moderately full-bodied. Full acidity. Moderately extracted. Heavily oaked. Mildly tannic. Red fruits, vanilla, leather, earth. Big, powerful aromas show concentration and intensity. Exotic and full in the mouth with a tart acidic backbone. Quite youthful in structure, with a hint of overripeness to the flavors, this should develop for years. Needs some time to soften.

Marques de Riscal

Reserva, Rioja 1994 $10.99.   86

Bright ruby with a fade to the rim. Medium-bodied. Balanced acidity. Moderately extracted. Mildly oaked. Mildly tannic. Spice, minerals. A subtle woody fragrance leads a lean palate with plenty of grip. Angular and firm with a drying finish.

Baron de Chirel Reserva, Rioja 1988 $40.99.   91

Solid orange red. Medium-bodied. Highly extracted. Moderately oaked. Quite tannic.
Oaky austere aromas lead a solid, tightly wound palate of concentrated currant and
cherry flavors. An astringent, though layered finish shows a still solid structure. This
needs more time in bottle to soften.

Marques del Puerto
Blanco, Rioja 1996 $9.99.   NR
Crianza, Rioja 1994 $9.99.   86

Bright cherry red with a faint purple hint. Medium-bodied. Moderately extracted. Mildly
oaked. Moderately tannic. Bright red fruit flavors of cherries and raspberries lead a taut,
brightly acidic palate with a quick middle and clean finish. Well balanced, with enough
acidity to be versatile at the table.

Reserva, Rioja 1991 $12.99.   83
Gran Reserva, Rioja 1989 $16.99.   89

Pale ruby. Moderately light-bodied. Moderately extracted. Mildly tannic. Lightly
perfumed vanilla aromas lead a bright faded cherry flavored palate with plenty of
new oak flavors. Drinking well now, this is a lighter style of Gran Reserva.

Roman Paladino Gran Reserva, Rioja 1978 $55.   90

Pale bright ruby with a browning cast. Medium-bodied. Moderately extracted. Moderately
oaked. Mildly tannic. Faintly leathery, dusty, oak spiced nose leads an elegant refined
palate with faded, dry fruit flavors and a lingering brown spice finish. Acids are still lively.
This is very much alive, and still quite structured.

Bodegas Martinez Bujanda
Valdemar, Vino Tinto, Rioja 1997 $6.   84
Conde de Valdemar, Crianza, Rioja 1995 $8.50.   88

Bright ruby cast. Moderately light-bodied. Full acidity. Moderately extracted. Moderately
oaked. Mildly tannic. Sweet oak, minerals, red fruits. Generous woody aromas lead a lean
and angular palate feel. Flavorful and zesty through the wood-accented finish.

Conde de Valdemar, Reserva, Rioja 1993 $12.   86

Bright ruby cast. Medium-bodied. Full acidity. Moderately extracted. Moderately oaked.
Mildly tannic. Vanilla, red fruits. Quite modern in style, with a fragrant, fruit-centered
personality and toasty oak accents. Lean and zesty through the finish.

Finca Valpiedra, Reserva, Rioja 1994 $25.   86

Saturated opaque ruby purple cast. Moderately full-bodied. Balanced acidity. Highly
extracted. Moderately oaked. Moderately tannic. Anise, chocolate. High toned aromas
lead to a thick, rich palate feel. Full and luxuriant with tannins that grab hold on the
finish. Needs time in the cellar to mellow and develop tertiary complexities.

Conde de Valdemar, Gran Reserva, Gold Label, Rioja 1991 $21.   88

Pale brick hue. Medium-bodied. Full acidity. Moderately extracted. Moderately oaked.
Mildly tannic. Brown spices, minerals. Attractive aromas have a decided sweet wood
accent. Lean and angular in the mouth with a sense of lightness. Racy acidity makes
for a crisp finish.

Bodegas Montecillo
Viña Cumbrero Crianza, Rioja 1995 $8.99.   83
Viña Monty, Gran Reserva, Rioja 1989 $16.99.   86

Bright brick hue with orange highlights. Medium-bodied. Full acidity. Subtly extracted.
Heavily oaked. Mildly tannic. Cedar, pipe tobacco, spice. Exotically fragrant with a spicy
array of flavors. Light in the mouth with a lean and angular structure. Crisp and flavorful
through the finish.

Bodegas Muga

Reserva, Rioja 1994 $15.50.   88

Deep blackish ruby cast. Medium-bodied. Full acidity. Highly extracted. Mildly oaked. Mildly tannic. Spice, minerals, chocolate. Lean aromas show a woody accent. Full and firm in the mouth with an angular finish.

Torre Muga, Reserva Especial, Rioja 1994 $48.   92

Deep ruby cast. Moderately full-bodied. Full acidity. Moderately extracted. Heavily oaked. Mildly tannic. Toasted coconut, vanilla, black fruits. Quite aromatic with a generous overlay of sweet oak flavors and a core of ripe fruit. Rich and extracted in the mouth with acidity lending a zesty quality to the finish. Intense and flavorful.

Bodegas Palacio

Glorioso, Rioja 1995 $14.   84

Glorioso, Reserva, Rioja 1994 $10.   84

Puelles

Crianza, Rioja 1995 $14.   83

Remelluri

Rioja 1995 $19.   86

Inky blackish ruby cast. Full-bodied. Balanced acidity. Highly extracted. Mildly oaked. Moderately tannic. Chocolate, roasted nuts. Unusually deep and brooding in color, flavor, and texture, making for an unusual interpretation of Rioja. Thick and rich in the mouth with tannins that clamp down on the finish. Should open with age.

Señorio de San Vicente

Tempranillo, Rioja 1995 $26.   NR

Siglo

Crianza, Rioja 1994 $9.99.   81

Reserva, Rioja 1988 $12.99.   88

Pale garnet orange. Medium-bodied. Moderately extracted. Moderately oaked. Mildly tannic. Sweet cinnamon aromas. Sweet cherries and oak flavors expand on the palate with a hint of powdery dry tannin on the finish. Very elegantly proportioned.

Gran Reserva, Rioja 1986 $16.99.   82

Bodegas Solabal

Crianza, Rioja 1995 $10.   85

Bodegas Solar de Carrion

Antaño, Tempranillo 1997 $6.   NR

Don Antaño Crianza, Rioja 1994 $7.   NR

R. Lopez de Heredia Viña Tondonia

Viña Gravonia, Rioja 1988 $12.   80

Viña Tondonia Reserva, Rioja 1985 $17.   NR

Viña Tondonia Rose, Rioja 1988 $12.   90

Dark orange hue. Medium-bodied. Moderately extracted. Moderately oaked. Maderized, complex, mature aromas lead a surprisingly smooth, dusty palate with little primary fruit flavors and soft acids. Quite juicy, with gentle brown spice flavors lingering on the finish. For lovers of older wines.

Viña Cubillo, Rioja 1993 $10.   82

Viña Bosconia, Rioja 1990 $14.   85

Viña Tondonia Reserva, Rioja 1990 $17.   **87**

Bright garnet red. Medium-bodied. Moderately extracted. Moderately oaked. Mildly tannic. Fragrant brown spice aromas lead a bright dried cherry flavored palate with very fine-grained tealike tannins keeping this dry though the finish. By the standards of this producer, this is quite youthful.

Viña Tondonia Gran Reserva, Rioja 1978 $34.   **86**

Fading reddish orange. Medium-bodied. Moderately extracted. Moderately oaked. Perfumed aromas of earth and brown spice and tomato are very complex and mature in character. Stewed, complex favors have juicy acids to back them up. Rustic tannins are very faded on the finish. Very mature.

Bodegas Vinegra
Don Teofilo I Crianza, Rioja Alavesa 1994 $17.   **82**

thirty-six

❧

Spain
Ribera del Duero
and the Provinces

❧

Ribera and the Provinces: Amazing Spanish Diversity

Spanish wine means much more than Rioja and Sherry. Wine is produced all over the country and Spain's legendary sunshine makes much of the country a viticultural Eden. As more and more investment is being made in the Spanish wine industry, a number of regions are emerging as stars of the future. Some of the key up and coming regions include:

Ribera del Duero: Spain's fastest developing region, Ribera del Duero, lies halfway between Madrid and the coast as the crow flies. It consists of a 69-mile stretch of the Duero River. Ribera del Duero is overwhelmingly a red wine region. Rioja's Tempranillo is grown under the title Tinta del Pais, and it accounts for an increasing majority of vineyard acreage in the Ribera. In the best hands, Tinta del Pais produces more long-lived and powerful wines than does Tempranillo in Rioja. One of the world's great wine estates and Ribera's flag-bearer, Vega Sicilia, has been producing wine for almost one and a half centuries. Located towards the west of the region, it stood alone as an estate of note until the arrival of Alejandro Fernandez in the early seventies, the quality of whose Tinto Pesquera wines have subsequently resulted in an enormous investment in the region as a whole. At their best Ribera's wines are reputedly the longest-lived in Spain. There seems little reason to doubt this when Vega Sicilia has released wines that still seem fresh and young 20 years or more after the vintage, seeming to defy the aging process. Nonetheless, they are not tough at all, but have an opulent, thick, velvety character. Riberas are unique and delicious reds, and the best part is that a number of these wines still offer excellent value!

Penedes: The region of Penedes, near Barcelona, is best known for Cava—sparkling wines made in the Champagne Method. Until recently the red wines of this region warranted little attention. Today they are among the very best in Spain. The Torres firm must be credited for much of Penedes's quality transformation. They introduced modern techniques such as temperature-controlled fermentation and careful varietal and clonal selection in the vineyards. The region's principal red varieties are Garnacha, Cariñena, Tempranillo, and Monastrell with a relatively small but growing presence of Cabernet Sauvignon and other international varietals. The wines range in style from light and fruity—reminiscent of Beaujolais—to rich and full-bodied with complex flavors of cedar, leather, and brown spices.

Navarra: The region of Navarra adjoins Rioja to the east. It is best known both for its reds and rosés. Garnacha is the principal variety with Tempranillo, Cabernet Sauvignon, and Merlot used to a lesser degree. Tempranillo is becoming more widely planted recently, being bottled both as a single variety and in a blend with Cabernet Sauvignon. These wines can be quite lovely, showing good fruit concentration with the classic Spanish flavors of earth, tobacco, and cedar.

Spain in Focus: Legendary Vega Sicilia

In the world of wine, Ribera del Duero's legendary Vega Sicilia is a paradox. How is it that a vineyard of such repute could lie in the remote and dusty plains of that country's interior? The climate at the winery is indeed extreme. At more

Scale: Superlative (96-100), Exceptional (90-95), Highly Recommended (85-89), Recommended (80-84), Not Recommended (Under 80)

than 2,000 feet in elevation, the nights are so cool that frost is a considerable danger. In 1971 the entire crop was destroyed, and many subsequent vintages have been greatly reduced. Rain is sparse, yet well retained by the chalky soil. The grapes are rarely picked before the end of October and in 1984 the harvest was still being completed at the end of November, with no leaves left on the vines!

Vega Sicilia's 250-acre vineyard was replanted in 1864 to incorporate Bordeaux varietals after *Phylloxera* had ravaged the existing vines. Today the blend continues to be an unorthodox Franco-Spanish collaboration of 60 percent Tempranillo, 25 percent Cabernet Sauvignon, 10 percent Merlot, four percent Malbec, and one percent Albillo (an indigenous white grape). The average age of the vines is greater than 40 years, with some being as old as 80, and the resulting yield is quite small, a fraction of that of the top wines of Bordeaux.

The winemaking remains completely traditional and the steps taken to insure quality border on the draconian. Upon arrival at the bodega, a rigorous selection of grapes is made, and only free run juice is used; no wine from the press is incorporated. After a few months in American oak vats, the wines are transferred to a combination of small American and French oak barrels and aged longer than any of the world's great wines. Unico, a reserve wine made six to seven times a decade, spends at least four and up to ten years in cask, while Valbuena, the "standard" wine, spends at least two and a half years in oak and a further two years in the bottle before it is released.

Rich and exotically opulent, with enormous fruit and a perfect balance between oak, extract, tannin, and acidity, these are consistently sensational wines on release that age well into the future. They are wines to seek out despite the scarcity—less than 20 percent of the production is allowed to leave Spain—and serve as a benchmark and a metaphor for the rise of lesser-known Spanish regions. In much of Spain, the sky is truly the limit.

Ribera del Duero and The Provinces at a Glance

Wines Reviewed:
191

Producers/Brands Represented:
79

Value Rating:
Good Overall
(Ribera del Duero/Priorat, Poor to Average)

Reviews

Bodegas 1890
Mayoral, Jumilla 1997 $5.　　　　83

Abadia Retuerta
Sardon de Duero, Castilla Leon 1996 $24.　　　　87

Saturated purple hue. Moderately full-bodied. Highly extracted. Moderately tannic. Olives, herbs, black fruits. Impressively aromatic, showing a classic olivey syrah note. Dense and flavorsome, this is very approachable now, with more than a hint of Northern Rhone style.

Cuvee El Palomar, Sardon de Duero, Castilla Leon 1996 $43.　　　　81
Cuvee El Campanario, Sardon de Duero, Castilla Leon 1996 $49.　　　　86

Opaque, saturated ruby. Moderately full-bodied. Highly extracted. Moderately tannic. Earth, olives, black fruits. Impressively rich, brooding aromas. Dense olivey, black fruit flavors are rather dry and constrained by inky tannins at present.

Adegas Valmiñor
Albariño, Rias Baixas 1997 $16.　　　　84

Full yellow hue. Moderately full-bodied. Moderately extracted. Apples, melon. Fruit-laden aromas strike an apple chord that follows through on the broad palate with viscous texture.

Alion
Ribera del Duero 1992 $25.　　　　90

Deep red with an opaque purplish cast. Full-bodied. Mild acidity. Medium fruit. Moderately oaked. Moderately tannic. Black fruits, tar, leather flavors. Rich and extracted with a reined-in nose, this is a dense wine without any rough edges. It will require time in the cellar.

Ribera del Duero 1993 $25.　　　　89

Full ruby red appearance. Moderately full-bodied. Highly extracted. Reminiscent of dill pickle, black currants, black tea. Rich oak-accented aromas lead a full spicy palate with deep black fruit flavors. This is still showing good tannic grip and a dry finish, but is quite drinkable now with the right sort of food.

Ribera del Duero 1994 $27.99.　　　　92

Opaque reddish-purple. Moderately full-bodied. Highly extracted. Moderately tannic. Rich blackberry and black currant aromas. Very full generous fruit flavors explode on the palate. Great depth and power. Very ripe and plush. Velvety dry tannins give the finish a silky texture.

Bodegas Antaño
Viña Mocen, Rueda Superior 1996 $9.99.　　　　88

Bright yellow-straw hue. Medium-bodied. Moderately extracted. Bright ripe Sauvignon-like aromas have a leafy accent. Green flavors fill the palate with fresh acidity in good balance. Squeaky clean, with a bright character.

Bodegas Aragonesas
Coto de Hayas Crianza, Campo de Borja 1994 $7.　　　　84

Bright crimson with a pinkish hue. Medium-bodied. Moderately extracted. Moderately tannic. Mildly portlike aromas. Firm, well-extracted, subtle black fruit flavors have a dry character, restrained by dry tannins. Robust style that needs food.

Bodegas Arzuaga Navarro
Crianza, Ribera del Duero 1995 $20.   90

Ruby red with a fading rim. Medium-bodied. Moderately extracted. Moderately tannic. Markedly oak aromas lead a cedary, supple palate with soft red fruit flavors and a firm tannic grip through the finish. Very stylish and substantial.

Reserva, Ribera del Duero 1994 $40.   94

Rich ruby with a lightening rim. Moderately full-bodied. Moderately extracted. Moderately oaked. Moderately tannic. Red fruits, cedar, vanilla. Very aromatic, with ripe berry fruit and toasty oak aromas. Supple, harmonious and fleshy on the palate. Tannins are of the textured, chewy character making for a hedonistic style.

Bodegas As Laxas
Albariño, Rias Baixas 1997 $14.99.   87

Full yellow-straw hue. Delightfully floral, perfumed aromas. A moderately full-bodied, moderately extracted palate with a succulent, buttery mouthfeel features, juicy acids and generously fruity peach and apricot flavors. Powerful, flavorful style.

Albariño, Bãgoa do Miño, Rias Baixas NV $19.99.   84

Medium yellow straw. Medium-bodied. Moderately extracted. Minerals, citrus. Stony, floral aromas lead a crisp, vibrant palate with zesty flavors through the finish. A lighter style.

Bodegas Ayuso
Viña Q, La Mancha NV $4.99.   NR

Estola Reserva, La Mancha 1993 $6.75.   84

Pale cherry red. Medium-bodied. Moderately extracted. Mildly tannic. Leather, soft red fruits. Elegant spice, faint leather aromas. Mature and elegant, with muted tannins lingering on the finish.

Estola Gran Reserva, La Mancha 1987 $24.50.   NR

Burgans
Albariño, Rias Baixas 1997 $9.   84

Bright yellow-gold. Buttery aromas follow through on a medium-bodied, viscous palate with relatively low, balanced acids and a rounded mouthfeel showing pineapple and tropical fruit flavors.

Bodegas Felix Lorenzo Cachazo
Carrasviñas, Rueda Superior 1996 $11.   82

J. Garcia Carrion
Castillo San Simon, Jumilla 1997 $5.   NR
Castillo San Simon Reserva, Jumilla 1992 $8.   82
Castillo San Sinon Gran Reserva, Junilla 1989 $10.   81
Mayor de Castilla, Ribera del Duero 1997 $9.   84

Ruby red with a fading rim. Medium-bodied. Moderately extracted. Mildly tannic. Pepper, red fruits. Moderately aromatic. Light on the palate with lean, crisp flavors that have subtle fruit character.

Mayor de Castilla Crianza, Ribera del Duero 1994 $12.   84

Dark ruby red with a subtle fading rim. Medium-bodied. Moderately extracted. Moderately tannic. Herbal, olive-tinged, dark fruit aromas are quite complex. Juicy fruit and mouthwatering acids carry the flavors through a slightly short finish.

Casa Castillo
Monastrell, Jumilla 1997 $8.50.   84
Saturated purple. Medium-bodied. Highly extracted. Quite tannic. Black fruits. Inky, floral-scented nose leads a tightly wound core of black fruit flavors with powdery, dry tannins clamping down on the finish.

Casa de la Viña
Cencibel, Valdepeñas 1996 $4.99.   83
Cencibel, Valdepeñas 1996 $5.99.   83

Casa Solar
Tempranillo, Sacedon-Mondejar 1995 $4.   81
Red Wine, Sacedon-Mondejar 1994 $5.   80

Bodegas Castaño
Viña Las Gruesas, Yecla 1996 $8.   NR
Hecula, Yecla 1994 $9.   85
Medium cherry red. Medium-bodied. Moderately extracted. Moderately tannic. Black cherry and leather aromas follow through on the palate. Fine depth of flavors with chewy black fruits and a dry finish showing some tannic grip.
Hecula Crianza, Yecla 1994 $12.   86
Pale garnet-cherry red. Moderately light-bodied. Moderately extracted. Mildly tannic. Red fruit aromas lead a palate of cherry and raspberry flavors with a touch of vanilla coming through on the finish. Quite dry and very quaffable.

Castillo de Valdestrada
Vino de la Tierra de Barros 1991 $9.99.   86
Pale cherry red. Medium-bodied. Moderately extracted. Mildly tannic. Vanilla, red fruits. Mellow oak-accented aromas lead a supple, brightly acidic palate with precise fruit acids persisting through a vanilla-scented finish. Harmonious.

Castillo San Simon
Jumilla 1996 $4.99.   NR

Cavas Murviedro
Valencia 1995 $4.99.   80
Crianza, Valencia 1993 $6.99.   82

Cellers d'Scala Dei
Cartoixa d'Scala Dei, Priorat 1996 $19.   88
Opaque dark purple red hue. Full-bodied. Highly extracted. Quite tannic. Floral aromas. Very solid grip with austere grainy tannins overwhelming the finish. Ripe black fruits flavors in the background, though more bottle age should harmonize this.

Bodegas Chivite
Chardonnay, Gran Feudo, Navarra 1997 $7.   NR
Gran Feudo Crianza, Navarra 1995 $7.   NR
Gran Feudo Reserva, Navarra 1994 $10.   NR
Coleccion 125 Reserva, Navarra 1994 $25.   82

Scale: Superlative (96-100), Exceptional (90-95), Highly Recommended (85-89), Recommended (80-84), Not Recommended (Under 80)

Clos Erasmus
Priorat 1996 $35.   92

Opaque dark purple hue. Full-bodied. Highly extracted. Quite tannic. Earth, black fruits. Complex earthy, woody aromas follow through on a solid, well extracted mouthful of dry flavors with drying tannins clamping on the finish. An underlying sense of mineral gives this an extra dimension.

Condado de Haza
Ribera del Duero 1996 $15.99.   91

Full ruby purple. Moderately full-bodied. Moderately extracted. Moderately tannic. Fleshy, ripe and very fruity with velvety, textured tannins making this supple and attractive through the finish. Has enough structure to cellar further although drinking well now.

Ribera del Duero 1995 $16.99.   91

Opaque purple-red. Medium-bodied. Highly extracted. Moderately tannic. Expansive raspberry and cherry fruit aromas follow through well on the palate. Very bright, concentrated red fruit profile is matched with dry fine-grained tannins that are not too dry for current drinking.

Corte Real
Cabernet Sauvignon-Tempranillo, Vino de Extremadura 1992 $12.99.   87

Pale cherry red. Medium-bodied. Moderately extracted. Mildly tannic. Spice, minerals, cherries. Scented spice box and cherry aromas follow through on an elegant, subtle palate with a lingering finish. Very harmonious, drinking well now.

Bodegas de Sarria
Señorio de Sarria Crianza, Navarra 1992 $7.99.   81
Señorio de Sarria Gran Reserva, Navarra 1987 $14.99.   85

Bright browning garnet. Medium-bodied. Moderately extracted. Moderately tannic. Mature, complex aromas of tomato and dill lead a smooth, bright palate of elegant faded flavors that persist surprisingly on the dry finish. For fans of mature Spanish wines.

Don Coyote
Chardonnay, Don Coyote, Pueblo Valley 1995 $5.99.   81
Cabernet Sauvignon, Don Coyote, Pueblo Valley 1994 $5.99.   83
Merlot, Don Coyote, Pueblo Valley 1994 $5.99.   85

Bright cherry red with purple highlights. Moderately light-bodied. Moderately extracted. Mildly tannic. Vanilla and berry fruit aromas. Crisp raspberry and cherry flavors have a sweetness on the entry that is balanced by bright acids that keep this fresh through the clean, astringent finish.

El Grifo
Malvasia Dulce, Lanzarote 1997 $15.   86

Pale green-gold. Medium-bodied. Ginger, flowers. Floral, spicy aromas follow through on a subtly sweet palate with crisp acids. Not quite sweet enough for dessert purposes, more of an aperitif style.

Bodegas Farina
Blanco Zamora, Vino de la Tierra de Zamora 1997 $5.99/L.   84

Medium yellow-gold. Medium-bodied. Moderately extracted. Minerals, apple. Mature, apple scented aromas lead a dulled, muted palate with a dry finish. Showing signs of mild oxidation as manifested in a nutty quality.

Colegiata Blanco, Toro 1997 $7.99.　　　　　　　84

Deep golden hue. Moderately full-bodied. Moderately extracted. Pears, peach, minerals. Waxy aromas lead a soft mouthful of pear and peach-like flavors, with a lingering finish. Pleasant, if rather neutral.

Tinto Zamora, Vino de la Tierra de Zamora 1996 $5.99/L.　　81

Toro 1997 $6.99.　　　　　　　81

Colegiata Tinto, Toro 1996 $7.99.　　　　　　　83

Dama de Toro Reserva, Toro 1990 $11.99.　　　　　　84

Browning cherry red. Medium-bodied. Moderately extracted. Heavily oaked. Cinnamon spice nose indicates maturity and extended barrel aging that is confirmed on the palate. Nice prune and raisin flavors linger through the finish. Drinking nicely now.

Dama de Toro Reserva, Toro 1991 $11.99.　　　　　82

Fin del Rio Reserva, Toro 1991 $12.99.　　　　　82

Gran Colegiata Crianza, Toro 1995 $12.99.　　　　NR

Gran Colegiata Reserva, Toro 1990 $12.99.　　　　85

Reddish brick-garnet. Medium-bodied. Moderately extracted. Moderately oaked. Mildly tannic. Spicy cinnamon and clove aromas lead a soft spicy palate with gentle red fruit flavors through a lingering spicy finish. Very well integrated, showing some faded austerity.

Gran Colegiata Reserva, Toro 1991 $14.99.　　　　82

Glamour de España
Reserva, Cariñena 1988 $9.95.　　　　　　　85

Pale cherry red with a faded rim. Moderately light-bodied. Moderately extracted. Mildly tannic. Light, faintly perfumed aromas. Juicy, refreshingly crisp palate has a cleanness of fruit flavors allied to a suggestive vanilla accent through the finish. Very elegant and quaffable.

Bodegas Godeval
Viña Godeval, Valdeorras 1997 $13.　　　　　　81

Bodegas Gormaz
Doce Linajes Tinto, Ribera del Duero 1997 $7.99.　　　83

Doce Linajes Crianza, Ribera del Duero 1995 $11.99.　　88

Ruby hue with brightening rim. Medium-bodied. Moderately extracted. Moderately tannic. Attractively aromatic with cedary, minerally complexity. Well-developed, juicy, generously fruity flavors with leathery tannins through the finish make this very approachable.

Bodegas Guelbenzu
Tinto, Navarra 1995 $9.99.　　　　　　　NR

Evo, Navarra 1994 $18.99.　　　　　　　82

Hijos de Antonio Barcelo
Peñascal, Castilla Leon 1995 $6.　　　　　　　84

Bright pink-crimson. Medium-bodied. Moderately extracted. Mildly tannic. Raspberries, minerals. Juicy, forward fruity flavors conclude with light tannins and clean fruit acids. Best suited to early drinking.

Tempranillo, Realeza, Castilla Leon 1997 $6.　　　　82

Viña Mayor Crianza, Ribera del Duero 1995 $11.　　　90

Ruby red with a fading rim. Medium-bodied. Moderately extracted. Moderately tannic. Blackberries. Chunky black fruit flavors are generous and juicy, with modestly dry tannins lingering on the finish. Has a firm edge, though it is supple enough for current drinking.

Scale: Superlative (96-100), Exceptional (90-95), Highly Recommended (85-89), Recommended (80-84), Not Recommended (Under 80)

802

Ibernoble

Ribera del Duero 1996 $12.   86

Deep reddish-purple. Medium-bodied. Moderately extracted. Mildly tannic. Floral, perfumed, youthful aromas lead a palate of bright juicy raspberries with supple, mild tannins on the finish. Drinking very nicely now.

Ribera del Duero 1997 $13.99.   85

Bright ruby purple. Medium-bodied. Moderately extracted. Mildly tannic. Herbs, red berries. Soft, ripe, fleshy aromas. Rounded and supple with ripe flavors and velvety tannins making for an attractive, forward, lighter style that is drinking well now.

Crianza, Ribera del Duero 1994 $22.50.   87

Deep blood red-ruby. Medium-bodied. Highly extracted. Moderately oaked. Moderately tannic. Minty, black fruit aromas. Crisp fruity flavors are bolstered by bright acids and rich grainy tannins. This comes across as very ripe with decent structure, drinkable now but better in a year or two.

Crianza, Ribera del Duero 1995 $23.99.   86

Blackish ruby with an opaque cast. Moderately full-bodied. Moderately extracted. Moderately tannic. Black fruits, earth. Fruity, woody nose. Solidly structured with inky fruit and dry, velvety tannins through the finish. Supple and generous, drinking well now.

Reserva, Ribera del Duero 1991 $39.95.   89

Dark ruby hue. Medium-bodied. Highly extracted. Moderately tannic. Dusty, brooding black fruit aromas follow through well on the palate, showing concentrated flavors and bright acids. This is still quite youthful with good cellaring structure.

Reserva, Ribera del Duero 1992 $28.   87

Blood red with a fading rim. Medium-bodied. Moderately extracted. Moderately tannic. Developed, dusty aromas follow through on the palate with crisp cherry fruit flavors and dry grippy tannins clamping on the finish. This could use more bottle age.

Bodegas Ismael Arroyo

Val Sotillo, Ribera del Duero 1996 $22.   84

Dark ruby purple. Moderately full-bodied. Highly extracted. Moderately tannic. Very youthful primary fruit aromas. Youthful and tight at present with powdery tannins attenuating the bright fleshy fruit flavors. A youthful style.

Jean Leon

Chardonnay, Penedes 1995 $29.99.   92

Medium yellow-straw luster. Medium-bodied. Moderately extracted. Heavily oaked. Wonderful toasted oak aromas lead a nutty fresh palate with cleanly defined fruit flavors well integrated with smoky oak notes that persist through the finish. Acids keep this fresh and lively, bringing out the complexity.

Cabernet Sauvignon, Reserva, Penedes 1990 $24.49.   90

Opaque with a blood-red rim showing orange tints. Moderately full-bodied. Highly extracted. Moderately oaked. Moderately tannic. Rich dark fruit aromas have a mature character. Solid, concentrated palate has an austere feel with black cherriy flavors and dry fine-grained tannins on the finish. Drinking well now.

Cabernet Sauvignon, Penedes 1991 $28.   90

Bright brick-cherry red. Medium-bodied. Highly extracted. Moderately oaked. Moderately tannic. Concentrated dried red cherry flavors have a freshness on the palate. Vanilla oak notes are well balanced by crisp, almost juicy acids. Powdery dry tannins give some grip through the finish. This is nice now.

Lezcano
Docetanidos, Cigales 1996 $9.   84

Deep strawberry hue. Medium-bodied. Moderately extracted. Fresh and fruity raspberry aromas follow through on the palate. Plenty of tart cherry-berry fruit flavors here with a cleanly astringent finish. Unsubtle but appealing.

Lusco de Miño
Albariño, Rias Baixas 1996 $19.99.   88

Medium golden luster. Medium-bodied. Highly extracted. Tart grapefruit zest aromas lead a rounded weighty palate with minerally backbone and plenty of character in the form of a tart citrus accent. An assertive style of Albariño.

Bodegas Marco Real
Homenaje, Navarra 1996 $6.99.   81
Homenaje Crianza, Navarra 1995 $7.99.   82
Cabernet Sauvignon, Homenaje, Navarra 1996 $9.   NR
Merlot, Homenaje, Navarra 1996 $9.   83
Homenaje Reserva, Navarra 1994 $12.   83

Marques de Alella
Clasico Blanco, Alella 1997 $9.   80

Marques de Griñon
Durius Blanco, Castilla y Leon 1996 $9.   89

Pale yellow-gold. Medium-bodied. Moderately extracted. Grassy, fresh aromas reveal melon and citrus flavors that expand on the palate with a lingering finish suggestive of Loire Sauvignon Blanc.

Syrah, Domino de Valdepusa, Toledo 1996 $21.   94

Bright red-purple. Moderately full-bodied. Moderately extracted. Mildly tannic. Berry fruits, vanilla. Explosively aromatic. Vibrant, concentrated berry fruit flavors explode on the palate, with mild powdery tannins giving some grip on the finish. This could cellar though is approachable now.

Marques de Riscal
Blanco, Rueda 1996 $5.99.   NR
Rueda 1995 $6.99.   85

Full golden straw. Medium-bodied. Highly extracted. Heavily oaked. Nutty, complex nose. Citrus oil flavors have a spicy edge that persists through a long finish. Rich, rounded mouthfeel is a plus.

Marques del Puerto
Rosado, Rioja 1996 $9.99.   84

Reddish with subtle orange highlights. Medium-bodied. Moderately extracted. Apple and floral aromas. Clean, bright, juicy acids with a hint of dried flowers and dried red fruits. This is refreshing and has a lengthy finish.

Mayor de Castilla
Ribera del Duero 1996 $9.99.   82

Monasterio de Tentudia
Vino de Extremadura 1989 $11.   81

Scale: Superlative (96-100), Exceptional (90-95), Highly Recommended (85-89), Recommended (80-84), Not Recommended (Under 80)

Tradicion, Vino de Extremadura 1989 $13.95.   84

Pale ruby cast. Medium-bodied. Full acidity. Subtly extracted. Heavily oaked. Mildly tannic. Vanilla, brown spices, red fruits. An extraordinarily fragrant nose features an array of spicy wood flavors. Lean and crisp in the mouth with a lengthy flavorful finish.

Emilio Moro

Cosecha, Ribera del Duero 1996 $19.   86

Dark ruby purple hue. Moderately full-bodied. Moderately extracted. Moderately tannic. Fleshy intense fruit aromas follow through on the palate, with firm tannins supplying structural weight through the finish. Fruit-forward, weighty style. Drinking well now.

Bodegas Nekeas

Cabernet-Tempranillo, Vega Sindoa, Navarra 1996 $7.   83

Tempranillo-Merlot, Vega Sindoa, Navarra 1997 $7.   NR

Old Vines Grenache, "El Chaparral," Vega Sindoa, Navarra 1997 $8.   82

Merlot, Vega Sindoa, Navarra 1996 $9.   86

Deep ruby purple. Medium-bodied. Full acidity. Moderately extracted. Mildly oaked. Mildly tannic. Vanilla, minerals, red fruits. Forward aromas show a core of lean fruit flavors and an oak accent. Clean, crisp and linear in the mouth. Angular finish has grip.

Bodegas Ochoa

Tinto, Navarra 1996 $6.99.   80

Cabernet Sauvignon, Navarra 1994 $10.99.   86

Dark ruby red. Medium-bodied. Moderately extracted. Moderately oaked. Moderately tannic. Enticing aromas of cedar, spice, and black currant follow through well on the palate. Plenty of Cabernet character, with an earthy note and some angular tannins for grip on the finish.

Cabernet Sauvignon, Navarra 1995 $11.99.   NR

Merlot, Navarra 1995 $11.99.   NR

Tempranillo, Navarra 1995 $11.99.   83

Reserva, Navarra 1992 $13.99.   80

Gran Reserva, Navarra 1991 $14.99.   NR

Moscatel, Vino Dulce, Navarra 1997 $14.99/500 ml.   87

Medium pale gold. Moderately full-bodied. Low acidity. Moderately extracted. Flowers, sweet fruits. Pronounced muscat floral aromas. Generously sweet and juicy on the palate. Mildly cloying on the finish, though tart fruit accompaniment would liven this up.

Palacio de Monsalud

Vino de la Tierra de Barros 1994 $8.99.   NR

Palacio de Valdeinfante

Private Collection, Spain 1992 $11.99.   81

Bodegas Hermanos Perez Pascuas

Viña Pedrosa, Ribera del Duero 1994 $27.   90

Dark ruby red. Highly extracted. Moderately tannic. Hugely complex herbal, rosemary-like aromas. Rich, deep, and chewy on the palate with prune and crisp cherry flavors. Dry grainy tannins give this fine structure at present.

Pazo de Barrantes
Albariño, Rias Baixas 1997 $15.99.   88

Bright yellow gold. Medium-bodied. Full acidity. Moderately extracted. Peach, lemon, minerals. Bright floral, fresh aromas lead a fruity mouthful of flavors that linger through a long finish.

Pazo de Villarei
Albariño, Rias Baixas 1997 $13.99.   84

Full golden yellow. Aromas show a mature character, confirmed on the moderately full-bodied palate that has a rather soft texture. Highly extracted flavors of baked apples, citrus. Drink it up.

Bodegas Peñalba López
Torremilanos Crianza, Ribera del Duero 1995 $13.99.   88

Saturated dark ruby with a brickish hue. Medium-bodied. Moderately extracted. Moderately tannic. Black fruits, earth, anise. Dusty, attractive aromas. Earthy, fleshy flavors, solidly structured. The finish is well gripped by dry, grainy tannins.

Pesquera
Ribera del Duero 1990 $16.   86

Portlike young purple color; slightly meaty nose, with black cherries at the center and cedar and tobacco around the edges. Full palate impression, with ample tannins for aging, yet softness in the supple plummy fruit style. An exciting, modern wine.

Ribera del Duero 1992 $13.99.   88

Dark purple to the rim. Full-bodied. Moderate acidity. Lots of fruit. Heavily oaked. Quite tannic. Reminiscent of black fruits, earth, brown spices. Densely extracted and brooding, this is an unusually inaccessible young Pesquera. The tightly wound core of fruit flavors is bound by full tannins. Opens considerably with aeration, but should be cellared for the mid-term. At present it is an excellent foil for rich game or lamb dishes.

Ribera del Duero 1994 $21.99.   92

Opaque black cherry color. Moderately full-bodied. Highly extracted. Quite tannic. Plums, earth, black tea. Brooding dark aromas lead an inky compact palate with a tight core and plenty of noble tannins through the finish. Youthful, though not entirely inaccessible.

Reserva, Ribera del Duero 1989 $35.   96

Deep ruby appearance. Outrageously deep and extracted, loaded with tannins that will age gracefully. Mouthwatering acidity. Crushed, dark fruits such as raspberry, blackberry, and blueberry, touched with herbs, and generously endowed with forest floor nuances. A blockbuster.

Reserva, Ribera del Duero 1991 $25.99.   92

Deep purplish hue to the rim. Full-bodied. Lots of fruit. Heavily oaked. Moderately tannic. Reminiscent of brown spices, black fruits, dried herbs. Intoxicatingly aromatic, this is a complex and extracted young Reserva. Though approachable, it would benefit from a tour of duty in the cellar.

Gran Reserva, Ribera del Duero 1985 $75.   97

Full-bodied with austere but finely integrated tannins. Good acidity. Huge redwood, herb, and mocha notes ripple through a dark cherry core, accented by brown spices and a touch of ginger. Marvelously fragrant and perfectly balanced.

Gran Reserva, Ribera del Duero 1992 $82.   90

Ruby blood red hue. Moderately full-bodied. Highly extracted. Moderately tannic. Minerals, earth, black fruits. Stunning earthy complexity shows a note of complex terroir. Dry, and well gripped at present, with stroppy tannins lingering. This needs more time.

Janus, Ribera del Duero 1994 $89.99.　　　　　　　　　　　　　　**94**

Inky opaque black-purple. Moderately full-bodied. Highly extracted. Heavily oaked. A hugely concentrated monster of a wine with great presence and balance. The tightly wound palate shows deep black and red fruit flavors with a big overlay of rich fine-grained tannins. This is one for the cellar.

Bodegas Piedemonte

Merlot, Navarra 1997 $7.50.　　　　　　　　　　　　　　　　　　**82**

Cabernet Sauvignon, Crianza, Navarra 1995 $10.50.　　　　　**86**

Deep ruby cast. Medium-bodied. Balanced acidity. Moderately extracted. Mildly tannic. Minerals, red fruits. Unusual high-toned aromas carry a berryish quality. Full though lean in the mouth, with an angular spicy finish.

Reserva, Navarra 1994 $13.50.　　　　　　　　　　　　　　　　**NR**

Moscatel, Vino Blanco Dulce, Navarra NV $5.99/500 ml.　　　**83**

Bodega Poboleda

Siu, Priorato 1997 $60.　　　　　　　　　　　　　　　　　　　　**88**

Bright purple hue. Medium-bodied. Highly extracted. Moderately tannic. Ripe berries, cordial. Floral, intense berry aromas. Super-ripe fruit flavors on entry follow through on the palate. Very, dusty tannins linger on the generously alcoholic finish. A concentrated, structured wine with enough acidity to balance.

Rene Barbier

Mediterranean White, Penedes NV $5.99.　　　　　　　　　　　**NR**

Mediterranean Red, Penedes NV $4.99.　　　　　　　　　　　　**83**

Cabernet Sauvignon, Mediterranean Select, Penedes 1994 $6.　　**84**

Dark opaque ruby. Medium-bodied. Moderately extracted. Mildly tannic. Mature, spicy aromas of black fruits follow through on the palate that is kept lively by bright citrus-like acids highlighting the minerally, dry finish. Very quaffable, particularly with food.

Merlot, Mediterranean Select, Penedes 1993 $6.　　　　　　　**80**

Tempranillo, Mediterranean Select, Penedes 1993 $6.　　　　**NR**

Bodegas Reyes

Teofilo Reyes, Ribera del Duero 1996 $26.　　　　　　　　　　**89**

Saturated ruby purple. Moderately full-bodied. Highly extracted. Moderately tannic. Muted aromas with fleshy undertones. Youthful and tight on the palate with powdery tannins gripping the finish. Has a rich, glycerous texture on the palate. Needs further bottle age.

Teofilo Reyes, Tinto Cosecha, Ribera del Duero 1994 $26.　　**88**

Full brick red with a fading rim. Moderately full-bodied. Moderately extracted. Moderately tannic. Red fruits, oak spice. Heavily wood accented aromas. Supple, rounded and well developed flavors show red berry fruit flavors and a good dose of dry, spicy oak accents on the finish. Drinking well now.

Bodegas Riberalta

Vega Izan, Ribera del Duero 1996 $8.99.　　　　　　　　　　　**80**

Joan Raventos Rosell

Chardonnay, Heretat Vall-Ventos, Penedes 1997 $12.　　　　**84**

Medium straw. Medium-bodied. Moderately extracted. Apples, pears, citrus zest. Juicy, clean fruity aromas lead a clean, well textured mouthfeel with good weight and texture through the finish. Very drinkable, with fine grip. Good varietal character.

Merlot, Heretat Vall-Ventos, Penedes 1997 $13.50. 86

Pale fading ruby hue. Medium-bodied. Moderately extracted. Mildly tannic. Leather, red fruits. Perfumed, leathery aromas follow through on the crisp palate with subtle berry fruit flavors and a lean finish.

Cabernet Sauvignon, Heretat Vall-Ventos, Penedes 1997 $15. 86

Bright ruby purple. Medium-bodied. Moderately extracted. Moderately oaked. Moderately tannic. Vanilla, cedar, black currants. Crisp, aromatic fruity nose with vanilla oak accents. Aromas follow through on the palate with nice primary fruit flavors lingering through the vanilla finish.

Pedro Rovira

Macabeu, "Alta Mar," Blanc de Nectar, Terra Alta 1997 $6.99.	NR
Raquel Rosé, Tarragona 1996 $6.99.	82
Mediterraneo Vino Tinto, Tarragona NV $3.99.	NR
Marques de Campo Real, Crianza, Tarragona 1993 $6.39.	NR
Tempranillo, Viña Mater, Reserva, Tarragona 1991 $8.99.	NR
Sacramental Wine, Terra Alta NV $10.99.	82
Moscatel, Tarragona NV $11.49.	83

Santiago Ruiz

O'Rosal, Rias Baixas 1996 $22. NR

Bodega S. Arroyo

Bodega San Jorge, Tinto Arroyo Crianza, Ribera del Duero 1995 $16. 89

Dark ruby hue with a slight fade. Medium-bodied. Moderately extracted. Mildly tannic. Cherries, minerals. Supple and attractive with soft, rounded fruit flavors and velvety tannins on the finish. Drinking very nicely now.

Bodega San Jorge, Tinto Arroyo Reserva, Ribera del Duero 1994 $35. 89

Bright brick red with a fading rim. Medium-bodied. Moderately extracted. Moderately tannic. Chocolate, raisin. Ripe spiced aromas. Mature tasting, with well developed flavors and nice minerally accent underneath. Quite complex with some exotic flavors.

Bodegas Salnesur

Albariño, Condes de Albarei, Rias Baixas 1997 $9. 90

Bright golden yellow. Creamy, zesty aromas lead a moderately full-bodied palate offering a generously fruity mouthful of flavors with fine minerally clarity through the finish. Moderately extracted flavors of minerals, peach and apple. A vividly flavored style.

Bodegas Sarda

Gran Vinya Sarda Reserva, Penedes 1985 $11.99. 80

Bodegas Señorio de Nava

Viña Marian, Rueda 1996 $8.39. 88

Straw color with brilliant clarity. Moderately light-bodied. Full acidity. Moderately extracted. Citrus, dried herbs, chalk. Pleasantly aromatic with a very crisp citrus presence on the palate. The vibrant acidity accents the classic Sauvignon flavors and provides an angular, youthful structure.

Tinto Joven, Ribera del Duero 1996 $8.99. 85

Bright ruby to the rim with brilliant clarity. Medium-bodied. Moderately extracted. Mildly tannic. Youthful and inviting in style, with a well-balanced palate. Deep, plummy fruit notes are made all the more complex by virtue of a pleasant sweet herbal accent.

Scale: Superlative (96-100), Exceptional (90-95), Highly Recommended (85-89), Recommended (80-84), Not Recommended (Under 80)

Crianza, Ribera del Duero 1995 $13.29.   87

Deep ruby hue. Medium-bodied. Moderately extracted. Moderately oaked. Mildly tannic. Well balanced if somewhat austere in the mouth with a solid core of black fruit flavors with vanilla and pepper notes through the finish.

Reserva, Ribera del Duero 1994 $20.99.   89

Deep ruby with a slight fade to the rim. Medium-bodied. Moderately extracted. Heavily oaked. Mildly tannic. Quite aromatic with a ripe black fruit character and generous oak accents. In the mouth the wine is well balanced with an angular finish.

Jaume Serra

Tempranillo, Penedes 1995 $5.   86

Pale cherry red. Medium-bodied. Balanced acidity. Subtly extracted. Mildly tannic. Cherries, spice. Berry fruit aromas follow through with crisp cherry flavors. Well balanced and highly drinkable, with bright acids lingering through the finish.

Torres

Viña Sol, Penedes 1997 $6.99.   NR

Chardonnay, Gran Viña Sol, Penedes 1996 $10.49.   85

Bright yellow-straw hue. Medium-bodied. Moderately extracted. Mildly oaked. Full peach and apple aromas follow through on the palate. Flavors are concentrated with good varietal definition and a subtle oak influence. Straightforward and quaffable.

Chardonnay, Gran Viña Sol, Penedes 1997 $10.99.   84

Pale green-straw. Medium-bodied. Full acidity. Moderately extracted. Butter, vanilla, apples. Juicy, mellow and fruity with a clean, smooth flavor profile enhanced by subtle oak nuances.

Viña Esmeralda, Penedes 1997 $10.99.   88

Pale platinum straw. Moderately light-bodied. Balanced acidity. Lychee, grapefruit. Ginger and citrus aromas are appealing, following through to a lightly framed, clean racy palate.

Fransola, Penedes 1996 $16.49.   85

Bright yellow-gold. Medium-bodied. Moderately extracted. Heavily oaked. Clean fresh lemon and apple flavors expand on the palate and linger through the finish. No oak influence discernible. This is a very versatile style.

Milmanda, Penedes 1994 $43.   84

Brilliant yellow-straw hue. Medium-bodied. Moderately extracted. Nutty, oaky aromas. Fresh apple flavors have a strong smoky, yeasty counterpart with a decidedly buttery note through the finish. A nice mouthfeel, but the acids do not quite carry the weight of this wine.

Tempranillo, Coronas, Penedes 1996 $7.99.   86

Pale cherry red with a fading rim. Medium-bodied. Moderately extracted. Moderately oaked. Mildly tannic. Pleasing oaky aromas follow through on the palate with juicy fruit flavors up-front, and lingering fruit acids. Drinking well now, showing some bottle development.

Gran Sangre de Toro, Penedes 1993 $10.49.   83

Garnacha-Cariñena, Gran Sangre de Toro, Reserva, Penedes 1995 $10.99.   84

Bright cherry red. Medium-bodied. Moderately extracted. Mildly oaked. Vanilla, red berries. Subtle oaky aromas reveal a supple, generously fruity mouthful of lingering flavors.

Merlot, Las Torres, Penedes 1997 $11.49.   89

Bright purple. Medium-bodied. Moderately extracted. Vanilla, cassis. Floral, black fruit aromas lead oaky, bright cherry flavors that have a direct, simple appeal. Highly quaffable.

Merlot, Viña Las Torres, Penedes 1996 $11.49.   **84**

Bright purple-red. Moderately light-bodied. Moderately extracted. Mildly oaked. Mildly tannic. Floral juicy fruit aromas lead an easygoing candied berry-flavored palate with a clean finish showing mild astringency. Nouveau-like and very accessible.

Cabernet Sauvignon, Gran Coronas Reserva, Penedes 1993 $14.49.   **87**

Dark brick red. Medium-bodied. Highly extracted. Black currant aromas have a hint of herbal character that comes through on the palate. Solid and flavorsome with a dry finish that shows some toasty oak and fine-grained tannins. Good now with rich foods though this should keep a few more years.

Pinot Noir, Mas Borras, Penedes 1993 $22.   **90**

Medium cherry-brick red. Medium-bodied. Moderately extracted. Mildly tannic. Leathery, herbal aromas indicate good varietal character. Dried cherry flavors expand on the palate with fine mouthfeel and dry, fine grained tannins through the finish. Very earthy style of Pinot Noir.

Cabernet Sauvignon, Gran Coronas Mas La Plana, Reserva,
Penedes 1994 $25.   **83**

Gran Coronas Gran Reserva Black Label, Penedes 1990 $37.   **92**

Dark brick red. Moderately full-bodied. Highly extracted. Moderately oaked. Moderately tannic. Developed black currant aromas are enticing. Concentrated, silky flavors of black cherries and cassis linger through the finish. Plenty of tannic grip still, but can be enjoyed now or cellared.

Valdamor

Albariño, Rias Baixas 1996 $24.99.   **89**

Bright yellow-straw. Medium-bodied. Balanced acidity. Moderately extracted. Peach, orange, minerals. Perfumed aromas also reveal mineral notes. Bold fruity flavors upfront yield to a dry, leaner styled finish.

Valdegema

Vino de la Tierra de Extremadura 1994 $11.99.   **NR**

Valdemar

Vino Rosado, Rioja 1997 $8.   **84**

Pale pinkish red. Medium-bodied. Balanced acidity. Moderately extracted. Cherry skins, minerals. Cherry skin aromas lead a rounded mouthfeel, showing cherrylike fruit flavors that finish in a dry manner.

Bodegas Valduero

Crianza, Ribera del Duero 1994 $14.99.   **84**

Dark purple-red. Medium-bodied. Highly extracted. Quite tannic. Crisp black berry fruit aromas with an herbal accent that follows through on the palate. Very structured with strapping tannins at present making the finish very dry.

Bodegas Valtravieso

Crianza, Ribera del Duero 1996 $25.   **86**

Saturated purple hue. Medium-bodied. Moderately extracted. Mildly tannic. Red berry fruits. Attractive ripe fruity aromas lead a supple, fleshy palate with full, forward fruity character and a hint of drying tannins. Drinking well now.

Reserva, Ribera del Duero 1995 $50.   **89**

Opaque dark ruby red, saturated to the rim. Moderately full-bodied. Highly extracted. Quite tannic. Black fruits, chocolate malt, oak. Intensely aromatic. Powerfully concentrated with minerally backbone and dense black fruit flavors. Wood spice is evident, with astringent tannins gripping the finish.

Scale: Superlative (96-100), Exceptional (90-95), Highly Recommended (85-89), Recommended (80-84), Not Recommended (Under 80)

Vega Adriana
Vino de La Tierra de Barros 1991 $9.99.   82

Vega Sicilia
Valbuena, Ribera del Duero 1989 $70.   97

Ink black appearance. Very full-bodied and smooth with velvety tannins. Medium acidity. A host of plums, cherries, mint, violets, and brown spices are packed into the glass. A beautiful wine for special feasts.

Valbuena, Ribera del Duero 1991 $90.   94

Deep and saturated crimson red hue with purplish highlights. Full-bodied. Lots of fruit. Heavily oaked. Moderately tannic. Reminiscent of smoke, red fruits, vanilla. Greater in extract than the 1989 or 1988, this Valbuena is rich and chunky. In need of cellaring to round itself out, it is nonetheless a profound wine with excellent length.

Valbuena, Ribera del Duero 1992 $75.   95

Dark reddish ruby . Moderately full-bodied. Highly extracted. Moderately tannic. Reminiscent of brown spice, dried herbs, concentrated cherries. Bright complex aromatics lead a packed palate with great uplifting acidity and a lush fruity center supported by generous soft tannins that give this a long chewy finish. Quite irresistible now, but will develop with cellaring.

Valbuena, Ribera del Duero 1993 $75.   93

Opaque blackish-ruby hue. Moderately full-bodied. Highly extracted. Moderately tannic. Highly aromatic nose of dried herbs, bramble fruits, and earth. Rounded generous and ripe flavors fill the palate. Rich, thick mouthfeel is enhanced by well-integrated plush tannins. This is drinking rather nicely now.

Unico, Ribera del Duero 1970 $175.   98

Deep crimson hue with brilliant clarity. Moderately full-bodied. Lots of fruit. Moderately oaked. Reminiscent of black fruits, oriental spices, vanilla. Only recently released, this wine was held by the winery for a quarter century till it was deemed ready. Extraordinary in its extraction and purity of ripe fruit flavors, it is a monumental wine that tastes only a few years old. Velvety and lush with a seamless structure, all components are in perfect balance. Though it drinks beautifully now, it will obviously hold well into the next century.

Unico, Ribera del Duero 1981 $150.   95

Dark brick red-garnet. Medium-bodied. Highly extracted. Heavily oaked. Moderately tannic. Perfumed brown spice aromas lead an elegant and rich mouthful of mature fruit flavors with plenty of smoky notes lingering on the long finish. Drinking very nicely now, though this has lost only the first blush of youth.

Unico, Ribera del Duero 1983 $110.   99

Deep garnet appearance. Very full-bodied with lots of tannin and medium acidity. Gorgeous perfume with prominent oak and sandalwood tones wafting over a melange of earthiness, chocolate, herbs, and berries. An unbelievably complex wine, well integrated, and still young.

Unico, Ribera del Duero 1985 $150.   96

Deep opaque ruby hue. Moderately full-bodied. Lots of fruit. Moderately oaked. Mildly tannic. Reminiscent of black fruits, vanilla, earth. Liquid silk, this is a beautifully integrated though densely extracted wine. Built for the ages, it is nonetheless accessible now, a Vega hallmark. Though the winery's practice is to release Unico only when ready to drink, this is clearly many years away from true maturity. Drink your '70s and wait for the new millennium.

Unico, Ribera del Duero 1986 $125.   **96**

Opaque blackish red. Moderately full-bodied. Highly extracted. Moderately tannic. Pronounced spicy, toasty nose. Hugely concentrated plum and black fruit flavors expand on the palate, deferring to smoky vanilla oak flavors on the finish. Outstanding mouthfeel and length, though it is a little reined-in at present. Extra cellar age would benefit this wine.

Bodegas Angel Rodriguez Vidal

Verdejo, Martinsancho, Rueda Superior 1996 $9.99.   **87**

Pale greenish straw. Moderately light-bodied. Moderately extracted. Faintly melony, vanilla aromas have a Riesling-like quality that comes through on a fresh fruity palate with apple and melon flavors persisting through a clean finish. Refreshing, aperitif style. Very quaffable.

Vinicola del Priorat

Onix, Priorat 1997 $9.   **85**

Bright opaque purple. Medium-bodied. Highly extracted. Mildly tannic. Cherries, red fruits. Ripe, almost overripe aromas lead a richly extracted and well-gripped palate, with generous alcohol and supple tannins suggesting early drinking. Quaffable.

Vinicola Navarra

Las Campanas Rosado, Navarra 1996 $6.99.   **88**

Reddish with subtle pink highlights. Medium-bodied. Moderately extracted. Mildly floral nose. Subtle raspberry fruit flavors have very good persistence through the finish. Very clean, juicy and fresh.

thirty-seven

Spain
Cava

Cava: All That Sparkles Is Not Champagne

Unfortunately for fans of bubbly, it is not a buyer's market for sparkling wines. With significant price increases in both French Champagne and the heretofore affordable sparkling wines of the United States, it is becoming more and more difficult to find quality bubbly at reasonable prices. In the case of sparkling wines, if they cost $5 per bottle, they will usually taste like they were $5 per bottle, as their light and delicate natures magnify flaws. All is not gloom and doom, however. In tasting sparklers from around the world, one region in particular has maintained an admirable level of consistency while keeping a lid on prices. These are the Méthode Champenoise wines of Spain, known as Cava.

What is Cava?

In the U.S., Cava is probably best known and defined by the two largest brands, Freixenet and Codorniu. Indeed, these firms are respectively the largest and second largest producers of sparkling wines in the world, and combined produce more than 85% of all Spanish Cavas. The remaining 15% of production is split between some 200 other producers, many of whom are small artisanal brands, which are only recently being imported.

The term Cava is Spanish for "cellar," but when used in connection with Spanish sparkling wines, it refers to the fact that any bottle labeled as "Cava" was made by the traditional method of Champagne production. The general adoption and acceptance of the term long ago gave the Spanish industry an individual identity separate and distinct from that of French Champagne. While the sparklers of California usually shy away from what the French consider a proprietary term, they have as yet to come up with an industry wide alternative. Somehow "California Sparkling Wine" doesn't quite roll off the tongue like "Cava."

Cava by the Glass

As for the wines themselves, while they are often overmatched when tasted side by side with French Champagne, they will compare

Cava
at a Glance

Wines Reviewed:

38

Producers/Brands Represented:

18

Value Rating:

Excellent

favorably with many U.S.-produced sparklers, and have been the definition of consistency—rarely great but almost always very good. Light and crisp in style, they tend to be very precise with vibrant bubbles. In fact, one might say that these wines will perform better and be more versatile than the richer French wines in simple "by the glass" settings. They make ideal aperitifs, pleasant yet undemanding, and their vibrancy also makes them ideal for Kir Royales or Mimosas.

Reviews

Catalana de Vins Artesans
NV Heredad Freixedas Cava Brut, Penedes $10.99. NR
NV Heredad Freixedas Cava Brut Nature, Cava $13.99. NR

Paul Cheneau
NV Blanc de Blancs Cava, Penedes $8.99. 81
1992 Grande Reserve Brut Cava, Penedes $14.95. 80

Codorniu
NV Blanc de Blancs Cava, Penedes $9. 85
Pale gold with emerald highlights. Medium-bodied. Moderately extracted. Reminiscent of citrus zest, pear, yeast. Crisp mouthfeel with clean flavors and some mild astringency through the finish that make this refreshing in style.
NV Brut Cava, Penedes $9. 88
Bright yellow-gold appearance. Moderately full-bodied. Highly extracted. Reminiscent of tropical fruits, citrus, cream of tartar. Attractive tropical aromas lead a richly fruity style with a full, rounded palate that should have a wide appeal.

Covides
NV Xenius Brut Reserva Cava, Penedes $10. 82

Cristalino
NV Brut Cava, Spain $7.50. 80

Freixenet
NV Carta Nevada Cava Brut, Penedes $6.99. 86
Bright yellow-gold. Medium-bodied. Balanced acidity. Yellow apples and butter aromas follow through well on the palate with sweet juicy flavors. Finishes with an intriguing spicy note.
NV Brut Rosé, Penedes $7.99. 87
Pale copper-red appearance. Medium-bodied. Moderately extracted. Reminiscent of dried herbs, yeast, red fruits. Subtle but aromatic smoky, herbal notes lead a flavorsome palate with some complexity through a lingering finish.
NV Cordon Negro Brut Cava, Penedes $7.99. 86
Pale greenish straw hue. Medium-bodied. Balanced acidity. Mildly floral aromas. Juicy, appealing, simple flavors have an appley and lemon cream character. The mouthfeel shows a degree of creamy richness.
NV Brut de Noirs Cava, Penedes $8.99. 81

Juvé y Camps
1992 Reserva Vintage Brut Cava, Penedes $12.95. NR

1992 Reserva de la Familia Extra Brut Cava, Penedes $17.95.   **84**

Bright golden appearance. Medium-bodied. Moderately extracted. Reminiscent of tropical fruit, yeast. Assertive full-flavored style with plenty of extracted flavor. Any lack of elegance is compensated by force of character. This should go well with food.

1992 Gran Juvé Camps Brut Cava, Penedes $34.95.   **87**

Very pale yellow with emerald highlights. Medium-bodied. Moderately extracted. Reminiscent of burnt coffee, citrus zest. Fine autolyzed yeast aromas. Assertively flavored with well-extracted flavors showing development. Quite a traditional style that would partner with food.

Cavas Lavernoya

Lacrima Baccus, Semi Sec Especial Cava, Penedes $10.   **87**

Bright golden straw. Medium-bodied. Moderately extracted. Moderately oaked. Mild sweetness. Nice sweet citrus, peach, and floral notes. Very attractive juicy flavors on entry with a lingering sweet finish. Ripe full flavored style.

NV Lacrima Baccus, Brut Especial Cava, Penedes $10.49.   **89**

Pale golden color. Moderately light-bodied. Moderately extracted. Reminiscent of quince, flowers, nuts. Very particular fruity aromas lead a lighter styled palate with a clean finish. This has original flavors with a hint of maturity. Fine balance overall.

Lacrima Baccus, Semi Sec Reserva Cava, Penedes $11.   **88**

Bright pale yellow color. Moderately full-bodied. Moderately extracted peach, ripe citrus, yeast flavors. Ripe fruit aromas lead a rich rounded palate with a creamy feel and well-balanced sweetness lingering through the long finish.

NV Lacrima Baccus, Brut Reserva Cava, Penedes $11.25.   **89**

Pale yellow appearance. Medium-bodied. Moderately extracted. Tropical fruits, yeast, minerals. Fruity aromas with mature nuances reveal a balanced palate showing some mature complexity through the finish.

NV Lacrima Baccus, Brut Rosé Cava, Penedes $11.25.   **87**

Bright copper-orange color. Medium-bodied. Moderately extracted. Reminiscent of red fruits, apple skins. Assertive aromas lead a fruity palate with slightly astringent notes with plenty of skin extract that gives this a long dry finish. This could match with lighter foods.

NV Lacrima Baccus, Brut Nature Gran Reserva Cava, Penedes $12.75.   **82**

NV Primerisimo, Lacrima Baccus Grand Cuvée, Brut Cava, Penedes $17.   **90**

Pale golden color. Medium-bodied. Moderately extracted. Cantaloupe, cream of tartar, and lemon flavors. Attractive fruity aromas lead a crisp entrance, with a lively and zesty mouthfeel and a lingering juicy finish. A very fresh style.

NV Summum, Lacrima Baccus, Brut Nature Cava, Penedes $17.   **85**

Pale golden appearance. Medium-bodied. Moderately extracted. Apples, citrus zest. Discernible mild oxidation on the nose. Crisp and bone dry on the palate with mild astringency through the finish.

LLopart

1992 Leopardi Cava Brut, Penedes $19.   **83**

Marques de Gelida

NV Cava Brut, Penedes $7.50.   **81**

Mont-Marcal

1994 Cava Brut, Penedes $10.49.   **81**

Montsarra
NV Cava Brut, Penedes $11.99.   88
Bright deep yellow-gold. Moderately full-bodied. Balanced acidity. Spicy, mature aromas show an oxidized character that follows through on the richly flavored, nutty palate with an elegant bead and a lingering, complex finish.

Joan Raventos Rosell
NV Brut Nature Cava, Penedes $14.   89
Bright golden color. Moderately full-bodied. Highly extracted. Interesting combination of yeast, browned butter, and tropical fruit flavors. Complex mature aromatics lead a full-flavored palate with rich nuances through the finish. A ripe and rounded style.

NV Brut Reserva Heretat Cava, Penedes $25.   88
Yellow-golden luster. Moderately full-bodied. Highly extracted. Yeast and maderized flavors. Assertive mature aromas. Full flavored and rich palate with plenty of extracted flavors lingering on the finish. Maybe a tad too traditional for some tastes but this shows plenty of character.

Bodegas Sarda
NV Cava Sarda Reserva Brut, Spain $12.99.   84
Moderately light-bodied. Moderate acidity. Mild fruit. Nice flavors of toast, minerals, limes, quinine. Faint oxidized notes accent austere, minerally fruit with crisp character.

Segura Viudas
NV Brut Reserva Cava, Penedes $6.99.   85
Pale straw appearance. Medium-bodied. Moderately extracted. Citrus, cream of tartar, dill. Fresh lemony flavors on the palate work well with a frothy mouthfeel that carries through on a full-flavored finish. Easy to drink this wine with anything, anytime.

NV Aria Cava Brut, Penedes $8.99.   86
Bright green-gold. Medium-bodied. Full acidity. Fresh green apple aromas lead a fruit-forward palate with a juicy, direct appeal and a clean finish. A snappy aperitif style.

NV Reserva Heredad Cava Brut, Penedes $15.   81

Jaume Serra
NV Cristalino Cava Brut, Penedes $8.   87
Brilliant yellow-straw color. Medium-bodied. Moderately extracted. Rich flavors of green apples and peach with a rounded mouthfeel. The lingering finish shows some mature yeasty notes. Full and generous style.

Sumarroca
NV Cava Brut, Penedes $8.99.   84
Pale platinum cast. Medium-bodied. Full acidity. Apples, minerals. Clean, direct and juicy with straightforward flavors and medium-beaded carbonation.

NV Cava Extra Brut, Penedes $8.99.   86
Pale green-straw. Medium-bodied. Full acidity. Big beaded carbonation. Lively mouthfeel with juicy, direct flavors. Finishes with lean minerally notes. Well-balanced, refreshing style.

Jané Ventura

NV Extra Brut Cava, Spain $14.   85

Moderately light-bodied. Moderate acidity. Mild fruit. Mineral, bread, flowers flavors. Steely and lean structured, with zesty acidity that makes the mouth water. Strong toasty bread notes emerge with aeration.

NV Gran Reserva Extra Brut Cava, Spain $18.   88

Moderately light-bodied. Moderate acidity. Mild fruit. Mild sweetness. Toast, grapefruit, chalk. Light, leanish fruit shows attractive, elegant toast notes and fine balance. Mild sweet notes add softening influence.

thirty-eight

❧

Spain
Sherry

❧

Sherry: The World's Best Wine Value

Produced only in a tiny and strictly defined area in the southwest corner of Spain, Sherry is one of the worlds greatest yet least understood wines. Its zone of production is known as the Sherry Triangle. This triangle has its vertices at three towns, in which stocks for the entire world are vinified and aged. The most important of these centers is the hot and dusty city of Jerez de la Frontera, which lies some 15 miles inland from the Atlantic Ocean. Indeed, the term Sherry itself is the 18th century Anglicization of this city's name. It is here that the majority of wineries, or bodegas, have their cellars.

The other two towns, Puerto de Santa Maria and Sanlucar de Barrameda, are situated on the coast. While Jerez is sweltering through the long Andalucian summer, the moderating influence of the ocean's breezes offers welcome relief for the coastal towns which lie just down the road. During the hottest months, many of the wealthy families of Jerez retreat to the relative comfort of their summer homes in Sanlucar. This is the best illustration of the conditions that create the not so subtle differences between wines produced in towns only miles apart from each other.

With its hot climate, Jerez has long been known for producing the rich and heavily roasted "brown Sherries," which have been favored for so long by people in colder climates. At the opposite end of the scale is Sanlucar, whose Sherries are matured steps from the open ocean. It is here that one of the preferred drinks of the Andalucians themselves is produced, Manzanilla. Distinctly light and fresh, with a characteristic tang, this delicious wine is only recently being discovered outside the region. As for the third town, unlike Sanlucar, Puerto's view of the sea is slightly more sheltered as one looks across the bay to a peninsula on which lies the ancient city of Cadiz. Thus, the sea's influence is somewhat tempered, and the resulting wines lie somewhere in style between Jerez and Sanlucar. Puerto Fino is its best known product, a lighter style of Sherry that makes an excellent aperitif in addition to pairing well with the region's abundant supply of fresh seafood.

A Wealth of Styles

Sherry is a fortified wine that is produced almost exclusively from the Palomino Fino grape. There are two basic types of Sherry—Fino and Oloroso—with all styles being variations thereof. The dividing line between the two can be largely attributed to one unique indigenous type of yeast known as *flor*. Flor grows spontaneously on the surface of wines in the Fino family while they are in barrel, and forms a layer that provides a barrier to oxidation. The resultant wines will retain a sense of freshness, and the flor will impart a distinctive set of aromas and flavors. It grows more evenly throughout the year in the cooler coastal towns and has a particular affinity for Sanlucar.

Those wines that do not develop flor belong to the Oloroso family, and are matured in contact with the outside air. This controlled method of oxidation results in darker, richer, mellower wines. After the vintage, experienced tasters evaluate the newly made white wines and classify them according to their expected development. This is the first step a young Sherry takes on its way to being bottled in one of a range of styles that are derived from the two basic types. These include:

Scale: Superlative (96-100), Exceptional (90-95), Highly Recommended (85-89), Recommended (80-84), Not Recommended (Under 80)

Manzanilla

Manzanilla is a variation of Fino that can only be made in Sanlucar. It is the lightest, palest, and most delicate of all Sherries. Cellared next to the sea, it is often characterized by a distinctive salty tang and vibrant acidity. These are fabulous aperitifs and pair brilliantly with shellfish in particular. As a matter of course, these wines should be served chilled.

Manzanillas should be consumed as soon as possible after bottling, as they degrade rather quickly in the bottle. Bottles that have been languishing on shelves for over a year will bare little resemblance to the original, and should be avoided. This may be tricky however, as the bottling dates are not on the labels. This is where a conscientious retailer with a high volume turnover becomes invaluable. Do not be afraid to ask how long your prospective bottle has been in stock. If your Manzanilla or Fino tastes overly maderized or is dark in color, it should be returned.

Fino

Finos are the flor-affected wines produced in Puerto and to a lesser degree in Jerez. They are a shade fuller than Manzanillas and have a characteristic bitter almond note. Jerez Finos tend to be the fullest of these lighter styled Sherries. Like Manzanillas, they make excellent aperitifs, but are versatile companions to the table as well.

Tio Pepe and La Ina are two famous brand names that are actually Fino Sherries. The freshness caveat about Manzanilla applies equally to Finos and it is imperative to purchase Fino in the freshest state possible and serve it chilled.

Amontillado

If a Fino Sherry is left to age, the flor will gradually consume nutrients in the wine until it can no longer replenish itself. This can take six to eight years and sometimes longer under optimum conditions. Once the flor dies, the old Fino will begin to oxidize, and evaporation will gradually raise the alcohol content. Depending upon the length of this second phase of aging, the wine will attain a natural

Sherry
at a Glance

Wines Reviewed:

115

Producers/Brands
Represented:

18

Value Rating:

Excellent

level of alcohol between 16 and 23 percent. The resultant Sherry will gradually darken in color and take on a perfumed nutty character.

At this point it is an Amontillado, the result of many years of labor intensive aging. Totally dry in its natural state, some Amontillados are sweetened with Pedro Ximenez or Moscatel to one degree or another, while others are bottled dry. The drier and moderately sweet Amontillados can be revelations at the table and pair well with a range of foods. Sweeter versions are a delight taken after a meal as a digestif. Both should be served at room temperature in order to maximize the bouquet.

Palo Cortado

Palo Cortado is a very rare Sherry, which is a style of Oloroso in that it breeds little or no flor. In other ways, however, it is a bit of a hybrid. Its bouquet is deep and complex while the wine retains a sense of clarity and crispness on the palate, showing great similarity to a fine Amontillado.

In order to avoid confusion, it must be noted that a Palo Cortado produced in Sanlucar will be labeled Jerez Cortado and some houses choose to classify their Palo Cortados by age using the designations *dos*, *tres*, or *cuatro* Cortado and so on. This designation varies from house to house however, and is not an accurate guide between varying producers' wines. Most Palo Cortados are bottled dry although a few are lightly sweetened. All will match beautifully with a wide range of foods, while richer versions will make ideal sipping wines. They are best enjoyed at room temperature.

Oloroso

Oloroso, in Spanish, means fragrant, and a good Oloroso will be intensely aromatic in a way that is similar to an Amontillado yet more rounded. Unlike an Amontillado, however, which had a sense of lightness imparted by its development as a Fino, an Oloroso is richer and develops further viscosity with age. Some are bottled dry, and these make particularly fine matches for richly flavored foods, though most exports are destined to be sweetened, and these make appealing after dinner drinks as well. Those that have been lightly sweetened are known to the Spanish as *Amorosos*, but are not often labeled as such. These are ideal as winter warmers and have long been favored by the British in warding off their chilly climate. Like Amontillados, Olorosos show best at room temperature.

Cream

A Cream Sherry is generally an Oloroso that has been sweetened quite heavily. It was originally developed in Bristol, England and made famous as Harvey's Bristol Cream. These are truly dessert Sherries, in that, unlike an Amoroso, the initial complexity of the Oloroso is largely masked by the Pedro Ximenez or Moscatel that is used to sweeten it. Developed for export, this style is most often consumed much as a port would be after a meal.

A relatively recent phenomenon, Pale Cream Sherry, was pioneered only in the 1970s by the then newly established firm of Croft's. In order to make a light colored blend with a sweetness level akin to traditional cream Sherries, Fino replaces Oloroso as the base wine. This lightens up the style overall, and adds the interesting nuances that are generated by a flor accented wine. For one who is very familiar with dry Finos, the taste can be quite disarming, if a trifle odd.

Pedro Ximenez and Moscatel

Pedro Ximenez and Moscatel are the minor grape varieties grown in the Sherry triangle and more prominently in provinces to the east. They are extremely rich sweet wines that form the preferred base for sweetening dry Sherries. Much more rarely they are bottled on their own, and Pedro Ximenez in particular makes one of the world's best hedonic dessert wines.

Once picked the grapes are generally left to shrivel in the hot sun for a period of time, thus concentrating their intense sugars. Pedro Ximenez of great age, such as those from the rare soleras of Osborne and Gonzalez Byass, reach an unbelievable level of viscosity that can be compared to motor oil, and the straightforward raisined character turns deeper, becoming complex and brooding. These wines can best be described as desserts in their own right.

The Solera

Once a Sherry's general style has been established it needs to be aged. In the Sherry towns, this is accomplished in a unique and ingenious way known as the solera system. Developed as a method of fractional blending, it assures a consistent house style from year to year and avoids the vagaries of vintage. Thus, the solera system is the reason Sherries are virtually never vintage dated.

A solera consists of a series of 500-liter oak casks arranged in rows with several levels. The row closest to the floor is referred to, somewhat confusingly, as the *solera* level, while the rows on top of the solera level are referred to as *criaderas*. The first row above the solera level, or second above the ground, is the first criadera, while the second is the second criadera, and so on. The solera as a whole will only contain wines of a certain type, such as Fino, Amontillado, Oloroso, e.t.c. Depending upon the type of Sherry being produced, a solera will have a variable amount of criaderas. Manzanillas for instance will often have 10 or 11 levels in the solera.

Several times a year, a small amount of wine will be drawn from the barrels in the solera level for bottling. These are replenished with an equal amount of Sherry from the first criadera, which in turn will be replenished by the next level up. The last criadera will be replenished by younger wines that have been chosen for their likeness to the wines in this particular solera. In the case of Fino and Manzanilla, this may be wine from the new vintage, while an Amontillado solera may be refreshed by a suitable wine that has made its way through the scales of an entire Fino solera.

This fractional blending of younger wines into older wines is what produces uniformity and consistency. The wine that is ultimately bottled from the solera will thus have an average age that varies from one solera to the next. Where freshness and lightness is a key, as in the case of Finos and Manzanillas, the Sherries are moved through the criaderas at a rapid pace, and the resultant wine is still relatively young, though imparted with great complexity derived from contact with the flor. Where oxidation is the key to aging, the pace is more relaxed and some soleras will have average ages upwards of fifty years or more, containing wines from the previous century. Many of these great soleras were founded in the 1700s and 1800s, and as such would take generations to replace. Understandably, a shipper's old soleras are his most prized and invaluable possessions. Many of these wines used to be reserved for family and friends, but some are now bottled in minute quantities and offered for sale as single solera wines. Lustau Almacenistas, Osborne and Gonzalez Byas's Rare Soleras, and certain Valdespinos are examples, and offer some of the greatest values in the world. Wines of similar ages from Bordeaux or Oporto would fetch hundreds of dollars per bottle, yet these Sherries are often sold between $20 and $40 per bottle... at the moment.

Glassware...A Final Note

Just as consumers as a whole are recognizing that table wines show best when served in proper glassware, the same needs to be said for Sherry. Like port, it should never be relegated to tiny liqueur or cordial glasses. The secret of Sherry lies in its inimitable and complex bouquet, and in order to experience it, one must use the proper glass. The best glass is similar to that which has been designed for port, having a tulip shape that narrows slightly at the top. This type of glass is known to the Jerezanos as a copita. A white wine glass will often work nearly as well, but the glass should not be filled beyond one half to one third full.

Reviews

Alvear

Alvear Fino, Montilla-Moriles. $8.   84

Alvear Amontillado, Montilla-Moriles. $7.50.   83

Alvear Solera Abuelo Diego, Amontillado, Montilla-Moriles. $14.   87

Full golden-straw color. Medium-bodied. Notes of brown spice, roasted almonds, smoke. Spicy, subtly oxidized nose. Long dry palate with delicate roasted flavors that linger through a teasingly long finish that does not become too dry.

Alvear Solera Fundacion, Amontillado Muy Viejo, Montilla-Moriles. $50. 93

Rich amber. Moderately full-bodied. Notes of blanched almond, salt, citrus peel. Hugely concentrated flavors with a thick viscous mouthfeel give this an imposing presence on the palate. Strikes an intriguing balance between richness and dry flavors on the mid palate. The finish, with a salty, spicy quality lingers for minutes.

Alvear Solera Abuelo Diego Oloroso, Montilla-Moriles. $14.   86

Bright amber cast. Medium-bodied. Roasted nuts, brown spices, orange peel. Subtle aromatics have pleasant fruit cake type overtones. Lighter in the mouth with good grip and intensity. Drying through the finish.

Alvear Festival Pale Cream, Montilla-Moriles. $7.   82

Alvear Cream, Montilla-Moriles. $7.50.   88

Light chestnut-amber. Moderately full-bodied. Notes of raisins, caramel, toasted nuts. Full, rich sweet smoky nose leads a rounded lush palate with a sweet entry. Tapers to a surprisingly dry finish, with plenty of rich flavors on the mid palate. Not the least bit cloying.

Alvear Moscatel, Montilla-Moriles. $7.50.   87

Dark chestnut brown appearance. Medium-bodied. Caramelized brown sugar, sweet peach, brown spice. Big caramel aromas with floral nuances that are well expressed on the surprisingly fresh and balanced palate, with a certain lightness to the mouthfeel. Not cloying. Best served with a slight chill.

Alvear Solera Abuelo Diego, Pedro Ximenez, Montilla-Moriles. $14.   **92**

Deep chestnut amber. Full-bodied. Notes of brown sugar, golden raisins, caramel. Sweet heavy caramel aromas lead a thick mouthful of intensely rich flavors with a sweetness that will find any lurking cavities. Long lingering sweet finish. All the concentrated character one expects from a PX, with a very pure expression of flavors.

Alvear Pedro Ximenez 1830, Dulce Muy Viejo, Montilla-Moriles. $80.   **97**

Motor oil black. Full-bodied. Notes of black licorice, rum raisin. Pours like syrup. Inimitable burnt oily aromas. Thick and viscous on the palate with a mouthcoating sweet quality revealing layers of flavors. Too cloying to be drunk in large quantities. Best sipped and savored as a dessert.

Argueso

Argueso San Leon Manzanilla, Sanlucar de Barrameda. $14.   **NR**

Argueso Pedro Ximenez Cream Sherry, Jerez de la Frontera. $17.   **92**

Deep mahogany with a hint of brightness and a golden edge. Full-bodied. Notes of brown spices, dried herbs, caramel, coffee. Brightly flavored with an attractive complexity. Modest acidity actually gives a sense of liveliness to this rich and highly focused elixir. Extraordinary length to the finish.

Antonio Barbadillo

Antonio Barbadillo Very Dry Manzanilla Sherry,
Sanlucar de Barrameda. $7.99.   **84**

Antonio Barbadillo Fino Dry Sherry, Jerez de la Frontera. $8.99.   **84**

Antonio Barbadillo Medium Dry Amontillado Sherry,
Jerez de la Frontera. $7.99.   **84**

Antonio Barbadillo Principe, Dry Amontillado Sherry,
Jerez de la Frontera. $75.   **91**

Amber with orange highlights. Medium-bodied. Notes of brown spice, roasted nuts. Tight, full flavored palate with some richness on the mouthfeel. Distinguished by a long complex finish with developing nutty flavors. Needs some time to open up.

Antonio Barbadillo Palo Cortado del Obispo Gascon Sherry,
Jerez de la Frontera. $125.   **92**

Deep amber with reddish-copper highlights. Moderately full-bodied. Notes of brown spice, roasted nuts, salt. Full burnt salty nose. Assertive and austere with a dry lengthy finish and real complexity. Very demanding on the palate.

Antonio Barbadillo Dry Oloroso Sherry, Jerez de la Frontera. $7.99.   **85**

Antonio Barbadillo Very Old Oloroso Sherry, Jerez de la Frontera. $11.99.   **88**

Dark amber with reddish highlights. Moderately full-bodied. Medium sweetness. Notes of dates, brown spice, raisins. Rich caramelized aromas lead an unctuous palate. Relatively viscous in the mouth, the sweetness of the palate is balanced by a touch of acidity. Subtle burnt herbal overtones add complexity to this straightforward wine.

Antonio Barbadillo Pale Cream Sherry, Jerez de la Frontera. $7.99.   **82**

Antonio Barbadillo Cream Sherry, Jerez de la Frontera. $7.99.   **84**

Antonio Barbadillo Pale Sweet Moscatel Sherry,
Jerez de la Frontera. $7.99.   **89**

Bright yellow-gold. Medium-bodied. Balanced acidity. This curious Sherry delivers the orange-blossom and ginger aromas of a good muscat, and the sweetness of a cream Sherry. A little low in acidity, this is more of a contemplative sipper.

Antonio Barbadillo Rich Sweet Pedro Ximenez Sherry,
Jerez de la Frontera. $10.99.   **80**

Croft

Croft Original Rare Pale Cream Sherry, Jerez de la Frontera. $10.   **86**

Golden with a bright yellow hue. Medium-bodied. Notes of blanched almonds, dried herbs, petrol, lacquer. A classic petrol note often associated with Fino sherries from Puerto de Santa Maria is distinctly evident in the nose. The palate has a well-balanced marriage of sweetness and acidity which results in a refreshing sense of crispness.

Jose de Soto

Jose de Soto Tio Soto Fino Sherry, Jerez de la Frontera. $7.99.   **80**

Jose de Soto Amontillado Sherry, Jerez de la Frontera. $7.99.   **NR**

Jose de Soto Cream Sherry, Jerez de la Frontera. $7.99.   **80**

Bodegas del Principe

Bodegas del Principe A. Soler Extra Amontillado Sherry, Jerez de la Frontera. $3.95.   **NR**

Bodegas del Principe A. Soler Extra Cream Sherry, Jerez de la Frontera. $3.59.   **NR**

Pedro Domecq

Pedro Domecq La Ina Very Pale Dry Fino Sherry, Jerez. $16.40.   **84**

Pedro Domecq Primero Amontillado Sherry, Jerez de la Frontera. $15.   **NR**

Pedro Domecq "51-1a," Very Rare Amontillado, Jerez de la Frontera. $73.   **93**

Very deep bronzed tawny hue. Moderately full-bodied. Aromatic with an intriguing briny quality. Quite viscous, yet comes across the palate with a sense of lightness due to its vibrant acidity. Snappy, with a clean drying finish and exceptional complexity.

Pedro Domecq Palo Cortado Sherry, Bottled 1986, Jerez de la Frontera. $35.   **82**

Pedro Domecq "Sibarita," Very Rare Palo Cortado, Jerez de la Frontera. $73.   **98**

Deep mahogany color. Moderately full-bodied. Exotic and complex aromas of toasted coconut and salted nuts lead to a forceful and mouth filling character on the palate. Excellent grip cleanses the palate and makes way for a finish of extravagant length and intensity. A hint of sweetness serves to balance the vibrant acidity.

Pedro Domecq Rio Viejo Rare Dry Oloroso Sherry, Jerez de la Frontera. $25.   **86**

Amber with a subtle greenish cast. Medium-bodied. Notes of black tea, yeast, dried flowers. Pungent and fully flavored with unusual aromatics. Features a subtle burnt character. Well-balanced acidity. Should find favor with those who prefer a fairly aggressive style.

Gonzalez Byass

Gonzalez Byass Elegante Manzanilla Sherry, Jerez de la Frontera. $5.99.   **85**

Gonzalez Byass Tio Pepe Fino Sherry, Jerez de la Frontera. $12.99.   **89**

Pale straw with traces of green. Medium-bodied. Moderate acidity. Notes of blanched almonds, petrol, beechwood. Attractive aromatics lead to a broad range of flavors on the mildly weighty palate. Well-balanced acidity.

Gonzalez Byass Elegante Medium Dry Amontillado Sherry, Jerez de la Frontera. $5.99.   **83**

Scale: Superlative (96-100), Exceptional (90-95), Highly Recommended (85-89), Recommended (80-84), Not Recommended (Under 80)

Gonzalez Byass Amontillado Del Duque,
Rare Old Solera Amontillado Viejo, Jerez de la Frontera. $40.   94

Rich, brilliant mahogany with a slight green edge. Moderately full-bodied. Notes of salted nuts, toasted coconut, exotic spices. Impressively fragrant, firmly structured, and quite rich with noticeable viscosity. The flavors are deep, warm, and lingering with a very drying finish. Crisp acidity maintains a sense of freshness, despite its forceful character.

Gonzalez Byass Apostoles, Rare Old Solera Oloroso Abocado,
Jerez de la Frontera. $40.   93

Brilliant deep amber with a subtle green cast. Medium-bodied. Notes of smoke, earth, salted pecans. Distinctly aromatic with a pungent character. Zesty acidity downplays the sweetness on the palate and keeps this exotically flavored Sherry from becoming too aggressive. The finish is lengthy and lends itself to fully flavored meats and cheeses.

Gonzalez Byass San Domingo, Pale Cream Sherry,
Jerez de la Frontera. $12.99.   89

Light golden with a subtle green hue. Moderately full-bodied. Notes of minerals, blanched almonds, stone fruits, savory spices. Distinctively aromatic, with a range of classic Fino flavors. Mouth filling, with just a hint of sweetness and an attractive nutty complexity which rides out a lingering finish. Strikes a pleasant balance between richness and lightness. This is an impressive, all purpose sipping Sherry.

Gonzalez Byass Elegante Cream Sherry, Jerez de la Frontera. $5.99.   87

Glossy deep brown with ruby highlights. Medium-bodied. Notes of ginger, molasses, toasted grains. Moderately complex aromatics play out on a well-balanced palate. Crisp acidity reigns in the sweetness for an uplifting finish.

Gonzalez Byass NOE, Rare Old Solera Pedro Ximenez,
Jerez de la Frontera. $40.   97

Opaque black with a tawny rim. Full-bodied. Notes of cocoa, molasses, toasted coconut, saddle leather. Has the consistency of high performance motor oil and literally coats the glass. Absolutely extraordinary aromatics have raced past the line from dried fruits to dark and roasted flavors. It is obviously the product of extreme age. Thick and concentrated, this is a tour de force of winemaking from a solera with few peers in Jerez.

Harvey's

Harvey's Dune, Pale Dry Fino Sherry, Jerez de la Frontera. $12.99.   83
Harvey's Harvey's Club Classic Medium Dry Sherry, Jerez. $12.99.   80
Harvey's Harvey's Isis Pale Cream Sherry, Jerez de la Frontera. $12.99.   84
Harvey's Harvey's Bristol Cream Sherry, Jerez de la Frontera. $12.99.   81
Harvey's 1796 Rare Oloroso Sherry, Jerez de la Frontera. $50.   88

Deep mahogany with a ruby cast. Moderately full-bodied. Notes of golden raisins, molasses, orange peel. Lushly textured and hedonistically flavored with a rich and sweet character that is well-balanced and doesn't overwhelm. Not terribly complex, but very attractive on the whole. A very pleasant after-dinner drink.

Hidalgo

Hidalgo La Gitana Manzanilla, Sanlucar de Barrameda. $9.99.   95

Very pale straw. Medium-bodied. Notes of citrus zest, petrol, brine. Crisp, fragrant, rancio aromas with petrol hints lead a crisp palate, clean as a whistle with a hint of mild astringency and a subtle salty note through the finish.

Hidalgo Manzanilla Pasada, Sanlucar de Barrameda. $15.49.   90

Pale gold. Medium-bodied. Notes of salty blanched almonds, brine. Complex rancio aromas lead a full flavored palate with a subtle oily-salty note and a lengthy finish with some fresh astringency. Steely edge.

Hidalgo Fino Superior "El Cuadrado," Jerez de la Frontera. $15.49.   **90**

Brilliant light gold. Medium-bodied. Notes of blanched almonds, minerals. Full fresh floral nose. Almost juicy, fresh palate with hint of softness and a lengthy juicy finish with briny notes.

Hidalgo Napoleon Amontillado, Sanlucar de Barrameda. $11.99.   **90**

Bright amber with a greenish copper tinge. Moderately light-bodied. Moderate acidity. Notes of sea salt, dried herbs, smoked peat. The maritime influence in the nose of this Sherry belies its years of cellaring in Sanlucar on the bay of Cadiz as opposed to inland Jerez. It has definite similarities in its crispness and austerity to the Manzanillas of Sanlucar. A product of further aging, it has subtle peaty notes which are not unlike an Islay whiskey yet nonetheless very light and fresh. Not for everyone, but it would make an excellent fully flavored aperitif.

Hidalgo Amontillado Viejo, Jerez de la Frontera. $63.99.   **93**

Deep burnished amber with dark orange highlights. Moderately full-bodied. Notes of salted almonds, leather, brown spice. Rich, thick palate with an almost fruity acidic note up front balanced by expansive brown spicy notes that linger. The finish develops for some time after swallowing with a salty, nutty tang. This needs plenty of time to aerate and reveal its potential aromas.

Hidalgo Jerez Cortado, Sanlucar de Barrameda. $17.99.   **90**

Rich chestnut. Medium-bodied. Moderate acidity. Notes of browned butter, dried limes, raisins. Darkly aromatic with a broad presence on the palate. Somewhat angular through the finish.

Hidalgo Oloroso Especial, Sanlucar de Barrameda. $15.99.   **89**

Brilliant pale copper with a subtle greenish cast. Medium-bodied. Moderate acidity. Notes of salted almonds, peat smoke, citrus zest. Features a pronounced sea salt and peat smoke character which is evocative of its lengthy aging only steps from the Atlantic. Racy acidity makes for an Oloroso which is quite unusual in its fresh and lively character. A medicinal tinge to the finish is vaguely suggestive of an Islay whiskey. Brimming with character this would still make an ideal aperitif in addition to being paired with fully seasoned seafoods.

Hidalgo Pedro Ximenez Viejo, Sanlucar de Barrameda. $16.99.   **89**

Deep opaque mahogany with ruby highlights. Full-bodied. Notes of leather, dates, orange peel. Extremely broad and rich with admirable viscosity. The flavors are pure hedonism with a lengthy finish. Just a touch of acidity keeps it from becoming cloying.

Emilio Lustau

Emilio Lustau Jarana, Light Fino Sherry, Jerez de la Frontera. $9.95.   **90**

Very pale straw. Moderately light-bodied. Notes of flowers, citrus zest, green olives. Fresh and lively, with a delectable perfumed character. Finishes crisply to round out the package.

Emilio Lustau Puerto Fino, Puerto de Santa Maria. $10.95.   **91**

Pale gold with green highlights. Moderately light-bodied. Notes of petrol, earth, blanched almonds. Complex and flavorful, with a fresh and lively palate feel. Has a fine finish with a lingering faintly roasted note. An ideal table companion.

Emilio Lustau Dry Amontillado Solera Reserva Los Arcos,
Jerez de la Frontera. $9.95.   **87**

Tawny amber with bronze highlights. Medium-bodied. Notes of toasted pecans, honey, minerals. A pleasantly perfumed nose leads to a fuller warming mouthfeel, with an attractively roasted character. Crisp acidity makes for a clean drying finish. Would make an excellent companion to the table.

Scale: Superlative (96-100), Exceptional (90-95), Highly Recommended (85-89), Recommended (80-84), Not Recommended (Under 80)

Emilio Lustau Rare Amontillado Solera Reserva Escuadrilla,
Jerez de la Frontera. $15.   90

Pale amber with a copper green cast. Notes of brown spices, toasted nuts, flowers. Very enticing overall with a well integrated character. Fully flavored yet quite crisp in the mouth with snappy acidity that lends a fresh green note. Fine lengthy finish. A definite match for rich seafoods and smoked meats.

Emilio Lustau Amontillado del Puerto, Solera Gran Reserva
"San Bartolome," Puerto de Santa Maria. $17.99.   89

Deep copper hue with brilliant clarity. Moderately light-bodied. Bewitching praline and salted nut aromatics are well translated on the palate and come through in the lingering finish. Dry, clean and crisp with good bite and fresh character throughout.

Emilio Lustau Palo Cortado Peninsula, Jerez de la Frontera. $14.95.   85

Emilio Lustau Solera Reserva, Don Nuño Dry Oloroso,
Jerez de la Frontera. $14.95.   83

Emilio Lustau Very Rare Oloroso Solera, Reserva Emperatriz Eugenia,
Jerez de la Frontera. $23.95.   94

Deep tawny amber with a golden rim. Moderately full-bodied. Notes of roasted nuts, leather, dried fruits. The concentrated aromas leap from the glass. Well-balanced acidity maintains a sense of liveliness through the lengthy finish. Would make a beautiful accompaniment to blue veined cheeses.

Emilio Lustau Deluxe Cream Solera Reserva Capataz Andres,
Jerez de la Frontera. $10.95.   91

Deep mahogany with a tawny rim. Moderately full-bodied. Notes of salted pecans, brown spices, chocolate. Aromatic and flavorful with a lovely roasted character. Zesty acidity balances the sweetness and maintains a sense of freshness. Rich in the mouth, but features a delicate warming finish. Pair with cheeses to enjoy after a meal.

Emilio Lustau Rare Cream Solera Reserva Superior,
Jerez de la Frontera. $14.95.   89

Deep mahogany with ruby highlights and a greenish rim. Moderately full-bodied. Notes of dried fruits, leather, salted nuts. Aromatic and flavorful with a well-balanced marriage of sweetness and acidity. Pleasant and lingering through the finish.

Emilio Lustau East India Solera Sherry, Jerez de la Frontera. $16.95.   89

Deep mahogany with ruby highlights. Moderately full-bodied. Notes of molasses, orange peel, dried fruits. Classic, smooth, and rich, the mouthfeel is quite viscous. A touch of acidity in the finish keeps the sweetness in check. Enjoy with or as dessert.

Emilio Lustau 1986 Vendimia Cream Sherry, Jerez de la Frontera. $18.99.   84

Emilio Lustau Moscatel Superior Emilin, Jerez de la Frontera. $14.95.   88

Deep dark mahogany with ruby overtones. Moderately full-bodied. Notes of raisins, molasses, flowers. Aromatic with a full, viscous palate feel. A touch of acidity lightens up the lengthy finish.

Emilio Lustau "Las Cruces," Centenary Selection Moscatel,
Jerez de la Frontera. $19.99.   92

Very deep mahogany hue. Full-bodied. Aromatic. Viscous quality to the palate with notes of golden raisins, dates, and black tea, offset by a solid level of acidity. Rich, long and flavorful. An exceptional dessert wine.

Emilio Lustau Pedro Ximenez, Solera Reserva San Emilio,
Jerez de la Frontera. $14.95.   90

Deep mahogany with a tawny rim. Moderately full-bodied. Notes of golden raisins, dates, exotic spices, blackened nuts. Intriguing and complex, with a highly roasted character. Viscous mouthfeel with a zesty note throughout that keeps it from becoming overwhelming. A brilliant after-dinner drink.

Emilio Lustau Almacenista

Emilio Lustau Almacenista Jurado Manzanilla Pasada de Sanlucar,
Sanlucar de Barrameda. $18.99.   89

Pale gold. Medium-light-bodied. Well-balanced. Crisp and lean acidity. Palate dominated by nutty flavor elements and a subtle ginger note. Complex and lingering.

Emilio Lustau Almacenista Jose Luis Gonzalez Obregon,
Fino del Puerto, Puerto de Santa Maria. $13.95.   86

Deep straw. Moderately light-bodied. Notes of dried herbs, toast, sake. Distinctively pungent in aromatics with a softer palate feel. Quite a bit richer than most Finos.

Emilio Lustau Almacenista Miguel Fontadez Florido,
Amontillado de Jerez, Jerez de la Frontera. $20.   88

Pale copper with greenish highlights and brilliant clarity. Moderately light-bodied. Full acidity. Notes of leather, toast, roasted nuts, flowers. Perfumed and ephemeral in the nose, with a delicate and restrained overall character. Vibrant acidity lends snap to a sharp clean finish.

Emilio Lustau Almacenista Manuel Cuevas Jurado, Manzanilla
Amontillada, Sanlucar de Barrameda. $19.95.   93

Golden with faded copper highlights. Moderately light-bodied. Moderate acidity. Notes of sea salt, roasted nuts, toffee. Features a subtle roasted character, which is admirably offset by its crisp and refreshing framework. A marvelous interplay between delicacy and richness of flavor. Quite complex through the finish. Highly recommended as an accompaniment to smoked fish or scallops.

Emilio Lustau Almacenista Alberto Lorento Piaget,
Amontillado Fino de Jerez, Jerez de la Frontera. $20.   89

Copper-toned amber with brilliant clarity. Moderately light-bodied. Full acidity. Notes of smoke, roasted almonds, malt. Enticingly aromatic with an elegant slightly roasted character. These elements are admirably shown against a racy framework with vibrant acidity and a snappy finish. A wonderful marriage between complexity of flavor and a refreshing sense of lightness.

Emilio Lustau Almacenista Vides, Palo Cortado de Jerez,
Jerez de la Frontera. $20.   92

Brilliant tawny amber. Medium-bodied. Full acidity. Notes of roasted salted nuts, orange peel, brown spices. Invitingly perfumed and complex with an attractive medicinal note. Ample acidity balances the rich flavors in allowing for a refreshing overall character.

Emilio Lustau Almacenista Rosario Farfante, Dos Cortados de Jerez,
Jerez de la Frontera. $21.95.   90

Deep amber with brilliant clarity. Medium-bodied. Moderate acidity. Notes of brown spices, leather, salted nuts. Attractively perfumed with an explosion of flavors on the palate. Angular and zesty through the finish with attractive acidity which maintains a sense of lightness.

Emilio Lustau Almacenista Vides, Single Cask Palo Cortado,
Jerez de la Frontera. $35.   87

Bright copper hue with a subtle greenish cast. Medium-bodied. Very subtle aromas delicately open on the palate. Very dry, with a snappy, sea salt note on the finish. Will show best with food, as the complexities will be drawn out.

Emilio Lustau Almacenista Juan Garcia Jarana,
Oloroso Pata de Gallina, Jerez de la Frontera. $21.95.   93

Deep and inviting brilliant amber hue with a greenish cast. Medium-bodied. Full acidity. Notes of dates, toffee, roasted walnuts. Assertively flavored with an attractive roasted character. Crisp acidity makes for a lively and fresh mouthfeel. Lengthy through the finish. A powerful wine to be savored, it would be a fitting end to a meal.

Scale: Superlative (96-100), Exceptional (90-95), Highly Recommended (85-89),
Recommended (80-84), Not Recommended (Under 80)

Emilio Lustau Almacenista Aranda y Latorre Oloroso Anada 1918,
Jerez de la Frontera. $21.99.   94

Bright and glossy deep amber. Medium-bodied. Well-balanced acidity. Relatively dry
with a very subtle impression of sweetness in the finish. Palate is a blend of raisins,
walnuts, smoke, and orange. Somewhat tight at first, it opens up beautifully with
aeration. Complex.

Emilio Lustau Almacenista Dona Pilar Aranda, Single Cask Oloroso,
Jerez de la Frontera. $35.   86

Deep, brilliant mahogany color. Medium-bodied. Subtle, deceptively complex aromas.
Crisp and dry on the palate with flavors of molasses, dates, and orange peel. Will
perform best with food.

Osborne

Osborne Manzanilla Sherry, Jerez de la Frontera. $7.99.   NR

Osborne Fino Sherry, Jerez de la Frontera. $7.99.   NR

Osborne Rare Sherry, Fino-Amontillado La Honda,
Jerez de la Frontera. $30.   90

Pale amber with greenish highlights. Moderately light-bodied. Full acidity. Notes of
lacquer, dried flowers, salted nuts. This Sherry's unmistakable Fino-like aromatics belie
it's origins in a rare Fino solera with over 50 years of age. The wine itself has an average
age of 18 years, thus its having taken on Amontillado-like characteristics. Delicately
wrought and lively, yet pungent and fully flavored, it is a very interesting marriage of
the two styles. A definite candidate for the dinner table, where it should be able to not
only stand up to fully flavored foods, but refresh the palate as well.

Osborne Dry Amontillado Solera AOS Rare Sherry,
Jerez de la Frontera. $35.   90

Brilliant pale copper hue. Pungent aromas of rancio, salted nuts, and Christmas spices
are intoxicating and exotic. A lush entry leads to a moderately full-bodied palate with
a firm structure and outstanding complexity. Bone dry through the lengthy finish.
Drink now.

Osborne Rare Palo Cortado, Solera PΔP, Jerez de la Frontera. $35.   99

Deep tawny brown. Medium-bodied. Rich and viscous. Perfectly balanced sweetness is
almost overlooked because of the incredible complexity of flavors. Pralines, leather, figs,
allspice; the adjectives are widely divergent and non-stop as new nuances are revealed
with every return to the glass. Takes well to aeration and is very much a moving target.
It continues to develop complexity after being open for some time. Though initially
stunning, it seems to be at its best on the second or third day.

Osborne Rare Sherry, Oloroso, Solera India, Jerez de la Frontera. $30. 92

Opaque dark brown with ruby highlights. Full-bodied. Notes of treacle, black tea, pipe
tobacco, spearmint. Pungent, large scaled, and moderately viscous, this is a Sherry to be
reckoned with. The flavors are unique and exotic with ample acidity that makes for a
drying finish. Not for everyone, but this wine is truly unique and exhilarating. Would
stand up to wild game meats or full-bodied cigars, and becomes more accessible after
being decanted and left to sit for several days.

Osborne Rare Oloroso Amoroso, Solera Alonso el Sabio,
Jerez de la Frontera. $30.   98

Deep mahogany with brilliant ruby highlights. Moderately full-bodied. Notes of
toasted coconut, dried fruits, salted almonds. Seductive in nature with lushly perfumed
aromatics. The sweetness on the palate is perfectly balanced by the wine's acidity. The
overall impression is one of seamless harmony and elegance with warming, pleasantly
woody overtones that linger on the palate for several minutes. This is a truly remarkable
Sherry which deserves to be enjoyed on a cold night while sitting by the fireplace.

Osborne Dark Mahogany Olorosa Solera BC 200 Rare Sherry,
Jerez de la Frontera. $35. **93**

Deep mahogany hue. Intense treacle, pecan, and sandalwood aromas show great complexity. A lush entry leads to a full-bodied, concentrated palate with great structure. The flavors build through the finish, but seem to end on a delicate note. Drink now.

Osborne Cream Sherry, Jerez de la Frontera. $7.99. **83**

Osborne Pedro Ximenez, Jerez de la Frontera. $10.99. **89**

Dark opaque brown with a tawny rim and subtle greenish highlights. Full-bodied. Notes of golden raisins, mocha, dates. Broadly aromatic with deep and attractive flavors. Large scaled but not cloying. Lovely and quite lengthy through the finish.

Osborne Rare Pedro Ximenez Viejo, Jerez de la Frontera. $35. **96**

Opaque, nearly black in color. Full-bodied and extraordinarily viscous, it literally paints the side of the glass. Very sweet, but balanced out by the complexity of competing components. Dense chocolate, mocha, and date notes. An unbelievably concentrated Sherry that shows breeding by its ability to maintain balance and avoid becoming clumsy or cloying, given its scale. Long, lingering finish.

Bodegas Robles

Bodegas Robles Robles Extra Cream, DO Montilla-Moriles. $7. **87**

Deep tawny hue with a bronzed cast. Medium-bodied. Complex and interesting aromatics lead to a well-balanced and vibrant palate. A hint of sweetness is offset by acidity, making for a refreshing and flavorful finish.

Bodegas Robles Robles Seleccion Pedro Ximenez,
DO Montilla-Moriles. $12. **88**

Very deep mahogany. Full-bodied. Rich and viscous. Features straightforward golden raisin, molasses and date flavors with an interesting vinous quality. A solid Pedro Ximenez of midterm age.

Sanchez Romate

Sanchez Romate Manzanilla, Sanlucar de Barrameda. $8.99. **92**

Pale gold. Medium-bodied. Notes of roasted nuts, toast, sweet herbs. Fuller in body and a touch darker than a standard manzanilla, this wine is exhibiting slight oxidative characteristics, perhaps a function of the age of the samples. Nonetheless, the flavors are fully developed and quite attractive, with a thoroughly cleansing brisk finish.

Sanchez Romate Fino Sherry, Jerez de la Frontera. $6.99. **86**

Pale straw. Medium-bodied. Balanced acidity. Notes of flowers, citrus, blanched almonds. Light floral aromas. Crisp greenish entrance with a clean character and delicate flavors through a simple finish. Best served well chilled as an aperitif.

Sanchez Romate Amontillado Sherry, Jerez de la Frontera. $6.99. **80**

Sanchez Romate Cream Sherry, Jerez de la Frontera. $5.99. **84**

Sandeman

Sandeman Don Fino, Superior Dry Fino, Jerez de la Frontera. $11.99. **93**

Very pale clear straw. Moderately light-bodied. Full acidity. Notes of citrus, flowers, savory herbs. Should it be possible to describe color with aroma, this wine would serve as green in the aromatic dictionary. Bright, fresh, lively, and crisp, this is a Sherry of superlatives. Exquisite snap with an attractive astringency to the finish. Just the thing to tame the oppressive heat of an Andalusian summer afternoon.

Sandeman Character, Medium Dry Amontillado,
Jerez de la Frontera. $13.99. **89**

Brilliant pale amber with a subtle bronze cast. Medium-bodied. Notes of citrus peel, vanilla, dried herbs. Fresh and lively with a crisp green note to the nose. Refreshing and elegantly wrought with a touch of sweetness that is met with a dash of acidity in the finish, where it picks up a warming roasted note. Clean, crisp, and complex.

Scale: Superlative (96-100), Exceptional (90-95), Highly Recommended (85-89), Recommended (80-84), Not Recommended (Under 80)

Sandeman Royal Ambrosante Rare Palo Cortado,
Jerez de la Frontera. $20.   88

Nut brown. Medium-bodied and viscous. Sweet and quite rich. Brown sugar, mocha, and golden raisin notes. Full flavored and very enticing.

Sandeman Armada, Rich Cream Oloroso, Jerez de la Frontera. $11.99.   92

Tawny amber with a greenish cast. Medium-bodied. Notes of leather, salted pecans, dried herbs. Full and complex in the nose with a pungent note, the palate is nonetheless fairly delicate. Moderate sweetness is well accented by pleasant acidity. Lengthy through the clean finish. Enjoy after a meal with cheeses and nuts.

Sandeman Royal Corregidor, Very Old Rare Rich Oloroso,
Jerez de la Frontera. $24.99.   88

Deep and brilliant mahogany with ruby highlights. Moderately full-bodied. Notes of figs, caramel, roasted nuts. Lush and seamless with an elegant overall character. The sense of sweetness on the palate plants this wine into an after dinner category, but subtle acidity keeps it from becoming cloying.

Sandeman Imperial Corregidor Rarest V.V.O. Oloroso,
Jerez de la Frontera. $25.   91

Deep brown. Medium-bodied. Very sweet and lush. Smoky dried date, chocolate, and caramel flavors are well defined and decadent. Rich, chewy finish. A densely styled dessert Oloroso.

Valdespino

Valdespino Inocente Fino Sherry, Jerez de la Frontera. $14.   87

Light straw. Medium-bodied. Notes of citrus, green apple, smoke. Quite pungent on the attack, with well-balanced acidity and a tangy finish. Forceful in style.

Valdespino Hartley & Gibson's Amontillado, Jerez de la Frontera. $7.99.   89

Rich and inviting mahogany. Notes of salted pecans, molasses, smoke. A classically roasted Amontillado character is displayed on a moderately viscous and warm palate. Fully flavored, with a hint of sweetness which is admirably offset by fresh acidity. Very lengthy and elegant through the finish. Could go with food but may be best as a more delicate Oloroso-alternative for the fireplace.

Valdespino Amontillado, Jerez de la Frontera. $13.99.   90

Deep and rich tawny amber. Moderately full-bodied. Notes of sweet malt, caramel, roasted nuts. Attractively perfumed with a viscous and slightly sweet presence on the palate. It is warm and quite complex with a drier finish due to its sprightly acidity. Classically roasted in character.

Valdespino Amontillado Coliseo, Jerez de la Frontera. $40.   92

Deep tawny brown with ruby highlights. Full-bodied. Notes of peat, charred wood, dried apricots, toasted coconut. This thrilling Sherry emanates from Valdespino's famous old Coliseo solera. Quite pungent and very fully flavored with a highly extracted character, the vibrant acidity keeps it from seeming overly weighty. It features a medicinal character which is not unlike that found in an Islay whiskey. Best after a meal, possibly accompanied by fine tobacco. Becomes more accessible after being open for one or two days, and should last a week.

Valdespino Palo Cortado Sherry del Carrascal, Jerez de la Frontera. $20.   88

Deep amber. Moderately full-bodied. Moderate acidity. Mild sweetness. Notes of toffee, charred wood, exotic spices. Darkly flavored, the subtle sense of sweetness marries well with the acidity to lend an overall sense of complex harmony.

Valdespino Cardenal Palo Cortado Sherry, Jerez de la Frontera. $29.   **90**

Rich mahogany. Moderately full-bodied. Notes of redwood, burned salted pecans with medicinal backnotes. Very unusual in style, unlike any other Palo Cortado. Exhibits a full blown heavily roasted character with rich exotic flavors akin to those found in old cognacs or Islay whiskies. It is obviously the product of extreme barrel age, with a very dry palate and lingering finish which begs for a rich cigar. Outstanding, or just too demanding, depending upon your perspective.

Valdespino Solera 1842, Oloroso Viejo Dulce, Jerez de la Frontera. $19.   **90**

Deep and brilliant mahogany with a subtle green cast. Full-bodied. Notes of coffee, brown spices, charred wood. Fully flavored and intense with vibrant acidity on the palate and a big warming finish. Attractively woody in overall character. Equally at home with richly flavored meats and cheeses or served as an ideal after-dinner digestif.

Valdespino Don Gonzalo Old Dry Oloroso Sherry, Jerez de la Frontera. $20.   **90**

Deep and rich tawny amber with brilliant clarity. Full-bodied. Notes of leather, brown spices, charred wood. Fully flavored and rich with an almost viscous character on the palate. Heavily roasted woody tones are emphasized by vibrant acidity. Full throttle and lengthy, this is a warming sipping Sherry to be savored after a meal.

Valdespino Hartley & Gibson's Cream Sherry, Jerez de la Frontera. $7.99.   **90**

Chestnut with a greenish hue. Medium full-bodied. Notes of oriental spices, dried fruits, redwood. Exotically perfumed, the nose is quite enticing. Moderately sweet and very flavorful. Lengthy and lingering finish.

Williams & Humbert

Williams & Humbert Dry Sack Superior Medium Dry Sherry, Jerez de la Frontera. $13.99.   **86**

Brilliant amber with copper highlights. Moderately full-bodied. Notes of wild mushrooms, toast, honey. Straightforward and well made with an unusual but enticing nose. The mild sweetness is balanced nicely by a touch of acidity, which keeps the finish fresh.

thirty-nine

❧

Portugal

❧

The Great Fortified Wines of Portugal

Port

By Portuguese law, port is the fortified wine made from vineyards along the Douro River and shipped from the city of Oporto near the point where the river meets the Atlantic Ocean. In the United States these wines are distinguished from other port wines by use of the term Oporto. Popularized by the British in the 18th century, they have become world famous and are now made in an array of styles.

Vintage Port

Vintage port is the flagship wine of the region. In the best of years, the port shippers will set aside the best lots of wine to make a vintage port. A "vintage year" will usually be declared by agreement among most of the shippers, but not always. On average, three to four vintage years will be declared in any given decade. Wines selected as vintage ports were generally shipped to England two years after the vintage and bottled immediately. In 1974, however, this practice was dropped and all vintage ports must now be bottled in Portugal. These wines will always throw a heavy sediment as they mature, and it is advisable to stand the bottle upright for 24 hours and decant before serving. They will usually require a minimum of 10 to 15 years to mature, while the best can last and improve for 50 years or more. As vintage ports age slowly in glass, other styles have developed which are more mature upon release.

Single-Quinta Vintage Port

Shippers will often bottle vintage ports from their best vineyards, or quintas, when a general vintage could have been declared but was not. In the late 1980's this was due in large part to a saturated market. These wines are handled in the same way as vintage ports with the exception of the fact that they are not blended from various vineyards. Some will argue that blending is an integral part of producing the greatest vintage ports, and thus, single-quintas are inherently inferior. In a top year, however, single-quintas can indeed be exceptional and often rival the quality of declared vintage ports.

Late Bottled Vintage Port

This is a blend of ports from different vineyards in the same vintage. They are handled like vintage ports but are usually bottled after five to seven years in wood as opposed to two. This serves to accelerate the aging process so that these wines are ready to drink upon release. LBVs will generally have the bottling date as well as the vintage on the label. They will throw a minimal sediment as most will have precipitated in cask.

Ruby Port

These ports are the standard house blends of wine form several vintages that generally spend an average of two to three years in cask. Rich in color, fruity, and sweet, these are the basic port drinker's wines as they are immediately accessible and often provide good value.

Scale: Superlative (96-100), Exceptional (90-95), Highly Recommended (85-89), Recommended (80-84), Not Recommended (Under 80)

Vintage Character Port

These wines are top quality ruby ports whose ingredients were almost up to vintage standards. They are a blend of several vintages that spend four or five years in cask. Ready when bottled, they will still throw some sediment. They are in essence fine ruby ports that have been aged like LBVs but do not come from a single vintage.

Tawny Port

Tawny ports differ radically from other types of port. They are a blend of several vintages that have undergone a prolonged maturation in cask. In this way the shippers try to maintain a consistent house style. As the wines age, they turn from a deep purple color to ruby to a golden brown shade, for which the style is named, tawny. The aging process renders a lighter bodied more mellow and aromatic wine. They are ideal for those that find vintage and vintage character ports to be too heavy. Less expensive tawnies may just be a blend of red and white ports, whereas the best will often have an indication of average age on the label. Most of these are bottled at 10, 20, or 30 years average age with the wines becoming progressively more delicate with greater time in wood. A further type, Colheita, is actually a vintage dated tawny with all grapes coming from a single year. These are rarely seen, but in character correspond roughly with 10, 20, and 30-year tawnies of similar ages. Once bottled, tawny ports will not improve with further aging.

Portugal
at a Glance

Wines Reviewed:

184

Producers/Brands
Represented:

28

Value Rating:

Average

Port Reviews

Porto

Barros

Barros Ruby Porto, Oporto. $8.99.   **84**

Barros Tawny Porto, Oporto. $8.99.   **82**

Barros Quinta D. Matilde Tawny Porto, Oporto. $13.99.   **86**

Pale amber-rosé. Moderately light-bodied. Notes of dried strawberries, vanilla. Fragrant aromatics. A light and delicate style with subtle nuances.

Barros 20 Anos Tawny Porto, Oporto. $33.99.   **90**

Light brownish-amber color. Moderately full-bodied. Notes of caramel, Grand Marnier, leather. Intense aromatics precede a silky mouthwatering palate kept lively with fine acids to balance the sugars.

Barros 1991 Vintage Porto, Oporto. $20.99.   **91**

Black-ruby to a purple rim. Moderately full-bodied. Notes of bramble fruits, flowers, vanilla. Intense ripe fruit nose leads into a deep black fruit palate with good viscosity. Well integrated and balanced.

Borges 1992 Late Bottled Vintage Porto, Oporto. $16.   **84**

Borges 1994 Vintage Porto, Oporto. $25.   **91**

Deep purple-red. Very youthful, with floral, jammy fruit aromas. Sweet and juicy on the entry with fleshy, young flavors and good body. The tannins are soft and plush on the finish. Hedonistic, but it needs some years to mesh together.

Churchill's

Churchill's 1990 Dry White Porto, Oporto. $16.99.   **80**

Churchill's VC Reserve Porto, Oporto. $11.99.   **85**

Churchill's 10 Year Old Tawny Porto, Oporto. $26.99.   **84**

Churchill's 1990 Late Bottled Vintage Porto, Oporto. $19.99.   **86**

Blackish-garnet color. Medium-bodied. Moderately extracted. Brown spices, caramel, black fruits. Rich and aromatic with complex flavors that taper off on a lighter-styled palate feel. Drying on the finish.

Churchill's 1990 Quinta da Agua Alta Single Quinta Vintage Porto, Oporto. $26.95.   **85**

Churchill's 1992 Quinta da Agua Alta Single Quinta Vintage Porto, Oporto. $24.95.   **88**

Deep purple. Full-bodied. Notes of smoke, bramble fruits, tobacco. Straightforward and direct with forward fruit and an ample framework.

Churchill's 1995 Quinta da Agua Alta Single Quinta Vintage Porto, Oporto. $34.99.   **89**

Opaque blackish hue with a purple rim. Moderately full-bodied. Shoe polish, lacquer, black fruits. Aromatic and quite complex in flavor, though somewhat lighter in structure for such a youthful Port. Should be an exceptional drink within a decade.

Churchill's 1991 Vintage Porto, Oporto. $51.99.   **85**

Churchill's 1994 Vintage Porto, Oporto. $39.99.   **87**

Black-ruby with a purple rim. Full-bodied. Highly extracted. Notes of flowers, oriental spice, black fruits. Pronounced floral aromatics. Ripe grape character with a strong exotic spicy component. Quite approachable now but will be even better in the short term when components come together.

Scale: Superlative (96-100), Exceptional (90-95), Highly Recommended (85-89), Recommended (80-84), Not Recommended (Under 80)

Cockburn's

Cockburn's Special Reserve, Oporto. $9.99.   85

Cockburn's 10 Year Old Tawny Porto, Oporto. $25.   86

Light copper. Medium-bodied. Moderately extracted. Brown spices, caramel. Lighter
in style, with a flavorful wood-accented palate feel. Has a sense of delicacy to the
well-balanced, sweet finish.

Cockburn's Directors' Reserve, 20 Year Old Tawny Porto, Oporto. $45.   92

Deep mahogany hue. Moderately full-bodied. Moderately extracted. Caramel, toasted
wood. Pleasantly aromatic, with forceful character on the palate. Deeply flavored and
rich with fine length and intensity.

Cockburn's 1992 Late Bottled Vintage Porto, Oporto. $20.   87

Cherry red. Medium-bodied. Notes of sweet dried cherries, sweet berries. Oak accented
aromas lead a spicy rounded palate with a bright fruity entry that expands on the palate.
Finish shows some mildly dry astringency.

Cockburn's 1992 Quinta dos Canais, Oporto. $38.   88

Deep blackish hue with a ruby rim. Moderately full-bodied. Black fruits, lacquer.
Aromatic and flavorful, still dominated by primary fruit flavors. Rich and firmly
structured on the palate with a mouth filling character. Fine length and grip.
Could use at least a decade to come into its own.

Cockburn's 1995 Quinta dos Canais, Oporto. $38.   91

Deep, opaque blackish hue with a purple rim. Moderately full-bodied. Shoe polish,
lacquer, black fruits. Aromatic and profoundly complex with a very sturdy structure.
Well-balanced and firm. Should be be drinking quite well in 10 to 15 years.

Cockburn's 1991 Vintage Porto, Oporto. $30.   87

Deep purple. Full-bodied. Notes of plums, pomegranate, vanilla. A rich mouthfeel
carries the suggestion of overripe fruits in a firmly structured framework.

Cockburn's 1994 Vintage Porto, Oporto. $40.   89

Deep ruby with full purple highlights. Moderately full-bodied. Notes of violets,
chocolate, bramble fruits. Violet-scented nose reveals a very solid palate with tightly
wound concentrated fruit flavors on the mid palate. Finish dominated by spirity
heat and spice.

Croft

Croft Distinction, Tawny Reserve, Oporto. $20.   81

Croft 1990 Late Bottled Vintage Porto, Oporto. $21.99.   87

Deep brick red. Moderately full-bodied. Notes of plums, dried fruits, oak spice. Attractive
oak accented aromas reveal a rich, rounded mouthful of sweet plummy flavors.

Croft 1995 Quinta de Roeda Vintage Porto, Oporto. $40.   88

Deep and opaque blackish hue with a ruby edge. Moderately full-bodied. Black fruits,
licorice, chocolate. Deeply aromatic with a wave of dark flavors on the palate. A youthful
wine, still dominated by its primary flavors. It should develop nicely with at least a decade
of cellaring.

Croft 1994 Vintage Porto, Oporto. $59.99.   92

Opaque blackish hue with a ruby edge. Full-bodied. Black fruits, licorice, lacquer.
Aromatic, with a rich and flavorful mouthfeel. Dark and powerful flavors have fine
grip and intensity, while the full-throttle character of the wine's other components
bodes well for decades of cellaring.

Delaforce

Delaforce His Eminence's Reserve Tawny Porto, Oporto. $20.   82

Delaforce Curious & Ancient 20 Year Old Tawny Porto, Oporto. $40.   **94**

Deep copper. Medium-bodied. Moderately extracted. Brown spices, toasted wood, bacon fat. Deeply aromatic with a hint of rancio and a wave of complex flavors on the palate. Good length and grip with real intensity.

Delaforce 1991 Late Bottled Vintage Porto, Oporto. $22.99.   **84**

Delaforce 1991 Quinta da Corte Vintage Porto, Oporto. $34.99.   **87**

Saturated ruby-black color. Medium-bodied. Notes of licorice, earth, oak spice, black fruits. Spirity, oaky nose hints at dark fruits. Rich sweet fruit flavors on entry give way to a solid underlay of firm oak spice and earth. This needs three to four more years for its components to settle.

Delaforce 1995 Quinta da Corte Vintage Porto, Oporto. $40.   **90**

Very deep and opaque blackish hue with a ruby rim. Full-bodied. Black fruits, anise, chocolate. Profoundly aromatic, very deep and lush, with a powerful mouth-filling character. A forceful wine that should require up to 15 or 20 years to come into its own.

Delaforce 1992 Vintage Porto, Oporto. $35.   **85**

Dow's

Dow's Christmas Porto, Oporto. $13.99.   **80**

Dow's Boardroom Tawny Porto, Oporto. $17.   **82**

Dow's 10 Year Old Tawny Porto, Oporto. $26.   **81**

Dow's 20 Year Old Tawny Porto, Oporto. $44.99.   **94**

Dark ruby-brown. Very rich aromas of brown spice and rancio. Rich on the entry with golden raisin flavors and rich brown spice character that emerges on the finish along with a touch of sea salt.

Dow's 30 Year Old Tawny Porto, Oporto. $75.   **91**

Deep reddish-amber. Medium light-bodied. Mild acid. Notes of roasted nuts, brown spices. Subtle and delicate with a complex layer of wood tinged flavors. Smooth and lingering.

Dow's 1982 Single Year Tawny Reserve, Oporto. $29.   **86**

Brilliant deep amber hue with ruby overtones. Forward red fruit and brown spice aromas show a harmonious wood accent. A rich entry leads a medium-bodied palate with mild sweetness. The finish is lean and flavorful. Drink now.

Dow's 1991 Late Bottled Vintage Porto, Oporto. $17.   **83**

Dow's 1992 Late Bottled Vintage Porto, Oporto. $16.99.   **81**

Dow's 1992 Quinta do Bomfim Vintage Porto, Oporto. $12/375 ml.   **89**

Dense purple hue. Supple, full-bodied. Bracing layer upon layer of opulent red fruit, raisins, and soft tannins. Lingering finish.

Dow's 1995 Quinta do Bomfim Vintage Porto, Oporto. $38.   **87**

Saturated deep purplish-red. Moderately full-bodied. Highly extracted. Mildly tannic. Notes of elderberry, plums, oak spice. Spicy rich fruity aromas have a distinct floral note. Rich rounded black fruit flavors show a silky quality on the palate. Solid spicy finish.

Dow's 1991 Vintage Porto, Oporto. $45.   **90**

Opaque blackish-purple. Full-bodied. Notes of pepper, black cherries, cassis. Tightly wound and closed in with a daunting structure. Difficult to evaluate now, but all components seem to be in place for serious aging.

Dow's 1994 Vintage Porto, Oporto. $38.   **98**

Opaque blackish-ruby with a purple rim. Full-bodied. Notes of black fruits, spice. Deep and brooding aromatics translate well onto an extracted and concentrated youthful palate with great structure. A Port for long term cellaring—20 years or more.

Scale: Superlative (96-100), Exceptional (90-95), Highly Recommended (85-89), Recommended (80-84), Not Recommended (Under 80)

Feist

Feist Baronial Fine White Port, Oporto. $12.	83
Feist Baronial, Oporto. $12.	84
Feist Vintage Character, Oporto. $14.	80
Feist Fine Baronial Tawny Porto, Oporto. $12.	80
Feist 10 Year Old Tawny Porto, Oporto. $18.	85
Feist 20 Year Old Tawny Porto, Oporto. $30.	87

Pale amber with rich reddish-gold highlights. Moderately full-bodied. Notes of rancio, toffee, boiled sweets, brown spice. Complex hints of Amontillado Sherry on the nose lead a rich toffee-like palate with suggestively fruity sweetness that expands on the palate. Lingering rancio notes on the finish.

Feist 30 Year Old Tawny Porto, Oporto. $60. **92**

Full reddish-amber color. Moderately full-bodied. Notes of rancio, Amontillado, caramel, brown spice. Complex aged Sherry-like aromas lead a rich rounded palate with outstanding spicy flavors and a lingering finish that reminds one of the finest Amontillado sherries. Complex and exotic.

Feist 40 Year Old Tawny Porto, Oporto. $100. **91**

Dark chestnut brown color. Full-bodied. Notes of dates, brown spice, licorice. Sweet rich aromas show have mature spicy accents. Rich chewy mouthful of spicy sweet flavors has a velvety viscous feel. Impressively aged with a weighty and assertive character through the finish.

Feist 1974 Colheita, Oporto. $38. **87**

Deep copper color. Medium-bodied. Brown sugar, caramel. Rather reserved aromatically, with a pleasant roasted quality on the palate. Well-balanced with good grip on the finish.

Feist 1967 Colheita, Oporto. $63. **93**

Deep copper color. Moderately full-bodied. Moderately extracted. Roasted nuts, treacle. Fragrant, with a full and rich roasted character on the palate. Concentrated and well integrated through the finish with fine grip and intensity.

Feist 1966 Colheita, Oporto. $70. **88**

Bright copper. Medium-bodied. Brown spices, toasted wood. Slightly hot in the nose, with a lean, comparatively light palate feel featuring vibrant acidity through the finish.

Feist 1965 Colheita, Oporto. $72. **90**

Deep copper cast. Moderately full-bodied. Roasted nuts, molasses. Pleasantly aromatic, with a rich and slightly viscous mouthfeel. Flavorful and well-balanced through the finish with good grip and intensity.

Feist 1963 Colheita, Oporto. $76. **92**

Deep copper color. Moderately full-bodied. Brown spices, caramel. Reserved aromatically, but quite rich and flavorful on the palate with deep and supple flavors. Fine grip and length with excellent intensity.

Feist 1957 Colheita, Oporto. $106. **89**

Bright copper hue. Medium-bodied. Orange peel and dried wood. Features some heat and a decided note of rancio richness to the nose. Drying on the palate, with a lean personality and mild astringency to the intense finish.

Feist 1991 Late Bottled Vintage Porto, Oporto. $18.	84
Feist 1991 Vintage Porto, Oporto. $26.	85

Fonseca

Fonseca Bin 27 Fine Reserve Porto, Oporto. $17.99. **88**

Deep, saturated ruby-purple hue. Brooding lacquer, black fruit and chocolate aromas are classic and intense. A firm entry leads a moderately full-bodied palate with mild sweetness and a firm structure. The finish is deep and balanced. Drink now.

Fonseca 10 Year Old Tawny Porto, Oporto. $27.99.   **86**

Fading brown with a subtle ruby highlight. Muted aromas have a salty, old barrel character. Sweet entry, with a rounded mouthfeel and flavors of caramel and dates, and notes of rancio and sea salt on the finish.

Fonseca 20 Year Old Tawny Porto, Oporto. $48.99.   **91**

Medium ruby-brown. Assertively oaky aromas with rancio notes. Sweet and generous on the attack, with complex and harmoniously integrated brown spice flavors carrying through to an impressively long finish.

Fonseca 1990 Late Bottled Vintage Porto, Oporto. $17.49.   **87**

Black-ruby color. Moderately full-bodied. Moderately extracted. Notes of raisins, plums, vanilla. Mild dried fruit aromas lead into a smooth and supple palate with a focused fruit core. Lingering fruity finish.

Fonseca 1995 Guimaraens Vintage Porto, Oporto. $38.99.   **92**

Very deep blackish hue with a purple rim that paints the side of the glass. Full-bodied. Notes of black fruits, chocolate, lacquer. Somewhat reined in aromatically, with a very backward and powerful personality. Very rich, with great grip and intensity and a lash of tannin. Has decades of life in front of it. Probably needs a minimum of 10 to 15 years to become approachable.

Fonseca 1994 Vintage Porto, Oporto. $50.   **96**

Completely saturated blackish-purple. Full-bodied. Notes of violets, blackberry, chocolate. Attractive floral accents on the nose lead a heavyweight palate with solid, tightly-wound fruit flavors showing great generosity up front. The finish is dominated by imposing tannins. A long term keeper that shows great promise. Cellar 20 years or more.

Graham's

Graham's Six Grapes Porto, Oporto. $19.   **86**

Deep blackish-ruby hue with a purple cast. Moderately full-bodied. Briar fruits, lacquer. Aromatic, with a pure and concentrated character on the palate. Clean and lengthy finish with good grip and intensity.

Graham's 10 Year Old Tawny Porto, Oporto. $27.99.   **91**

Pale ruby with a copper hue. Caramel and date aromas. The generous entry shows sweet fruit with a good follow-through and well-integrated oak-spice complexity. Very harmonious and long, with notable depth.

Graham's 20 Year Old Tawny Porto, Oporto. $45.99.   **96**

Ruby-copper hue with brown highlights. Rich, generous aromas and a concentrated attack with golden raisin flavors and a rich mouthfeel. The finish shows complexity and sweet persistence with rancio and brown spice flavors. This is a fatter style, with Amontillado-like complexity.

Graham's 30 Year Old Tawny Porto, Oporto. $81.   **90**

Dark reddish-amber. Medium light-bodied. Notes of toast, hazelnuts, dried cherries. Refined and subtle flavors have a definite sense of sweetness through the finish.

Graham's 1990 Late Bottled Vintage Porto, Oporto. $17.   **89**

Black-ruby color. Moderately full-bodied. Notes of black fruits, smoke, pine. Pronounced wood aromas lead into a rich, jammy and generously proportioned style. Long lingering fruity finish.

Graham's 1991 Late Bottled Vintage Porto, Oporto. $18.   **87**

Deep blackish-ruby hue. Moderately full-bodied. Moderately extracted. Black fruits, minerals, lacquer. Reserved aromatically, though rich and supple on the palate with a fruit-accented personality. Chunky and flavorful through the finish.

Graham's 1992 Late Bottled Vintage Porto, Oporto. $17.99.   **83**

Scale: Superlative (96-100), Exceptional (90-95), Highly Recommended (85-89), Recommended (80-84), Not Recommended (Under 80)

Graham's 1992 Malvedos Vintage Porto, Oporto. $13.50/375 ml.   90

Deep purple. Full-bodied. A lush, densely layered palate brimming with berries, oak, and herbs. Excellent large structure with a firm tannic grip and solid acidity. Long, buttery finish. A long term cellar selection.

Graham's 1995 Malvedos Vintage Porto, Oporto. $43.   86

Saturated deep purplish-red. Moderately full-bodied. Highly extracted. Notes of plums, licorice, brown spice. Rich sweet plummy aromas. Rounded and fleshy on the palate with generous flavors and some earthy dry tannins on the finish. Solidly structured.

Graham's 1991 Vintage Porto, Oporto. $49.   95

Very dark purple. Full-bodied. Notes of black cherries, vanilla, black pepper. Fully extracted and lengthy with exceptional balance and grip.

Graham's 1994 Vintage Porto, Oporto. $46.   95

Deep opaque black with a ruby rim. Full-bodied. Notes of sandalwood, black fruit, to ruby rim. Dark brooding aromas lead into a firm extracted palate. Currently quite closed but it shows richness and depth of flavors. For long term cellaring.

Harvey's

Harvey's Gold Cap Fine Ruby, Oporto. $17.   NR

Harvey's Fine Tawny, Oporto. $14.99.   88

Dark garnet. Medium-bodied. Notes of walnuts, raisins, baked cherries. Well-balanced with focused flavors. Lingering dried fruit notes on the finish.

Harvey's Hunting Tawny, Oporto. $17.   82

Harvey's Director's Bin, 20 Year Old Tawny Porto, Oporto. $32.50.   85

Martinez Fine Ruby Porto, Oporto. $11.   80

Martinez

Martinez Master's Reserve Porto, Oporto. $16.   83

Martinez Fine Tawny Porto, Oporto. $11.   81

Martinez 10 Year Old Tawny Porto, Oporto. $26.   83

Martinez 20 Year Old Tawny Porto, Oporto. $46.   84

Martinez 1995 Single Quinta da Chousa Vintage Porto, Oporto. $40.   86

Bright ruby hue with a lightening rim. Wonderfully aromatic with full floral, sweet fruit aromas. Sweet and rich on the entry with medium body and sugar plum flavors. Well-balanced, in a lighter style. Still needs more time.

Martinez 1995 Quinta da Eira Velha Vintage Porto, Oporto. $45.   84

Osborne

Osborne Ruby Porto, Oporto. $10.99.   82

Osborne 1992 Vintage Porto, Oporto. $22.50.   87

Deep purple. Medium to full-bodied. Notes of black cherries, cassis, sandalwood. Relatively restrained in style with a tightly wound core of fruit flavors. Not overly sweet.

Osborne 1994 Vintage Porto, Oporto. $28.   88

Dark ruby with a purple cast. Medium-bodied. Notes of dark fruit, currants, minerals. Floral aromatics reveal a rich core of brooding dark fruit. Finely extracted with good acidic backbone. Should cellar well, although surprisingly approachable now.

Pitters

Pitters Premium d'Or, Oporto. $19.95.   NR

Quinta de Roriz

Quinta de Roriz 1988 Late Bottled Vintage Porto, Oporto. $16.99.   86
Ruby with a garnet cast. Moderately light-bodied. Notes of dried fruits, brown spices,
Light perfumed aromas. A mature example in a lighter and more delicate style.

Quinta de Roriz 1991 Vintage Porto, Oporto. $32.49.   87
Black-ruby. Moderately full-bodied. Highly extracted. Notes of black fruits, bitter sweet
chocolate. Subdued and somewhat closed nose. Nice rich center with a sweetish finish
with spirity heat. Simple, easy, pleasant style.

Quinta do Noval

Quinta do Noval Old Coronation Ruby Porto, Oporto. $10.99.   82
Quinta do Noval Porto L.B. House Reserve, Oporto. $14.99.   84
Quinta do Noval Tawny, Oporto. $10.   80
Quinta do Noval 10 Year Old Tawny Porto, Oporto. $25.99.   87
Reddish-amber. Medium-bodied. Notes pine, earth, dried red fruits. Wood influenced
aromas reveal a firmly structured, slightly lean style with a dryish finish.

Quinta do Noval 20 Year Old Tawny Porto, Oporto. $82.99.   91
Reddish-amber. Medium-bodied. Notes of dried fruit, butterscotch. Rich aromas lead
into a succulent assertively fruity palate with layers of nutty complexity through to an
elegant textured finish.

Quinta do Noval 1984 Colheita Old Tawny Porto, Oporto. $23.75.   86
Deep tawny with garnet highlights. Medium-bodied. Balanced acidity. Notes of earth,
cherries, raisins. Warm aromas reveal a generous although not over complex palate
that finishes with a pleasing tangy note.

Quinta do Noval 1982 Colheita Old Tawny Porto, Oporto. $28.49.   88
Deep orangey-amber. Medium-bodied. Notes of dried fruits, nuts, vanilla. Fruity
aromas translate well on the palate with a textured, velvety mouthfeel. A little warmth
on the finish.

Quinta do Noval 1976 Colheita Old Tawny Porto, Oporto. $50.49.   93
Deep amber. Medium-bodied. Notes of dried fruit, earth, nuts. Fragrant mildly earthy
nose leads into a generous palate with a nutty, creamy character. Fruit is showing well.

Quinta do Noval 1971 Colheita Old Tawny Porto, Oporto. $74.99.   95
Deep amber. Medium-bodied. Notes of raisins, nuts, caramel, leather. Complex and
mildly tangy aromas lead into an expansive sweet palate with a hint of structure.
'Woody' character is nicely offset by fruit acidity.

Quinta do Noval 1968 Colheita Old Tawny Porto, Oporto. $83.49.   92
Deep amber. Moderately full-bodied. Notes of dried fruits, caramel, brown spice.
Complex aromatics lead into an unctuous mouthfeel and warm spicy palate. Lingering
sweet nutty finish.

Quinta do Noval 1967 Colheita Old Tawny Porto, Oporto. $88.99.   94
Rich tawny amber. Medium-bodied. Notes of dried fruits, almonds, dark chocolate.
Full and complex aromas lead into a rounded palate and mouthfeel with a long
roasted finish.

Quinta do Noval 1966 Colheita Old Tawny Porto, Oporto. $98.49.   93
Tawny amber. Medium-bodied. Notes of dried apricot, orange peel, nuts. Vibrant in
the mouth with a pronounced nutty character backed up by fine acidity. Complex and
lengthy with a lingering finish.

Quinta do Noval 1989 Late Bottled Vintage Porto, Oporto. $18.99.   87
Ruby with tawny highlights. Medium-bodied. Notes of raisins, plums, brown spice.
A more delicate mature style with fragrant aromatics and soft textured mouthfeel.
Well integrated flavors.

Quinta do Noval 1995 Quinta de Silval Vintage Porto, Oporto. $40. **86**

Opaque blackish hue with a purple cast to the rim. Moderately full-bodied. Black fruits. Reined in aromatically. Quite flavorful in a fruit-driven way. For a youthful vintage Port, it retains a sense of lightness on the palate, and is quite sweet through the finish. A good candidate for midterm cellaring of a decade or so.

Quinta do Noval 1991 Vintage Porto, Oporto. $29.25. **92**

Blackish-purple. Full-bodied. Notes of black fruits, toasty vanilla, cassis. Rich and concentrated with fully extracted classic flavors and a weighty framework.

Quinta do Noval 1991 Nacional Vintage Porto, Oporto. $250. **98**

Very dark purple. Notes of earth, black cherry, spicy plums. Elegant and supple with an unmistakable note of terroir. The structure is subtle and tactfully wrought. Though almost approachable now, it will clearly improve.

Quinta do Noval 1994 Vintage Porto, Oporto. $35. **90**

Opaque black-ruby with a purple rim. Moderately full-bodied. Notes of black fruits, flowers, tar. Floral accented aromas. Dense and finely extracted palate with some ripe opulent fruit. Still very spirity and tight knit. A medium-long term cellar wine for more than 10 years.

Quinta do Noval 1995 Vintage Porto, Oporto. $55. **93**

Deep and opaque blackish hue with a purple rim. Full-bodied. Balanced acidity. Black fruits, lacquer. Deep and powerful with a rich and complex palate feel. Currently tightly wound, with all the components to sustain decades of cellaring. Try in 10 to 15 years.

Ramos Pinto

Ramos Pinto Fine Ruby, Oporto. $13.75. **80**

Ramos Pinto Quinta da Urtiga, Oporto. $18. **88**

Dark ruby-brick. Medium-bodied. Notes of earth, brown spice, black fruits. Chewy black fruits on entry reveal a full flavored earthy style with a hint of tannin on the finish. Shows both substance and character.

Ramos Pinto Superior Tawny, Oporto. $13.75. **80**

Ramos Pinto Quinta da Ervamoira,
10 Year Old Tawny Porto, Oporto. $30. **86**

Medium ruby-brick red color. Medium-bodied. Notes of subtle red fruits, brown spice, earth. Piquant aromas reveal an assertive, flavorful palate that shows gutsy character with some earthy nuances and a fine spicy finish. Should be a good match for cigars.

Ramos Pinto Quinta do Bom Retiro,
20 Year Old Tawny Porto, Oporto. $56. **94**

Rich golden-orange with red tinges. Full-bodied. Notes of toffee, earth, brown spice, brown sugar. Opulent and thick mouthfeel gives this a hugely generous palate presence with big toffee-like flavors showing complexity and nuances. Some subtle earthy notes provide a contrast. Very flavorful through the finish. A blockbuster.

Ramos Pinto 1989 Late Bottled Vintage Porto, Oporto. $19.50. **84**

Ramos Pinto 1994 Quinta da Ervamoira Vintage Porto, Oporto. $44. **86**

Deep, opaque blackish hue with a ruby rim. Moderately full-bodied. Black fruits, lacquer. Ripe and generous with a sense of lushness to the palate. Fruit-centered flavors dominate the palate, and a lighter structure suggests that this will be approachable within a decade.

Ramos Pinto 1991 Vintage Porto, Oporto. $35. **87**

Very dark purple. Full-bodied. Notes of black fruits, pepper, brown spices. Lush and jammy on the palate with a firm character.

Ramos Pinto 1994 Vintage Porto, Oporto. $50. **88**

Opaque blackish hue with a purple rim. Moderately full-bodied. Black fruits, lacquer. Aromatic with a wave of rich, complex flavors on the palate. Deep, but still maintains a sense of lightness to the structure. This wine should be drinking nicely in 10 to 15 years.

Ramos Pinto 1995 Vintage Porto, Oporto. $35.   87

Saturated bright ruby-purple. Youthful dark fruit aromas show a floral accent. Lean on the entry, with a moderately full body and sugar plum fruit on the midpalate. The finish is short, with mean tannins showing. Rather structured. Age will improve this but not make it elegant. Can be consumed now or put in the cellar for the long haul.

Rozes

Rozes Special Reserve, Oporto. $14.99.   80

Rozes Infanta Isabel, 10 Year Old Tawny Porto, Oporto. $25.   88

Deep mahogany color. Moderately full-bodied. Roasted nuts, toasted wood. Flavorful and complex, with a distinctive note of rancio. Deeply flavored with good grip and fine length.

Rozes 20 Year Old Tawny Porto, Oporto. $45.   89

Deep mahogany with a ruby cast. Medium-bodied. Moderately extracted. Toasted wood. Lean and flavorful in style, with a deep and intense personality. Focused through the lengthy finish.

Rozes Over 40 Years Old, Wood Matured, Oporto. $125.   92

Deep copper hue with a big fade to the rim. Medium-bodied. Toasted wood, rancio, sea salt. Aromatic with a flavorful and complex palate feel. Well-balanced and deep through the lean finish. Excellent grip and intensity.

Rozes 1992 Late Bottled Vintage Porto, Oporto. $23.   80

Rozes 1994 Vintage Porto, Oporto. $46.   84

Sandeman

Sandeman Founders Reserve Porto, Oporto. $15.   80

Sandeman 20 Year Old Tawny Porto, Oporto. $34.   89

Deep copper hue. Medium-bodied. Moderately extracted. Toasted wood, caramel. Pleasantly aromatic with a sense of richness to the flavorful palate. Long and lively finish with good grip.

Smith Woodhouse

Smith Woodhouse Lodge Reserve Vintage Character Porto, Oporto. $13.99.   84

Smith Woodhouse 10 Year Old Tawny Porto, Oporto. $25.99.   82

Smith Woodhouse 1982 Madalena Vintage Porto, Oporto. $33.99.   88

Bright ruby-garnet hue. Baked fruit aromas. Sweet and juicy on the attack with a mature note of coffee. Finishes in a dry, somewhat lean manner. A lighter style, this is drinking well now and does not need further cellaring.

Smith Woodhouse 1995 Madalena Vintage Porto, Oporto. $32.   88

Saturated deep purplish-red color. Moderately full-bodied. Highly extracted. Mildly tannic. Notes of black fruits, plums, brown spice. Assertive spicy nose leads a palate of ripe rounded fruit flavors that are complimented by a solid spiced oak note through the finish. Well-balanced, though this will need some time in the cellar.

Smith Woodhouse 1992 Vintage Porto, Oporto. $12/375 ml.   91

Inky purple hue. Full-bodied. An elegant marriage of toasty oak and rich, dark fruits. Soft tannins in a fine, long finish.

Smith Woodhouse 1994 Vintage Porto, Oporto. $31.   89

Opaque black-ruby to a purple rim. Medium-bodied. Notes of black fruit, flowers, chocolate. Aromatic, soft and lush with a surprisingly open-knit structure. Pleasant floral style makes for short term cellaring.

Scale: Superlative (96-100), Exceptional (90-95), Highly Recommended (85-89), Recommended (80-84), Not Recommended (Under 80)

Symington's

Symington's 1992 Quinta do Vesuvio Vintage Porto, Oporto. $38.   **93**

Deep purple. Full-bodied. Notes of black cherries, brown spices, citrus peel. Elegant and refined with a well integrated character and all components in balance for the long haul.

Symington's 1994 Quinta do Vesuvio Vintage Porto, Oporto. $50.   **96**

Deep opaque with a crimson rim. Medium-bodied. Notes of black fruits, tobacco, flowers. Peachy aromas. Stunningly extracted fruit with a waves of complexity. Very accessible, deriving much of its structure from soft tannins. Should drink well in the near term.

Symington's 1995 Quinta do Vesuvio Vintage Porto, Oporto. $61.   **90**

Saturated deep purplish-red. Moderately full-bodied. Notes of vanilla, flowers, plums, black tea. Floral vanilla aromas. Sweet and generous on entry but solid extraction and hefty dry tannins on the finish. Tightly wound with impressive structure. Cellar 10 years or more.

Symington's 1996 Quinta do Vesuvio Vintage Porto, Oporto. $60.99.   **95**

Brilliant, opaque violet purple. Very aromatic with full floral, violet and ripe fruit character. Explosively fruity on the attack, with a medium body and soft, lush tannins. Notably hedonistic for such youth. Should be drinkable over the medium term (10 years).

Taylor Fladgate

Taylor Fladgate First Estate Reserve Porto, Oporto. $15.49.   **83**

Taylor Fladgate 10 Year Old Tawny Porto, Oporto. $26.99.   **86**

Fading pale ruby-brown. Mulled, spiced fruit aromas with a whiff of rancio. Juicy and bright on the entry, with a smooth midpalate and a finish that features oak spice and lingering rancio notes.

Taylor Fladgate 20 Year Old Tawny Porto, Oporto. $46.99.   **90**

Pale ruby-copper hue. Aromatically subdued with a salty note. Bright and sweet on entry with light flavors on the palate and a taut frame. Well-balanced though not as intense as typical 20 year old tawny Port.

Taylor Fladgate 1990 Late Bottled Vintage Porto, Oporto. $16.49.   **85**

Taylor Fladgate 1991 Late Bottled Vintage Porto, Oporto. $19.99.   **89**

Deep blood red. Rich plummy yet mildly earthy aromas. A rich entry leads a moderately full-bodied palate with well-stuffed flavors and a hint of tannic backbone. A solid style.

Taylor Fladgate 1991 Quinta de Vargellas Vintage Porto, Oporto. $37.49.   **93**

Dark ruby-black. Silky texture accentuates the medium body. Filled with tones of currants, chocolate, and a berry core. Approachable now, this will develop nicely for several years. A more delicate style for the usually macho Taylor.

Taylor Fladgate 1995 Quinta de Vargellas Vintage Porto, Oporto. $38.99.   **90**

Opaque blackish hue with a ruby-purple rim. Moderately full-bodied. Black fruits, licorice, lacquer. Quite aromatic with a flavorful fruit-accented palate feel. Lighter in style, though still quite rich. Should be approachable in 10 years or so.

Taylor Fladgate 1994 Vintage Porto, Oporto. $50.   **92**

Saturated deep reddish-purple color. Moderately full-bodied. Notes of flowers, fleshy black fruits, brown spice. Brooding dark fruity nose has floral accents. Rich, ripe and very well extracted with generosity up front, though the finish turns very spirity and hot. Very attractive, though youthfully awkward. Cellar 10 years.

Warre's

Warre's Fine Selected Ruby Porto, Oporto. $10.99.   **82**

Warre's Warrior Porto, Oporto. $14.99.   **84**

Warre's Sir William, 10 Year Tawny Porto, Oporto. $22.99.   **82**

Warre's 1976 Reserve Tawny, Oporto. $46.99.   86

Deep mahogany cast. Moderately full-bodied. Dried fruits, brown spices. Still fairly rich and youthful with dried fruit overtones throughout. Flavorful and straightforward with a touch of heat to the finish.

Warre's 1982 Late Bottled Vintage Porto, Oporto. $24.50.   85

Warre's 1984 Late Bottled Vintage Porto, Oporto. $21.99.   83

Warre's 1995 Quinta da Cavadinha Vintage Porto, Oporto. $32.99.   92

Saturated deep purplish-red. Medium-bodied. Highly extracted. Notes of citrus, plums, oak spice. Youthful, generous fruity aromas. High-toned sweet fruity flavors belie a sense of tightness with some oak spice and spirity feel on the finish. Outstanding acidity runs through this wine. Young and awkward but with great structure and promise for the future.

Warre's 1991 Vintage Porto, Oporto. $35.   92

Blackish-purple. Full-bodied. Notes of ripe black fruits, orange peel, pepper. Lush and lengthy, with supple tannins and well extracted flavors.

Warre's 1994 Vintage Porto, Oporto. $40.   94

Opaque, blackish-ruby to the rim. Moderately full-bodied. Notes of flowers, chocolate, black fruit. Lush and layered mouthfeel with complex flavors on the palate. Displaying some rough edges of its infancy, it quite approachable. Warrants medium term cellaring. 10 years plus.

Madeira

Madeira is the fortified wine produced on the Portuguese island of the same name that lies 360 miles off the northwest coast of Africa. Discovered in 1419, the new Portuguese colonists were exporting their wines to Europe by 1460. Due to chronic political difficulties with France the British turned to Madeira (as well as port) as a substitute for their beloved claret. By the late 1600's Madeira was firmly entrenched in British society and due to a taxation loophole became a particular favorite of the North American colonies.

To begin with, the wines were unfortified, but because of hostilities during the reign of Queen Anne, few British vessels put in on the island, and the storage dilemma became so acute that merchants began to distill surplus wine into brandy. This brandy was later added to the wine, enabling it to better withstand the long sea voyages across the Atlantic. Finally, as casks of Madeira would be taken as ballast for trips along the Imperialist routes, it was found that the gentle rocking along with the intense heat of the equator helped to soften and refine the wine. Thus, whatever the final destination, it became the practice to send Madeira on a long sea voyage. The effects of this practice are now achieved by the use of huge stoves, or estufas, which gradually heat the wines to a temperature of 104 to 114 degrees Fahrenheit for six months. This is the artificial equivalent of a voyage around the world.

When the wine comes from the estufa it rests for 18 months before being added to a solera system like that used for sherry. Of any of the world's wines, Madeira continues to improve with age, and rare vintage dated wines from the 19th and even 18th centuries that are consumed today provide testament to their amazing vitality. There are four distinct types of Madeira, all of which are named after the type of grape from which they are produced. These range from dry to full rich with steps between.

Scale: Superlative (96-100), Exceptional (90-95), Highly Recommended (85-89), Recommended (80-84), Not Recommended (Under 80)

Sercial and Verdelho

These are the drier Madeiras. Sercial, the driest, is thought to have originated from a Riesling grape but bears little resemblance to other wines made from it. It is pale to golden in color and light in body with a striking nose and vibrant acidity. It is often chilled and served as an aperitif or as an accompaniment to soup. Sercial is not unlike a richer more complex Fino Sherry. Verdelho is sweeter and slightly stronger than sercial but has a surprisingly dry and clean finish. This versatile wine may be consumed as an aperitif or even with a slice of cake. It is traditionally seen as the ideal compliment to turtle soup.

Bual and Malmsey

As opposed to sercial or verdelho, which have brandy added to them after fermentation, bual and malmsey are made by adding spirits during the fermentation. This leaves a considerable amount of sugar in the wines, making them sweeter and fuller-bodied. Both are usually drunk as dessert wines, but, the Portuguese prefer to consume bual with cheese. Malmsey, being the richest, is almost always held till after dinner. Though rich and luscious they have the characteristic acidity which keeps all Madeiras fresh and lively.

Madeira Reviews

Blandy's

Blandy's Rainwater, Madeira. $13.99.   82

Blandy's 5 Year Old Sercial, Madeira. $19.   86

Bright pale copper hue. Medium-bodied. Caramel, salted pecans. Quite aromatic with a lighter-styled, zesty palate feel. Crisp acidity lends a refreshing note to the clean and flavorful finish. Excellent grip.

Blandy's 5 Year Old Verdelho, Madeira. $19.   85

Blandy's 5 Year Old Malmsey, Madeira. $17.99.   84

Blandy's 10 Year Old Malmsey, Madeira. $32.99.   88

Brilliant copper-amber hue. Complex brown spice, chocolate, and toffee aromas. A rich entry is followed by a moderately full-bodied palate with marked sweetness and vibrant acidic balance. Supple, flavorful finish.

Blandy's 15 Year Old Malmsey, Madeira. $42.99.   94

Very deep tawny amber-copper hue. Forceful roasted nut, rancio and treacle aromas. A viscous entry leads a full-bodied palate with marked sweetness offset by vibrant acidity. The finish is exotic and lengthy. A very stylish wine with great complexity and depth.

Cossart Gordon

Cossart Gordon Rainwater, Madeira. $14.   82

Cossart Gordon 5 Year Old Bual, Madeira. $20.   88

Very deep copper with a greenish cast. Moderately full-bodied. Roasted nuts, molasses. Aromatic, with a viscous quality to the mouthfeel that is offset nicely by balancing acidity. Rich and lengthy with solid grip through the finish.

Cossart Gordon 10 Year Old Bual, Madeira. $32.99.   87

Brilliant amber hue. Intense toffee and salted pecan aromas show a distinctive rancio quality. A lean entry leads a medium-bodied palate with vibrant acidity and mild sweetness. Lean, flavorful finish with good bite. Shows complexity and depth of flavor with admirable balance.

Cossart Gordon 15 Year Old Bual, Madeira. $44.   92

Deep amber with brown highlights. Moderately full-bodied. Notes of raisins, toffee, orange peel. Rich aromas lead into a succulent and assertive palate with some fine acidity to keep the finish from cloying. A rich style showing great balance.

Cossart Gordon 5 Year Old Malmsey, Madeira. $20.   85

Cossart Gordon 10 Year Old Malmsey, Madeira. $32.   89

Blackish-brown. Full-bodied. Notes of raisins, sea salt, molasses. Fragrant and zesty on the palate with solid balance.

Henriques & Henriques

Henriques & Henriques 5 Year Old Sercial, Madeira. $17.49.   90

Deep amber. Medium-bodied. Notes of nuts, yeast, citrus. Very pungent with vibrant acidity and a Sherry-like character through the finish.

Henriques & Henriques 10 Year Old Sercial, Madeira. $29.95.   96

Very dark reddish-amber. Medium-bodied. Notes of brown spices, nuts, citrus peel. Extraordinarily intense and lengthy with a complex array of flavors and refreshing acidity making for a very clean finish.

Henriques & Henriques 5 Year Old Verdelho, Madeira. $17.49.   89

Dark chestnut hue. Medium-bodied. Notes of cinnamon, nuts, tobacco. Light and pleasant with a complex array of flavors and buttery mouthfeel.

Henriques & Henriques 10 Year Old Verdelho, Madeira. $29.95.   91

Dark reddish-amber. Medium-bodied. Notes of dried fruits, roasted nuts, caramel. Lengthy and well-balanced with a vibrant character.

Henriques & Henriques 5 Year Old Bual, Madeira. $17.49.   85

Henriques & Henriques 10 Year Old Bual, Madeira. $29.95.   92

Dark amber with reddish tinge. Medium-bodied. Notes of caramel, toffee, orange marmalade. Lively and full on the palate with an amazingly lengthy finish.

Henriques & Henriques 5 Year Old Malmsey, Madeira. $17.49.   83

Henriques & Henriques 10 Year Old Malmsey, Madeira. $29.95.   85

Leacock's

Leacock's Rainwater, Madeira. $12.   82

Leacock's 5 Year Old Sercial, Madeira. $17.99.   86

Deep amber with subtle copper highlights. Moderately full-bodied. Notes of Amontillado Sherry, brown spice, caramelized fruits. Baked spicy aromas show a touch of rancio. Dry caramel flavors on the palate linger through the finish. Appealing for it richness, though not enormously complex on the palate.

Leacock's 10 Year Old Bual, Madeira. $32.99.   87

Very deep tawny amber hue. Generous coffee and date aromas. A rich entry leads a moderately full-bodied palate with solid acidic bite. Lush, zesty finish with a hint of rancio.

Leacock's 5 Year Old Malmsey, Madeira. $17.99.   90

Deep blackish-brown. Medium to full-bodied. Notes of coffee, redwood, malt, dates. Intense and lively, yet still viscous and syrupy with an expansion of flavors on the palate.

Miles

Miles 5 Year Old Malmsey, Madeira. $16.99.   82

Scale: Superlative (96-100), Exceptional (90-95), Highly Recommended (85-89), Recommended (80-84), Not Recommended (Under 80)

forty

❧

Germany

❧

German Riesling:
One of the World's Great Wines

What is most surprising about German wines is how little attention they receive in the American wine market. Few know that Germany has experienced an unbroken string of good to excellent vintages since 1988. What's more, production of high-quality wine is up, vineyard acreage has expanded, and more wines are being produced from Riesling, Germany's finest grape. Yet, exports to the U.S. dropped by half during the 1980s, and have since shown steady single-digit market declines. Some top producers have done better, thanks to importers pushing their highest-quality lines, but too many indifferent German wines from the 1970s, combined with a worldwide move toward drier styles, has engendered lackadaisical sales overall.

The upshot is that good-quality German wines will sometimes be tough to find, but those who are willing to search them out will be rewarded by some of the best wine values in today's marketplace. Estate bottled German Rieslings at the Auslese and Spatlese levels are some of the world's finest white table wines, and they can often be purchased for less than your average start-up boutique winery's new Chardonnay; a great value to say the least.

Important German Riesling Categories

Kabinett & Spatlese: The lightest, and generally driest, of the German quality grades are Spatlese and Kabinett. Spatlese is literally a "late harvest" wine, and is often the best balanced for modern tastes. Kabinetts, the subtlest of all the German styles, offer crisp, refreshing characters and, at their best, a vital richness. Both styles prove extremely useful during meals and before them as an aperitif. They are also a particularly good match with Pacific Rim cuisine.

Auslese: In spite of the glamour of show wines like those that follow, Auslese is, to some critics, the most important category in the German hierarchy. It is made from specially selected, very ripe grapes, and has traditionally been made in an unctuous, sweet style. In the 1990s, however, there has been a shift among the more progressive winemakers toward a greater emphasis on acidity rather than residual sugar; that makes the wines easier to pair with food.

Beerenauslese & Trockenbeerenauslese: Trockenbeerenausleses or TBAs are made from a rigorous selection of grapes that have partially raisined on the vine and been attacked by *Botrytis cinerea*, or "noble rot." The rot penetrates the grape skins and dehydrates the fruit within, intensifying its sweetness and overall flavor. Because the ideal climatic conditions for making TBA wines occur so rarely, little of it is ever made, and its cost is inevitably high. One step down in ripeness from TBA is Beerenauslese, or BA. These are made from specially selected, super-ripe grapes that usually have seen some *Botrytis* but have not reached TBA type levels.

Scale: Superlative (96-100), Exceptional (90-95), Highly Recommended (85-89), Recommended (80-84), Not Recommended (Under 80)

Eiswein: Eiswein is an extraordinary style of sweet wine, made from late-harvested grapes that have actually frozen on the vine. The night of the first frost in the vineyards, the grapes are hastily picked and crushed, and their water, now in the form of ice crystals, is removed. What's left is an intensely concentrated nectar with amazingly crisp acids and graceful structure.

Is This Wine Sweet?

Note that ripeness (the above categories) is not the same as sweetness, which measures how much sugar is left in the wine after fermentation. Furthermore, the perception of sweetness in German wine is really a function of its acidity and residual sugar. For example, if a wine carries 3-4% residual sugar (RS), but is balanced by very high acidity, it may taste dry. Consequently, a Spatlese can actually be drier than a Kabinett. A careful review of the accompanying tasting note is essential if one wants to avoid any surprises!

Reviews

RS indicates residual sweetness

Weingut Werner Anselmann

Riesling, Edesheimor RosengartenSpatlese, Pfalz 1997 7.46% rs. $12.50.   **NR**

Spatburgunder, Edesheimer Ordensgut, Pfalz 1997 .2% rs. $12.75.   **NR**

Baron zu Knyphausen

Riesling, Rheingau 1997 1.53% rs. $9.95.   **83**

Riesling, Kabinett, Rheingau 1997 2.42% rs. $12.50.   **81**

Riesling, Kiedricher Sandgrub Spatlese, Rheingau 1997 5.9% rs. $19.50.   **88**

Deep straw cast. Full-bodied. Full acidity. Highly extracted. Citrus, melon, minerals. Aromatic and flavorful, with a ripe, well-extracted palate feel. Big and rich through the finish, with sweetness tempered by vibrant acidity.

Germany at a Glance

Wines Reviewed:

137

Producers/Brands Represented:

43

Value Rating:

Good to Excellent

Weingut Basserman-Jordan

Riesling, Deidesheimer Paradiesgarten Kabinett, Pfalz 1996 $16.   90

Full gold luster. Medium-bodied. Full acidity. Highly extracted. Minerals, tart peach. Muted aromas have a minerally quality. Very concentrated and angular on the palate. A serious wine with a bone-dry, assertive character. This needs some time to evolve.

Riesling, Ruppertsberger Nussbien Spatlese, Pfalz 1996 $20.   89

Deep straw cast. Medium-bodied. Full acidity. Moderately extracted. Earth, minerals, citrus. Big, with a sturdy, well-extracted palate feel. Sweetness really shines through in the finish, but is checked by zesty acidity. A full and weighty style.

Bergstrasser Winzer

Gewürztraminer, Bensheimer Paulus Spatlese,
Hessische Berstrasse 1997 4.65% rs. $14.99.   83

Riesling, Heppenheimer Stemmler Eiswein,
Hessiche Bergstrasse 1995 20.9% rs. $32.99.   88

Deep yellow-gold. Full-bodied. Low acidity. Mushy pears, peach. Rich, honeyed aromas. Thick, fat, and viscous, with generous fruit flavors and very high levels of sweetness that overcome the natural acids. A dessert in and of itself.

George Breuer

Riesling, Montosa, Charta, Rheingau 1996 .7% rs. $21.99.   88

Full yellow-gold. Medium-bodied. Full acidity. Moderately extracted. Minerals, citrus. Very aromatic, with minerally accents. Full, firm, and structured on the palate, with fine acids gripping the finish. This is nice now and will be better in a few years.

Riesling, Rudesheim Berg Schlossberg, Rheingau 1995 .7% rs. $37.99.   93

Full golden yellow. Medium-bodied. Balanced acidity. Moderately extracted. Petrol, citrus, minerals. Outstanding aromas have a petrol-like note that suggests ripeness and onset of maturity. Flavors do not disappoint, with rounded, mature Riesling character showing through.

Riesling, Rudesheimer Berg Rottland Auslese, Gold Kapsel,
Rheingau 1995 9.5% rs. $44.99/375 ml.   94

Yellow-gold. Moderately full-bodied. Balanced acidity. Fusel, minerals, oil. Exciting aromas show mineral-oil quality that is fully revealed on the complex, gripping palate. Concentrated flavors keep an attractive degree of sweetness throughout.

Riesling, Rudesheimer Berg Schlossberg Auslese,
Gold Kapsel, Rheingau 1996 16.7% rs. $117.99/375 ml.   96

Brilliant yellow-gold sheen. Full-bodied. Full acidity. Nectarine, pineapple, honey. Lush, tropical aromas convey a sense of richness that is delivered on the palate. Glycerous and intensely sweet, with a hint of petrol showing already. Lively acids struggle to make an impression. Delicious, though this needs time to deepen and develop.

Weingut Dr. Bürklin-Wolf

Forster Riesling, Kabinett, Pfalz 1997 2.08% rs. $11.50.   86

Bright medium gold. Medium-bodied. Balanced acidity. Moderately extracted. Citrus zest, minerals. Quite aromatic, with a rich, rounded entrance that is generous up front, though the finish turns lean and dry. This will show best with food.

Wachenheimer Riesling, Spatlese, Pfalz 1997 3.25% rs. $19.   87

Deep straw cast. Full-bodied. Full acidity. Highly extracted. Melon, petrol, citrus. Extravagantly fragrant, with real complexity. Rich and round on the palate, with a drying finish. Accessible, but should continue to develop well.

Forster Riesling, Spatlese, Pfalz 1997 2.78% rs. $21.   81

Riesling, Ruppertsberger Gaisbohl Spatlese, Trocken,
Pfalz 1997 .88% rs. $31.65.   **90**

Deep straw cast. Moderately full-bodied. Low acidity. Moderately extracted. Melon, minerals. Aromatically reserved, with a fat, rich entry that fills the mouth with fruit flavor up front, then turns assertive and dry on the finish, with alcohol warmth evident. Reminiscent of an Austrian Riesling style.

Riesling, Wachenheimer Rechbachel Auslese, "R,"
Pfalz 1990 5.97% rs. $31.65.   **94**

Deep yellow-gold. Moderately full-bodied. Full acidity. Petrol, peach. Intense aromas show petrol-like aromas. Rich, fruit-laden flavors fill the palate, making this very attractive now. Further time in bottle will be rewarded.

Wachenheimer Mandelgarten Scheurbe Trockenbeerenauslese,
Pfalz 1990 26.81% rs. $150/375 ml.   **96**

Deep golden luster. Full-bodied. Full acidity. Ripe pears, peach. Spicy botrytis aromas have a floral accent. Thick and viscous, yet this has some sprightly acids to enliven the finish. Powerful and nectarous, this is drinking well now.

Weingut Castell

Kerner, Schloss Castell, Franken 1997 .95% rs. $11.95.   **83**

Muller Thurgau, Casteller Bausch Spatlese, Trocken,
Franken 1997 .27% rs. $18.75.   **87**

Bright pale straw. Medium-bodied. Balanced acidity. Highly extracted. Citrus, talc, minerals. Austere, lean and intense through the finish, with a mild alcohol warmth. Shows fine structure, with a drying finish. Has the stuffing to drink with food, or to keep for a few years.

Rieslaner, Casteller Kugelspiel Spatlese, Franken 1997 2.8% rs. $23.35.   **82**

Friedrich Wilhelm Gymnasium

Riesling, Graacher Himmelreich Kabinett,
Mosel-Saar-Ruwer 1996 3.6% rs. $12.   **86**

Brilliant platinum-straw hue. Medium-bodied. Full acidity. Moderately extracted. Citrus, white peach, minerals. Vibrant and juicy, with great balance between acids and sugars. This balance lends a piercing quality through the finish.

Riesling, Graacher Domprobst Spatlese, Halbtrocken,
Mosel-Saar-Ruwer-Halbtrocken 1997 1.6% rs. $16.   **81**

Riesling, Graacher Himmelreich Spatlese,
Mosel-Saar-Ruwer 1996 4.2% rs. $16.   **88**

Pale straw cast. Moderately full-bodied. Full acidity. Highly extracted. Tangerines, minerals. Pleasantly aromatic, with a ripe, rounded palate feel on entry that turns lean and flavorful through the finish.

Riesling, Graacher Himmelreich Auslese,
Mosel-Saar-Ruwer 1997 5.7% rs. $22.   **89**

Pale platinum straw. Moderately light-bodied. Balanced acidity. Moderately extracted. Talc, flowers, citrus. Floral, zesty aromas lead a mouthful of vibrant flavors, with an angular, minerally feel through the finish. Youthful and snappy.

Riesling, Trittenheimer Apotheke Auslese,
Mosel-Saar-Ruwer 1997 5.9% rs. $22.   **89**

Bright straw cast. Moderately full-bodied. Full acidity. Highly extracted. Citrus, tropical fruits, talc. Ripe and fragrant, with a full, rounded mouthfeel. Crisp, juicy acidity lends structure through the angular finish.

Riesling, Graacher Himmelreich Beerenauslese,
Mosel-Saar-Ruwer 1994 12.6% rs. $40/375 ml.　　　　　95

Bright yellow-gold. Medium-bodied. Full acidity. Highly extracted. Petrol, minerals, honey. Vibrant, high-toned, honeyed petrol aromas. Intense, juicy fruit flavors finish dryly. Shows evident botrytis character. This should improve with age, though it is drinking well now.

Weingut Geil

Gewürztraminer, Mettenheimer Michelsberg Kabinett,
Rheinhessen 1997 3.84% rs. $14.99.　　　　　84

Medium straw cast. Medium-bodied. Low acidity. Moderately extracted. Ripe apples. Ripe, fruity aromas lead a softer-styled palate, with rounded, mildly sweet flavors lingering on the finish.

Siegerrebe, Spatlese, Rheinhessen 1996 4.6% rs. $18.99.　　　　　88

Pale straw. Medium-bodied. Balanced acidity. Moderately extracted. Smoke, leaves, nectarines. Attractive aromas lead a sweet, herbal array of flavors, enhanced by an oily mouthfeel showing viscous character.

Graf Neipperg

Rotwein, Wurttemberg 1997 .08% rs. $9.35.　　　　　NR
Neipperger Schlossberg Lemberger, Wurttemberg 1997 .06% rs. $13.95.　　　　　81

Carl Graff

Riesling, Graacher Himmelreich Kabinett,
Mosel-Saar-Ruwer 1997 3.3% rs. $7.95.　　　　　83

Riesling, Piesporter Goldtropfchen Kabinett,
Mosel-Saar-Ruwer 1997 3.67% rs. $11.95.　　　　　81

Riesling, Piesporter Michelsberg Spatlese,
Mosel-Saar-Ruwer 1997 4.53% rs. $8.75.　　　　　86

Bright platinum cast. Moderately full-bodied. Full acidity. Highly extracted. Minerals, citrus, talc. Aromatic and complex, with a firm, racy palate feel. Crisp acidity is offset by a hint of sweetness in a juicy finish.

Riesling, Graacher Himmelreich Spatlese,
Mosel-Saar-Ruwer 1997 4.28% rs. $10.　　　　　86

Bright platinum cast. Moderately full-bodied. Full acidity. Moderately extracted. Talc, minerals. Quite fragrant, with a lean, clean, racy palate feel. Zesty acidity balances a hint of sweetness in the finish.

Riesling, Wehlener Sonnenuhr Spatlese,
Mosel-Saar-Ruwer 1997 4.22% rs. $10.35.　　　　　81

Riesling, Erdener Pralat Auslese, Mosel-Saar-Ruwer 1997 5.26% rs. $16.　　84

Pale straw. Medium-bodied. Full acidity. Moderately extracted. Tropical fruits, apples. Grapey, floral aromas reveal a juicy, fruit-centered palate with a lush finish. Drinking well now.

Maximin Grunhauser

Riesling, Herrenberg Kabinett, Mosel-Saar-Ruwer 1997 5.82% rs. $21.50.　　88

Bright pale gold. Medium-bodied. Full acidity. Moderately extracted. Flowers, apples. Fresh, floral aromas lead a bright, juicy palate with precise flavors and great sugar/acid balance. A zesty, racy style showing a degree of intensity.

Riesling, Abtsberg Kabinett, Mosel-Saar-Ruwer 1997 6.6% rs. $24.　　　　93

Pale gold. Medium-bodied. Balanced acidity. Moderately extracted. Peach, apples. Tart, fruity aromas follow through well. Generous, sweet, fruity flavors. Rounded and full, showing exceptional purity of flavor, with a minerally backbone providing grip.

Riesling, Abtsberg Spatlese, Mosel-Saar-Ruwer 1997 7.32% rs. $26.95.   93
Bright straw cast. Medium-bodied. Full acidity. Highly extracted. Citrus, minerals.
Fragrant and full, with a precise, focused palate feel. Piercing acidity counterbalances
moderate levels of sweetness. Built for aging, this will be much better in a few years.

Riesling, Abtsberg Auslese, Mosel-Saar-Ruwer 1997 6.89% rs. $36.   92
Very pale straw. Medium-bodied. Full acidity. Moderately extracted. Minerals, lemons,
apples. Pure aromas show a degree of intensity that is confirmed on the palate. Very
bright acids subdue the sweetness, making for a structured wine that will age gracefully.

Weingut Herrenberg

Riesling, Bert Simon, Serrig Herrenberg Kabinett,
Mosel-Saar-Ruwer 1997 4.84% rs. $13.99/375 ml.   88
Bright pale gold. Medium-bodied. Balanced acidity. Moderately extracted. Green apples,
peach. Very attractive fruity aromas lead a flavorsome, fruity palate with a lingering finish.
Sweetness levels are very natural.

Riesling, Bert Simon, Serrig Wurtzberg Spatlese,
Mosel-Saar-Ruwer 1996 5.04% rs. $16.99/375 ml.   87
Deep straw cast. Full-bodied. Full acidity. Highly extracted. Melon, minerals.
Aromatic and full, with a ripe, generous mouthfeel. Still well structured, with juicy
acidity tempering a touch of sweetness. Fine length and intensity. Should develop well.

Weingut Heyl zu Herrnshelm

Riesling, Rheinhessen 1996 .95% rs. $15.60.   86
Bright yellow-gold. Medium-bodied. Balanced acidity. Moderately extracted. Herbs,
citrus, minerals. Mineral accents on the nose are confirmed on the palate, with steely
qualities giving this presence and length.

Niersteiner, Rheinhessen 1997 1.56% rs. $21.50.   83

Riesling, Niersteiner Oelberg Kabinett, Rheinhessen 1997 2.22% rs. $12.50. 86
Pale platinum cast. Moderately light-bodied. Full acidity. Subtly extracted. Apples,
citrus. Mildly floral aromas. Lean, fresh character with clean, bright flavors and a
sense of structure in a lighter frame.

*Riesling, Niersteiner Pettental Spatlese, Rheinhessen 1997 1.52% rs. $18.50.*85
Bright straw cast. Moderately full-bodied. Full acidity. Highly extracted. Citrus, minerals.
Aromatic and complex, with a full, ripe impression on the palate. Zesty acidity lends
structure through the finish.

Weingut Johannishof

Riesling, Johannisberger Goldatzel Kabinett,
Rheingau 1996 3.29% rs. $12.50.   86
Very pale gold. Medium-bodied. Balanced acidity. Moderately extracted. Citrus, minerals.
Lean, minerally flavors make for a refreshing style that has some grip and pairs easily with
lighter foods.

Riesling, Rudesheimer Spatlese, Rheingau 1997 5.63% rs. $21.   87
Deep straw cast. Full-bodied. Full acidity. Highly extracted. Melon, tropical fruits.
Extravagantly aromatic, with a ripe, forward quality throughout. Firm, zesty acidity
lends structure and balances some sweetness in the finish. Full-throttled style.

Weingut Kesselstatt

Riesling, Kaseler Nies'chen Kabinett,
Mosel-Saar-Ruwer 1997 4.06% rs. $15.80.   83

Riesling, Piesporter Goldtropfchen Kabinett,
Mosel-Saar-Ruwer 1997 4.32% rs. $16.80.   **87**

Bright pale gold. Medium-bodied. Balanced acidity. Moderately extracted. Petrol, earth, herbs. Aromas show an oily note. Strong earthy, herbal flavors give an assertive though flavorsome character, with richness and marked residual sweetness through the finish.

Riesling, Kaseler Nies'chen Spatlese,
Mosel-Saar-Ruwer 1997 5.11% rs. $20.50.   **85**

Bright straw cast. Medium-bodied. Full acidity. Moderately extracted. Minerals, citrus zest. Has a marked spritzy quality, with a hefty sulfurous note that seems quite stubborn. Racy, lean, and crisp in the mouth. Rather ungenerous at present.

Riesling, Scharzhofberger Spatlese,
Mosel-Saar-Ruwer 1997 4.76% rs. $21.50.   **87**

Bright straw cast. Moderately full-bodied. Full acidity. Highly extracted. Flowers, citrus, minerals. Fragrant and generous, with a bright, zesty palate feel. Classic Mosel, with a racy, delicate quality and a hint of sweetness to the finish. Will gain complexity with mid-term cellaring.

Weinkellerei Leonard Kreusch

Liebfraumilch, Rheinhessen 1997 3.5% rs. $5.99.   **NR**

Piesporter Michelsberg, Mosel-Saar-Ruwer 1997 3.5% rs. $6.99.   **81**

Zeller Schwarze Katz, Mosel-Saar-Ruwer 1997 $8.   **NR**

Dexheimer Doktor Kabinett, Rheinhessen 1997 4.84% rs. $8.99.   **86**

Medium straw. Medium-bodied. Moderately extracted. Peach, minerals. Fresh, juicy, mildly plasticy aromas follow through on the palate with crisp, fruity flavors. Shows concentration and depth.

Kabinett, Rheinhessen 1997 3.78% rs. $8.99.   **81**

Dexheimer Doktor Spatlese, Rheinhessen 1996 4.88% rs. $9.99.   **84**

Medium straw. Medium-bodied. Moderately extracted. Peach, minerals. Fresh, fruity aromas have a plastic note, leading a juicy palate with a mildly sweet entry and crisp acids that linger on the finish.

Spatlese, Rheinhessen 1997 4.32% rs. $9.99.   **NR**

Auslese, Rheinhessen 1996 5.24% rs. $10.99.   **82**

Riesling, Twisted River, Bin 169, Mosel-Saar-Ruwer 1997 1.69% rs. $7.99. **NR**

Riesling, Piesporter Michelsberg Kabinett,
Mosel-Saar-Ruwer 1996 3.2% rs. $9.99.   **81**

Riesling, Piesporter Michelsberg Spatlese,
Mosel-Saar-Ruwer 1996 4.32% rs. $10.99.   **NR**

Riesling, Piesporter Michelsberg Auslese,
Mosel-Saar-Ruwer 1996 4.5% rs. $11.99.   **84**

Pale straw hue. Medium-bodied. Full acidity. Highly extracted. Minerals, fusel, lemons. Assertive, mineral-accented aromas. Vibrant flavors have plenty of zesty character in a dry style.

Sybille Kuntz

Riesling, Trocken, Mosel-Saar-Ruwer 1997 .9% rs. $8.99.   **84**

Pale straw cast. Medium-bodied. Full acidity. Moderately extracted. Minerals, citrus zest. Lean and crisp, with solid structure evident in the minerally backbone and austere flavors. Straightforward and refreshing.

Scale: Superlative (96-100), Exceptional (90-95), Highly Recommended (85-89), Recommended (80-84), Not Recommended (Under 80)

Riesling, Bernkastel Kueser Weisenstein Auslese,
Bernkastel-Kueser 1996 .8% rs. $19.99. **86**

Bright yellow-straw color. Medium-bodied. Full acidity. Moderately extracted. Apples, tart peach. Vibrant tropical flavors are bolstered by zesty acids and a sense of mineral depth though the finish. Further cellar age will enhance this.

Riesling, Bernkastel-Kueser Weisensein Auslese,
Trocken, Mosel-Saar-Ruwer 1996 .25% rs. $19.99. **84**

Pale straw. Medium-bodied. Full acidity. Moderately extracted. Mineral, herbs. Lean and dry, with austere mineral flavors and an herbal note throughout. Impressively structured, though austere and tart. Food should provide a foil for this.

Riesling, Bernkastel-Kueser Weisenstein Beerenauslese,
Bernkastel-Kueser 1996 13.2% rs. $49.99/375 ml. **90**

Yellow-gold. Moderately full-bodied. Full acidity. Petrol, spice, peach. Intensely aromatic, showing a spicy accent. Juicy, tropical fruit flavors are lush, yet balanced by acids. This is already drinking very well.

Hans Lang

Riesling, Spatlese, Rheingau 1997 6.75% rs. $16.99. **93**

Bright platinum cast. Moderately full-bodied. Full acidity. Highly extracted. Citrus, stone fruits, minerals. Aromatically reserved, but piercing and pure on the palate, with an intense and flavorful finish. Shows excellent balance and acidity, with some moderate sweetness. Built to age.

Riesling, Auslese, Rheingau 1997 9.35% rs. $25.99. **90**

Pale straw. Medium-bodied. Apricot, peach. Lovely tropical aromas follow through on the palate, revealing high levels of sweetness. A fruit-centered style, with a lush finish that invites early drinking.

Weingut Ulrich Langguth

Riesling, Piesporter Gunterstay Kabinett,
Mosel-Saar-Ruwer 1997 3.52% rs. $15.99. **86**

Pale gold. Medium-bodied. Balanced acidity. Moderately extracted. Apples, minerals. Rich, glycerous nose. Sweet fruit flavors fill the palate with enough acidity to keep this fresh, though not racy. A softer style.

Dr. Loosen

Riesling, Mosel-Saar-Ruwer 1997 $10. **88**

Bright straw cast. Medium-bodied. Balanced acidity. Moderately extracted. Minerals, earth, peaches. Generous mineral-accented aromas. Round and forward in the mouth, with a hint of sweetness balanced by crisp acidity. Shows some complexity.

Riesling, Wehlener Sonnenuhr Kabinett,
Mosel-Saar-Ruwer 1997 $16.50/375 ml. **91**

Pale platinum. Moderately light-bodied. Balanced acidity. Moderately extracted. Minerals, green apples. Sweet, floral nose. Crisp and lively on the palate. Mild residual sweetness is well balanced by acids. Delicate, minerally finish. Exceptional balance; could be drunk now, though will show better in a year or two.

Riesling, Urziger Wurzgarten Spatlese, Mosel-Saar-Ruwer 1997 $25.50. **90**

Deep straw cast. Moderately full-bodied. Full acidity. Highly extracted. Minerals, earth, petrol. Quite aromatic, with a forward, complex range of flavors. Firm and full in the mouth, with angular acidity and a hint of sweetness. Excellent grip, length, and intensity.

Riesling, Wehlener Sonnenuhr Auslese, Mosel-Saar-Ruwer 1997 $30. **90**

Pale straw. Medium-bodied. Full acidity. Highly extracted. Minerals, pineapple. Reserved aromas hint of tropical richness. Very angular and awkward on the palate, with concentrated flavors and a dry, mineral-dominated finish. Still youthful, this needs time.

Riesling, Urziger Wurzgarten Auslese, Mosel-Saar-Ruwer 1997 $33/375 ml. 90
Pale straw. Moderately full-bodied. Balanced acidity. Moderately extracted. Nectarine,
apples. Fat, lush aromas lead a huge mouthful of sweet and intense flavors that are not
dominated by acids. This is very generous now, though age may well bring out further
complexity.

Riesling, Wehlener Sonnenuhr Beerenauslese,
Mosel-Saar-Ruwer 1997 $68/375 ml. 92
Pale yellow-gold. Moderately full-bodied. Full acidity. Nectarine, honey. Inviting, honeyed
aromas. Angular and sweet, with bright, tropical fruit flavors that finish sweetly. Generous
and attractive now, though this will appreciate with further cellaring.

Georg Messer
Kabinett, Trocken, Pfalz $8.90. NR
Riesling, Auslese, Halbtrocken, Pfalz 1997 $25. 89
Pale emerald straw. Medium-bodied. Balanced acidity. Minerals, fusel, tart peach.
Elegant, perfumed aromas show a purity on the palate that remains tight and steely
through the finish. Very impressive.
Matura, Rhein 1993 .59% rs. $12.90. 81

Pauly-Bergweiler
Riesling, Bernkasteler alte Badstube am Doctorberg Trockenbeerenauslese,
Mosel-Saar-Rower 1995 $99. 94
Bright yellow-straw color. Medium-bodied. Full acidity. Moderately extracted. Pineapple,
peach, spice. Heavy, botrytis-influenced, plastic aromas. Rich, viscous mouthfeel has
tropical richness. Nice now, though this will gain more complexity with age.
Riesling, Bernkasteler Lay Eiswein, Mosel-Saar-Rower 1996 $135. 90
Bright orange-gold. Full-bodied. Full acidity. Highly extracted. Honey, orange zest,
lemon. Deep, expressive aromas lead a bracingly acidic, sweet, viscous palate with huge
concentration. Impossible to drink at present, yet deeply impressive.

Herbert Pazen
Riesling, Mosel-Saar-Ruwer 1996 % rs. $10. NR
Riesling, Zeltinger Himmelreich Kabinett,
Mosel-Saar-Ruwer 1996 $12/375 ml. 83
Riesling, Zeltinger Himmelreich Spatlese,
Mosel-Saar-Ruwer 1996 $13.50. NR

Prinz von Hessen
Riesling, Johannisberger Klaus Kabinett, Rheingau 1996 $16.50. 80
Riesling, Johannisberger Klaus Spatlese, Rheingau 1996 $16.50. 89
Bright yellow-golden cast. Moderately full-bodied. Full acidity. Highly extracted. Minerals,
bread, hazelnuts. Quite aromatic, with an unusual nutty note. Firm and extremely
intense in the mouth, with piercing acidity through the weighty finish.

Prinz zu Salm-Dalberg'sches Weingut
Prinz Salm, Nahe 1997 5.13% rs. $11.20. 81
Riesling, Schloss Wallhausen Kabinett, Nahe 1997 3.62% rs. $14. 86
Very pale gold. Medium-bodied. Full acidity. Moderately extracted. Green apples,
minerals. Crisp and snappy, with brisk flavors showing a very bright, clean character.
An ideal, delicate aperitif style.

Weingut Rappenhof

Riesling, Niersteiner Pettenthal Auslese, Rheinhessen 1996 $24.   86

Yellow-gold. Medium-bodied. Full acidity. Minerals, limes, tart peach. Tart and zesty, with angular acids and a dry finish. Has all the structural elements to improve. A vibrant, austere style.

Bruno Reiss

Himmelstadter Kelter Bacchus Kabinett, Franken 1996 1.66% rs. $6.   86

Pale straw. Medium-bodied. Full acidity. Citrus, talc. High-toned, perfumed aromas. Oily, textured character with bone-dry flavors that never turn severe, remaining juicy through the finish.

Thüngersheimer Scharlachberg Rieslaner Spätlese, Franken 1994 1.2% rs. $12.   82

Würzburger Pfaffenberg Auslese, Optima, Franken 1996 7.1% rs. $23/375 ml.   87

Deep golden orange. Moderately full-bodied. Balanced acidity. Brown spice, ripe apples. Honeyed, rich aromas. Distinguished by a silky mouthfeel with glycerous richness and only a hint of sweetness through a juicy, fruit-acid finish.

Pfaffenberg Trocken, Domina, Franken 1994 .1% rs. $14.   NR

Rothrock

Chardonnay, Spatlese, Dry, Rheinhessen 1996 .4% rs. $12.   81

Riesling, Wormser Liebfrauenmorgen Spatlese, Rheinhessen 1997 2.2% rs. $10.99.   85

Bright platinum cast. Medium-bodied. Full acidity. Highly extracted. Citrus, minerals. Crisp and aromatic, with a straightforward, zesty structure. On the delicate side, with a slight hint of sweetness to the racy finish.

Ortega, Wormser Liebfrauenmorgen Beerenauslesse, Rheinhessen 1997 8% rs. $20/375 ml.   84

Pale straw. Moderately full-bodied. Low acidity. Pineapple, mango. Sweaty, honeyed fruit aromas lead a big, fat mouthful of flavors and a thick mouthfeel. Not one for the cellar.

Rudolf Muller

Riesling, "The Bishop of Riesling," Bereich Bernkastel, Mosel-Saar-Ruwer 1997 2.8% rs. $6.49.   81

Schloss Saarstein

Riesling, Trocken, Mosel-Saar-Ruwer 1997 $12.   84

Bright straw cast. Medium-bodied. Full acidity. Highly extracted. Minerals. Aromatically muted, with a lighter-styled though well-structured palate feel. Clean, crisp and rather lean.

Riesling, Serriger Schloss Saarsteiner Spatlese, Mosel-Saar-Ruwer 1997 $18.   93

Bright straw cast. Moderately full-bodied. Full acidity. Highly extracted. Flowers, acacia, white citrus. Perfumed and delicate, with a complex range of flavors. Firm and zesty in the mouth, with a lighter frame. Juicy acidity serves to balance a hint of sweetness.

Weingut Heinrich Schmitges

Riesling, Wehlener Sonnenuhr Auslese, Trocken, Mosel-Saar-Ruwer 1997 $22.   88

Pale yellow-gold. Moderately full-bodied. Full acidity. Highly extracted. Peach, citrus, minerals. Quite dry and firmly structured, with a juicy entry and a strong mineral backbone accentuated by angular acidity. Fruit sweetness is restrained by the acid and mineral flavors.

Riesling, Mosel-Saar-Ruwer 1997 $10.   86

Bright straw cast. Moderately full-bodied. Full acidity. Highly extracted. Talc, green
apples, peaches. Pleasantly aromatic, with a full and rounded palate feel. A hint of
sweetness is offset nicely by angular acidity. Should develop nicely with mid-term aging.

Riesling, Erdener Treppchen Kabinett,
Mosel-Saar-Ruwer 1997 4.5% rs. $13.50.   82

Riesling, Erdener Treppchen Spatlese, Trocken,
Mosel-Saar-Ruwer 1997 $18.   89

Bright straw cast. Moderately full-bodied. Full acidity. Highly extracted. Peaches,
minerals. Aromatic and concentrated, with a pure fruit tone throughout. Lean and
focused in the mouth, with a racy, well-structured palate. Absolutely dry through
the finish. Should develop nicely with mid-term aging.

Riesling, Wehlener Sonnenuhr Spatlese, Halbtrocken,
Mosel-Saar-Ruwer 1997 $18.   89

Bright straw cast. Medium-bodied. Full acidity. Highly extracted. Peaches, minerals,
citrus. Quite aromatic and very firm, with a highly structured, lean palate feel. Finishes
with a dry, refreshing crispness. Will gain further complexity with age.

Rivaner, Trocken, Mosel-Saar-Rower 1997 $10.   83

Weingut Schreiber Zink
Gewürztraminer, Dalsheimer Steig, Rheinhessen 1997 3% rs. $7.   90

Medium straw hue. Medium-bodied. Balanced acidity. Lychee, pineapple. Sweet, nutty
aromas are varietally pure. Glycerous, sweet fruit flavors fill the mouth, with a nutty note
pervading through the finish.

Selbach-Oster
Riesling, Graacher Domprobst Spatlese, Mosel-Saar-Ruwer 1996 $20.   94

Deep yellow-straw cast. Moderately full-bodied. Full acidity. Highly extracted. Petrol,
minerals, citrus. Quite aromatic, with real complexity to the range of flavors. Full and
ripe in the mouth, though firmly structured with sound acidity, to balance a hint of
sweetness through the finish.

Riesling, Graacher Himmelreich Spatlese, Mosel-Saar-Ruwer 1997 $20.   84

Bright straw cast. Moderately full-bodied. Balanced acidity. Moderately extracted.
Minerals, stone fruits, talc. Pleasantly aromatic, with a delicate, rounded quality. Ripe
and full, with juicy acidity and a hint of sweetness to the finish.

H. Sichel Sohne Gmbh
Blue Nun White, Rheinhessen 1996 $5.99.   82

St. Ursula
Silvaner, Trocken, Pfalz $9.   82
Riesling, Devil's Rock, Pfalz 1997 $6.99.   81
Riesling, Dry, Pfalz 1997 $6.99.   NR

Weingut Studert-Prum
Riesling, Wehlener Sonnenuhr Auslese,
Mosel-Saar-Ruwer 1997 6.8% rs. $19.99.   96

Medium straw luster. Medium-bodied. Full acidity. Moderately extracted. Tart peach,
green apple. Fresh, aromatic, tart fruit aromas. Palate displays youthful exuberance, with
piercing flavors focused by outstanding acid/sugar balance through a long finish. A few
years' cellaring will be well rewarded.

Scale: Superlative (96-100), Exceptional (90-95), Highly Recommended (85-89),
Recommended (80-84), Not Recommended (Under 80)

Riesling, Wehlener Sonnenuhr Kabinett,
Mosel-Saar-Ruwer 1997 3.7% rs. $9.99.   89

Bright pale gold. Medium-bodied. Balanced acidity. Moderately extracted. Minerals, sweet citrus, peach. Floral, high-toned aromas. Mild residual sweetness is well balanced by bright acids that give a snappy finish, making for a very refreshing style.

Weingut Tesch

Riesling, Laubenheimer St. Remigiusberg Auslese,
Nahe 1994 7.53% rs. $24.99.   93

Deep golden yellow. Moderately full-bodied. Full acidity. Highly extracted. Petrol, fusel, tart peach. Exciting, pure Riesling aromas show petrol-like whiffs. On the palate, epic proportions of acid and fruit flavors compete for attention. Still youthful; cellar time will improve this wine.

Riesling, Langenlonsheimer Konigsschild Spatlese,
Halbtrocken, Nahe 1996 1.6% rs. $18.99.   NR

Weingut Dr. H. Thanisch

Riesling, Mosel-Saar-Ruwer 1997 3.6% rs. $14.99.   85

Bright pale straw cast. Medium-bodied. Full acidity. Moderately extracted. Citrus zest, minerals. Pleasantly aromatic, with an angular, crisp quality throughout. Flavorful and pure, with zesty acidity balancing a hint of sweetness for a refreshing finish.

Riesling, Hochgewachs, Wehlener Sonnenuhr,
Mosel-Saar-Ruwer 1996 3.8% rs. $15.99.   91

Pale yellow-gold. Moderately full-bodied. Full acidity. Highly extracted. Earth, apricots, minerals. Seems to show a touch of botrytis in the nose, with fairly complex flavors in the mouth. Firm and rich, with angular acidity through the drying finish. Should develop well with age.

Riesling, Bernkasteler Doctor Badstube Kabinett,
Mosel-Saar-Ruwer 1997 4.5% rs. $29.99.   86

Very pale straw. Moderately light-bodied. Full acidity. Moderately extracted. Green apples, flowers, minerals. Fragrant, floral aromas. Delicate, fresh flavors with a fine acid/sugar balance that persists through the finish.

Riesling, Berncasteler Doctor Spatlese,
Mosel-Saar-Ruwer 1996 4.5% rs. $39.99.   92

Deep straw cast. Full-bodied. Full acidity. Highly extracted. Minerals, stone fruits. Aromatically reserved, but full and impressive in the mouth. Quite ripe, though still firm, with angular acidity through the finish. This will be better with near to mid-term aging.

Riesling, Brauneberger-Juffer-Sonnenuhr Auslese, Mosel-Saar-Ruwer 1995
5.8% rs. $24.99.   89

Pale straw. Medium-bodied. Full acidity. Moderately extracted. Minerals, limes. Strong mineral accents on the nose, with marked citrus notes. These follow through to an intense and vibrant palate, with concentrated, tightly wound flavors.

Weingut Ulrich Langguth

Riesling, Piesporter Goldtropfchen Auslese,
Mosel-Saar-Ruwer 1995 6.15% rs. $29.99.   89

Pale yellow-straw hue. Medium-bodied. Balanced acidity. Moderately extracted. Plastic, sweet limes, peach. Pronounced plastic aromas lead a mildly sweet, vibrant palate showing fine varietal flavors that further age will enhance.

Weinkellerei P.J. Valckenberg

Gewürztraminer, Pfalz 1997 2.7% rs. $8.95.   86

Pale straw hue. Medium-bodied. Balanced acidity. Moderately extracted. Glycerin, peach. Oily, rich aromas follow through to the palate, showing a glycerous presence. Not varietally intense, though still generous.

Liebfraumilch, Madonna, Rheinhessen 1997 3.1% rs. $6.25.   81

Madonna Spatlese, Rheinhessen 1997 5% rs. $8.35.   81

Pinot Blanc, Rheinhessen 1997 1.1% rs. $7.50.   82

Pinot Gris, Pfalz 1997 1% rs. $8.95.   80

Chardonnay, Eiswein, Rheinhessen 1996 21% rs. $43/375 ml.   86

Pale gold. Moderately full-bodied. Full acidity. Pears, green apples. Waxy, pearlike aromas. Vibrant acidity gets the better of the high-toned fruit flavors. Very clean.

Von Lade

Riesling, Dry, Rheingau 1996 $9.99.   81

Maximilian von Othegraven

Riesling, Kanzem-Altenberg Kabinett,
Mosel-Saar-Ruwer 1996 1.36% rs. $15.99.   83

Riesling, Kanzemer Altenberg Auslese,
Mosel-Saar-Ruwer 1983 4.6% rs. $45.   95

Deep golden yellow. Medium-bodied. Full acidity. Moderately extracted. Earth, petrol, minerals. Exciting aromas have a developed, figgy character. Very ripe on the palate, with the flavors already accessible, complex, and broad through a long, dry finish. Fully mature.

J.L. Wolf

Riesling, Wachenheimer Belz Auslese, Pfalz 1997 $24.   88

Pale straw. Medium-bodied. Full acidity. Tart pineapple, mineral. Racy and angular, with piercing acids and juicy flavors. Not at its best now; this needs time.

Riesling, Deidesheimer Herrgottsacker Kabinett, Pfalz 1996 $13.50.   81

Riesling, Wachenheimer Gerumpel Spatlese, Pfalz 1996 $16.50.   85

Deep straw cast. Full-bodied. Full acidity. Highly extracted. Minerals, petrol. Aromatically reserved, with a firm, steely palate feel. Shows great extract and weight, with a drying finish. Will gain complexity with mid-term cellaring.

Scale: Superlative (96-100), Exceptional (90-95), Highly Recommended (85-89), Recommended (80-84), Not Recommended (Under 80)

forty-one

~

Austria

~

Austria: The Next Big Thing?

Though Austria may be better known to Americans as the setting for *The Sound of Music*, it is rapidly forging a reputation among connoisseurs for producing an exciting range of wines. Though there are a number of excellent table wines to be sure, their dessert wines in particular have taken the world by storm. Though little known in the United States, Austrian wines have actually been gaining more and more notoriety on the world scene in recent years. In tasting the finest examples across a range of styles, one cannot help but be impressed with the overall level of quality. It all leads one to inquire as to where these wines have been all along.

The Ups and Downs of Austria

Austria is actually one of the oldest wine-producing nations in Europe, with vineyards dating back to the heyday of the Roman Empire. In fact, the Roman emperor Probus actually dispatched the legions to help with plantings on Austria's Pannonian plain as early as 280 A.D. By the 1700s, wines from the Habsburg Empire, of which Vienna was the capital, were sought after across northern Europe. The sweet wines of Tokay, which is now a part of Hungary, and those produced on the banks of Lake Neusiedl in Austria proper, had become legendary.

Unfortunately, like many areas of Europe, the Austrian wine industry was particularly hard hit by *Phylloxera* in the last quarter of the 19th century. When the vineyards were replanted, many growers were tempted by higher profits and planted varietals such as Welschriesling, which ultimately produced larger crops of inferior quality. For the rest of the 20th century, much of the Austrian wine trade focused on producing semi-sweet Lieblich wines that were made in imitation of German Rieslings. The nadir came in 1985 when a wine scandal erupted as several merchants were caught doctoring their wines with diethyline glycol, so as to pass them off as being of a higher degree of alcohol (and hence ripeness).

This event actually turned out to be a blessing in disguise, as it forced the government and growers to agree on new regulations and take the industry in completely new directions. The all-powerful middlemen were largely ruined and the growers were left to reclaim the international reputation that their wines had once enjoyed. Almost immediately the flabby, semi-sweet wines of yore were scrapped in favor of crisp dry whites. Riesling, Gruner Veltliner, Sauvignon Blanc, and even Chardonnay are now the buzz words in Austrian wine and in an amazingly short period of time the industry with roots in ancient Rome has reinvented itself and risen from the ashes. Featuring wines that are well suited to international palates and behind aggressive promotion by Austria's Wine Marketing Board, these wines have begun to gain footholds not only in Europe but also on this side of the Atlantic as well.

World's Greatest Stickies?

Austria makes some of the, if not the, finest sweet wines in the world. Though American consumers are still largely unfamiliar with them, it will only be a matter of time before these wines become as coveted here as they are already in parts of Europe. For connoisseurs of the exotic and rare *Botrytis*-affected wines

Scale: Superlative (96-100), Exceptional (90-95), Highly Recommended (85-89), Recommended (80-84), Not Recommended (Under 80)

of the world, Austria's Neusiedlersee, or Lake Neusiedl, will soon become a household world.

The lake itself is the key to the wine's production. It is shallow and warm with an area of nearly 60 square miles, and it is situated in the warmest part of Austria on the Hungarian border. Indeed, this area was a part of Hungary until 1921. The land surrounding the lake is flat, marshy, and humid, and in no other area of the world with the possible exception of Hungary's Tokay, does the noble rot, *Botrytis cinerea*, attack grapes so reliably, year in and year out. While *Botrytis* visits the great sweet wine areas of France and Germany only once in every few vintages, it is rare for the Neusiedlersee to have a year without *Botrytis*.

Great sweet wines have been made here for several hundred years, but the problems of *Phylloxera*, two world wars, and a Russian occupation of the region until 1956 were followed by the wine scandal of the '80s. Unfortunately, the 20th century has not been kind to the growers of Neusiedlersee. Once the Russians left in 1956, however, the way was cleared for a heavy reinvestment in the vineyards, and the general renaissance of Austrian wine and winemaking as a whole has only served to raise the quality of the area's wines that much further. As the 21st century dawns, it is possible to say that from a quality perspective, Neusiedlersee has retaken its rightful place in the world of viticulture.

Due to the certainty of the conditions, production of Beerenauslese, Trockenbeerenauslese, and Eiswein is relatively regular and the supplies (compared to Germany, for instance) are abundant. This means that the wines, though still somewhat expensive, are often offered at a fraction of the price of their French and German counterparts. Additionally, the Neusiedlersee produces an indigenous type of sweet wine that is one of the world's most exotic, Ausbruch.

In the traditional production of Ausbruch, the winemaker adds fresh non-*Botrytis* affected grapes or fresh must to the fermenting wine. This helps to keep the fermentation going when there is inherently so much sugar and so

❧

Austria at a Glance

Wines Reviewed:

296

Producers/Brands Represented:

144

Value Rating:

Poor to Average

❧

little liquid in the must. The result is a wine with a higher (and better-balanced) alcohol level, and a more vinous character than corresponding German wines. Furthermore, Ausbruchs are often aged in casks until they develop a touch of *rancio*, an oxidized Sherry-like character. The resultant wine can be mind-bogglingly complex, with tobacco, herb, and yeast nuances overlaid with the more typical ripe fruit flavors associated with *Botrytis*. Additionally, acidity is nowhere near the piercing levels that accompany many German wines of similar sweetness (usually eisweins), often making them far more pleasant in youth.

Key Dry Whites: Gruner & Riesling

Although Austria is currently producing some of the world's best dessert wines, they tend to be released in tiny quantities, and are fairly expensive. Of greater interest for everyday drinking would be the new generation of dry whites, many of which are both world class and widely distributed. While Riesling and Gruner Veltliner are undoubtedly the classics, Sauvignon Blanc and Chardonnay are showing promise.

Most dry whites come from Lower Austria, a region that has become closely associated with these styles. Confusingly, Lower Austria is actually the region in the northeast corner of the country around Vienna. The Lower Austrian sub-regions of Wachau, Kremstal, and Kamptal are on or near the Danube River to the west of Vienna, and figure most prominently in white wine production. Dry wines are emphasized in the Wachau in particular, and they are classified in three different quality grades in ascending order of ripeness: Steinfeder, Federspiel, and Smaragd. The finest Rieslings tend to show weight, concentration, and sophistication with an austere character that would make an excellent foil for seafood and shellfish in particular. They have very little in common with German renditions of the grape.

As for Gruner Veltliner, it may not be unique to Austria, but it belongs to Austria the way Gewürztraminer belongs to Alsace. It accounts for 36% of Austrian vine plantings, and hence produces the bulk of Austria's table wines. Its character can be crisp and refreshing though it tends to be richer and spicier than Riesling when it is at its finest. It is quite possibly the most versatile and distinctive of Austrian wines. In noting the differences between Gruner Veltliner and Riesling, Hugh Johnson said that to "compare it with Riesling is like comparing a wild flower with a finely bred garden variety in which scent, color, size, and form have been studied and improved for many years." Often with an exotic herbal note, Gruner would make an ideal companion to herb-accented pork or poultry dishes.

What About Austrian Reds?

At first thought one would probably think of Austria's climate as being quite cool. In the Alps and the western and northern reaches of the country this is true. The eastern plains that border Hungary and Slovenia, however, are a different story all together. Right in the heart of this region is Mittelburgenland, and this is Austria's red wine country, with 95% of the vineyards planted to red wine varietals.

Scale: Superlative (96-100), Exceptional (90-95), Highly Recommended (85-89), Recommended (80-84), Not Recommended (Under 80)

Traditional wines such as Blaufrankisch, Saint Laurent, and Zweigelt dominate production, but varieties like Cabernet Sauvignon and Merlot are being seen with greater regularity. Though the region is indeed warm, proper ripeness tends to be a chronic problem for Cabernet Sauvignon in particular, despite the fact that many growers have taken it up as the Holy Grail. More dependable wines tend to be made from Blaufrankisch and Saint Laurent.

Blaufrankisch has often been confused with Gamay, but it was probably brought from Hungary as opposed to France. The wines tend to be light in body, though certainly fuller than most Gamays. As with many Austrian reds, the use of new oak barrels is not uncommon, and the ripe raspberry qualities of the grape tend to incorporate the spice of the wood in an attractive way. Blaufrankisch also tends to be lighter in tannin and accessible upon release. As for Saint Laurent, the Austrians think that it is a member of the Pinot family, and its characteristics lend some credence to this theory. Indeed, Saint Laurent, like Pinot Noir, is lighter in body with an ethereal, heady, and exotic bouquet. Though tricky to grow, successful examples are consistently among the finest Austrian reds.

Reviews

Weingut Achs-Tremmel
Aurum, Trockenbeerenauslese, Neusiedlersee 1996 23% rs. $30/375 ml.   86
Dark orange-amber. Full-bodied. Low acidity. Yeast, orange liqueur. Yeasty, complex aromas. Thick, luxurious mouthfeel has a syrupy quality through the finish. Very hedonistic; only one glass is the limit.

Weingut Karl Aigner
Herzog Albrecht I, Brut, Donauland 1% rs. $13.   NR

Wolfgang Aigner
Feinburgunder, Kremser Sandgrube, Trocken, Kremstal 1997 .1% rs. $15.   83
Kremser, Privatfullung, Sandgrube, Kremstal 1997 1% rs. $17.   NR

Weingut Allram
Gruner Veltliner, Strasser Hasel, Alte Reben, Kamptal 1997 .08% rs. $16.   81
Weissburgunder, Strasser Hasel, Trocken, Kamptal 1997 .35% rs. $18.50.   83

Weinbau Alphart
Rotgipfler, Trockenbeerenauslese, Thermenregion 1995 22% rs. $35/375 ml. 88
Brilliant deep orange luster. Full-bodied. Full acidity. Highly extracted. Sweet peach, apples. Piquant aromas lead a lush, nectarous mouthfeel, with vibrant acidity coming through on the finish. Full-throttled style lacking only in aromatic grace.

Matthias Altenburger
Chardonnay, Pannonischer Reigen Spatlese, Altweibersommer,
Neusiedlersee 1997 4.22% rs. $12.50.   84
Bright pale yellow. Moderately full-bodied. Balanced acidity. Moderately extracted. Sweet apples, grapes. Sweet, juicy fruit flavors linger through the finish. A soft, accessible style with lower acids bringing out the sweetness.

Arachon-Vereinte Winzer
Arachon Passion, T-FX-T, Mittelburgenland 1996 .11% rs. $30. **NR**

Weingut Familie Auer
Cuvée Noir, Thermenregion 1996 .12% rs. $25. **86**
Bright cherry red. Medium-bodied. Balanced acidity. Moderately extracted. Red fruits, spice. Spicy aromas follow through well on the palate. Crisp, juicy berry flavors with minerally dryness.
Pinot Noir, Tattendorfer Trocken, Thermenregion 1996 .75% rs. $15. **NR**

Weingut Norbert Bauer
Blauer Portugieser, Weinviertel 1997 .34% rs. $9. **NR**
Blauer Burgunder, Trocken, Weinviertel 1993 .34% rs. $9. **85**
Dark ruby purple. Moderately full-bodied. Balanced acidity. Moderately extracted. Mildly tannic. Blueberries, chocolate. Extraordinarily aromatic, with deep, dark flavors that feature a haunting blueberry quality. Rich and supple in the mouth, with fantastic concentration. Seductive.

Weinbau Johann & Christine Baurel
Gruner Veltliner, Jochinger-Pichl Point, Smaragd, Wachau 1997 .16% rs. $21. **86**
Medium yellow-straw hue. Medium-bodied. Balanced acidity. Moderately extracted. Yeast, pears, minerals. Engaging aromas. Fresh, fruity, clean flavors open up and linger on the finish.

Weinbau Beck
Sylvaner, Trockenbeerenauslese, Neusiedlersee 1995 19.5% rs. $29/375 ml. **83**

Weingut Beck
Pannobile, Weiss, Trocken, Neusiedlersee 1995 .13% rs. $18. **90**
Brilliant yellow-gold. Moderately full-bodied. Full acidity. Highly extracted. Moderately oaked. Oak spice, figs, butter. Rich, spicy aromas do not disappoint on the palate. Concentrated flavors, with a dry finish. Linear, clean acidity.

Weingut Braunstein
Oxhoft Red, Trocken, Neusiedlersee 1994 .15% rs. $11. **83**

Weingut Paul Braunstein
Gewürztraminer, Trocken, Neusiedlersee 1997 .2% rs. $9. **83**
Oxhoft, Weiss, Trocken, Neusiedlersee 1996 .15% rs. $9. **86**
Bright golden yellow. Moderately full-bodied. Balanced acidity. Moderately extracted. Moderately oaked. Vanilla, smoke, citrus. Attractive smoky aromas follow through on the palate, with a toasty flavor profile and razor-sharp lemony flavors through the finish.
Blaufrankisch, Oxhoft, Neusiedlersee 1993 .15% rs. $13. **87**
Deep black ruby cast. Full-bodied. Full acidity. Highly extracted. Heavily oaked. Mildly tannic. Vanilla, minerals, red fruits. Shows a hefty oak overlay to the nose, with a flavorful, though firmly structured palate. Lean and intense through the finish. Will work well at the table.

Weingut Brundlmayer
Gruner Veltliner, Alte Reben, Trocken, Kamptal 1997 .3% rs. $29. **93**
Bright yellow-gold. Medium-bodied. Balanced acidity. Moderately extracted. Nectarines, sweet herbs, flowers. Delightfully fruity aromas. Rich, rounded and glycerous, yet not fat. Drinking nicely now.

Riesling, Alte Reben, "Zobinger Heiligenstein," Trocken,
Kamptal 1996 .3% rs. $35.   86

Pale yellow-gold. Medium-bodied. Full acidity. Moderately extracted. Tropical fruits, lemons, minerals. Rather ripe and expressive aromas follow through on the palate, with dry mineral character distinguishing the finish.

Winzerhof R. Brundlmayer

Pinot Blanc, Ried Holzweg, Donauland 1997 .08% rs. $25.   84

Very pale straw. Moderately light-bodied. Full acidity. Subtly extracted. Yeast. Interesting yeasty qualities. Floral nose. Tart, angular, and lean.

Domane Chorherren

Chardonnay, Ried Jungherren, Auslese, Lieblich, Wien 1996 2.35% rs. $21.   94

Dark golden yellow. Moderately full-bodied. Full acidity. Highly extracted. Exotic botrytis aromas have a powerful, spicy accent. Lush, rich, and rounded, with extravagant mouthfeel and depth, yet almost bone dry without being austere.

Traminer, Ried Gebhardin, Auslese, Wien 1996 2.61% rs. $23.   91

Deep golden yellow. Moderately full-bodied. Balanced acidity. Moderately extracted. Ripe lychee, spice, tropical fruits. Lush, ripe aromas. Generous, glycerous mouthfeel suggests an Alsatian late-harvest style. Outstanding.

Weingut Christ

Gruner Veltliner, Trocken, Wien 1997 .09% rs. $12.70.   NR
Weissburgunder, Spatlese Jungwinzer-Edition, Wien 1997 % rs. $18.   83
Sauvignon Blanc, Breiten, Trocken, Wien 1997 .34% rs. $17.30.   NR

Weingut Deiblhof

Blauer Burgunder/ St. Laurent, Langenlois, Trocken,
Kamptal 1997 .09% rs. $25.   NR

Dinstlgut Loiben

Riesling, Loibner Loibenberg, Lieblich, Wachau 1997 1.38% rs. $30.   88

Pale green straw. Medium-bodied. Balanced acidity. Moderately extracted. Green herbs, citrus, fusel. Herbal-tinged aromas lead a flavorsome, ripe palate showing some residual sweetness that makes for a rounded style.

Hans Diwald

Gruner Veltliner, Spatlese, Trocken, Donauland 1997 .11% rs. $11.50. 84

Pale straw hue. Medium-bodied. Full acidity. Moderately extracted. Dried herbs, minerals, citrus. Perfumed nose. Very lively and tart, with a snappy, mineral-dominated finish.

Peter Dolle

Gruner Veltliner, Strasser Gaisberg, Trocken Auslese,
Kamptal 1996 .61% rs. $12.   88

Deep gold. Full-bodied. Full acidity. Highly extracted. Spiced pears, lemons, earth. Sensational late-harvest aromas. Exotic botrytized flavors are kept in check by bright acids. Profoundly complex and assertive in style.

Weissburgunder, Trocken, Kamptal 1996 .55% rs. $10.   NR
Riesling, Strasser Gaisberg, Trocken, Kamptal 1997 .36% rs. $13.   89

Brilliant pale gold. Moderately full-bodied. Full acidity. Moderately extracted. Tart pineapple, citrus, minerals. Exotic floral aromas lead a wonderfully concentrated, pure palate with a lingering finish. This has the structure to age.

Riesling, Strasser Gaisberg "Oscar," Trocken, Kamptal 1997 .67% rs. $16. **88**
Bright yellow-gold. Moderately full-bodied. Full acidity. Highly extracted. Green apples, dried herbs. Crisp aromas lead a solid, glycerous mouthfeel with bright fruit-zest flavors lingering through the finish.

Weinbau Dopler

Cabernet Sauvignon, Selection, Barrique, Thermenregion 1996 .51% rs. $35. **83**
Blauer Portugieser, Halbtrocken, Thermenregion 1997 $11. **84**
Bright red-purple. Medium-bodied. Subtly extracted. Mildly tannic. Raspberry. Light-framed, supple, and juicy, with bright red fruit flavors lingering briefly. A quaffer.

Weingut Josef Ehmoser

Gruner Veltliner, Hohenberg Vollreife Trauben,
Donauland 1997 .1% rs. $16. **86**
Pale golden hue. Medium-bodied. Balanced acidity. Moderately extracted. Peach, nectarine, sweet herbs. Succulent and juicy, showing a sweet herbal note, with some fruit sweetness that gives way to a lean, minerally finish.

Josef und Rosalia Ernst

Goldburger, Ausbruch, Neusiedlersee-Hugelland 1994 19.3% rs. $22/375 ml. **84**
Yellow. Moderately light-bodied. Low acidity. Subtly extracted. Glazed apple, pear, earth. Soft texture. A bit funky, with gamey, wild aromatics. The slight dirty feel seems to overcast the pretty fruit flavors.

Erzherzog Johann Weine

Pinot Gris, Exklusiv, Steirischer, Kabinett, Trocken,
Sudsteiermark 1997 .8% rs. $15. **84**
Bright pale gold. Medium-bodied. Balanced acidity. Moderately extracted. Apples, minerals. Crisp, juicy and snappy. A lighthearted style, very appealing.

Weingut Fabian

Chardonnay, Trocken, Neusiedlersee 1997 .41% rs. $8. **NR**

Weingut Feiler-Artinger

Neuburger, Auslese, Neusiedlersee 1993 2.45% rs. $19. **90**
Full golden yellow. Moderately full-bodied. Balanced acidity. Moderately extracted. Lychee, spice. Spicy, aromatic varietal aromas show a degree of ripeness that follows through on the palate. Generous texture and flavors. Oily mouthfeel is a plus.

Weissburgunder, Auslese, Suss, Neusiedlersee 1993 4.83% rs. $20. **92**
Bright golden yellow. Moderately full-bodied. Balanced acidity. Moderately extracted. Honey, apples. Lush, juicy flavors. Unctuous. Mouthfilling and weighty, with serious concentration of flavors.

Ruster Ausbruch, Neusiedlersee 1996 11.88% rs. $38/375 ml. **95**
Deep yellow-gold. Medium-bodied. Full acidity. Moderately extracted. Burnt butter, glazed pear, dried herbs, earth. Soft texture. Rancio notes fill the palate. Elegant, slightly buttery entry brings a measure of lush fruit with brighter acidity. Rich and smooth into the finish. Certainly one that will age beautifully.

Pinot Noir, Ruster Ausbruch Essenz,
Neusiedlersee 1995 26.2% rs. $96/375 ml. **90**
Dark golden orange. Full-bodied. Candied tropical fruits. Thick, viscous, and cloying, with glycerin the keynote. Piercing acids do not quite cut through the richness of this wine, making for a rich, fat style that's a dessert in itself.

Weinberghof Fritsch

Gruner Veltliner, Ried Schlossberg Stockstall Trocken, Perfektion, Donauland 1997 .2% rs. $20. **86**

Deep golden hue. Medium-bodied. Balanced acidity. Moderately extracted. Peach, apples, minerals. Floral nose. Fresh, cleanly made. Mildly sweet up front, with a snappy, minerally finish.

Riesling, Perfektion, Trocken, Donauland 1997 .25% rs. $18. **86**

Pale straw. Medium-bodied. Full acidity. Moderately extracted. Citrus, minerals. Zesty, chalky aromas reveal a squeaky-clean palate with a lean, crisp character through the finish.

Blauer Burgunder, Perfektion, Donauland 1996 .1% rs. $30. **81**

Familie Gangl

Blaufrankisch, Schilfwein, Neusiedlersee 1994 16.8% rs. $30/375 ml. **89**

Deep amber cast. Full-bodied. Full acidity. Moderately extracted. Roasted nuts, caramel. Shows a slight Sherried note to the nose. Full, rich, and flavorful on the palate, with a distinctive nutty quality. Firm acidity counterbalances the sweetness through the finish.

Welschriesling, Trockenbeerenauslese, Neusiedlersee 1991 24.9% rs. $30/375 ml. **NR**

Weingut Gesellmann

Zweigelt, Mittelburgenland 1997 .11% rs. $10. **81**

Opus Eximium, Cuvée no.9, Mittelburgenland 1996 .14% rs. $20. **81**

Pinot Noir, Siglos, Mittelburgenland 1995 .18% rs. $25. **83**

Chardonnay, Trockenbeerenauslese, Mittelburgenland 1995 21.46% rs. $42/375 ml. **95**

Bright golden orange. Full-bodied. Full acidity. Pineapple, mandarins. Complex aromas. Cheesy, yeasty nose, slightly muted. High-toned acids, with thick, syrupy sweetness. Plenty of glycerin and weight, with a lingering, juicy, sweet finish. Great acidity on the finish. Searingly bright acids cut through the honeyed richness. Bold, complex.

Geyerhof

Malvasier, Kremstal 1997 .14% rs. $15. **83**

Weingut Walter Glatzer

Gruner Veltliner, Dornen Vogel, Carnuntum 1997 .18% rs. $15. **84**

Pale straw hue. Medium-bodied. Full acidity. Moderately extracted. Dried herbs, minerals, earth. Aromatically complex, with earthy depth that follows through well on the lighter-styled palate. Bright citrus flavors, with a lingering goüt de terroir.

Weissburgunder, Reservé, Trocken, Carnuntum 1996 .14% rs. $22. **88**

Deep golden yellow. Moderately full-bodied. Full acidity. Highly extracted. Smoke, butter, vanilla. Rich, rounded, and full, with a distinctly buttery flavor, cut by acidity. Quite an unusual wine.

Gotinsprun, Carnuntum 1996 .2% rs. $30. **89**

Saturated purple. Moderately full-bodied. Highly extracted. Mildly tannic. Cassis, black fruits. Jammy, herbal aromas. Well macerated and extracted. Thick, glycerous mouthfeel. Deep, ripe expression.

Weingut Familie Goldenits

Goldburger, Trockenbeerenauslese, Neusiedlersee 1995 13.72% rs. $30/375 ml. **96**

Brilliant yellow-gold. Full-bodied. Full acidity. Spice, caramelized fruit. Pungent botrytis nose follows through on the palate. Warm, spicy finish. Acids give this balance and structure. Very complex; not overly sweet.

Weingut Sepp Grassl

Chardonnay, Bodenglauber Trockenbeerenauslese,
Neusiedlersee 1995 25.3% rs. $70/375 ml.   82

Ewald Gruber

Gruner Veltliner Spatlese, Weinvertel 1997 .33% rs. $14.50.   82

Weingut Harald Haimer

Weissburgunder, Poysdorfer, Kabinett, Trocken,
Weinviertel 1997 .25% rs. $10.   82

Weinbau Hammer

Ruster Ausbruch, Pinot Cuvée, Neusiedlersee 1995 13% rs. $50/375 ml.   83
Ruster Ausbruch, Pinot Cuvée, Neusiedlersee 1993 12% rs. $55/375 ml.   95

Deep orange-gold. Moderately full-bodied. Full acidity. Spice, caramelized fruit. Toasty, botrytis-influenced aromas. Concentrated and very spicy through the finish. Finishes with dryness and acidity standing out. Very structured and intense, this should develop with further age.

Hasenohrl

Rotgipfler Auslese, Thermenregion 1995 22% rs. $40.   88

Deep yellow-gold luster. Moderately full-bodied. Full acidity. Highly extracted. Pears, sweet lemon cream. Rich, honeyed aromas follow through on the palate, showing glycerous mouthfeel and very bright acidity that tames the sweetness. Well structured, this should age gracefully.

Haus Marienberg

St. Laurent, Neusiedlersee 1994 .16% rs. $23.   86

Saturated ruby purple. Medium-bodied. Highly extracted. Moderately tannic. Dried herbs, red berries. Powerful, herbal aromas. Solid and structured, showing thick red berry flavors and dry tannins on the finish.

HM-I Cuvée, Neusiedlersee 1995 .2% rs. $24.   86

Full ruby cast. Medium-bodied. Moderately extracted. Mildly tannic. Sweet red fruits. Elegant aromas. Concentrated flavors, with a supple, textured mouthfeel and juicy flavors through the finish.

Welschriesling, Eiswein, Neusiedlersee 1996 13% rs. $32/375 ml.   84

Bright gold. Moderately light-bodied. Low acidity. Subtly extracted. Apple, pear, cream. Fat, soft texture. Quite smooth and oily, with a flat profile. Nearly cloying, yet rich fruit is not too sugared.

Chardonnay, Trockenbeerenauslese, Neusiedlersee 1996 20% rs. $30/375 ml. 89

Bright golden yellow. Full-bodied. Balanced acidity. Honey, topical fruit. Rich, honeyed aromas. Thick and nectarous, with a honeyed, viscous texture and fine concentration of tropical flavors. One glass only.

Weingut Ludwig Hiedler

Weissburgunder, Langenloiser Schenkenbichl, Halbtrocken,
Kamptal 1992 1.2% rs. $25.   85

Bright golden cast. Moderately full-bodied. Balanced acidity. Moderately extracted. Earth, wool, cream. Quite aromatic, with a complex, funky range of flavors that seem to have a touch of botrytis. Soft, lush, and generous in the mouth, with a big, full finish.

Familienweingut Egmont Hofinger

Gruner Veltliner, Gobelsburger Spatlese, Kamptal 1997 .09% rs. $14. 86

Full gold. Moderately full-bodied. Balanced acidity. Moderately extracted. Peach, grapefruit. Ripe aromas. Mildly sweet and generously fruity flavors linger through the finish. Distinguished by a fine glycerous mouthfeel.

Gruner Veltliner, Gobelsburger Kabinett, Kamptal 1997 .07% rs. $16. NR

Riesling, "Zobinger Heiligenstein" Kabinett, Kamptal 1997 .11% rs. $18. 83

Hofkellerei Stiftung Furst Liechtenstein

Gruner Veltliner, Clos Domaine, Weinviertel 1997 .1% rs. $18. NR

Rheinriesling, Spatlese, Clos Domaine, Weinviertel 1997 .3% rs. $18. 81

Anberola Merlot, Clos Domaine, Weinviertel 1995 .18% rs. $27. 82

Weingut A. Hollerer

Eiswein Cuvée, Riede Stein, Engabrunn, Krems 1992 10.1% rs. $30/375 ml. 89

Deep gold. Medium-bodied. Balanced acidity. Highly extracted. Tropical fruits, flowers, fresh sweet herbs, minerals, walnuts. Soft, smooth texture. Lovely fresh, floral, spicy aromatics. Silky and unctuous, with a splendid range of lush flavors. Quite dramatic as it slowly intensifies.

Hopler

Gewürztraminer, Trocken, Neusiedlersee 1996 .5% rs. $13. 88

Bright yellow-gold. Medium-bodied. Balanced acidity. Moderately extracted. Nuts, lychee, citrus. Spicy, varietally expressive aromas show a touch of earth, leading a taut yet flavorsome palate with a bright acids lingering on the finish.

Gruner Veltliner, Rieden-Verschnitt Kabinett, Trocken, Neusiedlersee 1996 .09% rs. $9. 86

Bright green-gold. Medium-bodied. Full acidity. Moderately extracted. Yeast, dried herbs, citrus. Complex earthy aromatics follow through on the palate, with a focused, flavorful character. Taut and precise through the finish.

Pinot Blanc, Privat Reservé, Halbtrocken, Neusiedlersee 1995 .97% rs. $12. 89

Deep golden straw hue. Moderately full-bodied. Balanced acidity. Highly extracted. Caramelized apples, spices. Rich, late-harvest aromas. Juicy, luscious and ripe, showing generous flavors. Somewhere between a dessert wine and a table wine.

Sauvignon Blanc, Kabinett, Trocken, Neusiedlersee 1997 .3% rs. $12. NR

Pinot Noir, Trocken, Neusiedlersee 1996 .5% rs. $12. NR

Ausbruch, Noble Reservé, Neusiedlersee 1981 13.5% rs. $20/375 ml. 99

Dark reddish gold, with a copper cast. Medium-bodied. Balanced acidity. Moderately extracted. Dark honey, citrus peel, Mission fig, apricot. Moderately rich texture. Forward and somewhat lively entry of rich, honeyed fruits and light mineral notes. For all the sweetness, there is an elegant, bright side that makes this most attractive. Great depth and maturity is evident. Has an Oloroso Sherry-like profile.

Pinot Blanc, Trockenbeerenauslese, Neusiedlersee 1995 15.1% rs. $30/375 ml. 89

Deep golden straw. Full-bodied. Full acidity. Smoke, tropical fruits. Elegant, smoky aromas follow through on the palate. Wonderfully complex and integrated, this is drinking well now, though bright acids will allow it to cellar.

House of Hafner

Samling 88, Trockenbeerenauslese, Burgenland 1995 19.5% rs. $72/375 ml. 88

Bright golden yellow. Moderately full-bodied. Full acidity. Highly extracted. Apricots, honey. Spicy, honeyed aromas. Vibrant and sweet in a juicy manner that lingers through a long finish. Fine balance and structure.

Samling 88, Trockenbeerenauslese, Burgenland 1996 18.6% rs. $78/375 ml.   **88**
Brilliant orange-gold. Full-bodied. Full acidity. Earth, smoke, caramelized fruit. Complex, smoky aromas lead a vibrant, structured palate with intense flavors through the finish. A pungent, forceful style that may overwhelm some palates.

Chardonnay, Barrique, Trockenbeerenauslese,
Burgenland 1996 17.1% rs. $86/375 ml.   **99**
Bright golden yellow. Full-bodied. Full acidity. Smoke, citrus. Astonishingly smoky and complex on the nose. Lush and vibrant, showing fine structure and length. This is drinking well now, but the acids suggest that it will improve. Intense and structured, with layers of oak spice and smoke. Exotic.

Weingut Hermann Huber

Strasser Chardonnay, Trocken, Kamptal 1997 .18% rs. $13.30.   **87**
Pale straw cast. Medium-bodied. Full acidity. Moderately extracted. Lemons, tart citrus fruits. Eye-closing acidity and strong, austere citrus flavors make this assertive. Serious purity and intensity of flavors are the keynotes.

Riesling, Stasser Gaisberg, Trocken, Kamptal 1997 .65% rs. $17.10.   **86**
Very pale green-gold. Moderately light-bodied. Full acidity. Subtly extracted. Lemons. Floral, perfumed aromas lead a very tart, angular palate with piercing acids.

Strasser Sauvignon Blanc, Ried Grub, Trocken, Kamptal 1997 .18% rs. $14. **82**

Weingut Hutter

Riesling, Ried Loibenberg Smaragd, Trocken, Wachau 1997 .1% rs. $40.   **86**
Pale gold. Medium-bodied. Full acidity. Moderately extracted. Grapefruit, minerals. Perfumed, zesty aromas lead a concentrated, citrusy palate with intensity of flavors through the finish.

Weingut Josef Jamek

Weissburgunder, Spatlese Ried Hochrain, Wachau 1997 .07% rs. $30.   **84**
Pale straw. Moderately full-bodied. Balanced acidity. Moderately extracted. Lemons, minerals. Full, alcohol-influenced mouthfeel, with a warm, spicy finish. Neutral in flavor, though it remains bright.

Johanneshof Reinisch

Chardonnay, Reservé, Trocken, Thermenregion 1996 .01% rs. $21.   **81**
Pinot Blanc, Trocken, Thermenregion 1996 .01% rs. $10.50.   **81**
Zweigelt, Thermenregion 1996 .01% rs. $12.   **86**
Pale cherry red. Moderately light-bodied. Subtly extracted. Mildly tannic. Herbs, minerals. Vapid flavors. Lean and crisp, with little intensity or richness. Ripe flavors on entry turn herbal and lean through the finish.

Chardonnay, Trockenbeerenauslese,
Thermenregion 1995 13% rs. $58/375 ml.   **95**
Dark orange. Full-bodied. Full acidity. Highly extracted. Lees, marmalade, caramelized fruit. Earthy, spicy aromas. Full-throttled style with piercing acidity and an impressively sweet entry that fades on the finish, leaving a drier sensation. Wonderful leesy, smoky nose. Complexity of aromas is fully reflected on the palate. Bright acidity. Lots of spice comes through on the finish. Evident oak influence.

Weingut Juris

Chardonnay, Golser Altenberg, Neusiedlersee 1997 .29% rs. $22.   **81**
St. Georg, Neusiedlersee 1996 .18% rs. $37.   **86**
Bright cherry red. Medium-bodied. Moderately extracted. Mildly tannic. Red cherries, vanilla. Fragrant, ripe aromas show oak accents. Rich, supple, and juicy, with a sweet oak note on the finish. For near-term drinking.

Scale: Superlative (96-100), Exceptional (90-95), Highly Recommended (85-89), Recommended (80-84), Not Recommended (Under 80)

St. Laurent, Neusiedlersee 1996 .22% rs. $40. 89

Magenta appearance. Medium-bodied. Full acidity. Moderately extracted. Herbs, tart red fruits. Crisp, ripe aromas follow through on the palate. Short, minerally finish. Generous mouthfeel is a plus.

Pinot Noir, Trocken, Neusiedlersee 1996 .19% rs. $40. 84

Pale ruby. Moderately light-bodied. Moderately extracted. Mildly oaked. Minerals, red fruits, oak spice. Lean, vibrant style, with zesty acids. Tannins are very muted, but this has good acidic, minerally grip.

Kaisergarten

Trockenbeerenauslese, Neusiedlersee 1995 17.22% rs. $29/375 ml. 84

Deep golden straw. Full-bodied. Full acidity. Tropical fruit. Cheesy, complex aromas. Thick, luxurious mouthfeel. Fine, juicy fruit flavors stay on the right side of cloying.

Symphonie, Trockenbeerenauslese, Neusiedlersee 1997 21.9% rs. $30/375 ml. 89

Bright yellow-straw color. Full-bodied. Balanced acidity. Apples, pears. Thick, syrupy, and luxurious, with an accent on clean, tropical flavors. Flavors are impressive but straightforward.

Seewinkler Impressionen, Trockenbeerenauslese, Neusiedlersee NV 14.1% rs. $32/375 ml. 84

Dark copper-orange. Full-bodied. Balanced acidity. Highly extracted. Earth, sweet orange. Aromas are unpromising, yet the flavors are better, showing a thick, caramelized character.

Weinhaus Kaisergarten

Ausbruch, Seewinkler Impressionen, Neusiedlersee 1991 17.76% rs. $11/375 ml. 86

Dark reddish gold, with an amber cast. Full-bodied. Balanced acidity. Highly extracted. Dark honey, molasses, apricot, golden raisin. Fat, broad texture. Quite viscous and heavy on the palate. Supports a good measure of rich flavors, with a nice spike of brown spice. Almost one to serve in a spoon.

Paul Kerschbaum

Blaufrankisch, Ried Durrau Trocken, Mittelburgenland 1996 .09% rs. $18. NR

Weingut Kollwentz-Romerhof

Steinzeiler, Neusiedlersee 1995 .02% rs. $55. 88

Saturated red-purple. Medium-bodied. Highly extracted. Mildly tannic. Flowers, tart red berries, minerals. High-toned, floral aromas lead a dense palate of red fruit flavors, with edgy tannins on the finish. Solid and structured, this will complement rich foods.

Weissburgunder, Beerenauslese, Burgenland 1996 13% rs. $40/375 ml. 99

Deep golden orange. Full-bodied. Balanced acidity. Peach, pineapple, bacon fat. Rich, complex, luxurious, smoky aromas show strong botrytis influence. Very thick and decadently sweet flavors fill the palate, with juicy fruit flavors lingering. Very intense, yet well balanced. Not overly sweet, with an exotic toasted-oak component that will please dessert-wine connoisseurs.

Chardonnay-Welschriesling, Trockenbeerenauslese, Neusiedlersee 1996 21% rs. $80/375 ml. 97

Deep orange-yellow. Moderately full-bodied. Balanced acidity. Tropical fruits, yeast. Smoky, yeasty aromas. Thick and succulent, sweet and nectarous. Extravagantly yeasty throughout. Sublime balance. Smoky, oak aromas follow through on the palate, with a lingering burnt-wood note. Very complex and distinctive. Fantastically rich. Outstanding structure.

Weingut Gunter Krikler

Weissburgunder, Trocken, Neusiedlersee 1997 .47% rs. $18.　　　81
Eiswein Cuvée, Neusiedlersee 1997 11.1% rs. $30/375 ml.　　　87

Yellow, with a pale orange cast. Medium-bodied. Balanced acidity. Moderately extracted. Apple, melon, orange. Mild texture. The lovely fresh floral fragrance offers a sensuous backdrop for lively, brisk fruit flavors. Somewhat like a fresh fruit salad, this will make delightful service for summertime refreshment.

Weingut Krutzler

Perwolff, Sudburgenland 1996 .09% rs. $29.　　　84

Saturated red-purple. Medium-bodied. Moderately extracted. Moderately tannic. Dried herbs, minerals. Lean herbal aromas follow through on the palate. Finishes with minerally austerity.

Weingut Kummer-Schuster

Weissburgunder, Beerenauslese, Neusiedlersee 1995 8.87% rs. $20/375 ml.　　89

Bright golden yellow. Moderately full-bodied. Full acidity. Pineapples, citrus. Honeyed aromas lead a luxuriant mouthfeel, with bright acids giving this focus. Spice and warmth come through on the finish.

Lackner-Tinnacher

Weissburgunder, Kabinett, Lage Steinbach, Trocken,
Sudsteiermark 1997 .6% rs. $20.　　　81
Grauburgunder, Eiswein, Sudsteiermark 1997 13.9% rs. $51/375 ml.　　　90

Medium gold. Moderately light-bodied. Balanced acidity. Moderately extracted. Fresh herbs, cantaloupe, pear. Moderately vibrant texture. A late-harvest style, without the richness of a dessert wine. Quite juicy and succulent, with the briskness of a table wine.

Lang

Chardonnay, Ausbruch, Neusiedlersee 1995 11.95% rs. $29/375 ml.　　　88

Bright golden straw. Moderately full-bodied. Full acidity. Honey, peach, rancio. Spicy, honeyed aromas. Outstanding acidity tears through the sugars, leaving a spicy finish that lingers. Delicious now, though this has the structure to improve.

Ausbruch, Chardonnay Barrique,
Neusiedlersee 1994 14.43% rs. $40/375 ml.　　　100

Deep bright gold. Medium-bodied. Balanced acidity. Moderately extracted. Earth, minerals, apples, pear, brown spice, browned butter. Soft texture. Broad palate replete with smoky, rich spices and a deep, earthy profile. Offers ample creamy fruit flavors and light nuttiness. Has intensity, into a lush finish. Rich rancio notes add character to the sheer power. Quite complex and fascinating.

Pinot Blanc, Ausbruch, Neusiedlersee 1991 11.85% rs. $40/375 ml.　　　97

Dark gold. Moderately full-bodied. Full acidity. Smoke, spice, tropical fruits. Botrytis-influenced aromas reveal an angular yet sweet palate with a snappy finish. Powerful, smoky, and intense.

Welschriesling, Trockenbeerenauslese,
Neusiedlersee 1995 26.2% rs. $32/375 ml.　　　95

Dark golden orange. Full-bodied. Balanced acidity. Honey, caramelized tropical fruits. Generous, fat aromas have a honeyed character. Thick and nectarous, yet with enough acidity to remain juicy on the finish. Pungently spicy nose. Complex and intense. Syrupy, yet has juicy acids. A full-throttled style that may develop further.

Samling 88, Trockenbeerenauslese,
Neusiedlersee 1994 18.53% rs. $33/375 ml.   **89**

Deep golden straw. Moderately full-bodied. Pears, apples, caramelized fruit. Exotic, fruity aromas. Clean, pure, concentrated fruit flavors with supporting acids.

Chardonnay, Trockenbeerenauslese,
Neusiedlersee 1995 24.66% rs. $35/375 ml.   **94**

Medium golden orange. Full-bodied. Full acidity. Caraway. Pungently spicy, rather unusual. Fantastically concentrated and unctuous. Acids keep a sense of liveliness through the finish. Heavy botrytis influence. High-toned acids are matched by intense fruit-salad flavors. Very unctuous and sweet.

Welschriesling, Trockenbeerenauslese,
Neusiedlersee 1994 22.5% rs. $35/375 ml.   **94**

Deep golden orange. Full-bodied. Low acidity. Tropical fruits, smoke, orange blossom. Decadent aromas. Rich and luxuriant, showing an unctuous texture and whopping sweetness, with smoky complexity. Cloying but nectarous. A sweet, honeyed, viscous style. Luxurious, but not for keeping.

Samling 88, Trockenbeerenauslese,
Neusiedlersee 1995 28.76% rs. $56/375 ml.   **88**

Bright orange-gold. Full-bodied. Low acidity. Apricots, papaya. Heavy, honeyed aromas. A huge mouthful of butter and glycerin, with whopping sugar levels. Very impressive, though one small glass is all you need.

Weingut Josef Leberl

Sauvignon Blanc, Beerenauslese, Neusiedlersee 1996 6% rs. $28/375 ml.   **87**

Medium yellow-gold. Moderately full-bodied. Balanced acidity. Citrus zest, minerals. Zesty, clean aromas follow through on the palate. High-toned citric sweetness is accompanied by minerally snap that keeps the sweetness subdued on the finish.

Melitta & Matthias Leitner

Pannobile, Weiss, Trocken, Neusiedlersee 1995 .02% rs. $25.   **86**

Dark yellow-gold. Moderately full-bodied. Balanced acidity. Highly extracted. Butter, oak spice. Rich, developed aromas follow through on a thick, rounded palate with some bright acids cutting through the butter and oak spice flavors.

Pannobile, Rot, Neusiedlersee 1995 .21% rs. $25.   **84**

Bright ruby red. Medium-bodied. Moderately extracted. Red fruits, herbs. High-toned aromas follow through well. Lively, bright, fruity flavors linger through the finish. Nice mouthfeel.

Weingut Franz Lentsch

Beerenauslese, Cuvée-Barrique, Neusiedlersee 1995 10.73% rs. $25/375 ml.   **93**

Bright orange-gold. Moderately full-bodied. Moderately extracted. Tropical fruits, peaches. Full, sweaty aromas. Juicy, thick mouthfeel is contrasted by good acids. Finishes with minerally persistence. Well balanced. Exotically spicy and smoky. Not too sweet. This is outstanding now, yet may develop with further age. Should appeal to all Sauternes lovers.

Trockenbeerenauslese Cuvée, Neusiedlersee 1995 15.3% rs. $28/375 ml.   **89**

Bright golden yellow. Moderately full-bodied. Full acidity. Tropical fruits, ginger. Exotic and pure, with outstanding concentration that makes for a very long finish. Has a spicy theme. Well structured.

Weingut Leth

Traminer, Classic, Halbtrocken, Donauland 1997 1.1% rs. $19.　　84

Pale yellow-gold. Medium-bodied. Balanced acidity. Moderately extracted. Butter, flowers. Soft, perfumed aromas lead a rounded, spicy palate with a buttery feel through a warm finish.

Gruner Veltliner, Felser Scheiben Trocken, Donauland 1997 .19% rs. $18.　89

Bright golden straw. Moderately full-bodied. Full acidity. Moderately extracted. Pear, grapefruit, minerals. Fragrant, citrus-edged aromas. Full-flavored style with a glycerous mouthfeel and a touch of sweetness that balances well with the lively acids.

Weissburgunder, Classic, Trocken, Donauland 1997 .67% rs. $18.　　82

Weingut Othmar u. Josefine Mad

Weissburgunder, Kabinett "Ambrosi,"
Neusiedlersee-Hugelland 1997 .1% rs. $10.　　83

Cabernet-Merlot, Ambrosi, Barrique Trocken,
Neusiedlersee 1995 .21% rs. $18.　　82

Weingut Malat

Rheinriesling, Trockenbeerenauslese, Kremstal 1996 22.1% rs. $70/375 ml.　95

Bright golden orange. Full-bodied. Full acidity. Pineapple, figs. Sherried aromas have a figgy note. Fine acids give a refreshing finish for such sweetness. Outstanding concentration, with a long, long finish.

Weingut Mantlerhof

Gruner Veltliner, Loss-Terrassen Auslese, Gedersdorf-Kremstsl 1997 $31.　94

Deep golden yellow. Moderately full-bodied. Full acidity. Highly extracted. Citrus, earth, minerals. Rich, ripe aromas. Rounded, oily texture with lively acids through the finish. Broad-shouldered, opulent style.

Markowitsch

Gruner Veltliner, Beerenauslese Gedersdorf, Kremstal 1995 $30/375 ml.　86

Deep golden orange. Moderately full-bodied. Full acidity. Caramelized orange, minerals, smoke. Rich, faintly sweaty aromas. Smoky, minerally backbone with caramelized fruit flavors through a dry finish. Acids remain bright through the finish.

Markowitsch

Chardonnay, Reservé, Trocken, Carnuntum 1996 .19% rs. $17.　　81
Riesling, Spatlese, Steindl, Kremstal 1996 .58% rs. $31.　　93

Brilliant yellow-gold. Moderately full-bodied. Full acidity. Highly extracted. Fusel, tart apricots. Exotic, tropical Riesling aromas with petrol notes. Solidly structured and forceful in the mouth, this will age benignly.

Sauvignon Blanc, Trocken, Carnuntum 1997 .39% rs. $15.　　84

Very pale straw cast. Medium-bodied. Full acidity. Moderately extracted. Tart tropical fruits, minerals, herbs. High-toned tropical Sauvignon Blanc aromas follow through on a very acidic palate, with intense flavors that fade quickly.

Rosenberg, Carnuntum 1996 .19% rs. $19.　　86

Saturated red-purple. Medium-bodied. Highly extracted. Mildly tannic. Herbs, red fruits, pepper. Very herbal, yet ripe aromas follow through on the palate. Lively and juicy, with an open-knit structure.

Weingut Familie Maurer

Chardonnay, Stoitzendorf-Sangerleiten, Trocken,
Weinviertel 1993 .12% rs. $12.　　NR

Scale: Superlative (96-100), Exceptional (90-95), Highly Recommended (85-89), Recommended (80-84), Not Recommended (Under 80)

Chardonnay, Stoitzendorf-Sangerleiten, Trocken,
Weinviertel 1997 .09% rs. $14.　　　　　　　　　　　81

Mayer am Pfarrplatz
Chardonnay, Nussberger Trocken, Wien 1997 .42% rs. $19.　　　82

Rheinriesling, Nussberger, Ried Preussen Trocken, Wien 1997 .36% rs. $21.　84

Pale gold. Medium-bodied. Full acidity. Moderately extracted. Apples, flowers, minerals. Floral aromas reveal clean flavors bolstered by lively acids. A lean and refreshing style.

Metternich-Sandor
Weissburgunder, Trocken, Kremstal 1997 .45% rs. $20.50.　　　89

Bright pale straw. Moderately full-bodied. Full acidity. Moderately extracted. Fusel, fresh herbs, lemons. Extraordinarily aromatic. Razor-sharp acids are perfectly balanced by the inherent oily richness of this wine. Focused, though not tart.

Weingut Sepp Moser
Chardonnay, Schnabel Barrique, Trocken, Kremstal 1996 .21% rs. $28.　　81

Gruner Veltliner, Breiter Rain, Kremstsl 1996 .18% rs. $34.　　　93

Bright yellow-gold. Medium-bodied. Balanced acidity. Moderately extracted. Sweet herbs, nectarine, ripe citrus. Exotic herbal aromas. Rich, rounded mouthfeel with good balancing acidity. Lifted by wonderful, pure, persistent fruit and herbal flavors.

Riesling, Beerenauslese, Kremstal 1995 12.96% rs. $80.　　　84

Bright golden yellow. Moderately full-bodied. Pears, apples. Clean, fruity aromas lead a thick, smooth mouthfeel with concentration of fruit flavors and acids giving fine intensity. Long finish. Acidity is a plus.

E & M Muller
Chardonnay, Ried Deutsche Weingarten, Spatlese,
Ottenberg 1993 .15% rs. $35.　　　　　　　　　　　NR

Pinot Gris, Kabinett, Ried Burgegg, Weststeiermark 1993 .13% rs. $30.　　95

Bright yellow-straw hue. Medium-bodied. Balanced acidity. Moderately extracted. Minerals, citrus oil. Very aromatic, smoky. Rounded, oily-textured mouthfeel, with bright acids through the finish. Showing some maturity.

Weingut Muller-Grossmann
Riesling, "Gottweiger Berg," Spatlese, Kremstal 1997 .63% rs. $25.　　NR

Johann Mullner
Gruner Veltliner Auslese, Weinzierlberg, Kremstal 1997 .15% rs. $25.　　89

Pale straw. Medium-bodied. Balanced acidity. Moderately extracted. Dried herbs, citrus, minerals. Ripe aromas reveal very intense, focused flavors, showing purity and length. Mouthfeel and texture are a standout, giving this palate presence.

Weingut Munzenrieder
Welschriesling, Trockenbeerenauslese,
Neusiedlersee 1995 16% rs. $53/375 ml.　　　　　　　89

Deep golden cast. Full-bodied. Balanced acidity. Highly extracted. Apricots, golden raisins, honey. Quite aromatic, with a wave of attractive flavors. Rich, fat, and round in the mouth, with a viscous quality. Lengthy finish.

G & R Nastl
Cuvée Scitamenta Vinitoris, Kamptal 1997 .42% rs. $22.　　　81

Naturnaher Weinbau Alfred Deim

Riesling, Schonberger, "Stoamandl "Trocken, Kamptal 1997 .06% rs. $15.   83

Weinbau Nekowitsch

The Red One, Schilfwein, Neusiedlersee 1996 29.3% rs. $55/375 ml.   83

Samling 88, Trockenbeerenauslese, Neusiedlersee 1996 29.3% rs. $38/375 ml. 87

Bright golden straw. Medium-bodied. Full acidity. Highly extracted. Smoke, peach. Smoky tropical aromas lead a smooth, juicy mouthfeel with a sense of balance that does not push it into the full-blown dessert category. This would show well with fruit-based desserts.

Weingut Ludwig Neumayer

Gruner Veltliner, Der Wein vom Stein, Traisental 1997 .5% rs. $32.   81

Weissburgunder, Halbtrocken, Traisental 1997 1.4% rs. $29.   90

Bright golden yellow. Medium-bodied. Balanced acidity. Tropical fruits, spice. Sweet and juicy up front, with a deft balance of acidity that keeps this in check through the finish. A soft, generous, ripe style.

Riesling, Trocken, Traisental 1997 .7% rs. $36.   84

Pale yellow-gold. Medium-bodied. Full acidity. Moderately extracted. Green apples. Crisp aromas. Very juicy flavors expand in the mouth. Refreshing, drinking well now.

Sauvignon Blanc, Auslese, Trocken, Traisental 1997 .8% rs. $30/375 ml.   94

Bright yellow-straw color. Medium-bodied. Balanced acidity. Moderately extracted. Gooseberries, herbs. Pure Sauvignon Blanc aromas. Extravagantly fruity flavors show a touch of sweetness that works well with the acidity. Oily mouthfeel.

Weingut Neumeister

Roter Traminer, Steintal Selektion, Sudoststeiermark 1997 .37% rs. $17.   83

Grauburgunder, Selektion, Trocken, Sudoststeiermark 1997 .5% rs. $16.   84

Medium straw. Moderately full-bodied. Balanced acidity. Moderately extracted. Citrus, glycerin. Weighty and rich in the mouth. Solidly structured, with a clean, acidic snap on the finish.

Morillon, Selektion, Trocken, Sudoststeiermark 1997 .47% rs. $17.   83

Sauvignon Blanc, Selektion, Sudoststeiermark 1997 .45% rs. $19.   84

Pale straw. Medium-bodied. Balanced acidity. Moderately extracted. Lemon zest, minerals. Rounded, glycerous mouthfeel, with puckering acidity on the finish. Clean and refreshing.

Weingut Neustifter

Gruner Veltliner, Exklisiv, Riede Hermannschachern,
Weinviertel 1997 .11% rs. $20.   90

Bright yellow-gold. Medium-bodied. Full acidity. Moderately extracted. Citrus, flowers, minerals. Exotic aromas display herbal, earthy complexity that follows through well on the palate. Intensely flavorful and concentrated, showing breed and class.

Nigl

Riesling, Senftenberger Piri Privat, Trocken, Kremstal 1997 $42.   84

Bright pale gold. Medium-bodied. Full acidity. Moderately extracted. Lemon zest. Floral, perfumed aromas lead a crisp mouthful of flavors that leave the palate refreshed.

Weingut Nittnaus

Pannobile, Golser Rotwein, Neusiedlersee 1993 .17% rs. $28.50. **89**

Saturated dark ruby. Moderately full-bodied. Highly extracted. Mildly tannic. Lead pencil, vanilla, black fruits. Deep aromas. Very concentrated and flavorsome, yet tannins are balanced and soft, with acids supplying the grip.

Weinbau Ochs

Welschriesling, Weiden am See, Eiswein,
Neusiedlersee 1997 11.58% rs. $15/375 ml. **86**

Platinum. Moderately light-bodied. Balanced acidity. Subtly extracted. Apple, green grape, minerals. Moderately light texture. Nearly crisp and lively feel with rich apple flavors, somewhat like cider. Fairly straightforward.

Blaufrankisch, Weiden am See, Eiswein,
Neusiedlersee 1997 10.88% rs. $16/375 ml. **82**

Weingut Opitz

Opitz One, Trockenbeerenauslese, Neusiedlersee 1994 18% rs. $80/375 ml. **84**

Deep red luster. Full-bodied. Low acidity. Earthy aromas. Thick, sweet, and nectarous. A cloying style with earthy undertones.

Goldackerl, Trockenbeerenauslese, Neusiedlersee 1995 16.5% rs. $85/375 ml. **89**

Deep golden yellow. Moderately full-bodied. Full acidity. Peaches, oranges. Honeyed aromas. Sensational concentration and depth, with purity of flavors and juicy acidity through the finish.

Weingut Martin Pasler

Gruner Veltliner, Neusiedlersee 1997 .11% rs. $11. **83**
Beerenauslese, Neusiedlersee 1996 10% rs. $13/375 ml. **82**
Trockenbeerenauslese, Neusiedlersee 1995 22.2% rs. $69/375 ml. **93**

Brilliant orange-gold. Full-bodied. Full acidity. Papaya, smoke. Honeyed, sweet, unctuous aromas follow through on the palate. Mellow and luxurious, this is for current drinking. Astoundingly deep, spicy aromas. Rich, lush, and unctuous flavors and mouthfeel, with enough acids to support the considerable weight.

Weingut R & A Pfaffl

Gruner Veltliner, Hundsleiten/Sandtal Trocken,
Weinvertel 1997 .21% rs. $15. **88**

Bright yellow-gold. Medium-bodied. Full acidity. Moderately extracted. Tropical fruits, minerals, spice. Deep aromas. Lean, intense and flavorful, with razor-sharp acids and a goût de terroir that shows breeding.

Riesling, Terrassen Sonnleiten, Lieblich, Weinviertel 1997 .19% rs. $15. **89**

Brilliant yellow-gold. Moderately full-bodied. Full acidity. Highly extracted. Earth, citrus oil, herbs. Aromatically deep. Broad, mouthfilling flavors show fine concentration and persistence. This has an ageworthy structure.

Sauvignon Blanc, Trocken, Spatlese, Weinviertel 1997 .54% rs. $16. **85**

Bright pale gold. Medium-bodied. Balanced acidity. Moderately extracted. Minerals, citrus zest, herbs. Bright, spicy aromas that show fine Sauvignon Blanc character. Rich, textured mouthfeel with an oily generosity and a broad, herbal flavor profile.

Weingut F.X. Pichler

Gruner Veltliner, M, Smaragd, Wachau 1997 .32% rs. $70. **89**

Medium yellow-straw hue. Medium-bodied. Balanced acidity. Moderately extracted. Sweet herbs, peach, minerals. Floral, high-toned aromas. Crisp minerally flavors with a spritzy mouthfeel. Lively and refreshing.

Weingut Gerhard Pittnauer
St. Laurent, Neusiedlersee 1995 .14% rs. $15.   **NR**

Weingut Pleil
Weissburgunder, Kabinett, Trocken, Weinviertel 1996 .13% rs. $16.   **80**

Weingut Josef Pleil
Chardonnay, Kabinett, Trocken, Weinviertel 1997 .66% rs. $17.   **89**

Pale metallic straw. Medium-bodied. Full acidity. Moderately extracted. Grapefruit zest, minerals. Riesling-like aromas. Bright and zesty, with un-Chardonnay character that does not lessen its appeal.

Chardonnay, Riede Gaisberg, Weinviertel 1997 $17.   **89**

Bright yellow-gold. Moderately full-bodied. Balanced acidity. Moderately extracted. Ripe apples, minerals. Rich and rounded, with sweet, fruity flavors lingering through the finish. Fine concentration of flavors and an emphasis on fruit.

Erich & Walter Polz
Sauvignon Blanc, Hochgrassnitzberg, Fassprobe 1997 .25% rs. $35.   **87**

Medium straw. Medium-bodied. Balanced acidity. Moderately extracted. Lemon cream, dried herbs. Fine, varietally expressive aromas. Lush, round, and almost fat by Austrian standards. This shows plenty of glycerin, with softer acids making for an easy-drinking style.

Weingut Prager
Gruner Veltliner, Weissenkirchner Ried Achleiten, Smaragd, Wachau 1997 .14% rs. $30.   **84**

Medium yellow-straw hue. Moderately full-bodied. Balanced acidity. Moderately extracted. Tropical fruit, citrus. Ripe aromas follow through on the palate with an oily, rich texture and a warm finish. This is substantial and thick. Lower acids exaggerate the thickness.

Riesling, Smaragd, Weissenkirchner Ried Klaus, Trocken, Wachau 1997 .39% rs. $38.   **87**

Medium yellow-gold. Medium-bodied. Full acidity. Moderately extracted. Minerals, citrus zest. Fresh, zesty aromas follow through on the palate, with a minerally backbone stretching through the finish. Well structured, this should age benignly.

Riesling, Smaragd Weissenkirchner Ried Steinriegl, Trocken, Wachau 1997 .7% rs. $38.   **88**

Pale straw. Medium-bodied. Full acidity. Moderately extracted. Green apples, minerals. Fresh, floral aromas lead a crisp, juicy palate with cleansing acidity lingering on the finish.

Weingut Familie Prieler
Chardonnay, Lage Seeberg-Schutzen, Trocken, Neusiedlersee 1995 .4% rs. $23.   **86**

Bright yellow-gold. Moderately full-bodied. Balanced acidity. Moderately extracted. Moderately oaked. Nuts, toasted oak, citrus. Attractive toasty aromas. Rich, spicy flavors show judicious oak influence. Textured, rounded mouthfeel. Long finish.

Cabernet Sauvignon, Neusiedlersee 1995 .13% rs. $13.   **90**

Full bright ruby red. Medium-bodied. Moderately extracted. Mildly tannic. Lead pencil, red fruits, minerals. Very aromatic, with high-toned fruity notes. Ripe, generous flavors and supple mouthfeel, with soft, balanced tannins lingering on the finish. Stylish, with acids providing grip and structure.

Blaufrankisch, Lage Goldberg, Trocken, Neusiedlersee 1994 .13% rs. $31.   **83**

Radetzky

Pinot Gris, Eiswein, Neusiedlersee 1995 9% rs. $20/375 ml.   **94**

Rich gold. Moderately full-bodied. Balanced acidity. Highly extracted. Creamy baked apple, flowers, dried herbs, citrus peel, earth. Rich texture. Lush and full on the palate. Smoky, earthy notes provide complexity. Loaded with rich flavors, this has great presence and concentration, with diverse components and nuances.

Trockenbeerenauslese Cuvée, Neusiedlersee 1995 12.5% rs. $20/375 ml.   **96**

Brilliant orange-gold. Full-bodied. Full acidity. Spice, caramelized tropical fruits. Exotic, spicy nose. Very complex and deep. Intense and concentrated, with wood spice and acids giving structure and complexity. Sauternes-style. Exotic, smoky aromas. Not too sweet, with bright acids, caramelized flavors, and a complex, smoky finish. Very stylish.

Pinot Blanc, Marsch, Trockenbeerenauslese,
Neusiedlersee 1995 13.5% rs. $25/375 ml.   **96**

Bright orange-gold. Full-bodied. Full acidity. Tropical fruit, citrus, spice. Honeyed, tropical aromas. Intense and spicy, with acids and sugars making for a focused, structured style. Highly impressive, showing a good acid/sugar balance.

Weinbau Christian Rainprecht

Chardonnay, Auslese, Suss, Neusiedlersee 1997 8.7% rs. $12/500 ml.   **84**

Bright yellow-gold. Medium-bodied. Moderately extracted. Honey, apples, nectarine. Attractive, honeyed aromas lead ripe, fruit-salad flavors with lush sweetness that maintains a natural balance with acids. Hedonistic.

Rulander, Auslese, Neusiedlersee 1995 6.7% rs. $12.   **85**

Dark golden luster. Moderately full-bodied. Full acidity. Dried herbs, grapefruit. Juicy acids and sweaty flavors make strange bedfellows. Herbal edge, with very pure citrus flavors. Shows a thick, viscous texture. A very distinctive style.

Neuburger, Trockenbeerenauslese, Neusiedlersee 1991 21.6% rs. $32/375 ml.   **93**

Deep orange-straw. Full-bodied. Full acidity. Peaches, apricots. Powerfully spicy, botrytized aromas lead a lush, tropical palate with a juicy theme. Racy acids support the thickness and sweetness. Flavors show a clean, fruity accent, though this has whopping sugar levels.

Franz Reindl

Weissburgunder, Spatlese, Trocken, Thermenregion 1997 .31% rs. $16.   **87**

Bright pale straw. Medium-bodied. Full acidity. Flowers, apples. Full floral aromas. Clean, fresh, and vibrant. Drinking well now, with plenty of youthful appeal.

Weinbau Hans Reinprecht

Muskat Ottonel, Spatlese, Lieblich,
Neusiedlersee-Hugelland 1996 5.2% rs. $10.50.   **93**

Dark gold. Full-bodied. Full acidity. Highly extracted. Blossom, tart pineapple. Rich, blossomy aromas lead a tropical, thick mouthful of flavors, with juicy acids giving great balance.

Die Quintessenz, Neusiedlersee 1993 .05% rs. $26.   **83**

Pinot Blanc, Ried Altenberg, Trockenbeerenauslese,
Oggau 1995 18% rs. $22/375 ml.   **NR**

Weingut Rosenhof

Weissburgunder, Glockner, Trocken, Neusiedlersee 1996 .16% rs. $20.   **82**
Blaufrankisch, Trocken, Neusiedlersee 1995 .18% rs. $20.   **81**

Weingut Sattlerhof

Sauvignon Blanc, Steirische Klassik, Trocken,
Sudsteiermark 1997 .2% rs. $20.   **86**

Pale straw. Medium-bodied. Full acidity. Moderately extracted. Citrus, grass, minerals. Grassy, varietally expressive aromas. Lean and angular on the palate, with cleansing acidity through the finish.

Sauvignon Blanc, Kranachberg, Trocken, Sudsteiermark 1997 4.1% rs. $30. **94**

Pale straw. Gooseberries, herbs. Great purity of varietal aromas. Intensely flavorful and ripe, with an exotic herbal streak across the palate.

Peter Schandl

Furmint Ausbruch, Neusiedlersee 1991 12.2% rs. $100/500 ml.   **97**

Deep gold, with a light orange cast. Moderately full-bodied. Balanced acidity. Highly extracted. Glazed tropical fruits, earth, flowers. Rich, soft texture. Lush, deep entry of rich, grilled/smoky flavors is balanced well by bright acidity and light floral nuances. Carries bold, concentrated structure into a plush, long finish. Quite exotic.

Weingut Schildhof

Riesling, Lieblich, Langenloiser 1997 1.8% rs. $11.50.   **84**

Yellow-gold. Medium-bodied. Full acidity. Moderately extracted. Apples, dried herbs. Crisp, juicy aromas follow through convincingly on the palate. Drinking well now.

Weingut Schloss Gobelsburg

Gruner Veltliner, Kamptal 1997 .5% rs. $30.   **88**

Bright pale gold. Medium-bodied. Balanced acidity. Moderately extracted. Spiced pears, citrus, dried herbs. Fragrant, floral aromas follow through on the palate, with distinctively pure fruit flavors.

Riesling, Alte Reben, Trocken, Kamptal 1997 .8% rs. $39.   **94**

Deep golden yellow. Medium-bodied. Full acidity. Moderately extracted. Minerals, ripe citrus. Powerful, ripe aromas. Weighty and intense, with oily, well-extracted flavors and a dry, phenolic finish. This has all the structural elements to cellar benignly.

Schlosskellerei Halbturn

Samling 88, Eiswein, Neusiedlersee 1997 18.2% rs. $30/375 ml.   **87**

Medium yellow. Medium-bodied. Balanced acidity. Moderately extracted. Apples, melon, maple sugar. Moderately rich texture. Brightly fragrant nose. Sugary sweet, fruit-pie entry. Nicely balanced, with lively acids and a brown-spice note.

Goldburger, Trockenbeerenauslese, Neusiedlersee 1995 19% rs. $29/375 ml. **91**

Deep orange-gold. Moderately full-bodied. Balanced acidity. Tropical fruits, minerals, bacon fat. Spicy, smoky nose. Thick mouthfeel, with juicy flavors persisting through the finish. Great contrast between lush sweetness and minerally flavors. Powerful botrytis. This is not too sweet, and has a strong overlay of smoke and spice. Further age will see it becoming more caramelized and drier.

Schlossweingut Graf Hardegg

Weissburgunder, "Max," Osterreich 1997 .2% rs. $19.   **86**

Bright pale yellow. Medium-bodied. Full acidity. Moderately extracted. Apples, minerals, spice. Subtly smoky aromas. Full-flavored and rich on the palate, with glycerin and spice through the finish.

Riesling, Steinbugel-Seefeld, Auslese, Weinviertel 1997 6% rs. $19.   **83**

Riesling, Steinbugel-Seefeld, "Max," Trocken, Weinviertel 1997 .7% rs. $19. **82**

Scale: Superlative (96-100), Exceptional (90-95), Highly Recommended (85-89), Recommended (80-84), Not Recommended (Under 80)

Merlot-Cabernet, Max, Weinviertel 1995 .2% rs. $19. **91**

Deep, dark ruby. Moderately full-bodied. Moderately extracted. Mildly tannic. Beets, black fruits, earth. Rich, thick, chewy style showing succulent fruit and velvety tannins. Drinking nicely now, but this will improve.

Riesling, Eiswein, Steinbugel 1996 25% rs. $30/300 ml. **93**

Deep gold, with an amber cast. Moderately full-bodied. Full acidity. Highly extracted. Glazed pear, apricot, amber honey, flowers. Fat, rich texture. Viscosity holds forth as a powerful burst of juicy, sweet fruit coats the mouth. Ample acidity drives the bold flavors forward. Luscious and decadent.

Schlumberger

Brut, Wein .4% rs. $12.66. **NR**

Cabernet Sauvignon/ Merlot, Privatkeller,
Thermenregion 1994 .11% rs. $11.66. **83**

Heidi Schrock

Fumé, Ruster Ausbruch, Neusiedlersee-Hugelland 1995 10% rs. $45/500 ml. **91**

Dark gold, with a pale copper cast. Medium-bodied. Balanced acidity. Moderately extracted. Golden raisin, clover honey, minerals, earth. Moderately full texture. Shows a Tokay-like profile with a lovely sweet palate, slight maderization, and ample acidity. Nicely spiced and lively into the finish. Highly aromatic and sensuous.

Ruster Ausbruch, Neusiedlersee-Hugelland 1995 10% rs. $45/500 ml. **89**

Deep gold. Medium-bodied. Balanced acidity. Moderately extracted. Marmalade, grapefruit, minerals. Moderately rich texture. Lively, fairly rich entry, with snappy citrus flavors and bright acidity. Sweet, delicate feel in the finish.

Ruster Ausbruch, Neusiedlersee-Hugelland 1996 9% rs. $45/500 ml. **89**

Deep gold, with a pale amber cast. Moderately full-bodied. Full acidity. Highly extracted. Earth, minerals, pear, dried flowers, citrus peel. Rich, smooth texture. Iron fist in a velvet glove. Lovely, rich, succulent flavors are buttressed by sweet fragrance. Classy and refined.

Schuckert

Gruner Veltliner, Novemberlese, Auslese Trocken,
Weinviertel 1997 .8% rs. $18. **88**

Pale straw. Medium-bodied. Full acidity. Moderately extracted. Sweet grapefruit. Mildly sweet, with tart tropical flavors lingering through the finish. Very attractive and accessible style that should have wide appeal.

Gruner Veltliner, Eiswein, Weinviertel 1993 8.51% rs. $40/375 ml. **89**

Deep gold, with a light amber cast. Medium-bodied. Balanced acidity. Moderately extracted. Brown spice, earth, minerals, honey, pear. Soft, oily texture. Fat, smooth entry with a petrol and bacon-fat component. Complex and intriguing, with a melange of flavors and curiosity throughout.

Friedrich Seiler

Chardonnay, Rieglband, Neusiedlersee 1997 .14% rs. $16. **83**

Ruster Ausbruch, Neusiedlersee-Hugellans 1995 17.7% rs. $37/375 ml. **89**

Bright yellow. Moderately full-bodied. Balanced acidity. Highly extracted. Honey, pear, lemon cream. Soft, mild texture. Rich, nearly fat entry, with soft spice and rounded flavors. Quite smooth and polished, with a light touch of rancio.

Weingut Setzer

Gruner Veltliner Trocken, Ried Eichholz, Weinvertel 1997 .5% rs. $20. **88**

Very pale straw. Medium-bodied. Full acidity. Moderately extracted. Apples, pears, spice. Clean, pure, fruity aromas follow through well on the mouthfilling palate. Flavorful, spicy finish persists. Generous style.

Skoff

Chardonnay, Morillon Edition, Sudsteiermark .2% rs. $15.   NR
Muskateller, Sudsteiermark .3% rs. $13.   84

Pale gold. Medium-bodied. Balanced acidity. Moderately extracted. Flowers, pears, minerals. Attractive floral aromas. Rounded and juicy, with relatively softer acids and clean flavors through to a minerally, spicy finish.

Weissburgunder, Kabinett, Osterreich .35% rs. $13.   84

Pale straw. Moderately full-bodied. Balanced acidity. Moderately extracted. Apples, minerals. Straightforward flavors. Nice, rounded glycerine-rich mouthfeel. Solid through the finish, with fine balance of acidity.

Sauvignon, Edition, Kabinett, Osterreich .5% rs. $17.   89

Bright orange straw. Moderately full-bodied. Full acidity. Moderately extracted. Pears, gooseberries. Distinctive, floral-tinged aromas follow through on the palate. Forceful and angular, with impressive texture and depth. Unusual style.

Weingut Leopold Sommer

Gruner Veltliner Trocken, Neusiedlersee 1997 .2% rs. $9.   86

Pale straw hue. Medium-bodied. Balanced acidity. Moderately extracted. Dried herbs, tart peach, citrus. Muted aromas show a mild floral note. Good oily weight, with lemony richness that prevails on the finish.

Sonnhof

Chardonnay, Ried Ladner, Langenloiser Trocken, Kamptal 1997 .09% rs. $17.   81

Gruner Veltliner, Langenloiser Steinhaus Trocken, Kamptal 1997 .09% rs. $17.   84

Pale green gold. Medium-bodied. Full acidity. Moderately extracted. Lemons, minerals. Aromatically reserved. Bright acids carry citrus flavors through the finish. Lean, reserved style. Youthful.

Gruner Veltliner, Loiserberg Trocken, Kamptal 1997 .47% rs. $20.   89

Pale straw. Medium-bodied. Balanced acidity. Moderately extracted. Tart peaches, minerals. Floral aromas. Juicy and forward, with a hint of sweetness through a lean, quick finish. Concentrated and youthful, this has the structure to develop.

Gruner Veltliner, Alte Reben Halbtrocken, Kamptal 1997 1% rs. $27.   81
Urgesteinsriesling, Alte Reben, Halbtrocken, Kamptal 1997 .96% rs. $32.   86

Bright pale gold. Medium-bodied. Full acidity. Moderately extracted. Green apples, citrus. Tart, crisp, and juicy through the finish. Very refreshing style.

Stadlmann Franz

Welschriesling, Eiswein, Neusiedlersee 1994 10.4% rs. $31/375 ml.   89

Bright golden yellow. Moderately full-bodied. Highly extracted. Peach, minerals. Peach-skin aromas. Bright, tropical burst of flavors is carried well by juicy acids. Shows a minerally note on the finish.

Weissburgunder, Trockenbeerenauslese, Neusiedlersee 1995 14% rs. $30/375 ml.   84

Dark golden orange. Full-bodied. Full acidity. Caramelized orange, spice. Smoky aromas. Thick and viscous, with depth of flavor and a minerally finish. Structured and complex.

Welschriesling, Trockenbeerenauslese, Neusiedlersee 1995 15% rs. $30/375 ml.   84

Bright yellow-gold. Medium-bodied. Balanced acidity. Apple, peach. Lighter in style. Pure fruit flavors finish cleanly. Lacks the weight and concentration of its peers.

888

Scale: Superlative (96-100), Exceptional (90-95), Highly Recommended (85-89), Recommended (80-84), Not Recommended (Under 80)

Weingut Stadlmann

Zierfandler, Mandel Hoh, Trocken, Thermenregion 1997 .05% rs. $20.   **84**

Bright yellow-gold. Medium-bodied. Balanced acidity. Moderately extracted. Pears, apples. Straightforward flavors are enhanced by a silky, rounded mouthfeel. Generous.

Zierfandler, Trockenbeerenauslese,
Thermenregion 1996 17.5% rs. $48/375 ml.   **88**

Orange gold. Moderately full-bodied. Full acidity. Mandarin, fruit punch, spice. Botrytis character shows through in the aromas and color. Fine concentration with superb balance of acids makes for a structured wine that is drinking well now.

Richard Stierschneider

Riesling, Smaragd, Trocken, Wachau 1997 .12% rs. $30.   **83**

Weingut Karl Stierschneider

Gruner Veltliner, Ultimo, Smaragd Trocken, Wachau 1996 .33% rs. $23.75.   **94**

Deep golden yellow. Moderately full-bodied. Full acidity. Highly extracted. Pears, earth, citrus, spice. Very ripe, late-harvest aromas. Fabulously rich and lengthy in the mouth, showing an earthy depth in the flavors. Lively acidity keeps this fresh. Long, spicy finish.

Feinburgunder, Smaragd, Weitenberg, Trocken,
Wachau 1995 .82% rs. $21.75.   **87**

Deep yellow-gold. Moderately full-bodied. Full acidity. Highly extracted. Spice, tropical fruit. Marked, complex botrytis aromas. Assertive flavors. Chewy and glycerous, with zippy acids through the finish. Austere flavors have a dry, spicy theme.

Riesling, Smaragd Achleithen, Trocken, Wachau 1997 .68% rs. $21.75.   **87**

Bright yellow-gold. Medium-bodied. Full acidity. Moderately extracted. Green apples, minerals. Buttery aromas reveal a suprisingly tart, zesty palate with minerally intensity. Weighty, big-shouldered style that will age well.

Stiftsweingut Heiligenkreuz Freigut

Zierfandler, Auslese, Ried Wiege, Thermenregion 1997 3.2% rs. $18.   **NR**

Stiftsweingut Heiligenkreuz Weingut Thallern

Chardonnay, Ried Pilzing, Spatlese, Thermenregion 1997 .14% rs. $16.   **NR**

E & M Tement

Sauvignon Blanc, Grassnitzberg, Sudsteiermark 1997 $28.   **86**

Bright yellow-gold. Medium-bodied. Balanced acidity. Moderately extracted. Gooseberries, citrus fruits. Varietally expressive aromas follow through well on the palate. Ripe, fruity flavors are well carried by acids and structure.

Sauvignon Blanc, Zieregg, Sudsteiermark 1997 $35.   **91**

Full yellow-gold luster. Moderately full-bodied. Balanced acidity. Moderately extracted. Tropical fruits, mango, minerals. Exotically ripe aromas. Rich, rounded mouthfeel with glycerous texture and stunning oily flavors that linger through the finish. Acids are in fine balance.

Richard Thiel

Rotgipfler, Gumpoldskirchner Spatlese, Thermenregion 1997 2.2% rs. $28.   **84**

Bright green-straw. Medium-bodied. Full acidity. Moderately extracted. Sweet citrus, apples. Juicy, sweet, citrus zest aromas follow through well on the palate, with a succulent finish. Acids remain lively throughout. Sweet-and-sour character.

Riesling, Gumpoldskirchner, "Das Beste vom Riesling," Trocken,
Thermenregion 1997 .42% rs. $24. **86**

Pale yellow-straw hue. Medium-bodied. Full acidity. Moderately extracted. Yeast, citrus zest, minerals. Distinctive aromas lead a tart, juicy mouthful of flavors through a dry, minerally finish. Angular.

Zierfandler, Gumpoldskirchner Rotgipfler, Beerenauslese,
Thermenregion 1996 7.6% rs. $32/375 ml. **84**

Brilliant yellow-gold. Moderately full-bodied. Full acidity. Citrus, minerals. High-toned, clean aromas follow through on the palate. Bright flavors; fairly thick mouthfeel with glycerin, not sugar, being the key point. Very lively through the finish.

Tinhof

Auslese, Lieblich, Neusiedlersee 1997 1.77% rs. $20. **87**

Deep golden yellow. Full-bodied. Balanced acidity. Baked pears, spice. Complex, spicy botrytis aromas follow through on the dry palate. Thick, glycerous mouthfeel.

Tobias Friedrich

Weidener Ausbruch, Neusiedlersee 1995 12.8% rs. $48/375 ml. **96**

Brilliant yellow-gold. Moderately full-bodied. Full acidity. Spice, peach. Exotically spicy, botrytized aromas. Intensely concentrated flavors strike a great balance between acidity and sugar.

Ernst Triebaumer

Chardonnay, Rust, Trocken, Neusiedlersee 1997 .12% rs. $21.80. **86**

Bright yellow-gold. Medium-bodied. Balanced acidity. Moderately extracted. Mildly oaked. Vanilla, smoke, citrus. Attractive vanilla-edged aromas follow though to a toasty palate, with bright acids and citrus zest flavors lingering on the finish.

Weissburgunder, Trocken, Neusiedlersee-Hugelland 1997 .11% rs. $17.50. **81**

Ruster Ausbruch, Neusiedlersee-Hugelland 1995 10.6% rs. $55.50/500 ml. **97**

Bright golden straw. Full-bodied. Brown spice, tropical fruits. Very flavorsome and hugely spicy style. The impression of sweetness is contrasted with an earthy, angular note on the finish; this persists, making for a complex, exotic style.

Ruster Beerenauslese, Neusiedlersee 1996 7.9% rs. $23.80/375 ml. **88**

Bright yellow-gold. Moderately full-bodied. Balanced acidity. Spice, pineapple, lemons. Very heavy, spicy, botrytis-influenced aromas. Thick, rich, and glycerous, with a fat and lavish texture. Acids remain bright and piercing throughout.

Paul Triebaumer

Ruster Ausbruch, Neusiedlersee-Hugelland 1996 10.3% rs. $37/375 ml. **89**

Deep gold, with a pale amber cast. Moderately full-bodied. Balanced acidity. Highly extracted. Flowers, glazed pear, minerals. Soft, lush texture. Sensationally silky, with richness and great balance. Packed with ample sweet flavors, and beautifully enhanced by deft fragrance and light mineral accents. Glides across the palate and just keeps building.

Weingut Umathum

Haideboden, Neusiedlersee 1996 .11% rs. $18. **93**

Saturated red-purple. Moderately full-bodied. Highly extracted. Mildly tannic. Cherries, red fruits. Ripe, Porty aromas. Bright, high-toned acids keep the flavors juicy and balanced, though this is a thick wine. Very mild tannins make for a hedonistic style.

Blauburgunder, Junger Berg, Trocken, Donauland 1996 .1% rs. $15. **81**

Chardonnay, Trockenbeerenauslese, Frauenkirchen 1995 13% rs. $38/375 ml. **89**

Brilliant golden straw. Moderately full-bodied. Full acidity. Highly extracted. Earth, peach. Earthy, pungent aromas follow through on the palate. Thick and sweet, yet with enough juicy acids to balance. Very smoky.

Scheurebe, Trockenbeerenauslese, Frauenkirchen 1995 25% rs. $38/375 ml. **89**

Brilliant yellow-gold. Moderately full-bodied. Balanced acidity. Peach, apple. Fragrant. Exotically fruity late-harvest aromas follow through to wonderfully pure fruit-salad flavors that linger through a thick finish. Very nectarous and fruit-centered. Delicate.

Weingut Undhof

Riesling, Spatlese, Steiner Pfaffenberg, Trocken, Kremstal 1990 1.46% rs. $32. **96**

Full golden luster. Moderately full-bodied. Balanced acidity. Moderately extracted. Petrol, apricots. Stunning ripe, oily aromas reveal a mouthfilling, weighty palate with a touch of residual sweetness balancing the acids, making for a juicy style. Quite mature.

Weingut Dr. Wolfgang Unger

Chardonnay, Ried Silberbugl, Spatlese, Wachau 1995 .32% rs. $28. **NR**

Riesling, Spatlese, Ried Silberbugel, Wachau 1997 .6% rs. $28. **89**

Brilliant pale yellow-gold. Medium-bodied. Full acidity. Moderately extracted. Dried herbs, apples, minerals. Crisp, fruity aromas follow through on a lively, refreshingly juicy palate. Well-structured style; this should improve.

Riesling, Auslese, Ried Silberbugel, Wachau 1995 3.4% rs. $42. **94**

Deep golden straw. Moderately full-bodied. Balanced acidity. Highly extracted. Honey, tropical fruits, petrol. Outstanding petrol-like, late-harvest aromas lead a lush, complex array of flavors that linger through the finish. Despite the aromas, this has only marginal sweetness.

Velich Apetlon

Seewinkel, Beerenauslese, Neusiedlersee 1996 12.3% rs. $18/375 ml. **90**

Brilliant golden orange. Full-bodied. Full acidity. Smoke, nectarine, pineapple. Honeyed, spicy aromas with huge botrytis influence. Fantastically concentrated and juicy, with a nectarous mouthfeel and a long, fruit-acid finish that leaves a longing for more. Oak spice, bright acids, and wonderful apricot fruit flavors. Elegant and classy. Good botrytis character.

Muskat Ottonel, Trockenbeerenauslese, Neusiedlersee 1996 15.3% rs. $25/375 ml. **89**

Brilliantly deep orange-gold. Full-bodied. Full acidity. Smoke, caramelized fruits. Burnt, caramelized aromas. High-toned acids and alcohol warmth combine with a fat, buttery mouthfeel make for a truly full-throttled style. Not overly sweet.

Markowitsch

Gruner Veltliner, Alte Reben, Carnuntum 1997 .4% rs. $13. **82**

Weinrieder

Chardonnay, Poysdorfer Hohenleiten, Halbtrocken, Weinviertel 1997 3.3% rs. $30. **83**

Chardonnay, Poysdorfer Hohenleiten, Lieblich, Weinviertel 1997 3% rs. $34. **86**

Bright medium gold. Medium-bodied. Full acidity. Moderately extracted. Sweet lemon cream, citrus. Very ripe, late-harvest aromas follow through to sweet, tropical flavors countered by tart acids on the finish.

Welschriesling, Birthal, Eiswein, Poysdorfer 1997 14% rs. $46/375 ml. **87**

Yellow, with a pale green cast. Moderately light-bodied. Full acidity. Subtly extracted. Oil-petrol, pine, pear, peach. Brisk texture. Vibrant acidity pushes tart and sweet flavors, as slight fragrance emerges.

Riesling, Schneiderberg, Eiswein, Poysdorfer 1997 16.9% rs. $52/375 ml.   91

Yellow. Full-bodied. Balanced acidity. Moderately extracted. Herbs, cream, apple, lemon-lime. Broad texture. A very large profile with a measure of grip and power. Neither fat nor cloying, yet there is ample weight throughout. Seems youthful. Should cellar wonderfully.

Josef u. Herta Werner

Gewürztraminer, Spatlese, Suss, Neusiedlersee 1997 5.63% rs. $60.   84

Pale yellow-gold. Medium-bodied. Balanced acidity. Moderately extracted. Peaches, flowers. Ripe, juicy aromas follow through on the palate. Lush, rounded, and very appealing.

Weingut Wieninger

Chardonnay, Classic, Wien 1997 .13% rs. $16.   NR

Gruner Veltliner, Herrenholz, Wien 1997 .12% rs. $15.   NR

Weinbau Franz Wimmer

**Weissburgunder Ausbruch, Ried Kapellenhaide,
Neusiedlersee 1995 13% rs. $20/375 ml.**   84

Bright gold. Medium-bodied. Balanced acidity. Moderately extracted. Minerals, dried herbs, apple, pineapple. Mild texture. Quite herbal, with a lighter feel on the palate. Straw and soft spice notes dominate fruit flavors. Fairly brisk throughout.

**Muller Thurgau, Ried Neufeldacker, Trockenbeerenauslese,
Neusiedlersee 1995 16.7% rs. $24/375 ml.**   93

Bright golden orange. Moderately full-bodied. Full acidity. Highly extracted. Spice, caramelized fruits. Spicy, botrytis aromas reveal succulent, caramelized flavor with great concentration of sugars and acidity. Sensational mouthfeel, with softer acids making for a more harmonious, very luxurious style.

Weingut Wimmer-Czerny

Gruner Veltliner, Alte Reben, Weelfel, Trocken, Donauland 1997 1% rs. $14. 84

Bright yellow-gold. Moderately light-bodied. Full acidity. Moderately extracted. Green herbs, minerals, spice. Lean herbal and mineral aromas follow through, with a hot, spicy finish elevated by bright acids. Mildly spritzy.

Winkler-Hermaden

Traminer, Ried Kirchleiten, Sudoststeiermark 1997 .4% rs. $20.   88

Deep golden cast. Full-bodied. Full acidity. Highly extracted. Spice, grapefruit, minerals. Quite aromatic, with a complex, herb-tinged array of flavors that say classic Gewürztraminer. Full, ripe, and round in the mouth, with ample acidity to provide balance and a lengthy, dry finish.

Sauvignon Blanc, Kapfensteiner Kogel, Sudoststeiermark 1997 .1% rs. $18. 83

Blauer Zweigelt, Olivin, Sudoststeiermark 1995 .01% rs. $23.   84

Bright red-purple. Medium-bodied. Moderately extracted. Mildly tannic. Cherries, minerals. Lean aromas lead a bright cherry-flavored entry, with a minerally backbone giving this an austere finish. Angular.

Winzer Krems

Gruner Veltliner Kabinett Trocken, Goldberg, Kremstal 1997 $10.   86

Pale yellow-straw cast. Medium-bodied. Balanced acidity. Moderately extracted. Citrus, minerals, flowers. Buttery, tropical aromas. Rounded, satisfying texture, though the flavors are straightforward citrus with floral hints.

Winzerhaus WeinvertriebsgesmbH

Riesling, Loibner Loibenberg Trockenbeerenauslese,
Wachau 1996 28.2% rs. $100/375 ml.　　　　　　　　　　　　**95**

Bright golden yellow. Moderately full-bodied. Full acidity. Honey, peaches, ginger.
Opulent aromas, very pure. Searingly high acids cut through the waves of sugary
sweetness on thick palate, creating a tug between acidity and sugar. Much like a
German TBA. Huge, buttery, and lush. One glass is all you need. A showpiece.
Three years more would add to the complexity.

Wohlmuth

Chardonnay, Summus, Trocken, Sudsteiermark 1997 .03% rs. $24.　　　**82**

Traminer, Summus, Lieblich, Sudsteiermark 1997 2.4% rs. $25.　　　　**88**

Bright pale gold. Moderately full-bodied. Balanced acidity. Moderately extracted. Lychee,
spice, apricot. Fine, varietally pure aromas follow through on the palate, with a touch of
residual sugar countering the bright acids. Intense and well-balanced.

Muskateller, Summus, Trocken, Sudsteiermark 1997 .02% rs. $23.　　　**83**

Pinot Blanc, Elitar, Lieblich, Sudsteiermark 1997 2.8% rs. $32.　　　　**93**

Medium yellow-gold. Medium-bodied. Balanced acidity. Moderately extracted. Apricots,
marzipan, honey. Honeyed aromas. Hint of residual sweetness, with acids playing on the
finish. Fine mouthfeel.

Sauvignon Blanc, Summus Ernte, Trocken,
Sudsteiermark 1997 .15% rs. $28.　　　　　　　　　　　　　　　**83**

Weingut Harald Zierer

Rotgipfler, Beerenauslese, Thermenregion 1996 9.5% rs. $30/500 ml.　　**86**

Bright golden yellow. Moderately full-bodied. Full acidity. Peach, citrus. Perfumed aromas
lead an intensely concentrated palate, with vibrant acids matching the sugars, giving a
juicy character. Clean.

R. Zimmermann

Chardonnay, Kabinett, Trocken, Wien 1997 .55% rs. $10.　　　　　**85**

Pale straw cast. Medium-bodied. Full acidity. Moderately extracted. Citrus, minerals,
slate. Aromatically reserved, but firm and concentrated on the palate, with a Chablis-like
intensity. Clean, racy acidity makes for a zesty finish. Should mature nicely.

Weingut Alois Zimmermann

Gruner Veltliner, Rohrehdorfer Rosshimmel, Kremstal 1997 .07% rs. $14.　**84**

Pale straw cast. Medium-bodied. Balanced acidity. Moderately extracted. Dried herbs,
citrus, minerals. Aromatically muted. Straightforward flavors are manifested in a lean
style, veering toward austerity on the finish.

Riesling, "Kremser Krax'n," Trocken, Kremstal 1997 .09% rs. $20.　　**86**

Bright pale gold. Moderately full-bodied. Full acidity. Moderately extracted. Green
apples, dried herbs, minerals. Muted aromas lead an imposing, assertive palate with
generous proportions. This has all the structural elements to age well.

Weingut Zull

Gruner Veltliner, Trocken, Schrattenthal Odfeld 1997 .08% rs. $13.　　**83**

Riesling, Innere Bergen, Trocken, Weinviertel 1997 .44% rs. $14.　　　**81**

forty-two

Australia

The Wines of Australia
Current Market Overview

To the U.S. consumer, the wines of Australia have already achieved a solid reputation for value. The common wisdom seems to be that Australian wines offer great value in the marketplace and tend to be very consistent. In general terms, these assumptions are correct. The Australian wine industry did a great deal to help pioneer the methods that brought mechanization and improved quality control to large-scale commercial viticulture. As the Australian industry is (in quantity) dominated by a handful of very large wineries with a great interest in export markets, this has meant that the world has received Australian wines of both consistently high quality and attractive prices.

There has, however, been a sea change in Australian viticulture. Aussie wines have gone decidedly upscale. As the large firms have gained acceptance in export markets for Australian wines, many of the country's hundreds of boutique producers have begun to export as well, and none of the varietals they produce has made a bigger splash than Shiraz. While Australia certainly produces fine varietals of all stripes, the world has woken up to its Shiraz in particular. Big, rich, and intense, Aussie Shiraz is a wine like no other in the world, and while being one of the world's acknowledged great originals, it is immensely enjoyable in youth. Consumers at any level of the market can find great pleasure in it. Beyond Shiraz, Australia is also making world-class Cabernet, Chardonnay, Riesling, Semillon, Grenache, and Dessert Wines.

While the selection of Aussie wines available in the U.S. has never been wider, quantities can still be a problem. The most coveted boutique producers sell out quickly. Savvy consumers will need a plan to acquire show wines such as Grange, Henschke, Clarendon Hills, Eileen Hardy, or Ebenezer. Fostering a relationship with a quality retailer will virtually be a prerequisite, but the wines are well worth the effort. Any would make a welcome addition to a well-stocked cellar. While these wines are indeed getting more and more expensive, prices are still quite reasonable when compared to the shenanigans going on in Bordeaux or Burgundy, particularly when one considers the limited quantities in question.

If you don't have the inclination to play the allocation game, there are still a number of outstanding wines to be found from Australia that are made in large quantities, including wines from the coveted trilogy of Shiraz, Cabernet, and Chardonnay. Additionally, most prices are still quite reasonable. On the other hand, when it comes to less popular varietals such as Semillon or Riesling, the wines can be almost embarrassingly cheap. Just as Shiraz has leapt up in price since the rest of the world caught on, the savvy consumer shouldn't wait forever to lap up some of these bargains—they won't be there forever.

What to Expect: Key Aussie Varietals & Wine Styles

Shiraz: Shiraz has been the most widely planted red grape in Australia since the 19th century, when cuttings were brought from Rhône Valley Syrah vines in France. Shiraz prospers in many Australian wine-producing regions and the country has at its disposal a healthy amount of old Shiraz vines producing spicy, concentrated wines in the same manner as old vines produce the finest northern Rhône wines. Penfold's Grange, made since the 1950s, has garnered a

Scale: Superlative (96-100), Exceptional (90-95), Highly Recommended (85-89),
Recommended (80-84), Not Recommended (Under 80)

reputation as one of the world's greatest wines, and has served as a role model for the heights that Shiraz can achieve within Australia. In recent years U.S. consumers have woken up to the greatness of Australian red wines and Shiraz wines in particular. This has driven prices of super premium wines up to and beyond the $100 mark. While the new boutique wines are generating a great deal of interest at the high end, prices have not increased for all Shiraz across the board (as has happened with California Cabernet). The large firms are still making extremely attractive Shiraz at very reasonable prices and Australian red wine is still at the very top of the "value for money" list. At the value end of the market, the "base" Shiraz from wineries such as Penfold's, Peter Lehmann, Maglieri, Wynns, Rosemount, or Lindemans are not only great values but are also made in fairly large quantities.

Cabernet Sauvignon & Merlot: Until quite recently, the average Australian wine drinker would place a greater emphasis on Cabernet Sauvignon than Shiraz. This may sound surprising to others around the world who think of Australia and Shiraz as being virtually synonymous, but, as is often the case, familiarity can breed contempt. Shiraz dominated Australian viticulture well into the '60s and '70s, yet it was thought of more as a rustic, indigenous wine (California Zinfandel, anyone?). World class meant mastering Cabernet Sauvignon, and so Australia blindly followed the worldwide Cabernet phenomenon. It was only through the intense international praise lavished upon Aussie Shiraz that the Australians themselves have begun to rediscover their national grape. What happened in the meantime however, was the creation of a new national wine style, Cabernet Sauvignon.

Australia actually adopted Cabernet at an early stage of its development as a quality wine producer, and Merlot is now increasingly popular due to its high demand at present. Cabernet and Shiraz blends found favor and acclaim before the more classical Bordeaux blend of Cabernet and Merlot. With Merlot

Australia
at a Glance

Wines Reviewed:

302

Producers/Brands Represented:

112

Value Rating:

Good to Excellent

vines now bearing fruit in the cooler regions of Australia, Merlot varietal wines and Bordeaux blends are appearing on the marketplace in commercial quantities. The sources of Australia's finest Bordeaux varietal wines are the country's cooler regions, notably Coonawarra and the upcoming Padthaway region, although the Barossa Valley produces rich Cabernets with higher alcohol levels and richer flavors. In relation to premium California wines, Aussie Cabernets will often have a more restrained character, sporting 12–13% alcohol, though they are distinctly New World in their fruity generosity of flavors.

Chardonnay: Australia is home to some of the world's outstanding Chardonnays and a huge volume of competitively priced, competently made bottlings are produced. Most fighting varietal brands will carry the wide ranging South Eastern Australia appellation that plays host to many of the country's viticultural districts, though premium estate wines will carry such familiar appellations as Padthaway, McLaren Vale, and Eden Valley, to name but a few. In recent years Australians have had a rethink about Chardonnay styles. The fashion is now for cooler climate areas, far less oak influence, and more vibrant citrus fruit flavors. The cool Padthaway region is now closely associated with this fresher style of Australian Chardonnay. Many wines now proudly state on the label that they are unwooded. With Australia at the forefront of technological advancement in viticulture and enology, and driven by a diversity of enormous commercial exporting producers and boutique wineries, Aussie Chardonnays will continue to compete effectively for the attention of U.S. consumers.

Semillon: While Semillon outside Australia is best known as the "other" grape in white Bordeaux and an essential component in Sauternes, inside Australia it is justly famous for making exceptional and distinctive white table wines. The style was pioneered in the warm Hunter Valley near Sydney, where the wines are typically unoaked. Taping into a young bottle, the novice consumer would be pardoned for asking what all the fuss is about. Young Hunter Semillons tend to be reserved and crisp with a linear acidic backbone. In five to ten years, however, the wines begin to develop outrageous waxy, lanolin-like flavors and deep colors while retaining their firm acidic structures. They continue to age for years, with tasty 30- and 40-year-old examples being not unheard of. The wines of Lindemans in particular typify this style. For those without the cellar-patience required, an increasing number of oaked Semillons have been on offer as of late, from the Barossa Valley as well as the Hunter. These versions are much more developed on release, but don't seem to work quite as well with food as their more traditional counterparts. Nonetheless, either version provides a welcome respite from yet another Chardonnay. At present, fine Semillon is amazingly underpriced, with examples often going for less than $10!

Riesling: Though many wine drinkers think of Australia as a hot and dusty country (correctly), there are a handful of regions which do quite well with Riesling. The Eden and Clare valleys, in particular, produce an exceptional style. These wines tend to feature great underlying acidity allied to solid ripeness levels. Flavors tend to be very precise with a classic, pithy, lime-like quality. All but the cheapest commercial wines are dry and most age quite well. Being unoaked, they pair brilliantly with food. Like Semillon, they are grossly underappreciated, particularly in the U.S., and fine examples can be had for laughable prices. They cannot be recommended highly enough.

Scale: Superlative (96-100), Exceptional (90-95), Highly Recommended (85-89), Recommended (80-84), Not Recommended (Under 80)

Dessert Wines: Quality fortified wine industries cannot be started overnight, as aged stocks of fortified wine are required for blending the final product. Australia used to be a nation of fortified sweet-wine drinkers before the modern wine boom started. To this day many of Australia's top producers are those firms with a century or more of history in making sweet fortified wines.

Australian tawny "port" is sometimes compared to Portuguese tawny Portos, though they have their own distinctive identity and are generally made in a sweeter, richer style. In many ways the finest Australian tawnies show a greater degree of complexity than the wood-dominated Portuguese originals. At the pinnacle of Australian sweet wines, however, are the nectarous Liqueur Muscats and Tokays. These extraordinary wines take their place among the most exquisite dessert wines of the world. Reduced and concentrated by long periods of aging in old wood barrels, these wines tend to be thick and rich with mind-boggling aromatics and great complexity of flavor. Vintage ports are also produced in Australia, frequently from the Shiraz grape variety. They are bold and fruity, requiring some cellaring, though in no way comparable to Portuguese Vintage Portos.

Sparklers: The Australian wine industry manages to make Méthode Champenoise wines of serious quality at prices that would make Champagne producers turn as green as their unripe grapes. Fruity, generous wines that can show fine yeasty notes often associated with more expensive wines typify the Australian sparkling wine style. Nearly all Aussie sparklers use Champagne grape varieties (Pinot Noir and Chardonnay) and most can be purchased for $10 or less. An esoteric specialty that is unique to Australia is Sparkling Shiraz. This is a fruity red sparkling wine that has flavors more commonly associated with Shiraz red table wines. Few examples are imported, but more adventurous drinkers may wish to seek them out.

Australia In Focus:
Coonawarra, McLaren Vale, and the Barossa

While all one seems to hear these days in Australia is cool climate this and cool climate that, one thing is certain, the vast majority of Australia's best Shiraz is coming from warm climate regions. As a spin-off to the Wine Australia '98 convention, organizers decided to highlight Aussie Shiraz by holding a competition. Over 130 wines were reviewed by some of Australia's best-known judges. The results sent a clear message. Nine of the top ten wines were from McLaren Vale or the Barossa Valley. This is not unusual; year after year, we find old vine examples from these two regions to be among the finest bottlings. Penfolds, Hardy's, Henschke, Clarendon Hills, Ebenezer—the names sound like a hall of fame roll call for some of the world's best Syrah. While the newer regions are certainly developing names for themselves, and there will always be exceptions, savvy consumers in search of great Shiraz should keep a keen eye out for bottlings from these two regions in particular.

Similarly, Coonawarra, a cooler region well to the south of the Barossa, can be looked to for consistently outstanding Cabernet Sauvignon. The famous Terra Rossa, or red earth, of the region combines with a host of other factors to make for ideal Bordeaux varietal conditions. In the cooler (for Australia) conditions, Cabernet takes on a deep varietal personality with excellent intensity and ripe, fruity, minty flavors. The best examples show exceptional balance and ageability, without the toughness the varietal is known for. The wines tend to show a bit more finesse than their California cousins without coming across as shy or wimpy. Just as the consumer in search of Shiraz should start with Barossa or McLaren, so should the consumer in search of an introduction to fine Aussie Cabernet turn to Coonawarra.

Recent Vintage Overview

1998: An El Niño year, reports state that 1998 was warmer than usual throughout Australia, with little rain to interfere with the harvest. Growers in the Barossa and Coonawarra in particular are optimistic with Geoff Schrapel, chairman of the Barossa Winemakers' Committee, ranking it alongside 1990 and 1996 as one of the best vintages of the decade. Reaction in Coonawarra has ranged from "best of the 1990s" to "best for 20 years." From South Australia to the Hunter and Yarra valleys everyone reports great ripeness, with reds in particular looking rich and intense. Though alcohol levels are high, acidity was not reported as being a problem. Whites should also be muscular and intense. This is certainly a vintage to watch over the next two to four years as the premium bottlings begin to reach the market.

1997: The 1997 vintage was marked by excessive heat in many Australian regions, particularly in the critical period before harvest. Overall, supply will be limited as quantities were down. Quality, however, seems to be fairly good, with a few notable exceptions. In cool regions such as the Yarra Valley, growers are excited as the unseasonable heat and lack of rain seems to have produced outstanding reds and whites. Other regions, such as Coonawarra, the Adelaide Hills, and the Barossa seem to have produced very good wines, though Eden Valley Riesling in particular was reported to be below average as it suffered from sunburn! Whites from the area seem to be rich and blowsy—tasty but not really for keeping. As for the Hunter, 11–13 inches of rain late in the season caused a range of problems. While Hunter reds suffered, some success is being claimed with Semillon. Overall, 1997 should be looked to for some good to excellent reds in South Australia's glamour appellations and excellent wines from Yarra Valley and normally cool Victorian regions...a mixed bag elsewhere.

1996: Most regions seem to have made good- to excellent-quality wines in large quantities. Supplies should be abundant. Barossa and Coonawarra reds are big and bold, but some other South Australian regions (such as the Vales) experienced some problematic rain at harvest. Beyond South Australia, a number of Victorian reds, including those from the Yarra Valley in particular, seem to lack somewhat for depth. Nonetheless, a bevy of outstanding reds from South Australia has already been released. These wines only portend more excellent releases over the next two years.

1995: Though the initial word was that 1995 was a difficult Australian vintage in general, there has been a wave of outstanding wines from South Australia, Victoria, and Western Australia. The Barossa Valley and McLaren Vale in particular seem to have led the way—a testament, no doubt, to the wealth of old vineyards in these areas. High-end releases of reds are now on the market and deserve to be highly recommended.

Scale: Superlative (96-100), Exceptional (90-95), Highly Recommended (85-89), Recommended (80-84), Not Recommended (Under 80)

Best Producers: Australia, Shiraz

Premier Australian Shiraz Producers (***)

- Barossa Valley Estate
  (Ebenezer & EE Black Pepper)
- Jim Barry (The Armagh)
- Clarendon Hills (Astralis)
- d'Arrenberg (The Dead Arm)
- Elderton
- Hardy's (Eileen Hardy)
- Henschke (Hill of Grace & Keyneton Estate)
- Leasingham (Classic Clare)
- Maglieri (Steve Maglieri)
- Mitchelton (Print Series)
- Orlando (Lawsons)
- Penfolds (Grange & Magill Estate)
- Rosemount (Balmoral)
- St Hallet (Old Block)
- Tatachilla (Foundation)
- Wynns (Michael)
- Yalumba (Octavius)

Great Australian Shiraz Producers (**)

- Tim Adams
- Jim Barry (McCrae Wood)
- Barwang
- Wolf Blass
- Bowen
- Briar Ridge
- Cimicky (Signature)
- Coriole
- d'Arrenberg (The Footbolt)
- Richard Hamilton (Hamilton Ewell Reserve)
- Hillstowe (Buxton)
- Kaesler (Old Vine)
- Leasingham
- Peter Lehmann
- Maglieri
- Penfolds (Bin Numbers)
- Plantagenet
- Chateau Reynella (Basket Pressed)
- Stanley Brothers (John Hancock)
- Tatachilla
- Warrabilla
- David Wynn (Patriarch)
- Wynns (Coonawarra)
- Yalumba

Dependable Australian Shiraz Producers (Recommended)

These producers have impressed us. Some are new. Some are older but improving steadily. Some have done well in the past but we have not tasted enough vintages to classify them as Premier or Great yet.

- Allandale
- Arrowfield
- Basedow
- Cassegrain
- Evans & Tate
- Fern Hill
- Lindemans
- Marienberg
- McGuigan
- Morris
- Mount Langi Ghiran
- Pepper Tree
- Pikes
- Redbank
- Rosemount (Diamond Label)
- Seaview
- Sheldrake
- Taltarni
- Tyrrell's
- Yarraman Road

Reviews

Abbey Vale

1997 Chardonnay, Margaret River $14.   81

1997 Sauvignon Blanc, Margaret River $14.   92

Pale straw cast. Moderately full-bodied. Balanced acidity. Moderately extracted.
Asparagus, smoke, minerals. Quite aromatic, with an attractive and complex array of
varietal flavors. Ripe and full in the mouth with an assertive, crisp finish. Impressively
intense varietal character.

1995 Cabernet-Merlot, Margaret River $15.   84

Bright ruby red with a slight fade. Medium-bodied. Balanced acidity. Moderately
extracted. Mildly tannic. Dried herbs, minerals, red fruits, earth. Shows a distinct
herbal/earthy note in the nose. Light in style and lean in the mouth, with a peppery
quality to the finish.

1996 60% Merlot-40% Shiraz, Margaret River $15.   86

Deep blackish ruby cast. Medium-bodied. Balanced acidity. Highly extracted. Moderately
oaked. Moderately tannic. Vanilla, red fruits, dried herbs. Pleasantly aromatic with a core
of fruit flavors enlivened by an herbal edge and sweet oak nuances. LA light style with a
lean structure, though the finish is lengthy.

Tim Adams

1997 The Fergus, Grenache, Clare Valley $11.   81

1996 Shiraz, Clare Valley $18.   88

Deep purple cast. Medium-bodied. Balanced acidity. Moderately extracted. Mildly tannic.
Chocolate, licorice, red fruits. Vibrant aromas show a high-toned spicy quality and merge
with a core of ripe fruit flavors. Crisp and lively with a deeply flavored finish.

Alice White

1997 Chardonnay, South Eastern Australia $7.   84

Bright golden cast. Moderately full-bodied. Balanced acidity. Moderately extracted. Bread
dough, pears. Understated aromas lead a ripe, almost fat mouthfeel that flattens toward
the finish. Texturally nice though the fruit flavors do not quite match the weight.

Allandale

1997 Chardonnay, Hunter River Valley $17.99.   86

Bright golden straw. Medium-bodied. Balanced acidity. Highly extracted. Smoke, butter,
ripe citrus. Rich, oaky, well-smoked aromas lead a nutty, rounded palate with low acids
making for a fat character. Finishes in a nutty manner.

1996 Matthew, Shiraz, Hunter River Valley $18.99.   83

Allanmere

1996 Chardonnay, Durham $17.99.   89

Bright yellow-straw cast. Moderately full-bodied. Balanced acidity. Highly extracted.
Moderately oaked. Brown spices, hazelnuts, minerals. Forward aromas feature a complex
nutty quality and leesy overtones. Ripe and full in the mouth with attractive acidity
through the flavorful finish.

Anderson

1993 French Oak White, Australia $16.99.   80

Bald Hill Creek

1996 Cabernet Sauvignon, Mornington Peninsula $17.99.   81

Scale: Superlative (96-100), Exceptional (90-95), Highly Recommended (85-89),
Recommended (80-84), Not Recommended (Under 80)

Banrock Station

1998 Semillon-Chardonnay, South Eastern Australia $5.99.　　　84

Bright straw cast. Medium-bodied. Full acidity. Moderately extracted. Melon, minerals. Subdued melony aromas lead a rounded mouthfeel supported by zesty acidity. Crisp and lively through the finish.

1998 Shiraz-Cabernet Sauvignon, South Eastern Australia $6.99.　　　NR

Barossa Valley Estate

1995 Ebenezer, Shiraz, Barossa Valley $25.　　　93

Deep blackish-ruby with a purple tinge. Moderately full-bodied. Balanced acidity. Moderately extracted. Heavily oaked. Mildly tannic. Menthol, red fruits. Perfumed throughout with a dominant minty component and a core of sweet fruit flavors. Rich and generous in the mouth with a seamless velvety quality. Drinking well now.

1995 E&E, Black Pepper Shiraz, Barossa Valley $70.　　　98

Deep blackish-ruby cast. Full-bodied. Balanced acidity. Highly extracted. Heavily oaked. Mildly tannic. Vanilla, mint, black fruits. Intense and generous aromatics are sweet and luscious. Rich and opulent in the mouth with a lush and velvety character. The personification of a show-style Shiraz. Exceptionally balanced and drinking beautifully now.

Jim Barry

1995 McCrae Wood, Cabernet Sauvignon-Malbec, Clare Valley $31.　　　84

Opaque blackish-ruby hue. Moderately full-bodied. Balanced acidity. Highly extracted. Mildly oaked. Mildly tannic. Black fruits, chocolate. Flavorful and lush with a velvety quality in the mouth. Rich and generous if a tad fat through the finish.

1995 The Armagh, Shiraz, Clare Valley $75.　　　90

Opaque blackish-purple hue. Full-bodied. Full acidity. Highly extracted. Heavily oaked. Quite tannic. Menthol, coffee, black fruits. Exotic aromas show an intense old-vine character. Huge and dense in the mouth with a large-framed and racy structure. Oozing with flavor, but the tannins clamp down hard on the finish.

Barwang

1996 Winemaker's Reserve, Cabernet Sauvignon, New South Wales $18.　　　88

Deep ruby-purple cast. Moderately full-bodied. Balanced acidity. Moderately extracted. Heavily oaked. Mildly tannic. Mint, vanilla, coffee. Forward aromas show a bright, oak-dominated quality. Intensely flavored and lean with a slight herbal quality throughout. Unusual.

1996 Winemaker's Reserve, Shiraz, New South Wales $18.　　　88

Bright ruby cast. Medium-bodied. Balanced acidity. Moderately extracted. Mildly tannic. Red fruits, minerals. Generous aromas have a lean minerally quality. Angular and austere in the mouth with a firm structure. Crisp and vibrant finish.

Basedow

1997 Semillon, Barossa Valley $11.　　　84

Dull yellow gold. Moderately full-bodied. Full acidity. Highly extracted. Moderately oaked. Vanilla, spice, minerals. Quite aromatic, with a hefty oak accent. Weighty but lean in the mouth, with a continuation of the oak-dominant flavor profile through the angular finish.

1995 Shiraz, Barossa $16.　　　86

Deep ruby with a slight fade. Medium-bodied. Balanced acidity. Subtly extracted. Mildly tannic. Anise, minerals, black fruits. Shows an unusual range of high-toned flavors. Surprisingly light in the mouth with a crisp and angular finish.

Benjamin
Tawny Port, Australia $12.99.   85

Light amber color. Moderately full body. Medium acid. Medium fruit. Medium oak. Mild tannin. Sweet. Reminiscent of caramel, brown sugar, dried fruits, nuts. Has very good balance, an impression of high alcohol, and moderate length. A blend of Cabernet Sauvignon, Shiraz and Merlot.

Black Marlin
1997 Chardonnay, South Eastern Australia $8.99.   NR

Black Opal
1997 82% Cabernet-18% Merlot, South Eastern Australia $10.50.   82

Blue Pyrenees
1996 Chardonnay, Australia $25.99.   87

Bright yellow-straw cast. Moderately full-bodied. Full acidity. Highly extracted. Moderately oaked. Vanilla, yeast, citrus. Quite fragrant, with a generous array of flavors. Big but well balanced in the mouth with zesty acidity that enlivens the palate. Finishes with an attractive leesy quality.

1995 Estate, 75% Cabernet-15%Shiraz-10% Merlot, Victoria $25.99.   89

Deep ruby-purple cast. Moderately full-bodied. Balanced acidity. Highly extracted. Moderately oaked. Quite tannic. Vanilla, black fruits, minerals. Forward aromas show a fancy oak overlay. Firm and angular in the mouth with concentrated flavors and a very firm structure. Tannins clamp down on the finish. Rather unyielding at present. Needs time.

Bowen
1996 Shiraz, Coonawarra $16.99.   89

Bright ruby-purple cast. Moderately full-bodied. Full acidity. Highly extracted. Mildly oaked. Mildly tannic. Mint, sweet herbs, game. Shows a distinctive Northern Rhone-like, old-vine medicinal quality to the complex and exotic flavors. Lush and supple in the mouth with a seamless quality through the gamey finish. Lighter in style and drinking beautifully.

Briar Ridge
1997 Hand Picked, Chardonnay, Hunter Valley $18.99.   82
1996 Cabernet Sauvignon, Hunter Valley $18.99.   NR
1996 Old Vines, Shiraz, Hunter Valley $16.99.   88

Bright purple cast. Medium-bodied. Full acidity. Moderately extracted. Mildly oaked. Mildly tannic. Briar fruits, minerals. Bright fruity aromas are ripe and zesty. Lighter in the mouth with fine fruit intensity through the finish.

Bulletin Place
1998 Chardonnay, South Eastern Australia $9.99.   84

Bright yellow-gold. Moderately full-bodied. Full acidity. Moderately extracted. Butter, citrus, pears. Quite fragrant, with a rich palate feel balanced by zesty acidity. The finish is angular and vibrant.

1997 Shiraz, South Eastern Australia $9.99.   81

Scale: Superlative (96-100), Exceptional (90-95), Highly Recommended (85-89), Recommended (80-84), Not Recommended (Under 80)

Burramurra

1995 Cabernet-Merlot, Victoria $29.   88

Opaque blackish-purple cast. Full-bodied. Balanced acidity. Highly extracted. Moderately oaked. Quite tannic. Menthol, red fruits, minerals. Generous aromas lead a big, full-throttled palate feel. Firm and intense with a big wave of tannins that bite down on the finish. Powerful, but in need of mid-term to long-term cellaring.

Callara

1997 Reserve Bin, Chardonnay, South Eastern Australia $7.   84

Deep gold. Moderately full-bodied. Balanced acidity. Moderately extracted. Bread, cream, tropical fruits. Rich and lush, with a weighty, ripe palate feel. Not overly flavorful, but extravagantly textured. Lobster, anyone?

1996 Reserve Bin, Cabernet Sauvignon, South Eastern Australia $7.   83

Campbells

NV Liquid Gold Tokay, Rutherglen $36/500 ml.   95

Bright amber cast. Moderately full-bodied. Balanced acidity. Moderately extracted. Dates, tea, olives, caramel. Perfumed and exotically aromatic with a rich and unctuous palate feel. Shows fine intensity and length. Powerful without being overbearing or cloyingly sweet.

Cassegrain

1997 Semillon-Chardonnay, Hastings River $9.99.   89

Deep yellow-straw cast. Moderately full-bodied. Full acidity. Moderately extracted. Lanolin, minerals, citrus. Aromatic and flavorful, with a lean and intense quality. Big and firm, with a lengthy finish dominated by classic waxy Semillon flavors.

1997 49% Cabernet Sauvignon-45% Shiraz-6% Merlot, Hastings River $10.99. 83
1996 78% Cabernet Sauvignon-22% Merlot, Hastings River $14.99.   83
1997 Reserve, Pinot Noir, Hastings River $22.99.   80
1997 Shiraz, Hastings River $14.99.   86

Bright purple. Medium-bodied. Balanced acidity. Moderately extracted. Moderately tannic. Black fruits, minerals. Aromatically reserved, with a firm and angular palate feel. Youthful and powerful, but rather unyielding. Perhaps time will help.

Chateau Reynella

1996 Chardonnay, McLaren Vale $12.99.   84

Deep straw cast. Moderately full-bodied. Balanced acidity. Moderately extracted. Heavily oaked. Brown spices, citrus. Quite fragrant, with a big toasty oak overlay that runs through the palate. Full but zesty in the mouth, with crispness through the finish.

1995 Basket Pressed, Cabernet-Merlot, McLaren Vale $15.   85

Opaque blackish ruby cast. Moderately full-bodied. Balanced acidity. Highly extracted. Moderately oaked. Moderately tannic. Black fruits, mint, minerals. Austere aromatics lead a rich but severe mouthfeel. Rather monolithic and a tad tough, with drying tannins biting into the core of dark flavors.

1995 Basket Pressed, Shiraz, McLaren Vale $24.99.   89

Opaque blackish-purple cast. Moderately full-bodied. Full acidity. Moderately extracted. Mildly oaked. Mildly tannic. Black fruits, minerals. Somewhat reserved aromatically, with a high-toned, intense mouthfeel. Crisp and angular through the finish. Well balanced-should marry well with food.

1992 Vintage Port, McLaren Vale $12.   86

Moderately full body. Medium acid. Medium fruit. Medium oak. Medium tannin. Medium sweetness. Reminiscent of cherries, blueberries, pepper. Nice length, a viscous mouthfeel and an impression of high alcohol make this a powerful after-dinner drink.

Old Cave Fine Tawny Port, McLaren Vale $18.99.   93

Dark brown-amber. Full-bodied. Salt, rancio, oak spice. Salty, rancio aromas lead a
powerfully flavored palate with heavy brown spice and sweet caramel flavors upfront
and a dry finish. Extraordinarily complex and not overly sweet.

Cimicky

1997 Gnarled Vine, Grenache, Barossa Valley $23.99.   NR
1996 Signature, Shiraz, Barossa Valley $23.99.   95

Deep blackish-purple hue. Moderately full-bodied. Balanced acidity. Highly extracted.
Heavily oaked. Mildly tannic. Mint, black fruits, vanilla. Intensely aromatic with a hefty
oak overlay. Rich, yet zesty acidity lends a sense of vibrance and highlights the crisp and
intense fruit flavors. Very lengthy finish. Drinking well now.

Clarendon Hills

1996 Astralis, Shiraz, Australia $120.   100

Opaque blackish-purple, paints the side of the glass. Full-bodied. Full acidity. Highly
extracted. Heavily oaked. Moderately tannic. Confectioners sugar, menthol, black fruits.
Generous aromas are complex and unusual with a definitive old-vine Syrah medicinal
note. Thick and full in the mouth with an intense and opulent quality. Finishes with a
wave of lush tannins. Well balanced and approachable with food, but probably in need
of mid-term cellaring.

Cockatoo Ridge

1998 Chardonnay, Australia $9.   89

Pale straw cast. Moderately full-bodied. Full acidity. Moderately extracted. Bananas,
peaches, minerals. Shows an attractive tropical note to the nose. Full in the mouth with
an overlay of acidity. The finish is clean and crisp.

1997 Cabernet Sauvignon-Merlot, Australia $10.   82
1997 Grenache-Shiraz, Australia $10.   84

Pale ruby-purple. Moderately light-bodied. Balanced acidity. Subtly extracted. Mildly
tannic. Black pepper, minerals, green herbs. Forward peppery aromas carry a green
edge. Light and lively in the mouth with a crisp finish. A light, undemanding style.

Coldstream Hills

1996 Chardonnay, Yarra Valley $17.   89

Bright yellow-golden cast. Moderately full-bodied. Full acidity. Moderately extracted.
Mildly oaked. Tropical fruits, toasted coconut, minerals. Generous and fragrant with
extremely ripe tropical aromas and a judicious overlay of oak. Clean and well structured
in the mouth, with an angular, zesty finish.

1997 Reserve, Chardonnay, Yarra Valley $27.   90

Yellow-gold luster. Moderately full-bodied. Highly extracted. Moderately oaked. Ripe
apples, minerals, oak spice. Reserved, brooding aromas have an oaky note. Weighty, well
gripped, and flavorful on the palate with lingering dry flavors. This is well structured and
could develop further in bottle.

1995 Briarston, Cabernet Sauvignon-Merlot-Cabernet Franc,
Yarra Valley $17.   87

Very deep ruby cast. Moderately full-bodied. Balanced acidity. Moderately extracted.
Moderately oaked. Mildly tannic. Chocolate, minerals, brown spices. Fragrant and spicy
with a lean quality in the mouth. Firm and well structured through the flavorful finish.

1997 Pinot Noir, Yarra Valley $17.   84

Deep ruby with a slight fade. Medium-bodied. Balanced acidity. Moderately extracted.
Moderately oaked. Mildly tannic. Brown spices, red fruits. Forward aromas show a hefty,
spicy oak accent. Lush and lively in the mouth with generous fruit character through the
finish. Drinking well now, this is not for keeping.

1997 Reserve, Pinot Noir, Yarra Valley $27.   **88**

Bright ruby with a slight fade. Moderately full-bodied. Balanced acidity. Moderately extracted. Mildly oaked. Mildly tannic. Red fruits, minerals, spice. Aromatically reserved with a youthful and firmly structured palate feel. Lean and intense with an angular finish.

Coriole

1996 Cabernet Sauvignon, McLaren Vale $25.   **82**

1996 Redstone, 55% Shiraz-22% Cabernet-22% Grenache,
McLaren Vale $18.   **90**

Opaque blackish-purple cast. Moderately full-bodied. Balanced acidity. Highly extracted. Heavily oaked. Mildly tannic. Chocolate, mint, black fruits. Flashy aromatics reveal a hefty wood accent. Intensely flavored and generously proportioned with acidity enlivening the finish.

Cranswick

1997 Riverina, Semillon-Chardonnay, South Eastern Australia $7.99.   **86**

Deep gold. Moderately full-bodied. Full acidity. Highly extracted. Lanolin, spice, minerals. Shows a spicy accent with a core of austere Semillon flavors. Big and full in the mouth with an angular edge through the finish.

1997 Shiraz-Merlot, Rivernia $7.99.   **NR**

d'Arenberg

1996 The Custodian, Grenache, McLaren Vale $20.   **90**

Dark ruby cast. Full-bodied. Balanced acidity. Highly extracted. Mildly oaked. Quite tannic. Black fruits, minerals. Forward aromas are deep and intense. Big, rich, and firm in the mouth with big tannins that clamp down on the finish. Needs time to show its best.

1996 The Footbolt, Old Vine Shiraz, McLaren Vale $14.   **86**

Deep purple. Moderately full-bodied. Balanced acidity. Moderately extracted. Mildly oaked. Mildly tannic. Earth, red fruits. Shows a rather unusual rubbery quality in the nose that seems to blow off with aeration. Light in the mouth with a lean structure. Intense and deeply fruited finish.

Deakin Estate

1996 Alfred, Chardonnay, Victoria $8.   **88**

Deep gold. Moderately full-bodied. Balanced acidity. Moderately extracted. Toasted oak, butter. Heavily oak- accented aromas with a buttery note that follows through on the palate. Quite flavorful and textured.

Diamond Ridge

1997 Chardonnay, South Eastern Australia $8.   **81**

1997 Merlot, South Eastern Australia $9.   **85**

Deep ruby cast. Moderately full-bodied. Full acidity. Highly extracted. Moderately oaked. Quite tannic. Cocoa, minerals. Lean chocolatey aromas lead a firm and intense palate given some clout by big, aggressive tannins that bite down on the finish.

Elderton

1995 Cabernet Sauvignon-Shiraz-Merlot, Barossa Valley $30.   **93**

Deep blackish-ruby hue. Full-bodied. Balanced acidity. Highly extracted. Heavily oaked. Moderately tannic. Cassis, mint, vanilla. Quite aromatic, with a firm core of Cabernet-accented flavors. Deep and complex, showing full yet soft extraction and real complexity. Will cellar...if you can wait.

1996 Shiraz, Barossa Valley $29.   **94**

Bright blackish-purple hue. Full-bodied. Balanced acidity. Highly extracted. Moderately oaked. Mildly tannic. Plums, chocolate, spice. Opulent aromas carry a Portlike level of richness and intensity. Round, lush, and voluptuous in the mouth with a thick and seamless quality. All curves—no corners. Drinking beautifully.

Evans Wine Co.

1996 Chardonnay, Hunter Valley $12.99.   **84**

Bright yellow-straw cast. Medium-bodied. Full acidity. Moderately extracted. Yeast, citrus, minerals. Aromas show yeast complexity and vibrant notes that follow through on the palate. Quite structured, with a firm backbone. This might improve over the short to medium term.

1997 Verdelho, Hunter Valley $11.49.   **83**

1997 Semillon, Hunter Valley $11.49.   **NR**

1997 Shiraz-Cabernet, South Eastern Australia $12.99.   **NR**

Fergusson

1997 Shiraz, South Eastern Australia $12.99.   **81**

Fern Hill

1997 Chardonnay, South Australia $16.   **84**

Bright straw cast. Moderately full-bodied. Full acidity. Moderately extracted. Minerals, citrus. Aromatically reserved with a lean minerally note. Crisp and intense in the mouth with a vibrant finish. Very clean and refreshing.

1995 Cabernet Sauvignon, South Australia $16.   **83**

1995 Shiraz, South Australia $16.   **86**

Dark ruby with a slight fade. Moderately full-bodied. Balanced acidity. Moderately extracted. Mildly oaked. Mildly tannic. Mint, red fruits, minerals. Forward and intense aromatics carry an attractive minty quality to a core of ripe fruit flavors. Rich and velvety in the mouth with a juicy finish.

Gleeson's Ridge

1996 Riesling, Clare Valley $14.99.   **92**

Bright gold-straw cast. Moderately full-bodied. Full acidity. Highly extracted. Petrol, lanolin, minerals. Exotically fragrant with an intense Riesling bouquet. Full and weighty in the mouth with an angular and vibrant character. This has all the classic elements for cellaring.

Goundrey

1997 Unwooded, Chardonnay, South East Australia $14.   **84**

Pale straw cast. Medium-bodied. Balanced acidity. Moderately extracted. Citrus, dried herbs, minerals. Crisp and lively with a ripe yet angular mouthfeel. Generous and flavorful through the finish.

1997 Reserve Selection, Chardonnay, Mount Barker-Western Australia $24.   **84**

Medium straw. Medium-bodied. Balanced acidity. Moderately extracted. Butter, oak spice. Attractive highly toasted aromas lead a buttery, oak-driven mouthful of flavors that finish quite quickly. A notably oak-dominated style.

1997 Shiraz-Grenache, South East Australia $14.   **81**

Grant Smith

1997 Vintner's Reserve Bin 138, Chardonnay, Riverina $6.99.   **NR**

Scale: Superlative (96-100), Exceptional (90-95), Highly Recommended (85-89), Recommended (80-84), Not Recommended (Under 80)

Grosset

1996 Gaia, Cabernet Sauvignon, Clare Valley $29.99.   89

Opaque blackish-purple hue. Moderately full-bodied. Balanced acidity. Highly extracted. Moderately tannic. Black pepper, cassis. Shows an unusual high-toned quality to the nose, which merges with a core of ripe fruit flavors. Lean and intense with a firm and zesty structure.

Hardys

NV Sparkling Shiraz, Australia $18.99.   86

Dark ruby red. Medium-bodied. Balanced acidity. Moderately extracted. Mint, blackberries. Richly aromatic, showing oak accents that follow through on a textured, finely beaded palate. Very supple, clean finish. Highly drinkable.

1997 Signature, Chardonnay, South Eastern Australia $9.99.   82

1997 Nottage Hill, Cabernet Sauvignon-Shiraz,
South Eastern Australia $7.99.   88

Bright ruby red with a slight fade. Medium-bodied. Balanced acidity. Moderately extracted. Mildly oaked. Mildly tannic. Red fruits, vanilla. Ripe fruity aromas carry an overlay of wood seasoning. Light in the mouth with a generous supple quality and a lengthy finish. Very tasty.

1993 Thomas Hardy, Cabernet Sauvignon, Coonawarra $70.   95

Opaque blackish-ruby hue. Full-bodied. Balanced acidity. Highly extracted. Heavily oaked. Moderately tannic. Menthol, cedar, chocolate. Features an outrageously forward and pungent nose with a complex minty quality. Big and rich in the mouth, but exquisitely balanced. Pushes the boundaries of weight without becoming overbearing. Approachable now, but certainly cellarworthy.

1995 Signature, 60% Cabernet Sauvignon-40% Shiraz,
South Eastern Australia $10.99.   83

1997 Nottage Hill, Shiraz, South Eastern Australia $7.99.   81

1995 Eileen Hardy, Shiraz, McLaren Vale-Padthaway $70.   99

Opaque blackish-purple cast. Full-bodied. Balanced acidity. Highly extracted. Heavily oaked. Mildly tannic. Mint, vanilla, chocolate, black fruits, violets. Outrageous aromas are complex, sweet, and generous. Large scaled and rich in the mouth, yet lush and incredibly supple. Showing great length and intensity. Fully approachable, but should age wonderfully.

Tall Ships Tawny Port, South Australia $12.99.   82

Whiskers Blake Tawny Port, Australia $13.99.   81

Whiskers Blake Tawny Port, Australia $14.   88

Pale red-amber color. Medium-bodied. Reminiscent of caramel, brown spice, baked apple. Baked, caramelized aromas. Sweet, juicy rich flavors expand on the palate with delicate spice on the finish. Well balanced.

Heggies

1996 Chardonnay, Eden Valley $16.95.   86

Pale straw hue. Medium-bodied. Full acidity. Moderately extracted. Smoke, lemon. Full smoky, lemony aromas follow through on the lean, focused palate with a firm, oak spiced finish. Quite angular and well gripped by acids.

1996 Viognier, Eden Valley $23.   82

1994 Merlot, Eden Valley $23.   86

Deep blackish-ruby cast with a slight fade. Moderately full-bodied. Balanced acidity. Highly extracted. Moderately oaked. Moderately tannic. Earth, minerals, black fruits. Lean aromas carry a slightly earthy quality and a touch of heat. Rich and chewy in the mouth with tannins that rear up on the finish.

1997 Botrytis Riesling, Eden Valley $14/375 ml.   **86**

Dull old-gold hue. Moderately full-bodied. Balanced acidity. Highly extracted. Pineapple, citrus, honey. Forward aromas carry a pure, piercing citric quality. Rich but zesty in the mouth with acidity enlivening the sweet finish.

Henschke

1997 Croft, Chardonnay, Lenswood $41.   **NR**

1997 Green's Hill, Riesling, Lenswood $25.   **91**

Bright straw cast. Moderately full-bodied. Full acidity. Highly extracted. Minerals, lime pith. Aromatically reserved with an intense and focused palate feel. Tightly wound with racy acidity and a core of classic pithy flavors. Will develop beautifully with mid-term aging.

1994 Cyril, Cabernet Sauvignon, Eden Valley $81.   **94**

Opaque blackish-ruby cast. Full-bodied. Balanced acidity. Highly extracted. Heavily oaked. Mildly tannic. Spice, leather, black fruits. Forward aromas show richness and intensity. Generous and flavorful in the mouth with a firm minerally structure and an exotic minty accent. Finishes for a mile. No need to cellar this, though it will develop nicely.

1995 Keyneton Estate, Shiraz-Cabernet-Merlot, Barossa $38.   **88**

Deep ruby cast. Moderately full-bodied. Balanced acidity. Highly extracted. Mildly tannic. Minerals, chocolate. Aromatically reserved, with a full, rounded, and lush mouthfeel. Generous and velvety through the finish.

1995 Abbotts Prayer, Merlot-Cabernet Sauvignon-Cabernet Franc, Lenswood $56.50.   **91**

Deep ruby-garnet cast. Moderately full-bodied. Balanced acidity. Moderately extracted. Moderately oaked. Mildly tannic. Roasted meats, brown spices, red fruits. Forward aromas show great complexity. Seamless and exceptionally smooth in the mouth with an elegant structure. Lengthy and fine through the finish. Drinking well now.

1996 Giles, Pinot Noir, Lenswood $41.   **91**

Deep ruby-garnet with a slight fade. Medium-bodied. Balanced acidity. Moderately extracted. Moderately oaked. Mildly tannic. Dried herbs, black cherries, bacon. Generous and enticing aromas show a classic Pinot melange of flavors. Ripe and rich in the mouth, yet delicate in structure. Packed with flavor, and finishes for a mile.

1995 Keyneton Vineyard, Shiraz, Mount Edelston $38.   **93**

Deep blackish-purple hue. Full-bodied. Balanced acidity. Highly extracted. Moderately oaked. Mildly tannic. Mint, black fruits, tar. Complex and intense aromatics show an exotic old-vine character. Rich and mouthfilling, yet well balanced. Carries its weight effortlessly. Deeply flavored and luxuriant through the finish. Drinking beautifully.

1993 Hill of Grace, Shiraz, Australia $150.   **100**

Opaque blackish-ruby hue. Full-bodied. Balanced acidity. Highly extracted. Mildly oaked. Moderately tannic. Grilled meats, game, roasted red fruits. Aromatically complex, with a succulent gamey quality to the flavors. Rich and opulent in the mouth with great intensity and depth. Well structured with firm tannins. Approachable with food, but should age beautifully. Finishes for a mile.

Hermitage Road

1996 Chardonnay, South Eastern Australia $10.   **83**

1997 Shiraz, South Eastern Australia $10.   **83**

Scale: Superlative (96-100), Exceptional (90-95), Highly Recommended (85-89), Recommended (80-84), Not Recommended (Under 80)

Highbank
1996 Cabernet Sauvignon-Merlot-Cabernet Franc, Coonawarra $36.　　87

Opaque blackish-purple cast. Full-bodied. Balanced acidity. Highly extracted. Mildly oaked. Quite tannic. Black fruits, minerals. Aromatically reserved, with a firm and youthful palate feel. Lean and intense with tough tannins on the finish. May come around, but rather tough at present.

Hill of Content
1996 Cabernet Sauvignon, McLaren Vale $12.99.　　92

Deep blackish ruby cast. Moderately full-bodied. Balanced acidity. Moderately extracted. Moderately oaked. Moderately tannic. Cedar, chocolate, black fruits. Ripe, rich and lush with an attractive spicy wood accent and a ripe core of fruit flavors that persist through the lingering, supple finish.

Hollick
1994 Cabernet Sauvignon-Merlot, Coonawarra $20.　　91

Dark ruby-garnet cast. Moderately full-bodied. Balanced acidity. Moderately extracted. Mildly tannic. Red fruits, minerals, sweet herbs. Unusual aromas carry a high-toned herbal accent to a core of ripe fruit flavors. Lean and well structured with exceptional balance. Carries a little Bordeaux-like edge.

Jacob's Creek
1998 Chardonnay, South Eastern Australia $7.99.　　86

Bright yellow-straw cast. Medium-bodied. Balanced acidity. Moderately extracted. Minerals, yeast, citrus. Bright leesy aromas lead a clean, angular mouthfeel with a vibrant, crisp, moderately weighty finish.

1998 Dry Riesling, Australia $7.99.　　86

Pale straw cast. Moderately light-bodied. Full acidity. Moderately extracted. Citrus, flowers, minerals. Quite fragrant, with a high-toned range of fruity flavors. Light and crisp in the mouth, with a zesty, drying finish.

1997 Cabernet Sauvignon, South Eastern Australia $8.99.　　86

Bright ruby cast. Medium-bodied. Balanced acidity. Moderately extracted. Moderately oaked. Mildly tannic. Sweet herbs, red fruits, brown spices. Generous aromas carry a spicy, herbal tinge that adds a degree of complexity. Ripe and supple through the finish.

1997 Merlot, South Eastern Australia $8.99.　　83

1997 65% Shiraz-35% Cabernet, South Eastern Australia $7.99.　　81

Jamiesons Run
1996 74% Cabernet-22% Shiraz-4% Merlot, Australia $10.99.　　89

Deep blackish purple. Full-bodied. Balanced acidity. Highly extracted. Heavily oaked. Moderately tannic. Chocolate, mint, black fruits. Forward aromas carry an attractive oak accent and lead a core of dark fruit flavors. Ripe and generous, with a flavorful finish that persists.

Jenke
1997 Merlot, Barossa Valley $16.99.　　86

Bright ruby cast. Medium-bodied. Balanced acidity. Moderately extracted. Mildly oaked. Mildly tannic. Red fruits, brown spices, minerals. Pleasantly aromatic with spicy nuances and a core of fruit flavors. Lush and supple in the mouth with a velvety quality through the finish.

Kaesler

1995 Old Vine, Shiraz, Barossa Valley $37.99. **90**

Deep ruby with a slight fade. Moderately full-bodied. Balanced acidity. Moderately extracted. Mildly tannic. Chocolate, earth, black fruits. Aromatically reserved and brooding, with a velvety mouthfeel and well-developed flavors that seem mature despite the a crisp acidity lending vibrancy to the finish. Very distinctive.

Katnook Estate

1997 Sauvignon Blanc, Coonawarra $9. **88**

Deep straw cast. Moderately full-bodied. Balanced acidity. Moderately extracted. Gooseberries, dried herbs, melon. Powerful, varietally expressive aromas lead a ripe and lush mouthfeel buttressed by crisp acidity. Generous and flavorful through the finish.

1996 Cabernet Sauvignon, Coonawarra $22. **92**

Opaque blackish-purple cast. Full-bodied. Balanced acidity. Moderately extracted. Moderately oaked. Moderately tannic. Black fruits, cedar, minerals. Complex and forward aromas lead a rich and chunky mouthfeel. Big and intense through the finish. Approachable with food, but best with mid-term cellaring.

1992 Odyssey, Cabernet Sauvignon, Coonawarra $38. **92**

Bright blackish ruby cast. Full-bodied. Balanced acidity. Highly extracted. Heavily oaked. Moderately tannic. Vanilla, mint, brown spices. Shows a lovely spicy nose, which portends a rather wood-dominated flavor profile. Rich and quite intense in the mouth with a drying finish. This needs more time to show its best.

Koppamurra

1996 Classic Cabernet Blend, South Australia $20. **84**

Deep blackish-ruby cast. Moderately full-bodied. Balanced acidity. Highly extracted. Mildly oaked. Moderately tannic. Smoke, game, black fruits. Generous aromas feature an unusual gamey note. Firm and lean in the mouth with grippy tannins through the finish.

Leasingham

1996 Domain, Chardonnay, Clare Valley $9.99. **NR**

1997 Bin 7, Riesling, Clare Valley $7.99. **86**

Bright straw cast. Medium-bodied. Full acidity. Moderately extracted. Minerals, citrus zest. Aromatically reserved, with a tight and focused mouthfeel. Crisp and intense, if rather unyielding through the finish.

1995 Classic Clare, Cabernet Sauvignon, Clare Valley $29.99. **91**

Opaque blackish-ruby cast. Medium-bodied. Full acidity. Highly extracted. Heavily oaked. Moderately tannic. Menthol, minerals, red fruits. Exotically fragrant with a big minty overtone. Full, but lean in structure with a sense of crispness. Finishes with an attractive edge. Should keep well over the long term.

1996 Bin 61, Shiraz, Clare Valley $14.99. **88**

Bright dark purple. Moderately full-bodied. Balanced acidity. Moderately extracted. Moderately oaked. Mildly tannic. Vanilla, red fruits. Features a hefty oak overlay and a core of ripe fruit flavors. Full but lean in structure with an edgy, flavorful finish.

1995 Classic Clare, Shiraz, Clare Valley $29.99. **92**

Opaque blackish-purple hue. Full-bodied. Balanced acidity. Highly extracted. Moderately oaked. Moderately tannic. Menthol, black fruits, kippers. Pungent and distinctive aromas feature a ripe old-vine Syrah medicinal edge. Rich and intense in the mouth with a powerful mouthfeel and fine structure. Tannins bite down on the finish. Should age well over the middle to long term.

Peter Lehmann

1997 Semillon, Barossa $13.   89

Deep straw cast. Moderately full-bodied. Full acidity. Moderately extracted. Wax, lanolin, minerals. Shows a pleasant, classic, waxy edge to the flavors. Full but firm in the mouth with a lean edge that turns rather dry through the long finish. This should develop well with further age.

1996 Cabernet Sauvignon, Barossa $18.   88

Deep ruby cast. Moderately full-bodied. Balanced acidity. Highly extracted. Moderately oaked. Moderately tannic. Black fruits, minerals, chocolate. Rich and flavorful, with an intense, spicy, dark fruit quality. Supple and velvety in the mouth and showing fine length through the finish.

1994 Mentor, Barossa $40.   93

Opaque ruby-purple cast. Full-bodied. Balanced acidity. Highly extracted. Heavily oaked. Moderately tannic. Black fruits, mint, toast. Outstanding aromatics show a bright, high-toned, spicy quality. Firm and intense in the mouth with an extremely flavorful finish featuring persistent mint and deeply wrought black fruit flavors.

1996 Shiraz, Barossa $15.   92

Deep blackish ruby hue. Moderately full-bodied. Balanced acidity. Moderately extracted. Moderately oaked. Mildly tannic. Game, chocolate, black fruits. Exotic aromas are generous and complex. Lush and supple in the mouth, with a seamless velvety quality. Rich and intense, with a lengthy chocolatey finish. Drinking well now.

Leydens Vale

1996 Chardonnay, Victoria $22.99.   84

Deep straw cast. Medium-bodied. Balanced acidity. Moderately extracted. Minerals, citrus, cream. Aromatically reserved, with a full but zesty mouthfeel. Clean and vibrant through the finish. Well balanced, and should open with age.

1996 Cabernet Sauvignon, South Eastern Australia $22.99.   82

1996 Pinot Noir, South Eastern Australia $23.99.   82

Lindemans

1997 Chardonnay, Padthaway $12.   91

Bright gold-yellow. Medium-bodied. Balanced acidity. Moderately extracted. Vanilla, minerals, citrus zest. Bright smoky aromas follow through to a crisp, zesty palate with subtle smoky notes pervading the finish. Well balanced and intensely flavorful, with very stylish winemaking evident.

1997 Bin 77, Semillon-Chardonnay, South Eastern Australia $8.   81

1997 Bin 45, Cabernet Sauvignon, South Eastern Australia $9.   86

Bright ruby cast. Medium-bodied. Balanced acidity. Moderately extracted. Mildly tannic. Black fruits, minerals. An austere, compact style that is rather reserved aromatically. Firm and dense through the finish with a solid, chewy midpalate.

1996 Special Selection, Cabernet Sauvignon, Coonawarra $15.   90

Opaque blackish purple cast. Full-bodied. Balanced acidity. Highly extracted. Heavily oaked. Quite tannic. Vanilla, briar fruits. A showy style with big, extracted color, flavor and texture accented by a hefty dose of new oak. Packed and youthful, with tannic grip. Has the balance to take needed long-term cellaring.

1997 Bin 40, Merlot, South Eastern Australia $9.   86

Bright ruby red with a slight fade. Medium-bodied. Balanced acidity. Moderately extracted. Mildly tannic. Red cherries, minerals. Ripe, fruity aromas lead a lighter-styled palate. Crisp and lively through a finish that is framed with bright acidity.

1996 Cabernet-Merlot, Padthaway $15   86

Opaque blackish-purple. Full-bodied. Balanced acidity. Highly extracted. Mildly oaked. Moderately tannic. Black fruits, minerals, pipe tobacco. Forward aromas lead a full and intense palate feel. Quite firm in the mouth, with gripping tannins biting into the finish.

1997 Bin 99, Pinot Noir, South Australia $8.   NR

1997 Pinot Noir, Padthaway $15.   NR

1997 Bin 50, Shiraz, South Australia $9.   84

Bright ruby-purple. Medium-bodied. Balanced acidity. Moderately extracted. Mildly tannic. Red fruits, minerals. Pleasant fruit-centered aromatics carry a slightly earthy note. Light in the mouth with bright brambly flavors and a straightforward herb-tinged finish.

Lowe

1997 Chardonnay, Mudgee $18.   85

Bright yellow-straw hue. Medium-bodied. Full acidity. Yeast, smoke, minerals. Complex smoky aromas show a fine yeasty character. Brightly acidic, yet juicy and well structured through the finish. Rather elegant.

1998 Semillon, Hunter Valley $17.   81

1997 Merlot, Hunter Valley $18.50.   80

1997 Orange Cabernet Sauvignon-Merlot, Hunter Valley $18.99.   93

Deep ruby with a slight fade. Full-bodied. Balanced acidity. Highly extracted. Heavily oaked. Mildly tannic. Menthol, black fruits. Rather Shiraz-like exotic aromas, with a pungent minty quality and a core of ripe fruit flavors. Generous and intense, though showing a great edge to the structure. Exceptionally well balanced.

Magpie

1997 Mourvedre-Grenache, Barossa Valley $17.   88

Deep ruby cast. Moderately full-bodied. Full acidity. Moderately extracted. Moderately oaked. Mildly tannic. Pepper, cocoa, black fruits. Exotic flavors are generous and complex. Smooth and velvety in the mouth with an extremely supple quality. Lush and tasty with fine length.

Marienberg

1996 Reserve, Chardonnay, South Eastern Australia $12.   84

Deep yellow-gold. Moderately full-bodied. Balanced acidity. Highly extracted. Heavily oaked. Brown spices, roasted nuts, blanched almonds. Forward aromas carry a developed, nutty quality. In the mouth it is large framed and marked by oak flavors through a drying, angular finish.

1995 Reserve, Cabernet Sauvignon, South Australia $12.   83

1995 Cottage Classic Red, 65% Cabernet Sauvignon-25% Mourvedre-10% Grenache, South Australia $10.   83

1995 Reserve, Shiraz, South Australia $12.   84

Bright ruby-garnet cast. Moderately full-bodied. Low acidity. Moderately extracted. Moderately oaked. Moderately tannic. Brown spices, chocolate, sandalwood. Forward aromas carry a prominent spicy accent. Generous, lush and velvety, with a sense of richness. Chewy tannins rear up on the finish.

12 Year Old Tawny Port, Australia $13.   85

Bright chestnut hue. Medium-bodied. Moderately extracted. Apricot, nuts. Sweet, spicy, fruity aromas lead a caramel and raisin palate with sweetness remaining on the right side of cloying. Very attractive.

McAlister

1995 The McAlister, South East Gippsland $40.   81

McGuigan

1997 Cold Fermented, Bin 7000, Chardonnay, South Eastern Australia $12. 81

1997 Personal Reserve, Chardonnay, South Eastern Australia $20. 83

1998 Cold Fermented, Bin 8000, Sauvignon Blanc,
South Eastern Australia $10. 84

Very pale straw cast. Moderately light-bodied. Full acidity. Moderately extracted. Dried herbs, minerals. Clean, varietally correct aromas. Lean and fresh with a racy, lighter-styled palate feel. The finish is angular and vibrant.

1998 Oak Aged, Bin 4000, Cabernet Sauvignon,
South Eastern Australia $12. 86

Bright purple. Moderately light-bodied. Balanced acidity. Moderately extracted. Mildly tannic. Black fruits. Forward grapey aromas are effusive. A straightforward, generous quaffing style with a bright fruity center. Drinking well now.

1997 Personal Reserve, Cabernet Sauvignon, South Eastern Australia $20. 89

Bright purple cast. Moderately full-bodied. Balanced acidity. Highly extracted. Heavily oaked. Mildly tannic. Vanilla, red fruits. Ripe and perfumed with a hefty overlay of oak seasoning and a generous mouthfilling quality. Big and chunky with a flavorful finish.

1998 Bin 3000, Merlot, South Eastern Australia $12. 84

Deep ruby-purple. Medium-bodied. Balanced acidity. Moderately extracted. Mildly tannic. Black fruits, raspberries. Bright grapey aromas portend a ripe and fruity style. Lighter in the mouth than the nose suggests. Bright primary fruit flavors and slight tannins show on the finish. Very user friendly.

1998 Bin 2000, Shiraz, South Eastern Australia $12. 84

Bright purple. Medium-bodied. Full acidity. Subtly extracted. Mildly tannic. Black fruits, violets. Primary grapey aromas lead a fresh and lively palate feel. Straightforward, fruity and deeply flavored, with very slight tannins on the finish.

1996 Personal Reserve, Shiraz, South Eastern Australia $20. 88

Deep ruby cast. Moderately full-bodied. Full acidity. Moderately extracted. Moderately tannic. Plums, black fruits. Rich and ripe aromas have a generous Portlike quality. Thick and supple in the mouth, with zesty acidity lending a sense of balance. Quite intensely flavored, framed with good acids.

Meadowbank

1995 Pinot Noir, Tasmania $20.99. NR

Charles Melton

1997 Rosé of Virginia, Barossa Valley $12. 84

Brilliant pale ruby-purple hue. Medium-bodied. Full acidity. Moderately extracted. Red fruits, minerals. Bright, cheerful aromas lead a crisp and zesty palate feel. Shows rather substantial flavors on a lighter frame.

Mitchell

1995 Semillon, Clare Valley $15.99. 93

Very deep golden hue. Full-bodied. Full acidity. Highly extracted. Lanolin, lacquer, blanched almonds. Classic Aussie Semillon with a pungent and expressive array of flavors. Rich and full in the mouth, yet well balanced by an angular edge of acidity. Firm and lengthy phenolic finish. Will continue to develop.

Mitchelton

1995 Print Series, Shiraz, Victoria $45. 93

Dark luminous blackish-purple hue. Moderately full-bodied. Balanced acidity. Highly extracted. Moderately oaked. Moderately tannic. Minerals, dusty red fruits, berries. Forward aromas carry an intense sweet oak overtone. Firm and concentrated in the mouth with firm tannins. Flavorful but still a bit tough. Round it out with mid-term to long-term cellaring.

Mount Langi Ghiran

1996 Billi-Billi Creek Red, South Eastern Australia $15.　　　86

Deep ruby-garnet cast. Medium-bodied. Full acidity. Moderately extracted. Moderately tannic. Pepper, red fruits, minerals. Lean peppery aromas lead a firm and forceful palate feel. Crisp and zesty with fine intensity of flavor through the finish.

1996 Shiraz, Victoria $30.　　　86

Deep ruby-purple cast. Moderately full-bodied. Balanced acidity. Highly extracted. Moderately tannic. Black pepper, earth, minerals. Shows a dominant peppery quality throughout. Ripe and rich, yet lean in structure, with an edge to the finish. Intense and grippy.

Mount Prior

1997 Chenin Blanc, South Eastern Australia $12.99.　　　84

Deep straw cast. Moderately full-bodied. Low acidity. Moderately extracted. Tropical fruits, citrus. Rather subdued aromatically with a ripe, lush palate feel. Generous and weighty with just enough acidity on the finish to lend a sense of balance.

1996 Ibis, South Eastern Australia $14.　　　NR

1995 Noble Gold, South Eastern Australia $12/375 ml.　　　82

Mountadam

1995 Chardonnay, Eden Valley $24.　　　NR

Noon's

1995 55% Cabernet Sauvignon-45% Shiraz, South Australia $19.99.　　　82

Orlando

NV Carrington Extra Brut, Australia $8.99.　　　NR

NV Carrington Rosé Brut, Australia $8.99.　　　88

Pale red-pink hue. Medium-bodied. Red fruits, citrus. Raspberry and strawberry aromas lead a crisp citric acid palate with red fruit accents that linger on the finish. Very tasty and straightforward.

1998 St. Helga, Riesling, Eden Valley $15.　　　88

Pale straw hue with a greenish edge. Moderately full-bodied. Full acidity. Moderately extracted. Citrus zest, minerals, talc. Features a high-toned Germanic accent to the floral-edged flavors. Zesty and intense in the mouth with a very firm core of acidity. Lean and vibrant finish. Should open with age.

1994 St. Hugo, Cabernet Sauvignon, Coonawarra $28.　　　89

Opaque blackish-ruby cast. Moderately full-bodied. Balanced acidity. Moderately extracted. Mildly oaked. Moderately tannic. Black fruits, chocolate, olives. A big, rich style with complex, high-toned flavors. Lush and supple with a chewy quality. Youthful and rather closed through the finish.

Oxford Landing

1998 Chardonnay, Australia $8.　　　82

1998 Sauvignon Blanc, Australia $8.　　　83

1997 Merlot, South Eastern Australia $9.　　　NR

1997 57% Cabernet Sauvignon-43% Shiraz, South Eastern Australia $9.　　　82

Scale: Superlative (96-100), Exceptional (90-95), Highly Recommended (85-89), Recommended (80-84), Not Recommended (Under 80)

Parker

1996 Terra Rossa, Cabernet Sauvignon, Coonawarra $26.   89

Pale ruby cast. Medium-bodied. Balanced acidity. Moderately extracted. Moderately oaked. Mildly tannic. Olives, mint, red fruits. Generous aromas have a roasted southern French quality, and a big overlay of oak. Lighter in the mouth with herbal accents that lend complexity through the lengthy finish.

1996 Terra Rossa First Growth, Coonawarra $63.   90

Opaque ruby-purple cast. Moderately full-bodied. Balanced acidity. Moderately extracted. Mildly oaked. Mildly tannic. Mint, black fruits, vanilla, dill pickle. Generous aromas feature an attractive core of complex fruit flavors and a generous oak overlay. Full, but clean and well structured in the mouth with a lengthy flavorful finish.

Pauletts

1997 Dry Riesling, Clare Valley $16.99.   93

Bright straw cast. Moderately full-bodied. Full acidity. Highly extracted. Flowers, lacquer, lime pith. Aromatic and complex with an exotic array of flavors. Firm and forceful in the mouth with a well-structured and focused mouthfeel. Should develop beautifully with age.

Penfolds

1997 Koonunga Hill, Chardonnay, South Eastern Australia $9.   81

1997 The Valleys, Chardonnay, South Australia $12.   88

Bright yellow-straw cast. Moderately full-bodied. Balanced acidity. Moderately extracted. Mildly oaked. Lemon cream, butter, yeast. Forward aromas show a pleasant nutty, leesy quality. Generous in the mouth with lemony acidity lending balance. Rounded and buttery through the finish.

1996 Adelaide Hills, Trial Bin, Chardonnay, South Australia $30.   89

Bright golden cast. Moderately full-bodied. Balanced acidity. Moderately extracted. Mildly oaked. Butter, citrus, cream. Aromatically generous with spicy overtones and a ripe creamy mouthfeel. Forward and lush through the lengthy finish.

1994 Reserve Bin 94A, Chardonnay, South Eastern Australia $35.   93

Deep golden cast. Full-bodied. Balanced acidity. Highly extracted. Heavily oaked. Butter, citrus, brown spices, hazelnuts. Outrageous, opulent aromas are mature and exotic. Big and full in the mouth, yet acidity lends a sense of balance. Actually finishes on the crisp side with exceptional length and intensity. A show style.

1995 Yattarna, Chardonnay, South Australia $60.   92

Deep golden cast. Moderately full-bodied. Full acidity. Highly extracted. Mildly oaked. Cream, minerals, citrus. Somewhat reserved aromatically, with spicy, leesy nuances. Full and focused in the mouth with a racy, flavorful quality. Still youthful in structure. Well balanced and should blossom with age.

1997 Koonunga Hill, Semillon-Chardonnay, South Australia $8.   88

Bright yellow-straw cast. Moderately full-bodied. Full acidity. Highly extracted. Lanolin, lacquer, minerals. Pleasantly fragrant, with Semillon-dominated aromas. Full and rich in the mouth, with a lean quality to the finish. Very well balanced and refreshing.

1996 Adelaide Hills, Trial Bin, Semillon, South Australia $29.   91

Deep golden hue. Moderately full-bodied. Full acidity. Highly extracted. Mildly oaked. Lanolin, minerals, toast. Fragrant and intense with an exotic, varietally expressive array of flavors. Rich but firm in the mouth with a lean edge through the finish. Should develop beautifully with age.

1995 Bin 407, Cabernet Sauvignon, South Australia $19.   88

Opaque blackish-ruby hue. Full-bodied. Balanced acidity. Highly extracted. Moderately oaked. Moderately tannic. Chocolate, brown spices, minerals. Dark, reserved aromas lead to a full, rich, and intense mouthfeel. Ripe and chunky with a note of austerity to the finish. This should be better after a few years in bottle.

1996 Shiraz-Cabernet Sauvignon, South Australia $9.   86

Deep blackish ruby with a purple cast. Moderately full-bodied. Balanced acidity. Moderately extracted. Mildly tannic. Black fruits. Fruit forward and lush, with a straightforward, supple mouthfeel. Light in style, but seamless and eminently drinkable.

1996 Bin 2, Shiraz-Mourvedre, South Eastern Australia $10.   86

Dark ruby cast. Medium-bodied. Balanced acidity. Moderately extracted. Mildly tannic. Earth, dried herbs, minerals. Features a Rhonelike roasted, earthy edge to the flavors. Light in the mouth, but flavorful and concentrated. Lengthy finish.

1995 Old Vine, Shiraz-Mourvedre-Grenache, Barossa Valley $17.   88

Dark ruby cast. Medium-bodied. Balanced acidity. Moderately extracted. Mildly tannic. Minerals, black fruits. Aromatically reserved, with a firm and concentrated palate feel. Shows real density of flavor but rather closed in at present. Should open with mid-term aging.

1995 Bin 389, Cabernet-Shiraz, South Australia $19.   87

Deep blackish-ruby hue. Moderately full-bodied. Balanced acidity. Highly extracted. Mildly oaked. Mildly tannic. Chocolate, mint, black fruits. Quite aromatic with a ripe and jammy quality to the fruit flavors. Mint and wood nuances add a measure of complexity. Seductive and velvety through the finish.

1994 St. Henri, Shiraz-Cabernet, South Australia $27.   90

Deep blackish-ruby hue. Moderately full-bodied. Balanced acidity. Highly extracted. Mildly tannic. Mint, black fruits, minerals. Forward aromas are generous and very seductive. Rich and lush in the mouth with a seamless velvety quality through the lengthy intense finish. Will develop nicely, though very fine now.

1995 Bin 128, Shiraz, Coonawarra $17.   86

Deep ruby with a slight fade. Medium-bodied. Full acidity. Moderately extracted. Mildly tannic. Roasted meats, game, earth. Shows a distinctive roasted edge to the flavors. Surprisingly light in the mouth with acidity lending a sense of vibrance. Crisp through the finish.

1995 Kalimna Bin 28, Shiraz, South Australia $19.   88

Deep ruby-purple cast. Moderately full-bodied. Balanced acidity. Moderately extracted. Moderately oaked. Mildly tannic. Chocolate, minerals. Still quite youthful with a reserved quality to the nose. Lush, supple, and opulent in the mouth with a rich and intense character. Structurally approachable, but could use a short tour in the cellar to allow the aromatics to more fully develop.

1994 Magill Estate, Shiraz, Adelaide $45.   92

Deep ruby cast. Moderately full-bodied. Full acidity. Moderately extracted. Heavily oaked. Mildly tannic. Cedar, red fruits, vanilla. Forward aromas show a distinctive cedary quality. Lean and well balanced in the mouth with acidity lending a sense of buoyancy. Leans more toward a claret style, making this easy to drink and pair with food.

1993 Grange, Shiraz, South Australia $125.   98

Opaque blackish-ruby hue. Full-bodied. Balanced acidity. Highly extracted. Moderately oaked. Moderately tannic. Menthol, grilled meats, coffee, black fruits. Unbelievably complex and generous aromas lead a rich and exotic mouthfeel. Concentrated, intense, and amazingly deep in flavor. Well balanced despite its size, with firm tannins through the finish. Approachable with food, but structured for long-term aging.

Club Tawny Port, South Autralia $9.   84

Amber-brown hue. Moderately full-bodied. Caramel, toffee, raisins. Sweet and nectarlike, with raisiny flavors that join sweet toffee notes lingering on the finish. Very generous.

Club Port, Reserve, South Australia $11.   86

Chestnut appearance. Moderately full-bodied. Fig, toffee. Heavily spiced aromas lead a toffee- and caramel-like entry, with sweetness lingering through the finish. Rancio qualities are quite subtle.

910

Scale: Superlative (96-100), Exceptional (90-95), Highly Recommended (85-89), Recommended (80-84), Not Recommended (Under 80)

Grandfather, Finest Tawny Port, Barossa Valley $60.   98

Dark chestnut. Full-bodied. Rancio, spice. Powerful aromas of caramel and brown spice
lead a very tangy palate with vibrant acids keeping the considerable sugars in check
through the finish. Thick, syrupy mouthfeel does not betray any cloying character.
Complex salty, rancio notes linger.

Penley
1996 Phoenix, Cabernet Sauvignon, Coonawarra $20.99.   94

Deep blackish-purple cast. Moderately full-bodied. Balanced acidity. Moderately
extracted. Moderately oaked. Mildly tannic. Olives, mint, black fruits. Complex, very
expressive aromas lead a ripe and supple palate feel. Generous and succulent with
great balance through the finish.

Pepper Tree
1996 Shiraz, Hunter-McLaren Vale $18.99.   87

Bright ruby with a slight fade. Medium-bodied. Balanced acidity. Moderately extracted.
Mildly oaked. Mildly tannic. Coffee, earth, minerals. Forward spicy aromatics lead a lush
palate feel. Edgy acidity makes for a crisp finish.

Pibbin
1995 Pinot Noir, Adelaide Hills $20.99.   81

Pikes
1996 Cabernet Sauvignon, Clare Valley $15.99.   91

Bright ruby-purple cast. Medium-bodied. Balanced acidity. Moderately extracted.
Moderately oaked. Mildly tannic. Menthol, red fruits, minerals. Forward, complex
aromatics show an intense minty quality. Intensely flavorful, lean, and zesty in the
mouth with exceptional balance and a real edge to the lengthy finish.

Plantagenet
1997 Omrah, Shiraz, Western Australia $17.   86

Deep ruby cast. Medium-bodied. Balanced acidity. Moderately extracted. Quite tannic.
Black pepper, black fruits. Forward peppery aromas lead to a lighter-styled but intense
mouthfeel. Lean and edgy with big grippy tannins through the finish.

Plunkett
1997 Strathbogie Ranges, Unwooded, Chardonnay, Victoria $16.99.   89

Bright straw cast. Moderately full-bodied. Full acidity. Moderately extracted. Yeast,
tropical fruits, lemon pie. Attractive aromatics show a forward, complex yeasty quality.
Ripe and full but zesty, with good grip and intensity.

Queen Adelaide
Woodley Tawny Port, South Australia $8.   89

Red-amber color. Medium-bodied. Balanced acidity. Moderately extracted. Medium
sweetness. Reminiscent of earth, nuts, caramel apples. A balanced, remarkably
easy-sipping style with attractive caramel undertones. Sweet notes play in the finish,
as alcohol provides pleasing warmth.

Redbank
1997 Long Paddock, Chardonnay, Victoria $9.   89

Bright straw cast. Medium-bodied. Balanced acidity. Moderately extracted. Minerals,
apples, vanilla. Understated but generous, with a precise set of clean fruit flavors. Elegant
and well balanced through the finish.

1997 Long Paddock, Shiraz, Victoria $9.   88

Deep ruby-purple. Moderately full-bodied. Balanced acidity. Moderately extracted. Moderately oaked. Mildly tannic. Black fruits, mint, tar. Ripe aromas show complexity and depth. Full and rich in the mouth, yet well balanced, with acidity lending an attractive edge to the finish.

Riddoch

1996 Shiraz, Coonawarra $9.   88

Bright ruby cast. Medium-bodied. Full acidity. Moderately extracted. Mildly oaked. Mildly tannic. Red fruits, vanilla. Fruit centered and light in style with a crisp character. Tasty and lush through the attractive finish.

Rosemount

1997 Show Reserve, Chardonnay, Hunter Valley $17.99.   89

Pale straw. Medium-bodied. Oak spice, tropical fruits. Toasty oak aromas lead a mildly tropical palate with toasted accents. Finishes rather hot and lean, though the oak is quite restrained.

1998 Traminer-Riesling, Australia $7.99.   82

1996 Show Reserve, Semillon, Hunter Valley $17.   88

Bright straw cast. Moderately full-bodied. Full acidity. Moderately extracted. Minerals, cream, toasted nuts. Forward aromas show an attractive toasty quality. Ripe and full in the mouth with a sturdy edge of acidity.

1997 Grenache-Shiraz, Australia $7.99.   84

Bright ruby-garnet cast. Medium-bodied. Balanced acidity. Subtly extracted. Mildly tannic. Black pepper, minerals, red fruits. Bright peppery aromas lead a lush but light palate feel. Generous and flavorful through the finish.

1997 Diamond, Pinot Noir, South Eastern Australia $9.99.   82

Rymill

1995 Cabernet Sauvignon, Coonawarra $16.   93

Opaque blackish-ruby hue. Full-bodied. Balanced acidity. Highly extracted. Mildly oaked. Mildly tannic. Olives, cedar, black fruits. Exotic and complex aromatics have a southern French-like "garrigue" quality. On the palate, deep and tarry with a rich but balanced mouthfeel. Finishes with great flavor intensity.

1995 Shiraz, Coonawarra $16.   92

Deep blackish-ruby cast. Moderately full-bodied. Balanced acidity. Highly extracted. Mildly oaked. Mildly tannic. Roasted meat, chocolate, nuts. Extravagant meaty aromas show complexity and depth. Lush and supple in the mouth with a sense of lightness. Fine length and intensity through the finish.

Salitage

1995 Red Blend, Pemberton, Western Australia $35.   92

Opaque blackish-ruby hue. Full-bodied. Balanced acidity. Highly extracted. Moderately tannic. Black fruits, minerals, spice. Forward aromas show a generous spicy accent. Full and rich in the mouth with a firm core of fruit flavors. Intense and well structured but somewhat closed in. Should age nicely.

Sandalford

1996 Cabernet Sauvignon, Margaret River $19.   89

Deep saturated ruby cast. Moderately full-bodied. Balanced acidity. Moderately extracted. Moderately oaked. Mildly tannic. Black fruits, mint, minerals. Quite fragrant, with complex herbal nuances and a firm core of fruit flavors. Full but angular in the mouth with a refreshing lean structure. Complex and well balanced.

Scale: Superlative (96-100), Exceptional (90-95), Highly Recommended (85-89), Recommended (80-84), Not Recommended (Under 80)

1996 Shiraz, Mount Barker-Margaret River $19. 81

Seabrook & Seabrook
1997 Merlot, McLaren Vale $23.99. 88

Dark ruby cast. Moderately full-bodied. Balanced acidity. Highly extracted. Moderately tannic. Black fruits, minerals, mint. Fairly subdued aromatics lead a rich and flavorful mouthfeel. Shows firm structure through the finish with solid grip and intensity of flavors.

Seaview
1997 Brut, South Eastern Australia $8. 89

Pale yellow-straw cast. Medium-bodied. Balanced acidity. Moderately extracted. Bread, biscuit, citrus. Mature toasty aromas follow through on the palate, showing a rounded style and a touch of phenolic dryness on the finish. Very flavorful and appealing.

NV Sparkling Shiraz-Cabernet, South Eastern Australia $12. 87

Bright ruby-purple. Medium-bodied. Moderately extracted. Pepper, black fruits, vanilla. Youthful Shiraz aromas have an oaky backnote. Flavorful and crisp, with dark bramble fruit flavors that finish with a note of dry tannins. Intense.

1997 Chardonnay, McLaren Vale $8. 84

Bright straw cast. Medium-bodied. Full acidity. Moderately extracted. Mildly oaked. Citrus, yeast, spice. Pleasantly aromatic with a core of citric flavors and gentle spicy nuances. Rounded yet crisp in the mouth with a lengthy, flavorful finish.

1996 Edwards & Chaffey, Chardonnay, McLaren Vale $26. 87

Deep yellow-straw cast. Moderately full-bodied. Full acidity. Highly extracted. Heavily oaked. Yeast, brown spices, butter. Quite fragrant, with a generous and opulent array of flavors. Big but well balanced in the mouth, with brisk acidity enlivening the finish. Fine length and intensity.

1996 Cabernet Sauvignon, South Australia $10. 85

Opaque blackish ruby hue. Full-bodied. Balanced acidity. Highly extracted. Moderately tannic. Minerals, licorice, black fruit. Aromatically reserved, with a big, rich, chunky mouthfeel. Thick and intense through the finish, but rather unyielding due to big firm tannins.

Seppelt
1997 Reserve Bin, Terrain Series, Chardonnay, South Eastern Australia $8. 84

Bright gold. Medium-bodied. Full acidity. Moderately extracted. Minerals, citrus zest, spice. Rather subdued aromatically with a hint of spice. Lean and angular in the mouth with a crisp, refreshing finish.

1997 Corella Ridge, Chardonnay, Victoria $14. 90

Bright yellow-straw cast. Moderately full-bodied. Full acidity. Moderately extracted. Moderately oaked. Brown spices, yeast, citrus. Forward aromatics show a measure of complexity. Ripe and zesty with a big yeasty quality throughout. Fine grip and intensity through the finish.

1996 Black Label, Terrain Series, Cabernet Sauvignon, South Eastern Australia $10. 84

Very dark ruby cast. Moderately full-bodied. Balanced acidity. Highly extracted. Moderately tannic. Black cherries, minerals. Generous aromas lead a concentrated, fruit-driven palate. Ripe and tasty through the finish with soft, lingering tannins.

1997 Sunday Creek, Pinot Noir, Victoria $18. 89

Deep ruby-purple cast. Moderately full-bodied. Balanced acidity. Highly extracted. Heavily oaked. Moderately tannic. Vanilla, red fruits, minerals. Deeply colored and modern with a rush of wood flavors to match a core of ripe berry fruit. Full and well structured in the mouth with grippy tannins through the finish. A big, showy Pinot, but stylish and tasty.

Trafford Tawny Port, Barossa Valley $11. **91**

Rusty amber color. Medium-bodied. Reminiscent of brown spice, dates. A subtle, mature spicy nose hints at the elegance of age. Sweet and spicy flavors are refined and and finish like a dry Amontillado Sherry.

Para Port Tawny, Australia $24.99. **93**

Deep mahogany hue. Attractve, exotic fig, toffee, and roasted nut aromas show the type of complexity that only comes with extreme age. A rich attack leads to a moderately full-bodied palate with mild sweetness and a wave of roasted flavors. Intense and firm. Develops in the glass with aeration and keeps some time in the bottle. Drink now.

Sheldrake

1996 Chardonnay, Western Australia $12. **87**

Dark gold. Medium-bodied. Balanced acidity. Moderately extracted. Butterscotch, pear. Developed aromas lead a bright, textured palate with pearlike flavors persisting through the finish. A rich and flavorful style that is drinking well now.

1996 Stirling Estate, Merlot, Western Australia $13. **83**

1995 Shiraz, Western Australia $13. **87**

Deep ruby hue with a slight fade. Moderately full-bodied. Full acidity. Moderately extracted. Mildly oaked. Moderately tannic. Game, roasted meat, earth. Generous aromas feature a distinctive roasted, gamey quality. Ripe and full in the mouth, with juicy acidity buoying the finish. Intense, well balanced and fairly concentrated.

Tawny Port, Australia $13/500 ml. **82**

St. Hallett

1996 Faith, Shiraz, Barossa $18. **86**

Bright purple cast. Medium-bodied. Balanced acidity. Moderately extracted. Mildly tannic. Minerals, red fruits, violets. Aromatically reserved with a crisp and lean structure. Fruit centered and eminently drinkable, finishing cleanly.

1994 Old Block, Shiraz, Barossa $35. **89**

Deep blackish-ruby hue. Moderately full-bodied. Full acidity. Moderately extracted. Mildly oaked. Mildly tannic. Minerals, briar fruits. Aromatically reserved with buoyant acidity lending a sense of liveliness to the palate. Racy through the finish. Balanced and tasty but lacks a bit of stuffing on the midpalate to qualify for a heavyweight.

Stanley Brothers

1995 Thoroughbred, Cabernet Sauvignon, Barossa Valley $20.99. **84**

Deep ruby with a slight fade. Moderately full-bodied. Balanced acidity. Highly extracted. Mildly oaked. Moderately tannic. Minerals, black fruits. Ripe and intense with a big core of fruit flavor. Well structured and sizable on the palate, with a touch of heat to the finish.

1996 John Hancock, Shiraz, Barossa Valley $24.99. **88**

Deep ruby with a purple edge. Moderately full-bodied. Full acidity. Moderately extracted. Moderately oaked. Mildly tannic. Briar fruits, minerals. Ripe fruity aromas are accentuated by vibrant acidity. Rich, yet crisply structured, with fine length and intensity.

Charles Sturt

1995 55% Cabernet Sauvignon-30% Syrah-15% Merlot, Australia $13.99. **89**

Deep blackish ruby cast. Full-bodied. Balanced acidity. Highly extracted. Mildly oaked. Quite tannic. Spice, minerals. Somewhat reserved aromatically, with a concentrated and well-structured mouthfeel. Firm and intense through the finish. Well balanced, should gain complexity with age.

Taltarni

NV Brut Taché, Victoria $18.99.   83

1995 Clover Hill Brut, Tasmania $28.   81

1998 Sauvignon Blanc, Victoria $13.   90

Bright platinum hue. Moderately light-bodied. Balanced acidity. Subtly extracted. Gooseberries, dried herbs. Aggressive aromas are pure and varietally expressive. Surprisingly light in the mouth though wonderfully pure, flavorsome and juicy. This is a stylish wine.

1996 Shiraz, Victoria $15.   86

Deep ruby cast. Medium-bodied. Balanced acidity. Moderately extracted. Mildly tannic. Black pepper, minerals. Forward peppery aromas are present throughout. Lean and angular in style, with gripping tannins through the finish.

Tatachilla

1997 Chardonnay, McLaren Vale $13.99.   80

1997 Grenache-Shiraz, McLaren Vale $13.99.   84

Bright ruby cast. Medium-bodied. Balanced acidity. Moderately extracted. Mildly tannic. Black pepper, raspberries, minerals. Quite aromatic, with a convincing array of complex Rhonelike flavors. Light in structure but concentrated in flavor. Interesting.

1997 Wattle Park, Shiraz, South Australia $9.99.   86

Bright ruby cast. Medium-bodied. Balanced acidity. Moderately extracted. Mildly tannic. Red fruits, minerals. Ripe and fruity, with a generous array of flavors. Light in the mouth, with an edgy, minerally quality through the finish.

1996 Shiraz, McLaren Vale $17.99.   89

Deep ruby cast. Moderately full-bodied. Balanced acidity. Moderately extracted. Moderately oaked. Mildly tannic. Plums, sweet herbs, dill pickle. Ripe aromas carry a distinctive herbal edge. Full and rich in the mouth, yet buoyed by zesty acidity. Lengthy and intense finish. Quite interesting.

1995 Foundation, Shiraz, McLaren Vale $34.99.   94

Deep ruby-purple cast. Full-bodied. Balanced acidity. Highly extracted. Heavily oaked. Mildly tannic. Vanilla, sandalwood, black fruits. Perfumed aromas show an extravagant sweet oak quality. Rich, ripe, and unctuous in the mouth with great intensity and persistence of flavor. Fine length. Drinking well, but with the acidity to age.

Trentham

1995 Chardonnay, Riverland $15.99.   91

Brilliant yellow-gold hue. Moderately full-bodied. Highly extracted. Butterscotch, vanilla, butter. Rich, heavy aromas follow through on a rounded, low acid palate showing thick texture and silky finish. Shows a generous, supple, and attractive character.

1996 60% Cabernet Sauvignon-40% Merlot, Australia $16.99.   89

Blackish-ruby hue with a slight fade. Moderately full-bodied. Balanced acidity. Highly extracted. Moderately oaked. Mildly tannic. Dill pickle, spice, chocolate. Spicy aromatics show an oak-dominant quality to the flavors. Rich and ripe in the mouth with a core of lush fruit flavors that offset the wood. Generous and well balanced through the finish.

Tyrrell's

1997 Old Winery, Chardonnay, South Eastern Australia $9.99.   86

Deep gold. Moderately full-bodied. Full acidity. Moderately extracted. Bread dough, citrus, cream. Subtle bready aromas lead a surprisingly zesty palate with an overlay of crisp acidity. Tart and juicy through the finish.

1997 Shee-Oak, Chardonnay, Hunter Valley $18.99.   NR

1997 Old Winery, Cabernet-Merlot, South Australia $10.99. 84

Deep ruby cast. Moderately full-bodied. Balanced acidity. Highly extracted. Mildly oaked. Moderately tannic. Vanilla, black fruits. Quite youthful, with a firm and extracted structure and reserved flavors. Lean through the lengthy cassis-accented finish.

1997 Old Winery, Pinot Noir, South Eastern Australia $10.99. 85

Pale ruby-garnet cast. Moderately light-bodied. Balanced acidity. Moderately extracted. Moderately oaked. Quite tannic. Sweet oak, overripe red fruits. Shows a jammy quality to the nose. Straightforward and tasty flavors play out until firm tannins take over on the finish.

1996 Eclipse, Pinot Noir, Hunter Valley $18.99. 84

Bright ruby with a slight fade. Moderately full-bodied. Balanced acidity. Moderately extracted. Moderately oaked. Mildly tannic. Brown spices, minerals, red fruits. Forward aromas show a spicy woody quality. Full and round in the mouth with a drying finish.

1996 Old Winery, Shiraz, South Eastern Australia $9.99. 84

Dark ruby with a slight garnet fade. Moderately full-bodied. Full acidity. Moderately extracted. Moderately oaked. Mildly tannic. Dried herbs, minerals, earth. Distinctive aromatics lead a rich mouthfeel offset by zesty acidity. Finishes on a lingering herb-tinged note.

1996 Brokenback, Shiraz, Hunter Valley $18.99. 84

Pale ruby-purple cast. Medium-bodied. Balanced acidity. Moderately extracted. Mildly tannic. Minerals, red fruits. Aromatically reserved with a lean and zesty quality in the mouth. Ripe and flavorful with an edgy finish showing a tannic spike.

Wakefield

1994 Cabernet Sauvignon, Clare Valley $16.49. 81

Warrabilla

1997 Merlot, King Valley $30. 87

Opaque blackish-ruby hue. Full-bodied. Balanced acidity. Highly extracted. Heavily oaked. Moderately tannic. Pickle barrel, black fruits, sweet herbs. Pungent and oak dominated with an intense pickley quality. Rich and full in the mouth with a continuation of the unusual flavors. Interesting, but not for everyone.

1997 Brimin, 62% Cabernet-38% Shiraz, Victoria $24. 90

Opaque blackish-purple hue. Full-bodied. Balanced acidity. Highly extracted. Moderately oaked. Mildly tannic. Chocolate, spice, black fruits. Ripe and full with forward aromatics and a thick, chunky mouthfeel. Deeply flavored and well balanced. Drinking well now.

1997 Shiraz, Victoria $30. 92

Opaque blackish-purple hue. Full-bodied. Balanced acidity. Heavily oaked. Moderately tannic. Coffee, chocolate, briar fruits. Exotic aromas carry an intense spicy quality throughout. Rich and velvety in the mouth with fine weight and intensity. Very lengthy and approachable now, but built to age.

Wilton

1995 Botrytis Semillon, New South Wales $18/375 ml. 86

Deep brilliant amber cast. Medium-bodied. Full acidity. Moderately extracted. Caramel, dates, figs. Exotic aromas lead a surprisingly light and angular palate feel with moderate sweetness. Finishes on the lean side.

Wolf Blass

1998 Chardonnay, South Australia $11.99. 85

Pale straw cast. Medium-bodied. Full acidity. Moderately extracted. Blanched almonds, minerals. Developed aromatics hint at a degree of maturity. Lean and austere in the mouth, with a touch of bitterness through the finish.

Scale: Superlative (96-100), Exceptional (90-95), Highly Recommended (85-89), Recommended (80-84), Not Recommended (Under 80)

1997 Yellow Label, Cabernet Sauvignon, South Australia $11.99.   **89**
Deep ruby cast. Medium-bodied. Balanced acidity. Moderately extracted. Mildly oaked. Mildly tannic. Red fruits, brown spices, minerals. Generous aromas show an attractive spicy accent. Well balanced and well structured with a lean edge to the firm, flavorful finish.

Wyndham

1997 Bin 222, Chardonnay, South Eastern Australia $8.99.   **83**
1998 Bin 777, Semillon-Chardonnay, South Eastern Australia $7.99.   **83**
1996 Bin 444, Cabernet Sauvignon, South Eastern Australia $9.99.   **84**
Deep ruby hue. Medium-bodied. Balanced acidity. Moderately extracted. Mildly oaked. Mildly tannic. Cassis, minerals, chocolate. Firm and complex in flavor with a deep core of dark fruit flavors and a spicy herbal accent. Aromatic and generous through the finish.
1998 Bin 333, Pinot Noir, South Eastern Australia $9.99.   **81**
1996 Bin 555, Shiraz, Australia $9.99.   **85**
Bright ruby-garnet cast. Moderately full-bodied. Low acidity. Moderately extracted. Moderately tannic. Stewed fruits, sweet herbs, pine. Spicy aromatics, with a rich, ripe, stewed quality. Shows a touch of heat on the palate which cuts the finish a bit short.

David Wynn

1997 Chardonnay, South Eastern Australia $13.   **87**
Bright gold. Moderately full-bodied. Balanced acidity. Moderately extracted. Moderately oaked. Brown spices, cream, citrus. Quite fragrant, with a spicy oak overlay and a ripe, creamy palate feel. Shows some crispness toward the finish ,with fine acid intensity.
1996 Cabernet Sauvignon, Eden Valley $15.   **86**
Deep blackish ruby cast. Moderately full-bodied. Balanced acidity. Moderately extracted. Moderately oaked. Mildly tannic. Chocolate, minerals, black fruits. Aromatically reserved, with a full palate feel showing ripe fruit flavors and velvety chocolatey notes that turn firm through the finish.
1995 Patriarch, Shiraz, Eden Valley $35.   **86**
Deep ruby cast. Medium-bodied. Balanced acidity. Moderately extracted. Moderately oaked. Mildly tannic. Vanilla, sweet herbs, chocolate. Forward aromas show a complex herbal character that merges with a core of ripe chocolate flavors in the mouth. Surprisingly delicate in the mouth with buoyant acidity lending a sense of lightness to the crisp finish.

Wynns

1997 Coonawarra Estate, Chardonnay, Coonawarra $12.   **86**
Pale yellow-straw hue. Medium-bodied. Full acidity. Moderately extracted. Citrus zest, apples, minerals. In the nose this is crisp and lively, though it shows some drier flavors on the intense, zesty finish. Well structured.
1995 Cabernet Sauvignon, Coonawarra $14.   **86**
Opaque blackish ruby hue. Moderately full-bodied. Balanced acidity. Moderately extracted. Mildly tannic. Cassis, minerals, chocolate. Aromatically reserved, though rich and flavorful in the mouth with a focused dark fruit character. A lush, supple style.
1994 John Riddoch, Cabernet Sauvignon, Coonawarra $40.   **89**
Opaque blackish-purple cast. Full-bodied. Balanced acidity. Highly extracted. Heavily oaked. Moderately tannic. Vanilla, cassis, mint. Forward aromatics are showy and opulent. Big but firmly structured and linear. Grippy acidity lends some buoyancy to the finish. Big tannins in the finish suggest the need for mid-term to long-term cellaring.
1996 Coonawarra Estate, Shiraz, Coonawarra $13.   **84**
Deep ruby-purple. Medium-bodied. Full acidity. Moderately extracted. Mildly tannic. Black pepper, dried herbs. Shows a distinctive peppery quality throughout. Light in the mouth with a sense of crispness through the finish. Attractive and eminently quaffable.

1994 Michael, Shiraz, Coonawarra $40.   92

Opaque blackish-ruby cast. Moderately full-bodied. Balanced acidity. Highly extracted. Heavily oaked. Mildly tannic. Vanilla, mint, black fruits. Forward and generous aromas show a firm core of berry flavors and attractive sweet oak nuances. Concentrated, yet surprisingly light in the mouth, with a vibrant and zesty quality through the finish. Drinking well now.

Yalumba

1997 Chardonnay, Barossa $12.   NR

1997 Limited Release, Viognier, Barossa $15.   91

Bright yellow-straw hue. Moderately full-bodied. Balanced acidity. Moderately extracted. Stone fruits, honey. Elegant floral, honeyed aromas lead a sumptuous, thick mouthfeel with peachy flavors that linger through the finish. Very attractive and displays fine varietal character.

1996 Cabernet Sauvignon, South Australia $15.   86

Bright ruby red. Medium-bodied. Balanced acidity. Moderately extracted. Mildly oaked. Mildly tannic. Red fruits, dill pickle. Crisp and aromatic with a bright fruity quality in the mouth. Straightforward and lively through the finish.

1995 The Menzies, Cabernet Sauvignon, Coonawarra $29.   86

Deep ruby with a slight fade. Moderately full-bodied. Balanced acidity. Highly extracted. Moderately oaked. Mildly tannic. Dill pickle, cassis, chocolate. Forward aromas carry a big spicy quality. Lighter in the mouth with a mature cast to the flavors. Pleasant, supple finish.

1996 Bush Vine, Grenache, Barossa $14.   89

Bright ruby cast. Moderately full-bodied. Balanced acidity. Highly extracted. Mildly tannic. Briar fruits, minerals. Ripe, jammy aromas lead a full, rich palate feel. Lush and generous through the flavorful finish.

**1994 The Signature, Cabernet Sauvignon-Shiraz,
Barossa Valley-Coonawarra $40.**   92

Opaque blackish-purple cast. Full-bodied. Balanced acidity. Highly extracted. Heavily oaked. Moderately tannic. Cedar, mint, cassis. Exotic and outrageous aromatics show a profound core of black fruit flavors and a hefty overlay of sweet oak nuances. Deep and rich in the mouth with a thick velvety quality. Sizable but well balanced. Approachable now, though it should cellar well.

1996 Shiraz, Barossa $15.   89

Deep ruby-purple. Moderately full-bodied. Balanced acidity. Moderately extracted. Moderately oaked. Mildly tannic. Dusty red fruits, minerals, spice. Pleasantly aromatic with a sweet, spicy quality to the nose. Full but crisp in structure, with an edge providing balance toward the well-gripped and intense finish.

1994 Octavius, Edition V, Shiraz, Barossa $60.   94

Opaque dark purple cast. Full-bodied. Full acidity. Highly extracted. Heavily oaked. Moderately tannic. Mint, black fruits, vanilla. Extravagant sweet aromas lead a full-throttled palate feel. Amazingly deep and dense with intense waves of flavor. Tannins still have a bite on the finish, indicating mid-term cellaring would be appropriate. A classic show Shiraz.

Clocktower Tawny Port, Australia $9.99.   86

Tawny-amber color. Medium-bodied. Moderately extracted. Reminiscent of caramel, baked fruits, mild brown spice. Mildly vinous quality on the nose reveals flavors of sweet caramelized fruits that expand on the palate and linger through the finish. Vinous fruit flavors are more apparent than spicy wood.

Galway Pipe Tawny Port, Australia $22.99.   90

Brownish amber color. Medium-bodied. Reminiscent of walnut, ginseng, dried fruits. Sweet exotically spicy nose shows great harmony that is confirmed on the palate of nectarous spicy flavors. Elegant lingering finish has persistent delicate spice flavors.

Scale: Superlative (96-100), Exceptional (90-95), Highly Recommended (85-89),
Recommended (80-84), Not Recommended (Under 80)

1997 Botrytis Semillon-Sauvignon Blanc, Griffith-Barossa $15/375 ml.   **84**
Deep golden hue. Moderately full-bodied. Low acidity. Moderately extracted. Melon, pears. Forward fruity aromas with a touch of honeyed character leads a fat and rounded mouthfeel with mildly cloying sweetness levels and a viscous finish.

NV Antique Tawny, Museum Release, New South Wales $16/375 ml.   **97**
Deep mahogany cast. Moderately full-bodied. Balanced acidity. Highly extracted. Roasted salted nuts, caramel, brown spices. Wonderfully aromatic and flavorful with an aged, roasted-salty quality to the flavors. Rich and enticing with a touch of warming heat throughout. Complex and very intense.

Yarra Ridge
1998 Pinot Noir, Yarra Valley $11.99.   **84**
Pale ruby-purple. Moderately full-bodied. Balanced acidity. Highly extracted. Moderately tannic. Briar fruits, minerals. Jammy fruit flavors lead a light palate with light varietal fruit flavors that taper to a mildly astringent finish. A ripe manifestation of Pinot Noir.

Yarra Yering
1996 Dry Red Wine No.1, Victoria $42.   **88**
Deep ruby cast. Medium-bodied. Balanced acidity. Highly extracted. Moderately oaked. Moderately tannic. Dried herbs, minerals. Herbal aromas lead a firm and nervy palate feel. Displays an austere minerally backbone with grippy tannins on the finish. Features an almost Italian edge to the structure. Should develop over the long term.

1996 Dry Red Wine No.2, Victoria $42.   **84**
Very deep ruby hue. Medium-bodied. Full acidity. Moderately extracted. Mildly tannic. Red fruits, pepper. Attractive aromas lead an edgy and intense palate feel. Lots of acidity makes for a mouth-puckering palate and a racy finish. Zesty, bright, and intense.

Yarraman Road
1996 Barrington, Chardonnay, Hunter Valley $19.   **89**
Medium straw. Medium-bodied. Balanced acidity. Moderately extracted. Yeast, smoke, minerals. Complex yeast and oak aromas do not follow through with a similar degree of depth. Finishes rather quickly showing melony flavors behind the oak spice.

1995 Cabernet-Shiraz, South Eastern Australia $20.   **84**
Bright ruby-garnet cast. Medium-bodied. Balanced acidity. Moderately extracted. Mildly oaked. Mildly tannic. Mint, cedar, red fruits. Attractive nuanced aromas are showing an edge of maturity. Well balanced and crisp in the mouth with acidity enlivening the finish.

1994 Shiraz, South Eastern Australia $20.   **86**
Bright blackish-garnet hue. Moderately full-bodied. Full acidity. Moderately extracted. Moderately oaked. Moderately tannic. Chocolate, brown spices, overripe red fruits. Spicy aromas lead a big, rich palate. Full and rounded, with solid balancing acidity and grippy tannins through the finish. A very ripe style.

Yering Station
1995 Cabernet Sauvignon-Merlot-Cabernet Franc, Yarra Valley $18.99.   **82**

forty-three

❧

New Zealand

❧

The Wines of New Zealand:
Current Market Overview

Situated in the deep end of the South Pacific, New Zealand is famously remote, with Australia serving as her only neighbor, over 1000 miles to the west. Fortunately for the New Zealanders (or Kiwis, in the local parlance), the topography is as dramatic as the nation is remote. New Zealand stretches for over 1000 miles from north to south and, as such, has a widely varying climate. If it were transposed onto European latitudes, the nation would stretch from the Baltic Sea and Denmark to the African nation of Tunisia. This means that New Zealand's vineyard regions are as varying in latitude as the Rhine Valley in Germany and Andalucia in the south of Spain.

Latitude, however, is only part of the story. Europe's vineyard areas are either influenced by continental weather patterns, or moderated by the warm waters of the Mediterranean and the Atlantic's Gulf Stream. New Zealand, on the other hand, is an island nation (or, more accurately, a two-island nation) and the climate is strictly maritime. Moreover, the waters surrounding New Zealand have a bracingly cold Antarctic influence, so that a wine region of the equivalent Northern Hemisphere latitude as Bordeaux (the South Island's Central Otago) has a climate as chilly as the Mosel Valley in Germany. Outside of the handful of vineyards in the near subtropical north of the country near Auckland, however, what really drives New Zealand viticulture is rain.

The prevailing weather patterns move big storms from west to east and dump large amounts of rain on the western coast. The effect of this rain, however, is moderated by the mountainous interior, and the rains tend to dissipate before reaching the big vineyard areas on the East Coast of the North Island (Gisbourne & Hawke's Bay). Unfortunately, these same areas are vulnerable to the big easterly cyclonic storms that can blow in from the South Pacific in the autumn, right around harvest. This penchant for rain, combined with an extraordinarily intense sun (New Zealand weather forecasts give sunburn advisories which can be measured in less than ten minutes) and fertile soils can make high-quality viticulture difficult, as vines in these growing conditions have a tendency to turn into something resembling dense jungle. Addressing this problem has put New Zealand's vintners on the forefront of developments in trellising and canopy management, and these advances have led to some very good wines from both Hawke's Bay and Gisbourne, particularly Chardonnay.

Mad About Marlborough:
The World's Best Sauvignon Blanc?

In 1973, New Zealand's biggest wine company, Montana (Brancott in the U.S.), was looking to expand. While land in the established vineyard region of Hawke's Bay was going for NZ $2000 an acre, land in Marlborough, a drab pastureland at the northern tip of the South Island could be had for as little as NZ $250 an acre. Rolling the dice, they bought 14 farms totaling 4000 acres, and set about planting Muller-Thurgau, which at the time was the most popular New Zealand varietal. On a hunch, after tasting New Zealand's first ever Sauvignon Blanc, a Matua Valley 1974, Montana took another chance and planted 60 acres of the Marlborough property to the varietal. The rest, as they say, is history.

Scale: Superlative (96-100), Exceptional (90-95), Highly Recommended (85-89), Recommended (80-84), Not Recommended (Under 80)

The resultant wines were unlike anything the world had ever seen before. Marlborough Sauvignon had "out-Sancerred" Sancerre. Amazingly crisp and vibrant with an extraordinary herbal pungency, these were wines that couldn't be ignored. They were polarizing, and met with critical acclaim or revulsion, but they certainly demanded a reaction. These first wines led to a planting boom, and Marlborough is still growing at a breakneck pace, while the world is awakening to the wines. Why did this hitherto unknown region prove so successful?

Marlborough has a unique geographic position, which has allowed it to overcome the pitfalls alluded to earlier, which had plagued New Zealand viticulture on the North Island. Again, first and foremost is the issue of rain. Like the Northern regions, western storms are broken up in the mountainous interior, but unlike the Northern Regions, Marlborough is sheltered from the autumnal cyclones by the southern tip of the Northern Island to the east. This allows vintners the luxury of a lengthy ripening season, as the fruit can hang well into April and even May. Indeed, rainfall from February to April (New Zealand's harvest period) is drier than anywhere else in the country, and the critical month of March is Marlborough's driest of the year.

Marlborough is also the sunniest place in New Zealand, helping with ripeness, while acidity is preserved by the cold maritime summer nights. Finally, unlike the other regions, the soils are fairly infertile and very stony, helping to retain heat and affording excellent drainage. The drainage is so good, in fact, that irrigation is essential.

Today, Marlborough is home to many wineries and others on the North Island are sourcing Marlborough grapes. Despite the continual increases in plantings, however, these quintessential Sauvignons have been under increasing worldwide demand, and shipments to the United States have been minimal. This has meant that, up until this point, New Zealand wines have maintained a relatively low profile in the U.S. market. While wines such as Cloudy Bay are on strict allocation in Britain,

New Zealand at a Glance

Wines Reviewed:

61

Producers/Brands Represented:

24

Value Rating:

Average to Good

for instance, bottles can often be found sitting on U.S. retailer's shelves. To be sure there are cult fans, but the chilly reception the style has received in the U.S. mass media has tempered any impending explosion of interest.

Things may be set to change, however. Increased production has allowed more New Zealand wine than ever to be exported to the U.S. While slightly more than 250,000 bottles of New Zealand wine were exported to the U.S. between June 30, 1995, and June 30, 1996, the figure had risen to nearly 700,000 bottles for the year ending June 30, 1997. Sales increases of that magnitude are sure to grab attention, and the media will be sure to follow. In the end New Zealand Sauvignon Blanc is may not be for everyone, but to many it will prove to be irresistible.

Reviews

Brancott
1997 Reserve, Chardonnay, Gisborne $16.   90

Yellow-gold luster. Moderately full-bodied. Balanced acidity. Moderately oaked. Vanilla, butterscotch. Lavishly rich, ripe aromas follow through on the palate with juicy, fruit-centered flavors showing honeyed richness and lushly oaked character. Drinking well now, with balanced acids.

1997 Reserve, Sauvignon Blanc, Marlborough $16.   91

Pale straw. Medium-bodied. Moderately extracted. Gooseberries, herbs, greengage. Intense varietally pure aromas follow through on the palate with a fine intensity of classic flavors. The finish is well gripped by acids and a touch of dryness.

Kim Crawford
1997 Tietjen, Chardonnay, Gisborne $20.   86

Deep yellow-straw cast. Full-bodied. Full acidity. Highly extracted. Lanolin, minerals, brown spices. Shows an unusual waxy undercurrent to the core of oak-spiced flavors. Full but lean in the mouth with a structured quality to the flavorful finish.

1997 Sauvignon Blanc, Marlborough $15.   84

Deep straw cast. Moderately full-bodied. Balanced acidity. Moderately extracted. Gooseberries, minerals, citrus zest. Generous varietal aromas lead a rounded palate feel supported by edgy acidity through the finish. Shows an impressive mouthfeel.

1996 Sauvignon Blanc, Awatere $20.   87

Bright golden cast. Moderately full-bodied. Full acidity. Highly extracted. Minerals, spice, dried herbs. Spicy flavors seem to suggest some oak influence. Edgy and intense in the mouth with an herbal quality through the racy finish.

Fairhall Downs
1997 Sauvignon Blanc, Marlborough $15.99.   95

Deep straw cast. Moderately full-bodied. Full acidity. Highly extracted. Gooseberries, asparagus, tropical fruits. Outrageous aromatics are both pungent and complex. Lean, racy, and intense in the mouth, yet ripe and opulent. A classic example of powerful, aromatic New Zealand Sauvignon Blanc.

Framingham
1997 Sauvignon Blanc, Marlborough $13.50.   84

Deep straw cast. Medium-bodied. Balanced acidity. Moderately extracted. Wool, citrus, minerals. Shows a slightly funky Loire-like quality to the nose. Rounded and lush in the mouth with a rush of acidity to the finish.

1998 Late Harvest, Reserve, Riesling, Marlborough $30/375 ml.   **82**

Giesen
1998 Sauvignon Blanc, Marlborough $12.   **86**
Bright straw cast. Medium-bodied. Full acidity. Moderately extracted. Gooseberries, minerals, dried herbs. Attractive varietal aromas lead a racy, crisp palate feel. Lean and stylish, with a mildy phenolic finish.

Goldwater
1997 Roseland, Chardonnay, Marlborough $19.99.   **86**
Deep yellow-straw cast. Moderately full-bodied. Full acidity. Highly extracted. Minerals, tropical fruits. Aromatically reserved with an angular, lanolin-like, waxy sensation in the mouth. Firm and sharp through the finish.

1998 Dog Point, Sauvignon Blanc, Marlborough $17.99.   **86**
Deep straw cast. Moderately full-bodied. Full acidity. Moderately extracted. Cream, minerals. Aromatically reserved, but opulent and rich in the mouth with a sturdy backbone of zesty acidity. Ripe and intense.

1996 Cabernet Sauvignon-Merlot, Waiheke Island $50.   **84**
Deep ruby hue. Medium-bodied. Balanced acidity. Highly extracted. Moderately tannic. Minerals, dried herbs, spice. Lean aromas show a slight herbal edge. Firm and somewhat austere in the mouth. Well balanced and should open with time.

Grove Mill
1997 Chardonnay, Marlborough $20.   **88**
Bright yellow-straw cast. Moderately full-bodied. Full acidity. Moderately extracted. Minerals, cream, melon. Rather reserved aromatically, but ripe and rounded in the mouth with a creamy, leesy quality. Lush and generous through the finish.

1996 Lansdowne, Chardonnay, Marlborough $30.   **90**
Bright yellow-straw cast. Medium-bodied. Full acidity. Highly extracted. Minerals, citrus zest, cream. Subtle creamy aromas lead a rounded mouthfeel where the flavors are complex and substantial. Firmly structured and angular toward the lengthy finish. Should age nicely.

1998 Sauvignon Blanc, Marlborough $18.   **84**
Brilliant pale straw cast. Medium-bodied. Full acidity. Moderately extracted. Minerals, dried herbs. Aromatically reserved with delicate herbal overtones. Lighter in the mouth and perhaps lacking somewhat for intensity of flavor, but clean and racy through the finish.

House of Nobilo
1998 Fall Harvest, Chardonnay, Gisborne $9.99.   **83**
1998 White Cloud, Medium Dry White, Hawkes Bay-Gisbourne $6.99.   **84**
Pale straw cast. Moderately full-bodied. Full acidity. Subtly extracted. Green apple, citrus peel, flowers. Bright aromatic flavors have an overtone of sweetness. Clean, racy, and fairly dry in the mouth, with a lean pithy quality to the finish.

1998 Fall Harvest, Sauvignon Blanc, Marlborough $9.99.   **83**

Hunter's
1997 Sauvignon Blanc, Marlborough $16.   **87**
Deep straw cast. Moderately full-bodied. Full acidity. Moderately extracted. Gooseberries, dried herbs, minerals. Varietally intense aromas lead a lean and racy palate feel. Crisp and sturdy with an edgy phenolic quality to the finish. Six months extra in bottle should help.

Kumeu River Vineyard

1996 Chardonnay, Kumeu $32.   84

Bright golden cast. Moderately full-bodied. Full acidity. Moderately extracted. Mildly oaked. Menthol, vanilla, minerals. Forward aromas have an intriguing herbal minty quality. Ripe and full in the mouth with a firm edge of acidity. Angular through the finish. Interesting.

1996 Matés Vineyard, Chardonnay, Kumeu $41.   83
1997 Sauvignon Blanc, Kumeu $19.   NR

Lawson's

1996 Dry Hills, Chardonnay, Marlborough $18.99.   86

Deep mat-gold cast. Moderately full-bodied. Full acidity. Moderately extracted. Minerals, citrus zest, yeast. Angular and reserved in style with a firm and extracted structure. Finishes with a slight pithy quality.

1998 Dry Hills, Sauvignon Blanc, New Zealand $12.99.   84

Bright straw cast. Moderately full-bodied. Full acidity. Moderately extracted. Cream, minerals, citrus. Rather subtle in flavor, but rich and ripe in the mouth. Supported by an edgy streak of acidity that makes for a refreshing finish.

Martinborough Vineyard

1996 Chardonnay, Martinborough $25.99.   81

Matua

1997 Judd Estate, Chardonnay, Gisborne $17.   83
1998 Sauvignon Blanc, Hawkes Bay $14.   83
1997 Reserve, Sauvignon Blanc, Waimauku $20.   87

Deep yellow-straw cast. Moderately full-bodied. Balanced acidity. Moderately extracted. Tropical fruits, lanolin, spice. Forward aromas show an attractive leesy, yeasty note. Ripe and rich in the mouth with a rounded quality. Crisp through the finish. A luxurious style.

1996 Smith-Dartmoor Estate, Cabernet Sauvignon, Hawkes Bay $16.75.   83
1996 Smith Dartmoor Estate, Merlot, Hawkes Bay $16.75.   NR
1996 Late Harvest, Muscat, Hawkes Bay $11/375 ml.   81

Mills Reef

1996 Sauvignon Blanc, Hawkes Bay $16.   81

Nautilus

1997 Chardonnay, Marlborough $18.   83
1998 Sauvignon Blanc, Marlborough $14.   87

Bright platinum cast. Moderately full-bodied. Full acidity. Highly extracted. Minerals, citrus zest, dried herbs. Aromatically reserved with subtle herbal overtones. Clean and intense in the mouth with a solid degree of ripeness. Powerful yet restrained, with a pithy quality to the finish.

Palliser

1998 Sauvignon Blanc, Martinborough $17.   94

Bright straw cast. Moderately full-bodied. Full acidity. Highly extracted. Sweet herbs, gooseberries, tropical fruits. Powerful varietal aromas lead a rich and ripe palate feel. Firmly structured and racy in the mouth with a zesty acidic edge. Crisp and intense with a very lengthy finish.

Scale: Superlative (96-100), Exceptional (90-95), Highly Recommended (85-89), Recommended (80-84), Not Recommended (Under 80)

1997 Pinot Noir, Martinborough $22. **95**

Deep ruby cast. Moderately full-bodied. Balanced acidity. Moderately extracted. Mildly oaked. Mildly tannic. Red fruits, iron, spice. Outstanding complex aromas show classic Pinot complexity. Firm ironlike qualities remind one of a Vosne-Romanee. Full, intense, and well structured, with a lengthy and flavorful finish.

Sacred Hill

1997 Chardonnay, Hawkes Bay $16. **86**

Bright old-gold hue. Moderately full-bodied. Full acidity. Highly extracted. Minerals, cream, spice. Shows a subtle spicy hint to the nose. Full but well structured in the mouth with an intense racy quality provided by elevated acidity.

1997 Riflemans, Chardonnay, Hawkes Bay $34. **91**

Deep yellow-straw cast. Moderately full-bodied. Full acidity. Highly extracted. Minerals, citrus zest, yeast. Ripe minerally aromas lead to a full but sharp palate feel. Angular and concentrated through the finish with an intense leesy quality that gives this an extra dimension.

1996 Reserve, Sauvignon Blanc, Hawkes Bay $16. **86**

Deep yellow-straw color. Moderately full-bodied. Full acidity. Highly extracted. Lanolin, spice, minerals. Shows an unusual, almost maderized aroma that resembles maturing Semillon. Lean and racy in the mouth with a phenolic finish.

1997 Whitecliff, Sauvignon Blanc, Hawkes Bay $16. **86**

Bright straw cast. Medium-bodied. Balanced acidity. Moderately extracted. Wool, minerals. Shows a subtle, funky, Loire-like edge to the nose. Lighter in the mouth, with a pithy, phenolic quality to the finish.

1997 Whitecliff, Merlot, Hawkes Bay $16. **84**

Deep saturated ruby cast. Medium-bodied. Balanced acidity. Highly extracted. Moderately tannic. Minerals, dried herbs. Lean minerally aromas lead an angular mouthfeel that carries a degree of austerity. Firm through the finish with some mild astringency.

1997 Basket Press, Reserve, Cabernet Sauvignon-Merlot, Hawkes Bay $22. **89**

Deep ruby with a slight purple overtone. Medium-bodied. Balanced acidity. Moderately extracted. Mildly tannic. Dried herbs, mint, minerals. Pungent aromas show a distinctive and aggressive herbal quality. Lean and well structured in the mouth, yet quite flavorful. Well balanced and quite Bordeaux-like.

Saint Clair

1998 Unoaked, Chardonnay, Marlborough $14.99. **83**

1997 Sauvignon Blanc, Marlborough $12.99. **91**

Bright straw cast. Moderately full-bodied. Full acidity. Highly extracted. Asparagus, tropical fruits, minerals. Expressive aromatics show both complexity and intensity. Rich and ripe in the mouth with a generous texture buttressed by racy acidity. Flavorful and zesty finish.

Shingle Peak

1997 Chardonnay, Marlborough $14. **84**

Deep yellow-straw cast. Moderately full-bodied. Full acidity. Highly extracted. Tropical fruits, minerals, cream. Shows subtle tropical nuances in the nose. Ripe and rich in the mouth, but firmly structured and angular through the finish.

1997 Pinot Gris, Marlborough $14. **84**

Deep straw cast. Moderately full-bodied. Full acidity. Moderately extracted. Orange blossom, wool, minerals. Rather muted aromatically with subtle citrusy overtones. Full and extremely racy in the mouth. Clean, crisp finish.

1998 Sauvignon Blanc, Marlborough $13.50.   87

Bright straw cast. Medium-bodied. Full acidity. Moderately extracted. Minerals, citrus, dried herbs. Shows attractive varietal aromas that lead to a racy and intense palate feel. Ripe and full through the zesty finish.

1997 Pinot Noir, Marlborough $13.50.   84

Pale ruby hue with a slight fade. Medium-bodied. Full acidity. Subtly extracted. Mildly oaked. Mildly tannic. Minerals, red fruits, spice. Quite light in style, with subtle herb-tinged aromatics. Lean and angular through the finish with slight but dry tannins.

1997 Botrytis Riesling, Marlborough $15/375 ml.   84

Deep golden cast. Balanced acidity. Highly extracted. Tropical fruits, citrus, pineapple. Ripe, fruity aromas lead to a viscous mouthfeel with just enough acidity to lend a sense of balance. Clean and precise flavors continue through the sweet finish.

Spencer Hill

1996 Evan's Vineyard, Chardonnay, Moutere $16.   84

Deep old gold cast. Moderately full-bodied. Full acidity. Highly extracted. Hazelnuts, minerals, toasted coconut. Generous aromas show a high degree of maturity. Lean and angular in the mouth with a drying finish. Interesting, but drink up.

1996 Tasman Bay, Chardonnay, Marlborough $16.   87

Bright straw cast. Moderately full-bodied. Balanced acidity. Moderately extracted. Moderately oaked. Vanilla, yeast, toast. Generous aromas feature a complex leesy quality. Ripe and rounded in the mouth with a pleasant interplay between fruit and wood accents. Crisp structure makes for a buoyant, lengthy finish.

1997 Tasman Bay, Nelson, Sauvignon Blanc, Nelson $12.   90

Bright yellow-straw cast. Moderately full-bodied. Balanced acidity. Moderately extracted. Moderately oaked. Vanilla, asparagus, spearmint. Attractive aromatics show a judicious touch of wood and a core of very ripe Sauvignon Blanc flavors. Rounded and luxuriant in the mouth, with both complexity and intensity.

St. Jerome

1994 60% Cabernet Sauvignon–40% Merlot, Henderson $42.99.   85

Deep blackish-ruby hue. Full-bodied. Low acidity. Highly extracted. Quite tannic. Charred wood, earth. Dense aromas with a smoky edge lead a deeply extracted palate with flavors that turn rather lean and dry through the finish. This should improve with some cellaring though it will always be tough.

Te Mata Estate

1996 Elston, Chardonnay, Hawkes Bay $34.99.   88

Deep straw cast. Medium-bodied. Full acidity. Moderately extracted. Moderately oaked. Brown spices, minerals, citrus. Shows a generous wood accent to the nose that merges with a crisp citric impression in the mouth. Ripe and zesty.

1996 Awatea, Cabernet-Merlot, Hawkes Bay $34.99.   83

1996 Coleraine, Cabernet-Merlot, Hawkes Bay $42.99.   84

Deep ruby with a slight purple overtone. Moderately full-bodied. Balanced acidity. Highly extracted. Moderately tannic. Mint, anise, red fruits. Powerful aromas have an interesting high-toned herbal quality. Full throttled in the mouth with ripe flavors encased in a very firm structure. Lean tannins stand out in the finish.

Vavasour

1997 Dashwood, Sauvignon Blanc, Marlborough $12.99.   89

Brilliant platinum cast. Medium-bodied. Full acidity. Moderately extracted. Minerals, citrus zest, gooseberries. Attractive varietal aromas are forward and complex. Light in the mouth with a crisp and racy palate feel. Zesty and angular through the finish.

Scale: Superlative (96-100), Exceptional (90-95), Highly Recommended (85-89),
Recommended (80-84), Not Recommended (Under 80)

1997 Sauvignon Blanc, Awatere Valley $21.99. **90**

Bright straw hue. Full-bodied. Full acidity. Highly extracted. Gooseberries, minerals, lime. Powerful aromas show intense varietal character. Intense and edgy in the mouth with a full-throttled, racy quality. Lean and vibrant through the flavorful finish.

1997 Single Vineyard, Sauvignon Blanc, Awatere Valley $21.99. **89**

Brilliant yellow-straw cast. Full-bodied. Full acidity. Highly extracted. Moderately oaked. Vanilla, minerals, citrus zest. Dominated by a rush of oak aromas on the nose that merge with an array of very ripe fruit flavors in the mouth. Big and rich in style with an edgy finish.

Wairau River

1997 Sauvignon Blanc, Marlborough $20. **86**

Deep straw cast. Moderately full-bodied. Full acidity. Moderately extracted. Dried herbs, minerals. Aromatically reserved with a lean and racy palate feel. Crisp and zesty through the finish. Well structured but rather unyielding.

1997 Reserve, Sauvignon Blanc, Marlborough $25. **85**

Bright golden cast. Medium-bodied. Full acidity. Highly extracted. Moderately oaked. Vanilla, minerals, citrus. Shows a touch of oak aromas to the nose. Lean and austere in the mouth with an angular quality. Finishes with a touch of bitterness.

forty-four

❧

South America
Chile

❧

Cheap Chile...
going, going, gone?

Chile has provided good hunting for U.S. consumers seeking unbeatably priced and extravagantly fruity wines. This notwithstanding, the U.S. market has seen the introduction of a $50 Chilean red wine called Seña, and in its wake, a slew of Cabernet-based wines bearing $25 price tags. However, there still seems to be a core of reasonably priced wines to fill the $10 and under price bracket, a level at which California is offering fewer and fewer alternatives of comparable quality.

Generous color, ripe yet abundant tannins, and explosively fruity personalities broadly characterize Chile's best modern-styled reds. Chile's white wines have been best received in the form of Chardonnay—in its riper, oaked manifestation—and tropical-styled Sauvignon Blanc that rarely sees oak.

Culturally, the Chileans may have an affinity with Europe, but viticulturally speaking, Chilean wines have more in common with California. Both are warm climates moderated by the cool waters of the Pacific, and have consistent Mediterranean-style climates. In short, Chile, like California, is grape-growing heaven. This fact was not lost on the legions of outside investors (Mondavi, Kendall-Jackson, Marnier-Lapostolle, and the owners of Chateau Lafite, to name a few) who have provided the necessary capital and know-how to turn the Chilean industry into what it is today.

Chileans often like to point out that they are one of the last bastions of ungrafted *Vinifera* (European wine grape) vines. Unlike almost every other great region of wine production, they have not experienced any major outbreaks of the troublesome louse, *Phylloxera*, which has forced French and Californians alike to graft their vines onto *Phylloxera*-resistant native American rootstock. In this, their isolation—behind the towering peaks of the Andes on one side and the Pacific Ocean on the other—serves them well.

It was only a matter of time before Chile made a play for the luxury market in Bordeaux vari-

Chile
at a Glance

Wines Reviewed:

145

Producers/Brands Represented:

32

Value Rating:

Good

Scale: Superlative (96-100), Exceptional (90-95), Highly Recommended (85-89), Recommended (80-84), Not Recommended (Under 80)

etal wines. Seña, the product of the long-term partnership between Robert Mondavi and Errazuriz, is a Cabernet-Merlot blend designed to be "the benchmark for the best that Chile has to offer." The Seña 1995 Aconcagua Valley is the finest Chilean red wine to date, and by a long way the most expensive at $50. It marks the point at which Chile will start to command top prices for the finest wines from its best vineyards. Expect others to follow the road of diminishing returns to ultimate quality. The difference between a very good wine and one that is acknowledged as "truly great," as any serious collector knows, is measured in many dollars.

Casa Lapostolle produces what could well be Chile's best wines for under $20. Cuvée Alexandre, the top-label, comes in three flavors: Merlot, Cabernet Sauvignon, and Chardonnay. All of the current releases are outstanding. The Cuvée Alexandre Merlot could fairly be tagged a pocket-Pomerol, and the Cuvée Alexandre Chardonnay has Burgundian flair with New World generosity. These French allusions are particularly appropriate, as Casa Lapostolle is the product of French investment from the Marnier-Lapostolle group and the consulting expertise of Merlot wizard Michel Rolland—a man whose advice has forged a distinct style for some estates on Bordeaux's Right Bank.

However, even $20 still buys a lot of hedonistic Chilean wine. Unlike most of the world, $10 is still a useful denomination for buying Chilean wine. The ease with which irrigated grape-growing is done in Chile and the increasing capacity of Chile's industry seem certain to assure that Chile will be offering great values for some time to come.

Reviews

Calina

1998 Chardonnay, Valle de Itata $9.   84

Pale straw. Lean green apple aromas show no oak infuence. A crisp entry leads a moderately light-bodied palate with crisp flavors that finish quickly. Clean and quaffable. Drink now.

1997 Valle del Rapel, Cabernet Sauvignon, Chile $9.   84

Deep, saturated ruby purple. Subdued black fruit and mineral aromas. A firm attack leads a full-bodied palate with big chewy tannins. Rich, weighty finish. Though it shows good fruit intensity, it is just a touch monolithic. Drink now or later.

Caliterra

1998 Chardonnay, Valle Central $8.99.   84

Bright golden yellow. Clean mild aromas of ripe citrus and apple. A crisp entry leads a medium-bodied palate with straightforward, clean varietal flavors. Shows little oak influence. Drink now.

1997 Sauvignon Blanc, Valle Central $7.99.   80
1996 Cabernet Sauvignon, Valle Central $8.99.   84

Bright garnet hue with a slight fade. Forward brown spice and mineral aromas. A lean entry leads a medium-bodied palate with firm tannins that have some grip. Intense, flavorful finish. Drink now.

1998 Merlot, Valle Central $8.99.   86

Deep violet red. Moderately aromatic with crisp red fruit character. A bright entry leads a medium-bodied palate with high-toned flavors and light, drying tannins. Youthful and straightforward. Drink now.

Carmen

1997 Chardonnay, Valle Central $7.99.   NR
1996 Reserve, Chardonnay, Maipo Valley $13.99.   81
1995 Reserve, Chardonnay-Semillon, Maipo Valley $9.99.   84

Bright golden hue. Moderately full-bodied. Low acidity. Moderately extracted. Lanolin, vanilla. Quite aromatic with classic Semillon flavors. Full and waxy on the palate with a rounded slightly viscous quality. Could use a bit more grip on the finish, but quite tasty nonetheless.

1997 Sauvignon Blanc, Valle Central $7.99.   80
1997 Reserve, Sauvignon Blanc, Casablanca Valley $13.99.   85

Deep straw color. Medium-bodied. Full acidity. Moderately extracted. Gooseberries, dried herbs. Quite pungent, with typical and forceful Sauvignon aromatics. The palate is racy and angular. Finishes with a hint of bitterness.

1996 Cabernet Sauvignon, Central Valley $7.99.   NR
1996 Reserve, Cabernet Sauvignon, Maipo Valley $13.99.   82
1996 Reserve, Grande Vidure Cabernet, Maipo Valley $13.99.   80
1995 Gold Reserve, Cabernet Sauvignon, Maipo Valley $24.   85

Dark red with a violet rim. Medium-bodied. Moderately extracted. Heavily oaked. Moderately tannic. Oak, cassis. Big oaky nose follows through on the palate with cassis and dry oak flavors being the main impression. Quite generous, though conventional.

1996 Merlot, Valle Central $7.99.   82
1996 Reserve, Merlot, Rapel Valley $13.99.   89

Saturated blackish-ruby hue with a purple cast. Medium-bodied. Balanced acidity. Moderately extracted. Moderately oaked. Mildly tannic. Brown spices, black fruits, dried herbs. Pleasantly aromatic with fruit-centered flavors and herbal nuances throughout. Lighter in structure with a clean character and a lingering finish.

1995 Petite Syrah, Maipo Valley $13.99.   90

Deep blackish hue. Moderately full-bodied. Balanced acidity. Highly extracted. Heavily oaked. Moderately tannic. Black fruits, vanilla. Emphatically New World with a wave of extract and huge fruit and oak flavors. Quite deep and dense though not overly structured, with firm tannins balanced by the weight of the wine. Well balanced overall.

1996 Late Harvest, Semillon, Maipo Valley $7.99/375 ml.   80

Casa Lapostolle

1997 Chardonnay, Casablanca Valley $10.   86

Deep gold. Assertively aromatic with browned butter, yeast and oak aromas. A rich attack leads a moderately full-bodied palate with generous mouthfeel and overtly buttery character through the finish. Drink now.

1996 Cuvée Alexandre, Chardonnay, Casablanca Valley $16.   90

Dark gold. Richly aromatic with a generous, leesy, heavily oaked character. Very rich on the attack with a full body and lush texture. Quite overstated, in a California sort of way, but undeniably hedonistic and yet very stylish. Acid balance gives this wine good structure, but it is very appealing now.

1997 Sauvignon Blanc, Rapel Valley $9.   84

Pale straw hue. Aromatically muted with a mild buttery, tropical note. A flat entry leads a medium-bodied palate that shows soft acids and flavors.

1996 Cabernet Sauvignon, Rapel Valley $10.   86

Bright ruby hue. Generous overripe red fruit, spice and plum aromas. A lush entry leads a very ripe, medium-bodied palate with subtle tannins. Delicate, flavorful finish. Drink now.

1996 Cuvée Alexandre, Cabernet Sauvignon, Rapel Valley $16.   91

Deep, saturated ruby hue. Forward brown spice and red fruit aromas show a hefty oak accent. A ripe entry is followed by a moderately full-bodied palate with lush tannins. Spicy, wood-driven finish. Drink now.

1997 Merlot, Rapel Valley $10.   83

1997 Cuvée Alexandre, Merlot, Rapel Valley $16.   90

Saturated purple-red. Rich, deep aromas of black fruit and oak. A concentrated attack leads a moderately full-bodied palate with generous fruit flavors and plenty of toasty oak through the finish. A year or two in the cellar should harmonize this.

Cavas del Raco
1997 Oak Melody, Chardonnay, Alto Maipo $8.   NR

Chateau La Joya
1997 Gran Reserva, Chardonnay, Colchagua Valley $9.99.   82
1996 Gran Reserva, Cabernet Sauvignon, Colchagua Valley $9.99. 81
1996 Gran Reserva, Merlot, Colchagua Valley $9.99.   83

Concha y Toro
1998 Casillero del Diablo, Chardonnay, Casablanca Valley $10. 86

Medium straw hue. Clean, fresh aromas of citrus and butter. A juicy entry leads a medium-bodied palate with bright varietal flavors that linger through the finish. Oak is very subtle. Drink now.

1997 Amelia, Chardonnay, Casablanca Valley $18.   89

Deep gold. Generous aromas of browned butter and tropical fruits. A rich attack leads a moderately full-bodied palate with lush flavors, juicy acids and well-integrated oak. The finish lingers. This is a stylish wine. Drink now.

1997 Casillero del Diablo, Cabernet Sauvignon, Maipo Valley $10. 86

Bright ruby hue. Generous red fruit and mineral aromas. A lush entry leads a medium-bodied palate with velvety tannins. Shows complexity and fruit persistence through the finish. Stylish. Drink now.

1995 Don Melchor, Private Reserve, Puente Alto Vineyard, Cabernet Sauvignon, Maipo Valley $26. 90

Deep ruby purple. Intense licorice, black fruit and spice aromas show a modest wood accent. A solid entry leads a full-bodied palate with firm tannins and bright acidity. Intense, flavorful finish. Drink now.

1997 Casillero del Diablo, Merlot, Rapel Valley $10.   83
1996 Marques de Casa Concha, Peumo Vineyard, Merlot, Rapel Valley $14. 89

Saturated blood red. Austere earthy aromas. A solid entry leads a moderately full-bodied palate with dry, minerally flavors and a lingering austere finish. There is little fruit generosity, but it shows nice "terroir" notes. Drink now.

Cousiño Macul
1996 Antiguas Reservas, Cabernet Sauvignon, Valle del Maipo $14. 86

Bright cherry red with a slight fade. Forward cedar, red fruit and mineral aromas. A lean entry leads a medium-bodied palate with firm tannins and some grip. Complex, flavorful finish. Very stylish in an unusual rustic way. Drink now.

1995 Finis Terrae, Maipo Valley $31.   **90**

Deep ruby hue. Unusual mineral and anise aromas carry a harmonious wood accent. A lush entry leads a medium-bodied palate with velvety tannins. Flavorful, character-filled finish. Shows an interesting note of terroir. Drink now.

De Martino

1996 Sauvignon Blanc, Maipo Valley $9.   **81**

1996 Prima Reserva, Sauvignon Blanc, Maipo Valley $10.   **84**

Bright golden cast. Medium-bodied. Balanced acidity. Moderately extracted. Moderately oaked. Vanilla, citrus. Oak treatment is readily apparent on the nose and combines with a core of citric flavors on the palate. Brisk in style with an edge of acidity through the finish.

1995 Cabernet Sauvignon, Maipo Valley $9.   **84**

Bright cherry violet. Moderately light-bodied. Moderately extracted. Moderately oaked. Mildly tannic. Vanilla, raspberries, red fruits. Floral, oak-scented aromas. The lighter-styled palate shows crisp red fruit flavors through a clean, lightly oaky finish. Well balanced and quaffable.

1995 Prima Reserva, Cabernet Sauvignon, Maipo Valley $12.   **82**

1995 Reserva de Familia, Cabernet Sauvignon, Maipo Valley $30.   **89**

Dark red with a solid violet rim. Moderately full-bodied. Highly extracted. Moderately oaked. Moderately tannic. Chocolate, cassis, vanilla. Ripe, rich aromatics. Textured, generous mouthfeel shows well-extracted Cabernet flavors and ample soft tannins through the finish. Rather nice now, though well structured.

1996 Merlot, Maipo Valley $9.   **NR**

1996 Prima Reserva, Merlot, Maipo Valley $12.   **NR**

Doña Consuelo

1998 Chardonnay, Maule Valley $7.   **NR**

1997 Reserve, Viña Segú Ollé, Cabernet Sauvignon, Maule Valley $10.   **82**

1998 Viña Segú Ollé, Merlot, Maule Valley $7.   **87**

Bright neon violet hue. Muted floral aromas. A crisp entry leads a medium-bodied palate with crisp fruit flavors and drying tannins. Well structured and classic, if not overly flavorful.

Errazuriz

1996 Chardonnay, Casablanca Valley $8.99.   **NR**

1995 Reserva, Chardonnay, Casablanca Valley $13.99.   **82**

1995 Sauvignon Blanc, Curico Valley $8.99.   **NR**

1995 Cabernet Sauvignon, Curico Valley $8.99.   **80**

1994 Reserva, Cabernet Sauvignon, Aconcagua Valley $13.99.   **82**

1997 El Ceibo Estate, Cabernet Sauvignon, Aconcagua Valley $25.   **86**

Very deep ruby hue. Generous spice and black fruit aromas. A rich entry, then a moderately full-bodied palate with lean, firm tannins. A well-structured wine that shows modest complexity. Drink now.

1996 Merlot, Curico Valley $8.99.   **82**

1996 Don Maximiano Estate, Merlot, Aconcagua Valley $25.   **87**

Saturated dark ruby hue. Very aromatic with deep fruity aromas and toasted oak, and a touch of Brettanomyces. A rich entry leads a moderately full-bodied palate with concentrated flavors that show a dirty note that either adds to the complexity or detracts from the wine, depending on your perspective. Rich, weighty and structured.

Scale: Superlative (96-100), Exceptional (90-95), Highly Recommended (85-89), Recommended (80-84), Not Recommended (Under 80)

La Palma

1997 Gran Reserva, Chardonnay, Rapel $14. **86**

Deep gold. Ripe aromas of butter and yellow apples. A crisp entry leads a medium-bodied palate with varietally expressive fruit flavors and subtle oak. Finishes with crisp fruit flavors. Drink now.

1997 Cabernet Sauvignon, Rapel Valley $7. **88**

Deep ruby hue. Aromatically subdued with ripe black fruit overtones. A lush entry is followed by a moderately full-bodied palate with ripe, rounded tannins. Chewy, flavorful finish. Drink now.

1997 Reserve, Cabernet Sauvignon, Rapel $11. **86**

Deep, saturated ruby hue. Generous red fruit and brown spice aromas show a big oak accent. A lush attack leads a medium-bodied palate with supple tannins. Rounded, flavorful finish. Drink now.

1997 Merlot, Rapel $7. **84**

Bright neon violet-pink hue. Youthful aromas show dark, ripe fruits and a floral note. Bright and juicy on the attack, followed by a medium-bodied palate with light but dry tannins giving some grip. Drink now.

1997 Reserva, Merlot, Rapel $11. **86**

Bright purple-red. Vanilla and black fruit aromas show a youthful character. Crisp on the attack with a moderately full-bodied palate and solid tannins. Fruit flavors are generous and rich throughout. Nice now, though it will keep a few years.

1997 Gran Reserva, Merlot-Cabernet Sauvignon, Rapel $14. **NR**

La Playa

1998 Chardonnay, Maipo Valley $6.99. **81**

1997 Estate Reserve, Chardonnay, Maipo Valley $9.99. **82**

1996 Cabernet Sauvignon, Maipo Valley $6.99. **89**

Deep, saturated ruby red with purple highlights. Forward wood spice, black fruit and mineral aromas. A lush entry leads a medium-bodied palate with ripe, rounded tannins. Flavorful, generous finish. Drink now.

1995 Estate Reserve, Cabernet Sauvignon, Maipo Valley $9.99. **84**

Deep ruby hue. Forward anise and spice aromas show a big woody influence. A lush entry leads a medium-bodied palate with firm tannins. Fades toward the finish. Drink now.

1996 Merlot, Maipo Valley $6.99. **81**

1996 Estate Reserve, Merlot, Maipo Valley $10.99. **NR**

Los Vascos

1997 Cabernet Sauvignon, Colchagua $8.99. **88**

Bright ruby purple. Complex mineral, lead pencil,and red fruit aromas. A lean entry leads a firm, medium-bodied palate with lean tannins. Structured, flavorful finish. Drink now or later.

Montes

1998 Chardonnay, Curico Valley $10. **NR**

1996 Alpha, Cabernet Sauvignon, Curico Valley $18. **88**

Semi-saturated ruby hue. Very aromatic with spicy oak and cassis fruit aromas. A firm entry leads a moderately full-bodied palate with concentrated cassis flavors, firm but judicious tannins, and a notably spicy oak note through the finish. Drink now or later.

1998 Special Cuvée, Merlot, Curico Valley $10. **83**

Pionero

1998 Chardonnay, Central Valley $7.   NR

1998 Sauvignon Blanc, Central Valley $6.   86

Bright green-straw hue. Varietally pure aromas with ripe lemon and herbal notes. A crisp entry leads a medium-bodied palate with bright lemony flavors through a clean, medium-length finish.

1998 Cabernet Sauvignon, Central Valley $7.   84

Bright purple. Muted aromas carry gentle red fruit and herb undertones. A firm entry leads a moderately light-bodied palate. Tannins have some grip. The finish is fruity and straightforward. A quaffer. Drink now.

1998 Merlot, Central Valley $8.   84

Bright ruby hue with a pink rim. Aromatically lean with tart berry fruit aromas. A crisp attack leads a medium-bodied palate with bright acids and a lean minerally finish. Drink now.

Santa Alicia

1996 El Cipres, Gran Riserva, Chardonnay, Maipo Valley $9.99.   81

1994 Los Maitenes, Gran Riserva, Cabernet Sauvignon, Maipo Valley $9.99. NR

1995 El Pimiento, Gran Reserva, Merlot, Maipo Valley $9.99.   84

Bright ruby red. Fruit forward, plummy aromas. A fruity entry leads a medium-bodied palate with nice varietally correct fruit flavors and supple tannins, with good acidity working on the finish. Drink now.

Santa Amelia

1998 Chardonnay, Chile $6.50.   80

1998 Reserve Selection, Chardonnay, Maule Valley $7.50.   83

1998 Sauvignon Blanc, Maule Valley $6.50.   81

1997 Cabernet Sauvignon, Maule Valley $6.50.   83

1997 Reserve Selection, Cabernet Sauvignon, Maule Valley $7.50.   84

Deep ruby purple. Forward grapey aromas show a touch of overripeness and a gentle wood accent. A lush entry leads a medium-bodied palate with firm tannins. Structured, flavorful finish. Drink now.

1998 Merlot, Maule Valley $6.50.   84

Saturated purple. Ungenerous aromas have pommace-like note. A firm entry leads a moderately full-bodied palate with tannic grip and cherry flavors. The style is rather rustic.

1998 Reserve Selection, Merlot, Maule Valley $7.50.   NR

Santa Carolina

1997 Reserva, Chardonnay, Maipo Valley $9.   81

Santa Ema

1997 Reserve, Chardonnay, Maipo Valley $12.   81

1995 Reserve, Cabernet Sauvignon, Maipo Valley $12.   84

Bright ruby with with subtle purple highlights. Quite aromatic with oaky accents. A spicy entry leads a medium-bodied palate with good cassis flavors and vanilla notes coming through on the finish. Has a note of tannic grip, though it is drinking well now.

1996 Reserve, Merlot, Maipo Valley $12.   NR

1996 Cabernet-Merlot, Maipo Valley $10.   81

Scale: Superlative (96-100), Exceptional (90-95), Highly Recommended (85-89), Recommended (80-84), Not Recommended (Under 80)

Santa Marvista

1998 Reserva, Chardonnay, Central Valley $6.   NR

1998 Reserva, Merlot, Central Valley $6.   90

Saturated deep violet red. Very aromatic with a ripe, plummy character. Rich on the entry, with a moderately full-bodied palate and lush tannins with juicy acids to complement the generous plummy fruit flavors. Drink now.

Santa Monica

1997 Chardonnay, Rancagua $7.99.   NR

1995 Cabernet Sauvignon, Rancagua $7.99.   NR

1996 Cabernet Sauvignon, Rapel Valley $7.99.   80

1996 Merlot, Rancagua $7.99.   81

Santa Rita

1997 120, Chardonnay, Lontue Valley $7.49.   NR

1996 Reserva, Chardonnay, Maipo Valley $11.49.   81

1996 Medalla Real, Chardonnay, Casablanca Valley $13.99.   84

Deep straw color. Medium-bodied. Balanced acidity. Moderately extracted. Mildly oaked. Melon, citrus, vanilla. Pleasantly aromatic, with a lighter-styled and relatively vibrant character on the palate. Straightforward and clean through the finish.

1997 120, Sauvignon Blanc, Lontue Valley $7.49.   81

1997 Reserva, Sauvignon Blanc, Maule Valley $11.49.   88

Deep straw color. Medium-bodied. Full acidity. Moderately extracted. Dried herbs, gooseberries. Aromatic and quite typically Sauvignon-like in flavor throughout. Vibrant, fresh, and racy on the palate, with a clean and refreshing finish.

1995 120, Cabernet Sauvignon, Rapel Valley $7.49.   80

1996 Reserva, Cabernet Sauvignon, Maipo Valley $11.49.   84

Dark cherry red with a solid brick rim. Medium-bodied. Moderately extracted. Moderately oaked. Moderately tannic. Licorice, black fruits, brown spice. Well structured, dry palate with some concentrated dark fruit flavors and a long dry finish.

1995 Medalla Real Special Reserve, Cabernet Sauvignon,
Maipo Valley $13.99.   88

Dark red with a violet rim. Medium-bodied. Moderately extracted. Moderately oaked. Moderately tannic. Dried herbs, black cherries, blackberries. Ripe black fruit aromas lead a chunky, generous palate with plenty of varietal character and textured, mouth-drying tannins coming through on the finish. OK now, but the structure should let this develop and improve further.

1995 Casa Real, Old Vines Vineyard, Cabernet Sauvignon,
Maipo Valley $29.99.   91

Deep almost opaque red. Medium-bodied. Highly extracted. Moderately oaked. Quite tannic. Lacquer, cassis, minerals. Aromatically intense. Very concentrated tightly wound flavors have a solid mineral theme with a taut, tight tannins drying out the lengthy finish. Very persistent fruity flavors. Seriously structured; best to wait a few years for this one.

1996 Petite Syrah-Merlot, Central Valley $12.99.   80

1996 Late Harvest, Semillon, Maipo Valley $10.99/375 ml.   87

Deep golden hue. Medium-bodied. Low acidity. Moderately extracted. Moderately oaked. Honey, Semillon. Sauternes-like in style with hefty botrytis and barrel influences making for a flavorful and elegant wine. Lighter in style on the palate with a finish that tapers off. Quite good but better acidic structure would have made it excellent.

Seña

1995 Red Table Wine, Aconcagua Valley $50.   94

Deep, saturated ruby hue. Generous earth and black fruit aromas show a big wood accent and a touch of barnyard. A lush entry leads a full-bodied palate with outstanding intensity of flavor, firm tannins and balanced acidity. Harmonious and velvety through the flavorful finish. Very stylish and rather reminiscent of a Napa Valley show style. Drink now or later.

1996 Red Table Wine, Aconcagua Valley $50.   89

Deep, saturated ruby hue. Subdued mineral and black fruit aromas show a subtle earthy accent. A firm entry leads a full-bodied palate with lush tannins and a sense of intensity. The finish is soft and harmonious. Well structured and rich. Drink now.

Miguel Torres

1997 Chardonnay, Curico $6.99.   NR

1997 Sauvignon Blanc, Curico District $6.49.   87

Bright straw color. Moderately light-bodied. Full acidity. Moderately extracted. Dried herbs, gooseberries. Expressive, classic Sauvignon Blanc flavors are forceful and persistent. Vibrant and racy on the palate, with zippy acidity and good snap to the finish.

1995 Manso de Velasco, Cabernet Sauvignon, Curico $16.   89

Dark brick with a solid violet edged rim. Medium-bodied. Moderately extracted. Moderately oaked. Moderately tannic. Herbs, black fruits, pencil lead. Exotic aromas show intensity. Flavors are quite concentrated and have an earthy, minerally quality that is reinforced through the finish. Medoc-like. Elegant.

Undurraga

1998 Chardonnay, Maipo Valley $7.99.   81

1996 Reserva, Chardonnay, Talagante, Maipo Valley $11.99.   NR

1998 Sauvignon Blanc, Lontue Valley $7.99.   80

1997 Cabernet Sauvignon, Colchagua Valley $7.99.   86

Bright ruby red. Forward grapey, red fruit aromas. A lush entry leads a medium-bodied palate with ripe, fruit-centered flavors and supple tannins. The finish is ripe and rounded. A stylish quaffer. Drink now.

1995 Reserva, Cabernet Sauvignon, Maipo Valley $11.99.   81

1998 Pinot Noir, Maipo Valley $9.99.   83

Veramonte

1997 Chardonnay, Alto de Casablanca $10.   84

Bright straw hue. Smoky, buttery aromas. A soft entry leads a medium-bodied palate with a nice mouthfeel and obvious oak accents. Finishes quickly. Drink now.

1997 Cabernet Sauvignon, Alto de Casablanca $10.   88

Deep, saturated ruby red. Forward black fruit and spice aromas carry a hefty wood accent. A lush entry leads a medium-bodied palate that shows firm tannins. Ripe, rounded finish. Drink now.

1997 Merlot, Alto de Casablanca $10.   87

Deep ruby-brick red. Rich, complex aromas show mature fruit character with complex cedar notes. An elegant attack leads a moderately full-bodied palate with harmonious flavors of cedar and fruits that linger through the finish. Drink now.

Scale: Superlative (96-100), Exceptional (90-95), Highly Recommended (85-89), Recommended (80-84), Not Recommended (Under 80)

Viña Calina

1997 Selección de las Lomas, Chardonnay, Chile $15.   87

Bright yellow-straw hue. Overtly oaky aromas with citrus zest. A lively attack leads a medium-bodied palate with bright citrus flavors and oak spice through the finish. Straightforward. Drink now.

1997 Selección de las Lomas, Cabernet Franc, Maule $18.   86

Deep purple. Forward spicy aromas with wood dominant. A lush entry leads a medium-bodied palate with ripe tannins. Fruit emerges on the supple finish. Drink now.

1996 Selección de las Lomas, Cabernet Sauvignon, Chile $18.   89

Deep, saturated ruby hue. Forward spice and red fruit aromas. A lush entry leads a medium-bodied palate with firm tannins. Flavorful and intense through the finish. Drink now or later.

1996 Vicuña Vineyard, Cabernet Sauvignon, Rapel Valley $18.   90

Deep ruby red. Opulent brown spice and red fruit aromas show an attractive oak influence. A rich entry leads a moderately full-bodied palate with chewy tannins and excellent flavor intensity. Persistent, well-balanced finish. Drink now or later.

1997 Selección de las Lomas, Merlot, Chile $20.   87

Saturated deep purple. Oak-accented aromas. A firm entry leads a moderately full-bodied palate with structuring tannins and brisk acidity, and fruit flavors that are concentrated and bright. An impressive effort, but youthful; it will be better in a few years.

Viña Santa Carolina

1997 Chardonnay-Sauvignon Blanc, Colchagua Valley $8/1.5 L.   86

Medium green-straw hue. Bright, ripe aromas of citrus and tropical fruits. A fresh entry leads a medium-bodied palate with good acids to keep the fruit flavors bright through the finish.

1996 Reserva, Cabernet Sauvignon, Maipo Valley $9.   83

1996 Reserva, Merlot, Maule Valley $9.   87

Bright red-pink color. Candied berry aromas with a note of vanilla. A crisp entry leads a medium-bodied palate with bright, mildly candied berry flavors and soft tannins on the finish. Shows some depth of flavor. Drink now.

1996 Cabernet Sauvignon-Merlot, Colchaqua Valley $8/1.5 L.   NR

1996 Merlot-Cabernet Sauvignon, Colchagua Valley $8/1.5 L.   NR

Viña Tarapaca

1998 Chardonnay, Maipo Valley $7.   84

Pale yellow. Weak aromas of tinned fruit. A weak attack leads a medium-bodied palate with sweet fruit flavors. This has marked residual sugar and is rather confected. Cocktail for the masses.

1998 Sauvignon Blanc, Maipo Valley $7.   83

1998 La Isla Vineyard, Sauvignon Blanc, Maipo Valley $12.   84

Medium pale straw hue. Muted, buttery aromas show a suggestion of grass. A thick attack leads a medium-bodied palate with broad texture though rather dull fruit flavors.

1996 Reserva, Cabernet Sauvignon, Maipo Valley $11.   81

1997 Merlot, Maipo Valley $7.   NR

1996 Zavala, Maipo Valley $25.   88

Deep, saturated garnet hue. Forward forest, mineral and cedar aromas show complexity and maturity. A firm entry leads a moderately full-bodied palate with velvety tannins. The finish is mellow and smoky. This is a heavily wooded but rich Spanish style. Drink now.

Viu Manent

1997 Reserva, Chardonnay, Colchagua Valley $12.   89

Pale straw hue. Aromatically muted, with a note of citrus. Ripe, warm aromas show a vanilla note. Mildy viscous on the attack with a soft texture and rounded mouthfeel and good length. Smooth, though not hugely flavorful. Drink now.

1997 Reserva, Fume Blanc, Colchagua Valley $10.   85

Pale golden cast. Medium-bodied. Balanced acidity. Moderately extracted. Mildly oaked. Minerals, bread dough. Subtly wooded and quite round in the mouth with a sense of lushness. Clean and crisp through the finish.

1995 Reserva, Cabernet Sauvignon, Colchagua Valley $12.   85

Deep blackish-ruby color with a slight haze. Medium-bodied. Moderately extracted. Moderately oaked. Mildly tannic. Green pepper, dried herbs, red fruits. Quite aromatic with a big herbal accent to the flavors. Lighter in style on the palate with a clean and flavorful wood-tinged finish.

1996 Reserva, Malbec, Colchagua Valley $12.   82

1997 Reserva, Oak Aged, Malbec, Colchagua Valley $12.   88

Deep purple. Fantastically aromatic, with chocolate and blueberry aromas showing a toasty oak influence. A rich attack leads a moderately full body with forward chocolate and fleshy fruit flavors that finish with firm tannins and a long toasty note. Probably best drunk in its youth for its seductive, vivid flavors.

Walnut Crest

1997 Estate Selection, Chardonnay, Casablanca Valley $9.50.   84

Deep golden yellow. Rather fat, buttery aromas show oak influences. A thick attack leads a moderately full-bodied palate with tart acids on the finish. Very buttery, and short on fruit flavors. Drink now.

1996 Estate Selection, Merlot, Maipo Valley $9.50.   81

forty-five

❧

South America
Argentina

❧

Argentina: Sleeping Giant

Although Argentina is behind Chile in the development of its wine industry—a much lesser proportion of Argentine wine is exported—it is a source for very good values in red wine. Argentina, amazingly, is the fourth-largest wine producer in the world. The wines that we do not see are consumed locally, and typically are the product of extended aging in old oak vessels.

The Argentine Cabernets and Merlots that are exported to the United States are generally lighter in style, and display less varietal intensity than many equivalent Chilean wines. However, for reasons not completely clear, Malbec prospers in Argentina. It is Malbec, the variety otherwise known as being the backbone of Cahors, from southwestern France, that makes Argentina's best red wines. Modern styles of Malbec are inky and darkly colored, yet show plush, softer tannins with dark fruit flavors. Argentine whites, particularly Chardonnays, are of the rounder, fatter style. Some good examples are to be found, but many others are not so memorable.

As with Chile, the Andes, which separate the two countries, are the most important geographic influence on the vineyards. These mountains effectively insulate Argentina's wine-producing regions from the cooling effects of Pacific Ocean air, and deprive them of moisture, producing both hot and arid conditions for viticulture. Water for irrigation is, however, plentifully provided by run-off streams from the same mountains.

Mendoza is Argentina's most important wine-producing region. It is located roughly on a parallel with the Maipo Valley to the west, across the Andes in Chile. The best red wines of Mendoza are mostly attributed to Malbec, though Cabernet Sauvignon, Merlot, and Syrah also play a part. As much as 90% of exportable fine wine comes from Mendoza.

Wine is a serious local industry in Mendoza, with well over a thousand wineries in the area. However, only a very small number of these have been able, yet, to make the investment in

Argentina at a Glance

Wines Reviewed:

50

Producers/Brands Represented:

15

Value Rating:

Average to Good

Scale: Superlative (96-100), Exceptional (90-95), Highly Recommended (85-89), Recommended (80-84), Not Recommended (Under 80)

modern facilities and vineyards planted with appealing varietals for the export market. What is found on the U.S. market at present is only the tip of the iceberg in terms of quantity and future potential.

Reviews

Altos de Medrano

1997 Viña Hormigas Reserva, Malbec, Mendoza $25.   92

Saturated purple. Youthful floral, violet and black fruit aromas. A rich attack leads a moderately full body with concentrated flavors and weighty texture. Tannins are plentiful and supple. This is a modern well-extracted style with plenty of fruit generosity.

Balbi

1997 Chardonnay-Semillon, Mendoza $8.   NR

1997 Malbec, Mendoza $12.   84

Bright ruby red. Moderately aromatic with subtle oak spice. Crisp on the entry, with a medium-bodied palate showing bright acids and clean black fruit flavors through the crisp finish. Very direct and appealing.

1997 Malbec-Syrah, Mendoza $8.   81

Catena

1997 Agrelo Vineyards, Chardonnay, Mendoza $18.   88

Bright yellow-gold. Quite aromatic with sweet pine character. A smooth entry leads a moderately full-bodied palate with a buttery mouthfeel and alcohol warmth on the finish. A generous if rather obvious style.

1996 Lunlunta Vineyards, Malbec, Mendoza $21.   91

Saturated dark ruby-purple. Generous aromas of ripe black fruits and toasted oak. A rich entry is followed by a moderately full-bodied palate with generously extracted, concentrated fruit flavors, supple tannins and toasty oak. Very modern and appealing.

Bodegas Escorihuela

1997 Don Miguel Gascón, Viognier, Mendoza $11.99.   83

1997 Don Miguel Gascón, Malbec, Mendoza $11.99.   90

Saturated dark purple. Brooding anise and blackberry aromas. A rich attack leads a moderately full-bodied palate with fine-grained, rich tannins and concentrated flavors. Acids are rather soft. This wine will be best drunk in youth with rich foods.

Etchart

1997 Chardonnay, Cafayate $12.99.   NR

1996 Rio de Plata, Malbec, Mendoza $6.99.   NR

Marcus James

1997 Special Reserve, Chardonnay, Mendoza $6.99.   NR

1995 Special Reserve, Cabernet Sauvignon, Mendoza $6.99.   NR

1995 Special Reserve, Malbec, Mendoza $6.99.   NR

1995 Merlot, Mendoza $6.99.   NR

Mariposa

1997 Cabernet Sauvignon, Mendoza $9.   NR

1997 Malbec, Mendoza $9.   80

1997 Tapiz Reserve, Malbec, Mendoza $15. 86

Saturated purple-pink. Deep black fruit aromas. A firm entry leads a moderately full-bodied palate with dark fruit flavors and moderate tannic grip through the finish. Shows good varietal character. Try with rich foods.

1997 Merlot, Mendoza $9. 81

Bodega Norton

1996 Malbec, Mendoza $9. 84

Pale ruby red. Fennel aromas, with medicinal aromas that are very distinctive. A crisp entry leads a tart, moderately light-bodied palate that has crisp red fruit flavors and a distinct herbal accent. Drink now.

1995 Privada, Mendoza $13. 84

Garnet-ruby hue. Ripe, mildly stewed aromas show bottle development. A thick entry leads a moderately full-bodied palate with rustic flavors of spice, and faded fruit. Rather warm on the finish. Drink now.

Santa Julia

1998 Chardonnay, Mendoza $7. 81

1998 Sauvignon Blanc, Mendoza $7. 83

1998 Torrontes, Mendoza $6. 86

Pale straw hue. Pungent, Muscat-like flower, grapefruit and spice aromas. A rich entry leads a moderately full-bodied palate with zesty acidity. Rich, persistent finish. Aggressively flavorful and showing excellent varietal intensity. Drink now.

1997 Cabernet Sauvignon, Mendoza $7. NR

1996 Oak Reserve, Cabernet Sauvingon, Mendoza $10. 83

1997 Malbec, Mendoza $7. 82

1996 Oak Reserve, Malbec, Mendoza $10. 84

Pale ruby red. Attractively spiced aromas lead a moderately light-bodied palate with plenty of oak spice and subtle fruit flavors. Acids are crisp through the finish. A quaffer.

1997 Merlot, Mendoza $7. 81

1997 Malbec-Cabernet Sauvignon, Mendoza $7. NR

1997 Pinot Noir, Mendoza $7. NR

1997 Sangiovese, Menoza $7. NR

1997 Tempranillo, Mendoza $7. 83

Sichel

1996 Blue Nun, Merlot, Mendoza $7. NR

Trapiche

1997 Oak Cask, Chardonnay, Mendoza $8.99. 83

1997 Fond de Cave, Chardonnay, Mendoza $14.99. 83

1995 Oak Cask, Cabernet Sauvignon, Mendoza $8.99. 85

Deep ruby red. Generous spice and mineral aromas show a hefty oak accent. A lush entry leads a moderately full-bodied palate with lean, firm tannins that carry through the finish. Drink now.

1996 Fond de Cave, Cabernet Sauvignon, Mendoza $14.99. 81

1995 Oak Cask, Malbec, Mendoza $8.99. 84

Bright ruby red. Very aromatic with a fleshy toasted-oak accent. A bright attack leads a medium-bodied palate with light cherry-berry flavors and soft tannins. Finishes with attractive toasted-oak notes. Drink now.

Scale: Superlative (96-100), Exceptional (90-95), Highly Recommended (85-89), Recommended (80-84), Not Recommended (Under 80)

Tri Vento

1997 Malbec, Mendoza $7.   83

Trumpeter

1996 Cabernet Sauvignon, Maipu $10.   86

Bright ruby red. Forward dill pickle and spice aromas show a strong oak influence. A lush entry leads a medium-bodied palate with soft tannins. The finish is flavorful and harmonious. Well balanced with a stylish mouthfeel. Drink now.

Vinterra

1997 Chardonnay, Mendoza $6.99.   83

1997 Cabernet Sauvignon, Mendoza $6.99.   NR

1997 Malbec, Mendoza $6.99.   80

1997 Merlot, Mendoza $6.99.   NR

Weinert

1997 Carrascal White, Mendoza $10.99.   81

1995 Cabernet Sauvignon, Mendoza $16.95.   86

Deep garnet hue with a slight fade. Generous wood spice and black fruit aromas. A lush entry leads a medium-bodied palate with soft, rounded tannins. Supple, mellow finish in a Spanish style. Drink now.

1994 Malbec, Mendoza $13.50.   NR

1995 Merlot, Mendoza $13.50.   NR

1995 Carrascal, Mendoza $10.99.   81

1993 Cavas de Weinert Gran Vino, Mendoza $17.95.   83

forty-six

❧

South Africa

❧

South Africa: "Good Hope" Turning Into Reality

Though thought of as distinctly New World, South Africa's wine industry is actually over 300 years old. With recent governmental changes, South Africa has left its long period of international isolation, and wine drinkers in the U.S. are beginning to see more and more of the fabled "Cape" wines on the domestic market. These wines actually share more in common with Old World styles than do their New World counterparts. Growing in a cooler climate, with a distinct maritime influence, South African wines are generally a couple of degrees lower in alcohol than Australian or Californian wines, and have higher levels of acidity with lean, taut structures. All in all, the national style shares much in common with that of France. Balance and moderation are the buzzwords, making these wines exceptionally friendly at the table. South African wines do have some unique signatures, however. Fans of these wines note a distinctive minerally flavor present particularly in the reds, which is usually described as iron-like. This nuance can often be found in a wine unique to the area known as Pinotage. A cross between Pinot Noir and Cinsault, an obscure grape from the south of France, Pinotage is a light- to mid-weight red with lots of character. It is one of the few wines in the world that when fully ripe smells like blueberries.

Other specialties are also centered on classic French varietals. South African Chardonnays are quite different from the high-alcohol, full-blown, buttery versions found in the New World. Rather, they tend to be crisp and well structured with a piquant character lent by elevated levels of acidity. Further, the spicy flavors imparted by oak aging tend to be fairly subtle. Indeed, oak-dominated wines are a rarity in South Africa, though KWV's Cathedral Cellar line is a notable, high-volume exception.

While their Chardonnays are often of excellent quality, it is with the great red Bordeaux varietals, Cabernet Sauvignon and Merlot, that South Africans produce their finest wines. Examples from high-quality, estate producers tend to be refined, well structured, and flavorful with an elegance and restraint hauntingly similar to that of good Bordeaux. These wines come nowhere near the sheer fruit intensity or weight of familiar California examples, and they are probably more drinkable on a regular basis because of it. This is not to diminish their aging potentials, however. Certain South African Cabernets, even in the $10 to $15 range, have shown the ability to age beautifully for a decade or more. This would be an almost unheard-of phenomenon in virtually any other wine region.

As a final note, many of the best estates produce a reserve-style blend of Bordeaux varietals and market it as their flagship wine, à la Bordeaux. These wines will almost always represent shocking value for money when compared to Bordeaux or even California Meritage. When searching for the pinnacle of South Africa's Bordeaux varietals, these blends are often the best bet. Producers such as Meerlust, Rust en Vrede, Eikendal, and Warwick usually lead the pack.

Scale: Superlative (96-100), Exceptional (90-95), Highly Recommended (85-89), Recommended (80-84), Not Recommended (Under 80)

In sum it all comes back to value. World class wines or not, South Africa produces a wide range of distinctive styles to tempt the adventurous wine drinker, and the rampant price escalation that has affected many of the world's other premium wine regions has not been nearly as severe in South Africa. The end result? Many of the better South African wines also represent some of the world's best wine values.

Reviews

Backsberg

1997 Chardonnay, Paarl $12.99.   83

1995 Cabernet Sauvignon, Paarl $13.   85

Dark blackish-ruby hue. Moderately full-bodied. Balanced acidity. Moderately extracted. Heavily oaked. Moderately tannic. Brown spices, dill pickle, minerals. Quite aromatic with a wood-driven personality that lends a sense of sweetness to the palate. Well structured and flavorful with a fairly astringent finish.

1996 Merlot, Paarl $12.99.   NR

1995 Shiraz, Paarl $12.   85

Bright blackish-ruby hue. Moderately light-bodied. Balanced acidity. Moderately extracted. Moderately oaked. Mildly tannic. Black fruits, vanilla, black pepper. Pleasantly aromatic with a solid oak overlay and a core of fruit flavors on the palate. Lighter in the mouth but well structured with a snappy, mildly astringent finish.

Baobab

1997 Chardonnay, Western Cape $8.99.   81

1997 Merlot, Western Cape $8.99.   89

Deep, saturated ruby hue. Intense lead pencil, iron and red fruit aromas show character and style. A firm entry leads a moderately full-bodied palate with lean tannins and outstanding flavor intensity. The finish is lengthy and complex. Drink now or later.

Beyerskloof

1998 Pinotage, Stellenbosch $10.99.   88

Bright purple. Forward grapey aromas hint at carbonic maceration (Beaujolais-like flavors). A ripe entry leads a medium-bodied palate with intense fruity, spicy flavors and subtle tannins, and a flavorful finish. A sturdy quaffer. Drink now.

South Africa at a Glance

Wines Reviewed:

113

Producers/Brands Represented:

37

Value Rating:

Average to Good

Boland

1997 Chardonnay, Paarl $10.   84

Bright straw cast. Moderately light-bodied. Full acidity. Moderately extracted. Minerals, citrus. Clean, crisp, and racy in a Chablis style with a focused, pure mouthfeel and angular acidity. Refreshing zippy finish.

1997 Chenin Blanc, Paarl $9.   82

1994 Cabernet Sauvignon, Paarl $11.   80

1995 Cabernet Sauvignon, Paarl $11.99.   80

1995 Pinotage, Paarl $9.   NR

1997 Rooi Muskadel, Paarl $11.99.   90

Bright ruby-tinged chestnut color. Full-bodied. Balanced acidity. Highly extracted. Black tea, dates. Slightly hot on the nose, with a complex vinous character reminiscent of an Australian Show Tokay. Lush and viscous in the mouth, with a sense of richness and a lingering finish. Fine intensity.

1996 Port, Paarl $10.99.   85

Bright blackish-ruby color with a purple cast. Medium-bodied. Balanced acidity. Highly extracted. Mildly tannic. Black fruits, chocolate. Lighter in style, with a straightforward fruit-centered palate. Finishes with some very mild astringency. Somewhat simple, but quite tasty, and approachable now.

Boplaas

1995 Carel Nel, Cabernet Sauvignon, Western Cape $12.   81

1994 Vintage Reserve Port, Western Cape $25.   88

Opaque blackish-ruby hue. Medium-bodied. Full acidity. Highly extracted. Moderately tannic. Lacquer, chocolate, black fruits. Somewhat reined in aromatically at present. Ripe and expansive on a lighter-styled palate, with all the classic components of a good young Port. Finishes with some astringent tannins. Will reward mid-term cellaring.

Boschendal

1997 Reserve, Chardonnay, South Africa $14.99.   84

Bright straw hue. Powerful spicy aromas show a big wood accent. A firm entry leads a medium-bodied palate that shows angular acidity. Clean, wood-accented finish. Drink now.

1998 Sauvignon Blanc, Coastal Region $11.99.   88

Very pale straw hue. Generous herbal aromas are pure and varietally intense. A rounded attack leads a medium-bodied palate with lush acidity. Brimming with flavor. Drink now.

Bouwland

1997 Cabernet Sauvignon-Merlot, Stellenbosch $10.99.   93

Deep purple-red. Generous red fruit and mineral aromas show a gentle oak overlay. A lush entry leads a medium-bodied palate with ripe tannins and excellent flavor intensity that are persistent and harmonious through the finish. Drink now.

Chamonix

1997 Chardonnay, Franschhoek $15.   86

Bright pale gold. Fresh, tart aromas of passion fruit and citrus. A crisp entry is followed by a medium-bodied palate with toasty oak spice through the finish. Shows good fruit concentration.

1998 Gemini, Franschhoek $15.   83

1998 Sauvignon Blanc, Franschhoek $10.   84

Bright pale gold. Fresh, tart aromas of passion fruit and citrus. A crisp entry leads a medium-bodied palate with toasty oak spice through the finish. Shows good fruit concentration. The steely finish has nice grip.

Scale: Superlative (96-100), Exceptional (90-95), Highly Recommended (85-89), Recommended (80-84), Not Recommended (Under 80)

1996 Cabernet Sauvignon, Franschhoek $15.   **86**

Bright ruby hue with a fading rim. Nice minerally, somewhat lean aromas. A bright entry leads a medium-bodied palate with clean cherry fruit flavors and wiry, flavorful tannins that linger on the finish. Fine acids and grip. Drink now or later.

1995 Merlot, Franschhoek $12.   **87**

Deep saturated ruby hue with a purplish cast. Medium-bodied. Full acidity. Moderately extracted. Mildly oaked. Mildly tannic. Chocolate, red fruits, earth. Quite aromatic, with complex flavors that play out on a firmly structured angular palate feel. Lean and focused through a very precise finish.

Clos Malverne

1995 Cabernet Sauvignon, Stellenbosch $15.   **90**

Dark blackish-ruby hue. Medium-bodied. Balanced acidity. Moderately extracted. Moderately oaked. Mildly tannic. Black fruits, brown spices, minerals. Pleasantly aromatic and deeply flavored, with a sense of lushness to the supple palate. Complex throughout with well-integrated fruit and wood notes and a distinctive accent of terroir. Fine length and intensity.

1998 Basket Pressed, Pinotage, Stellenbosch $12.99.   **81**

1996 Pinotage, Stellenbosch $14.   **80**

De Wetshof

1997 Lesca, Chardonnay, Robertson $11.99.   **81**

Delheim

1998 Chardonnay, Stellenbosch $13.   **82**

1996 Cabernet Sauvignon, Stellenbosch $15.   **89**

Bright garnet hue. Intense lead pencil and game aromas show complexity. A firm entry is followed by a moderately full-bodied palate with exotic flavors, sharp acidity and firm tannins. Supple, flavorful finish. Drink now.

1995 Grand Reserve, Stellenbosch $18.   **89**

Deep garnet hue. Subdued forest, earth and cedar aromas. The entry is soft, followed by a medium-bodied palate that shows wood-tinged flavors and velvety tannins. The finish is rounded and supple. Drink now.

1996 Shiraz, Stellenbosch $13.   **89**

Deep, saturated ruby hue. Pungent, exotic game and olive aromas. A brisk entry leads a full-bodied palate with sharp acidity and firm tannins. Shows great intensity of flavor. A smoky and wild style, it is not everyone's cup of tea, but is extremely interesting. Drink now or later.

Eikendal

1997 Chardonnay, Stellenbosch $14.99.   **90**

Pale golden hue. Medium-bodied. Full acidity. Moderately extracted. Mildly oaked. Yeast, citrus. Quite aromatic with a leesy quality that really comes through on the palate. Crisp and very zesty with piquant acidity and a flavorful finish. Could use a year or so to round out the acidic edges.

1995 Cabernet Sauvignon, Stellenbosch $15.99.   **83**

1996 Merlot, Stellenbosch $15.99.   **87**

Bright blackish-ruby hue. Medium-bodied. Balanced acidity. Moderately extracted. Mildly oaked. Mildly tannic. Earth, iron, dried herbs, black fruits. Quite aromatic, with real complexity to the wave of flavors on the palate. Well structured with a sense of lightness and delicacy in the mouth. Elegant and well balanced through the lingering finish.

1994 Classique, Stellenbosch $16.99.   86

Deep blackish-ruby hue. Medium-bodied. Balanced acidity. Moderately extracted. Moderately oaked. Mildly tannic. Cedar, minerals, black fruits. Quite aromatic, with a mellow oak overlay. Lush and round in the mouth, though firmly structured with some mild astringency to the lengthy finish.

1995 Classique, Stellenbosch $16.99.   90

Deep blackish-ruby hue. Medium-bodied. Balanced acidity. Moderately extracted. Mildly oaked. Mildly tannic. Cassis, minerals, cedar. Quite aromatic, with a concentrated, well-structured, elegant palate feel. Features a core of very pure flavors through the lengthy finish. Well balanced with fine intensity.

Neil Ellis

1996 Chardonnay, Elgin $14.   85

Bright golden hue. Medium-bodied. Balanced acidity. Moderately extracted. Mildly oaked. Bread dough, minerals, white pepper. Fairly reserved and elegant in style with complex flavors that are slightly left of center. Focused and somewhat austere on the palate with a lingering finish.

1997 Sauvignon Blanc, Groenekloof $12.   90

Bright straw color. Medium-bodied. Full acidity. Moderately extracted. Gooseberries, dried herbs. Aromatic and varietally expressive, with classic Sauvignon Blanc flavors. Crisp but fairly round in the mouth, with a clean and flavorful finish. Well balanced with fine intensity.

1998 Sauvignon Blanc, Groenekloof $11.99.   86

Very pale straw hue. Generous herb and mineral aromas. A lean entry is followed by a medium-bodied palate with angular acidity. Taut varietal finish with a hint of pithiness. Drink now.

1995 Cabernet Sauvignon, Stellenbosch $17.50.   84

Bright blackish-ruby hue. Medium-bodied. Balanced acidity. Moderately extracted. Mildly oaked. Mildly tannic. Minerals, brown spice. A little reined in aromatically with a well balanced, elegant palate feel. Quite reserved in style with a relatively firm structure and a sense of vibrancy to the finish.

Fairview

1996 Chardonnay, Paarl $14.99.   88

Deep straw color. Medium-bodied. Balanced acidity. Moderately extracted. Heavily oaked. Vanilla, butter, yeast. California comes to South Africa. Oak driven in flavor, with a flavorful, though soft and lush character in the mouth. Finishes with a velvety and extremely buttery quality. Quite pleasant, but could use a bit more grip.

1997 Pinot Gris, South Africa $8.99.   NR

1996 Merlot, Paarl $15.   85

Bright blackish-ruby hue. Medium-bodied. Balanced acidity. Moderately extracted. Mildly tannic. Red fruits, minerals. Pleasantly aromatic, with fruit-centered flavors and a sense of austerity to the firmly structured palate. Clean, vibrant, and lingering finish.

1997 Zinfandel-Cinsault, Paarl $12.   84

Bright purple color. Moderately full-bodied. Balanced acidity. Moderately extracted. Moderately tannic. Briar fruits. Intensely fruity in character, with an aromatic and flavorful quality throughout. Lush and rich on the palate, this bears more than a passing resemblance to a California Zin...just a bit higher in acidity and lighter in body. Fairly astringent through the finish.

1996 Shiraz, Paarl $13.99.   87

Bright ruby purplish hue. Medium-bodied. Balanced acidity. Moderately extracted. Moderately oaked. Mildly tannic. Briar fruits, vanilla, black pepper. Quite aromatic with an extremely flavorful presence on the palate. Lighter in style though fairly well structured with a buoyant lengthy finish.

Scale: Superlative (96-100), Exceptional (90-95), Highly Recommended (85-89), Recommended (80-84), Not Recommended (Under 80)

Fleur du Cap

1996 Chardonnay, Coastal Region $10.50.   83

1995 Merlot, Coastal Region $10.50.   80

1996 Noble Late Harvest, Coastal Region $12.50/375 ml.   89

Brilliant yellow-gold. Intense honey and sweet tropical fruit aromas. A rich entry leads a medium-bodied moderately sweet palate with enough acidity to lend a sense of balance. The finish is clean and not at all cloying. Drink now.

Groot Constantia

1994 Rood, Constantia $8.   NR

Haute Provence

1997 Angels' Tears, Coastal Region $8.99.   82

Kanonkop

1997 Kadette, Stellenbosch $9.99.   83

KWV

1997 Chardonnay, Western Cape $7.99.   83

1997 Cathedral Cellar, Chardonnay, Coastal Region $11.99.   88

Deep yellow-straw hue. Generous brown spice and citrus aromas show a hefty oak accent. A rich entry leads a moderately full-bodied palate with crisp acids. The finish is flavorful and well structured. Drink now.

1998 Steen, Western Cape $6.99.   83

1997 Sauvignon Blanc, Western Cape $7.49.   81

1995 Cathedral Cellar, Cabernet Sauvignon, Coastal Region $12.99.   86

Deep, saturated purple-red. High-toned anise and mineral aromas carry a subtle wood accent. A lush entry leads a medium-bodied palate that shows fine-grained tannins. Integrated and harmonious with a mellow woody quality through the finish. Drink now.

1996 Merlot, Western Cape $8.99.   NR

1995 Cathedral Cellar, Merlot, Coastal Region $12.99.   82

1996 Roodeberg, Western Cape $11.99.   88

Bright garnet hue. Subtle herb and cedar aromas. A soft entry leads a moderately light-bodied palate with mild tannins, and a rounded, complex finish. Drink now.

1997 Pinotage, Western Cape $8.99.   83

1995 Cathedral Cellar, Pinotage, Coastal Region $12.99.   85

Deep ruby hue. Generous spice aromas carry a hefty wood accent. A lush entry leads a medium-bodied palate with soft tannins. The finish is rounded and gentle. A modern oaky style. Drink now.

L'Ormarins

1997 Chardonnay, Franschhoek Valley $11.   81

1996 Blanc Fumé, Franschhoek $11.50.   83

La Motte

1991 Cabernet Sauvignon, Franschhoek Valley $18.   88

Bright garnet hue. Soft tobacco, earth and forest aromas show distinctive mature overtones. A lush entry leads a medium-bodied palate marked by gentle tannins. Complex, rounded finish. Drink now.

1994 Estate Red, Franschhoek Valley $15.   88

Deep garnet hue. Generous forest, earth and spice aromas. A lush entry leads a medium-bodied palate with velvety tannins and a supple, flavorful finish. Mature and stylish. Drink now.

Le Bonheur

1997 Chardonnay, Simonsberg-Stellenbosch $11.   NR
1991 Cabernet Sauvignon, Simonsberg-Stellenbosch $18.   88

Deep, saturated garnet red. Firm mineral and red fruit aromas. A lean entry, a medium-bodied mouthfeel, and firm tannins. The finish is persistent and well balanced. Drink now.

Meerlust

1994 Merlot, Stellenbosch $22.   90

Bright blackish-ruby hue. Medium-bodied. Balanced acidity. Moderately extracted. Moderately oaked. Mildly tannic. Brown spices, red fruits, earth. Pleasantly aromatic and quite flavorful, striking a nice balance between wood and fruit derived flavors. Well structured with a sense of austerity and a bright zesty finish. Fine intensity.

1995 Merlot, Stellenbosch $24.   89

Deep, saturated ruby hue. Restrained aromas show a firm minerally backbone and a subtle wood accent. A structured attack leads a moderately full-bodied palate with grainy tannins and an intense, brooding finish. Well structured, and though unyielding at present, it should open with age. Midterm cellar candidate (3–6 years).

1994 Rubicon, Stellenbosch $25.   92

Deep garnet hue. Generous vanilla, mineral and red fruit aromas show a well-integrated oak influence. A lush entry leads a medium-bodied palate with firm tannins. Rich and harmonious through the supple finish. Drink now or later.

Middelvlei

1993 Pinotage, Stellenbosch $12.50.   NR

Neethlingshof

1995 Chardonnay, Stellenbosch $10.99.   NR
1997 Chardonnay, Stellenbosch $14.   82
1995 Neethlingshoffer White, Stellenbosch $9.99.   85

Bright golden hue. Medium-bodied. Full acidity. Moderately extracted. Petrol, minerals, earth. Quite aromatic, with a clean and vibrant mouthfeel. Steely through the finish with good complexity of flavor.

1996 Weisser Riesling, Stellenbosch $10.99.   81
1996 Sauvignon Blanc, Stellenbosch $10.99.   NR
1997 Sauvignon Blanc, Stellenbosch $14.   87

Bright straw color. Moderately light-bodied. Full acidity. Moderately extracted. Dried herbs, gooseberries. Extremely aromatic, with an expressive, classic Sauvignon Blanc flavor profile. Clean, crisp, and racy in the mouth, with a vibrant and refreshing finish.

1993 Cabernet Sauvignon, Stellenbosch $10.99.   80
1994 Merlot, Stellenbosch $10.99.   NR
1995 Merlot, Stellenbosch $14.   83
1993 Pinotage, Stellenbosch $11.99.   82
1995 Pinotage, Stellenbosch $14.   86

Bright blackish-ruby hue. Moderately light-bodied. Full acidity. Moderately extracted. Mildly tannic. Minerals, red fruits. Aromatic, with a reserved steely style on the palate. Firmly structured though flavorful with some mild astringency through the finish. Has very good grip.

1997 Noble Late Harvest, Weisser Riesling, Stellenbosch $27.50/375 ml.   **89**

Deep burnished copper hue. Full-bodied. Full acidity. Highly extracted. Tropical fruits, earth. Quite aromatic with a slight funky note. Extremely thick and viscous on the palate with enough acidity to keep this weighty wine from becoming cloying. Flavorful and lingering finish. A little goes a long way, but impressive.

Robert's Rock

1998 Chenin Blanc-Chardonnay, Western Cape $5.99.   **83**

1997 Shiraz-Malbec, Western Cape $6.99.   **89**

Bright cherry red. Generous red fruit aromas carry a subtle oak accent. A lean entry leads a medium-bodied palate with firm tannic grip and enlivening acidity. Crisp, intense finish. Drink now or later.

Rooiberg

1996 Rhine Riesling, South Africa $7.   **82**

1994 Cape Ruby, Eilandia $14.99.   **83**

Rust en Vrede

1996 Merlot, Stellenbosch $14.   **84**

Deep blackish-ruby hue. Moderately light-bodied. Full acidity. Moderately extracted. Mildly tannic. Earth, minerals. Quite earthy in aromatics, with a well-structured, reserved character on the palate. Firm and well balanced through the finish, with vibrant acidity.

1993 Estate Selection, Stellenbosch $25.   **91**

Dark blackish-ruby hue. Moderately full-bodied. Balanced acidity. Highly extracted. Heavily oaked. Moderately tannic. Cedar, minerals, black fruits. Extremely aromatic with a big oak overlay and a firm core of fruit and mineral flavors that show a sense of terroir. Somewhat austere and reserved though elegant and well balanced. Exhibiting fine grip and intensity, this is approachable now but should improve with age.

Saxenburg

1997 Sauvignon Blanc, Stellenbosch $10.   **87**

Pale straw color. Medium-bodied. Full acidity. Moderately extracted. Dried herbs, gooseberries. Forcefully aromatic with an extremely pure and expressive palate feel. Clean and quite crisp, with a very snappy finish.

1995 Cabernet Sauvignon, Stellenbosch $14.   **88**

Dark blackish-ruby color. Medium-bodied. Balanced acidity. Moderately extracted. Mildly oaked. Mildly tannic. Minerals, black fruits. Pleasantly aromatic with a sense of richness to the palate. Well structured though unusually lush with a deeply flavored and lingering finish.

1996 Merlot, Stellenbosch $13.   **88**

Very deep blackish-ruby hue. Medium-bodied. Balanced acidity. Moderately extracted. Mildly oaked. Mildly tannic. Red fruits, brown spices, iron. Quite aromatic and flavorful with a solid interplay between fruit, wood, and mineral notes. Elegant and well structured on the palate with a sense of leanness. Well balanced with fine intensity and length.

1996 Pinotage, Stellenbosch $13.   **85**

Bright saturated ruby color. Medium-bodied. Full acidity. Moderately extracted. Mildly tannic. Iron, red fruits. Quite aromatic, as signature mineral notes combine with fruit-derived qualities on the palate. Solidly structured, with a snappy, vibrant mouthfeel, and some mild astringency to the finish.

Simonsvlei

1995 Reserve, Pinotage, Coastal Region $13.99.   87

Bright ruby-garnet color. Moderately light-bodied. Balanced acidity. Moderately extracted. Mildly tannic. Iron, earth. Forcefully aromatic, with signature mineral-edged classic Pinotage flavors. Lighter in style on the palate, though well balanced with a lively finish. Could use a bit more structure, but is a great expression of terroir.

Stellenryck

1997 Chardonnay, Coastal Region $12.   88

Deep yellow-straw color. Generous brown spice aromas show a hefty wood accent. A rich entry leads a moderately full-bodied palate with firm acidity. Clean, structured finish. Drink now.

1992 Cabernet Sauvignon, Coastal Region $16.   89

Deep purple-red. Generous spice and red fruit aromas show a hefty oak accent. A firm entry leads a medium-bodied palate with lean tannins. Angular and stylish through the finish. Shows excellent grip and intensity. Drink now.

Stellenzicht

1997 Chardonnay, Stellenbosch $17.50.   87

Pale golden cast. Medium-bodied. Full acidity. Moderately extracted. Mildly oaked. Vanilla, minerals. Reined in and youthful at the moment, with tightly wound acidity. Well-crafted wood and fruit flavors peer out from behind the solid structure and seem well balanced. All bodes well for a harmonious wine to emerge after near-term cellaring.

1997 Sauvignon Blanc, Stellenbosch $17.50.   88

Bright straw color. Medium-bodied. Full acidity. Moderately extracted. Dried herbs, minerals, citrus. Aromatic, though very tightly wound and quite youthful on the palate. Clean and snappy through the finish with fine intensity. Should open up nicely with near-term cellaring.

1994 Cabernet Sauvignon, Stellenbosch $15.99.   86

Deeply saturated blackish-ruby color. Moderately full-bodied. Balanced acidity. Moderately extracted. Mildly oaked. Moderately tannic. Black fruits, minerals, brown spices. Fruit centered and tightly wound on the palate with a dense core of flavor. Quite firmly structured with real astringency to the finish. Well balanced, it should mellow and gain complexity with mid-term cellaring.

1995 Cabernet Sauvignon, Stellenbosch $17.50.   82

1994 Merlot, Stellenbosch $17.50.   82

1995 Stellenzicht, Stellenbosch $26.   89

Deep blackish-ruby hue. Medium-bodied. Balanced acidity. Moderately extracted. Mildly oaked. Mildly tannic. Cassis, minerals, brown spices. Elegant and lean in style, with a decided accent to fruit-derived qualities. Oak plays in the background along with complex terroir-driven mineral and earth flavors. Firm and angular finish with fine intensity.

1995 Syrah, Stellenbosch $15.   89

Bright blackish-ruby hue. Moderately full-bodied. Full acidity. Moderately extracted. Heavily oaked. Mildly tannic. Cedar, chocolate, black fruits. Quite aromatic with a hefty oak overlay and a solid core of fruit derived flavors. Well structured and complex, with vibrant acidity and a lengthy finish.

Van Loveren

1997 Pinot Gris, Robertson $9.   86

Deep straw color with a very slight copper cast. Moderately full-bodied. Low acidity. Moderately extracted. Earth, melon. Fairly aromatic, with a rich, oily, highly textured mouthfeel. Lush and almost viscous through the finish. Solid, but could use a bit more grip.

Scale: Superlative (96-100), Exceptional (90-95), Highly Recommended (85-89), Recommended (80-84), Not Recommended (Under 80)

1997 Special Late Harvest, Gewurztraminer, Robertson $9. NR

Villiera
NV Tradition Carte Rouge Brut, South Africa $12. 86

Brilliant straw hue with finely beaded bubbles and a thin mousse. Attractive yeast and cream aromas. A crisp entry leads a rich, creamy, moderately full-bodied mouthfeel with vibrant acidity. Clean, lengthy finish. Drink now.

1998 Chardonnay, Paarl $12. 82

Warwick
1995 Cabernet Sauvignon, Stellenbosch $14. 88

Deep blackish-ruby hue. Moderately full-bodied. Full acidity. Moderately extracted. Moderately oaked. Mildly tannic. Chocolate, black pepper, leather. Quite aromatic, with a dense and flavorful quality on the palate. Firmly structured, with a vibrant note to the oak-tinged finish.

1995 Trilogy, Stellenbosch $18. 86

Blackish-ruby color. Medium-bodied. Balanced acidity. Moderately extracted. Heavily oaked. Mildly tannic. Red fruits, dried herbs, pickle barrel. Quite aromatic, with flavors that are almost like Pinot Noir. Lush and round in the mouth, with an accent on barrel character. Firmly structured through the finish.

Weltevrede
1997 Chardonnay, Robertson $12. NR

Zandvliet
1996 Special Reserve, Cabernet Sauvignon, Robertson Wine of Origin $20. 82
1996 Special Reserve, Merlot, Robertson $20. 85

Dark blackish-ruby hue. Medium-bodied. Balanced acidity. Moderately extracted. Heavily oaked. Mildly tannic. Dill pickle, dried herbs, sandalwood. Quite aromatic with a distinctive pickle note that is often the result of long-term aging in some types of American oak. The full flavors on the palate are also largely wood driven, but the wine is well structured and vibrant. Well balanced with fine length through the finish.

Brand Index

Brand Index

A

A.F. Gros, 579
Abadia Retuerta, 798
Abbey Vale, 902
Abel Mendoza, 787
Acacia, 26, 394, 402, 404
Ackerman, 309, 491, 496
Acorn, 26, 427-428
Ada Nada, 673
Adastra, 26, 444
Adegas Valmiñor, 798
Adelaida, 27, 346-347, 394, 410, 427-428, 438, 447
Adelsheim, 261, 393, 396
Adler Fels, 27, 462-463
Aficionado Cellars, 27
Ahlgren, 27, 432-433
Aia della Macina, 721
Aile d'Argents, 525
Alain Cailbourdin, 624
Alain Graillot, 645
Alba, 298, 309, 491, 496
Alban, 27, 32, 420, 422-423, 446, 452, 467
Albert Mann, 501, 509
Albertoni, 28, 428
Albino Armani, 759
Albino Rocca, 709
Albola, 758
Alderbrook, 28, 359, 410, 462, 490
Aldo Conterno, 685
Aldo Marenco, 699
Alessandro de Conciliis, 766
Alexander Valley Vineyards, 28, 361
Alfred Gratien, 599, 606
Alice White, 902
Alion, 798
Allandale, 902
Allanmere, 902
Altamura, 29, 346, 350, 427-428
Altos de Medrano, 953
Alvear, 824, 825
Amador Foothill Winery, 29, 428, 457
Ambra, 721, 737, 746
Amiot-Servelle, 570
Amistani di Guarda, 758
Amity, 261, 396, 398, 462, 490
Anapamu, 29, 439
Anderson, 902
Anderson's Conn Valley Vineyards, 30, 346, 352-353, 394, 444
André Perret, 651
Andrea Oberto, 702
Andrew Will, 226, 252, 346, 368, 377, 380-382, 389
Andron Blanquet, 526
Aney, 526

Angeline, 30
Angelo Boffa, 676
Angelo Negro, 702
Angelo Sassetti, 748
Anselma, 674
Antares, 30, 378
Antichi Poderi dei Gallina, 674
Antinori, 758, 720, 722
Antonelli, 758
Antonio Barbadillo, 825
Antonio Gallino, 692
Antonio Viglione, 715
Apex, 229, 346, 368, 377, 381-382, 389, 438, 448, 490-491
Arachon-Vereinte Winzer, 870
Arbor Crest, 229, 369, 456
Archery Summit, 261, 394, 397
Arciero, 30, 464
Argiano, 723
Argiolas, 758
Argueso, 825
Argyle, 261, 394, 461, 473-474
Armand Rousseau, 590
Armando Cuniberto, 688
Armando Piazzo, 705
Arnauld, 527
Arrowood, 31, 345-346, 359, 377, 438, 442, 452
Artadi, 787
Artigues, 527
Ashland, 262
Atlas Peak Vineyards, 31, 356, 428, 441
Attilio Ghisolfi, 693
Au Bon Climat, 31, 393, 399, 405, 438, 446-447, 452
Audubon, 32, 384
Aurelio Nota, 702
Aurelio Settimo, 711
Autumn Hill, 299
Autumn Wind, 262, 396
Avignonesi, 723
Ayala, 599, 600, 619
Az. Agr. Conterno (Cascina Sciulun), 686

B

B.R. Cohn, 65, 362
Babcock, 32, 394, 399, 427-428, 439, 446
Backsberg, 959
Badger Mountain, 230, 432
Badia a Coltibuono, 723
Badia a Passignano, 723
Bagnoli, 759
Baileyana, 33, 447
Baily, 33
Balbi, 680, 953
Bald Hill Creek, 902
Balestard la Tonnelle, 527
Baltieri, 759
Bandiera, 33

E

G

M

W

Bibliography

Baldy, Marian W. 1997. *The University Wine Course.* San Francisco, Calif.: The Wine Appreciation Guild.

Boulton, Roger B., Vernon L. Singleton, Linda F. Bisson, Ralph E. Kunkee. 1996. *Principles and Practices of Winemaking.* New York: Chapman and Hall.

Clarke, Oz. 1991. *Oz Clarke's New Classic Wines.* New York: Simon and Schuster.

_____. 1995. *Oz Clarke's Wine Atlas.* London: Little, Brown and Company.

Gladstones, John. 1997. *Viticulture and Environment.* Adelaide, South Australia: Winetitles.

Halliday, James. 1991. *Wine Atlas of Australia and New Zealand.* North Ryde, New South Wales: Angus and Robertson.

_____. 1993. *Wine Atlas of California.* New York: Viking.

Hanson, Anthony. 1995. *Burgundy.* London: Faber and Faber.

Johnson, Hugh, and James Halliday. 1992. *The Vintner's Art.* New York: Simon and Schuster.

Macaluso, Roberto. 1994. *La vite ed il vino nella provincia Granda.* Brescia: Edizione Internazionale.

Meredith, Ted Jordan. 1990. *Northwest Wine.* Kirkland, Wash.: Nexus Press.

Morton, Lucie T. 1985. *Winegrowing in Eastern America.* Ithaca, N.Y.: Cornell University Press.

Robinson, Jancis. 1994. *The Oxford Companion to Wine.* Oxford: Oxford University Press.

Vine, Richard P., Ellen M. Harkness, Theresa Browning, and Cheri Wagner.1997. *Winemaking.* New York: Chapman and Hall.

Winkler, A.J., James A. Cook, W.M. Kliewer, and Lloyd A. Lider. 1974. *General Viticulture.* Los Angeles: University of California Press.